Macmillan
ILLUSTRATED
ANIMAL
ENCYCLOPEDIA

Macmillan
ILLUSTRATED
ANIMAL
ENCYCLOPEDIA

Edited by Dr. Philip Whitfield
American Consultant: Professor Edward S. Ayensu
Foreword by Gerald Durrell

MACMILLAN PUBLISHING COMPANY
NEW YORK
PRINTED IN ITALY

Consultant Editor: **Dr. Philip Whitfield,**
Zoology Department, King's College, University of London

American Consultant: **Professor Edward S. Ayensu,**
Office of Biological Conservation, Smithsonian Institution, Washington D.C.

Consultants:

Mammals: **Dr. D. M. Stoddart,**
Zoology Department, King's College, University of London

Birds: **I. C. J. Galbraith,**
Ornithology Department, British Museum (Natural History), Tring, Hertfordshire

Reptiles and Amphibians: **Professor Barry Cox,**
Zoology Department, King's College, University of London

Fishes: **Alwyne Wheeler,**
British Museum (Natural History), London.

Artists:

Mammals: **Graham Allen**
        Dick Twinney (pp. 83, 85, 125–57, 191, 193)

Birds: **Michael Woods**
        Malcolm Ellis (pp. 303, 325, 327, 357, 361, 363, 379, 399, 401)
        Keith Brewer (pp. 273, 275, 359)

Reptiles and Amphibians: **Alan Male**

Fishes: **Colin Newman**

Conceived, edited and designed by
Marshall Editions Limited, 71 Eccleston Square, London SW1V 1PJ

Editor: **Jinny Johnson**
Text Editor: **Gwen Rigby**
Art Director: **John Bigg**   Production: **Barry Baker**
Researcher: **Pip Morgan**   **Janice Storr**

PRINTED IN ITALY

Macmillan Publishing Company
866 Third Avenue, New York, N.Y. 10022
Collier Macmillan Canada, Inc.

Library of Congress Catalog Card Number: 84–3956
      ISBN 0-02-627680-1

Reader's Digest Fund for the Blind is publisher of the Large-Type Edition of *READER'S DIGEST*. For subscription information about this magazine, please contact Reader's Digest Fund for the Blind, Inc., Dept. 250, Pleasantville, N.Y. 10570.

Macmillan books are available at special discounts for bulk purchases for sales promotions, premiums, fund raising, or educational use. Special editions or book excerpts can also be created to specification. For details contact:
Special Sales Director, Macmillan Publishing Company,
866 Third Avenue, New York, N.Y. 10022

10 9 8 7 6 5 4 3 2 1

Contents

7 Foreword by Gerald Durrell

8 Introduction

Mammals

10

12 Spiny Anteaters, Platypus
14 Opossums, Colocolo, Rat Opossums
16 Dasyurid Marsupials
18 Numbat, Koala and other marsupials
20 Bandicoots, Phalangers, Pygmy Possums, Ringtails
22 Kangaroos
26 Anteaters, Sloths
28 Armadillos, Pangolins, Aardvark
30 Tenrecs, Solenodons
32 Golden Moles, Hedgehogs
34 Shrews
36 Moles, Elephant Shrews, Flying Lemurs
38 Old World Fruit Bats
40 Mouse-tailed Bats, Sheath-tailed Bats
42 Hog-nosed Bat, Slit-faced Bats, False Vampire Bats
44 Horseshoe Bats, Old World Leaf-nosed Bats
46 Fisherman Bats, Mustached Bats, Vampire Bats, Free-tailed Bats
48 American Leaf-nosed Bats
50 Evening Bats
52 Funnel-eared Bats and relatives
54 Tree Shrews
56 Mouse-lemurs, Lemurs, Aye-aye
58 Lorises, Tarsiers
60 Marmosets and Tamarins
62 New World Monkeys
66 Old World Monkeys
74 Apes
78 Dogs
82 Bears
84 Raccoons, Pandas
86 Mustelids
92 Civets
98 Hyenas

100 Cats
106 Sea Lions, Walrus
108 Seals
110 Seals, Dugong, Manatees
112 River Dolphins, Porpoises
114 Dolphins
116 Sperm Whales, White Whales
118 Beaked Whales
120 Gray Whale, Rorquals, Right Whales
122 Elephants, Hyraxes
124 Horses
126 Tapirs, Rhinoceroses
128 Pigs
130 Peccaries, Hippopotamuses
132 Camels
134 Chevrotains, Musk Deer, Deer
136 Deer
138 Deer, Giraffes, Pronghorn
140 Bovids
158 Squirrels
162 Pocket Gophers, Pocket Mice
164 Mountain Beaver, Beavers, Springhare, Scaly-tailed Squirrels
166 New World Rats and Mice
168 Hamsters, Mole-rats
170 Crested Rat, Spiny Dormice and relatives
172 Voles and Lemmings
174 Gerbils
176 Climbing Mice, Pouched Rats, Island Water Rats
178 Old World Rats and Mice
180 Dormice, Jumping Mice, Jerboas
182 Porcupines
184 Guinea Pigs, Capybara, Pacas and Agoutis
186 Chinchillas and relatives
188 Spiny Rats, Cane Rats and relatives
190 Pikas, Rabbits and Hares
192 Rabbits and Hares

Birds

194

196 Ratites, Tinamous
198 Penguins, Grebes, Loons

200 Albatrosses, Petrels
202 Storm-petrels, Diving-petrels
204 Tropicbirds, Gannets and Boobies, Pelicans
206 Darters, Cormorants, Frigatebirds
208 Herons and Bitterns
210 Storks, Flamingos, Ibises, Hammerkop, Shoebill
212 Screamers, Ducks
214 Ducks
216 New World Vultures, Secretary Bird, Osprey
218 Hawks
224 Falcons
226 Megapodes, Curassows, Hoatzin
228 Pheasants
232 Grouse, Turkeys, Guineafowl, American Quail
234 Cranes and relatives
236 Rails
238 Finfoots, Bustards and relatives
240 Jacanas, Plovers, Painted-snipes, Oystercatchers
242 Sandpipers
244 Avocets, Crab Plover, Thick-knees
246 Pratincoles, Seedsnipes, Sheathbills
248 Skuas, Gulls, Skimmers
250 Auks
252 Sandgrouse, Pigeons
254 Pigeons
258 Lories, Cockatoos, Parrots
260 Parrots
264 Cuckoos
266 Cuckoos, Turacos
268 Barn Owls, Owls
270 Owls
272 Frogmouths, Potoos and relatives
274 Nightjars
276 Swifts, Crested Swifts
278 Hummingbirds
280 Trogons, Mousebirds
282 Kingfishers
284 Motmots, Bee-eaters and relatives
286 Hoopoe, Woodhoopoes, Hornbills
288 Jacamars, Barbets and relatives

continued

290 Toucans
292 Woodpeckers
296 Ovenbirds
298 Antbirds
300 Woodcreepers, Gnateaters, Tapaculos
302 Manakins, Cotingas
304 Sharpbill, Plantcutters, Tyrant Flycatchers
306 Tyrant Flycatchers
310 Broadbills, Pittas and relatives
312 Larks
314 Swallows
316 Pipits
318 Cuckoo-shrikes and Minivets
320 Bulbuls
322 Bulbuls, Leafbirds
324 Shrikes
326 Vangas, Waxwings, Palm Chat
328 Wrens
330 Mockingbirds, Dippers, Accentors
332 Thrushes
338 Babblers
342 Babblers, Parrotbills and relatives
344 Gnatcatchers, Old World Warblers
346 Old World Warblers
348 Australian Warblers
350 Old World Flycatchers
352 Monarch Flycatchers
354 Fantail Flycatchers, Whistlers
356 Penduline Tits, Titmice
358 Treecreepers, Philippine Creepers, Nuthatches
360 Flowerpeckers, White-eyes
362 Sunbirds
364 Honey Eaters
368 Buntings
372 Plush-capped Finch, Cardinals and Grosbeaks, Swallow-tanager
374 Tanagers
378 American Wood Warblers
380 Hawaiian Honeycreepers, Vireos
382 Icterids
384 Finches
386 Waxbills
388 Weavers
392 Starlings

394 Orioles, Drongos, Wattlebirds
396 Butcherbirds, Wood Swallows, Mudnest Builders
398 Bowerbirds, Birds of Paradise
400 Crows

402 **Reptiles**

404 Emydid Turtles
406 Land Tortoises
408 Snapping Turtles, Mud Turtles, River Turtles
410 Leatherback, Marine Turtles
412 Softshell Turtles, Greaved Turtles, Matamatas
414 Crocodiles, Alligators and Caimans, Gavial
416 Tuatara, Iguanas
418 Iguanas
420 Agamid Lizards
422 Chameleons
424 Geckos
426 Geckos, Scaly-foot Lizards
428 Night Lizards, Teiid Lizards
430 Skinks
434 Lacertid Lizards
436 Girdled and Plated Lizards
438 Old World Burrowing Lizards, Anguid Lizards, Legless Lizards
440 Crocodile Lizards, Gila Monster, Monitors
442 Amphisbaenids
444 Slender Blind Snakes, Blind Snakes, Pipe Snakes, Shieldtail Snakes, Sunbeam Snake
446 Pythons and Boas, Wart Snakes
448 Colubrine Snakes
454 Cobras and Sea Snakes
456 Vipers
458 Pit Vipers

460 **Amphibians**

462 Salamanders
464 Mole Salamanders
466 Amphiumas, Olm and Mudpuppies, Sirens
468 Lungless Salamanders
470 Caecilians

472 Mexican Burrowing Toad, Pipid Frogs, Narrow-mouthed Frogs
474 Discoglossid Frogs, Tailed Frogs, Spadefoot Toads
476 Myobatrachid Frogs, Ghost Frogs, Leptodactylid Frogs, Mouth-brooding Frog
478 Bufonid Toads, Gold Frog
480 Treefrogs
482 True Frogs
484 True Frogs, Hyperoliid Frogs, Sooglossid Frogs

486 **Fishes**

488 Lampreys, Hagfishes, Sharks
490 Sharks
494 Skates and Rays
496 Chimaeras, Lungfishes, Coelacanth
498 Sturgeons, Gars, Bowfin, Bichirs
500 Osteoglossiform, Elopiform and Mormyriform Fishes
502 Herrings
504 Eels, Spiny Eels
506 Salmon
510 Cypriniform Fishes
518 Siluriform Fishes
524 Lanternfishes, Beardfishes, Trout-perches
526 Codfishes
530 Toadfishes, Angler Fishes
532 Atheriniform Fishes
538 Lampridiform Fishes, Zeiform Fishes
540 Beryciform Fishes
542 Syngnathiform Fishes, Sticklebacks and Tube-snouts
544 Flying Gurnards, Scorpaeniform Fishes
546 Scorpaeniform Fishes
548 Perchlike Fishes
574 Gobiesociform Fishes, Flatfishes
576 Flatfishes
580 Tetraodontiform Fishes

584 Classification: lists of vertebrate orders and families
588 Index
600 Acknowledgments

Foreword

The value of a natural history such as this, so concise and beautifully illustrated, can hardly be overestimated, both as a reference work for identification, and as a teaching tool. I sometimes think that we in the West are somewhat complacent about magnificent books like this — we tend to take them for granted. We should not. Not long ago I was in Madagascar, probably one of the most interesting areas, biologically speaking, in the world. I was horrified to find that the only means of identification of some of their unique fauna available to the ordinary Malagasy was a series of blurred and not very well drawn pictures of lemurs on the backs of matchboxes.

It is a sobering thought that within the next 80 to 100 years, many of the fascinating creatures so beautifully described here will vanish unless world governments start thinking in terms of conservation and not desecration. It is the appearance of books like this that, hopefully, will help stem the tide of extermination now sweeping the world.

With its fine illustrations and its careful and unusual layout, this is an excellent encyclopedia. It really is a sort of who's who of the animal world showing who is related to whom. It is so deftly written and arranged that it will be of immense value to both the professional and amateur naturalist, and certainly every school should have a copy.

I am delighted to recommend it to all who value the fascinating planet on which we live.

Gerald Durrell

The Jersey Wildlife Preservation Trust

Introduction

Human beings are vertebrate animals, as are all our essential domesticated creatures and most of the dominant large animals in every earthly ecosystem. The few large invertebrate animals that do exist, giant squid, for example, serve to emphasize by their very rarity the preeminent position of vertebrates. Between them, the mammals, birds, reptiles, amphibians and fishes rule the sea and the land. In rivers, lakes, swamps and even in the air, it is vertebrate animals that provide the obvious animal segment of living communities.

One particular feature links creatures as diverse as lampreys, sharks, salmon, frogs, alligators, eagles and chimpanzees and makes them a natural grouping — an organic and interrelated assemblage. All vertebrates have vertebrae, that is, a longitudinal series of skeletal elements along their main nerve tract, the spinal cord. Not all, however, have a backbone exactly like ours, consisting of distinct, bony blocks, although all the higher, most recently developed types do. These latter animals include the bony fishes, amphibians, reptiles, birds and mammals. The cartilaginous fishes — sharks, rays and skates, for example — have vertebrae, but these consist of cartilage rather than bone, and the even more primitive lampreys and hagfishes have only simple rudiments of vertebral structures close to the spinal cord.

When compared with invertebrate groups, such as corals, flatworms, worms, mollusks, crustaceans, spiders and insects, there is little doubt that the vertebrate type of body organization provides the potential for the most intricate and sophisticated animals. Animals have been called the most exquisite and complicated machines in the known universe, and the higher vertebrates represent the very pinnacle of complexity and subtlety. In this perspective, zoology, which might otherwise appear to be an esoteric speciality, becomes one of the most demanding and vital of disciplines — the attempt to understand and learn more about these extraordinary machines.

The *Macmillan Illustrated Animal Encyclopedia* sets out to provide a comprehensive catalog of the staggering range of animal types within the vertebrate group. From the 43,500 or so species of living vertebrates, a selection has been made to represent their diversity to best effect. It is clearly impossible to be comprehensive at the species level, so we have looked at a higher level in the classification hierarchy and organized the book at family level, at which it is possible to be comprehensive.

The classification of animals into groups often seems a mystifying or intimidating exercise, as does the scientific naming of animals that goes with it. But both are merely an attempt to organize the creatures into recognizable groups which show their relationships. The Latin- or Greek-based names are enormously useful because of their stability: the scientific name of an animal remains the same all over the world, but there may be dozens of common names. An animal species is a group of animals that can, at least potentially, breed with one another and produce fertile offspring. This is a natural grouping based on the intrinsic attributes and activities of the animals themselves. Each species is given a unique, two-part name in which the second component is specific to that species. The tiger, for example, is called *Panthera tigris*. *Panthera* is its generic name — the genus *Panthera* contains 5 different species of big cat — while *tigris* is its specific name, which refers only to the tiger. The generic and specific names are always printed in italics.

The species names are only the first two levels of a taxonomical hierarchy. Many more levels are required in order to encompass the patterns of similarity which exist. In ascending order, the most commonly used levels are species, genus, family, order, class and phylum; ultimately all animals are grouped together in the kingdom Animalia.

To return to the tiger, this animal and all other cats belong to the cat family, Felidae, and all have certain physical and behavioral characteristics in common. This family is grouped with other families of related animals, such as dogs, viverrids and mustelids, in the order Carnivora, and this and all other orders of mammals belong to the class Mammalia. It is at the vital family level that this book is comprehensive. A discussion of the major characteristics of each family is accompanied by a number of representative examples of the family; thus, if a given species is not shown, a close relative of it will be. Each order is also mentioned. Some of the larger families, such as the Old World rats and mice, Muridae, are split up into many subfamilies, since this facilitates the description of the various groups and avoids the gross generalization that would otherwise result in these cases.

Only in the Fish section has this level of comprehensiveness been changed. Here, because of the enormous number of families — many of them little known — it has not been possible to deal with fish diversity in terms of a comprehensive analysis of all fish families. Instead, every order of fish is described, and, where relevant, important families are considered separately.

In something so complex as taxonomy, there is bound to be argument, and there are many areas of disagreement in the ordering and grouping of particular species and families; in this book the consultants have followed what they believe to be the best guidelines. Where there is particular controversy over the placing of a particular species, the problem is mentioned in the text.

The tiger is a species of cat, and almost everyone knows — or would claim to know — what a tiger looks like. However, species do not consist of identical individuals. Enormous genetic diversity exists within a species, as a cursory examination of the common house cat reveals. In many animal species it is possible to identify groupings known as subspecies or races. These often represent geographically distinct forms of a species that show characteristic differences from one another. This accounts, for example, in the birds for the sometimes quite striking differences in plumage between individuals of the same species. The tiger, too, has half a dozen geographically distinct subspecies, which vary in size and in fur coloration and patterning. Subspecies of a species can still interbreed. All subspecies, however, are human-defined, and they are essentially arbitrary, unlike the species themselves, which correspond more or less precisely to actual interbreeding groups of animals.

This book is a catalog and, as with any catalog, part of its organization emphasizes similarities. Similar animals are grouped into their family assemblages, and this format enables the shared habits and structures of related animals to be easily grasped. Ultimately though, there is another way of responding to the patterns of animal organization delineated here. Instead of emphasizing the shared characteristics, one can marvel at the almost infinite range of life-styles and physical structures of vertebrate animals that is a joy in itself. There is space and opportunity enough in this book to savor the amazing diversity of mammals, birds, reptiles, amphibians and fishes and to find fascination in the contrasts, even between members of the same family.

Philip Whitfield

CONSERVATION STATUS

Many of the world's animal species are in danger of extinction or are becoming rare, often as a direct result of human activity. All animals, particularly threatened species, are monitored by the International Union for Conservation of Nature and Natural Resources (IUCN) and listed in the Red Data books that are produced by this organization.

The status of threatened species is indicated in this book by symbols, the meaning of which is given below. This information is printed with the kind assistance of the IUCN Conservation Monitoring Centre, Cambridge, England.

ENDANGERED Ⓔ
Species in grave danger of extinction, which can survive only if effective conservation measures are adopted and the causes of their difficulties cease.

VULNERABLE Ⓥ
Species which may become endangered if their numbers continue to diminish at the present rate.

RARE Ⓡ
Species which are at risk because their population is already small, e.g., those with restricted distribution.

OUT OF DANGER Ⓞ
Species which were once included in one of the above categories but, because of effective conservation measures, are now no longer in danger.

INDETERMINATE Ⓘ
Species which are suspected of being endangered, vulnerable or rare but about which there is insufficient information to permit classification.

NAMES
Common and scientific names are given for each species. Common names tend to vary greatly, but the most generally accepted version is used. In some instances, where there are two names of equal importance, both are given thus: Little Grebe/Dabchick. Where there is an alternative name that is subordinate to the main choice, this is given in parentheses: (European) Bee-eater.

RANGE AND HABITAT
The normal range of a species is explained as fully as possible, given the limitations of space. The animal's particular habitat helps to clarify its precise occurrence within a large range. The book notes instances where a species has been introduced outside its native range by human agency.

SIZE
Sizes are given as approximate total lengths unless otherwise stated; in birds this is the length from bill tip to tail tip; in turtles and tortoises the length of the shell is given. Exceptions are made where individual circumstances demand: for example, where a bird has an exceptionally long tail, this measurement may be given separately. In the Mammals section, two separate measurements are given: head and body length and tail length. The vast range of sizes of the animals has meant that the drawings cannot be to a single scale.

Mammals – the peak of vertebrate adaptability

There are 4,008 species of mammal, which are the most adaptable and diverse group of vertebrates on our planet today. Whales, dolphins and seals are important members of the animal community in the seas, while forms such as otters and beavers are successful in freshwater habitats. On dry land, a huge diversity of mammal types prospers underground, on the land surface and in trees and other vegetation. Mammals have even taken to the air in the form of bats, the night-flying insectivores. In all these types, mammals reveal a startling variability in feeding strategies. Some feed only on plant material, others on small invertebrates. Many kill and eat other vertebrates, including mammals, while some eat almost anything. To begin to understand the reasons for the adaptability and success of mammalian lines of evolution, it is necessary to look at what a mammal is, how it is constructed, how it operates physically and behaviorally and what its ancestors were like.

A mammal is a warm-blooded, four-limbed, hairy vertebrate (an animal with a backbone). Male mammals inseminate females internally, using a penis, and females, typically, retain their developing fetuses within the uterus, where the bloodstreams of mother and offspring come close together (but do not fuse) in a placenta. The time spent in the womb by the developing fetus is known as the gestation period and varies from group to group. Some mammals, such as rabbits, rodents and many carnivores, are born naked, blind and helpless, while others, such as cattle and deer, are small, but fully formed and capable versions of the adult. Mothers produce milk for their young from skin-derived mammary glands.

The vast majority of mammals possess these characteristics, but a few exceptions, real and apparent, must be taken into account. Whales and their relatives and manatees have only forelimbs. Examination of their skeletal structure, however, leaves no doubt that these highly modified aquatic animals are derived from four-legged ancestors. However, the monotremes — the platypus and spiny anteaters — are highly uncharacteristic mammals. They have retained the egg-laying habits of their reptilian ancestors and do not form placentas. The pouched mammals, or marsupials, also have an unorthodox method of reproduction compared with that of the normal placenta-forming mammals. Kangaroos, wallabies and their relatives retain a thin shell around the developing young inside the mother's body, but the shell dissolves away before the offspring emerges to crawl into the pouch and attach itself to a milk-delivering nipple. Some species do have a primitive placenta. The marsupial young is born in a far less advanced state than most mammals and finishes its development in the pouch.

Knowledge of the ancestry of mammals is based largely on the study of fossil remains of parts of skeletons and, to some extent, on surviving primitive mammalian types, such as the platypus. Mammals evolved from reptiles, but because the only evidence is in fossil bones, there is no point in the geological record where we can say: Here, reptiles changed into mammals. A more realistic statement is that there is a long evolutionary history of a group of reptiles that possessed mammal-like skeletal characteristics. These reptiles were very successful in the Permian and Triassic periods but were reduced to a mere remnant of their former diversity in the Late Triassic and Jurassic times. During the 90 million years between the Early Jurassic and the Late Cretaceous, however, this mammal-like stock of reptiles gave rise to small forms which must be regarded as real mammals in the modern sense. From the Late Cretaceous period (around 70 million years ago) until now, the mammals have continued their explosive expansion into different ways of life and environments to become the dominant group of land-dwelling vertebrates and an important part of aquatic life.

Apart from reproductive sophistication, mammals are remarkable in a number of other ways. They have large, complex brains and acute and well-integrated sensory systems. They employ a range of vocal, visual and olfactory means of communication with other species and with members of their own species — communication with the latter is important in the organization of family and social groupings. The keratinous hairs that grow out of mammalian skin insulate the body and are part of a complex of temperature-regulation mechanisms with which mammals maintain a constant high body temperature, irrespective of external climatic conditions. Metabolic heat, especially that produced by brown fat in the body, can be used to offset heat losses and can be transferred around the body via the circulatory system, which is powered by the four-chambered heart. The body can be cooled by the evaporation of sweat secretions at the body surface. All this temperature-control "machinery" is under the control of the hypothalamus in the brain. When temperature-control demands exceed energy resources, for example in low temperatures, some mammals are able to hibernate. During hibernation, the animal's body temperature drops to close to that of the surroundings, and its heart and respiration slow dramatically so that it uses the minimum of energy. Thus it is able to survive for as long as several months on stored fat.

The astonishing diversity of present-day mammals is illustrated in the following pages, which review each living family and describe representative examples. Briefly, the range of types is as follows. The primitive monotremes and marsupials, the majority found in Australia, have already been mentioned. Australia separated from the southern continents before it could receive any placental mammals. Thus the mammal fauna was able to radiate into a diverse range of forms, which mirrors the range of placental mammals found in the rest of the world. There are burrowing, tree-dwelling, ant-eating, herbivorous and predatory marsupials, and

marsupial analogues exist or have existed for almost all placental mammals except bats, whales and seals.

The placental mammals break down into four broad groups. The first contains the most primitive creatures: the insectivores such as shrews, hedge-hogs and moles, as well as the bats, sloths, anteaters, armadillos and pangolins and the primate group, to which human beings belong. The second group contains two orders of small, largely herbivorous mammals with gnawing teeth: the rodents, and the rabbits and related forms. In the third group is a single dramatically specialized order: the whales, dolphins and porpoises, which, more than any other animals, have renounced their terrestrial ancestry and become as fully aquatic as any air-breathing animal can be. The fourth and final group contains a complex mixture of orders which are believed to have some common ancestry, despite the different evolutionary paths they have taken. It includes all the carnivores (animals such as cats, dogs, mustelids and bears), the aardvark, elephants, hyraxes, seals, manatees and the dugong, as well as the two major groups of hoofed mammals, the uneven-toed types, such as tapirs, horses and rhinoceroses, and the even-toed (cloven-hoofed) types, such as pigs, peccaries, camels, deer, cattle, sheep and goats.

The evolutionary success of the mammals is hard to evaluate. In measurements of the dominance of a particular group or its species diversity, success is seen as the result of an amalgam of intrinsic biological merit and chance. Still, no other major class of vertebrates has ever conquered such a variety of habitats so completely. The advent of our own species has probably increased the rate of mammalian extinctions in some groups, but others, such as rodents, are evolving into new ecological niches created by human activities. At the present time, the mammals are an overwhelmingly successful group, and human beings — the most dominant species — may come to control the future of the planet.

Spiny Anteaters, Platypus

ORDER MONOTREMATA

Two families with a combined total of only 3 living species make up this order. Although well adapted for their environments, monotremes are considered primitive mammals in that they retain some reptilian characteristics of body structure and they lay eggs. However, they also possess the essential mammalian characteristics of body hair and mammary glands. Monotremes are probably a parallel development, rather than a stage in the evolution of mammals. A problem in understanding the origins of this order is that no fossil monotremes have been found.

TACHYGLOSSIDAE:
Spiny Anteater Family

There are 2 species of spiny anteater, or echidna. Both are covered with coarse hairs, and their backs are set with spines. They have elongated, slender snouts and strong limbs and are powerful diggers. Like anteaters, they have no teeth and very weak jaws. Termites, ants and other small arthropods are swept into the mouth by a long, sticky tongue, which can reach well beyond the tip of the snout. The insects are then crushed between the tongue and the roof of the mouth.

NAME: Long-nosed Spiny Anteater, *Zaglossus bruijni*
RANGE: New Guinea
HABITAT: forest
SIZE: body: 45–77 cm (17¾–30¼ in)
  tail: vestigial Ⓥ

The long-nosed spiny anteater is larger than the short-nosed and has fewer, shorter spines scattered among its coarse hairs. The snout is two-thirds of the head length and curves slightly downward. There are five digits on each foot, but on the hind feet only the three middle toes are equipped with claws. Males have a spur on each of the hind legs. This spiny anteater is primarily a nocturnal animal that forages for its insect food on the forest floor.

The breeding female has a temporary abdominal brood patch, in which her egg is incubated and in which the newborn young remains in safety, feeding and developing. Little is known about the life of this rarely seen animal, but it is believed to have similar habits to those of the short-nosed spiny anteater.

There were once thought to be 3 species in this genus, but now all are believed to be races of this one species. The population of spiny anteaters in New Guinea is declining because of forest clearance and overhunting, and the animal is much in need of protection.

NAME: Short-nosed Spiny Anteater, *Tachyglossus aculeatus*
RANGE: Australia, Tasmania, S.E. New Guinea
HABITAT: grassland, forest
SIZE: body: 30–38 cm (11¾–15 in)
  tail: vestigial

The short-nosed spiny anteater has a compact, round body closely set with spines. At the end of its naked snout is a small, slitlike mouth, through which its long tongue can be extended 15 to 18 cm (6 to 7 in) beyond the snout. The tongue is coated with sticky saliva, so any insect it touches is trapped. Spiny anteaters have no teeth but break up their food between horny ridges in the mouth; termites, ants and other small invertebrates form their main diet.

Spiny anteaters have five digits, all with strong claws, on each foot. Males also have spurs on each hind leg which may be used in defense. They are excellent diggers and, if in danger, rapidly dig themselves into the ground. They do not live in burrows but in hollow logs or among roots and rocks. Their ability to regulate their body temperature is poor, and in cool weather they hibernate.

On her abdomen, the breeding female has a temporary patch, or groove, which develops at the start of the breeding season. When she has laid her leathery-shelled egg, she transfers it to the patch, where it incubates for 7 to 10 days. The egg is coated with sticky mucus to help it stay in the groove. When the young hatches, it is only 1.25 cm (½ in) long and helpless, so it must remain on the mother's abdomen while it develops.

The female has plenty of milk from mammary glands but no nipples, so the baby feeds by sucking special areas of abdominal skin through which the milk flows. Once the spines develop, at about 3 weeks, the young is no longer carried by its mother.

ORNITHORHYNCHIDAE:
Platypus Family

The single species of this family is an extraordinary animal in appearance but perfectly adapted for its way of life. The platypus was discovered 200 years ago, and when the first specimen arrived at London's Natural History Museum, scientists were so puzzled by it that they believed the specimen to be a fake.

Platypuses are now protected by law and are quite common in some areas.

NAME: Platypus, *Ornithorhynchus anatinus*
RANGE: E. Australia, Tasmania
HABITAT: lakes, rivers
SIZE: body: 46 cm (18 in)
  tail: 18 cm (7 in)

The platypus is a semiaquatic animal, and many of its physical characteristics are adaptations for its life as a freshwater predator. Its legs are short but powerful, and the feet are webbed, though the digits retain large claws, useful for burrowing. On the forefeet the webs extend beyond the claws and make efficient paddles; on land, the webs can be folded back to free the claws for digging. On each ankle the male platypus has a spur connected to poison glands in the thighs; these spurs are used against an attacker or against a competing platypus but never against prey. The poison is not fatal to man but causes intense pain.

The platypus's eye and ear openings lie in furrows which are closed off by folds of skin when the animal is submerged. Thus, when hunting underwater, the platypus relies on the sensitivity of its tactile, leathery bill to find prey. The nostrils are toward the end of the upper bill but can only function when the head is in air. Young platypuses have teeth, but adults have horny, ridged plates on both sides of the jaws for crushing prey.

The platypus feeds mainly at the bottom of the water, making dives lasting a minute or more to probe the mud with its bill for crustaceans, aquatic insects and larvae. It also feeds on frogs and other small animals and on some plants. Platypuses have huge appetites, consuming up to 1 kg (2¼ lb) of food each night.

Short burrows dug in the riverbank above the water level are used by the platypus for refuge or during periods of cool weather. In the breeding season, however, the female digs a burrow 12 m (40 ft) or more in length, at the end of which she lays her 2 or 3 eggs on a nest of dry grass and leaves; the rubbery eggs are cemented together in a raft. She plugs the entrance to the burrow with moist plant matter, and this prevents the eggs from drying out during the 7- to 14-day incubation period. When the young hatch, they are only about 1.25 cm (½ in) long and helpless. Until they are about 5 months old, they feed on milk, which issues from slits in the mother's abdominal wall. Unlike spiny anteaters, they do not draw up tucks of skin into pseudonipples but lap and suck the milk off their mother's abdominal fur.

Short-nosed Spiny Anteater

Long-nosed Spiny Anteater

Platypus

Opossums, Colocolo, Rat Opossums

ORDER MARSUPIALIA

There are some 250 species of marsupial mammal in North and South America and in Australasia east of Wallace's line (an imaginary line between Borneo and Sulawesi, and Bali and Lombok). They evolved at about the same time as the true, or placental, mammals, but were replaced by them over much of their range. Only in Australia, which separated from the southern continents of Gondwanaland after it had been populated by some early marsupials but before it received any placental mammals, has the true potential of this order been realized. There, marsupials have adapted to a variety of ecological niches and have exploited all available habitats.

The principal characteristic of marsupial mammals is their method of reproduction. Instead of retaining young inside the uterus until they are well developed, as occurs in placental mammals, gestation is extremely short — as brief as 11 days — and the young finish their development inside a pouch on the mother's belly.

DIDELPHIDAE: Opossum Family

There are over 70 species in the opossum family, found from the southern tip of South America northward to southeast Canada. They are all basically rat-shaped animals with scaly, almost hairless tails and rather unkempt fur. Some species possess a proper pouch, while others carry their young between two flaps of skin on the belly.

Most opossums are forest dwellers, although one exceptional species has taken to an aquatic way of life. They feed on leaves, shoots, buds and seeds, and insects may also be eaten.

NAME: South American Mouse-opossum, *Marmosa mitis*
RANGE: Belize to N.W. South America; Trinidad, Tobago, Grenada
HABITAT: forest, dense scrubland
SIZE: body: 16.5–18.5 cm ($6\frac{1}{2}$–$7\frac{1}{4}$ in)
tail: 26–28 cm ($10\frac{1}{4}$–11 in)

With a long, pointed nose and huge eyes, which indicate its nocturnal way of life, the mouse-opossum is more shrewlike than mouselike in appearance. It has no permanent home but constructs temporary daytime nests in tree holes or in old bird's nests. An agile climber, the mouse-opossum has a long, prehensile tail, which acts as a fifth limb.

Mouse-opossums breed two or three times a year, and litters of up to 10 young are born after a gestation of 17 days. The young must cling to the mother's fur, since mouse-opossums do not have proper pouches.

NAME: Virginia Opossum, *Didelphis virginiana*
RANGE: S.E. Canada through USA to Central America: Nicaragua
HABITAT: forest, scrubland
SIZE: body: 32.5–50 cm ($12\frac{3}{4}$–$19\frac{3}{4}$ in)
tail: 25.5–53.5 cm (10–21 in)

The only marsupial found north of Mexico and the largest of the opossum family, the Virginia opossum may weigh up to 5.5 kg (12 lb). It is a successful creature, which has adapted to modern life, scavenging in refuse cans and dumps. Should it be threatened by a dog, bobcat, eagle or mink, it may feign death — it "plays possum" — and the predator generally loses interest.

In Canada, opossums breed once a year, in spring, but in the south of the range, two or even three litters of 8 to 18 young may be produced in a year. Usually only about 7 of a litter survive pouch life. In the southern USA, opossums are trapped for their fur and flesh.

NAME: Water Opossum, *Chironectes minimus*
RANGE: Mexico, south through Central and South America to Argentina
HABITAT: freshwater lakes and streams
SIZE: body: 27–32.5 cm ($10\frac{1}{2}$–$12\frac{3}{4}$ in)
tail: 36–40 cm ($14\frac{1}{4}$–$15\frac{3}{4}$ in)

The water opossum, or yapok, is the only marsupial to have adapted to aquatic life. It lives in bankside burrows, emerging after dusk to swim and search for fish, crustaceans and other invertebrates. Prey is eaten on the bank. The opossum's long tail aids its movements in water, but it uses the broadly webbed hind feet for propulsion.

In December, water opossums mate, and a litter of about 5 young is born some 2 weeks later. The pouch is made watertight by a strong ring of muscle, and the young remain quite dry, even when the mother is totally immersed in water. It is not known how the young obtain sufficient oxygen in their hermetically sealed environment.

NAME: Short-tailed Opossum, *Monodelphis brevicaudata*
RANGE: Suriname to N. Argentina
HABITAT: forest
SIZE: body: 11–14 cm ($4\frac{1}{4}$–$5\frac{1}{2}$ in)
tail: 4.5–6.5 cm ($1\frac{3}{4}$–$2\frac{1}{2}$ in)

Although the short-tailed opossum lives in forested country, it is a poor climber and tends to stay on the forest floor. During the day, it shelters in a leafy nest, which it builds in a hollow log or tree trunk. It emerges at night to feed on seeds, shoots and fruit, as well as on insects, carrion and some small rodents, which it kills with a powerful bite to the back of the head.

Litters of up to 14 young are born at any time of year and must cling to their mother's nipples and the surrounding fur, since she has no pouch. When they are older, they ride on her back.

MICROBIOTHERIIDAE: Colocolo Family

There is a single species in this family, which appears to be closely related to the opossums.

NAME: Colocolo, *Dromiciops australis*
RANGE: Chile, W. Argentina
HABITAT: forest
SIZE: body: 11–12.5 cm ($4\frac{1}{4}$–5 in)
tail: 9–10 cm ($3\frac{1}{2}$–4 in)

An adaptable animal, the colocolo occurs in both high-altitude and lowland forest. It feeds largely on the leaves and shoots of Chilean bamboo but also eats insects and earthworms. In the colder parts of the range, colocolos hibernate in winter, but in more temperate regions, they remain active all year round.

Colocolos breed in spring, producing litters of up to 5 young. They have no true pouch, and the young must cling to the mother's fur.

CAENOLESTIDAE: Rat Opossum Family

There are only 7 known species of rat opossum, all of which live in inaccessible forest and grassland regions of the High Andes. None is common, and the family is poorly known. Rat opossums are small, shrewlike animals, with thin limbs, a long, pointed snout and slender, hairy tail. Their eyes are small, and they seem to spend much of their lives in underground burrows and on surface runways. It is likely that there are more species yet to be discovered.

NAME: Rat Opossum, *Caenolestes obscurus*
RANGE: Colombia, Venezuela
HABITAT: montane forest
SIZE: body: 9–13 cm ($3\frac{1}{2}$–5 in)
tail: 9–12 cm ($3\frac{1}{2}$–$4\frac{3}{4}$ in)

The rat opossum lives on the forest floor and shelters in hollow logs or in underground chambers during the day. At dusk, it emerges to forage in the surface litter for small invertebrate animals and fruit.

Rat opossums may be far more common than is generally thought, but the inhospitableness of their habitat makes their study and collection extremely difficult. Nothing is known of their reproductive habits.

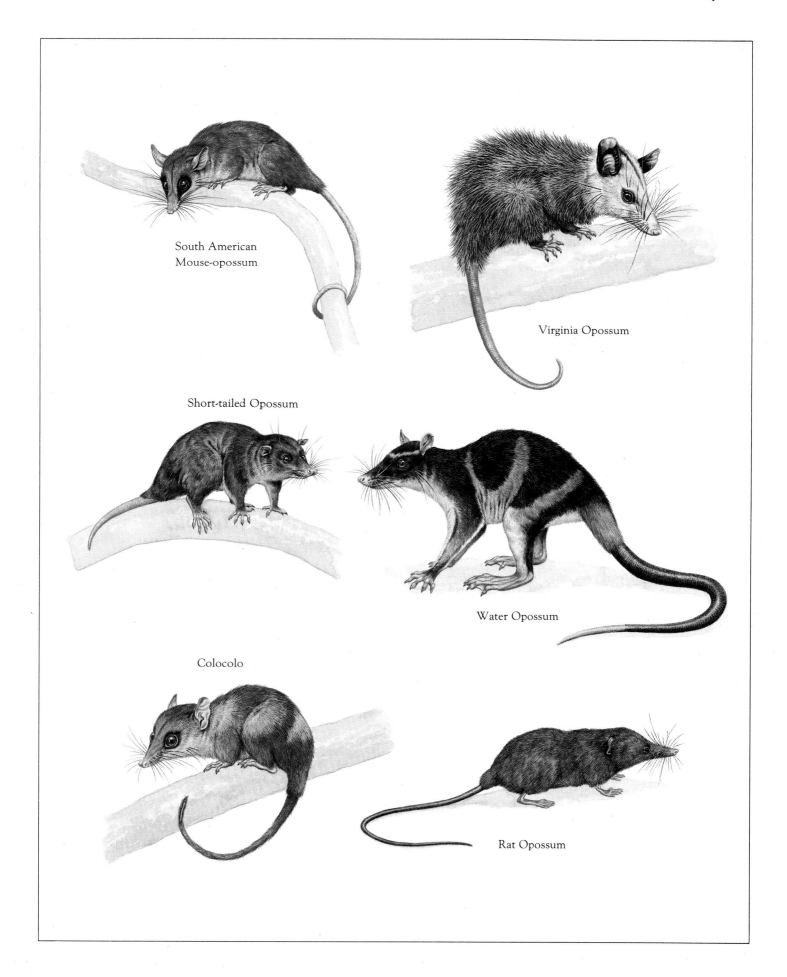

South American
Mouse-opossum

Virginia Opossum

Short-tailed Opossum

Water Opossum

Colocolo

Rat Opossum

Dasyurid Marsupials

NAME: Pygmy Planigale, *Planigale maculata*
RANGE: N. and N.E. Australia
HABITAT: arid bush and scrub
SIZE: body: 5–5.5 cm (2–2¼ in)
tail: 5.5 cm (2¼ in)

The pygmy planigale shelters in a burrow during the day and emerges at night to search for food. Although it is smaller than a white mouse, it feeds on large insects, such as grasshoppers, which it kills by biting off the head. Small birds are also caught, and in one night, a pygmy planigale may eat its own weight in food.

Little is known of the reproduction and social organization of these animals. They appear to be solitary and to give birth to up to 12 young between December and March.

NAME: Brown Antechinus, *Antechinus stuarti*
RANGE: E. seaboard of Australia
HABITAT: forest
SIZE: body: 9.5–11 cm (3¾–4¼ in)
tail: 10–12 cm (4–4¾ in)

A secretive, nocturnal animal, the brown antechinus is common in the forests surrounding Australia's major cities. It climbs well and probably searches for insect food up in eucalyptus and acacia trees.

Mating, a violent procedure in this species lasting about 5 hours, occurs in August, and a litter of 6 or 7 young is born after a gestation of 30 to 33 days. They cling to the nipples on the mother's belly until they become so large that they impede her movements; they are then left in an underground nest while she hunts. They themselves breed almost a year after birth. As a result of a hormone imbalance, males can mate only once before they die.

NAME: Mulgara, *Dasycercus cristicauda*
RANGE: central Australia
HABITAT: desert, spinifex bush
SIZE: body: 12.5–22 cm (5–8½ in)
tail: 7–13 cm (2¾–5 in)

Perfectly adapted for life in one of the world's most inhospitable environments, the mulgara never comes out of its burrow until the heat of the day has passed, and even then it tends to stay in places that have been in shadow. Its kidneys are highly developed to excrete extremely concentrated urine in order to preserve water, and it never drinks. All the mulgara's nutritional needs are provided by its prey. Insects are its staple diet, but lizards and even newborn snakes are also eaten.

Mulgaras breed from June to September, and the usual litter contains 6 or 7 young. The pouch is little more than two lateral folds of skin.

DASYURIDAE

This family of approximately 49 species contains a wide variety of marsupials, from tiny mouse-sized creatures which live on the forest floor to large, aggressive predators. Many zoologists regard it as the least advanced family of Australian marsupials because all members have fully separated digits — fused digits are a characteristic of advanced families of marsupials. Yet its success is undoubted, for representatives are found in all habitats, from desert to tropical rain forest.

Most dasyurids have poorly developed pouches and resort to carrying their young about underneath them, like bunches of grapes. Unlike the American opossums, which carry older young on their backs, dasyurids deposit their young in nests when they become too large to carry around.

NAME: Kowari, *Dasyuroides byrnei*
RANGE: central Australia
HABITAT: desert, grassland
SIZE: body: 16.5–18 cm (6½–7 in)
tail: 13–14 cm (5–5½ in)

A small marsupial, adapted for life in the desert heart of Australia, the kowari lives in underground burrows, singly or in small groups. At night, it emerges to search among the grass tussocks for insects, lizards or even small birds.

Kowaris breed in winter, from May to October, and produce litters of 5 or 6 young after a gestation of 32 days.

NAME: Fat-tailed Dunnart, *Sminthopsis crassicaudata*
RANGE: W. Australia, east to W. Queensland, W. New South Wales and W. Victoria
HABITAT: woodland, heath, grassland
SIZE: body: 8–9 cm (3–3½ in)
tail: 5.5–8.5 cm (2¼–3¼ in)

The fat-tailed dunnart, like some species of dormouse and sheep, has the ability to store fat in its tail. During the wet season, when insects and spiders are abundant, the dunnart stores excess fat in special cells at the base of its tail. These reserves are used up during periods of drought, and the tail gradually slims down. If the drought persists longer than is usual, the fat-tailed dunnart is able to enter a state of torpor, in which its body temperature falls and its meager food reserves last longer because its energy needs are less.

Young dunnarts start to breed when they are about 4 months old and produce litters at intervals of about 12 weeks. Their courtship is aggressive, and males compete in vicious fights for females in heat.

NAME: Quoll, *Dasyurus viverrinus*
RANGE: E. Australia
HABITAT: forest
SIZE: body: 35–45 cm (13¾–17¾ in)
tail: 21–30 cm (8¼–11¾ in)

The quoll is one of 4 species of cat-sized, predatory dasyurid, specialized for life as carnivores. At one time ruthlessly destroyed by poultry keepers, quolls are now known to do as much good as they do harm, by killing rodents, rabbits and invertebrate pests and helping to keep the ecological balance. Quolls live in rock piles or in hollow logs and emerge only at night to search for food.

The breeding season lasts from May to August, and up to 18 young are born after a gestation of about 14 days. The young stay in a well-developed pouch, which they leave before they are weaned at 4½ months. During the latter part of the time for which the young are dependent on their mother, they clamber all over her, clinging to her fur as she feeds. The quoll is one of the few marsupials known in which the litter size at birth is far higher than the number that can be supported. Within 48 hours of birth, 10 or more of the young will die, leaving the mother with about 8, which she can support.

NAME: Tasmanian Devil, *Sarcophilus harrisi*
RANGE: Tasmania
HABITAT: dry forest
SIZE: body: 52.5–80 cm (20½–31½ in)
tail: 23–30 cm (9–11¾ in)

This powerfully built marsupial has the reputation of being a vicious and ruthless killer of sheep; in fact, it is more of a scavenger of dead sheep than a killer of live ones. Its massive head and enormous jaws, resembling those of the hyena, allow it to smash through the bones of a carcass. Tasmanian devils live in dens in rock piles and under tree stumps and are normally nocturnal. Sometimes they emerge during the day to lie in the sun. They are more common now than they were a century or more ago, when great numbers were hunted and killed by farmers. Before the thylacine, or Tasmanian wolf, became extinct, the devils lived almost exclusively on the discarded carcasses left by that predator. Hunting may be a new way of life.

Tasmanian devils live for about 8 years and breed in the second year. A litter of about 4 young is born in early winter (May or June), and they quickly crawl into the mother's well-developed pouch, where they remain for 15 weeks. They feed on her milk until they are about 20 weeks old.

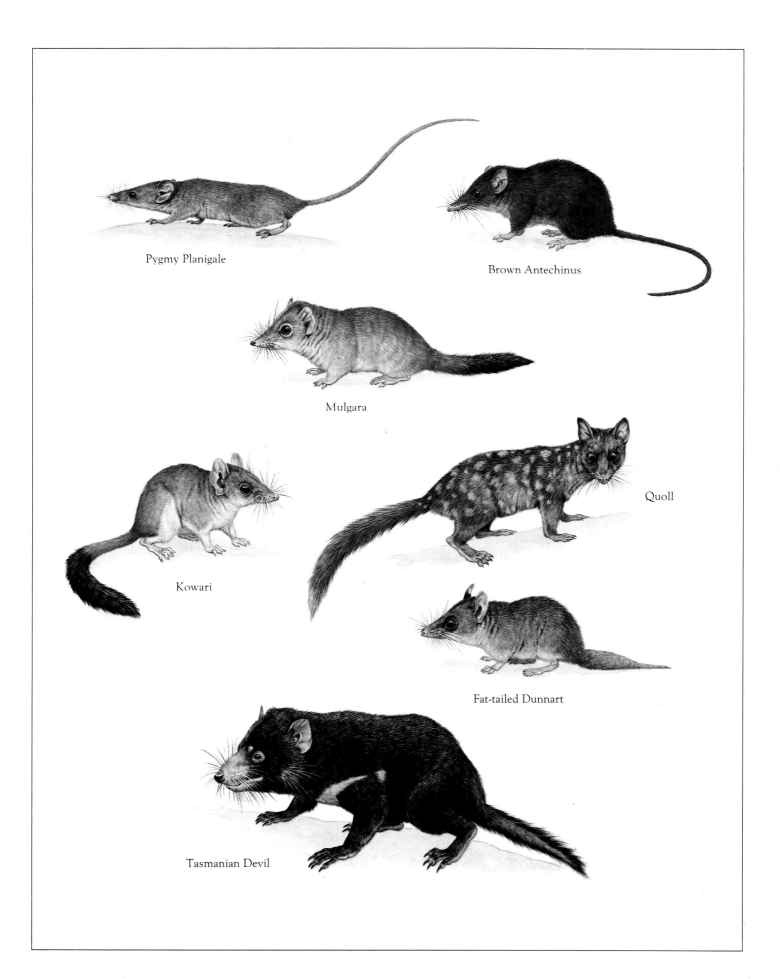

Pygmy Planigale

Brown Antechinus

Mulgara

Kowari

Quoll

Fat-tailed Dunnart

Tasmanian Devil

Numbat, Koala and other marsupials

MYRMECOBIIDAE: Numbat Family

The single species in this Australian family is a small marsupial which is adapted to the niche filled by anteaters in other parts of the world. It was formerly called the banded anteater and feeds in a similar manner to anteaters.

NAME: **Numbat,** *Myrmecobius fasciatus*
RANGE: **S.W. Australia**
HABITAT: **forest**
SIZE: **body: 17.5–27.5 cm (6¾–10¾ in)**
   tail: 13–17 cm (5–6¾ in)   Ⓔ

The numbat feeds principally on termites, although ants and some other small invertebrates are also eaten. Like the anteaters, it has a sticky tongue, about 10 cm (4 in) in length, with which it sweeps insects into its mouth. Its teeth are poorly developed and capable of doing little more than crushing and stilling the wriggling insects. A captive numbat was observed to eat 10 thousand to 20 thousand termites daily.

Between January and May, the female numbat produces a litter of 4 young. She has no pouch, so the young must cling to her nipples, and she drags them around as she searches for food.

NOTORYCTIDAE: Marsupial Mole Family

The single species in this Australian marsupial family has a clear resemblance to the placental moles and leads a similar existence.

NAME: **Marsupial Mole,** *Notoryctes typhlops*
RANGE: **S.W. Australia**
HABITAT: **desert**
SIZE: **body: 9–18 cm (3½–7 in)**
   tail: 1.25–2.5 cm (½–1 in)

The marsupial mole is superbly adapted to a burrowing way of life, having large, shovel-like forepaws, no eyes and silky fur, which helps it move easily through the sand. Unlike true moles, marsupial moles do not dig permanent burrows, for as they travel through the soft sand, the tunnel falls in immediately behind them. They feed on earthworms and other underground invertebrates, such as beetle larvae, and come to the surface quite frequently, although they move awkwardly on land.

Nothing is known of their reproductive habits, but since the pouch contains only two nipples, they presumably bear only 2 young at a time. The testes of the male marsupial mole never descend into a scrotum but remain in the body, close to the kidneys.

PHASCOLARCTIDAE: Koala Family

The single species in this family is one of Australia's best-known marsupials and also one of the most specialized for life in the trees.

During the first three decades of this century, koalas were hunted for their skins, and in 1924 alone, over 2 million were exported. Today the koala is no longer threatened, and with strict conservation measures, populations are increasing throughout its range.

NAME: **Koala,** *Phascolarctos cinereus*
RANGE: **E. Australia**
HABITAT: **dry forest**
SIZE: **body: 60–85 cm (23½–33½ in)**
   tail: vestigial

The tree-dwelling koala seldom comes down to the ground and then only to pass from one tree to another. Its diet is limited, consisting of the leaves and shoots of a few species of *Eucalyptus*. An adult will consume just over 1 kg (2¼ lb) of leaves a day.

Koalas live singly or in small groups consisting of a single male with a harem of females. They breed in summer, and the female produces a single young after a gestation of about a month. The tiny koala enters the pouch, which opens backward, and remains there for 5 or 6 months. After this period of pouch life, it rides on its mother's back. After weaning, the mother feeds her young on semidigested leaves. Many koalas suffer from the infectious fungal disease cryptococcosis, which causes lesions or abscesses in the lungs, joints and brain and which they can transfer to man, often with fatal results. It is thought that the source of the fungal infection is soil, which koalas regularly eat, apparently as an aid to digestion.

VOMBATIDAE: Wombat Family

The 3 species of wombat all live in Australia; 1 is also found in Tasmania. They are strong, powerfully built marsupials which superficially resemble badgers. With their long, bearlike claws, they excavate vast burrow systems and tear up underground roots and tubers for food. They are strictly vegetarian and often raid cultivated fields to feed on the soft, developing ears of grain.

Wombats share with koalas the curious phenomenon of a backward-opening pouch.

NAME: **Wombat,** *Vombatus ursinus*
RANGE: **E. Australia, Tasmania**
HABITAT: **forest, scrub**
SIZE: **body: 70 cm–1.2 m (27½ in–4 ft)**
   tail: vestigial

The wombat is a common forest animal along Australia's eastern seaboard and is often found at high altitudes in the Snowy Mountains. Its burrows may stretch more than 13 m (42 ft) from the entrance and go down more than 2 m (6½ ft). It is not known whether wombats are gregarious below ground, but the number of burrows occurring together suggests that they are. Above ground, the wombat follows regularly used pathways through the forest.

The female gives birth in late autumn, usually to a single young; the newborn remains in the pouch, where there are two nipples, for about 3 months. Once out of the pouch, it forages with its mother for several months before living independently. It is not unusual for wombats to live for more than 20 years.

TARSIPEDIDAE: Honey Possum Family

The only member of its family, the honey possum is a zoological enigma because it has no obvious close relatives. In general appearance it resembles the other small possums, but its feet are quite different. The second and third digits on each hind foot are totally fused, but the two tiny claws at the tip of the fused digit are evidence of its original state.

NAME: **Honey Possum,** *Tarsipes spencerae*
RANGE: **S.W. Australia**
HABITAT: **heathland with bushes and trees**
SIZE: **body: 7–8.5 cm (2¾–3¼ in)**
   tail: 9–10 cm (3½–4 in)

The honey possum feeds on pollen and nectar of the large flowers of *Banksia*, a flowering shrub found in the southwestern corner of Australia. It often hangs upside down while feeding, using its prehensile tail as a fifth limb. The tongue, with its bristly tip, resembles that of a hummingbird or nectar-feeding bat and can be extended about 2.5 cm (1 in) beyond the tip of the nose. The teeth are poorly developed, but tough ridges on the palate are used to scrape the nectar and pollen off the tongue. Occasionally the honey possum will eat small insects, discarding their tough wings.

In midwinter, the honey possums mate, and females give birth to 2 young after a gestation of about 4 weeks. The young remain in the pouch until they are about 4 months old.

18

Numbat

Marsupial Mole

Koala

Wombat

Honey Possum

Bandicoots, Phalangers, Pygmy Possums, Ringtails

PERAMELIDAE: Bandicoot Family
There are about 17 species of bandicoot, widely distributed over Australia and New Guinea in a range of habitats from desert to rain forest. All have long, powerful claws on their forefeet and are good diggers.

NAME: **Gunn's Bandicoot, *Perameles gunni***
RANGE: **Australia: S. Victoria; Tasmania**
HABITAT: **woodland, heathland**
SIZE: **body: 25–40 cm (9¾–15¾ in)**
tail: 7.5–18 cm (3–7in)

Like most bandicoots, Gunn's bandicoot is a very aggressive, belligerent creature which lives alone. Males occupy large territories and consort with females for only as long as is necessary for mating. Primarily a nocturnal animal, it emerges from its nest at dusk to forage for earthworms and other small invertebrates. Probing deep into the soil with its long nose, the bandicoot digs eagerly when a food item is located.

Although the female bandicoot has 8 nipples, she seldom produces more than 4 or 5 young. The gestation period of 11 days is one of the shortest of any mammal and is followed by 8 weeks in the pouch.

NAME: **Brown Bandicoot, *Isoodon obesulus***
RANGE: **S. Australia, Queensland; Tasmania**
HABITAT: **scrub, forest**
SIZE: **body: 30–35 cm (11¾–13¾ in)**
tail: 7.5–18 cm (3–7 in)

The brown bandicoot occurs in areas of dense ground cover and can survive in quite dry places, as long as it has somewhere to hide from eagles and foxes. It appears to locate prey, such as earthworms and beetle larvae, by scent and leaves small conical marks with its long nose as it forages about. Ant larvae and subterranean fungi are also eaten, as well as scorpions.

Reproduction is closely linked to the local rainfall pattern, and many brown bandicoots breed all year round. A litter of up to 5 young is born after an 11-day gestation and is weaned at 2 months.

THYLACOMYIDAE:
Rabbit-bandicoot Family
Only a single species survives of this family, the lesser rabbit-bandicoot, *Macrotis leucura*, having become extinct within the last century. The remaining species is extremely rare, and stringent conservation measures are in force.

NAME: **Rabbit-bandicoot, *Macrotis lagotis***
RANGE: **central and N.W. Australia**
HABITAT: **woodland, arid scrub**
SIZE: **body: 20–55 cm (7¾–21½ in)**
tail: 11.5–27.5 cm (4½–10¾ in) Ⓔ

The rabbit-bandicoot lives alone in a burrow system, which it excavates with its powerful forepaws. The burrow descends 2 m (6½ ft) or more, and the bandicoot is thus protected from the heat of the day. After dark, when the air is cool, the rabbit-bandicoot emerges to feed on termites and beetle larvae, which it digs from the roots of wattle trees. It may also eat some of the fungi that grow around the roots.

Courtship is brief and aggressive, as with most bandicoots. The 3 young are born between March and May and spend 8 weeks in the pouch.

PHALANGERIDAE:
Phalanger Family
The 12 species in this family occur in Australia, New Guinea and Sulawesi. The totally Australian species are known as possums, those from the islands are called phalangers. All species are about the size of domestic cats and are tree-dwelling and nocturnal. They have a prehensile tail, used as a fifth limb when climbing. Leaves, gum from wattle trees and insects are their main foods, but small birds and lizards may also be eaten if available.

NAME: **Brush-tailed Possum, *Trichosurus vulpecula***
RANGE: **Australia, Tasmania; introduced into New Zealand**
HABITAT: **forest, woodland**
SIZE: **body: 32–58 cm (12½–22¾ in)**
tail: 24–35 cm (9½–13¾ in)

The brush-tailed possum is the only native marsupial to have benefited from man's encroachment on virgin land, for it has become adapted to living near habitation and to feeding on refuse. In natural conditions, it eats young shoots, flowers, leaves and fruit, with some insects and young birds.

Breeding occurs once or twice a year, normally with 1 young in each litter. The gestation period is 17 days, and the young possum then stays in the pouch for about 5 months.

BURRAMYIDAE:
Pygmy Possum Family
There are 7 species of these tiny, mouse-sized possums in Australia and New Guinea. All are arboreal, often living in the tallest trees.

NAME: **Pygmy Glider, *Acrobates pygmaeus***
RANGE: **E. and S.E. Australia**
HABITAT: **dry forest**
SIZE: **body: 6–8.5 cm (2¼–3¼ in)**
tail: 6.5–8.5 cm (2½–3¼ in)

The pygmy glider lives at the top of tall forest trees and has evolved a flight membrane, which enables it to glide from one tree to another. As it leaps, the flaps of skin between wrists and heels are stretched out, and the featherlike tail provides directional stability. The tips of its digits are broad and deeply furrowed to help it cling to surfaces on landing. It feeds on insects, gum, nectar and pollen.

The litter of 2 to 4 young is born in July or August.

PETAURIDAE: Ringtail Family
There are about 22 species of ringtail, in Australia and New Guinea. They are tree-dwellers and make good use of the prehensile abilities of their long tails.

NAME: **Sugar Glider, *Petaurus breviceps***
RANGE: **E. and N. Australia; New Guinea**
HABITAT: **woodland**
SIZE: **body: 11–15 cm (4¼–6 in)**
tail: 12–18 cm (4¾–7 in)

The habit of feeding on the sugary sap that oozes from any wound inflicted on the bark of wattle and gum trees is the origin of this animal's common name. Sugar gliders regularly damage the bark of such trees and return for several days running to lick up the exudates. They are sociable animals, which live in groups of up to 20 in holes in trees. With their gliding membranes outstretched, they can glide for up to 55 m (180 ft), flipping upward at the end of the descent to land, head upward, on a tree trunk.

A litter of 2 or 3 young is born after a 21-day gestation. They leave the pouch when 3 to 4 months old.

NAME: **Greater Glider, *Schoinobates volans***
RANGE: **E. Australia**
HABITAT: **forest**
SIZE: **body: 30–48 cm (11¾–18¾ in)**
tail: 45–55 cm (17¾–21½ in)

The largest of Australia's gliding marsupials, the greater glider can weigh up to 1.4 kg (3 lb). It lives in holes high up in the trees, and feeds exclusively on leaves and shoots. Greater gliders can glide 100 m (330 ft) or more from tree to tree, moving their long bushy tails to steer themselves.

In midwinter, the female gives birth to 1 young, which then spends 4 months in the pouch.

Gunn's Bandicoot

Brown Bandicoot

Rabbit-bandicoot

Brush-tailed Possum

Pygmy Glider

Sugar Glider

Greater Glider

Kangaroos

NAME: Musk Rat-kangaroo,
Hypsiprymnodon moschatus
RANGE: Australia: N.E. Queensland
HABITAT: rain forest
SIZE: body: 23.5–33.5 cm ($9\frac{1}{4}$–$13\frac{1}{4}$ in)
tail: 13–17 cm (5–$6\frac{3}{4}$ in)

The musk rat-kangaroo is a unique member of its family in two ways: first, it has a well-formed first digit, or thumb, on each hind foot, and second, it is the only kangaroo regularly to give birth to twins. It is also unusual in other respects; for example, it often moves around on four legs in the manner of a rabbit. Both male and female produce a pungent musky odor, but the reason for this is not known. Their diet includes a wide range of plant matter, from palm berries to root tubers, and they also eat insects and earthworms.

Little is known of the social habits of the musk rat-kangaroos, but they seem to move singly or in pairs. The young are usually born in the rainy season (February to May), but this can vary.

NAME: Potoroo, *Potorous tridactylus*
RANGE: E. Australia, S.W. corner of
W. Australia; Tasmania
HABITAT: low, thick, damp scrub
SIZE: body: 30–40 cm ($11\frac{3}{4}$–$15\frac{3}{4}$ in)
tail: 15–24 cm (6–$9\frac{1}{2}$ in)

Despite its small size and rabbitlike appearance, the potoroo has all the characteristics of reproduction and the gait of the larger kangaroos. Although it may occasionally move on all fours, it usually bounds along on its strong hind legs, covering 30 to 45 cm ($11\frac{3}{4}$ to $17\frac{3}{4}$ in) with each hop. It is nocturnal, emerging at dusk to forage for plants, roots, fungi and insects.

Potoroos breed at any time of year, and the single young spends 17 weeks in the pouch.

NAME: Rufous Rat-kangaroo,
Aepyprymnus rufescens
RANGE: E. Australia: Queensland to
N.E. Victoria
HABITAT: grassland, woodland
SIZE: body: 38–52 cm (15–$20\frac{1}{2}$ in)
tail: 35–40 cm ($13\frac{3}{4}$–$15\frac{3}{4}$ in)

The largest of the rat-kangaroos, the rufous rat-kangaroo builds a grassy nest in which to spend the heat of the day. It has little fear of man and will enter foresters' camps and even feed from the hand. This lack of fear makes the animals vulnerable to attack by introduced dogs and red foxes, and while their populations are in no immediate danger, the future survival of these little kangaroos is a cause for concern. They breed slowly — a maximum of 2 young a year — but nothing more is known of their breeding habits.

MACROPODIDAE:
Kangaroo Family

There are about 57 species of kangaroo, and the family is regarded by most authorities as the most advanced of all the 15 surviving families of marsupials, for both the teeth and feet are greatly modified. The hind feet are extremely large — the origin of the family's scientific name — and the thumb is totally absent; digits 2 and 3 are slender and bound together by skin; digit 4 is massive and armed with a long, tough claw, and digit 5 is only a little smaller. A kangaroo has fewer teeth than other marsupials, and these are high-crowned and deeply folded. They are similar to those of the placental mammals of the family Bovidae (sheep and cattle). Most kangaroos eat only plant matter, but some of the small species also feed on invertebrates.

The main characteristic of kangaroos is their method of moving on two legs. They make a series of great bounds, during which the long hind legs propel the body forward with considerable force. The long, powerful tail acts as a counterbalance, providing the necessary stability when they land. Although hopping may seem an awkward form of locomotion, at speeds of more than 20 km/h (12 mph), it is more efficient in terms of energy use than quadrupedal running. Kangaroos often have to travel long distances to find food, so speed and efficiency are important, and the selective pressures for fast movement are great.

Members of the kangaroo family occur in Australia and New Guinea and also in Tasmania and the Bismarck Islands. Some are forest-dwellers, but others live in extremely hot, arid areas, and during the worst of the day's heat they seek the shade of a rocky outcrop and regularly salivate over their upper arms to aid evaporative cooling. If intense drought continues for so long that the females can no longer make milk for their young, the sucklings are expelled from the pouch and perish. When the rains arrive and food supplies return, a reserve embryo, which has been held in a suspended state of development, is implanted in the uterus, and a new pregnancy begins without the female having to mate again. In this way, kangaroos cope successfully with their harsh environment. Most kangaroos produce only 1 young at a time. Males and females generally look alike, except for the pouch structure of the female; in some of the larger species, the male is slightly larger than his mate.

NAME: Red-legged Pademelon,
Thylogale stigmatica
RANGE: Australia: E. Queensland,
E. New South Wales
HABITAT: wet forest
SIZE: body: 53–62 cm ($20\frac{3}{4}$–$24\frac{1}{2}$ in)
tail: 32–45 cm ($12\frac{1}{2}$–$17\frac{3}{4}$ in)

The red-legged is one of 3 species of pademelon, all of which are solidly built forest-dwellers, slightly heavier in the hindquarters than the graceful kangaroos of the open plains. They are adaptable creatures which can occupy a variety of habitats, provided there is plenty of cover. At dusk, they emerge to forage for leaves, buds, shoots and fruit. Pademelons sometimes occur in herds, but there are also solitary individuals.

A single young is the rule, although twins have been recorded.

NAME: Spectacled Hare-wallaby,
Lagorchestes conspicillatus
RANGE: N. and central Australia
HABITAT: desert grassland
SIZE: body: 40–50 cm ($15\frac{3}{4}$–$19\frac{3}{4}$ in)
tail: 35–45 cm ($13\frac{3}{4}$–$17\frac{3}{4}$ in)

There are 4 species of small hare-wallaby living in the arid and desert grasslands of Australia. They make rough, grassy nests among the tough spinifex vegetation and, if disturbed, behave much like hares, leaping off in a zigzag manner. The spectacled hare-wallaby leads a solitary life, only coming together with another for mating. This isolation is necessary because of the extreme difficulty of eking out an existence in the inhospitable environment.

A single young is produced at any time of year and is itself sexually mature at about a year old.

NAME: Ring-tailed Rock Wallaby,
Petrogale xanthopus
RANGE: central and E. Australia
HABITAT: rocky outcrops, boulder piles
SIZE: body: 50–80 cm ($19\frac{3}{4}$–$31\frac{1}{2}$ in)
tail: 40–70 cm ($15\frac{3}{4}$–$27\frac{1}{2}$ in) $\circledV$

Long exploited for its high-quality fur, the ring-tailed rock wallaby is now found in only a few isolated areas. It is the most handsomely marked of the rock wallabies, all of which live in the most inhospitable regions of the outback. Like all rock wallabies, its feet, with broad, soft pads and strong claws, are adapted for scrambling around on the rocks, and it is remarkably agile. Its long tail does not have a thickened base and is not used as a prop as in true kangaroos. Rock wallabies feed on whatever plant material they can find.

Breeding takes place throughout the year, but if drought conditions persist too long, the rock wallabies sacrifice any young in their pouches.

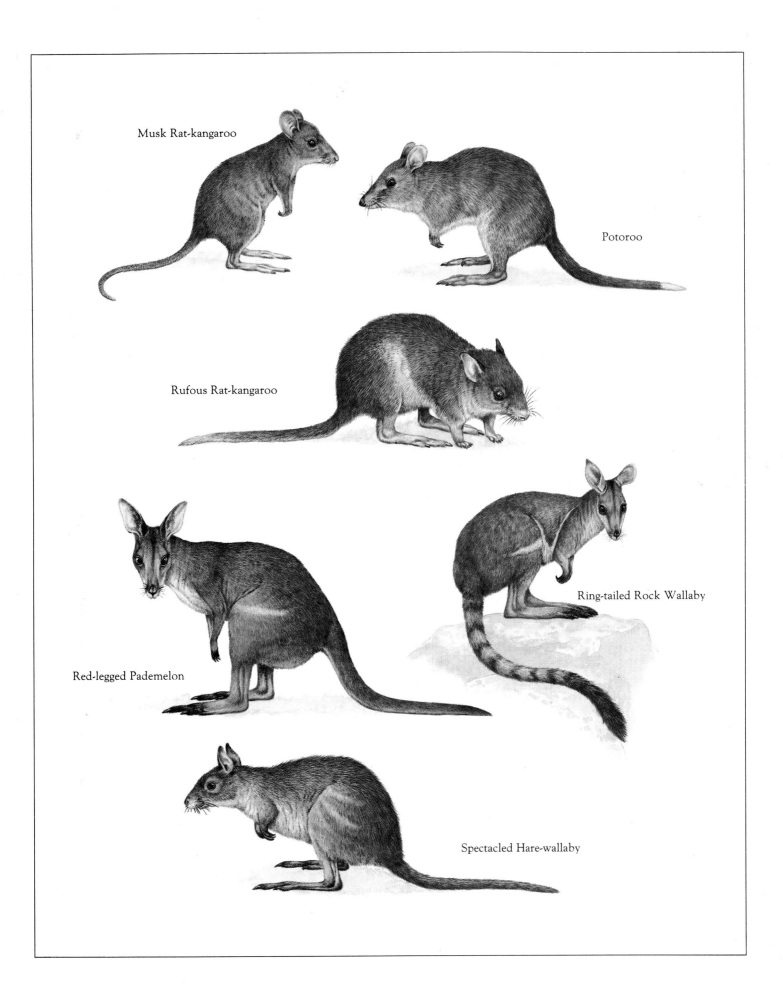

Musk Rat-kangaroo

Potoroo

Rufous Rat-kangaroo

Red-legged Pademelon

Ring-tailed Rock Wallaby

Spectacled Hare-wallaby

Kangaroos

NAME: Quokka, *Setonyx brachyurus*
RANGE: S.W. Australia
HABITAT: dense vegetation
SIZE: body: 47.5–60 cm (18¾–23½ in)
tail: 25–35 cm (9¾–13¾ in)

The quokka was once widespread over the southwest of Australia, but shooting for sport quickly reduced the population to a low level. Today the quokka occurs in only a few swampy valleys in the Darling Range, near Perth, but it is abundant on Rottnest and Bald islands, just off the coast. Quokkas have a good nose for fresh water: on Rottnest Island they travel as far as 2.5 km (1½ mi) to find it. They have learned to scavenge on refuse dumps for food in times of drought and sparse plant supply, and are also able to supplement their protein intake by utilizing urea, a urinary waste product. In this respect, they resemble desert mammals.

The female quokka gives birth to 1 tadpole-sized young after a gestation of 17 days and mates again the following day. The embryo resulting from this second mating is held free in the uterus and will implant and start development only after the earlier offspring has left the pouch. Quokkas first breed when about 2 years old.

It is to be hoped that the development of Rottnest Island as an important recreational site for the people of Perth can be achieved without destroying the habitat of this intelligent little wallaby.

NAME: Lumholtz's Tree Kangaroo, *Dendrolagus lumholtzi*
RANGE: Australia: N.E. Queensland
HABITAT: forest
SIZE: body: 52–80 cm (20½–31½ in)
tail: 42–93 cm (16½–36½ in)

Only 3 species of kangaroo, 2 of which occur in Australia and a third in New Guinea, have taken to life in the trees. Unlike most arboreal mammals, they have few adaptations for this specialized way of life; their hind feet are singularly undeveloped for climbing, but their front feet are better adapted for grasping than those of other kangaroos. They are, however, remarkably agile in trees, and their long tails, although not prehensile, give considerable stability. Grass, leaves and fruit are their main foods, and they frequently climb backward down trees to the ground to graze.

Small groups live together and sleep in the same tree. Little is known of their breeding habits other than that they produce 1 young at any time of year. Tree kangaroos are not rare, but their secretive way of life and the denseness of their forest habitat make them hard to observe.

NAME: Red Kangaroo, *Macropus rufus*
RANGE: central Australia
HABITAT: grassy arid plains
SIZE: body: 1–1.6 m (3¼–5¼ ft)
tail: 90 cm–1.1 m (35½ in–3½ ft)

The red kangaroo is the largest living marsupial; an old male can attain a weight of about 70 kg (154 lb). Only the male sports the deep russet-red coat; the female has a bluish-gray coat and is often referred to as the "blue flier." Red kangaroos live on the arid grassland of the desert in small herds, which consist of an adult male and several females. During the heat of the day, they shelter by rocky outcrops or in the shade of stunted trees and emerge during the evening to feed and drink. Although, weight for weight, kangaroos eat as much as sheep, they convert their food more efficiently — a kangaroo is 52 percent meat, a sheep 27 percent.

Breeding occurs throughout the year, and the gestation lasts 30 to 40 days. A few hours before the birth, the mother starts to clean and nuzzle at her pouch. Sitting back, with her tail bent forward between her hind legs, and holding the pouch open with her forelimbs, she licks it inside and out, often continuing until the moment of birth. The newborn offspring weighs only 0.75 gm (1/40 oz) and is 1/30,000 of its mother's weight. Although so tiny, it has well-developed front claws, which it uses to clamber up from the mother's genital opening to the pouch. Once safely in the pouch, it takes one of the nipples into its mouth. The nipple grows with the baby and is about 10 cm (4 in) long at the time of weaning. The quality of the mother's milk changes as the baby grows, becoming richer and more fatty during the later phase of lactation.

The young kangaroo spends about 240 days in the pouch and then accompanies its mother for a further 120 days, occasionally putting its head into her pouch to suck, even though it may contain a younger sibling. During intense drought conditions, most pouch young (known as "joeys") will die, but the loss is made up from a stock of reserve embryos carried in the mother's uterus.

Until recently, red kangaroos were hunted on a massive scale, but this is now subject to strict controls.

NAME: New Guinea Forest Wallaby, *Dorcopsis veterum*
RANGE: New Guinea
HABITAT: lowland rain forest
SIZE: body: 49–80 cm (19¼–31½ in)
tail: 30–55 cm (11¾–21½ in)

In most respects, the New Guinea forest wallaby appears to resemble the Australian pademelons, but very little is known of this species. One difference is that the tip of the tail is armed with a few broad, tough scales, the function of which remains a mystery.

Whenever possible, forest wallabies feed on grass, but they also eat a variety of other plant materials. They are seldom observed by day and may lie up in leafy nests until dusk. Nothing is known of their breeding habits, except that only 1 young is carried at a time.

NAME: Bridled Nail-tailed Wallaby, *Onychogalea fraenata*
RANGE: Australia: central Queensland
HABITAT: thick scrub
SIZE: body: 45–67 cm (17¾–26¼ in)
tail: 33–66 cm (13–26 in) Ⓔ

The 3 species of nail-tailed wallaby derive their name from a scale, like a small fingernail, hidden in the thick hair at the tip of the long, thin tail. Its function is unknown. In the middle of the nineteenth century, the bridled nail-tailed wallaby was abundant over much of eastern and southeastern Australia, but in this century, it was unrecorded for several decades until a population was discovered in central Queensland, in 1974. Competition by rabbits for food, predation by red foxes and hunting are major causes of its decline. Conservation measures are in hand and will need to be applied for many years if this species is to survive in the wild.

Thick scrub is used for food and cover by nail-tailed wallabies. Nothing is known of their breeding habits except that they produce 1 young at a time.

NAME: Swamp Wallaby, *Wallabia bicolor*
RANGE: E. and S.E. Australia
HABITAT: dense thickets, rocky gullies
SIZE: body: 45–90 cm (17¾–35½ in)
tail: 33–60 cm (13–23½ in)

Swamp wallabies occur in small herds but are often hard to see because of their habit of lying down when danger threatens. Only when the danger is imminent do the wallabies break cover and scatter in different directions with explosive speed. Their diet is varied, and they readily switch from one plant species to another. This flexibility means that they can become pests of agricultural crops, and some measure of control is often necessary locally.

Breeding takes place throughout the year, and the female produces 1 young, which stays in her pouch for about 300 days. It continues to feed for 60 days after leaving the pouch.

Quokka

Red Kangaroo

Lumholtz's Tree Kangaroo

New Guinea Forest Wallaby

Bridled Nail-tailed Wallaby

Swamp Wallaby

Anteaters, Sloths

ORDER EDENTATA

This order includes 3 families of mammals, all of which exhibit evolutionary tooth reduction or loss in connection with their specialized diet of insects such as ants and termites. The families are the anteaters, the sloths and the armadillos. The name of the order means, appropriately, "the toothless ones."

MYRMECOPHAGIDAE:
Anteater Family

There are 4 species of anteater, found in Mexico and Central and South America as far south as northern Argentina. They normally inhabit tropical forests but also occur in grassland. All forms have extremely elongate snouts and no teeth. Their tongues are long and covered with a sticky salivary secretion, which enables them to trap insects easily. The anteaters break into ant or termite nests by means of their powerful clawed forefeet, each of which has an enlarged third digit. The largest species, the giant anteater, is ground-dwelling, while the other, smaller species are essentially arboreal.

NAME: **Giant Anteater,** *Myrmecophaga tridactyla*
RANGE: **Central America, South America to N. Argentina**
HABITAT: **forest, savanna**
SIZE: **body: 1–1.2 m (3¼–4 ft)**
   tail: 65–90 cm (25½–35½ in)   Ⓥ

The largest of its family, the remarkable giant anteater has a long snout, a distinctive black stripe across its body and a bushy, long-haired tail. Using its powerful foreclaws, the anteater demolishes ant or termite mounds and feeds on huge quantities of the insects and their eggs and larvae. Its long tongue can be extended as much as 61 cm (24 in) and is covered with sticky saliva, so insects adhere to it. As it wanders in search of food supplies, the anteater walks on its knuckles, thus protecting the sharp foreclaws. Unlike other anteaters, it does not climb trees, although it readily enters water and can swim. Except for females with young, giant anteaters usually live alone. In areas far from human habitation, the giant anteater is active in the daytime, but nearer human dwellings, it is active only at night.

The female produces 1 young after a gestation of about 190 days. The offspring is carried on the mother's back and stays with her until her next pregnancy is well advanced.

NAME: **Tamandua,** *Tamandua mexicana*
RANGE: **S. Mexico, through Central and South America to Bolivia and Brazil**
HABITAT: **forest**
SIZE: **body: 54–58 cm (21¼–22¾ in)**
   tail: 54.5–55.5 cm (21½–21¾ in)

A tree-dwelling animal, this anteater is smaller than its giant relative and has a prehensile tail, which it uses as a fifth limb; the underside of the tail is naked, which improves its grip. On the ground, the tamandua moves slowly and clumsily. It is active mainly at night, when it breaks open the nests of tree-living ants and termites and feeds on the insects. Like all anteaters, it has a long, protrusible tongue, which is covered with sticky saliva, enabling it to trap its prey. If attacked, it will strike out at its adversary with its powerful foreclaws.

The female gives birth to 1 young; the length of the gestation is unknown. The youngster is carried on its mother's back but may be set down on a branch while she feeds.

NAME: **Two-toed Anteater,** *Cyclopes didactylus*
RANGE: **S. Mexico, through Central and South America to Bolivia and Brazil**
HABITAT: **forest**
SIZE: **body: 15–18 cm (6–7 in)**
   tail: 18–20 cm (7–7¾ in)

An arboreal animal, the two-toed anteater climbs with agility, using its prehensile tail and long feet with special joints, which enable the claws to be turned back under the foot when grasping branches so that they do not become blunted. This anteater rarely comes down to the ground but sleeps in a hollow tree or on a branch during the day and is active at night, searching for ants and termites. Like its relatives, it uses its sharp, powerful foreclaws for breaking into ant and termite nests and its long, sticky tongue for gobbling up the insects. These anteaters are themselves often attacked by large birds of prey.

Little is known about the two-toed anteater's breeding habits. The female produces 1 young, which both parents feed on regurgitated insects.

BRADYPODIDAE: Sloth Family

The 5 species of sloth all live in tropical forests of Central and South America. These highly adapted mammals are so specialized for life in the trees that they are unable to walk normally on the ground. However, most of their life is spent among the branches, where they hang upside down by means of their curved, hooklike claws. They feed on plant material.

NAME: **Three-toed Sloth,** *Bradypus tridactylus*
RANGE: **Honduras, south to Brazil, Paraguay and N. Argentina**
HABITAT: **forest**
SIZE: **body: 50–60 cm (19¾–23½ in)**
   tail: 6.5–7 cm (2½–2¾ in)

The three-toed sloth is so well adapted to living upside down, hanging from branches by its hooklike claws, that its hair grows in the opposite direction from that of other mammals and points downward when the sloth is hanging in its normal position. Each of the outer hairs is grooved, and microscopic green algae grow in these grooves, giving the sloth a greenish tinge which helps to camouflage it amid the foliage. This sloth's head is short and broad and its neck particularly mobile — it has two more neck vertebrae than normal for mammals — allowing great flexibility of head movement. It climbs slowly, moving one limb at a time, and swims quite well but can move on the ground only by dragging its prone body forward with its hooked limbs. Sloths rarely come to the ground, but the three-toed sloth does descend about once a week to defecate in a hole it makes with its tail. Leaves and tender buds, particularly those of *Cecropia* trees, are the three-toed sloth's main foods. Its sight and hearing are poorly developed, and it depends on smell and touch for finding food.

The female produces 1 young after a gestation of 120 to 180 days; she even gives birth hanging in the trees. The offspring is suckled for about a month and then fed on regurgitated food.

NAME: **Two-toed Sloth,** *Choloepus didactylus*
RANGE: **Venezuela, N. Brazil, Guyana, Suriname, French Guiana**
HABITAT: **forest**
SIZE: **body: 60–64 cm (23½–25¼ in)**
   tail: absent or vestigial

The two-toed sloth eats, sleeps, gives birth and even defecates while hanging upside down in the trees by means of its hooklike claws. On each forefoot are two digits, closely bound together with skin, each of which bears a large, curved claw. Although all its movements are extremely slow, it can strike out quickly to defend itself and can inflict a serious wound with its claws. On the ground, it can only drag itself along, but it swims easily. Mainly active at night, the two-toed sloth sleeps during the day, keeping still to avoid detection by enemies. It feeds on leaves, twigs and fruit.

The female gives birth to a single offspring after a gestation of at least 263 days. The young sloth clings to its mother while she hangs in the trees.

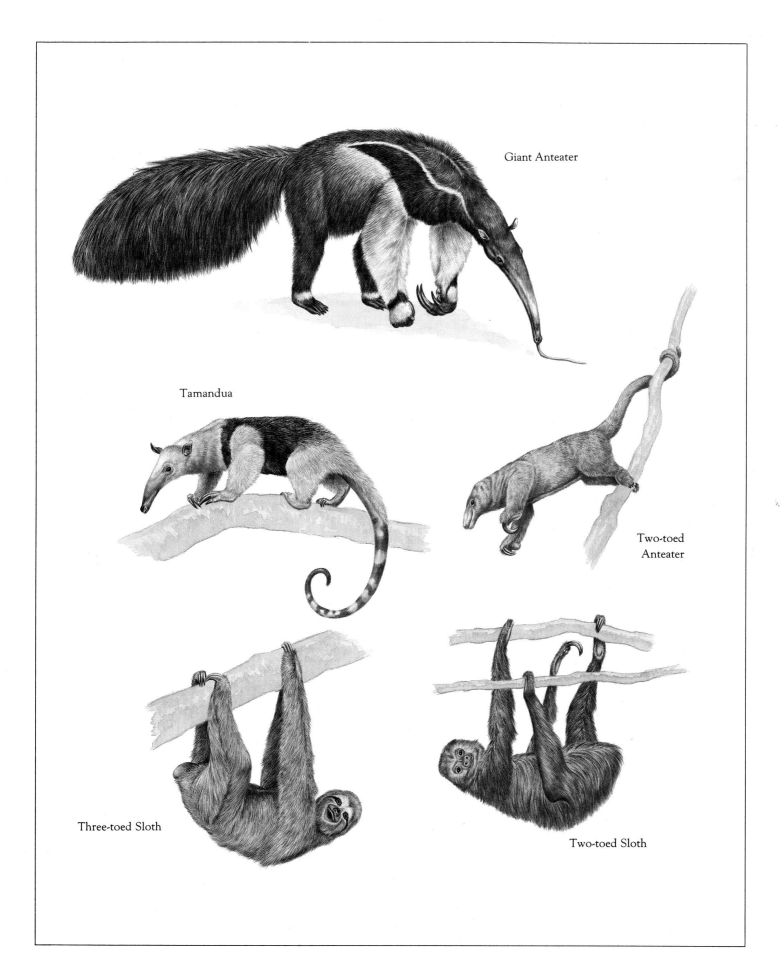

Giant Anteater

Tamandua

Two-toed Anteater

Three-toed Sloth

Two-toed Sloth

Armadillos, Pangolins, Aardvark

DASYPODIDAE: Armadillo Family

The 20 species of armadillo all occur in the New World, from the southern states of the USA through Central and South America to Chile and Argentina.

Armadillos are digging animals, usually active at night. Their skin is dramatically modified to form extremely tough, hornlike, articulated plates, which cover the top of the tail, back, sides, ears and front of the head and provide the animal with excellent protection. Some armadillo species can curl themselves up into a ball so that their limbs and vulnerable underparts are protected by the armor.

NAME: Giant Armadillo, *Priodontes maximus*
RANGE: Venezuela to N. Argentina
HABITAT: forest
SIZE: body: 75 cm–1 m (29½ in–3¼ ft)
**   tail: 50 cm (19¾ in)** Ⓥ

The largest of its family, the giant armadillo may weigh up to 60 kg (132 lb). Its body is armored with movable horny plates, and there are only a few hairs on the skin between the plates. There may be as many as 100 small teeth, but these are gradually shed with age. The claws on the forefeet are particularly long, those on the third digits measuring as much as 20 cm (7¾ in). A fairly agile animal, the giant armadillo can support itself on its hind legs and tail while digging or smashing a termite mound with its powerful forelimbs. It feeds on ants, termites and other insects and also on worms, spiders, snakes and carrion. If attacked, it can only partially roll itself up and is more likely to flee.

The breeding habits of this armadillo are little known. The female produces 1 or 2 young.

NAME: Nine-banded Armadillo, *Dasypus novemcinctus*
RANGE: S. USA, through Central and South America to Uruguay
HABITAT: arid grassland, semidesert
SIZE: body: 45–50 cm (17¾–19¾ in)
**   tail: 25–40 cm (9¾–15¾ in)**

The most common, widespread armadillo, this species has 8 to 11, usually 9, bands of horny plates across its body. It spends the day in a burrow, which may house several individuals, and emerges at night to root about in search of food. It digs with its powerfully clawed forefeet or investigates holes and crevices with its tapering snout to find food such as insects, spiders, small reptiles, amphibians and eggs.

A litter nearly always consists of 4 young, which the mother suckles for about 2 months.

NAME: Pink Fairy Armadillo, *Chlamyphorus truncatus*
RANGE: central W. Argentina
HABITAT: dry sandy plains
SIZE: body: 12.5–15 cm (5–6 in)
**   tail: 2.5 cm (1 in)** Ⓥ

This tiny armadillo, with its pale pink armor, emerges from its burrow at dusk to feed on ants in particular but also on worms, snails and plant material. It digs with its forefeet and supports its rear on its rigid tail, thus freeing its hind limbs for kicking away earth. It has five claws on each foot. These little armadillos have proved difficult to keep in captivity, and their breeding habits are not known.

ORDER PHOLIDOTA
MANIDAE: Pangolin Family

The pangolin family is the only one in its order; it contains 7 species of nocturnal ant- and termite-eating animals, found in Africa, southern Asia and Southeast Asia. The typical pangolin has the same general body shape as that of the American giant anteater but is covered with enormous overlapping scales, like the bracts of a pinecone. The scales are movable and sharp edged. The pangolin has no teeth in its elongate head but does have an extremely long, protrusible tongue, with which it catches its prey.

NAME: Giant Pangolin, *Manis gigantea*
RANGE: Africa: Senegal, east to Uganda, south to Angola
HABITAT: forest, savanna
SIZE: body: 75–80 cm (29½–31½ in)
**   tail: 50–65 cm (19¾–25½ in)**

The largest of its family, the giant pangolin is a ground-dwelling, nocturnal animal. The female is smaller than the male. This pangolin sleeps by day in a burrow and is active mainly between midnight and dawn, when it searches for various species of ants and termites. Using its powerful foreclaws, it can break into nests above or below ground. Its movements are slow and deliberate, and it can walk on its hind limbs, its long tail helping it to balance, or on all fours; it can also swim. If threatened, the giant pangolin can roll itself into a ball, a ploy that protects it from most enemies. If necessary, however, it will lash out with its sharp-scaled tail and spray urine and anal gland secretions.

There is 1 young, born in an underground nest after a gestation of about 5 months. The newborn pangolin has soft scales, which harden in about 2 days. After a month or so, the youngster accompanies its mother on feeding trips, sitting on the base of her tail.

NAME: Tree Pangolin, *Manis tricuspis*
RANGE: Africa: Senegal to W. Kenya, south to Angola
HABITAT: rain forest
SIZE: body: 35–45 cm (13¾–17¾ in)
**   tail: 49–60 cm (19¼–23½ in)**

On its back, this pangolin has distinctive scales with three pronounced points on their free edge. In older animals the points of the scales become worn. An adept climber, the tree pangolin has a very long prehensile tail, with a naked pad on the underside of the tip that aids grip. During the day, it sleeps on the branch of a tree or in a hole, which it digs in the ground, and emerges at night to feed on tree-dwelling ants and termites, which it detects by smell. It tears open arboreal nests with its powerful forelimbs and sweeps up the insects with deft movements of its long tongue. Like all pangolins, it shows a strong preference for particular species of ant and termite and will reject others. The food is ground down in the pangolin's muscular, horny-surfaced stomach.

The female gives birth to a single young after a gestation of 4 to 5 months. Its scales harden after a couple of days, and at 2 weeks of age, it starts to go on feeding trips with its mother.

ORDER TUBULIDENTATA
ORYCTEROPODIDAE:
Aardvark Family

There is one family in this order, containing a single species that lives in Africa. Its relationship to other mammal groups is obscure. The aardvark's teeth are unique, quite unlike those of any other mammal: they have no enamel and consist of dentine columns, interspersed with tubes of pulp.

NAME: Aardvark, *Orycteropus afer*
RANGE: Africa, south of the Sahara
HABITAT: all regions with termites, from rain forest to dry savanna
SIZE: body: 1–1.6 m (3¼–5¼ ft)
**   tail: 44.5–60 cm (17½–23½ in)**

The aardvark is a solitary, nocturnal, insect-eating animal. Its sight is poor, but its other senses are excellent; it has large ears, which are normally held upright but can be folded and closed, and highly specialized nostrils for sniffing out its prey. Dense hair surrounding the nostrils seals them off when the aardvark digs. The animal uses its powerful forelimbs to smash down the nests of the ants and termites that are its main foods. It sweeps up the prey with its long, sticky tongue.

The female gives birth to a single young after a gestation of 7 months. The offspring is suckled for 4 months.

Giant Armadillo

Nine-banded Armadillo

Pink Fairy Armadillo

Giant Pangolin

Tree Pangolin

Aardvark

Tenrecs, Solenodons

ORDER INSECTIVORA

This order includes about 344 species found all over the world, except in Australia and the southern half of South America. Most are ground-dwelling or burrowing animals which feed on insects and invertebrates.

TENRECIDAE: Tenrec Family

This family of insectivores includes the 30 species of shrewlike or hedgehoglike tenrecs, all restricted to Madagascar and the nearby Comoro Islands, and the 3 West African otter shrews. Tenrecs are a most interesting family zoologically because they have become adapted to a number of different ways of life: *Tenrec* resembles the North American opossum; *Setifer*, the hedgehogs; *Microgale*, the shrews; and *Oryzorictes* has several molelike characteristics.

All tenrecs retain some reptilian features, regarded as primitive in mammals, such as the cloaca, where the urogenital and anal canals open into a common pouch.

NAME: **Tailless Tenrec,** *Tenrec ecaudatus*
RANGE: **Madagascar, Comoro Islands**
HABITAT: **brushland, dry forest clearings, highland plateaus**
SIZE: **body: 27–39 cm (10½–15¼ in)**
   tail: 10–16 mm (½–¾ in)

The tailless tenrec has a superficial resemblance to a hedgehog, with its sparse coat set with stiff hairs and spines. It is active at night, probing rotting vegetation and leaf litter for insects, worms and roots. Fruit, too, forms part of its diet. In the dry season, tailless tenrecs hibernate in deep burrows which they plug behind them with soil. Prior to hibernation, the tenrec builds up its brown fat reserves to sustain it through the 6-month sleep.

In early October, immediately after hibernating, the tenrecs mate and produce a litter of up to 25 young in November; usually about 16 survive.

NAME: **Greater Hedgehog Tenrec,** *Setifer setosus*
RANGE: **Madagascar**
HABITAT: **dry forest, highland plateaus**
SIZE: **body: 15–19 cm (6–7½ in)**
   tail: 10–16 mm (½–¾ in)

The greater hedgehog tenrec is set with short sharp spines, which cover its back like a dense, prickly mantle. If disturbed, it rolls itself into a tight ball while emitting a series of squeaks and grunts. The female produces a litter of up to 6 young in January. Like baby hedgehogs, the young have soft spines at birth, but by 2 weeks old the spines have hardened.

NAME: **Streaked Tenrec,** *Hemicentetes semispinosus*
RANGE: **Madagascar**
HABITAT: **scrub, forest edge**
SIZE: **body: 16–19 cm (6¼–7½ in)**
   tail: vestigial

Although less densely spined than the hedgehog tenrec, this species can still protect itself by partially curling up. When alarmed, a small patch of heavy spines in the middle of the back is vibrated rapidly, making a clicking noise. Striped tenrecs do not hibernate, but they do remain inactive during spells of cool weather. Like other tenrecs, they feed on insects and other invertebrates. Females are sexually mature at 8 weeks and produce a litter of 7 to 11 young between December and March after a gestation of at least 50 days.

NAME: **Shrew Tenrec,** *Microgale longicaudata*
RANGE: **Madagascar**
HABITAT: **forest: sea level to montane**
SIZE: **body: 5–15 cm (2–6 in)**
   tail: 7.5–17 cm (3–6½ in)

The shrew tenrec, as its name implies, occupies the ecological niche filled by shrews in other parts of the world. The coat is short, but dense, and quite lacking in the spines so common in this family. Although it climbs well and the distal third of its long tail is prehensile, the shrew tenrec seems to feed mostly on grubs, worms and small insects on the forest floor. Like shrews, these tenrecs are active at all hours of the day and night, but each individual maintains its own pattern of rest and activity. Little is known of the breeding habits; shrew tenrecs are believed to produce litters of 2 to 4 young. They do not appear to hibernate.

NAME: **Rice Tenrec,** *Oryzorictes hova*
RANGE: **Madagascar**
HABITAT: **marshy areas**
SIZE: **body: 8–13 cm (3–5 in)**
   tail: 3–5 cm (1¼–2 in)

Rice tenrecs, so called because they occupy the banks beside rice fields, spend most of their lives underground; their forelimbs are well adapted for digging. They feed on invertebrates, but there is some evidence that they also eat mollusks and crustaceans. Although seen above ground only at night, they may be active underground at all hours. Nothing is known of their breeding habits, but they are sufficiently abundant to achieve pest status in the rice-growing areas of Madagascar.

NAME: **Giant Otter Shrew,** *Potomogale velox*
RANGE: **W. and central equatorial Africa**
HABITAT: **streams: sea level to 1,800 m (6,000 ft)**
SIZE: **body: 29–35 cm (11½–14 in)**
   tail: 24–29 cm (9½–11½ in)

Although geographically separated from the other tenrecs, the 3 otter shrews are believed to be a subfamily of the Tenrecidae. The giant otter shrew is, overall, the largest living insectivore and does bear a strong superficial resemblance to the otter, with its flattened head and heavy tail. Its coat is dense with a glossy overlayer of guardhairs.

Giant otter shrews live in burrows with entrances below water level. They emerge at dusk to hunt for crabs, fish and frogs, which they pursue through the water with great agility. They live solitary lives but consort in pairs shortly before mating. Litters of 2 to 3 young are born throughout the year.

SOLENODONTIDAE: Solenodon Family

There are 2 species only of solenodons alive today: *Solenodon cubanus* on Cuba and *S. paradoxus* on the neighboring island of Hispaniola. They are rather ungainly, uncoordinated creatures and, although the size of rats, look more like shrews with their probing snouts. Their eyes are small and rheumy, and they are far more nocturnal than the wide-eyed rats.

Solenodons grow and breed slowly, and this, combined with the predatory attacks of introduced dogs and cats, means that their survival is now threatened. Conservation areas are being established for these animals, but their future is far from secure.

NAME: **Cuban Solenodon,** *Solenodon cubanus*
RANGE: **Cuba**
HABITAT: **montane forest**
SIZE: **body: 28–32 cm (11–12½ in)**
   tail: 17–25 cm (6½–10 in)   ®

Solenodons have a varied diet. At night they search the forest floor litter for insects and other invertebrates, fungi and roots. They climb well and feed on fruits, berries and buds but have more predatory habits too. With venom from modified salivary glands in the lower jaw, the solenodon can kill lizards, frogs, small birds or even rodents. Solenodons seem not to be immune to the venom of their own kind, and there are records of cage mates dying after fights. They produce litters consisting of 1 to 3 young.

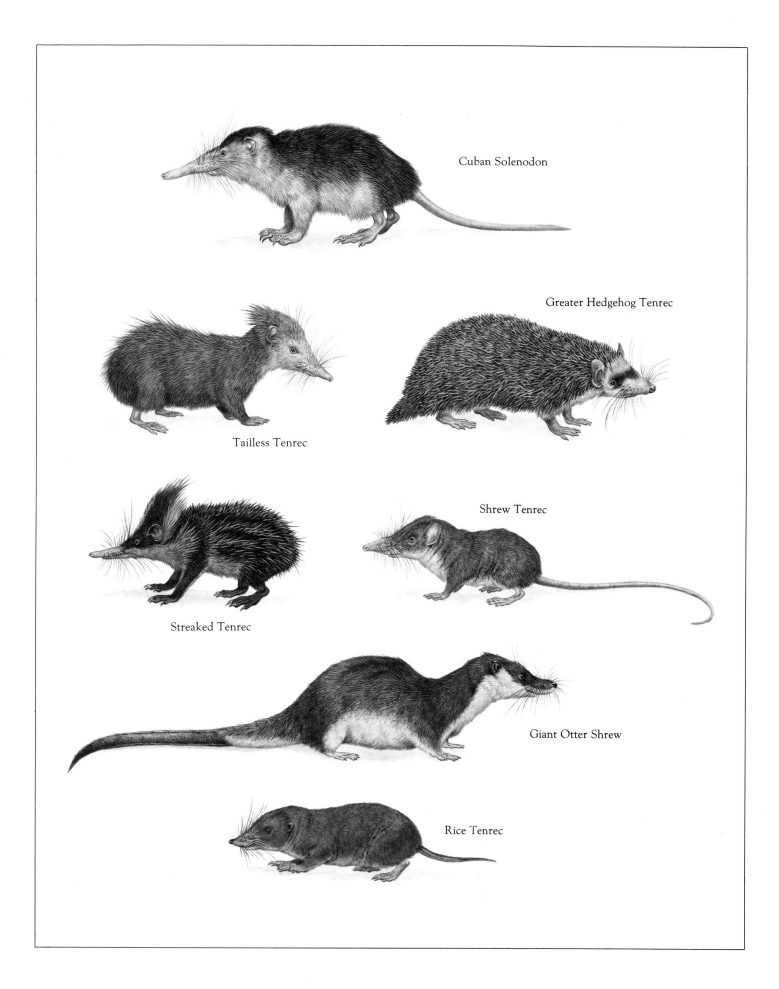

Cuban Solenodon

Greater Hedgehog Tenrec

Tailless Tenrec

Shrew Tenrec

Streaked Tenrec

Giant Otter Shrew

Rice Tenrec

Golden Moles, Hedgehogs

CHRYSOCHLORIDAE: Golden Mole Family

Golden moles bear a close resemblance to the true moles but are, in fact, only distantly related. They have cylindrical bodies, short powerful limbs and no visible tail. Their fur is thick and dense, and the metallic luster it imparts gives the group its name. Golden moles are blind, their eyes being reduced to mere vestiges covered by fused hairy eyelids. The shovel-like paws on their forelimbs are used for digging, and the enlarged flattened claws on the "index" and middle digits act as cutting edges.

The 17 species of golden mole are found only in Africa, south of a line linking Cameroon with Tanzania. They occur in all types of habitat from rugged mountainous zones to sandy plains.

NAME: Cape Golden Mole, *Chrysochloris asiatica*
RANGE: Zaire, E. Africa, Zimbabwe to western Cape Province
HABITAT: workable soil up to 2,800 m (9,000 ft)
SIZE: body: 9–14 cm (3½–5½ in)
tail: absent

The Cape golden mole is a frequent visitor to gardens and farmland in much of southern Africa. Its presence is usually revealed by raised, cracked tunnel tracks radiating outward from a bush or shed. At night golden moles may travel on the surface, and in damp weather they root about for beetles, worms and grubs.

Once a year, in the rainy season, females produce litters of 2 to 4 young. Shortly before the birth, the mother makes a round, grass-lined nest in a special breeding chamber. The young suckle for almost 3 months until their teeth erupt.

NAME: Hottentot Golden Mole, *Amblysomus hottentotus*
RANGE: W. South Africa
HABITAT: sand or peat plains
SIZE: body: 8.5–13 cm (3¼–5 in)
tail: absent

The Hottentot golden mole differs from other species in that it has only two claws on each forepaw. When these animals occur in orchards and young plantations, their burrowing may seriously disturb roots and kill the trees, but generally they do more good than harm by eating insects, beetle larvae and other invertebrate pests.

Pairs breed between November and February when rainfall is high; they produce a litter of 2 young.

NAME: Giant Golden Mole, *Chrysospalax trevelyani*
RANGE: South Africa: eastern Cape Province
HABITAT: forest
SIZE: body: 20–24 cm (8–9½ in)
tail: absent ®

As its name implies, the giant golden mole is the largest of its family and weighs up to 1.5 kg (3¼ lb). It is a rare species and on the brink of extinction.

Giant golden moles frequently hunt above ground for beetles, small lizards, slugs and giant earthworms. When disturbed they dart unerringly toward their burrow entrance and safety, but how they are able to locate it is not known. During the winter rainy season, they are believed to produce a litter of 2 young.

ERINACEIDAE: Hedgehog Family

This family contains 17 species of two superficially quite distinct types of animal: the hedgehogs and the gymnures, or moonrats. Members of the hedgehog subfamily occur right across Europe and Asia to western China and in Africa as far south as Angola. Moonrats live in Indo-China, Malaysia, Borneo, the Philippines and northern Burma. All feed on a varied diet of worms, insects and mollusks, as well as some berries, frogs, lizards and birds.

In the northern part of their range, hedgehogs hibernate during the winter months, but in warmer areas this is not necessary.

NAME: Western European Hedgehog, *Erinaceus europaeus*
RANGE: Britain, east to Scandinavia and Romania; introduced in New Zealand
HABITAT: scrub, forest, cultivated land
SIZE: body: 13.5–27 cm (5½–10½ in)
tail: 1–5 cm (½–2 in)

One of the most familiar small mammals in Europe, the hedgehog gets its name from its piglike habit of rooting around for its invertebrate prey in the hedgerows. It is quite vocal and makes a range of grunting, snuffling noises. The upper part of the head and the back are covered in short, banded spines. If threatened, the hedgehog rolls itself up, and a longitudinal muscle band, running around the edge of the prickly cloak, acts as a drawstring to enclose the creature within its spiked armor. The chest and belly are covered with coarse, springy hairs.

Hedgehogs produce one, sometimes two, litters of about 5 young each year; the young are weaned at about 5 weeks. In the north of their range, hedgehogs hibernate throughout the winter.

NAME: Desert Hedgehog, *Paraechinus aethiopicus*
RANGE: N. Africa, Middle East to Iraq
HABITAT: arid scrub, desert
SIZE: body: 14–23 cm (5½–9 in)
tail: 1–4 cm (½–1½ in)

The desert hedgehog resembles its slightly larger European cousin, but its coloration is more variable. Generally the spines are sandy-buff with darker tips, but dark and white forms are not uncommon. Desert hedgehogs dig short, simple burrows in which they pass the day. At night, when the air is cool, they emerge to search for invertebrates and the eggs of ground-nesting birds. Scorpions are a preferred food; the hedgehogs nip off the stings before eating them. In common with most desert mammals, these hedgehogs probably have highly adapted kidneys, enabling them to exist for long periods without water.

In July or August desert hedgehogs breed, producing a litter of about 5 young.

NAME: Moonrat, *Echinosorex gymnurus*
RANGE: Cambodia, east to Burma
HABITAT: forest, mangrove swamps
SIZE: body: 26–44 cm (10–17¼ in)
tail: 20–21 cm (8–8¼ in)

One of the largest insectivores, the moonrat has a long snout, an unkempt appearance and an almost naked, scaly tail. It can defend itself by producing a foul, fetid odor from a pair of anal glands which repels all but the most persistant predators. Moonrats live in crevices between tree roots or in hollow logs; they emerge around dusk to forage for mollusks, insects and worms. Some fruit, and fish and crabs too, may be eaten. Little is known of the moonrat's breeding habits, but they seem to breed throughout the year, producing 2 young at a time.

NAME: Mindanao Moonrat, *Podogymnura truei*
RANGE: Philippines: Mindanao
HABITAT: upland forest and forest edge at 1,600–2,300 m (5,250–7,500 ft)
SIZE: body: 13–15 cm (5–6 in)
tail: 4–7 cm (1½–2¾ in) Ⓥ

This curious creature is restricted to a small natural range and has never been common. Now, because of logging operations and slash-and-burn agriculture, much of its habitat is being destroyed, and its survival is seriously threatened. It has long soft fur and a tail with more hairs than that of *Echinosorex*. It feeds on insects, worms and even carrion, which it finds in grasses and among stands of moss. Nothing is known of the breeding habits of Mindanao moonrats.

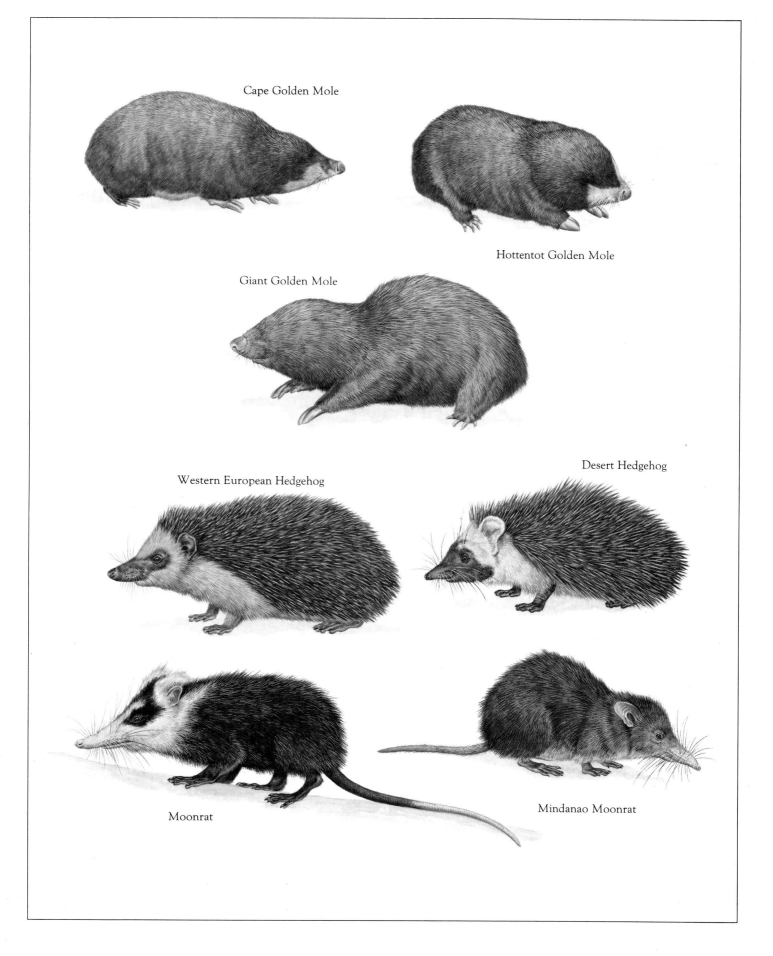

Cape Golden Mole

Hottentot Golden Mole

Giant Golden Mole

Desert Hedgehog

Western European Hedgehog

Moonrat

Mindanao Moonrat

Shrews

NAME: Masked Shrew, *Sorex cinereus*
RANGE: northern N. America to New Mexico
HABITAT: moist forest
SIZE: body: 4.5–9.5 cm (1¾–3¾ in)
  tail: 2.5–8 cm (1–3 in)

The masked shrew is a common species throughout North America, though less abundant in the arid regions to the south. It inhabits the surface layer of forest, living in and around burrows made by itself and other woodland animals. It is active day and night, with about seven periods of feeding activity in each 24 hours. Earthworms and snails are preferred foods, but masked shrews eat a wide range of invertebrate prey.

Generally solitary animals, male and female pair only for mating. Several litters of up to 10 young are born during the late spring and summer. The young are weaned after about a month, but the family may remain together for another month, the only time during which these shrews are sociable.

NAME: Short-tailed Shrew, *Blarina brevicauda*
RANGE: E. USA
HABITAT: almost all terrestrial habitats
SIZE: body: 7.5–10.5 cm (3–4 in)
  tail: 1.5–3 cm (½–1¼ in)

This abundant and widespread species is unusual in two ways: first, it seems to be partly gregarious since, in captivity, it seeks out the company of other shrews; second, it often climbs trees for food — most shrews climb only rarely.

In much of the USA, the short-tailed shrew is an important controlling influence on larch sawflies and other destructive forest pests on which it feeds. It builds a grassy nest under a stump or log and produces three or four litters a year of up to 9 young each. The gestation period is 17 to 21 days.

NAME: Merriam's Desert Shrew, *Megasorex gigas*
RANGE: W. coastal strip of Mexico
HABITAT: rocky or semidesert, dry forest
SIZE: body: 8–9 cm (3–3½ in)
  tail: 4–5 cm (1½–2 in)

Merriam's desert shrew has large prominent ears. In common with most desert mammals, it is active only at night, when it emerges from crevices between boulders or under rocks to search for insects and worms. Although it eats up to three-quarters of its own weight every 24 hours, it seems only to feed at night, unlike other shrews which feed throughout the period. Its breeding habits are not known.

SORICIDAE: Shrew Family

There are more than 200 species of shrew, distributed throughout most of the world, except Australia and New Zealand, the West Indies and most of South America. Shrews are insectivores, and most lead inoffensive lives among the debris of the forest floor or on pastureland, consuming many types of invertebrate. Water shrews are known to overpower frogs and small fish, which they kill with venomous bites — the saliva of many shrews contains strong toxins. Carrion may also be included in the shrew's diet.

Shrews are active creatures with high metabolisms. Their hearts may beat more than 1,200 times every minute, and, relative to their body size, they have enormous appetites. Even in cold northern regions, they do not hibernate in winter; it would be impossible for them to build up sufficient reserves. Although shrews are heavily preyed upon by owls and hawks, acrid-smelling secretions from well-developed flank glands seem to deter most mammalian predators.

Some species of shrew are reported to eat their own feces and perhaps those of other creatures. By doing so, they boost their intake of vitamins B and K and some other nutrients. This habit may be related to the shrews' hyperactive life and enhanced metabolism. Shrews rely heavily on their senses of smell and hearing when hunting; their eyes are tiny and probably of little use.

NAME: Ceylon Long-tailed Shrew, *Crocidura miya*
RANGE: Sri Lanka
HABITAT: damp and dry forest, savanna
SIZE: body: 5–6.5 cm (2–2½ in)
  tail: 4–4.5 cm (1½–1¾ in)

This shrew, with its long, lightly haired tail, spends much of its life among the debris of the forest floor, where damp, cool conditions encourage a rich invertebrate population on which it feeds. It also eats small lizards and young birds on occasion. Strong-smelling scent glands seem to protect the shrew itself from much predation.

The breeding season of the long-tailed shrew lasts from March until November; a female produces about five litters in this time, each of about 6 young. After 8 days, the young leave the nest for the first time, each gripping the tail of the one in front in its mouth as the caravan, led by the mother, goes in search of food. This habit seems to be restricted to this genus of shrews.

NAME: Pygmy White-toothed Shrew, *Suncus etruscus*
RANGE: S. Europe, S. Asia, Africa
HABITAT: semiarid grassland, scrub, rocky hillsides
SIZE: body: 3.5–5 cm (1¼–2 in)
  tail: 2.5–3 cm (1–1¼ in)

Usually regarded as the world's smallest terrestrial mammal, a fully grown pygmy shrew weighs about 2 g (1/14 oz). How such a tiny mammal can survive is not fully understood, but it must have a constant and reliable source of food, and that is one reason why it is restricted to the warmer parts of the Old World. Its coat is dense to prevent undue heat loss from its tiny body.

Pygmy shrews feed on spiders and insects almost as large as themselves, including grasshoppers and cockroaches. Nothing is known of their breeding habits, but they remain quite abundant, and it may be that their small size protects them from heavy predation, since they share their habitat with larger, more tempting species.

NAME: Mouse Shrew, *Myosorex varius*
RANGE: South Africa, north to the Limpopo
HABITAT: moist areas, forest, scrub, river banks
SIZE: body: 6–11 (2¼–4¼ in)
  tail: 3–5.5 cm (1¼–2¼ in)

Perhaps the most primitive of existing shrews, the mouse shrew has two more teeth in its lower jaw than normal and thus resembles the extinct early mammals, although otherwise it is like most shrews. Mouse shrews do not appear to make or use burrows but seek holes and hollows for daytime shelter. Nests of shredded grass are made for sleeping and for use as nurseries. Females produce up to six litters a year of 2 to 4 young each.

NAME: Armored Shrew, *Scutisorex somereni*
RANGE: Africa: Uganda, near Kampala
HABITAT: forest
SIZE: body: 12–15 cm (4¾–6 in)
  tail: 7–9.5 cm (2¾–3¾ in)

One of the most puzzling members of the shrew family, the armored shrew has a spine which is fortified and strengthened by a mesh of interlocking bony flanges and rods. Despite this, it moves much like other shrews, although its predatory behavior is characterized by rather ponderous and apparently well-thought-out movements. There are reports that an armored shrew can support the weight of a grown man without being crushed.

Armored shrews appear to eat plant material and invertebrates. They are believed to breed throughout the year.

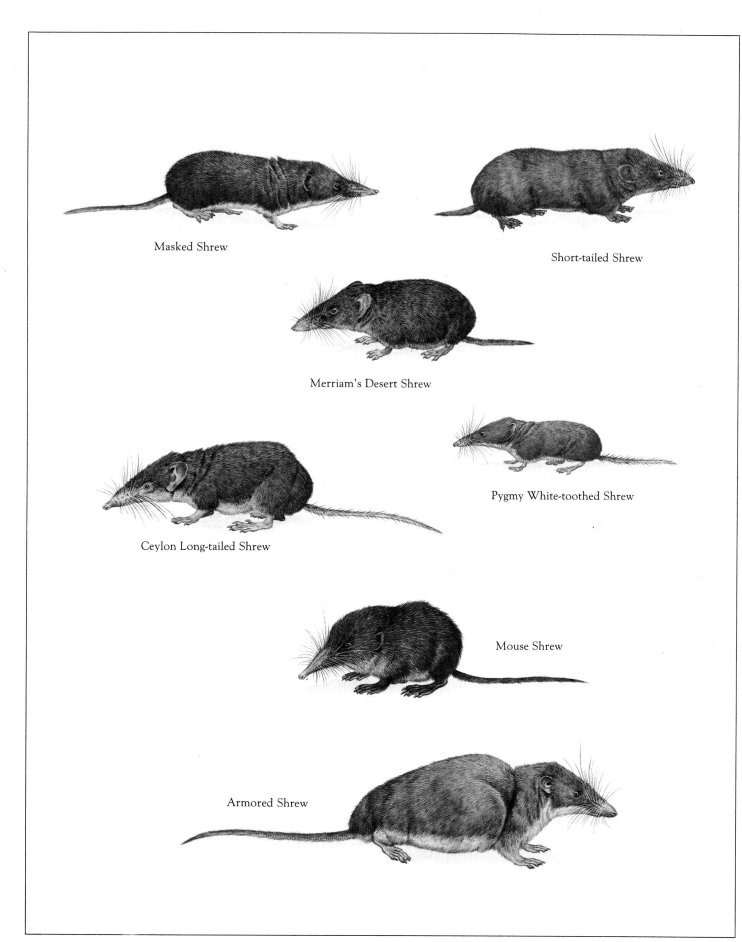

Masked Shrew

Short-tailed Shrew

Merriam's Desert Shrew

Pygmy White-toothed Shrew

Ceylon Long-tailed Shrew

Mouse Shrew

Armored Shrew

Moles, Elephant Shrews, Flying Lemurs

TALPIDAE: Mole Family

The majority of the 20 species of mole lead an underground life, but 2 species of desman and the star-nosed mole are adapted for an aquatic life. Moles are widespread throughout Europe and Asia, south to the Himalayas, and from southern Canada to northern Mexico. They need habitats with soft soil so that they are able to dig their extensive burrow systems.

All moles have highly modified hands and forearms, which act as pickax and shovel combined. Moles seldom come above ground, and their eyes are tiny and covered with hairy skin. Their tactile sense is highly developed, however, and their facial bristles respond to the tiniest vibrations. Moles can move backward or forward with equal ease — when reversing, the stumpy tail is held erect, and the sensory hairs on it provide warning of any approaching danger.

NAME: **Coast Mole,** *Scapanus orarius*
RANGE: **N. America: British Columbia to Baja California**
HABITAT: **well-drained deciduous forest**
SIZE: **body: 11–18.5 cm (4¼–7¼ in)**
   tail: 2–5.5 cm (¾–2¼ in)

The coast, or Pacific, mole, and its close relatives, the broad-footed mole and Townsend's mole, all have nostrils which open upward. Their eyes are much more visible than those of other species, but this does not necessarily mean that their sight is better. Like other moles, they live underground and rarely venture up to the surface.

Coast moles feed on earthworms and soil-dwelling larvae and do much good by devouring the larvae of insect pests. Between 2 and 5 young are born in early spring after a 4-week gestation.

NAME: **European Mole,** *Talpa europaea*
RANGE: **Europe, E. Asia**
HABITAT: **pasture, forest, scrub**
SIZE: **body: 9–16.5 cm (3½–6½ in)**
   tail: 3–4 cm (1¼–1½ in)

The extensive burrow systems in which European moles live are excavated rapidly: a single individual can dig up to 20 m (66 ft) in one day. The moles feed primarily on earthworms but also eat a wide range of other invertebrates, as well as snakes, lizards, mice and small birds.

In early summer the female produces a litter of up to 7 young, born in a leaf-lined underground nest and weaned at about 3 weeks. Occasionally there is a second litter.

NAME: **Hairy-tailed Mole,** *Parascalops breweri*
RANGE: **S.E. Canada, N.E. USA**
HABITAT: **well-drained soil in forest or open land**
SIZE: **body: 11.5–14 cm (4½–5½ in)**
   tail: 2–3.5 cm (¾–1½ in)

As its name implies, this species is characterized by its almost bushy tail. Otherwise it is similar to other moles in habits and appearance. Hairy-tailed moles dig extensive tunnels at two levels: an upper level just beneath the surface, used in warm weather, and a lower tunnel, used as a winter retreat. The moles mate in early April and litters of 4 or 5 young are born in mid-May.

The eastern mole, *Scalopus aquaticus*, also a North American species, closely resembles the hairy-tailed, but has a nearly naked tail.

NAME: **Star-nosed Mole,** *Condylura cristata*
RANGE: **S.E. Canada, N.E. USA**
HABITAT: **any area with damp soil**
SIZE: **body: 10–12.5 cm (4–5 in)**
   tail: 5.5–8 cm (2¼–3¼ in)

This species of mole has a fringe of 22 fingerlike tentacles surrounding the nostrils, which it uses to search for food on the bottoms of ponds and streams. Although star-nosed moles dig and use tunnel systems, they seldom feed within them. They are excellent swimmers and divers and feed largely on aquatic crustaceans, small fish, water insects and other pond life. Their fur is heavy and quite waterproof. The female gives birth to a litter of 2 to 7 young in spring. The young are born with well-developed nostril tentacles.

NAME: **Russian Desman,** *Desmana moschata*
RANGE: **E. Europe to central W. Asia**
HABITAT: **pools and streams in densely vegetated areas**
SIZE: **body: 18–21.5 cm (7–8½ in)**
   tail: 17–21.5 cm (6¾–8½ in) Ⓥ

The largest member of the mole family, the desman has forsaken the underground for the aquatic life, although it does excavate short burrows as bank-side residences. When swimming, the desman's flattened tail acts as a rudder and propulsive force; its webbed feet, supplied with fringing hairs, make most effective paddles. Desmans feed on a variety of aquatic life from fishes and amphibians to insects, crustaceans and mollusks.

Now much reduced in numbers, this species is the subject of intensive conservation measures, and there are projects to reintroduce desmans into parts of their former range where they have been eliminated.

MACROSCELIDIDAE: Elephant Shrew Family

The 16 species of African elephant shrews have extraordinary trunklike noses. They remain a zoological enigma and are classified among the Insectivora on account of their dentition.

NAME: **Elephant Shrew,** *Macroscelides proboscideus*
RANGE: **Africa: Namibia, South Africa: Cape Province**
HABITAT: **plains, rocky outcrops**
SIZE: **body: 9.5–12.5 cm (3¾–5 in)**
   tail: 9.5–14 cm (3¾–5½ in)

The abundant elephant shrews are active by day and night. They catch and eat termites and sometimes dig burrows into termite mounds. Seeds, fruit and berries, too, are part of their diet, and to reach these the elephant shrews hop and jump from twig to branch on their powerful hind legs, using their long tails as counterbalances.

A litter of 1 or 2 well-developed young is born during the rainy season. The young can walk and jump almost as soon as they are born and appear to suckle for only a few days.

ORDER DERMOPTERA CYNOCEPHALIDAE: Flying Lemur Family

There are only 2 species of flying lemur, or colugo, and, like elephant shrews, they are a puzzle, having characteristics of lemurs and of insectivores. For this reason they have their own order.

NAME: **Philippine Flying Lemur/Colugo,** *Cynocephalus volans*
RANGE: **Philippines**
HABITAT: **forest**
SIZE: **body: 38–42 cm (15–16½ in)**
   tail: 22–27 cm (8¾–10½ in)

The flying lemur "flies" with the aid of its gliding membrane, or patagium, which stretches from the neck to the wrists and ankles and to the tip of the tail. With limbs and membrane outstretched, the flying lemur can glide through the trees for up to 135 m (450 ft). Almost helpless on the ground, it is an agile climber and feeds on shoots, buds, fruit and flowers from a great range of forest trees. Its great enemy is the Philippine eagle, which feeds almost exclusively on flying lemurs.

In February flying lemurs mate, and after a 2-month gestation, the female gives birth to a single young, occasionally to twins. She carries her young with her until it grows too large and heavy.

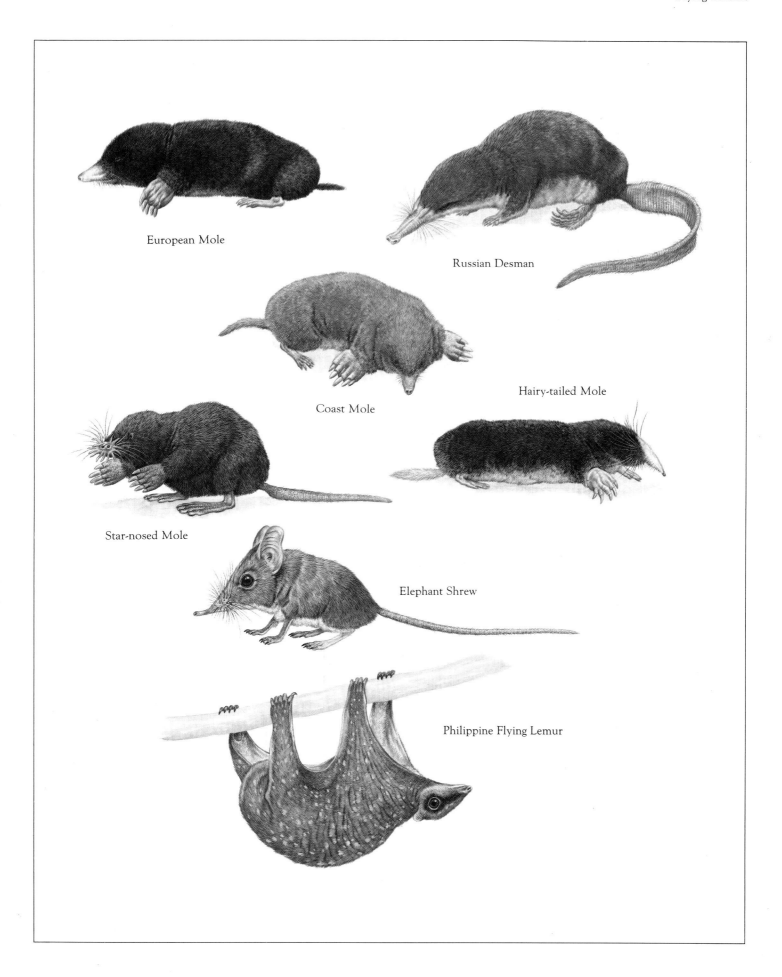

European Mole

Russian Desman

Coast Mole

Hairy-tailed Mole

Star-nosed Mole

Elephant Shrew

Philippine Flying Lemur

Old World Fruit Bats

NAME: Greater Fruit Bat, *Pteropus giganteus*
RANGE: S. and S.E. Asia
HABITAT: forest, scrub
SIZE: body: 35–40 cm (13¾–15¾ in)
   wingspan: 1.5 m (5 ft)
   tail: absent

The wingspan of the greater fruit bat is the largest of any bat. It is a highly sociable creature and roosts by day in large trees in flocks of several thousand. At dusk the flocks take to the air and disperse in search of food. The bat crushes fruit between its peglike teeth to obtain the juice and spits out the seeds and flesh. Soft flesh, such as banana, is swallowed.

There is no general breeding season for this species, but in each part of its huge range births are more or less synchronized. One young is born after a gestation of about 6 months and is carried about by its mother until it is 8 weeks old.

NAME: Hammer-headed Bat, *Hypsignathus monstrosus*
RANGE: Africa: the Gambia to Uganda and Angola
HABITAT: mangrove and other swamps
SIZE: body: 25–30 cm (10–12 in)
   wingspan: 70–95 cm (27–37 in)
   tail: absent

The hammer-headed bat derives its name from a curious nasal swelling, the function of which remains a mystery. It is one of the noisiest bats; males gather in special trees and chorus to one another for hours.

Hammer-headed bats roost in small numbers. They feed on the juices of mangoes and soursops and may also have carnivorous tendencies. Females produce a single young after a gestation of 5½ months.

NAME: Dog Bat, *Rousettus aegyptiacus*
RANGE: Africa, east to India and Malaysia
HABITAT: forest; caves, tombs, temples
SIZE: body: 11–13 cm (4¼–5 in)
   wingspan: 30–45 cm (12–18 in)
   tail: 1.5 cm (½ in)

Dog bats roost deep in caves or tombs and seem to rely on echolocation for flight navigation in these places. They are the only fruit bats to use this phenomenon, so important to the insectivorous bats. They feed on fruit juices and flower nectar and play a useful role as pollinators.

The breeding season of dog bats is from December to March. Females produce 1 young after a gestation of 15 weeks. The young bat clings to its mother and is transported everywhere until it can itself fly. It begins to feed on fruit at the age of 3 months.

ORDER CHIROPTERA

One species in every four mammals is a bat, yet remarkably little is known of this order. Bats are the only mammals capable of sustained flight, as opposed to gliding, which they achieve by means of their well-designed wings. The four elongated fingers of each hand support the flight membrane, which is also attached to the ankles and sometimes incorporates the tail.

PTEROPODIDAE:
Old World Fruit Bat Family

There are about 130 species of these large, fruit-eating bats, sometimes known as flying foxes, found in the tropical and subtropical regions of the Old World. Their eyes are large, their ears simple in structure like those of rodents, and they have a keen sense of smell. On each hand there is a sturdy thumb, equipped with a robust claw; some species have an extra claw at the tip of the second digit where it protrudes from the wing membrane. Using these claws and their hind feet, fruit bats make their way along the branches of their feeding trees in search of fruit; some also feed on pollen and nectar. Males and females look alike.

NAME: Franquet's Fruit Bat, *Epomops franqueti*
RANGE: Africa: Nigeria to Angola, east to Zimbabwe and Tanzania
HABITAT: forest, open country
SIZE: body: 13.5–18 cm (5–7 in)
   wingspan: 23–25 cm (9–10 in)
   tail: absent

Franquet's fruit bat is also known as the epauleted bat on account of the distinct patches of white fur on each shoulder. Rather than crushing fruit to release the juice, this bat sucks it out. It encircles the fruit with its lips, pierces the flesh with its teeth and, while pushing the tongue up against the fruit, it sucks, using the action of its pharyngeal pump.

Franquet's bats breed throughout the year, producing a single young at a time after a 3½-month gestation.

NAME: Harpy Fruit Bat, *Harpyionycteris whiteheadi*
RANGE: Philippines, Sulawesi
HABITAT: forest, up to 1,700 m (5,600 ft)
SIZE: body: 14–15 cm (5½–6 in)
   wingspan: 23–30 cm (9–12 in)
   tail: absent

The prominent incisor teeth of the harpy fruit bat appear to operate almost like the blades of a pair of scissors, and the bat seems to use them to snip off figs and other fruit from the trees.

NAME: Tube-nosed Fruit Bat, *Nyctimene major*
RANGE: Sulawesi to Timor, New Guinea, N. Australia, Solomon Islands
HABITAT: forest
SIZE: body: 7–12 cm (3–4¾ in)
   wingspan: 20–28 cm (8–11 in)
   tail: 1.5–2.5 cm (½–1 in)

This bat has a pair of nasal scrolls which stand out on each side of the head like snorkel tubes. Their exact function is not clear, but they may help the bat locate ripe fruit by bestowing a "stereo" effect on the nose. Guavas, figs and even the pulp of young coconuts make up the diet of the tube-nosed bat. Pieces of fruit are torn out with the teeth and then chewed and kneaded against the chest and belly. Only the juice is consumed, the rest is dropped to the ground.

Tube-nosed bats seem less social than other fruit bats and usually roost alone. They cling to the trunks of trees and are afforded some camouflage by their spotted wings. They breed in September and October and produce 1 young.

NAME: Long-tongued Fruit Bat, *Macroglossus minimus*
RANGE: Burma, east to Malaysia and Bali
HABITAT: forest, plantations
SIZE: body: 6–7 cm (2¼–2¾ in)
   wingspan: 14–17 cm (5½–6¾ in)
   tail: vestigial

One of the smallest fruit bats, the long-tongued has adopted a solitary way of life, thus making itself less obvious to predators. By day it roosts in rolled-up banana or hemp leaves, emerging at dusk to feed on pollen and nectar from plants. It feeds on fruit, too, and is considered a plantation pest in some parts of its range. These bats are quite vocal and make a shrieking noise at night. They breed in August and September, producing a single young after a gestation of 12 to 15 weeks.

NAME: Queensland Blossom Bat, *Syconycteris australis*
RANGE: S. New Guinea, south to Australia to New South Wales
HABITAT: wet and dry forest
SIZE: body: 5–6 cm (2–2½ in)
   wingspan: 12–15 cm (4¾–6 in)
   tail: vestigial

The smallest fruit bat, the Queensland blossom bat inhabits eucalyptus and acacia forests and seems to feed almost exclusively on the pollen and nectar of the many species of these trees. The bat feeds by inserting its long brushlike tongue deep into the long-necked blooms. Females give birth to a tiny infant in summer, that is, in November or December.

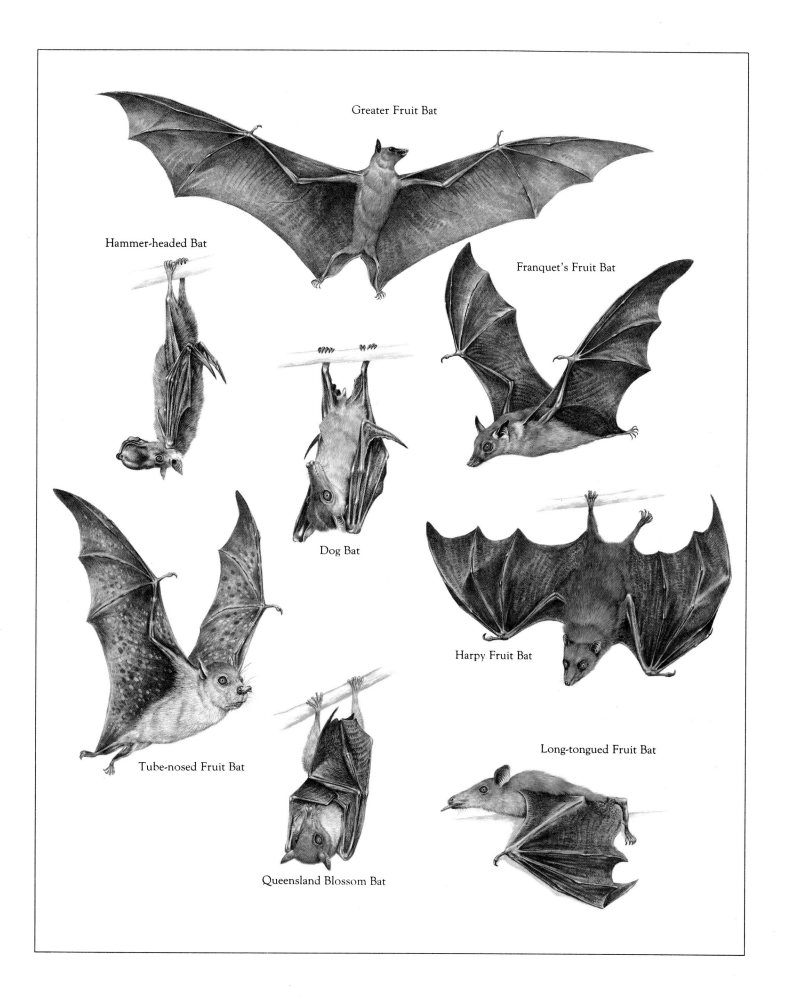

Greater Fruit Bat

Hammer-headed Bat

Franquet's Fruit Bat

Dog Bat

Harpy Fruit Bat

Tube-nosed Fruit Bat

Long-tongued Fruit Bat

Queensland Blossom Bat

Mouse-tailed Bats, Sheath-tailed Bats

RHINOPOMATIDAE:
Mouse-tailed Bat Family

Mouse-tailed bats derive their name from their long, naked tails, which equal the head and body in length. There are 4 species, found from the Middle East through India to Thailand and Sumatra. These bats have occupied certain pyramids in Egypt for 3 millenniums or more.

NAME: Greater Mouse-tailed Bat,
Rhinopoma microphyllum
RANGE: **Middle and Near East**
HABITAT: **treeless arid land**
SIZE: **body: 6–8 cm (2¼–3 in)**
   wingspan: 17–25 cm (6¾–10 in)
   tail: 6–8 cm (2¼–3 in)

Colonies of thousands of mouse-tailed bats occupy roosts in large ruined buildings, often palaces and temples. They feed exclusively on insects, and in those areas where a cool season temporarily depletes the food supply, the bats may enter a deep sleep resembling torpor. Prior to this, they lay down thick layers of fat which may weigh as much as the bats themselves, and with this they survive for many weeks with neither food nor water. As they sleep, the accumulated fat is used up, and by the time the cold season is passed, nothing of it remains.

Mouse-tailed bats mate at the beginning of spring, and the female produces a single offspring after a gestation of about 4 months. The young bat is weaned at 8 weeks but does not attain sexual maturity until its second year.

EMBALLONURIDAE:
Sheath-tailed Bat Family

There are 40 species of bat in this family, and all have a characteristic membrane which spans the hind legs; the tail originates beneath the membrane and penetrates it through a small hole. The advantages of this arrangement are not clear, but the bat is able to adjust this versatile "tailplane" during flight by movements of its legs only, and it may improve its aerial abilities.

Sheath-tailed bats range over tropical and subtropical regions of the world in a variety of habitats, but never far from trees. They are primarily insect eaters but may supplement their diet with fruit.

Scent-producing glandular sacs on the wings, in the crooks of the elbows, are another characteristic of these bats. The thick, pungent secretions of these glands are more profuse in males than females and may assist females in their search for mates.

NAME: Brazilian Long-nosed Bat,
Rhynchonycteris naso
RANGE: **S. Mexico to central Brazil**
HABITAT: **forest, scrub; near water**
SIZE: **3.5–4.5 cm (1¼–1¾ in)**
   wingspan: 12–16 cm (4¾–6¼ in)
   tail: 1–2 cm (½ in)

Characteristic features of the Brazilian long-nosed bat are its long snout and the tufts of gray hair on its forearms. These bats are slow fliers, ill suited for hunting up in the treetops where they would be easy prey for birds, so they have developed the habit of feeding on insects which live just above the surface of ponds, lakes and rivers. They sometimes roost in rocky crevices but often just cling to rocks or to concrete, where their color pattern gives them a resemblance to patches of lichen. Individuals roost a considerable distance from one another, perhaps to enhance the effect of the camouflage.

Between April and July, females give birth to 1 young. Until the young bat is about 2 months old and able to fend for itself, its mother chooses a dark safe roost inside a log, or deep within a pile of stones, in which to leave it.

NAME: Lesser White-lined Bat,
Saccopteryx leptura
RANGE: **Mexico to Bolivia and Brazil**
HABITAT: **lowland forest**
SIZE: **4–5 cm (1½–2 in)**
   wingspan: 18–22 cm (7–8¾ in)
   tail: 1 cm (½ in)

One of the most strikingly marked of all bats, the lesser white-lined bat has a pair of wavy white lines running down its back from the nape of the neck to the rump. The lines serve to break up the body shape of the bat and also provide some camouflage. The male has a pair of well-developed saclike glands in the wing membrane, just above the crooks of the arms.

In Mexico, these bats have been observed roosting under concrete bridges and on the walls of buildings. Each individual seems faithful to its roosting place, returning each morning to the precise spot that it left the evening before. Females give birth to young in the rainy season when their food supply — beetles and moths — is most plentiful. The young are weaned before they are 2 months old.

NAME: Old World Sheath-tailed Bat,
Emballonura monticola
RANGE: **Thailand to Malaysia, Java, Sumatra, Borneo and Sulawesi**
HABITAT: **rain forest**
SIZE: **body: 4–6 cm (1½–2¼ in)**
   wingspan: 16–18 cm (6¼–7 in)
   tail: 1 cm (½ in)

Old World sheath-tailed bats generally roost in rock fissures or caves in the forest in groups of a dozen or so. At dusk they all depart simultaneously to feed and then return together at dawn. They appear to feed in the top layer of the tallest trees and to supplement their insect diet with fruit and even flowers. Although little is known of the breeding habits of these bats, they are likely to breed throughout the year, producing 1 young at a time.

NAME: Tomb Bat, *Taphozous*
longimanus
RANGE: **Madagascar, east to S. Asia**
HABITAT: **coconut groves, scrub, ruined tombs and palaces**
SIZE: **body: 7–9 cm (2¾–3½ in)**
   wingspan: 25–33 cm (9¾–13 in)
   tail: 2–3.5 cm (¾–1½ in)

Tomb bats are fond of roosting in man-made structures and are often found in tombs. Tomb bats appear in Chinese paintings of 2,000 years ago — almost the oldest recorded artistic impression of any bat. Neat little creatures with short shiny coats, tomb bats fly up as high as 100 m (330 ft) at dusk in search of their insect prey. As the night progresses, they gradually descend. While hunting, tomb bats emit loud cries, easily audible to human ears.

NAME: Northern Ghost Bat, *Diclidurus*
virgo
RANGE: **S. Mexico, Central America**
HABITAT: **forest, open land**
SIZE: **body: 5–8 cm (2–3¼ in)**
   wingspan: 18–30 cm (7–11¾ in)
   tail: 1.5–2.5 cm (½–1 in)

The northern ghost bat, with its white fur and wing membrane, is a truly spectral creature. Since almost all other bats are dark, it is a mystery as to why this species should be white. However, it is just as successful at hunting insect prey as its dark relatives, which suggests that there is no evolutionary disadvantage in the light coloration. Another curious feature of this species is the presence of saclike glands in the tail membrane; there are no wing glands. The northern ghost bat roosts in caves or crevices, usually alone, occasionally in pairs. It appears to breed throughout the year.

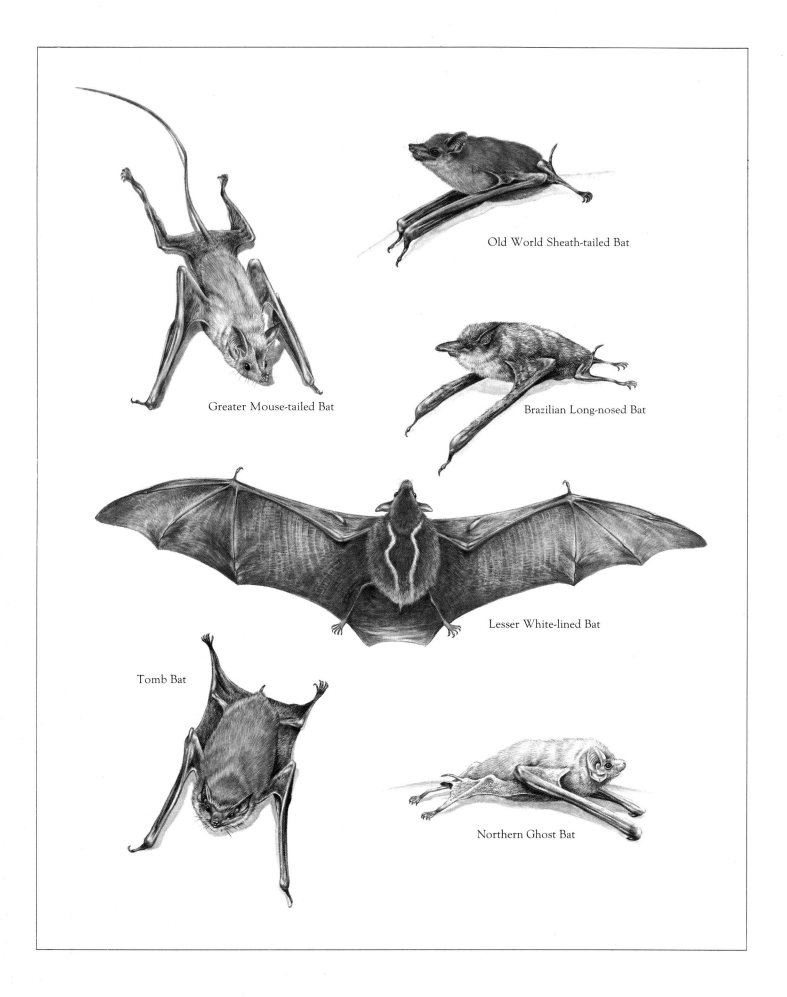

Old World Sheath-tailed Bat

Greater Mouse-tailed Bat

Brazilian Long-nosed Bat

Lesser White-lined Bat

Tomb Bat

Northern Ghost Bat

Hog-nosed Bat, Slit-faced Bats, False Vampire Bats

CRASEONYCTERIDAE:
Hog-nosed Bat Family
The single species in this family was first discovered in 1973 in the karst region of western Thailand. It is the smallest bat yet recorded and may be the world's smallest mammal. Its distribution may be far wider than at present known.

NAME: **Hog-nosed Bat,** *Craseonycteris thonglongyai*
RANGE: **Thailand**
HABITAT: **limestone caves**
SIZE: **body: 3–3.5 cm (1¼ in)**
  wingspan: 11–12.5 cm (4¼–5 in)
  tail: absent

A fully grown, adult hog-nosed bat weighs no more than 2 g (1/14 oz). Its piglike nose is thought to be an adaptation for gleaning small insects and other invertebrates off the surface of leaves. At dusk, hog-nosed bats emerge from their roosting caves and forage around the tops of bamboo clumps and in the dense foliage of teak trees, which their tiny bodies can easily penetrate. Nothing is known of their breeding habits.

NYCTERIDAE:
Slit-faced Bat Family
There are 10 species in this family. All are distinguished by a pair of slits in the sides of the face which extend laterally from the nostrils to just above the eyes. Like most complex facial features in bats, these slits are thought to play a part in beaming ultrasonic "radar" signals. Another unusual feature of the slit-faced bat is the tail, which extends to the end of the tail membrane and then terminates in a "T" shaped bone, unique among mammals.

NAME: **Egyptian Slit-faced Bat,** *Nycteris thebaica*
RANGE: **Middle East, Africa, south of the Sahara; Madagascar**
HABITAT: **dry plains, forest**
SIZE: **body: 4.5–7.5 cm (1¾–3 in)**
  wingspan: 16–28 cm (6¼–11 in)
  tail: 4–7.5 cm (1½–3 in)

Slit-faced bats feed on a variety of invertebrate animals which they catch in trees or even on the ground; scorpions seem to be a particularly favored food. The bats generally give birth to a single offspring in January or February and are thought to produce a second later in the year.

MEGADERMATIDAE:
False Vampire Bat Family
In the struggle for survival among the many bat species, this one family has evolved as specialist predators on other bats. The false vampire swoops silently down on a smaller bat and seems to chew it for a while before devouring the meat — a habit that led to the belief that these bats sucked blood. This is now known not to be the case, and, in fact, not all false vampires are even carnivorous; those that are use their predatory skills only to supplement an insectivorous diet. There are 5 species of false vampire, all with long ears and fluted nose leaves.

NAME: **Greater False Vampire Bat,** *Megaderma lyra*
RANGE: **India to Burma, S. China, Malaysia**
HABITAT: **forest, open land**
SIZE: **body: 6.5–8.5 cm (2½–3¼ in)**
  wingspan: 23–30 cm (9–11¾ in)
  tail: absent

The greater false vampire regularly supplements its diet of insects, spiders and other invertebrates with prey such as bats, rodents, frogs and even fish. Groups of 3 to 50 false vampires roost together and are usually the sole inhabitants of their caves. Presumably their predatory tendencies deter other bats from sharing their abode.

False vampires mate in November, and 1 young is born after a gestation of 20 weeks. Shortly before females are due to give birth, males leave the roost and return 3 or 4 months later, to resume communal roosting.

NAME: **Heart-nosed Bat,** *Cardioderma cor*
RANGE: **E. central Africa: Ethiopia to Tanzania**
HABITAT: **forest, scrub**
SIZE: **body: 7–9 cm (2¾–3½ in)**
  wingspan: 26–35 cm (10¼–13¾ in)
  tail: absent

The heart-nosed bat closely resembles the greater false vampire in appearance and way of life but has a wider, heart-shaped nose leaf. Like its relatives, it feeds on vertebrate animals as well as insects. Before the heat of the day has passed, the heart-nosed bat emerges from its roost and swoops to catch lizards; it will even enter houses in pursuit of rodents or wall lizards. It is a strong flier and can take off from the ground carrying a load as big as itself. Heart-nosed bats attack smaller bats in flight, "boxing" them with their powerful wings to upset their directional stability.

NAME: **Australian False Vampire Bat,** *Macroderma gigas*
RANGE: **N. and W. tropical Australia**
HABITAT: **forest with rock caves**
SIZE: **body: 11.5–14 cm (4½–5½ in)**
  wingspan: 46–60 cm (18–23½ in)
  tail: absent

On account of its pale coloration, the Australian false vampire is popularly known as the ghost bat. It is one of the most carnivorous of bats and feeds almost exclusively on mice, birds, geckos and other bats. Its method of attack is to flop down on the unsuspecting prey and enmesh it in its strong wings, then to deliver a single killing bite to the back of the prey's neck. It can rise from the ground carrying a dead rodent and fly to a feeding perch in cave or tree. Like all false vampires, this species has long ears which are joined by a membrane extending about halfway up their length.

Males forsake the communal roost in September or October, just before the young are due to be born. By January the young bats are as big as their mothers and accompany them on hunting trips. The males move back into the roosts by April. This handsome species is now rare, and active conservation measures are urgently required to ensure its survival.

NAME: **Yellow-winged Bat,** *Lavia frons*
RANGE: **Africa: Senegal to Kenya**
HABITAT: **swamps, lakes in forest and open country**
SIZE: **body: 6.5–8 cm (2½–3 in)**
  wingspan: 24–30 cm (9½–11¾ in)
  tail: absent

The fur color of the yellow-winged bat is variable, but the ears and wings are always yellowish-red. It roosts in trees and bushes, and only the flickering of its long ears gives away its presence. These bats often fly in the daytime but seem to feed only at night. In contrast to the other false vampires, yellow-winged bats appear to restrict themselves to insect food. Their method of hunting is rather like that of the flycatcher birds: they wait until an insect flies near them before swooping down from the perch to snap it up.

Yellow-winged bats breed throughout the year; males do not leave the communal roost for the birth season.

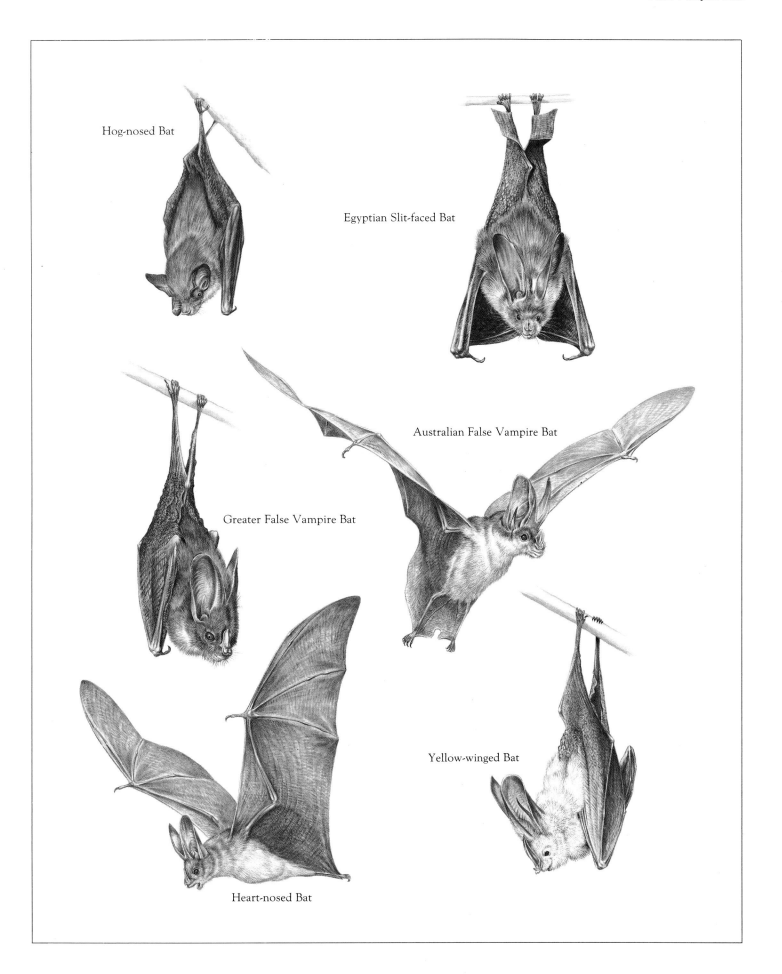

Hog-nosed Bat

Egyptian Slit-faced Bat

Australian False Vampire Bat

Greater False Vampire Bat

Yellow-winged Bat

Heart-nosed Bat

Horseshoe Bats, Old World Leaf-nosed Bats

RHINOLOPHIDAE:
Horseshoe Bat Family

The shape of the fleshy structure surrounding the nose distinguishes the horseshoe bat from other insectivorous bats. While most small bats emit their ultrasonic cries through open mouths, horseshoe bats "shout" through their nostrils. The nose leaf acts as an adjustable megaphone, enabling the bat to direct its "radar" beam wherever it wishes. Two other structures on the face, the lancet above the nostrils and the sella, which partially separates them, are immensely muscular and can vibrate at the same frequency as the sound pulse. Horseshoe bats are also distinctive in that, instead of folding their wings to their sides when roosting, they wrap them around their bodies, which makes them appear like the cocoons of enormous insects.

There are 51 species of horseshoe bat, found in temperate and tropical parts of the Old World as far east as Japan and Australia. Male and female generally look alike.

NAME: Greater Horseshoe Bat, *Rhinolophus ferrumequinum*
RANGE: Europe, Asia, N. Africa
HABITAT: forest, open and cultivated land
SIZE: body: 11–12.5 cm ($4\frac{1}{2}$–5 in)
 wingspan: 33–35 cm (13–14 in)
 tail: 2.5–4 cm (1–$1\frac{1}{2}$ in)

The greater horseshoe bat is rather slow and fluttering in flight and not adept at catching insects in the air. It feeds largely on the ground, swooping down on beetles with unerring accuracy. These bats hibernate from October to March and often choose winter quarters deep within caves, crevices or potholes. Thousands hibernate together and make long migrations to reach these quarters. The female gives birth to 1 young in April and carries it about until it is 3 months old.

NAME: Lesser Horseshoe Bat, *Rhinolophus hipposideros*
RANGE: Europe, Asia, N. Africa
HABITAT: open country with caves
SIZE: body: 7–10 cm ($2\frac{3}{4}$–4 in)
 wingspan: 22.5–25 cm (9–10 in)
 tail: 1.5–2.5 cm ($\frac{1}{2}$–1 in)

The lesser horseshoe bat is similar to the greater and equally fluttering in flight, but it is more maneuverable and hunts far more in the air. In summer it roosts in trees, hollow logs and houses, making incessant chattering noises. In winter the bats make short migrations to winter hibernation quarters in caves, which are frost-free but not necessarily dry.

NAME: Philippine Horseshoe Bat, *Rhinolophus philippinensis*
RANGE: Philippines
HABITAT: primary forest, broken land
SIZE: body: 7–9 cm ($2\frac{3}{4}$–$3\frac{1}{2}$ in)
 wingspan: 23–26 cm (9–$10\frac{1}{4}$ in)
 tail: 1.5–2.5 cm ($\frac{1}{2}$–1 in)

Within the rich bat fauna of its native islands, the Philippine horseshoe bat occupies its own special niche. It feeds on large slow-flying insects and on heavily armored ground beetles and, using its sharp teeth, can slice through the thick wing cases and wings before devouring the insects.

Hibernation is not necessary in the Philippines climate, and the bats remain active throughout the year. Breeding also occurs throughout the year. Young mature in their second year, and males are smaller than females.

HIPPOSIDERIDAE: Old World Leaf-nosed Bat Family

The 40 species of Old World leaf-nosed bats resemble the horseshoe bats and are sometimes classified with them as a subfamily. They have a horseshoe-shaped nose leaf, and the area above the nostrils is often highly modified into prongs and forks, creating curious facial structures. The family is distributed in tropical and subtropical regions of Africa and southern Asia, east to Australia and the Solomon Islands. These bats are extremely numerous and of incalculable benefit to mankind, since they feed entirely on insects and destroy many insect pests.

NAME: Persian Trident Bat, *Triaenops persicus*
RANGE: Egypt, east to Iran, south to the Gulf of Aqaba
HABITAT: arid land, semidesert
SIZE: body: 3.5–5.5 cm ($1\frac{1}{2}$–$2\frac{1}{4}$ in)
 wingspan: 15–19 cm (6–$7\frac{1}{2}$ in)
 tail: 1.5 cm ($\frac{1}{2}$ in)

The Persian trident bat and the other 2 species in its genus are distinguished from the rest of their family by the structures above the nose disk. These bats roost in underground cracks and tunnels. They emerge while it is still light to fly fast and low over the ground until they reach their feeding areas where, high in the foliage, small insects are hunted down.

Trident bats breed some time between December and May, the actual timing of the births coinciding with the rains. A single young is born and is left in the roost while its mother hunts.

NAME: Flower-faced Bat, *Anthops ornatus*
RANGE: Solomon Islands
HABITAT: forest, mixed agricultural land
SIZE: body: 4.5–5 cm ($1\frac{3}{4}$–2 in)
 wingspan: 14–16.5 cm ($5\frac{1}{2}$–$6\frac{1}{2}$ in)
 tail: 0.5–1.5 cm ($\frac{1}{4}$–$\frac{1}{2}$ in)

The flower-faced bat is known only from a handful of specimens collected early this century. It derives its name from the flowerlike appearance of the nose disk. This crenellated structure has several layers, superimposed one upon the other like the whorls of petals in a flower. Why such a bizarre device is required by this species is not known.

NAME: Trident Leaf-nosed Bat, *Asellia tridens*
RANGE: N. Africa, east to India
HABITAT: arid scrub
SIZE: body: 5–6 cm (2–$2\frac{1}{4}$ in)
 wingspan: 21–22 cm ($8\frac{1}{4}$–$8\frac{3}{4}$ in)
 tail: 2–2.5 cm ($\frac{3}{4}$–1 in)

The trident bat has a three-pronged nasal lancet. Hundreds of these bats roost together in underground tunnels and cracks. They emerge in early evening to skim over the surface of the land toward palm groves where, in the shade and moisture, insects abound. Beetles and moths are favored foods.

NAME: Large Malay Leaf-nosed Bat, *Hipposideros diadema*
RANGE: Thailand, east to Malaysia
HABITAT: forest, often near human habitation
SIZE: body: 7–10 cm ($2\frac{3}{4}$–4 in)
 wingspan: 22.5–25 cm (9–10 in)
 tail: 2.5–3 cm (1–$1\frac{1}{4}$ in)

This sociable bat roosts in groups of many hundreds in caves or old buildings. At dusk the bats depart to hunt; they forage around flowers, snapping up insects, and occasionally tear open figs to dig out insect larvae, at the same time consuming fig pulp and seeds. The single young is usually born in November or December.

NAME: Tailless Leaf-nosed Bat, *Coelops frithi*
RANGE: Bangladesh through Indo-China to Java
HABITAT: forest
SIZE: body: 3–4.5 cm (1–$1\frac{3}{4}$ in)
 wingspan: 11–13 cm ($4\frac{1}{4}$–$5\frac{1}{4}$ in)
 tail: absent

The tailless leaf-nosed bat has a much less complex nose disk than its relatives. Its ears are shorter and more rounded than is usual in this family. Small groups of a dozen or more bats shelter during the day in hollow trees or in human dwellings. In Java, it has been observed that births occur toward the end of February.

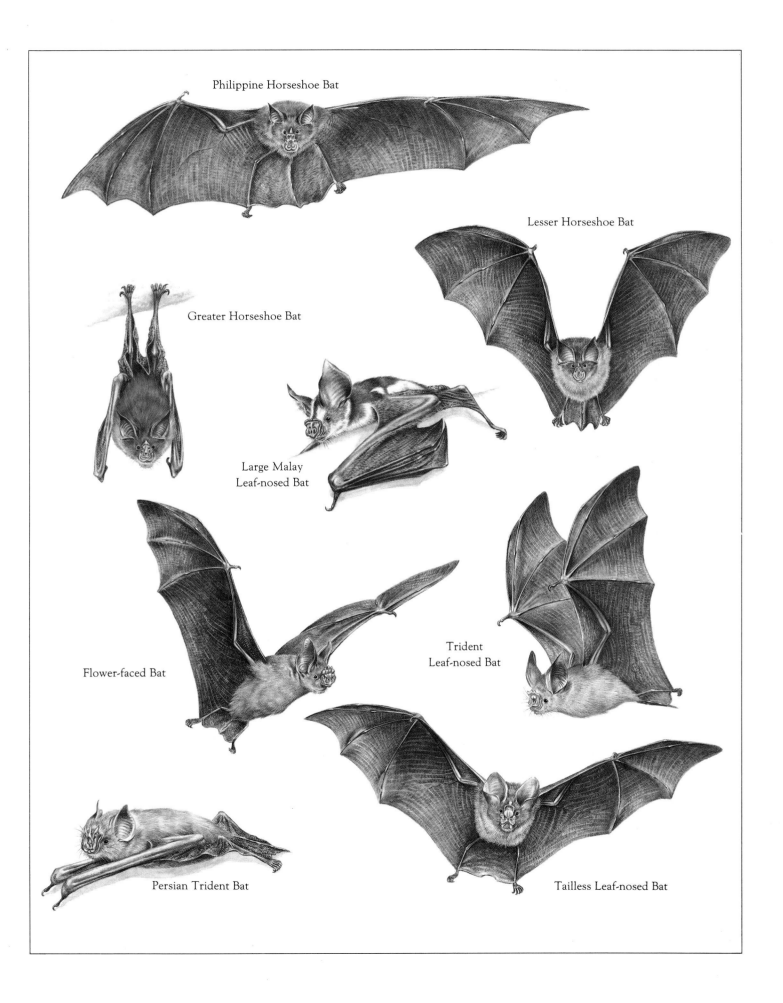

Philippine Horseshoe Bat

Lesser Horseshoe Bat

Greater Horseshoe Bat

Large Malay
Leaf-nosed Bat

Flower-faced Bat

Trident
Leaf-nosed Bat

Persian Trident Bat

Tailless Leaf-nosed Bat

Fisherman Bats, Mustached Bats, Vampire Bats, Free-tailed Bats

NOCTILIONIDAE:
Fisherman Bat Family
There are 2 species in this family, both found in Central America and northern South America. They inhabit swampy forests and mangroves and, as their name implies, feed on fish.

NAME: **Fisherman Bat**, *Noctilio leporinus*
RANGE: **Mexico, south to Argentina; Antilles, Trinidad**
HABITAT: **forest, mangrove swamps**
SIZE: **body: 10–13 cm (4–5¼ in)**
    wingspan: 28–30 cm (11–12 in)
    tail: 1–2.5 cm (½–1 in)

With powerful, stiff-winged flight, the fisherman bat swoops to within an inch of the water, dipping briefly to impale a small fish with its long sharp claws and scoop it into its mouth. Fisherman bats also use their feet to catch insects, both in the water and the air, and these make up a substantial part of their diet in some regions. Just how they locate their prey is unknown, but, since they emit floods of ultrasound while hunting, it is thought that they can detect tiny ripples made by a surfacing fish.

In November or December fisherman bats mate, and a single young is born after a gestation of about 16 weeks.

MORMOOPIDAE:
Mustached Bat Family
There are 8 species in this family which ranges from southern Arizona to Brazil. The bats derive their name from the fringe of hairs surrounding the mouth. Some species have wing membranes which meet and fuse in the middle of the back, which gives the back a naked appearance.

NAME: **Parnell's Mustached Bat**, *Pteronotus parnelli*
RANGE: **N. Mexico to Brazil; West Indies**
HABITAT: **lowland tropical forest**
SIZE: **body: 4–7.5 cm (1½–3 in)**
    wingspan: 20–33 cm (8–13 in)
    tail: 1.5–3 cm (½–1¼ in)

In addition to the fringe of hairs surrounding its mouth, this bat has a plate-like growth on its lower lip and small fleshy papillae projecting down from the upper lip. This mouth structure aids the bat in the collection of its insect food.

Mustached bats are gregarious and roost in large groups in caves. They lie horizontally and do not hang in the usual manner of bats. Young are usually born in May when the bats' food supply is most abundant. Most females have just 1 young a year.

NAME: **Peters' Ghost-faced Bat**, *Mormoops megalophylla*
RANGE: **Arizona to northern South America; Trinidad**
HABITAT: **forest, scrub, near water**
SIZE: **body: 6–6.5 cm (2–2½ in)**
    wingspan: 25–28 cm (10–11 in)
    tail: 2.5 cm (1 in)

A pair of fleshy flaps on the chin and peglike projections on the lower jaw distinguish this species. Ghost-faced bats shelter in caves, tunnels and rock fissures. They hunt somewhat later than most bats, emerging after dark to look for insects. They fly close to the ground and often feed near pools and swamps.

DESMODONTIDAE:
Vampire Bat Family
Highly specialized mammals, vampire bats are totally adapted to a diet of blood. They are the only mammals to qualify for the title of parasite. There are 3 species.

NAME: **Vampire Bat**, *Desmodus rotundus*
RANGE: **N. Mexico to central Chile, Argentina and Uruguay**
HABITAT: **forest**
SIZE: **body: 7.5–9 cm (3–3½ in)**
    wingspan: 16–18 cm (6¼–7 in)
    tail: absent

The vampire, like most bats, hunts at night. It alights on the ground a few feet away from its victim and walks over on all fours. With its four razor-sharp canine teeth, the vampire makes a small incision on a hairless or featherless part of the animal. The edges of the bat's long, protruded tongue are bent downward and form a tube, through which saliva is pumped out to inhibit clotting and blood is sucked in.

About half an hour's feeding each night is sufficient for a vampire bat, and although the host loses only a small amount of blood, the bat may transmit various diseases in its saliva, including rabies.

MOLOSSIDAE:
Free-tailed Bat Family
The 80 species of free-tailed bat occur in the warmer parts of the Old and New World. The typical free-tailed bat has a rodentlike tail, which extends well beyond the free edge of the tail membrane, and rather narrow wings, which beat more rapidly than those of other insectivorous bats. Free-tailed bats feed entirely on insects, favoring hard-shelled species. They roost in vast hordes, and their droppings create guano used in the fertilizer industry.

NAME: **Egyptian Free-tailed Bat**, *Tadarida aegyptiaca*
RANGE: **N. Africa, Middle East**
HABITAT: **arid scrub land**
SIZE: **body: 5.5–7 cm (2¼–2¾ in)**
    wingspan: 17–19 cm (6¾–7½ in)
    tail: 3–5 cm (1¼–2 in)

One of the commonest mammals in the Middle East today, the Egyptian free-tailed bat roosts in groups of many thousands. Almost any sizable crevice suffices, even if it is already occupied by a bird or another mammal. The bats mate in late winter, and the female gives birth to a single young after a gestation of 77 to 84 days. A second pregnancy may follow immediately.

NAME: **Wroughton's Free-tailed Bat**, *Otomops wroughtoni*
RANGE: **S. India, Sri Lanka**
HABITAT: **open, partially forested land**
SIZE: **body: 9.5–11 cm (3¾–4¼ in)**
    wingspan: 28–30 cm (11–12 in)
    tail: 3–5 cm (1¼–2 in)

This species roosts in small groups or even alone, and although few specimens have been collected, it is probably not as rare as it seems. Females give birth to a single young in December.

NAME: **Black Mastiff Bat**, *Molossus ater*
RANGE: **S. Mexico, Central America, Trinidad**
HABITAT: **scrub, savanna, forest**
SIZE: **body: 6–9 cm (2½–3½ in)**
    wingspan: 26–28 cm (10–11 in)
    tail: 3–4 cm (1¼–1½ in)

This species has dense, short-piled fur of velvety texture. It hunts insects and catches as many as possible at a time, cramming them into capacious cheek pouches. On returning to its roost, the bat devours the contents of the pouches. This hunting behavior may have evolved to reduce the amount of time the bats are out and at risk from the attentions of predators. One or two litters are born in summer.

NAME: **Greater Mastiff Bat**, *Eumops perotis*
RANGE: **S.W. USA, Mexico, northern South America**
HABITAT: **forest, near human habitation**
SIZE: **body: 7–10 cm (2¾–4 in)**
    wingspan: 28–30 cm (11–12 in)
    tail: 4–6 cm (1½–2¼ in)

Greater mastiff bats emerge from their roost after dark and hunt small insects, usually ants, bees and wasps, wherever they may be found. In the mating season, the throat glands of males swell enormously, and the odorous secretions of these glands may attract females. Young are born in late summer, and twins are not uncommon.

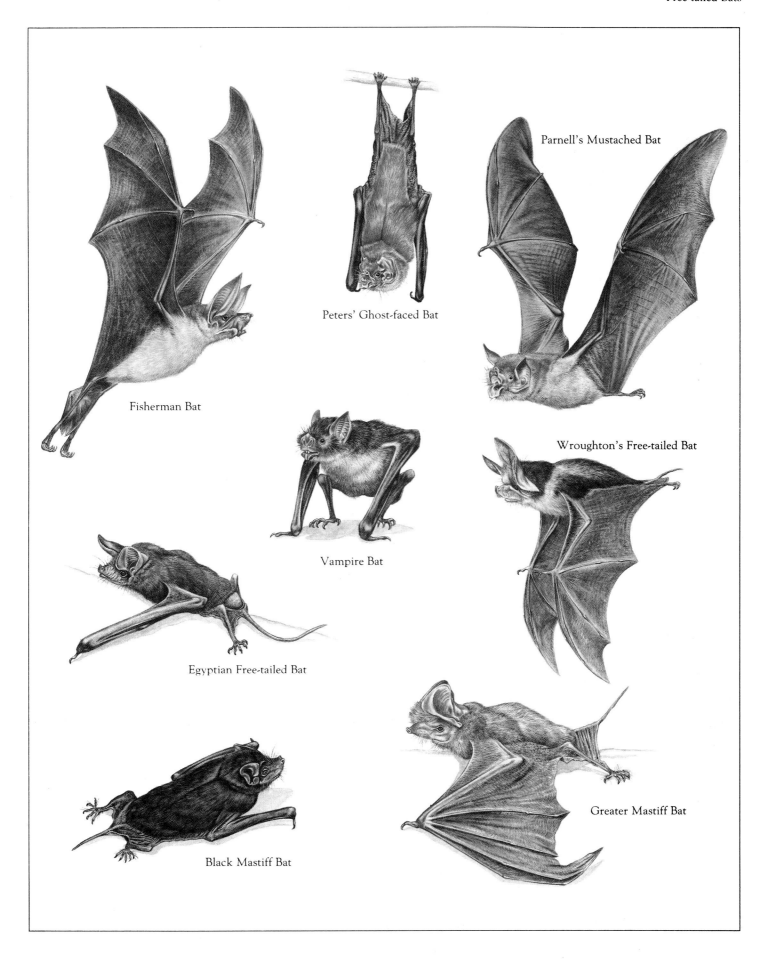

Fisherman Bat

Peters' Ghost-faced Bat

Parnell's Mustached Bat

Vampire Bat

Wroughton's Free-tailed Bat

Egyptian Free-tailed Bat

Black Mastiff Bat

Greater Mastiff Bat

American Leaf-nosed Bats

NAME: **Pallas' Long-tongued Bat,**
Glossophaga soricina
RANGE: **N. Mexico to Brazil, Paraguay**
and Argentina; West Indies
HABITAT: **woodland, often arid areas**
SIZE: **body: 5–6.5 cm (2–2½ in)**
wingspan: 20–24 cm (7¾–9½ in)
tail: 0.5 cm (¼ in)

The mammalian equivalent of the hummingbird, this bat hovers in front of flowers and scoops up pollen and nectar from deep within them with the aid of its long tongue. Tiny bristles on its surface help the pollen to stick fast.

Females form maternity colonies in summer, rejoining their original roosts when the young are born. Twins do occur, but a single young is more common.

NAME: **Linnaeus' False Vampire,**
Vampyrum spectrum
RANGE: **S. Mexico to Peru and Brazil;**
Trinidad
HABITAT: **forest, often near human**
habitation
SIZE: **body: 12.5–13.5 cm (5–5¼ in)**
wingspan: 80 cm–1 m (31½ in–3¼ ft)
tail: absent

This species, formerly believed to be a blood-sucker, is now known to kill and eat rodents, birds and other bats. It is surprisingly agile on all fours and stalks mice stealthily; it then kills by an accurate pounce, which breaks the prey's neck or shatters its skull. The bats breed in June, and the females are most solicitous parents, licking their young incessantly and feeding them pieces of chewed mouse flesh as they approach weaning.

NAME: **Tent-making Bat,** *Uroderma*
bilobatum
RANGE: **S. Mexico to Peru and Brazil;**
Trinidad
HABITAT: **forest, plantations**
SIZE: **body: 5.5–7.5 cm (2¼–3 in)**
wingspan: 20–24 cm (7¾–9½ in)
tail: absent

The tent-making bat is alert and active by day and has developed a simple way of creating a shady refuge. Fan-shaped palm leaves are partially bitten through in a semicircular line, a third of the way along a frond. The end of the frond collapses, making a tent-shaped refuge, from which the bats fly out in search of ripe fruit. A colony of 20 or 30 bats may share a tent. Pregnant females establish maternity tents, and young are born between February and April. The young remain in the maternity tent until they are able to fly. Males live alone or in small groups during the breeding season, returning to the females when the young are weaned.

PHYLLOSTOMATIDAE:
American Leaf-nosed Bat Family

As night descends over the Central and South American jungles, leaf-nosed bats emerge from their roosts to feed on the pollen and nectar of flowers, as well as on the insects attracted to the blooms. There is such a variety of plants that about 140 species of leaf-nosed bat have evolved to exploit this particular way of life. Generally the bats are small, but Linnaeus' false vampire has a wingspan which may exceed 1 m (3¼ ft), making it the largest New World bat.

Leaf-nosed bats may be tailless or have tiny tails embedded in the tail membrane. The characteristic linking most members of the family is the presence of a nose leaf — a flap of tissue above the nostrils. Unlike the leaves of the Old World leaf-nosed bats (Hipposideridae), these are little more than simple flaps of skin.

These abundant little bats do much good by transferring pollen from one flower to another, and a number of plants have become specially adapted to pollination by bats by flowering at night and producing a heavy, musky odor, which attracts them.

NAME: **Spear-nosed Bat,** *Phyllostomus*
hastatus
RANGE: **Belize to Peru, Bolivia and**
Brazil; Trinidad
HABITAT: **forest, broken country**
SIZE: **body: 10–13 cm (4–5¼ in)**
wingspan: 44–47 cm (17¼–18½ in)
tail: 2.5 cm (1 in)

One of the larger American bats, the spear-nosed has virtually abandoned an insectivorous diet for a carnivorous one. It feeds on mice, birds and small bats and occasionally on insects and fruit. Huge flocks of these bats shelter in caves and abandoned buildings and at dusk depart together for their feeding grounds. Young are born in May and June in the communal roost.

NAME: **Yellow-shouldered Bat,** *Sturnira*
lilium
RANGE: **N. Mexico to Paraguay and**
Argentina; Jamaica
HABITAT: **lowland forest**
SIZE: **body: 6–7 cm (2¼–2¾ in)**
wingspan: 24–27 cm (9½–10½ in)
tail: absent

The yellow-shouldered bat feeds on ripe fruit and roosts alone or in small groups in old buildings, hollow trees or in the crowns of palm trees. In the north of their range, these bats breed throughout the year, but in the south, the young are born between May and July. Females generally produce 1 young at a time.

NAME: **Brazilian Large-eared Bat,**
Micronycteris megalotis
RANGE: **S.W. USA to Peru, Brazil;**
Trinidad, Tobago and Grenada
HABITAT: **dry scrub to tropical rain forest**
SIZE: **body: 4–6.5 cm (1½–2½ in)**
wingspan: 16–20 cm (6¼–7¾ in)
tail: 0.5–1 cm (¼–½ in)

Brazilian large-eared bats roost in small groups in a great variety of shelter holes. They emerge as dusk is falling and swoop around fruit trees, chasing heavy, slow-flying insects, such as cockchafers, or plucking cockroaches from the ground. They appear to supplement this diet with the pulp of fruit such as guavas and bananas. Young are born between April and June, most females having a single offspring.

NAME: **Seba's Short-tailed Bat,** *Carollia*
perspicillata
RANGE: **S. Mexico to S. Brazil**
HABITAT: **forest, plantations**
SIZE: **body: 5–6.5 cm (2–2½ in)**
wingspan: 21–25 cm (8¼–9¾ in)
tail: 0.5–1.5 cm (¼–½ in)

This bat feeds almost entirely on ripe fruit, such as bananas, figs, guavas and plantains, which it locates by smell. There is no defined breeding season for this species, and females produce their single youngster at any time of the year.

NAME: **Jamaican Fruit-eating Bat,**
Artibeus jamaicensis
RANGE: **N. Mexico to Brazil and**
N. Argentina; West Indies
HABITAT: **scrub, forest**
SIZE: **body: 7.5–9 cm (3–3½ in)**
wingspan: 23–26 cm (9–10¼ in)
tail: absent

This bat is one of the most efficient mammalian food processors: it feeds on fruit, which passes through its gut in as little as 15 minutes. There is no time for bacterial action to destroy material, so the bat is an important disseminator of seeds. The breeding season lasts from February to July, and females give birth to 1, sometimes 2, young.

NAME: **Cuban Flower Bat,** *Phyllonycteris*
poeyi
RANGE: **Cuba**
HABITAT: **primary forest, cultivated land**
SIZE: **body: 7.5–8 cm (3–3¼ in)**
wingspan: 21–23 cm (8¼–9 in)
tail: 1–1.5 cm (½ in)

The Cuban flower bat has little or no nose leaf. It is a gregarious bat and roosts in thousands in caves and rock fissures. With its long, slender tongue, it sucks and laps up nectar and pollen from many types of flowers, and it also feeds on fruit. These bats breed throughout the year; young are left in the roost until they are able to fly.

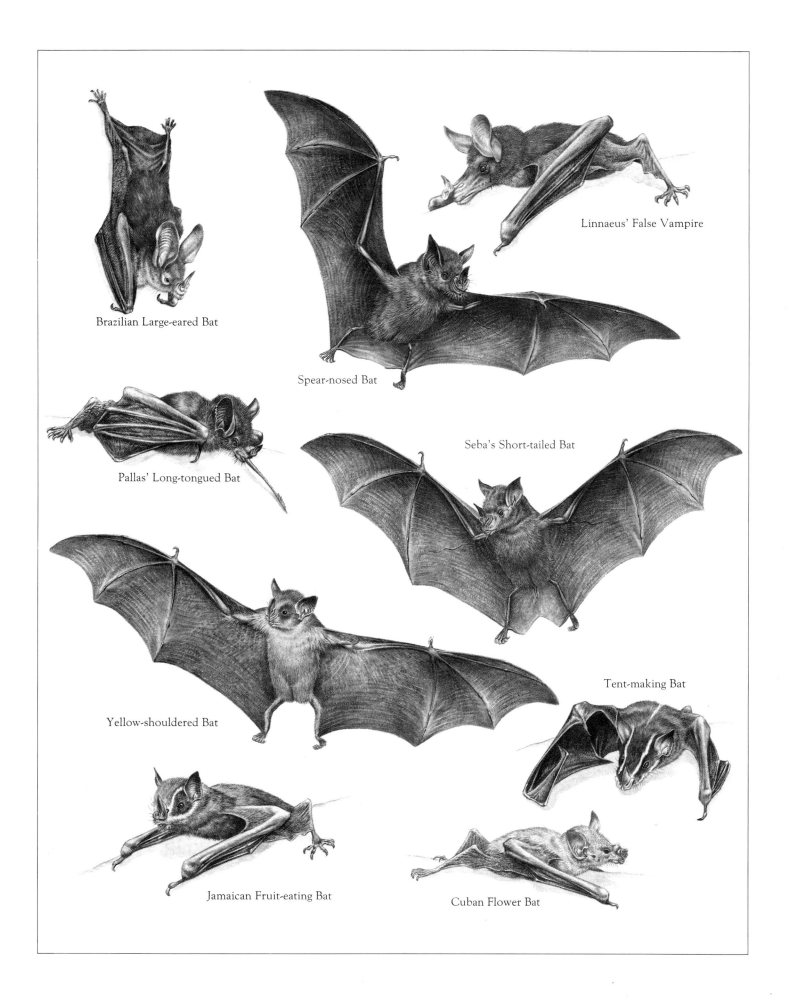

Brazilian Large-eared Bat

Linnaeus' False Vampire

Spear-nosed Bat

Pallas' Long-tongued Bat

Seba's Short-tailed Bat

Yellow-shouldered Bat

Tent-making Bat

Jamaican Fruit-eating Bat

Cuban Flower Bat

Evening Bats

NAME: Little Brown Myotis, *Myotis lucifugus*
RANGE: N. America: from 62°N, south to Mexico
HABITAT: forest, built-up areas
SIZE: body: 4 cm (1½ in)
  wingspan: 14–18 cm (5½–7 in)
  tail: 2.5 cm (1 in)

A common species in North America, this bat adapts equally well to cold and hot climates. It feeds on whatever insects are abundant locally. In summer, the females segregate themselves and roost in maternity sites. A single young, sometimes twins, is born in May or June after a gestation of 50 to 60 days. The young are mature at 1 year.

In the warmer parts of their range, these bats do not hibernate, but northern populations may migrate hundreds of miles to suitable hibernation sites.

NAME: Fish-eating Bat, *Pizonyx vivesi*
RANGE: coasts of Baja California and W. Mexico
HABITAT: caves, coastal rock piles
SIZE: body: 7–8.5 cm (2¾–3¼ in)
  wingspan: 25–32 cm (9¾–12½ in)
  tail: 5–6.5 cm (2–2½ in)

A bat specialized for feeding on fish, this species has feet with long rakelike toes, ending in razor-sharp claws. Late in the evening, the bat flies low over the sea and takes small fish and crustaceans from the surface by impaling them on its claws. It is not known how it locates its prey, but its "radar" system might be capable of noting irregularities in the water caused by a fish moving close to the surface.

The female bat bears a single young in May or June and carries her infant with her until it is half-grown. It is then left in a secure roost with other young, while the mother hunts.

NAME: Common Long-eared Bat, *Plecotus auritus*
RANGE: N. Europe, east to N.E. China and Japan
HABITAT: sheltered, lightly wooded areas
SIZE: body: 4–5 cm (1½–2 in)
  wingspan: 23–28 cm (9–11 in)
  tail: 3–4.5 cm (1¼–1¾ in)

The distinguishing feature of this bat is its long ears, which are three-quarters the length of its head and body. In summer, these bats roost in buildings and trees and hunt primarily for the night-flying noctuid moths. They also feed on midges, mosquitoes and other flies, often picking them off vegetation in dive-bombing, swooping flights.

The female gives birth to a single young in June, and females and young form nursery roosts. Long-eared bats are mature at about a year old.

VESPERTILIONIDAE: Evening Bat Family

There are some 275 species in this family, found around the world from the tropics to as far as about 68° North. Many species hibernate for 5 or 6 months to survive the winter in harsh northern latitudes. Nearly all species are insectivorous, although one or two feed on fish which they scoop from the water. Insects are usually caught in the air, the bat tossing the insect into its tail membrane with its wing. All these bats make use of echolocation for finding prey and for plotting their flight course.

Evening bats are extremely numerous in the cool, northern parts of the world. Without their massive consumption of blackflies, midges and mosquitoes, life for humans during the short northern summers would be distinctly more uncomfortable.

NAME: Common Pipistrelle, *Pipistrellus pipistrellus*
RANGE: Europe, east to Kashmir
HABITAT: open land
SIZE: body: 3–4.5 cm (1¼–1¾ in)
  wingspan: 19–25 cm (7½–9¾ in)
  tail: 2.5–3 cm (1–1¼ in)

Perhaps the commonest European bats, pipistrelles roost in groups of up to a thousand or more in lofts, church spires, farm buildings and the like. In winter, these bats migrate to a suitable dry cave to hibernate in colonies of 100,000 or more. They feed on insects, eating small prey in flight but taking larger catches to a perch to eat. Births occur in mid-June and twins have been recorded. The bats actually mate in September, prior to hibernation, and the sperm is stored in the female for 7 or 8 months before fertilization occurs and gestation starts.

NAME: Big Brown Bat, *Eptesicus fuscus*
RANGE: N. America: Alaska to Central America; West Indies
HABITAT: varied, often close to human habitation
SIZE: body: 5–7.5 cm (2–3 in)
  wingspan: 26–37 cm (10¼–14½ in)
  tail: 4.5–5.5 cm (1¾–2¼ in)

Big brown bats eat almost all insects except, it seems, moths, and also manage to catch water beetles. They have been recorded flying at a speed of 25 km/h (15½ mph). They will enter houses to hibernate, although huge numbers migrate to caves in Missouri and other southern states for this purpose. Young are born from April to July; a single young is the rule west of the Rockies, but twins are common in the east.

NAME: Red Bat, *Lasiurus borealis*
RANGE: N. America, West Indies, Galápagos Islands
HABITAT: forested land with open space
SIZE: body: 6–8 cm (2¼–3¼ in)
  wingspan: 36–42 cm (14¼–16½ in)
  tail: 4.5–5 cm (1¾–2 in)

The red bat's fur varies in shade from brick-red to rust, suffused with white. Males are more brightly colored than females. The species is unique among bats in the size of its litters, regularly giving birth to 3 or 4 young in June or early July. The female carries her young with her at first, even though their combined weights may exceed her own body weight. North American red bats migrate southward in autumn and north again in spring.

NAME: Noctule, *Nyctalus noctula*
RANGE: Europe, east to Japan
HABITAT: forest, open land
SIZE: body: 7–8 cm (2¾–3¼ in)
  wingspan: 32–35.5 cm (12½–14 in)
  tail: 3–5.5 cm (1¼–2¼ in)

One of the largest evening bats, the noctule feeds mainly on maybugs, crickets and dorbeetles, and there are reports of its killing house mice. In winter, noctules hibernate in trees or lofts, usually in small groups, but roosts of a few hundred do occur. They breed in June, producing 1, or sometimes 2 or even 3, young.

NAME: Barbastelle, *Barbastella barbastellus*
RANGE: Europe, east to central USSR
HABITAT: open land, often near water
SIZE: body: 4–5 cm (1½–2 in)
  wingspan: 24.5–28 cm (9½–11 in)
  tail: 4–4.5 cm (1½–1¾ in)

In early evening, often before sunset, barbastelles emerge to hunt for insects, flying low over water or bushes. Males and females segregate for the summer, and females form maternity colonies. From late September, barbastelles congregate in limestone regions to hibernate in deep, dry caves.

NAME: Painted Bat, *Kerivoula argentata*
RANGE: Africa: S. Kenya, Namibia, Natal
HABITAT: arid woodland
SIZE: body: 3–5.5 cm (1¼–2¼ in)
  wingspan: 18–30 cm (7–11¾ in)
  tail: 3–5.5 cm (1¼–2¼ in)

Small groups of painted bats are often found in the most unlikely roosts, such as in the suspended nests of weaver finches and sunbirds or under the eaves of African huts. Doubtless the bright and broken coloration of these bats is a form of camouflage to protect them while they roost in vulnerable sites. Nothing is known of their breeding biology.

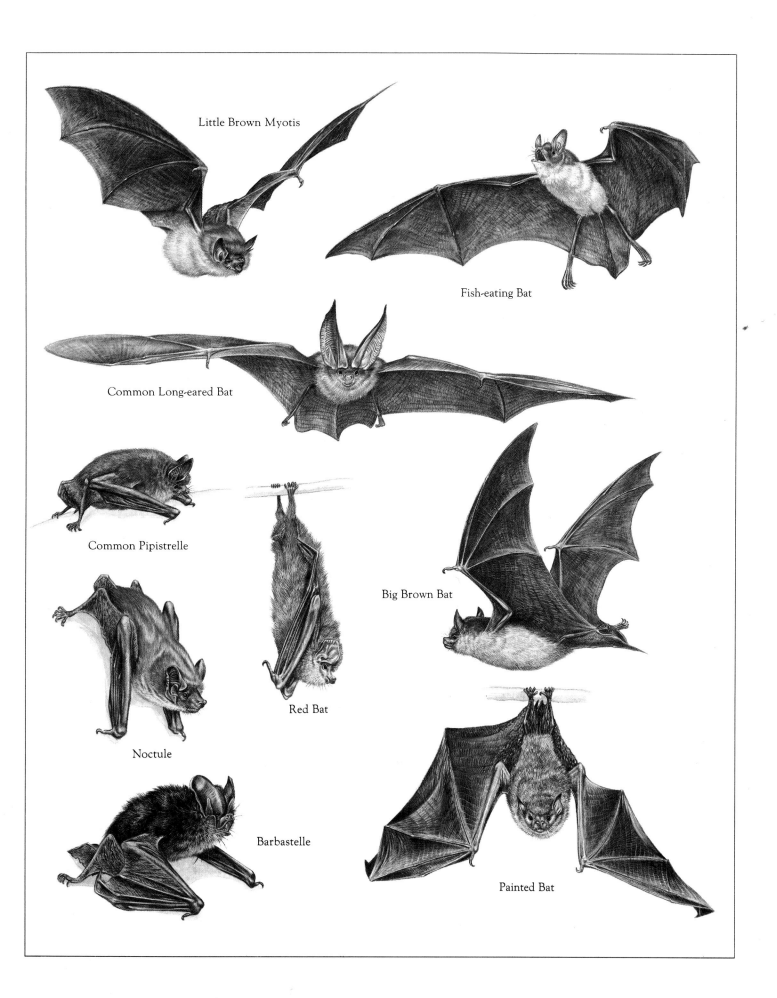

Little Brown Myotis

Fish-eating Bat

Common Long-eared Bat

Common Pipistrelle

Big Brown Bat

Red Bat

Noctule

Barbastelle

Painted Bat

Funnel-eared Bats and relatives

NATALIDAE:
Funnel-eared Bat Family

The 3 species of funnel-eared bat occur in cavernous country in tropical South America. The family name comes from the large funnel-shaped ears, the outer surfaces of which bear glandular projections. Males and females look alike, except that on their muzzles males have thick glandular, or sensory, pads whose function is not known.

NAME: **Mexican Funnel-eared Bat,** *Natalus stramineus*
RANGE: **N. Mexico to Brazil; Lesser Antilles**
HABITAT: **tropical lowlands**
SIZE: **body: 3–5.5 cm (1¼–2¼ in)**
  wingspan: 18–24 cm (7–9½ in)
  tail: 5–6 cm (2–2¼ in)

Funnel-eared bats roost in caves and mines, sometimes in huge numbers but more often in groups of about a dozen. The bats emerge at dusk to search for slow-flying insects, and they themselves fly with fluttering, rather mothlike movements. Breeding takes place at any time of the year, and the sexes segregate just before the young are born.

FURIPTERIDAE:
Smoky Bat Family

There are 2 species in this family, both characterized by their smoky coloration, by being thumbless and by having extremely long tail membranes. The family occurs in tropical South America and in Trinidad.

NAME: **Eastern Smoky Bat,** *Furipterus horrens*
RANGE: **Costa Rica, northern South America; E. Peru, Guianas, Brazil; Trinidad**
HABITAT: **forest**
SIZE: **body: 4–6 cm (1½–2¼ in)**
  wingspan: 22–30 cm (8½–11¾ in)
  tail: 4–6 cm (1½–2¼ in)

Unlike other bats, the eastern smoky bat has no clawed thumbs, so that when it alights on the wall of its cave or tunnel roost, it must perform an aerial somersault to grasp the surface with its hind feet. Another curious feature of this bat and its fellow species is the high forehead: the snout and the brow join almost at right angles.

Practically nothing is known of the biology of either species of smoky bat because few zoologists have studied them. They certainly feed on insects, but how they avoid competing with the many other species of insect-eating bat within their range is not understood.

THYROPTERIDAE:
Disk-winged Bat Family

The 2 species in this family occur in Central America and in tropical South America, as far as Peru and southern Brazil. They derive their name from suction pads at the base of each thumb and on the ankles. These disks are attached to the bat by short stalks and enable it to climb rapidly up smooth leaves and bare tree trunks. A curious characteristic of disk-winged bats is that they usually hang head upward when roosting — a feat made possible by the powerful suction disks.

NAME: **Peters' Disk-winged Bat,** *Thyroptera discifera*
RANGE: **Belize, south to Ecuador and Peru**
HABITAT: **forest**
SIZE: **body: 3–5 cm (1¼–2 in)**
  wingspan: 18–25 cm (7–9¾ in)
  tail: 2.5–3 cm (1–1¼ in)

This small insect-eating bat has a similar high forehead to that of the smoky bat, but again the reasons for this are not known. It can climb up smooth surfaces, even glass, by means of its sucker disks; the suction pressure from a single disk is quite sufficient to support the entire weight of the bat. Suction is applied or released by specialized muscles in the forearms.

Disk-winged bats have unusual roosting habits: they roost in the young, curled leaves of plants such as bananas. These leaves, before they unfurl, form long tubes, and several bats may roost in a single leaf, anchored by their suckers to the smooth surface. The bats must find a new leaf practically every day as the previous roost unfurls.

Breeding takes place throughout the year, and the sexes do not appear to segregate before the females give birth. A single young is the normal litter, and the mother carries it about with her until it weighs more than half her body weight. Her flying ability is not impaired by this extra load. Subsequently the young bat is left in the roost while she hunts.

MYZOPODIDAE:
Sucker-footed Bat Family

The single species of sucker-footed bat is restricted to the island continent of Madagascar. The Myzopodidae is the only family of bats found solely on that island and represents a relict species, cut off from Africa when Madagascar broke free from that land mass.

NAME: **Sucker-footed Bat,** *Myzopoda aurita*
RANGE: **Madagascar**
HABITAT: **forest**
SIZE: **body: 5–6 cm (2–2¼ in)**
  wingspan: 22–28 cm (8½–11 in)
  tail: 4.5–5 cm (1¾–2 in)

Superficially the sucker-footed bat resembles the disk-winged bats of the New World, for there are large suction disks at the base of each thumb and on each ankle. But the disks of this bat are quite immobile, in sharp contrast to those of the disk-winged bat which are connected to the body by mobile stalks, and they appear to be less efficient. The bat roosts inside curled leaves or hollow plant stems, and sometimes the smooth trunk of a tree may also serve it as a temporary nest.

Nothing is known of the breeding or feeding habits of these bats and they seem to be rather rare. Logging and the destruction of large areas of their forest habitat may be posing a threat to their survival.

MYSTACINIDAE: New Zealand Short-tailed Bat Family

The sole member of its family, the short-tailed bat is one of New Zealand's two native species of mammal (the other is a vespertilionid bat called *Chalinolobus tuberculatus*).

NAME: **New Zealand Short-tailed Bat,** *Mystacina tuberculata*
RANGE: **New Zealand**
HABITAT: **forest**
SIZE: **body: 5–6 cm (2–2¼ in)**
  wingspan: 22–28 cm (8½–11 in)
  tail: 1.5–2 cm (½–¾ in)

The short-tailed bat has a thick mustache fringing its small mouth; each bristle of the mustache has a spoon-shaped tip. Its thumbs bear not only the usual heavy claws but also have tiny secondary talons at their base, and its hind feet are equipped with razor-sharp claws.

An agile bat on all fours on the ground, the short-tailed bat runs rapidly, even up steeply sloping objects. To assist it in this, the wing membranes are furled in such a way that the forearms can be used as walking limbs. Beetles and other ground-dwelling insects seem to form the bulk of the diet of this species. They do not hibernate (the other New Zealand bat does) and roost in small groups in hollow trees. A single young is born in October.

Mexican Funnel-eared Bat

Eastern Smoky Bat

Peters' Disk-winged Bat

Sucker-footed Bat

New Zealand Short-tailed Bat

Tree Shrews

NAME: **Common Tree Shrew,** *Tupaia glis*
RANGE: **S. and S.E. Asia: India to Vietnam and Malaysia, S. China, Indonesia**
HABITAT: **rain forest, woodland, bamboo scrub**
SIZE: **body: 14–23 cm ($5\frac{1}{2}$–9 in)**
tail: **12–21 cm ($4\frac{3}{4}$–$8\frac{1}{4}$ in)**

A squirrel-like creature, with a long, bushy tail, the common tree shrew is active and lively, climbing with great agility in the trees but also spending much of its time on the ground, feeding. Its diet is varied and includes insects (particularly ants), spiders, seeds, buds and probably also small birds and mice. It normally lives alone or with a mate.

Breeding seems to occur at any time of year, and a rough nest is made in a hole in a fallen tree or among tree roots. In Malaysia, where breeding of this species has been most closely observed, females produce litters of 1 to 3 young after a gestation of 46 to 50 days. The newborn young are naked, with closed eyes, but are ready to leave the nest about 33 days after birth.

NAME: **Mountain Tree Shrew,** *Tupaia montana*
RANGE: **Borneo**
HABITAT: **montane forest**
SIZE: **body: 11–15 cm ($4\frac{1}{4}$–6 in)**
tail: **10–15 cm (4–6 in)**

The mountain tree shrew has a long, bushy tail and a slender, pointed snout. Although agile in trees, it spends much of its time on the ground, searching for food. Insects, fruit, seeds and leaves are all included in its diet, and it will sit back on its haunches to eat, holding the food in both its forepaws. This species is thought to be slightly more social than others of its genus and may live in small groups.

Breeding takes place at any time of year, and a litter, normally of 2 young, is born after a 49- to 51-day gestation.

NAME: **Madras Tree Shrew,** *Anathana ellioti*
RANGE: **central and S. India**
HABITAT: **rain forest, thorny woodland**
SIZE: **body: 16–18 cm ($6\frac{1}{4}$–7 in)**
tail: **16–19 cm ($6\frac{1}{4}$–$7\frac{1}{2}$ in)**

The Madras tree shrew is squirrel-like and similar in most aspects to the tree shrews of the *Tupaia* genus. It is identified, however, by its larger ears, heavier snout and the pale stripe on each shoulder. Active during the day, it moves in trees and on the ground, searching for insects and probably fruit to eat. Little is known about its breeding habits, but they are probably similar to those of the *Tupaia* tree shrews.

ORDER SCANDENTIA
TUPAIIDAE: Tree Shrew Family

There is a single family in the order Scandentia, containing approximately 16 species of tree shrew, which live in the forests of eastern Asia, including Borneo and the Philippines. These biologically interesting, but visually undistinguished, mammals have affinities with the order Insectivora, because of their shrewlike appearance, and with the order Primates, because of their complex, convoluted brains; they have been included in both of these orders. Most modern zoologists agree, however, that tree shrews should be placed in a distinct order so that their uniqueness is emphasized, rather than hidden in a large, diverse order. Until much more is known of their biology, tree shrews will remain an enigma.

Tree shrews resemble slim, long-nosed squirrels in general appearance, and their ears are squirrel-like in shape and relative size. Their feet are modified for an arboreal existence, having naked soles equipped with knobbly pads, which provide tree shrews with a superb ability to cling to branches. This ability is enhanced by the presence of long, flexible digits, with sharp, curved claws. The 16 species range from 10 to 22 cm (4 to $8\frac{1}{2}$ in) in body length, with tails of 9 to 22.5 cm ($3\frac{1}{2}$ to $8\frac{3}{4}$ in). They run rapidly through the forest canopy, and most are active in the daytime, searching for insects and fruit to eat. They drink frequently and are also fond of bathing.

Despite their name, tree shrews are not exclusively arboreal, and many species spend a good deal of time on the ground. Their senses of smell, sight and hearing are good. Tree shrews usually live in pairs, and males, particularly, are aggressive toward one another. The borders of a pair's territory are marked with urine and glandular secretions.

There are 1 to 4 young in a litter, usually 1 or 2, born in a separate nest from the normal sleeping quarters. The female visits her young only once a day or even every other day, but they are able to take sufficient milk in a short period to sustain them during her long absences. Males and females look similar, but males are usually larger.

Tree shrews bear a close resemblance to fossils of the earliest mammals, so it may be assumed that the first true mammals looked, and possibly behaved, like these fascinating little animals.

NAME: **Bornean Smooth-tailed Tree Shrew,** *Dendrogale melanura*
RANGE: **Borneo**
HABITAT: **montane forest above 900 m (3,000 ft)**
SIZE: **body: 11–15 cm ($4\frac{1}{4}$–6 in)**
tail: **9–14 cm ($3\frac{1}{2}$–$5\frac{1}{2}$ in)**

The smallest of the tree shrews, this species is distinguished by its smooth, short-haired tail, which ends in a point. Its body fur, too, is short and close, dark reddish-brown on the back and lighter orange-buff on the underparts. More arboreal than the other members of its family, it finds much of its insect food on the lower branches of trees. Its breeding habits are not known.

NAME: **Philippine Tree Shrew,** *Urogale everetti*
RANGE: **Philippines: Mindanao**
HABITAT: **rain forest, montane forest**
SIZE: **body: 17–20 cm ($6\frac{1}{4}$–$7\frac{3}{4}$ in)**
tail: **11–17 cm ($4\frac{1}{4}$–$6\frac{3}{4}$ in)**

A particularly elongate snout and a rounded, even-haired tail are characteristics of the Philippine tree shrew. Its fur is brownish, but with orange or yellow underparts. Active during the day, it climbs well and runs fast on the ground. Its diet is varied and includes insects, lizards, young birds and bird's eggs and fruit.

In the wild, Philippine tree shrews are thought to nest on the ground or on cliffs. Their breeding habits have been observed in captivity, where females have produced 1 or 2 young after a gestation of 54 to 56 days.

NAME: **Feather-tailed Tree Shrew,** *Ptilocercus lowi*
RANGE: **Malaysia, Sumatra, Borneo**
HABITAT: **rain forest**
SIZE: **body: 12–14 cm ($4\frac{3}{4}$–$5\frac{1}{2}$ in)**
tail: **16–18 cm ($6\frac{1}{4}$–7 in)**

This tree shrew is easily identified by its unusual tail, which is naked for much of its length but has tufts of hair on each side of the terminal portion, making it resemble a feather. Other features characteristic of this species are its ears, which are large and membranous and stand away from the head, and its hands and feet, which are larger, relative to body size, than those of other tree shrews. Said to be nocturnal, the feather-tailed tree shrew spends much of its life in trees and is a good climber, using its tail for balance and support and spreading its toes and fingers wide for grip. Insects, fruit and some lizards are its main foods.

Feather-tailed tree shrews nest in holes in trees or branches, well off the ground, but their breeding habits are not known. They generally live in pairs.

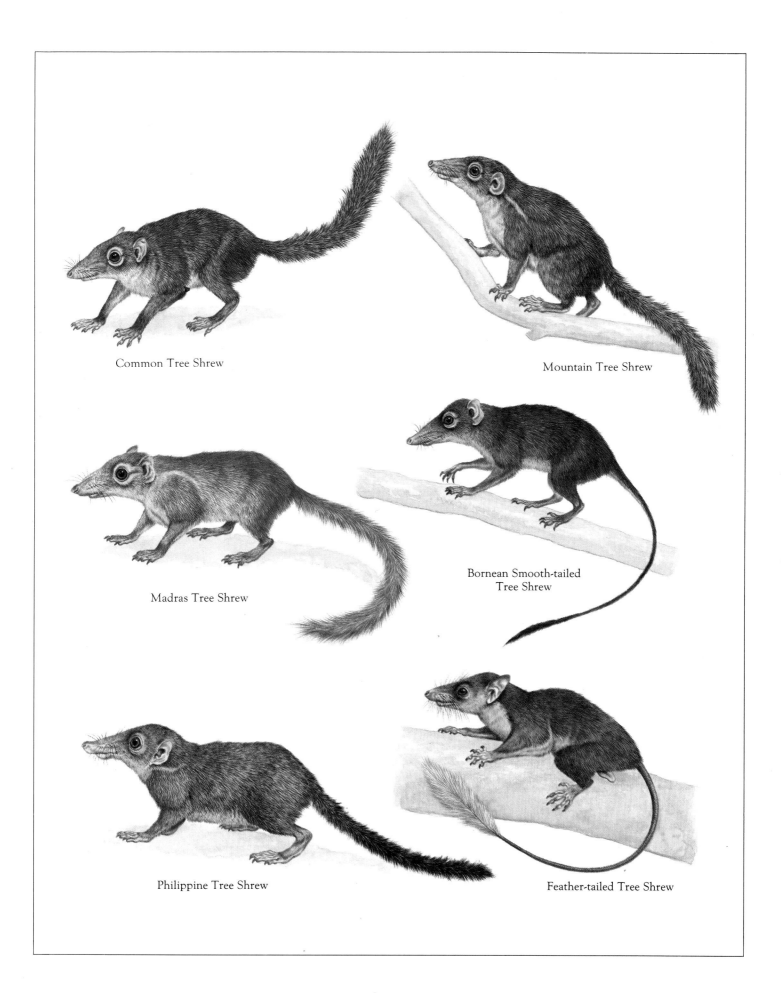

Common Tree Shrew

Mountain Tree Shrew

Madras Tree Shrew

Bornean Smooth-tailed
Tree Shrew

Philippine Tree Shrew

Feather-tailed Tree Shrew

Mouse-lemurs, Lemurs, Aye-aye

ORDER PRIMATES

There are about 179 species of primate, divided into two main groups: first, the prosimians, or primitive primates, which include lemurs, the aye-aye, lorises and tarsiers; and second, the higher primates such as marmosets, monkeys, apes and man.

CHEIROGALEIDAE:
Mouse-lemur Family

The 7 species of mouse-lemur occur in forest areas throughout Madagascar and are among the smallest primates.

NAME: **Russet Mouse-lemur,** *Microcebus rufus*
RANGE: **E. Madagascar**
HABITAT: **forest**
SIZE: **body: 12.5–15 cm (5–6 in)**
    tail: 12.5–15 cm (5–6 in)

Mainly nocturnal in its habits, this tiny primate moves swiftly and nimbly on fine branches amid dense foliage, using its tail as a balancing organ, and will leap across gaps between trees. It also comes down to the ground to forage in leaf litter for beetles. Insects and small vertebrates are its main foods, supplemented by fruit and buds. Though they normally move and hunt alone, russet mouse-lemurs often sleep in small groups in nests made in hollow trees or constructed from leaves.

LEMURIDAE: Lemur Family

There are about 16 species of lemur, all found in Madagascar and the nearby Comoro Islands. Most live in wooded areas and are agile tree-climbers.

NAME: **Ring-tailed Lemur,** *Lemur catta*
RANGE: **S. Madagascar**
HABITAT: **dry, rocky country with some trees**
SIZE: **body: 45 cm (17¾ in)**
    tail: 55 cm (21½ in)

The ring-tailed lemur has a pointed muzzle, large eyes and triangular ears. Its fur is thick and soft, and its bushy, distinctively ringed tail accounts for more than half its total length. Both sexes have special scent glands on the lower forelimbs; males have larger glands than females, with a horny spur near each. Males also have scent glands on the upper arms, under the chin and by the penis, while females have scent glands in the genital region. The lemurs use the secretions in these glands to mark territory boundaries, but will also mark whenever excited or disturbed. Troops of up to 20, sometimes 40, animals occupy a territory, with females and young

forming the core, while males move from troop to troop. Females are dominant over all males. Ring-tailed lemurs are active throughout the day, sometimes climbing up trees but also spending much time on the ground on all fours, with tail erect. They feed on fruit, leaves, bark, grass and resin, which they chisel from the trees with their lower incisors.

Females usually produce 1 young at a time, sometimes 2 or 3, after a gestation of about 136 days. The young is born well haired and with eyes open and is independent at 6 months.

NAME: **Ruffed Lemur,** *Varecia variegata*
RANGE: **N.E. and E. Madagascar**
HABITAT: **rain forest**
SIZE: **body: 60 cm (23½ in)**
    tail: 60 cm (23½ in)

Distinguished by its long ruff, this lemur has white and black, brown or rufous fur. It is a nimble climber, most active at dusk and during the first part of the night, when it forages for fruit, leaves and bark; it rarely descends to the ground.

In November, the female produces 1 to 3 young in a nest in a hole in a tree or on a forked branch, which she lines with her own fur. The gestation period is 99 to 102 days.

INDRIIDAE:
Leaping Lemur Family

The 4 species of leaping lemur occur in the scrub country and forests of Madagascar. In all of these lemurs the snout is shortened and bare of fur, giving them a resemblance to monkeys.

NAME: **Verreaux's Sifaka,** *Propithecus verreauxi*
RANGE: **W. and S. Madagascar**
HABITAT: **dry and rain forest**
SIZE: **body: 45 cm (17¾ in)**
    tail: 55 cm (21½ in)   Ⓔ

This large, long-limbed sifaka has a naked black face, large eyes, and ears nearly concealed by fur. Coloration is highly variable, ranging from yellowish-white to black or a reddish-brown. Troops of up to 10 animals occupy a well-defined territory, the boundaries of which are marked with urine or with secretions of the male's throat gland. They feed in the morning and afternoon on leaves, buds and fruit and are relaxed in their movements, spending much of the day resting and sun-bathing. Sifakas are primarily arboreal but sometimes come down to the ground.

Young are born from the end of June to August after a gestation of about 130 days. Females usually produce 1 young, which is suckled for about 6 months.

NAME: **Woolly Lemur,** *Avahi laniger*
RANGE: **E. and N.W. Madagascar**
HABITAT: **forest**
SIZE: **body: 30–45 cm (11¾–17¾ in)**
    tail: 33–40 cm (13–15¾ in)   Ⓥ

A nocturnal animal, the long-limbed woolly lemur sleeps up in the trees by day and is active at night, when it searches for fruit, leaves and buds to eat. It is an agile climber and only occasionally descends to the ground, where it moves in an upright position.

Young are usually born in late August or September after a gestation of about 150 days. The female normally produces a single young, which she suckles for about 6 months.

NAME: **Indri,** *Indri indri*
RANGE: **N.E. Madagascar**
HABITAT: **forest up to 1,800 m (6,000 ft)**
SIZE: **body: 61–71 cm (24–28 in)**
    tail: 3–6 cm (1¼–2¼ in)   Ⓔ

The largest of the lemurs, the indri is immediately identified by its stumpy tail. It has a longer muzzle than the sifakas and a naked black face. Indris live in family groups and are active during the day at all levels of the forest, searching for leaves, shoots and fruit.

Mating takes place in January or February, and females give birth to 1 young after a gestation of 4½ to 5½ months.

DAUBENTONIIDAE:
Aye-aye Family

The single species of aye-aye is a nocturnal, arboreal animal, found in the dense forests of Madagascar.

NAME: **Aye-aye,** *Daubentonia madagascariensis*
RANGE: **formerly N.E. Madagascar, now only in nature reserves**
HABITAT: **rain forest**
SIZE: **body: 36–44 cm (14¼–17¼ in)**
    tail: 50–60 cm (19¾–23½ in)   Ⓔ

Well adapted for life in the trees, the extraordinary aye-aye has specialized ears, teeth and hands. It emerges from its nest at night to search for food, mainly insect larvae, plant shoots, fruit and eggs. All its digits are long and slender, but the third is particularly long, and using this, it taps on a tree trunk to locate wood-boring insects. It listens for movement with its large, sensitive ears, and when a grub is located, it probes with its long finger to extract the prey. Sometimes it will first tear open the wood with its powerful teeth. It also uses its teeth to open eggs or coconuts.

Every 2 or 3 years, females produce a single young, which they suckle for over a year.

Russet Mouse-lemur

Ruffed Lemur

Ring-tailed Lemur

Woolly Lemur

Verreaux's Sifaka

Indri

Aye-aye

Lorises, Tarsiers

LORISIDAE: Loris Family

The 12 species that make up this family of primates occur in Africa, southern India, Southeast Asia and neighboring islands. Most specialists divide the family into two groups: first, the lorises, potto and angwantibo, which have short tails or no tails at all and are slow and deliberate in their movements; and second, the bush babies and galagos, which have long limbs and tails and are expert leapers.

NAME: **Slender Loris, *Loris tardigradus***
RANGE: **Sri Lanka, S. India**
HABITAT: **rain forest, open woodland, swamp forest**
SIZE: **body: 18–26 cm (7–10¼ in)**
   tail: absent or vestigial

The slender loris spends most of its life in trees, where it moves slowly and deliberately on its long, thin limbs. It has a strong grip with its efficient grasping hands, and its thumbs and great toes are opposable. A nocturnal animal, it spends the day sleeping up in the trees, its body rolled up in a ball. Toward evening, it becomes active and hunts for insects — particularly grasshoppers — lizards, small birds and their eggs, as well as some shoots and leaves. It approaches prey stealthily, with its usual deliberate movements, and then quickly grabs it with both hands.

In India, the slender loris is known to breed twice a year, births occurring most often in May and December. Usually 1 young, sometimes 2, is born, which makes its own way to the mother's teats, clinging to her fur.

NAME: **Slow Loris, *Nycticebus coucang***
RANGE: **S. and S.E. Asia: E. India to Malaysia; Sumatra, Java, Borneo, Philippines**
HABITAT: **dense rain forest**
SIZE: **body: 26–38 cm (10¼–15 in)**
   tail: vestigial

A plumper, shorter-limbed animal than its relative the slender loris, the slow loris is, however, similar in its habits. It spends the day sleeping up in a tree, its body rolled into a tight ball. At night, it feeds in the trees on insects, bird's eggs, small birds and shoots and fruit, seldom coming down to the ground. A slow, but accomplished, climber, its hands and feet are strong and capable of grasping tightly. It can even hang by its feet. The thumb and great toe are opposable to the other digits.

Breeding takes place at any time of year, and 1 young, sometimes 2, is born after a gestation of 193 days. Slow lorises are thought to live in family groups.

NAME: **Potto, *Perodicticus potto***
RANGE: **W., central and E. Africa**
HABITAT: **forest, forest edge**
SIZE: **body: 30–40 cm (11¾–15¾ in)**
   tail: 5–10 cm (2–4 in)

A thickset animal with dense fur, the potto has strong limbs and grasping feet and hands; the great toe and thumb are opposable. At the back of its neck are four horny spines, projections of the vertebrae that pierce the thin skin. The potto sleeps up in the trees during the day and hunts at night. Although slow and careful in its movements, the potto can quickly seize insect prey with its hands; snails, fruit and leaves are also eaten.

The female gives birth to 1 young a year, after a gestation of 6 to 6½ months. Although weaned at 2 or 3 months, the young may stay with its mother for up to a year.

NAME: **Angwantibo, *Arctocebus calabarensis***
RANGE: **W. Africa: Nigeria, Cameroon, south to Congo River**
HABITAT: **dense rain forest**
SIZE: **body: 25–40 cm (9¾–15¾ in)**
   tail: about 1.25 cm (½ in)

Also known as the golden potto because of the sheen to its fur, the arboreal angwantibo has strong hands and feet, adapted for grasping branches. Its first finger is a mere stump, and the second toe is much reduced. A skilled, but slow climber, the angwantibo is active at night, when it feeds mostly on insects, especially caterpillars, and also on snails, lizards and fruit. Outside the breeding season, it is usually solitary.

The female gives birth to 1 young after a gestation of 131 to 136 days. Her offspring is weaned at 4 months and fully grown at 7.

NAME: **Greater Bush Baby, *Otolemur crassicaudatus***
RANGE: **Africa: Somalia, Kenya, south to South Africa: Natal**
HABITAT: **forest, wooded savanna, bushveld, plantations**
SIZE: **body: 27–47 cm (10½–18½ in)**
   tail: 33–52 cm (13–20½ in)

The greater bush baby is a strongly built animal, with a pointed muzzle and large eyes. Its hands and feet are adapted for grasping, with opposable thumbs and great toes. Much of its life is spent in the trees, where it is active at night and feeds on insects, reptiles, birds and bird's eggs and plant material. It makes a rapid pounce to seize prey and kills it with a bite. It has a call like the cry of a child (hence the name bush baby) made most frequently in the breeding season.

The female gives birth to a litter of 1 to 3 young between May and October, after a gestation of 126 to 136 days.

NAME: **Lesser Bush Baby, *Galago senegalensis***
RANGE: **Africa: south of the Sahara to the Vaal River (not Guinea or central African rain forest)**
HABITAT: **savanna, bush, woodland**
SIZE: **body: 14–21 cm (5½–8¼ in)**
   tail: 20–30 cm (7¾–11¾ in)

More active and lively than its relative the greater bush baby, this species moves with great agility in the trees and hops and leaps with ease. Like all its family, it sleeps up in the trees during the day and hunts for food at night. Spiders, scorpions, insects, young birds, lizards, fruit, seeds and nectar are all included in its diet. It lives in a family group, the members of which sleep together but disperse on waking.

Breeding habits vary slightly in different areas of the range. In regions where there are two rainy seasons, females have two litters a year, each usually of only 1 offspring; where there is only one rainy season, females produce one litter, often, but not always, of twins. The gestation period varies between 128 and 146 days, and the young are fully grown at about 4 months.

TARSIIDAE: Tarsier Family

The 3 species in this family occur in the Philippines and Indonesia. These little prosimian primates are primarily nocturnal and arboreal and climb and jump with great agility. They are better adapted to leaping than any other primates, with their elongate hind legs and feet. Their long tails are naked.

NAME: **Western Tarsier, *Tarsius bancanus***
RANGE: **Sumatra, Borneo**
HABITAT: **secondary forest, scrub**
SIZE: **body: 8.5–16 cm (3¼–6¼ in)**
   tail: 13.5–27 cm (5¼–10½ in)

The western tarsier, like its two relatives, is identified by its long, naked tail and extremely large, round eyes. Its forelimbs are short and its hind limbs long because of the adaptation of the tarsus, or ankle bones; this enables the tarsier to leap. The specialized tarsus is, of course, the origin of both the common and scientific names. A nocturnal, mainly arboreal animal, the tarsier sleeps during the day, clinging to a branch with its tail. At dusk, it wakes to prey on insects, its main food, which it catches by making a swift pounce and seizing the insect in its hands.

Breeding occurs at any time of year, and females give birth to 1 young after a gestation of about 6 months. The young tarsier is born well furred, with its eyes open, and is capable of climbing and hopping almost immediately.

Slender Loris

Slow Loris

Potto

Angwantibo

Greater Bush Baby

Lesser Bush Baby

Western Tarsier

Marmosets and Tamarins

NAME: Goeldi's Marmoset, *Callimico goeldii*
RANGE: upper Amazon basin
HABITAT: scrub, forest
SIZE: body: 18–21.5 cm (7–8½ in)
tail: 25–32 cm (9¾–12½ in) Ⓘ

Few Goeldi's marmosets have been seen or captured, and details of their habits are not well known. This marmoset is identified by the long mane around its head and shoulders and by some long hairs on its rump. It forages in all levels of the trees and bushes, searching for plant matter, such as berries, and for insects and small vertebrates. An agile animal, it walks and runs well and leaps expertly from branch to branch. It often goes down to the ground and will seek refuge on the ground when alarmed by a predator such as a bird of prey.

Strong, long-lasting pair bonds exist between mates, and Goeldi's marmosets usually live in family groups of parents and offspring. The female bears a single young as a rule, after a gestation of 150 days. These marmosets are highly vocal and communicate with a variety of trills and whistles.

The exact state of the population of this species of marmoset is uncertain, but it is known to be rare and to have a patchy, localized distribution. In recent years it has suffered badly from the destruction of large areas of forest and from illegal trapping. More information is needed on these marmosets in order to set up suitable reserves and to ensure the survival of the species.

NAME: Pygmy Marmoset, *Cebuella pygmaea*
RANGE: upper Amazon basin
HABITAT: tropical forest
SIZE: body: 14–16 cm (5½–6¼ in)
tail: 15–20 cm (6–7¾ in)

The smallest marmoset and one of the smallest primates, the pygmy marmoset is active in the daytime but may rest at noon. Particularly vulnerable to attack by large birds of prey because of its size, it tries to keep out of sight to avoid danger and moves either extremely slowly or in short dashes, punctuated by moments of frozen immobility. Its cryptic coloration also helps to hide it from predators. It is primarily arboreal and sleeps in holes in trees but does come down to the ground occasionally to feed or to move from one tree to another. It eats fruit, insects, small birds and bird's eggs and is also thought to feed on sap from trees, which it obtains by gnawing a hole in the bark.

Pygmy marmosets live in troops of 5 to 10 individuals in which the females are dominant.

CALLITRICHIDAE:
Marmoset and Tamarin Family

Marmosets and tamarins make up 1 of the 2 families of primates to occur in the New World. Together with the monkeys, family Cebidae, they are known as the flat-nosed, or platyrrhine, monkeys. There are about 17 species of marmoset and tamarin, but more may sometimes be listed, depending on whether some variations are regarded as subspecies or species in their own right. Apart from the mouse-lemurs, marmosets are the smallest primates, varying from mouse- to squirrel-size. Their fur is soft, often silky, and many have tufts or ruffs of fur on their heads. Their tails are furry and not prehensile.

Active in the daytime, marmosets and tamarins are primarily tree-dwelling but do not have grasping hands or opposable thumbs like most primates. Neither do they swing from branch to branch, but they are rapid and agile in their movements and bound swiftly through the trees in a similar manner to squirrels. Their diet is varied, including both plant and animal material. At night, marmosets sleep curled up in holes in trees.

They are social animals and live in small family groups. The usual number of young is 2, and the male assists his mate by carrying one of the twins on his back. Often extremely vocal, marmosets make a variety of high-pitched cries.

NAME: Silvery/Black-tailed Marmoset, *Callithrix argentata*
RANGE: Brazil, Bolivia
HABITAT: forest, tall grass
SIZE: body: 15–30 cm (6–11¾ in)
tail: 18–40 cm (7–15¾ in) Ⓥ

Recognized by its silky, silvery-white body fur, this marmoset has no hair on its face and ears, which are reddish in color; there is often some gray on its back, and its tail is black. With quick, jerky movements, the silvery marmoset runs and hops in trees and bushes, looking for food such as fruit, leaves, insects, spiders, small birds and bird's eggs. It usually moves in groups of 2 to 5. Like most marmosets, it has a range of expressions, including grimaces and raising of the eyebrows, which are used to threaten rivals or enemies.

The female gives birth to 1 or 2 young, occasionally 3, after a gestation of 140 to 150 days. The male assists at the birth and is largely responsible for the care of the young.

NAME: Golden Lion Tamarin, *Leontopithecus rosalia*
RANGE: S.E. Brazil
HABITAT: coastal forest
SIZE: body: 19–22 cm (7½–8½ in)
tail: 26–34 cm (10¼–13¼ in) Ⓔ

A beautiful animal, this tamarin has a silky golden mane covering its head and shoulders and concealing its ears. In common with the other members of its family, it leaps from branch to branch with great agility as it searches for fruit, insects, lizards, small birds and bird's eggs to eat. It lives in small groups and is highly vocal.

The female gives birth to 1 or 2 young, rarely 3, after a gestation of 132 to 134 days. The father assists in the care of the young, giving them to the mother at feeding time and later preparing their first solid food by squashing and softening it in his fingers.

NAME: Emperor Tamarin, *Saguinus imperator*
RANGE: W. Brazil, E. Peru, N. Bolivia
HABITAT: lowland forest
SIZE: body: 18–21 cm (7–8¼ in)
tail: 25–32 cm (9¾–12½ in) Ⓘ

Easily identified by its flowing white mustache, the emperor tamarin is one of 11 species included in this genus. It is an active, agile animal, moving with quick, jerky movements in the shrubs and trees as it searches for fruit, tender vegetation, insects, spiders, small vertebrate animals and bird's eggs. It lives in small groups and makes a great variety of shrill sounds.

The female produces twin offspring after a gestation of about 5 months. The father assists at the birth and cleans the newly born young. Like many other marmosets, he also helps at feeding time by handing the baby to the mother.

NAME: Black and Red Tamarin, *Saguinus nigricollis*
RANGE: S. Colombia to adjacent areas of Ecuador and Brazil
HABITAT: primary and secondary forest
SIZE: body: 15–28 cm (6–11 in)
tail: 27–42 cm (10½–16½ in)

This tamarin is typical of its genus, with its unspecialized, short, broad hands, equipped with claws, and a small body. The hairs around its mouth are white, but the skin under the mustache is pigmented, as are the genitalia. Family groups consisting of a male, a female and 1 or 2 young live in a defined territory — the female marks branches on the boundaries of the territory with secretions of her anal glands and urine. Insects, leaves and fruit are the main foods of these tamarins.

The female gives birth to 2 young after a gestation of 140 to 150 days.

Silvery Marmoset

Pygmy Marmoset

Goeldi's Marmoset

Emperor Tamarin

Golden Lion
Tamarin

Black and Red Tamarin

New World Monkeys

NAME: Three-banded Douroucouli/ Night Monkey, *Aotus trivirgatus*
RANGE: Panama to Paraguay (patchy distribution)
HABITAT: forest
SIZE: body: 24–37 cm (9½–14½ in)
  tail: 31–40 cm (12¼–15¾ in)

The three-banded douroucouli has a heavily furred body and tail and is characterized by its large eyes and round head. It is usually grayish in color, with dark markings on the head, and has an inflatable sac under the chin that amplifies its calls. A nocturnal monkey, it can see very well at night and moves with agility in the trees. It rarely descends to the ground. Fruit, leaves, insects and spiders are its main foods, but it also takes some small mammals and birds. Douroucoulis usually live in pairs, accompanied by their offspring. Several families may group together during the day to sleep in a hollow tree or in a nest among foliage.

The female gives birth to a single young, which clings to its mother for the first few weeks of life before it starts to climb alone.

NAME: Monk Saki, *Pithecia monachus*
RANGE: upper Amazon basin
HABITAT: forest
SIZE: body: 35–48 cm (13¾–18¾ in)
  tail: 31–51 cm (12¼–20 in)

The monk saki has long, shaggy hair framing its face and on its neck and a thick, bushy tail. A shy, wary animal, it is totally arboreal, living high in the trees and sometimes descending to lower levels but not to the ground. It generally moves on all fours but may sometimes walk upright on a large branch and will leap across gaps. During the day, it moves in pairs or small family groups, feeding on fruit, berries, honey, some leaves, small mammals, such as mice and bats, and birds.

The female gives birth to 1 young.

NAME: Black-bearded Saki, *Chiropotes satanas*
RANGE: N. South America to Brazil
HABITAT: forest
SIZE: body: 36–52 cm (14¼–20½ in)
  tail: 36–50 cm (14¼–19¾ in)

The black-bearded saki is identified by its prominent beard and the long black hair on its head; the rest of the coat is reddish-chestnut or blackish-brown. The tail is thick and heavily furred. Little is known of the habits of this monkey in the wild other than that it lives in large trees and feeds mainly on fruit. It requires many square kilometres of undisturbed habitat for successful breeding, however, and the widespread lumbering of primary forest poses a threat to its long-term survival.

CEBIDAE:
New World Monkey Family

Most of the New World monkeys of the family Cebidae are much larger in size than any of the marmosets and tamarins — the other group of flat-nosed (platyrrhine) American monkeys. There are about 32 species, including capuchins, howler monkeys, woolly monkeys, sakis and ouakaris. Typically these monkeys have long, hairy tails, which in some species are prehensile and of great importance in arboreal locomotion.

With a few exceptions, cebid monkeys conform to the flat-nosed appearance so characteristic of New World monkeys. The nostrils are wide apart and open to the sides, whereas Old World monkeys have nostrils placed close together and opening forward. The long, thin fingers of the hands are useful manipulative organs and bear strong nails, but the thumbs are not opposable. The big toe, however, is large and can be opposed against the other toes for gripping branches. Thus equipped, cebid monkeys are excellent runners and leapers in wooded habitats in Central and South America, from Mexico in the north to Argentina in the south. They are gregarious and live in family-based groups with much vocal and visual communication. Diet is predominantly vegetarian.

NAME: White-fronted Capuchin, *Cebus albifrons*
RANGE: parts of Colombia, Venezuela, upper Amazon area; Trinidad
HABITAT: forest
SIZE: body: 30–38 cm (11¾–15 in)
  tail: 38–50 cm (15–19¾ in)

A lively, intelligent monkey, like all the capuchins, this species is slender and long-limbed, with a partially prehensile tail. There is considerable variation in color over the range, but these capuchins are usually different shades of brown. Alert and fast-moving, they are inquiring by nature, have great manual dexterity and investigate all sorts of plants and fruit in the hope that they may be edible. Shoots, fruit, insects, young birds and bird's eggs are all part of their diet. Primarily arboreal, these capuchins do sometimes descend to the ground and may venture across open country. They are gregarious and live in territories in groups of 20 to 30.

The female usually gives birth to 1 young, although twins have been known. The offspring is suckled for several months and is carried around by both parents.

NAME: Dusky Titi, *Callicebus moloch*
RANGE: Colombia to Bolivia
HABITAT: forest, thickets
SIZE: body: 28–39 cm (11–15¼ in)
  tail: 33–49 cm (13–19¼ in)

An inhabitant of densely vegetated areas, the dusky titi often occurs in damp, waterlogged forest. It can move quite fast if necessary but rarely does so and generally stays within a fairly small area, feeding on fruit, insects, spiders, small birds and bird's eggs. Active in the daytime, it moves in pairs or family groups, which communicate by means of a wide repertoire of sounds. Dusky titis have rounded heads and thick, soft coats and frequently adopt a characteristic posture with the body hunched, limbs close together and tail hanging down.

The female gives birth to 1 young.

NAME: Squirrel Monkey, *Saimiri sciureus*
RANGE: Colombia to Amazon basin
HABITAT: forest, cultivated land
SIZE: body: 26–36 cm (10¼–14¼ in)
  tail: 35–42 cm (13¾–16½ in)

A slender monkey with a long, mobile tail, the squirrel monkey has a short, brightly colored coat. It is highly active and lively, feeding during the day on fruit, nuts, insects, spiders, young birds and eggs, and it occasionally comes to the ground to feed. Squirrel monkeys sometimes raid fruit plantations for food. They are gregarious and live in bands of 12 to 30 or more.

The female gives birth to 1 young after a gestation of 24 to 26 weeks. The newborn infant is able to climb soon after birth and receives little attention from its parents.

NAME: Bald Ouakari, *Cacajao calvus*
RANGE: W. Brazil
HABITAT: forest
SIZE: body: 51–57 cm (20–22½ in)
  tail: 15–16 cm (6–6¼ in) ⓥ

A distinctive monkey, the bald ouakari has a naked face, long, shaggy hair and a beard. Its white hair appears reddish in the sunlight. Its tail is fairly short — the 3 species of ouakari are the only New World monkeys to have short tails. Extremely agile on all fours, this ouakari rarely leaps, since it does not have the long, counterbalancing tail of other types of cebid monkey. It frequents the treetops, feeding largely on fruit but also on leaves, insects, small mammals and birds, and seldom descends to the ground. Active in the daytime, bald ouakaris live in small troops consisting of several adult males and females and their young of different ages.

White-fronted Capuchin

Three-banded Douroucouli

Dusky Titi

Monk Saki

Squirrel Monkey

Black-bearded Saki

Bald Ouakari

New World Monkeys

NAME: Red Howler Monkey, *Alouatta seniculus*
RANGE: Colombia to mouth of Amazon River, south to Bolivia
HABITAT: forest, mangrove swamps
SIZE: body: 80–90 cm (31½–35½ in)
tail: 80–90 cm (31½–35½ in)

One of the largest New World monkeys, the red howler has reddish-brown fur and a sturdy body and legs. Its tail is prehensile, with an extremely sensitive naked area on the underside near the tip. All male howler monkeys are renowned for the incredibly loud calls produced by their specialized larynxes, and this apparatus is most developed in the red howler. The chief adaptation of the larynx is the greatly expanded hyoid bone surrounding it that makes a resonating chamber for the sound. The jaw is expanded and deepened to accommodate the bulbous larynx and sports a thick beard. The male red howler occupies a territory and leads a troop of, usually, 6 to 8 animals. In order to defend his territory, he shouts for long periods at rival groups to signal his possession. Most shouting is done in the early morning and late afternoon, but red howlers may be heard at any time of day — from over 3 km (1¾ mi) away.

Red howlers live and move adeptly in the trees, although they frequent large branches because of their sturdy build. Their digits are organized in such a way as to facilitate the grasping of branches, with the first two fingers separated and opposable to the other three; this arrangement does, however, make delicate manipulation of food items difficult. Red howlers leap well and use their prehensile tails for support. They sometimes go down to the ground and will even cross open land; they are good swimmers. Leaves and some fruit are the red howler's staple diet. At night, these monkeys sleep in the trees on branches.

Breeding appears to occur at any time of year, and the female gives birth to 1 young after an average gestation of 20 weeks. The young howler clings to its mother's fur at first and later rides on her back; it is suckled for 18 months to 2 years.

NAME: Black Howler Monkey, *Alouatta caraya*
RANGE: S. Brazil to N. Argentina
HABITAT: forest
SIZE: body: 80–90 cm (31½–35½ in)
tail: 80–90 cm (31½–35½ in)

Only male black howlers are actually black; females have brown coats. These howlers live in troops, probably containing more than 1 male, and occupy territories, which they defend by their powerful shouts in the same way that red howlers do. The bulbous larynx, concealed under the bushy beard, amplifies the shouts. Black howlers tend to have quieter voices and smaller territories than red howlers.

A strongly built monkey with powerful limbs and a prehensile tail, the black howler lives in the trees, feeding on leaves and fruit. The female gives birth to 1 young after a gestation of about 20 weeks, and her offspring stays with her for up to 2 years.

NAME: Black Spider Monkey, *Ateles paniscus*
RANGE: northern South America to Brazil and Bolivia
HABITAT: forest
SIZE: body: 40–60 cm (15¾–23½ in)
tail: 60–80 cm (23½–31½ in) Ⓥ

Only surpassed by the gibbons for grace and agility in the trees, the black spider monkey, with its extremely long limbs and tail, is the most adept and acrobatic of all New World monkeys. Light in build, with a small head, the spider monkey has the most highly developed prehensile tail of all mammals and uses it as a fifth limb to grasp branches or food items as it moves through the trees. The monkey's whole weight can be supported by the tail, and when hanging by the tail with the long arms outstretched, the animal has an amazing reach. Part of the underside of the tail nearest the tip is naked and patterned with fine grooves, resembling human fingerprint patterns. These increase friction and thus aid grip. Spider monkeys frequently swing through the trees, using their hands like hooks to hang onto the branches. The hands are accordingly modified, with long, curved digits and only vestigial thumbs. While this structure makes the hands ideal for swinging in trees, it impedes delicate manipulation of food, but the monkey often uses its highly sensitive tail to gather food and to hold items, such as fruit, while it takes off the skin with its teeth.

Black spider monkeys rarely come to the ground and feed in trees, mainly on fruit and some nuts. They live in groups of 15 to 30 animals in a home range, but a group may split into smaller parties while foraging during the day. Most feeding is done in the early morning and the afternoon.

The female gives birth to 1 young after an average gestation of about 20 weeks. The young is dependent on its mother for 10 months or so.

NAME: Woolly Spider Monkey, *Brachyteles arachnoides*
RANGE: S.E. Brazil
HABITAT: coastal forest
SIZE: body: about 61 cm (24 in)
tail: about 67 cm (26¼ in) Ⓔ

The woolly spider monkey usually has a yellowish-gray to brown or reddish coat, and the naked facial skin is often red, especially when the animal is excited. Its body is powerful and its limbs long and slender, and, like the spider monkeys, it has a highly efficient prehensile tail, which it uses as a fifth limb. The underside of the tail near the tip is naked and extremely sensitive. Woolly spider monkeys often move by swinging from branch to branch, and their thumbs, of little use for such locomotion, are vestigial.

Active in the daytime, woolly spider monkeys feed in trees, mainly on fruit. They are gregarious, but little more is known of their habits in the wild.

NAME: Common Woolly Monkey, *Lagothrix lagothricha*
RANGE: upper Amazon basin
HABITAT: forest up to 2,000 m (6,600 ft)
SIZE: body: 50–68 cm (19¾–26¾ in)
tail: 60–72 cm (23½–28¼ in) Ⓥ

Heavier in build than the spider monkeys, the common woolly monkey has short, thick hair. Its head is rounded, its body robust, and it has a prominent belly. Fast and agile in the trees, it moves on all fours and by swinging hand over hand, but it is less graceful than the spider monkeys. Its thumbs and toes are well developed for grasping branches, and it has a strong prehensile tail, with a sensitive naked area near the tip.

Woolly monkeys are highly gregarious and live in troops of up to 50. They forage in the daytime for plant material, mostly fruit, but are less active than many other New World monkeys. Primarily arboreal, they do, nevertheless, often come down to the ground, where they walk upright, using their long tails as counterbalances.

The female gives birth to 1 offspring after a gestation of 18 to 20 weeks. The young monkey holds onto the fur of its mother's belly or back at first and is carried around, but after a few weeks it is able to clamber about the branches unaided. The female suckles her young for 12 months or more. Common woolly monkeys are sexually mature at about 4 years old.

Black Howler Monkey (male)

Red Howler Monkey
(male)

Black Spider Monkey

Woolly Spider Monkey

Common Woolly Monkey

Old World Monkeys

NAME: **Barbary Ape,** *Macaca sylvanus*
RANGE: **Gibraltar; Africa: Morocco,
N. Algeria**
HABITAT: **rocky areas, forest clearings on
mountains**
SIZE: **body: 55–75 cm (21½–29½ in)
tail: absent** Ⓥ

The barbary ape is a robust, tailless monkey, with a rounded head and short muzzle. Males are larger than females and have longer hair on the crown. Formerly found elsewhere in southwest Europe, barbary apes now occur outside Africa only on Gibraltar, where the population is reinforced by bringing in animals from North Africa. Barbary apes live in troops of 10 to 30 males, females and young in a defined territory. The monkeys sleep in trees or among rocks and feed in the early morning and afternoon, taking a rest at midday. They climb well and forage in trees and on the ground for grass, leaves, berries, fruit, roots, insects and spiders. They will also plunder gardens and crops.

The female gives birth to a single young, rarely twins, after a gestation of about 7 months. Births take place at any time of year but peak from May to September. Males help females to look after and carry the young in the first few days. The offspring suckles for about 3 months and stays with its mother for up to 6 months.

NAME: **Stump-tailed Macaque,** *Macaca
arctoides*
RANGE: **Burma, S. China to Malaysia**
HABITAT: **forest, cultivated land**
SIZE: **body: 50–70 cm (19¾–27½ in)
tail: 4–10 cm (1½–4 in)**

Distinguished by its pink-tinged face, shaggy hair and short tail, the stump-tailed macaque is an aggressive, fearless monkey that often invades gardens and cultivated fields. It spends much of its time on the ground but also climbs up into trees to sleep or to find food or a safe refuge, although it is not a particularly agile animal. Leaves, fruit, roots and crops, such as potatoes, are its main foods, and it usually picks up the items with its hands. Two cheek pouches are used for storing food, which is later removed and chewed at leisure. Stump-tailed macaques are active in the daytime and live in groups of 25 to 30, led by a dominant individual. Members of the group constantly chatter and squeal to each other, and they also communicate by means of a wide range of facial expressions. Males are larger than females.

Little is known about the reproduction of these macaques in the wild, but females are thought to produce an infant every other year.

CERCOPITHECIDAE:
Old World Monkey Family

The monkeys and apes of the Old World are usually grouped together as the catarrhine primates — those with closely spaced nostrils that face forward or downward. The Old World monkeys themselves are the largest group of catarrhines, with about 76 species known, in Africa, Asia and Indonesia. There are a few general differences between Old and New World monkeys. The Old World species are generally larger and often have bare buttock pads, which may be brightly colored, and their tails, although often long, are seldom, if ever, fully prehensile.

The family includes the macaques, baboons, mandrills, mangabeys, guenons, langurs, colobus and leaf monkeys and many other forms. Almost all are diurnal animals, with excellent vision, hearing and sense of smell. Most are arboreal, but baboons are ground-feeding specialists, and the macaques are found both in the trees and on the ground. Generally Old World monkeys live in family or larger groups and communicate by a variety of visual and vocal signals. Males are often considerably larger than females.

NAME: **Japanese Macaque,** *Macaca fuscata*
RANGE: **Japan**
HABITAT: **high-altitude forest**
SIZE: **body: 50–75 cm (19¾–29½ in)
tail: 25–30 cm (9¾–11¾ in)**

The only monkey found in Japan, the Japanese macaque is the sole primate other than humans able to withstand a cold, snowy winter and near-freezing temperatures. In some parts of its range, it spends long periods immersed up to the neck in thermal pools. It is a medium-sized, well-built monkey, with dense fur and long whiskers and beard. Active both on the ground and in trees, it feeds mainly on nuts, berries, buds, leaves and bark.

Social groups of up to 40 individuals live together, led by an older male. The relationship between females and their mothers is extremely important; as long as their mother lives, females remain in association with her, even when they have their own young, and such female groups are the core of a troop. Males stay with their mothers and kin until adolescence, when they may join a peripheral group of males that drifts between troops. After a period in such a group, or alone, the male joins a troop, usually not that of his birth.

Females give birth to 1 young after a gestation of between 6 and 7 months.

NAME: **Bonnet Macaque,** *Macaca radiata*
RANGE: **S. India**
HABITAT: **forest, scrub, cultivated and
suburban areas**
SIZE: **body: 35–60 cm (13¾–23½ in)
tail: 48–65 cm (18¾–25½ in)**

The common name of this long-tailed macaque is derived from the unruly cap of dark hairs on its crown. Its face is normally pale pink, but the faces of lactating females are dark red. Males are much larger than females. An agile, active monkey, the bonnet macaque spends the bulk of its time in the trees, although it moves readily on the ground and also swims well. It has a voracious appetite and feeds on leaves, fruit, nuts seeds, insects, bird's eggs and, occasionally, lizards.

The female gives birth to 1 young, sometimes twins, after a gestation of about 150 days.

NAME: **White-cheeked Mangabey,**
Cercocebus albigena
RANGE: **Africa: Cameroon to Uganda,
Kenya, Tanzania**
HABITAT: **forest**
SIZE: **body: 45–70 cm (17¾–27½ in)
tail: 70 cm–1 m (27½ in–3¼ ft)**

A slender, elegant monkey, the white-cheeked mangabey is distinguished by its conspicuous eyebrow tufts and the mane of long hairs on its neck and shoulders. Its tail is immensely long and mobile and covered with rather shaggy hairs; it is semiprehensile. Males are larger than females and have longer tails. These mangabeys sleep and spend nearly all their time in trees; they feed during the day on fruit, nuts, leaves, bark and insects. Troops of 10 to 30 animals live together and are extremely noisy, constantly chattering and shrieking to one another.

The female gives birth to 1 young after a gestation of 174 to 180 days. The young is suckled for up to 10 months.

NAME: **Agile Mangabey,** *Cercocebus
galeritus*
RANGE: **Africa: S.E. Nigeria, Zaire to
E. Kenya**
HABITAT: **rain and swamp forest**
SIZE: **body: 45–65 cm (17¾–25½ in)
tail: 45–75 cm (17¾–29½ in)** Ⓔ

A slender, but strongly built monkey, the agile mangabey has long legs and tail and a fringe of hairs on its forehead. There are several races, which vary slightly in coloration; one has no fringe on the forehead. The details of this mangabey's daily habits are poorly known, but it is thought to be active on the ground and in trees and to feed on leaves, fruit, crops and insects. It lives in troops of 12 to 20, consisting of several old males, mature females and young.

Stump-tailed Macaque

Japanese Macaque

Bonnet Macaque

Barbary Ape

White-cheeked Mangabey

Agile Mangabey

Old World Monkeys

NAME: Olive Baboon, *Papio anubis*
RANGE: Africa: Senegal, east to N. Zaire,
  Ethiopia, Kenya, Uganda, N. Tanzania
HABITAT: savanna
SIZE: body: up to 1 m ($3\frac{1}{4}$ ft)
  tail: 45–75 cm ($17\frac{3}{4}$–$29\frac{1}{2}$ in)

The olive baboon is a large, heavily built baboon, with a sloping back and a well-developed, doglike muzzle, equipped with powerful teeth. Males have a mane of long hair around neck and shoulders and are larger than females. The tail has a tuft at its end, and the buttock area is naked, with broad callosities.

These baboons live in troops of 20 to 150 individuals, organized in a strict hierarchy. Although mainly ground-living animals, olive baboons sleep at night in the safety of trees or rocks and emerge in the morning to travel to feeding grounds in a well-ordered procession. Older juveniles lead the way, followed by the females and younger juveniles; the older males with the mothers and infants come next, and young males bring up the rear and scout ahead of the party to warn of any danger. Olive baboons are omnivorous, feeding on grass, seeds, roots, leaves, fruit, bark, insects, invertebrates, bird's eggs and young, lizards and young mammals such as antelope and lambs.

The female gives birth to 1 young, rarely 2, after a gestation of about 187 days. At first the young clings to its mother's belly but at 4 or 5 weeks begins to ride on her back. It takes its first solid food at 5 or 6 months and is weaned and independent at 8 months, although it is guarded by the mother until it is about 2 years old.

NAME: Hamadryas Baboon, *Papio*
  hamadryas
RANGE: Africa: Ethiopia, Somalia;
  S. Saudi Arabia
HABITAT: dry rocky country, savanna,
  semidesert
SIZE: body: 50–95 cm ($19\frac{3}{4}$–$37\frac{1}{2}$ in)
  tail: 40–60 cm ($15\frac{3}{4}$–$23\frac{1}{2}$ in)

The male hamadryas baboon is as much as twice the size of the female and has a heavy mane around its neck and shoulders. Females and younger males lack the mane and have brownish hair. Like all baboons, this species has a dog-like muzzle and a sloping back. Family troops of an old male and several females and their young live together, sleeping in trees or among rocks at night and wandering in search of food during the day. They eat almost any plants, insects and small animals.

The peak breeding season is May to July, and the female produces 1, rarely 2, young after a gestation of between 170 and 175 days.

NAME: Chacma Baboon, *Papio ursinus*
RANGE: Africa: Angola, Zambia to South
  Africa
HABITAT: savanna, rocky areas
SIZE: body: up to 1 m ($3\frac{1}{4}$ ft)
  tail: 40–75 cm ($15\frac{3}{4}$–$29\frac{1}{2}$ in)

A large, yet slender baboon, with a prominent muzzle and a sloping back, the chacma baboon carries its tail in a characteristic posture as if "broken" near the base. It lives in troops of about 30 to 100 individuals, sleeping among rocks or in trees at night and searching for food during the day. These baboons feed early and late in the day and rest at midday. Almost any plant and animal matter, such as leaves, fruit, insects, small invertebrates, lizards, birds and young mammals, is included in their diet, but they are predominantly vegetarian.

When in heat, the bare skin around the female's genital region swells, and at the peak of her fertile period only high-ranking males may mate with her. This is common to all savanna baboons.

The female gives birth to a single young, very rarely twins, after a gestation of 175 to 193 days, and suckles her offspring for about 8 months.

NAME: Drill, *Mandrillus leucophaeus*
RANGE: Africa: S.E. Nigeria, Cameroon
HABITAT: forest
SIZE: body: 45–90 cm ($17\frac{3}{4}$–$35\frac{1}{2}$ in)
  tail: 6–12 cm ($2\frac{1}{4}$–$4\frac{3}{4}$ in) Ⓔ

A powerfully built forest baboon, with a large head and a short, stumpy tail, the drill has a long muzzle, a ridged face and large nostrils. Males are much larger than females, sometimes twice the size, and have heavy manes on neck and shoulders. The skin of the buttock pads and the area around them is brightly colored, and the hue becomes more pronounced when the animal is excited. Although it climbs well and sleeps in low branches, the drill is ground-dwelling and moves on all fours. It lives in family troops of 20 or more animals, which may join with other troops to form bands of as many as 200. The baboons communicate with a variety of deep grunts and sharp cries, as well as with up and down movements of the head with mouth closed, to express threat, or side to side movements with teeth exposed, to express friendship. Old males dominate the troop and guard its safety; they are formidable animals, well equipped for fighting, with their sharp teeth and strong limbs. They feed on plant matter, insects and small invertebrate and vertebrate animals.

Young are born at all times of the year. The female produces 1 young after a gestation of about 7 months.

NAME: Mandrill, *Mandrillus sphinx*
RANGE: Africa: Cameroon, Gabon
HABITAT: forest
SIZE: body: 55–95 cm ($21\frac{1}{2}$–$37\frac{1}{2}$ in)
  tail: 7–10 cm ($2\frac{3}{4}$–4 in)

The male mandrill is a large, heavily built forest baboon, with an elongate snout marked with deep, often colorful ridges. Adult females are much smaller and have less pronounced ridges and facial coloration. Although mandrills sleep in trees, they live and feed on the ground in troops of about 20 to 50 animals, led and protected by one or more old males. They feed on fruit, nuts, leaves, insects and small invertebrate and vertebrate animals.

Births occur at any time of year but peak from December to February. The female produces a single young after a gestation of about $7\frac{1}{2}$ months.

NAME: Gelada, *Theropithecus gelada*
RANGE: Africa: Ethiopia
HABITAT: mountains: rocky ravines,
  alpine meadows
SIZE: body: 50–75 cm ($19\frac{3}{4}$–$29\frac{1}{2}$ in)
  tail: 45–55 cm ($17\frac{3}{4}$–$21\frac{1}{2}$ in)

The impressive gelada has a distinctive head, with a somewhat upturned muzzle marked with ridges, and the nostrils are located well back, not at the end of the muzzle as in other baboons. Long side-whiskers project backward and upward, and there is a heavy mane over the neck and shoulders which may reach almost to the ground in old males. On the chest and throat are three areas of bare red skin, which the male expands and brings into full view in his aggressive threat posture. Females are about half the size of males and have much lighter manes.

The gelada is a ground-dweller and even sleeps on rocky ledges and cliffs. It lives in family groups of several females and their young, led by a large mature male; these family groups may sometimes gather into large troops of several hundred animals. Young and unattached males may form their own units. In the morning, the geladas leave the cliffs where they have slept and move off to alpine meadows, where they feed largely on plant material, such as grasses, seeds and fruit, and on insects and other small animals. They do not have a specific territory, and the male keeps his family together by means of a variety of calls and facial expressions. Geladas have excellent vision, hearing and sense of smell.

Most young are born between February and April. The female produces a single offspring, rarely twins, after a gestation of 147 to 192 days and suckles it for up to 2 years. After giving birth, she does not have a period of heat for 12 to 18 months.

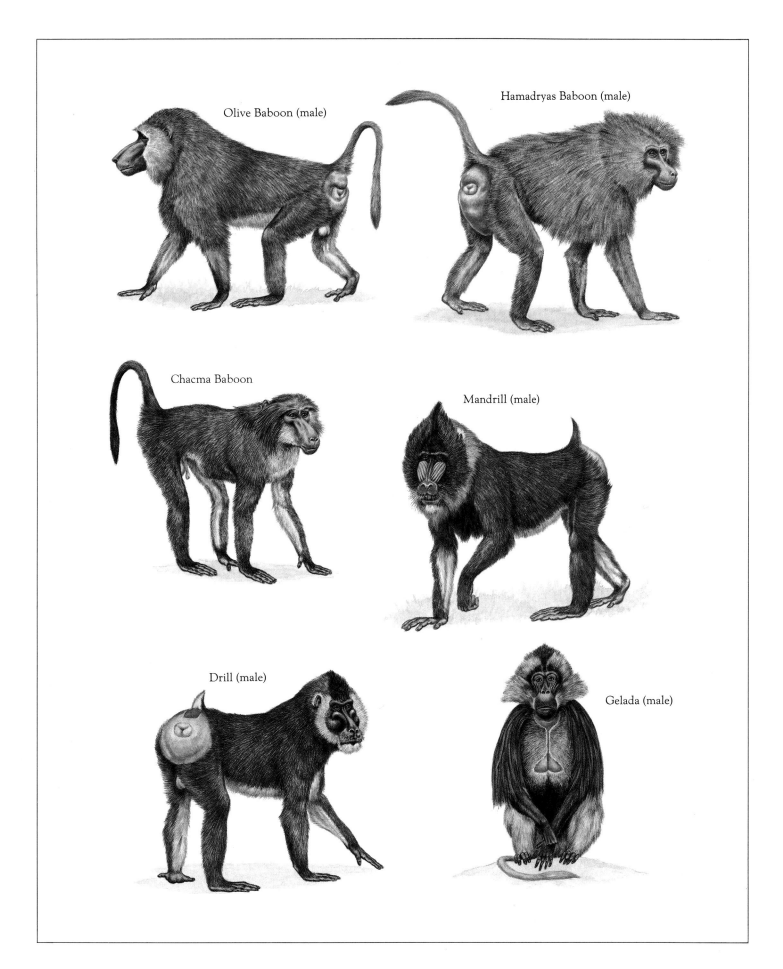

Olive Baboon (male)

Hamadryas Baboon (male)

Chacma Baboon

Mandrill (male)

Drill (male)

Gelada (male)

Old World Monkeys

NAME: Vervet Monkey, *Cercopithecus aethiops*
RANGE: Africa: Senegal to Somalia, south to South Africa
HABITAT: savanna, woodland edge
SIZE: body: 40–80 cm (15¾–31½ in)
  tail: 50–70 cm (19¾–27½ in)

There are many races of this medium- to large-sized monkey, which vary in their facial markings and whiskers. Generally, however, they have black faces, white whiskers and grayish or yellowish-olive hair. Although they sleep and take refuge in trees, these adaptable monkeys forage in open country and will run some distance on the ground. They also climb, jump and swim well. Family troops of an old male and several females and young live together and may join with other troops during the day. Generally rather quiet monkeys, males utter a harsh cry, and others may scream when frightened. Mainly vegetarian animals, they feed on leaves, shoots, fruit, flowers, seeds and bark but also eat some insects, spiders, lizards, bird's eggs and young birds.

Breeding occurs at any time of year. The female gives birth to a single young after a gestation of 175 to 203 days and suckles it for about 6 months. For the first few weeks, the baby clings to its mother's belly but starts to leave her at 3 weeks and to climb at 4 weeks old. When males become sexually mature, their scrotums adopt a blue-green hue.

NAME: De Brazza's Monkey, *Cercopithecus neglectus*
RANGE: Africa: Cameroon, south to Angola, east to Uganda
HABITAT: rain and swamp forest, dry mountain forest near water
SIZE: body: 40–60 cm (15¾–23½ in)
  tail: 53–85 cm (20¾–33½ in)

The robust, heavily built De Brazza's monkey has a conspicuous reddish-brown band, bordered with black, on its forehead, and a well-developed white beard. Its back slopes upward to the tail so that the rump is higher than the shoulders. Females look similar to males but are smaller. Active during the day, this monkey is a good climber and swimmer and also moves with speed and agility on the ground, where it spends a good deal of its feeding time. Leaves, shoots, fruit, berries, insects and lizards are its main foods, and it will also raid crops. It lives in small family groups of an old male and several females with young or sometimes in larger troops of 30 or more animals.

The female gives birth to 1 young after a gestation of 177 to 187 days. After a week, the baby first starts to let go of its mother's body, and by 3 weeks, it is starting to climb and run.

NAME: Red-bellied Monkey, *Cercopithecus erythrogaster*
RANGE: Africa: Nigeria
HABITAT: forest
SIZE: body: about 45 cm (17¾ in)
  tail: about 60 cm (23½ in)

This apparently rare monkey has a dark face with a pinkish muzzle, fringed with white side-whiskers. The breast and belly are usually reddish-brown, hence the common name, but can be gray in some individuals. Females look similar to males but have grayish underparts, arms and legs. Few specimens of this monkey have been found, and its habits are not known.

NAME: Diana Monkey, *Cercopithecus diana*
RANGE: Africa: Sierra Leone to Ghana
HABITAT: rain forest
SIZE: body: 40–57 cm (15¾–22½ in)
  tail: 50–75 cm (19¾–29½ in)

A slender, elegant monkey, the Diana monkey has most striking coloration, with its black and white face, white beard and chest and distinctive patches of bright chestnut on its back and hind limbs. There are also conspicuous white stripes on the otherwise dark hair of each thigh. Females are smaller than males but in other respects look similar. An excellent climber, the Diana monkey spends virtually all its life in the middle and upper layers of the forest and is noisy and inquisitive. Troops of up to 30 animals live together, led by an old male, and are most active in the early morning and late afternoon, when they feed on leaves, fruit, buds and other plant matter and also on some insects and bird's eggs and young.

The female bears a single young after a gestation of about 7 months and suckles it for 6 months.

NAME: Talapoin, *Miopithecus talapoin*
RANGE: Africa: Gabon to W. Angola
HABITAT: rain forest, mangrove swamps, always near water
SIZE: body: 25–40 cm (9¾–15¾ in)
  tail: 36–52 cm (14¼–20½ in)

One of the smallest African monkeys, the talapoin has a slender body, a round head, which is large relative to body size, and prominent ears. Its legs are longer than its arms, and its tail exceeds its head and body length. Talapoins live in family troops of 12 to 20 or so individuals, and each troop has its own territory, although several troops may sometimes unite into a larger group. These monkeys sleep in bushes and mangroves and are active in the daytime, particularly in the early morning and late afternoon. Good climbers and runners, they enter water readily and swim and dive well. Leaves, seeds, fruit,

water plants, insects, eggs and small animals are all included in their diet, and they will raid plantation crops.

Most births occur between November and March. After a gestation of about 6½ months, the female produces a single young, which is born well haired and with its eyes open. The young talapoin develops quickly and takes its first solid food at 3 weeks; it is largely independent at 3 months, although it continues to suckle until it is 4 or 5 months old.

NAME: Patas Monkey, *Erythrocebus patas*
RANGE: Africa: Senegal, east to Ethiopia, south to Tanzania
HABITAT: grassland, dry savanna, forest edge, rocky plateaus
SIZE: body: 50–75 cm (19¾–29½ in)
  tail: 50–75 cm (19¾–29½ in)

The slender, long-legged patas monkey is among the fastest moving of all primates on the ground: it can attain speeds of up to 50 km/h (31 mph). The male may be as much as twice the size of the female, and the lower parts of his limbs are pure white; the limbs of females are fawn or yellowish-white. Patas monkeys live in troops, consisting of an old male and up to 12 females and their young, and occupy a large territory. Although they sleep in trees, usually at the edge of forest, these monkeys spend virtually all of their day on the ground, searching for fruit, seeds, leaves, roots, insects, lizards and bird's eggs. While the troop feeds, the male leader keeps a lookout for danger and warns his harem of the approach of any enemies.

Most births occur from December to February, and females produce 1 young after a gestation of 170 days. The baby takes its first solid food at about 3 months old.

NAME: Allen's Swamp Monkey, *Allenopithecus nigroviridis*
RANGE: Africa: E. Congo, Zaire
HABITAT: swampy forest
SIZE: body: 40–50 cm (15¾–19¾ in)
  tail: 45–55 cm (17¾–21½ in)

Allen's swamp monkey is a sturdily built primate with relatively short limbs and tail. Its head is rounded, and there are ruffs of whiskers from the ears to the mouth. Males are slightly larger than females, but otherwise the two look similar. Little is known about the habits of these monkeys. They live in troops and feed mainly on leaves, fruit and nuts but apparently also eat snails, crabs, fish and insects. They climb and jump well and enter water readily.

The female produces a single young, which clings to her belly and suckles for 2 or 3 months.

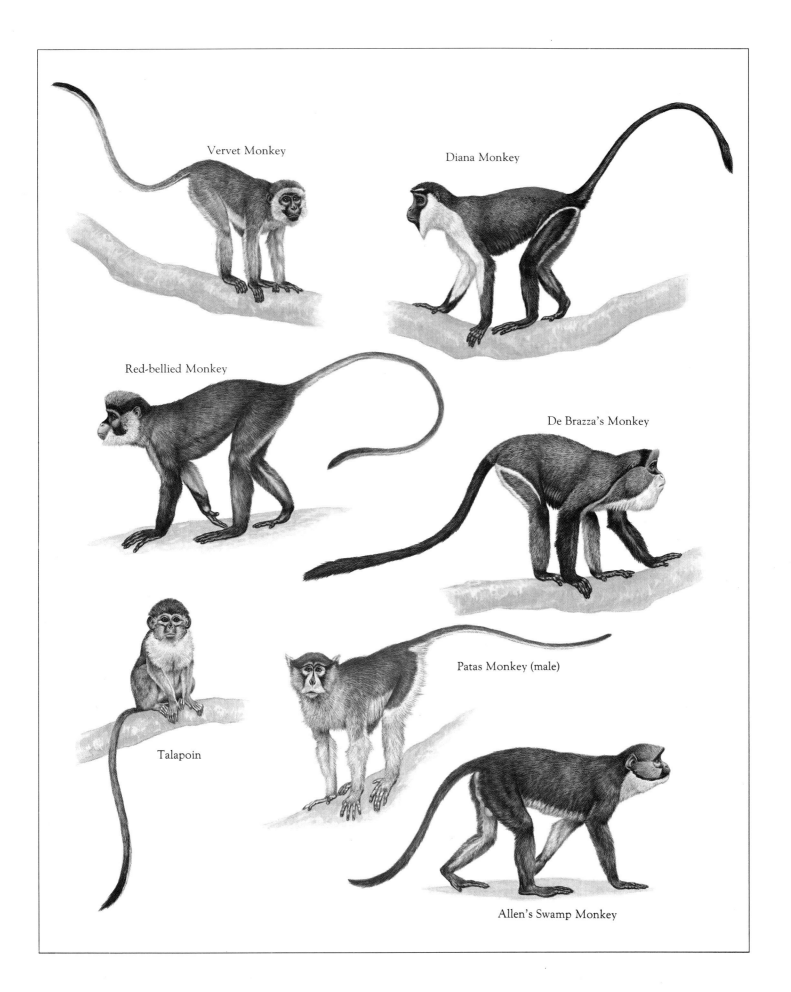

Vervet Monkey

Diana Monkey

Red-bellied Monkey

De Brazza's Monkey

Patas Monkey (male)

Talapoin

Allen's Swamp Monkey

Old World Monkeys

NAME: Angolan Black and White
Colobus Monkey, *Colobus angolensis*
RANGE: Africa: Angola to Kenya
HABITAT: forest
SIZE: body: 50–67 cm (19¾–26¼ in)
tail: 63–90 cm (24¾–35½ in)

All colobus monkeys have long limbs
and tails and robust bodies. They have
only four fingers on each hand, their
thumbs being vestigial or absent. The
Angolan black and white colobus is one
of several black and white species and,
with its sturdy body and rounded head,
is typical of its genus. It is identified by
the characteristic long white hairs on its
shoulders, but the many races of this
species differ slightly in the extent of the
white on shoulders and tail.

These monkeys live in family troops
of several females and their young, led
and guarded by an old male. As young
males mature, they either go off alone or
found their own troops. Each troop has
its own territory, with feeding areas and
sleeping trees, but may sometimes join
with other troops to form a group of 50
or so. The animals are active in the daytime, with a period of rest or grooming
at midday. Much of their food, such as
leaves, fruit, bark and insects, is found
in the trees, where they run and leap
with astonishing agility, so they rarely
need to descend to the ground.

Breeding takes place all year round,
females giving birth to 1 young after a
gestation of 147 to 178 days. The baby
starts to climb at 3 weeks but suckles
and stays with its mother for well over
a year. Females will suckle young other
than their own.

NAME: Red Colobus Monkey, *Colobus badius*
RANGE: Africa: Senegal to Ghana,
Cameroon, Zaire, Uganda, Tanzania
HABITAT: rain, swamp and secondary
forest, usually near water
SIZE: body: 46–70 cm (18–27½ in)
tail: 42–80 cm (16½–31½ in) Ⓔ

There are many races of this slender,
long-tailed colobus monkey, with
coloration ranging from orange-red to
reddish-brown, often with black on the
back and shoulders; the underparts are
reddish-yellow to grayish or white.
Females are smaller than males but
otherwise look similar. The red colobus
monkey lives in a troop of 50 to 100
animals made up of many small family
groups, each with a male and several
females and young. Active during the
day, they feed among the branches on
flowers, shoots, fruit and leaves, leaping
acrobatically from tree to tree.

The female produces 1 young after a
gestation of 4 to 5½ months. She alone
nurses the infant until it is weaned at 9
to 12 months.

NAME: Olive Colobus Monkey,
Procolobus verus
RANGE: Africa: Sierra Leone to Ghana
HABITAT: rain, swamp and secondary
forest
SIZE: body: 43–50 cm (17–19¾ in)
tail: 57–64 cm (22½–25¼ in) Ⓡ

The smallest of the colobus monkeys,
the olive colobus has a little, rounded
head, a short muzzle and rather subdued
coloration. Male and female are about
the same size, but the female lacks the
crest of upright hairs the male has on his
crown. This colobus lives in a family
troop of an old male and several females
and their young, usually 6 to 10 in all.
Sometimes the group may be bigger,
up to 20, with several adult males.
The monkeys sleep and take refuge in
the middle layers of the forest but feed
on the lowest branches. They do not
climb into the treetops and only rarely
come to the ground. Leaves and some
flowers are their staple diet. They are
rather quiet monkeys and make few
sounds.

Reproductive details are not known
except that the mother carries her baby
in her mouth for the first few weeks
after birth — a habit shared only with
other species of colobus.

NAME: Proboscis Monkey, *Nasalis larvatus*
RANGE: Borneo
HABITAT: mangrove swamps, riverbanks
SIZE: body: 53–76 cm (20¾–30 in)
tail: 55–76 cm (21½–30 in) Ⓥ

The sturdily built proboscis monkey
lives in the treetops of mangrove swamp
jungles, where the trees are strong and
rigid and do not attain enormous
heights. It is an agile animal and runs
and leaps in the branches, using its long
tail as a counterbalance; its long fingers
and toes aid grip. The male is considerably larger than the female, perhaps
twice her weight, and has an extraordinarily long, bulbous nose. When he
makes his loud, honking call, the nose
straightens out. The female has a much
smaller nose and a quieter cry.

Proboscis monkeys live in small
groups of 1 or 2 adult males and several
females and their young. They are most
active in the morning, when they feed
on leaves and shoots of mangrove and
pedada trees, as well as on the fruit and
flowers of other trees. Much of the rest
of the day is spent basking in the treetops, where they also sleep at night.

Mating takes place at any time of
year, and the female produces a single
young after a gestation of about 166
days. These monkeys are difficult to
keep in captivity and are becoming increasingly rare in the wild.

NAME: Snub-nosed Monkey, *Pygathrix roxellana*
RANGE: S.W. and S. China, Tibet,
E. India
HABITAT: mountain forest; winters in
lower valleys
SIZE: body: 50–83 cm (19¾–32½ in)
tail: 51 cm–1 m (20 in–3¼ ft) Ⓡ

This large, long-tailed monkey has a distinctive upturned nose, hence its common name, and golden hairs on its
forehead, throat and cheeks. Because of
their remote, mountainous range, few
snub-nosed monkeys have yet been observed. They are said to live in troops of
100 or more and to feed on fruit, buds,
leaves and bamboo shoots.

NAME: Langur, *Presbytis entellus*
RANGE: India, Sri Lanka
HABITAT: forest, scrub, arid rocky areas
SIZE: body: 51 cm–1 m (20 in–3¼ ft)
tail: 72 cm–1 m (28¼ in–3¼ ft)

This large, long-limbed monkey has a
black face and prominent eyebrows. It
adapts well to many different habitats
and will live near human habitation and
raid shops and houses for food. In the
Himalayas, the langur is believed to
make regular migrations, moving up the
mountains in summer and down again
in winter. Although an agile climber, the
langur spends more than half of its time
on the ground, where it finds much of its
food. It is almost entirely vegetarian,
feeding on leaves, shoots, buds, fruit
and seeds; very rarely, it eats insects.

Langurs live in groups of 1 or more
adult males with females and juveniles,
usually about 15 to 35 individuals in all,
although in some areas groups of 80 or
90 have been observed. There are also
smaller, all-male groups containing 4 to
15 animals. In groups with a single male,
he is in sole charge of the movements
and daily routine, and life is peaceful;
in larger groups, the males contest
and squabble, even though there is a
dominant male.

Breeding takes place at any time of
year except in areas with marked
seasonal changes, where births are concentrated into the 2 or 3 most climati-
cally favorable months. The female
gives birth to 1, occasionally 2, young
after a gestation of 6 or 7 months. Other
females in the troop show a great
interest in the newborn infant, and the
mother allows them to touch it shortly
after birth. For the first few weeks, the
infant clings tightly to its mother, but
at 4 weeks it starts to move short distances independently and, at 3 months,
is allowed to play with other infants and
to take some solid food. It continues
to suckle for 10 to 15 months but
nevertheless undergoes much stress
during the weaning period.

Angolan Black and White Colobus Monkey

Red Colobus Monkey

Olive Colobus Monkey (male)

Snub-nosed Monkey

Proboscis Monkey (male)

Langur

Apes

NAME: **Black Gibbon,** *Hylobates concolor*
RANGE: **Indo-China, Hainan**
HABITAT: **rain forest**
SIZE: **body: 45–63 cm (17¾–24¾ in)**
  tail: absent ⓘ

There are several subspecies of black, or crested, gibbon, occurring in various parts of Indo-China; they differ in details of fur coloration. The black male is slightly larger than the female and has a tuft of hair on the crown; the female is buff colored. Like most gibbons, the male of this species has a throat sac, which amplifies his voice.

Black gibbons feed on a variety of foods, mostly fruit, buds and insects, although occasionally small vertebrates may be eaten.

NAME: **Siamang,** *Hylobates syndactylus*
RANGE: **Malaysia, Sumatra**
HABITAT: **mountain forest**
SIZE: **body: 75–90 cm (29½–35½ in)**
  tail: absent

The largest of the gibbons, the siamang has entirely black fur and no pale brow band. It is also distinguished by the web that unites the second and third toes of each foot. Siamangs are tree-dwelling and extremely agile, despite their large size. They swing from branch to branch and may walk upright on strong boughs. At night, they sleep on high, strong branches. Fruit, especially figs, is a staple food of the siamangs, and they also eat flowers, leaves and shoots, some insects and even bird's eggs.

Adult siamang pairs live together in a territory with their offspring of different ages, but unmated adults live alone. Families communicate by short barks and a distinctive whooping call, which is amplified by the inflatable throat sac. The female siamang gives birth to a single young after a gestation of 230 to 235 days. The newborn baby is almost hairless and clings to its mother for safety and warmth.

NAME: **Kloss's Gibbon,** *Hylobates klossi*
RANGE: **Mentawi Islands west of Sumatra**
HABITAT: **hill and lowland rain forest**
SIZE: **body: 65–70 cm (25½–27½ in)**
  tail: absent Ⓥ

Kloss's gibbon looks like a small version of *H. syndactylus* and is very similar in its habits. It is the smallest of all the gibbons and is thought to represent the form and structure of ancestral gibbons. Strictly tree-dwelling, it leaps and swings in the trees with tremendous dexterity and feeds on fruit, leaves, shoots and, perhaps, insects.

Family groups, each consisting of an adult pair and up to 3 offspring, occupy a territory and sleep and feed together. Females give birth to a single young.

PONGIDAE: Ape Family

The 10 species of primate in this family are found in Africa, Southeast Asia, Sumatra, Java and Borneo. All members of the family lack an external tail and have protruding jaws, but they divide into two distinct groups: the agile, slender gibbons and the robust great apes.

The gibbons are specialized arboreal forms, very different externally from the great apes and probably having the most remarkable adaptations of all mammals for rapid locomotion in trees. They use their extremely elongate arms and hooked hands to swing through the forest canopy and are spectacularly skillful climbers. All 6 species of gibbon have long, slender hands, with the thumb deeply divided from the index finger, which gives additional flexibility. When standing upright, the gibbon's long arms touch the ground, so they are often carried above its head. Gibbons are primarily vegetarian but also eat insects, young birds and eggs.

While the slender gibbons weigh from 5 to 13 kg (11 to 28 lb), the great apes are much larger, adult male gorillas weighing as much as 270 kg (595 lb), and even chimpanzees between 48 and 80 kg (106 and 176 lb). All great apes are able to move on their hind legs, if briefly, although they are normally on all fours. Gorillas and chimpanzees are largely terrestrial, but the orangutan spends much of its time in trees, where it swings from branch to branch with surprising agility. While gorillas are vegetarian animals, the chimpanzees and orangutans are omnivorous.

Members of this family are generally gregarious and live in family-based groups, which forage together during the day and build sleeping nests at night. Male great apes are considerably larger than females and may have other special characteristics such as the fatty chin and facial flaps of the mature male orangutan. Male and female gibbons are mostly similar in size.

NAME: **Lar Gibbon,** *Hylobates lar*
RANGE: **S. Burma, Malaysia, Thailand, Cambodia, Sumatra**
HABITAT: **rain forest, dry forest**
SIZE: **body: 42–58 cm (16½–22¾ in)**
  tail: absent

The lar gibbon may be black or pale buff, but the hands, feet, brow band and sides of the face are always pale. Like all gibbons, it is tree-dwelling and rarely descends to the ground. It moves in the trees by swinging from branch to branch by means of its long arms or by running upright along large branches. Largely vegetarian, the lar gibbon feeds on fruit, leaves, shoots, buds and flowers and occasionally on insects. Lar gibbons live in family groups of 2 to 6 individuals — an adult male and female and their young of different ages.

Females give birth to 1 young at intervals of 2 to 4 years. The gestation period is 7 to 7½ months. Young gibbons remain with their mothers for at least 2 years and are suckled throughout this period.

NAME: **Pileated Gibbon,** *Hylobates pileatus*
RANGE: **S.E. Thailand**
HABITAT: **forest**
SIZE: **body: 43–60 cm (17–23½ in)**
  tail: absent Ⓔ

The pileated, or capped, gibbons derive their name from the black cap on the heads of both sexes. Like all gibbons, they are born white and pigmentation gradually spreads down from the head. By the time they are sexually mature, male pileated gibbons are completely black, while females are buff with a black cap.

Pileated gibbons are strongly territorial, and males shout abuse to one another across territory boundaries; they seldom fight, however. They feed on a mixed diet of leaves, buds, resin and insects.

NAME: **Hoolock,** *Hylobates hoolock*
RANGE: **Bangladesh, E. India, S. China, N. Burma**
HABITAT: **hill forest**
SIZE: **body: 46–63 cm (18–24¾ in)**
  tail: absent

The hoolock has the long limbs and the shaggy fur characteristic of gibbons. Males and females are thought to be about the same size, but adult males are blackish-brown in color and females yellow-brown. Newborn hoolocks are grayish-white and gradually darken, to become black at a few months old. The female's color fades at puberty — 6 or 7 years of age. Almost entirely arboreal, the hoolock sleeps in the trees and, in the daytime, swings itself from branch to branch and tree to tree, searching for food. Fruit, leaves and shoots are its staple foods, but it also eats spiders, insects, larvae and bird's eggs.

Family groups of a mated pair and their young live together, but several families may gather in feeding areas, though normally each family feeds in its own territory. The hoolock's loud calls are important, both for communication with its own group and between groups. Mating occurs at the start of the rainy season, and females bear a single young between November and March.

Black Gibbon
(male)

Hoolock
(male)

Kloss's Gibbon

Lar Gibbon

Pileated Gibbon

Siamang

Apes

NAME: Orangutan, *Pongo pygmaeus*
RANGE: Sumatra, Borneo
HABITAT: rain forest
SIZE: height: 1.2–1.5 m (4–5 ft)
   tail: absent   Ⓔ

The orangutan, with its reddish-brown, shaggy hair, has a strong, heavily built body and is the second-largest primate. The arms are long and powerful and reach to the ankles when the animal stands erect; there is a small thumb on each broad hand that is opposable to the first digit. The orangutan's legs are relatively short and weaker than the arms. Males are much larger and heavier than females and are also identified by the cheek flaps that surround the face of the mature adult. All adults have fatty throat pouches.

Orangutans live alone, in pairs or in small family groups and are active in the daytime at all levels of the trees. They walk along large branches on all fours or erect and sometimes swing by their hands from branch to branch. On the ground, they walk on all fours or stand erect. Fruit is their staple diet, but they also feed on leaves, seeds, young birds and eggs. The orangutan sleeps in the trees in a platform nest made of sticks; it may make a new nest every night.

After a gestation period of more than 9 months, the female gives birth to a single young. She cares for her offspring for some time — one captive young was suckled for 6 years — and it clings to her fur as she moves around in the trees.

NAME: Gorilla, *Gorilla gorilla*
RANGE: Africa: S.E. Nigeria to W. Zaire;
  E. Zaire into adjacent countries
HABITAT: rain forest up to 3,000 m
  (10,000 ft)
SIZE: male height: 1.7–1.8 m (5½–6 ft)
  female height: 1.4–1.5 m (4½–5 ft)
  tail: absent   Ⓥ

The largest and most robust of the primates, the gorilla is also a gentle, intelligent and sociable animal which lives a peaceful, quiet existence if undisturbed. Its body, covered with coarse black hair, is massive, with a short, broad trunk and wide chest and shoulders. The head is large, with a short muzzle, and the eyes and ears small; old males have high crowns. The muscular arms are longer than the short, thick legs, and the broad hands are equipped with short fingers and thumbs. Males are bigger and heavier than females, and those over 10 years old have silvery-gray hair on their backs — hence the name silverback, given to old males. There are two races: the lowland and the mountain gorilla, also referred to as the western and eastern races, respectively.

On the ground, gorillas normally move in a stooped posture, with the knuckles of the hands resting on the ground, but they do stand erect on occasion. Females and juveniles climb trees, but males rarely do so because of their great bulk. Gorillas live in a close-knit group of a dominant male, 1 or 2 other males, several females and young; some groups may contain only the dominant male, 2 or 3 females and young. The group wanders in a home range of 10 to 40 sq km (4 to 15½ sq mi), which is not defended or marked at the boundaries. There may be some conflict with neighboring groups, but encounters are generally avoided by communications such as drumming on the ground from a distance. Old males will threaten rivals by standing erect and beating the chest while roaring and barking and sometimes by tearing up and throwing plants. When the leader of a troop dies, younger males contest for dominance.

Gorillas are active in the daytime. The troop rises between 6 A.M. and 8 A.M., feeds for a while on plant material, such as leaves, buds, stalks, berries, bark and ferns, and then has a period of rest and relaxation. Gorillas do not appear to drink but get the water they need from their juicy diet. They feed again in the afternoon and then retire for the night in nests made of twigs and leaves. Young gorillas under 3 years old sleep with their mothers, but all others have their own nests.

Breeding appears to take place at any time of year. The female gives birth to a single young after a gestation of more than 9 months. The young is completely dependent and clings to its mother's fur at first, but it is able to sit up at 3 months and to walk and climb at 5 months. It suckles for 12 to 18 months and remains with its mother for about 3 years.

NAME: Pygmy Chimpanzee, *Pan*
  paniscus
RANGE: Africa: Zaire
HABITAT: rain forest
SIZE: body: 55–60 cm (21½–23½ in)
  tail: absent
  height: up to 1 m (3¼ ft)   Ⓥ

Similar to the chimpanzee, this species (sometimes regarded as only a subspecies) has longer, thinner legs, a more slender body and a narrow face. Its hair and facial skin are black. It moves in the trees and on the ground, feeding mainly on fruit but also on leaves and shoots. A gregarious animal, the pygmy chimpanzee lives in a family group, and several families may gather in a good feeding area. Otherwise its habits are much the same as those of the chimpanzee.

The female bears 1 young after a gestation of 227 to 232 days. Her offspring stays with her for up to 3 years.

NAME: Chimpanzee, *Pan troglodytes*
RANGE: Africa: Guinea to Zaire, Uganda
  and Tanzania
HABITAT: rain forest, savanna with
  woodland
SIZE: body: 68–94 cm (26¾–37 in)
  tail: absent
  height: 1.2–1.7 m (4–5½ ft)   Ⓥ

The intelligent, social chimpanzee has a wide range of sounds and gestures for communication and is probably one of the most expressive of all animals. Thickset and robust, but more lightly built than the gorilla, the chimpanzee has a strong body and long limbs, the powerful arms being longer than the legs. Its hands and feet are narrow and long, with opposable thumbs on the hands. Males are slightly larger than females. There is great variability in the color of hair and facial skin, but the hair is generally blackish and the face light, darkening in older individuals. The rounded head bears broad, prominent ears, and the lips are mobile and protrusible.

Chimpanzees climb well but spend most of the time on the ground, where they generally walk on all fours, even though they stand erect on occasion, as when their hands are full of food. Their social structure is more variable than that of the gorilla. Rain forest animals live in troops of males, of females with young, of males and females with young, or of adults of both sexes without young. The composition of the troop often changes. Savanna chimpanzees generally live in more stable troops of 1 or more males, several females and their young. They occupy a home range, the size of which depends on the size of the troop and on the food supply. Neighboring troops meet with much noise and communication, but there is usually little aggression.

Active in the daytime, chimpanzees rise at dawn and feed mainly on plant material, such as fruit, nuts, leaves, shoots and bark, and on eggs and insects. They will use stems or twigs as tools, to extract termites or ants from their hiding places. Savanna chimpanzees will kill young animals for food by holding them by the hind limbs and striking their heads on the ground. At night, chimpanzees usually sleep in the trees, each making its own nest with interwoven, broken and bent branches. Young under 3 years old sleep with their mothers.

Females have regular periods of heat, with swelling of the genital region, and may mate with all the males in the troop. Usually 1 young is born, sometimes twins, after a gestation of 227 to 232 days. The young animal lives closely with its mother for 2 to 3 years.

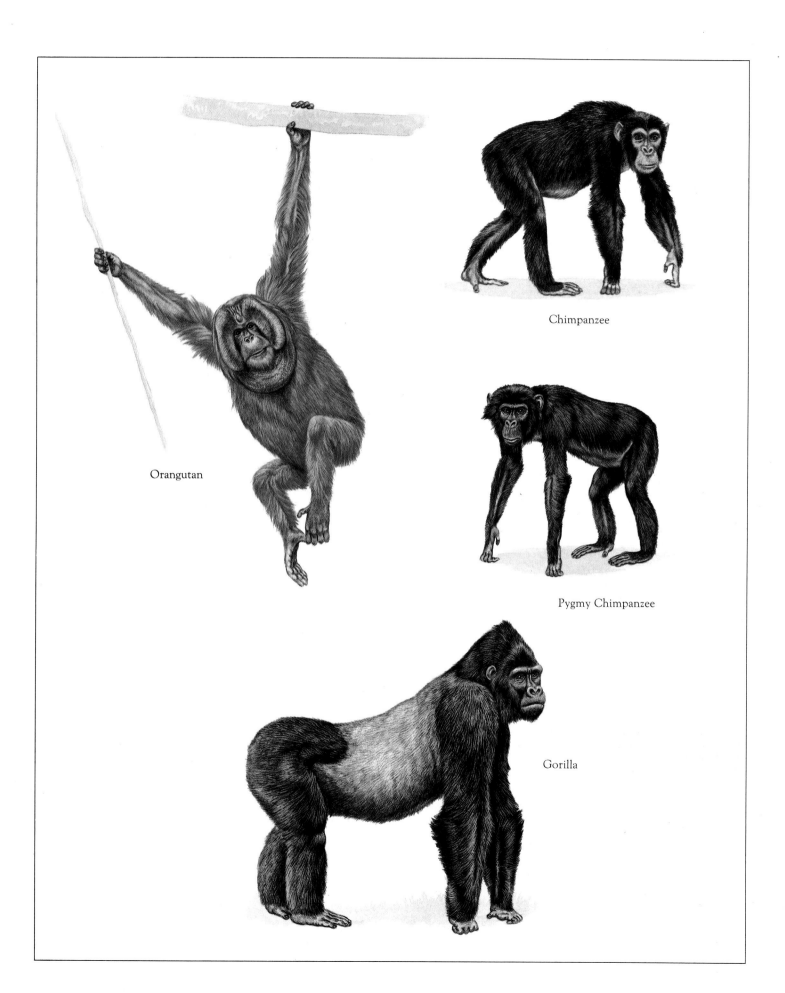

Chimpanzee

Orangutan

Pygmy Chimpanzee

Gorilla

Dogs

NAME: Coyote, *Canis latrans*
RANGE: Alaska, Canada, USA (formerly absent from S.E. but now spreading there); Mexico, Central America
HABITAT: prairie, open woodland
SIZE: body: 85–95 cm (33½–37½ in)
tail: 30–38 cm (11¾–15 in)

A highly adaptable animal, the coyote has managed to thrive, even to increase its population, despite being trapped and poisoned for many years. Although the coyote probably does kill some sheep, young cattle and poultry, its diet consists mainly of rodents and rabbits, and in this way it is of service to the farmer. It also eats snakes, insects, carrion, fruit, berries and grasses and will enter water to catch fish, frogs and crustaceans.

Coyote pairs mate in late winter, and a litter of 5 to 10 young is born after a gestation of 63 to 65 days. The male brings all the food for the female and young at first, but later both parents hunt for food. The young leave when about 6 or 7 months old to find their own home range.

The coyote is the North American equivalent of the jackals, which occur in Asia and Africa.

NAME: Gray Wolf, *Canis lupus*
RANGE: E. Europe (isolated populations in Spain and Italy), east to India, USSR; Canada, USA: some N. states and isolated western populations; Mexico
HABITAT: tundra, steppe, open woodland and forest
SIZE: body: 1–1.4 m (3¼–4½ ft)
tail: 30–48 cm (11¾–18¾ in) ⓥ

One of the ancestors of the domestic dog, the gray wolf is a powerful, muscular animal with a thick, bushy tail. Wolves vary in color from almost white in the Arctic to yellowish-brown or nearly black farther south. Intelligent social animals, wolves live in family groups or in packs that sometimes include more than one family or other individuals besides the family. The pack members hunt together, cooperating to run down prey such as deer, caribou and wild horses, and they also eat small animals such as mice, fish and crabs. Social hierarchy in the pack is well organized and is maintained by ritualized gestures and postures; the leading male signals his rank by carrying his tail higher than the others do. Pairs remain together for life.

The female gives birth to 3 to 8 pups after a gestation of about 63 days. Born blind and hairless, the pups first venture outside the den at 3 weeks, and the whole pack helps to care for them.

ORDER CARNIVORA

There are 8 families in this order: the dogs, bears, raccoons, pandas, mustelids, civets, hyenas and cats. Typically these animals are flesh-eating predators, but not all are totally carnivorous, and a specialized few feed only on plant matter.

CANIDAE: Dog Family

Dogs and their close relatives the jackals, wolves, coyotes and foxes represent one of the most familiar groups of carnivorous mammals. This familiarity is partly due to the fact that dogs were the first animals to be fully domesticated by man.

The family contains about 35 recognized species and is distributed almost worldwide. Domesticated animals aside, dogs are absent only from New Zealand, New Guinea, Madagascar and some other islands. The dingo was introduced into Australia by aboriginal man. All dogs have the well-known muscular, long-legged body, generally with a bushy tail. The ears are usually large, triangular in outline and erect, and the muzzle is long.

Canids are excellent runners, able to sustain a high speed for considerable distances, and long pursuits are an important part of the hunting technique of many species. Some canids hunt down large prey in packs, while others, such as foxes, are typically solitary hunters. Males and females generally look alike, although males are often slightly larger than females.

NAME: Dingo, *Canis dingo*
RANGE: Australia
HABITAT: sandy desert to wet and dry sclerophyll forest
SIZE: body: about 1.5 m (5 ft)
tail: about 35 cm (13¾ in)

The dingoes are descended from domesticated dogs introduced by the aboriginal human inhabitants of Australia many thousands of years ago. In anatomy and behavior dingoes are indistinguishable from domestic dogs, but the two have interbred for so long that there are now few pure dingoes. They live in family groups but may gather into bigger packs to hunt large prey. Originally they fed on kangaroos, but when white settlers started to kill off the kangaroos, dingoes took to feeding on introduced sheep and rabbits.

A litter of 4 or 5 young is born in a burrow or rock crevice after a gestation of about 9 weeks. The young are suckled for 2 months and stay with their parents for at least a year.

NAME: Arctic Fox, *Alopex lagopus*
RANGE: Arctic regions of Europe, Asia and N. America
HABITAT: tundra, open woodland
SIZE: body: 46–68 cm (18–26¾ in)
tail: up to 35 cm (13¾ in)

One of the few truly arctic mammals, the arctic fox has well-furred feet and small, rounded ears. It feeds on ground-dwelling birds, lemmings and other small rodents and also eats the leftovers from polar bear kills and carrion, such as stranded marine animals. Burrows, usually in the side of a hill or cliff, provide shelter, but arctic foxes do not hibernate and can withstand temperatures as low as −50°C (−58°F).

A litter of 4 to 11 young is born in May or June after a gestation of 51 to 57 days. They are cared for by both parents.

NAME: Red Fox, *Vulpes vulpes*
RANGE: Canada, USA; Europe (except Iceland); Asia to Japan and Indo-China; introduced in Australia
HABITAT: woodland, open country; recently increasing in urban areas
SIZE: body: 46–86 cm (18–33¾ in)
tail: 30.5–55.5 cm (12–21¾ in)

The versatile, intelligent red fox adapts well to different conditions and has excellent senses and powers of endurance. Although sometimes about at all hours, it is typically active at night, resting during the day in a burrow abandoned by another animal or dug by itself. It lives alone outside the breeding season and is a skillful hunter, preying largely on rodents but also on rabbits, hares, birds, insects and invertebrates. Fruit and berries are also eaten in autumn, and the red fox has taken to scavenging on refuse in urban areas.

A litter of 4 young is born after a gestation of 51 to 63 days. The male brings food for his family until the female is able to leave the cubs or take them out foraging.

NAME: Fennec Fox, *Vulpes zerda*
RANGE: N. Africa: Morocco to Egypt, south to N. Niger, Sudan; east to Sinai Peninsula and Kuwait
HABITAT: desert, semidesert
SIZE: body: 37–41 cm (14½–16 in)
tail: 19–21 cm (7½–8¼ in)

The smallest of the foxes, the fennec fox is identified by its relatively huge ears. It shelters in burrows it digs in the sand and is generally active at night, when it preys on small rodents, birds, insects and lizards.

Fennec foxes are sociable animals which mate for life; each pair or family has its own territory. A litter of 2 to 5 young is born in spring after a gestation of 50 to 51 days.

Coyote

Gray Wolf

Arctic Fox

Red Fox

Fennec Fox

Dingo

Dogs

NAME: **Dhole,** *Cuon alpinus*
RANGE: **central and E. Asia, south to Sumatra and Java**
HABITAT: **forest, woodland; open country in north of range**
SIZE: **body: 76 cm–1 m (30 in–3¼ ft)**
tail: 28–48 cm (11–18¾ in) Ⓥ

Dholes, or Asiatic wild dogs, are gregarious animals which live in family groups or in packs of up to 30 that contain several families. Most of their hunting is done in the daytime, and although they are not particularly fast runners, dholes pursue their prey in a steady, relentless chase, finally exhausting the victim. Both smell and sight are important to them when tracking their prey. Because they hunt in packs, dholes are able to kill animals much larger than themselves, such as deer, wild cattle, sheep and pigs, water buffaloes and bantengs.

After a gestation of about 9 weeks, a litter of 2 to 6 young is born in a sheltered spot among rocks or a hole in a bank. Several females may breed near one another. Dholes are now becoming rare after many years of persecution, and they are also affected by the greatly reduced populations of many of their prey animals. They are now protected in some parts of their range.

NAME: **Bush Dog,** *Speothos venaticus*
RANGE: **Central and South America: Panama to Peru, Brazil and Paraguay**
HABITAT: **forest, savanna**
SIZE: **body: 57.5–75 cm (22½–29½ in)**
tail: 12.5–15 cm (5–6 in) Ⓥ

Stocky and terrierlike, the bush dog has short legs and tail. It is now rare throughout its range, and little is known of its habits in the wild. A nocturnal dog, it is believed to hunt in packs, preying mainly on rodents, including large species such as pacas and agoutis. Bush dogs swim well, probably better than any other wild canid, and readily pursue prey into water. During the day, they take refuge in a hole or crevice, often the abandoned burrow of an armadillo. They mark the boundaries of their territory with urine and secretions from anal glands.

A litter is thought to contain 4 or 5 young, which are born in a burrow, and both parents tend the young.

NAME: **Maned Wolf,** *Chrysocyon brachyurus*
RANGE: **South America: Brazil, Bolivia, Paraguay, Uruguay, N. Argentina**
HABITAT: **grassland, swamp edge**
SIZE: **body: 1.2 m (4 ft)**
tail: about 30 cm (11¾ in) Ⓥ

Similar to a red fox in appearance, with its long legs and muzzle, the maned wolf has a yellowish-red coat of fairly long hair, with an erectile mane on the neck and shoulders. The tail may be white or white-tipped. A wary, solitary animal, the maned wolf lives in remote areas and is active mainly at night. It runs fast, with a loping gallop, but has less stamina than many canids and does not usually run down its prey. Large rodents, such as pacas and agoutis, birds, reptiles and frogs are all caught by the maned wolf, and it also feeds on insects, snails and some fruit.

A litter of up to 5 young is born after a gestation of about 2 months. At first, the young have short legs and muzzles, which gradually grow longer during their first year of life.

NAME: **Crab-eating Fox,** *Dusicyon thous*
RANGE: **South America: Colombia to N. Argentina**
HABITAT: **open woodland, grassland**
SIZE: **body: 60–70 cm (23½–27½ in)**
tail: 30 cm (11¾ in)

The first specimen of this fox ever examined had a crab in its mouth, hence the common name, but, in fact, crabs are only one item in a wide-ranging diet. This fox is also known as the common zorro. Mainly nocturnal and solitary, the crab-eating fox spends the day in a shelter, often a burrow abandoned by another animal. It hunts small rodents, such as mice and rats, lizards, frogs and crabs and also feeds on insects and fruit and digs for turtle eggs. Poultry also figures in the diet of the crab-eating fox.

The female gives birth to a litter of 2 to 6 young.

NAME: **Raccoon Dog,** *Nyctereutes procyonoides*
RANGE: **E. Siberia, N.E. China, Japan, N. Indo-China; introduced in E. and central Europe**
HABITAT: **forest and rocky banks near rivers and lakes**
SIZE: **body: 50–55 cm (19¾–21½ in)**
tail: 13–18 cm (5–7 in)

Foxlike in build, but with shorter legs and tail, the raccoon dog has a dark patch on each side of its face, reminiscent of the raccoon's black mask. It lives alone or in family groups of 5 or 6 and is primarily nocturnal. During the day, it shelters in a den among rocks or bushes, in a hollow tree or in a burrow abandoned by another animal. A raccoon dog may sometimes dig its own burrow. Usually found near water, the raccoon dog is an excellent swimmer, and frogs and fish are major food items; it also eats rodents, acorns, fruit and berries and scavenges on carrion and refuse around human habitation.

A litter of 6 to 8 young is born after a gestation of about 2 months. The pups are independent at about 6 months old.

NAME: **Hunting Dog,** *Lycaon pictus*
RANGE: **Africa, south of the Sahara to South Africa: Transvaal; (not in rain forest areas of W. and central Africa)**
HABITAT: **savanna, plains, semidesert, mountains up to 3,000 m (10,000 ft)**
SIZE: **body: 80 cm–1.1 m (31½ in–3½ ft)**
tail: 30–40 cm (11¾–15¾ in) Ⓥ

Recognized by its dark-brown, black or yellowish coat, well mottled with light patches, the hunting dog has long legs and a short, extremely powerful muzzle. Hunting dogs live in packs of 6 to 30 or more, sometimes up to 90, with a high degree of social cooperation and interaction between individuals in the pack; they communicate by means of gestures and body postures and a few calls. Nomadic animals, hunting dogs roam over a wide area looking for their prey; only when the young are too small to travel do they remain in one place for more than a few days.

During much of the day, the dogs rest and groom themselves in the shade; most hunting is done in the early morning and evening or on bright moonlit nights. After a mass greeting ceremony between pack members, the dogs move off to search for prey such as gazelles, impalas and zebras. Once prey is located by sight, the dogs follow it slowly for a while before starting the final chase. They may concentrate on one victim or follow several members of a herd before all switching to one particular animal. When close enough, the dogs start to bite the prey wherever they can, often seizing its legs and tail and causing it to fall. They disembowel it and immediately start tearing it to pieces and feeding. The pack shares the kill without aggression, allowing young animals to feed first and disgorging meat to latecomers. Some pack members return to the den and disgorge meat for the adults guarding the young. By expert cooperation, by taking turns in the chase and by combined attack, hunting dogs can successfully bring down prey much bigger than themselves, even wildebeests.

The female gives birth to 2 to 16 young, usually 7, after a gestation of 69 to 72 days. The litter is born in a burrow, such as an abandoned aardvark or warthog hole, and more than one female may share the den. The young are blind at birth, but their eyes open at about 2 weeks, and they soon begin to venture out of the den. They are suckled for about 3 months and fed on regurgitated food by pack members from the age of 2 weeks. The whole pack takes an interest in the young and will feed any motherless pups. At 6 months the young begin to learn to hunt and accompany the pack.

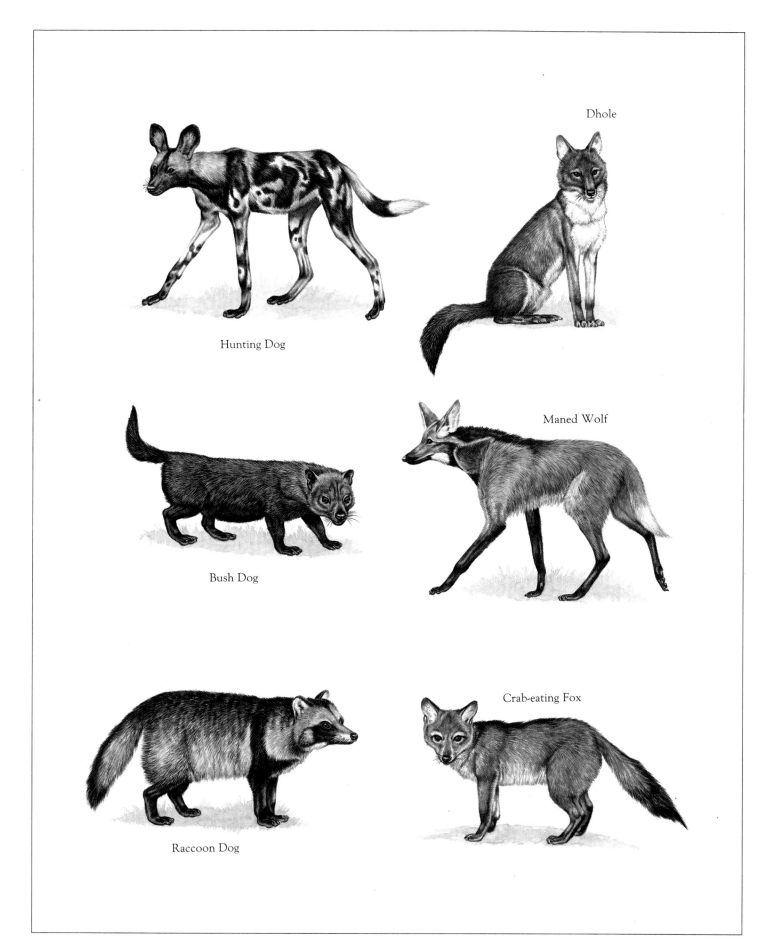

Dhole

Hunting Dog

Maned Wolf

Bush Dog

Crab-eating Fox

Raccoon Dog

Bears

NAME: **Spectacled Bear,** *Tremarctos ornatus*
RANGE: **South America: Venezuela, Colombia, Ecuador, Peru, W. Bolivia**
HABITAT: **forest, savanna, mountainous areas up to 3,000 m (10,000 ft)**
SIZE: **body: 1.5–1.8 m (5–6 ft) tail: 7 cm (2¾ in)** Ⓥ

The only South American bear, this species is generally black or dark brown in color, with white markings around the eyes and sometimes on the neck. Mainly a forest dweller, although it also ranges into open country, this bear feeds largely on plant material such as leaves, fruit and roots. It is also thought to prey on deer and vicuñas. It is a good climber and sleeps in a tree in a large nest it makes from sticks.

The spectacled bear lives alone or in a family group. The female produces a litter of up to 3 young after a gestation of 8 to 8½ months.

NAME: **Big Brown Bear/Grizzly Bear,** *Ursus arctos*
RANGE: **Europe: Scandinavia to Balkans, scattered populations in France, Italy and Spain; USSR; Asia, north of Himalayas; Alaska, W. Canada, mountainous areas of W. USA**
HABITAT: **forest, tundra**
SIZE: **body: 1.5–2.5 m (5–8¼ ft) tail: absent**

Many subspecies are covered by the scientific name *U. arctos*, including the Kodiak bear and the grizzly bears. At least 2 races of grizzly are rare or endangered. The races vary in color from pale yellowish-fawn to dark brown or nearly black, but all are large, immensely strong bears, and they are among the biggest carnivores. They live alone or in family groups and are active night or day, although in areas where bears have been persecuted, they are nocturnal. The diet varies greatly from area to area but may include plant material, such as fruit, nuts, roots and seaweed, as well as insects, fish, small vertebrates and carrion. Alaskan brown bears feed heavily on migrating salmon. Most individuals are too slow to catch wild, hoofed mammals, although they have been known to kill bison, and many are too heavy to climb trees. In late summer and autumn, the bears fatten up on vast quantities of fruit and berries in preparation for the winter sleep — a period of torpor, not true hibernation.

Females breed every 2 or 3 years and produce litters of 1 to 4 young after a gestation of 6 to 8 months. The newborn young are blind and tiny, usually weighing only about 300 to 700 g (10½ to 25 oz). They remain with the mother for a year, sometimes longer.

URSIDAE: Bear Family

The 7 species of bear are an offshoot of doglike ancestors. Dogs and their relatives consume a certain amount of plant material in their largely carnivorous diet, and this omnivorous tendency is increased in the bears, which are adaptable consumers of a wide range of foods, including insects, small vertebrates, grass, leaves, fruit and nuts. Bears' teeth lack the shearing blades of those of cats and dogs.

Bears are large, sturdily built animals with big heads, short limbs and exceptionally short tails. They have flat, five-toed feet with long, curving claws. Only the polar bear inhabits Arctic regions; the others all occur in temperate and tropical areas of the northern hemisphere, and 1 species lives in northern South America. In cold winter weather, many bears undergo a period of torpor; this winter sleep is not true hibernation, since temperature and respiration rate do not fall drastically, as they do in true hibernators. Male and female look alike.

NAME: **Black Bear,** *Ursus americanus*
RANGE: **Alaska, Canada, USA: patchy distribution in New England through Pennsylvania to Tennessee, Florida to Louisiana, mountainous areas of the west; N. Mexico**
HABITAT: **wooded areas, swamps, national parks**
SIZE: **body: 1.5–1.8 m (5–6 ft) tail: 12 cm (4¾ in)**

Black bears actually vary in color from glossy black to dark brown, reddish-brown or almost white. There is often a small white patch on the chest. Originally found throughout much of the USA, this bear now lives only in the wilder, uninhabited areas and in national parks, where it is thriving and on the increase. Occasionally seen in daytime, black bears are usually active at night, when they roam for long distances in search of food such as fruit, berries, nuts, roots and honey. They also feed on insects, rodents and other small mammals, stranded fish and even carrion and refuse. Their sense of smell is good, but their hearing and eyesight are only fair. In autumn, black bears gorge on the ample supplies of fruit to fatten themselves for their long sleep during the coldest weather.

After mating, pairs separate, and except for females with cubs, black bears are usually solitary. A litter of 1 to 4 young is born in January or February after a gestation of about 7 months.

NAME: **Asiatic Black Bear,** *Selenarctos thibetanus*
RANGE: **Afghanistan to China, Siberia, Japan, Korea, Taiwan, Hainan, S.E. Asia**
HABITAT: **forest and brush up to 3,600 m (11,800 ft)**
SIZE: **body: 1.3–1.6 m (4¼–5¼ ft) tail: 7–10 cm (2¾–4 in)**

Although usually black, with some white markings on the snout and chest, some Asiatic black bears may be reddish or dark brown. They feed largely on plant matter and will raid crop fields for food or climb trees to obtain fruit and nuts; they also eat insect larvae and ants. However, they can be aggressive predators and sometimes kill cattle, sheep and goats.

The female has a litter of 2 cubs, which are blind and extremely small at birth. They stay with their mother until almost fully grown.

NAME: **Polar Bear,** *Thalarctos maritimus*
RANGE: **Arctic Ocean to southern limits of ice floes**
HABITAT: **coasts, ice floes**
SIZE: **body: 2.2–2.5 m (7¼–8¼ ft) tail: 7.5–12.5 cm (3–5 in)** Ⓥ

A huge bear with an unmistakable creamy-white coat, the polar bear is surprisingly fast and can easily outrun a caribou over a short distance. It wanders over a larger area than any other bear and, of course, swims well. Seals, fish, seabirds, arctic hares, caribou and musk oxen are the polar bear's main prey, and in the summer it also eats berries and leaves of tundra plants.

Normally solitary animals outside the breeding season, polar bears mate in midsummer. A litter of 1 to 4 young is born after a gestation of about 9 months, and the young bears remain with their mother for about a year. Thus females breed only every other year.

NAME: **Sun Bear,** *Helarctos malayanus*
RANGE: **S.E. Asia, Sumatra, Borneo**
HABITAT: **mountain and lowland forest**
SIZE: **body: 1.1–1.4 m (3½–4½ ft) tail: absent**

The smallest bear, the sun bear nevertheless has a strong, stocky body and powerful paws, with long, curved claws that help it climb trees. It spends the day in a nest in a tree, sleeping and basking in the sun, and searches for food at night. Using its strong claws, the sun bear tears at tree bark to expose insects, larvae and the nests of bees and termites; it also preys on junglefowl and small rodents. Fruit and coconut palm, too, are part of its diet.

There are usually 2 young, born after a gestation of about 96 days and cared for by both parents.

Polar Bear

Black Bear

Spectacled Bear

Asiatic Black Bear

Sun Bear

Big Brown Bear

Raccoons, Pandas

PROCYONIDAE: Raccoon Family

There are about 18 species in this family, all of which inhabit temperate and tropical areas of the Americas. They are all long-bodied, active animals, thought to be closely linked to the dog-bear line of carnivore evolution. They are good climbers and spend much of their life in trees. Males are usually longer and heavier than females, but otherwise the sexes look alike.

NAME: **Raccoon,** *Procyon lotor*
RANGE: **S. Canada, USA, south to Panama**
HABITAT: **wooded areas, often near water, swamps**
SIZE: **body: 41–60 cm (16–23½ in)**
tail: 20–40 cm (7¾–15¾ in)

Familiar, adaptable mammals, raccoons have coped well with the twentieth century and today are even spotted in cities, scavenging for food. The raccoon is stocky but agile, with thick, grayish fur and a bushy tail ringed with black bands; its pointed face has a characteristic "bandit" mask across the eyes. On the forepaws are long, sensitive digits, which the raccoon uses with great dexterity when handling food. Mainly active at night, the raccoon is a good climber and can swim if necessary. Its wide-ranging diet includes aquatic animals such as frogs and fish, small land animals, such as rodents, birds, turtle eggs, nuts, seeds, fruit and corn.

A litter of 3 to 6 young is born in spring after a gestation of about 65 days. The young raccoons' eyes are open at about 3 weeks old; they start to go out with their mother at about 2 months old, remaining with her until autumn.

NAME: **Bushy-tailed Olingo,** *Bassaricyon gabbi*
RANGE: **Central America, south to Venezuela, Colombia and Ecuador**
HABITAT: **forest**
SIZE: **body: 35–47.5 cm (13¾–18¾ in)**
tail: 40–48 cm (15¾–18¾ in)

An expert climber, the bushy-tailed olingo spends much of its life in trees and rarely descends to the ground. Using its long tail to help it balance, it leaps from tree to tree and runs along the branches. It is primarily nocturnal, and although it lives alone or in pairs, it joins in groups with other olingos and with kinkajous to search for food. Fruit is its staple diet, but it also eats insects, small mammals and birds.

Breeding takes place at any time of year, and usually 1 young is born after a gestation of 73 or 74 days. The female chases her mate away shortly before the birth and rears her offspring alone.

NAME: **Coati,** *Nasua nasua*
RANGE: **South America (not Patagonia)**
HABITAT: **woodland, lowland forest**
SIZE: **body: 43–67 cm (17–26¼ in)**
tail: 43–68 cm (17–26¾ in)

The coati is a muscular, short-legged animal with a long, banded tail and a pointed, mobile snout. It lives in groups of up to 40 individuals, which hunt together day and night, resting in the heat of the day. With its mobile snout, the coati probes holes and cracks in the ground, rocks or trees, searching for the insects, spiders and other small ground-dwelling invertebrates that are its staple diet. Fruit and larger animals, such as lizards, are also eaten.

After mating, the group splits up and females go off alone to give birth. A litter of 2 to 7 young is born after a gestation of about 77 days, usually in a cave or a nest in a tree. Once the young are about 2 months old, the females and their offspring regroup with yearlings of both sexes. Males over 2 years old are allowed to accompany the group only for the few weeks of the mating period and even then are subordinate to females.

NAME: **Kinkajou,** *Potos flavus*
RANGE: **E. Mexico, through Central and South America to Brazil**
HABITAT: **forest**
SIZE: **body: 41–57 cm (16–22½ in)**
tail: 40–56 cm (15¾–22 in)

The tree-dwelling kinkajou is an agile climber, using its prehensile tail as a fifth limb to hold on to branches, which leaves its hands free for picking food. During the day, the kinkajou rests, usually in a hole in a tree, and then emerges at night to forage in the trees. It feeds mainly on fruit and insects and occasionally on small vertebrates, and its long tongue is adapted for extracting the soft flesh from fruit, such as mangoes, avocados and guavas, and for licking up nectar, insects and even honey from bee's nests. The nocturnal kinkajous often feed in the same fruit trees that are used by monkeys during the daytime.

The female gives birth to 1 young, rarely 2, in a tree hollow after a gestation of 112 to 118 days. The young kinkajou takes its first solid food at about 7 weeks and is independent when about 4 months old. It is able to hang by its prehensile tail after only 8 weeks or so.

AILUROPODIDAE: Panda Family

The giant panda and the lesser, or red, panda are the only members of this small family, which has evolutionary links with both bears and raccoons.

NAME: **Giant Panda,** *Ailuropoda melanoleuca*
RANGE: **mountains of central China**
HABITAT: **bamboo forest**
SIZE: **body: 1.2–1.5 m (4–5 ft)**
tail: 12.5 cm (5 in) ®

One of the most popular, newsworthy mammals, the giant panda is a rare, elusive creature, and surprisingly little is known of its life in the wild. It is large and heavily built, with a massive head, stout legs and a thick, woolly black and white coat, often with a brownish tinge to the black. The panda's forepaw is specialized for grasping bamboo stems, its main food: it has an elongated wrist bone that effectively provides a sixth digit, against which the first and second digits can be flexed. The panda consumes huge amounts of bamboo in order to obtain sufficient nourishment and thus spends 50 to 75 percent of its day feeding. It is also thought to eat some other plants and, occasionally, small animals. Normally solitary, unless breeding or caring for young, pandas are primarily ground-dwelling but regularly climb trees for shelter or refuge.

The male leaves his territory to find a mate and courts her by uttering whines and barks. He will drive off any rival males before mating. The female gives birth to 1 blind, helpless young, which weighs only about 140 g (5 oz) — tiny in comparison to its mother, which may weigh as much as 115 kg (253 lb). The cub grows rapidly, however, and by 8 weeks is more than 20 times its birth weight.

NAME: **Lesser/Red Panda,** *Ailurus fulgens*
RANGE: **Nepal to W. Burma, S.W. China**
HABITAT: **bamboo forest**
SIZE: **body: 51–63.5 cm (20–25 in)**
tail: 28–48.5 cm (11–19 in)

The lesser panda, with its beautiful rusty-red coat and long, bushy tail, resembles a raccoon more than it does its giant relative. Primarily nocturnal, it spends the day sleeping, curled up on a branch with its tail over its head or its head tucked onto its chest. It feeds on the ground on bamboo shoots, grass, roots, fruit and acorns and may occasionally eat mice, birds and bird's eggs. A quiet creature unless provoked, when it rears up on its hind legs and hisses, it lives in pairs or family groups.

In the spring, the female gives birth to 1 to 4 young, usually only 1 or 2, after a gestation of 90 to 150 days. The longer gestations recorded are thought to include a period of delayed implantation, during which the fertilized egg lies dormant in the womb, only starting to develop at the time that will ensure birth at the optimum season for the young's survival. The young stay with their mother for up to a year.

Bushy-tailed Olingo

Kinkajou

Lesser Panda

Raccoon

Giant Panda

Coati

Mustelids
Weasels, Martens

NAME: **Ermine,** *Mustela erminea*
RANGE: **Europe, Asia, N. USA, Greenland; introduced in New Zealand**
HABITAT: **forest, tundra**
SIZE: **body: 24–29 cm (9½–11½ in)**
   tail: 8–12 cm (3–4¾ in)

The ermine is a highly skilled predator. It kills by delivering a powerful and accurate bite to the back of the prey's neck. Rodents and rabbits are the ermine's main diet, but it will also kill and eat other mammals — including some bigger than itself — as well as birds, eggs, fish and insects. At the beginning of winter, in the northern part of its range, the ermine loses its dark fur and grows a pure white coat, only the black tail tip remaining. This white winter pelt is prized by the fur trade.

Ermines produce a litter of 3 to 7 young in April or May. The male assists in caring for and feeding the young, which are helpless at birth. Their eyes do not open until they are about 3 weeks old, but at 7 weeks young males are already larger than their mother

There are 15 species of *Mustela,* including the minks now farmed for their dense fur.

NAME: **Black-footed Ferret,** *Mustela nigripes*
RANGE: **N. America: Alberta to N. Texas**
HABITAT: **prairie**
SIZE: **body: 38–45 cm (15–17¾ in)**
   tail: 12.5–15 cm (5–6 in)   Ⓔ

The black-footed ferret feeds mainly on prairie dogs, but these animals are considered farm pests and large numbers are poisoned. This destruction of their natural prey has caused a drastic decline in the numbers of ferrets — and their indirect poisoning. The black-footed ferret is now protected by law, but it is still in great danger of extinction and its survival depends either on the conservation of prairie dogs or on its ability to adapt to other areas and prey. It is generally a nocturnal animal. In June it produces a yearly litter of 3 to 5 young.

NAME: **Least Weasel,** *Mustela nivalis (rixosa)*
RANGE: **Europe, N. Africa, Asia, N. America; introduced in New Zealand**
HABITAT: **farmland, woodland**
SIZE: **body: 18–23 cm (7–9 in)**
   tail: 5–7 cm (2–2¾ in)

This weasel is the smallest carnivore. It undergoes the same winter color change as the ermine in the northern part of its range. The least weasel preys mostly on mice and is small enough to pursue them into their burrows. It is most active by night but will hunt in the daytime. One or two litters a year, of 4 or 5 young each, are born in an underground nest.

MUSTELIDAE: Mustelid Family

The mustelid family of carnivores is an extremely successful and diverse group of small to medium-sized mammals. There are about 67 species in 23 genera from all regions of the world except Australia and Madagascar; 2 species have been introduced into New Zealand to control rodents. Although there is a moderate range of physique, most mustelids conform to the pattern of long, supple body, short legs and longish tails. Males are almost invariably larger than females.

This blueprint of shape has proved adaptable in terms of niche utilization. Mustelids have become expert burrowers, tree climbers and swimmers. One species, the sea otter, is almost entirely marine.

Anal scent glands are well developed in mustelids, and the secretions are used for marking territory boundaries. Some species, notably polecats and skunks, have particularly foul-smelling secretions which they spray as a defensive technique.

NAME: **Western Polecat,** *Mustela putorius*
RANGE: **Europe**
HABITAT: **forest**
SIZE: **body: 38–46 cm (15–18 in)**
   tail: 13–19 cm (5–7½ in)

The western polecat is a solitary, nocturnal creature. It hunts rodents, birds, reptiles and insects, mostly on the ground; it only rarely climbs trees. Like all mustelids, the polecat has anal scent glands, but the secretions are particularly offensive and are used as a defense, as well as for marking territory. It breeds once or twice a year, bearing litters of 5 to 8 young. The domestic ferret is probably descended from this polecat.

NAME: **Marten,** *Martes americana*
RANGE: **Canada, N. USA**
HABITAT: **forest, woodland**
SIZE: **body: 35.5–43 cm (14–17 in)**
   tail: 18–23 cm (7–9 in)

An agile, acrobatic creature with a bushy tail, the marten spends much of its time in trees, where it preys on squirrels. It also hunts on the ground and eats small animals and insects, fruit and nuts. Martens den in hollow trees and produce a yearly litter of 2 to 4 young, usually in April. The young are blind and helpless at birth; their eyes open at 6 weeks, and they attain adult weight at about 3 months.

The closely related fisher, M. *pennanti,* is one of the few creatures that preys on American porcupines.

NAME: **Sable,** *Martes zibellina*
RANGE: **Siberia; Japan: Hokkaido**
HABITAT: **forest**
SIZE: **body: 38–45 cm (15–18 in)**
   tail: 12–19 cm (5–7½ in)

The sable, one of the 7 species of marten, has long been hunted for its luxuriant fur. Conservation measures have now been introduced in Russia to save the decreasing wild population, and sables are farmed for pelts. The sable is a ground-dweller and feeds on small rodents and other small mammals, as well as on fish, insects, honey, nuts and berries. A yearly litter of 2 to 4 is produced, usually in April.

NAME: **Zorilla,** *Ictonyx striatus*
RANGE: **Africa: Senegal and Nigeria to South Africa**
HABITAT: **savanna, open country**
SIZE: **body: 28.5–38.5 cm (11–15 in)**
   tail: 20.5–30 cm (8–12 in)

Also known as the striped polecat, the single species of zorilla can eject a nauseating secretion from its anal glands when alarmed. It is primarily a nocturnal animal and feeds on rodents, reptiles, insects and bird's eggs. By day, it rests in a burrow which it digs itself or takes over from another animal or in a rock crevice or pile of stones. The litter of 2 or 3 young is born in a burrow.

NAME: **Grison,** *Galictis vittata*
RANGE: **S. Mexico to Peru and Brazil**
HABITAT: **forest, open land**
SIZE: **body: 47–55 cm (18½–21½ in)**
   tail: 16 cm (6 in)

The grison is an agile animal, good at climbing and swimming. It feeds on frogs and worms as well as other ground-living creatures. The abandoned burrow of another animal or a rock or tree root crevice serves it as a den, and a litter of 2 to 4 young is produced in October. There are 3 species of grison, all living in Central and South America. The local population uses grisons in the same way as ferrets, for flushing out chinchillas.

NAME: **Tayra,** *Eira barbara*
RANGE: **S. Mexico to Argentina; Trinidad**
HABITAT: **forest**
SIZE: **body: 60–68 cm (24–27 in)**
   tail: 38–47 cm (15–18½ in)

The single species of tayra runs, climbs and swims well. It preys on small mammals, such as tree squirrels and rodents, and also feeds on fruit and honey. Tayras move in pairs or small family groups and are active at night and in the early morning. They are believed to produce a yearly litter of 2 to 4 young.

Zorilla

Black-footed Ferret

Western Polecat

Least Weasel

Marten

Grison

Sable

Ermine

Tayra

Mustelids
Wolverine, Badgers

NAME: **Wolverine,** *Gulo gulo*
RANGE: **Scandinavia, Siberia, Alaska,**
    Canada, W. USA
HABITAT: **coniferous forest, tundra**
SIZE: **body: 65–87 cm (25½–34¼ in)**
    tail: 17–26 cm (6½–10 in)

The single species of wolverine is a heavily built animal, immensely strong for its size and capable of killing animals larger than itself. Although largely carnivorous, wolverines also feed on berries. They are solitary animals, mainly ground-dwelling, but they can climb trees. Each male holds a large territory with 2 or 3 females and mates in the summer. The female wolverine bears 2 or 3 young in the following spring, usually after a period of delayed implantation.

Delayed implantation is an interesting phenomenon allowing animals to mate at the ideal time and bear young at the ideal time, even though the intervening period is longer than their actual gestation. The fertilized egg remains in a suspended state in the womb, and development starts only after the required period of dormancy. The young suckle for about 2 months and remain with their mother for up to 2 years, at which time they are driven out of her territory. They become sexually mature at about 4 years of age.

NAME: **Ratel,** *Mellivora capensis*
RANGE: **Africa; Middle East to N. India**
HABITAT: **steppe, savanna**
SIZE: **body: 60–70 cm (23½–27½ in)**
    tail: 20–30 cm (7¾ to 11¾ in)

The stocky ratel is also known as the honey badger because of its fondness for honey, and in Africa a honey-eating association has developed between the ratel and a small bird, the honey guide. Calling and flying just ahead, the bird leads the ratel to a wild bees' nest. With its powerful foreclaws, the ratel then breaks open the nest, and both partners share the spoils. The unusually tough hide of the ratel protects it from bee stings and is also a good defense in another way: the skin is so loose on the body that the animal can twist about in its skin and even bite an attacker which has a hold on the back of its neck. In addition to honey and bee larvae, the ratel eats small animals, insects, roots, bulbs and fruit and will occasionally attack large animals such as sheep and antelope.

Although sometimes active in the daytime, ratels are generally nocturnal animals. They live singly or in pairs and produce a litter of 2 young in an underground burrow or a nest among rocks. The gestation period is 6 or 7 months.

NAME: **Eurasian Badger,** *Meles meles*
RANGE: **Europe to Japan and S. China**
HABITAT: **forest, grassland**
SIZE: **body: 56–81 cm (22–32 in)**
    tail: 11–20 cm (4–7¾ in)

The gregarious Eurasian badger lives in family groups in huge burrows with networks of underground passages and chambers and several entrances. A burrow system, or sett, may be used by successive generations of badgers, each making additions and alterations. Bedding material of grass, hay and leaves is gathered into the sleeping chambers and occasionally dragged out to air in the early morning. Around the sett are play areas, and the boundaries of the group's territory are marked by latrine holes.

Badgers are generally nocturnal and emerge from the sett around dusk. They are playful creatures, and at this time the young and adults will indulge in boisterous romping. Such play helps to strengthen the social bonds, crucial to group-living animals. Badgers feed on large quantities of earthworms as well as on small animals, bulbs, fruit and nuts. They mate in the summer when social acitivity is at its height, but gestation of the fertilized eggs does not start until such a time as to ensure that the 2 to 4 young are not born until the following spring.

NAME: **Badger,** *Taxidea taxus*
RANGE: **S.W. Canada to central Mexico**
HABITAT: **open grassland, arid land**
SIZE: **body: 42–56 cm (16½–22 in)**
    tail: 10–15 cm (4–6 in)

The single species of *Taxidea* is the only New World badger. It has a rather flattened body shape but is otherwise similar to other badgers. A solitary creature, the badger is generally active at night, although it will come out of its burrow during the day. It is an excellent digger and burrows rapidly after disappearing rodents — its main food. It sometimes buries a large food item for storage. Birds, eggs and reptiles make up the rest of its diet.

The badgers mate in late summer, but the 6-week gestation period does not begin until February, so the litter is born only the following spring. The 1 to 5 young, usually 2, are born on a grassy bed in the burrow and are covered with silky fur. Their eyes open at 6 weeks and they suckle for several months.

In northern parts of its range and at high altitudes, the badger sleeps for much of the winter, surviving on its stored fat. However, it does not truly hibernate and becomes active in mild spells.

NAME: **Hog Badger,** *Arctonyx collaris*
RANGE: **N. China, N.E. India, Sumatra**
HABITAT: **wooded regions in uplands and**
    lowlands
SIZE: **body: 55–70 cm (21½–27½ in)**
    tail: 12–17 cm (5–6½ in)

Similar in shape and size to the Eurasian badger, the hog badger is distinguished by its white throat and mostly white tail. The common name refers to the badger's mobile, piglike snout, used for rooting for plant material and animals. A nocturnal animal, it spends its day in a rock crevice or deep burrow; its habits are much the same as those of the Eurasian badger. Like all badgers, the hog badger has anal scent glands with potent secretions, and its black and white markings constitute a warning that it is a formidable opponent.

The breeding habits of the hog badger are not well known, but in one observation the female gave birth to 4 young in April.

NAME: **Stink Badger,** *Mydaus javanensis*
RANGE: **Sumatra, Java, Borneo**
HABITAT: **dense forest**
SIZE: **body: 37.5–51 cm (15–20 in)**
    tail: 5–7.5 cm (2–3 in)

The 2 species of stink badger have particularly powerful anal gland secretions, said to be as evil-smelling as those of skunks. When threatened or alarmed, the stink badger raises its tail and ejects a stream of the fluid. However, like musk, although foul in concentration, the secretion can be sweet-smelling in dilution and was formerly used in the making of perfume. This nocturnal creature lives in a burrow and feeds on worms, insects and small animals. The second species, the Palawan badger, M. *marchei*, inhabits the Philippine and Calamian islands.

NAME: **Chinese Ferret Badger,** *Melogale*
    moschata
RANGE: **N.E. India, S. China, Indo-**
    China, Java, Borneo
HABITAT: **grassland, open forest**
SIZE: **body: 33–43 cm (13–17 in)**
    tail: 15–23 cm (6–9 in)

Distinctive masklike face markings distinguish the Chinese ferret badger from other oriental mustelids. This badger lives in burrows or crevices and is active at dusk and at night. It is a good climber and feeds on fruit, insects, small animals and worms. Ferret badgers are savage when alarmed and their anal secretions are foul-smelling. A litter of up to 3 young is born in May or June. There are 2 other species of ferret badger, both in Southeast Asia.

Wolverine

Ratel

Eurasian Badger

Hog Badger

Stink Badger

Badger

Chinese Ferret Badger

Mustelids
Skunks, Otters

NAME: **Striped Skunk,** *Mephitis mephitis*
RANGE: **S. Canada to N. Mexico**
HABITAT: **semiopen country, woods, grassland**
SIZE: **body: 28–38 cm (11–15 in)**
  tail: 18–25 cm (7–10 in)

Notorious for its pungent anal gland secretions, the striped skunk is one of the most familiar mustelids. Like others of its family, it does not use these secretions against rival skunks, only against enemies. The fluid is an effective weapon because the smell temporarily stops the victim's breathing. The striped skunk is a nocturnal animal, spending the day in a burrow or in a den beneath old buildings, wood or rock piles. It feeds on mice, eggs, insects, berries and carrion. A litter of 5 or 6 young is born in early May in a den lined with vegetation. The hooded skunk, *M. macroura*, is a similar and closely related species; the black and white markings of both skunks are highly variable and constitute a warning display.

NAME: **Hog-nosed Skunk,** *Conepatus mesoleucus*
RANGE: **S. USA to Nicaragua**
HABITAT: **wooded and open land**
SIZE: **body: 35–48 cm (13¾–19 in)**
  tail: 17–31 cm (6½–12 in)

This nocturnal, solitary, slow-moving animal has the coarsest fur of all skunks. The common name derives from the animal's long piglike snout, which it uses to root in the soil for insects and grubs. Snakes, small mammals and fruit also feature in its diet. The hog-nosed skunk dens in rocky places or abandoned burrows and produces a litter of 2 to 5 young. There are 7 species of hog-nosed skunk, all found in the southern USA and South America.

NAME: **Spotted Skunk,** *Spilogale gracilis*
RANGE: **W. USA to central Mexico**
HABITAT: **wasteland, brush and wooded areas**
SIZE: **body: 23–34.5 cm (9–13½ in)**
  tail: 11–22 cm (4¼–8½ in)

The white stripes and spots of the spotted skunk are infinitely variable; no two animals have quite the same markings. A nocturnal, mainly terrestrial animal, this skunk usually dens underground, but it is a good climber and occasionally shelters in trees. Rodents, birds, eggs, insects and fruit are the main items in its diet.

In the south of the spotted skunk's range, young are born at any time of year, but farther north, the 4 or 5 young are produced in spring. The gestation period is about 4 months.

NAME: **Eurasian Otter,** *Lutra lutra*
RANGE: **Europe, N. Africa, Asia**
HABITAT: **rivers, lakes, sheltered coasts**
SIZE: **body: 55–80 cm (21½–31½ in)**
  tail: 30–50 cm (12–19½ in) Ⓥ

Although agile on land, otters have become well adapted for an aquatic life. The Eurasian otter has the slim mustelid body, but its tail is thick, fleshy and muscular for propulsion in water. All four feet are webbed, and the nostrils and ears can be closed when the otter is in water. Its fur is short and dense and keeps the skin dry by trapping a layer of air around the body. An excellent swimmer and diver, the otter moves in water by strong undulations of its body and tail and strokes of its hind feet. It feeds on fish, frogs, water birds, voles and other aquatic creatures.

Otters are solitary, elusive creatures, now rare in much of their range. They den in a riverbank in a burrow called a holt and are most active at night. Even adult otters are playful animals and enjoy sliding down a muddy bank. A litter of 2 or 3 young is born in the spring — or at any time of year in the south of the otter's range. There are 8 species of *Lutra*, all with more or less similar habits and adaptations.

NAME: **Giant Otter,** *Pteronura brasiliensis*
RANGE: **Venezuela to Argentina**
HABITAT: **rivers, slow streams**
SIZE: **body: 1–1.5 m (1¼–5 ft)**
  tail: 70 cm (27½ in) Ⓔ

The giant otter is similar in appearance to *Lutra* species but is larger and has a flattened tail with crests on each edge. It generally travels in a group and is active during the day. Giant otters feed on fish, eggs, aquatic mammals and birds. They den in holes in a riverbank or under tree roots and produce yearly litters of 1 or 2 young. Now endangered, the giant otter is protected in some countries, but enforcement of the law in the vast, sparsely inhabited areas of the animal's range is extremely difficult and numbers are still decreasing.

NAME: **African Clawless Otter,** *Aonyx capensis*
RANGE: **Africa: Senegal, Ethiopia, South Africa**
HABITAT: **slow streams and pools; coastal waters, estuaries**
SIZE: **body: 95 cm–1 m (37 in–3¼ ft)**
  tail: 55 cm (21½ in)

The African clawless otter swims and dives as well as other otters, although its feet have only small connecting webs. As its name suggests, this otter has no claws other than tiny nails on the third and fourth toes of the hind feet. It has less dense fur than most otters so has not been hunted as extensively. Crabs

are the most important item of the clawless otter's diet, and it is equipped with large, strong cheek teeth for crushing the hard shells; it also feeds on mollusks, fish, reptiles, frogs, birds and small mammals. Like most otters, it comes ashore to eat and feeds from its hands rather than from the ground. Indeed, clawless otters seem particularly skillful in their hand movements.

Clawless otters do not dig burrows but live in crevices or under rocks in family groups, pairs or alone. The litter of 2 to 5 young stays with the parents for at least a year.

NAME: **Sea Otter,** *Enhydris lutris*
RANGE: **Bering Sea; USA: California coast**
HABITAT: **rocky coasts**
SIZE: **body: 1–1.2 m (1¼–4 ft)**
  tail: 25–37 cm (10–14½ in)

The most highly adapted of all otters for an aquatic existence, the sea otter spends nearly all its life at sea, always in water less than 20 m (66 ft) deep. Its body is streamlined and legs and tail are short. The hind feet are webbed and flipperlike, and the forefeet are small. Unlike most other marine mammals, it does not have an insulating layer of fat but must rely on a layer of air trapped in its fur for protection against the cold water. Much time and effort is spent on grooming the dense, glossy fur for its insulating qualities are lessened if it becomes unkempt.

Sea otters feed on clams, sea urchins, mussels, abalone and other mollusks which they collect from the seabed and eat while lying in the water. In order to cope with the hard shells of much of its food, the sea otter has discovered how to use rocks as tools. When diving for food, the sea otter also brings up a rock from the seabed. Placing the stone on its chest as it lies on its back in the water, the otter bangs the prey against the stone until the shell is broken, revealing the soft animal inside. At dusk, the sea otter swims into the huge kelp beds found in its range and entangles itself in the weed so that it does not drift during the night while it is asleep.

Sea otters breed every two years or so and give birth to 1 pup after a gestation period of 8 or 9 months. The pup is born in an unusually well-developed state, with eyes open and a full set of milk teeth. The mother carries and nurses the pup on her chest as she swims on her back. At one time sea otters were hunted for their beautiful fur and became rare, but they have been protected by law for some years.

Striped Skunk

Hog-nosed Skunk

Spotted Skunk

Eurasian Otter

Giant Otter

African Clawless Otter

Sea Otter

Civets

NAME: **African Linsang,** *Poiana richardsoni*
RANGE: **Africa: Sierra Leone to Zaire**
HABITAT: **forest**
SIZE: **body: 33 cm (13 in)**
  tail: 38 cm (15 in)

A nocturnal animal, the African linsang is a good climber and spends more time in the trees than on the ground. During the day, it sleeps in a nest built of green vegetation in a tree and then emerges at night to hunt for insects and young birds; it also feeds on fruit, nuts and plant material. Elongate and slender, this linsang is brownish-yellow to gray, with dark spots on the body and dark bands ringing the long tail.

Little is known of the breeding habits of the African linsang, but females are thought to produce litters of 2 or 3 young once or twice a year.

NAME: **Banded Linsang,** *Prionodon linsang*
RANGE: **Thailand, Malaysia, Sumatra, Borneo**
HABITAT: **forest**
SIZE: **body: 37.5–43 cm (14¾–17 in)**
  tail: 30.5–35.5 cm (12–14 in)

The slender, graceful banded linsang varies from whitish-gray to brownish-gray in color, with four or five dark bands across its back and dark spots on its sides and legs. It is nocturnal and spends much of its life in trees, where it climbs and jumps skillfully, but it is just as agile on the ground. Birds, small mammals, insects, lizards and frogs are all preyed on, and this linsang also eats bird's eggs.

The breeding habits of this species are not well known, but it is believed to bear two litters a year of 2 or 3 young each. Young are born in a nest in a hollow tree or in a burrow.

NAME: **Masked Palm Civet,** *Paguma larvata*
RANGE: **Himalayas to China, Hainan, Taiwan, S.E. Asia, Sumatra, Borneo**
HABITAT: **forest, brush**
SIZE: **body: 50–76 cm (19¾–30 in)**
  tail: 51–64 cm (20–25¼ in)

The masked palm civet has a plain gray or brownish-red body with no stripes or spots but with distinctive white mask-like markings on the face. It is nocturnal and hunts in the trees and on the ground for rodents and other small animals, as well as for insects, fruit and plant roots. The secretions of its anal glands are extremely strong-smelling and can be sprayed considerable distances to discourage any attacker.

A litter of 3 or 4 young is born in a hole in a tree. The young are grayer than adults and do not have conspicuous face masks at first.

VIVERRIDAE: Civet Family

There are about 72 species of civet, mongoose, genet and linsang in this family. All are small to medium-sized carnivores which live in the Old World, with a distribution stretching from southern Europe through Africa, Madagascar and Asia. Most viverrids have long, sinuous bodies, elongate skulls, short legs and long tails. There are generally five claws on each foot, and these claws are partly retractable. Many species of viverrid emit a strong-smelling secretion from anal scent glands, the active ingredient of which, civetone, is used in the manufacture of perfumes.

Viverrids have adapted to a variety of habitats, such as open savanna and dense forest, while some species are semiaquatic in fresh water. Males and females generally look alike, but males are sometimes larger and heavier.

NAME: **African Palm Civet,** *Nandinia binotata*
RANGE: **Africa: Guinea, east to S. Sudan, south to Mozambique**
HABITAT: **forest, savanna, woodland**
SIZE: **body: 44–60 cm (17¼–23½ in)**
  tail: 48–62 cm (18¾–24½ in)

Active at night, the African palm civet is a skillful climber and spends much of its life in trees. Its diet is varied, ranging from insects, lizards, small mammals and birds to many kinds of fruit (which may sometimes be its sole food), leaves, grass and some carrion. A solitary animal, it spends the day resting in the trees. The male is larger and heavier than the female, and both have short legs and long, thick tails. The short muzzle is adorned with long whiskers. Usually grayish-brown to dark reddish-brown in color, this civet has a pale creamy spot on each shoulder — the origin of its other common name of two-spotted palm civet.

The female gives birth to a litter of 2 or 3 young after a gestation of about 64 days.

NAME: **Congo Water Civet,** *Osbornictis piscivora*
RANGE: **Africa: N.E. Zaire**
HABITAT: **rain forest near streams**
SIZE: **body: 45–50 cm (17¾–19¾ in)**
  tail: 35–42 cm (13¾–16½ in)

The rarely seen Congo water civet is thought to lead a semiaquatic life and to feed largely on fish and aquatic creatures. It has a slender body, short legs, with the hind legs longer than the forelegs, and a thick, bushy tail. Its coat is reddish-brown, with darker hair on the backs of the ears and the middle of the back and tail.

NAME: **African Civet,** *Viverra civetta*
RANGE: **Africa, south of the Sahara to South Africa: Transvaal**
HABITAT: **forest, savanna, plains, cultivated areas**
SIZE: **body: 80–95 cm (31½–37½ in)**
  tail: 40–53 cm (15¾–20¾ in)

Large and doglike, the African civet has a broad head, strong neck and long legs; the hind legs are longer than the forelegs. Its coat is generally gray, with darker legs, chin and throat, and the back and flanks are patterned with dark stripes and patches; the size and spacing of these dark markings is highly variable. By day, the African civet sleeps in a burrow or under cover of vegetation or rocks. It rarely climbs trees except to escape from an enemy, but it swims well. Mammals up to the size of young antelope, birds, including poultry and their eggs, reptiles, frogs, toads and insects are all hunted, and this civet also takes some carrion, as well as feeding on fruit and berries.

The female gives birth to 1 to 4 young, usually 2, after a gestation of 63 to 68 days. The young take their first solid food at 3 weeks and are weaned at 3 months. There may be as many as three litters a year.

NAME: **Small-spotted Genet,** *Genetta genetta*
RANGE: **S.W. Europe: S.W. France, Spain and Portugal; Africa, Middle East**
HABITAT: **semidesert, scrub, savanna**
SIZE: **body: 50–60 cm (19¾–23½ in)**
  tail: 40–48 cm (15¾–18¾ in)

A slender, short-legged animal, this genet is marked with dark spots, which may form lines down its whitish to brownish-gray body. Its head is small and muzzle pointed, and its long tail is encircled with black bands. An agile, graceful animal, the small-spotted genet moves on land with its tail held straight out behind and climbs well in trees and bushes. It spends the day sleeping in an abandoned burrow of another animal, in a rock crevice or on the branch of a tree and starts to hunt at dusk. Sight, hearing and sense of smell are good, and the genet stalks its prey, crouching almost flat before pouncing. Most prey, such as rodents, reptiles and insects, is taken on the ground, but the genet will climb trees to take roosting or nesting birds; it also kills poultry. It normally lives alone or in pairs.

A litter of 2 or 3 young is born in a hole in the ground or in a tree or in a rock crevice after a gestation of 68 to 77 days. The young are born blind, and their eyes open after 5 to 12 days. They are suckled for up to 3 months and are fully independent by 9 months.

African Linsang

Small-spotted Genet

Banded Linsang

African Civet

Congo Water Civet

African Palm Civet

Masked Palm Civet

Civets

NAME: Binturong, *Arctictis binturong*
RANGE: S.E. Asia, Palawan, Sumatra, Java, Borneo
HABITAT: forest
SIZE: body: 61–96.5 cm (24–38 in)
tail: 56–89 cm (22–35 in)

A large viverrid with long, coarse fur, the binturong has distinctive ear tufts and a prehensile tail, which it uses as a fifth limb when climbing. It is the only carnivore other than the kinkajou, a member of the raccoon family, to possess such a tail. During the day, it sleeps up in the trees and emerges at night to climb slowly, but skillfully, among the branches, searching for fruit and other plant matter, as well as insects, small vertebrates and carrion.

After a gestation of 90 to 92 days, the female produces a litter of 1 or 2 young. Both parents care for the young, which are born blind and helpless.

NAME: Falanouc, *Eupleres goudoti*
RANGE: N. Madagascar
HABITAT: rain forest, swamps
SIZE: body: 46–50 cm (18–19¾ in)
tail: 22–24 cm (8½–9½ in) ⓥ

The falanouc, also known as the small-toothed mongoose, with its long, slender body, pointed muzzle and short legs, does resemble a mongoose in build. The hind legs are longer than the forelegs, and the rear is consequently higher than the front of the body. The tail is thick and bushy. Active at dusk and during the night, the falanouc does not climb or jump well but slowly hops along the ground, searching for earthworms (its main food), insects, aquatic snails, frogs and sometimes even small mammals and birds. It readily wades into water in pursuit of prey. When food is abundant, the falanouc lays down a store of fat near the base of its tail on which it lives during the dry season, when worms are scarce.

Falanoucs pair for life, and each pair lives in a territory, the boundaries of which they mark with secretions of the anal and head glands. After a gestation of about 12 weeks, the female bears 1 young, which is born with a full covering of hair and with its eyes open; it is weaned at 9 weeks.

These animals are becoming rare outside nature reserves because of the destruction of forest land, competition with an introduced civet, *Viverricula indica*, and overhunting by local people.

NAME: Otter-civet, *Cynogale bennetti*
RANGE: Indo-China, Malaysia, Borneo, Sumatra
HABITAT: swamps, near rivers
SIZE: body: 57–67 cm (22½–26¼ in)
tail: 13–20 cm (5–7¾ in)

The otter-civet spends much of its life in water and has several adaptations for its aquatic habits. Like many aquatic mammals, it has short, dense underfur, which is waterproof, covered by a layer of longer, coarse guard hairs. Its nostrils open upward and can be closed off by flaps, and the ears can also be closed. The otter-civet's feet are supple and have broad webs; these webs are only partial and do not extend to the tips of the digits, so the animal is able to move as well on land as in water.

With only the tip of its nose above the water, the otter-civet is almost invisible as it swims and so is able to ambush creatures that come to the water's edge to drink; it also takes prey in water. Fish, small mammals, birds and crustaceans are all included in the otter-civet's diet, and it also eats fruit. It has long, sharp teeth for seizing prey and broad, flat molars, which it uses to crush hard-shelled items such as crustaceans. On land, it climbs well and may take refuge in a tree if attacked, rather than making for water.

A litter of 2 or 3 young is born in a burrow or hollow tree. They are not independent until about 6 months old.

NAME: Meerkat, *Suricata suricatta*
RANGE: Africa: Angola to South Africa
HABITAT: open country, savanna, bush
SIZE: body: 25–31 cm (9¾–12¼ in)
tail: 19–24 cm (7½–9½ in)

The meerkat, also known as the suricate, has the long body and short legs typical of many mongooses. Its coat is mainly grayish-brown to light gray in color, marked with dark bands across the body, but it has dark ears and nose and a light-colored head and throat. The fur on the belly is thin and helps the meerkat to regulate its body temperature. It sits up sunning itself or lies on warm ground to increase its temperature and reduces it by lying belly-down in a cool, dark burrow.

Gregarious animals, meerkats live in family units, sometimes several families living together in a group of 30 or so. The colony occupies a home range, which contains shelters, such as burrows or rock crevices, and feeding sites. The animals need to move to a different area several times a year when food supplies dwindle. Meerkats are good diggers and make burrows with several tunnels and chambers. Active in the daytime, they forage in pairs or small groups, often sitting up on their hind legs to watch for prey or for danger. They run fast for short distances but cannot climb or jump well. Insects, spiders, scorpions, centipedes, small mammals, lizards, snakes, birds and their eggs, snails, roots, fruit and other plant material are all included in their varied, wide-ranging diet. Meerkats have good hearing and sense of smell and excellent eyesight; they keep constant watch for birds of prey, their main enemies, and they instantly dive for a burrow or other cover if alarmed.

Breeding takes place mainly between October and April. The female gives birth to 2 to 5 young, usually 2 or 3, in a grass-lined underground chamber after a gestation of about 77 days. The young are born blind, but their eyes open 12 to 14 days after birth, and they take their first solid food at 3 or 4 weeks.

NAME: Banded Palm Civet, *Hemigalus derbyanus*
RANGE: Malaysia, Sumatra, Borneo
HABITAT: forest
SIZE: body: 41–51 cm (16–20 in)
tail: 25–38 cm (9¾–15 in)

The banded palm civet has a slender, elongate body and a tapering, pointed snout. It is usually whitish to orange-buff in color, with dark stripes on the head and neck, behind the shoulders and at the base of the tail.

A nocturnal animal, the banded palm civet is a good climber, with strong feet well adapted to arboreal life, and it forages for its prey in trees, on the forest floor and beside streams. Worms and locusts are its main foods, but it also eats ants, spiders, crustaceans, land and aquatic snails and frogs.

Little is known of its breeding habits.

NAME: Salano, *Salanoia concolor*
RANGE: N.E. Madagascar
HABITAT: rain forest
SIZE: body: 35–38 cm (13¾–15 in)
tail: 18–20 cm (7–7¾ in)

Salanos are gregarious animals; they pair for life and live in family groups in a territory, marking the boundaries with secretions of the anal glands. At night, the salano rests in a burrow that it digs or takes over from other animals or in a hollow tree. During the day, it searches for insects (its main food), amphibians, reptiles and, occasionally, small mammals and birds. It also eats the contents of eggs, which it cracks by taking them in its hind feet and hurling them backward against a stone or tree.

The female gives birth to 1 young, but other details of the salano's breeding habits are not known.

Binturong

Falanouc

Otter-civet

Meerkat

Banded Palm Civet

Salano

Civets

NAME: **Indian Mongoose,** *Herpestes auropunctatus*
RANGE: **Iraq to India, south to Malaysia; introduced in West Indies, Hawaii and Fiji**
HABITAT: **desert, open scrub, thin forest, dense forest**
SIZE: **body: 35 cm (13¾ in)**
 tail: 25 cm (9¾ in)

This widespread mongoose varies in size and appearance according to its environment; desert populations are the smallest and palest. Generally, however, the soft, silky fur is olive-brown, and the tail is shorter than the head and body length.

At night, the Indian mongoose rests in a burrow, which it digs itself, and during the day it hunts for food, treading the same paths consistently and keeping in cover of vegetation. It feeds on almost anything it can catch, such as rats, mice, snakes, scorpions, centipedes, wasps and other insects, and is much appreciated for its ability to keep pest species, such as rats, at bay. Indeed, this adaptable mongoose has been introduced into areas outside its native range specifically for the purpose of destroying the rats and snakes that were infesting crops.

Females may produce two litters a year, each of 2 to 4 young, which are born after a gestation of about 7 weeks. The newborn are blind and hairless, and their mother carries them about in her mouth and defends them fiercely.

NAME: **Marsh Mongoose,** *Atilax paludinosus*
RANGE: **Africa, south of the Sahara**
HABITAT: **marshland, tidal estuaries, swamps**
SIZE: **body: 45–60 cm (17¾–23½ in)**
 tail: 30–40 cm (11¾–15¾ in)

The large, sturdily built marsh mongoose is an expert swimmer and diver and is probably the most aquatic of all the mongooses. Despite its expertise in water, its feet are not webbed but have short, strong claws. Mainly nocturnal, this mongoose swims or roams along streambanks or in marshes, searching for food such as crabs, aquatic insects, fish, frogs and snakes. It often uses its forepaws to feel in mud or under stones for prey. To crush hard-shelled animals, such as crabs, it will dash the creature against a rock or tree. The marsh mongoose shows complicated and balletic scent-marking behavior. Standing on its forepaws, with its tail over its back, it marks the underside of branches with secretions of its anal glands.

Marsh mongooses live alone or in pairs or small family groups. The female gives birth to 1 to 3 young in a burrow or in a nest amid a pile of vegetation.

NAME: **Banded Mongoose,** *Mungos mungo*
RANGE: **Africa, south of the Sahara**
HABITAT: **savanna, often near water**
SIZE: **body: 30–45 cm (11¾–17¾ in)**
 tail: 20–30 cm (7¾–11¾ in)

The banded mongoose has a stout body and a rather short snout and tail. It varies in coloration from olive-brown to reddish-gray, and light and dark bands alternate across its back from shoulders to tail. It is active in the daytime — in hot weather only in the morning and evening — and also sometimes emerges on moonlit nights. A good climber and swimmer if necessary, the banded mongoose is a generally bold, adventurous animal in its search for food. It often digs and forages in the ground and in leaf litter, hunting for prey such as insects, spiders, scorpions, centipedes, small frogs, lizards, snakes and small mammals and birds. It also eats fruit, plant shoots and eggs, which it hurls against stones to smash their shells.

Family troops of up to 30 animals live together, moving their range every few days except in the breeding season. They shelter in hollow trees or rock crevices or in burrows, which they dig or take over from other animals. If attacked, they defend themselves courageously, growling and spitting and arching their backs.

A litter of 2 to 6 young is born in a burrow after a gestation of about 8 weeks. Their eyes open at 10 days, and they first venture out about 3 weeks after birth.

NAME: **Cusimanse,** *Crossarchus obscurus*
RANGE: **Africa: Sierra Leone to Cameroon**
HABITAT: **rain forest**
SIZE: **body: 30–40 cm (11¾–15¾ in)**
 tail: 15–25 cm (6–9¾ in)

The cusimanse has a particularly long, narrow head and snout, the nose protruding beyond the lower lip. Like most mongooses, it is gregarious and lives in family groups of up to 12 animals, which keep in touch with chattering calls while they wander in search of food. They dig in the soil for worms, wood lice, spiders, snails and insects and also prey on crabs, frogs, reptiles, small mammals and birds and their eggs. To break eggs and hard-shelled prey, the cusimanse throws them against a tree or stone. At night, cusimanses sleep in burrows, which they dig, often in an old termite mound. They rarely climb trees, unless forced to do so in order to escape from an enemy.

The female cusimanse bears several litters a year, each of 2 to 4 young. The gestation period is about 70 days.

NAME: **White-tailed Mongoose,** *Ichneumia albicauda*
RANGE: **Africa, south of the Sahara**
HABITAT: **savanna, dense bush, forest edge, often near water**
SIZE: **body: 47–69 cm (18½–27¼ in)**
 tail: 36–50 cm (14¼–19¾ in)

This large, long-legged mongoose has a distinctive bushy tail, which is gray at its base, usually becoming white or off-white at the tip; some individuals may have an entirely blackish tail. It lives alone or in pairs and is normally active only at night, but in very secluded areas it may emerge in the late afternoon. A poor climber, the white-tailed mongoose is able to swim, although it rarely does so, and most of its hunting is done on the ground. It preys on insects, frogs, reptiles, rodents and ground-living birds and uses its strong teeth to crush snails and crabs. Eggs, berries and fruit are also included in this varied diet.

The female gives birth to a litter of 2 or 3 young.

NAME: **Bushy-tailed Mongoose,** *Bdeogale crassicauda*
RANGE: **E. Africa: Kenya to Zimbabwe and Mozambique**
HABITAT: **coastal forest, savanna**
SIZE: **body: 40–50 cm (15¾–19¾ in)**
 tail: 20–30 cm (7¾–11¾ in)

A robust mongoose with a broad muzzle and sturdy legs, this species does indeed have a broad, heavily furred tail. It is an elusive, nocturnal animal and rests by day in a burrow, often one taken over from another animal, or in a hole in a hollow tree. At night, it hunts for insects, including termites, and lizards, snakes, rodents and other small creatures.

NAME: **Fossa,** *Cryptoprocta ferox*
RANGE: **Madagascar**
HABITAT: **forest**
SIZE: **body: 60–75 cm (23½–29½ in)**
 tail: 55–70 cm (21½–27½ in) ⓥ

The largest Madagascan carnivore, the fossa resembles a cat as much as a viverrid and has a rounded, catlike head but with a longer muzzle. Its body is slender and elongate, and its hind legs are longer than its forelegs. Active at dusk and at night, it is an excellent climber and is equally agile in trees and on the ground. It lives alone and hunts for mammals up to the size of lemurs, as well as for birds, lizards, snakes and insects; it also kills domestic poultry.

The female bears 2 or 3 young in a burrow, a hole in a tree or a den among rocks after a gestation of about 3 months. She cares for them alone. The young are weaned at 4 months and are fully grown and independent at 2 years.

96

Indian Mongoose

Marsh Mongoose

Banded Mongoose

Cusimanse

Bushy-tailed Mongoose

White-tailed Mongoose

Fossa

Hyenas

NAME: Aardwolf, *Proteles cristatus*
RANGE: Africa: Sudan, south to South Africa, Angola
HABITAT: open dry plains, savanna
SIZE: body: 65–80 cm (25½–31½ in)
tail: 20–30 cm (7¾–11¾ in)

A smaller and more lightly built version of the hyena, the aardwolf has a pointed muzzle, slender legs and an erectile mane on the neck and along the back. There are dark stripes on its yellowish- to reddish-brown body and legs. Unless in a family group with young, the aardwolf lives alone in a territory centered on a den, which may be the abandoned burrow of an aardvark or a hole it digs itself. The boundaries of the territory are marked by anal gland secretions. Active at night, the aardwolf has extremely acute hearing and can detect the movements of termites, its main food. These are lapped from the ground or grass by means of the aardwolf's long tongue, which is covered with sticky saliva, making the task easier. It also eats other insects, bird's eggs, small mammals and reptiles.

A litter of 2 to 4 young is born in a burrow. After weaning, both parents feed the young on regurgitated termites.

NAME: Striped Hyena, *Hyaena hyaena*
RANGE: Africa: Senegal to Tanzania; Middle East to India
HABITAT: dry savanna, bush country, semidesert, desert
SIZE: body: 1–1.2 m (3¼–4 ft)
tail: 25–35 cm (9¾–13¾ in)

The striped hyena is identified by the dark stripes on its gray or yellowish-gray body and by the erectile mane around its neck and shoulders that extends down the middle of its back. Males are usually larger than females, and both have the heavy head and sloping back typical of the hyenas.

Although they live in pairs in the breeding season, striped hyenas are generally solitary. Each has a home range, which must contain some thick cover, and the boundaries are marked by anal gland secretions rubbed onto grass stems. Active at night, the striped hyena feeds on carrion, such as the remains of the kills of big cats, and preys on young sheep and goats, small mammals, birds, lizards, snakes and insects; it will also eat fruit. Striped hyenas stay well away from the larger spotted hyenas.

After a gestation of about 3 months, a litter of 2 to 4 young is born in a hole in the ground or among rocks. Both parents help to care for the young, which are blind at birth and are suckled for up to a year.

HYAENIDAE: Hyena Family

The hyenas of Africa and southwest Asia and the aardwolf of southern Africa together constitute a small family of land-dwelling carnivores that is related to the viverrids and the cats. This relationship is somewhat surprising in terms of superficial appearance, since all members of the hyena family have an extremely doglike body form.

The 3 species of hyena, particularly, resemble dogs but are more heavily built in the forequarters than the hindquarters. They have massive heads; indeed the jaws of the spotted hyena, the largest member of the group, are the most powerful of any mammal. All hyenas are able to crush the biggest bones of their prey to extract the marrow. Hyenas specialize in feeding on carrion, often the kills of lions and other large carnivores, and are able to drive smaller predators, such as cheetah, away from their kills. They are, however, also predators in their own right, particularly spotted hyenas, and by hunting in cooperative packs can bring down animals as large as zebras. In fact, in one area of Tanzania, spotted hyenas are more successful killers than lions. Near villages and towns, hyenas are useful scavengers and feed on any refuse left out at night.

The aardwolf is a highly adapted offshoot of the hyena stock. It is more lightly built and has a narrow, pointed head, large ears and tiny teeth. It feeds mostly on termites.

Males and females look alike in all members of the family, but males may be larger.

NAME: Brown Hyena, *Hyaena brunnea*
RANGE: Africa: Angola to Mozambique, south to N. South Africa
HABITAT: dry savanna, plains, semidesert
SIZE: body: 1.1–1.2 m (3½–4 ft)
tail: 25–30 cm (9¾–11¾ in) Ⓥ

Typical of its family, with a bulky head and back sloping toward the rear, the brown hyena has long, rough hair over much of its body, with a mane of even longer hair on the neck and shoulders. This hyena is usually dark brown to brownish-black in color, with a lighter-brown mane and legs.

Unless in a family group, the brown hyena is solitary, but it sometimes gathers with others in a hunting pack or at a big carcass. It lives in a large territory, which it marks with secretions from anal scent glands and with feces. During the day, it sleeps in a burrow, often one left by another animal such as an aardvark, or among rocks or tall grass and emerges at night to find carrion or to hunt prey such as rodents, birds, including poultry, reptiles or wounded large animals. Near the coast, brown hyenas also feed on dead fish, mussels and the stranded corpses of seals and whales.

A litter of 2 to 4 young is born in a burrow after a gestation of 92 to 98 days. The young are suckled for about 3 months but remain with their parents for up to 18 months, during which the male brings them food. Although protected in game reserves, brown hyenas are considered pests because of their habit of attacking livestock, and large numbers have been killed by farmers.

NAME: Spotted Hyena, *Crocuta crocuta*
RANGE: Africa, south of the Sahara
HABITAT: semidesert to moist savanna
SIZE: body: 1.2–1.8 m (4–6 ft)
tail: 25–30 cm (9¾–11¾ in)

The largest of the hyenas, the spotted hyena has a big, powerful head, slender legs and a sloping back. Its tail is bushy, and a short mane covers its neck and shoulders. The head and feet are always a lighter brown than the rest of the body, and irregular dark spots are scattered overall; these vary greatly in color and arrangement.

The spotted hyena is an inhabitant of open country and does not enter forest. Packs of 10 to 30 animals are the usual size, each pack occupying a territory. The boundaries of the territory are marked with urine, droppings and anal gland secretions and carefully guarded to keep out rival packs. Males are dominant in the pack. Hyenas sleep in burrows, which they dig themselves, or among tall grass or rocks and emerge at dusk. They are normally active only at night but may hunt during the day in some areas. As well as feeding on carrion, spotted hyenas hunt large mammals such as antelope, zebras, and domestic livestock. The victim is often brought down by a bite in the leg and then torn to pieces by the pack while still alive. Spotted hyenas are extremely noisy animals, making a variety of howling screams when getting ready for the hunt, as well as eerie sounds like laughter when they kill and when mating.

When courting, spotted hyenas eject strong-smelling anal gland secretions, and the male prances around the female and rolls her on the ground. The gestation period is 99 to 130 days, and the 1 or 2 young are born in a burrow with eyes open and some teeth already present. The young are suckled for a year to 18 months, by which time they are able to join the hunting pack.

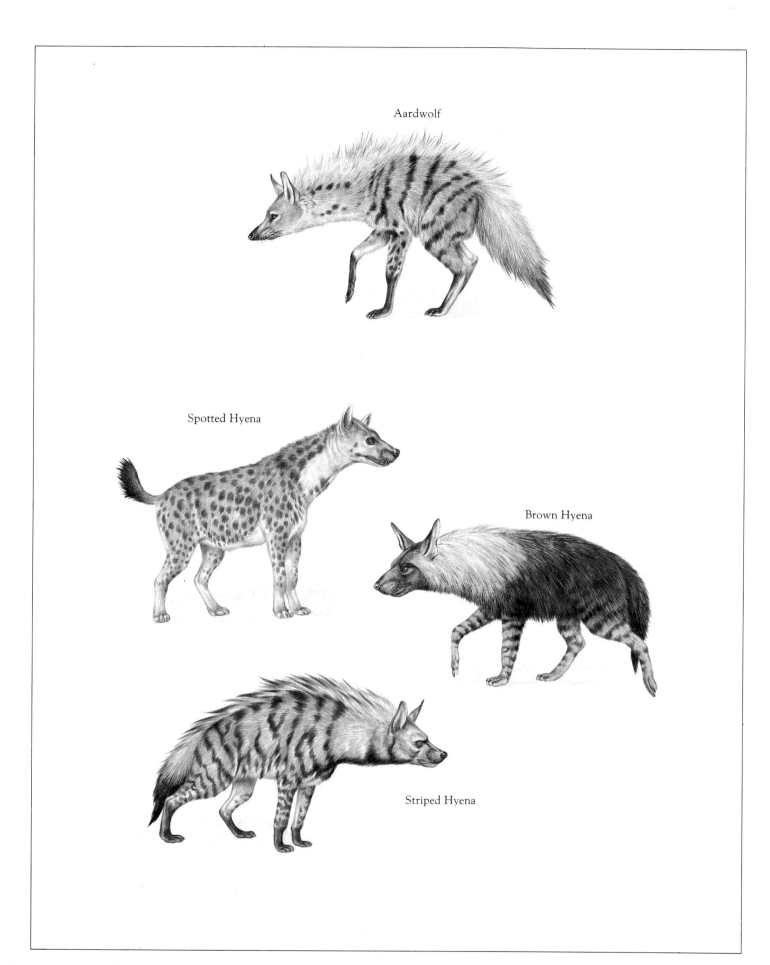

Aardwolf

Spotted Hyena

Brown Hyena

Striped Hyena

Cats

NAME: Golden Cat, *Felis aurata*
RANGE: Africa: Senegal to Zaire
(not Nigeria), Kenya
HABITAT: forest, forest edge
SIZE: body: 72–93 cm (28¼–36½ in)
tail: 35–45 cm (13¾–17¾ in)

A robust, medium-sized cat, the golden cat has rather short, sturdy legs and small, rounded ears. Coloration varies enormously from brownish-red to slate-gray on the upperparts; some golden cats have distinct spots all over the body, some only on the underside.

An inhabitant of dense forest, this cat spends much of its life in trees and is active mainly at night. During the day it sleeps up in a tree. It is a solitary, elusive creature, and little is known of its habits. It preys on mammals up to the size of small antelope and on birds up to the size of guineafowl.

NAME: Leopard Cat, *Felis bengalensis*
RANGE: S.E. Asia, Sumatra, Borneo,
Java, Philippines
HABITAT: forest
SIZE: body: about 60 cm (23½ in)
tail: about 35 cm (13¾ in)

A nocturnal, rarely seen creature, the leopard cat rests during the day in a hole in a tree. It is an agile climber and preys on small birds and on mammals up to the size of squirrels and hares; it may occasionally kill a small deer. The coloration and pattern of the leopard cat are variable, but it is usually yellowish, gray or reddish-brown on the upperparts of the body, with a whitish belly, and is dotted overall with dark spots. These spots are in regular lines and may merge to form bands.

The breeding habits of this cat are not well known, but the female is thought to produce litters of 3 or 4 young in a cave or a den under fallen rocks.

NAME: Pampas Cat, *Felis colocolo*
RANGE: South America: Ecuador, Peru,
Brazil to S. Argentina
HABITAT: open grassland, forest
SIZE: body: 60–70 cm (23½–27½ in)
tail: 29–32 cm (11½–12½ in)

A small, but sturdily built animal, the pampas cat has a small head and thick, bushy tail. Its long fur is variable in color, ranging from yellowish-white to brown or silvery-gray. In the north of its range, it lives in forest and, although primarily ground-dwelling, will take refuge in trees. Farther south, it inhabits the vast grasslands, where it takes cover among the tall pampas grass. Active at night, it hunts small mammals, such as cavies, and ground-dwelling birds, such as tinamous.

The female gives birth to litters of 1 to 3 young after a gestation thought to be about 10 weeks.

FELIDAE: Cat Family

There are approximately 35 species in the cat family as classified here, but numbers differ according to source, and there is considerable disagreement as to the organization of the family. Of all predators, cats are probably the most efficient killers. Coloring, size and fur patterning vary within the family, but all species from the smallest to the largest are basically similar in appearance and proportions to the domestic cat — an ideal predatory body form.

Cat bodies are muscular and flexible, and the head is typically shortened and rounded, with large forward-directed eyes. Limbs can be proportionately short or long, but in all species except the cheetah there are long, sharp, completely retractile claws on the feet for the grasping of prey. The overpowering of prey however, practically always involves a bite from the powerful jaws, which are armed with well-developed, daggerlike canines. Shearing cheek teeth, or carnassials, are used for slicing through flesh.

This successful family is distributed almost worldwide, being absent only from Antarctica, Australasia, the West Indies and some other islands, and Madagascar, which is inhabited by cat-like viverrids. Male and female look alike in most species, but males are often slightly larger.

Sadly, the fine fur of the cats has long been coveted by man, and many species have been hunted until they are rare and in danger of extinction.

NAME: Caracal, *Felis caracal*
RANGE: Africa (except rain forest belt);
Middle East to N.W. India
HABITAT: savanna, open plains,
semidesert, sand desert
SIZE: body: 65–90 cm (25½–35½ in)
tail: 20–30 cm (7¾–11¾ in)

The caracal is identified by its long, slender legs, rather flattened head and long, tufted ears. A solitary animal, it occupies a home range, which it patrols in search of prey. It is most active at dusk and at night but may also emerge in the daytime. A wide variety of mammals, ranging from mice to reedbuck, are included in its diet, and it also feeds on birds, reptiles, and domestic sheep, goats and poultry.

The male caracal courts his mate with yowls similar to those of the domestic cat. In a well-concealed den in a rock crevice, tree hole or abandoned burrow, the female bears a litter of 2 or 3 young after a gestation of 69 or 70 days. The young suckle for 6 months and are not independent until 9 to 12 months old.

NAME: Mountain Lion, *Felis concolor*
RANGE: S.W. Canada, W. USA, Mexico,
Central and South America
HABITAT: mountainsides, forest, swamps,
grassland
SIZE: body: 1–1.6 m (3¼–5¼ ft)
tail: 60–85 cm (23½–33½ in) Ⓔ

The widespread mountain lion, also known as the cougar or puma, is now becoming increasingly rare and some subspecies are in danger of extinction. It varies greatly in color and size over its range, but tawny and grayish-brown are the predominant colors. A solitary creature, the mountain lion occupies a defined territory. A male's home range may overlap with the territories of one or more females but not with the territory of another male. Normally active in the early morning and evening, the mountain lion may emerge at any time. Its main prey are mule deer and other deer, but it also eats rodents, hares and, occasionally, domestic cattle. Having stalked its prey, the mountain lion pounces and kills with a swift bite to the nape of the neck.

Young are born in the summer in the temperate north and south of the range or at any time of year in the tropics. Male and female pair for the season, maybe longer, and during his mate's period of sexual receptivity, or heat, the male fights off any rivals. After a gestation of 92 to 96 days, the litter of 2 to 4 young is born in a den, among rocks or in thick vegetation. At 6 or 7 weeks old, the young start to take solid food brought to them by their mother, and they remain with her for 1 or even 2 years.

NAME: Lynx, *Felis lynx*
RANGE: Europe: Scandinavia to Spain
and Portugal, east through Asia to
Siberia; Alaska, Canada, N. USA
HABITAT: coniferous forest, scrub
SIZE: body: 80 cm–1.3 m (31½ in–4¼ ft)
tail: 4–8 cm (1½–3 in)

The lynx is recognized by its short tail and its tufted ears and cheeks. Its coat varies in coloration over its wide range, particularly in the degree of spotting, which may be faint or conspicuous. Although strictly protected in most countries, lynx are becoming scarce, and some races are in danger of extinction. A solitary, nocturnal animal, the lynx stalks its prey on the ground or lies in wait for it in low vegetation. Hares, rodents, young deer and ground-living birds, such as grouse, are its main prey.

Breeding normally starts in the spring, and a litter of 2 or 3 young is born in a den among rocks or in a hollow tree after a gestation of about 63 days. The cubs remain with their mother throughout their first winter.

Golden Cat

Leopard Cat

Caracal

Pampas Cat

Mountain Lion

Lynx

Cats

NAME: Ocelot, *Felis pardalis*
RANGE: USA: Arizona, Texas; Mexico, Central and South America to N. Argentina
HABITAT: humid forest, thick bush, marshy areas
SIZE: body: 95 cm–1.3 m (37½ in–4¼ ft)
tail: 27–40 cm (10½–15¾ in) (V)

The characteristic dark markings that pattern the ocelot's coat are so variable that no two animals are quite alike. Generally nocturnal, the ocelot sleeps on a branch or under cover of vegetation during the day and emerges at night to hunt for small mammals, such as young deer and peccaries, agoutis, pacas and other rodents, as well as birds and snakes. It is an extremely secretive animal and rarely shows itself in open country. Males and females live in pairs in a territory but do not hunt together.

Ocelots mate at night, and courting males make loud, screeching calls similar to those of domestic cats. After a gestation of about 70 days, a litter of 2 young, sometimes 4, is born in a safe den in a hollow tree or in thick vegetation. These beautiful cats have become rare, both because of the destruction of their forest habitat and because they have long been hunted for their fur. It is now illegal in many countries to trade in ocelot skins, but such laws are hard to enforce when the demand continues and the black market price is high.

NAME: Bobcat, *Felis rufus*
RANGE: S. Canada, USA, Mexico
HABITAT: chaparral, brush, swamp, forest
SIZE: body: 65 cm–1 m (25½ in–3¼ ft)
tail: 11–19 cm (4¼–7½ in)

The bobcat is short-tailed, like the lynx, but is generally smaller than the latter and has less conspicuous ear tufts. It varies considerably in size, the largest individuals occurring in the north of the range and the smallest in Mexico. Adaptable to a variety of habitats, the bobcat is ground-dwelling but does climb trees and will take refuge in a tree when chased. It is solitary and nocturnal for the most part but may hunt in the daytime in winter. Small mammals, such as rabbits, mice, rats and squirrels, are its main prey, and it also catches ground-dwelling birds, such as grouse. It hunts by stealth, slowly stalking its victim until near enough to pounce.

The female bobcat gives birth to a litter of 1 to 6 young, usually 3, after a gestation of about 50 days. The young first leave the den at about 5 weeks and start to accompany their mother on hunting trips when they are between 3 and 5 months old.

NAME: Pallas's Cat, *Felis manul*
RANGE: central Asia: Iran to W. China
HABITAT: steppe, desert, rocky mountainsides
SIZE: body: 50–65 cm (19¾–25½ in)
tail: 21–31 cm (8¼–12¼ in)

Pallas's cat has a robust body and short, stout legs. Its head is broad, and its ears low and wide apart, protruding only slightly from the fur. The fur varies in color from pale gray to yellowish-buff or reddish-brown and is longer and more dense than that of any other wild cat. An elusive, solitary creature, this cat lives in a cave or rock crevice or a burrow taken over from another mammal, such as a marmot, usually emerging only at night to hunt. It preys on small mammals, such as mice and hares, and on birds.

Mating occurs in spring, and females give birth to litters of 5 or 6 young in summer.

NAME: Serval, *Felis serval*
RANGE: Africa, south of the Sahara to South Africa: S. Transvaal
HABITAT: savanna, open plains, woodland
SIZE: body: 65–90 cm (25½–35½ in)
tail: 25–35 cm (9¾–13¾ in)

A slender, long-legged cat with a small head and broad ears, the serval has a graceful, sprightly air. Coloration varies from yellowish-brown to dark olive-brown; lighter-colored animals tend to have rows of large black spots on their fur, while darker individuals are dotted with many fine spots. The serval is usually active in the daytime and lives in a small territory, the boundaries of which are marked with urine. It is generally solitary, but a female may enter a male's territory. Mammals from the size of rodents up to small antelope are its main prey, but it also eats birds, poultry, lizards, insects and some fruit. Servals have excellent sight and hearing.

A litter of 1 to 4, usually 2 or 3, young is born in a safe den among rocks or vegetation or in a burrow taken over from another mammal. The gestation period is 67 to 77 days.

NAME: Wild Cat, *Felis silvestris*
RANGE: Scotland, S. Europe; Africa (not Sahara), Middle East to India
HABITAT: forest, scrub, savanna, open plains, semidesert
SIZE: body: 50–65 cm (19¾–25½ in)
tail: 25–38 cm (9¾–15 in)

One of the ancestors of the domestic cat, the wild cat is similar in form but slightly larger and has a shorter, thicker tail, which is encircled with black rings. Coloration varies according to habitat, cats in dry sandy areas being lighter than forest-dwelling cats. Largely solitary and nocturnal, the wild cat lives in a

well-defined territory. Although it is an agile climber, it stalks most of its prey on the ground, catching small rodents and ground-dwelling birds.

Rival courting males howl and screech as they vie for the attention of a female, and it is she who eventually makes the selection. She bears 2 or 3 young after a gestation of 63 to 69 days. The young first emerge from the den, sited in a cave, hollow tree or fox hole, when they are 4 or 5 weeks old and leave their mother after about 5 months.

NAME: Cheetah, *Acinonyx jubatus*
RANGE: Africa, east to Asia: E. Iran, Turkmenistan, Afghanistan
HABITAT: open country: desert, savanna
SIZE: body: 1.1–1.4 m (3½–4½ ft)
tail: 65–80 cm (25½–31½ in) (V)

Superbly adapted for speed, the cheetah is the fastest of the big cats, able to attain speeds of 112 km/h (69½ mph). Its body is long and supple, with high muscular shoulders, and its legs are long and slender. The tail aids balance during the cheetah's high-speed sprints.

Cheetahs live in territories in open country, alone, in pairs or in family groups. They are active in the daytime, and sight is the most important sense in hunting. Having selected its prey when in hiding, the cheetah stalks its victim and then attacks with a short, rapid chase, knocking over the prey and killing it with a bite to the throat. Hares, jackals, small antelope, the young of larger antelope, and birds, such as guineafowl, francolins, bustards and young ostriches, are the cheetah's main prey. Several adults may, however, cooperate to chase and exhaust larger animals, such as zebras.

Rival males compete in bloodless struggles for the attention of a female. She bears a litter of 2 to 4 young after a gestation of 91 to 95 days and brings them up alone. The young stay with the mother for up to 2 years.

NAME: Clouded Leopard, *Neofelis nebulosa*
RANGE: Nepal to S. China, Taiwan, Sumatra, Borneo
HABITAT: forest
SIZE: body: 62–106 cm (24½–41¾ in)
tail: 61–91 cm (24–35¾ in) (V)

The rare, elusive clouded leopard has a long, powerful body, relatively short legs and a long tail. It is a good climber and hunts by pouncing from trees, as well as by stalking prey on the ground. Birds, pigs, small deer and cattle are the clouded leopard's main victims, and it kills with a single bite from its exceptionally long canine teeth.

A litter of 1 to 5 cubs is born after a gestation of 86 to 92 days.

Pallas's Cat

Ocelot

Bobcat

Serval

Wild Cat

Cheetah

Clouded Leopard

Cats

NAME: Lion, *Panthera leo*
RANGE: Africa, south of the Sahara;
N.W. India; formerly more
widespread in Asia
HABITAT: open savanna
SIZE: body: 1.4–2 m (4½–6½ ft)
tail: 67 cm–1 m (26¼ in–3¼ ft)

A splendid, powerfully built cat, the lion has a broad head, thick, strong legs and a long tail tipped with a tuft of hair that conceals a clawlike spine. The male is larger than the female and has a heavy mane on the neck and shoulders. Body coloration varies from tawny-yellow to reddish-brown, and the mane may be light yellow to black.

This impressive creature actually spends 20 or more hours a day resting. Lions normally hunt during the day, but in areas where they themselves are hunted, they are active only at night. They live in groups, known as prides, consisting of up to 3 adult males and up to 15 females and their young in a territory that is defended against intruders, particularly other mature male lions. A small group of young males without prides may live together. Lions prey on mammals, such as gazelles, antelope and zebras, and may cooperate to kill larger animals, such as buffaloes and giraffes. Smaller animals and birds and even crocodiles may also be eaten. Lionesses do most of the hunting, often in groups, some acting as beaters to drive prey toward other lionesses lying in wait. Lions attack by stalking their prey and approaching it as closely as possible before making a short, rapid chase and pounce. They kill by a bite to the neck or throat.

Breeding occurs at any time of year. A litter of 1 to 6 young, usually 2 or 3, is born after a gestation of 102 to 113 days. They are suckled for about 6 months, but after the first 3 months, an increasing proportion of their food comes from the kills of adults. The cubs are left behind with one or two adults while the rest of the pride goes off to hunt, but if a kill is made, a lioness will return and lead them to it. Once they are over 4 months old, the cubs accompany their mothers everywhere, even following behind on hunting trips. They are not sexually mature until about 18 months old; young males are driven from the pride at about this age, but females remain with their family.

NAME: Jaguar, *Panthera onca*
RANGE: S.W. USA, N. Mexico, Central
and South America to N. Argentina
HABITAT: forest, savanna
SIZE: body: 1.5–1.8 m (5–6 ft)
tail: 70–91 cm (27½–35¾ in) Ⓥ

The largest South American cat, the powerful jaguar has a deep chest and massive, strong limbs. Its coloration varies from light yellow to reddish-brown, with characteristic dark spots. Although not quite as graceful and agile as the leopard, the jaguar climbs trees, often to lie in wait for prey and is also an excellent swimmer. Like lions, jaguars cannot sustain high speeds and depend on getting close to prey for successful kills. Peccaries and capybaras are frequent prey, and jaguars also kill mountain sheep, deer, otters, rodents, ground-living birds, turtles, caimans and fish.

Normally solitary animals, male and female jaguars stay together for a few weeks when breeding. After a gestation of 93 to 105 days, a litter of 1 to 4 young is born in a secure den in vegetation, among rocks or in a hole in a riverbank. The female is aggressive in her protection of the young from any intruder, including the father.

NAME: Leopard, *Panthera pardus*
RANGE: Asia: Siberia to Korea, Sri Lanka
and Java; Middle East; Africa
HABITAT: desert to forest, lowland plains
to mountains
SIZE: body: 1.3–1.9 m (4¼–6¼ ft)
tail: 1.1–1.4 m (3½–4½ ft) Ⓥ

Formerly widespread, the leopard is now patchily distributed and many of its subspecies are extinct or endangered. A strong, but elegant cat, it has a long body and relatively short legs. Most leopards are buff or tawny, with characteristic rosette-shaped black spots, but some are entirely black and are known as panthers. Panthers and leopards are otherwise identical.

Leopards are solitary and normally hunt day or night. In areas where they are persecuted, however, leopards are nocturnal. They swim and climb well and often lie basking in the sun on a branch. Their sight and sense of smell are good, and their hearing is exceptionally acute. Prey includes mammals up to the size of large antelope, young apes — particularly baboons and monkeys — birds, snakes, fish and domestic livestock. Large items may be dragged up into a tree for safety while the leopard feeds; it will also feed on carrion.

Females have regular fertile periods, and males may fight over sexually receptive females. The litter of 1 to 6, usually 2 or 3, young is born in a rock crevice or hole in a tree after a gestation of about 90 to 112 days. The young are suckled for 3 months and are independent at 18 months to 2 years. The mother hunts alone, but if she makes a kill, she hides it while she goes to fetch her cubs. Older cubs may catch some small prey for themselves.

NAME: Tiger, *Panthera tigris*
RANGE: Siberia to Java and Bali
HABITAT: forest
SIZE: body: 1.8–2.8 m (6–9¼ ft)
tail: about 91 cm (35¾ in) Ⓔ

The largest of the big cats, the tiger has a massive, muscular body and powerful limbs. Males and females look similar, but males have longer, more prominent cheek whiskers. Coloration varies from reddish-orange to reddish-ocher, and the pattern of the dark, vertical stripes is extremely variable. Tigers of the northern subspecies tend to be larger and paler than tropical subspecies.

Tigers are shy, nocturnal creatures and usually live alone, although they are not unsociable and seldom fight among themselves. They climb well, move gracefully on land and are capable of galloping at speed when chasing prey. Wild pigs, deer, and cattle, such as gaur and buffaloes, are the tiger's main prey, and it also kills other mammals, such as the sloth bear.

Male and female associate for only a few days for mating. The female gives birth to a litter of, usually, 2 or 3 young after a gestation of 103 to 105 days. The young may stay with their mother for several years.

Most races of these magnificent animals are now rare, and the Bali and Java tigers may be extinct because of indiscriminate killing earlier this century and the destruction of forest habitats.

NAME: Snow Leopard, *Panthera uncia*
RANGE: Pakistan, Afghanistan, north to
USSR; Himalayas, east to China
HABITAT: mountain slopes, forest
SIZE: body: 1.2–1.5 m (4–5 ft)
tail: about 90 cm (35½ in) Ⓔ

In summer, the snow leopard, also known as the ounce, lives in alpine meadows above the tree line, amid snow and glaciers; but in winter it follows the migrations of prey animals down to forest and scrub at about 2,000 m (6,600 ft). A powerful, agile animal capable of huge leaps over ravines, the snow leopard stalks prey such as ibex, markhor, wild sheep and goats, boars and ground-dwelling birds, such as pheasants, partridges and snowcocks; in winter it will also take domestic livestock. Females may be accompanied by young, but otherwise snow leopards live alone, constantly roaming around their huge territories. They are active mainly in the early morning and late afternoon.

The female gives birth to 2 or 3 cubs, rarely 4 or 5, after a gestation of 98 to 103 days. The young start to accompany their mother on hunting trips when about 2 months old.

Lion (male)

Leopard

Jaguar

Tiger

Snow Leopard

Sea Lions, Walrus

ORDER PINNIPEDIA

The 3 families in this order — sea lions and fur seals, earless seals and the walrus — are all carnivores adapted to life in water. Their limbs have become flippers, but pinnipeds are still able to move, albeit awkwardly, on land, where they all spend part of their lives.

OTARIIDAE: Sea Lion Family

There are approximately 14 species of fur seal and sea lion. The main features that distinguish these animals from the seals, family Phocidae, are the presence of external ears and the ability to tuck the hind flippers forward to facilitate locomotion on land. Sea lions occur in the southern Atlantic and Indian oceans and in the North and South Pacific, and come to land, or haul out, on coasts and islands.

Generally gregarious, these animals haul out in large numbers at traditional breeding sites, called rookeries, where males compete for the best territories.

Females give birth to the young conceived the previous year and mate again some days later. Mating and giving birth are synchronized in this convenient manner as a result of the phenomenon of delayed implantation. The embryo lies dormant for a period before development starts, thus ensuring the correct timing of the birth without producing young of undue size. Males are considerably larger than females and have big, bulbous heads.

NAME: **South American Fur Seal, *Arctocephalus australis***
RANGE: **South Pacific and Atlantic Oceans, from Brazil around to Peru**
HABITAT: **breeds on coasts and islands**
SIZE: **1.4–1.8 m (4½–6 ft)**

The South American fur seal usually has deep reddish-brown underfur; the male has a coarse mane. It feeds on marine invertebrates, squid, fish and penguins and prefers to haul out on rocky coasts.

These fur seals are extremely territorial in the breeding season. Males take up their territories in November, competing for the prime spots and rigorously enforcing boundaries, since those with the best and largest sites mate with the most females. Males are joined 2 weeks later by the females, who give birth to their young within a few days. The female remains with her pup for up to 12 days, during which period she mates with the male whose territory she is in, then goes to sea to feed, returning at intervals to suckle the pup. The males rarely leave their territories until all the mating is over.

NAME: **Northern Fur Seal, *Callorhinus ursinus***
RANGE: **Bering Sea, Sea of Okhotsk**
HABITAT: **breeds on islands in range such as Aleutian and Pribilof Islands**
SIZE: **1.5–1.8 m (5–6 ft)**

Northern fur seals have larger rear flippers than other species in the family Otariidae, and both male and female have a pale patch on the neck. The male may be four times the female's weight. Usually alone or in pairs at sea, these fur seals feed on fish and squid and rarely come to land outside the breeding season.

Males establish territories on the breeding beaches before females arrive to give birth to their young. The female stays with her single offspring for 7 days before going off on brief feeding trips, returning to suckle it at intervals.

NAME: **California Sea Lion, *Zalophus californianus***
RANGE: **Pacific coasts: British Columbia to Mexico; Galápagos Islands**
HABITAT: **breeds on coasts and islands in south of range**
SIZE: **1.7–2.2 m (5½–7¼ ft)**

This attractive sea lion takes well to training and is the most commonly seen species in circuses and marine shows. Females and juveniles are tan-colored when dry, while the larger males are brown; males are also distinguished by the horny crest on their heads. Social animals, these sea lions occur in groups and often come onto land outside the breeding season. They feed on fish, octopus and squid.

Males gather at a breeding site but only establish territories when the females arrive and start to give birth; territories are ill defined and somewhat unstable. The female produces 1 young and mates again a few days later.

NAME: **Australian Sea Lion, *Neophoca cinerea***
RANGE: **off S. and S.W. Australia**
HABITAT: **coasts and islands**
SIZE: **up to 2.4 m (7¾ ft)**

A nonmigratory species, this sea lion does not travel far from the beach of its birth and often comes out onto land throughout the year. It moves quite easily on land and may travel several kilometers. A gregarious species, it is usually found in small groups. Fish, squid and penguins are its main foods.

The males establish well-defined territories, which they defend vigorously, and usually manage to prevent females on their sites from leaving. The female produces 1 young and remains with it for 14 days, during which time she mates. She then goes to sea, returning at 2-day intervals to suckle the pup.

NAME: **Northern/Steller Sea Lion, *Eumetopias jubata***
RANGE: **N. Pacific Ocean**
HABITAT: **breeds on Pribilof and Aleutian Islands, Kuril Islands, islands in Sea of Okhotsk, coast of N. America to San Miguel Island off S. California**
SIZE: **2.4–2.8 m (7¾–9¼ ft)**

The largest member of the family Otariidae, the northern sea lion overlaps in its range with the California sea lion but is distinguished by its size and lighter color. It feeds on fish, squid and octopus, and stomach contents have revealed that it dives to 180 m (600 ft) or more to find food.

Males establish well-defined territories at breeding grounds and maintain the boundaries with ritual threat displays. They remain there throughout the breeding period, mating with the females in their area, and do not feed for about 2 months. Shortly after arriving, the female gives birth to 1 young. She remains with the pup constantly for the first 5 to 13 days before going briefly to sea to feed, leaving her pup in the company of other young.

ODOBENIDAE: Walrus Family

The 1 species of walrus resembles the sea lions in that its hind flippers can be brought forward to help it move on land. It cannot move as fast or adeptly as a sea lion, however, and will often just drag itself forward.

NAME: **Walrus, *Odobenus rosmarus***
RANGE: **Arctic Ocean; occasionally N. Atlantic Ocean**
HABITAT: **pack ice, rocky islands**
SIZE: **male: 2.7–3.5 m (8¾–11½ ft); female: 2.2–2.9 m (7¼–9½ ft)**   ①

The largest, heaviest pinniped, the male walrus is a huge animal with heavy tusks, formed from the upper canine teeth which extend downward. Females also have tusks, but they are shorter and thinner. Walruses feed on bottom-living invertebrates, particularly mollusks, of which they consume only the soft muscular foot or siphon. They are thought to extract these portions by some form of suction. They also feed on crustaceans, starfish, fish and even mammals.

Walruses are gregarious throughout the year. During the mating season, they congregate in traditional areas, where males compete for space near potential mates and display. There is a period of delayed implantation of 4 or 5 months and a gestation of 11 months, so females can breed only every other year at most. Usually 1 young is born, rarely 2, and it may be suckled for up to 2 years.

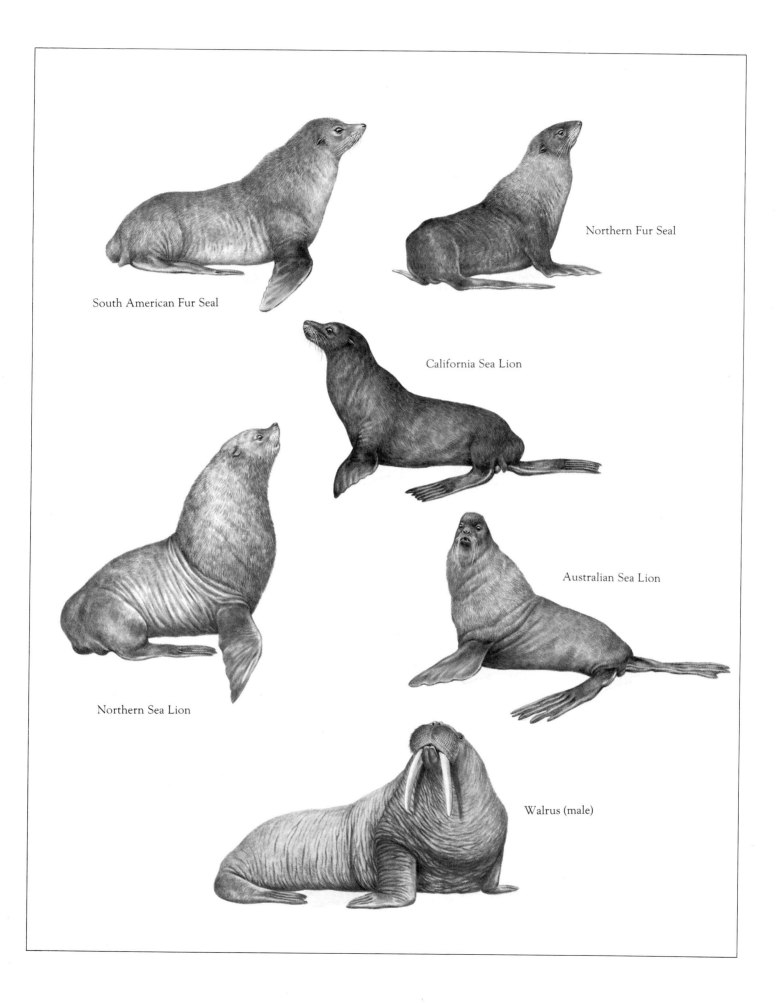

South American Fur Seal

Northern Fur Seal

California Sea Lion

Northern Sea Lion

Australian Sea Lion

Walrus (male)

Seals

NAME: **Gray Seal,** *Halichoerus grypus*
RANGE: **N. Atlantic Ocean**
HABITAT: **breeds on rocky coasts of Scandinavia and Britain; Iceland and Faeroe Islands; Labrador, Gulf of St. Lawrence, Newfoundland**
SIZE: **1.6–2.3 m (5¼–7½ ft)**

The largest of the seals, excepting the elephant seals, a male gray seal may weigh up to 300 kg (660 lb) and be more than twice as heavy as a female. The male is also identified by his massive shoulders, covered with thick skin, which forms heavy folds and wrinkles, and by the elongated snout, rounded forehead and wide, heavy muzzle. The female has a flatter profile and a daintier, more slender muzzle. Gray seals travel far from breeding sites but stay mostly in coastal waters, feeding on fish and also on some crustaceans, squid and octopus.

The timing of breeding differs in the three areas of the range, but females always arrive at breeding grounds first and give birth before the males appear. The males take up positions on the beach, the older, experienced individuals getting the best places, but there is little fighting, and males may move sites from day to day. Having suckled her pup for about 3 weeks, the female mates and then leaves the area.

NAME: **Harp Seal,** *Pagophilus groenlandicus*
RANGE: **N. Atlantic and Arctic Oceans: N. USSR to Scandinavia and Greenland; Labrador, Newfoundland**
HABITAT: **subarctic and arctic waters**
SIZE: **1.6–1.9 m (5¼–6¼ ft)**

The harp seal is identified by its black head and the dark band along its flanks and over its back; the rest of the body is usually pale gray, but this is highly variable. An expert, fast swimmer, the harp seal spends much of the year at sea and makes regular north-south migrations; it can also move fast over ice if necessary. Fish and crustaceans are the harp seal's main foods, and it is renowned for its ability to dive long and deep. It is generally a gregarious species, and only old males live alone.

Females form whelping groups on the ice and give birth to their young in late February and early March. The pups are suckled for 2 to 4 weeks, growing rapidly on the nourishing milk, which is rich in fat. They are then left by the mothers, who go off to feed for a few weeks before migrating north to summer feeding grounds. Courting males fight rivals with their teeth and flippers and probably mate with females 2 or 3 weeks after they have given birth.

PHOCIDAE: Seal Family

Often known as earless seals because they lack external ears, the 19 species in this family have made the most complete transition from a terrestrial to an aquatic way of life of all the pinnipeds. Their hind flippers cannot be turned forward like those of other pinnipeds, and locomotion on land is, therefore, more restricted, since they must drag themselves forward with the fore flippers. In water, however, they are highly skillful swimmers and divers, moving with undulatory movements of the hind portion of the body and the hind flippers. Seals have particularly sophisticated mechanisms to enable them to dive deep for food and to stay underwater for long periods. Most impressive are the adaptations related to the blood circulation. During a dive, the heart rate may drop from 120 to about 4 beats a minute, but without any corresponding drop in blood pressure. This is achieved by reducing the blood supply to body parts other than the muscles of the heart itself and the brain, thus reserving the seal's blood oxygen for only the most vital organs.

The body of a seal is typically torpedo shaped, thick layers of fatty blubber under the skin accounting for much of its weight. The flippers as well as the body are furred, and the seals undergo an annual molt.

In some species, males are much bigger and heavier than females, but in others, females are the larger sex. Some are monogamous, but others, such as the elephant seals, are gregarious and polygamous. In most species there is a delay between fertilization and the actual start of gestation — a phenomenon known as delayed implantation. This ensures that both birth and mating can be accomplished within the short period when the seals are all together on dry land.

NAME: **Leopard Seal,** *Hydrurga leptonyx*
RANGE: **Antarctic Ocean**
HABITAT: **pack ice, coasts, islands**
SIZE: **3–3.5 m (9¾–11½ ft)**

An unusually slender seal, the leopard seal is built for speed and has a large mouth, well suited to grasping the penguins, and sometimes other seals, that are its main prey. It catches penguins underwater or as they move off the ice and, using its teeth, tears away the skin with great efficiency before eating them. Squid, fish and crustaceans are also caught.

Mating is thought to take place from January until March, but there is little information available.

NAME: **Harbor Seal,** *Phoca vitulina*
RANGE: **N. Atlantic and N. Pacific Oceans**
HABITAT: **temperate and subarctic coastal waters**
SIZE: **1.4–1.8 m (4½–6 ft)**

The harbor seal has a proportionately large head and short body and flippers. Although often gray with dark blotches, these seals vary considerably in coloration, and spots may be light gray to dark brown or black. Males are larger than females. Generally nonmigratory, the harbor seal often hauls out on protected tidal rocks and even travels up rivers and into lakes. It feeds mostly during the day on fish, squid and crustaceans and has been known to make dives lasting 30 minutes, although they normally last only 4 or 5 minutes.

Courtship and mating take place in water. The single pup is closely guarded by its mother and suckles for 2 to 6 weeks. Born in an advanced state of development, the pup can swim from birth and dive for 2 minutes when 2 or 3 days old. After weaning, the pup is left alone, and the mother mates again.

NAME: **Crabeater Seal,** *Lobodon carcinophagus*
RANGE: **Antarctic**
HABITAT: **edge of pack ice**
SIZE: **2–2.4 m (6½–7¾ ft)**

Crabeater seals may well be the most abundant of all pinnipeds, and in their remote habitat they have few enemies other than killer whales. Capable of rapid movement over the ice, the crabeater seal thrusts with alternate forelimbs and the pelvis, and it is thought to achieve speeds of as much as 25 km/h (15½ mph). It feeds mainly on krill, small shrimplike crustaceans, which it strains from the water by means of its trident-shaped teeth.

Births and mating probably occur from October to the end of December. The pup is well developed at birth and suckles for about 5 weeks.

NAME: **Bearded Seal,** *Erignathus barbatus*
RANGE: **Arctic Ocean**
HABITAT: **shallow waters; breeds on ice floes**
SIZE: **2.1–2.4 m (6¾–7¾ ft)**

Numerous long bristles on the snout are the identifying feature of the bearded seal and the source of its common name. It is a robust, heavily built species in which females are slightly longer than males. Bottom-dwelling invertebrates, such as crustaceans and mollusks, and fish are its main foods.

The female gives birth to 1 pup, which can swim immediately. The pup suckles for 12 to 18 days, during which time the female usually mates again.

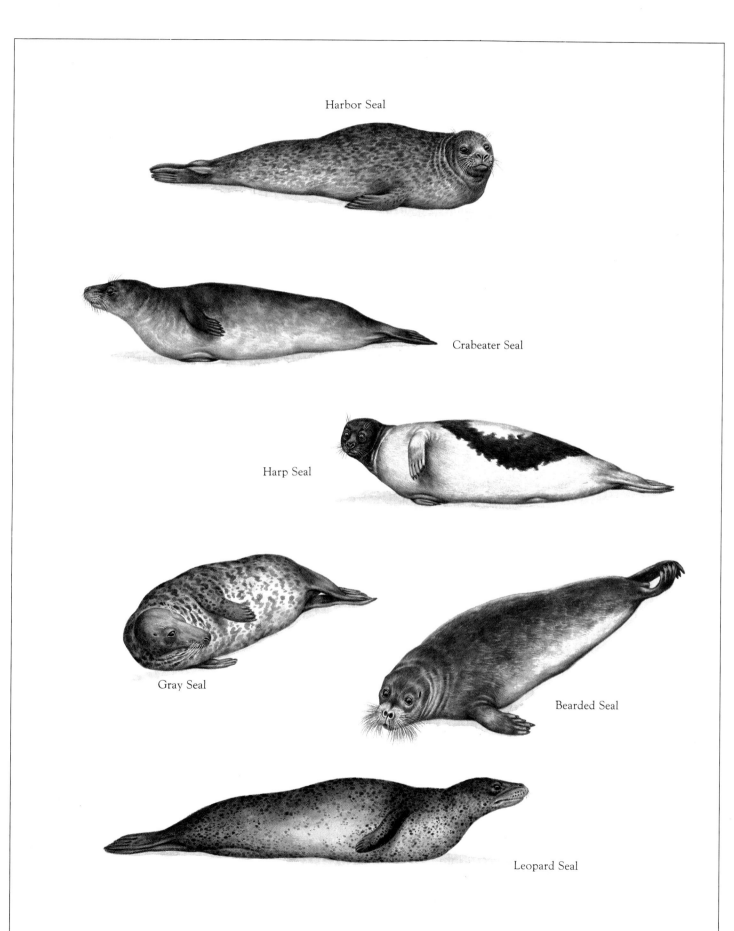

Harbor Seal

Crabeater Seal

Harp Seal

Gray Seal

Bearded Seal

Leopard Seal

Seals, Dugong, Manatees

NAME: **Northern Elephant Seal,**
  Mirounga angustirostris
RANGE: **Pacific coast of N. America:**
  Vancouver Island to central Baja
  California
HABITAT: **breeds on offshore islands**
SIZE: **male: up to 6 m (19¾ ft)**
  female: up to 3 m (9¾ ft)

The largest pinniped in the northern hemisphere, the male elephant seal may weigh a massive 2,700 kg (6,000 lb), much of it accounted for by the thick layer of blubber. Females rarely weigh more than 900 kg (2,000 lb). Because of its size, this species was a major target for commercial sealers, and by the end of the nineteenth century the population was dangerously low. Only one of the breeding islands appeared to be used, and that by only a hundred or so seals. With strict protection, numbers have increased since then, and between 1957 and 1976, the population tripled to over 47,000 — a remarkable recovery.

Northern elephant seals feed on fish and squid and make long, deep dives. Adult males haul out for breeding in late November and fight for dominance in the social hierarchy — high-ranking males mate with the most females. With the aid of the greatly enlarged nasal chamber, which creates the elephantine snout, males utter loud, vocal threats against rivals. Females arrive a couple of weeks after males, and each gives birth to a single pup, which is suckled for about a month. The bond between mother and young is close, and the female defends the pup from other adults and rarely leaves the breeding colony, existing on her blubber until the pup is weaned. She then mates again and leaves the breeding ground. Weaned pups gather in a group on the beach, where they remain for another month, living on fat reserves built up while suckling.

NAME: **Mediterranean Monk Seal,**
  Monachus monachus
RANGE: **W. Atlantic Ocean: Canary**
  Islands to Mediterranean Sea; Turkish
  coast of Black Sea
HABITAT: **breeds on rocky islets and cliffs**
SIZE: **2.3–2.7 m (7½–8¾ ft)** Ⓔ

The Mediterranean monk seal is becoming rare now that its previously remote hauling-out spots on islets and cliffs are accessible to humans with motorboats and scuba diving equipment. These seals often become entangled in fishing nets. They are extremely upset by any disturbance, and mothers and pregnant females particularly are nervous of any approach, and pregnancies may be spontaneously aborted.

Births occur from May to November, with a peak in September and October; pups are suckled for about 6 weeks.

NAME: **Weddell Seal,** *Leptonychotes*
  weddelli
RANGE: **Antarctic**
HABITAT: **edge of pack ice**
SIZE: **up to 2.9 m (9½ ft)**

One of the larger seals, the Weddell has a small head in proportion to its body and an appealing, short-muzzled face; the female is longer than the male. Weddell seals make deeper, longer dives than any other seal, the maximum recorded depth being 600 m (2,000 ft), and the longest duration 73 minutes. Dives to 300 and 400 m (1,000 and 1,300 ft) are common, and antarctic cod, abundant at these depths, are one of the Weddell seal's main food species. During a dive, the heart rate slows to 25 percent of the predive rate.

Weddell seals are normally solitary outside the breeding season, but young animals may form groups. In the breeding season, males seem to set up underwater territories, which females can enter freely. The female gives birth on land to 1 pup, with which she stays constantly for about 12 days; she then spends about half her time in water until the pup is weaned at about 6 weeks. When only 7 weeks old, the pup can dive to 90 m (300 ft). Females mate once their pups are weaned.

NAME: **Hooded Seal,** *Cystophora cristata*
RANGE: **N. Atlantic Ocean: arctic and**
  subarctic waters
HABITAT: **edge of pack ice**
SIZE: **2–2.6 m (6½–8½ ft)**

Hooded seals spend much of their lives in open seas, diving deep for fish and squid. They make regular migrations to areas of pack ice in the Denmark Strait and east of Greenland, where all adults gather to haul out and molt. After molting, the seals disperse to reassemble at breeding grounds in different areas the following spring.

Pups are born in March on ice floes and are suckled for 7 to 12 days. During this period, the female is courted by a male, who stays in the water near her and her pup, chasing away any rivals. If necessary, he hauls out and displays or fights, making threat calls that are amplified by the huge, inflatable nasal sac. The female mates about 2 weeks after giving birth.

ORDER SIRENIA

The sirenians are the only completely aquatic herbivorous mammals. There are 2 families, the dugong and the manatees, containing a total of 4 species. All have streamlined bodies and flipper-like forelimbs. Their hind limbs have been lost in the formation of a tail with a horizontal fluke.

DUGONGIDAE: Dugong Family

There is now only 1 species in this family, the other member, Steller's sea cow, having been exterminated in the eighteenth century by excessive hunting, only 25 years after its discovery.

NAME: **Dugong,** *Dugong dugon*
RANGE: **coast of E. Africa, Indian Ocean,**
  Red Sea to N. Australia
HABITAT: **coastal waters**
SIZE: **up to 3 m (9¾ ft)** Ⓥ

The dugong is a large, but streamlined animal, identified by its tail, which has a crescent-shaped fluke. Its head is heavy, with a fleshy, partially divided snout. The male has two tusks formed from the incisor teeth, but these are often barely visible under the fleshy lips. A shy, solitary animal, the dugong leads a sedentary life, lying on the seabed for much of the time and only rising to the surface to breathe every couple of minutes. Its nostrils are placed on the upper surface of the muzzle, so the dugong can breathe, while remaining almost submerged. Seaweed and sea grass are its main foods.

Little is known of the dugong's reproductive habits, but the gestation is thought to be about a year. The single young is born in the water and is helped to the surface by its mother.

TRICHECHIDAE: Manatee Family

There are 3 species of manatee; 2 live in fresh water in West Africa and the Amazon, and the third in coastal waters of the tropical Atlantic Ocean.

NAME: **American Manatee,** *Trichecus*
  manatus
RANGE: **Atlantic Ocean: Florida to**
  Guyana
HABITAT: **coastal waters**
SIZE: **up to 3 m (9¾ ft)** Ⓥ

The manatee has a heavier body than the dugong and is also distinguished by its oval tail fluke. There are three nails in each of its flippers, which it uses to gather food. The manatee feeds at night, foraging by touch and smell. Its diet is quite varied, since it eats any sort of vegetation and also often takes in small invertebrate animals with the plants. For much of the day, the manatee lies on the seabed, rising every couple of minutes to breathe at the surface. Manatees are social animals and live in family groups, sometimes gathering in larger herds.

The gestation period is about a year. One young is born in water and is helped by its mother to the surface to breathe.

Weddell Seal

Mediterranean Monk Seal

Northern Elephant Seal (male)

Hooded Seal

American Manatee

Dugong

River Dolphins, Porpoises

ORDER CETACEA

There are 76 species of whale, dolphin and porpoise. They are the only aquatic mammals to spend their entire lives in water. All are streamlined animals with strong, horizontally set tail flukes. Their front limbs are modified into flippers and there are no visible hind limbs. As a general rule, cetaceans produce only one young at a time although twins are known.

There are two groups within the order. First, the toothed whales, with 66 species of small whale, dolphin and porpoise, all of which prey on fish and squid. To help locate their prey, they use a form of ultrasonic sonar: they emit high-frequency clicking sounds which bounce off objects, the echoes informing the whale with astonishing accuracy of the size, distance and speed of travel of the object. All of these whales have teeth, some a pair, some as many as 200.

In the second group are the 10 largest whales, known as the baleen whales. These marine giants feed on tiny planktonic animals, which they extract from the sea by filtering water through plates of fringed horny material hanging from their upper jaws. These baleen plates act as sieves to trap the plankton. The group has 3 families: gray whales, rorquals and right whales.

PLATANISTIDAE: River Dolphin Family

The 5 species in this family all inhabit rivers in South America and Asia. They look alike and are grouped as a family, but the resemblance may be more to do with evolutionary pressures of similar habitat than close relationship. All the river dolphins are small for cetaceans, with long slender beaks and prominent rounded foreheads. The rivers these dolphins inhabit are muddy and full of sediment, and visibility is poor; as a result they rely heavily on echolocation to find food and avoid obstacles, and their eyes have become much reduced.

NAME: **Boutu,** *Inia geoffrensis*
RANGE: **Amazon basin**
HABITAT: **rivers, streams**
SIZE: **1.8–2.7 m (6–9 ft)**

The boutu has a strong beak studded with short bristles and a mobile, flexible head and neck. Most boutus have a total of 100 or more teeth. Their eyes, although small, seem to be more functional than those of other river dolphins. Boutus feed mainly on small fish and some crustaceans, using echolocation clicks to find their prey. Boutus live in pairs and seem to produce young between July and September.

NAME: **Ganges Dolphin,** *Platanista gangetica*
RANGE: **India: Ganges and Brahmaputra river systems**
HABITAT: **rivers, streams**
SIZE: **1.5–2.4 m (5–8 ft)**

The Ganges dolphin has a beak, which can be as long as 46 cm (18 in), and has up to 120 teeth. Its forehead curves up steeply from the beak. An agile animal, it generally swims on its side and returns to the normal upright position to breathe. It can dive for a maximum of 3 minutes at a time but usually remains under for about 45 seconds.

The Ganges dolphin is blind — its eyes have no lenses — but it finds its food by skillful use of echolocation signals. It feeds mainly on fish and some shrimps and hunts in the evening and at night. The dolphins are usually seen in pairs and may gather in groups of 6 or so to feed. They mate in autumn, and calves are born the following summer after a gestation of about 9 months.

NAME: **Whitefin Dolphin,** *Lipotes vexillifer*
RANGE: **China: Yangzte River; formerly Lake Tungting**
HABITAT: **muddy-bottomed rivers**
SIZE: **2–2.4 m (6½–8 ft)**   ①

Since 1975 this species has been protected by law in China, but although the total numbers are not known, population still seems to be low. The whitefin dolphin has a slender beak, which turns up slightly at the tip, and a total of 130 to 140 teeth. With little or no vision, it relies on sonar for hunting prey, mainly fish, but may also probe in the mud with its beak for shrimps.

Groups of 2 to 6 dolphins move together, sometimes gathering into larger groups for feeding. In the rainy summer season, they migrate up small swollen streams to breed, but no further details are known of their reproductive behavior.

PHOCOENIDAE: Porpoise Family

Although the name porpoise is sometimes erroneously applied to members of other families, strictly speaking, only the 6 members of this family are porpoises. They are small, beakless whales, rarely exceeding 2.1 m (7 ft) in length. They have 60 to 80 spatular teeth and feed mainly on fish and squid.

Porpoises live in coastal waters throughout the northern hemisphere, often ascending the estuaries of large rivers. One species, the spectacled porpoise, *Phocoena dioptrica*, occurs off the coasts of South America.

NAME: **Harbor Porpoise,** *Phocoena phocoena*
RANGE: **N. Atlantic, N. Pacific Oceans; Black and Mediterranean Seas**
HABITAT: **shallow water, estuaries**
SIZE: **1.4–1.8 m (4½–6 ft)**

Gregarious, highly vocal animals, porpoises live in small groups of up to 15 individuals. There is much communication within the group, and porpoises will always come to the aid of a group member in distress. Porpoises feed on fish, such as herring and mackerel, and can dive for up to 6 minutes to pursue prey, which are pinpointed by the use of echolocation clicks.

Breeding pairs mate in July and August and perform prolonged courtship rituals, caressing one another as they swim side by side. Gestation is 10 or 11 months, and calves are suckled for about 8 months. While her calf feeds, the mother lies on her side at the surface so that it can breathe easily.

NAME: **Dall's Porpoise,** *Phocoenides dalli*
RANGE: **temperate N. Pacific Ocean**
HABITAT: **inshore and deeper oceanic waters**
SIZE: **1.8–2.3 m (6–7½ ft)**

Dall's porpoise is larger and heavier than most porpoises; its head is small, and the lower jaw projects slightly beyond the upper. It lives in groups of up to 15, which may gather in schools of 100 or more to migrate north in summer and south in winter. It feeds on squid and fish, such as hake, and most probably uses echolocation when hunting. Pairs mate at any time of the year, and the young are suckled for as long as 2 years.

NAME: **Finless Porpoise,** *Neophocaena phocaenoides*
RANGE: **E. and S.E. Asia: Pakistan to Borneo and Korea; Yangtze River, E. China Sea**
HABITAT: **coasts, estuaries, rivers**
SIZE: **1.4–1.8 m (4½–6 ft)**

The finless porpoise is different from other porpoises in that it has a prominent, rounded forehead, which gives the appearance of a slight beak, and a ridge of small rounded projections just behind where the dorsal fin should be. Finless porpoises dive for less than a minute in search of prey and are quick and agile in the water. They feed largely on crustaceans, squid and fish and are skillful echolocators. Although finless porpoises generally move in pairs, groups of up to 10 are sometimes seen. Little is known of their breeding behavior, but young calves travel clinging to the projections on their mothers' backs.

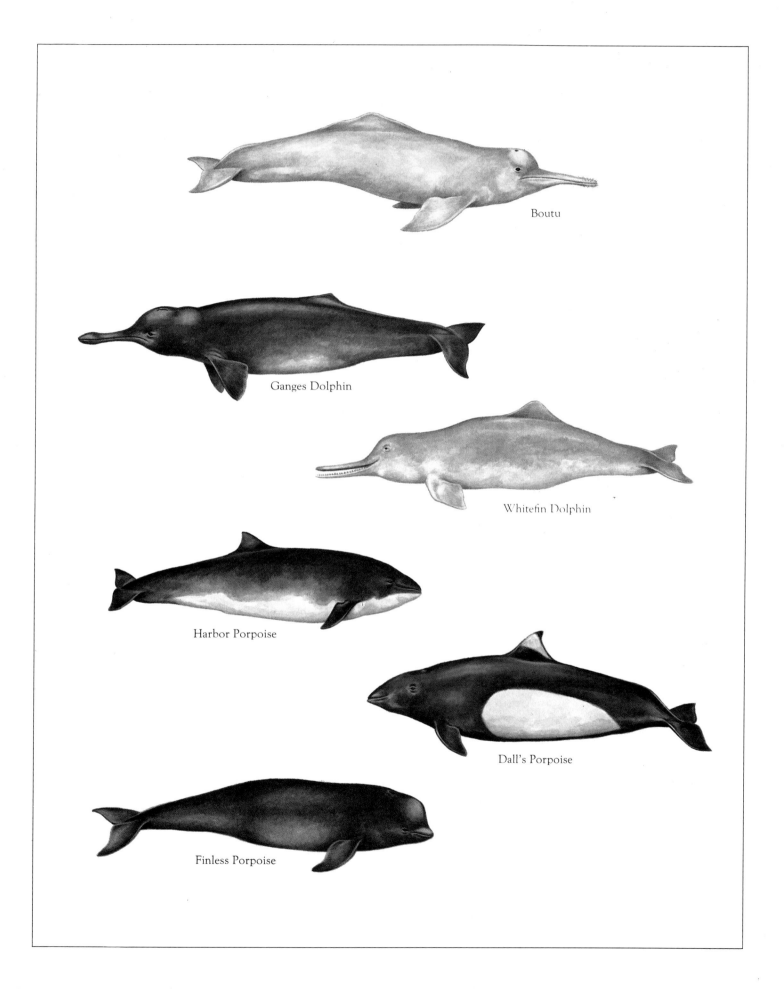

Boutu

Ganges Dolphin

Whitefin Dolphin

Harbor Porpoise

Dall's Porpoise

Finless Porpoise

Dolphins

NAME: **Indo-Pacific Humpbacked Dolphin,** *Sousa chinensis*
RANGE: **Indian Ocean, S.W. Pacific Ocean, Yangtze River**
HABITAT: **coasts, estuaries, swamps**
SIZE: **2–3 m (6½–10 ft)**

The young of this species all have the normal streamlined body shape, but adults have humps of fatty tissue on the back. The beak is long, and there is a total of at least 120 teeth. These dolphins feed in shallow water on fish, mollusks and crustaceans and use echolocation when searching for prey. They are gregarious creatures, living in groups of up to 20 individuals.

NAME: **Striped Dolphin,** *Stenella coeruleoalba*
RANGE: **Atlantic and Pacific Oceans, temperate and tropical areas**
HABITAT: **deep offshore waters**
SIZE: **2.4–3 m (8–10 ft)**

Color is variable in this species, but there is always a dark stripe running along the side and usually a dark band curving from the dorsal fin toward the eye. Striped dolphins have between 90 and 100 teeth and feed on small fish, squid and shrimps. They move in large schools of several hundred, even several thousand, individuals, which are organized into age-segregated groups. Females breed about every 3 years. The gestation period is 12 months, and calves are nursed for from 9 to 18 months.

NAME: **Common Dolphin,** *Delphinus delphis*
RANGE: **worldwide, temperate and tropical oceans**
HABITAT: **coastal and oceanic waters**
SIZE: **2.1–2.6 m (7–8½ ft)**

The classic dolphin depicted by artists for centuries, the common dolphin is a beautifully marked animal, with a long beak and pointed flippers. The markings are the most complex of any whale and are extremely variable. There are a number of geographically recognizable forms of this widespread species.

Dolphins live in hierarchical groups of 20 to 100 or more; groups sometimes join together, forming huge schools. There are many reports of these highly intelligent social animals coming to the aid of injured companions. Active animals, they roll and leap in the water and often swim at the bows of ships. Although they normally breathe several times a minute, they can dive for as long as 5 minutes to depths of 280 m (920 ft) to feed on fish and squid and certainly make good use of echolocation when hunting. Young are born in the summer, after a gestation of 10 or 11 months.

DELPHINIDAE: Dolphin Family

There are 32 species in this, the largest, most diverse cetacean family, which is found in all oceans and some tropical rivers. Most have beaked snouts and slender streamlined bodies and they are among the smallest whales. Typically, the dolphin has a bulging forehead, housing the melon, a lens-shaped pad of fat thought to help focus the sonar beams. A few species, notably the killer whale, are much larger and do not have beaks. Male dolphins are usually larger than females, and in some species the sexes differ in the shape of their flippers and dorsal fins. Dolphins swim fast and feed by making shallow dives and surfacing several times a minute. They are extremely gregarious and establish hierarchies within their social groups.

NAME: **Atlantic Bottle-nosed Dolphin,** *Tursiops truncatus*
RANGE: **worldwide, temperate and tropical oceans**
HABITAT: **coastal waters**
SIZE: **3–4.2 m (10–14 ft)**

Now the familiar performing dolphin in zoos and on screen, this dolphin is a highly intelligent animal which is, tragically, still hunted and killed by man in some areas. It is a sturdy creature with a broad, high fin and a short, wide beak. Its lower jaw projects beyond the upper, and this, combined with the curving line of the mouth, gives it its characteristic smiling expression.

Bottle-nosed dolphins live in groups of up to 15 individuals, sometimes gathering into larger schools, and there is much cooperation and communication between the group members. They feed mainly on bottom-dwelling fish in inshore waters but also take crustaceans and large, surface-swimming fish. They are highly skillful echolocators, producing a range of click sounds in different frequencies to analyze any object at a distance with great precision. Up to 1,000 clicks a second are emitted.

Breeding pairs perform gentle courtship movements, caressing one another before copulation. Gestation lasts 12 months, and two adult females assist the mother at the birth and take the calf, which is normally born tail first, to the surface for its first breath. The mother feeds her calf for about a year, so there must be at least a 2-year interval between calves. Like all whales, the bottle-nosed dolphin produces extremely rich milk, with a fat content of over 40 percent, to satisfy the high energy demands of her fast-growing youngster.

NAME: **Killer Whale,** *Orcinus orca*
RANGE: **worldwide, particularly cooler seas**
HABITAT: **coastal waters**
SIZE: **7–9.7 m (23–32 ft)**

The largest of the dolphin family, the killer whale is a robust yet streamlined animal, with a rounded head and no beak. The characteristic dorsal fin of an adult male is almost 2 m (6½ ft) high; and while the fins of females and juveniles are much smaller and curved, they are still larger than those of most other cetaceans. Adults have a total of 40 to 50 teeth.

Killer whales are avid predators and feed on fish, squid, sea lions, birds and even other whales. Their echolocation sounds are unlike those of other dolphins and are probably used to find food in turbid water.

Extended family groups of killer whales live together and cooperate in hunting. They have no regular migratory habits but do travel in search of food.

NAME: **Long-finned Pilot Whale,** *Globicephala melaena*
RANGE: **N. Atlantic Ocean; temperate southern oceans**
HABITAT: **coastal waters**
SIZE: **4.8–8.5 m (16–28 ft)**

The long-finned pilot whale has an unusual square-shaped head and long, rather narrow flippers. Pilot whales have a vast repertoire of sounds, some of which are used for echolocation purposes. Squid is their main food, but they also feed on fish such as cod and turbot. Social groups are made up of 6 or more whales, and they have particularly strong bonds. Groups may join into larger schools. Gestation lasts about 16 months, and the mother feeds her young for well over a year.

The range of this species is unusual in that it occurs in two widely separated areas.

NAME: **Risso's Dolphin/Grampus,** *Grampus griseus*
RANGE: **worldwide, temperate and tropical oceans**
HABITAT: **deep water**
SIZE: **3–4 m (10–13 ft)**

Most adult Risso's dolphins are badly marked with scars, apparently caused by members of their own species, since the marks correspond to their own tooth pattern. The body of this dolphin is broad in front of the fin and tapers off behind it. It has no beak, but there is a characteristic crease down the center of the forehead to the lip. There are no teeth in the upper jaw and only three or four in each side in the lower jaw. Squid seems to be its main food.

Striped Dolphin

Indo-Pacific Humpbacked Dolphin

Common Dolphin

Atlantic Bottle-nosed Dolphin

Killer Whale (male)

Long-finned Pilot Whale

Risso's Dolphin

Sperm Whales, White Whales

PHYSETERIDAE:
Sperm Whale Family

There are 3 species of sperm whale, 1 of which is the largest of all toothed whales, while the other 2 are among the smallest whales. Their characteristic feature is the spermaceti organ, located in the space above the toothless upper jaw; this contains a liquid, waxy substance which may be involved in controlling buoyancy when the whale makes deep dives. All sperm whales have underslung lower jaws but have little else in common.

NAME: **Pygmy Sperm Whale,** *Kogia breviceps*
RANGE: **all oceans**
HABITAT: **tropical, warm temperate seas**
SIZE: **3–3.4 m (10–11 ft)**

Its underslung lower jaw gives the pygmy sperm whale an almost sharklike appearance, belied by its blunt, square head. Unlike its large relative with its disproportionately huge head, the pygmy sperm whale's head accounts for only about 15 percent of its total length. There are 12 or more pairs of teeth in the lower jaw. The short, broad flippers are located far forward, near the head, and there is a small dorsal fin, behind which the body tapers off markedly.

Pygmy sperm whales are thought to be shy, slow-moving animals. They feed on squid, fish and crabs from both deep and shallow water so may be less of an exclusively deepwater species than the sperm whale. Pygmy sperm whales have often been sighted alone, but evidence suggests that they form social units of 3 to 5 individuals.

Little is known of the reproductive habits of pygmy sperm whales. Gestation is believed to last about 9 months; calves are born in the spring and fed by the mother for about a year.

NAME: **Dwarf Sperm Whale,** *Kogia simus*
RANGE: **all oceans**
HABITAT: **tropical and subtropical seas**
SIZE: **2.4–2.7 m (8–9 ft)**

Superficially similar to the pygmy sperm whale, the dwarf sperm whale tends to have a more rounded head than its relative although there is considerable individual variation in head shape. Its lower jaw is set back, and it has up to 11 pairs of teeth.

Little is known of the biology and habits of this whale, but fish and squid are believed to be its main items of diet. Species found in the stomachs of dwarf sperm whales are all known to live at depths of more than 250 m (820 ft), so there seems little doubt that these whales make prolonged dives for food.

NAME: **Sperm Whale,** *Physeter catodon*
RANGE: **all oceans**
HABITAT: **temperate and tropical waters**
SIZE: **11–20 m (36–66 ft)**

The largest of the toothed whales, the sperm whale has a huge head, as great as one-third of its total body length, and a disproportionately small lower jaw, set well back from the snout. On its back is a fleshy hump and behind this are several smaller humps. Its flippers are short, but the tail is large and powerful and useful for acceleration. Surrounding the nasal passages in the huge snout is a mass of the waxy substance known as spermaceti. When the whale dives, it allows these passages to fill with water, and by controlling the amount and temperature of the water taken in at different depths, it can alter the density of the wax and thus the buoyancy of its whole body. This facility enables the whale to make its deep dives and to remain down, at neutral buoyancy, while searching for prey. Sperm whales are known to dive to 1,000 m (3,300 ft) and may even dive to more than twice this depth. They feed mainly on large, deepwater squid, as well as on some fish, lobsters and other marine creatures. Their sonar system is essential for finding prey in the black depths of the ocean.

All sperm whales migrate toward the poles in spring and back to the equator in autumn, but females and young do not stray farther than temperate waters. Adult males, however, travel right to the ice caps in high latitudes. They return to the tropics in winter and contest with each other to gather harem groups consisting of 20 to 30 breeding females and young. Males under about 25 years old do not generally hold harems, but gather in bachelor groups.

The gestation period for sperm whales is about 14 to 16 months. When a female gives birth, she is surrounded by attendant adult females, waiting to assist her and to help the newborn to take its first breath at the surface. As with most whales, usually only 1 young is produced at a time, but twins have been known. Mothers suckle their young for up to 2 years.

MONODONTIDAE:
White Whale Family

There are 2 species in this family, both of which live in arctic waters. They are distinctive whales with many features in common. Both have more flexible necks than is usual for whales, and their tails, too, are highly maneuverable. They have no dorsal fins. In both species males are larger than females.

NAME: **White Whale,** *Delphinapterus leucas*
RANGE: **Arctic Ocean and subarctic waters**
HABITAT: **shallow seas, estuaries, rivers**
SIZE: **4–6.1 m (13–20 ft)**

Often known as the beluga, the white whale has a rounded, plump body and just a hint of a beak. There is a short raised ridge on its back where the dorsal fin would normally be. At birth, these whales are a dark brownish-red; they then turn a deep blue-gray and gradually become paler until, at about 6 years old, they are a creamy-white color. They have about 32 teeth.

White whales feed on the bottom in shallow water, mainly on crustaceans and some fish. They actually swim under pack ice and can break their way up through the ice floes to breathe.

Sexual maturity is attained when the whales are 5 to 8 years old. The whales mate in spring and calves are born in the summer, after a gestation of about 14 months. Since the young are suckled for at least a year, white whales are able to breed only every 3 years or so. All white whales are highly vocal and make a variety of sounds for communication, as well as clicks used for echolocation. Their intricate songs caused them to be known as sea canaries by the nineteenth-century whalers. White whales congregate in vast herds of hundreds of individuals to migrate south in winter and then return to rich northern feeding grounds in summer.

NAME: **Narwhal,** *Monodon monoceros*
RANGE: **high Arctic Ocean (patchy distribution)**
HABITAT: **open sea**
SIZE: **4–6.1 m (13–20 ft)**

The male narwhal has an extraordinary spiral tusk which is actually its upper left incisor. The tooth grows out of a hole in the upper lip to form the tusk, which may be as much as 2.7 m (9 ft) long. The female may sometimes have a short tusk. It is not known what the purpose of the tusk is, but it is probable that it is a sexual characteristic, used by males to dominate other males and impress females.

Narwhals feed on squid, crabs, shrimps and fish. Groups of 6 to 10 whales form social units and may gather into larger herds when migrating. They do make click sounds, as well as other vocal communications, but it is not certain whether or not these are used for echolocation. Narwhals mate in early spring, and gestation lasts 15 months. Mothers feed their calves for up to 2 years. At birth, calves are a dark blue-gray but as they mature this changes to the mottled brown of adults.

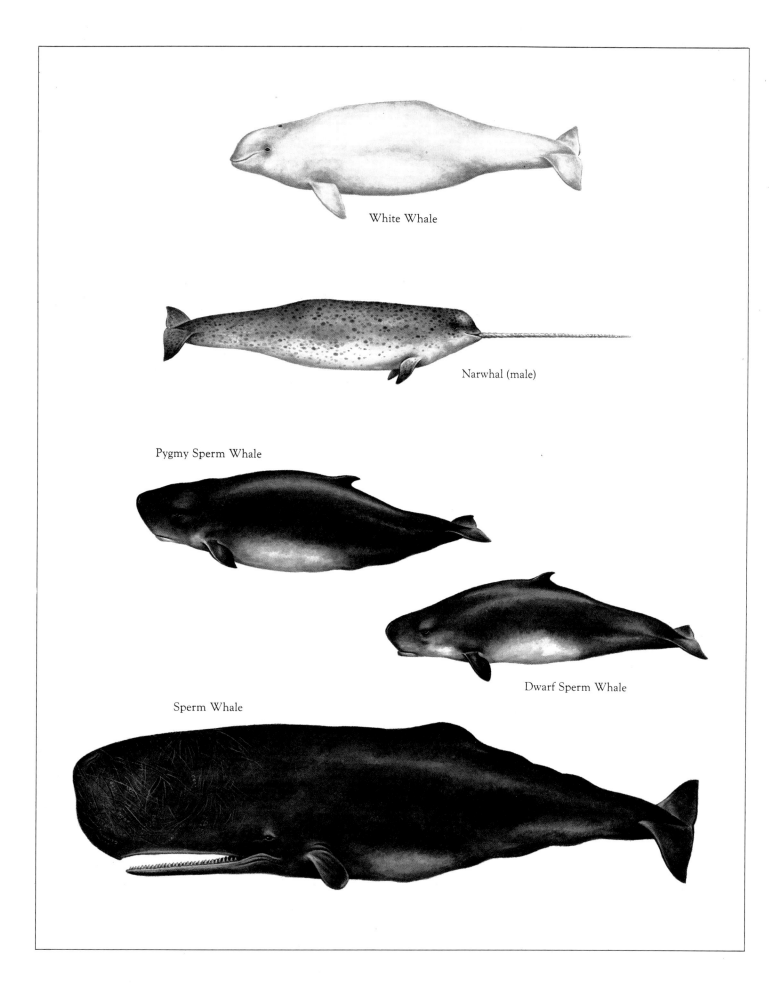

White Whale

Narwhal (male)

Pygmy Sperm Whale

Dwarf Sperm Whale

Sperm Whale

Beaked Whales

NAME: Northern Bottle-nosed Whale,
Hyperoodon ampullatus
RANGE: Arctic, N. Atlantic Oceans
HABITAT: deep offshore waters
SIZE: 7.3–10 m (24–33 ft) Ⓥ

A sturdy, round-bodied whale, the northern bottle-nosed has a prominent, bulbous forehead that is particularly pronounced in older males. Males are generally larger than females. The adult male has only two teeth, which are in the lower jaw, but these are often so deeply embedded in the gums that they cannot be seen. Adult females also have only two teeth, and these are always embedded in the gum. Some individuals have further vestigial, unusable teeth in the gums.

Squid, some fish such as herring and sometimes starfish make up the diet of the northern bottle-nosed whale. A member of a deep-diving family, it is believed to dive deeper than any other whale and certainly remains under water for longer. These are gregarious whales, and they collect in social units of 4 to 10 individuals, a group usually consisting of a male and several females with young. Pairs mate in spring and summer, and gestation lasts about 12 months. The whales are sexually mature at between 9 and 12 years of age.

Since commercial whaling of this species began in 1887, populations have been seriously depleted.

NAME: Cuvier's Beaked Whale, *Ziphius cavirostris*
RANGE: all oceans, temperate and tropical areas
HABITAT: deep waters
SIZE: 6.4–7 m (21–23 ft)

Cuvier's beaked whale has the typical tapering body of its family and a distinct beak. Adult males are easily distinguished by the two teeth which protrude from the lower jaw; in females these teeth remain embedded in the gums. The coloring of this species is highly variable: Indo-Pacific whales are generally various shades of brown, many with darker backs or almost white heads, while in the Atlantic, the whales tend to be gray or gray-blue. All races are marked with scars and with discolored oval patches caused by the feeding of parasitic lampreys.

Squid and deepwater fish are their main food, and these whales make deep dives, lasting up to 30 minutes, to find prey. There is no definite breeding season, and calves are born at any time of the year. Groups of up to 15 individuals live and travel together.

ZIPHIIDAE: Beaked Whale Family

There are 18 species of beaked whale, found in all oceans. Most are medium-sized whales with slender bodies and long narrow snouts; some species have bulging, rounded foreheads. A particular characteristic of the family is the pair of grooves on the throat. Although Shepherd's beaked whale has more than 50 teeth, all other beaked whales have only one or two pairs, and the arrangement and shape of these are a useful means of identification.

Beaked whales feed largely on squid. They are deep divers and are believed to dive deeper and to remain submerged for longer periods than any other marine mammals. They generally move in small groups, but adult males are often solitary.

Although the second-largest family of whales (the dolphin family is the largest with 32 species), beaked whales are a little-known group. Some species are known to exist only from a few skulls and bones. The 12 species in the genus *Mesoplodon* are particularly unresearched but interesting. Only males have functional teeth, with a single pair protruding from the lower jaw. The shape and length of these differ from species to species, culminating in M. *layardi*, in which the backward-pointing teeth grow upward out of the mouth like tusks.

NAME: Sowerby's Beaked Whale,
Mesoplodon bidens
RANGE: N. Atlantic Ocean
HABITAT: deep, cool coastal waters
SIZE: 5–6 m (16½–20 ft)

There are 12 closely related species of beaked whale in the genus *Mesoplodon*. Most tend to live in deep water, staying clear of ships, so they are rarely seen and their habits are little known. All have fairly well-rounded bodies, with small flippers in proportion to body size. Males are larger than females. Mature whales are generally marked with many scars; some of these are caused by parasites and others are, perhaps, the result of fights between individuals of the same species.

Sowerby's beaked whale was the first beaked whale to be recognized officially and described as a species, in 1804. The male has a pointed tooth at each side of the lower jaw. Females have smaller teeth in this position or no visible teeth at all. Squid and small fish are the main food of Sowerby's beaked whale. Its breeding habits are not known, but it is thought to migrate south in winter and to give birth in its wintering area.

NAME: Shepherd's Beaked Whale,
Tasmacetus shepherdi
RANGE: New Zealand seas; off coasts of Argentina and Chile
HABITAT: coasts, open ocean
SIZE: 6–6.6 m (20–22 ft)

Shepherd's beaked whale was not discovered until 1933, and very few individuals have since been found or sighted. Until recently, the species was believed to occur only around New Zealand, but in the 1970s identical specimens were found off Argentina and Chile.

Unique in its family for its tooth pattern, Shepherd's beaked whale has a pair of large teeth at the tip of its lower jaw, with 12 or more pairs behind them, and about 10 pairs in the upper jaw. It resembles the rest of the family in habits and appearance. Squid and fish are believed to be its main food.

NAME: Baird's Beaked Whale, *Berardius bairdi*
RANGE: temperate N. Pacific Ocean
HABITAT: deep water over 1,000 m (3,300 ft)
SIZE: 10–12 m (33–39 ft)

The largest of the beaked whales, Baird's beaked whale has a distinctive beak, with the lower jaw extending beyond the upper. A pair of large teeth protrudes at the tip of the lower jaw, and behind these is a pair of smaller teeth. Female whales are generally larger than males and lighter in color but have smaller teeth. Adult males are usually marked with scars, caused by their own species, suggesting that there is much rivalry and competition for leadership of groups of breeding females.

The normal social unit is a group of 6 to 30, led by a dominant male. The whales mate in midsummer, and gestation lasts for 10 months, sometimes longer. The migration pattern of this species is the exact opposite of the normal migration habits of whales. They spend the summer in warm waters to the south of their range off California and Japan, then move northwards in winter to the cooler waters of the Bering Sea and similar areas. These movements are probably connected with the local abundance of food supplies. Deep divers, Baird's beaked whales feed on squid, fish, octopus, lobster, crabs and other invertebrates.

Arnoux's beaked whale, B. *arnouxii*, which occurs in the temperate South Pacific and South Atlantic, is the closely related southern counterpart of Baird's beaked whale. Although rarely seen, it is believed to be similar in both appearance and habits.

Northern Bottle-nosed Whale

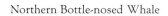

Cuvier's Beaked Whale

Sowerby's Beaked Whale (male)

Shepherd's Beaked Whale

Baird's Beaked Whale (male)

Gray Whale, Rorquals, Right Whales

ESCHRICHTIDAE:
Gray Whale Family

There is a single species in this family, which is in some ways intermediate between the rorqual and right whales, the other 2 baleen whale families. The gray whale differs from both of these in that it has two or sometimes four throat grooves, instead of the 100 or more in the other baleen whales.

NAME: **Gray Whale,** *Eschrichtius robustus*
RANGE: **N.E. and N.W. Pacific Ocean**
HABITAT: **coastal waters**
SIZE: **12.2–15.3 m (40–50 ft)** (V)

The gray whale has no dorsal fin, but there is a line of bumps along the middle of its lower back. Its jaw is only slightly arched and the snout is pointed. Males are larger than females. Like all baleen whales, it feeds on small planktonic animals by filtering water through rows of fringed horny plates, suspended from the upper jaw. Any creatures in the water are caught on the baleen plates, and the water is expelled at the sides of the mouth. Using its tongue, the whale takes the food from the baleen to the back of its mouth to be swallowed. The gray whale feeds at the bottom of the sea, unlike other baleen whales, stirring up the sediment with its pointed snout, then sieving the turbulent water.

Gray whales perform migrations of some 20,000 km (12,500 mi) between feeding grounds in the north and breeding grounds in the south. They spend the summer months in the food-rich waters of the Arctic, when they do most of their feeding for the year. At the breeding grounds, they gather to perform courtship rituals, and breeding animals pair off with an extra male in attendance. They lie in shallow water, and as the pair mate, the second male lies behind the female, apparently supporting her. The gestation period is 12 months, so the calf is born at the breeding grounds a year after mating has taken place and travels north with its mother when it is about 2 months old.

BALAENOPTERIDAE:
Rorqual Family

There are 6 species of rorqual whale. All except the humpback whale are similar in appearance, but they differ in size and color. Most have about 300 baleen plates on each side of the jaws, which are not highly arched, and there are a large number of grooves on the throat. Females are larger than males.

NAME: **Minke Whale,** *Balaenoptera acutorostrata*
RANGE: **all oceans, temperate and polar areas**
HABITAT: **shallow water, estuaries, rivers, inland seas**
SIZE: **8–10 m (26–33 ft)**

The smallest of the rorqual family, the minke whale has a distinctive, narrow pointed snout and 60 to 70 throat grooves. In polar areas, minke whales feed largely on planktonic crustaceans, but temperate populations eat fish and squid more often than any other baleen whale. Out of the breeding season, these whales tend to occur alone or in pairs, but they may congregate in rich feeding areas. Gestation lasts 10 to 11 months and calves are suckled for 6 months.

NAME: **Sei Whale,** *Balaenoptera borealis*
RANGE: **all oceans (not polar regions)**
HABITAT: **open ocean**
SIZE: **15–20 m (49–65½ ft)**

A streamlined, flat-headed rorqual, the sei whale is a fast swimmer, achieving speeds of 50 km/h (26 kn). Almost any kind of plankton, as well as fish and squid, are eaten by sei whales, and they usually feed near the surface. Family groups of 5 or 6 whales move together, and pair bonds are strong and may last from year to year. The gestation period is 12 months, and the calf is fed by its mother for 6 months.

NAME: **Blue/Sulphur-bottomed Whale,** *Balaenoptera musculus*
RANGE: **all oceans**
HABITAT: **open ocean**
SIZE: **25–32 m (82–105 ft)** (E)

The largest mammal that has ever existed, the blue whale may weigh more than 146 metric t (161 US t). Its body is streamlined and, despite its enormous bulk, it is graceful in the water. It has 64 to 94 grooves on its throat. These gigantic whales feed entirely on small planktonic crustaceans and, unlike many baleen whales, are highly selective, taking only a few species. They feed during the summer months, which they spend in nutrient-rich polar waters, and over this period take up to 4.1 metric t (4.4 US t) of small shrimps apiece each day.

In autumn, when ice starts to cover their feeding grounds, the blue whales migrate toward the equator but eat virtually nothing while in the warmer water. They mate during this period, and, after a gestation of 11 to 12 months, the calves are born in warm waters the following year.

Even though blue whales have been protected since 1967, populations of this extraordinary animal are still low, and it is in danger of extinction.

NAME: **Humpback Whale,** *Megaptera novaeangliae*
RANGE: **all oceans**
HABITAT: **oceanic, coastal waters**
SIZE: **14.6–19 m (48–62 ft)** (E)

The humpback has a distinctly curved lower jaw and an average of 22 throat grooves. Its most characteristic features are the many knobs on the body and the flippers, which are about 5 m (16 ft) long and scalloped at the front edges. Humpback whales are more gregarious than blue whales and are usually seen in family groups of 3 or 4, although they may communicate with many other groups.

In the southern hemisphere, humpbacks feed on planktonic crustaceans, but in the northern hemisphere they eat small fish. Populations in both hemispheres feed in polar regions in summer and then migrate to tropical breeding areas for the winter. The gestation period is 11 to 12 months, and a mother feeds her calf for almost a year.

Humpbacks perform the most extraordinary, complex songs of any animal. The songs may be repeated for hours on end and are specific to populations and areas. They may change from year to year.

BALAENIDAE:
Right Whale Family

It is in the 3 species of right whale that the baleen apparatus is most extreme. Right whales have enormous heads, measuring more than a third of their total body length, and highly arched upper jaws to carry the long baleen plates. They have no throat grooves.

Regarded by whalers as the "right" whales to exploit, they have been killed in such numbers by commercial whalers over the last century that they are rare today.

NAME: **Bowhead Whale,** *Balaena mysticetus*
RANGE: **Arctic Ocean**
HABITAT: **coastal waters**
SIZE: **15–20 m (49–65½ ft)** (E)

The bowhead has a massive head and a body that tapers sharply toward the tail. Its jaws are strongly curved to accommodate the 4.5 m- (15 ft-) long baleen plates, the longest of any filter-feeding whale.

Bowheads feed on the smallest planktonic crustaceans, which they catch on the fine fringes of their baleen. They mate in early spring, the gestation period is 10 to 12 months, and the calf is fed for almost a year. Occasionally twins are produced.

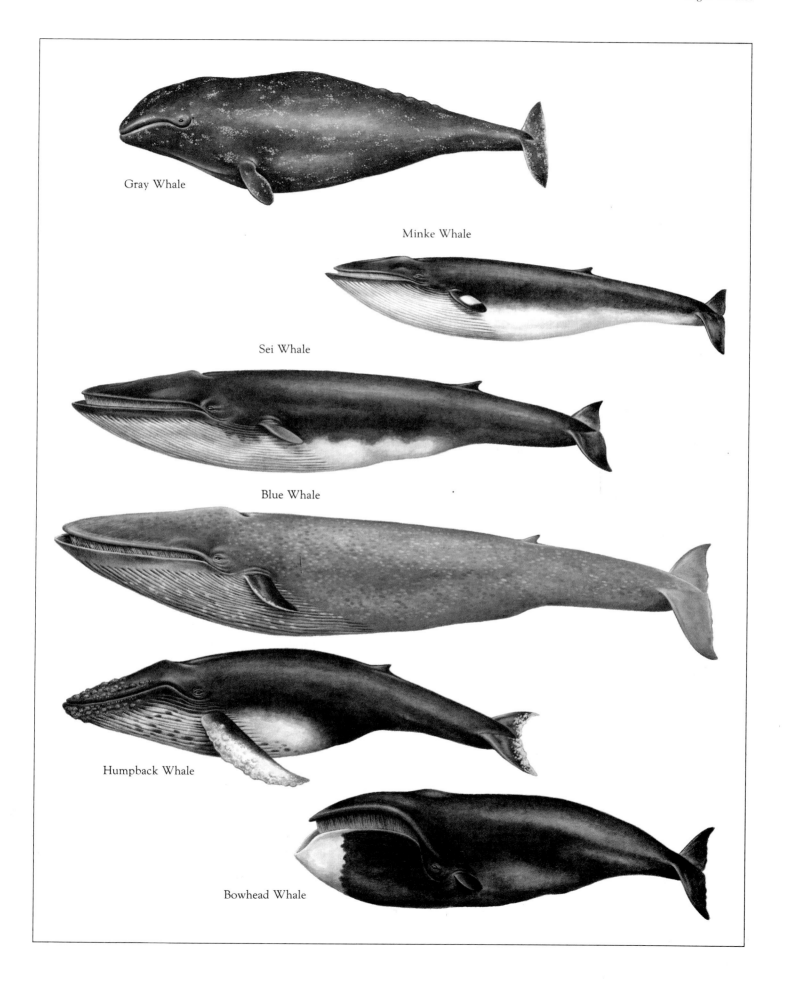

Gray Whale

Minke Whale

Sei Whale

Blue Whale

Humpback Whale

Bowhead Whale

Elephants, Hyraxes

ORDER PROBOSCIDEA

The elephants are the only surviving representatives of this once diverse and widespread group, which formerly contained many species of huge herbivorous mammal.

ELEPHANTIDAE: Elephant Family

The two species of elephant are by far the largest terrestrial mammals: they may stand up to 4 m (13 ft) at the shoulder and weigh as much as 5,900 kg (13,000 lb). One species lives in Africa, the other in India and Southeast Asia. Elephants are quite unmistakable in appearance; they have thick, pillarlike legs, and their feet are flattened, expanded pads. On the head are huge ears, which are fanned to and fro to help dissipate excess body heat, and the most remarkable of adaptations, the trunk. This is an elongated nose and upper lip which is extremely flexible and has a manipulative tip. An extraordinarily sensitive organ, it is used for gathering food, drinking, smelling and fighting.

Both species of elephant have suffered badly from destruction of forest and vegetation in their range, and large numbers have been killed for their ivory tusks. Although hunting is now strictly controlled, poaching continues, since the demand for ivory persists.

NAME: **African Elephant**, *Loxodonta africana*
RANGE: **Africa, south of the Sahara**
HABITAT: **forest, savanna**
SIZE: **body: 6–7.5 m (19¾–24½ ft)**
 tail: 1–1.3 m (3¼–4¼ ft) Ⓥ

The huge, majestic elephant is perhaps the most imposing of all the African mammals. It has larger ears and tusks than the Asian species and two finger-like extensions at the end of its trunk. Females are smaller than males and have shorter tusks. Elephants rest in the midday heat and have one or two periods of rest at night but are otherwise active at any time, roaming with their swinging, unhurried gait in search of food. Depending on its size, an elephant may consume up to 200 kg (440 lb) of plant material a day, all of which is grasped with the trunk and placed in the mouth. The diet includes leaves, shoots, twigs, roots and fruit from many plants, as well as cultivated crops on occasion.

Elephants are social animals, particularly females, and are known to demonstrate concern for others in distress. A troop usually comprises several females and their young of various ages. As they mature, young males form separate troops. Old males may be shunned by the herd when they are displaced by younger males.

Breeding occurs at any time of year, and a female in heat may mate with more than one male. The gestation period is about 22 months, and usually only 1 young is born. The female clears a secluded spot for the birth and is assisted by other females. The calf is suckled for at least 2 years and remains with its mother even longer. She may have several calves of different ages under her protection and gives birth only every 2 to 4 years.

NAME: **Indian Elephant**, *Elephas maximus*
RANGE: **India, Sri Lanka, S.E. Asia, Sumatra**
HABITAT: **forest, grassy plains**
SIZE: **body: 5.5–6.5 m (18–21¼ ft)**
 tail: 1.2–1.5 m (4–5 ft) Ⓥ

Although an equally impressive animal, the Indian elephant has smaller ears than its African counterpart, a more humped back and only one fingerlike extension at the end of its mobile trunk. The female is smaller than the male and has only rudimentary tusks. The main social unit is a herd led by an old female and including several females, their young and an old male, usually all related. Other males may live alone but near to a herd and will sometimes feed or mate with members of the herd. The herd rests in the heat of the day but spends much of the rest of the time feeding on grass, leaves, shoots, fruit and other plant material, all of which they search out and grasp with highly sensitive trunks. Their hearing and sense of smell are excellent, and eyesight poor.

During the heat period, called musth, which is often accompanied by profuse secretion of scented liquid from a gland on the side of the head, normally docile animals become excited and unpredictable. The gestation period is about 21 months, and the female usually gives birth to a single young.

ORDER HYRACOIDEA
PROCAVIIDAE: Hyrax Family

Small herbivorous mammals found in Africa and the Middle East, the hyraxes, conies or dassies have the general appearance of rabbits with short, rounded ears. There are about 5 species, and the family is the only one in its order. Some hyraxes are agile climbers in trees, while others inhabit rocky koppies, or small hills. On the feet are flattened nails, resembling hoofs, and a central moist cup that functions as an adhesive pad when the hyrax is climbing.

NAME: **Tree Hyrax**, *Dendrohyrax arboreus*
RANGE: **Africa: Kenya to South Africa: Cape Province**
HABITAT: **forest**
SIZE: **body: 40–60 cm (15¾–23½ in)**
 tail: absent

The tree hyrax is an excellent climber and lives in a tree hole or rock crevice, where it rests during the day. It emerges in the afternoon or evening to feed in the trees and on the ground on leaves, grass, ferns, fruit and other plant material. Insects, lizards and bird's eggs are also eaten on occasion. Tree hyraxes normally live in pairs and are extremely noisy animals, uttering a wide range of screams, squeals and grunts.

A litter of 1 or 2 young is born after a gestation of about 8 months.

NAME: **Small-toothed Rock Hyrax**, *Heterohyrax brucei*
RANGE: **Africa: Egypt to South Africa: Transvaal; Botswana and Angola**
HABITAT: **open country, plains to mountains, forest, savanna**
SIZE: **body: 40–57 cm (15¾–22½ in)**
 tail: absent

Despite its name, this hyrax lives among rocks or trees, depending on its habitat, sheltering in crevices or holes. Sociable animals, rock hyraxes form colonies of up to 30, each colony consisting of several old males, many breeding females and their young. They feed during the day, mainly on leaves of trees but also on small plants and grass.

The female gives birth to 1 or 2 young, rarely 3, after a gestation of 7½ to 8 months.

NAME: **Large-toothed Rock Hyrax**, *Procavia capensis*
RANGE: **Arabian Peninsula; Africa: Senegal to Somalia and N. Tanzania, S. Malawi, S. Angola to South Africa: Cape Province**
HABITAT: **rocky hillsides, rock piles**
SIZE: **body: 43–47 cm (17–18½ in)**
 tail: absent

This hyrax lives among rocky outcrops and is an agile climber. It feeds mostly on the ground on leaves, grass, small plants and berries but readily climbs to feed on fruits such as figs; in winter, it eats bark. Much of the rest of the day it spends lying in the sun or shade to maintain its body temperature, and at night the hyraxes huddle together to minimize loss of body heat. These hyraxes are sociable and live in colonies of 50 or more individuals.

Males are aggressive at mating time and reassert their dominance over rivals and younger males. The female gives birth to 1 to 6 young, usually 2 or 3, after a gestation of 7 to 8 months.

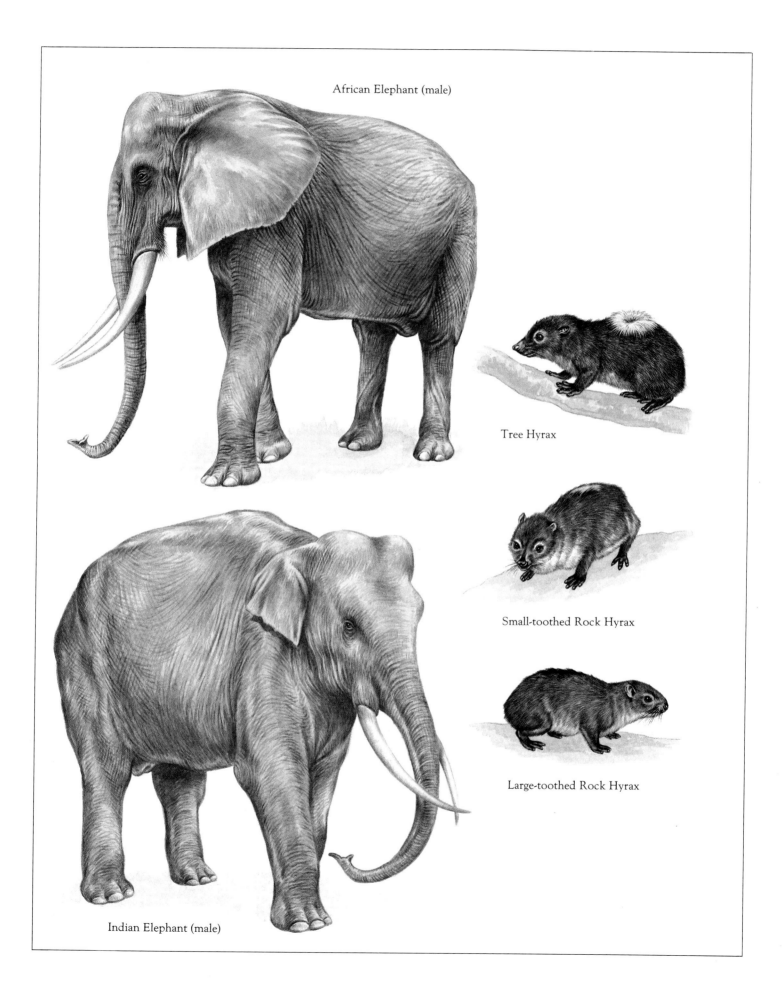

African Elephant (male)

Tree Hyrax

Small-toothed Rock Hyrax

Large-toothed Rock Hyrax

Indian Elephant (male)

Horses

NAME: Common Zebra, *Equus burchelli*
RANGE: E. and S. Africa
HABITAT: grassy plains, lightly wooded savanna, hills
SIZE: body: 1.9–2.4 m (6¼–7¾ ft)
tail: 43–57 cm (17–22½ in)

Great variation in marking occurs in these zebras, both between individuals and the various subspecies; toward the south of the range, the stripes on the hind parts of the body generally become lighter. The body is rounded, and the legs slender, and there is a small erect mane on the back of the neck. The base color of the body varies from white to yellowish, and stripes may be light to dark brown or black.

Active in the daytime, these zebras leave their resting place at dawn and move to grazing grounds to feed on grass and sometimes on leaves and bark. They must drink regularly. Zebras live in families of up to 6 females and their young, led by an old male. When the male is 16 to 18 years old, he is peacefully replaced by a younger male of 6 to 8 years and then lives alone. Several families share a home range and may join in large herds, but they can always recognize each other by pattern, voice and scent.

The female gives birth to a single young, rarely twins, after a gestation of about a year. Until the foal learns to recognize its mother — in 3 or 4 days — she drives other animals away. It suckles for about 6 months and is independent at about a year old.

NAME: Grevy's Zebra, *Equus grevyi*
RANGE: E. Africa: Kenya, Ethiopia
HABITAT: savanna, semidesert
SIZE: body: 2.6 m (8½ ft)
tail: 70–75 cm (27½–29½ in) (V)

The largest of its family, Grevy's zebra has a long head, broad, rounded ears and a relatively short, strong neck; an erect mane runs from its crown down the back of its neck. Its body is white with black stripes, which are narrower and more numerous than those of the common zebra. Grevy's zebra grazes during the day, resting in the shade if possible in the noon heat, and likes to drink daily. Mature males live alone, each in his own territory, while males without territories live in troops. Females and their young live in separate troops of a dozen or more. In the dry season, male and female troops migrate, but territorial males stay on unless there is a severe drought.

The female gives birth to a single young after a gestation thought to be about a year. The young is able to recognize its mother after the first few days. It suckles for 6 months and remains with its mother for up to 2 years.

ORDER PERISSODACTYLA

There are only 3 surviving families of perissodactyl, or odd-toed, hoofed mammals: horses, tapirs and rhinoceroses. Nine other families, now extinct, are known from fossils.

EQUIDAE: Horse Family

The horses, asses and zebras together make up a small family of about 8 species of hoofed mammal, highly adapted for fast, graceful running. In this group the foot has evolved to the point of being a single hoof on an elongate third digit. The family has a natural distribution in Asia and Africa, but the wild horse itself has been domesticated by man and has since spread to other parts of the world.

In the wild, all equids live in herds, make regular migrations and feed in the main on grass. Their teeth are adapted for grass-cropping and grinding, with chisel-shaped incisors and very large premolars and molars with convoluted surfaces. The skull is elongate to accommodate the large cheek teeth.

NAME: African Ass, *Equus africanus*
RANGE: N.E. Africa
HABITAT: open grassy plains, rugged rocky country, semidesert, mountains
SIZE: body: about 2 m (6½ ft)
tail: 42.5 cm (16¾ in) (E)

The ancestor of the domestic ass, the African ass is now rare in the wild, and it is thought that many of those which remain are crossbreeds with domestic stock. They have suffered from excessive hunting and from competition from increasing numbers of domestic livestock. Of the 4 subspecies, 1 is now extinct and 2 nearly so.

The African ass has a large head with long, narrow ears and short, smooth hair, which varies from yellowish-brown to bluish-gray in color. A good climber, it is adept at moving over rocks and rugged country as it wanders, feeding on grass and herbage. It may sometimes browse on foliage and needs to drink regularly. Most active at dusk and nighttime and in the early morning, it spends much of the heat of the day resting, in shade if possible. Female African asses live in loose-knit troops with their young or in mixed troops of young animals of both sexes. Older males live alone or in male troops. The asses' senses are good, and they defend themselves by kicking and biting.

The female gives birth to 1 young after a gestation of 330 to 365 days. She keeps all other animals away from her newborn offspring for several days until it has learned to recognize her.

NAME: Przhevalski's Horse, *Equus ferus*
RANGE: Mongolia, W. China
HABITAT: plains, semidesert
SIZE: body: 1.8–2 m (6–6½ ft)
tail: 90 cm (35½ in) (E)

The ancestor of the domestic horse, Przhevalski's horse is distinguished by its erect mane and lack of forelock. It interbreeds with domestic stock, and few purebred animals remain. Populations have declined drastically because of hunting, cold winters and competition with domestic livestock for water and pasture, and the species may soon be extinct in the wild.

When their numbers were greater, Przhevalski's horses moved in large herds, but now they live in small herds, each led by a dominant male. Young are born in April or May.

NAME: Onager, *Equus hemionus*
RANGE: Iran, Afghanistan, USSR
HABITAT: steppe, gorges, river margins
SIZE: body: about 2 m (6½ ft)
tail: 42.5 cm (16¾ in) (V)

Also called the Asiatic wild ass, the onager has declined in numbers because of human settlement in its range, grazing by domestic stock and hunting. In summer, it lives on high grassland and migrates in winter to lower levels to find water and pasture. It feeds on many types of grass, and the availability of fresh water is critical to its survival. A sociable animal, it lives in troops of up to 12 females and young, led by a dominant male, but in autumn, troops may gather in larger herds to migrate.

The female gives birth to a single young after a gestation of about a year.

NAME: Kiang, *Equus kiang*
RANGE: Tibet
HABITAT: high plateaus
SIZE: body: 2.2 m (7¼ ft)
tail: 49 cm (19¼ in)

The largest of the wild asses, the kiang is the only one that still occurs in large, although dwindling, numbers. It remains on the high plateaus throughout the year and does not migrate, but in autumn it does put on an enormous amount of fat, as much as 40 kg (88 lb), which helps to sustain it through the winter and also forms an insulating layer against the cold. With their hard lips and horny gums, kiangs are well equipped for feeding on the tough grasses in their habitat, and they will eat snow if they cannot find water.

Kiangs live in herds in which a specific dominance order is maintained, but they are generally aggressive, and in the breeding season, males fight one another over females. The female gives birth to 1 young after a gestation of about a year.

Common Zebra

Grevy's Zebra

Przhevalski's Horse

African Ass

Kiang

Onager

Tapirs, Rhinoceroses

TAPIRIDAE: Tapir Family

The 4 living species of tapir are thought to resemble the ancestors of the perissodactyls. They are stocky, short-legged animals with four toes on the forefeet and three on the hind feet. The body is covered with short, bristly hairs, giving the tapir a smooth-coated appearance. The snout and upper lip are elongated to form a short, mobile trunk with nostrils at its tip.

Tapirs are mainly nocturnal, forest-dwelling animals and feed on vegetation. Of the 4 species, 3 occur in Central and South America and 1 in Southeast Asia.

NAME: Malayan Tapir, *Tapirus indicus*
RANGE: S.E. Asia: Burma to Malaysia, Sumatra
HABITAT: humid, swampy forest
SIZE: body: 2.5 m (8¼ ft)
   tail: 5–10 cm (2–4 in)   Ⓔ

The Malayan tapir differs from other tapirs in its striking grayish-black and white coloration. It also has a longer, stronger trunk than the tapirs from South America. A shy, solitary animal, it is active only at night, when it feeds on aquatic vegetation and the leaves, buds and fruit of low-growing land plants. It swims well and if alarmed, makes for water.

The female gives birth to a single young after a gestation of about 395 days. The body of the young tapir is patterned with camouflaging stripes and spots, which disappear at about 6 to 8 months. Malayan tapirs have been badly affected by the destruction of large areas of forest and the changes wrought by human settlement and are now extremely rare.

NAME: Brazilian Tapir, *Tapirus terrestris*
RANGE: South America: Colombia, Venezuela, south to Brazil and Paraguay
HABITAT: rain forest, near water or swamps
SIZE: body: 2 m (6½ ft)
   tail: 5–8 cm (2–3 in)

Nearly always found near water, the Brazilian tapir is a good swimmer and diver but also moves fast on land, even over rugged, mountainous country. It is dark brown in color and has a low, erect mane running from the crown down the back of the neck. Using its mobile snout, this tapir feeds on leaves, buds, shoots and small branches that it tears from trees, fruit, grasses and aquatic plants.

The female gives birth to a single spotted and striped young after a gestation of 390 to 400 days.

RHINOCEROTIDAE: Rhinoceros Family

Of the living perissodactyl mammals, only the rhinoceroses show the massive, heavy-bodied structure that was so common among the earlier, now extinct families of the order. There are 5 species of rhinoceros, found in Africa and Southeast Asia, and all have huge heads with one or two horns and a prehensile upper lip, which helps them browse on tough plant material. The legs are short and thick, with three hoofed toes on each foot, and the skin is extremely tough, with only a few hairs. Male and female look much alike, but females tend to have smaller horns.

NAME: Indian Rhinoceros, *Rhinoceros unicornis*
RANGE: Nepal, N.E. India
HABITAT: grassland in swampy areas
SIZE: body: 4.2 m (13¾ ft)
   tail: 75 cm (29½ in)   Ⓔ

The largest of the Asian species, the Indian rhinoceros has a thick, dark-gray hide studded with many small protuberances. The skin falls into deep folds at the joints, giving the rhinoceros an armor-plated appearance. Both sexes have a single horn on the head, but the female's horn is smaller. Generally a solitary animal, the Indian rhinoceros feeds in the morning and evening on grass, weeds and twigs and rests during the remainder of the day.

The female gives birth to a single young after a gestation of about 16 months. The young rhinoceros is active soon after birth and is suckled for up to 2 years.

NAME: Sumatran Rhinoceros, *Dicerorhinus sumatrensis*
RANGE: Burma, Thailand, Malaysia, Sumatra, Borneo, possibly Laos
HABITAT: dense forest, near streams
SIZE: body: 2.5–2.8 m (8¼–9¼ ft)
   tail: about 60 cm (23½ in)   Ⓔ

The smallest member of its family, the Sumatran rhinoceros has two horns; those of the female are smaller than the male's. Bristlelike hairs are scattered over the thick skin and fringe the edges of the ears. Sumatran rhinoceroses are usually solitary, although a male and female pair may live together. They feed mostly in the early morning and evening on leaves, twigs, fruit and bamboo shoots and may trample down small trees to browse on their foliage. Like other rhinoceroses, this species has good hearing and sense of smell, but its sight is poor.

The female bears a single young after a gestation of about 7 to 8 months.

NAME: Square-lipped/White Rhinoceros, *Ceratotherium simum*
RANGE: Africa: N.W. Uganda and adjacent regions; Zimbabwe to N. South Africa
HABITAT: savanna
SIZE: body: 3.6–5 m (11¾–16½ ft)
   tail: 90 cm–1 m (35½–3¼ ft)

The largest living land animal after the elephant, the square-lipped rhinoceros has a pronounced hump on its neck and a long head, which it carries low. Its muzzle is broad, with a squared upper lip. This rhinoceros is generally grayish in color but takes on the color of the mud in which it has been wallowing, so may, in fact, be any shade of grayish- or reddish-brown.

Despite its size, the square-lipped rhinoceros is a placid animal and tends to flee from trouble, rather than attack. Each old male occupies his own territory, which may be shared by younger males, but the female is sociable and is usually accompanied by another female with young or by her own young and several others. They feed only on grass, grazing and resting from time to time throughout the day and night.

The female gives birth to a single young after a gestation of about 16 months. The calf suckles for at least a year and stays with its mother for 2 or 3 years, leaving her only when her next calf is born.

NAME: Black Rhinoceros, *Diceros bicornis*
RANGE: Africa: S. Chad and Sudan to South Africa
HABITAT: bush country, grassland, woodland
SIZE: body: 3–3.6 m (9¾–11¾ ft)
   tail: 60–70 cm (23½–27½ in)   Ⓥ

The black rhinoceros is, in fact, gray in color but varies according to the mud in which it wallows. It has no hump on its neck but has a large head, held horizontally, which bears two horns and sometimes a third small horn. Its upper lip is pointed and mobile, which helps the animal to browse on the leaves, buds and shoots of small trees and bushes. Less sociable than the square-lipped rhinoceros, black rhinoceroses live alone, except for mothers and young. Adults live in overlapping home ranges, with boundaries marked by dung heaps.

Male and female remain together for only a few days when mating. The female gives birth to a single young after a gestation of about 15 months. The young rhinoceros suckles for about a year and stays with its mother for 2 or 3 years, until her next calf is born.

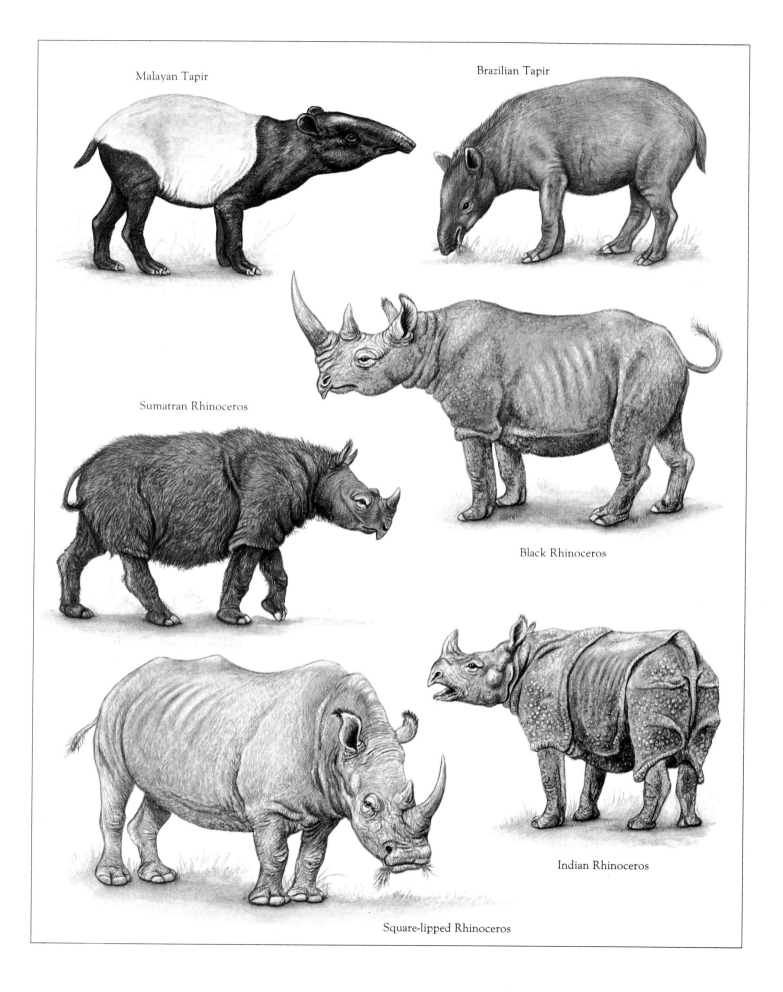

Malayan Tapir

Brazilian Tapir

Sumatran Rhinoceros

Black Rhinoceros

Indian Rhinoceros

Square-lipped Rhinoceros

Pigs

NAME: Bush Pig, *Potamochoerus porcus*
**RANGE: Africa, south of the Sahara;
Madagascar**
**HABITAT: forest, bush, swamps, thickets
in savanna**
**SIZE: body: 1–1.5 m (3¼–5 ft)
tail: 30–45 cm (11¾–17¾ in)**

Also known as the red river hog, this pig has an elongate snout and long, tufted ears. Its bristly coat varies from reddish-to grayish-brown, with a white dorsal mane and whiskers. Bush pigs are gregarious animals and live in groups of up to 12 or so, led by an old male. They wander over a wide range to seek food and eat almost anything, including plant matter, such as grass, roots, fruit and grain crops, and small mammals, young birds and carrion. Normally active in the daytime, bush pigs are nocturnal in areas where they are hunted.

Breeding occurs throughout the year, particularly at times of abundant food supplies. The female gives birth to 3 to 6 young in a grassy nest, after a gestation of 120 to 130 days.

**NAME: Warthog, *Phacochoerus
aethiopicus***
**RANGE: Africa: Ghana to Somalia, south
to South Africa: Natal**
HABITAT: savanna, treeless open plains
**SIZE: body: 1.1–1.4 m (3½–4½ ft)
tail: 35–50 cm (13¾–19¾ in)**

The warthog has long legs, a large head and a broad muzzle that bears tusks derived from the canine teeth. On each side of the big head are two wartlike protuberances — the origin of the animal's common name. Its bristly coat is sparse, but there is a mane of long bristles running to the middle of the back, and there are whiskers on the lower jaw. The female is smaller than the male and has shorter tusks.

Generally gregarious, warthogs live in family groups in a territory that may be shared by more than one family. They prefer to have water for drinking and wallowing within their range and also some form of shelter, such as aardvark burrows or holes among rocks, where they rest in the heat of the day and at night. As well as grazing on short grass, warthogs feed on fruit and, in dry spells, will probe the ground with their tusks to obtain bulbs, tubers and roots. They occasionally prey on small mammals and will take carrion.

Timing of the breeding season tends to be associated with the local rainy seasons. The female gives birth to 2 to 4 young after a gestation of 170 to 175 days. The young suckle for up to 4 months but, after a week, start to leave the burrow in which they are born to feed on grass.

ORDER ARTIODACTYLA

This is the largest and most diverse order of hoofed herbivorous mammals, containing the pigs, peccaries, hippopotamuses, camels, deer, antelope, cattle, sheep and goats. Artiodactyls have an even number of toes, the weight of the body being carried on digits 3 and 4, which are, typically, encased in pointed hoofs. The first digit is always absent, and digits 2 and 5 are always more or less reduced.

Artiodactyls can run rapidly and have specialized teeth for cutting and grinding vegetation. Plant material is digested in a complex, four-chambered stomach with the aid of enzymes and symbiotic microorganisms.

SUIDAE: Pig Family

Pigs are more omnivorous than other artiodactyls and lack some of their specializations. There are about 8 species, native to Europe, Asia and Africa, inhabiting forested or brush areas. Pigs are stocky animals, with long heads terminating in mobile snouts, which are tough, sensitive and flattened at the tip. The snout is used for plowing up forest litter or soil to find food. The upper canine teeth usually grow outward and upward to form tusks. On each foot are four toes, but only the third and fourth reach the ground and have functional hoofs.

NAME: Wild Boar, *Sus scrofa*
**RANGE: S. and central Europe, N.W.
Africa; through Asia to Siberia, south
to Sri Lanka, Taiwan and S.E. Asia;
introduced in USA**
HABITAT: forest, woodland
**SIZE: body: 1.1–1.3 m (3½–4¼ ft)
tail: 15–20 cm (6–7¾ in)**

The ancestor of the domestic pig, the wild boar has a heavy body covered with dense, bristly hair, thin legs and a long snout. The male has prominent tusks derived from the canine teeth. Wild boars live alone or in small groups of up to 20, with males separate from, but remaining close to, the females. Active at night and in the morning, they forage over a wide area for food, digging for bulbs and tubers and also eating nuts and a variety of other plant material, as well as insect larvae and, occasionally, carrion. An agile, fast-moving animal, the wild boar is aggressive if alarmed; males use their strong tusks for defense.

The breeding season varies according to regional climate, but in Europe, wild boars mate in winter and give birth to a litter of up to 10 striped young in spring or early summer after a gestation of about 115 days.

NAME: Bearded Pig, *Sus barbatus*
RANGE: Malaysia, Sumatra, Borneo
**HABITAT: rain forest, scrub, mangrove
swamps**
**SIZE: body: 1.6–1.8 m (5¼–6 ft)
tail: 20–30 cm (7¾–11¾ in)**

A large pig with an elongate head and a narrow body, the bearded pig has abundant whiskers on its chin and a bristly, wartlike protuberance beneath each eye. These warts are more conspicuous in males than in females. Fallen fruit, roots, shoots and insect larvae are the bearded pig's staple foods, and it also invades fields of root crops. It often follows gibbons and macaques to pick up the fruit they drop.

After a gestation of about 4 months, the female makes a nest of plant material and gives birth to 2 or 3 young, which stay with her for about a year.

**NAME: Giant Forest Hog, *Hylochoerus
meinertzhageni***
**RANGE: Africa: Liberia, Cameroon, east
to S. Ethiopia, Tanzania, Kenya**
HABITAT: forest, thickets
**SIZE: body: 1.5–1.8 m (5–6 ft)
tail: 25–35 cm (9¾–13¾ in)**

The largest of the African pigs, the giant forest hog has a huge elongate head, a heavy body and rather long legs for its family. Its muzzle is broad, and there are glandular swellings in the skin under its eyes and across its cheeks. Males are bigger and heavier than females. These pigs live in family groups of up to 12, and pairs remain together for life. They wander over a large, but undefined range, feeding on grass, plants, leaves, buds, roots, berries and fruit. Mostly active at night and in the morning, they rest during the heat of the day.

The female gives birth to 1 to 4 young, sometimes up to 8, after a gestation of 4 to 4½ months.

NAME: Babirusa, *Babyrousa babyrussa*
RANGE: Sulawesi, Sula Islands
**HABITAT: moist forest, lakeshores and
riverbanks**
**SIZE: body: 87–107 cm (34¼–42 in)
tail: 27–32 cm (10½–12½ in)** Ⓥ

The babirusa has unusual upper tusks which grow upward through the muzzle and curve back toward the eyes. Only males have prominent lower tusks, and these are thought to be a sexual characteristic. Elusive animals, babirusas prefer dense cover near water and are fast runners and good swimmers, even in the sea. They move in small groups, the male doing most of the rooting and unearthing of food, while females and young trail behind, feeding on items such as roots, berries, tubers and leaves.

The female gives birth to 2 young after a gestation of 125 to 150 days.

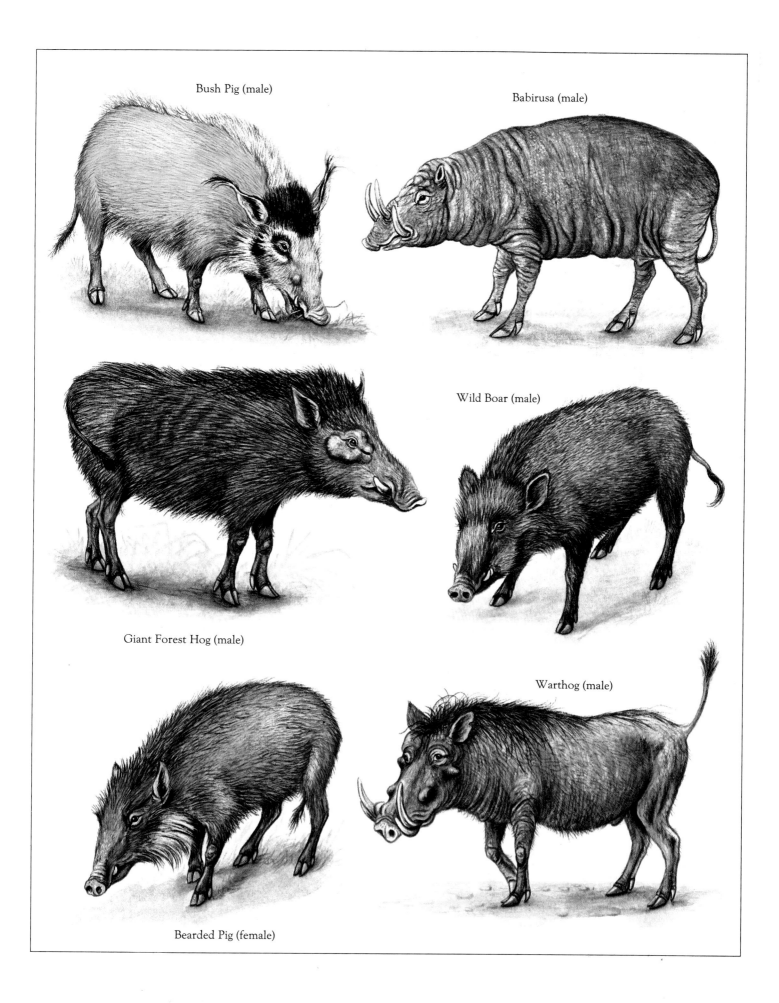

Bush Pig (male)

Babirusa (male)

Wild Boar (male)

Giant Forest Hog (male)

Warthog (male)

Bearded Pig (female)

Peccaries, Hippopotamuses

TAYASSUIDAE: Peccary Family

The 3 species of peccary occur only in the New World, from the southwestern USA to central Argentina. The New World equivalent of pigs in their habits, peccaries resemble pigs but are smaller and differ from them in a number of ways. First, they have only three toes on each hind foot (pigs have four); second, peccaries have a prominent musk gland on the back about 20 cm (7¾ in) in front of the tail; and third, their tusks are directed downward, not upward like those of pigs.

NAME: **Chaco Peccary, *Catagonus wagneri***
RANGE: Bolivia, Argentina, Paraguay
HABITAT: semiarid thorn scrub, grassland
SIZE: body: about 1 m (3¼ ft)
tail: 87 cm (34¼ in) (V)

Once thought to be extinct, the Chaco peccary is now believed to be reasonably abundant in areas where it is undisturbed, although the species as a whole is vulnerable. The animals have suffered from excessive hunting and from the loss of much of their thorn scrub habitat, which has been cleared for cattle ranching.

A long-tailed, long-legged animal, this species is active during the day and has better vision than other peccaries. It moves in small groups of up to 6 animals, among which there are strong social bonds, and feeds largely on cacti and the seeds of leguminous plants.

NAME: **White-lipped Peccary, *Tayassu pecari***
RANGE: Mexico, Central and South America to Paraguay
HABITAT: forest
SIZE: body: 95 cm–1 m (37½ in–3¼ ft)
tail: 2.5–5.5 cm (1–2¼ in)

The white-lipped peccary has a heavy body, slender legs and a long, mobile snout. A gregarious animal, it gathers in groups of 50 to 100 individuals of both sexes and all ages. Active in the cooler hours of the day, these peccaries are fast, agile runners, even on rugged ground. Using their sensitive snouts, they dig around on the forest floor, searching for plant material, such as bulbs and roots, and for small animals. Although their sight is poor and hearing only fair, these peccaries have such an acute sense of smell that they can locate bulbs underground by scent alone.

The female gives birth to a litter of 2 young after a gestation period of about 158 days.

NAME: **Collared Peccary, *Tayassu tajacu***
RANGE: S.W. USA, Mexico, Central and South America to Patagonia
HABITAT: semidesert, arid woodland, forest
SIZE: body: 75–90 cm (29½–35½ in)
tail: 1.5–3 cm (½–1¼ in)

Collared peccaries are robust, active animals, able to run fast and swim well. They live in groups of 5 to 15 individuals, and the musky secretions of the gland on each animal's back seem to play a part in maintaining the social bonds of the herd, as well as being used for marking territory. With their sensitive snouts, collared peccaries search the ground for roots, herbs, grass and fruit; they also eat insect larvae, worms and small vertebrates. In summer, they feed only in the morning and evening, but in winter they are active all day long, treading well-worn, regular paths through their home range. Hearing is the most acute of this peccary's senses.

Several males in a herd may mate with a female in heat, and there is rarely fighting or rivalry. After a gestation of 142 to 149 days, the female leaves the herd and gives birth to 2 or 3 young in a sheltered spot. The young are active soon after birth, and the mother returns to the herd with them within a couple of days.

HIPPOPOTAMIDAE: Hippopotamus Family

There are 2 species of hippopotamus, found only in Africa, although fossil evidence shows that the family was once more widely distributed in the southern parts of the Old World. Both species are amphibious, spending much of their lives in water, and they have various adaptations for this mode of life, including nostrils that can be closed and specialized skin glands that secrete an oily, pink substance which protects their virtually hairless bodies.

NAME: **Hippopotamus, *Hippopotamus amphibius***
RANGE: Africa, south of the Sahara to Namibia and South Africa: Transvaal
HABITAT: rivers or lakes in grassland
SIZE: body: (male) 3.2–4.2 m (10½–13¾ ft)
(female) 2.8–3.7 m (9¼–12 ft)
tail: 35–50 cm (13¾–19¾ in)

One of the giants of Africa, the hippopotamus has a bulky body and a massive head and mouth equipped with an impressive set of teeth; the canine teeth form tusks. Its legs are short and thick, and there are four webbed toes on each foot. When the hippopotamus is in water, it lies with much of its vast body submerged; often only the bulging eyes, ears and nostrils are visible. It swims and dives well and can walk along the river or lake bottom. Daytime hours are spent resting in water or on the shore; then, in the evening, the hippopotamus emerges to graze on land, taking short grass and other plants and fallen fruit. Hippopotamuses play a vital role in the ecology of inland waters, both by keeping down bankside vegetation and by excreting tons of fertilizing manure into the water, which encourages the growth of plankton and invertebrates and thus sustains the whole ecosystem.

Hippopotamuses are gregarious animals and live in groups of up to 15 or so, sometimes more, led by an old male. Males are aggressive and will fight for prime positions on the riverbank or for dominance of the group. To threaten or challenge a rival, the male opens his mouth in a huge, yawning gape and bellows. All adults are fierce in defense of their young.

Mating takes place in water at any time of year but is generally timed so that births coincide with the rains and, thus, the luxuriant growth of grass. A single young is born on land or in shallow water after a gestation of 233 to 240 days. The young is suckled for about a year, and females usually give birth every 18 months to 2 years.

NAME: **Pygmy Hippopotamus, *Choeropsis liberiensis***
RANGE: Guinea to Nigeria
HABITAT: rain forest, swamps and thickets near water
SIZE: body: 1.7–1.9 m (5½–6¼ ft)
tail: 15–21 cm (6–8¼ in) (V)

The pygmy hippopotamus is much less aquatic than its giant relative and has a proportionately smaller head and longer legs; only the front toes are webbed. It lives near water but stays on land for much of the time, feeding at night on leaves, swamp vegetation and fallen fruit and also on roots and tubers, which it digs up. Usually alone, except for breeding pairs or females with young, it occupies a territory, which it defends against rivals. When alarmed, the pigmy hippopotamus seeks refuge in dense cover or in water.

The female gives birth to a single young after a gestation of 180 to 210 days. The young stays with its mother for up to 3 years. Rare over almost all its range, the pygmy hippopotamus may have disappeared entirely from some areas. The population has suffered from excessive hunting, combined with the destruction of large areas of its forest habitat.

Collared Peccary

White-lipped Peccary

Hippopotamus

Pygmy Hippopotamus

Chaco Peccary

Camels

NAME: **Guanaco,** *Lama guanicoe*
RANGE: **South America: Peru to Patagonia**
HABITAT: **semidesert to about 5,000 m (16,500 ft)**
SIZE: **body: 1.2–1.7 m (4–5½ ft)**
tail: 25 cm (9¾ in)

The guanaco is a slender, long-limbed animal, capable of fast movement over rugged terrain and able to leap nimbly up mountain trails. Adaptable to heat or cold, it lives in open country and feeds on grass. Males are polygamous and lead harems of 4 to 10 females with their young, which they defend, fighting off any rivals or intruders that try to steal one of their females. Young males and males without harems also form herds.

The female gives birth every other year, producing a single young after a gestation of 10 or 11 months. The young guanaco is active soon after birth and is able to run with speed and grace.

Llamas and alpacas are domesticated forms of the guanaco and are bred as pack animals and fleece producers, respectively. They interbreed readily with one another and with wild guanacos.

NAME: **Vicuña,** *Vicugna vicugna*
RANGE: **South America: Peru to N. Chile**
HABITAT: **semiarid grassland at altitudes over 4,000 m (13,000 ft)**
SIZE: **body: 1.4–1.6 m (4½–5¼ ft)**
tail: 15 cm (6 in) Ⓥ

The vicuña's tawny-brown coat is thick and woolly and longest on the sides; it enables the animal to tolerate the cold, snow and ice of its mountain habitat. Gregarious animals, vicuñas live in groups of up to 15 females led by a male or in all-male herds. The harem band lives in a territory which is fiercely guarded by the adult male; at the first sign of any danger he alerts the females so that they can escape. Male troops consist mainly of young animals and do not have a specific territory but wander nomadically. Since most of the best grazing is appropriated by the territorial family males, these nomads are continually trespassing and being driven away. Rival males have a characteristic habit of spitting at each other as they fight. Vicuñas are fast, graceful animals, capable of maintaining speeds of 47 km/h (29 mph) over long distances, even at high altitudes. They feed on grass and small plants. Eyesight is their most acute sense; hearing is fair and sense of smell poor.

The female gives birth to 1 young after a gestation of 10 to 11 months. The young can stand and walk soon after birth and suckles for about 10 months. Vicuñas have long been killed for their fine wool and meat, but despite this, a few years ago the vulnerable population was said to be on the increase.

CAMELIDAE: Camel Family

The 4 surviving species in this formerly more diverse family are the most primitive of the ruminants, or cud-chewing animals. Of the 4, dromedaries and most of the bactrian camels are wholly domesticated. There are still wild bactrians in the Gobi Desert, and guanacos and vicuñas maintain wild populations in South America.

Camels and their relatives have highly specialized feet. They have evolved to the point of having only two toes on each foot, but the foot bones are expanded sideways to produce the support for two broad, flat pads on each foot, with a nail on the upper surface of each toe. This foot structure is particularly well developed in the camel species, and it enables them to walk on soft, sandy soil, where conventional hoofs would sink in deeply.

The head of a camelid is relatively small, with an elongate snout terminating in a cleft upper lip. Vegetation is cropped by using long, forward-pointing lower incisors that work against tough upper gums. Camelids have complex, three-chambered stomachs and ruminate, or chew the cud.

The humps of the 2 species of camel are fat stores which provide food reserves — vital in the unpredictable conditions of the camel's desert habitat.

NAME: **Bactrian Camel,** *Camelus ferus*
RANGE: **central Asia: China, Mongolia**
HABITAT: **desert, steppe**
SIZE: **body: about 3 m (9¾ ft)**
tail: about 53 cm (20¾ in) Ⓥ

The bactrian, or two-humped, camel has been domesticated but has not spread outside its native range to the extent that the dromedary has. Only a small number of bactrian camels lives wild in the Gobi Desert, and even these may be part domestic stock. It is thought, however, that Mongolian stocks may be slowly increasing.

Apart from its two humps, the main characteristic of the bactrian camel is its long, shaggy hair, which keeps it warm in winter but is shed in summer, leaving the body almost naked. Docile, slow-moving animals, these camels move with a rolling gait, which is the result of their ability to raise both legs on one side at the same time. They feed on virtually any vegetation, such as grass, the foliage of trees and bushes, and small plants.

After a gestation of 370 to 440 days, the female gives birth to 1 young, which is active within only 24 hours. It is suckled for about a year and fully grown when about 5 years old.

NAME: **Dromedary,** *Camelus dromedarius*
RANGE: **N. Africa, Middle East; introduced in Australia**
HABITAT: **semiarid and arid grassland, desert, plains**
SIZE: **body: 2.2–3.4 m (7¼–11 ft)**
tail: 50 cm (19¾ in)

The dromedary, or one-humped camel, now exists only as a domesticated animal, which it has been, so it is thought, since 4000 B.C. Before then it probably lived in North Africa and Arabia. Today there are two main types: a heavily built, slow-moving animal, used as a beast of burden, and a light, graceful, fast-running racer, used for riding. Both have short, coarse hair, longest on the crown, neck, throat and hump. Dromedaries feed on grass and any other available plants and can survive in areas of sparse, tough vegetation.

Certain adaptations fit the dromedary for life in hot, dry climates; the most significant of these is its ability to go for long periods without drinking, linked with its ability to conserve water in the body. Its hump is its most important specialization, for it gives protection from the sun by absorbing heat and carries fat stores, which are metabolized to provide energy and water. The camel does not store water in the hump but can do so in the stomach lining. The kidneys are able to concentrate urine, thus avoiding water loss, and moisture can be absorbed from fecal material. Moreover, the body temperature of the camel drops at night and rises so slowly during the day that the animal does not need to sweat for a long time to cool itself. During an extended period without water, the camel is able to lose up to 27 percent of its body weight without detrimental effect. This loss can be recovered in 10 minutes by drinking. In one experiment, a thirsty camel drank 104 litres (27 US gal) in a few minutes.

Females breed only every other year. After a gestation of 365 to 440 days, the female moves away from the herd to give birth to her single young. When it is able to walk, after a day or so, the mother rejoins the herd with her young. Although the calf is suckled for almost a year, it starts to nibble plants as soon as it is born and by 2 months old is regularly feeding on vegetation. Mother and young keep in touch by calling, the calf giving distress calls if it becomes separated from her.

Dromedary

Guanaco

Vicuña

Bactrian Camel

Chevrotains, Musk Deer, Deer

TRAGULIDAE: Chevrotain Family

There are 4 species of chevrotain, or mouse deer, found in tropical forest and mangrove swamps in Africa and Asia. They are tiny, delicate creatures which look like minute deer with mouselike heads but which are probably related to both camels and pigs. They stand only 20 to 35 cm (7¾ to 13¾ in) high at the shoulder and weigh only 2.3 to 4.6 kg (5 to 10¼ lb). Active at night, they feed largely on plants and fruit.

NAME: Water Chevrotain, *Hyemoschus aquaticus*
RANGE: Africa: Guinea to Cameroon, Zaire, Gabon, Central African Republic
HABITAT: forest, near water
SIZE: body: 75–85 cm (29½–33½ in)
tail: 10–15 cm (4–6 in)

About the size of a hare, with a hunched back, small head and short, slender legs, the water chevrotain has a variable pattern of white spots on its back and up to three white stripes along its flanks. It rests during the day in thick undergrowth or in a hole in a riverbank and emerges at night to forage for grass, leaves and fruit, as well as some insects, crabs, fish, worms and small mammals. Water chevrotains are solitary except in the breeding season, each individual occupying its own territory. Chevrotains always live near water and are good swimmers; if danger threatens, they often escape by diving underwater.

At breeding time, the male simply finds the female by scent, and they mate without aggression. The female gives birth to 1 young after a gestation of about 4 months. The young is suckled for 8 months but takes some solid food at 2 weeks old.

NAME: Lesser Malay Chevrotain, *Tragulus javanicus*
RANGE: S.E. Asia, Indonesia
HABITAT: lowland forest, usually near water
SIZE: body: 40–47 cm (15¾–18½ in)
tail: 5–8 cm (2–3¼ in)

The tiny, deerlike lesser Malay chevrotain has a robust body on extremely slender legs. It has no horns, but in males, the canine teeth in the upper jaw are enlarged into tusks. A nocturnal creature, it inhabits the dense undergrowth, making little tunnel-like trails through which it moves; it feeds on grass, leaves, fallen fruit and berries. It lives alone except when breeding.

The female gives birth to 1 young after a gestation of about 5 months.

MOSCHIDAE: Musk Deer Family

The 3 species of musk deer, all in the genus *Moschus*, occur in central and northeastern Asia. Sometimes classified with the chevrotains or with the true deer, musk deer are in several respects intermediate between these two groups. They stand about 50 to 60 cm (19¾ to 23½ in) high at the shoulder and have no horns, but they do possess large tusks, formed from the upper canine teeth. The name musk deer comes from the waxy secretions produced by a gland on the abdomen of the male.

NAME: Forest Musk Deer, *Moschus chrysogaster*
RANGE: Himalayas to central China
HABITAT: forest, brushland at 2,600–3,600 m (8,500–11,800 ft)
SIZE: body: about 1 m (3¼ ft)
tail: 4–5 cm (1½–2 in)

Long, thick, bristly hairs cover the body of the forest musk deer and help protect the animal from the often harsh weather conditions of its habitat. Male and female look more or less alike, but the male has larger tusks, developed from the upper canine teeth, and a gland on the abdomen which secretes musk in the breeding season. Only mature males have these glands. Usually solitary, musk deer may occasionally gather in groups of up to 3. They are active in the morning and evening, feeding on grass, moss and shoots in summer and lichens, twigs and buds in winter.

At the onset of the breeding season, males fight to establish dominance and thus access to the largest number of females. They wrestle with their necks, trying to push one another to the ground, and may inflict deep wounds with their tusks. The female gives birth to a single young.

CERVIDAE: Deer Family

There are about 34 species of true deer, distributed over North and South America, Europe, northwest Africa and Asia. Found in habitats ranging from the Arctic to the tropics, deer are slim, long-legged, elegant herbivores. Their most obvious characteristic is the pair of antlers, possessed by males of all species except the Chinese water deer. Most deer shed and regrow their antlers in an annual cycle, shedding them in late winter or early spring and growing them in summer, before the autumn rutting contests for dominance. The cycle is primarily under hormonal control and is influenced by changes in the length of daylight

NAME: Chinese Water Deer, *Hydropotes inermis*
RANGE: China, Korea; introduced in England
HABITAT: riverbanks with reedbeds and rushes, grassland, fields
SIZE: body: 77.5 cm–1 m (30½ in–3¼ ft)
tail: 6–7.5 cm (2¼–3 in)

The only true deer to lack antlers in the male, the Chinese water deer has tusks, formed from enlarged upper canine teeth; these are larger in males than in females. Both male and female have small scent glands on each side of the groin and are the only deer to possess such glands. A nocturnal animal, this deer usually lives alone or in pairs and rarely gathers in herds. It feeds on reeds, coarse grass and other vegetation.

Males contest in fierce fights for dominance, in the rutting season before breeding. After a gestation of about 6 months, the female gives birth to 4 young — this is the largest litter produced by any deer.

NAME: Chinese Muntjac, *Muntiacus reevesi*
RANGE: S.E. China, Taiwan; introduced in England and France
HABITAT: dense vegetation, hillsides; parkland in introduced range
SIZE: body: 80 cm–1 m (31½ in–3¼ ft)
tail: 11–18 cm (4¼–7 in)

The antlers of the male Chinese muntjac are small, rarely exceeding 15 cm (6 in) in length, but this deer also has tusks, formed from the upper canine teeth; females have smaller tusks than males. The Chinese muntjac lives in a territory, which it rarely leaves, and prefers to stay under cover of vegetation. It lives alone or in pairs and seldom forms herds. Primarily nocturnal, it may be active in the morning in quiet, undisturbed areas. It feeds on grass, low-growing leaves and shoots.

In dominance contests, males fight with their tusks, rather than their antlers, and make doglike barking noises. The female usually gives birth to 1 young after a gestation of about 6 months.

NAME: Tufted Deer, *Elaphodus cephalophus*
RANGE: S. China, N. Burma
HABITAT: dense undergrowth, near water
SIZE: body: about 1.6 m (5¼ ft)
tail: 7–12 cm (2¾–4¾ in)

The male tufted deer is characterized by the tuft of hair on the forehead at the base of the antlers; the antlers themselves are short and often almost hidden by the tuft. A nocturnal, normally solitary deer, this species feeds on grass and other plant material.

The female gives birth to 1 young after a gestation of about 6 months.

Forest Musk Deer
(male)

Water Chevrotain

Chinese Water Deer
(male)

Lesser Malay Chevrotain

Tufted Deer
(male)

Chinese Muntjac

Deer

NAME: Père David's Deer, *Elaphurus davidianus*
RANGE: originally China; now in wildlife parks and reintroduced in China
HABITAT: wildlife parks
SIZE: body: 1.5 m (5 ft)
  tail: 50 cm (19¾ in)

This interesting deer became extinct in the wild in about 1920. However, at the beginning of this century, some of the few remaining specimens left in China were brought to England to live on the grounds of Woburn Abbey, in Bedfordshire, where they have thrived. Populations of Père David's deer can now be found in zoos and parks around the world, and they have been reintroduced in China.

Père David's deer has a mane of thick hair around its neck and throat and a rather longer tail than most deer. One tine of each antler usually points backward, while the other points upward and forks. Although they feed mainly on grass, the deer supplement their diet with aquatic plants. For most of the year they live in herds led by a dominant male, but the male lives alone for 2 months before and 2 months after the rutting season.

During the rutting season, the male fights rivals to gain or retain dominance over a harem. Females give birth to 1 or 2 young after a gestation of about 250 days.

NAME: White-tailed Deer, *Odocoileus virginianus*
RANGE: S. Canada, USA, Central and South America to Peru and Brazil
HABITAT: forest, swamps, open brushland
SIZE: body: 1.5–2 m (5–6½ ft)
  tail: up to 28 cm (11 in)

One of the most adaptable animals in the world, the white-tailed deer is found from near-arctic regions to the tropics. Its adaptability is reflected in its feeding habits: it browses and grazes on many kinds of grasses, weeds, shrubs, twigs, fungi, nuts and lichens. A slender, sprightly creature, the white-tailed deer has a long tail, white on its underside, a white band across its nose and a white patch on the throat. White-tailed deer are shy, elusive animals and do not usually congregate in large herds; in severe winter weather, however, they may congregate in a group in a sheltered spot out of the wind.

It is not certain whether or not males are polygamous, but in the breeding season, they engage in savage battles over mates. The gestation period is 6½ to 7 months; young females usually produce only a single offspring, but older females may have litters of 2 or 3. Young are able to walk immediately and are suckled for about 4 months.

NAME: Moose, *Alces alces*
RANGE: N. Europe and Asia: Scandinavia to Siberia; Alaska, Canada, N. USA; introduced in New Zealand
HABITAT: coniferous forest, often near lakes and rivers
SIZE: body: 2.5–3 m (8¼–9¾ ft)
  tail: 5–7.5 cm (2–3 in)

The largest of the deer, the moose is identified by its size, its broad, overhanging muzzle and the flap of skin, known as the bell, hanging from its throat. The massive antlers of the male are flattened and palmate, with numerous small branches. The moose is less gregarious than other deer and is usually alone outside the breeding season. In winter, it feeds on woody plants, but in summer, water plants provide the bulk of its food. It wades into water to feed and swims well.

Bellowing males display to attract females, and they engage in fierce contests with rivals. Following an 8-month gestation, the female gives birth to a single calf, very rarely to twins. The calf is suckled for about 6 months but stays with its mother for a year.

NAME: Caribou/Reindeer, *Rangifer tarandus*
RANGE: N. Europe and Asia: Scandinavia to Siberia; Alaska, Canada, Greenland
HABITAT: tundra
SIZE: body: 1.2–2.2 m (4–7¼ ft)
  tail: 10–21 cm (4–8¼ in)

Once divided into several species, all caribou and reindeer, including the domesticated reindeer, are now considered races of a single species. The races vary in coloration from almost black to brown, gray and almost white. The caribou is the only deer in which both sexes have antlers, although those of the female are smaller. The antlers are unique in that the lowest, forward-pointing tine is itself branched. Females are gregarious and gather in herds with their young, but adult males are often solitary. Some populations migrate hundreds of miles between their breeding grounds on the tundra and winter feeding grounds farther south. Grass and other tundra plants are their main food in summer, but in winter caribou feed mainly on lichens, scraping away the snow with their hoofs to expose the plants.

In autumn, males fight to gather harems of 5 to 40 or so females. The female produces 1, occasionally 2, young after a gestation of about 240 days. Young caribou are able to run with the herd within a few hours of birth.

NAME: Wapiti, *Cervus canadensis* **(conspecific with** *C. elaphus*)
RANGE: W. Europe, N.W. Africa, Asia to W. China, N.W. America; introduced in New Zealand
HABITAT: open deciduous woodland, mountains, plains, moorland
SIZE: body: 1.6–2.5 m (5¼–8¼ ft)
  tail: 12–15 cm (4¾–6 in)

Known as the wapiti in North America and the red deer in Britain, this deer is reddish-brown in summer but grayish-brown in winter. Most older males have antlers with two forward-pointing tines near the base, while young males usually have one tine. In autumn and winter, the male has a mane of longer hair on the neck. A gregarious species, wapiti live in herds and are active in the morning and late afternoon or evening, feeding on grass, heather, leaves and buds.

In the autumn, males take part in fierce, antler-clashing fights in order to obtain territories and harems. They defend their females throughout the breeding season and then return to all-male herds in the winter. Females give birth to 1 calf, rarely 2, after a gestation of about 8 months. The young deer is able to walk a few minutes after birth.

NAME: Roe Deer, *Capreolus capreolus*
RANGE: Europe and Asia: Britain to S.E. Siberia, S. China
HABITAT: woodland
SIZE: body: 95 cm–1.3 m (37½ in–4¼ ft)
  tail: 2–4 cm (¾–1½ in)

The smallest of the native European deer, the roe deer is unique in having almost no tail. It has a pale rump, and the rest of its coat is reddish-brown in summer and grayish-brown in winter; fawns are spotted. The antlers of the male never have more than three points apiece. These shy, graceful deer are generally solitary, except in the breeding season, but may gather in small groups in the winter. Active at night, they browse on shrubs and broad-leaved trees.

In the breeding season, the male takes a territory and marks its boundaries by rubbing the trunks of trees with his antlers until the bark is frayed and the wood exposed. He has only 1 mate and defends her and his territory against rivals. The period until birth is 9 or 10 months, which is much longer than that of most deer and includes a period of delayed implantation — once the egg is fertilized, it lies dormant in the uterus for about 4½ months before true gestation begins. This ensures that both mating and birth take place at the optimum time. Before giving birth to her 1 or 2 young, the female roe deer chases away her offspring of the previous year.

Moose (male)

Wapiti (male)

White-tailed Deer
(male)

Caribou (male)

Roe Deer (male)

Père David's Deer (male)

Deer, Giraffes, Pronghorn

NAME: **Pampas Deer,** *Ozotoceros bezoarticus*
RANGE: **South America: Brazil, Paraguay, Uruguay, N. Argentina**
HABITAT: **grassland, open plains**
SIZE: **body: 1.1–1.3 m (3½–4¼ ft)**
    tail: 10–15 cm (4–6 in)   Ⓔ

The slender, long-legged pampas deer once lived only among tall pampas grass, but now that much of this land has been turned over to grain, the deer may frequent even wooded country. As with most deer, only the male has antlers; the front prong of these is not divided, while the hind portion branches once or twice. Males also have glands in the feet which give off a strong garlicky smell, noticeable more than 1 km (0.6 mi) away. In winter, pampas deer live alone or in pairs, but in spring they may form larger groups. They rest in cover during the day and emerge in the evening to feed on grass. Some races of this deer are now extremely rare due to uncontrolled hunting and the loss of their habitat to agriculture.

Unlike most deer, the male pampas deer stays with the female after her single offspring is born and helps her to guard it from predators.

NAME: **Northern Pudu,** *Pudu mephistophiles*
RANGE: **South America: Colombia to N. Peru**
HABITAT: **forest, swampy savanna at 2,000–4,000 m (6,600–13,000 ft)**
SIZE: **body: 65 cm (25½ in)**
    tail: 2.5–3.5 cm (1–1¼ in)   Ⓘ

The smallest of the native New World deer, the northern pudu has short, delicate legs, a rounded back and small, simple antlers. Its dark-brown hair is thick and dense. It is a shy, inconspicuous creature, and little is known of its habits as its high, remote habitat has made it hard to observe. It is thought to live in small groups or alone and to feed on leaves, shoots and fruit.

Females produce a single young, sometimes twins, normally between November and January.

GIRAFFIDAE: Giraffe Family
The giraffe family is an interesting and specialized offshoot of the deer family. It appears to have originated in the Old World and is now reduced to only 2 species: the giraffe itself and the okapi, both found in Africa.

Both animals have unique, skin-covered, blunt horns, which are never shed. The giraffe has an extraordinarily elongate neck and legs, which make it the tallest terrestrial animal.

NAME: **Giraffe,** *Giraffa camelopardalis*
RANGE: **Africa, south of the Sahara**
HABITAT: **savanna**
SIZE: **body: 3–4 m (9¾–13 ft)**
    tail: 90 cm–1.1 m (35½ in–3½ ft)

The giraffe, with its long legs and its amazingly long neck, when erect stands up to 3.3 m (11 ft) at the shoulder and nearly 6 m (19½ ft) at the crown. Its characteristic coloration of a light body and irregular dark spots is very variable, both geographically and between individuals; some animals may be almost white or black, or even unspotted. Both male and female have skin-covered horns, one pair on the forehead and sometimes a smaller pair farther back, on the crown. Some animals have yet another small horn, or bump, between these pairs. The tail ends in a tuft of long hairs.

Gregarious animals, giraffes usually live in troops of up to 6, sometimes 12, and may occasionally gather in larger herds. A troop consists of females and their offspring, led by a male. Males fight for possession of females, wrestling with their heads and necks. The troop ambles around its territory, feeding mostly in the early morning and afternoon on the foliage, buds and fruits on the top of acacia and thorn trees. The giraffes may also eat grass, plants and grain crops. At midday, giraffes rest in shade and at night lie down for a couple of hours or rest standing.

Females give birth to a single offspring, rarely twins, after a gestation of over a year — usually 400 to 468 days. Births invariably occur at first light. The young is suckled for 6 to 12 months and continues to grow for 10 years.

NAME: **Okapi,** *Okapia johnstoni*
RANGE: **Zaire**
HABITAT: **rain forest**
SIZE: **body: 1.2–2 m (4–6½ ft)**
    tail: 30–42 cm (11¾–16½ in)

An inhabitant of dense forest, the okapi, although long hunted by the local Pygmy tribes, was only made known to the outside world in 1901, when it was discovered by the then governor of Uganda. He thought it was related to the zebra because of its stripes, but, in fact, it bears a remarkable resemblance to primitive ancestors of the giraffe, known only from fossils. The okapi has a compact body, which slopes down toward the hindquarters, and distinctive stripes on its legs. Only males possess short, skin-covered horns, similar to those of the giraffe. The tongue is so long that the okapi can use it to clean its own eyes and eyelids.

Okapis live alone, each in its own home range, and meet only in the breeding season. They feed on leaves, buds and shoots of trees, which they can reach with their long tongues, and on grass, ferns, fruit, fungi and manioc.

Pairing usually takes place between May and June or November and December but may occur at any time. The female gives birth to 1 young after a gestation of 421 to 457 days. The young okapi suckles for up to 10 months and is not fully developed until 4 or 5 years of age.

ANTILOCAPRIDAE: Pronghorn Family
The North American pronghorn, found in Canada, USA and northern Mexico, is the sole living representative of a New World group of antelopelike ruminants. There is also, however, a body of opinion that suggests this animal should be included in the family Bovidae, but it is kept apart on account of its curious horn structure.

NAME: **Pronghorn,** *Antilocapra americana*
RANGE: **central Canada, W. USA, Mexico**
HABITAT: **open prairie, desert**
SIZE: **body: 1–1.5 m (3¼–5 ft)**
    tail: 7.5–10 cm (3–4 in)   Ⓔ

Both male and female pronghorns have true, bony horns, although those of females are small and inconspicuous. The horns are covered with sheaths of specialized, fused hairs, and pronghorns are unique in that these sheaths are shed annually. The small, forward-pointing branch on each horn, the prong, is in fact part of this sheath.

One of the fastest running mammals in North America, the pronghorn can achieve speeds of up to 65 km/h (40 mph). It is also a good swimmer. In summer, it moves in small, scattered groups but congregates in larger herds of up to 100 animals in winter. Pronghorns are active during the day but feed mostly in the morning and evening, taking grasses, weeds and shrubs such as sagebrush. White hairs on the pronghorn's rump become erect if the animal is alarmed and act as a warning signal to other pronghorns.

Some males collect harems, fighting rival males for the privilege. The female gives birth to her young after a gestation of 230 to 240 days; there is usually only 1 in a female's first litter, but in subsequent years, she produces 2, or even 3, young. Only 4 days after birth, pronghorns can outrun humans.

Pronghorns are now rare due to overhunting, competition for food from domestic livestock and the destruction of their natural habitat.

Northern Pudu (male)

Okapi (male)

Pronghorn (male)

Giraffe

Pampas Deer (male)

Bovids

NAME: **Greater Kudu**, *Tragelaphus strepsiceros*
RANGE: **Africa: Lake Chad to Eritrea, Tanzania; Zambia to Angola and South Africa; introduced in N. Mexico**
HABITAT: **thick acacia bush; rocky, hilly country; dry riverbeds, near water.**
SIZE: **body: 1.8–2.45 m (6–8 ft)**
tail: 35–55 cm (13¾–21½ in)

The most elegant of antelope, the greater kudu is large and slender. The male has long horns, which spread widely in two to three open spirals; the female occasionally has small horns. When running, the bull lays his horns flat along his back. Over the kudu's wide range, there are variations in coloration and the number of stripes on the sides. Kudu are browsers, feeding early and late on leaves, shoots and seeds and, in dry areas, wild melons. They also make night raids on cultivated fields and can jump over a 2 m (6½ ft) fence. Their hearing and sense of smell are good, although their sight seems poor.

Kudu live mostly in small herds of 6 to 12 females with young, sometimes with 1 or 2 older bulls. Otherwise males are solitary or form bachelor herds. After a gestation of about 7 months, the female produces 1 calf, which suckles for about 6 months.

NAME: **Eland**, *Tragelaphus oryx*
RANGE: **Africa: Ethiopia, E. Africa to Angola and South Africa; mostly in game parks in Namibia, N. Cape Province, Natal, Mozambique**
HABITAT: **open plains, savanna, mopani bush, montane forest to 4,500 m (14,750 ft), semidesert**
SIZE: **body: 2.1–3.5 m (6¾–11½ ft)**
tail: 50–90 cm (19¾–35½ in)

The size of an ox, the eland is the largest of the antelopes, and a fully grown bull may weigh as much as 900 kg (2,000 lb). The cow is smaller and more slightly built, with lighter horns and no mat of hair on the forehead. Eland live in troops of 6 to 24 animals and are always on the move, depending on the availability of food and water. In times of drought, they wander widely and form large herds. Old solitary bulls are common; young bulls form single-sex troops. Eland are browsers, feeding in the morning and at dusk, and even on moonlit nights, on leaves, shoots, melons, tubers, bulbs, onions and thick-leaved plants. They have a good sense of smell and eyesight and will move upwind of danger.

There is usually 1 calf, born after a gestation of 8½ to 9 months; it lies hidden for a week, then follows the female, who suckles it for about 6 months.

BOVIDAE: Bovid Family

This biologically and economically important family of herbivorous ungulates contains about 123 species, of which domesticated cattle, sheep and goats must be the best-known members. The family probably originated in Eurasia and moved only recently to North America; it is absent from South America and most diverse in Africa.

Over their wide range, bovids utilize almost all types of habitat, from grassland, desert and tundra to dense forest. Coupled with this diversity of habitat is great diversity of body form and size, and bovids range between buffaloes and tiny antelope. There are, however, common features within the group. Fore and hind toes are reduced to split, or artiodactyl (even-toed), hoofs, based on digits 3 and 4. There is a complex four-chambered stomach in which vegetable food is degraded by microorganism symbiosis. As part of this digestive system, bovids chew the cud, bringing up food from the first stomach and rechewing it. Normally both male and female have defensive hollow horns, which are larger in the male.

NAME: **Bongo**, *Tragelaphus euryceros*
RANGE: **Africa: Sierra Leone to Sudan (not Nigeria), Kenya, Tanzania**
HABITAT: **forest, bush, bamboo jungle**
SIZE: **body: 1.7–2.5 m (5½–8¼ ft)**
tail: 45–65 cm (17¾–25½ in)

The adult male bongo is the largest of the forest-dwelling antelopes and may weigh up to 227 kg (500 lb); the chestnut-colored coat darkens with age in the male. Both sexes have narrow, lyre-shaped horns, which they lay along their slightly humped backs when running, to prevent them from catching in branches. Shy animals, bongos rest in dense cover during the day, browsing at dawn and dusk on leaves, shoots, bark, rotten wood and fruit; they also dig for roots with their horns. At night they will venture into clearings and plantations to feed on grass.

They live in pairs or small groups of females and young with a single male; old males are solitary. One young is born after a gestation of 9½ months.

NAME: **Nyala**, *Tragelaphus angasi*
RANGE: **Africa: Malawi to South Africa: Natal**
HABITAT: **dense lowland forest, thickets in savanna, near water**
SIZE: **body: 1.35–2 m (4½–6½ ft)**
tail: 40–55 cm (15¾–21½ in)

These antelope live in the densest cover, emerging only at dusk and dawn. The males are large and slenderly built, with big ears and shaggy coats. Females and juveniles are reddish-brown and lack the long fringe of hair underneath the body, the horns and the white facial chevron that distinguish the male; females are much smaller than males. Nyala live in parties of 8 to 16 cows and young, alone or with one or more bulls. Solitary bulls and parties of bulls are also found, and toward the end of the dry season, herds of up to 50 animals may form. They browse on leaves, shoots, bark and fruit of trees, standing on their hind legs to reach high leaves. They also eat new, tender grass.

The single young is born after a gestation of 8½ months; females mate again a week after the birth.

NAME: **Nilgai**, *Boselaphus tragocamelus*
RANGE: **peninsular India (not Sri Lanka)**
HABITAT: **forest, low jungle**
SIZE: **body: 2–2.1 m (6½–6¾ ft)**
tail: 46–54 cm (18–21¼ in)

The nilgai is the only member of its genus and is the largest antelope native to India. It has slightly longer front legs than hind ones and a long, pointed head. The male has short horns and a tuft of hair on the throat; both sexes have short wiry coats, reddish-brown in the male and lighter in the female. Females and calves live in herds; males are usually solitary or form small parties. Nilgai are browsers but also like fruit and can do considerable damage to sugarcane crops.

Females commonly produce 2 calves after a gestation of about 9 months and mate again immediately after calving. Bulls fight each other on their knees for available females.

NAME: **Four-horned Antelope**, *Tetracerus quadricornis*
RANGE: **peninsular India (not Sri Lanka)**
HABITAT: **open forest**
SIZE: **body: 1 m (3¼ ft)**
tail: 12.5 cm (5 in)

This little antelope is the only one in its genus. The male is unique among Bovidae in having two pairs of short, unringed, conical horns: the back pair 8 to 10 cm (3¼ to 4 in) long, the front pair 2.5 to 4 cm (1 to 1½ in) long; the latter may be merely black, hairless skin. These are not gregarious antelope — normally only two are found together, or a female with her young. They graze on grasses and plants and drink often, running for cover at the least hint of danger with a peculiar, jerky motion.

Four-horned antelope mate during the rainy season and usually produce 1 to 3 young after a gestation of about 6 months.

Bongo

Nyala (male)

Nilgai (male)

Four-horned Antelope
(male)

Greater Kudu (male)

Eland (male)

Bovids

NAME: Gaur, *Bos gaurus*
RANGE: India, S.E. Asia
HABITAT: hill forest
SIZE: body: 2–2.5 m (6½–8¼ ft)
　　tail: 60–80 cm (23½–31½ in) Ⓥ

Once common in hilly, forested areas throughout their range, gaur now only occur in scattered herds in remote areas and in parks and reserves. Gaur are legally protected, but this is hard to enforce except in reserves, and the population is still threatened.

The gaur is a strong, heavily built animal, with a massive head, thick horns and a prominent muscular ridge on its shoulders that slopes down to the middle of its back. Females are smaller than males and have shorter, lighter horns. Gaur range in color from reddish to dark brown or almost black, with white hair on the lower half of the legs. In small herds of up to 12 animals, they take shelter in the shade and seclusion of forest in the heat of the day and at night, but they venture into the open to feed in the early morning and late afternoon, when they graze and also sometimes browse on the leaves and bark of trees.

During the breeding season, the timing of which varies from area to area, bulls roam through the forest searching for females in heat. When a male finds a mate, he defends her from other males. The female moves slightly away from the herd to give birth to her offspring in a safe, secluded spot; they rejoin the herd a few days later.

NAME: Banteng, *Bos javanicus*
RANGE: Bali, Burma to Java, Borneo
HABITAT: forested, hilly country to 2,000 m (6,600 ft)
SIZE: body: 2 m (6½ ft)
　　tail: 85 cm (33½ in) Ⓥ

The banteng is blue-black, with white stockings and rump, and is quite cow-like in its appearance; females and young are a bright reddish-brown. Bulls may reach 1.5 m (5 ft) at the shoulder, and they have a hairless shield on the crown between the horns. Wary and shy, bantengs are found in thickly forested areas where there are glades and clearings in which they can graze during the night. In the monsoon season, they move up the mountains and browse on bamboo shoots.

Gregarious animals, bantengs live in herds of 10 to 30 animals, although occasionally large bulls may become solitary. They mate during the dry season, and females produce 1 or 2 calves after a gestation of 9½ to 10 months. Small populations of two subspecies are known: *B. j. biarmicus* in Burma, Thailand and parts of Indo-China; and *B. j. lowi* in Borneo.

NAME: Water Buffalo, *Bubalus arnee*
RANGE: India, S.E. Asia; introduced in Europe, Africa, Philippines, Japan, Hawaii, Central and South America, Australia
HABITAT: dense growth, reed grass in wet areas
SIZE: body: 2.5–3 m (8¼–9¾ ft)
　　tail: 60 cm–1 m (23½ in–3¼ ft)

A large, thickset, clumsy creature, with huge splayed hoofs, the water buffalo stands 1.5 to 1.8 m (5 to 6 ft) at the shoulder. It has a long, narrow face, and the span of its flattened, crescent-shaped horns is the largest of all bovids — they can measure as much as 1.2 m (4 ft) along the outer edge. Its bulky body is sparsely covered with quite long, coarse, blackish hair, and there is a tuft of coarse hair in the middle of the forehead. Water buffaloes feed early and late in the day and at night on the lush grass and vegetation that grows near and in lakes and rivers. When not feeding, they spend much of their time submerged, with only their muzzles showing above water, or wallowing in mud, which, when dried and caked, gives them some protection from the insects that plague them.

Water buffaloes are gregarious and live in herds of various sizes. In the breeding season, males detach a few cows from the main herd and form their own harems. Each cow produces 1 or 2 calves after a gestation of 10 months; calves suckle for almost a year. Water buffaloes live for about 18 years.

Tame and docile, these animals have been domesticated and used as beasts of burden in India and Southeast Asia since about 3000 B.C. They also yield milk of good quality and their hides make excellent leather. It is estimated that the domestic population in India and Southeast Asia alone is now at least 75 million, and water buffaloes have been widely introduced in countries where conditions are suitable. Some of these introduced populations have become feral, as in Australia. Truly wild stocks number no more than 2,000.

NAME: Anoa, *Bubalus depressicornis*
RANGE: Sulawesi
HABITAT: lowland forest
SIZE: body: 1.6–1.7 m (5¼–5½ ft)
　　tail: 18–31 cm (7–12¼ in) Ⓔ

The anoa is the smallest of the buffaloes, an adult male standing only 69 to 106 cm (27 to 42 in) at the shoulder. However, it is stockily built, with a thick neck and short, heavy horns, which are at most 38 cm (15 in) long. Although wary, the anoa is aggressive when cornered. Juveniles have thick, woolly, yellow-brown hair, which becomes dark brown or blackish, blotched with white, in adults; old animals may have almost bare skins. Perhaps because of this, anoas appear to enjoy bathing and wallowing in mud. They feed alone during the morning, mainly on water plants and young cane shoots, then spend the rest of the day lying in the shade, generally in pairs. They only form herds just before the females are due to calve. Usually 1 young is born after a gestation of 9½ to 10 months.

When unmolested, anoas have a life span of 20 to 25 years, but destruction of their normal habitat has driven them into inaccessible, swampy forest, and their survival is further threatened by unrelenting hunting, for their horns, meat and thick hides.

NAME: Yak, *Bos mutus*
RANGE: W. China, Tibetan plateau, N. India, Kashmir
HABITAT: desolate mountain country to 6,100 m (20,000 ft)
SIZE: body: up to 3.25 m (10½ ft) (male)
　　tail: 50–80 cm (19¾–31½ in) Ⓔ

Originally these massive animals were found throughout their range, but centuries of hunting and persecution have forced them to retreat into areas of mountain tundra and ice desert, and now they cannot live in warm, lowland areas. Sturdy and sure-footed and covered with long, blackish-brown hairs, which form a fringe reaching almost to the ground, they are, however, well equipped to cope with the rigors of terrain and climate in their habitat. Males may stand up to 2 m (6½ ft) at the shoulder; females are smaller and weigh only about one-third as much as males. Both have heavy, forward-curving horns, which they use for defense; when threatened, they form a phalanx, facing outward with horns lowered, with the calves encircled for protection.

Yaks feed morning and evening on whatever vegetation they can find, spending the rest of the time relaxing and chewing the cud. They are usually found in large groups consisting of females and young with a single bull; bachelor bulls roam in groups of 2 or 3. The female produces 1 calf in the autumn, after a gestation of 9½ to 10 months.

Wild yaks are an endangered species. Domesticated yaks, however, have been used for centuries in Tibet as draft and pack animals. They also provide milk, meat, hair and wool for cloth, and hides. Domestic yaks are usually about half the size of wild ones and are often without horns. Their coats are redder, mottled with brown, black and sometimes white.

Banteng (male)

Anoa (male)

Gaur (male)

Water Buffalo
(male)

Yak (male)

Bovids

NAME: **Bison**, *Bison bison*
RANGE: **N. America**
HABITAT: **prairie, open woodland**
SIZE: **body: 2.1–3.5 m (6¾–11½ ft)**
   tail: 50–60 cm (19¾–23½ in)

Although there were once millions of bison roaming the North American grasslands, wholesale slaughter by the early European settlers brought them almost to extinction by the beginning of the twentieth century. Since then, due largely to the efforts of the American Bison Society, herds have steadily been built up in reserves, where they live in a semiwild state, and it is estimated that there are now some 20,000 animals. The male may be as much as 2.9 m (9½ ft) at the shoulders, which are humped and covered with the shaggy, brownish-black fur that also grows thickly on the head, neck and forelegs. The female looks similar to the male but is smaller; young are more reddish-brown. Both sexes have short, sharp horns.

Primarily grazers, bison live in herds that vary from a family group to several thousand; huge numbers formerly made seasonal migrations in search of better pasture. They feed morning and evening, and during the day, they rest, chewing the cud or wallowing in mud or dust to rid themselves of parasites.

During the mating season, bulls fight for cows, which give birth to a single calf, away from the herd, after a gestation of 9 months. Within an hour or two, mother and calf rejoin the herd. The calf is suckled for about a year and remains with its mother until it reaches sexual maturity at about 3 years old.

NAME: **European Bison/Wisent**, *Bison bonasus*
RANGE: **Poland, USSR**
HABITAT: **open woodland, forest**
SIZE: **body: 2.1–3.5 m (6¾–11½ ft)**
   tail: 50–60 cm (19¾–23½ in)

Like its American counterpart, the European bison, which was formerly found throughout Europe, has been reduced to semiwild herds in reserves: three in Poland and eleven in USSR, with the largest in the Białowieża Forest on the border between the two countries. The drop in numbers has been caused by the almost total eradication of forests, for these bison are browsers, living mainly on leaves, ferns, twigs, bark and, in autumn, almost exclusively on acorns.

The European bison closely resembles the American, but is less heavily built, with longer hind legs. It has scantier, shorter hair on the front of the body and head, and the horns, too, are lighter and much longer, reaching as much as 51 cm (20 in) in the male. The female produces a single calf after a gestation of 9 months.

NAME: **African Buffalo**, *Synceros caffer*
RANGE: **Africa, south of the Sahara**
HABITAT: **varied, always near water**
SIZE: **body: 2.1–3 m (6¾–9¾ ft)**
   tail: 75 cm–1.1 m (29½ in–3½ ft)

There are 2 subspecies of African buffalo: the smaller, reddish, forest-dwelling buffalo, *S. c. nanus*, and *S. c. caffer*, described here, which lives in savanna and open country. This powerfully built animal has a huge head with a broad, moist muzzle, large drooping ears and heavy horns, the bases of which may meet across the forehead. An aggressive animal and a formidable fighter, it is extremely dangerous to hunt, since it may charge without provocation or, if wounded, wait in thick bush and attack a pursuing hunter. Apart from man, its enemies are the lion and occasionally the crocodile, both of which usually succeed in killing only young or sick animals.

African buffaloes have adapted to live in a variety of conditions, from forest to semidesert, wherever there is adequate grazing and plenty of water, for they drink morning and evening and enjoy lying in water and wallowing in mud. They feed mainly at night, on grass, bushes and leaves, resting in dense cover during the day. Although their eyesight and hearing are poor, they have a strongly developed sense of smell. Buffaloes are gregarious, living in herds which range from a dozen or so to several hundred animals, often led by an old female but dominated by a mature bull. Old bulls are ousted from the herd and live alone in groups of 2 to 5.

Although normally silent, buffaloes bellow and grunt during the mating season, which varies throughout the range and appears to be related to climate. A single calf is born after a gestation of 11 months; it is covered with long, blackish-brown hair, most of which is lost as it matures. African buffaloes live for about 16 years.

NAME: **Bay Duiker**, *Cephalophus dorsalis*
RANGE: **Africa: Sierra Leone to E. Zaire and N. Angola**
HABITAT: **thick forest and jungle**
SIZE: **body: 70 cm–1 m (27½ in–3¼ ft)**
   tail: 8–15 cm (3–6 in)

The subfamily Cephalophinae contains two groups: the forest duikers, of which the bay duiker is one, and the bush duikers. The bay duiker is typical of its group, with rather slender legs, a slightly hunched back and a smooth glossy coat. Both male and female have small, backward-pointing horns, which are sometimes obscured by the crest of hairs on the forehead. Duikers are timid and when disturbed dash for thick cover — the name duiker means "diver".

They are mainly active at night, when they feed on grass, leaves and fruit, even scrambling up into bushes or onto logs to reach them.

Bay duikers live singly or in pairs and produce 1 young after a gestation of 7 to 8 months. The young is independent at about 3 months old.

NAME: **Yellow Duiker**, *Cephalophus sylvicultor*
RANGE: **Africa: Senegal to Kenya, Zambia, N. Angola**
HABITAT: **moist highland forest**
SIZE: **body: 1.15–1.45 m (3¾–4¾ ft)**
   tail: 11–20.5 cm (4¼–8 in)

Another forest duiker and the largest of its subfamily, the yellow duiker is remarkable for the well-developed crest of hairs on its forehead and for the yellowish-orange patch of coarse, erectile hairs that grow in a wedge shape on its back. Both sexes have long, thin, sharp-pointed horns. The young loses its dark coloration at about 8 months.

Yellow duikers live in pairs or alone, keeping to thick cover. They are active at night and have a varied diet that includes leaves, grass, herbs, berries, termites, snakes, eggs and carrion. They are hunted by humans for their meat and have many other enemies, ranging from leopards and jackal to pythons and large birds of prey.

NAME: **Common/Gray Duiker**, *Sylvicapra grimmia*
RANGE: **Africa, south of the Sahara**
HABITAT: **all types except desert and rain forest, up to 4,600 m (15,000 ft)**
SIZE: **body: 80 cm–1.15 m (31½ in–3¾ ft)**
   tail: 10–22 cm (4–8½ in)

This bush duiker is slightly different from the forest duikers, with its straighter back and thicker, grizzled coat. The crest is quite well developed, and the male has sharp horns, which the female does not always have. Common duikers are adaptable and can survive in almost any habitat from scrub country to open grassland, even invading cultivated lands. The male establishes a fiercely defended territory, in which the animals have regular running, defecating and resting areas. They browse at night on leaves and twigs, which they will stand on their hind legs to reach. They also eat fruit, berries, termites, snakes, eggs and, especially, guineafowl chicks.

Usually found alone or in pairs, they may form small groups in the breeding season, which varies throughout the range and appears to be linked to the rains. The female produces 1 young after a gestation of 4 to 4½ months; normally 2 young are born each year.

Yellow Duiker

Bison (male)

European Bison (female)

Common Duiker (male)

Bay Duiker

African Buffalo (male)

Bovids

NAME: Lechwe, *Kobus leche*
RANGE: Africa: Zaire, Zambia, Angola,
Botswana, South Africa
HABITAT: flood plains, swamps, lakes
SIZE: body: 1.3–1.7 m (4¼–5½ ft)
tail: 30–45 cm (11¾–17¾ in) Ⓥ

There are 3 races of lechwe, whose
coloration varies from bright chestnut to
grayish-brown. In all races, the male has
thin, lyre-shaped horns, up to 91 cm (3 ft)
long, which form a double curve; they
are particularly fine in *K. l. kafuensis*.
With their long, pointed and wide-
spreading hoofs, lechwes are perfectly
adapted to an aquatic way of life and cannot move quickly on dry ground. They
come out of the water only to rest and
calve, spending most of their time
wading in water up to about 50 cm (20 in)
deep, where they feed on grasses and
water plants. They swim well and will
even submerge, with only the nostrils
showing, if threatened. Apart from humans, they are preyed on mainly by lions,
cheetahs, hyenas and hunting dogs.

Lechwes are sociable and form herds
of several hundred during the breeding
season, when males fight fiercely, even
though they are not territorial. At other
times, young males form large, single-
sex herds. After a gestation of 7 to 8
months, the female produces a single
calf, which suckles for 3 to 4 months.

NAME: Uganda Kob, *Kobus kob thomasi*
RANGE: Africa: Uganda to south of Lake
Victoria
HABITAT: open grassy plains, lightly
wooded savanna, near permanent
water
SIZE: body: 1.2–1.8 m (4–6 ft)
tail: 18–40 cm (7–15¾ in)

A graceful, sturdily built, medium-sized
antelope, the Uganda kob is a subspecies of the nominate species, which it
closely resembles except that the white
on the face completely encircles the
eyes. Male and female look alike, but
only the male has horns, which are lyre
shaped, with an S-curve when seen from
the side. Kob usually live in single sex
herds of 20 to 40, sometimes up to 100.
They are grazers, feeding usually in the
morning and at dusk, although during
the day they will go into the water and
eat water plants. They are preyed on
mainly by lions, leopards, spotted hyenas and hunting dogs. Solitary animals
often lie flat and hide when threatened.

In the breeding season, each rutting
male has an area 9 to 15 m (30 to 50 ft) in
diameter, which he defends against
other males. Females move freely
through these rutting areas, mating with
several males. One young is born after
a gestation of 8½ to 9 months, and, since
the female mates again almost at once,
two births are possible in a year.

NAME: Common/Defassa Waterbuck,
Kobus ellipsiprymnus
RANGE: Africa, south of the Sahara to the
Zambezi, east to Ethiopia
HABITAT: savanna, woodland, stony hills,
near water
SIZE: body: 1.8–2.2 m (6–7¼ ft)
tail: 22–45 cm (8½–17¾ in)

The many races of this waterbuck vary
in coloration from a yellowish- or a
reddish-brown to gray and grayish-
black; some have a white ring or patch
on the rump. This waterbuck has large,
hairy ears, which are white inside and
tipped with black, and the male has
heavy, much-ringed horns, which sweep
back in a crescent shape. A large animal,
standing 1.2 to 1.4 m (4 to 4½ ft) at the
shoulder, it weighs 159 to 227 kg (350 to
500 lb). Glands in the skin exude a
musky-smelling, oily secretion, and the
meat is easily tainted when the animal is
skinned, so it is not much hunted. The
chief predators are lions, leopards and
hunting dogs. True to their name, waterbuck spend much time near water and
drink often; they take refuge in reedbeds when threatened. They are grazers,
feeding on tender, young grass shoots.

Common waterbuck move in small
herds of up to 25, usually females and
young with a master bull; young bulls
form bachelor herds. The female
produces 1 young after a gestation of
about 9 months.

NAME: Reedbuck, *Redunca arundinum*
RANGE: Africa: Zaire, Tanzania, south to
South Africa
HABITAT: open plains, hilly country with
light cover, near water
SIZE: body: 1.2–1.4 m (4–4½ ft)
tail: 18–30 cm (7–11¾ in)

A medium-sized antelope — about
91 cm (3 ft) at the shoulder — the reedbuck is a graceful animal, with distinctive movements. It runs with a rocking
motion, flicking its thick, hairy tail, and
the male marks and defends his territory
by displaying his white throat patch and
making bouncing leaps with his head
raised. Reedbuck also make a characteristic clicking sound when running
and whistle through their noses when
alarmed or on the defense. The female
resembles the male but is smaller and
lacks his ridged, curved horns; juveniles
are a grayish-brown. As their name suggests, reedbuck are always found near
water, although not in it, and they spend
much time lying in reedbeds or tall
grass. They graze on grass and shoots
and will raid crops.

Reedbuck are usually found alone or
in pairs or small family groups. A single
young is born after a gestation of 7¾
months.

NAME: Roan Antelope, *Hippotragus
equinus*
RANGE: Africa, south of the Sahara
HABITAT: open woodland, dry bush,
savanna, near water
SIZE: body: 2.4–2.6 m (8–8½ ft)
tail: 60–70 cm (23½–27½ in)

There are approximately 6 races of roan
antelope, which vary in coloration from
gray to reddish-brown. The roan is a
large antelope, the largest in Africa after
the eland and kudu, and as the name
suggests, it superficially resembles a
horse, with its long face and stiff, well-
developed mane. The male's backward-
curving horns are short but strong; the
female's are lighter. Roan antelope usually live in herds of up to 20 females and
young, led by a master bull, often alongside oryx, impalas, wildebeests, buffaloes, zebras and ostriches. Young males
form bachelor herds. They are preyed
on mainly by lions, leopards, hunting
dogs and hyenas. At least 90 percent of
the roans' food is grass, and they rarely
eat leaves or fruit, so they need to drink
often.

Roan antelope are aggressive, and
males will fight on their knees with
vicious, backward sweeps of their
horns. In the breeding season, the bull
detaches a cow from the herd and they
live alone for a while. The female produces 1 calf after a gestation of 8½ to 9
months; it attains sexual maturity at 2½
to 3 years old.

NAME: Rhebok, *Pelea capreolus*
RANGE: South Africa
HABITAT: grassy hills and plateaus with
low bush and scattered trees
SIZE: body: 1–1.2 m (3¼–4 ft)
tail: 10–20 cm (4–7¾ in)

A small, graceful antelope, weighing
22.5 kg (50 lb) at most, the rhebok is
covered with soft, woolly hair. The male
has upright, almost straight horns, 15 to
27 cm (6 to 10½ in) long. Rhebok feed on
grass and the leaves of shrubs and are
very wary, bounding off the moment
they are disturbed, with a run that jerks
up their hindquarters. They are found
in family parties consisting of a master
buck with a dozen or more females and
young; immature males are normally
solitary. The male is highly territorial
and marks out his fairly extensive range
by tongue clicking, display and urination. Despite his small size, the buck
is extremely pugnacious and is known
to attack and even kill sheep, goats and
mountain reedbuck; he will also attack
smaller predators.

In the breeding season, males stage
fierce mock battles without actually
doing any harm, and they will also chase
each other. One, sometimes 2, young
are born after a 9½-month gestation.

Lechwe (male)

Rhebok (male)

Reedbuck (male)

Uganda Kob (male)

Roan Antelope (male)

Common Waterbuck (male)

Bovids

NAME: **Arabian Oryx,** *Oryx leucoryx*
RANGE: **S.E. Saudi Arabia: Rub' al Khali area**
HABITAT: **desert**
SIZE: **body: 1.6 m (5¼ ft)**
　　tail: 45 cm (17¾ in)　　　　　Ⓔ

This is the smallest and rarest of the oryx and the only one found outside Africa. It lives in extreme desert conditions, feeding on grass and shrubs and traveling widely to find food. It is well adapted to its arid habitat, for it can live without drinking, obtaining the moisture it needs from its food; it also uses its hoofs and horns to scrape out a hollow under a bush or alongside a dune in which to shelter from the sun.

Although generally sociable, male oryx fight among themselves in the breeding season; if cornered, they will attack. One young is born after an 8-month gestation.

The present endangered status of the Arabian oryx is the result of overhunting, for its slender horns, its hide and its meat are all prized. Although protected by law, it may already be extinct in the wild, since none has been seen since 1972. It is hoped, however, to breed from captive animals and so reintroduce this oryx to the wild.

NAME: **Blue Wildebeest,** *Connochaetes taurinus*
RANGE: **Africa: S. Kenya to N. South Africa**
HABITAT: **open grassland, bush savanna**
SIZE: **1.7–2.4 m (5½–8 ft)**
　　tail: 60 cm–1 m (23½ in–3¼ ft)

The clumsy appearance of the blue wildebeest, the lugubrious expression given by its black face and tufty beard, its rocking-horse gait and its constant snorts and grunts have earned it a reputation as a "clown." Nevertheless, it is a most successful species.

Wildebeests are extremely gregarious, and herds numbering tens of thousands may be seen in East Africa during the dry season, when they make migrations of as much as 1,600 km (1,000 mi) in search of water and grazing. Breeding herds usually consist of up to 150 females and young, with 1 to 3 males. The bulls patrol the outside of their herd, keeping it closely grouped and defending a zone around it, even when migrating. Wildebeests feed almost exclusively on grass and need to drink often. They are frequently seen in association with zebras and ostriches; perhaps the wariness of the former offers them some protection from common predators: lions, cheetahs, hunting dogs and hyenas.

The female looks like the male but is smaller. After a gestation of 8½ months, she produces 1 calf, which can stand within 3 to 5 minutes of birth.

NAME: **Addax,** *Addax nasomaculatus*
RANGE: **Africa: E. Mauritania, W. Mali; patchy distribution in Algeria, Chad, Niger and Sudan**
HABITAT: **sandy and stony desert**
SIZE: **body: 1.3 m (4¼ ft)**
　　tail: 25–35 cm (9¾–13¾ in)　　Ⓥ

With its heavy head and shoulders and slender hindquarters, the addax is a clumsy-looking animal. Its coloration varies widely between individuals, but there is always a mat of dark-brown hair on the forehead, and both sexes have thin, spiral horns. Addax are typical desert-dwellers, with their large, wide-spreading hoofs, adapted to walking on soft sand, and they never drink, obtaining all the moisture they need from their food, which includes succulents. Their nomadic habits are closely linked to the sporadic rains, for addax appear to have a special ability to find the patches of desert vegetation that suddenly sprout after a downpour. They are normally found in herds of 20 to 200.

The female produces 1 young after a gestation of 8½ months.

NAME: **Hartebeest,** *Alcelaphus buselaphus*
RANGE: **Africa, south of the Sahara**
HABITAT: **grassy plains**
SIZE: **body: 1.7–2.4 m (5½–8 ft)**
　　tail: 45–70 cm (17¾–27½ in)

The nominate race, the bubal hartebeest, is extinct, but there are 12 subspecies, a further 2 of which (*A. b. swayne* and *A. b. tora*) are endangered, due to disease, hunting and destruction of their habitat.

Hartebeests are odd-looking animals, with backs that slope down slightly from high shoulders and long heads, with a pedicel on top from which spring the horns. Both male and female have horns, which show great intraspecific variation in both size and shape. Coloration also varies from deep chocolate to sandy fawn; females are paler than males.

These sociable antelope are found in herds of from 4 to 30, consisting of females and young with a master bull. He watches over his herd, often from a vantage point on top of a termite mound. Although hartebeests can go for long periods without water, they drink when they can and enjoy wallowing; they also use salt licks with avidity. They are partial to the young grass that grows after burning and often graze with zebras, wildebeests and gazelles and, like these, are preyed on largely by lions.

A single calf is born after a gestation of 8 months. It remains with its mother for about 3 years, at which time young males form a troop of their own.

NAME: **Bontebok,** *Damaliscus dorcas*
RANGE: **South Africa: W. Cape Province**
HABITAT: **open grassland**
SIZE: **body: 1.4–1.6 m (4½–5¼ ft)**
　　tail: 30–45 cm (11¾–17¾ in)　　Ⓞ

The strikingly marked bontebok was at one time almost extinct but is now fully protected and out of danger, and the population in game reserves numbers several thousand. The very similar blesbok, *D. d. phillipsi* (= *albifrons*), was also endangered, but it, too, is now flourishing, since it has been established in many reserves.

The sexes look alike, but females and juveniles are paler. Bontebok are grazers, active morning and evening. When disturbed, they move off swiftly upwind in single file. They are remarkably agile and can clamber over fences or wriggle under or through them.

The female produces a single calf after a 7½-month gestation, and young remain with their mothers until they are about 2 years old, when young males form bachelor herds. Outside the breeding season, bontebok live in mixed herds of from 20 to 500 animals.

NAME: **Sassaby,** *Damaliscus lunatus*
RANGE: **Africa, south of the Sahara, east to Ethiopia, Somalia**
HABITAT: **open plains, flood plains, grassland with scattered bush**
SIZE: **body: 1.5–2 m (5–6½ ft)**
　　tail: 40–60 cm (15¾–23½ in)

The nominate race of sassaby is found from Zambia to northern South Africa; it is probably conspecific with *D. korrigum*, known as the tiang or topi, which is found elsewhere. Together, sassabies and topis are the most numerous of all antelope in Africa. In shape they are similar to the true hartebeests, but neither the slope of the back nor the length of the head is so exaggerated. Coloration and horns vary from race to race and between sexes; females are usually paler than males. Sassabies are active early and late in the day, when they feed on grass and herbage and also drink. They can, however, go without water for as long as 30 days.

Sassabies are not as gregarious as the hartebeests and generally move in parties of 8 to 10, which may join to form herds of up to 200 in the dry season. The mature male is highly territorial and marks his central stamping ground with dung and with scent, which he rubs from his face and neck onto bushes, grass stems and the ground. He defends his territory from rivals and predators.

The female produces a single calf after a gestation of 7½ to 8 months.

Bontebok

Blue Wildebeest (male)

Sassaby

Hartebeest

Addax

Arabian Oryx (male)

Bovids

NAME: **Klipspringer**, *Oreotragus oreotragus*
RANGE: **Africa: N. Nigeria, east to Somalia, south to South Africa**
HABITAT: **rocky outcrops, hillsides, mountains to 4,000 m (13,000 ft)**
SIZE: **body: 75 cm–1.15 m (29½ in–3¾ ft)** **tail: 7–23 cm (2¾–9 in)**

The klipspringer always occurs where there are rocky outcrops interspersed with grassy patches and clumps of bush. It is a fairly small antelope with strong legs and blunt-tipped hoofs the consistency of hard rubber; it fills a niche similar to that of the chamois. As it leaps about among the rocks, it is cushioned from bumps by its long, thick, bristly coat. The female is slightly heavier than the male and except in 1 race, *O. o. schillingsi*, does not have horns.

Klipspringers are sometimes found in small parties, more often in pairs, in a territory marked out by glandular secretions and defended against interlopers. They feed morning and evening and on moonlit nights and will stand on their hind legs to reach the leaves, flowers and fruit that form the bulk of their diet. They also eat succulents, moss and some grass and drink when water is available.

Klipspringers probably mate for life. The female produces 1 young after a gestation of about 7 months, and there may be 2 young born in a year.

NAME: **Beira Antelope**, *Dorcatragus megalotis*
RANGE: **Africa: Somalia**
HABITAT: **dry, bush-clad mountains, stony hills**
SIZE: **body: 80–90 cm (31½–35½ in)** **tail: 6–7.5 cm (2¼–3 in)** ⓥ

A rare antelope, the beira is often mistaken for the klipspringer, although it has a slightly longer head, much bigger ears and longer, slimmer legs. The hind legs, especially, are long, with the result that the rump is higher than the shoulders. There is no crest, and only the male has horns; the female is larger than the male.

Beiras live in pairs or small family parties on extremely stony hillsides close to a grassy plain. Their highly specialized hoofs have elastic pads underneath which give a good grip on the stones. Beiras feed in the early morning and late afternoon on leaves of bushes, particularly mimosa, grass and herbage and do not need to drink.

Little is known of their habits or biology, for not only are they rare but their coloration blends so well with the background that they are impossible to spot unless they move. The female gives birth to a single young.

NAME: **Oribi**, *Ourebia ourebi*
RANGE: **Africa: Sierra Leone to Ethiopia, Tanzania, Zambia, South Africa**
HABITAT: **wide, grassy plains with low bush, near water**
SIZE: **body: 92 cm–1.1 m (3–3½ ft)** **tail: 6–10.5 cm (2¼–4¼ in)**

The oribi is small and graceful, with a long neck and slender legs, longer behind than in front. The silky coat has a sleek, rippled look, and the black-tipped tail is conspicuous when the animal runs. Below each large, oval ear there is a patch of bare skin that appears as a black spot. The female has no horns and is larger than the male.

Pairs or small parties of up to 5 animals live in a territory, which the male marks out by rubbing glandular secretions on twigs and grass stems. Here the oribis have regular running, resting and defecating places. They are active early and later in the day and on moonlit nights, when they feed on grass, plants and leaves. During the day and when danger threatens, they lie quietly in long grass or by a bush or rock.

The female gives birth to 1 young after a gestation of 6½ to 7 months.

NAME: **Royal Antelope**, *Neotragus pygmaeus*
RANGE: **Africa: Sierra Leone, Liberia, Ivory Coast, Ghana**
HABITAT: **forest, forest clearings**
SIZE: **body: 35–41 cm (13¾–16 in)** **tail: 5–6 cm (2–2¼ in)**

This dainty, compact little animal, the smallest African antelope, weighs 3 to 4.5 kg (7 to 10 lb) — not much more than a rabbit. Indeed, it is called "king of the hares" by local tribespeople and thus "royal" antelope by Europeans. It has a rounded back and a short tail, which it holds tightly against its rump. The male has tiny, sharp horns, which the female lacks; young are darker in color than adults. Royal antelopes live in pairs or alone in a small territory, which they usually mark out with dung heaps. They are timid and secretive and are mainly active at night, when quite large numbers may feed together on leaves, buds, shoots, fungi, fallen fruit, grass and weeds. They sometimes venture into vegetable plots and cocoa and peanut plantations. Although they are preyed on by a wide range of mammals, birds and even large snakes, their small size often enables them to slip away unseen from danger, with their bellies almost on the ground. Their vulnerability is also compensated for by their astounding abilility to leap, like springboks, as much as 3 m (10 ft) into the air.

Royal antelopes probably pair for life; the female produces 1 young.

NAME: **Kirk's Dik-dik**, *Madoqua kirki*
RANGE: **Africa: Somalia to Tanzania; S.W. Angola, Namibia**
HABITAT: **bush country with thick undergrowth and scattered trees**
SIZE: **body: 55–57 cm (21½–22½ in)** **tail: 4–6 cm (1½–2¼ in)**

There are 7 races of this small, dainty antelope, which occur in two widely separated regions. Coloration of the soft coat varies from pale gray-brown in dry areas to a much darker shade in wet areas. The nose is slightly elongated and the legs long and thin, with the hind legs always bent, so the hindquarters slope downward. Males have tiny horns, with a crest of long hair between them; the slightly larger female lacks horns.

Dik-diks are found alone or in pairs, often with their 2 most recent young. Males scent-mark and fiercely defend the boundaries of a clearly defined territory, within which there are regularly used paths and places for resting and defecating. Shy, secretive animals, dik-diks browse at sunset and at night on leaves, shoots, buds and flowers, especially those of the acacia. They also eat fallen fruit, dig up roots and tubers with their horns and hoofs and frequent salt licks; they do not need to drink. Their enemies include leopards, caracals, servals, wild cats, eagles and humans.

Dik-diks pair for life and produce 1 young after a gestation of 6 months; there are two litters a year.

NAME: **Grysbok**, *Raphiceros melanotis*
RANGE: **Africa: Tanzania to South Africa**
HABITAT: **grassy plains, bush savanna at the foot of hills**
SIZE: **body: 60–75 cm (23½–29½ in)** **tail: 5–8 cm (2–3 in)**

This rough-coated, stocky little antelope has relatively short legs, slightly longer behind, which gives it a sloping back. Males have short, sharply pointed horns and generally darker coloration than females. Solitary outside the breeding season, the grysbok establishes a fairly small territory, which is marked out by means of scent and defecation sites. It feeds in the morning and late in the afternoon on the foliage of trees and bushes and is particularly fond of grapevine leaves. During the day, the grysbok rests in the shade of a bush or rock or in long grass. Its main predators are leopards, caracals and crowned eagles, and when threatened, the antelope lies flat, zigzagging away when the enemy is near, only to dive suddenly for cover and disappear again.

The breeding biology of the grysbok is not well known, but it is thought to be similar to that of the steenbok, which produces 1 young after a gestation of 5½ months.

Royal Antelope (male)

Grysbok (male)

Oribi (male)

Kirk's Dik-dik (male)

Klipspringer (male)

Beira Antelope (male)

Bovids

NAME: Impala, *Aepyceros melampus*
**RANGE: Africa: Kenya, Uganda, south to
N. South Africa**
**HABITAT: light mopani woodland, acacia
savanna**
**SIZE: body: 1.2–1.6 m (4–5¼ ft)
tail: 30–45 cm (11¾–17¾ in)**

A graceful, medium-sized antelope with
a glossy coat, the impala is identified by
the unique bushy tuft of dark hairs
above the hind "heels," the vertical
dark stripes on white on the back of the
thighs and tail and, in the male, the long,
elegant, lyre-shaped horns. The impala is
remarkable also for its fleetness and for
the amazing leaps it makes — as far as
10 m (33 ft) and as high as 3 m (10 ft) —
seemingly for enjoyment, as well as to
escape from predators.

Impalas are extremely gregarious, and
in the dry season troops may join to
form herds of 200 or so. They are active
day and night and eat quantities of grass
and leaves, flowers and fruit. In the
breeding season, the ram establishes a
territory and a harem of 15 to 20 females,
which he defends fiercely; immature
males form separate troops. After a
gestation of 6½ to 7 months, the female
produces 1 young, which is born at midday, when many predators are som-
nolent, and remains hidden until it is
strong enough to join the herd.

NAME: Blackbuck, *Antilope cervicapra*
RANGE: India and Pakistan
HABITAT: open grassy plains
**SIZE: body: 1.2 m (4 ft)
tail: 18 cm (7 in)**

The only species in its genus, the blackbuck is one of the few antelope in which
the coloration of male and female is
dissimilar. The dominant male in the
herd is dark, almost black on back and
sides and has long, spirally twisted
horns; the female is yellowish-fawn and
lacks horns. Subordinate males have
smaller horns and retain female coloration. They only darken and develop
large horns if they assume the dominant
position in a herd, following the death
of the leading male.

Blackbucks feed largely on grass and
are active morning and evening, resting
in the heat of the day. The female is
unusually alert, and it is she who first
gives warning of danger. When alarmed,
blackbucks flee with leaps and bounds,
then soon settle into a swift gallop.

Blackbucks are normally found in
groups of 15 to 50, consisting of a
dominant male with females and young;
as males mature, they are driven out and
form their own small parties. The breeding male sets up a territory and defends
it and his harem against rivals. One
young, sometimes 2, is born after a
gestation of 6 months.

NAME: Springbok, *Antidorcas
marsupialis*
**RANGE: Africa: Angola, South Africa,
Botswana (Kalahari Desert)**
HABITAT: treeless grassland (veld)
**SIZE: body: 1.2–1.4 m (4–4½ ft)
tail: 19–27 cm (7½–10½ in)**

The brightly colored, striking springbok has a most unusual glandular pouch
in its skin that stretches from the middle
of the back to the base of the tail. When
the animal is excited or alarmed, the
pouch opens and reveals a crest of long,
stiff, white hairs. Male and female look
alike, both with ridged, strong horns.
The springbok's name is derived from
its ability to bound as high as 3.5 m
(11½ ft) into the air, half a dozen times in
succession, either in alarm or play, with
back curved, legs stiff and crest
displayed.

Springboks eat the leaves of shrubs
and bushes and grass and are independent of water. They were once exceedingly numerous, and in times of
drought, herds of up to a million would
make long migrations in search of fresh
grazing, devastating the pasture and
farmland that lay in their path. As a
result, thousands were slaughtered, but
they have now been reintroduced
throughout their range and are again
thriving. In the breeding season, the
male may establish a territory and a
harem of 10 to 30, but large mixed herds
are the norm. The female produces 1
young after a gestation of about 6
months.

NAME: Dibatag, *Ammodorcas clarkei*
RANGE: Africa: Somalia, E. Ethiopia
**HABITAT: sandy or grassy plains with
scattered bushes**
**SIZE: body: 1.5–1.6 m (5–5¼ ft)
tail: 30–36 cm (11¾–14¼ in)** Ⓥ

Although superficially it resembles the
gerenuk, the dibatag is much grayer, and
the male has shorter and quite different
horns. The long, thin, black-tufted tail is
generally held upright when the animal
is running and gives it its name, which
derives from the Somali words *dabu*
(tail) and *tag* (erect). These animals live
in pairs or family parties consisting of an
adult male and 3 to 5 females with
young. They move seasonally with the
rains, wherever food supplies are plentiful. They are active morning and evening, browsing on leaves and young
shoots of bushes, which, like the
gerenuk, they reach on their hind legs.
They also eat flowers, berries and new
grass; they do not need to drink.

As a rule, 1 calf is born in the rainy
season after a gestation of 6 to 7 months,
but it is possible for a female to produce
2 young in a year.

NAME: Gerenuk, *Litocranius walleri*
**RANGE: Africa: Somalia, Ethiopia to
Kenya, Tanzania**
HABITAT: dry thornbush country, desert
**SIZE: body: 1.4–1.6 m (4½–5¼ ft)
tail: 23–35 cm (9–13¾ in)**

This large, graceful-looking gazelle is
remarkable chiefly for its long neck
(gerenuk means giraffe-necked in
Somali) and for its long legs. It has a
small, narrow head, large eyes and
mobile lips; there are tufts of hair on the
knees, and the short, almost naked tail
is held close against the body except in
flight, when it is curled up over the
animal's back. The male has horns and
is larger than the female.

Gerenuks are usually found in pairs
or family parties consisting of a male
and 2 to 5 females with young. They are
browsers, living almost entirely on
leaves and young shoots of thorny
bushes and trees, which they reach by
standing against the trunk on their hind
legs and stretching their necks, using a
foreleg to pull down the branches. They
feed morning and evening, standing still
in the shade at midday. They are quite
independent of water. Their main
predators are cheetahs, leopards, lions,
hyenas and hunting dogs.

A single young is born, usually in the
rainy season after a gestation of about
6½ months.

NAME: Thomson's Gazelle, *Gazella
thomsoni*
**RANGE: Africa: Sudan, Kenya,
N. Tanzania**
HABITAT: open plains with short grass
**SIZE: body: 80 cm–1.1 m (31½ in–3½ ft)
tail: 19–27 cm (7½–10½ in)**

This graceful, small gazelle has a distinctive broad, dark stripe along its sides,
in marked contrast to the white underparts. The male is larger than the female
and has much stronger horns. There are
about 15 races of Thompson's gazelle,
which show only minor variations of
coloring or horn size. They feed morning and evening, mainly on short grass
and a small amount of foliage; they need
to drink only when the grazing is dry.
Their chief predators are cheetahs, lions,
leopards, hyenas and hunting dogs.

These gazelles live in loosely struc-
tured groups which may vary between 1
old ram with 5 to 65 females and young,
herds of young males with 5 to 500 members and groups of pregnant and recently
calved females. When grazing is good, a
mature male may establish a territory,
which he marks by urination and droppings and by the scraping and smearing
of ground and bushes with horns and
glandular secretions. Females calve at
any time of year after a 6-month gestation and may produce 2 calves a year.

Thomson's Gazelle
(male)

Blackbuck (male)

Gerenuk
(male)

Impala
(male)

Springbok

Dibatag
(male)

Bovids

NAME: **Saiga,** *Saiga tatarica*
RANGE: **Volga River to central Asia**
HABITAT: **treeless plains**
SIZE: **body: 1.2–1.7 m (4–5½ ft)**
 tail: 7.5–10 cm (3–4 in)

The saiga is a migratory species, well adapted to its cold, windswept habitat. It has a heavy fawnish-cinnamon coat with a fringe of long hairs from chin to chest, which in the winter changes to a uniformly creamy-white and becomes exceedingly thick and woolly. It is thought, too, that the saiga's enlarged, proboscislike nose with downward-pointing nostrils may be an adaptation for warming and moisturizing inhaled air. The nasal passages are lined with hairs, glands and mucous tracts, and in each nostril there is a sac lined with mucous membranes; such sacs appear in no other mammal but the whale. The male has horns, regarded as being of medicinal value by the Chinese; this led to overhunting, but saigas have been protected since 1920, and there are now over a million of them.

Saigas feed on low-growing shrubs and grass, and in autumn large herds gather and move off southward to warmer, lusher pastures. When spring comes, groups of 2 to 6 males begin to return northward, followed by the females. In May, after a gestation of about 5 months, the female gives birth to 1 to 3 young, which are suckled until the autumn.

NAME: **Serow,** *Capricornis sumatraensis*
RANGE: **N. India to central and S. China; S.E. Asia to Sumatra**
HABITAT: **bush and forest at 600–2,700 m (2,000–9,000 ft)**
SIZE: **body: 1.4–1.5 m (4½–5 ft)**
 tail: 8–21 cm (3–8¼ in) Ⓔ

The slow, but extremely sure-footed serow has short, solid hoofs; it is found on rocky slopes and ridges of thickly vegetated mountains. It is active early and late in the day, feeding on grass and leaves; it lies in the shelter of an overhanging rock for the rest of the time. The hairs on its back and sides are light colored at the base and black at the tip, giving the coat an overall dark appearance; there is a completely black stripe along the center of the back, and the mane varies from white to black on different individuals. Both male and female have horns, which they use to defend themselves, particularly against the dogs with which they are hunted by the Chinese, who believe that different parts of the serow have great healing properties.

Little is known of their breeding habits except that 1, more often 2, young are born after a gestation of about 8 months.

NAME: **Common Goral,** *Nemorhaedus goral*
RANGE: **S.E. Siberia to Manchuria, Korea**
HABITAT: **mountains at 1,000–2,000 m (3,300–6,600 ft)**
SIZE: **body: 90 cm–1.3 m (35½ in–4¼ ft)**
 tail: 7.5–20 cm (3–7¾ in)

These animals are mountain-dwellers, found generally where there are grassy hills and rocky outcrops near forests. They have long, sturdy legs, and their long coats of guard hairs overlaying a short, woolly undercoat give them a shaggy appearance. Male and female look alike, both with horns, but the male has a short, semierect mane.

Apart from old bucks, which live alone for most of the year, gorals normally live in family groups of 4 to 8. They feed on grass in the early morning and late afternoon, resting on a rocky ledge in the middle of the day. The female gives birth to 1, rarely 2, young after a gestation of about 6 months.

NAME: **Mountain Goat,** *Oreamnos americanus*
RANGE: **N. America: Rocky Mountains from Alaska to Montana, Idaho, Oregon; introduced in South Dakota**
HABITAT: **rocky mountains above the tree line**
SIZE: **body: 1.3–1.6 m (4¼–5¼ ft)**
 tail: 15–20 cm (6–7¾ in)

This splendid-looking animal is not a true goat but a goat-antelope and is the only species in its genus. It is found among boulders and rocky screes above the tree line and is well adapted to its cold, harsh habitat. It has thick, woolly underfur and a long, hairy, white coat, which is particularly thick and stiff on the neck and shoulders, forming a ridge, or hump. The hoofs have a hard, sharp rim enclosing a soft, spongy inner pad, which gives the mountain goat a good grip on rocks and ice. Both sexes have beards and black, conical horns.

Mountain goats are slow-moving but amazingly sure-footed, climbing to dizzying heights and seemingly inaccessible ledges in their search for grass, sedges and lichens to eat. They also browse on the leaves and shoots of trees and will travel considerable distances to search out salt licks. In winter, they come down to areas where the snow is not too deep, even to the coast in places. In severe weather, they may take refuge under overhanging rocks or in caves.

Mountain goats are probably monogamous, and the female produces 1 or 2 kids in the spring after a gestation of about 7 months. The young kids are remarkably active and within half an hour of birth are able to jump about among the rocks.

NAME: **Chamois,** *Rupicapra rupicapra*
RANGE: **Europe to Middle East**
HABITAT: **mountains**
SIZE: **body: 90 cm–1.3 m (35½ in–4¼ ft)**
 tail: 3–4 cm (1¼–1½ in)

For nimbleness, audacity and endurance, the chamois is unparalleled among mountain-dwellers. It thrives in wild and inhospitable surroundings where weather conditions may be savage and has been known to survive as long as 2 weeks without food. It is the only species in its genus. It is slimly built, with distinctive horns that rise almost vertically, then sweep sharply backward to form a hook. The legs are sturdy, and the hoofs have a resilient, spongy pad underneath, which gives the chamois a good grip on slippery or uneven surfaces. The coat is stiff and coarse, with a thick, woolly underfleece.

Chamois graze on the tops of mountains in summer on herbs and flowers; in winter, they come farther down the slopes and browse on young pine shoots, lichens and mosses. They are wary animals, and a sentinel is always posted to warn of danger. Females and young live together in herds of 15 to 30; old males are solitary except in the rutting season in the autumn. Fighting is common among males, with older rams locking horns with young animals in a struggle to assert their supremacy. The female usually has 1 kid, but 2 or 3 are fairly common.

NAME: **Ibex,** *Capra ibex*
RANGE: **Switzerland, Italy**
HABITAT: **Alps to 3,000 m (10,000 ft)**
SIZE: **body: 1.5 m (5 ft)**
 tail: 12–15 cm (4¾–6 in)

From Roman times, different parts of these animals have been regarded as possessing miraculous healing powers, and ibex were hunted to the point of extinction. Today, however, a few small, protected herds survive in reserves. The most remarkable feature of the male ibex is the long, backward-sweeping horns; the female has shorter horns. The coat is a brownish-gray, with longer hair on the back of the neck forming a mane in old males. The male has a small beard on the chin.

Ibex live above the tree line, descending to the upper limits of forest only in the harshest winter conditions. In summer, they climb up into alpine meadows, where they graze on grass and flowers. At this time, females are found with young and subadults, and males form their own groups, within which token fights often take place to establish an order of rank. Only in the winter rutting season do males rejoin female herds. The female gives birth to 1 young after a gestation of 5 to 6 months.

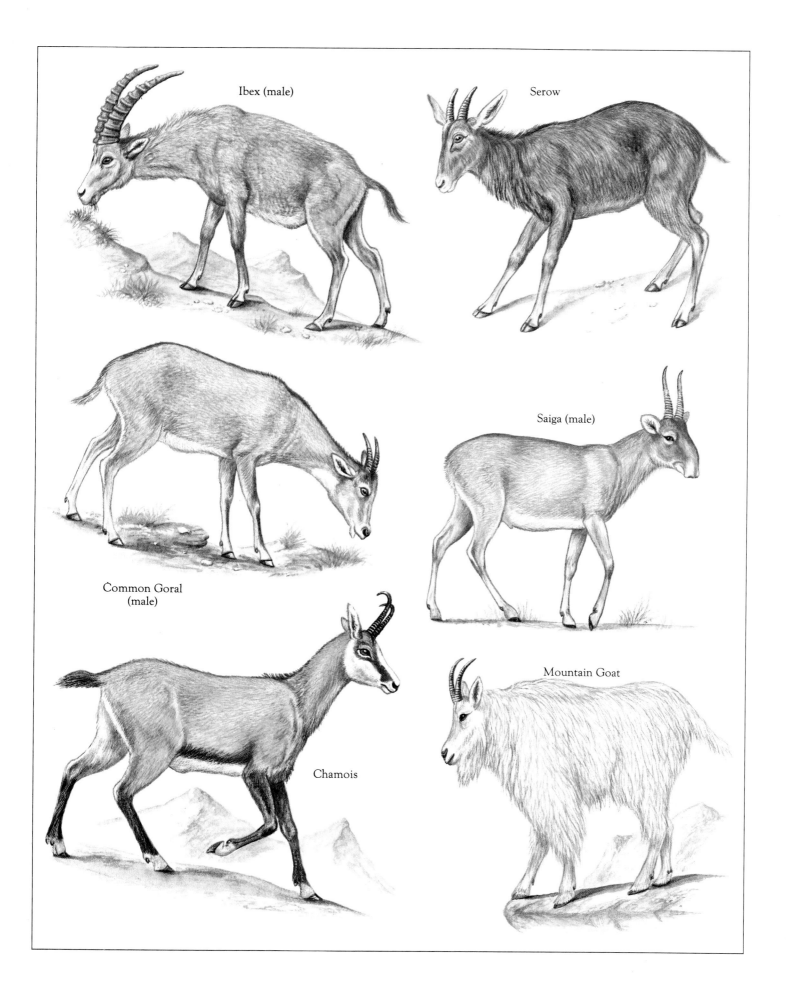

Ibex (male)

Serow

Saiga (male)

Common Goral
(male)

Chamois

Mountain Goat

Bovids

NAME: **Musk Ox,** *Ovibos moschatus*
RANGE: **N. Canada, Greenland**
HABITAT: **tundra**
SIZE: **body: 1.9–2.3 m (6¼–7½ ft)**
    tail: 9–10 cm (3½–4 in)

In prehistoric times, the musk ox occurred throughout northern Europe, Siberia and North America. It was largely exterminated, surviving only in northern Canada and Greenland; however, it has now been successfully reintroduced in Norway and Alaska. It is the only species in its genus. The musk ox is superbly equipped for life in harsh arctic conditions, for it has a dense undercoat which neither cold nor water can penetrate and an outer coat of long, coarse hair that reaches almost to the ground and protects it from snow and rain. The broad hoofs prevent it from sinking in soft snow. Both sexes have heavy horns that almost meet at the base, forming a broad frontal plate. Facial glands in the bull emit a strong, musky odor in the rutting season, hence the animal's name.

Musk oxen are gregarious, living in herds of as many as 100. In the mating season, young bulls are driven out by old, master bulls and form small bachelor groups or remain solitary. The female produces 1 young after a gestation of 8 months. When threatened, musk oxen form a circle, facing outward with horns lowered, with the young in the middle; this is an effective defense against wolves, their natural enemies, but not against humans with guns. Musk oxen feed mainly on grass, but they also eat mosses, lichens and leaves and will dig through snow for food.

NAME: **Himalayan Tahr,** *Hemitragus jemlahicus*
RANGE: **India: Kashmir (Pir Panjal Mountains), Punjab; Nepal, Sikkim**
HABITAT: **tree-covered mountain slopes**
SIZE: **body: 1.1 m (3½ ft)**
    tail: 9 cm (3½ in)

Although the tahr appears much like a goat, with its heavy, shaggy coat that forms a mane around the shoulders, it differs from true goats in having a naked muzzle and no beard; the horns, too, are long and not twisted, and there are scent glands on the feet.

Tahrs are goatlike in their habits as well, for they live on precipitous mountainsides, where they climb and leap about with supreme ease. They are gregarious, living in herds of 30 to 40 and feeding on almost any vegetation they can reach. Wary animals, they always post a sentinel to watch for danger approaching from below.

The breeding season peaks in the winter. The female gives birth to 1 or 2 young after a 6- to 8-month gestation.

NAME: **Takin,** *Budorcas taxicolor*
RANGE: **Asia: Burma; China: Szechwan and Shensi Provinces**
HABITAT: **dense thickets in mountain forest, 2,400–4,250 m (7,900–14,000 ft)**
SIZE: **body: 1.2 m (4 ft)**
    tail: 10 cm (4 in)   ®

The takin lives in dense bamboo and rhododendron thickets near the upper limits of the tree line in some of the most rugged country in the world. It is a clumsy-looking, solidly built animal, with thick legs and large hoofs with dewclaws. The coat ranges from yellowish-white to blackish-brown, always with a dark stripe along the back. Both males and females have horns.

Although old bulls are generally solitary, in summer they join large herds, which graze in the evening on grass and herbage near the tops of mountains; in winter takins move down to the valleys, where they live in smaller groups, eating grass, bamboo and willow shoots. They are shy animals, spending most of their time under cover in dense thickets, in which there are regularly used paths leading to their grazing grounds and salt licks.

The female produces 1 young after a gestation of about 8 months; it is strong and active and able to follow its mother after about 3 days.

NAME: **Barbary Sheep,** *Ammotragus lervia*
RANGE: **N. Africa: Atlantic coast to Red Sea, south to N. Mali and Sudan; introduced in S.W. USA**
HABITAT: **dry, rocky, barren regions**
SIZE: **body: 1.3–1.9 m (4¼–6¼ ft)**
    tail: 25 cm (9¾ in)

The Barbary sheep is the only sheep indigenous to Africa and the only species in its genus. The mane of long, soft, thick hairs on its throat, chest and upper forelegs differentiates it from other wild sheep, but, like them, both sexes have horns, those of the female being almost as heavy as the male's.

Small family parties consisting of a breeding pair and their offspring of various litters wander about in search of food: grass, herbaceous plants, and leaves and twigs of low-growing bushes. They obtain all the water they need from this diet and from dew. Having no cover in which to hide when danger threatens, Barbary sheep rely on the camouflage effect of their sandy-colored coats and remain perfectly still. They are hunted for their flesh, hides, hair and sinews.

In captivity, Barbary sheep produce one litter a year of 1 or 2 young. They have been successfully crossed with domestic goats, and the offspring with chamois.

NAME: **Mountain Sheep/Bighorn,** *Ovis canadensis*
RANGE: **S.W. Canada, W. USA**
HABITAT: **upland and mountainous areas**
SIZE: **body: 1.2–1.8 m (4–6 ft)**
    tail: 15 cm (6 in)   Ⓥ

The mountain sheep is found on high mountain pastures in summer, when groups of males or females with young graze independently on grass and herbage. In winter, they form mixed herds and move to lower pastures. A high-ranking male mountain sheep is a most impressive animal, with massive spiral horns up to 1.15 m (3¾ ft) long. Horn size is of great significance in establishing rank order among males; smaller-horned, lower-ranking males are treated as females by dominant males, which perhaps prevents their being driven out of the herd. In the rutting season, high-ranking males of comparable horn size have fierce battles, rushing at each other and crashing their horns together; the fighting may go on for hours, and occasionally an animal is killed. Females have very short horns.

The ewe produces 1 or 2 lambs after a gestation of about 6 months and is assiduous in her care of the young.

NAME: **Mouflon,** *Ovis orientalis*
RANGE: **Sardinia, Corsica; reintroduced in Germany, Hungary, Austria and Czechoslovakia**
HABITAT: **rugged mountains**
SIZE: **body: 1.2 m (4 ft)**
    tail: 7 cm (2¾ in)

The mouflon, the wild sheep of Europe, is now found only in reserves in Sardinia and Corsica, but even there it is inadequately protected. The male has long, spiral horns, often with the tips curving inward; those of the female are short. The mouflon has an extremely woolly underfleece, covered in winter by a coarse, blackish-brown top coat, with a distinctive white saddle patch in the male; in the summer this patch disappears. The female and young are gray or darker brown, with no patch.

Mouflon are active early and late in the day and do not wander far, even when food is scarce. They appear to be able to eat every type of vegetation: grass, flowers, buds and shoots of bushes and trees, even poisonous plants such as deadly nightshade. They live in separate groups composed of females with young or males on their own in the summer. In the rutting season, a mature ram will detach a female from the herd and mate with her. Fierce fighting may take place if an old ram is challenged, but there are seldom casualties. The ewe produces 1 lamb after a gestation of 5 months.

Musk Ox

Himalayan Tahr

Mouflon
(male)

Barbary Sheep

Takin

Mountain Sheep
(male)

Squirrels

NAME: European Red Squirrel, *Sciurus vulgaris*
RANGE: Europe, east to China, Korea and Japan: Hokkaido.
HABITAT: evergreen forest
SIZE: body: 20–24 cm (7¾–9½ in)
tail: 15–20 cm (6–7¾ in)

Until the arrival of the North American gray squirrel in Britain at the beginning of this century, the only European species was the red squirrel. Populations are now declining in Britain, but red squirrels are still abundant in Europe and Asia. Conifer cones are their main food, although in summer they also eat fungi and fruit.

The length of the breeding season is dictated by local climate: in a good year a female may produce two litters of about 3 young each. The young are born in a tree nest, called a drey, which also doubles as winter quarters.

NAME: Gray Squirrel, *Sciurus carolinensis*
RANGE: S.E. Canada, E. USA; introduced in Britain and South Africa
HABITAT: hardwood forest
SIZE: 23–30 cm (9–11¾ in)
tail: 21–23 cm (8¼–9 in)

The gray squirrel's natural home is the oak, hickory and walnut forests of eastern North America, where its numbers are controlled by owls, foxes and bobcats. It feeds on seeds and nuts — an adult squirrel takes about 80 g (2¾ oz) of shelled nuts each day — and on eggs, young birds and insects. Occasionally gray squirrels strip the bark from young trees to gain access to the nutritious sap beneath.

Two litters are produced each year, in early spring and summer. There are up to 7 young in a litter, but usually only 3 or 4 survive. Males are excluded from the nest and take no part in rearing the young. In the south of England, the introduced gray squirrel is ousting the native red squirrel.

NAME: African Giant Squirrel, *Protoxerus stangeri*
RANGE: W. Africa, east to Kenya; Angola
HABITAT: palm forest
SIZE: body: 22–33 cm (8½–13 in)
tail: 25–38 cm (9¾–15 in)

Sometimes called the oil-palm squirrel, this species feeds primarily on nuts from the oil palm. In regions where calcium is scarce, it has been observed to gnaw bones and ivory. The African giant squirrel is a secretive creature, and its presence is usually only detected by a booming call, which it utters when disturbed. Little is known of its breeding habits, but it probably breeds throughout the year.

ORDER RODENTIA

The largest of the mammalian orders, Rodentia contains at least 1,591 species in 28 families.

SCIURIDAE: Squirrel Family

The differences between squirrels and other families of rodents are not immediately noticeable; most of them are technical and of interest only to zoologists. There are about 246 species of squirrel, and generally they are alert, short-faced animals. Some have taken to burrowing and live in vast subterranean towns (prairie dogs); others run and hop about over logs and stones (chipmunks); and many have taken to life in the trees (tree and flying squirrels). Most forms are active by day and are among the most brightly colored of all mammals. Their eyes are large and vision, including color vision, good. The few nocturnal species, such as the flying squirrels, are more drab in appearance. Males and females generally look alike.

Squirrels have a wide distribution, occurring in all parts of the world except for southern South America, Australia, New Zealand, Madagascar and the deserts of the Middle East. In temperate climates they undergo periods of dormancy in cold weather. Dormancy differs from true hibernation in that the creature wakes every few days for food. True hibernation occurs in a limited number of squirrel species. Squirrels are social animals and have evolved a complex system of signaling with their bushy tails. They are also quite vocal, and most can make a variety of sounds.

NAME: Indian Striped Squirrel, *Funambulus palmarum*
RANGE: India, Sri Lanka
HABITAT: palm forest
SIZE: body: 11.5–18 cm (4½–7 in)
tail: 11.5–18 cm (4½–7 in)

With their distinctive stripes, these little squirrels superficially resemble chipmunks. They are highly active animals, foraging by day for palm nuts, flowers and buds. They may damage cotton trees by eating the buds, but when they feed on the nectar of the silky oak flowers, they do good by pollinating the flowers they investigate.

Males are aggressive and fight for females, but once mating has taken place, they show no further interest in females or young. About three litters, each containing about 3 young, are born during the year. The gestation period is 40 to 45 days. Young females are sexually mature at 6 to 8 months old.

NAME: Black Giant Squirrel, *Ratufa bicolor*
RANGE: Burma to Indonesia
HABITAT: dense forest
SIZE: body: 30–45 cm (11¾–17¾ in)
tail: 30–50 cm (11¾–19¾ in)

The 4 species of giant squirrel are, as their name implies, very large, and they can weigh up to 3 kg (6½ lb). Black giant squirrels are extremely agile, despite their size, and can leap 6 m (20 ft) or more through the trees; as they do so, their tails trail down like rudders. They feed on fruit, nuts, bark and a variety of small invertebrate animals. Singly or in pairs, they shelter in nests in tree holes.

In the breeding season a huge nest is made in which the female produces 1, sometimes 2, young after a gestation of about 4 weeks.

NAME: African Palm Squirrel, *Epixerus ebii*
RANGE: Ghana, Sierra Leone
HABITAT: dense forest; near swamps
SIZE: body: 25–30 cm (9¾–11¾ in)
tail: 28–30 cm (11–11¾ in) ①

The African palm squirrel is one of the rarest rodents on record. Forest clearance and swamp-draining activities present an intolerable disturbance to this species, from which it may not recover. However, the inaccessibility of its habitats affords it a measure of protection in some parts of its range, and this may allow time for a thorough survey to be made of its status, which at present is not really known. It is believed to feed largely on the nuts of the raphia swamp palm, but it probably eats other foods as well. Nothing is known of its breeding habits nor the reasons for its rarity.

NAME: Prevost's Squirrel, *Callosciurus prevosti*
RANGE: S.E. Asia
HABITAT: forest
SIZE: body: 20–28 cm (7¾–11 in)
tail: 15–25 cm (6–9¾ in)

The sharp contrast of colors in the coat of Prevost's squirrel makes it one of the most distinctive members of the family (the generic name means "beautiful squirrel"). These squirrels forage by day for seeds, nuts, buds, shoots and, occasionally, bird's eggs and insects. They live singly or in pairs. Shortly before giving birth, the female leaves her normal nest in a hollow tree and builds a nest of sticks, twigs and leaves high up in the branches. Here, safe from the attentions of ground-living predators, she gives birth to a litter of 3 or 4 young. It is not known exactly how many litters each female produces in a year, but in some parts of the range there may be as many as four.

Indian Striped Squirrel

European Red Squirrel

Black Giant Squirrel

African Giant Squirrel

Prevost's Squirrel

African Palm Squirrel

Gray Squirrel

Squirrels

NAME: **African Ground Squirrel,** *Xerus erythropus*
RANGE: **Africa: Morocco to Kenya**
HABITAT: **forest, scrub, savanna**
SIZE: **body: 22–30 cm ($8\frac{1}{2}$–$11\frac{3}{4}$ in)**
   tail: 18–27 cm (7–$10\frac{1}{2}$ in)

Rather like that of its North American counterpart, the fur of the African ground squirrel is harsh and smooth, with practically no underfur. It lives in extensive underground burrow systems, which it digs with its strong forepaws. Very tolerant of humans, it carries out its routine of searching for seeds, berries and green shoots by day. These squirrels are a social species and greet one another with a brief "kiss" and a flamboyant flick of the tail.

Mating occurs in March or April, and litters of 3 or 4 young are born after a gestation of about 4 weeks. In some areas, African ground squirrels are thought to inflict a poisonous bite; the basis for this mistaken belief is that their salivary glands contain streptobacilli, which cause septicemia.

NAME: **Thirteen-lined Ground Squirrel,** *Spermophilus tridecemlineatus*
RANGE: **S. central Canada, central USA**
HABITAT: **prairie, pastureland**
SIZE: **body: 17–29 cm ($6\frac{3}{4}$–$11\frac{1}{2}$ in)**
   tail: 6–14 cm ($2\frac{1}{4}$–$5\frac{1}{2}$ in)

These strikingly marked little rodents are active during the day and are often seen in considerable numbers, although their social groups are far looser than those of prairie dogs.

Like other ground squirrels, they have keen eyesight and frequently rear up on their haunches to survey the scene, searching for predators such as hawks, bobcats and foxes. If danger threatens, the squirrels disappear into their burrows. Although some squirrels live among piles of boulders, most dig burrows, which vary in size and complexity. Large squirrels may dig tunnels, which are 60 m (200 ft) or more in length, with side chambers, but younger individuals make smaller, shallower burrows. Seeds, nuts, fruit, roots and bulbs form the main bulk of the diet of these squirrels, but they sometimes eat insects, bird's eggs and even mice. In winter, they hibernate, having gained layers of body fat to sustain them through the winter. Their body temperature falls to about 2°C (35.6°F), and their hearts beat only about 5 times a minute, compared to 200 to 500 times in an active animal.

After hibernation, the squirrels mate; the gestation period is about 4 weeks, and a litter of up to 13 blind, helpless young is born in early summer. The eyes of the young open at about 4 weeks, and they are independent of the mother at about 6 weeks.

NAME: **Black-tailed Prairie Dog,** *Cynomys ludovicianus*
RANGE: **central USA**
HABITAT: **grassland (prairie)**
SIZE: **body: 28–32 cm (11–$12\frac{1}{2}$ in)**
   tail: 8.5–9.5 cm ($3\frac{1}{4}$–$3\frac{3}{4}$ in)

The prairie dog derives its common name from its stocky, terrierlike appearance and from its sharp, doglike bark, which it utters to herald danger. One of the most social rodent species, prairie dogs live in underground burrows, called towns, containing several thousand individuals. They emerge by day to graze on grass and other vegetation and can often cause serious damage to cattle ranges. Feeding is regularly interrupted for bouts of socializing, accompanied by much chattering.

Females give birth to litters of up to 10 young during March, April or May, after a 4-week gestation. After being weaned at 7 weeks, the young disperse to the edge of the town. Prairie dogs are commonly preyed on by eagles, foxes and coyotes.

NAME: **Eastern Chipmunk,** *Tamias striatus*
RANGE: **S.E. Canada, E. USA**
HABITAT: **forest**
SIZE: **body: 13.5–19 cm ($5\frac{1}{4}$–$7\frac{1}{2}$ in)**
   tail: 7.5–11.5 cm (3–$4\frac{1}{2}$ in)

The chipmunk is one of the best-known small mammals in North America, for its lack of fear of man and its natural curiosity make it a frequent sight at camping and picnic sites. Chipmunks dig burrows under logs and boulders, emerging in the early morning to forage for acorns, cherry stones, nuts, berries and all manner of seeds. Occasionally they are sufficiently numerous to cause damage to crops. During the autumn they store food supplies; they do not truly hibernate but merely become somewhat lethargic during winter.

A single litter of up to 8 young is born each spring. Although weaned at 5 weeks, the young stay with their mother for some months. They have a lifespan of about 5 years.

NAME: **Woodchuck,** *Marmota monax*
RANGE: **Alaska, Canada, south to E. USA**
HABITAT: **forest**
SIZE: **body: 45–61 cm ($17\frac{3}{4}$–24 in)**
   tail: 18–25 cm (7–$9\frac{3}{4}$ in)

The woodchuck, or groundhog as it is called in some regions, is a heavily built, rather belligerent rodent. Woodchucks feed in groups, and, ever fearful of the stealthy approach of a mountain lion or coyote, one member of the group keeps watch while the others search for edible roots, bulbs, tubers and seeds.

The young — 4 or 5 in a litter — are born in late spring and grow very fast. By autumn they have achieved adult size and are forced away from the parental nest by the aggression of the male. Woodchucks may live for as long as 15 years.

NAME: **Red Giant Flying Squirrel,** *Petaurista petaurista*
RANGE: **Asia: Kashmir to S. China; Sri Lanka, Java, Borneo**
HABITAT: **dense forest**
SIZE: **body: 40–58 cm ($15\frac{3}{4}$–$22\frac{3}{4}$ in)**
   tail: 43–63 cm (17–25 in)

The broad membrane that joins the ankles to the wrists of this handsome creature does not allow true flight, but the squirrel can glide up to 450 m (1,500 ft). Gliding enables the squirrel to move from one tall tree to another without having to descend to the ground each time. By day, these squirrels rest in hollow trees, coming out at dusk to search for nuts, fruit, tender twigs, young leaves and flower buds to eat. They live singly, in pairs or in family groups.

Little is known of the reproductive habits of these squirrels, but they appear to have just 1 or 2 young in each of two or three litters a year. Because the young are not seen to ride on the mother's back, it is assumed that they are deposited in a safe refuge while the mother feeds. These substantial rodents are hunted by local tribespeople for their flesh.

NAME: **Northern Flying Squirrel,** *Glaucomys sabrinus*
RANGE: **S. Canada, W. USA**
HABITAT: **forest**
SIZE: **body: 23.5–27 cm ($9\frac{1}{4}$–$10\frac{1}{2}$ in)**
   tail: 11–18 cm ($4\frac{1}{4}$–7 in)

By stretching out all four limbs when it jumps, the flying squirrel opens its flight membrane, which extends from wrists to ankles, and is able to glide from one tree to another. Speeds of as much as 110 m/min (360 ft/min) may be achieved. Normally the squirrels forage about in the treetops for nuts, living bark, lichens, fungi, fruit and berries, only taking to the air should an owl or other predator appear. In autumn, stocks of nuts and dried berries are laid up in hollow trees, for the flying squirrels do not hibernate in winter.

At any time from April onward, young are born in a softly lined nest in a hollow tree. There are normally between 2 and 6 in a litter, and the young suckle for about 10 weeks, unusually long for small rodents. It is thought that this is because an advanced level of development is necessary before gliding can be attempted.

African Ground Squirrel

Black-tailed Prairie Dog

Thirteen-lined Ground Squirrel

Eastern Chipmunk

Red Giant Flying Squirrel

Woodchuck

Northern Flying Squirrel

Pocket Gophers, Pocket Mice

GEOMYIDAE:
Pocket Gopher Family

There are some 30 species of pocket gopher distributed throughout North America, from 54° North to Panama and from coast to coast. They spend most of their lives underground, in complex and wide-ranging burrow systems which they dig with their chisel-like incisor teeth and strong, broad paws. Gophers occur wherever the soil is soft and supports rich vegetation — roots and tubers form the main diet.

The burrowing activities of these animals tend to be detrimental to grassland, and great efforts are made to exterminate pocket gophers, which, however, reproduce at a prodigious rate.

NAME: **Plains Pocket Gopher,** *Geomys bursarius*
RANGE: **central USA: Canadian border to Mexico**
HABITAT: **sandy soil in sparsely wooded areas**
SIZE: **body: 18–24 cm (7–9½ in)**
    tail: 10–12.5 cm (4–5 in)

Pocket gophers get their common name from the two deep, fur-lined cheek pouches, which can be crammed full of tubers or shoots for transport back to the nest. Plains pocket gophers lead solitary lives, the male leaving its burrow only to seek out a female during the breeding season; after mating, he returns to his burrow. A litter of 2 or 3 young is born after a gestation of 18 or 19 days. The young are weaned at 10 days but remain in their mother's burrow until they are about 2 months old. They are sexually mature at 3 months.

Although ranchers consider pocket gophers pests, their burrowing does aerate the soil and thus, in the long term, improves the productivity of the pastureland.

NAME: **Northern Pocket Gopher,** *Thomomys talpoides*
RANGE: **S.W. Canada to USA: Colorado**
HABITAT: **grassland and open forest to altitudes of 4,000 m (13,000 ft)**
SIZE: **body: 25–30 cm (9¾–11¾ in)**
    tail: 6–9.5 cm (2¼–3¾ in)

The northern pocket gopher often lives in areas which experience intense winter weather, but it does not hibernate. It builds up huge piles of roots and bulbs in underground larders and survives during the winter on these food stores. Pairs mate in early spring and litters of up to 10 young are born after a gestation of 18 days. Females may mate again almost immediately, giving birth a few days after the first litter is weaned.

HETEROMYIDAE:
Pocket Mouse Family

There are about 70 species of pocket mouse and kangaroo rat, with considerable variations in external appearance. Some are mouselike and live in dense forest, others have long hind legs, bound along like kangaroos and live in deserts and arid plains. They eat seeds, as well as insects and other invertebrates, and have deep, fur-lined cheek pouches in which food can be transported. They are fertile animals, some species producing three or four litters a year. The family occurs in North, Central and South America.

NAME: **Silky Pocket Mouse,** *Perognathus flavus*
RANGE: **USA: Wyoming, south to Texas; Mexico**
HABITAT: **low arid plains**
SIZE: **body: 10–12 cm (4–4¾ in)**
    tail: 4.5–6 cm (1¾–2¼ in)

The silky pocket mouse has dense soft fur which it keeps in immaculate condition. Although nocturnal, it emerges from its burrows when the sand is still very hot; the soles of its feet are covered by thick pads of soft fur which keep them from burning and which also act like snowshoes, spreading the body weight more evenly. The silky pocket mouse moves on all fours or on its hind legs only.

Breeding seasons are from April to June and August to September, and there are normally 4 young in a litter. They are born deep in the burrow system and first emerge to forage for seeds at about 3 weeks old.

NAME: **Californian Pocket Mouse,** *Perognathus californicus*
RANGE: **USA: California; south to Mexico: Baja California**
HABITAT: **arid sandy plains**
SIZE: **body: 19–23 cm (7½–9¼ in)**
    tail: 10–14.5 cm (4–5¾ in)

Californian pocket mice dig extensive burrow systems in the sandy soil of their habitat. The entrance is usually sited underneath a small shrub or bush to provide some shade and protection from predators. The mice feed largely on seeds, transporting them back to the burrow in their cheek pouches. They also eat green plants on occasion but seldom, if ever, drink; their bodies are adapted to survive without drinking. The breeding season lasts from April to September, but there is a marked decline in activity during the hottest part of the summer. Up to 7 young are born in each litter, after a gestation of about 25 days.

NAME: **Pale Kangaroo Mouse,** *Microdipodops pallidus*
RANGE: **USA: W. central Nevada**
HABITAT: **windswept sand dunes**
SIZE: **body: 6.5–8 cm (2½–3¼ in)**
    tail: 6.5–10 cm (2½–4 in)

To help it cover the great distances it must travel to find the sparse food supplies in its barren habitat, this rodent has powerful hind legs for bounding, with broad flat feet, fringed with stiff hairs. As the mouse hops, its long tail streams out, counterbalancing it and giving it the appearance of a small kangaroo.

Kangaroo mice are long-lived and breed more slowly than other members of their family. In particularly hot, dry summers, they do not breed at all.

NAME: **Desert Kangaroo Rat,** *Dipodomys deserti*
RANGE: **USA: Nevada, south to Mexico**
HABITAT: **arid brush and grassland**
SIZE: **body: 30.5–38 cm (12–15 in)**
    tail: 18–21.5 cm (7–8½ in)

Desert kangaroo rats dig their burrows in well-drained, easily dug soils. They are nocturnal and travel great distances in search of food. Since their kidneys are four times more efficient than a human's, they can live their whole lives without ever drinking.

Breeding occurs in any month of the year. Litters of up to 5 young are born after about 30 days' gestation.

NAME: **Mexican Spiny Pocket Mouse,** *Liomys irroratus*
RANGE: **USA: S.W. tip of Texas; Mexico**
HABITAT: **arid woodland**
SIZE: **body: 19–30 cm (7½–11¾ in)**
    tail: 9.5–17 cm (3¾–6¾ in)

The coat of this species bears stiff, grooved hairs which form a protective shield around the body, helping to deter some predators. It prefers lush, succulent vegetation to eat, but also forages for seeds and roots which it carries back to its burrow in its cheek pouches. Breeding takes place at any time of year, and litters usually contain about 4 young.

NAME: **Forest Spiny Pocket Mouse,** *Heteromys anomalus*
RANGE: **Colombia, Venezuela; Trinidad**
HABITAT: **tropical rain forest**
SIZE: **body: 12.5–16 cm (5–6¼ in)**
    tail: 13–20 cm (5–7¾ in)

This shy, nocturnal rodent lives in burrows on the forest floor. It collects seeds, buds, fruit, leaves and shoots and carries them back to the burrows for eating. Litters of about 4 young are born at any time of the year, but mostly in spring and early summer.

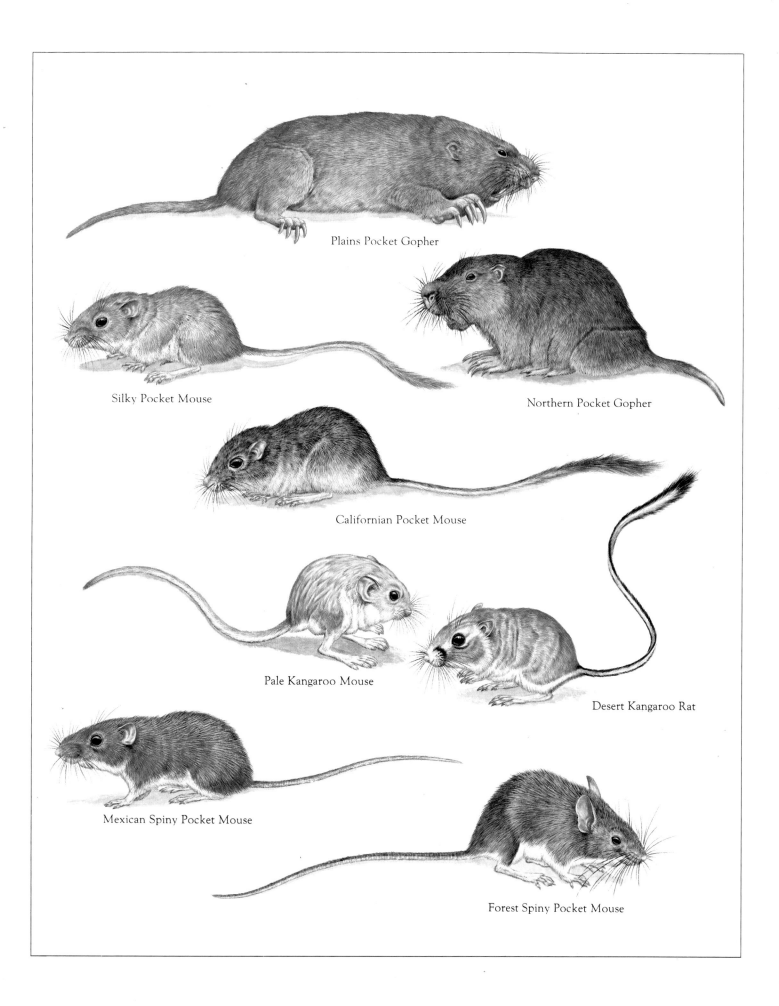

Plains Pocket Gopher

Silky Pocket Mouse

Northern Pocket Gopher

Californian Pocket Mouse

Pale Kangaroo Mouse

Desert Kangaroo Rat

Mexican Spiny Pocket Mouse

Forest Spiny Pocket Mouse

Mountain Beaver, Beavers, Springhare, Scaly-tailed Squirrels

APLODONTIDAE: Mountain Beaver Family

This rodent family contains a single species, the mountain beaver. Its common name is particularly inappropriate because this heavy-bodied, burrowing animal is neither a beaver nor associated with high country. Indeed, its ancestry and evolution are poorly understood, despite the fact that the fossil record suggests that the family is an ancient one.

NAME: **Mountain Beaver/Aplodontia,** *Aplodontia rufa*
RANGE: **N.W. USA**
HABITAT: **moist forest**
SIZE: **body: 30–43 cm (11¾–17 in)**
  tail: 2.5 cm (1 in)

The mountain beaver is a solitary creature, and each adult digs its own burrow system of underground nest and tunnels. Although it climbs poorly, rarely going up trees, almost any plant material, including bark and twigs, is eaten by the mountain beaver, and it makes stores of food for the winter months. In spring, beavers produce a litter of 2 or 3 young, which are born in a nest lined with dry vegetation.

CASTORIDAE: Beaver Family

The 2 species of beaver both lead semiaquatic lives and are excellent swimmers. Their hind feet are webbed, and they have broad, flat, hairless tails. Males and females look alike, but males tend to have larger anal scent glands. These glands produce a musky-smelling secretion, probably used for marking territory boundaries.

Beavers are always found near waterways surrounded by dense growths of trees such as willow, poplar, alder and birch. They feed on the bark, twigs, roots and leaves of these trees and use their enormous incisor teeth to fell trees for use in the construction of their complex dams and lodges.

Beavers make dams to create their desired living conditions. A pair starts by damming a stream with branches and mud to create a lake, deep enough not to freeze to the bottom in winter, in which they hoard a winter food supply of branches. A shelter with sleeping quarters is made of branches, by the dam or on an island or bank, or a burrow is dug in the riverbank. When beavers have felled all the available trees in their territory, they dig canals into the woods to float back trees from farther afield. Most of the beavers' activity takes place at night.

NAME: **Beaver,** *Castor canadensis*
RANGE: **N. America: Alaska to Texas**
HABITAT: **rivers, lakes, with wooded banks**
SIZE: **body: 73 cm–1.3 m (28¾ in–4¼ ft)**
  tail: 21–30 cm (8¼–11¾ in)

One of the largest rodents, the beaver weighs up to 27 kg (60 lb) or more. It is well adapted for its aquatic habits: the dense fur provides both waterproofing and insulation, and its ears and nostrils can be closed off by special muscles when it is under water, allowing it to stay submerged for up to 15 minutes.

A beaver colony normally consists of an adult pair and their young of the present and previous years. Two-year-old young are driven out to form their own colonies. Autumn is a busy time for the beavers, when they must make repairs to the lodge and dam and stockpile food for the winter. They mate in midwinter, and the young, usually 2 to 4, are born in the spring. The young are well developed at birth and are able to swim and feed themselves after about a month.

NAME: **Eurasian Beaver,** *Castor fiber*
RANGE: **now only in parts of Scandinavia, Poland, France, S. Germany, Austria and USSR**
HABITAT: **rivers, lakes, with wooded banks**
SIZE: **body: 73 cm–1.3 m (28¾ in–4¼ ft)**
  tail: 21–30 cm (8¼–11¾ in)

The largest European rodent, the Eurasian beaver has the same habits and much the same appearance as the American beaver, and they are considered by some experts to be only one species. Like its American counterpart, this beaver builds complex dams and lodges but, where conditions are right, may simply dig a burrow in the riverbank which it enters underwater. It feeds on bark and twigs in the winter and on all kinds of vegetation in summer.

Beavers are monogamous animals, and females are believed to mate for life: the male may mate with females other than his partner. Pairs produce litters of up to 8, usually 2 to 4, young in the spring.

PEDETIDAE: Springhare Family

This African rodent family contains a single species, the springhare. Its forelegs are short but the hind legs are relatively long and powerful, and it leaps along in hops of at least 3 m (10 ft). The long bushy tail acts as a counterbalance when the animal is traveling at high speed.

NAME: **Springhare,** *Pedetes capensis*
RANGE: **Kenya to South Africa**
HABITAT: **dry open country**
SIZE: **35–43 cm (13¾–17 in)**
  tail: 37–47 cm (14½–18½ in)

When alarmed or traveling distances, springhares bound along like kangaroos, but when feeding, they move on all fours. A nocturnal animal as a rule, the springhare spends the day in its burrow, emerging at night to feed on bulbs, roots, grain and sometimes a few insects. Several burrows occur in the same area, some occupied by individuals, others by families. There is probably only one litter a year of 1, sometimes 2, young, born in the burrow.

ANOMALURIDAE: Scaly-tailed Squirrel Family

The 7 species of scaly-tailed squirrel are all tree-dwelling rodents, found in the forests of west and central Africa. Apart from a single "nonflying" species, they all have broad membranes at the sides of the body which can be stretched out to form a parachutelike structure, allowing the animal to glide through the air. Scaly-tailed squirrels are not closely related to true squirrels (Sciuridae).

NAME: **Beecroft's Flying Squirrel,** *Anomalurus beecrofti*
RANGE: **W. and central Africa**
HABITAT: **forest**
SIZE: **body: 30–40.5 cm (11¾–16 in)**
  tail: 23–43 cm (9–17 in)

Beecroft's flying squirrel travels from tree to tree, rarely descending to the ground. With flight membranes extended, it leaps off one branch and glides up to 90 m (300 ft), to land on another tree. It finds all its food up in the trees and feeds on berries, seeds and fruit, as well as on some green plant material. Most of its activity takes place at night. These rodents generally live singly or in pairs and make dens in tree holes. They produce two litters a year of 2 or 3 young each.

NAME: **Zenker's Flying Squirrel,** *Idiurus zenkeri*
RANGE: **Cameroon, Zaire**
HABITAT: **forest**
SIZE: **body: 6–10 cm (2¼–4 in)**
  tail: 7.5–13 cm (3–5 in)

This small flying squirrel has an unusual tail with long hairs projecting from each side, giving it a feathery appearance. Like its relatives, Zenker's flying squirrel is mainly nocturnal and feeds on berries, seeds and fruit. A gregarious species, it lives in holes in trees in groups of up to a dozen.

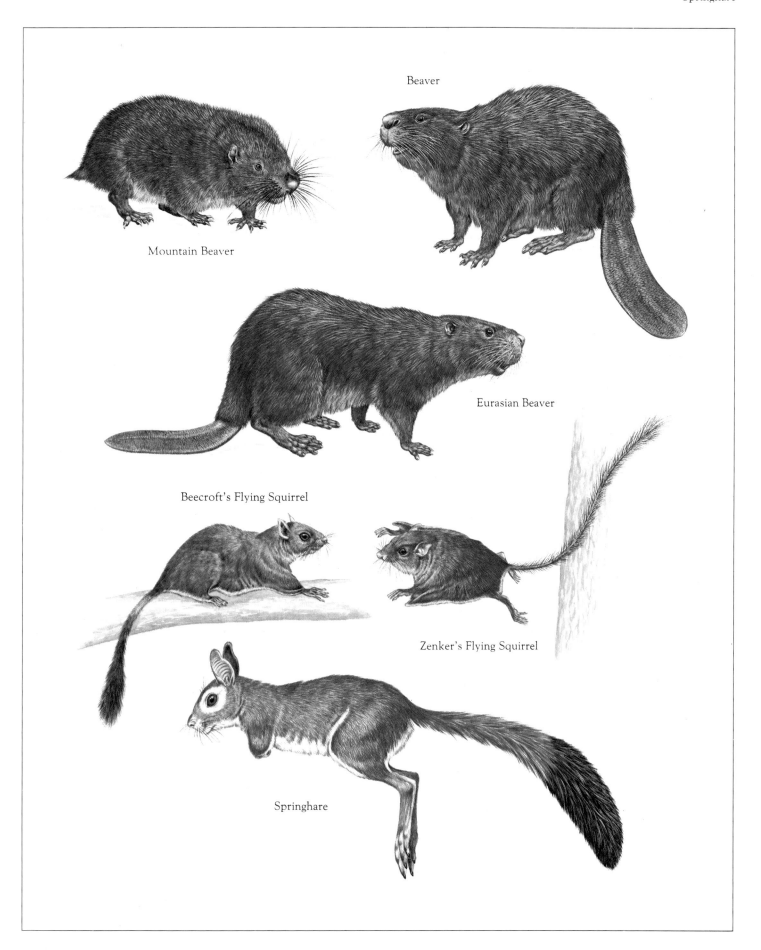

Beaver

Mountain Beaver

Eurasian Beaver

Beecroft's Flying Squirrel

Zenker's Flying Squirrel

Springhare

New World Rats and Mice

NAME: **Baja California Rice Rat,** ***Oryzomys peninsulae***
RANGE: **Mexico: tip of Baja California**
HABITAT: **damp land in dense cover**
SIZE: **body: 22.5–33 cm (9–13 in)**
tail: 11–18 cm (4¼–7 in)

There are 100 species of rice rat, all looking much like the Baja California species and leading similar lives. They feed mostly on green vegetation, such as reeds and sedges, but also eat fish and invertebrates. They can become serious pests in rice fields and can cause severe damage to the plants. They weave grassy nests on reed platforms above water level or, in drier habitats, excavate burrows in which they breed throughout the year, producing up to 7 young in each litter.

NAME: **Spiny Rice Rat,** ***Neacomys guianae***
RANGE: **Colombia, east to Guyana**
HABITAT: **dense humid forest**
SIZE: **body: 7–10 cm (2¾–4 in)**
tail: 7–10 cm (2¾–4 in)

This species is distinguished by the spiny coat, which grows thickly on the rat's back but sparsely on its flanks. Little is known of these rodents, which live on the floors of the most impenetrable forests, but it is thought that they breed the year round, producing litters of 2 to 4 young.

NAME: **Climbing Mouse,** ***Rhipidomys venezuelae***
RANGE: **N. Brazil, Venezuela, Guyana**
HABITAT: **dense forest**
SIZE: **body: 8–15 cm (3¼–6 in)**
tail: 18–25 cm (7–9¾ in)

This secretive, nocturnal mouse lives in the deepest forest. Although it makes its nest in a burrow beneath the roots of a tree, it spends much of its life high in the treetops, feeding on lichens, small invertebrates and plants such as bromeliads. Equipped with strong, broad feet and long, sharp claws, it is an agile climber, and its long tail acts as a counterbalance when it jumps from one branch to the next. Climbing mice breed throughout the year, and the usual litter is 2 to 5 young.

NAME: **Western Harvest Mouse,** ***Reithrodontomys megalotis***
RANGE: **USA: Oregon, south to Panama**
HABITAT: **grassland**
SIZE: **body: 5–14 cm (2–5½ in)**
tail: 6–9 cm (2¼–3½ in)

Harvest mice tend to prefer overgrown pastures to cultivated farmland. In summer, they weave globular nests, up to 17.5 cm (7 in) in diameter, attached to stalks of vegetation. Litters of about 4 young are born in these nests after a gestation period of about 23 days.

HESPEROMYINAE:
New World Rats and Mice Subfamily

This is one of the 14 subfamilies of the huge rodent family Muridae, which contains rats, mice, voles, gerbils, hamsters and others. There are about 350 species in this subfamily, and it is the largest mammalian group. Members occur in all habitats, from deserts to humid forests. These undistinguished but abundant little rodents are of immense importance as the primary consumers in their range and occupy a basic position in a number of food chains.

NAME: **Deer Mouse,** ***Peromyscus maniculatus***
RANGE: **Canada to Mexico**
HABITAT: **forest, grassland, scrub**
SIZE: **body: 12–22 cm (4¾–8½ in)**
tail: 8–18 cm (3¼–7 in)

Deer mice are agile animals, running and hopping with ease through what sometimes seems quite impenetrable bush. They construct underground nests of dry vegetation and may move house several times a year. They have a catholic diet, consisting almost equally of plant and animal matter. Young deer mice start to breed at 7 weeks, and litters of up to 9 young are born after a gestation of between 3 and 4 weeks.

NAME: **Golden Mouse,** ***Ochrotomys nuttalli***
RANGE: **S.E. USA**
HABITAT: **brushy and thicketed scrub**
SIZE: **body: 8–9.5 cm (3¼–3¾ in)**
tail: 7–9.5 cm (2¾–3¾ in)

This little mouse spends most of its life among the vines of wild honeysuckle and greenbrier. Here it weaves a solid-looking nest, which may house a whole family or just a single mouse. The mice also build rough feeding platforms in other spots, where they sit to consume seeds and nuts. Golden mice breed from spring to early autumn. The gestation period is about 4 weeks, and there are usually 2 or 3 young in a litter.

NAME: **Northern Grasshopper Mouse,** ***Onychomys leucogaster***
RANGE: **S. Canada to N. Mexico**
HABITAT: **semiarid scrub and desert**
SIZE: **body: 9–13 cm (3½–5 in)**
tail: 3–6 cm (1¼–2¼ in)

The northern grasshopper mouse is largely carnivorous: grasshoppers and scorpions are its main prey, but it may even overpower and eat one of its own kind. These mice nest in burrows, which they dig themselves or find abandoned, and breed in spring and summer, producing litters of 2 to 6 young after a 33-day gestation.

NAME: **South American Field Mouse,** ***Akodon arviculoides***
RANGE: **Brazil**
HABITAT: **woodland, cultivated land**
SIZE: **body: 11.5–14.5 cm (4½–5¾ in)**
tail: 4.5–6.5 cm (1¾–2½ in)

There are more than 60 species of South American field mouse. These mice are active day and night, although most above-ground activity takes place at night; they feed on a wide range of plant matter. There are usually two litters each year, in November and March, with up to 7 young in a litter. Special breeding chambers in the burrows are set aside for pregnant and nursing females.

NAME: **Arizona Cotton Rat,** ***Sigmodon arizonae***
RANGE: **USA: Arizona, south to Mexico**
HABITAT: **dry grassland**
SIZE: **12.5–20 cm (5–7¾ in)**
tail: 7.5–12.5 cm (3–5 in)

Cotton rats are so abundant that they are sometimes declared a plague. They normally feed on plants and small insects, but when populations are high, they take the eggs and chicks of bobwhites as well as crayfish and fiddler crabs. They breed prolifically, producing their first litter of up to 12 young when just 10 weeks old.

NAME: **White-throated Wood Rat,** ***Neotoma albigula***
RANGE: **USA: California to Texas, south to Mexico**
HABITAT: **scrub, lightly forested land**
SIZE: **body: 28–40 cm (11–15¾ in)**
tail: 7.5–18.5 cm (3–7¼ in)

A group of up to 100 of these rats will build a large nest of whatever material is available, such as twigs and pieces of cactus. The nest may be up to 2 m (6½ ft) in diameter and is usually situated in a pile of rocks or at the base of a tree. The rats dash in and out of the nest, foraging for shoots, fruit and other plant food. Litters contain 1 to 4 young.

NAME: **Fish-eating Rat,** ***Ichthyomys stolzmanni***
RANGE: **Colombia, south to Peru**
HABITAT: **near rivers and lakes**
SIZE: **body: 14.5–21 cm (5¾–8¼ in)**
tail: 14.5–19 cm (5¾–7½ in)

Fish-eating rats are highly specialized rodents, well adapted to feeding on fish and some aquatic invertebrates, for they have partially webbed feet and swim strongly. The upper incisor teeth are simple, spikelike structures, used to spear the fish, which is then dragged ashore for consumption. The rats breed in burrows, which they dig in a riverbank, and produce one or two litters of young each year.

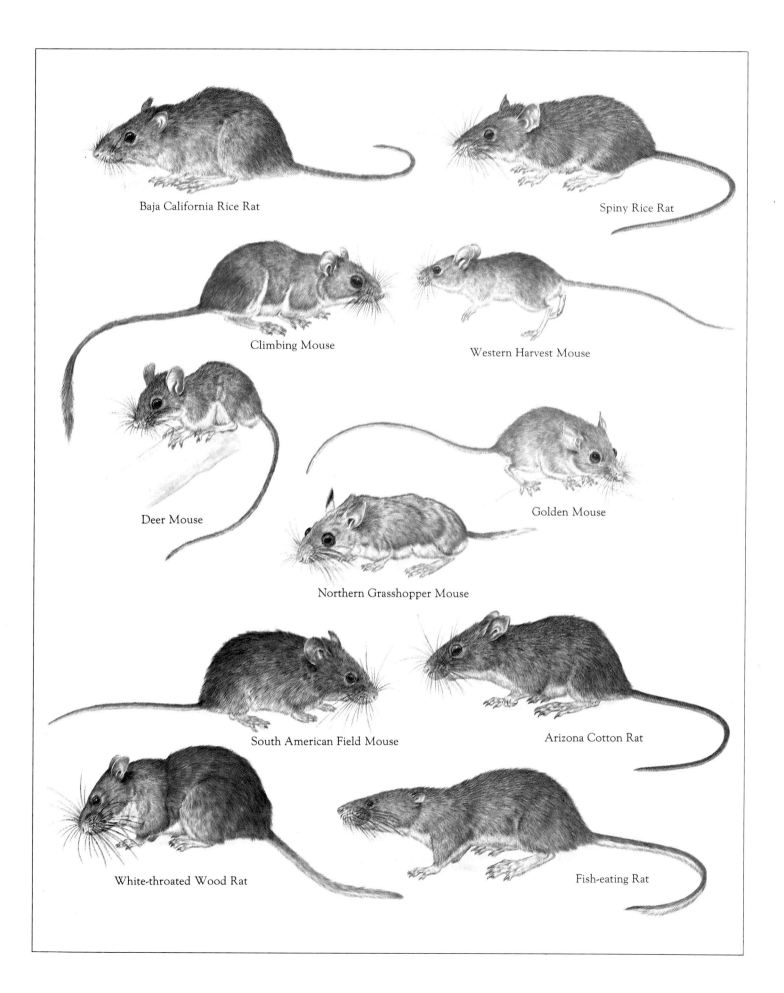

Baja California Rice Rat

Spiny Rice Rat

Climbing Mouse

Western Harvest Mouse

Deer Mouse

Golden Mouse

Northern Grasshopper Mouse

South American Field Mouse

Arizona Cotton Rat

White-throated Wood Rat

Fish-eating Rat

Hamsters, Mole-rats

CRICETINAE: Hamster Subfamily

The true hamsters are small burrowing rodents, found in the Old World from Europe eastward through the Middle East and central Asia. There are 15 species known, all of which are characterized by a body shape like that of a thickset rat with a short tail. All species have capacious cheek pouches, used for carrying food back to the burrow; when full, the pouches may extend back beyond the level of the shoulder blades.

NAME: **Common Hamster, *Cricètus cricetus***
RANGE: **W. Europe, USSR**
HABITAT: **grassland, cultivated land**
SIZE: **body: 22–30 cm (8½–11¾ in)**
  tail: 3–6 cm (1¼–2¼ in)

The common hamster occupies a burrow system with separate chambers for sleeping and food storage. It feeds on seeds, grain, roots, potatoes, green plants and insect larvae. In late summer, it collects food for its winter stores. Grain is particularly favored, and up to 10 kg (22 lb) may be hoarded. From October to March or April, the hamster hibernates, waking periodically to feed on its stores.

During the summer, females usually produce two litters, each of 6 to 12 young, which themselves bear when they are just 2 months old.

NAME: **Golden Hamster, *Mesocricetus auratus***
RANGE: **Middle East**
HABITAT: **steppe**
SIZE: **body: 17–18 cm (6¾–7 in)**
  tail: 1.25 cm (½ in)

Golden hamsters are primarily nocturnal creatures, but they may be active at times during the day. Adults live alone in burrow systems which they dig. They are omnivorous, feeding on vegetation, seeds, fruit and even small animals. Their cheek pouches are large and, when filled, double the width of head and shoulders.

Golden hamsters are highly aggressive and solitary creatures, and females must advertise clearly when they are sexually receptive. They do this by applying a specific vaginal secretion to rocks and sticks in their territories and cease to mark as soon as the receptive phase of the estrous cycle is over. The usual litter contains 6 or 7 young, and there may be several litters a year.

The domesticated strain of the species makes a popular pet.

NAME: **Striped Hamster, *Phodopus sungorus***
RANGE: **USSR, N. China**
HABITAT: **arid plains, sand dunes**
SIZE: **body: 5–10 cm (2–4 in)**
  tail: absent

This small, yet robust hamster is active at night and at dawn and dusk. Little is known about it, but its habits seem to be similar to those of other hamsters. It feeds on seeds and plant material and fills its cheek pouches with food to carry back to its burrow.

Striped hamsters are more sociable than their golden cousins and may occur in quite large colonies. They are so well adapted to their cool habitat that they do not breed well at room temperature. Litters contain 2 to 6 young, which are weaned at 21 days. Females mate again immediately after giving birth, so they can produce litters at three-week intervals.

SPALACINAE:
Blind Mole-rat Subfamily

This small subfamily of highly specialized burrowing rodents probably contains only the 3 species found in the eastern Mediterranean area, the Middle East, southern USSR and northern Africa. They are heavy-bodied rodents with short legs, small feet and a remarkable absence of external projections: there is no tail, external ears are not apparent, and there are no external openings for the tiny eyes that lie buried under the skin.

NAME: **Lesser Mole-rat, *Spalax leucodon***
RANGE: **S.E. Europe; Africa: Libya**
HABITAT: **grassland and cultivated land**
SIZE: **body: 15–30.5 cm (6–12 in)**
  tail: absent

Mole-rats live in complex burrow systems with many chambers and connecting tunnels, which they dig with their teeth and heads, rather than with their feet. They feed underground on roots, bulbs and tubers but may occasionally venture above ground at night to feed on grasses, seeds and even insects. One litter of 2 to 4 young is born in early spring, after a gestation of about 4 weeks.

MYOSPALACINAE:
Eastern Asiatic Mole-rat Subfamily

There are 4 species in this group, found in USSR and China. These mole-rats are stocky, burrowing rodents equipped with heavily clawed limbs for digging. They do not have external ears, but their tiny eyes are apparent, and there is a short, tapering tail.

NAME: **Common Chinese Zokor, *Myospalax fontanieri***
RANGE: **China: Szechwan to Hopeh Provinces**
HABITAT: **grassland, steppe**
SIZE: **body: 15–27 cm (6–10½ in)**
  tail: 3–7 cm (1¼–2¾ in)

The zokor lives in long burrows, which it digs with amazing speed among the roots of trees and bushes, using its long, sharp claws. As it goes, it leaves behind a trail of "mole hills" on the surface. Grain, roots and other underground parts of plants are its main foods, and the zokor ventures above ground only occasionally at night, when it runs the risk of being caught by an owl.

RHIZOMYINAE:
Mole-rat and Bamboo Rat Subfamily

There are 6 species in this subfamily, which fall into two closely related groups: 2 species of East African mole-rats and 4 species of Southeast Asian bamboo rats. All are plant-eating, burrowing rodents.

NAME: **Giant Mole-rat, *Tachyoryctes macrocephalus***
RANGE: **Africa: Ethiopia**
HABITAT: **montane grassland**
SIZE: **body: 18–25.5 cm (7–10 in)**
  tail: 5–8 cm (2–3 in)

The giant mole-rat has a stout, molelike body and small, yet functional eyes. It is a powerful burrower, equipped with short, strong limbs and claws. When a pile of soil has built up behind it, the animal turns and pushes the soil to the surface with the side of its head and one forefoot. It is active both day and night and feeds on plant material above and below ground.

Surprisingly for such a common species, nothing is known of the breeding habits of this mole-rat.

NAME: **Bamboo Rat, *Rhizomys sumatrensis***
RANGE: **Indo-China, Malaysia, Sumatra**
HABITAT: **bamboo forest**
SIZE: **body: 35–48 cm (13¾–18¾ in)**
  tail: 10–15 cm (4–6 in)

The bamboo rat has a heavy body, short legs and a short, almost hairless tail. Its incisor teeth are large and strong, and it uses these and its claws for digging. It burrows underground near clumps of bamboo, the roots of which are its staple diet. It also comes out of its burrow to feed on bamboo above ground and on other plants, seeds and fruit.

The usual litter is believed to contain 3 to 5 young, and there may be more than one litter a year.

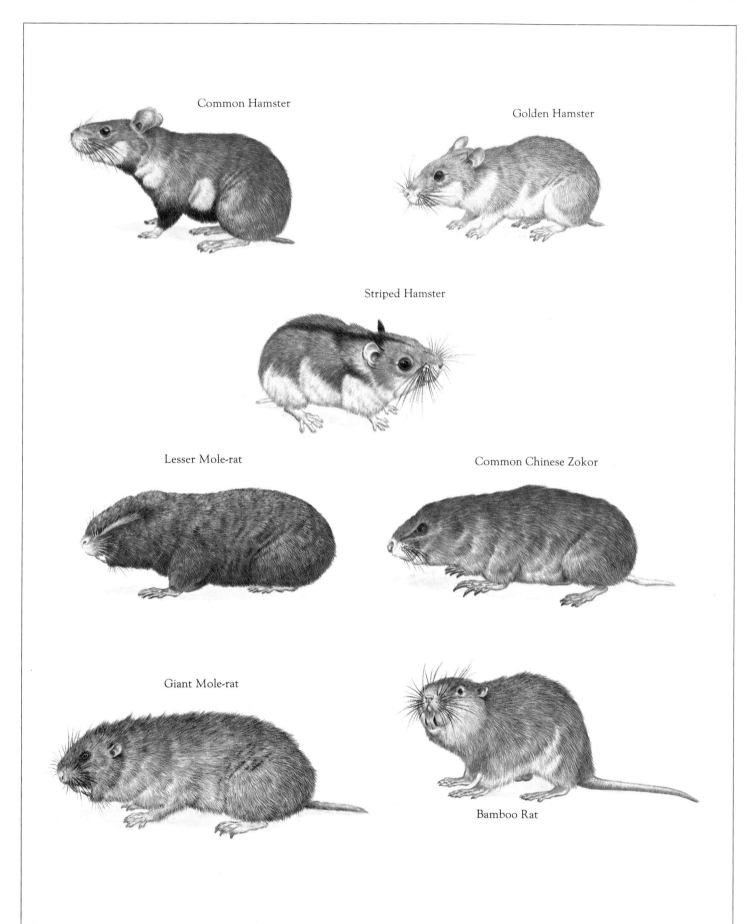

Common Hamster

Golden Hamster

Striped Hamster

Lesser Mole-rat

Common Chinese Zokor

Giant Mole-rat

Bamboo Rat

Crested Rat,
Spiny Dormice and relatives

LOPHIOMYINAE:
Crested Rat Subfamily

A single species is known in this group: the crested, or maned, rat, found in dense mountain forests. The animal's general appearance is not at all ratlike, for it is about the size of a guinea pig and has long, soft fur and a thick, bushy tail. The female is generally larger than the male.

NAME: **Crested Rat**, *Lophiomys imhausi*
RANGE: E. Africa
HABITAT: forest
SIZE: body: 25.5–36 cm (10–14¼ in)
 tail: 14–18 cm (5½–7 in)

Crested rats are skilled climbers, leaving their daytime burrows at night to collect leaves, buds and shoots among the trees. Along the neck, back and part of the tail is a prominent mane of coarse hairs, which can be erected when the animal is excited or alarmed. The raised crest exposes a long scent gland, which produces a stifling odor in order to deter predators. The hairs lining the gland have a unique, wicklike structure to help broadcast the odor. Another curious feature of these rodents is the reinforced skull, the significance of which is not known.

NESOMYINAE:
Madagascan Rat Subfamily

This subfamily includes 11 species, of which 10 are found only in Madagascar and 1 occurs in South Africa. It is a varied group, and the species seem to have become adapted to fill different ecological niches, but they do have some common features. It has been suggested, however, that they are not all of common ancestry and that a considerable amount of evolutionary convergence has occurred.

NAME: **Madagascan Rat**, *Nesomys rufus*
RANGE: Madagascar
HABITAT: forest
SIZE: body: 19–23 cm (7½–9 in)
 tail: 16–19 cm (6¼–7½ in)

This species of Madagascan rat is mouselike in appearance, with long, soft fur and a light-colored belly. Its hind feet are long and powerful, and the middle three toes are elongated. It seems likely that the Madagascan rat is an adept climber, using its sharp claws to grip smooth bark.

Although little is known of this creature's habits, it is probable that its diet is made up of small invertebrates, buds, fruit and seeds. Nothing is known of its breeding cycle.

NAME: **White-tailed Rat**, *Mystromys albicaudatus*
RANGE: South Africa
HABITAT: grassland, arid plains
SIZE: body: 14–18 cm (5½–7 in)
 tail: 5–8 cm (2–3 in)

The white-tailed rat is the only member of its group to occur outside Madagascar. It is a nocturnal creature and spends the day in an underground hole, emerging at dusk to feed on seeds and other plant material. It is said that the strong smell of these rodents repels mammalian predators, such as suricates and mongooses, but they are caught by barn, eagle and grass owls.

White-tailed rats appear to breed throughout the year, producing litters of 4 or 5 young. A curious feature of the early development of these rats is that the young become firmly attached to the female's nipples and are carried about by her. They only detach themselves when about 3 weeks old.

PLATACANTHOMYINAE:
Spiny Dormouse Subfamily

There are 2 species in this subfamily. Their common name originates from the flat, pointed spines that are intermixed with the fur, particularly on the back. Spiny dormice are well adapted for tree-climbing, for their feet are equipped with sharp claws and padded soles, and the digits spread widely.

NAME: **Malabar Spiny Dormouse**, *Platacanthomys lasiurus*
RANGE: S. India
HABITAT: forest, rocks
SIZE: body: 13–21 cm (5–8¼ in)
 tail: 7.5–10 cm (3–4 in)

The Malabar spiny dormouse lives in trees and feeds on seeds, grain and fruit. The long tail, with its dense, bushy tip, is used as a balancing aid when the animal is moving in trees. A nest of leaves and moss is made for shelter in a hole in a tree or among rocks. This rodent sometimes becomes an agricultural pest because of its diet, and it has been known to destroy quantities of crops such as ripe peppers.

Although spiny dormice are not uncommon, nothing is known of the breeding habits of these secretive rodents. The other species of the subfamily, the Chinese pygmy dormouse, *Typhlomys cinereus*, lives in forest in southeast China.

OTOMYINAE:
African Swamp Rat Subfamily

There are about 12 species in this group, all found in Africa, south of the Sahara to Cape Province. They inhabit a range of habitats and climatic zones, including mountains, arid regions and swampy areas, and are all competent swimmers. A characteristic of the group is that the members have only two pairs of mammary glands, situated in the lower abdomen.

NAME: **Swamp Rat**, *Otomys irroratus*
RANGE: Zimbabwe to South Africa
HABITAT: damp grassland, swamps
SIZE: body: 13–20 cm (5–7¾ in)
 tail: 5–17 cm (2–6¾ in)

A plump-bodied rodent, the African swamp rat has a rounded, volelike head and small ears. Characteristic features are the grooves on each side of the incisor teeth. Active day and night, this rat feeds on seeds, berries, shoots and grasses. It will enter water readily and even dive to escape danger. Its nest is usually above ground and is made of plant material, although in some areas swamp rats make use of burrows discarded by other species.

Young females reach sexual maturity at 10 weeks of age, males about 3 weeks later. Although swamp rats seldom damage crops, their parasites do transmit tick-bite fever and possibly bubonic plague. Swamp rats are an important food source for many larger predators.

NAME: **Karroo Rat**, *Parotomys brantsi*
RANGE: South Africa: Cape Province
HABITAT: sandy plains
SIZE: body: 13.5–17 cm (5¼–6¾ in)
 tail: 7.5–12 cm (3–4½ in)

Karroo rats are gregarious animals which live in colonies. They dig burrows and sometimes also build nests of sticks and grass above the burrows. They are nervous, wary animals and stay near their shelters most of the time. Leaves of the saltbush tree provide the bulk of their diet, and they generally feed during the day. Every 3 or 4 years, their population increases dramatically and they feed on agricultural crops, causing considerable damage.

Karroo rats are believed to breed about four times a year, producing litters of 2 to 4 young.

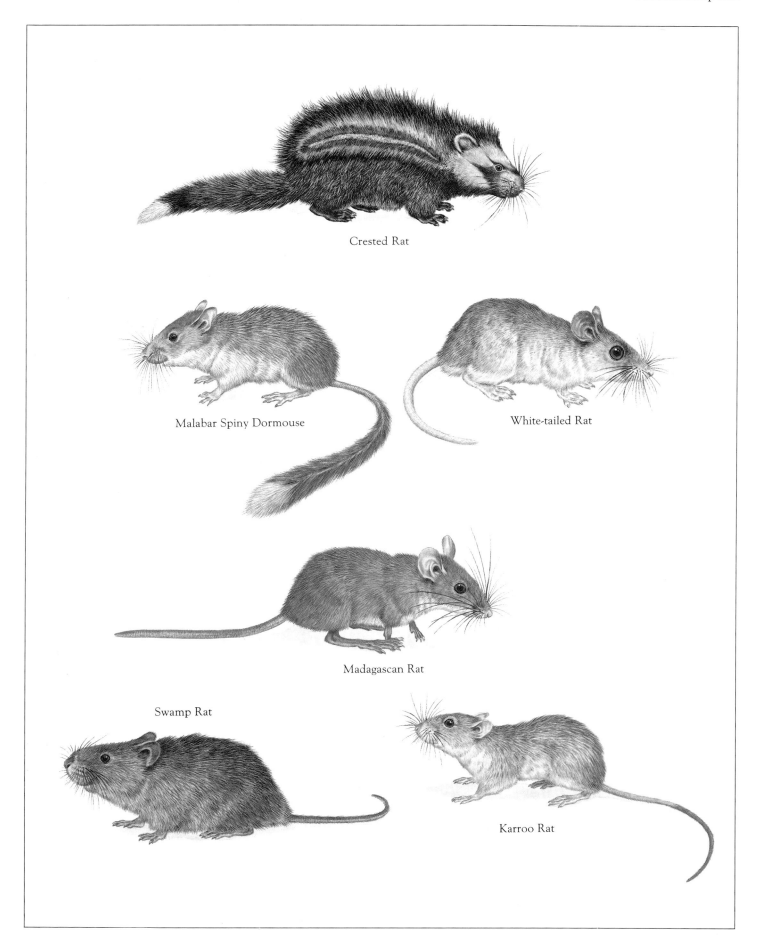

Crested Rat

Malabar Spiny Dormouse

White-tailed Rat

Madagascan Rat

Swamp Rat

Karroo Rat

Voles and Lemmings

NAME: **Norway Lemming,** *Lemmus*
lemmus
RANGE: **Scandinavia**
HABITAT: **tundra, grassland**
SIZE: **body: 13–15 cm (5–6 in)**
tail: 2 cm (¾ in)

The boldly patterned Norway lemming is active day and night, alternating periods of activity with short spells of rest. Grasses, shrubs and particularly mosses make up its diet; in winter it clears runways under the snow on the ground surface in its search for food. These lemmings start to breed in spring, under the snow, and may produce as many as eight litters of 6 young each throughout the summer.

Lemmings are fabled for their dramatic population explosions, which occur approximately every three or four years. It is still not known what causes these, but a fine, warm spring following two or three years of low population usually triggers an explosion that year or the next. As local populations swell, lemmings are forced into surrounding areas. Gradually more and more are driven out, down the mountains and into the valleys. Many are eaten by predators, and more lose their lives crossing rivers and lakes. Lemmings do not deliberately commit suicide.

NAME: **Southern Bog Lemming,**
Synaptomys cooperi
RANGE: **N.E. USA; S.E. Canada**
HABITAT: **bogs, meadows**
SIZE: **body: 8.5–11 cm (3¼–4¼ in)**
tail: 2 cm (¾ in)

Sociable animals, southern bog lemmings live in colonies of up to about 30 or so. They make burrows just under the ground surface and also clear a network of paths, or runways, on the surface, where they keep the grass cut and trimmed; little piles of cuttings punctuate these runways. Bog lemmings are active day and night. They have powerful jaws and teeth and feed largely on plant material. Breeding continues throughout the spring and summer, and females produce two or three litters a year of 1 to 4 young each.

NAME: **Sagebrush Vole,** *Lagurus curtatus*
RANGE: **W. USA**
HABITAT: **arid plains**
SIZE: **body: 9.5–11 cm (3¾–4¼ in)**
tail: 1.5–3 cm (½–1¼ in)

As its common name suggests, this pale-colored vole is particularly common in some areas of arid plains where the sagebrush is abundant. It makes shallow burrows near the ground surface and is active at any time of the day and night. It feeds on the sagebrush and on other green vegetation and produces several litters a year of 4 to 6 young each.

MICROTINAE:
Vole and Lemming Subfamily

There are about 110 species in this group of rodents, found in North America, northern Europe and Asia; lemmings tend to be confined to the more northerly regions. All species are largely herbivorous, and they usually live in groups or colonies. Many dig shallow tunnels, close to the ground surface, and clear paths through the grass within their range. Others are partly aquatic, and some species climb among low bushes.

Local populations of voles and lemmings are subject to cyclical variation in density, with boom years of greatly increased population occurring every few years.

NAME: **Southern Mole-vole,** *Ellobius*
fuscocapillus
RANGE: **central Asia**
HABITAT: **grassy plains**
SIZE: **body: 10–15 cm (4–6 in)**
tail: 0.5–2 cm (¼–¾ in)

The southern mole-vole is a more habitual burrower than other voles and lemmings and is more specifically adapted. Its snout is blunt, its eyes and ears small to minimize damage from the soil, and it has short, strong legs. It probably uses its teeth to loosen the soil when burrowing, for while its incisors are stronger than is usual in voles, its claws, although adequate, are not as strong as those of other burrowing rodents.

Southern mole-voles feed on roots and other underground parts of plants. Like moles, they make shallow tunnels in which to search for food and deeper, more permanent tunnels for nesting. They breed at any time of year, probably according to the availability of food, and produce 3 or 4 young at a time.

NAME: **Bank Vole,** *Clethrionomys*
glareolus
RANGE: **Europe (not extreme north or**
south), east to USSR
HABITAT: **woodland**
SIZE: **body: 8–11 cm (3¼–4¼ in)**
tail: 3–6.5 cm (1¼–2½ in)

The bank vole feeds on softer plant material than most voles. It will climb on bushes to find its food, eating buds, leaves and fruit, as well as some insects. It is active night and day, with several rest periods, and, like other voles, it clears well-defined runways in the grass and makes shallow tunnels. Nests are usually made under logs or among tree roots, and in summer females produce several litters of 3 to 5 young each.

NAME: **Meadow Vole,** *Microtus*
pennsylvanicus
RANGE: **Canada, N. USA**
HABITAT: **grassland, woodland, often**
near water
SIZE: **body: 9–12.5 cm (3½–5 in)**
tail: 3.5–6.5 cm (1¼–2½ in)

The meadow vole is a highly adaptable species, found in a wide range of habitats. It is a social animal, but each adult has its own territory. The voles clear runways in the grass, which they keep trimmed, and feed on plant material such as grass, seeds, roots and bark. A nest of grass is made in the ground or in a shallow burrow under the runways.

The female is a prolific breeder, producing at least three and often as many as twelve or thirteen litters a year of up to 10 young each. The gestation period is 3 weeks, and females start to breed at only 3 weeks old.

NAME: **Muskrat,** *Ondatra zibethicus*
RANGE: **Canada, USA; introduced in**
Europe
HABITAT: **marshes, freshwater banks**
SIZE: **body: 25–36 cm (9¾–14¼ in)**
tail: 20–28 cm (7¾–11 in)

An excellent swimmer, this large rodent spends much of its life in water and has webbed hind feet and a long, naked, vertically flattened tail which it uses as a rudder. It feeds on aquatic and land vegetation and occasionally on some mussels, frogs and fish. It usually digs a burrow in the bank of a river, but where conditions permit, it builds a lodge from plant debris in shallow water and inside it constructs a dry sleeping platform above water level. The lodge may shelter as many as 10 animals.

At the onset of the breeding season, the muskrats' groin glands enlarge and produce a musky secretion, believed to attract male and female to one another. They breed from April to August in the north, and throughout the winter in the south of their range. Two or three litters of 3 or 4 young are born after a gestation of 29 or 30 days.

NAME: **European Water Vole,** *Arvicola*
terrestris
RANGE: **Europe, east to E. Siberia**
HABITAT: **freshwater banks, grassland**
SIZE: **body: 14–19 cm (5½–7½ in)**
tail: 4–10 cm (1½–4 in)

Although competent in water, the European water vole is less agile than the more specialized muskrats and beavers. It makes a burrow in the bank of a river or stream or burrows into the ground, if far from water. Grasses and other plant material are its main food. Water voles breed in summer, producing several litters of 4 to 6 young.

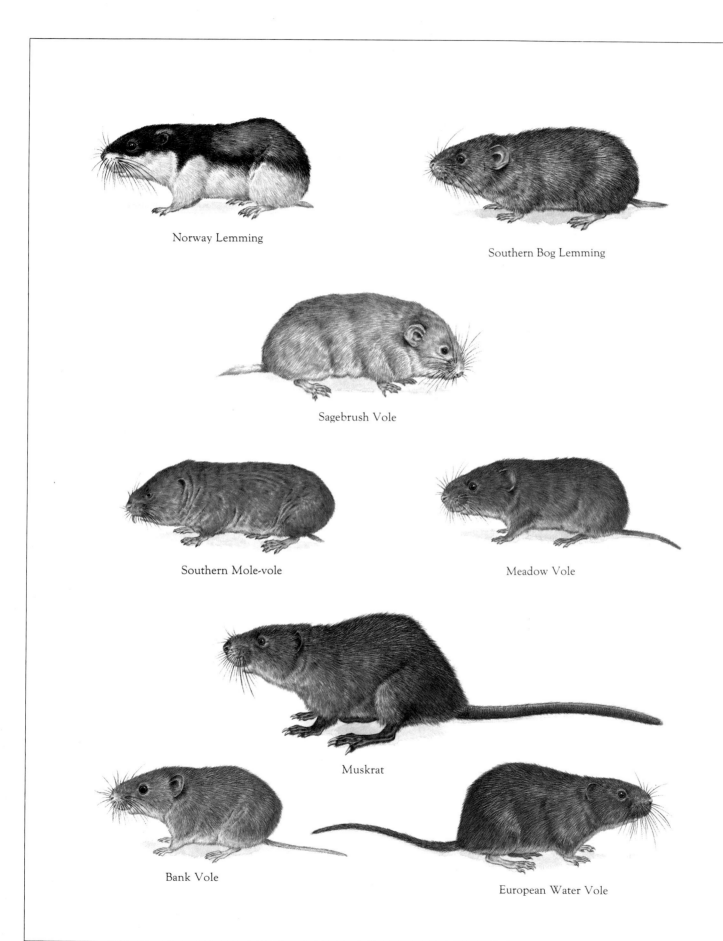

Norway Lemming

Southern Bog Lemming

Sagebrush Vole

Southern Mole-vole

Meadow Vole

Muskrat

Bank Vole

European Water Vole

Gerbils

NAME: Large North African Gerbil, *Gerbillus campestris*
RANGE: Africa: Morocco to Somalia
HABITAT: sandy desert
SIZE: body: 10–14 cm (4–$5\frac{1}{2}$ in)
tail: 11–12 cm ($4\frac{1}{4}$–$4\frac{3}{4}$ in)

There are about 25 species in the genus *Gerbillus*, all found from Morocco eastward to Pakistan. All occupy the driest deserts and eke out their existence in the most inhospitable environments. The large North African gerbil occurs in groups of 12 or more, living in simple, poorly made burrows, dug in the sand. The gerbils remain hidden by day, emerging at dusk to search for insects, seeds and windblown vegetable matter. They never have to drink but derive all the water they need from the fats contained in seeds. They breed throughout the year, producing litters of up to 7 young after a gestation period of 20 or 21 days.

NAME: South African Pygmy Gerbil, *Gerbillurus paeba*
RANGE: S. Africa: S.W. Angola to Cape Province
HABITAT: desert
SIZE: body: 8–9 cm ($3\frac{1}{4}$–$3\frac{1}{2}$ in)
tail: 6.5–7 cm ($2\frac{1}{2}$–$2\frac{3}{4}$ in)

Of the 4 species of pygmy gerbil which occur in the southwestern corner of Africa, *G. paeba* is the most widespread. It constructs simple burrows in sandy or gravelly soil, generally with one entrance higher than the other to improve ventilation. Pygmy gerbils feed on whatever plant and animal food is available. When desert plants bloom, the gerbils lay in stores of seeds and fruit in underground larders. They usually breed about twice a year, but in times of abundant food supplies may breed up to four times in a year. The young are fed by their mother for up to a month.

NAME: Greater Short-tailed Gerbil, *Dipodillus maghrebi*
RANGE: Africa: N. Morocco
HABITAT: upland, arid semidesert
SIZE: body: 9–12.5 cm ($3\frac{1}{2}$–5 in)
tail: 6.5–7 cm ($2\frac{1}{2}$–$2\frac{3}{4}$ in)

Among the many gerbil species in North Africa, the greater short-tailed gerbil occupies a specific and specialized ecological niche. It inhabits the foothills and midregions of the Atlas Mountains and lives among boulder fields and rock scree. Like all gerbils, it is an active animal, emerging at night to forage among the sparse vegetation for seeds, buds and insects. It may have to travel considerable distances each night to find food.

Litters of about 6 young are born in brood chambers underground.

GERBILLINAE: Gerbil Subfamily

There are some 70 or so members of this subfamily of rodents, all of which come from central and western Asia and Africa. They are all well adapted for arid conditions and many occur only in apparently inhospitable deserts. Chief among their adaptations is a wonderfully efficient kidney, which produces urine several times more concentrated than in most rodents, thus conserving moisture. Water loss from the lungs is a major problem for desert-dwelling animals, and all gerbils have specialized nose bones which serve to condense water vapor from the air before it is expired. This essential water is then reabsorbed into the system.

To keep their bodies as far as possible from the burning sand, gerbils have long hind legs and feet, the soles of which are insulated with dense pads of fur. Their bellies are pure white to reflect radiated heat. Finally, gerbils adapt to desert life by being strictly nocturnal, never emerging from their burrows until the heat of the day has passed.

Gerbils are all seed-eaters and make large stores of food during the brief periods when the desert blooms. They never occur in great densities, but they are abundant enough to be an important source of food for predators such as fennec foxes and snakes.

NAME: Great Gerbil, *Rhombomys opimus*
RANGE: Iran, east to Mongolia and China
HABITAT: arid scrubland
SIZE: body: 16–20 cm ($6\frac{1}{4}$–$7\frac{3}{4}$ in)
tail: 13–16 cm (5–$6\frac{1}{4}$ in)

The great gerbil occupies a wide range of habitats, from the cold central Asiatic mountains to the Gobi Desert, with its high summer temperatures. It is an adaptable animal, which changes its behavior to suit its environment. In winter, its activity is in inverse proportion to the depth of snow, and in some colonies the gerbils come to the surface only rarely. Large colonies can do much damage to crops and irrigation channels, and great gerbils are considered pests in parts of the USSR.

Great gerbils are herbivorous animals and build up winter stores of 60 kg (130 lb) or more of plant material in their burrows. During the winter, huge numbers of these gerbils are preyed on by owls, stoats, mink and foxes. In spring, however, their rapid breeding soon replenishes the colonies.

NAME: Indian Gerbil, *Tatera indica*
RANGE: W. India, Sri Lanka
HABITAT: plains, savanna, arid woodland
SIZE: body: 15–19 cm (6–$7\frac{1}{2}$ in)
tail: 20–25 cm ($7\frac{3}{4}$–$9\frac{3}{4}$ in)

The Indian gerbil is a sociable animal, living communally in deep burrow systems with many entrances. Often these entrances are loosely blocked with soil to discourage the entry of predatory snakes and mongooses. Sometimes the populations of this species increase to such an extent that the animals leave their normal habitat and invade fields and gardens in search of bulbs, roots, green vegetation, insects and even eggs and young birds. Indian gerbils breed throughout the year, producing litters of up to 8 young. It is thought that these animals are a reservoir of bubonic plague.

NAME: Fat-tailed Gerbil, *Pachyuromys duprasi*
RANGE: Africa: Algerian Sahara to S.W. Egypt
HABITAT: sandy desert
SIZE: body: 10.5–14 cm ($4\frac{1}{4}$–$5\frac{1}{2}$ in)
tail: 4.5–6 cm ($1\frac{3}{4}$–$2\frac{1}{4}$ in)

This little gerbil derives its name from its habit of storing fat in its stubby tail. During periods when food is abundant, the tail enlarges in size and may even become too fat to be carried; in lean times, the fat is used up and the tail decreases again. These gerbils spend their days in underground burrows, emerging at night to search for whatever seeds and grubs they can find in the scant vegetation. They have enormous ear bones and very acute hearing, which may help them to locate underground insects. Litters of about 6 young are produced throughout the year, and the gestation period is 19 to 22 days. The young gerbils are independent at about 5 weeks old.

NAME: Fat Sand Rat, *Psammomys obesus*
RANGE: Algeria, east to Saudi Arabia
HABITAT: sandy desert
SIZE: body: 14–18.5 cm ($5\frac{1}{2}$–$7\frac{1}{4}$ in)
tail: 12–15 cm ($4\frac{3}{4}$–6 in)

The fat sand rat overcomes the problem of the unpredictability of desert food supplies by laying down a thick layer of fat all over its body when food is abundant. It then lives off this fat when food is short. Active day and night, this gerbil darts about collecting seeds and other vegetation which it carries back to its burrow. In early spring, a brood chamber is made and lined with finely shredded vegetation, and the first litter of the year is born in March. There are usually 3 to 5 young in a litter, and the breeding season continues until late summer.

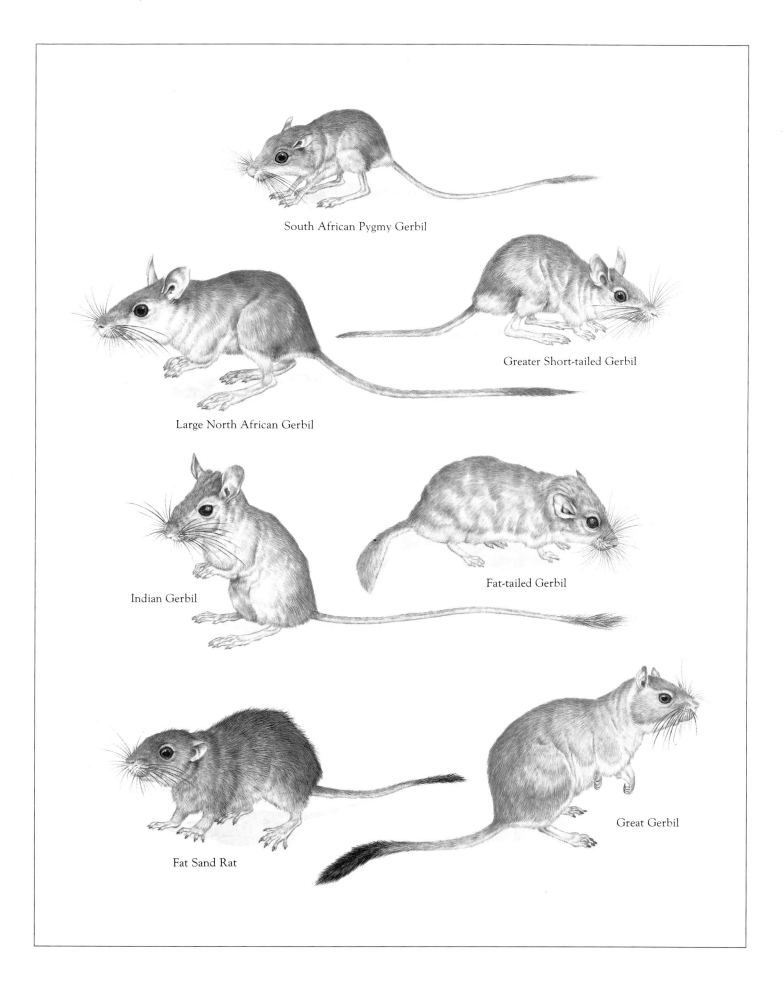

South African Pygmy Gerbil

Greater Short-tailed Gerbil

Large North African Gerbil

Indian Gerbil

Fat-tailed Gerbil

Fat Sand Rat

Great Gerbil

Climbing Mice, Pouched Rats, Island Water Rats

DENDROMURINAE:
African Climbing Mouse Subfamily

There are about 21 species of climbing mice, all of which occur in Africa, south of the Sahara. They are linked by certain skull and tooth characteristics, but otherwise they are quite a varied group. Most are agile climbers and have an affinity for tall vegetation, but some species are ground-living. Many forms have extremely long tails which they wrap around stems and twigs for extra stability. Although abundant, these rodents do not occur in the large groups characteristic of mice and voles. Many species live in extremely dense forest.

One climbing mouse, *Dendroprionomys rousseloti*, is known only from three specimens caught in Zaire, but this may indicate the degree of research effort rather than rarity.

NAME: **African Climbing Mouse,** *Dendromus mesomelas*
RANGE: **Cameroon to Ethiopia, south to South Africa**
HABITAT: **swamps**
SIZE: **body: 6–10 cm (2¼–4 in)**
   tail: 7–12 (2¾–4¾ in)

The most striking feature of this little rodent is its prehensile tail, which acts as a fifth limb when the mouse climbs the stems of plants. Climbing mice are strictly nocturnal and are always on the alert for owls, mongooses and other predators. They feed on berries, fruits and seeds, and occasionally search for lizards and the eggs and young of small birds. Sometimes they manage to climb into the suspended nests of weaver finches, and there are records of them establishing their own nests in these secure hammocks, although they usually build nests of stripped grass at the base of grass stems.

Climbing mice breed throughout the year, producing litters of 3 to 5 young.

NAME: **Fat Mouse,** *Steatomys krebsi*
RANGE: **Angola, Zambia, south to South Africa**
HABITAT: **dry, open, sandy plains**
SIZE: **body: 7–10 cm (2¾–4 in)**
   tail: 4–4.5 cm (1½–1¾ in)

Fat mice are adapted for life in the more seasonal parts of southern Africa. During the rainy season, when seeds, bulbs and insects are abundant, the mice gorge themselves, becoming quite fat. In the dry season, when plant growth stops, they live off their stores of fat. They live singly or in pairs in underground burrows, breeding in the wet season and producing litters of 4 to 6 young.

CRICETOMYINAE:
African Pouched Rat Subfamily

There are about 6 species of African pouched rat, all with a pair of deep cheek pouches for the transportation of food. They occur south of the Sahara and occupy a range of habitats, from sandy plains to the densest forests. One species has taken to living close to human refuse dumps, scavenging for a living.

Normally African pouched rats live alone in underground burrow systems, which they construct or else take over from other species. The burrows include separate chambers for sleeping, excreting and, if the inhabitant is female, breeding. Special larder chambers are used as food stores for the dry season. Despite the complexity of their homes, pouched rats move every few weeks to a new burrow.

NAME: **Giant Pouched Rat,** *Cricetomys emini*
RANGE: **Sierra Leone to Malawi**
HABITAT: **dense forest**
SIZE: **body: 25–45 cm (9¾–17¾ in)**
   tail: 36–46 cm (14¼–18 in)

As its name implies, the giant pouched rat is a substantial rodent, weighing up to about 1 kg (2¼ lb). It lives in dark forests or areas of dense scrub, emerging from its burrow at night to forage for roots, tubers, fruit and seeds. Some food is eaten where it is found, but much is taken back to the burrow in the rat's capacious cheek pouches. Giant pouched rats live singly, associating only briefly with others for mating, which occurs at all times of the year. Litters contain 2 or 3 young, born after a gestation of about 6 weeks.

NAME: **Long-tailed Pouched Rat,** *Beamys hindei*
RANGE: **S. Kenya**
HABITAT: **forest**
SIZE: **body: 10–11 cm (4–4¼ in)**
   tail: 9.5–10 cm (3¾–4 in)

The long-tailed pouched rat occurs in a restricted part of central Africa, although the related *B. major* extends as far south as northern Zimbabwe. This rat seems to spend much of its life underground in a complex burrow system which it constructs. It feeds mainly on the underground storage organs of plants — tubers and bulbs — although the presence of seeds in its food stores suggests that it spends some time above ground searching for food. Groups of up to two dozen rats live together, breeding at all times of the year. Litters contain 1 to 5 young, which are mature at about 5½ months.

HYDROMYINAE:
Island Water Rat Subfamily

There are about 17 species of these large rats, most of which inhabit rivers and swamps in Australia, New Guinea and its associated islands and the Philippines. All share certain family characteristics of teeth and skull. The origin of the family is uncertain, and it is not known how it spread over such a wide part of the globe. Some species, such as the Australian water rat, *Hydromys chrysogaster*, are common, while others, such as the false water rat of Australia, *Xeromys myoides*, are extremely rare. Little is known about most of these shy, retiring creatures.

NAME: **Australian Water Rat,** *Hydromys chrysogaster*
RANGE: **Tasmania, Australia, New Guinea; Aru, Kai and Bruni Islands**
HABITAT: **swamps, streams, marshes**
SIZE: **body: 20–35 cm (7¾–13¾ in)**
   tail: 20–35 cm (7¾–13¾ in)

This imposing rodent has a sleek, streamlined appearance, well suited to its aquatic habits. Its partially webbed hind feet enable it to perform complex maneuvers in the water. It feeds on small fish, frogs, crustaceans and water birds which it pursues and captures. Catches are often taken to a special food store for later consumption.

In the south of their range, water rats breed in early spring, producing a litter of 4 or 5 young; farther north they may breed all year round.

NAME: **Eastern Shrew Mouse,** *Pseudohydromys murinus*
RANGE: **N.E. New Guinea**
HABITAT: **montane forest**
SIZE: **body: 8.5–10 cm (3¼–4 in)**
   tail: 9–9.5 cm (3½–3¾ in)

The Eastern shrew mouse is known from only four specimens taken at between 2,100 and 2,700 m (6,900 and 9,000 ft) in dense forest. However, the species is probably not as rare as this suggests, since there has been little organized survey work in this remote area. Little is known about the natural history of this animal, but since it does not have webbed feet, it is probably less aquatic than its relatives. Its long, strong tail may aid in climbing, and it probably spends much of its time seeking food in the shrub layer of the rain forest.

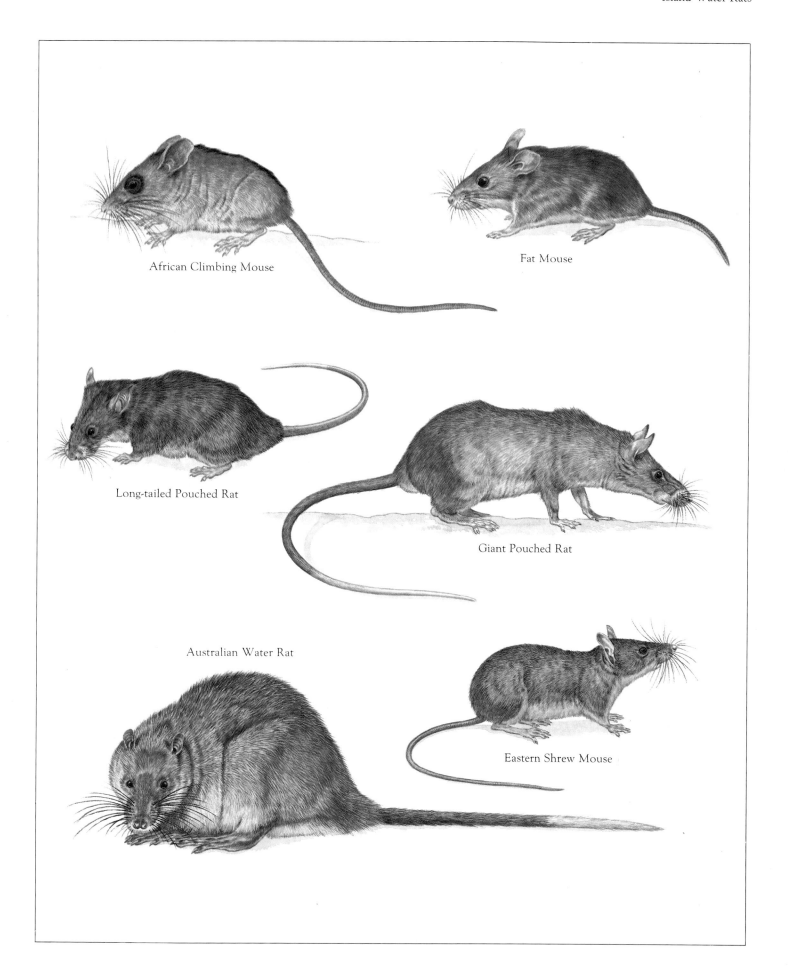

African Climbing Mouse

Fat Mouse

Long-tailed Pouched Rat

Giant Pouched Rat

Australian Water Rat

Eastern Shrew Mouse

Old World Rats and Mice

NAME: **Harvest Mouse,** *Micromys minutus*
RANGE: **Europe, east to the Urals**
HABITAT: **hedgerows, reedbeds**
SIZE: **body: 5.5–7.5 cm (2¼–3 in)**
    tail: 5–7.5 cm (2–3 in)

These attractive little mice are among the smallest rodents: a fully grown male weighs about 7 g (¼ oz). Harvest mice build tennis-ball-sized nests of finely stripped grass among reed stems or grass heads. Here, safe from the attentions of owls or weasels, the litter of up to 12 young is born and reared. Adult harvest mice feed on seeds and small insects. They are the only Old World mammals to have truly prehensile tails.

NAME: **Wood Mouse,** *Apodemus sylvaticus*
RANGE: **Ireland, east to central Asia**
HABITAT: **forest edge**
SIZE: **body: 8–13 cm (3¼–5¼ in)**
    tail: 7–9.5 cm (2¾–3¾ in)

The wood mouse is one of the commonest of the European small rodents. Strictly nocturnal, wood mice emerge from their nests under the roots of trees in the evening and often forage in pairs for seeds, insects and seasonal berries. They usually breed between April and November, but may continue throughout the winter, if food is abundant.

NAME: **Rough-tailed Giant Rat,** *Hyomys goliath*
RANGE: **New Guinea**
HABITAT: **forest**
SIZE: **body: 29–39 cm (11½–15¼ in)**
    tail: 25–38 cm (9¾–15 in)

This rat derives its common name from the thick overlapping scales covering the underside of its tail. As these scales are often worn down, it is thought that they act to prevent the tail from slipping when it is used as a brace when the rat is climbing. This shy, secretive species is poorly studied, but it appears to feed on epiphytic plants on the branches of trees and on insects.

NAME: **African Grass Rat,** *Arvicanthis abyssinicus*
RANGE: **W. Africa to Somalia and Zambia**
HABITAT: **savanna, scrub, forest**
SIZE: **body: 12–19 cm (4¾–7½ in)**
    tail: 9–16 cm (3½–6¼ in)

The grass rat is a highly social rodent, living in colonies which sometimes number up to a thousand. The rats dig burrows in the earth or, alternatively, may establish themselves in a pile of rocks. Their staple food is probably grass seeds, but they also eat sweet potatoes and cassava. They breed throughout the year.

MURINAE:
Old World Rats and Mice Subfamily

This subfamily of almost 400 species of rodents contains some of the world's most successful mammals. They are highly adaptable and extremely tolerant of hostile conditions. Many are pests, wreaking havoc on stored grain and root crops, while others act as reservoirs for disease. Rats and mice occur throughout the world and have followed man even to the poles.

NAME: **Four-striped Grass Mouse,** *Rhabdomys pumilio*
RANGE: **central Africa, south to the Cape of Good Hope**
HABITAT: **grass, scrub**
SIZE: **body: 9–13 cm (3½–5¼ in)**
    tail: 8–12.5 cm (3¼–5 in)

This common small rodent lives in a burrow that opens into thick vegetation and feeds on a wide variety of plant and animal food. In central Africa, these mice breed throughout the year, producing up to six litters annually, with 4 to 12 young per litter. In the south, the breeding season is limited to September through to May, and four litters are born.

NAME: **Black/House Rat,** *Rattus rattus*
RANGE: **worldwide (originally native to Asia)**
HABITAT: **associated with man**
SIZE: **body: 20–26 cm (7¾–10¼ in)**
    tail: 20–24 cm (7¾–9½ in)

It has been said that the black, or ship, rat, carrying such diseases as bubonic plague, typhus, rabies and trichinosis, has altered human destiny more than any individual in recorded history. Wherever man has gone, and in all his activities, his unchosen companion has been the black rat. The success of this species is due to its extremely wide-ranging diet and its rapid rate of reproduction. Litters of up to 10 young are born every 6 weeks or so throughout the year.

NAME: **Norway/Brown Rat,** *Rattus norvegicus*
RANGE: **worldwide (originally native to E. Asia and Japan)**
HABITAT: **associated with man**
SIZE: **body: 25–30 cm (9¾–11¾ in)**
    tail: 25–32 cm (9¾–12½ in)

The Norway rat is a serious pest, living alongside man wherever he lives and feeding on a wide range of food. These rats carry *Salmonella* and the bacterial disease tularaemia, but rarely the plague. They breed throughout the year, and the gestation period is 21 days.

NAME: **Stick-nest Rat,** *Leporillus conditor*
RANGE: **south-central Australia; Franklin Island, South Australia**
HABITAT: **arid grassland**
SIZE: **body: 14–20 cm (5½–7¾ in)**
    tail: 13–18 cm (5¼–7 in)

Stick-nest rats build huge nests of sticks and debris, each inhabited by a pair or by a small colony of rats. The rats are vegetarian but may occasionally eat insects. They breed during the wet season, producing litters of 4 to 6 young.

NAME: **Mosaic-tailed Mouse,** *Melomys cervinipes*
RANGE: **N.E. Australia**
HABITAT: **forest, usually near water**
SIZE: **body: 9–17 cm (3½–6¾ in)**
    tail: 11–17 cm (4¼–6¾ in)

The scales on the tails of most rats and mice are arranged in rings, but in this species they resemble a mosaic. These mice breed during the rainy season — November to April — and produce litters of up to 4 young. They are active climbers and often rest up in pandanus trees in nests made of finely shredded grass and leaves.

NAME: **House Mouse,** *Mus musculus*
RANGE: **worldwide**
HABITAT: **fields; associated with man**
SIZE: **body: 6.5–9.5 cm (2½–3¾ in)**
    tail: 6–10.5 cm (2¼–4¼ in)

Mice eat relatively little, but they spoil vast quantities of stored food such as grain. Wild mice are nocturnal and feed on grass seeds and plant stems and, occasionally, on insects.

NAME: **Hopping Mouse,** *Notomys alexis*
RANGE: **central Australia**
HABITAT: **dry grassland, spinifex scrub**
SIZE: **body: 9–18 cm (3½–7 in)**
    tail: 12–23 cm (4¾–9 in)

The Australian counterpart of the kangaroo rats of North Africa and North America, this rodent emerges from its cool, humid burrows only at night. It feeds on seeds, roots and any green vegetation. Hopping mice breed during the winter months, producing litters of 2 to 5 young.

NAME: **Greater Bandicoot Rat,** *Bandicota indica*
RANGE: **India to S. China; Taiwan, Java**
HABITAT: **forest, scrub; often near man**
SIZE: **body: 16–36 cm (6¼–14¼ in)**
    tail: 16–26 cm (6¼–10¼ in)

These rodents are serious pests in agricultural areas because they not only spoil grain but steal quantities of food for their own underground larders. They breed throughout the year and bear litters of 10 to 12 young.

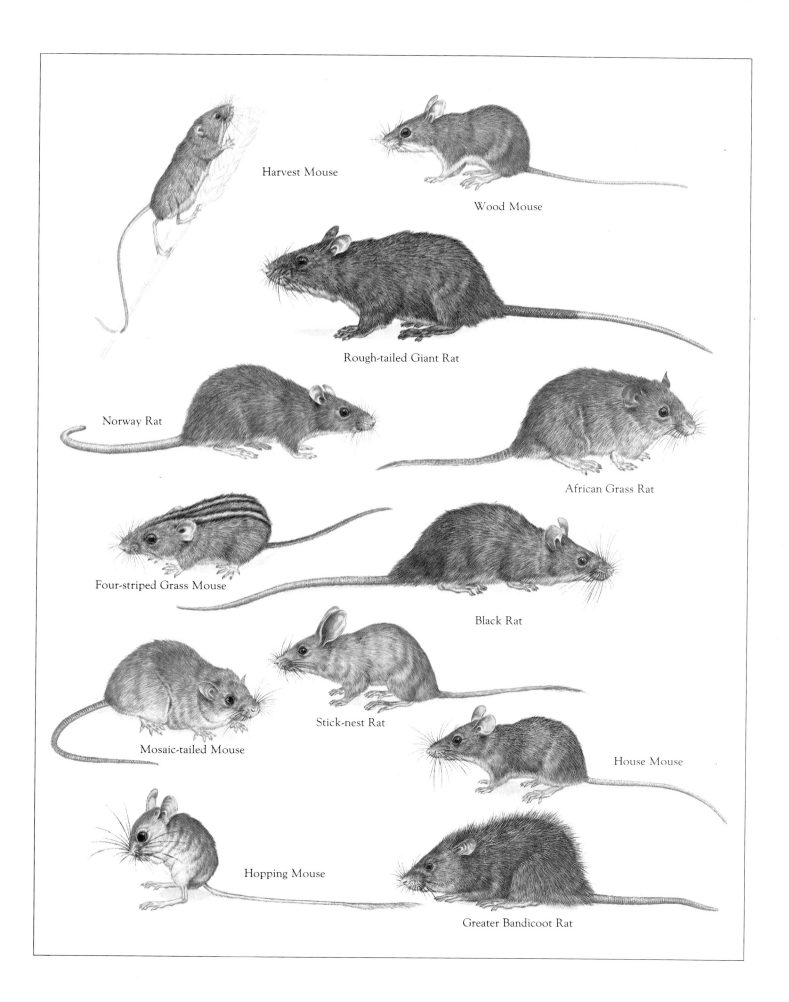

Harvest Mouse

Wood Mouse

Rough-tailed Giant Rat

Norway Rat

African Grass Rat

Four-striped Grass Mouse

Black Rat

Mosaic-tailed Mouse

Stick-nest Rat

House Mouse

Hopping Mouse

Greater Bandicoot Rat

Dormice, Jumping Mice, Jerboas

GLIRIDAE: Dormouse Family

There are 14 species of dormouse. Six species, all in the genus *Graphiurus*, occur in Africa, and others are found in Europe, northern Asia and Japan. These nocturnal rodents resemble short, fat squirrels and most have bushy tails. During late summer and autumn, most dormice build up their body fat reserves and then hibernate during the winter. They wake periodically to feed on the fruit and nuts that they store for winter consumption.

NAME: **Fat Dormouse, *Glis glis***
RANGE: **Europe, Asia**
HABITAT: **forest**
SIZE: **body: 15–18 cm (6–7 in)**
tail: 13–16 cm (5¼–6¼ in)

The largest of its family, the fat dormouse has a long bushy tail and rough pads on its paws to facilitate climbing. It feeds on nuts, seeds, berries and fruit and occasionally catches insects and small birds. In summer, it makes a nest of plant fiber and moss up in a tree, but its winter hibernation nest is usually made nearer the ground in a hollow tree or in an abandoned rabbit burrow. The female produces a litter of 2 to 6 young in early summer.

NAME: **Japanese Dormouse, *Glirurus japonicus***
RANGE: **Japan (except Hokkaido)**
HABITAT: **montane forest**
SIZE: **body: 6.5–8 cm (2½–3¼ in)**
tail: 4–5 cm (1½–2 in)

A tree-dwelling, nocturnal rodent, the Japanese dormouse spends its days in a tree hollow or in a nest built in the branches. It feeds at night on fruit, seeds, insects and bird's eggs. In winter it hibernates in a hollow tree or even in a man-made shelter such as an attic or nesting box. After hibernation, the dormice mate, and the female gives birth to 3 to 5 young in June or July. Occasionally a second litter is produced in October.

NAME: **African Dormouse, *Graphiurus murinus***
RANGE: **Africa, south of the Sahara**
HABITAT: **forest, woodland**
SIZE: **body: 8–16.5 cm (3¼–6½ in)**
tail: 8–13 cm (3¼–5¼ in)

African dormice are agile creatures which move swiftly over bushes and vegetation in search of seeds, nuts, fruit and insects. They shelter in trees or rock crevices and, although primarily nocturnal, may be active by day in dense dark forests. Up to three litters of 2 to 5 young are born in summer.

SELEVINIIDAE: Desert Dormouse Family

Only a single species, discovered in 1938, is known from this family.

NAME: **Desert Dormouse, *Selevinia betpakdalensis***
RANGE: **USSR: S.E. Kazakhstan**
HABITAT: **desert**
SIZE: **body: 7–8.5 cm (2¾–3¼ in)**
tail: 7–9.5 cm (2¾–3¾ in)

The desert dormouse digs a burrow for shelter in which it is believed also to hibernate. It feeds largely on insects but also eats plant matter and makes winter food stores of plant material in its burrow. It moves around by making short jumps on its hind legs. In late spring, desert dormice mate and produce a litter of up to 8 young.

ZAPODIDAE: Jumping Mouse Family

The 10 species in this family are all small, mouse-shaped rodents, with long hind limbs modified for jumping. Some of these species can leap up to 2 m (6½ ft) when startled. Members of the family are found in open and forested land, as well as in swamps, throughout eastern Europe, Asia and North America.

NAME: **Meadow Jumping Mouse, *Zapus hudsonius***
RANGE: **Canada, N.E. and N. central USA**
HABITAT: **open meadows, woodland**
SIZE: **body: 7–8 cm (2¾–3¼ in)**
tail: 10–15 cm (4–6 in)

Meadow jumping mice feed on seeds, fruit and insects for which they forage on the ground, bounding along in a series of short jumps. They are primarily nocturnal but in wooded areas may be active day and night under cover of the vegetation. In summer they make nests of grass and leaves on the ground, in grass or under logs; but in winter, they dig burrows or make small nests just above ground, on a bank or mound, in which to hibernate. They do not store food but, prior to hibernation, gain a substantial layer of body fat that sustains them. From October to April, the meadow jumping mouse lies in its quarters in a tight ball, its temperature only just above freezing, and its respiration and heart rates greatly reduced to conserve energy.

Meadow jumping mice produce two or three litters a year. Most mate for the first time shortly after emerging from hibernation, and the 4 or 5 young are born after a gestation of about 18 days.

NAME: **Northern Birch Mouse, *Sicista betulina***
RANGE: **N. and central Europe, E. Siberia**
HABITAT: **woodland**
SIZE: **body: 5–7 cm (2–2¾ in)**
tail: 8–10 cm (3¼–4 in)

This rodent is easily distinguished by the dark stripe down its back and by its tail, which is about one and a half times the length of its body. A nocturnal animal, it spends the day in its burrow, emerging at night to search for insects and small invertebrates to eat. It also feeds on seeds and fruit, particularly during the fattening-up period, prior to hibernating from October to April. Females produce a litter of 3 to 5 young in May or June, after a gestation of 4 or 5 weeks.

DIPODIDAE: Jerboa Family

The 27 species of jerboa form a family of jumping rodents, with hind limbs which are at least four times as long as their manipulative forelimbs. These rodents are found in deserts, semiarid zones and steppe country in North Africa and Asia, where they construct complex burrow systems.

NAME: **Northern Three-toed Jerboa, *Dipus sagitta***
RANGE: **central Asia: Caucasus to N. China**
HABITAT: **sand dunes, steppe, pine forest**
SIZE: **body: 10–13 cm (4–5¼ in)**
tail: 15–19 cm (6–7½ in)

The northern three-toed jerboa feeds on plants, seeds and insects. It needs very little water and is able to survive on the water contained in its food. In summer, it spends its days in a shallow burrow and emerges in the evening to travel to its feeding grounds, leaping along on its powerful hind limbs. In autumn, it digs a deeper burrow and hibernates from November to March. These jerboas mate soon after awakening and may have two litters of 2 to 5 young in a season.

NAME: **Great Jerboa, *Allactaga major***
RANGE: **USSR: Ukraine, east to China**
HABITAT: **steppe, semidesert**
SIZE: **body: 9–15 cm (3½–6 in)**
tail: 16–22 cm (6¼–8½ in)

The great jerboa and 8 of the 9 other species in the genus *Allactaga* have five toes on each hind foot. Great jerboas feed on seeds and insects, which they find by combing through the sand with the long slender claws on their front feet. They are nocturnal, spending the day in burrows; they also hibernate in burrows. One or two litters are produced each year.

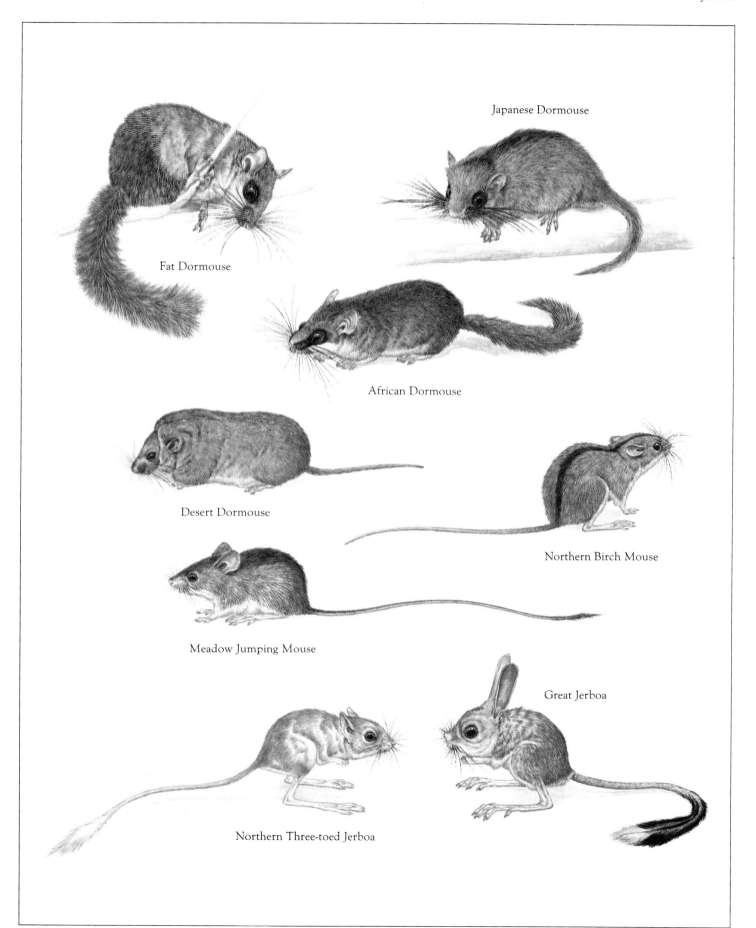

Japanese Dormouse

Fat Dormouse

African Dormouse

Desert Dormouse

Northern Birch Mouse

Meadow Jumping Mouse

Great Jerboa

Northern Three-toed Jerboa

Porcupines

HYSTRICIDAE:
Old World Porcupine Family

The 12 species in this family are all large rodents, unmistakable in their appearance, with long spines, derived from hairs, covering back, sides and parts of the tail. Porcupines live in desert, forest and savanna regions of Africa, parts of Asia and Indonesia and the Philippines. Most are primarily ground-living creatures; they move in a clumsy, shuffling manner which rattles their spines. They are generally nocturnal animals and live in burrows, which they dig, or in holes or crevices. They feed on plant material, such as roots, bulbs, tubers, fruit and bark, and on some carrion. Males and females look alike.

NAME: **Indonesian Porcupine,** *Thecurus sumatrae*
RANGE: **Sumatra**
HABITAT: **forest**
SIZE: **body: 54 cm (21¼ in)**
 tail: 10 cm (4 in)

The Indonesian porcupine's body is covered with flattened spines, interspersed with short hairs. The spines are longest on the back and sides, becoming smaller on the tail; on the underside of the body, the spines are rather more flexible than those elsewhere. The specialized "rattling" quills on the tail expand near the tips; these expanded portions are hollow so that the quills rattle when they are vibrated together as a warning to potential enemies.

NAME: **Crested Porcupine,** *Hystrix africaeaustralis*
RANGE: **Africa: Senegal to Cape Province**
HABITAT: **forest, savanna**
SIZE: **body: 71–84 cm (28–33 in)**
 tail: up to 2.5 cm (1 in)

The crested porcupine is a stout-bodied rodent, with sharp spines up to 30 cm (11¾ in) long on its back. Specialized hollow quills on the tail can be rattled in warning when the tail is vibrated. If, despite its warnings, a porcupine is still threatened, it will charge backward and drive the sharp, backward-curving spines into its enemy. The spines detach easily from the porcupine but cannot actually be "shot" as was once believed.

Crested porcupines are slow-moving animals that rarely climb trees. They dig burrows in which they spend the day, emerging at night to feed. They are thought to produce two litters a year of 2 to 4 young each. The young are born with soft spines and remain in the nest until their spines harden, when they are about 2 weeks old.

NAME: **Asian Brush-tailed Porcupine,** *Atherurus macrourus*
RANGE: **S.E. Asia: Assam to Malaya**
HABITAT: **forest, often near water**
SIZE: **body: 40–55 cm (15¾–21½ in)**
 tail: 15–25 cm (6–9¾ in)

A slender, ratlike porcupine, the brush-tailed has a distinctive long tail, tipped with a tuft of bristles. The spines of this species are flattened and grooved and most are short.

During the day, the brush-tailed porcupine shelters in a burrow, among rocks or even in a termite mound and emerges at night to hunt for food, mostly plants, roots, bark and insects. An agile creature, it will climb trees and runs well. It has partially webbed feet and is able to swim. Groups of up to 8 individuals shelter and forage together.

There are 3 other species of brush-tailed porcupine in this genus, all with similar appearance and habits.

NAME: **Long-tailed Porcupine,** *Trichys fasciculata*
RANGE: **S.E. Asia: Malaya, Sumatra, Borneo**
HABITAT: **forest**
SIZE: **body: 28–47 cm (11–18½ in)**
 tail: 17–23 cm (6¾–9 in)

The spines of the long-tailed porcupine are flattened and flexible, but shorter and less well developed than those of other species. The long tail breaks off easily, and many adults are found in this condition. These porcupines are good climbers and have broad paws, with strong digits and claws for holding on to branches.

ERITHIZONTIDAE:
New World Porcupine Family

The 9 species of New World porcupine are generally similar in appearance to the Old World species and have the same coarse hair and specialized spines. Unlike the Old World porcupines, they are largely tree-living, and the feet are adapted for climbing, with wide soles and strong digits and claws. Six of the species are in the genus *Coendou* and have prehensile tails — a prehensile tail is one equipped with muscles which allow it to be used as a fifth limb, for curling around and grasping branches. Males and females look alike.

New World porcupines are generally, but not exclusively, nocturnal and spend their days in hollows in trees or in crevices in the ground. Both male and female mark their home range with urine. The family occurs in North, Central and South America.

NAME: **Porcupine,** *Erithizon dorsatum*
RANGE: **Canada; USA: Alaska, W. states, south to New Mexico, some N.E. states.**
HABITAT: **forest**
SIZE: **body: 46–56 cm (18–22 in)**
 tail: 18–23 cm (7–9 in)

A thickset animal, this porcupine has spines on neck, back and tail and some longer spines, armed with minute barbs at their tips. It is slow and clumsy, but climbs trees readily to feed on buds, twigs and bark. In summer, it also feeds on roots and stems of flowering plants and even on some crops. It does not hibernate.

The porcupines mate at the beginning of winter, and the courting male often sprays the female with urine before mating, perhaps to prevent other males attempting to court her. After a gestation of 7 months, the young, usually only 1, is born in the late spring. It is well developed at birth, with fur, open eyes and soft quills which harden within an hour. A few hours after birth, the young porcupine can climb trees and feed on solid food.

NAME: **Tree Porcupine,** *Coendou prehensilis*
RANGE: **Bolivia, Brazil, Venezuela**
HABITAT: **forest**
SIZE: **body: 30–61 cm (11¾–24 in)**
 tail: 33–45 cm (13–17¾ in)

The body of the tree porcupine is covered with short, thick spines. Its major adaptation to arboreal life is its prehensile tail, which it uses to grasp branches when it is feeding. The tail lacks spines, and the upper part of its tip is naked, with a callused pad for extra grip. The hands and feet, too, are highly specialized for climbing, with long curved claws on each digit. Tree porcupines are mainly nocturnal, and slow but sure climbers. They feed on leaves, stems and some fruits. Females seem to produce only 1 young a year.

NAME: **Upper Amazon Porcupine,** *Echinoprocta rufescens*
RANGE: **Colombia**
HABITAT: **forest**
SIZE: **body: 46 cm (18 in)**
 tail: 10 cm (4 in)

The Upper Amazon porcupine has a short, hairy tail that is not prehensile. Its back and sides are covered with spines, which become thicker and stronger toward the rump. It is an arboreal animal and generally inhabits mountainous areas over 800 m (2,600 ft). Little has been discovered about the breeding habits and biology of this species of porcupine.

Crested Porcupine

Indonesian Porcupine

Asian Brush-tailed Porcupine

Long-tailed Porcupine

Tree Porcupine

Upper Amazon Porcupine

Porcupine

Guinea Pigs, Capybara, Pacas and Agoutis

CAVIIDAE:
Guinea Pig/Cavy Family

There are about 15 species in this interesting and entirely South American family of ground-living rodents. Within the group are forms known as guinea pigs or cavies, mocos or rock cavies, and the Patagonian "hares," locally called "maras." Cavies and rock cavies have the well-known chunky body shape of domestic guinea pigs, with short ears and limbs, a large head and a tail which is not externally visible. Maras have a more harelike shape, with long legs and upstanding ears.

Cavies feed on plant material, and their cheek teeth continue to grow throughout life to counteract the heavy wear caused by chewing such food. Most live in small social groups of up to 15 or so individuals; sometimes they join in larger groups of as many as 40. They do not hibernate, even in areas which experience low temperatures.

NAME: **Cavy**, *Cavia tschudii*
RANGE: **Peru to N. Argentina**
HABITAT: **grassland, rocky regions**
SIZE: **body: 20–40 cm (7¾–15¾ in)**
 tail: no visible tail

These nocturnal rodents usually live in small family groups of up to 10 individuals, but may form larger colonies in particularly suitable areas. Although their sharp claws are well suited for digging burrows, they often use burrows made by other species or shelter in rock crevices. They feed at dawn and dusk, largely on grass and leaves.

Cavies breed in summer, or throughout the year in mild areas, producing litters of 1 to 4 young after a gestation of 60 to 70 days. The young are well developed at birth and can survive alone at 5 days old. This species is the probable ancestor of the domestic guinea pig, which is kept as a pet and also widely used in scientific research laboratories. Cavies are still kept by upland Indians as a source of fine, delicate meat.

NAME: **Rock Cavy**, *Kerodon rupestris*
RANGE: **N.E. Brazil**
HABITAT: **arid rocky areas**
SIZE: **body: 20–40 cm (7¾–15¾ in)**
 tail: no visible tail

Similar in build to the cavy, the rock cavy has a longer, blunter snout and longer legs. It shelters under rocks or among stones and emerges in the afternoon or evening to search for leaves to eat. It will climb trees to find food.

The female rock cavy is believed to produce two litters a year, each consisting of 1 or 2 young.

NAME: **Mara**, *Dolichotis patagona*
RANGE: **Argentina**
HABITAT: **open arid land**
SIZE: **body: 69–75 cm (27¼–29½ in)**
 tail: 4.5 cm (1¾ in)

The mara has long, slender legs and feet, well adapted for running and bounding along at speeds as great as 30 km/h (18½ mph) in the manner of a hare or jackrabbit. Indeed, the mara fills the niche of the hare in an area where the latter is absent.

On each hind foot there are three digits, each with a hooflike claw; each forefoot bears four digits, armed with sharp claws. Maras are active in the daytime and feed on any available plant material. They dig burrows or take them over from other animals, and the litter of 2 to 5 young is born in a nest made in the burrow.

HYDROCHOERIDAE:
Capybara Family

This family contains only 1 species, the capybara, which is the largest living rodent. It resembles a huge guinea pig, with a large head and square muzzle, and lives in dense vegetation near lakes, rivers or marshes.

NAME: **Capybara**, *Hydrochoerus hydrochaeris*
RANGE: **Panama to E. Argentina**
HABITAT: **forest, near water**
SIZE: **body: 1–1.3 m (3¼–4¼ ft)**
 tail: vestigial

The capybara spends much time in water and is an excellent swimmer and diver; it has partial webs between the digits of both its hind feet and forefeet. When swimming, only its eyes, ears and nostrils show above the water. Capybaras feed on plant material, including aquatic plants, and their cheek teeth grow throughout life to counteract the wear and tear of chewing. They live in family groups and are active at dawn and dusk. In areas where they are frequently disturbed, capybaras may be nocturnal.

Males and females look alike, but there is a scent gland on the nose that is larger in the male. They mate in spring, and a litter of 2 young is born after a gestation of 15 to 18 weeks. The young are well developed at birth.

DINOMYIDAE: Pacarana Family

This South American family contains 1 apparently rare species, the false paca, or pacarana, so called because its striking markings are similar to those of the paca.

NAME: **Pacarana**, *Dinomys branicki*
RANGE: **Colombia to Bolivia**
HABITAT: **forest**
SIZE: **body: 73–79 cm (28¾–31 in)**
 tail: 20 cm (7¾ in)

The pacarana is a slow-moving, docile animal with short, strong limbs and powerful claws. It feeds on plant material, such as leaves, stems and fruit, and sits up on its haunches to examine and eat its food. Its cheek teeth are subject to considerable wear and grow throughout its life. It is most probably nocturnal.

Little is known of its breeding habits, but 2 young seems to be the normal number in a litter.

DASYPROCTIDAE:
Paca and Agouti Family

The 12 species in this family are distributed throughout Central and South America. All are medium to large ground-living rodents, with limbs well adapted for running.

The group splits naturally into three: the nocturnal pacas, the daytime-active agoutis, and the acuchis, about which little is known. All species have been hunted extensively for their flesh; they themselves eat leaves, fruit, roots and stems, all of which may be hoarded in underground stores.

NAME: **Paca**, *Cuniculus paca*
RANGE: **S. Mexico to Suriname, south to Paraguay**
HABITAT: **forest, near water**
SIZE: **body: 60–79 cm (23½–31 in)**
 tail: 2.5 cm (1 in)

The nocturnal paca is usually a solitary animal. It spends its day in a burrow, which it digs in a riverbank, among tree roots or under rocks, emerging after dark to look for food. The paca enters water willingly and will often escape from predators by swimming. It is believed to produce two litters a year of 1, rarely 2, young.

NAME: **Brazilian Agouti**, *Dasyprocta aguti*
RANGE: **Venezuela, E. Brazil; Lesser Antilles**
HABITAT: **forest, savanna**
SIZE: **body: 41–62 cm (16–24½ in)**
 tail: 1–3 cm (½–1¼ in)

Agoutis are social animals and are active in the daytime. They are good runners and can also jump up to 2 m (6½ ft) vertically, from a standing position. Agoutis dig burrows in a riverbank or under a tree or stone and tread well-defined paths from burrows to feeding grounds. They are believed to mate twice a year and bear litters of 2 to 4 young.

Cavy

Rock Cavy

Mara

Capybara

Pacarana

Paca

Brazilian Agouti

Chinchillas and relatives

CHINCHILLIDAE:
Viscacha and Chinchilla Family
There are about 6 species in this family which is found only in South America. All species have dense, beautiful fur, and the importance of the chinchillas, in particular, to the fur trade has led to their becoming relatively endangered as a wild species.

The hind limbs of the Chinchillidae are longer than their forelimbs, and the animals are good at running and leaping; they are also good climbers. They feed on plants, including roots and tubers, and their cheek teeth grow throughout life. Social animals, they live in small family groups which are part of larger colonies. Where the ground is suitable, they dig burrows, but otherwise they shelter under rocks.

NAME: **Plains Viscacha,** *Lagostomus maximus*
RANGE: **Argentina**
HABITAT: **grassland**
SIZE: **body: 47–66 cm (18½–26 in)**
   tail: 15–20 cm (6–7¾ in)
The plains viscacha is a robust rodent with a large head and blunt snout. Males are larger than females. Colonies of plains viscachas live in complex burrows, with networks of tunnels and entrances. They are expert burrowers, digging mainly with their forefeet and pushing the soil with their noses — their nostrils close off to prevent soil from entering them.

Females breed once a year or sometimes twice in mild climates. There are usually 2 young, born after a gestation of 5 months.

NAME: **Chinchilla,** *Chinchilla laniger*
RANGE: **Bolivia, Chile**
HABITAT: **rocky, mountainous areas**
SIZE: **body: 22.5–38 cm (8¾–15 in)**
   tail: 7.5–15 cm (3–6 in)   Ⓥ
Chinchillas are attractive animals, with long ears, large eyes and bushy tails. They live in colonies of 100 or more, sheltering in holes and crevices in rocks. They feed on any available vegetation, sitting up to eat and holding their food in their front paws.

Female chinchillas are larger than males and are aggressive toward one another. They breed in winter, usually producing two litters of 1 to 6 young. The gestation period is 111 days, and the young are suckled for 6 to 8 weeks.

The chinchilla's exceedingly soft, dense coat is the cause of its present extreme rarity in the wild, although it is now farmed all over the world for its valuable fur.

CAPROMYIDAE:
Hutia and Nutria Family
There are now about 12 living species in this family; several other species have become extinct relatively recently. The family divides into two groups: the 11 species of hutia, all found on West Indian islands, and the single species of nutria, or coypu, which is semiaquatic and a native of South America.

NAME: **Ingraham's Hutia,** *Capromys ingrahami*
RANGE: **Bahamas**
HABITAT: **forest**
SIZE: **body 30–50 cm (11¾–19¾ in)**
   tail: 15–30 cm (6–11¾ in)   Ⓔ
This hutia feeds mostly on fruit and leaves but occasionally eats small invertebrates and reptiles. It is a good climber and seeks some food in the trees. Active in the daytime, it shelters in a burrow or rock crevice at night. It is believed to breed all year round, provided the temperature stays above 15°C (60°F), and produces litters of 2 to 9 young.

Hutias have been unable to cope with man's introduction of mongooses and dogs to the West Indies, and many species may be heading for extinction.

NAME: **Nutria,** *Myocastor coypus*
RANGE: **Bolivia and S. Brazil to Chile and Argentina; introduced in N. America, Europe and Asia.**
HABITAT: **near marshes, lakes, streams**
SIZE: **body: 43–63 cm (17–24¾ in)**
   tail: 25–42 cm (9¾–16½ in)
The semiaquatic nutria is a skilled swimmer and diver and looks like a beaver with a rat's tail. Its hind feet are webbed and it has dense fur. Nutrias feed on aquatic vegetation and possibly on mollusks. They dig burrows in riverbanks, clear trails in their territory and are extremely destructive to plants and crops. By escaping from farms where they are bred for their fur, these animals have colonized new areas all over the world, and are sometimes considered pests because of the damage they do.

Two to three litters of up to 10 young are produced during the year, and the gestation period is 132 days. Young nutrias can swim only a few hours after birth.

OCTODONTIDAE:
Octodont Rodent Family
The 8 species of octodont rodent all occur in South America. Most resemble rats with round noses and long furry tails. They are all good burrowers.

NAME: **Degu,** *Octodon degus*
RANGE: **W. Peru, Chile**
HABITAT: **mountains, coastal regions**
SIZE: **12.5–19.5 cm (5–7½ in)**
   tail: 10–16 cm (4–6¼ in)
The degu is a stout, short-legged rodent with a large head for its size. Active during the day, it feeds on plants, bulbs and tubers. It is thought to breed all year round and may produce several litters a year of 2 young each.

CTENOMYIDAE:
Tuco-tuco Family
This family of 32 species, all found in South America, is believed by some authorities to be a group of relatives of the octodont rodents which has become highly specialized for a burrowing, underground existence.

NAME: **Tuco-tuco,** *Ctenomys talarum*
RANGE: **E. Argentina**
HABITAT: **grassland**
SIZE: **body: 17–25 cm (6¾–9¾ in)**
   tail: 6–11 cm (2¼–4¼ in)
Tuco-tucos look very much like North American pocket gophers (Geomyidae) and lead similar lives in complex burrow systems. Their front teeth are enormous relative to their body size and are used, when burrowing, to loosen the soil, which is then pushed out of the tunnel with the feet. Tuco-tucos spend nearly all their lives underground and feed on roots, tubers and stems.

In winter and spring, the tuco-tucos mate, and a single litter of 2 to 5 well-developed young is born after a gestation period of about 15 weeks.

ABROCOMIDAE:
Chinchilla-rat Family
There are 2 species only of chinchilla-rat, both native to South America. As their common name suggests, their fur resembles that of the chinchilla, although it is of poorer quality, and they have a ratlike body shape.

NAME: **Chinchilla-rat,** *Abrocoma bennetti*
RANGE: **Chile**
HABITAT: **high coastal plains**
SIZE: **body: 19–25 cm (7½–9¾ in)**
   tail: 13–18 cm (5¼–7 in)
A resident of cold, bleak mountain regions, the chinchilla-rat is a little-known creature. It feeds on plant matter and its cheek teeth grow throughout life. Mainly a ground-dweller, it can also climb trees in search of food. Chinchilla-rats live in burrows or rock crevices, apparently in small groups.

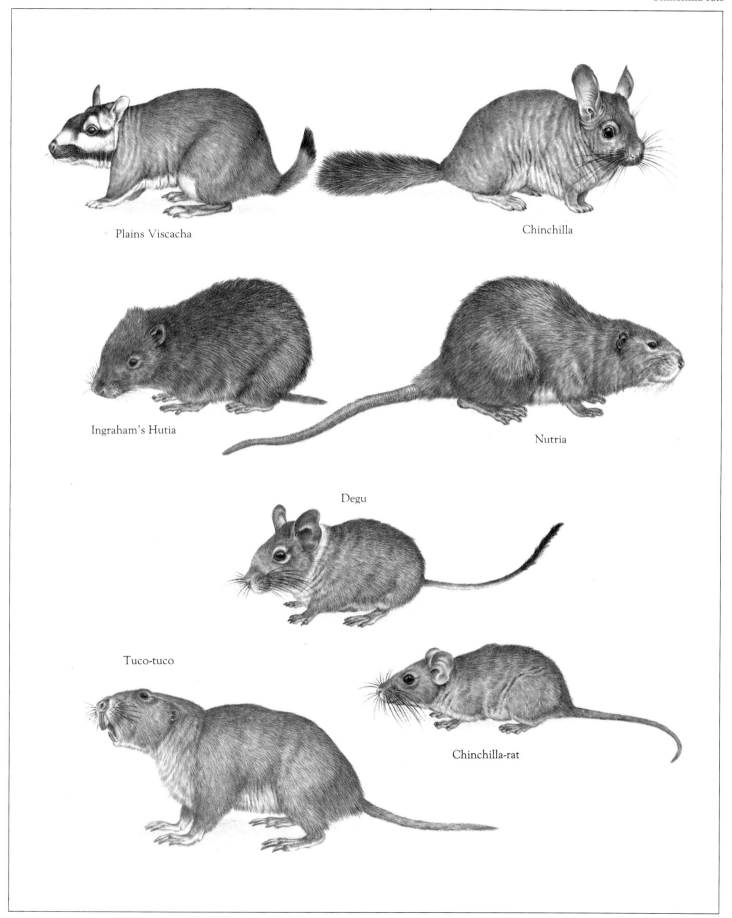

Plains Viscacha

Chinchilla

Ingraham's Hutia

Nutria

Degu

Tuco-tuco

Chinchilla-rat

Spiny Rats, Cane Rats and relatives

ECHIMYIDAE:
American Spiny Rat Family

The 45 species of American spiny rat are found from Nicaragua in the north to central Brazil in the south. Most are robust, ratlike creatures with a more or less spiny coat of sharp hairs. They are herbivorous, feeding on a variety of plant material. Most prefer to live close to rivers and streams.

Like many South American rodents, spiny rats have a long gestation and give birth to well-developed young which can run around when only a few hours old.

NAME: **Gliding Spiny Rat,** *Diplomys labilis*
RANGE: **Panama**
HABITAT: **forest**
SIZE: **body: 25–48 cm (9¾–19 in)**
tail: 20–28 cm (7¾–11 in)

Well adapted for arboreal life, the gliding spiny rat has long, strong toes and sharp, curved claws with which it can grip the smoothest of bark. Its common name derives from its habit of leaping from branch to branch, spreading its limbs to utilize its gliding membrane as it does so.

Gliding spiny rats make their nests in hollows in trees near water. They breed throughout the year, producing litters of 2 young after a gestation of about 60 days. The young are able to clamber around among the branches a few hours after they are born.

NAME: **Armored Rat,** *Hoplomys gymnurus*
RANGE: **Nicaragua, south to Colombia and Ecuador**
HABITAT: **rain forest, grassy clearings**
SIZE: **body: 22–32 cm (8¾–12½ in)**
tail: 15–25 cm (6–9¾ in)

The most spiny of all the spiny rats, the armored rat has a thick coat of needle-sharp hairs along its back and flanks. These rodents live in short, simple burrows in the banks of streams and emerge at night to forage for food. They breed throughout the year, producing litters of 1 to 3 young.

THRYONOMYIDAE:
Cane Rat Family

The 6 species of cane rat are found throughout Africa, south of the Sahara. They are substantial rodents, weighing up to 7 kg (15½ lb), and they are the principal source of animal protein for some tribes. In the cane fields they cause serious damage to the crop, stripping the cane of its outer bark to expose the soft central pith on which they feed.

NAME: **Cane Rat,** *Thryonomys swinderianus*
RANGE: **Africa, south of the Sahara**
HABITAT: **grassy plains, sugarcane plantations**
SIZE: **body: 35–61 cm (13¾–24 in)**
tail: 7–25 cm (2¾–9¾ in)

Cane rats do not normally live in burrows, preferring to construct a sleeping platform from chopped-up vegetation when needed. Occasionally, though, they take over disused aardvark or porcupine burrows or seek refuge among a pile of boulders. In southern Africa, cane rats are known to mate from April to June and to give birth to litters of 2 to 4 young after a gestation of 2 months. The young cane rats are born with their eyes open and are able to run around soon after birth.

PETROMYIDAE:
Dassie Rat Family

The single species in this family is an unusual rodent that looks more like a squirrel than a rat. Its common name links it in habit with the dassie, or rock hyrax, for both creatures share a love of the sun and spend much time basking on rocks, moving from place to place to catch the strongest rays. While the others bask, one member of the colony keeps a lookout for predators, such as mongooses, eagles or leopards, uttering a shrill warning call if danger threatens.

NAME: **Dassie Rat,** *Petromus typicus*
RANGE: **Africa: Angola, Namibia**
HABITAT: **rocky, arid hills**
SIZE: **body: 14–20 cm (5½–7¾ in)**
tail: 13–18 cm (5¼–7 in)

Dassie rats live in colonies and are active in the daytime. They feed on fruit, seeds and berries. They mate in early summer (October) and give birth in late December to a litter of 1 or 2 young.

BATHYERGIDAE:
Mole-rat Family

There are 9 species of mole-rat, all found in Africa, south of the Sahara. They are highly specialized for a subterranean life, for they are virtually blind and have powerful incisor teeth and claws for digging. Their skulls also are heavy and strong, and they use their heads as battering rams. The underground storage organs of plants — tubers and bulbs — are their main food, and worms and insect larvae may be eaten occasionally. Most have thick velvety coats which resemble that of the mole, but the naked mole-rat is quite hairless.

NAME: **Cape Dune Mole-rat,** *Bathyergus suillus*
RANGE: **South Africa to Cape of Good Hope**
HABITAT: **sand dunes, sandy plains**
SIZE: **body: 17.5–33 cm (6¾–13 in)**
tail: 4–7 cm (1½–2¾ in)

The largest member of its family, the Cape dune mole-rat may weigh up to 1.5 kg (3 lb). It has relatively huge incisor teeth, each one measuring 2 mm (1/12 in) across, and a fearsome bite. It builds extensive burrow systems, usually close to the surface, which can be a serious menace to root crops.

In November or December females give birth to 3 to 5 well-developed young.

NAME: **Naked Mole-rat,** *Heterocephalus glaber*
RANGE: **Somalia, Ethiopia, N. Kenya**
HABITAT: **arid steppe, light sandy soil**
SIZE: **body: 8–9 cm (3¼–3½ in)**
tail: 3.5–4 cm (1½ in)

This species, the smallest of its family, is one of the most curious mammals known. Each colony of about 100 rats is ruled by a single queen, who alone breeds. She is tended by a few nonworkers of both sexes, which are fatter and more sluggish than the workers. The latter dig the burrows and gather the roots and tubers for the whole colony to eat. The queen appears to be able to inhibit sexual maturation in all other females, but how this is achieved is not known. She breeds throughout the year and may produce up to 20 young in each litter. If she dies or is removed, a nonworker female assumes her role.

CTENODACTYLIDAE:
Gundi Family

The 5 species of gundi are found in Africa. They are extremely agile and can climb almost vertical rock faces. All members of the family are highly vocal and can utter a range of birdlike trills and twitters.

NAME: **Gundi,** *Ctenodactylus gundi*
RANGE: **Africa: Sahara**
HABITAT: **rocky outcrops**
SIZE: **body: 16–20 cm (6¼–7¾ in)**
tail: 1–2 cm (½–¾ in)

Shy animals, gundis feed only at night on a range of plant material which they usually take back to the safety of a rock crevice to consume. The gestation period of gundis is about 40 days, and the usual litter size is 1 or 2 young, which are able to run around immediately after birth.

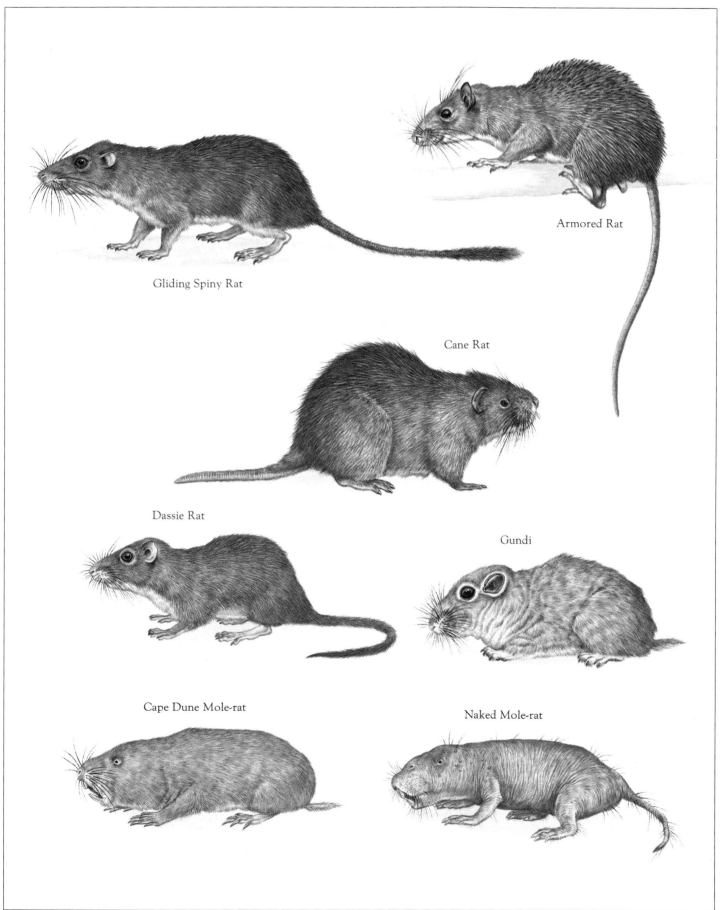

Armored Rat

Gliding Spiny Rat

Cane Rat

Dassie Rat

Gundi

Cape Dune Mole-rat

Naked Mole-rat

Pikas, Rabbits and Hares

ORDER LAGOMORPHA

There are 2 families and about 54 species in this order: the pikas and the rabbits and hares. For many years, these herbivores were regarded as a subgroup of the rodents, but a detailed examination of their structure, dentition and chewing mechanisms suggests that the two groups are distinct but related.

OCHOTONIDAE: Pika Family

There are about 14 species of pika, all in the same genus. They live in north and central Asia, and 1 species also occurs in North America. Pikas are smaller than rabbits and have short, rounded ears and no visible tail.

NAME: **Northern Pika**, *Ochotona alpina*
RANGE: **Siberia, N.E. China, Japan: Hokkaido; western N. America: Alaska to New Mexico**
HABITAT: **rocky mountain slopes, forest**
SIZE: **body: 20–25 cm (7¾–9¾ in)**

A small, short-legged animal, this pika cannot run fast like a rabbit but moves in small jumps. It lives in family groups and takes shelter in a den made among rocks or tree roots. Grass and slender plant stems are its main food, and, like all pikas, it gathers extra food in late summer and piles it in heaps like little haystacks to use in the winter. If they run short of food in winter, pikas tunnel through the snow to reach their stores.

There may be up to three litters a year, depending on the region; in North America there are two, both in the summer months. Each litter contains 2 to 5 young, born after a gestation of 30 or 31 days.

LEPORIDAE:

Rabbit and Hare Family

Found in forest, shrubby vegetation, grassland, tundra and on mountain slopes in the Americas, Europe, Asia and Africa, the rabbits and hares are an extremely successful family of small herbivorous mammals. The common rabbit has been introduced in Australia and New Zealand, where it has proved itself to be remarkably adaptable.

Compared with pikas, the 40 or so species of rabbit and hare have become highly adapted for swift running, with disproportionately well-developed hind limbs. They also have long, narrow ears and small tails. Their teeth are adapted for gnawing vegetation: they have chisel-shaped upper incisors, which grow throughout life, for biting and large cheek teeth for chewing.

NAME: **Brown Hare**, *Lepus capensis*
RANGE: **N., E. and S. Africa, Europe (not Iceland or N. Scandinavia), across temperate Asia to China; introduced in N. and South America, Australia and New Zealand**
HABITAT: **open country, farmland, woodland**
SIZE: **body: 44–76 cm (17¼–30 in)**
 tail: 7–11 cm (2¾–4¼ in)

A fast-running hare with long hind limbs, the brown hare is active mainly at dusk and at night. During the day, it remains in a shallow depression in the ground, known as a form, which is concealed among vegetation. It feeds on leaves, buds, roots, berries, fruit, fungi, bark and twigs and is usually solitary.

The female may have several litters a year, each of 1 to 6 young, which are born in the form, fully furred and active, with their eyes open. They are suckled for about 3 weeks and leave their mother about a month after birth.

NAME: **Black-tailed Jackrabbit**, *Lepus californicus*
RANGE: **USA: Oregon, east to South Dakota and Missouri, south to N. Mexico; introduced in some eastern states of USA**
HABITAT: **prairie, cultivated land, arid scrub**
SIZE: **body: 46.5–63 cm (18¼–24¾ in)**
 tail: 5–11.5 cm (2–4½ in)

Identified by its long ears and large, black-striped tail, this jackrabbit has powerful, elongate hind limbs and moves with a fast, bounding gait. For short periods, it may attain speeds of up to 56 km/h (35 mph) and tends to run rather than to take cover if threatened. In summer, it feeds on succulent green plants and grass, turning to more woody vegetation in winter. This jackrabbit, like all lagomorphs, ingests its fecal pellets, and it is thought to obtain additional nutrients when the material passes through the digestive system a second time.

There may be several litters a year, with 1 to 6 young in each; the average gestation period is 43 days. The young are born fully furred, with eyes open, in a shallow depression on the ground.

NAME: **Snowshoe Rabbit**, *Lepus americanus*
RANGE: **Alaska, Canada, N. USA**
HABITAT: **forest, swamps, thickets**
SIZE: **body: 36–52 cm (14¼–20½ in)**
 tail: 2.5–5.5 cm (1–2¼ in)

Also known as the varying hare, this animal has a dark-brown coat in summer that turns white in winter, except for a black edging on the ear tips. This coat is of undoubted camouflage value, although in fact only the visible tips of

the hairs are pure white. Usually active at night and in the early morning, the snowshoe rabbit feeds on juicy green plants and grass in summer and twigs, shoots and buds in winter. The population of these animals fluctuates tremendously on a roughly 10-year cycle, due to the availability of food and predator interactions.

Breeding begins in March, and there may be two or three litters, each of 1 to 7, usually 4, young, which are born well furred, with their eyes open.

NAME: **Natal Red Hare**, *Pronolagus crassicaudatus*
RANGE: **Africa: Namibia, South Africa, Botswana, Zimbabwe, Mozambique**
HABITAT: **stony country with scattered vegetation, forest edge**
SIZE: **body: 42–50 cm (16½–19¾ in)**
 tail: 6–14 cm (2¼–5½ in)

The Natal red hare lives alone in a small territory and is usually active at dusk and at night, feeding on grass and green-leaved plants. During the day, it rests in a shallow depression, or form, near cover of grass or rocks, and if alarmed, it darts into a rock crevice or hole. Like all hares, its hearing is acute, and its sight and sense of smell are also good.

The female gives birth to 1 or 2 fully haired young after a gestation of about a month.

NAME: **Volcano Rabbit**, *Romerolagus diazi*
RANGE: **Mexico: S.E. of Mexico City**
HABITAT: **slopes of volcanoes**
SIZE: **body: 28.5–31 cm (11¼–12¼ in)**
 tail: vestigial Ⓔ

This unusual rabbit, with its extremely restricted distribution, is now rare and strictly protected. It has short, rounded ears and trots, rather than hops, on its short legs as it moves along the runways it makes in the grass. Mainly active at night and at dusk, it feeds on grass and young shoots. Volcano rabbits live in colonies and dig burrows for shelter.

The wild population of this species may be as low as 1,300, but a captive colony exists in the zoo on Jersey in the Channel Islands.

NAME: **Hispid Hare**, *Caprolagus hispidus*
RANGE: **Nepal to N.E. India: Assam**
HABITAT: **forest, grassy bamboo thickets**
SIZE: **body: about 47 cm (18½ in)**
 tail: 2.5 cm (1 in) Ⓔ

Also known as the bristly or Assam rabbit, the hispid hare has an unusual coat of coarse, bristly fur; its ears are short and broad and its legs stout. It lives alone or sometimes in pairs and digs a burrow for shelter. Grass shoots, roots and bark are its main foods.

Volcano Rabbit

Black-tailed Jackrabbit

Hispid Hare

Snowshoe Rabbit

Northern Pika

Brown Hare

Natal Red Hare

Rabbits and Hares

NAME: **Swamp Rabbit, *Sylvilagus aquaticus***
RANGE: **south-central USA: Georgia to Texas**
HABITAT: **marshland, swamps, wet woodland**
SIZE: **body: 45–55 cm (17¾–21½ in)**
  tail: 6 cm (2¼ in)

The robust, large-headed swamp rabbit takes to water readily and is an expert swimmer and diver. It swims to avoid danger when pursued and also to reach islets or other new feeding areas. With its large, splayed toes, it also moves easily on damp, muddy land. Mainly nocturnal, it emerges from its shelter beneath a log or in a ground hollow at any time after heavy rain and feeds on grass, herbs and aquatic vegetation. It may also forage in grain fields where these are near swamps. Although usually docile, rival males will attack each other in ferocious, face-to-face fights, sometimes inflicting serious wounds.

After a gestation of about 40 days, a litter of 1 to 6 young, usually 2 or 3, is born in a shallow depression in the ground lined with grass and fur. The young are born furred, and their eyes open a few days after birth. There are thought to be two litters a year.

NAME: **Brush Rabbit, *Sylvilagus bachmani***
RANGE: **W. coast of N. America: British Columbia to Baja California**
HABITAT: **chaparral, thick brush or scrub**
SIZE: **body: 27–33 cm (10½–13 in)**
  tail: 2–4 cm (¾–1½ in)

The small, brown brush rabbit has a tiny tail and rounded ears. The rabbits living in hot inland regions to the south of the range tend to have longer ears than those living on the cooler, humid northern coast. Presumably this is because sound does not travel as well in hot, dry air as in moist, cool air and so the animals need the larger ears to pick up sounds more effectively. This shy, elusive rabbit stays hidden in dense undergrowth for much of the time, venturing out for only short distances to feed on a wide variety of green plants and taking almost anything within reach. It moves along well-trodden runways through the vegetation but does not make a burrow.

There are three or four litters a year, born between January and June. Each litter contains 3 to 5 young, born after a gestation of about 27 days. Births take place in a shallow hollow in the ground, which is lined with grass and fur. The young are born blind but with a covering of fine fur.

NAME: **Desert Cottontail, *Sylvilagus auduboni***
RANGE: **USA: California to Montana, south to Arizona and Texas; N. Mexico**
HABITAT: **open plains with scattered vegetation, wooded valleys, sagebrush lands**
SIZE: **body: 30–38 cm (11¾–15 in)**
  tail: 5–7.5 cm (2–3 in)

The desert cottontail is distinguished from the brush rabbit, with which it overlaps in the south of its range, by its larger size and ears and by its grayish coat. Often abroad at any time of day, it is, however, most active in the late afternoon and at night, when it feeds on grass, leaves of various plants, including cultivated plants, and fruit. It can do much damage to gardens and crops. Never far from some form of cover, it darts for safety if alarmed, the white underside of its tail momentarily revealed as it is flicked up. A burrow or a shallow depression in the ground is used for shelter.

Breeding takes place in spring or throughout the year, depending on the area. A litter of 1 to 5 blind, helpless young is born after a gestation of 26 to 30 days.

NAME: **Pygmy Rabbit, *Sylvilagus idahoensis***
RANGE: **N.W. USA: Oregon, Idaho, Montana, Utah, Nevada, N. California**
HABITAT: **arid areas with sagebrush**
SIZE: **body: 23–29 cm (9–11½ in)**
  tail: 2–3 cm (¾–1¼ in)

The smallest member of its genus, this species has thick, soft fur and short hind legs. It lives in a burrow that it excavates itself and does not often venture far from its home. During much of the day, it rests in the burrow, emerging at dusk to feed on sagebrush and any other available plant matter. Its main enemies are coyotes and owls, and if alarmed, the pygmy rabbit takes refuge in its burrow, which usually has 2 or 3 entrances.

Litters of 5 to 8 young, usually 6, are born between May and August.

NAME: **Common Rabbit, *Oryctolagus cuniculus***
RANGE: **Europe (except far north and east), N.W. Africa; introduced in many countries, including New Zealand, Australia, Chile**
HABITAT: **grassland, cultivated land, woodland, grassy coastal cliffs**
SIZE: **body: 35–45 cm (13¾–17¾ in)**
  tail: 4–7 cm (1½–2¾ in)

The ancestor of the domestic rabbit, this species has been introduced into many areas outside its native range and has been so successful as to become a major pest in some places. Smaller than

a hare, with shorter legs and ears, the common rabbit is brownish on the upperparts, with buffy-white underneath. The feet are equipped with large, straight claws.

Gregarious animals, these rabbits live in burrows, which they dig near to one another, and there may be a couple of hundred rabbits in a colony, or warren. They are most active at dusk and during the night but may emerge in the daytime in areas where they are undisturbed. Grass and leafy plants are their main foods, but rabbits also feed on vegetable and grain crops and can cause serious damage to young trees. In winter, they eat bulbs, twigs and bark if more succulent foods are unavailable. As a warning to others of approaching danger, a rabbit may thump the ground with its hind foot.

There may be several litters a year, born in the spring and summer in Europe. There are 3 to 9 young in a litter, and the gestation period is 28 to 33 days. Young are born naked, blind and helpless in a specially constructed burrow lined with vegetation and fur, which the mother plucks from her belly. They do not emerge from the burrow until about 3 weeks old. The female is in heat again 12 hours after the birth, but not all pregnancies last the term, and many embryos are resorbed. It is estimated that only about 40 percent of litters conceived are actually born, and the average number of live young produced by a female in a year is 11.

NAME: **Sumatran Rabbit, *Nesolagus netscheri***
RANGE: **S.W. Sumatra**
HABITAT: **forested mountain slopes at 600–1,400 m (2,000–4,600 ft)**
SIZE: **body: 36–40 cm (14¼–15¾ in)**
  tail: 1.5 cm (½ in) Ⓔ

The only member of its family to have a definitely striped coat, the Sumatran rabbit has buffy-gray upperparts with brown stripes and a line down the middle of its back from nose to tail. The tiny tail and the rump are reddish, while the limbs are grayish-brown. This unusual rabbit is now extremely rare, even in areas where it was once abundant, because of large-scale clearance of its forest habitat for cultivation.

Primarily nocturnal, the Sumatran rabbit spends the day in a burrow, but it is believed to take over an existing hole, rather than dig its own. It feeds on leaves and stalks of plants in the forest undergrowth.

Common Rabbit

Desert Cottontail

Pygmy Rabbit

Brush Rabbit

Swamp Rabbit

Sumatran Rabbit

Birds – feathered conquerors of the air

Distributed over the surface of the earth and inhabiting almost every possible area other than the deep ocean are about 8,600 species of bird. Ranging in size from tiny hummingbirds weighing only a few grams to the ostriches that stand taller than the average human being, birds have a special place in human consciousness. Birds are often boldly marked or colored, have complex family and group behavior, are easily observed and, above all, have the power of flight. Consequently they have always stimulated much interest, pleasure, wonderment, even envy, in human beings.

Birds are warm-blooded, air-breathing vertebrates with four limbs, the front pair of which are modified to form muscle-powered wings that, in the vast majority of living birds, give the potential for active flight. Birds can be unambiguously identified as such by their feathers — a feature which all birds possess and which no other animal shares.

Much of the unique nature of a bird's body structure is linked to its need for a low takeoff weight and a good power-to-weight ratio. Like mammals, birds are descended from reptilian ancestors. In the course of evolving, they have taken the heavy-boned, scaly, elongate body of a reptile and turned it into a light, compact flying machine with a feather-covered outer surface. The bones have become slim, thin-walled and filled with air sacs deriving from the walls of the lungs. All skeletal structures are pared down to produce maximum strength with minimum weight, and the heavy reptilian skull has changed to a light, almost spherical cranium, terminating in a toothless beak covered with horny plates. The number of bones is reduced, and some have been fused for greater rigidity.

Like reptilian scales and mammalian hairs, feathers are constructed largely from the tough protein keratin. They exist in a vast range of shapes, sizes and colors and have a variety of functions. First, they provide a light, flexible, thermally insulating protective layer over the bird's surface, crucial for maintaining the bird's high constant body temperature, which can reach 42°C (107.6°F). Second, the colors and patterns of feathers are the prime means of visual communication between birds. Third, and perhaps most importantly, the large, airfoil-shaped feathers of the wings and those of the tail provide the bird's flight surfaces. The wing feathers are attached to the highly modified bones of the forelimbs and provide the main lift and thrust for flight, while the tail feathers help the bird steer during flight. The tail feathers are attached to a stumpy remnant of a tail, quite unlike that of the birds' reptilian ancestors.

The earliest fossil bird, *Archaeopteryx*, dating from the Upper Jurassic period 140 million years ago, demonstrates an intriguing intermediate stage in the progressive loss of reptilian characteristics as birds evolved. *Archaeopteryx* had feathers and wings, but it also had teeth in its jaws and a typically reptilian set of tail vertebrae — it was essentially a feathered, winged reptile.

Although air offers relatively little resistance to motion, takeoff and active flight require a massive output of power from the bird. The relatively huge breast muscles of a bird, attached to a deep keel on the breastbone, deliver this power to the basal bone of the wing, the humerus. For these muscles to operate at the necessary high power output requires good blood circulation and an exceptionally efficient respiratory system, to supply oxygen at the required

194

rate. Birds have four-chambered hearts, similar to those of mammals but independently evolved, which can operate extremely rapidly: a sparrow's heart beats 500 times a minute, a hummingbird's up to 1,000 times a minute in flight.

A bird's respiratory system seems to take the air-breathing lung to the limits of its capability. The lungs are paired and operate in conjunction with an extensive system that includes numerous air sacs as well as thin tubes that efficiently pass oxygen into the bloodstream.

The ability to extract oxygen from the air much more rapidly and efficiently than a mammal is able to do helps to explain the astoundingly fast wing-beats of a hummingbird, the lightning flight of some swifts and the capacity of some birds to fly at altitudes where the atmosphere contains little oxygen.

In some bird families it is usual for males and females to have similar plumage; in others, the sexes differ in appearance. Although there are some interesting exceptions (for example, the females of many species of birds of prey are larger than the males), when the sexes differ, the male bird is normally the larger and more colorfully feathered, and the female has duller plumage, which may help to conceal her on the nest. For most, but not all, birds, there is a single breeding season in any year. Typically, in this period cock birds find and protect nesting territories and may sing or display to intimidate rival males and attract mates. Fertilization is internal, but apart from a few species, the male bird does not possess a penis but only a small erectile protuberance at the base of his cloaca (the reproductive opening) through which sperm passes into the female's cloaca.

Birds lay eggs containing large yolks, the food reserves for the developing embryo, surrounded by a tough, mineralized shell. The egg is formed as the ovum passes from the ovary down the oviduct to the outside world, successive layers of white inner and outer shell membranes being added on the way. Most birds lay their eggs in some form of nest, where they are incubated by one or both parents while the embryo develops. The young of some birds, such as ducks and pheasants, hatch covered with downy feathers and are able to walk immediately, while the young of others, such as blackbirds and most other songbirds, are born naked and helpless and need a period of feeding and care.

Among the 27 orders of living birds, a remarkable variety of modifications has taken place to the basic avian body, with the most crucial adaptations being to feet, legs, beaks and wings. There are large, long-legged walking birds, such as ostriches, rheas, emus and cassowaries, that have completely lost the power of flight. There are other flightless birds, such as the penguins, that have wings adapted as underwater paddles. At the opposite extreme are the insectivorous swifts, birds so aerial that it is possible that their only contact with the ground throughout life may be at the nest. There are highly specialized predators of the night (owls, nightjars) and of the daylight hours (eagles, hawks, falcons), with strong beaks and killing talons. Almost any type of small animal or vegetable food is the diet of some bird species — a shrike pouncing on a grasshopper, a hummingbird extracting nectar and a parrot feeding on jungle fruit, all testify to the breathtaking diversity of the world of birds.

Ratites, Tinamous

STRUTHIONIDAE: Ostrich Family

Ostriches are the largest living birds. There is now only a single species, living in Africa, but formerly the family's range extended from southern Europe to Mongolia as well as throughout Africa.

NAME: **Ostrich**, *Struthio camelus*
RANGE: **Africa**
HABITAT: **grassland, arid land**
SIZE: **1.75–2.75 m (6–9 ft) tall**

The ostrich is too big to fly but has become so perfectly adapted to high-speed running that it is the fastest creature on two legs. At speeds of up to 70 km/h (44 mph), it can easily outstrip most enemies. Powerful legs, flexible knees and supple, two-toed feet are its adaptations for speed. The ostrich has lost its strong wing feathers, but the male has soft, curling plumes, once much in demand for fashionable hats and boas. Female birds are slightly smaller than males and have brownish plumage and off-white wings and tails. Juveniles are grayish-brown.

Ostriches eat mostly plant matter but occasionally feed on small reptiles. They are nomadic, wandering in small groups in search of food. At breeding time, the male collects a harem of 2 to 5 females. One female scrapes a shallow pit in the ground in which to lay her eggs, and the rest of the harem probably uses the same nest. The eggs are the biggest laid by any bird — the equivalent in volume of about 40 hen's eggs. The male bird takes over the incubation of the eggs at night and shares in the care of the young.

DROMAIIDAE: Emu Family

The one surviving species in the emu family is the second-largest living bird. It is closely related to the cassowaries, although they are externally dissimilar.

NAME: **Emu**, *Dromaius novaehollandiae*
RANGE: **Australia**
HABITAT: **arid plains, woodland, desert**
SIZE: **2 m (6½ ft) tall**

Emus have remained common in Australia despite having been destroyed as serious pests on farmland. They can run at speeds of 48 km/h (30 mph) and swim well. Fruit, berries and insects make up the bulk of their diet. The female lays 7 to 10 dark-green eggs, with a characteristic pimply texture, in a hollow in the ground. The male incubates the eggs for about 60 days.

RATITES

"Ratites" is the informal name given to a mixed group of running birds with some dramatic morphological differences from all other birds. Apart from the fowl-sized kiwis of New Zealand, ratites are all extremely large, ground-living birds, with massive, muscular legs for powerful running. Their wings are much reduced in size and are not functional. The ratite breastbone is flat and small and has no central keel — in other birds this keel serves for the attachment of the flight muscles. The word "ratite" means "raftlike," as opposed to carinate, applicable to all other birds and meaning "keeled."

The living ratite families (ostrich, rheas, kiwis, emu and cassowaries) are grouped in 4 orders; cassowaries and the emu share the same order.

CASUARIIDAE: Cassowary Family

There are 3 species of cassowary, all in Australasia, but because of the isolating effects of island habitats, many races have evolved with minor differences. All are large powerful birds and are well adapted to forest life.

NAME: **Common Cassowary**, *Casuarius casuarius*
RANGE: **N. Australia, New Guinea, E. Indonesia**
HABITAT: **rain forest**
SIZE: **1.5 m (5 ft) tall**

The common cassowary is an impressive bird with long, hairlike quills which protect it from the forest undergrowth. Its wings are vestigial, but its legs are extremely powerful and armed with sharp-toed feet, capable of inflicting severe wounds. The bald but brightly colored head and neck bear brilliant wattles and a horny casque. As the cassowary moves through the dense forest in search of seeds, fruits and berries, it holds this prominent casque well forward to help break a path. Male and female look alike, but the female is larger. The female lays 3 to 6 green eggs in a shallow, leaf-lined nest on the ground.

RHEIDAE: Rhea Family

Rheas are the South American equivalents of the ostrich and the heaviest of the New World birds. Although they have larger wings than other ratites, they are still unable to fly, but they are good swimmers and fast runners.

NAME: **Greater Rhea**, *Rhea americana*
RANGE: **South America, east of the Andes**
HABITAT: **open country**
SIZE: **1.5 m (5 ft) tall**

Greater rheas live in flocks of 20 to 30 birds. Male and female look much alike. They feed on plants, seeds, insects and small animals. At breeding time, the male displays and gathers a harem of females. He leads his mated females to a shallow nest which he has prepared, and they all lay their eggs in this one nest, making a clutch of up to 18 eggs, which the male incubates.

APTERYGIDAE: Kiwi Family

Kiwis are flightless forest birds. There are 3 species, all living in New Zealand.

NAME: **Brown Kiwi**, *Apteryx australis*
RANGE: **New Zealand**
HABITAT: **forest**
SIZE: **50 cm (19¾ in)**

The brown kiwi, emblem of New Zealand, is a rarely seen, nocturnal creature. It has rudimentary wings concealed under coarse, hairlike body feathers. Its legs are short and stout, with powerful claws for scratching around the forest floor in search of insects, worms and berries. The nostrils are at the tip of the bird's pointed bill, and it seems to have a good sense of smell — rare among birds. Females are larger than males, but the sexes otherwise look similar. The female lays 1 or 2 eggs in a burrow, where they are incubated by the male. Each egg weighs about 450 g (1 lb) and is exceptionally large in proportion to the bird's body weight.

TINAMIDAE: Tinamou Family

Tinamous are fowl-like ground birds, found in a variety of habitats from Mexico to Argentina. They can fly but are weak and clumsy, and although built for running, their best defense is to remain still, relying on their protective coloring. They feed on seeds, berries and insects. There are 47 species of tinamou.

NAME: **Great Tinamou**, *Tinamus major*
RANGE: **S. Mexico, Bolivia, Brazil**
HABITAT: **rain forest, cloud forest**
SIZE: **46 cm (18 in)**

The great tinamou, like all members of its family, is polygamous, and females lay up to 12 eggs, often in different nests. With their vivid, clear colors — blue, green and pink — and highly glazed surface, these eggs are among the most beautiful of all birds' eggs.

Ostrich
(male)

Greater Rhea

Emu

Brown Kiwi

Common Cassowary

Great Tinamou

Penguins, Grebes, Loons

ORDER SPHENISCIFORMES
SPHENISCIDAE: Penguin Family

Penguins are a primitive and highly specialized group of marine birds. All 18 species are flightless and exquisitely adapted for marine existence. Their wings have been modified into flat, unfoldable paddles which are used propulsively for rapid underwater swimming in pursuit of fish and squid. Feathers are short and glossy and form a dense, fur-like mat which is waterproof, streamlined and a superb thermal insulating layer. Their short legs, with webbed feet, are set far back to act as swimming rudders, but this position means that the birds must stand upright on land or slide along on their bellies.

Penguins usually come ashore only to breed and molt; the rest of the year is spent entirely at sea. All forms, except the Galápagos penguin, breed on the Antarctic continent, subantarctic islands or the southern coasts of South America, southern Africa and Australia, often in extremely harsh conditions.

NAME: **Little Blue/Fairy Penguin,**
Eudyptula minor
RANGE: **New Zealand: South Island;**
Tasmania, S. Australia
HABITAT: **coastal waters**
SIZE: **40 cm (15¾ in) tall**

The smallest penguin, the little blue penguin lives around coasts and islands in its range, seeking food in shallow waters. Breeding birds tend to return each year to the same nesting sites and to the same mates. A brief courtship re-establishes the pair bond. The little blue nests in crevices or in a burrow, which it digs or takes over from other birds. The females lays 2 eggs, and both male and female incubate for 33 to 40 days.

NAME: **Galápagos Penguin,** *Spheniscus*
mendiculus
RANGE: **Galápagos Islands**
HABITAT: **coastal waters**
SIZE: **51 cm (20 in) tall**

The rarest of penguins and the only species to venture near the equator, the Galápagos penguin owes its presence there to the exceptional situation of its native islands. Although so close to the equator, the Galápagos are bathed by the cool waters of the Humboldt Current, which makes the area habitable for a cold-loving penguin. The current is also rich in nutrients, supplying plenty of food right up the food chain. The penguins breed from May to July and make a nest of stones in a cave or crevice on the coast. Two eggs are laid.

NAME: **Emperor Penguin,** *Aptenodytes*
forsteri
RANGE: **southern oceans**
HABITAT: **ocean and pack ice**
SIZE: **1.2 m (4 ft) tall**

Emperor penguins, largest of the penguin family, endure the worst breeding conditions of any bird. These penguins never actually come to land but gather in huge colonies on the pack ice of the antarctic seas. After pairing, the female lays her 1 egg at the beginning of winter and at once returns to the sea. Her partner incubates the egg on his feet, where it is protected by a flap of skin and feathers. All the males in the colony huddle together for warmth and protection during their vigil in the bitterly cold, totally dark antarctic winter. As the male cannot leave the egg, he fasts during the 64-day incubation period. When the chick is born, he feeds it from secretions in his crop, and the chick remains protected on his feet. By this time the ice is breaking up, and the female returns to take over while the male recovers and feeds. Both parents then care for their chick.

ORDER PODICIPEDIFORMES
PODICIPEDIDAE: Grebe Family

Nineteen species of these satin-plumaged water birds are found scattered around the world; some species are widespread. They all breed in fresh water, usually making a nest of floating, decaying vegetation. Like penguins, grebes are fast swimmers, with legs set well back on the body. The large grebes are highly streamlined birds which chase and catch fish underwater with their long pointed beaks. Other species feed on bottom-feeding mollusks and are smaller and more compact, with stubby thick bills. Males and females look similar, while juveniles have striped heads and necks.

NAME: **Little Grebe/Dabchick,**
Tachybaptus ruficollis
RANGE: **Europe, Africa and Madagascar,**
Asia, Indonesia, New Guinea
HABITAT: **lakes, ponds, rivers**
SIZE: **27 cm (10½ in)**

The little grebe is one of the smaller grebes and is rotund and ducklike in shape. It feeds on insects, crustaceans and mollusks. In winter its plumage is gray-brown and white, but in the breeding season it has a reddish throat and foreneck. The female lays 2 to 10 eggs in a floating clump of vegetation in shallow water or among aquatic plants. Both parents incubate the clutch for a total of 23 to 25 days.

NAME: **Great Crested Grebe,** *Podiceps*
cristatus
RANGE: **Europe, Asia, Africa, south of**
the Sahara; Australia, New Zealand
HABITAT: **lakes, ponds, rivers, coastal**
waters
SIZE: **51 cm (20 in)**

Easily recognized on water by its long slender neck and daggerlike bill, the great crested grebe is rarely seen on land, where it moves awkwardly, or in flight. It feeds mainly on fish, which it catches by diving from the surface of the water. The great crested is one of the largest grebes; adults are particularly striking in their breeding plumage, when they sport a double-horned crest on the head and frills on the neck. In winter this crest is much reduced, the frills lost and the head largely white. The sexes look alike, but males generally have longer bills and larger crests and frills. Before mating, these grebes perform an elegant mutual courtship dance to establish the pair bond. Both partners perform head-wagging and reed-holding displays and other ritualized movements. They mate on a reed platform near the nest, which is among the reeds. The female lays 2 to 7 eggs, which are incubated by both parents for 27 to 29 days.

ORDER GAVIIFORMES
GAVIIDAE: Loon Family

Loons are foot-propelled diving birds. All 4 or 5 species live in the high latitudes of the northern hemisphere and are the ecological counterparts of grebes in those areas. The birds feed primarily on fish, which they chase and seize under water. Males and females look alike.

NAME: **Red-throated Loon,** *Gavia stellata*
RANGE: **circumpolar: N. America,**
N. Europe, N. Asia
HABITAT: **lakes, ponds, seas**
SIZE: **53–69 cm (21–27 in)**

The red-throated loon has a thin grebe-like bill and a reddish throat patch at breeding time; in winter its back is spotted with white, and its head is gray and white. Like the others in the family, the red-throated loon flies strongly and, because it is smaller than other species, takes off from the water more easily. After a courtship display of bill-dipping and diving, the female lays 1 to 3 eggs in a heap of moss or other vegetation or in a shallow dip in the ground. Both parents share the 24- to 29-day incubation of the clutch and feed the young.

Emperor Penguin

Little Blue Penguin

Galápagos Penguin

Great Crested Grebe

Red-throated Loon

Little Grebe

Albatrosses, Petrels

ORDER PROCELLARIIFORMES

This order of birds contains 4 families, namely, the albatrosses, petrels, storm-petrels and diving-petrels. All are totally marine birds with webbed feet and hooked beaks surmounted by elongated tubular nostrils. Between 80 and 100 species (according to different classifications) of these "tubenoses" are distributed around the oceans of the world. Most species store stomach oil as a long-distance food reserve; this oil can also be discharged from mouth or nostrils as a foul-smelling chemical defense. Typical species in this order have low reproductive rates, long periods of immaturity and long life-spans.

DIOMEDEIDAE: Albatross Family

The 13 species of albatross are all large pelagic birds, noted for their spectacular gliding flight over vast ocean distances. Most occur in the southern hemisphere, but a few do live in the North Pacific. The birds have an unmistakable body form with extremely long narrow wings. The albatross bill is large and hooked. Male and female look alike in all species except the wandering albatross. Albatrosses feed on fish, squid and other marine animals which they catch at the surface of the water or just below it. Most species are migratory.

NAME: **Wandering Albatross,** *Diomedea exulans*
RANGE: **southern oceans, approximately 60° S to 25° S**
HABITAT: **oceanic**
SIZE: **110–135 cm (43–53 in)**
    wingspan: 290–324 cm (114–127½ in)

The wandering albatross is the largest species in its family and the longest-winged of all birds. Using the strong winds of the oceans of the southern hemisphere, it glides and soars for long periods. As well as feeding on fish and squid, these albatrosses follow ships and gather to scavenge when refuse is dumped. Female birds have brown flecks on the crown; juveniles have brown bodies and underwings, which gradually become mottled, then white.

    The wandering albatross comes to land on subantarctic islands in the South Pacific, Indian and South Atlantic oceans only to breed. Courtship displays and greeting ceremonies are elaborate: the birds rattle their bills, touch bill tips and spread their huge wings. The female lays 1 egg, which is incubated for about 80 days by both parents. Since both parents feed the chick intermittently for about a year, the birds can breed only every other year.

NAME: **Light-mantled Sooty Albatross,** *Phoebetria palpebrata*
RANGE: **southern oceans to about 33° S**
HABITAT: **oceanic**
SIZE: **72 cm (28 in)**

A small graceful albatross, the light-mantled sooty is far better able to maneuver in the air than the large seabirds. It breeds on antarctic and sub-antarctic islands and makes a neat cup-shaped nest of plant material. The female lays 1 egg, and both parents care for the chick for a few months. Eventually the parents desert the chick, which soon follows them out to sea.

PROCELLARIIDAE: Petrel Family

This family, with about 66 species, is the largest group of tubenoses and contains birds such as petrels, shearwaters, fulmars and prions. Most species have long slender wings and short tails. Males and females look alike. Representatives of the family occur in all oceans; most species are migratory. Except when breeding, these birds rarely come to land and spend most of their lives flying over the ocean. They are expert at flying through the most severe weather.

    Within the family, species have become adapted to different feeding methods. Fulmars feed on plankton and scavenge around fishing fleets; prions filter planktonic animals from the water; the gadfly petrels (such as *Pterodroma* sp.) catch squid and octopus at night, and shearwaters are surface predators of fish.

    Most species nest in burrows or rock crevices, although a few nest on cliff ledges or open ground. The female usually lays a single egg, which both parents incubate in shifts of 2 to 12 days. Petrels usually nest in colonies.

NAME: **Broad-billed Prion/Whale Bird,** *Pachyptila vittata*
RANGE: **southern oceans**
HABITAT: **oceanic**
SIZE: **31 cm (12¼ in)**

The 6 species of prion, all in the genus *Pachyptila*, are similar in appearance and size and virtually indistinguishable at sea. The broad-billed prion is slightly larger than the others and can be identified by its markedly broader bill. It feeds on small planktonic animals, which it filters from the water through the hairlike fringes of lamellae at the sides of the bill. The birds often form huge feeding flocks in areas of plankton-rich water. Colonies of broad-billed prions breed in summer on islands in the South Atlantic and southern Indian oceans and off New Zealand.

NAME: **Manx Shearwater,** *Puffinus puffinus*
RANGE: **Atlantic and Pacific Oceans, Mediterranean Sea**
HABITAT: **oceanic and coastal**
SIZE: **30–38 cm (11¾–15 in)**

There are several geographically distinct races of the Manx shearwater with slight plumage differences. Shearwaters feed by day, seizing fish, squid, crustaceans and debris at the water surface or diving in pursuit of prey. They have complex migration routes between feeding grounds and travel long distances. A shearwater removed from its burrow in Britain and taken to the USA returned home, a distance of about 4,500 km (2,800 mi) in 13 days. The birds nest in huge colonies on offshore islands. The female lays her egg in a burrow, and both parents care for the chick.

NAME: **Northern Fulmar,** *Fulmarus glacialis*
RANGE: **N. Atlantic, N. Pacific Oceans**
HABITAT: **oceanic**
SIZE: **45–50 cm (17¾–19¾ in)**

Fulmars exploit the waste from commercial fishing, and with the spread of this industry, these large, robust petrels have dramatically increased their numbers. They swim but seldom dive, catching most of their food at the water surface. Male and female birds look alike, but the males have bigger bills. They nest on cliff ledges on coasts or islands; the female lays 1 egg, incubated by both parents. The adults feed the chick and defend it by spitting stomach oil at predators.

NAME: **Scaled Petrel,** *Pterodroma inexpectata*
RANGE: **S. and N. Pacific Oceans to 55° N**
HABITAT: **oceanic**
SIZE: **36 cm (14¼ in)**

The scaled petrel is a fairly small species with long narrow wings. Its flight is fast, and it swoops and dives with great ease. Primarily a nocturnal bird, it feeds largely on squid and octopus. It breeds on Stewart and Snares islands near New Zealand and migrates north in winter to the western North Pacific. Like most petrels, it lays only 1 egg.

Wandering Albatross

Light-mantled Sooty Albatross

Scaled Petrel

Manx Shearwater

Northern Fulmar

Broad-billed Prion

Storm-petrels, Diving-petrels

HYDROBATIDAE:
Storm-petrel Family

These small seabirds occur in most oceans, mainly south of the Arctic Circle. There are about 21 species, which are divided into 2 distinct groups, each one characteristic of the northern or southern hemisphere; their ranges overlap in the tropics. The northern birds have short legs, long pointed wings and forked tails; they feed by swooping and skimming low over the water. The southern birds have long slender legs, short rounded wings and square tails; they are adapted for a particular method of feeding: "stepping" over the surface of the water with wings spread to seize items of food.

All storm-petrels are small birds, reaching a maximum length of about 25 cm (10 in). All have black, or black and brown, plumage with white rump feathers. Males and females look alike, and all have a distinctive musky smell. Juveniles are similar to adults. Most storm-petrels are deepwater birds and come to land and inshore waters only to breed. Some species are not known to settle on the sea and they seldom dive. Many storm-petrels follow ships and take refuse and animals disturbed by the wake.

Storm-petrels breed in colonies, usually on remote offshore islands. Long-term pair bonds are the rule, but this may be due largely to the birds' habit of returning to the same nest sites year after year. They often come to land at night to breed; consequently vocal displays are more important than visual. They nest in crevices and burrows. Most migrate after breeding.

NAME: **Black Storm-petrel,** *Oceanodroma melania*
RANGE: **eastern N. Pacific Ocean: California to Peru**
HABITAT: **coastal and offshore waters**
SIZE: **21–23 cm (8–9 in)**

With its deeply forked tail, the black storm-petrel is characteristic of the northern group of storm-petrels and is one of several species inhabiting the nutrient-rich waters of the Pacific. This storm-petrel feeds on plankton and on the larvae of the spiny lobster.

The black storm-petrel breeds on islands off the coast of Baja California. The female lays 1 egg in a nest in a burrow or rock crevice.

NAME: **Storm-petrel,** *Hydrobates pelagicus*
RANGE: **N.E. Atlantic Ocean, W. Mediterranean Sea**
HABITAT: **oceanic**
SIZE: **14–18 cm (5½–7 in)**

The storm-petrel is the smallest European seabird and one of the 3 Atlantic species of storm-petrel. It is more aerial than aquatic but will land and swim briefly on the sea in all weather. It feeds on fish, squid and crustaceans and often follows ships to feed on waste thrown into the water. The only time it comes to land is in the breeding season, to nest on remote islands and promontories. The nest is a burrow, dug by both partners, or a hole or cavity in the cliff face. The female lays 1 egg, and both parents share the incubation duties and the care of the chick. In the winter the birds migrate south of their breeding range to the Red Sea and the west coast of Africa.

NAME: **Wilson's Petrel,** *Oceanites oceanicus*
RANGE: **Antarctic, Atlantic and Indian Oceans**
HABITAT: **oceanic**
SIZE: **15–19 cm (6–7½ in)**

Wilson's petrel is typical of the southern group of storm-petrels. Its legs are long and toes short, and it is ideally suited for hopping and paddling over the water surface to pick up prey. On occasion it also hovers over the surface. This species feeds mostly on plankton and the oil and fat debris from whaling stations.

Breeding pairs nest in burrows or in crevices under rocks. In experiments, banded individuals were found to return to the same nest sites year after year, usually on islands off the tip of South America. The female lays 1 egg, which her mate helps to incubate. Both feed the chick. In winter the birds migrate north to the tropics or even north of the equator, and they can sometimes be seen off the Atlantic coast of North America. Some ornithologists believe Wilson's petrel to be the most abundant bird species in the world.

NAME: **Ringed Storm-petrel,** *Oceanodroma hornbyi*
RANGE: **Pacific coast of South America**
HABITAT: **oceanic**
SIZE: **20–22 cm (7¾–8½ in)**

The ringed storm-petrel has a distinctive plumage pattern, with a white collar around the neck and a dark band across the chest. Although a seabird, this species flies inland to breed in the Chilean Andes.

NAME: **White-faced Storm-petrel,** *Pelagodroma marina*
RANGE: **Atlantic, Indian and S. Pacific Oceans**
HABITAT: **oceanic**
SIZE: **20.5 cm (8 in)**

This species has distinctive black and white plumage. Like all southern storm-petrels, it lowers its long legs and splashes down on the sea to feed at the water surface. It takes plankton and also catches small squid. Colonies breed on many islands in the Atlantic and around the coasts of Australia and New Zealand. The female lays 1 egg in a burrow dug in soft ground. The white-faced storm-petrel's choice of ground nest sites, combined with its awkwardness on land, makes it vulnerable to severe predation by cats and by other birds during its breeding season.

PELECANOIDIDAE:
Diving-petrel Family

Diving-petrels are a highly distinctive group of 5 tubenose birds, all classified in a single genus: *Pelecanoides*. All species have a compact body form, with short neck, wings, legs and tail, and their overall appearance is similar to that of the auks (Alcidae). The similarities are linked to their shared basic feeding method: they dive from the air into the sea and use their short wings to swim underwater in search of prey. Their food includes crustaceans and small schooling fish such as anchovies. Diving-petrels fly with rapid wing beats. All species are found in the southern oceans and along the west coast of South America as far north as Peru.

NAME: **Subantarctic Diving-petrel,** *Pelecanoides urinatrix*
RANGE: **S. Atlantic and Indian Oceans**
HABITAT: **coastal waters**
SIZE: **18–21 cm (7–8¼ in)**

This diving-petrel, like its fellows, is a coastal rather than an oceanic seabird. It breeds, sometimes colonially, on South Atlantic islands, from the Falklands east to Australia and New Zealand. Breeding birds dig a burrow nest several feet long. The parents take turns incubating their 1 egg for a total of about 8 weeks, and they share the feeding of the chick. The chick leaves the nest when it is about 7 or 8 weeks old.

Black Storm-petrel

Storm-petrel

Wilson's Petrel

Ringed Storm-petrel

Subantarctic Diving-petrel

White-faced Storm-petrel

Tropicbirds, Gannets and Boobies, Pelicans

ORDER PELECANIFORMES

This order contains 60 species of birds grouped into 6 families: pelicans, gannets and boobies, tropicbirds, cormorants, darters and frigatebirds. All are medium to very large aquatic birds with webbed feet and are found in both marine and freshwater habitats.

PHAETHONTIDAE:
Tropicbird Family

Tropicbirds are elegant white seabirds, easily distinguished by their two elongated central tail feathers. The 3 species in the family all occur in tropical oceans, where they fly far out to sea and breed on islands. They are poor swimmers and tend to catch food by hovering above the water, then plunging down to seize the prey. Fish, squid and crustaceans are their main food. Male and female look alike.

NAME: **Red-tailed Tropicbird,** *Phaethon rubricauda*
RANGE: **Indian and Pacific Oceans**
HABITAT: **oceanic**
SIZE: **41 cm (16 in)**
  tail: 51 cm (20 in)

The red-tailed tropicbird, with its dark-red tail feathers, is a particularly striking species; in the breeding season, the bird's white plumage takes on a rosy tinge. Tropicbirds move awkwardly on land, so they tend to nest on ledges or cliffs where they are in a position for easy takeoff. Although usually solitary at sea, they are numerous at breeding grounds and fight over nest sites and partners. No actual nest is made; the single egg is laid on the ground. Both parents incubate the egg for about 42 days and feed the downy chick until it leaves the nest at 12 to 15 weeks.

SULIDAE:
Gannet and Booby Family

The 9 birds in this family fall into two distinct groups: the 6 species of booby and the 3 species of gannet. They occur in all the oceans of the world: the boobies in tropical and subtropical areas, and the gannets generally in temperate zones. All are impressive marine birds that feed by plunge-diving for prey. Most have stout bodies, long pointed wings and short legs. Male and female generally look alike, occasionally differing in bill and foot color. Juveniles have brownish feathers at first and develop the adult plumage over a few years.

NAME: **Brown Booby,** *Sula leucogaster*
RANGE: **tropical Atlantic and Pacific Oceans**
HABITAT: **mostly coastal**
SIZE: **64–74 cm (25–29 in)**

Boobies were apparently given their common name because of their folly in allowing sailors to approach and kill them for food. Like gannets, boobies plunge-dive for fish and squid but specialize in feeding in shallow water and in the catching of flyingfish. The brown booby stays nearer the coast than the gannet and breeds on cliffs and rocks or even on beaches and coral reefs. The female lays 1 or 2 eggs in a hollow on the ground or among rocks, and both parents share the incubation and feeding duties.

NAME: **Northern Gannet,** *Sula (= Morus) bassana*
RANGE: **N. Atlantic Ocean**
HABITAT: **coastal waters**
SIZE: **87–100 cm (34–39¼ in)**

Gannets are streamlined, heavily built seabirds with thick necks, strong legs and webbed feet. Offshore rather than oceanic birds, they are magnificent in the air and fly or soar over the water searching for fish and squid. Once prey is sighted, the gannet will plummet 30 m (100 ft) or more down to the sea, grasp the catch and bring it to the surface. The bird's stout bill and specially adapted skull, with resilient, air-filled spaces, take much of the initial impact of these expert dives. Other adaptations perfect gannets for marine life. First, there are no external nostrils. The nostril openings are covered by bony flaps so that water cannot be forced into them when the bird dives. The rear edge of the upper bill bows outward so that the gannet can breathe. Second, salt glands above the eye orbits produce a concentrated salt solution which enters the mouth by the internal nostrils and drips away from the beak, and this enables the gannet to feed on salty fish and to drink seawater without having to excrete vast quantities of urine to eliminate the salt.

Gannets are extremely gregarious birds, breeding in colonies of thousands of birds on rocks and islands. Attempts to breed gannets in small groups have failed, and it could be that the social stimulation of the colony is a crucial factor for breeding success. The birds display to establish and maintain pair bonds, and each pair occupies and defends a breeding territory. Nests are so closely packed that incubating birds can reach out and touch one another. The female lays 1 egg, which both parents incubate for 43 to 45 days.

PELECANIDAE: Pelican Family

The pelicans, which give this order its name, comprise 8 species found in large lakes and on seacoasts. They are gregarious, strong-flying birds which feed on fish, caught while the birds are swimming in shallow water or, in one case, by diving from the air. The most dramatic anatomical feature is the huge gular pouch beneath the long broad bill. Males and females look alike.

NAME: **Great White/Rosy Pelican,** *Pelecanus onocrotalus*
RANGE: **S.E. Europe, Asia, Africa**
HABITAT: **inland lakes, marshes**
SIZE: **140–175 cm (55–69 in)**

A large white bird with the characteristic pouched bill, the great white pelican is well adapted for aquatic life. The short strong legs and webbed feet propel it in water and aid the rather awkward takeoff from the water surface. Once aloft, the long-winged pelicans are powerful fliers, however, and often travel in spectacular V-formation groups. The pelican's pouch is simply a scoop. As the pelican pushes its bill underwater, the lower bill bows out, creating a large pouch which fills with water and fish. As the bird lifts its head, the pouch contracts, forcing out the water but retaining the fish. A group of 6 to 8 great white pelicans will gather in a horseshoe formation in the water to feed together. They dip their bills in unison, creating a circle of open pouches, ready to trap every fish in the area.

Large numbers of these pelicans breed together in colonies. The female lays 2 to 4 eggs in a nest of sticks in a tree or on the grass. The young are cared for by both parents.

NAME: **Brown Pelican,** *Pelecanus occidentalis*
RANGE: **USA, Caribbean, South America, Galápagos Islands**
HABITAT: **coasts**
SIZE: **127 cm (50 in)**

The brown pelican is the smallest pelican and is rather different from the rest of its family. It is a seabird and catches fish by diving into the water from as high as 15 m (50 ft). When it dives, it holds the wings back and the neck curved into an S-shape so that the front of the body, which is provided with cushioning air sacs, takes some of the impact of the plunge into the water. The successful bird generally returns to the surface to eat its catch.

The female brown pelican lays her 2 or 3 eggs in a nest which is built in a tree or sometimes on the ground.

Red-tailed Tropicbird

Northern Gannet

Brown Booby

Brown Pelican

Great White Pelican

Darters, Cormorants, Frigatebirds

ANHINGIDAE: Darter Family

These superb underwater fish-hunters look much like streamlined cormorants but have longer, slender necks and sharply pointed bills. Also known as anhingas, the 4 species of darter are found in a variety of freshwater habitats throughout the tropics. There are some differences in the plumage of males and females, and males have light plumes on head and neck in the breeding season.

NAME: **Anhinga/Snakebird**, *Anhinga anhinga*
RANGE: **S. USA to Argentina**
HABITAT: **lakes, rivers**
SIZE: **90 cm (35 in)**

Like cormorants, anhingas dive deep in pursuit of fish, keeping their wings in at their sides and paddling with their feet. While underwater, the anhinga keeps its long neck folded in, ready to dart out and impale prey with the sharp beak. The edges of the beak are serrated, providing a firm grip on the fish once it has been transferred from the impaled position. At the water surface, the anhinga often swims with all but its head and sinuous neck submerged — hence its other common name, "snakebird." Crustaceans, amphibians and insects also form part of the anhinga's diet.

Anhingas are colonial breeders, often nesting near other large water birds. They build nests in a tree near or overhanging water. The female lays 3 to 6 eggs, which both partners incubate.

PHALACROCORACIDAE: Cormorant Family

There are about 30 species of these mainly black, medium-sized water birds. Typically, cormorants have long necks and bodies, wings of moderate length, short legs and large webbed feet. Male and female resemble each other, with small plumage differences in the breeding season. All cormorants are specialist fish-eaters and are found in marine and freshwater habitats. They are coastal birds, rarely seen over open sea. They swim well and dive from the surface to catch prey. In flight, their necks are fully extended, and they often fly in lines or V-formations.

Cormorants are gregarious birds; they nest colonially and defend small nest territories. After feeding excursions they rest on rocks, trees or cliffs, often with their wings, which quickly become waterlogged, spread out to dry.

NAME: **Great Cormorant**, *Phalacrocorax carbo*
RANGE: **N. America, Europe, Africa, Asia, Australia**
HABITAT: **coasts, marshes, lakes**
SIZE: **80–100 cm (31–39¼ in)**

Also sometimes known as the black cormorant, this bird is the largest species in its family and also the most widely distributed. Habitats and nesting sites vary greatly over its enormous range. Male and female birds look alike, but the breeding male acquires some white feathers on the head and neck and a white patch on each flank. Immature birds have brownish plumage with pale underparts.

Cormorants feed primarily on fish, but they will also eat crustaceans and amphibians. Prey is caught underwater during dives lasting 20 or 30 seconds. The bird swims by using its webbed feet for propulsion and its long tail as a rudder. Most prey is brought back to the surface and shaken before being swallowed.

Breeding pairs make their nests in trees or on the ground, inland or on the coast, depending on the situation in their particular range. The usual clutch is 3 or 4 eggs. Both parents incubate the eggs and feed the chicks. The chicks make their first flight about 50 days after hatching but are not completely independent for another 12 to 13 weeks.

NAME: **Reed Cormorant/Long-tailed Shag**, *Halietor africanus*
RANGE: **Africa, Madagascar**
HABITAT: **rivers, lagoons**
SIZE: **58 cm (23 in)**

One of four small, long-tailed, shorter-necked cormorants, the reed cormorant is primarily an inland water bird but is also found on the west coast of southern Africa. Male and female generally look alike, but in the breeding season the male's plumage darkens and he also develops a tuft of feathers on the forehead and white plumes on face and neck. Young birds are brown and yellowish-white.

Reed cormorants feed on fish and some crustaceans, which they catch underwater by diving from the surface. Like other cormorants, they return to the surface to swallow their prey. In the breeding season, reed cormorants make their nests on the ground or in trees, and the female lays 2 to 4 eggs.

NAME: **Flightless Cormorant**, *Nannopterum harrisi*
RANGE: **Galápagos Islands**
HABITAT: **coastal waters**
SIZE: **91–99 cm (36–39 in)** ®

This large bird, clumsy on land but superb in the water, has lost all power of flight. Its wings are tiny, with only a few flight feathers remaining. The flightless cormorant is able to catch all the food it needs in the nutrient-rich waters around the island coasts, and there are no mammalian predators in the Galápagos. Thus, unlike its fellow cormorants, this species has no need to fly great distances in search of food or to escape from danger. However, the population of these birds is small and they are now rare.

FREGATIDAE: Frigatebird Family

Frigatebirds are the most aerial of all water birds and are graceful and spectacular in flight. They are masters of the air above the sea and soar over huge oceanic distances. They are large birds with extremely long, pointed wings and long forked tails. All 5 species inhabit tropical and subtropical areas. Females are generally larger than males and have white breasts and sides. Males have bright-red throat pouches, which they inflate to enormous size in their courtship displays.

NAME: **Magnificent Frigatebird**, *Fregata magnificens*
RANGE: **Central America; South America; Galápagos Islands**
HABITAT: **coastal waters, islands, bays, estuaries**
SIZE: **95–110 cm (37–43 in)**
wingspan: **215–245 cm (85–96 in)**

The male magnificent frigatebird has a particularly large and splendid throat pouch, and the species has the greatest wing area, relative to body size, of any bird. It feeds chiefly on fish, squid, crustaceans and jellyfish, which it catches by swooping down to the water surface. It rarely alights on the sea. Frigatebirds supplement their diet by stealing fish from other birds. Having spotted a booby or other seabird returning to land, the frigate gives chase and forces its quarry to regurgitate its catch, which it then grabs in midair.

The nest of the magnificent frigatebird is a flimsy construction of sticks. The female lays a single egg, which both parents incubate. Both feed and care for the chick for a total of about 7 weeks. Both parents bring the chick food until it is able to fly at 4 or 5 months old and continue feeding it intermittently for some weeks more.

Anhinga

Flightless Cormorant

Great Cormorant
(breeding plumage)

Reed Cormorant

Magnificent Frigatebird
(male)

Herons and Bitterns

NAME: American Bittern, *Botaurus lentiginosus*
RANGE: N. America; winters in South America
HABITAT: marshland
SIZE: 66 cm (26 in)

The American bittern has a distinctive cry, rather different from the characteristic boom of other bitterns. This strange, three-syllable cry has inspired one of the bird's common names: "thunder pumper." This bittern feeds alone, moving slowly and deliberately with bill always at the ready to jab quickly at fish, crabs, snakes, frogs, insects or small mammals. It is a migratory species; although birds in milder areas do not actually migrate, they do disperse after breeding. The clutch of 4 to 6 eggs is laid in a nest platform on land or in water, and the female bird seems to perform most of the parental duties.

NAME: Black-crowned Night Heron, *Nycticorax nycticorax*
RANGE: Europe, Asia, Africa, N. and South America
HABITAT: varied, usually near marshes
SIZE: 61 cm (24 in)

Probably the most numerous of all herons, the black-crowned night heron is an attractive, stocky bird with white, ribbonlike plumes extending from the back of its head; these are erected in courtship display. As its name suggests, this bird feeds mainly at night and at dusk; it preys on fish, reptiles, frogs and insects and also raids the nests of other birds.

At the beginning of the breeding season, the male finds a nest site, usually among reeds or in a bush or a tree, which he then uses as a base for his displays. His mate finishes the building of the nest and lays 3 to 5 eggs. Both parents feed and care for the chicks.

NAME: Gray Heron, *Ardea cinerea*
RANGE: Europe, Asia, Africa
HABITAT: varied, near shallow water
SIZE: 92 cm (36 in)

A large, long-legged, long-billed bird, the gray heron is familiar throughout most of the Old World except Australia. Its New World equivalent, the great blue heron, *A. herodias*, is similar but slightly larger, with reddish coloring on neck and thighs. The heron feeds on fish, eels, young birds, eggs, snakes and plants. To obtain its food, the heron fishes from the land, with its head stretched forward into the water, or wades in to forage. Once prey is spotted, the bird grasps it with a swift, lethal thrust of the bill.

Gray herons breed in colonies; the female lays 3 to 5 eggs, and both parents feed the young.

ORDER CICONIIFORMES

This order of wading birds contains 6 families. Four of these, the herons, storks, ibises and flamingos, are widespread groups with a variety of adaptations. The remaining 2 families are monotypic, represented by the shoebill and the hammerkop — both specialized African forms.

ARDEIDAE:
Heron and Bittern Family

The 60 or more species of heron, bittern and egret in this family are all moderate to large birds with slim bodies, long necks and legs, and large broad wings. Male and female look alike in most species. All herons have patches of powder-down feathers on the breast and rump — a feature probably associated with their mucus-laden diet of fish and amphibians. The powder produced by these specialized feathers is utilized in preening to remove slime from the plumage.

Herons hunt in water of varying depth, either while standing motionless or while wading. Prey is grasped (not impaled) with the powerful, dagger-shaped beak. Herons usually breed in colonies. During the breeding season, many species undergo changes of plumage color and develop long plumes on the head or back.

NAME: Cattle Egret, *Ardeola ibis*
RANGE: Iberia, Africa, Asia, Indonesia, N. and South America, Australia
HABITAT: open land, drier than the habitat of most herons
SIZE: 50 cm (19¾ in)

The cattle egret is an extremely successful species and has expanded its range all over the world. Its success is partly due to its association with herbivorous animals. The birds follow large grazing animals, wild or domesticated, and catch the insects, particularly grasshoppers, disturbed by them. Cattle egrets feeding in this way gain about 50 percent more food for less effort than birds feeding by other methods. The cattle do not really benefit from the association, since cattle egrets do not remove parasites; the cattle may, however, be warned of approaching danger by the birds. Cattle egrets have now learned that the same results can be achieved by following farm machinery. In water the egrets feed on frogs and fish in the main.

The male gathers material for the nest, and the female builds it, usually in a small tree. The pair copulate on the nest, and the female lays 2 to 5 eggs.

NAME: Black Heron, *Egretta ardesiaca*
RANGE: Africa, south of the Sahara
HABITAT: swamps, mangroves, mud flats
SIZE: 48–50 cm (18¾–19¾ in)

Physically, the black heron is much like a black-plumaged version of an egret, but it is well known for its odd feeding method. The heron stands in shallow waters, bill pointing downward, and spreads its wings in a circle, forming a canopy over its head. Specialized broad flight feathers aid the effectiveness of the canopy. The exact purpose of this habit is not known, but it has been suggested that fish are attracted to the seeming shelter of the patch of shade that is formed, thus becoming easy prey for the heron. Fish must also be more easily visible in the canopy's shade. When young birds first start to fish, they make one-winged canopies. The canopy posture is also used in the courtship display. Black herons build a nest of twigs above the water in a tree or bush. The clutch usually contains 3 or 4 eggs.

NAME: Great Egret, *Egretta alba*
RANGE: almost worldwide; absent from much of Europe
HABITAT: shallow water
SIZE: 90–120 cm (35–47 in)

This egret, also sometimes known as the American egret, is one of the most widespread of its family. Nonbreeding and immature birds have yellow bills, but as the breeding season approaches, the adult's bill becomes mostly black. It finds its food — fish, mollusks, insects, small mammals, birds and plants — either by standing and waiting in the water or by slowly stalking its prey. The nest is made in a tree or reedbed, and the female lays 2 to 5 eggs. Both parents incubate the clutch in shifts for a total of 25 or 26 days.

NAME: Boat-billed Heron/Boatbill, *Cochlearius cochlearius*
RANGE: Mexico to Peru and Brazil
HABITAT: swamps and wetlands
SIZE: 45–50 cm (17¾–19¾ in)

The classification of this species has been the subject of some dispute, and it is sometimes placed in a family on its own. Its only important distinction from other herons is the broad, scoop-like bill. Boat-billed herons generally feed at night on fish and shrimps. The bill seems to be extremely sensitive and opens at the merest touch, drawing in water and prey; it is also used with a scooping action. These birds perform bill-clattering and preening displays, accompanied by vocal signals, at mating time. They nest alone or in groups in trees and bushes. The female lays 2 to 4 eggs which both parents incubate.

Cattle Egret

Black Heron

(feeding posture)

Boat-billed Heron

American
Bittern

Gray Heron

Great Egret
(breeding plumage)

Black-crowned Night Heron

Storks, Flamingos, Ibises, Hammerkop, Shoebill

CICONIIDAE: Stork Family

Storks are large, long-legged birds with elongated necks and long broad wings. Although their feet are webbed at the base, denoting aquatic habits, storks tend to feed in drier areas than most other members of their order. They are strong fliers and are particularly striking in flight, with neck and legs stretched out, the legs trailing down slightly. Males and females look alike. There are 17 species, all but 3 in the Old World. Northern populations are migratory.

NAME: **White Stork,** *Ciconia ciconia*
RANGE: **E. Europe, W. Asia; winters in Africa**
HABITAT: **forest and near human habitation**
SIZE: **102 cm (40 in)**
   1.2 m (4 ft) tall

Legend has it that the white stork brings babies, and for this reason these birds have always been popular and protected to some degree. They are gregarious birds and tolerant of human habitation. They feed mostly on frogs, reptiles, insects and mollusks. The nest is a huge structure of sticks, which the stork builds up in a tree or on a building. The female lays 1 to 7 eggs, which both parents incubate. Although not vocal birds, white storks perform a greeting ceremony, making bill-clattering sounds as they change shifts at the nest. In doing so, they turn their heads around over their backs thus turning away their bills — or weapons. This action, in direct contrast to their bill-forward threat display, appeases any aggression between the partners. In winter white storks migrate south; most go to Africa by way of Gibraltar or Istanbul, so avoiding long journeys over open sea, for which their type of soaring flight is not suited.

NAME: **Openbill,** *Anastomus oscitans*
RANGE: **India to S.E. Asia**
HABITAT: **inland waters**
SIZE: **81 cm (32 in)**
   61 cm (24 in) tall

The openbill, as its name suggests, has a remarkable bill: there is a gap between the mandibles, which meet only at the tips. This feature, which develops gradually and is not present in juvenile birds, seems to be an adaptation for holding the large, slippery water snails on which the birds feed. Openbills are more aquatic than most storks but still make their nests in trees. The female lays 3 to 6 eggs, which are incubated by both parents. The African openbill, *A. lamelligerus*, has the same bill shape.

PHOENICOPTERIDAE: Flamingo Family

There are 5 species of flamingo. All are tall, pinkish-white birds with long necks, large wings and short tails. Their toes are short and webbed. All swim and fly well; the neck and legs are extended in flight. Males and females look alike. Huge numbers of flamingos live and breed in colonies; in Africa, a colony of lesser flamingos, *Phoeniconaias minor*, may number a million or more individuals. They are irregular breeders and may only breed successfully every two or three years.

Flamingos feed in the water, filtering out minute food particles with their highly specialized bills.

NAME: **American Flamingo,** *Phoenicopterus ruber*
RANGE: **Caribbean, Galápagos Islands**
HABITAT: **lagoons, lakes**
SIZE: **114 cm (45 in)**

The American flamingo has an air of frivolous fantasy, but, in fact, it is perfectly adapted for its way of life: the long legs enable it to stand in shallow water while it filter-feeds with the strangely shaped bill. The flamingo holds its bill so that it lies horizontally beneath the water, the upper half below the lower. Water flows into the bill and, by movements of the large, fleshy tongue, is pushed through hairlike lamellae which sieve out food particles before the water is expelled at the sides of the bill. Flamingos feed on mollusks, crustaceans, insects, fish and minute aquatic plants.

The nest is a mound of mud which the female scrapes together with her bill. She lays 1 or 2 eggs in a shallow depression at the top of the mound. The young birds are dependent on their parents for food until their filtering mechanism develops and they are able to fly — about 65 to 70 days.

THRESKIORNITHIDAE: Ibis Family

Ibises and spoonbills are medium-sized wading birds. The typical family member has a moderately long neck, long wings, short tail and toes webbed at the base. Male and female look more or less alike. In some species the face or even the whole head and neck is unfeathered. All ibises fly well, with neck extended. There are about 25 species of ibis, all with long curved bills, and 6 species of spoonbill, with broad spatulate bills. Most are gregarious birds. Northern species are migratory.

NAME: **Glossy Ibis,** *Plegadis falcinellus*
RANGE: **temperate and tropical Eurasia, Indonesia, Australia, Africa, West Indies, Caribbean**
HABITAT: **marshes, lakes**
SIZE: **55–65 cm (21½–25½ in)**

The glossy ibis is the most widespread member of the family. It feeds on insects and small aquatic life. The female lays 3 or 4 eggs in a nest in a tree or reedbed. Both parents incubate the eggs and care for the young. The range and numbers of this species have been reduced by the drainage of large areas of marshland.

SCOPIDAE: Hammerkop Family

The sole member of this family has been the subject of much dispute as to its classification.

NAME: **Hammerkop,** *Scopus umbretta*
RANGE: **Africa, Madagascar, Middle East**
HABITAT: **tree-lined streams**
SIZE: **50 cm (19¾ in)**

The hammerkop gets its common name from the resemblance of its head in profile — with its long, heavy, slightly hooked bill and backward-pointing crest — to a hammer. In flight the hammerkop holds its neck slightly curved back. Male and female birds look alike. Hammerkops are generally active at dusk and feed on amphibians, fish, insects and crustaceans. They live in pairs and build remarkable nests — elaborate roofed structures of sticks and mud, measuring up to 1.8 m (6 ft) across, placed in the branches of trees. The female lays 3 to 6 eggs, and both parents care for the downy young.

BALAENICIPIDAE: Shoebill Family

The single species in this family is a little-known, nocturnal bird which, like the hammerkop, has links and similarities to several groups.

NAME: **Shoebill,** *Balaeniceps rex*
RANGE: **E. central Africa**
HABITAT: **marshes**
SIZE: **117 cm (46 in)**

The shoebill is a large bird, its most obvious feature being a monstrous shovel-like bill with a hooked tip. The bird seems to use this bill for searching out food — fish, frogs, snakes, mollusks and carrion — in the mud of its marshland home.

A solitary bird, the shoebill can fly well and even soar, holding its neck drawn in, pelican-fashion. It lays 2 eggs on the ground in a nest made of rushes and grass.

White Stork

Openbill

Hammerkop

American Flamingo

Shoebill

Glossy Ibis

Screamers, Ducks

ORDER ANSERIFORMES:
A highly successful and diverse group of birds, this order contains 2 families: the Anatidae (ducks, geese and swans), and the Anhimidae (screamers).

ANHIMIDAE: Screamer Family
The 3 species of screamer are similar to geese in body size but have longer legs and large feet with only partial webbing. The toes are long, enabling the birds to walk on floating vegetation. All live in South America.

NAME: **Black-necked/Northern Screamer,** *Chauna chavaria*
RANGE: **N. Colombia, Venezuela**
HABITAT: **marshes, wet grassland**
SIZE: **71–91 cm (28–36 in)**

Like all screamers, the black-necked has a noisy trumpeting call (the origin of its common name) which it uses as an alarm signal. It feeds mostly on water plants. The female lays 4 to 6 eggs in a nest of aquatic vegetation, and both parents incubate the eggs.

ANATIDAE: Duck Family
This family contains an assemblage of water birds, found in all areas of the world except continental Antarctica and a few islands. There are about 140 species, grouped into 3 subfamilies: first, the Anseranatinae, with a single species, the magpie goose; second, the Anserinae, which contains the whistling-ducks, swans, true geese and the freckled duck; third, the Anatinae, with all the true ducks.

All members of the family are aquatic to some degree and feed on plant and animal life from the surface of the water or beneath it by up-ending or diving. The majority are broad-bodied birds with shortish legs, and feet with front toes connected by webs. Beaks vary according to feeding methods but are usually broad, flattened and blunt-tipped, with small terminal hooks. In many species males have brightly colored plumage and females plain, brownish feathers. Generally in such sexually dimorphic species, the female performs all parental duties.

Most ducks molt all their flight feathers simultaneously after the breeding season and undergo a flightless period of 3 or 4 weeks. During this period, males of some species adopt "eclipse" plumage, similar to the female's muted plumage. After breeding, many species migrate to winter feeding grounds.

NAME: **Magpie Goose,** *Anseranas semipalmata*
RANGE: **Australia, Tasmania, S. New Guinea**
HABITAT: **swamps, flood plains**
SIZE: **76–86 cm (30–34 in)**

An interesting, apparently primitive species, the magpie goose is the only true waterfowl to have only partially webbed feet. Its bill is long and straight, and the head is featherless back to the eyes. Females resemble males but are smaller. Plant material is its major food source, and the magpie goose forages by grazing and digging and by bending down tall grasses with its feet to reach the seeds. Magpie geese are gregarious birds and move in flocks of several thousand. Mates are usually kept for life, but a male may mate with two females. The female lays about 8 eggs in a nest of trampled vegetation; both partners incubate the clutch for a total of 35 days and feed the chicks.

NAME: **White-faced Whistling-duck,** *Dendrocygna viduata*
RANGE: **tropical South America, Africa, Madagascar**
HABITAT: **lakes, swamps, marshes**
SIZE: **43–48 cm (17–19 in)**

The 8 species of whistling-duck all live in the tropics. The white-faced whistling-duck feeds on aquatic insects, mollusks, crustaceans and plant matter such as seeds and rice; it will often dive for food. Much of the foraging activity takes place at night; during the day the birds roost near the water, often in flocks of several hundred, and preen themselves and others. Mutual preening plays an important part in the formation of pairs and maintenance of bonds. Between 6 and 12 eggs are laid in a nest made in a hole in a tree. Both partners incubate the eggs for 28 to 30 days.

NAME: **Tundra Swan (Bewick's/ Whistling Swan),** *Cygnus columbianus*
RANGE: **Holarctic**
HABITAT: **tundra, swamps and marshes**
SIZE: **114–140 cm (45–55 in)**

Bewick's swan and the whistling swan are sometimes treated as 2 separate species, but are so alike that they are now generally regarded as conspecific. Both breed in the far north of their range and migrate enormous distances to winter in Europe, China, Japan and the USA. Males and females look alike — the female is sometimes slightly smaller — and juveniles have mottled grayish plumage. The swans feed in shallow water on aquatic vegetation. The bonds between mates are strong and permanent and are formed and maintained by mutual displays. The female lays her clutch of 3 to 5 eggs in a nest of sedge and moss lined with down, usually near water. She incubates them for 35 to 40 days. The cygnets must make the long migration south when only 80 to 90 days old.

NAME: **Graylag Goose,** *Anser anser*
RANGE: **Europe, Asia**
HABITAT: **flood plains, estuaries**
SIZE: **76–89 cm (30–35 in)**

The graylag is the most numerous and widespread goose in Eurasia. Males of this sturdy, large-headed species are bigger than females, but otherwise the sexes look alike. The geese feed on plant materials, such as roots, leaves, flowers and fruit, both on the ground and in water. A nest of vegetation and twigs is made on the ground near a tree or bush or among reedbeds, and the female incubates the 4 to 6 eggs for 28 days. The male helps to defend the goslings.

NAME: **Canada Goose,** *Branta canadensis*
RANGE: **N. America; introduced in Europe and New Zealand**
HABITAT: **varied**
SIZE: **56–110 cm (22–43 in)**

Habitats of the 12 geographically distinct races of Canada goose vary from semidesert to temperate rain forest and arctic tundra. The races also vary greatly in size. Canada geese feed by day on grassland vegetation and aquatic plants. It is a migratory species and uses the same routes from generation to generation. There is a tendency, particularly in females, for Canada geese to return to their own birthplace to breed, thus quickly producing local races and variations. Pair and family bonds are strong and are maintained by displays. The female goose lays about 5 eggs in a shallow scrape on the ground, lined with down and plant material. While her mate stays nearby to defend her, she incubates the clutch for 25 to 30 days.

NAME: **Shelduck,** *Tadorna tadorna*
RANGE: **Europe, central Asia**
HABITAT: **coasts and estuaries**
SIZE: **61 cm (24 in)**

Shelducks are a group of large, goose-like ducks. The shelduck feeds on mollusks, particularly on the estuarine snail *Hydrobia*, as well as on fish, fish eggs, insects and their larvae, and algae. Females are smaller than males and have white feathers between eyes and bill. Pair bonds are strong and thought to be permanent, and at breeding grounds the pairs take up territories. The female lays about 9 eggs in a burrow or cavity nest or in the open. While she incubates the clutch for 28 to 30 days, the male defends her.

Black-necked Screamer

Tundra Swan (Whistling)

Tundra Swan (Bewick's)

Canada Goose

Graylag Goose

Magpie Goose

White-faced Whistling-duck

Shelduck (male)

Ducks

NAME: Falklands Steamer Duck,
Tachyeres brachypterus
RANGE: Falkland Islands
HABITAT: coasts
SIZE: 61–74 cm (24–29 in)

Steamer ducks are heavily built marine diving ducks; 2 of the 3 species are flightless. The female is smaller than the male and has a yellow-green bill and dark brown head with white rings around the eyes. These coastline foragers feed primarily on mollusks, bivalves, crabs and shrimps — there is a record of one bird found to have 450 mussel shells in its stomach and crop. The Falklands steamer duck makes a nest on grass or dry seaweed, or even in an abandoned penguin burrow, and lines it with down. The female lays 5 to 8 eggs; the male guards her attentively while she incubates.

NAME: Mallard, Anas platyrhynchos
RANGE: throughout northern hemisphere
HABITAT: almost anywhere near water
SIZE: 41–66 cm (16–26 in)

The mallard is a typical dabbling duck, often feeding tail-up in shallow water. Female mallards have plain brownish plumage, with distinctive blue feathers on the wings. Pair bonds are renewed each year with a prolonged period of intricate social displays, including the ritualized preening of the bright wing patches. The female lays her 8 to 10 eggs in a nest on the ground. Her mate deserts her early in the incubation period and flies off to undergo his annual molt with the other males. The mallard is the ancestor of all domestic ducks except muscovies.

NAME: Northern Shoveler, Anas clypeata
RANGE: Europe, Asia, N. America
HABITAT: inland marshes, coastal waters
SIZE: 43–56 cm (17–22 in)

The shoveler's distinctive spatulate bill is an adaptation for feeding on plankton. As the bird swims, it sucks water into the bill; the water is strained out through hairlike lamellae lining the bill which retain the tiny planktonic creatures. Female birds have much duller plumage than males; they are mostly brown but have blue and green feathers on the wings. Northern shovelers usually move in small groups or pairs for most of the year. The female makes a nest in a reedbed and lays 7 to 14 eggs, which she incubates for 23 to 25 days. The ducklings are born with normal bills; the spatulate shape develops as they mature.

NAME: Common Eider, Somateria
mollissima
RANGE: circumpolar (north)
HABITAT: coasts, inland rivers and lakes
SIZE: 56–71 cm (22–28 in)

Like most ducks, the female eider lines her nest with down plucked from her breast. The down of the eider is particularly soft and warm and has long been collected and used by man. The female duck has barred, brownish plumage, and both male and female have Y-shaped bill extensions of membrane reaching almost up to the eyes. During the breeding season, eiders frequent coasts and feed on mollusks, crustaceans and other small creatures. They nest in colonies but fight over nest sites, and each pair holds its own territory. The female incubates the clutch of about 5 eggs alone for 27 to 28 days, while her mate goes off with the other males to undergo his annual molt.

NAME: Greater Scaup, Aythya marila
RANGE: circumpolar (north)
HABITAT: coastal and inland waters
SIZE: 41–51 cm (16–20 in)

One of the group of ducks known as pochards, the scaup breeds in tundra regions and winters to the south. It feeds on small invertebrates such as mollusks and crustaceans. Like other pochards, such as the canvasback, A. valisineria, and the tufted duck, A. fuligula, it is an excellent diver and frequently dives as deep as 8 m (26 ft) in search of food. Scaups gather in huge flocks, and at breeding grounds pairs overlap their ranges. The female lays 8 to 10 eggs, which she incubates for 23 to 27 days.

NAME: Mandarin Duck, Aix galericulata
RANGE: E. Asia, Korea, China, Japan;
introduced in Britain and N. Europe
HABITAT: inland swamps, lakes and pools
SIZE: 43–51 cm (17–20 in)

The exquisite mandarin duck has been celebrated in Japanese and Chinese art for centuries. In China, mandarins were symbols of fidelity and were given as wedding gifts.

Mandarins are most active at dawn and dusk; they feed on vegetable matter, such as seeds, acorns and rice, and on insects, snails and small fish. They are social ducks, and the pair bond continues from year to year when possible. Their courtship displays are particularly elaborate, including ritualized preening of the enlarged sail-like feathers on the flanks and display drinking. The female lays 9 to 12 eggs, often in a tree-hole nest, and incubates them. The closely related wood duck, A. sponsa, of North America is also brilliantly marked.

NAME: Red-breasted Merganser, Mergus
serrator
RANGE: Holarctic
HABITAT: coastal and inland waters
SIZE: 48–66 cm (19–26 in)

Mergansers are fish-eating, diving ducks with long, thin, serrated bills, well adapted for catching fish underwater. They also feed on crustaceans. Courtship rituals are complex. The male stretches his neck and sprints over the water; before copulating he performs a series of drinking, preening and wing-flapping movements. The female lays her 9 or 10 eggs in a hole or cavity. The male deserts his mate early in the incubation period. Once the young have hatched, several females collect their young together into one brood, which they tend together.

NAME: Muscovy Duck, Cairina moschata
RANGE: Central America, tropical
South America
HABITAT: rivers and marshes in forest
SIZE: 66–84 cm (26–33 in)

These birds, familiar in their domestic form, are rare in their pure form outside the native range. The male has warty skin around the eyes and an enlarged bill base; the female's head is entirely feathered, and there is no bill enlargement. The wild form is attractive, but some of the domestic muscovies have evolved with grotesque warts and bill caruncles. Muscovies feed on plants, seeds, small fish and insects and are also fond of termites, which are plentiful in their forest habitat. As they are tropical birds, muscovies have no real migratory pattern but may move to coasts in dry seasons. They do not form large flocks, and pair and family bonds are weak. Courtship displays are simple and brief. The female lays 8 to 15 eggs in a hollow or among rushes and incubates them alone. The male plays no part in the care of the young.

NAME: Ruddy Duck, Oxyura jamaicensis
RANGE: USA, Central America, Andes;
introduced in Britain
HABITAT: inland lakes and rivers;
estuaries
SIZE: 35–48 cm (14–19 in)

The ruddy duck is one of a group of ducks known as stifftails. All are small, stocky, freshwater diving ducks with the distinctive habit of holding the tail up at an angle while swimming. Ruddy ducks are usually active at night and feed on aquatic plants, insects and small invertebrates. They are not highly developed socially and do not hold nesting territories. Females lay about 8 eggs in a ground nest but will sometimes lay more eggs in other nests.

Falklands Steamer Duck
(male)

Muscovy Duck (male)

Red-breasted
Merganser
(male)

Common Eider (male)

Mallard
(male)

Northern Shoveler (male)

Greater Scaup (male)

Ruddy Duck
(male)

Mandarin Duck (male)

New World Vultures, Secretary Bird, Osprey

ORDER FALCONIFORMES

Birds of prey are birds that hunt and kill other animals (particularly the higher vertebrates) for food. They include the specialist nocturnal predators — the owls — and the daytime hunters. The latter group makes up the order Falconiformes. The order contains almost 300 species spread around the world, with general names such as eagle, hawk, falcon and vulture. It contains 2 large and diverse families — the Accipitridae and the Falconidae — and 3 smaller and more specialized families, the Cathartidae (New World vultures), the Pandionidae and the Sagittariidae.

CATHARTIDAE: New World Vulture Family

There are 7 species of New World vultures and condors, with a geographical range from Tierra del Fuego and the Falkland Islands to as far north as southern Canada. The cathartid vultures are superficially similar to Old World vultures but are, in fact, a quite distinct family, as internal anatomical features show. Nonetheless, like their African cousins, these birds feed on carrion, and their unfeathered heads and necks enable them to plunge into messy carcasses without soiling plumage. The feet, with long toes and weakly hooked claws, are adapted for perching rather than grasping. Vultures and condors are solitary birds, although some do roost in colonies. Nests are usually made in hollow trees. Males and females look alike.

NAME: King Vulture, *Sarcoramphus papa*
RANGE: Mexico to Argentina
HABITAT: tropical forest, savanna
SIZE: 79 cm (31 in)

The king is a medium-sized vulture with broad wings and tail. The featherless skin on its head is marked with extraordinary, garish patterns. It is reputed to kill live animals but feeds mainly on carrion. As its name suggests, this big-billed bird takes precedence over other vultures at carcasses. Carrion can be hard to spot in the dense tropical forest, so the king vulture is one of the few birds that relies heavily on its sense of smell to detect food. Stranded fish on riverbanks are an important food item.

The breeding habits of this vulture are poorly known, but in one observation an egg was laid in a hollow tree stump and incubated by both parents. Young king vultures in their first full plumage have black feathers. The brilliant facial markings and creamy plumage develop over the first 2 years.

NAME: California Condor, *Gymnogyps californianus*
RANGE: USA: California
HABITAT: mountains
SIZE: 114–140 cm (45–55 in)   Ⓔ

One of the largest birds in the world, this immense vulture is also one of the heaviest flying birds at over 11 kg (25 lb). The range of this bird was once much larger, but the population has declined drastically because of the destruction of its habitat and the onslaught of hunters, and the species is now probably on the verge of extinction. The condor is fully protected under the United States Endangered Species Act and by California law. There are plans to breed the condors in captivity as a last attempt to save the species.

A spectacular bird in flight, with its extremely long, broad wings, the California condor soars at great heights and can glide as far as 16 km (10 mi) without wing movements. It must have the right air conditions for soaring and may stay at its roost in bad weather or on calm days. The California condor spends at least 15 hours a day at the roosting area; outside of the breeding season, roosting and foraging are its main activities. It feeds on carrion, mostly large animals, and is not known to attack living creatures.

At the start of the breeding season, the male displays to his prospective mate. The female lays her egg on the ground in a cave or hole in a cliff. Both parents incubate in shifts. The young bird is fed and tended by the parents for over a year; thus California condors can breed only every other year.

NAME: Turkey Vulture, *Cathartes aura*
RANGE: temperate and tropical N. and South America
HABITAT: plains, desert, forest
SIZE: 66–132 cm (26–52 in)

Also known as the turkey buzzard, this most widespread New World vulture soars over open country in search of carrion. It feeds on waste of all sorts, including sea lion excrement, rotten fruit and vegetables and carrion of small animals. Turkey vultures have been trapped and destroyed in many parts of their range because they are mistakenly believed to carry anthrax and other diseases of livestock. They are, however, pests on some Peruvian guano islands, where they take eggs and young birds.

At night groups of 30 or more birds roost together, but this is really the only time that turkey vultures are social. No real nest is made at breeding time; the female lays her 2 eggs in a cave or in a hollow log on the ground. Both parents incubate the eggs and care for the young.

SAGITTARIIDAE: Secretary Bird Family

This family contains only 1 species, an eaglelike bird with a distinctive crest, elongated tail feathers and long legs. Male and female look alike, but females are slightly smaller.

NAME: Secretary Bird, *Sagittarius serpentarius*
RANGE: Africa, south of the Sahara
HABITAT: open, grassy country
SIZE: 150 cm (59 in)

The secretary bird spends most of its time on the ground, walking with long strides, and may cover 30 km (20 mi) or so every day. It can run to catch prey, which it takes with a swift thrust of its head; it kills larger animals by stamping on them. Small mammals, insects, some birds and eggs, reptiles, in fact almost anything crawling on the ground, are the secretary bird's prey.

In the breeding season, pairs are strongly territorial and chase intruders off their breeding range. The nest is usually on top of a tree and is made of sticks and turf, lined with grass and leaves. The female incubates the 2 or 3 eggs.

PANDIONIDAE: Osprey Family

This family contains only 1 species, the hawklike osprey. Male and female look alike.

NAME: Osprey, *Pandion haliaetus*
RANGE: almost worldwide
HABITAT: lakes, rivers, coasts
SIZE: 53–62 cm (21–24 in)

The osprey, or fish hawk, feeds almost exclusively on fish; the soles of its feet are studded with small spikes to help grip the slippery prey. When hunting, the osprey flies over water and, when it sights a fish, may hover briefly. It then plunges into the water, feet forward, sometimes completely submerging, sometimes alighting quite gently. It grasps the fish in both feet and returns to feed at its perch. If fish are not available, the osprey feeds on small mammals and wounded birds.

At breeding time, the pair makes a large nest on the ground, using sticks, seaweed and other debris. The same nest may be repaired and used year after year and becomes huge. A clutch of 2 to 4 eggs, usually 3, is incubated mainly by the female. The male brings food during incubation and for the first 4 weeks of the fledgling period. After breeding, northern populations migrate south for the winter.

California Condor

Turkey Vulture

Osprey

Secretary Bird

King Vulture

Hawks

NAME: Egyptian Vulture, *Neophron percnopterus*
RANGE: S. Europe, Africa, Middle East, India
HABITAT: open country
SIZE: 60–70 cm (23½–27½ in)

The Egyptian vulture is a small species which defers to larger vultures at a carcass and so must often be content with scraps. It also feeds on insects and on ostrich and flamingo eggs and is one of the very few creatures to use a tool: in order to break into a huge ostrich egg, the vulture will drop rocks on it until it cracks open. This vulture often scavenges on all kinds of refuse, including human excrement.

Display flights of swoops and dives precede mating, and the pair builds a nest on a crag or on a building. The female lays 1 or 2 eggs, which both parents incubate for about 42 days.

NAME: Lammergeier/Bearded Vulture, *Gypaetus barbatus*
RANGE: S. Europe, Africa, India, Tibet
HABITAT: mountains
SIZE: 95–105 cm (37–41 in)

An uncommon and magnificent bird, the lammergeier descends from the mountains only to forage for food. It spends most of its day on the wing, soaring with unequaled grace. It feeds on carrion of all sorts, including human, but defers to larger vultures at carcasses. As one of the last in line, the lammergeier is often left with the bones, and it has developed the knack of dropping them on rocks to split them and reveal the marrow.

Each breeding pair holds a large territory, and the birds perform spectacular diving and swooping flight displays. They nest in cliff niches or on ledges and lay 1 or 2 eggs, which are incubated for 53 days. Normally only 1 chick is reared.

NAME: Lappet-faced Vulture, *Torgos tracheliotus*
RANGE: Africa
HABITAT: bush, desert
SIZE: 100–115 cm (39–45 in)

The lappet-faced is a typical Old World vulture with perfect adaptations for a scavenging life. Its powerful hooked bill cuts easily into carrion, and its bare head and neck save lengthy feather-cleaning after plunging deep into a messy carcass. The immense broad wings, with widely spaced primary feathers, are ideal for soaring and gliding for long periods, using few wing beats. No real mating display has been observed. A huge stick nest is made at the top of a tree or on a crag, and the female lays 1 egg.

ACCIPITRIDAE: Hawk Family

This is the largest family in the Falconiformes order and contains about 217 species of diverse predatory and carrion-eating birds. Representatives occur in almost all regions of the world except Antarctica, northern parts of the Arctic and small oceanic islands.

It is hard to generalize about the typical accipiter since the family contains so many different types and sizes of bird, and, in addition to the predatory forms, the family also includes the 14 or so carrion-feeding Old World vultures. Apart from the vultures, the family includes the "true hawks" (including buzzards and eagles), harrier eagles and serpent eagles, harriers, kites and fish eagles, honey buzzards and a few other specialized types.

Among these birds, the female is significantly larger than the male in almost every case, excluding the vultures. Characteristic physical features of this family are the down-curved, pointed beak, the base of which is covered with a fleshy cere carrying the external nostrils, and large wings with rounded tips and often barred or streaked underparts. All the birds have widely spaced toes and long, sharp, curving claws. On the soles of the feet are roughened, bulging pads to facilitate the seizing of prey.

Most species nest in trees, while some of the larger eagles and buzzards use cliff ledges. These large species are long-lived birds which reach breeding maturity slowly. They have small clutches of only 1 or 2 eggs.

NAME: Honey Buzzard, *Pernis apivorus*
RANGE: Eurasia, Indonesia
HABITAT: woodland
SIZE: 52–61 cm (20½–24 in)

The honey buzzard has broad, barred wings, a long tail and specially adapted feathers to protect it from the stings of bees and wasps whose nests it attacks. Larvae and honey are a major food source for this bird, and it also feeds on live wasps, skillfully nipping off the sting before swallowing them. Some small vertebrates and flying termites also feature in the honey buzzard's diet.

A mating pair holds a home territory, and the male performs a distinctive display flight, striking his wings together above his head. They make a tree nest of sticks and leaves. Both parents incubate the clutch of 1 to 3 eggs for 30 to 35 days and feed the young. Northern Eurasian populations migrate south to Africa in winter.

NAME: Red Kite, *Milvus milvus*
RANGE: Europe, W. Asia, N. Africa
HABITAT: woodland, open country
SIZE: 61–66 cm (24–26 in)

The red kite is a large bird with long wings and a distinctive, deeply forked tail. It breeds in woodland but hunts in open country. As it flies low over fields, it searches for prey. It can hover briefly and pursues its quarry with great agility. Small mammals up·to the size of a weasel, birds, reptiles, frogs, fish, insects and carrion are all eaten, and red kites also kill domestic poultry.

A breeding pair nests in a tree, often adding sticks and oddments to an old nest. Between 1 and 5 eggs, usually 3, are laid, and the female undertakes most of the 28- to 30-day incubation; the male brings her food and takes over from time to time.

NAME: Brahminy Kite, *Haliastur indus*
RANGE: India, S. China, Australasia
HABITAT: near water, coasts
SIZE: 46 cm (18 in)

The brahminy kite feeds on frogs, crabs, snakes, fish, insects and some carrion. It also scavenges around human habitation for all kinds of scraps and refuse. At the breeding site the birds perform display flights before starting to build a nest. The nest is made of sticks and lined with leaves and is sited in a tree or among mangroves. The female lays 1 to 4 eggs, which she incubates for 26 or 27 days while her mate keeps her supplied with food.

NAME: Everglade/Snail Kite, *Rostrhamus sociabilis*
RANGE: USA: Florida; Caribbean, Mexico, Central and South America
HABITAT: freshwater marshes
SIZE: 38 cm (15 in)

The Everglade kite feeds solely on water snails of the genus *Pomacea*; the elongated upper bill is an adaptation for this curious diet. The kite flaps slowly over the water on its large broad wings. When it sights a snail, it swoops down, grasps it with one foot and takes it back to a perch. Standing on one foot, the kite holds the snail in such a way that it can emerge from the shell. The instant the snail appears, the kite strikes it with its sharp bill; the blow damages the snail's nervous system and its impaled body goes limp. The kite shakes the snail free, and the empty shell falls to the ground.

Nests of breeding pairs are simple structures in marsh grass or bushes. The female lays 3 or 4 eggs, and both parents incubate the clutch and care for the young. This unusual bird is now rare, particularly in Florida, and is protected by conservation laws.

Red Kite

Lammergeier

Brahminy
Kite

Honey Buzzard

Lappet-faced Vulture

Everglade Kite

Egyptian Vulture

Hawks

NAME: **Bald Eagle,** *Haliaeetus leucocephalus*
RANGE: **N. America**
HABITAT: **coasts, rivers and lakes**
SIZE: **81–102 cm (32–40 in)**

The national symbol of the USA, the bald eagle is one of 8 species of eagle in the genus *Haliaeetus*, all with a liking for fish. Most of the others are called "sea" or "fish" eagles and are coastal birds. Dead and dying fish are the staple diet of the bald eagle, but it also takes live fish from the water and catches some birds and mammals. Groups of these impressive birds gather where food is available, particularly by rivers near the Alaskan coast, where they prey on exhausted salmon migrating upriver.

Bald eagles breed in northern North America on inland lakes, migrating south, if necessary, in the winter to find food. Pairs remain together and reestablish bonds each year with spectacular courtship displays, when the birds lock talons in midair and somersault down together. The nest is made of sticks and sited in a large tree or on rocks. It is added to, year after year, and can be as large as 2.5 m (8 ft) across and 3.5 m (11½ ft) deep, one of the largest of all birds' nests. Most of the time the female incubates the 1 to 3 eggs, but the male takes an occasional turn. The young remain in the nest for 10 or 11 weeks and are aggressive and competitive. Often the youngest of the brood is starved or killed.

All populations of this fine eagle have declined, seriously in some areas. It has suffered from the contamination of its habitat and prey by toxic chemicals, and with its slow breeding rate, it is hard for the species to recover.

NAME: **Palm-nut Vulture,** *Gypohierax angolensis*
RANGE: **Africa, south of the Sahara**
HABITAT: **forest, mangrove swamps, savanna**
SIZE: **71 cm (28 in)**

This curious bird resembles both vultures and sea eagles, and some authorities believe it to be a link between them. It feeds almost exclusively on the husk of the fruit of the oil palm, *Elaeis guineensis*, and its distribution virtually coincides with that of the plant. The diet is supplemented with fruit of the raphia palm, crabs, mollusks, snails and locusts, but all are rejected in favor of oil palm. A sedentary bird, the palm-nut vulture tends to stay around the same haunts and may remain near its breeding grounds all year. A pair builds a nest in a tree, using sticks and pieces of oil palm, or repairs an old nest. The female lays 1 egg, which is incubated for about 44 days.

NAME: **Bateleur,** *Terathopius ecaudatus*
RANGE: **Africa, south of the Sahara**
HABITAT: **savanna and plains**
SIZE: **80–85 cm (31½–33½ in)**
  wingspan: **170–180 cm (67–71 in)**

The most interesting bird in a group of birds of prey known as snake eagles or snake hawks, the bateleur has an unmistakable flight silhouette, with its exceptionally long wings and very short tail; its feet project beyond the tail tip in flight. Unlike other snake eagles, the bateleur feeds mostly on carrion but also kills for itself. It makes fierce attacks on other carrion-feeding birds, robbing them of their spoils. A spectacular bird in flight, it soars effortlessly for hours and probably travels about 320 km (200 mi) every day. Once it gets aloft by means of rapid flapping, the bateleur makes scarcely a wing beat, and it performs aerobatic feats such as complete rolls.

Breeding pairs nest in trees and make compact, cup-shaped nests of sticks. A third adult is often present throughout the whole breeding cycle — an unusual occurrence in the bird world which has not been fully explained. The third adult does not incubate or visit the actual nest but roosts nearby with the male and appears at the nest if an intruder troubles the parents. This habit may be a development of the tendency of juvenile and subadult birds to stay near the parents' nest during breeding. The single egg is normally incubated by the female for about 42 days. The young bird is particularly weak at first but has a long fledgling period, during which it is fed by both parents.

NAME: **Crested Serpent Eagle,** *Spilornis cheela*
RANGE: **India to S. China; S.E. Asia, Indonesia**
HABITAT: **forest**
SIZE: **51–71 cm (20–28 in)**

The crested serpent eagle is a variable species and the many races differ in size and plumage tones. The birds soar above the land, calling occasionally, but do not hunt in the air; they generally catch prey by dropping down on it from a perch. Like other snake eagles, the crested serpent eagle feeds mainly on reptiles, particularly tree snakes; its feet, with short, strong, rough-surfaced toes, are adapted for grasping its slippery prey.

A pair often remains together all year. In the breeding season, the birds perform flight displays, then build a small nest of sticks in a tree. The female incubates her 1 egg for about 35 days, and the male supplies her with food.

NAME: **African Harrier Hawk,** *Polyboroides typus*
RANGE: **Africa, south of the Sahara**
HABITAT: **forest**
SIZE: **63 cm (25 in)**

The African harrier hawk is a long-tailed, long-legged bird with a bare-skinned face. The young of other birds are its main source of food, although it also eats other creatures and the fruit of the oil palm. It clambers about on trees with great agility, searching for nests, and even hangs upside down, with wings flapping, to attack pendulous weaver-bird nests. The hawks' own nest is built in a tree, and both parents incubate the 1 to 5 eggs for about 40 days.

NAME: **Northern Harrier/Marsh Hawk,** *Circus cyaneus*
RANGE: **Holarctic**
HABITAT: **moors, marshes, plains**
SIZE: **44–52 cm (17–20½ in)**

A widely distributed bird, the northern harrier breeds in North America, Europe and Asia, then migrates south of its breeding grounds in winter. There are 10 species of harrier, all in the genus *Circus*. All hunt by flying low over the ground, carefully searching the area for prey. Once a creature is spotted, the harrier drops down on it and kills it on the ground.

Northern harriers feed on small mammals, birds, including those wounded by hunters, and some reptiles, frogs and insects. A nest is made on the ground in marshy land or among low vegetation, and the average clutch contains 4 to 6 eggs. The female incubates the eggs and the male brings food, both during this period and after the chicks hatch.

NAME: **Dark Chanting Goshawk,** *Melierax metabates*
RANGE: **W. central Africa; Middle East**
HABITAT: **bush, scrub**
SIZE: **38–48 cm (15–19 in)**

The handsome dark chanting goshawk perches on a vantage point in a tree or bush ready to glide swiftly down to take prey on the ground. The bird's long legs enable it to pursue quarry on the ground too, where it runs quickly, like a small secretary bird. Lizards, snakes and insects are the chief prey, but small mammals and ground birds are also caught.

At the onset of the breeding season, the male bird chants his melodious song to attract the female, and the two fly together over the breeding site. A small nest of sticks and mud is built in a tree, and the female lays 1 or 2 eggs.

The habits of the closely related pale chanting goshawk, *M. canorus*, are almost identical.

Bald Eagle

Crested Serpent Eagle

Bateleur

Palm-nut
Vulture

Dark Chanting
Goshawk

African Harrier Hawk

Northern Harrier

Hawks

NAME: **Goshawk**, *Accipiter gentilis*
RANGE: **N. America, Europe, Iran, Tibet, Japan**
HABITAT: **forest, woodland**
SIZE: **51–66 cm (20–26 in)**
  wingspan: **120 cm (47¼ in)**

These aggressive hawks are the largest birds in the genus *Accipiter* and are efficient killers. They fly through the forest, weaving skillfully in and out of trees, and sometimes soar over the tree-tops. They kill prey with a viselike grip of the powerful talons, then pluck it (if a bird) and eat it on the ground. A goshawk is capable of killing birds as large as pheasant and grouse and mammals the size of rabbits and hares. The birds are often trained for falconry.

Goshawk pairs usually mate for life. They winter alone and in the spring meet at the breeding grounds, where they perform flight displays. A new nest is made in a tree or an old nest is repaired. The pair roost together while building the nest and perform a scream-ing duet each day before sunrise. They mate about 10 times a day during the egg-laying period, which lasts 6 to 8 weeks.

The clutch contains from 1 to 5 eggs, usually 3, but the number is affected by the availability of suitable prey. The female incubates the clutch for 36 to 38 days; the male brings her food and takes over occasionally. Some northern popu-lations of goshawks migrate south after breeding.

NAME: **Cooper's Hawk**, *Accipiter cooperii*
RANGE: **S. Canada, USA, N. Mexico**
HABITAT: **woodland**
SIZE: **36–51 cm (14–20 in)**

Cooper's hawk is a medium-sized bird with rounded wings and tail and is a typical accipiter in its habits. It lives in the cover of woodland and ventures out to find prey. When hunting, Cooper's hawk usually perches and watches for prey, waits until its quarry is looking away, then quickly swoops down and seizes it. Bobwhites, starlings, black-birds, chipmunks and squirrels are common prey. The hawk also pursues creatures on the ground, half running and half flying.

At the breeding site, the male defends a territory, and when a female appears, he feeds her; both then perform court-ship flights. The clutch is usually 4 or 5 eggs, sometimes 6, and the female does most of the incubation. An attentive mother, she helps the chicks to emerge from their shells and feeds and guards them closely in the first weeks of life. Some northern populations migrate south after breeding.

NAME: **Fishing Buzzard**, *Busarellus nigricollis*
RANGE: **tropical lowlands, Mexico to Paraguay and Argentina**
HABITAT: **open country near water**
SIZE: **46–51 cm (18–20 in)**

A specialized hawk, the fishing buzzard has long, broad wings, a short, broad tail and a slightly hooked bill. The bottoms of its toes are covered with tiny prickly spines — an adaptation for catching and holding fish. In open areas the fishing buzzard can swoop down and catch its prey while scarcely wetting its plumage; elsewhere it will plunge into the water to fish, then sit drying its wings.

NAME: **Buzzard**, *Buteo buteo*
RANGE: **breeds in Europe, Asia to Japan; winters in E. Africa, India, Malaya and S. China**
HABITAT: **woodland, moorland**
SIZE: **51–56 cm (20–22 in)**

The buzzard is not a bold hunter and spends more time perching than on the wing; once aloft it soars well. It feeds mainly on small ground mammals up to the size of rabbits, reptiles, insects, car-rion and some ground birds. It kills most of its prey by dropping on it from its perch or from hovering flight and nearly always kills on the ground.

The size of the buzzard's breeding ter-ritory varies from year to year, accord-ing to food supplies. Courtship flights are uncharacteristically energetic, and the birds dive and swoop with vigor. A nest is made on a tree or crag, and the female lays 2 to 6 eggs.

NAME: **Red-tailed Hawk**, *Buteo jamaicensis*
RANGE: **N. and Central America, West Indies**
HABITAT: **varied: deserts, forest, mountains**
SIZE: **46–61 cm (18–24 in)**

A powerful, thickset, aggressive bird with a loud voice and a distinctive chest-nut tail, the red-tailed hawk tolerates a wide variety of habitats, probably more than any other North American hawk. It is an opportunistic hunter, and al-though its staple diet is rodents and rab-bits, it also eats snakes, lizards, birds and insects. It hunts on the wing or from a perch, swooping down on prey.

Pairs display over the breeding terri-tory. A nest is made of twigs high in a tree or, in the desert, on a cactus plant. The female hawk remains on or near the nest for some weeks before laying her clutch of 1 to 4 eggs. Her mate feeds her throughout this period. Both parents share the incubation, which lasts from 28 to 32 days. The young birds are able to feed themselves at 4 or 5 weeks.

NAME: **Harpy Eagle**, *Harpia harpyja*
RANGE: **S. Mexico to N. Argentina**
HABITAT: **lowland rain forest**
SIZE: **90 cm (35½ in)** ®

A formidable bird, the harpy is the world's largest eagle. It has huge feet, each the size of a man's hand, equipped with lethally sharp talons. Its broad wings are short for a bird of its size and enable it to maneuver through dense forest. The harpy flies from tree to tree, looking and listening for prey, and can give chase through the branches with great agility. Arboreal mammals, such as monkeys, sloths, opossums, coati and tree porcupines, are its primary source of food, and it occasionally catches large birds.

The harpy's nest is a platform of sticks placed high in the tallest trees. Because these nests are perhaps 45 m (150 ft) up from the forest floor, ob-servations of egg-laying and care of the young are few, but the bird is believed to lay 2 eggs. The young birds remain with their parents for a long time, per-haps a year, and it seems certain that harpy eagles breed only every other year. Now rare, harpy eagles have declined in numbers, largely because of the destruction of vast areas of their habitat. They have also been relentlessly shot by hunters. Although nominally protected by law, any measures are difficult to enforce in the remote areas where the harpy is likely to occur.

NAME: **Golden Eagle**, *Aquila chrysaetos*
RANGE: **Holarctic, as far south as N. Africa and Mexico**
HABITAT: **moor, mountain forest**
SIZE: **76–89 cm (30–35 in)**

These magnificent birds are probably the most numerous large eagles in the world. The golden eagle is a formidable predator, equipped with huge feet with long curved claws, a hooked bill and exceptionally sharp-sighted eyes. When hunting, the golden eagle soars for long periods searching for prey, then makes a rapid dive down to seize and kill the animal with its crushing talons. Most food is taken on the ground, and mam-mals such as hares and rabbits are the chief prey. Grouse and other birds are also caught, and carrion is an important food source.

Golden eagles perform spectacular flight displays over the nest site. The nest is made high on a ledge or tree and is often repaired and reused. Some pairs have several nests, used in rotation. The 2 eggs are usually incubated by the female, but the male takes an occasional turn. In 80 percent of observed cases, the first chick to hatch killed the young-er, unhindered by the mother.

Cooper's Hawk

Goshawk

Buzzard

Fishing
Buzzard

Red-tailed
Hawk

Harpy Eagle

Golden Eagle

Falcons

NAME: **Caracara**, *Polyborus plancus*
RANGE: S. USA; South America
HABITAT: open country
SIZE: 56–61 cm (22–24 in)

Caracaras are a group of neotropical birds quite unlike the rest of the falcons. They eat all kinds of animals, from insects to mammals, and also scavenge on carrion. Both members of a breeding pair build the nest, usually in a tree or on the ground. The female lays 2 to 4 eggs, and both parents incubate the eggs for a total of 28 days and care for the young. The young remain in the nest for 2 or 3 months, being fed by their parents.

NAME: **Barred Forest Falcon**, *Micrastur ruficollis*
RANGE: S. Mexico to N. Argentina
HABITAT: forest
SIZE: 33–38 cm (13–15 in)

One of a group of 5 neotropical forest falcons, the barred forest falcon is well adapted for life in dense jungle. A long-legged, short-winged bird, it flies deftly through the trees and waits in cover to attack prey. It feeds on small mammals, lizards and birds and often hunts the birds that follow army ants. Little is known of its breeding habits.

NAME: **Collared Falconet**, *Microhierax caerulescens*
RANGE: Himalayas, N. India, S.E. Asia
HABITAT: forest
SIZE: 19 cm (7½ in)

The 8 species of falconet are the smallest birds of prey. All have similar habits. The collared falconet hunts its food more in the manner of a flycatcher than a true falcon; it makes short flights from a perch to catch insects and, occasionally, small birds. It lays 4 to 5 eggs in a hole in a tree.

NAME: **Kestrel**, *Falco tinnunculus*
RANGE: Europe, Asia, Africa
HABITAT: open country, plains, cultivated land
SIZE: 34–38 cm (13¼–15 in)

Kestrels hunt over open ground and are the hovering specialists. They fly some 10 to 15 m (30 to 50 ft) above ground to search an area, hover and watch and, if something is sighted, drop gently down on it. The staple diet of kestrels consists of small mammals, but they also catch small birds, reptiles and insects. The clutch of 4 to 9 eggs is laid on a ledge, in a hole in a tree or in the old nest of another bird. The female does the greater share of the incubation, which lasts 27 to 29 days. She remains with the chicks when they are first hatched and the male brings food, but later she leaves them to assist her mate.

FALCONIDAE: Falcon Family

The 60 species of falcon are all daytime-hunting birds of prey. They are found nearly all over the world. In appearance they are close to similar-sized accipiters, having sharp curved claws and powerful hooked beaks. Most species, however, have long pointed wings in contrast to the more rounded, slotted outlines of accipiters. There are also specific skeletal differences between the groups, such as details of skull structure and breastbones. Many falcons have so-called "tomial" teeth — cutting edges on the upper bill with corresponding notches in the lower bill. Males and females look similar, but females are generally larger.

The family is divided into 4 subfamilies: caracaras, laughing falcons, forest falcons, and the main subfamily, Falconinae, which includes falconets, pygmy falcons and the typical falcons of the genus *Falco*, of which there are some 37 species. Falcons (except caracaras) do not build nests.

NAME: **Hobby**, *Falco subbuteo*
RANGE: Britain to China; winters in Africa and the Far East
HABITAT: open country, bush, savanna
SIZE: 30–36 cm (12–14 in)

Hobbies are small, long-winged falcons found all over the Old World. All are exceedingly swift in flight and catch almost all their prey on the wing. They are specialists in taking flying prey (birds, insects, bats) from a swarm or flock and can even catch swallows and swifts. In the breeding season, pairs perform mutual aerobatic displays with great speed and agility. The 2 or 3 eggs are laid in an old abandoned nest of another bird. The female does most of the incubation, and her mate feeds her.

NAME: **Brown Falcon/Hawk**, *Falco berigora*
RANGE: Australia, New Guinea, Tasmania, Dampier Island
HABITAT: open country
SIZE: 40–51 cm (15¾–20 in)

The brown falcon is one of the commonest birds of prey in Australia. Its appearance and behavior are more like those of an *Accipiter* hawk than a falcon, hence its name. Less active than other falcons, it spends much time perching but is capable of swift flight. It kills prey on the ground, mammals such as rabbits, young birds, reptiles and insects and some carrion making up its diet. The female lays her 2 to 4 eggs in the abandoned nest of another bird, and both parents incubate.

NAME: **Gyrfalcon**, *Falco rusticolus*
RANGE: Arctic Europe, Asia, N. America, Greenland, Iceland
HABITAT: mountains, tundra
SIZE: 51–63 cm (20–25 in)

An impressive bird and the largest of the falcons, the gyrfalcon has a stockier build than the peregrine. Plumage can be dark, white or gray. Most breed north of the timberline and remain in the Arctic all year, but some populations migrate south for the winter. When hunting, the gyrfalcon flies swiftly near the ground. It can make rapid dives on prey, like the peregrine, but this is less characteristic. Birds are its main prey, although it feeds on some mammals, particularly in winter. Rock ptarmigan and willow grouse make up the bulk of the gyrfalcon's diet, and their numbers can affect its breeding rate. In years when these birds are abundant, gyrfalcons produce large clutches, but in years of scarcity they lay only a couple of eggs or do not breed at all.

Gyrfalcons perform display flights when courting. The female lays 2 to 7 eggs on a ledge or in an old cliff nest. She incubates the clutch for 27 to 29 days, during which her mate brings her food. When the young hatch, both parents bring food to them.

NAME: **Peregrine Falcon**, *Falco peregrinus*
RANGE: almost worldwide
HABITAT: varied, often mountains and sea cliffs
SIZE: 38–51 cm (15–20 in)   Ⓥ

The 17 races of this widespread bird vary greatly in plumage color. The peregrine's wings are tapered and pointed and its tail slim and short; it is virtually without equal in the speed and precision of its flight. Birds are its chief prey. The peregrine makes a dramatic, high-speed, near-vertical dive at its prey, then kills it outright with its talons or seizes it and takes it to the ground to eat. The peregrine can also chase prey through the air, changing direction with supreme ease. It is the most highly prized bird for falconry.

At the onset of the breeding season, peregrines perform spectacular flight displays. The 2 to 6 eggs are laid on a ledge site, on the ground or even on a city building. The female does most of the incubation, but the male takes an occasional turn and brings food for his mate. When the young are 2 weeks old, the female leaves them in the nest and helps the male find food for them. The young fly at about 40 days old. These birds are seriously declining in numbers, partly because of the incidental ingestion of pesticides, which reach them via insect-feeding birds.

Collared Falconet

Caracara

Hobby

Peregrine Falcon

Barred Forest Falcon

Kestrel

Brown Falcon

Gyrfalcon

Megapodes, Curassows, Hoatzin

ORDER GALLIFORMES

This order includes the megapodes, curassows, hoatzin, and pheasants and their relatives. Most are ground-living birds, but curassows and hoatzins are arboreal.

MEGAPODIIDAE:
Megapode Family

The 12 species in this family all occur in Australasia and Indonesia. Males and females look more or less alike, and all have large, strong legs and feet. They feed on insects, small vertebrate animals, seeds and fruit.

Megapodes do not brood their eggs in the normal way but lay them in mounds of decaying vegetation or sand and allow them to be incubated by natural heat.

NAME: **Malleefowl,** *Leipoa ocellata*
RANGE: **S. Australia**
HABITAT: **mallee (arid eucalyptus woodland)**
SIZE: **55–61 cm (21½–24 in)**

Despite its arid habitat, the male malleefowl manages to create an efficient incubator mound, which he is engaged in tending for much of the year. In winter, he digs a pit and fills it with plant material. Once this has been moistened by the winter rains, he covers it with sand, and the sealed-off vegetation starts to rot and build up heat. The malleefowl keeps a constant check on the temperature by probing the mound with his beak and keeps it to about 33°C (91°F). He controls any fluctuations by opening the mound to cool it or by piling on more sand.

The laying season lasts some time, since the female lays her 15 to 35 eggs one at a time, at intervals of several days, in holes made in the mound by the male. The chicks hatch about 7 weeks after laying and struggle out unaided. They are wholly independent and can fly within a day.

NAME: **Common Scrubfowl,** *Megapodius freycinet*
RANGE: **E. Indonesia to Melanesia; N. and N.E. Australia**
HABITAT: **rain forest and drier areas**
SIZE: **45 cm (17¾ in)**

An active, noisy bird, the scrubfowl seldom flies but seeks refuge in trees if disturbed. In some areas these birds make simple incubation mounds in sand, which are then warmed by the sun or, on some islands, by volcanic activity. In rain forest, they make huge mounds, up to 5 m (16 ft) high, containing decomposing plant material. The eggs are laid in tunnels dug into the mound.

CRACIDAE: Curassow Family

There are about 44 species in this family, found in the neotropical zone from south Texas to Paraguay. All are nonmigratory forest birds, often adapted for a tree-dwelling life. Many species have crests or casques on their heads.

NAME: **Great Curassow,** *Crax rubra*
RANGE: **Mexico to Ecuador**
HABITAT: **tropical rain forest**
SIZE: **94 cm (37 in)**

Great curassows roost and nest in trees but also spend a good deal of time on the ground. They feed on fruit, leaves and berries. The males have a loud, booming ventriloquial call that seems to be amplified by the elongated trachea. This call is used in courtship display and to threaten other males.

Curassows make an untidy nest of twigs and leaves in a bush or tree. Both parents feed and care for the 2 chicks.

NAME: **Nocturnal Curassow,** *Nothocrax urumutum*
RANGE: **South America: upper Amazon basin**
HABITAT: **tropical rain forest**
SIZE: **66 cm (26 in)**

The nocturnal curassow is, in fact, active during the day, searching for its food. It sings only at night, however, making a booming call, and in males the voice is amplified by means of an extended trachea. The sexes look alike, with bare, brightly colored faces, ample crests and brown and rufous plumage.

NAME: **Crested Guan,** *Penelope purpurascens*
RANGE: **Mexico, south to Venezuela, Ecuador**
HABITAT: **lowland rain forest and drier areas**
SIZE: **89 cm (35 in)**

Primarily tree-living birds, crested guans forage in small groups up in the treetops, walking slowly along the branches and leaping across gaps. They will, however, come down to the ground to collect fallen fruit and seeds and to find drinking water. Male and female birds look alike.

In the breeding season, guans perform a wing-drumming display. While in flight, the bird begins to beat its wings at twice the normal speed, producing a whirring sound that is maintained for several seconds. A bulky nest is made from twigs and lined with leaves. The usual clutch is 2 or 3 eggs, and the female guan does most of the incubation.

NAME: **Chachalaca,** *Ortalis vetula*
RANGE: **USA: extreme S. Texas; Mexico, Central America**
HABITAT: **brush, thickets in rain forest; drier areas**
SIZE: **51–61 cm (20–24 in)**

The chachalaca's common name is derived from its three-syllable call, "cha-cha-lak," and, like the curassow's, its voice is amplified by its elongated trachea. Groups of birds set up a deafening chorus, morning and evening.

Primarily a tree-dwelling bird, the chachalaca feeds on berries, fruit, leaves and shoots and some insects. It also comes down to the ground to search for some of its food. A small, frail nest is made of twigs, up in a tree or bush, and the female incubates the clutch of 3 or 4 eggs. Male and female chachalacas look alike.

OPISTHOCOMIDAE:
Hoatzin Family

The hoatzin is the sole species in this family. It has some similarity to Galliformes, so has been placed in this order, but the grouping has recently been challenged, and because of its unique characteristics, it is suggested that the hoatzin be placed on its own.

NAME: **Hoatzin,** *Opisthocomus hoazin*
RANGE: **South America: Amazon and Orinoco basins**
HABITAT: **wooded riverbanks**
SIZE: **61 cm (24 in)**

The hoatzin is an unusual-looking bird, with large wings and tail, a long neck and a small head for its size, topped with a ragged crest. Male and female look alike. An arboreal bird, it is a poor flier and uses its wings more for support and balance when climbing and perching than for flying. Hoatzins live in flocks of 10 to 20 individuals and are most active in the mornings and evenings. They feed on fruit and leaves, particularly the tough leaves of mangrove and arum; their digestive tracts are enlarged, which enables them to cope with this bulky vegetation.

The hoatzin builds its untidy stick nest in a tree overhanging water so that, if threatened, the young birds, which can swim, can drop down into the water and so escape danger. There are 2 or 3 eggs in a clutch, and both parents are believed to incubate. The young hoatzin possesses a unique adaptation for arboreal life: there is a pair of hooked claws on the bend of each wing, which help the young bird to clamber nimbly among the trees. These claws are lost as the bird matures.

Common Scrubfowl

Malleefowl

Chachalaca

Great
Curassow

Nocturnal
Curassow

Crested Guan

Hoatzin

Pheasants

NAME: **European Quail**, *Coturnix coturnix*
RANGE: **Europe, Asia, east to Lake Baikal, N. India; Africa; winters Mediterranean coast, Africa, Asia to S. India, Thailand**
HABITAT: **grassland, farmland**
SIZE: **18 cm (7 in)**

One of the smallest birds in the pheasant family, the quail is a neat, rounded bird with a weak bill and legs. The female resembles the male in build but has an unmarked buff throat and a closely spotted breast. A rarely seen bird, the quail forages in the undergrowth and tends to run through vegetation to escape danger, rather than to fly, although it can fly considerable distances when migrating. It feeds mainly on seeds but eats some small invertebrates, particularly in the summer.

Breeding takes place in early summer, and the female lays one clutch of 9 to 15 eggs in a plant-lined scrape on the ground. She incubates her eggs for 16 to 21 days.

NAME: **Painted Quail**, *Excalfactoria chinensis*
RANGE: **India to S.E. China, Malaysia, Indonesia, Australia**
HABITAT: **swamp, grassland**
SIZE: **15 cm (6 in)**

A tiny but distinctive bird, the painted quail is typical of the eastern quails, which are more boldly patterned than the European birds. The female painted quail has duller plumage than the male, mainly buff-colored with a barred breast. Painted quails forage in vegetation and feed on seeds and insects.

The female lays 4 to 8 eggs in a shallow scrape on the ground. She incubates the clutch for about 16 days.

NAME: **Himalayan Snowcock**, *Tetraogallus himalayensis*
RANGE: **W. Himalayas**
HABITAT: **mountain slopes**
SIZE: **72 cm (28¼ in)**

The Himalayan snowcock is one of 7 species of snowcock, all found at high altitudes in Asia. Typical of its group, it is a large bird, with coloration which blends well with its environment. In the early morning, pairs or groups of up to 5 snowcocks fly down the hillsides from their roosts to find water to drink. The rest of the day is spent slowly coming back up, feeding on the way on roots, tubers, green plants, berries and seeds.

Breeding takes place between April and June. The courting males are particularly noisy at this time, making loud five-note whistles. The female lays 5 to 7 eggs in a hollow she scrapes in the ground among stones and rocks. She incubates the clutch for 27 or 28 days.

PHASIANIDAE: Pheasant Family

This large family contains 5 subfamilies: the grouse, guineafowl, turkey and American quail subfamilies (shown on p.232) and the largest, the pheasant subfamily.

There are about 154 species in the pheasant subfamily (Phasianinae), divided into 3 main groups: partridges, including snowcocks and francolins, Old World quails and the true pheasants. Most are plump, rounded birds which usually feed and nest on the ground but often roost for the night in trees. Their wings are short and powerful and capable of strong but not sustained flight. Most are seed-eating birds which scratch around for food with their stout, unfeathered legs and strong claws, but many also eat insects and other small invertebrates, as well as fruit and berries.

Males and females have different plumage coloration in many species, particularly the larger pheasants. Some of the smaller, plainer birds are monogamous, while in the more ornate species, the males tend to be polygamous. The nest is usually simple, often a scrape on the ground; chicks are born fully covered with down and can leave the nest soon after hatching.

The pheasant subfamily is an Old World group, but many species have been successfully introduced in areas outside their native range. Some are well known as game birds, hunted for sport and eaten by humans.

NAME: **Red-legged Partridge**, *Alectoris rufa*
RANGE: **S.W. Europe to S.E. France, N. Italy, Corsica; introduced in Britain, Azores, Madeira and Canary Islands**
HABITAT: **scrub, moorland, farmland**
SIZE: **32–34 cm (12½–13¼ in)**

A typical partridge, with a larger bill, stronger legs and longer tail than the quails, the red-legged partridge is distinguished by the white stripe above each eye, the black-bordered white throat and red bill and legs. Males and females look alike, but juveniles are less vividly colored. These birds roost in trees and bushes but feed on the ground, mainly on plants, although they occasionally eat insects and frogs. Reluctant to fly, they prefer to escape danger by running.

Breeding begins in April or May. Red-legged partridges are monogamous birds and make long-lasting pair bonds. The female lays 10 to 16 eggs in a shallow scrape, which the male makes on the ground and lines with leaves. The clutch is incubated by both parents for about 23 or 24 days.

NAME: **Red-necked Francolin**, *Francolinus afer*
RANGE: **Africa, south of the equator, except S.W.**
HABITAT: **bush, cultivated land, savanna**
SIZE: **41 cm (16 in)**

The francolins are all large game birds, with strong bills and characteristic patches of bare skin on head or neck. Mainly African birds — over 30 species occur in Africa — a few francolins live in Asia. The red-necked francolin, with the distinctive red skin around its eyes and on its neck, is typical of the group. Its breast is covered with broad dark streaks which help to camouflage it in the open bush country it frequents. Males and females look alike.

In small family groups, francolins forage for plant food and insects. They fly well and take refuge in trees if disturbed. They nest on the ground and females lay 5 to 9 eggs.

NAME: **Red Spurfowl**, *Galloperdix spadicea*
RANGE: **India**
HABITAT: **cultivated land, stony hills**
SIZE: **36 cm (14¼ in)**

A type of partridge, the male red spurfowl has distinctive scalloped plumage and naked red skin around each eye. The female's grayish plumage is barred and spotted with black. Pairs or groups of up to 5 spurfowl forage together, scratching in the undergrowth for seeds, tubers and berries, as well as slugs, snails and termites.

The timing of the breeding season varies from area to area, according to conditions; although this is usually between January and June, it can be at any time of year. The nest is a shallow scrape on the ground among bamboo or scrub, scantily lined with a few leaves or blades of grass. The female lays 3 to 5 eggs which she incubates alone. The male helps to care for the young.

NAME: **Roulroul Partridge**, *Rollulus rouloul*
RANGE: **Burma to Sumatra and Borneo**
HABITAT: **floor of dense forest on lowland or hills**
SIZE: **25.5 cm (10 in)**

The roulroul is the most attractive and unusual of the wood partridges. The male is instantly recognizable by his red, brushlike crest; he also has red skin around the eyes and a red patch on his bill. The female bird has a few long feathers on her head but lacks the crest.

These partridges move in mixed groups of up to 12, occasionally more, feeding on seeds, fruit, insects and snails. Little is known about their breeding habits, but they are thought to lay 5 or 6 eggs.

Red Spurfowl (male)

Red-legged Partridge

Himalayan Snowcock

Painted Quail (male)

Roulroul
Partridge (male)

Red-necked
Francolin

European Quail (male)

Pheasants

NAME: **Temminck's Tragopan,** *Tragopan temminckii*
RANGE: **mountains of W. China, N. Burma and S.E. Tibet**
HABITAT: **forest**
SIZE: **64 cm (25¼ in)**

Like all the 5 species of tragopan, the male Temminck's tragopan is a striking bird, with beautiful, elaborate plumage. The female is much plainer, with rufous to grayish-brown plumage on the upperparts and a buff or white throat and light-brown underparts. This tragopan is even more unsocial and more arboreal than other tragopans and prefers cool, damp forest. It feeds on seeds, buds, leaves, berries and insects.

At the start of the breeding season, the male courts his mate, displaying his brilliant plumage. The nest is made in a tree, and the female lays 3 to 6 eggs.

NAME: **Red Junglefowl,** *Gallus gallus*
RANGE: **Himalayas to S. China, S.E. Asia, Sumatra, Java; introduced in Sulawesi, Lesser Sunda Islands**
HABITAT: **forest, scrub, cultivated land**
SIZE: **43–76 cm (17–30 in) including tail of 28 cm (11 in) in male**

The ancestor of the domestic fowl, the red junglefowl is a beautiful, colorful bird. The female is much smaller and duller than the striking male, however, with mainly brown plumage and some chestnut on the head and neck. Over the range, several races of red junglefowl occur which vary slightly in appearance. They are gregarious birds, gathering in flocks of up to 50 or so to feed on grain, grass shoots and crops, fruit, berries, insects and their larvae.

The breeding season is usually March to May. The female scrapes a hollow in the ground near a bush or bamboo clump and lines it with leaves. She incubates the clutch of 5 or 6 eggs for 19 to 21 days.

NAME: **Gray Peacock Pheasant,** *Polyplectron bicalcaratum*
RANGE: **Himalayas to Hainan; S.E. Asia: Burma, Thailand, Indo-China**
HABITAT: **forest**
SIZE: **56–76 cm (22–30 in)**

The gray peacock pheasant is one of 6 species in the genus *Polyplectron*, all of which occur in India, Southeast Asia or Sumatra. The female is smaller than the decorative male and has fewer, smaller eyespots, which are black with white borders. They are secretive, yet noisy, birds and feed on grain, fruit, berries and insects.

The male displays to his mate, calling as he spreads his tail and wing coverts. The female lays 2 to 6 eggs in a nest on the ground and incubates the clutch for about 21 days.

NAME: **Golden Pheasant,** *Chrysolophus pictus*
RANGE: **W. China; introduced in Britain**
HABITAT: **scrub on rocky hillsides; introduced in woodland**
SIZE: **male: 98–108 cm (38½–42½ in)**
female: 63–65 cm (24¾–25½ in)

A spectacularly beautiful bird, the male golden pheasant has brilliant plumage and a crest of golden feathers. The female bird is much plainer, with various shades of brown plumage, streaked with black. In the wild, golden pheasants move in pairs or alone and are shy birds, alert to any danger. They have short wings and are reluctant to fly, preferring to run from any threat. Seeds, leaves, shoots and insects are their main foods.

Little is known of the breeding habits of this pheasant in its natural habitat, but in Britain, it makes a shallow scrape on the ground and lines it with plant material. The female lays 5 to 12 eggs, which she incubates for 22 days, apparently hardly ever, if at all, leaving the nest during this period.

NAME: **Ring-necked Pheasant,** *Phasianus colchicus*
RANGE: **Caspian area, east across central Asia to China, Korea, Japan and Burma; introduced in Europe, N. America, New Zealand**
HABITAT: **woodland, forest edge, marshes, agricultural land**
SIZE: **male: 76–89 cm (30–35 in)**
female: 53–64 cm (20¾–25¼ in)

Extremely successful as an introduced species, the ring-necked pheasant is probably the best known of all game birds. So many subspecies have now been introduced and crossed that the plumage of the male is highly variable, but a typical bird has a dark-green head and coppery upperparts, with fine, dark markings; many have a white collar. The female is less variable and has brown plumage.

In the wild, ringnecks feed on plant material, such as seeds, shoots and berries, and on insects and small invertebrates. They are ground-dwelling birds and spend much of their time scratching for food in undergrowth.

Male ringnecks are polygamous and have harems of several females. The female scrapes a shallow hollow in the ground, usually in thick cover, which she lines with plant material. She lays 7 to 15 eggs on consecutive days and begins the 22- to 27-day incubation only when the clutch is complete. The young are tended and led to food by the female, rarely with any help from the male. Ringnecks produce only one brood a season.

NAME: **Indian Peafowl,** *Pavo cristatus*
RANGE: **India, Sri Lanka**
HABITAT: **forest, woodland, cultivated land**
SIZE: **male: 92 cm–1.2 m (3–4 ft) without train; 2–2.25 m (6½–7¼ ft) in full plumage;**
female: 86 cm (33¾ in)

The magnificent Indian peafowl is so widely kept in captivity and in parks and gardens outside its native range that it is a familiar bird in much of the world. The cock is unmistakable, with his iridescent plumage, wiry crest and glittering train, adorned with eyespots. The smaller female, or peahen, has brown and some metallic green plumage and a small crest.

Outside the breeding season, peafowls live in small flocks of 1 male and 3 to 5 hens, but, after breeding, they may split into groups made up of adult males or females and young. They feed in the open, early in the morning and at dusk, and spend much of the rest of the day in thick undergrowth. Seeds, grain, groundnuts, shoots, flowers, berries, insects and small invertebrates are all eaten by these omnivorous birds, and they may destroy crops.

In the breeding season, the male bird displays, fully spreading his erect train to spectacular effect by raising and spreading the tail beneath it. With his wings trailing, he prances and struts in front of the female, periodically shivering the spread train and presenting his back view. The female may respond by a faint imitation of his posture. In the wild, the nest scrape is made in thick undergrowth, and the female incubates her 4 to 6 eggs for about 28 days.

NAME: **Congo Peacock,** *Afropavo congensis*
RANGE: **Africa: Congo basin**
HABITAT: **dense rain forest**
SIZE: **60–70 cm (23½–27½ in)**

First described in 1936, the Congo peacock is the only native African game bird larger than a francolin. The male bird has dark, glossy plumage and a crest of black feathers on the head, behind a tuft of white bristles. The female has a crest, but no bristles, and is largely rufous brown and black, with some metallic green plumage on her upperparts. The habits of Congo peacocks in the wild have seldom been documented, but they are believed to live in pairs and to take refuge and to roost in trees. They feed on grain and fruit.

Congo peacocks are monogamous in captivity and build a nest of sticks in a tree. The female incubates the 3 or 4 eggs for about 26 days.

Gray Peacock Pheasant (male)

Red Junglefowl (male)

Golden Pheasant
(male)

Temminck's Tragopan (male)

Ring-necked Pheasant
(male)

Indian Peafowl
(male)

Congo Peacock
(male)

Grouse, Turkeys, Guineafowl, American Quail

TETRAONINAE: Grouse Subfamily

The 18 species of grouse are all plump, rounded birds, found in temperate regions of North America, northern Europe and Asia. Many species are hunted for sport and eaten by man. Grouse have short wings and are capable of strong but not prolonged flight; their legs, and sometimes their toes, are feathered. They feed mostly on plant material and some insects.

Many species perform elaborate courtship displays, often communally. Sexes look different in some species. The young are born in a well-developed state, able to leave the nest only hours after hatching, and they require little attention from the parent birds.

NAME: **Black Grouse**, *Tetrao tetrix*
RANGE: **N. Europe, N. Asia**
HABITAT: **moor, forest**
SIZE: **41–51 cm (16–20 in)**

Social display is a particularly well-developed activity in the black grouse. In spring males, or blackcocks, gather at a traditional display ground, known as a lek and used year after year. Each day about sunrise, the males call, dance and posture — each in his own patch of the lek — to attract the watching females. The male black grouse has a distinctive lyre-shaped tail, which he spreads and displays in courtship. Females, or grayhens, are smaller than males and have mottled brown plumage and forked tails.

Black grouse are polygamous birds, and a successful dominant male may mate with many females. Each female lays a clutch of 6 to 11 eggs in a shallow, leaf-lined hollow on the ground. She incubates the eggs for 24 to 29 days.

NAME: **Greater Prairie Chicken,** *Tympanuchus cupido*
RANGE: **central N. America**
HABITAT: **prairie**
SIZE: **42–46 cm (16½–18 in)**

This increasingly rare bird was once common over a large area of North America. Male and female birds look similar, but females have barred tail feathers and smaller neck sacs. Prairie chickens feed on plant matter, such as leaves, fruit and grain, and in the summer they catch insects, particularly grasshoppers. Male birds perform spectacular courtship displays, inflating their orange neck sacs and raising crests of neck feathers. They give booming calls and stamp their feet as they posture, to make the display even more impressive. Female birds lay 10 to 12 eggs and incubate them for 21 to 28 days.

NAME: **Rock Ptarmigan,** *Lagopus mutus*
RANGE: **Holarctic**
HABITAT: **forest, tundra**
SIZE: **33–39 cm (13–15½ in)**

The ground-dwelling rock ptarmigans depend on camouflage for defense, and to achieve this in the changing background of their northerly range, they adopt different plumages. The summer plumage is mottled to blend with the forest, while during the winter snows ptarmigans have white plumage, only the tail feathers remaining dark. Rock ptarmigans feed on leaves, buds, fruits and seeds and on some insects in the summer.

They are monogamous birds; the male defends a small territory at the breeding grounds. The female lays 6 to 9 eggs in a leaf-lined hollow on the ground and incubates them for 24 to 26 days.

MELEAGRIDINAE: Turkey Subfamily

There are 2 species of wild turkey. Both are large birds with bare skin on head and neck. Males and females look similar, but females are smaller and have duller plumage and smaller leg spurs.

NAME: **Turkey,** *Meleagris gallopavo*
RANGE: **USA, Mexico**
HABITAT: **wooded country**
SIZE: **91–122 cm (36–48 in)**

The wild turkey has a lighter, slimmer body and longer legs than the domesticated version. Turkeys are strong fliers over short distances. They roost in trees but find most of their food on the ground and eat plant matter, such as seeds, nuts and berries, as well as some insects and small reptiles.

A breeding male has a harem of several females. Each female lays her eggs in a shallow, leaf-lined nest on the ground; sometimes two or more females use the same nest. The female incubates the clutch of 8 to 15 eggs for about 28 days and cares for the young. The sexes segregate after breeding.

NUMIDINAE: Guineafowl Subfamily

The 7 species of guineafowl are heavy-bodied, rounded game birds with short wings and bare heads. Males and females look virtually alike. All species occur in Africa and Madagascar. The helmeted guineafowl is the ancestor of the domestic guineafowl.

NAME: **Helmeted Guineafowl,** *Numida meleagris*
RANGE: **E. Africa**
HABITAT: **forest, dry brush**
SIZE: **63 cm (25 in)**

The helmeted guineafowl, named for the bony protuberance on its crown, has the distinctive spotted plumage of most species of guineafowl. It feeds on insects and on plant material such as seeds, leaves and bulbs. The female lays 10 to 20 eggs in a hollow scraped in the ground. She incubates the eggs and her mate helps care for the young.

ODONTOPHORINAE: American Quail Subfamily

There are about 33 species of American quail, distributed from Canada to northeast Argentina. Many are hunted for sport and food. They are larger, more diverse and more strikingly colored than the Old World quails and differ from them in certain anatomical features, the most important of which is the stronger, serrated bill, typical of the American birds.

NAME: **Bobwhite,** *Colinus virginianus*
RANGE: **USA to Guatemala; introduced in West Indies**
HABITAT: **brush, open woodland, farmland**
SIZE: **23–27 cm (9–10½ in)**

Bobwhites are gregarious birds for much of the year, moving in coveys of 30 or so. In spring the coveys break up, and the birds pair for mating. The nest is a hollow in the ground. The average clutch is 14 to 16 eggs, and both parents incubate the eggs. Male and female birds look alike, but the male has striking face markings, while the female's face is buff-brown. The common name of this species is an imitation of its call.

NAME: **California Quail,** *Lophortyx californica*
RANGE: **W. USA**
HABITAT: **rangeland and agricultural land**
SIZE: **24–28 cm (9½–11 in)**

The state bird of California, this quail is an attractive bird with a characteristic head plume. Females look similar to males and have head plumes but lack the black and white facial markings; they have buff-brown heads and chests. California quail move in flocks, mostly on foot; they do not fly unless forced to do so. They feed on leaves, seeds and berries, and some insects. The female lays her 12 to 16 eggs in a leaf-lined hollow on the ground, and generally she incubates them for 18 days.

Black Grouse (male)

Turkey

Greater Prairie Chicken
(male)

Rock Ptarmigan

California Quail (male)

Helmeted Guineafowl

Bobwhite (male)

Cranes and relatives

ORDER GRUIFORMES

A diverse assemblage of wading and ground-living birds, this order contains 12 families, several of which contain only 1 species.

MESITORNITHIDAE:
Mesite Family

The 3 species of mesite all live in Madagascan forests. They run well but rarely fly, and 1 species, Bensch's mesite, *Monias benschi*, has yet to be seen in flight. Males and females look alike in 2 species, but unalike in Bensch's mesite.

NAME: **White-breasted Mesite,** *Mesitornis variegata*
RANGE: **N.W. Madagascar**
HABITAT: **dry forest**
SIZE: **25.5 cm (10 in)** ®

The white-breasted mesite is a ground-dwelling bird and spends much of its life searching the forest floor for insects and seeds. Mesites generally move in pairs, heads bobbing as they walk.

The nest is made in a bush or low tree so the birds can climb up to it. It consists of a platform of twigs, lined with leaves; 1 to 3 eggs are laid. There is some doubt as to whether the male or female incubates the eggs.

TURNICIDAE: Buttonquail Family

The 14 species of buttonquail and hemipode are dumpy, ground-living birds which closely resemble quails but have only three toes on each foot. Their wings are short and rounded, and the birds seldom fly. Females are larger and more brightly plumaged than males. All species occur in tropical and subtropical regions of the Old World.

NAME: **Andalusian Hemipode/Little Buttonquail,** *Turnix sylvatica*
RANGE: **S. Spain, Africa; S. Asia to Indonesia, Philippines**
HABITAT: **grassland, scrub**
SIZE: **15 cm (6 in)**

A shy, secretive bird, the Andalusian hemipode spends much of its time in the undergrowth, although it is able to fly. It feeds on plants, seeds and insects. The female bird takes the dominant sexual role, displaying to the male and competing with other females. Both birds make the nest, which is usually a hollow in the ground, lined with grass. From 3 to 8 oval eggs, usually 4, are laid, and the male incubates the clutch for an average of 13 days — one of the shortest incubation periods for any bird.

PEDIONOMIDAE:
Plains-wanderer Family

The single species in this family is related to the buttonquails and was formerly included in that family. The plains-wanderer, however, has four toes on each foot and lays pointed, not oval, eggs. These and some structural differences are sufficient to place it in a separate family.

NAME: **Plains-wanderer/Collared Hemipode,** *Pedionomus torquatus*
RANGE: **S.E. Australia**
HABITAT: **open grassland**
SIZE: **15–17 cm (6–6¾ in)**

A small, compact bird with short rounded wings, the female plains-wanderer has a chestnut-colored breast and a distinctive collar of black spots. Plains-wanderers seldom fly, but search for their food — insects, seeds and plants — on the ground. The nest is a simple hollow in the ground, lined with grass. The female lays 3 or 4 eggs, which are incubated by the male.

GRUIDAE: Crane Family

The 15 species of crane are splendid, long-legged, long-necked birds, often with brightly colored bare skin on the face and decorative plumes on the head. The larger species stand up to 1.5 m (5 ft) tall. They are found over most of the world, except in South America, Madagascar, Malaysia, Polynesia and New Zealand.

Except during the breeding season, when they consort only in pairs, they are gregarious birds, and after breeding, they migrate in large flocks, flying in V-formation or in line, with necks extended and legs trailing. Males and females have similar plumage.

NAME: **Whooping Crane,** *Grus americana*
RANGE: **N. America**
HABITAT: **wetlands in prairies and other open habitats**
SIZE: **1.2–1.4 m (4–4½ ft) tall** Ⓔ

Exceedingly rare birds in the wild, whooping cranes have been at the point of extinction, although vigorously protected, since the 1930s, when they almost disappeared. They breed in Canada and winter on the Texas Gulf Coast, and their migrations are carefully monitored.

An omnivorous bird, the whooping crane feeds on grain, plants, insects, frogs and other small animals. It lays 2 eggs on a flat nest of sticks on the ground. Both parents incubate the eggs and care for the young.

NAME: **Crowned Crane,** *Balearica pavonina*
RANGE: **Africa, south of the Sahara**
HABITAT: **swamps**
SIZE: **1 m (3¼ ft) tall**

The common name of this elegant bird is derived from the magnificent crest of yellow feathers on its head. All cranes perform ceremonial dances in the breeding season and, in a simpler form, throughout the year; the crowned crane is particularly spectacular as it postures with wings outstretched to display its feathers, struts about and jumps into the air. Both parents incubate the clutch of 2 or 3 eggs and care for the young.

ARAMIDAE: Limpkin Family

The single species in this family is a marsh bird with similarities to both cranes and rails. It is now protected by law in the USA, after having been hunted almost to extinction early this century. Males and females look alike.

NAME: **Limpkin,** *Aramus guarauna*
RANGE: **USA: S. Georgia, Florida; Mexico, Central and South America; Caribbean**
HABITAT: **swamps**
SIZE: **59–71 cm (23¼–28 in)**

A long-legged bird, with long toes and sharp claws, the limpkin flies slowly and infrequently. It is most active at dusk and at night, when it uses its sensitive, slightly curved beak to probe the mud for freshwater snails.

Limpkins breed between January and August, depending on area, but in the USA the nesting season is usually March or April. A shallow nest is made of sticks, usually on the ground near water, and both parents incubate the 4 to 8 eggs.

PSOPHIIDAE: Trumpeter Family

The 3 species of trumpeter are soft-plumaged, largely black birds, with weak, rounded wings. They rarely fly, but run swiftly on their long legs. Males look like females but make loud, trumpeting calls.

NAME: **Common Trumpeter,** *Psophia crepitans*
RANGE: **South America: Amazon basin**
HABITAT: **forest**
SIZE: **53 cm (20¾ in)**

Common trumpeters are gregarious birds which move in flocks around the forest floor, feeding on fruit, berries and insects. Trumpeters perform dancelike courtship movements and are believed to nest in holes in trees. The 6 to 10 eggs are incubated by the female.

White-breasted Mesite

Limpkin

Whooping Crane

Plains-wanderer

Andalusian Hemipode

Crowned Crane

Common Trumpeter

Rails

236

NAME: **Takahe**, *Notornis mantelli*
RANGE: **New Zealand: now confined to Murchison Mountains, South Island**
HABITAT: **high valleys at 750–1,200 m (2,500–4,000 ft)**
SIZE: **63 cm (24¾ in)** Ⓔ

First discovered in 1849, the takahe was sighted only four times in the next 50 years and was assumed to be extinct until its rediscovery in 1948. Despite careful conservation, however, there were thought to be only 100 pairs alive in 1977. Competition from introduced deer for the plants it feeds on and predation by introduced ermines are major reasons for its decline.

A stout bird, the takahe runs well but is flightless. It may venture into shallow water but does not swim as a rule. It feeds on the coarse fibrous vegetation of its habitat, particularly on snow grass (*Danthonia*), taking the seed heads and stems. Holding down the clump with one foot, it cuts out stems with its heavy beak and consumes their tender bases.

Pairs remain together for life when possible and usually breed in November. After several trial nests, a nest of grass stalks is made between or under clumps of grass which give some shelter. Both parents incubate the 2 eggs for up to 28 days, but many nests are destroyed by bad weather or predators and only 1 chick from each clutch is ever reared.

NAME: **Common Moorhen/Common Gallinule**, *Gallinula chloropus*
RANGE: **worldwide (not Australasia)**
HABITAT: **swamps, marshes, ponds, slow rivers with cover on banks**
SIZE: **33 cm (13 in)**

A familiar water bird, the moorhen is one of the most adaptable, successful members of its family. It frequents almost any fresh water and adjacent land and readily adapts to man-made environments such as urban parks and farms. It is a lively, active bird, far less secretive than the rail or crake, and swims freely on open water. Plant matter, such as pond weeds, berries and fallen fruit, makes up the bulk of the moorhen's diet, but it also eats a small amount of insects.

In the breeding season, the timing of which varies over its vast range, the moorhen pair defends a territory and performs intricate displays on both land and water. Both sexes help to build a nest of dead reeds and other aquatic plants among reeds or in a bush at the water's edge. The 5 to 11 eggs are laid on consecutive days and incubated for 19 to 22 days by both parents. Some pairs may produce a second brood during the season. Northernmost populations migrate south in winter.

RALLIDAE: Rail Family

There are 132 species of rail, crake, wood rail, gallinule and coot in this distinctive, cosmopolitan family. They are ground-living birds, often found in or around water and marshy areas, and are well adapted for life in dense vegetation. Typical species are small to medium-sized birds — 14 to 51 cm (5½ to 20 in) long — with moderately long legs and toes and short rounded wings. Their bodies are laterally compressed, enabling them to squeeze through clumps of vegetation. Males and females look alike or nearly so in most species, although males are sometimes larger. Most are solitary, secretive birds.

There are two groups within the family: first, the rails, crakes and wood rails, with their camouflaging mottled plumage; and second, the darker gallinules and coots, which are much more aquatic in their habits. Most species fly reasonably well but may ordinarily be reluctant to take to the air, although many make long migrations between winter and summer habitats. Island-dwelling rails have been particularly prone to becoming flightless, which has then led to their extinction.

Diet is varied in the rail family. Species with long, thin bills probe in soft soil and leaf litter for insects, spiders, mollusks, worms and other invertebrates, while species with shorter, thicker bills feed on vegetation. Coots are aquatic feeders and dive or up-end for a variety of underwater plants and animals.

NAME: **Water Rail**, *Rallus aquaticus*
RANGE: **Europe, N. Africa, N. Asia to Japan**
HABITAT: **marshes, reedbeds**
SIZE: **28 cm (11 in)**

The slim-bodied water rail moves easily and skillfully through the tangled aquatic vegetation which it frequents. A shy bird, it runs for cover when alarmed, but is less retiring than the small rails and will come onto open land when the marshes freeze over in winter. It swims short distances near cover. Its varied diet includes plant material, such as roots, seeds and berries, as well as insects, crustaceans, small fish and worms.

April to July is the normal breeding season in most of the rail's range, and it sometimes produces two broods. The nest, made of dry reeds and other plants, is situated on the marsh. Both parents share the 19- to 21-day incubation of the 6 to 11 eggs.

NAME: **Giant Wood Rail**, *Aramides (=Eulabeornis) ypecaha*
RANGE: **South America: E. Brazil, Paraguay, Uraguay, E. Argentina**
HABITAT: **marshes, reedbeds, rivers**
SIZE: **53 cm (20¾ in)**

A large, handsome bird, the giant wood rail is an abundant species in its range. These birds feed alone during the day on plant and animal material, but at night they gather in small groups in the marshes and call in chorus.

The nest is made of grass and plant stems in a low bush just above the marsh surface. About 5 eggs are laid.

NAME: **American Coot**, *Fulica americana*
RANGE: **central and S. Canada, USA, Central and South America along Andes; Hawaiian Islands, Caribbean, Bahamas**
HABITAT: **marshes, ponds, lakes, rivers**
SIZE: **33–40 cm (13–15¾ in)**

A dark-plumaged, ducklike species with a white bill, the American coot is a conspicuous, noisy water bird. Its flight is strong and swift, although it seldom flies far unless migrating. It is a strong swimmer and good walker; as with all coots, its toes are lobed, which improves its swimming abilities.

Water plants are its main food, but it also eats aquatic insects, mollusks and some land plants. The coots often feed in flocks on the water, hundreds of birds swimming together like a moving black island.

In North America, the birds breed from April to May. After prolonged courtship rituals, a cup-shaped nest is made of dried marsh plants in a reedbed or on floating vegetation. The 8 to 12 eggs are incubated by both male and female for 21 or 22 days. Northernmost populations migrate south in winter.

NAME: **Corncrake**, *Crex crex*
RANGE: **Europe, W. Asia**
HABITAT: **grassland, cultivated land**
SIZE: **26.5 cm (10½ in)**

This small, slender rail seldom flies in its everyday life, although it migrates several thousand miles to winter in tropical Africa. It is a land-dwelling rail and runs swiftly through vegetation in search of seeds, grain and insects to feed on. Dawn and dusk are the corncrake's main periods of activity, but in spring the male makes his rasping call day and night. Only seen alone or in pairs, it is not a gregarious species except when migrating south.

The female corncrake constructs the nest, which is made on the ground from grass and weeds, and she incubates the 8 to 12 eggs for 14 to 21 days. The young birds are fed for a few days by the female or by both parents.

Takahe

Giant Wood Rail

Common Moorhen

American Coot

Water Rail

Corncrake

Finfoots,
Bustards and relatives

HELIORNITHIDAE:
Finfoot Family

There are 3 species of finfoot, one in each of the world's major tropical areas: Central and South America, Africa and Asia (India to Sumatra). They are probably the last relics of a once large, wide-ranging family. Male and female look more or less alike, but females may be smaller and differ slightly in plumage.

NAME: **African Finfoot,** *Podica senegalensis*
RANGE: **Africa, south of the Sahara**
HABITAT: **wooded streams, pools, mangrove swamps**
SIZE: **53–63.5 cm (20¾–25 in)**

An aquatic bird, the finfoot skulks at the edges of well-wooded streams, among overhanging vegetation. It swims low in the water, sometimes with only its head and neck visible, and dives well. Once aloft, it flies strongly and also leaves the water to clamber around in vegetation and climb trees. Insects and small invertebrates, amphibians and fish are its main foods. Male and female birds look similar, but the male is larger and has buff-gray plumage on the front of the neck, while the female's throat and neck are whitish.

The nest is made of twigs and rushes on a branch overhanging water or else among flood debris. The female lays 2 eggs.

NAME: **Sungrebe,** *Heliornis fulica*
RANGE: **S. Mexico, through Central and South America to N. Argentina**
HABITAT: **stagnant streams, wooded rivers**
SIZE: **28 cm (11 in)**

Although smaller than the African finfoot, the sungrebe has the same elongate body and lobed toes. Its common name is particularly unsuitable, since the bird frequents shady overgrown margins of streams and rivers and is rarely seen in the open. It feeds on insects, especially larvae found on leaves, and on small invertebrates, amphibians and fish. It flies strongly but tends to take cover in undergrowth to escape danger, rather than to fly.

The 4 eggs are laid in a bush or tree overhanging water.

EURYPYGIDAE: Sunbittern Family

The sunbittern, found in Central and South America, is the sole member of its family. It is related to rails and bustards, but its exact affinities are uncertain. Male and female look alike.

NAME: **Sunbittern,** *Eurypyga helias*
RANGE: **Central America, South America to Brazil**
HABITAT: **forest streams and creeks**
SIZE: **46 cm (18 in)**

The sunbittern is an elegant bird, with a long bill, slender neck and long legs. It frequents the well-wooded banks of streams, where it is perfectly camouflaged in the dappled sunlight by its mottled plumage. Fish, insects and crustaceans are its main foods, which it hunts from the bank or seizes with swift thrusts of its bill, while wading in the shallows.

In courtship display, the beautifully plumaged wings are fully spread, revealing patches of color, and the tips are held forward, framing the head and neck. The birds also perform a courtship dance, with tail and wings spread. Both partners help to build the large domed nest in a tree and incubate the 2 or 3 eggs for about 28 days.

RHYNOCHETIDAE: Kagu Family

The classification and relationships of the kagu, the sole member of its family, have been the subject of much dispute.

NAME: **Kagu,** *Rhynochetos jubatus*
RANGE: **New Caledonia**
HABITAT: **forest**
SIZE: **56 cm (22 in)**   Ⓔ

Once abundant, the nocturnal, virtually flightless kagu is now rare, largely due to the onslaught by introduced dogs, cats and rats. The kagu feeds on insects, worms and snails, which it finds on or in the ground by probing with its long, pointed bill. Male and female look more or less alike.

In display, the two birds face each other, spreading their wings to show off the black, white and chestnut plumage. They may perform remarkable dances, whirling round with the tip of the tail or wing held in the bill. A nest is made on the ground, and both parents incubate the single egg for about 36 days.

CARIAMIDAE: Seriema Family

The 2 species of seriema are long-legged, ground-living birds, both of which occur in South America. They are believed to be the only surviving descendants of some long-extinct carnivorous ground birds, known from fossils. Males and females look alike or nearly so.

NAME: **Red-legged Seriema,** *Cariama cristata*
RANGE: **E. Bolivia, Brazil, Paraguay, Uruguay, N. Argentina**
HABITAT: **grassland**
SIZE: **76–91 cm (30–35¾ in)**

A tall, graceful bird, the red-legged seriema runs fast but rarely flies, tending to rely on its speed on land to escape from danger. The sharp, broad bill, under the tufty crest, is powerful, reminiscent of the bill of a bird of prey, and is used to kill reptiles and amphibians, as well as for feeding on insects, leaves and seeds.

The nest is made of sticks and built in a tree. Both parents incubate the 2 or 3 eggs for 25 or 26 days.

OTIDIDAE: Bustard Family

Bustards are heavily built, ground-dwelling birds, which tend to run or walk rather than fly, although they are capable of strong flight. The majority of the 24 species occur in Africa, but there are bustards in southern Europe, Asia and Australia. Male birds are more boldly plumaged than females.

NAME: **Great Bustard,** *Otis tarda*
RANGE: **scattered areas of S. and central Europe, east across Asia to Siberia and E. China**
HABITAT: **grassland, grain fields**
SIZE: **75 cm–1 m (29½ in–3¼ ft)**

The male great bustard is a large, strong bird, with a thick neck and sturdy legs. The female is smaller and slimmer, lacking the male's bristly "whiskers" and chestnut breast plumage. Insects and seeds are their main foods, but they are omnivorous.

The male bustard performs a remarkable courtship display, raising his wings and tail and puffing himself out until he resembles a moving, feathery ball. The 2 or 3 eggs are laid in an unlined scrape on the ground and incubated by the female for 25 to 28 days.

NAME: **Little Black Bustard/Black Korhaan,** *Afrotis atra*
RANGE: **South Africa**
HABITAT: **grassland, bush**
SIZE: **53 cm (20¾ in)**

Male little black bustards are showy, conspicuous birds, with distinctive markings on the head and neck. Females are duller, with much of the plumage mottled with black, tawny and rufous spots and only the underparts pure black. They generally live in pairs in a well-defined territory and feed mainly on vegetable matter and some insects.

The female usually lays only 1 egg on the ground and incubates it herself.

Sunbittern

African Finfoot

Sungrebe

Kagu

Little Black Bustard
(male)

Red-legged Seriema

Great Bustard (male)

Jacanas, Plovers, Painted-snipes, Oystercatchers

ORDER CHARADRIIFORMES

This order contains over 300 species in 15 families grouped into 3 suborders. The first contains all the shorebirds, or waders, such as plovers, sandpipers and jacanas. In the second group are skuas, gulls and terns, and skimmers. The third suborder has a single family, the auks.

JACANIDAE: Jacana Family

The 8 species of jacana are all long-legged water birds found in tropical and subtropical areas worldwide. They have extraordinary feet which are an adaptation for their habit of moving over floating vegetation: their toes and claws are so exceedingly long that their weight is well distributed over a large surface area, and they are able actually to walk over precarious floating lily pads. Males and females look alike, but females are slightly larger.

NAME: **North American Jacana,** *Jacana spinosa*
RANGE: **Central America, Greater Antilles, USA: S. Texas**
HABITAT: **lakes, ponds**
SIZE: **25 cm (9¾ in)**

North American jacanas feed on insects and other aquatic life and on the seeds of water plants, all of which they take from the water surface or vegetation. They swim and dive well but fly slowly. A nest is made of aquatic plants, and the clutch of 3 to 5, usually 4, eggs is incubated by both parents for a total of 22 to 24 days.

CHARADRIIDAE: Plover Family

This family contains about 63 species of small to medium-sized, fairly plump wading birds. The typical plover has a short straight bill, round head and short legs. Males and females look alike or nearly so, but some species have seasonal differences in plumage.

NAME: **Lapwing,** *Vanellus vanellus*
RANGE: **Europe, W. and N. Africa, Asia**
HABITAT: **grassland, farmland**
SIZE: **30 cm (12 in)**

A distinctive bird with a crested head and broad rounded wings, the lapwing is also known as the peewit, after the cry it makes in flight. Lapwings feed mostly on insects but also on worms, snails and some plant matter. The male makes a ceremonial nest scrape to initiate breeding behavior in the female. She completes the nest and lays 3 to 5 eggs. The clutch is incubated for 24 to 31 days.

NAME: **American Golden Plover,** *Pluvialis dominica*
RANGE: **N. America, Asia; winters in South America, Hawaii and other Pacific islands, Australia, New Zealand, S. Asia**
HABITAT: **marshes, fields, open country**
SIZE: **23–28 cm (9–11 in)**

One of the champion long-distance migratory birds, this plover flies to wintering grounds 12,800 km (8,000 mi) south of its breeding grounds on the tundra of North America and Siberia.

American golden plovers feed on insects and some mollusks and crustaceans. They lay 3 or 4 eggs in a shallow dip in the tundra, lined with moss and grass. Both parents incubate, the male during the day and the female at night, for a total of 20 to 30 days. In winter this plover loses its distinctive facial markings, and its head and breast are a speckled golden color.

NAME: **Wrybill,** *Anarhynchus frontalis*
RANGE: **New Zealand**
HABITAT: **riverbeds, open country**
SIZE: **20 cm (8 in)**

The wrybill is a small plover with a unique bill, the tip of which turns to the right. To find its insect food, the wrybill tilts its head to the left and sweeps the tip of its bill over the mud with a horizontal scissoring action. Wrybills winter in North Island and travel to South Island to breed. They nest in large estuaries on a particular type of shingle, the stones of which are similar in color to the wrybill and its eggs, thus providing camouflage. The female lays 2 or 3 eggs among the shingle in October.

NAME: **Ringed Plover,** *Charadrius hiaticula* **(conspecific with Semi-palmated Plover)**
RANGE: **N. Europe, W. Asia, N. America**
HABITAT: **seashore**
SIZE: **19 cm (7½ in)**

A common northern shorebird, the ringed plover has distinctive head and breast markings in its summer plumage. It feeds on mollusks, insects, worms and some plants. The female lays 3 to 5 eggs and will defend eggs or young with a distraction display technique used by many plover species. If a predator approaches the nest, the parent bird flaps awkwardly away as if injured and unable to fly, all the time leading the enemy away from the young. Once the predator is well away from the nest, the plover flies up suddenly and escapes, to return to the nest later.

ROSTRATULIDAE: Painted-snipe Family

There are only 2 species in this family, one in the Old World and the other, the lesser painted-snipe, *Nycticryphes semicollaris*, in South America. It is an unusual family in that the normal sexual roles are reversed.

NAME: **Greater Painted-snipe,** *Rostratula benghalensis*
RANGE: **Africa, south of the Sahara; Madagascar, S. Asia, Australia**
HABITAT: **marshes**
SIZE: **24 cm (9½ in)**

The greater painted-snipe is a secretive crepuscular bird, rarely seen in the open. It feeds on insects, snails and worms, most of which it finds in muddy ground with its sensitive bill, and some plant matter.

The female bird is the showy partner, the male is smaller with brownish plumage. She performs an impressive courtship display, spreading her wings forward and expanding her tail to show the spots on the feathers. Females will fight over males. The male bird makes a pad of grass as a nest, and when the female has laid the 3 or 4 eggs, he incubates the clutch and cares for the young.

HAEMATOPODIDAE: Oystercatcher Family

Oystercatchers are large, noisy, coastal birds found throughout the world, except on oceanic islands and in polar regions. There is only 1 genus, with about 8 closely related species. There are only slight sexual and seasonal plumage differences.

NAME: **European Oystercatcher,** *Haematopus ostralegus*
RANGE: **virtually worldwide**
HABITAT: **coasts, estuaries**
SIZE: **46 cm (18 in)**

The European oystercatcher is by far the most widespread of its family, and there are several races. Like all oystercatchers, it has a long, blunt, flattened bill, which it uses to pry shellfish off rocks. Mollusks and crustaceans are its main food, but this bird has also learned to seek insects and worms on farmland farther inland.

Oystercatchers are gregarious birds and live and move in large flocks. Their nest is a hole in the ground, often lined with grass or decorated with moss. The female lays 2 to 4 eggs, and both partners incubate them for 24 to 27 days.

North American Jacana

Lapwing

Greater Painted-snipe
(female)

American Golden Plover
(summer plumage)

Wrybill

European
Oystercatcher

Ringed Plover
(summer plumage)

Sandpipers

NAME: **Whimbrel,** *Numenius phaeopus*
RANGE: **breeds in Canada, Alaska, Asia, N. Europe; winters in S. America, Africa, S.E. Asia, Australasia**
HABITAT: **breeds on moors, tundra; winters on muddy and sandy shores, estuaries, marshes**
SIZE: **40 cm (15¾ in)**

One of the group of birds known as curlews, the whimbrel has a distinctively striped crown and a long, curving bill. It feeds on small invertebrates, including crabs, which it often partially dismembers before swallowing. In spring and summer, it eats many insects, and berries are also an important food.

Whimbrels breed in subarctic and subalpine tundra and arrive at breeding grounds in the spring, often returning to the same territory year after year. As the snows disperse, males begin their courtship displays. The nest is made on the ground, usually in the open, and the female bird lays 4 eggs, which are incubated for 27 or 28 days by both parents. Once the chicks are fully fledged, at 5 or 6 weeks, the adults leave almost immediately, starting the migration south to wintering areas. The young birds follow a few weeks later.

NAME: **American Woodcock,** *Scolopax minor*
RANGE: **N. America: breeds from Manitoba to Louisiana and Florida; winters from southern part of breeding range to Gulf Coast**
HABITAT: **woodland, young forest**
SIZE: **28 cm (11 in)**

Woodcocks are inland wood and forest birds, far less aquatic than most others of their family. The American woodcock is a shy, secretive bird, with a long bill, rounded wings and chunky body. It finds its food by probing the soil with its slender bill, the tip of which is very flexible and can be opened under the soil. It prefers areas with low, shrubby vegetation where there are plenty of earthworms, for they constitute two-thirds of its total intake, although it also feeds on beetle and fly larvae.

Males generally arrive at breeding grounds in March and April, slightly before females, in order to establish display territories that are sufficiently large to allow their courtship flights. Females are attracted to the display area by the males' calls, and a male will mate with several females. The female bird makes a nest under a small tree or bush and lays 4 eggs. She incubates the clutch for 21 days, leaving the nest only once a day at dusk to feed. Chicks are almost fully grown at about 4 weeks. If a woodcock's chicks are in danger, the mother can take them, one at a time, between her legs and fly to a safe refuge.

SCOLOPACIDAE:
Sandpiper Family

There are about 82 species in this, the most diverse of all the families in the Charadriiformes order. Under a wide range of common names, such as sandpiper, curlew, turnstone, snipe, woodcock and redshank, species are found worldwide, on every continent and on almost every island of any size. Most species are ground-living wading birds that find much of their food in water. Males and females generally look alike, but some species develop special breeding plumage.

NAME: **Redshank,** *Tringa totanus*
RANGE: **breeds in Europe, N. USSR; winters in S. Europe, N. Africa, S. Asia**
HABITAT: **breeds on moorland, marshes; winters on mud flats, meadows, estuaries, shores**
SIZE: **28 cm (11 in)**

An abundant and widespread sandpiper, the redshank adapts well to almost any habitat near water. The bright red legs identify this species immediately; it also has dark stripes on head and neck, which become paler in winter. Insects predominate in its diet, but it also eats mollusks and crustaceans.

Redshanks arrive at breeding grounds between March and May and pair off after courtship displays. The 4 eggs are laid in a cup-shaped nest on the ground and are incubated for 23 days.

NAME: **Common Snipe,** *Gallinago gallinago*
RANGE: **breeds in Canada, N. USA, Europe to N.E. Asia; winters in Central and South America, Africa, India, Indonesia**
HABITAT: **marshes, wet meadows, moors**
SIZE: **25.5 cm (10 in)**

A shy, secretive bird, the common snipe has rather pointed wings, a long bill and striped and barred plumage, which provides effective camouflage among vegetation. Insects, particularly fly and beetle larvae, are the snipe's most important food items, but it also eats earthworms, small crustaceans, snails and small quantities of plant material.

Males arrive at breeding grounds before females and establish territories for display. In the most common display, the male dives through the air at great speed, causing a drumming sound as air rushes through his outer tail feathers. The nest is made on dry ground when possible and near clumps of grass, which the birds pull down over it. The 3 or 4 eggs are incubated for 17 to 19 days, usually by the female alone.

NAME: **Ruff,** *Philomachus pugnax*
RANGE: **breeds in N. Europe, Asia; winters in Europe, Africa, S. Asia**
HABITAT: **tundra, grassland, marshes**
SIZE: **23–30.5 cm (9–12 in)**

Male ruffs perform complex communal displays to attract mates. In the breeding season, males develop large frills of feathers around their heads and necks and gather at a traditional display ground, called a lek; there is great individual variation in the color of frills. Each older, dominant male holds an area within the lek and may be attended by several males, who must display with him and pay court to him in the hope of a chance to mate with one of his females.

Once mated, the female bird, called a "reeve," leaves the display ground and makes a nest in long grass. She incubates her 4 eggs for 20 to 23 days.

NAME: **Ruddy Turnstone,** *Arenaria interpres*
RANGE: **circumpolar: breeds on arctic coasts; winters south of breeding range**
HABITAT: **breeds on marshes, tundra; winters on rocky shores**
SIZE: **18–23 cm (7–9 in)**

In the breeding season, the turnstone has bold black, white and reddish-brown markings, which become duller in winter. Insects, particularly midges, and some plant material are its main food in summer, but in winter it forages on seashores, turning over stones and other debris with its bill to find mollusks, crustaceans and even carrion.

Breeding birds arrive from wintering areas in late May or early June. The 4 eggs are laid in a grass-lined hollow on the ground and incubated by both parents for 21 to 23 days.

NAME: **Red Phalarope,** *Phalaropus fulicarius*
RANGE: **breeds in N. America: Alaska to Hudson Bay and arctic islands; winters off W. Africa and Chile**
HABITAT: **breeds in tundra and wet meadows; winters at sea**
SIZE: **18 cm (7 in)**

The only swimming bird in its family, the toes of the phalarope are adapted for swimming, having flattened fringing scales, and it comes ashore only to breed. The female is the brightly colored sex in this species, with her breeding plumage of reddish throat and underparts, while the male is smaller and duller. In winter both sexes have grayish plumage. Phalaropes feed on beetles, flies, crustaceans and small fish.

Normal sexual roles are reversed in phalaropes, and the showy female takes the initiative in courtship and mating. The male incubates the 4 eggs for about 19 days and cares for the young.

Ruddy Turnstone (breeding plumage)

Whimbrel

Redshank

Common Snipe

Ruff (variations in male breeding plumage)

Red Phalarope
(female in breeding plumage)

American Woodcock

Avocets, Crab Plover, Thick-knees

IBIDORHYNCHIDAE: Ibisbill Family

The ibisbill, the single species in this family, differs from the avocets and stilts, with which it is sometimes grouped, both in its northerly, high-altitude habitat and in its downward-curving bill.

NAME: **Ibisbill,** *Ibidorhyncha struthersii*
RANGE: **high plateaus of central Asia; Himalayas**
HABITAT: **shingle banks, shingle islands in mountain streams**
SIZE: **38 cm (15 in)**

The ibisbill uses its down-curving bill to probe for food under stones in the shingly riverbeds it frequents. It often wades into the water and submerges its head and neck. Small groups of ibisbills generally live and feed together. The female bird lays 4 large eggs in a ground nest, and the clutch is incubated by both parents.

RECURVIROSTRIDAE: Avocet Family

This family includes 13 species of long-billed, long-legged wading birds, which are found throughout much of the world, except in northernmost regions. These birds fly and sometimes swim well and generally live near water. Their feet are usually at least slightly webbed. Aquatic insects, mollusks, fish, frogs and some plant matter are the main items of their diet. Many species have black and white plumage, and male and female look more or less alike.

NAME: **Black-winged Stilt,** *Himantopus himantopus*
RANGE: **Old World, to about 50°N**
HABITAT: **mainly freshwater swamps, marshes, lagoons**
SIZE: **38 cm (15 in)**

This distinctive stilt has long pink legs, longer in proportion to its body size than those of any bird except the flamingo; in flight, its legs project far beyond the tail. Stilts walk quickly, taking long strides, and wade into water to pick insects and small aquatic animals off vegetation and off the water surface. The long slender bill is ideally adapted for this purpose.

Colonies of stilts nest together near water. Some nests are substantial structures, built up in shallow water from sticks and mud; others are small flimsy ground nests. Between April and June the female lays 3 to 5 eggs, which both parents incubate for 26 days. The young leave the nest soon after hatching.

NAME: **Avocet,** *Recurvirostra avosetta*
RANGE: **Europe, W. and central Asia; northern populations winter in W. Africa and S. Asia**
HABITAT: **mud flats, estuaries, sandbanks**
SIZE: **42 cm (16½ in)**

An unmistakable bird, the avocet has striking black and white plumage and a long bill that curves upward. In flight, the long legs usually project beyond the tail. Avocets feed on insects, small aquatic animals and some plant matter, all of which they find by sweeping their bills from side to side at the surface of mud or shallow water. In deeper water, the avocet dips its head below the surface and will swim and up-end like a duck.

Avocets breed colonially; pairs mating after displays involving both partners. The nest is usually a simple scrape near water in which the female lays 3 to 5 eggs. Both parents incubate the eggs and later guard their chicks against predators. Juveniles have some brownish plumage but are otherwise similar to adults. The American avocet, *R. americana*, resembles this avocet, but has cinnamon plumage on head, neck and breast during the breeding season.

DROMADIDAE: Crab Plover Family

The sole species in this family, the crab plover may be related to stone curlews and thick-knees, which it resembles to some degree. However, the bird has several unique features, so it is at present placed in its own family. Female crab plovers are slightly smaller than males and have shorter black feathers.

NAME: **Crab Plover,** *Dromas ardeola*
RANGE: **breeds on islands from E. Africa to the Persian Gulf; winters on coasts and islands of the W. Indian Ocean**
HABITAT: **estuaries, reefs**
SIZE: **38 cm (15 in)**

A stocky bird with a heavy, compressed bill, the crab plover flies strongly and runs swiftly. Its black and white markings are striking and distinct in flight; the legs are long and the toes are partially webbed. Crabs are, indeed, the main item of its diet, but it also feeds on other crustaceans and on mollusks, which it breaks open with its strong, pointed bill. Crab plovers are noisy, gregarious birds and they nest in colonies. The female lays her single egg at the end of a burrow in a sandbank, often in a crab burrow. Although it is able to run around soon after hatching, the chick is cared for by both parents and fed in the burrow.

BURHINIDAE: Thick-knee Family

The 9 species in this family have a variety of common names, such as thick-knee, stone curlew and dikkop, and all have characteristic thickened joints between tarsus and shin. These birds are ploverlike in appearance but also resemble the bustards, Otididae, in some respects. They have three toes only on each foot, and these are partially webbed. Thick-knees are active at dusk and at night, and their unusually large yellow eyes are an adaptation for nocturnal activity. Male and female birds look alike. The family is widely distributed in the Old World, and there are 2 species in Central and South America.

NAME: **Great Shore Plover,** *Esacus magnirostris*
RANGE: **India, Sri Lanka; Australia and New Caledonia**
HABITAT: **coasts and rivers**
SIZE: **50 cm (19¾ in)**

A sturdy, large-headed bird, this thick-knee has a strong, slightly upturned bill and large yellow eyes. It feeds mostly at night on insects, worms, mollusks and crustaceans, and on some small vertebrate animals. Like all thick-knees, it runs fast, but in short dashes, and is a reluctant but strong flier. To avoid danger, it may crouch down or even flatten itself on the ground, head and neck outstretched.

In the breeding season, the great shore plover lays 2, or sometimes 3, eggs in a shallow hollow in the ground; these are incubated by the female, with some assistance from the male. Both parents care for the chicks which are, however, able to fend for themselves almost immediately.

NAME: **Stone Curlew,** *Burhinus oedicnemus*
RANGE: **S. England, Europe, N. Africa, S.W. Asia; winters to the south of its range**
HABITAT: **open country, heath, farmland**
SIZE: **41 cm (16 in)**

Although only some populations migrate, the stone curlew is nevertheless the only migratory thick-knee, northern birds wintering in East Africa. Like all its family, the stone curlew's plumage blends well with its surroundings, providing camouflage, but it has two bold wing bars which are conspicuous in flight. Its bill is short and straight, and it feeds mainly on invertebrates and on snails and worms. The female lays her 2 eggs on the ground in a hollow and incubates them with some assistance from her mate.

Avocet

Crab Plover

Black-winged Stilt

Great Shore Plover

Ibisbill

Stone Curlew

Pratincoles, Seedsnipes, Sheathbills

GLAREOLIDAE: Pratincole Family

This family contains 16 species: pratincoles, coursers and the Egyptian plover. All are fairly small, ploverlike birds with sharply pointed bills. The pratincoles and coursers differ in some general respects: the former have short beaks, narrow, pointed wings, forked tails, short legs and feet with four toes; the latter have longer bills, broader wings and tails and longer legs with three-toed feet (they have no hind toes). Birds of both groups feed on insects, mollusks, leeches, small lizards and seeds. The species occur in warmer areas of the Old World, including Australia. Males and females have similar plumage but may differ in size.

NAME: **Cream-colored Courser,**
Cursorius cursor
RANGE: **Africa, Canary and Cape Verde Islands; S.W. Asia, W. India**
HABITAT: **desert and semidesert**
SIZE: **23 cm (9 in)**

A slender, pale-plumaged bird with distinctive eye stripes, the cream-colored courser merges well with its desert surroundings. Although its flight is rapid, it tends to run rather than fly, often crouching down on the ground between bursts of movement.

Cream-colored coursers do not make regular migrations but do wander out of their range, often flying into Europe, although they do not breed there. The female lays 2 or 3 eggs on the ground, on sand or rock. She incubates the eggs at night, when the desert temperature drops, but may need to stand above them during the day to shield them from the sun.

NAME: **Egyptian Plover, Pluvianus**
aegyptius
RANGE: **N.E., W. and W. central Africa**
HABITAT: **shores and sandbanks of rivers and lakes**
SIZE: **20 cm (7¾ in)**

The Egyptian plover differs, in its more striking plumage and rather short legs, from the coursers, with which it belongs. It is usually found near water, and for centuries has been known as the crocodile bird because of the belief that it will feed on the debris and food particles remaining in the mouth of a basking crocodile. This behavior is unconfirmed, although the bird does often feed near crocodiles and on their body parasites; its main food is insects.

The female Egyptian plover lays 2 or 3 eggs, which it covers lightly with sand while they incubate; it will also cover chicks temporarily, to hide them from potential danger.

NAME: **Collared Pratincole, Glareola**
pratincola
RANGE: **S. Europe, S.W. Asia, Africa**
HABITAT: **open land, sun-baked mud flats, freshwater banks**
SIZE: **25 cm (9¾ in)**

The collared pratincole, with its deeply forked tail, is ternlike in its swift, agile flight, but can run easily on the ground like a plover. It has a characteristic creamy, black-bordered throat, but the border is less distinct in winter. Pratincoles are gregarious birds, and flocks gather at dusk to feed on insects which they chase and catch in the air, often in the vicinity of water.

They breed in colonies of anything from a few pairs to hundreds of birds and generally nest after the rainy or flood season in their area. Their 2 to 4 eggs are laid on the ground and are well camouflaged by their blotched, neutral coloration, which blends with the background, whether soil, sand or rock. Both parents incubate the eggs for a total of 17 or 18 days. The young are able to run around immediately after hatching. After breeding, European collared pratincoles migrate to Africa, south of the Sahara.

THINOCORIDAE:
Seedsnipe Family

The 4 species of seedsnipe all live in South America. The common name derives from the fact that all are seed-eating birds that have the rapid zigzagging flight of the snipes.

Seedsnipes are rounded, ground-feeding birds which range in size from 17 to 28 cm (6¾ to 11 in). The wings are long and pointed, the tail short and the bill strong and conical. The plumage is cryptic and partridgelike, and males and females show some differences in plumage.

NAME: **Least Seedsnipe, Thinocorus**
rumicivorus
RANGE: **Andes: Ecuador to Tierra del Fuego; east to Patagonia and Uruguay; Falkland Islands**
HABITAT: **dry plains, coastal and inland**
SIZE: **17 cm (6¾ in)**

The smallest of the seedsnipes, the least seedsnipe has the mottled, camouflaging plumage typical of its family; male birds have black markings which give a "necktie" effect. Primarily a ground-living bird, it can run rapidly, despite its short legs, and it blends so well with its surroundings that, if threatened, it will remain still and almost invisible, taking to the air at only the last minute.

The nesting season varies according to latitude. The 4 eggs are laid on the ground in a shallow hollow and are incubated by the female. If she has to leave the eggs for a time, she will half bury them in the sand. The young are able to run around soon after hatching.

CHIONIDIDAE: Sheathbill Family

The 2 species of sheathbill are medium-sized — 35.5 to 43 cm (14 to 17 in) — white-plumaged, shore-living birds, found on the islands of the far southern oceans. They are squat and heavy-bodied, resembling pigeons in build, and have a comblike covering over the upper beak which gives them their common name. Their legs are short and stocky and their feet powerful. Male and female sheathbills look alike, but females are usually smaller.

Ornithologists consider the sheathbills to resemble the common ancestors of the gulls and waders and to be a link between the two families.

NAME: **Snowy/Yellow-billed Sheathbill,**
Chionis alba
RANGE: **subantarctic islands of the S. Atlantic Ocean, extending to Graham Land and southern South America when not breeding.**
HABITAT: **coasts**
SIZE: **39 cm (15¼ in)**

Snowy sheathbills are gregarious and pugnacious birds, and except during the breeding season, they live in small flocks, feeding together and often fighting. Although they fly well and will make long journeys, even over sea, they spend most of their time on the ground. They swim well although their feet have only rudimentary webs. Sheathbills are avid scavengers and haunt seal and penguin colonies to seize afterbirths or weak young. They also search the shore for all kinds of fish, invertebrates, carcasses and almost any other debris that they can eat. They consume quantities of seaweed for the invertebrates that it harbors.

Sheathbills nest in isolated pairs in a crevice or among rocks. The 2 or 3 eggs are laid on feathers, seaweed and other soft material. Both male and female incubate the eggs for a total of 28 days, but it seems as if only 1 chick is actually reared as a general rule.

In winter, sheathbills in the extreme south of the range migrate north, but those on subantarctic islands usually remain there. The other species in this family, the black-billed sheathbill, C. minor, occurs in the subantarctic sector of the Indian Ocean.

Collared P. tincole

Cream-colored Courser

Snowy Sheathbill

Egyptian Plover

Least Seedsnipe (male)

Skuas, Gulls, Skimmers

STERCORARIIDAE: Skua Family

There are about 5 species of skua, or jaeger, as some are called in North America. They are dark-plumaged, gull-like seabirds, characterized by their piratical method of obtaining food: they chase other seabirds, such as gulls and terns, in the air and force them to disgorge their prey. Males and females are outwardly alike, but the females are sometimes larger.

NAME: Skua, *Catharacta skua*
RANGE: N. Atlantic Ocean: Iceland, Faeroes, Shetland and Orkney Islands; winters as far south as the Tropic of Cancer
HABITAT: oceanic, coastal waters
SIZE: 51–56 cm (20–22 in)

A strongly built bird with a hooked bill and sharply curved claws, the skua not only attacks other birds to steal their prey but also kills and eats ducks and gulls and preys on eggs and young at breeding grounds. It also follows ships to feed on scraps thrown overboard and takes carrion.

An otherwise solitary bird, it nests in colonies. A shallow scrape is made on a rocky slope or at the foot of a cliff, and 1 to 3 eggs, usually 2, are laid. Both partners incubate the eggs for 26 to 29 days and care for the chicks.

LARIDAE: Gull Family

This family of about 90 species of white seabird with black or gray markings is distributed worldwide. The family divides into two distinct groups: gulls and terns. Gulls are the classic shoreline birds; they seldom dive and few species catch fish. Powerfully built, with heavy bills and bodies, they have long wings which are broader and blunter than those of the terns. Terns are smaller, graceful birds, often with deeply forked tails. They dive for fish, and most species also catch insects in the air or on the water.

NAME: Ivory Gull, *Pagophila eburnea*
RANGE: Arctic coasts and islands; winters among ice floes, sometimes south of the Arctic Circle
HABITAT: coasts, pack ice
SIZE: 35.5–43 cm (14–17 in)

The only gull with all-white plumage, the ivory gull is a striking, plump-bodied bird with black legs. It seldom swims but can run over ice. It feeds on fish and invertebrates and scavenges on carrion and refuse. It breeds in colonies and lays 2 eggs on the ground or on a cliff ledge.

NAME: Herring Gull, *Larus argentatus*
RANGE: most of northern hemisphere
HABITAT: coasts, estuaries; inland water and fields
SIZE: 55–66 cm (21½–26 in)

The commonest coastal gull in North America and Europe, the herring gull feeds on small surface fish, scavenges on waste and sewage, steals eggs and preys on young birds and small mammals. It also flies inland to feed on worms and other invertebrates.

Herring gulls nest in colonies on cliff slopes, islands or beaches. The nest is usually made of weeds and grass in a hollow in the ground or is sometimes built in a tree or even on a building. The 2 or 3 eggs are incubated for 25 to 27 days by both parents. In their first year, the young have dark-brown plumage, and they do not attain full adult plumage for 3 years. Male and female adult birds look alike, but males are often larger.

NAME: Black-headed Gull, *Larus ridibundus*
RANGE: Iceland, N. Europe and Asia; winters south of range to N. Africa, S. Asia and Philippines
HABITAT: coasts, inland marshes
SIZE: 35.5–38 cm (14–15 in)

A small, active gull, the black-headed gull is often seen inland in winter (when it is not black-headed), and thrives in freshwater habitats, where it feeds on insects and invertebrates. It scavenges, especially at refuse dumps, and also feeds on the coast like other gulls.

Black-headed gulls breed colonially on marshes, moors and coasts in the spring. A pair builds a nest, usually on the ground and made of plant material, and the female lays 3 eggs, which are incubated for 20 to 24 days.

NAME: Black-legged Kittiwake, *Rissa tridactyla*
RANGE: N. Pacific, N. Atlantic Oceans, parts of Arctic Ocean
HABITAT: oceanic
SIZE: 41–46 cm (16–18 in)

This kittiwake is much more oceanic in its habits than the *Larus* gulls and normally comes ashore only to breed. It seldom walks, so its legs are much shorter than those of most gulls, and it has only three toes on each foot. It feeds on fish, small mollusks and crustaceans and also scavenges the waste dumped from fishing boats.

These kittiwakes nest in huge colonies of thousands of birds, normally on high cliffs. A pair builds a nest from plants, seaweed and guano, cementing it to the cliff ledge with mud. The usual clutch is 2 eggs, which are incubated for 23 to 32 days by both parents.

NAME: Common Tern, *Sterna hirundo*
RANGE: eastern N. America, N. Europe, Asia; winters south of range to the tropics
HABITAT: coastal islands, coasts; inland rivers and lakes
SIZE: 33–41 cm (13–16 in)

A common and widespread coastal bird, the common tern feeds on small fish and other marine creatures, which it catches by hovering over the prey and then diving rapidly into the water to seize it with its bill.

Terns nest in colonies of hundreds of thousands on isolated beaches, islands or cliffs. A pair scrapes a hollow in the ground which is then lined with vegetation. Both parents take turns, incubating the 2 or 3 eggs for 21 to 26 days.

NAME: Brown Noddy, *Anous stolidus*
RANGE: tropical oceans
HABITAT: offshore waters, islands
SIZE: 41–43 cm (16–17 in)

The 5 species of noddy tern are all birds of tropical seas. The noddy seldom dives, but will float on the surface of the water or perch on buoys, driftwood or reefs, watching for prey. It often flies just above the water and snatches small fish when they are driven to the surface by larger fish.

Brown noddies make their untidy twig nests in bushes or on the ground. Both parents incubate the single egg.

RYNCHOPIDAE: Skimmer Family

There are 3 species of skimmer: 2 are tropical freshwater birds; the third, from the Americas, is coastal in its habits. Skimmers have eyes with slitlike pupils, unique among birds.

NAME: Black Skimmer, *Rynchops niger*
RANGE: USA; winters in S. USA, Central and South America
HABITAT: coastal waters, rivers and lakes with sandbanks
SIZE: 41–51 cm (16–20 in)

Skimmers possess a unique structural modification: the lower half of the bill, which is laterally flattened and considerably longer than the upper half, is an adaptation for a special method of fishing. The skimmer flies just above a smooth water surface, with its bladelike lower bill cleaving a straight furrow through the water. When the bill strikes a small fish or crustacean, the skimmer clamps down its upper bill and pulls its head back to swallow the prey, while continuing to fly.

Black skimmers breed in spring in colonies of as many as 200 pairs. They scrape hollows in the sand, and the female lays 2 to 4 eggs.

Skua (arctic form)

Black-legged Kittiwake

Ivory Gull

Herring Gull

Common Tern

Black-headed Gull
(breeding plumage)

Brown Noddy

Black Skimmer

Auks

NAME: **Common Murre,** *Uria aalge*
RANGE: **N. Atlantic, N. Pacific Oceans**
HABITAT: **offshore waters, oceanic**
SIZE: **41–43 cm (16–17 in)**

One of the most common species in this family, the common murre has a longer, narrower bill than is usual for auks and a less bulky body. In breeding plumage, the head, neck and upperparts are dark brown, but in winter, the throat and front and sides of face and neck are white, with dark stripes extending back from the eyes. These birds feed on fish, mollusks and worms which they catch underwater.

At the end of May, colonies of birds gather in breeding areas on top of rocks or on cliffs. Each female lays 1 egg on bare rock; the egg is pear-shaped, and this led to the long-held belief that, if it moves, it rolls around in a circle, rather than off the ledge. However, this is probably not so, and the reason why the egg is this shape may well be related to its large size and the narrow pelvis of the mother bird. The eggs vary enormously in color and pattern, and this may help the birds to recognize their own eggs in the crowded breeding colony. Both parents incubate the egg for 28 to 30 days. In winter, the birds migrate south of their normal breeding range.

NAME: **Common Puffin,** *Fratercula arctica*
RANGE: **N. Atlantic Ocean: arctic coasts of eastern N. America and W. Eurasia**
HABITAT: **open sea, rocky coasts**
SIZE: **29–36 cm (11½–14¼ in)**

A small, round-bodied auk with a large head, the common puffin has a spectacular striped bill, which it uses to catch food and in display. In summer, the puffin's bill is colorful, the upper parts of the body and collar are black and the underparts white. In winter, the face is grayish and the bill smaller and duller. Young birds resemble adults in winter plumage, but have smaller, darker bills. The puffin feeds on fish and shellfish and can carry several items at a time in its capacious bill as it flies back to its nest. Its flight is strong and fast, but, like all auks, it has short legs set well back on the body and waddles along clumsily on land.

Common puffins breed from late May in colonies on turfed cliff tops or on islands. The female lays 1 egg, rarely 2, in a burrow abandoned by a shearwater or rabbit or in a hole which she digs herself with her feet. Both parents incubate the egg for 40 to 43 days. After breeding, most puffins winter at sea, offshore from the breeding range, but some populations migrate southward.

ALCIDAE: Auk Family

The auks are a small family of short-tailed, short-necked diving seabirds, found in the North Pacific, North Atlantic and Arctic oceans and along their coasts. They are truly marine birds, only coming to land to breed on coasts. The 22 species include the guillemots, razorbills, auklets, puffins, murres and auks. All have dark-brown or black plumage, usually with white underparts. Auks swim well and dive from the surface to pursue prey underwater, propelling themselves with their short, narrow wings. They stand upright on land, and this, combined with their general body shape and marine habits, makes them the northern equivalents of the penguins, found in the southern hemisphere.

Indeed, the name penguin was first applied by early mariners to the largest member of the family, the great auk; it was only later used for the similarly adapted birds we know today as penguins. The great auk was flightless, its short, powerful wings of use only for underwater propulsion. Because of this it could not easily escape from man, so great auks were constantly slaughtered for food and have now been extinct for more than a century.

Auks are not, however, closely related to penguins: the resemblance is an example of two groups of birds adapting in a similar way to fill the same niche in northern and southern hemispheres.

Gregarious birds, auks nest in colonies of hundreds or even thousands of birds on cliff tops and rocks. They fly fast, with rapid wing beats, but some of the small species are better adapted for swimming than flying. Some species migrate south of the normal range in winter. Males and females look alike, but there are some seasonal plumage changes. In their annual molt, most species lose all the flight feathers at once and are temporarily flightless.

NAME: **Crested Auklet,** *Aethia cristatella*
RANGE: **N. Pacific Ocean, Bering Sea**
HABITAT: **ocean, sea cliffs**
SIZE: **24–27 cm (9½–10½ in)**

In the breeding season, the crested auklet has a dark crest of long plumes that fall forward over its bright bill and white plumes behind the eyes. In winter, the crest and eye plumes are smaller, and the bill a dull yellow. Young birds have no crests. These small auklets feed mainly on crustaceans.

Colonies of crested auklets gather on cliffs to breed, and the female lays 1 egg in a rock crevice or among stones.

NAME: **Razorbill,** *Alca torda*
RANGE: **N. Atlantic Ocean**
HABITAT: **coasts, open sea**
SIZE: **40–42 cm (15¾–16½ in)**

A well-built auk, with a heavy head and a thick neck, the razorbill has a stout, compressed bill with distinctive white markings. In summer, the razorbill's head, neck and upper parts are black, with prominent white lines from bill to eyes. In winter, the cheeks and forehead are white. Razorbills feed on fish, crustaceans and mollusks.

Colonies of razorbills nest on sea cliffs and rocky shores on the Atlantic coasts of Europe and North America, often near guillemot colonies. The breeding season starts about mid-May, and the female lays 1 egg, rarely 2, in a hole or crevice. Both parents incubate the egg for about 25 days, and the young leaves the nest after about 15 days.

NAME: **Dovekie,** *Alle alle*
RANGE: **Arctic Ocean; winters in N. Atlantic Ocean**
HABITAT: **coasts, open sea**
SIZE: **20 cm (7¾ in)**

The smallest auk, the dovekie is a squat, rounded bird, with a short thick neck and a stout, strong bill. In winter the throat and breast, which are dark in summer plumage, become white. The dovekie feeds on crustaceans, small fish and mollusks. An excellent swimmer, it dives rapidly if alarmed.

From mid-June, thousands of dovekies gather in crowded colonies on arctic coasts and cliffs. They do not make nests, and the female lays 1 egg, occasionally 2, in a crack in the rock. Both sexes take turns to incubate the egg for 24 to 30 days. Dovekies spend the winter at sea, moving as far south as Iceland and Norway. They may even appear inland in particularly bad weather. This species occurs in vast numbers in its arctic habitat and is believed to be one of the most abundant birds in the world.

NAME: **Marbled Murrelet,** *Brachyramphus marmoratus*
RANGE: **N. Pacific Ocean**
HABITAT: **coasts, islands**
SIZE: **24–25 cm (9½–9¾ in)**

In the breeding season, the marbled murrelet has distinctly barred and speckled underparts, which become white in winter. It feeds, like the rest of the auks, on fish and other marine animals and, when on water, holds its slender bill and tail pointing upward.

Unusually for an auk, it flies inland to breed in mountains or forest areas and lays 1 egg on a twig platform, on moss, or in a nest abandoned by another species of bird.

Common Murre (breeding plumage)

Razorbill (breeding plumage)

Common Puffin
(breeding plumage)

Dovekie
(breeding plumage)

Marbled Murrelet
(breeding plumage)

Crested Auklet
(breeding plumage)

Sandgrouse, Pigeons

ORDER COLUMBIFORMES

This order includes 2 living families — the sandgrouse and the pigeons — and the now extinct dodo family.

PTEROCLIDIDAE: Sandgrouse Family

The 16 species of sandgrouse are all terrestrial birds, found in south Europe, Asia and Africa. Despite their name, they are not related to grouse. Sandgrouse are sturdy birds, with short necks, small heads and long, pointed wings; their legs are short and they cannot run but move fast with a waddling gait. Most are sandy colored, with many spotted and barred feathers, which provide good camouflage in the deserts and open plains in which they live. Females are usually smaller than males.

NAME: Pallas's Sandgrouse, *Syrrhaptes paradoxus*
RANGE: central Asia, S. Siberia, S. Mongolia to N. China
HABITAT: high-altitude semidesert, steppe
SIZE: 35–40 cm (13¾–15¾ in)

Pallas's sandgrouse is a rounded, short-legged bird about the size of a small pigeon. The central tail and outer wing feathers are long and pointed, an indication that it is a strong, fast flier. It is distinguished from other sandgrouse by the black patch on the belly. Adults feed on hard seeds and shoots of desert plants and also take much hard grit.

These sandgrouse nest in large colonies from April to June, laying 3 or 4 eggs in a scrape on the ground. Both parents incubate the eggs for 22 to 27 days and feed the young by regurgitation. There are probably two or three clutches a year.

COLUMBIDAE: Pigeon Family

There are about 295 species of pigeon and dove, found in most parts of the world except the Antarctic and some oceanic islands. The greatest variety occurs in Asia and Australasia, where there are many extremely beautiful species. The name "pigeon" is generally used to describe larger birds in the family, while "dove" is applied to smaller forms, but there are exceptions to this rule, such as the rock dove, which is pigeonlike in every way.

Pigeons and doves vary in size from birds about the size of a sparrow to a few almost as large as a turkey. Most have dense, soft plumage, rounded, compact bodies and relatively small heads. Male and female look alike in most species, but in a few birds, the male has more

striking plumage. Both share an unusual reproductive feature: the lining of the crop secretes "pigeon milk," with which they feed their young for the first few days. This nutritious fluid is high in protein and fats and smells like cheese. Pigeons and doves generally lay only 1 or 2 eggs in a flimsy, but effective, nest, made of sticks.

Many pigeons and doves spend much of their lives in and around trees, feeding on seeds, fruit, buds and other plant material. Others are ground-dwelling but have much the same diet. Pigeons and doves are strong fliers, with excellent homing abilities.

NAME: Ground Dove, *Columbina passerina*
RANGE: S. USA; Mexico, south to central Ecuador, N. Brazil; West Indies
HABITAT: open scrub, cultivated land
SIZE: 15–17 cm (6–6¾ in)

These tiny, ground-living doves walk about briskly in pairs or small groups, with heads nodding, picking up seeds, waste grain, insects and small berries and even scraps of human food. The ground dove is a plump, compact bird with a short, broad tail and rounded wings. The female is much duller than the male.

Mating takes place from February to October over the range. The male courts the female on the ground, pursuing her with his expanded neck bobbing in time to his monotonous cooing. A flimsy nest is made in a low bush or tree or on the ground, and 2 eggs are laid. They are incubated by both parents for 13 or 14 days.

NAME: Rock Dove/Pigeon, *Columba livia*
RANGE: islands and coasts of W. Britain, countries bordering Mediterranean; E. Europe, east to India and Sri Lanka
HABITAT: sea and inland cliffs; fields
SIZE: 33–35.5 cm (13–14 in)

This species is the ancestor of all the domestic pigeons, including the homing pigeon, and of the feral pigeons (wild birds descended from birds bred in captivity) found in towns almost worldwide. Rock doves generally move in pairs or small groups, although large flocks are quite frequent. They feed on open ground, mainly on seeds, especially cultivated grains, but also on grasses, snails and other mollusks.

Mating takes place throughout the year, after much bowing, nodding, billing and cooing. The nest is flimsily made of twigs and grass on a sheltered cliff ledge or in a hole in a cliff, building or, occasionally, a tree. Two eggs are laid, which are incubated for 17 or 18 days.

NAME: Band-tailed Pigeon, *Columba fasciata*
RANGE: western N. America, south to Mexico; Central America, Colombia
HABITAT: coniferous forest, oak woodland in mountainous areas
SIZE: 36–39 cm (14¼–15¼ in)

This is a heavily built pigeon. The tail, which is notable in flight and gives the bird its common name, is distinctly banded, with a pale end, a dark band across the middle and a blue-gray base. The band-tailed pigeon flies strongly and swiftly and spends much time perching in trees, where it also seeks most of its food: nuts, berries, seeds, buds and blossoms. It also eats grasshoppers and other insects and, in the autumn, gorges on acorns.

Depending on area, the pigeons mate from March to September, and the female lays 1 egg, occasionally 2, which both parents incubate for 18 to 20 days.

NAME: Mourning Dove, *Zenaida macroura*
RANGE: temperate areas in Canada; USA: all states; Mexico, Bahamas, Cuba, Hispaniola
HABITAT: woodland, grain fields with trees, semidesert, suburbs
SIZE: 28–33 cm (11–13 in)

The mourning dove has short legs, a rounded body, a neat head and a thin, delicate-looking bill. The central tail feathers are very long in the male, and the wings are long and pointed. The birds generally move in pairs or small groups, but large numbers may gather at feeding grounds. Ground-living birds, they eat mainly weed seeds or grain spilled in harvesting but also take snails and other invertebrates.

The common name derives from the sweet, melancholy cooing of the male, which is followed by a courtship flight. Mating begins in January in the south of the range to April in the north. The nest is loosely constructed of twigs in a tree or bush, a roof gutter or chimney corner or even on the ground. The female lays 2 eggs, which are incubated by both birds for 14 or 15 days.

NAME: Blue-headed Quail-dove, *Starnoenas cyanocephala*
RANGE: Cuba, formerly Jamaica
HABITAT: lowland forest and shrubbery; locally highland forest
SIZE: 30.5–33 cm (12–13 in)

Numbers of this medium-sized dove are becoming fewer, owing to destruction of its habitat, and little is known about it. It feeds on the ground in areas where it can walk freely, taking mainly seeds, snails and berries. The nest is made low in a tree or shrub or on the ground, and usually 2 eggs are laid.

Pallas's Sandgrouse

Band-tailed Pigeon

Rock Dove

Mourning Dove (male)

Ground Dove (male)

Blue-headed Quail-dove

Pigeons

NAME: **Collared Dove,** *Streptopelia decaocto*
RANGE: **Ireland, Britain, W. Europe (not Spain, Portugal); India, Sri Lanka, Burma; introduced in Middle East, China, Japan.**
HABITAT: **towns, villages, farmland; arid scrubland, palm groves (in India)**
SIZE: **31.5 cm ($12\frac{1}{2}$ in)**

This species has enormously expanded its range over recent years by adapting to live in close association with man in both towns and countryside. It now breeds regularly in Great Britain and can be identified by its gray-brown coloration and by its proportionately long white-edged tail and dark primary feathers. Ground-feeding birds, collared doves feed chiefly on seeds, often spilled grain, but take also human food, berries and other plant material. In Europe, to the dismay of fruit-growers, they raid cherry orchards.

In India, these birds breed throughout the year, whenever food supplies are plentiful; in Europe, from March to October. The male makes frequent and showy display flights, rising up with clapping wings then gliding down, often in a spiral, with its wings and tail spread out. The scanty twig nest is made in a tree or bush or on a ledge on a building, and the female lays 2 eggs which are incubated for 14 to 16 days.

NAME: **Nicobar Pigeon,** *Caloenas nicobarica*
RANGE: **Andaman and Nicobar Islands, east to Philippines, New Guinea and Solomon Islands**
HABITAT: **small, off-lying wooded islands**
SIZE: **40 cm ($15\frac{3}{4}$ in)**

The Nicobar pigeon is quite a large bird, with long legs, a short white tail and heavy bill. Its stance is rather like that of a vulture, and unlike most pigeons, it has short, hard plumage, except on the neck, where the feathers are elongated to form hackles that cover most of the body. The female is slightly smaller than the male, with a smaller bill cere, and the juvenile looks like the female, but duller and without the white tail.

These birds are found throughout their range only on small islands and tiny islets off larger islands, but their flight is swift and strong and they wander freely between groups of islands. Little is known about their habits, but they appear to be ground feeders, feeding on seeds, fruit and some invertebrates, mainly at dusk, or by day in the gloom of the forest. The white tail and large eyes seem to be adaptations for this way of life.

Nicobar pigeons may nest in large colonies, building their nests in trees or bushes. The female lays a single egg.

NAME: **Yellow-legged Green Pigeon,** *Treron phoenicoptera*
RANGE: **India, Sri Lanka, S.E. Asia to Vietnam (not Malaysia)**
HABITAT: **forest, scrubland, fruiting trees in open country, parks and gardens**
SIZE: **33 cm (13 in)**

This colorful bird is about the size of a feral pigeon but is rather more heavily built. Females look similar to males but are not quite as bright, while juveniles have no mauve shoulder patches and are much duller and paler. Yellow-legged green pigeons are swift, strong fliers and usually move about in groups of up to 10 birds, although they will gather in trees in huge flocks to feed. They clamber about the branches, clinging to them and even hanging upside down to reach particularly succulent berries and fruit (especially wild figs), buds and shoots. They also drink by clinging to branches which overhang or trail into the water.

In India, green pigeons breed from March to June. Before mating, the male parades up and down in front of the female with feathers puffed out, calling with a tuneful sequence of notes rather like a human whistle. The usual twiggy nest is built in a shrub or tree, often close to other green pigeons' nests, and the female lays 2 eggs which are incubated for about 14 days.

NAME: **Nutmeg/Torres Strait Pigeon,** *Ducula spilorrhoa*
RANGE: **New Guinea, islands and archipelagos to N.E. and E. Australia**
HABITAT: **woodland, mangrove swamps, savanna, forest edge, plantations, gardens**
SIZE: **39–44.5 cm ($15\frac{1}{4}$–$17\frac{1}{2}$ in)**

Nutmeg pigeons roost and breed in large numbers on small off-lying islands, but parties of them daily fly long distances over the sea to feed on larger islands or in coastal areas of the mainland. They search among the branches of trees and shrubs for fruit and berries, and as their name suggests, they eat wild nutmegs, although these are not an important part of their diet. Observations indicate that birds breeding on islands of the Great Barrier Reef off Australia fly high in large flocks when going to feed but return in the evening, just skimming the water, in a stream of small parties.

Flying also plays a part in the mating behavior of these birds, when males display to females by bowing and then shooting swiftly up into the air to glide down, time and again. The breeding season appears to be from September to January in New Guinea and October and November in Australia. The birds build a twiggy nest in a shrub or tree, and the female lays 1 egg, which is incubated by both parents for 26 to 28 days.

NAME: **Superb Fruit Dove/ Purple Crowned Pigeon,** *Ptilinopus superbus*
RANGE: **Sulawesi, Sulu Archipelago, islands and archipelagos of W. Papua and New Guinea to N.E. Australia**
HABITAT: **forest, forest edge, riverbanks, cultivated land with trees**
SIZE: **22–24 cm ($8\frac{1}{2}$–$9\frac{1}{2}$ in)**

This compact, medium-sized dove is truly superb, with its green and coppery plumage but, despite this, is remarkably inconspicuous when sitting in the treetops. The female is a more uniform blue-green, while the feathers of the juvenile are yellow-green. Superb fruit doves fly with a whirring flight from tree to tree, usually singly or in pairs, but dozens may congregate to feed on berries and small fruit as it ripens.

The nest is normally a small collection of twigs, set low in a tree or shrub, and the female lays a single egg. Both parents incubate the egg for about 14 days, the male during the day and the female at night.

NAME: **Diamond Dove,** *Geopelia cuneata*
RANGE: **N. and inland Australia; sometimes coastal areas of S. Australia**
HABITAT: **open woodland, mulga (acacia) scrub, open land with trees, near water**
SIZE: **19–21.5 cm ($7\frac{1}{2}$–$8\frac{1}{2}$ in)**

A delicate-looking, rather plump little bird about the size of a house sparrow, the diamond dove is the smallest pigeon of all. Diamond doves are gregarious birds and are only rarely seen alone. Normally they move about in pairs, not always of opposite sexes, or in groups of up to 20 or so. Although they usually roost and nest in trees, they feed on the ground and walk around with a quick toddling action, searching for tiny seeds of grasses and herbaceous plants. They also eat the larger seeds of the *Acacia* and probably leaves and shoots of weeds and grasses. They are great sun lovers and will often rest in the sunshine, even in the heat of the day. Characteristically their flight is fast and swooping, rather like that of parakeets.

Mating is accompanied by unusual behavior by the male: he displays to the female by lifting his wings, then mounts her and immediately dismounts and strikes above her head with his wing. He remounts and repeats the action on the other side of the female; he then mounts her for the third time and copulates. Once again, he appears to attack the female but does not actually touch her. The nest is a typical pigeon nest, although small, usually low down in a bush or tree or a tangle of fallen branches and dry grass, in which the female lays 2 eggs. The eggs hatch after 12 or 13 days, and the young can fly 11 or 12 days later.

Yellow-legged Green Pigeon

Diamond Dove

Nutmeg Pigeon

Superb Fruit Dove (male)

Collared Dove

Nicobar Pigeon (male)

Pigeons

NAME: Large Brown Cuckoo Dove/ Brown Pigeon, *Macropygia phasianella*
RANGE: E. Australia; Java and Sumatra and adjacent islands; N. Borneo to the Philippines
HABITAT: glades and clearings in forest
SIZE: 38–43.5 cm (15–17 in)

The large brown cuckoo dove has rich, reddish-brown plumage with faint gray barring and spotting on the neck, breast and underparts; the speckling is more marked in the female, and the juvenile is even more noticeably barred. In eastern Australia, this is one of the commonest pigeons in the remaining pockets of rain forest, but populations are being reduced by forest clearance and by hunting. The long tail gives the bird an awkward appearance when it is flying among the trees, but, in fact, it seems to be an adaptation to the bird's largely arboreal way of life, since the spread tail is often used as a balancing aid. Cuckoo doves eat fruit and berries, which they take from the ground, as well as from trees and shrubs.

In Queensland, Australia, where breeding has been observed, mating takes place between July and January. The female lays 1 egg which is incubated for 16 to 18 days.

NAME: Crested Pigeon, *Ocyphaps lophotes*
RANGE: Australia
HABITAT: arid areas: lightly wooded grassland, open country and agricultural land with some trees and shrubs, near water
SIZE: 31–35 cm (12¼–13¾ in)

This slimly built pigeon, with its longish tail, long dark crest, like that of a lapwing, and strikingly barred wing coverts, has a sprightly air. The impression of jauntiness is emphasized by its swift, distinctive flight, in which several rapid wing beats alternate with periods of gliding, with the wings held still and almost horizontal. Since these birds live in arid country, reliable watering places, such as steady streams, dams or even cattle troughs, are essential to them. They normally come to drink before feeding, about an hour after sunrise, and in dry periods a flock of up to a thousand may gather. Generally, however, crested pigeons move about in pairs or in groups of from 4 to 30 individuals, feeding on the ground on seeds of herbaceous plants and *Acacia* trees, young green shoots and small bulbs.

They nest mainly in spring and summer, but breeding can take place almost year-round, usually after heavy rains. The female lays 2 eggs which are incubated for 18 days. There may be up to 7 successive broods.

NAME: Luzon Bleeding-heart Pigeon, *Gallicolumba luzonica*
RANGE: Philippines: islands of Luzon and Polillo
HABITAT: forest
SIZE: 30.5 cm (12 in)

The most striking characteristic of this pigeon is the patch of hairy, blood-red feathers in the middle of the breast that gives the bird its common name. The illusion that the breast of the bird is bleeding is enhanced by the fact that the red feathers of the "wound" form an indentation in the surrounding white feathers. Both male and female have this "bleeding heart." The bleeding-heart pigeon has a plump, compact body, short to medium-length wings and tail, and long legs. When alarmed, it tends to fly only a short distance and then to land and run rapidly, or to crouch with its head lowered and tail raised. Although it roosts in trees, it is mainly a ground-living bird and feeds on seeds, fallen berries and probably many insects and other invertebrates: the pigeons in this genus appear to take more animal food than most other pigeons.

They are thought to nest fairly low down in bushes, trees or vines and to lay 2 eggs to a clutch.

Other closely related species of *Gallicolumba* are found on neighboring islands. There are 3 species in New Guinea, but generally most islands and archipelagos support only one species.

NAME: Victoria Crowned Pigeon, *Goura victoria*
RANGE: N. New Guinea: Siriwo River to Astrolabe Bay; introduced (?) in Japen and Biak Islands
HABITAT: rain forest, muddy lowland flats
SIZE: 58.5–73.5 cm (23–29 in)

The 3 species of crowned pigeon are remarkable chiefly for their size — about that of a large domestic fowl — and for their erect, laterally compressed, fan-shaped crests of feathers. These feathers are long, with slightly separated barbs at the ends, which give them a beautiful lacelike appearance. Male and female look alike; juveniles are duller.

Little is known of the habits of the Victoria crowned pigeon in the wild, but it probably behaves in much the same way as other closely related species in the same area, spending most of its time on the ground, feeding on fallen fruit, berries and possibly small invertebrates. In captivity, it will also eat lettuce, corn, carrots and peanuts and is particularly fond of wild figs. It perches on branches and flies up into trees when alarmed.

Courtship display seems to consist of bowing and "dancing" by the male bird.

The female responds by spreading her wings and raising them up high; she also runs around the male, with slightly bent legs, uttering short hissing cries. The proportionately large nest is built among the branches of a tree and is more compact and less makeshift than a typical pigeon nest. In captivity, the female has been observed to lay 1 egg, which was incubated by both parents for 30 days. The young bird left the nest at about 4 weeks but was fed by both parents until it was 13 weeks old.

NAME: Tooth-billed Pigeon, *Didunculus strigirostris*
RANGE: Samoa: Upolu and Savaii Islands
HABITAT: wooded mountainsides
SIZE: 38 cm (15 in) Ⓥ

This species takes its name from its unique bill, which is strong and curved, with two notches and three projections — or teeth — on each side of the lower mandible. The scientific name, *strigirostris*, means "owl bill." The tooth-billed pigeon is a thick-set bird about the size of a feral pigeon, with a short tail, rather long legs and tight plumage, which has a silvery sheen, on head and breast. In the female, the feathers have less sheen; the juvenile is much browner and its plumage is more barred.

These birds live on the ground, feeding on seeds, fruit, berries and the mountain plantain which grows in their habitat. When eating, they hold their food down with their feet and, with the bill, tear it apart or nibble it into pieces before swallowing it. It is thought that the shape of the bill may have evolved as a response to these specialized feeding habits. When numbers of these birds were still plentiful, they were usually found in groups of 10 to 20.

When flushed, tooth-billed pigeons will fly, with loudly beating wings, for about 30 m (100 ft), beneath the lowest branches of tall trees, and then glide for a comparable distance before settling in a tree. They fly with agility among undergrowth and perch in low trees, although they seem to roost in tall ones. It is said that formerly these birds nested on the ground, but they now nest in trees because of the destruction wrought by introduced pigs. No definite information about their nesting habits is available.

Large Brown
Cuckoo Dove (male)

Luzon Bleeding-heart Pigeon

Tooth-billed Pigeon

Crested Pigeon

Victoria Crowned Pigeon

Lories, Cockatoos, Parrots

ORDER PSITTACIFORMES

The 315 or so species of parrot make up one of the most easily identified groups of birds. Despite a size range of between 10 and 101 cm (4 and 40 in), all types have a general similarity of outward appearance and inner structure. There are 3 families within the order: first, the brush-tongued lories; second the cockatoos; and third, the parrots proper.

Most parrots are brightly colored tree-living birds. Their beaks are short, powerful and strongly hooked, with a bulging base, or cere. The upper part of the parrot's bill is hinged and moved by muscles, and the flexibility that this gives allows the bill to become almost like a third manipulative limb, which is used in climbing and feeding. Although many birds have hinged bills, this feature is more marked in the short-billed parrots. Males and females look alike in most species, but there are plumage differences in a few instances.

Parrots are distributed throughout the tropical and subtropical zones of both hemispheres, with the largest number of species found in Australasia and in the Amazon area of South America. In the forests of these regions, parrots feed largely on fruit, nuts, seeds, nectar and fungi. They manipulate their foods with their feet and with their beaks and strong, mobile tongues. Many parrots are extremely gregarious and vocal, making screaming and discordant calls. Although renowned as mimics in captivity, they are not known to mimic sounds in the wild.

LORIIDAE: Lory Family

Known as lories or lorikeets, the 54 species in the lory family are characterized by their brush-tipped tongues, with which they extract pollen and nectar from flowers. They are all gregarious, arboreal birds.

NAME: **Black-capped Lory,** *Lorius lory*
RANGE: **New Guinea, Papuan Islands**
HABITAT: **forest**
SIZE: 31 cm (12¼ in)

Several races of this lory, with slight plumage differences, occur on the various islands in its range. Shy birds, black-capped lories frequent the upper levels of the forest, usually moving in pairs or small groups of up to a dozen. They feed on pollen, nectar, flowers and fruit, and on insects and their larvae. Little is known of the breeding habits of this lory, but from the few observed cases, it appears that the female lays 2 eggs, which she incubates for a period of about 24 days.

NAME: **Rainbow Lory/Lorikeet,** *Trichoglossus haematodus*
RANGE: **E. and N. Australia, Tasmania; Bali, east to New Hebrides**
HABITAT: **forest, coconut plantations, gardens, parks**
SIZE: 26 cm (10¼ in)

One of the most attractively plumaged birds in the parrot order, the adaptable rainbow lorikeet inhabits almost any wooded land, even near human habitation. Usually seen in pairs or flocks of anything from 3 or 4 to 100 birds, rainbow lorikeets are active and noisy and continually fly about the trees, searching for food and calling loudly. Pollen, nectar, fruit, berries, seeds, leaves, insects and larvae are all included in their diet, and they will feed on grain crops and invade orchards.

Rainbow lorikeets nest in holes in trees, high above the ground. The female lays 2 eggs, rarely 3, which she incubates for about 25 days. Both parents feed the chicks, which stay in the nest until they are about 7 or 8 weeks old.

CACATUIDAE: Cockatoo Family

The 18 species of cockatoo are distinguished from other parrots mainly by skull characteristics, but their most obvious external feature is the erectile crest on the head. A cockatoo raises its crest when alarmed and when alighting.

NAME: **Cockatiel,** *Nymphicus hollandicus*
RANGE: **Australia**
HABITAT: **open country**
SIZE: 32 cm (12½ in)

The slender cockatiel has long wings and tail and a tapering crest on its head. Males and females differ slightly in plumage, males having brighter markings than females. In pairs or small flocks, cockatiels forage on the ground for grass seeds and also feed in the trees on fruit and berries.

Breeding usually takes place between August and December, but the exact timing depends on the conditions, particularly on rainfall. The 4 to 7 eggs are laid in a hole in a tree and are incubated by both parents for 21 to 23 days. The young leave the nest at 4 or 5 weeks, and males acquire their bright facial markings at about 6 months.

NAME: **Sulphur-crested Cockatoo,** *Cacatua galerita*
RANGE: **New Guinea and offshore islands, Aru Islands, N. and E. Australia, Tasmania; introduced in New Zealand**
HABITAT: **forest, savanna, farmland**
SIZE: 50 cm (19¾ in)

Noisy, gregarious birds, sulphur-crested cockatoos move in pairs or family groups in the breeding season, but join in flocks for the rest of the year. In open country, these flocks may number hundreds of birds. Each flock has a habitual roosting site, which the birds leave at sunrise to fly to daytime feeding grounds, where they eat seeds, fruit, nuts, flowers, leaves, insects and larvae.

After a brief courtship display, culminating in a spell of mutual preening, the sulphur-crested cockatoos nest in a hole in a tree. Both parents incubate the 2 or 3 eggs for about 30 days, and the young stay in the nest for 6 to 9 weeks.

PSITTACIDAE: Parrot Family

With about 243 species, this is the largest of the 3 families in the parrot order. It includes a wide variety of forms, none of which has a crest or a brush-tipped tongue.

NAME: **Kea,** *Nestor notabilis*
RANGE: **New Zealand: South Island**
HABITAT: **forest, open country**
SIZE: 48 cm (18¾ in)

The kea is a bold, stocky bird with a long, curving upper bill; the female's bill is shorter and less curved. Keas fly strongly, wheeling in wide arcs, even in stormy, windy weather. They feed in trees and on the ground on fruit, berries, leaves, insects and larvae. They will also scavenge on refuse dumps and eat carrion. The belief has long persisted that keas attack and kill sheep, and many birds have been destroyed by farmers for this reason. Although they may well attack sick, injured or trapped sheep, these activities are thought to have been exaggerated, and keas are now protected by law.

Nesting can take place at almost any time of year but usually occurs between July and January. Males are polygamous and may mate with several females. The nest is made in a crevice, under rocks, among the roots of a tree or in a hollow log. The female lays 2 to 4 eggs which she incubates for 21 to 28 days.

NAME: **Red-breasted Pygmy Parrot,** *Micropsitta bruijnii*
RANGE: **Buru, Ceram, New Guinea, Bismarck Archipelago, Solomon Islands**
HABITAT: **mountain forest**
SIZE: 9 cm (3½ in)

In pairs or small groups, these tiny parrots clamber over branches of trees, busily feeding on the lichens and fungus prevalent in high forest. The short tail has stiff shafts and can be used as a prop, in the manner of a woodpecker. Pygmy parrots may also feed on other plant material and insects.

Kea (male)

Sulphur-crested
Cockatoo

Black-capped
Lory

Red-breasted
Pygmy Parrot

Cockatiel (male)

Rainbow Lory

Parrots

NAME: Eclectus Parrot, *Eclectus
(=Larius) roratus*
**RANGE: New Guinea to Solomon and
Sumba Islands; Australia: extreme
N. Queensland;**
HABITAT: lowland forest
SIZE: 35 cm (13¾ in)

Male and female eclectus parrots differ
so radically in plumage that for years
they were thought to be separate
species. Both are glossy, brilliant birds,
males with primarily green plumage and
females with red. The body is stocky
and the tail short and square. They are
noisy, gregarious birds, roosting in
groups of as many as 80 and flying off at
sunrise in pairs or small groups to feed
on fruit, nuts, seeds, berries, leaves,
flowers and nectar.

The nest is made high up in a tree at
the edge of the forest or in a clearing.
The 2 eggs are laid in a hole in the tree
trunk, and the female incubates them
for about 26 days.

NAME: Gray Parrot, *Psittacus erithacus*
**RANGE: central Africa: W. coast to Kenya
and N.W. Tanzania**
**HABITAT: lowland forest, savanna,
mangrove swamps**
SIZE: 33 cm (13 in)

Flocks of gray parrots roost together in
tall trees at the forest edge or on small
islands in rivers and lakes. At sunrise
they fly off swiftly in pairs or small
groups to find food, following regular
routes to and from the roosting area.
Climbing from branch to branch, gray
parrots feed in the trees on seeds, nuts,
berries and fruit, particularly the fruit of
the oil palm.

The timing of the breeding season
varies according to area, and there may
occasionally be two broods a year.
There have been few observations of
nesting in the wild, but the female is
believed to lay 3 or 4 eggs in a hole in a
tree and to incubate them herself.

NAME: Peach-faced Lovebird, *Agapornis
roseicollis*
**RANGE: S.W. Africa: Angola, Namibia,
S. Africa: N. Cape Province**
HABITAT: dry open country
SIZE: 15 cm (6 in)

Flocks of these noisy, abundant lovebirds maneuver skillfully and swiftly
among the trees and bushes. They eat
seeds and berries and never move far
from some form of water supply.
Lovebirds are so called because of their
conspicuous mutual preening habits.

Colonies of lovebirds nest in crevices
in cliffs or in buildings, or take over
large parts of the communal, many-
chambered nests of weaver birds. The
female is thought to lay 3 to 6 eggs,
which she incubates for 23 days.

NAME: Kakapo/Owl Parrot, *Strigops
habroptilus*
**RANGE: New Zealand: formerly all
islands, now parts of South and
Stewart Islands (least threatened on
Stewart Island)**
**HABITAT: mountain forest (all altitudes to
1,250 m (4,100 ft)**
SIZE: 64 cm (25¼ in)   Ⓔ

Although the highest priority has been
given to its protection, the kakapo is in
serious danger of extinction. The population has declined steadily over the last
1,000 years, with the settlement of New
Zealand, the resulting land clearance
and the introduction of predators such
as ermines and rats. Efforts are being
made to establish kakapos on offshore
islands, which are free from predators.

A most unusual parrot, the kakapo is
a ground-living, flightless, nocturnal
bird. During the day it shelters among
rocks or bushes or in a burrow and
emerges at dusk to feed on fruit, berries,
nuts, seeds, shoots, leaves,, moss and
fungi. The kakapo climbs well, using its
beak and feet, and can flap its wings to
help balance itself as it climbs or jumps
from trees.

Courtship habits, too, are different
from those of other parrots, for the
males display communally in traditional areas, or leks. Each male excavates several shallow, bowl-shaped
areas in which he displays: the bowl
helps to amplify the booming calls
which accompany his show. The nest is
a burrow, made among rocks or tree
roots, and 1 or 2, rarely 3, eggs are laid.
The female is thought to incubate the
clutch and care for the young alone.
Kakapos do not appear to breed every
year, and breeding may be linked to the
availability of food.

NAME: Rose-ringed Parakeet, *Psittacula
krameri*
**RANGE: central Africa, India to Sri
Lanka; introduced in Mauritius,
Middle East, Singapore**
HABITAT: woodland, cultivated land
SIZE: 40 cm (15¾ in)

The bold, noisy rose-ringed parakeets
are usually seen in small flocks, although they may gather in hundreds at
feeding or roosting sites. They fly well
but tend not to travel far afield. Seeds,
berries, fruit, flowers and nectar are the
main items of their diet, and they are
relentless in their search, invading orchards and plantations, decimating sunflower crops and rice paddies and even
ripping open bags of stored grain.

Males and females differ slightly in
plumage: the female lacks the pink
collar and black facial markings and has
shorter central tail feathers. At the onset
of the breeding season, the pair perform

their courtship ritual, the female rolling
her eyes and head until the male
approaches, rubs bills with her and
feeds her. They nest in a hole in a tree,
which they excavate or take over from
woodpeckers or barbets, or under the
roof of a building. The female lays 3 to
5 eggs, which she incubates for 22 days.
The young leave the nest about 7 weeks
after hatching.

NAME: Crimson Rosella, *Platycercus
elegans*
**RANGE: E. and S.E. Australia; introduced
in New Zealand and Norfolk Island**
**HABITAT: coastal and mountain forest,
gardens, parks**
SIZE: 36 cm (14½ in)

Crimson rosellas are bold, colorful
birds, abundant in most of their range.
Adults live in pairs or groups of up to 5,
while juveniles band together in larger
groups. Much of their day is spent feeding, mainly on seeds but also on fruit,
blossoms, insects and larvae, on the
ground or in the treetops.

The breeding season starts in late
August or early September. In his courtship display, the male lets his wings
droop while he fans his tail out, moving
it from side to side. The female nests in
a hole in a tree and lays 5 to 8 eggs, which
she incubates for 21 days, leaving the
nest only briefly each morning to be fed
by her partner. The young leave the nest
at about 5 weeks but remain with their
parents for another 5 weeks before joining a flock of other young rosellas.

NAME: Budgerigar, *Melopsittacus
undulatus*
**RANGE: Australia (interior); introduced
in USA: Florida**
HABITAT: scrub, open country
SIZE: 18 cm (7 in)

So popular as a cage bird, with its many
color variations, the budgerigar is a
small parrot with predominantly green
plumage in the wild. Its numbers vary
with conditions, but it is generally common and, in years of abundant food
supplies, is one of the most numerous
Australian species. Active mainly in the
early morning and late afternoon, flocks
of budgerigars search on the ground for
grass seeds, their main food. They are
swift, agile birds in the air, and flocks are
nomadic, continually moving from one
area to another in search of food and
water.

Breeding takes place at any time of the
year, usually after rains which ensure
food supplies. A nest is made in a
hollow in a tree stump or log, and 4 to
6, sometimes 8, eggs are laid and incubated by the female for 18 days. The
young leave the nest after about 30 days.

Eclectus Parrot (female) (male)

Gray Parrot

Peach-faced Lovebird

Kakapo

Rose-ringed Parakeet (male)

Budgerigar

Crimson Rosella

Parrots

NAME: **Scarlet Macaw**, *Ara macao*
RANGE: **Mexico, Central America,**
northern South America to Brazil
HABITAT: **forest, savanna, plantations**
SIZE: **85 cm (33½ in)**

A spectacular, brilliantly plumaged bird, the scarlet macaw is one of the largest and most striking members of its family. A frequently photographed and painted species and the most familiar of South American parrots, it is nevertheless declining in numbers because of the widespread destruction of its rain forest habitat and the collection of large numbers of young birds and nestlings for the lucrative cage-bird trade. It is already rare in some parts of its range.

Scarlet macaws maintain strong pair bonds and are generally seen in pairs, family groups or flocks of up to 20. As they make their daily journeys from roosting areas to feeding grounds, pairs will fly together, wings almost touching. They feed up in the trees on seeds, fruit, nuts, berries and other plant matter and, although they eat in silence, they fly off, squawking noisily, at any disturbance.

Surprisingly little is known of the breeding habits of these splendid birds. Nests have been observed in holes in tree trunks well above the ground, but there is little reliable information on clutch size or incubation.

NAME: **Spectacled Parrotlet**, *Forpus*
conspicillatus
RANGE: **Central and South America:**
E. Panama, Colombia (not S.E.),
W. Venezuela
HABITAT: **open forest, thornbush**
SIZE: **12 cm (4¾ in)**

About 3 races of this little parrotlet occur within the range, all with slight plumage differences. Generally, however, males have dull, greenish upperparts, with yellow markings on the forehead, cheeks and throat and some blue markings. Females have brighter green upperparts than males and lack the blue markings. Out of the breeding season, spectacled parrotlets move in small flocks of 5 to 20, making constant chattering calls. Busy, active birds, they forage in trees and bushes for berries, fruit, buds and blossoms or search on the ground for the seeds of grasses and herbaceous plants. Their flight is swift and erratic.

During the breeding season, the parrotlets associate in pairs. Little is known of their breeding habits, but it is likely that they make their nests in natural holes in trees or posts. The female is believed to lay 2 to 4 eggs. There are several species of parrotlet in the genus *Forpus*, all with similar habits and appearance.

NAME: **Sun Conure**, *Aratinga solstitialis*
RANGE: **South America: Guyana,**
Suriname, French Guiana, N.E. Brazil
HABITAT: **open forest, savanna**
SIZE: **30 cm (11¾ in)**

A beautiful bird, with vibrant yellow plumage, the sun conure is not a common species, and little is known of its habits. Generally seen in small flocks, sun conures are noisy birds which make frequent screeching calls. They feed on seeds, fruit, nuts and berries, usually up in the treetops.

According to the few observations of breeding habits, the female lays 3 or 4 eggs and incubates them for 4 weeks. Both parents feed the chicks, which remain in the nest for about 8 weeks.

The golden-capped conure, *A. aurocapilla*, and the jendaya conure, *A. jendaya*, are both similar to the sun conure and may even be races of the same species.

NAME: **Yellow-headed Parrot/Yellow-**
crowned Amazon, *Amazona*
ochrocephala
RANGE: **Mexico, Central America, south**
to E. Peru, N. Bolivia and N. Brazil;
Trinidad
HABITAT: **forest, wide range of wooded**
habitats
SIZE: **35 cm (13¾ in)**

The yellow-headed parrot is one of the 29 or so species in the genus *Amazona*, all sometimes referred to as "amazons." Most are medium-sized parrots with predominantly green plumage and some brilliant markings. Like many amazons, this species is declining in numbers both because of the destruction of its forest habitat in some areas and because of the collection of large numbers of young for the cage-bird trade. Yellow-headed parrots are particularly sought after because of their reputation as good mimics and talkers.

During the day small groups of these parrots feed in the treetops on fruit, seeds, nuts, berries and blossoms and will also come down to within 2 m (6½ ft) of the ground to find food. They are strong fliers and travel well above the trees except when going only short distances. At dusk they return to regular roosting areas.

A breeding pair finds a hollow in a tree trunk, which both enlarge, and the female lays 3 or 4 eggs. She incubates them for 29 days, during which the male remains nearby. Twice a day the female leaves the eggs briefly to join her mate, who feeds her by regurgitation.

NAME: **Monk Parakeet**, *Myiopsitta*
monachus
RANGE: **South America: central Bolivia,**
S. Brazil to central Argentina;
introduced in Puerto Rico and
N.E. USA
HABITAT: **open woodland, palm groves,**
cultivated land, eucalyptus plantations
SIZE: **29 cm (11½ in)**

A popular cage bird and abundant in the wild, the monk parakeet is a medium-sized parrot, with long tail feathers and a heavy bill. It is an adaptable species and readily inhabits trees planted by man in orchards or on ranchland, even when near to human habitation. The highly gregarious monk parakeets occur in flocks of 10 to 100 or more and build enormous communal nests, unique in the parrot order. The nest is used for breeding and for roosting and so is inhabited throughout the year and is always the center of much activity as the birds come and go, shrieking noisily.

Monk parakeets leave the nest in small groups to find food, and if they are feeding in open country or fields, a few birds will sit up in nearby trees to act as sentinels. At the first sign of danger, they call a warning, and the feeding birds quickly disperse. Seeds, fruit, berries, nuts, blossoms, leaves, insects and larvae are all eaten, and monk parakeets can cause much damage by feeding on cereal crops and in orchards.

Although the nest is used all year round, at the start of the breeding season in October the birds add to it and repair any damage. The nest is usually situated at the top of a tree and is made of twigs, particularly thorny twigs, which hold together well and deter predators. It may start with only a few compartments, but it is gradually added to until it has anything up to 20 compartments, each occupied by a pair of birds. Each compartment has its own entrance at the bottom of the nest, leading into the brood chamber. The whole structure is so strong that other birds may nest on top of it.

The female parakeet lays 5 to 8 eggs, but because of the obvious difficulties of observing behavior in such a structure, little is known of the incubation of the clutch or the care of the chicks. The young birds leave the nest at about 6 weeks old.

Scarlet Macaw

Monk Parakeet

Sun Conure

Yellow-headed
Parrot

Spectacled Parrotlet (male)

Cuckoos

NAME: Common Koel, *Eudynamys scolopacea*
RANGE: India, Pakistan, Sri Lanka, S. China, S.E. Asia, New Guinea, Australia
HABITAT: forest edge, scrub, cultivated land, gardens
SIZE: 43 cm (17 in)

The koel is a solitary bird, keeping to leafy trees and seldom descending to the ground. It feeds on fruit, particularly figs, but also eats insects and small invertebrates such as snails. Male and female look unalike: the male is black and glossy, while the female has brownish plumage, spotted and barred with white and buff.

The female koel lays her eggs in the nest of the house crow, *Corvus splendens*, or of a friarbird or honey eater. Birds which use the crow as a foster parent lay several eggs which resemble those of the host but are smaller. The young koels are black like young crows.

NAME: Drongo Cuckoo, *Surniculus lugubris*
RANGE: India, S.E. Asia, S. China, Indonesia
HABITAT: forest, scrub, cultivated land
SIZE: 25.5 cm (10 in)

The drongo cuckoo resembles the drongo, *Dicrurus macrocercus*, in its plumage and forked tail, unique among cuckoos, and uses it as a foster parent in some areas. A solitary, mainly nocturnal bird, it feeds on insects, particularly grasshoppers and caterpillars, and on fruit such as figs. It also catches winged insects by leaping up into the air after them in the manner of the drongo.

The female lays her eggs in the nests of various drongo species and in those of other birds. Juveniles have white flecks in their black plumage, which disappear as the birds mature.

NAME: Channel-billed Cuckoo, *Scythrops novaehollandiae*
RANGE: Australia to New Guinea, Indonesia
HABITAT: forest, woodland
SIZE: 63.5 cm (25 in)

The largest cuckoo of the Australasian region, the channel-billed cuckoo, with its large, deep bill, is reminiscent of a toucan or hornbill. It will devour almost anything, but insects, fruit and berries are its preferred foods.

Channel-billed cuckoos migrate north in March, returning south in September to breed. The female lays 2 or more eggs in the nest of a crow, magpie or currawong. The 2 blind, naked cuckoo chicks attempt to push one another out of the nest at first, but are usually unable to do so, and normally both are reared.

ORDER CUCULIFORMES

This order contains only 2 families: the cuckoos and the turacos.

CUCULIDAE: Cuckoo Family

The 50 species of true cuckoo are the best-known members of this family, largely because of the practice of brood parasitism. The female bird lays her eggs in the nest of another species, which then incubates and rears her young. In some species this habit is now highly developed, and the cuckoo's eggs resemble those of the host species. Since parasitic cuckoos generally lay in the nests of much smaller passerine birds, their eggs must be smaller and hatch more quickly than those of the nonparasitic cuckoos.

There are 127 species in the family, including the Old World cuckoos, many of which are brood parasites, and the New World cuckoos, which, for the most part, are not. Other forms are the social-nesting guira, the anis, roadrunners, couas and coucals.

The family as a whole has a cosmopolitan distribution and contains many migratory forms. Cuckoos and their relatives range in size between 15 and 71 cm (6 and 28 in) in length, and most are slender bodied, with long tails and short legs. Males and females look alike in most species.

NAME: Cuckoo, *Cuculus canorus*
RANGE: Europe, N. Africa, N. and S.E. Asia; winters south of range in Africa and S. Asia
HABITAT: forest, woodland, moors
SIZE: 33 cm (13 in)

The male cuckoo's familiar song, the origin of its common name, heralds the arrival of spring, when the bird flies north to breed in Europe and Asia. A slim, long-tailed bird, it leads a solitary life outside the breeding season and haunts trees, hedges and thickets, where it feeds on large insects, particularly hairy caterpillars.

Breeding starts in mid-May, and each female has a well-defined territory in which she searches for nests in which to lay her eggs. She uses the same host species, usually small passerine birds such as dunnocks, wagtails or redstarts, throughout her life. The species she chooses is probably that of her own foster parents. On alternate days, she lays a single egg, each in a different nest, at the same time removing one of the host's eggs, until she has laid a total of 8 to 12 eggs. She must lay her egg stealthily, without the host bird's knowledge, for, if it is alarmed, it may reject the whole clutch. The young cuckoo

hatches in about 12 days; since it is much the bigger, stronger and faster-growing bird, it is able to oust the hosts' own young from the nest and claim all its foster parents' attention. The hosts have to work extremely hard in order to satisfy the demands for food made by the young cuckoo, which is much larger than they are.

NAME: African Emerald Cuckoo, *Chrysococcyx cupreus*
RANGE: Africa, south of the Sahara
HABITAT: forest edge and clearings
SIZE: 20 cm (7¾ in)

A shy bird, which haunts the dense foliage of tall forest trees, the emerald cuckoo is more often heard than seen, for it darts for cover at the slightest hint of danger. Considered to be one of the most beautiful of African birds, the male has a golden-yellow belly and an emerald-green back. The female has moss-green upperparts, a brown crown and a white belly, barred with moss-green. Emerald cuckoos feed on a variety of insects, including caterpillars, ants and beetles.

The female lays her eggs in the nests of such birds as bulbuls, orioles, puff-back shrikes and black-headed weavers.

The emerald cuckoo is thought to be migratory. A smaller relative, the shining cuckoo, *C. lucidus*, migrates some 3,200 km (2,000 mi) across the southwest Pacific Ocean from New Zealand to the Solomon Islands.

NAME: Yellow-billed Cuckoo, *Coccyzus americanus*
RANGE: breeds from Canada to Mexico and Caribbean islands; winters in Central and South America
HABITAT: woodland, orchards, thickets
SIZE: 28–33 cm (11–13 in)

A secretive, shy bird, the yellow-billed cuckoo frequents undergrowth and brush, searching for hairy caterpillars (its preferred food) and beetles, grasshoppers, tree crickets, army ants, wasps and flies. It also feeds on summer fruit and small frogs and lizards.

A nonparasitic cuckoo, it builds its own nest of sticks in a tree or bush and lines it with dry leaves, grass or even pieces of rag. The female lays 3 or 4 eggs, one every 2 or 3 days, and both parents incubate the eggs, each of which hatches 14 days after laying. The nestlings are almost naked when they hatch, with only a sparse covering of down. Both parents feed and tend the young.

Cuckoo

African Emerald Cuckoo (male)

Channel-billed Cuckoo

Common Koel (male)

Yellow-billed Cuckoo

Drongo Cuckoo

Cuckoos, Turacos

NAME: **Roadrunner,** *Geococcyx californianus*
RANGE: **S.W. USA: S. California, Utah, Kansas, south to Mexico**
HABITAT: **semiarid open country**
SIZE: **50–60 cm (19¾–23½ in)**

A slender, fowl-like bird, with a small shaggy crest, a long tail and long legs, the roadrunner is a fast-running ground-bird which can attain speeds of 24 km/h (15 mph) or more. But its short, rounded wings are functional, and it can fly, albeit clumsily. Like its cousin, the lesser roadrunner, *G. velox*, of Mexico and Central America, it lives in dry, open places and feeds on ground-living insects, such as crickets and grasshoppers, and on other small invertebrates, bird's eggs, lizards, snakes (even rattlesnakes) and fruits such as prickly pear. It usually kills by making a sudden pounce on prey. True to its name, this shy bird is often seen on roads, but if surprised, it runs rapidly away.

Roadrunners form permanent pair bonds and live in their territory all year round. They build neat, shallow nests of sticks, lined with leaves and feathers, in trees or cactus clumps. The female lays 2 to 6 eggs in April or May; they are incubated for about 20 days. The eggs hatch over several days, and if food supplies are scarce, the larger nestlings take all there is, leaving the younger, smaller birds to starve. Both parents care for the young, which hatch naked and helpless. Their eyes open after about 7 days, and they are able to feed themselves at about 16 days.

NAME: **Smooth-billed Ani,** *Crotophaga ani*
RANGE: **Central and South America, West Indies**
HABITAT: **forest edge, grassland, pasture**
SIZE: **33 cm (13 in)**

Anis are nonparasitic cuckoos, with long square-ended tails, heavy hooked bills and short wings. Their flight is weak, so they feed mainly on the ground on insects and some fallen fruit and berries. Anis are often seen on ranches near grazing cattle because the animals disturb ground insects, and this association helps the anis to find three times more food than they otherwise would.

Smooth-billed anis are gregarious birds, living in flocks of up to 25 and even building a communal nest, which is a bulky structure, made of sticks, weeds and grass and situated low in a small tree or bush. A group of females, each laying 3 or 4 eggs, fills the nest with 20 or more and will then share the incubation of the clutch. The young birds hatch after about 14 days, and the whole flock helps to feed them.

NAME: **Small Green-billed Malkoha,** *Rhopodytes viridirostris*
RANGE: **S. India, Sri Lanka**
HABITAT: **forest, scrub, bamboo forest**
SIZE: **38 cm (15 in)**

Also known as the blue-faced malkoha, this distinctive cuckoo, with its green bill and sky-blue eye patch, is a common Indian species. It flies feebly and reluctantly and spends most of the time under cover of bushes and undergrowth. Large insects, such as grasshoppers, mantids and caterpillars, form the bulk of its diet, and it occasionally catches small lizards.

A nonparasitic species, it builds a shallow nest, made of sticks and lined with leaves. The female lays 2 eggs.

NAME: **Running Coua,** *Coua cursor*
RANGE: **S.W. Madagascar**
HABITAT: **arid brush**
SIZE: **36 cm (14¼ in)**

The running coua is a terrestrial bird and usually moves on foot, although it can fly reasonably well, if laboriously. Single birds or small groups walk about looking for insects such as caterpillars; if alarmed, they run quickly, periodically interrupting their stride with hops.

Although a member of the cuckoo family, the coua builds its own nest, but little is known about its breeding habits.

NAME: **Buff-headed Coucal,** *Centropus milo*
RANGE: **Solomon Islands**
HABITAT: **forest**
SIZE: **66 cm (26 in)**

One of the largest cuckoos, the buff-headed coucal has short wings, a long tail and a big, curved bill. A poor flier, it spends most of its time on the ground and even there moves awkwardly. It will sometimes flap up into a tree, moving from branch to branch and then gliding clumsily down. It feeds on large insects, frogs and reptiles.

The coucal's nest is a rounded, domed structure, made of grass and built in the undergrowth just above ground level. The female lays 3 to 5 eggs.

NAME: **Striped Cuckoo,** *Tapera naevia*
RANGE: **S. Mexico, Central America, South America to N. Argentina**
HABITAT: **savanna, swamps**
SIZE: **30.5 cm (12 in)**

The striped cuckoo is a shy bird that perches on a tree, calling for hours at a time, often during the hottest part of the day. Its call is a melancholy, carrying whistle, which sounds like "sa-ci." The striped cuckoo is one of the 3 American cuckoos to have parasitic breeding habits, but little is known about them.

MUSOPHAGIDAE:
Turaco Family

The 19 species of turaco are fowl-like, tree-dwelling birds of tropical Africa. Except for the go-away birds, which are gray and white, turacos are glossy and brightly colored, with long, broad tails and short, rounded wings. Many species have hairy crests and bare skin around the eye area. The brilliant red of the head and wing feathers of some species is the result of a copper complex pigment, unique in the animal kingdom, which is soluble in alkalis. The quite different green pigment is also unique.

Turacos have short, stout bills and feed largely on insects and fruit. Males and females look alike.

NAME: **Red-crested Turaco,** *Tauraco erythrolophus*
RANGE: **Africa: Angola, Zaire**
HABITAT: **woodland, savanna**
SIZE: **40.5 cm (16 in)**

The red-crested turaco is a fruit-eating bird, which lives in trees and seldom descends to the ground. Like other turacos, it is a poor flier but is agile and swift in the trees and can run, hop and climb among the branches. In addition to fruit, it eats seeds, insects and snails.

This turaco is almost identical in appearance to Bannerman's turaco, *T. bannermani*, and the most obvious distinguishing feature is the nostrils: rounded in the red-crested and slit-shaped in Bannerman's turaco. Nothing is known of the breeding habits of either species.

NAME: **Common Go-away Bird,** *Corythaixoides concolor*
RANGE: **Africa: Tanzania, Congo River basin to South Africa**
HABITAT: **open bush, acacia scrub**
SIZE: **51 cm (20 in)**

Although wary, the common go-away bird is not timid, and at the hint of anything suspicious, it alerts all the animals in the area with its penetrating call, which sounds like "g'away, g'away." In pairs or small groups, the go-away birds perch on treetops or fly clumsily from one tree to another; they feed on berries, fruit and insects.

The breeding season is between October and January. The birds display, one partner perching in a treetop and the other hovering above it, and both help to build a nest of sticks in dense creepers or up in an acacia tree. The female lays 2 or 3 large eggs, which both parents incubate for, it is thought, a total of about 18 days.

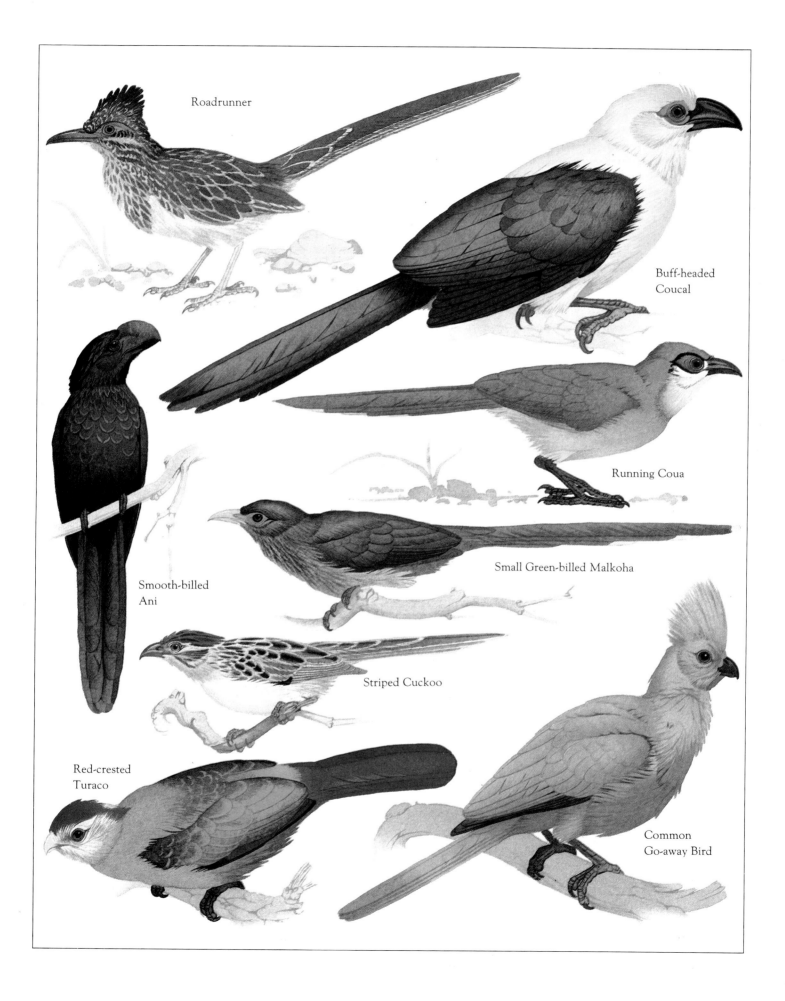

Roadrunner

Buff-headed
Coucal

Running Coua

Smooth-billed
Ani

Small Green-billed Malkoha

Striped Cuckoo

Red-crested
Turaco

Common
Go-away Bird

Barn Owls, Owls

ORDER STRIGIFORMES

Within this order are 2 very similar families of owls. With their flattened faces, enormous eyes, taloned feet and predatory, usually nocturnal habits, owls represent the nighttime equivalent of the hawks, eagles and falcons.

Owls kill with their talons: each toe is tipped with a sharp, hooked claw. They then swallow their prey whole and regurgitate the indigestible bones, fur and feathers in the form of pellets. Males and females look alike in most species, although the females are sometimes larger.

TYTONIDAE: Barn Owl Family

The 12 species of barn and bay owl differ from the typical owls in many minor details. They can be distinguished by the heart-shaped facial disk, relatively small eyes and long, slender legs. The long, hooked beak is mostly concealed by feathers, and the toes are strong with sharp, curved claws. All barn owls are nocturnal hunters.

NAME: **Oriental Bay Owl,** *Phodilus badius*
RANGE: **N. India, Sri Lanka, S.E. Asia, Greater Sunda Islands**
HABITAT: **forest**
SIZE: **29 cm (11½ in)**

The oriental bay owl is similar in shape and appearance to the barn owl with which it is now grouped. It is strictly nocturnal and is believed to feed mostly on insects, which it hunts in and around the trees. It lays 3 to 5 eggs, usually in a hole in a tree. An African species of bay owl has been discovered only recently.

NAME: **Barn Owl,** *Tyto alba*
RANGE: **worldwide, except temperate Asia and many Pacific islands**
HABITAT: **open country, woodland, inhabited areas**
SIZE: **34 cm (13¼ in)**

The barn owl is a long-legged, usually pale-plumaged bird with a white face. There are over 30 subspecies over its wide range, differing mainly in intensity of plumage coloration. Barn owls generally live alone or in pairs and roost during the day in farm buildings, hollow trees or caves. At night, they emerge to hunt, feeding primarily on small rodents, which they catch and kill on the ground, and also on small birds.

Breeding usually starts in April in the north. The female nests in an old building, a hollow tree trunk or a rock crevice and lays 4 to 7 eggs, which she incubates for about 33 days. The male brings food to her during this period, and both parents care for the young.

STRIGIDAE: Owl Family

The 134 species of typical owl are distributed all over the world, except on some oceanic islands. They are soft-feathered, short-tailed birds, with big heads and enormous eyes set in a circular facial disk. In all species the beak is hooked and partly hidden by feathers.

Most owls hunt at night and all feed entirely on animals, from insects and invertebrates to birds and medium-sized mammals such as rabbits. They have exceptionally keen eyesight and excellent hearing.

NAME: **Brown Fish Owl,** *Ketupa zeylonensis*
RANGE: **Middle East to S. China, Sri Lanka, S.E. Asia**
HABITAT: **forested streams and lakes**
SIZE: **56 cm (22 in)**

A specialized, semiaquatic owl, the brown fish owl is always found near water and feeds on fish, as well as on the more typical prey of owls. Its feet and ankles are unfeathered, an adaptation which allows it to wade in the shallows to catch fish without the plumage getting wet.

The breeding season of this species begins in February or March. It makes a nest platform in a tree by joining some branches together, or nests on a ledge or rock. Only 1 or 2 eggs are laid and are then incubated by both parents for a total of about 35 days.

NAME: **Elf Owl,** *Micrathene whitneyi*
RANGE: **S.E. USA, Mexico**
HABITAT: **wooded canyons, deserts with saguaro cactus**
SIZE: **12.5–15 cm (5–6 in)**

One of the smallest owls in the world, the elf owl is distinguished by its short tail from other small owls in its range. During the day, it roosts in a tree or bush and comes out at dusk to hunt. Insects are its main prey, many being caught in the owl's feet while it is in flight. It will also hover over foliage or dart out from a perch after prey like a flycatcher. Beetles, moths, grasshoppers, crickets and scorpions (the sting is removed or crushed) are frequent prey, and it occasionally catches small snakes and lizards.

Elf owls nest in deserted woodpecker holes in cactus plants or tree trunks. The male finds a suitable site and sings to attract a female, who responds and enters the nest. In April or May, she lays 1 to 5 eggs, which she incubates for 24 days. The male feeds the female while she incubates and also brings food for her to give to the young when they have hatched.

NAME: **Screech Owl,** *Otus asio*
RANGE: **N. America: Canada to Mexico**
HABITAT: **open woodland, cactus desert**
SIZE: **18–25.5 cm (7–10 in)**

A small owl with conspicuous ear tufts, the screech owl roosts during the day in a hollow tree or old building and starts to hunt at dusk. It catches insects and mice, shrews and other small mammals, as well as frogs, lizards and some birds. Breeding starts from February to July, according to area. Screech owls nest in a hole in a tree, such as an abandoned woodpecker hole, usually without any nesting material. Normally 4 or 5 eggs are laid, but there may be as many as 8. The male brings food while the female incubates, but once the eggs hatch, both parents feed the young.

NAME: **Snowy Owl,** *Nyctea scandiaca*
RANGE: **circumpolar: arctic Canada, Greenland, N. Eurasia**
HABITAT: **tundra, marshes, coasts**
SIZE: **52–65 cm (20½–25½ in)**

The snowy owl is a large species with distinctive, mainly white plumage; females have more dark, barred markings than males. It usually hunts during the day and takes prey up to the size of arctic hares and lemmings, as well as smaller rodents and birds such as ducks and gulls.

The snowy owl begins nesting in mid-May. It makes a shallow scrape in the ground or on a rock, lines it with moss and feathers and lays 4 to 10 eggs. Up to 15 eggs may be laid if food supplies are particularly good. The male brings food to the female while she incubates the eggs for 32 or 33 days.

NAME: **Great Horned Owl,** *Bubo virginianus*
RANGE: **N., Central and South America**
HABITAT: **varied: woodland, forest, city parks, suburbs**
SIZE: **46–64 cm (18–25¼ in)**

The great horned owls are among the biggest and most powerful of American owls. Their prominent ear tufts are simply feathers and are not connected with the hearing apparatus. They roost in trees, and while they do most of their hunting at night, they may hunt by day in unpopulated regions. They catch mammals up to the size of cats, birds, insects and reptiles.

The timing of nesting depends on area, but it can be as early as January or February. The owl uses the old nest of another bird species or nests in a cave, a hollow in a tree or on a cliff ledge. Usually 3 eggs are laid, but there can be as many as 6. The eggs are incubated for 30 to 35 days by both parents, who then feed and vigorously defend their young.

Barn Owl

Elf Owl

Great Horned Owl

Screech Owl

Oriental Bay Owl

Snowy Owl (male)

Brown Fish Owl

Owls

NAME: Morepork/Boobook, *Ninox novaeseelandiae*
RANGE: New Zealand, Australia, S. New Guinea, Lesser Sunda Islands
HABITAT: forest, scrub, open country with caves for roosting
SIZE: 29 cm (11½ in)

The morepork is the most widely distributed owl in New Zealand and Australia. It is usually seen at dusk when it begins to hunt for its food, which consists largely of insects, particularly moths, as well as spiders, lizards, small birds, rats and mice. It occasionally hunts during the day. The common names are derived from one of its calls, which sounds like "morepork" or "boobook." One subspecies, the Norfolk boobook, is now listed as rare.

The morepork nests in November and lays 3 or 4 eggs in a nest in a hollow tree or in a patch of thick vegetation. The female begins her 30- to 31-day incubation after laying the first egg, but lays the rest later, at 2-day intervals. After hatching, the young remain in the nest for about 5 weeks, guarded and fed by their parents.

NAME: Long-eared Owl, *Asio otus*
RANGE: N. America, Europe, Asia
HABITAT: coniferous forest, woodland, parks
SIZE: 33–40.5 cm (13–16 in)

The long-eared owl is of a slenderer build than the tawny owl and has distinctive ear tufts; these tufts are simply feathers and have no connection with the actual ears. In flight, the long-eared owl keeps its ear tufts flat against its head. One of the most nocturnal of owls, it preys on rats, mice, shrews, moles, bats, squirrels, rabbits and other small mammals, as well as on birds and insects. During the day, long-eared owls roost in trees, their mottled brown plumage helping them to blend with the surroundings.

Long-eared owls roost from March to May, according to area; when food supplies are abundant they may produce two broods. The female lays 3 to 10 eggs, usually 4 or 5, in an old nest of another bird species or even in a squirrel's nest. If no such nest is available, she will lay her eggs on the ground under a tree or bush. She incubates the eggs for 26 to 28 days, and her partner brings food to her both during this period and once the chicks are hatched. The young leave the nest 3 to 4 weeks after hatching.

Some northern populations of long-eared owls migrate south of their breeding areas in winter, to Mexico, northern Egypt and India, and northward again in spring.

NAME: Hawk Owl, *Surnia ulula*
RANGE: Canada, extreme N. USA, N. Asia, Scandinavia
HABITAT: open areas in coniferous forest
SIZE: 36–43 cm (14¼–17 in)

The hawk owl is easily recognized by its tail, which is longer than usual for owls, and by its pale facial disk, bordered with black. Its wings are fairly short and pointed, giving it a hawklike appearance in flight. It hunts by day, watching from a perch in the trees then flying down after prey. It feeds on mice, lemmings, squirrels and other small mammals, as well as on birds and some insects.

Nesting takes place from April to June, depending on the area, and the clutch size varies annually according to the food supply. The female lays her eggs, usually 5 or 6 but sometimes up to 9, in the hollow top of a tree stump or in an abandoned nest or woodpecker hole. The eggs are incubated for 25 to 30 days, mostly by the female.

NAME: Eurasian Pygmy Owl, *Glaucidium passerinum*
RANGE: N. Europe, east through USSR and central Asia to China
HABITAT: open forest
SIZE: 16 cm (6 in)

The smallest European owl, the pygmy owl has a small head and a long tail for its size. Its facial disk is less apparent than that of most owls. It hunts mainly at night and feeds on small rodents and on birds, many of which it catches in flight.

Pygmy owls breed from March to May and often nest in disused woodpecker holes. The male brings food to the female while she incubates the 2 to 7 eggs for about 28 days and to the young once they are hatched.

NAME: Little Owl, *Athene noctua*
RANGE: Europe, Africa, W. and central Asia, east to China; introduced in Britain and New Zealand
HABITAT: forest, open country, urban land
SIZE: 21 cm (8¼ in)

A small owl, with a flat-topped head, low forehead and large yellow eyes, the little owl has a stern, frowning expression. It is often active in the daytime. Insects and small rodents are its main foods, but it occasionally eats small birds and even carrion.

In Europe, the little owl nests from mid-April onward in a hole in a tree, on rocks or buildings, or even in an abandoned burrow or old nest of another bird. The female lays 3 to 5 eggs and incubates them for about 29 days. The male must bring all the food when the young are first hatched, but later both parents take a share in the hunting.

NAME: Tawny Owl, *Strix aluco*
RANGE: Britain, Europe, N. Africa, W. and central Asia to Korea
HABITAT: woods, gardens, parks, urban areas
SIZE: 38 cm (15 in)

The tawny owl is a strongly built bird, with mottled plumage, a rounded head and black eyes. One of the most common European owls, it is distinguished from the long- and short-eared owls by its lack of ear tufts and its dark eyes. It is strictly nocturnal, roosting in a tree during the day and hunting small rodents, birds and some insects at night.

Breeding starts in late March. The tawny owl nests in a hole in a tree or occasionally on the ground or in an old nest of another species. Usually 2 to 4 eggs are laid, but there can be as many as 8. The female alone incubates the clutch for 28 to 30 days. The male brings food for the newly hatched young for the first few weeks, but then both parents go out hunting. The young leave the nest at about 5 weeks.

NAME: Burrowing Owl, *Speotyto cunicularia*
RANGE: S.W. Canada, W. USA and Florida; Central and South America
HABITAT: semidesert, grassland without trees
SIZE: 23–28 cm (9–11 in)

The burrowing owl is a small, ground-living owl with a short tail and long legs, well suited to its terrestrial habits. It often lives in the abandoned burrows of prairie dogs and other mammals and usually adapts the burrow to its needs by digging with its feet to enlarge the hole and make a nesting chamber. Where there is a complex of burrows, such as those left by prairie dogs, a number of owls will take over, forming a colony. Contrary to popular belief, the owls do not share the burrows with prairie dogs.

Although burrowing owls usually hunt in the evening, they are often seen during the day standing at the burrow entrances. They feed on insects, such as moths, dragonflies, grasshoppers, beetles and crickets, and on small rodents, birds, frogs and reptiles. They frequently follow moving animals, such as dogs or horses, presumably to catch any prey the animals disturb.

Burrowing owls nest from March to July. The female lays 6 to 11 eggs, usually 8 or 9, in a chamber at the end of the burrow, which may be lined with dried animal droppings. Both parents incubate the eggs for about 28 days. Northern populations of burrowing owls migrate south of their breeding range in winter.

Morepork

Hawk Owl

Long-eared Owl

Eurasian Pygmy Owl

Little Owl

Tawny Owl

Burrowing Owl

Frogmouths, Potoos and relatives

ORDER CAPRIMULGIFORMES

This order comprises 5 families: the oilbird, frogmouths, potoos, nightjars and owlet-nightjars. Most of these birds are nocturnal.

PODARGIDAE: Frogmouth Family

The 13 species of frogmouth occur from India through Southeast Asia to New Guinea and Australia. Poor fliers, they have short, rounded wings and stumpy tails and tend to catch their prey by jumping onto it from a tree. They have large, flat bills with an enormous gape. Males and females look more or less alike.

NAME: **Tawny Frogmouth,** *Podargus strigoides*
RANGE: **Australia, Tasmania**
HABITAT: **forest, open woodland, trees in scrub, gardens, parks**
SIZE: **33–47 cm (13–18½ in)**

The nocturnal tawny frogmouth spends the day resting in a tree, where its mottled, streaked plumage blends perfectly with the lichen-covered branches. At any hint of danger, the bird stretches out its body, with head and bill pointing upward, and in this posture it is almost indistinguishable from a broken branch or stump. Much of the frogmouth's hunting is done at dusk, when it watches for prey from a tree or post, then descends silently to seize it on the ground. Insects, snails, frogs and even small mammals and birds are all included in its diet. There are at least 7 subspecies of tawny frogmouth, all varying slightly in size and shade of plumage.

The nest is a flimsy platform of sticks and leaves, made on a forked branch, or an old nest of another species may be used. The female incubates the 2 eggs for about 30 days, and both parents feed the young.

NAME: **Ceylon Frogmouth,** *Batrachostomus moniliger*
RANGE: **Sri Lanka, S.W. India**
HABITAT: **forest**
SIZE: **19–23 cm (7½–9 in)**

The Ceylon frogmouth is a tree-dwelling bird but takes most of its food on the ground after short flights from a perch; frogmouths of this genus seem to be more skillful in flight than those of the genus *Podargus*. Insects and small invertebrates are its main food. Like all frogmouths, this bird has mottled gray-brown plumage, which provides excellent camouflage as it sits on branches.

A single egg is laid in a small padlike nest, made from the bird's own down with a covering of lichen and cobwebs.

STEATORNITHIDAE: Oilbird Family

The single species of oilbird is sufficiently unusual to merit its own family. A large-eyed nocturnal bird, it has a patchy distribution in northern South America. Male and female birds look alike.

NAME: **Oilbird,** *Steatornis caripensis*
RANGE: **locally in Peru, through Ecuador, Colombia and Venezuela to French Guiana; Trinidad**
HABITAT: **seaside and mountain caves**
SIZE: **43 cm (17 in)**

A long-winged, long-tailed bird, the oilbird has small, almost useless legs and feet. It lives in deep, totally dark caves, where even its large eyes, specialized for nighttime vision, are ineffective. However, it can nest and fly about in these caves with ease by means of a system of echolocation similar to that used by bats. As it flies, the bird makes a series of high-pitched clicking sounds, which bounce off the walls of the cave and enable it to navigate. After dark, the oilbird emerges to feed on fruit, particularly that of palms. It seizes the fruit in its strong bill, swallows it whole and digests the entire night's intake the following day, back in its roost. The oilbird has a well-developed sense of smell and probably uses this, as well as its good nighttime vision, to find ripe fruit.

Oilbirds live in colonies of up to 50 pairs. The nest is made on a ledge from droppings, mixed with regurgitated fruit, and the female lays 2 to 4 eggs. Both parents incubate the eggs for about 33 days and feed the young on palm fruit. During their period on the nest, the young oilbirds become enormously fat, weighing at least half as much again as an adult, since they are not able to fly until they are about 4 months old. Local people used to capture these fledglings and render their fat for use as cooking oil — hence the common name — but this practice is now prohibited by law in most areas.

NYCTIBIIDAE: Potoo Family

The 5 species of potoo occur in the West Indies and adjacent areas of Central and South America. Although related to nightjars and similar to them in appearance, potoos feed like flycatchers, darting out from a perch to catch insects. Males and females look alike or nearly so.

NAME: **Common Potoo,** *Nyctibius griseus*
RANGE: **Jamaica, Hispaniola, Trinidad and Tobago; Mexico, Central America, tropical South America**
HABITAT: **forest edge, open forest, cultivated land with trees**
SIZE: **41 cm (16 in)**

The common potoo has a long tail, sometimes as much as half of its total length, and very short legs. Its grayish-brown plumage is heavily mottled and streaked, rendering it almost invisible among the lichen-covered branches of its habitat. During the day it sits in an extremely upright posture, often on a broken branch or stump, with its head and bill pointing upward so that it looks like part of the tree. At night, the potoo hunts for food, flying out from a perch to catch insects and returning to the same spot to consume them.

The single egg is laid on top of a tree stump and is incubated by both parents. If disturbed, the sitting bird adopts the upright posture and freezes or may retaliate by opening its eyes and bill wide and fluffing out its plumage in threat. Both parents feed the young, which sit in the upright posture in the nest. The young fly about 44 days after hatching.

AEGOTHELIDAE: Owlet-nightjar Family

Owlet-nightjars are small, dumpy birds, which resemble the related nightjars in many respects but have the flat-faced look of owls. They hunt at dawn and dusk, catching insects in the air or, more often, on the ground, where they move easily. There are 8 species, found in New Guinea, Australia and some nearby islands.

NAME: **Australian Owlet-nightjar,** *Aegotheles cristatus*
RANGE: **Australia, Tasmania, S. New Guinea**
HABITAT: **forest, woodland, scrub**
SIZE: **20–24 cm (7¾–9½ in)**

A shy, solitary bird, the Australian owlet-nightjar spends the day perched in an upright posture on a branch, disguised by its mottled and barred plumage. It starts to hunt for insects and invertebrates at dusk, taking much of its prey on the ground but also chasing aerial insects. Its bill is small and flat, but with a large gape, and is almost obscured by erect bristles.

The clutch of 3 or 4 eggs is laid in a hole in a tree or bank, lined with green leaves. The lining is renewed as the leaves wither. There may be more than one brood in a year.

Tawny Frogmouth

Common Potoo

Ceylon Frogmouth

Oilbird

Australian
Owlet-nightjar

Nightjars

NAME: Common Poor-will,
Phalaenoptilus nuttallii
**RANGE: breeds S.W. Canada, W. USA;
winters S. USA, Mexico**
**HABITAT: arid bush on hills and
mountains**
SIZE: 18–21.5 cm (7–8½ in)

A small, short-tailed nightjar, the common poor-will flits around at night, hunting moths, beetles and grasshoppers on or near the ground. During the day, it roosts in shrubbery or tall woods, at dawn and dusk calling out its cry of "poor-will" or "poor-jill."

The poor-will is the only bird known to hibernate. Each October it seeks out a rock crevice in which to spend the winter, often returning to the same spot year after year. Its body temperature falls from 40° to 41°C (104° to 106°F) to 18° to 19°C (64° to 66°F), and its heart and breathing rates drop to almost undetectable levels as its energy requirements drop to a minimum.

In early summer, poor-wills breed; the female lays 2 eggs on bare ground or gravel. The clutch is incubated by both parents.

NAME: Lyre-tailed Nightjar, *Uropsalis
lyra*
**RANGE: South America: Andes in
Venezuela, Colombia, Ecuador, Peru**
**HABITAT: mountain forest, savanna, open
woodland**
**SIZE: male: 79 cm (31 in);
female: 25.5 cm (10 in)**

The male lyre-tailed nightjar has two extremely long outer tail feathers, which account for up to 66 cm (26 in) of his total length. As the common name implies, these feathers are lyre-shaped and they are thought to be used in the male's courtship display. The female lacks these specialized features.

A solitary, nocturnal bird, this nightjar perches on low branches, often near water, and calls at dusk. Little is known of its feeding or breeding habits, but they are probably similar to those of other nightjars.

NAME: Greater Eared Nightjar,
Eurostopodus macrotis
**RANGE: India: Assam to S.E. Asia,
Philippines, Sulawesi**
HABITAT: forest, scrub
SIZE: 41 cm (16 in)

Mainly solitary birds, these large nightjars occasionally gather in small groups. They feed on insects caught in the air. Flying high around the treetops at dawn or dusk, they perform skillful aerobatics as they pursue their prey and call constantly, with a clear whistle. The female lays 1 egg on dead leaves, often in the shade at the foot of a tree.

CAPRIMULGIDAE:
Nightjar Family

Approximately 67 species of this specialized family of nocturnal birds are distributed almost worldwide: only New Zealand and some Pacific islands lack an example. They do not occur at high latitudes. Many have evocative names, such as nightjar, goatsucker, whip-poor-will and chuck-will's-widow, which are usually derived from their loud, repetitive calls.

Nightjars have long, pointed wings, and large eyes for good nighttime vision. The bill is short and weak, but it opens extremely wide and is fringed by sensory bristles. Most nightjars call for a period each evening at dusk, before they begin their aerial hunting. Flying silently and slowly, but making sudden darts after prey, they capture insects, which the bristles help to funnel into their wide, open mouths, and occasionally young birds. Nightjars are masterly in flight but have short, weak legs and avoid walking far on the ground.

During the daytime, nightjars roost in trees or on the ground, hidden from predators by their supremely efficient camouflaging plumage. In trees, they perch with their bodies lengthwise along the branch. All species have finely mottled gray, black and brown heads and backs, which blend perfectly with foliage or ground vegetation. Male and female look unalike in most species, having some plumage differences.

NAME: Standard-winged Nightjar,
Macrodipteryx longipennis
**RANGE: Africa: Chad, Sudan, Ethiopia,
N. Uganda, Kenya**
HABITAT: savanna, scrub
SIZE: 23 cm (9 in)

The standard-winged nightjar feeds on insects, which it catches in the air. A migratory species, it breeds in the southern part of its range from January to March and then moves north to Chad and northern Sudan.

In the breeding season, the male nightjar develops one elongated flight feather on each wing that grows to about 23 cm (9 in) in length. These are used in courtship displays, when the male flies around the female, raising his elongated feathers and arching and vibrating his wings. The male is believed to mate with more than one female, each of which lays 2 eggs on the ground; several birds may lay in the same area. The male bird then migrates, leaving the females to incubate the eggs and care for the young.

NAME: Pauraque, *Nyctidromus albicollis*
**RANGE: S.W. USA; Mexico; Central and
South America to N.E. Argentina**
**HABITAT: semiopen scrub, woodland
clearings**
SIZE: 28 cm (11 in)

Perching in a tree at night, the pauraque watches for prey, then launches into the air and flies close to the ground to catch insects, such as moths, wasps, bees and beetles, in its wide, gaping bill. During the day it roosts, hidden among the dead leaves on the woodland floor where it is virtually invisible. Male and female have some plumage differences: the female's outer wing and tail feathers are black, barred with rufous brown, while the male's are brown, barred with white, and are conspicuous in flight.

Pauraques live alone or in pairs. The female lays 2 eggs on bare ground, under the cover of bushes, and both parents incubate the clutch. They feed the nestlings by inserting the tip of the bill into a gaping mouth and regurgitating insects from the throat. The young birds begin to hop out of the nest at 2 or 3 days old, although they are not yet able to fly.

NAME: (European) Nightjar,
Caprimulgus europaeus
**RANGE: breeds in Europe, N. Africa,
W. and central Asia; winters in
tropical Africa**
**HABITAT: open country, forest edge,
moors, heaths, semidesert**
SIZE: 26 cm (10¼ in)

This long-winged, long-tailed bird is the only nightjar widespread in Europe, and it tolerates many different habitats. The male bird has some white spots on the outer wing tips and his tail feathers are tipped with white, but the sexes are otherwise similar in plumage.

After spending an inactive day perching on a branch, or on the ground, the nightjar takes wing at sunset and can be seen wheeling and gliding in the air and making sudden darts after moths and other nocturnal insects. It makes a churring call — the "jar" of its name.

The breeding season starts in mid-May. The male courts the female by clapping his wings together, and both birds sway their tails from side to side before mating. The female lays 2 eggs in a slight scrape on the ground or on top of vegetation. Both parents incubate, the female during the day and the male at night, and the eggs hatch after 18 days. Both parents care for the young, which are able to fly at about 17 or 18 days old. There are 2 broods in a season.

Standard-winged Nightjar (male)

Common Poor-will

Nightjar (male)

Lyre-tailed Nightjar (male)

Pauraque (male)

Greater Eared Nightjar (male)

Swifts, Crested Swifts

ORDER APODIFORMES

This order includes 3 families: swifts, crested swifts and hummingbirds. All are birds with highly developed flight abilities.

APODIDAE: Swift Family

Swifts are the most aerial of birds. The 67 species in this fast-flying family seem to be able to carry out every avian activity on the wing, other than nesting. They catch food, eat, drink, collect material for nest construction and even copulate while flying. Some species may also be able to sleep aloft. Although they can take off with difficulty from flat ground, swifts normally alight only on vertical surfaces, such as cliffs or buildings, and they cannot perch. They are usually active in the daytime and feed on insects.

Swifts range in length between 9 and 25.5 cm (3½ and 10 in), and male and female look alike. Owing to similarity of habits rather than close relationship, swifts have a superficial resemblance to swallows and martins, for they possess the same narrow, pointed, although longer, wings and short, normally forked tails. Their legs and feet are tiny since they seldom, if ever, walk, but they have strong, curved claws for gripping landing and nesting surfaces. In most species, all four toes point forward. The beak is typically short and slightly down-curving and has a wide gape.

All swifts glue their nests together with glutinous saliva from specialized salivary glands.

NAME: **Brown Needletail,** *Chaetura gigantea*
RANGE: **India through S.E. Asia to the Philippines**
HABITAT: **forest up to 1,800 m (6,000 ft)**
SIZE: **25.5 cm (10 in)**

One of the fastest-flying bird species, the brown needletail can reputedly attain speeds of 250 to 300 km/h (155 to 185 mph). It feeds on insects and will hover motionless, like a hawk, watching for prey. The female lays 3 to 5 eggs in a nest made on the ground.

NAME: **White-throated Swift,** *Aeronautes saxatalis*
RANGE: **W. Canada and USA to Mexico and El Salvador**
HABITAT: **vicinity of mountain and coastal cliffs, canyons, rugged foothills**
SIZE: **15–18 cm (6–7 in)**

The white-throated swift attains speeds of up to 300 km/h (185 mph) and is probably the fastest-flying bird in North America. It catches insects, such as flies, beetles, bees, wasps, flying ants and leaf-hoppers, on the wing. The swifts court in flight and copulate either on the wing, with bodies pressed together as they tumble downward, or in a nesting site. The nest, made in a crack or crevice in a coastal cliff or mountainside, is cup shaped and constructed of feathers and grass, glued together with saliva. The 4 or 5 eggs are laid in May and June and incubated by both parents.

NAME: **Palm Swift,** *Cypsiurus parvus*
RANGE: **W. Africa**
HABITAT: **open country**
SIZE: **18 cm (7 in)**

Palm swifts are gregarious birds which move in flocks and are easily distinguished by their unusually long tails. They are especially active at dusk, when many insects swarm.

The palm swift nests on the underside of a palm frond. The breeding pair makes a pad of feathers, which are glued together and to the leaf with saliva. They then glue the 1 or 2 eggs to the nest, also with saliva. Assuming a vertical posture and gripping the sides of the nest with their claws, both partners take turns at incubating the eggs. When the chicks hatch, they must immediately cling on to the nest with their claws and maintain their hold until they are fully fledged and ready to fly.

NAME: **Edible-nest Swiftlet,** *Collocalia fuciphaga*
RANGE: **Andaman and Nicobar Islands, S.E. Asia, Philippines**
HABITAT: **coasts, islands; feeds over forest and scrub**
SIZE: **12.5 cm (5 in)**

This swiftlet is one of 20 or more similar species in the genus *Collocalia*, all of which are found in Southeast Asia and the islands of the Pacific. The differentiation of the species is extremely difficult but has now been clarified by considering nest construction and sites and the ability to echolocate.

The swiftlets build their nests in caves, often in colonies of many thousands, and find their way in the darkness of the deeper caves by using echolocation, a rare ability among birds. As they fly, they make rapid clicking sounds and use the high-frequency echoes off the cave walls to navigate.

All swiftlets use saliva to make their nests and to glue them to cave walls, but the edible-nest swiftlet's nests are made almost entirely from hardened saliva with only a few feathers included — probably by accident. And it is these nests which give the bird its common name, for they are harvested in huge numbers to make the bird's-nest soup which Chinese gourmets consider a delicacy. The female lays 2 or 3 eggs.

NAME: **Common Swift,** *Apus apus*
RANGE: **breeds in Europe, east to China; N.W. Africa; winters in Africa**
HABITAT: **over open country, fresh water, urban areas**
SIZE: **16 cm (6¼ in)**

A common, gregarious bird, this swift is almost always seen in the air and only occasionally alights on walls, rocks or buildings. Uttering harsh, screaming cries, it flies in search of aerial insects, alternating rapid wing beats with long spells of gliding flight.

The breeding season starts in mid-May. The swifts select nest sites under the eaves of buildings or in rock crevices and make shallow, cup-shaped nests of grass and feathers, glued together with saliva. There are usually 3 eggs in a clutch, laid at 2- or 3-day intervals, and they are incubated for 14 to 20 days. Both parents feed the young, but may leave them for several days at a time. When this happens, the young burn up their fat stores and development slows down. If the fast is prolonged, the nestlings' body temperature may drop as much as 27.5°C (50°F), and they lapse into torpor, without any ill effects, until food is once again available.

HEMIPROCNIDAE: Crested Swift Family

The 4 species of crested swift all have crests and long, deeply forked tails. Their plumage is softer and brighter than that of other swifts, and they are less aerial in their habits. Unlike true swifts, they are able to perch. Males and females have some slight plumage differences. Crested swifts occur in India and Southeast Asia, south to the Solomon Islands.

NAME: **Crested Swift,** *Hemiprocne longipennis*
RANGE: **India, S.E. Asia, Indonesia to Sulawesi**
HABITAT: **forest edge, open woodland**
SIZE: **20.5 cm (8 in)**

The crested swift can perch on branches and telephone wires, from which it swoops down to feed on airborne insects. Males and females look similar, but the male has a chestnut patch behind the eye, while in the female this plumage is green.

The nest of the crested swift is a tiny, cup-shaped structure, made of thin flakes of bark, glued together with saliva and attached with saliva to the branch of a tree. There is just room on it for the 1 egg, which both parents take turns to incubate by sitting on the branch and puffing up their breast feathers to cover the egg. Both parents care for the chick.

Palm Swift

Common Swift

Edible-nest
Swiftlet

White-throated
Swift

Brown
Needletail

Crested Swift
(male)

Hummingbirds

NAME: Sword-billed Hummingbird,
Ensifera ensifera
RANGE: Andes: Venezuela, Colombia,
Ecuador, Peru, Bolivia
HABITAT: shrubby slopes at 2,500–3,000 m
(8,200–10,000 ft)
SIZE: bird: 7.5 cm (3 in)
bill: 12.5 cm (5 in)

The sword-billed hummingbird has the longest bill, relative to body size, of any bird. This bill allows the bird to probe deep into trumpet-shaped flowers to obtain nectar and to capture insects, which are themselves feeding on the nectar.

NAME: White-tipped Sicklebill,
Eutoxeres aquila
RANGE: Costa Rica, Panama, Colombia,
Ecuador, N.E. Peru
HABITAT: forest
SIZE: 12.5 cm (5 in)

This little hummingbird's strongly downward-curving bill is adapted to obtaining nectar from irregularly shaped flowers such as *Coryanthes* orchids. The bird will also cling awkwardly to *Heliconia* flowers and probe the blossoms with its bill.

NAME: Ruby-throated Hummingbird,
Archilochus colubris
RANGE: breeds in S.E. Canada, E. USA;
winters in Mexico, Central America
and West Indies
HABITAT: woodland, gardens
SIZE: 9 cm (3½ in)

This tiny bird migrates 800 km (500 mi) or more across the Gulf of Mexico to its wintering grounds — an extraordinary feat for such a small bird. The male has a distinctive ruby-red throat, and the female has white throat plumage and a rounded tail.

NAME: Bee Hummingbird, *Calypte
helenae*
RANGE: Cuba, Isle of Pines
HABITAT: forest
SIZE: 5.7 cm (2¼ in)

The smallest bird in the world, the bee hummingbird's actual body measures only 1.25 cm (½ in), and its bill, of similar size, and tail make up the total length. It weighs only 2 g (1/14 oz). Its tiny wings beat 50 to 80 times a second as it hovers to feed from flowers.

NAME: Giant Hummingbird, *Patagona
gigas*
RANGE: Ecuador to Chile and Argentina
HABITAT: arid land
SIZE: 21.5 cm (8½ in)

The largest hummingbird, this species weighs 20 g (¾ oz). It beats its wings only 8 or 10 times a second, and although it feeds at flowers, it also catches insects in flight.

TROCHILIDAE:
Hummingbird Family

Named for the drone produced by the extremely rapid beating of their wings, the spectacular hummingbirds occur all over the Americas, from Alaska to Tierra del Fuego and high in the Andes, but mainly in the tropics. The 319 or so species include the smallest, and some of the most striking, birds known.

Hummingbirds range in length from 5.7 to 21.5 cm (2¼ to 8½ in), but the tail often makes up as much as half of this length. Their wings are long and narrow relative to body size, and hummingbirds are quite unsurpassed in their aerial maneuverability. They can hover motionless in front of a flower, their wings beating so fast that they are virtually invisible; they can fly upward, sideways, downward and, uniquely, backward. The keel of the breastbone in a hummingbird is proportionately bigger than that of any other bird, to support the massive flying muscles needed to power their movements.

The hummingbird's main foods are insects and nectar, which it obtains by plunging its long, slender, often curved bill (which has become specially adapted for the task) deep inside the flower. It uses its tubular tongue to extract the nectar, and the shapes of both bill and tongue are often closely related to those of particular flowers.

There is a great variety of tail shapes among male hummingbirds, and these decorative feathers are used in courtship display; females have duller plumage than males and lack the ornamental tail feathers. Except in the breeding season, hummingbirds are solitary and defend their territory aggressively, even against much larger birds. The female builds a cup-shaped nest, which is placed on a branch or palm frond or on a rock, and normally lays 2 eggs. In all but 1 species, she alone incubates the eggs and cares for the young.

NAME: Frilled Coquette, *Lophornis
magnifica*
RANGE: E. and central Brazil
HABITAT: forest, scrub
SIZE: 7 cm (2¾ in)

The brilliant frilled coquette can easily be mistaken for a butterfly, either as it hovers, feeding from a flower, or when pairs are courting, for the male chases the female until she slows down, and they then hover together, fluttering up and down. The female builds a cup-shaped nest among low vegetation and covers the outside with cobwebs, pieces of bark and plant fibers, which camouflage it.

NAME: Ruby-topaz Hummingbird,
Chrysolampis mosquitus
RANGE: Colombia, Venezuela, the
Guianas, Brazil, N.E. Bolivia
HABITAT: forest, scrub, savanna
SIZE: 9 cm (3½ in)

The male of this species has glittering, colorful plumage, while the female's feathers are greenish and gray.

The birds feed on nectar and insects, both in low vegetation and tall trees.

NAME: Marvelous Spatule-tail,
Loddigesia mirabilis
RANGE: Andes in Peru
HABITAT: forest at 2,300–2,600 m
(7,500–8,500 ft)
SIZE: body: 12.5 cm (5 in)
tail: 14 cm (5½ in)

The male of this little-known hummingbird species has an extraordinary tail, with only four feathers, two of which are greatly elongated and wirelike and expanded into racket shapes at the ends. During his courtship display, the male bird frames his iridescent throat plumage with his decorative tail feathers and flies back and forth in front of his prospective mate.

NAME: Long-tailed Sylph Hummingbird,
Aglaiocercus kingi
RANGE: Venezuela to Bolivia, Peru and
Ecuador
HABITAT: forest, scrub
SIZE: male: 18 cm (7 in)
female: 9.5 cm (3¾ in)

The outer tail feathers of the male of this species are almost 12.5 cm (5 in) long and are used in courtship display. The female's tail feathers are not elongated, and she has a buff-white throat and cinnamon underparts.

NAME: Crimson Topaz, *Topaza pella*
RANGE: the Guianas, Venezuela, Brazil
HABITAT: rain forest
SIZE: 20 cm (7¾ in)

A glittering, colorful bird, the male crimson topaz has two elongated black tail feathers, which are 6 cm (2¼ in) longer than the rest of the tail. The female is less startling, but she, too, has some gleaming green and red plumage, as well as bronze and violet tail feathers.

NAME: Andean Hillstar, *Oreotrochilus
estella*
RANGE: Andes: from Ecuador to
Argentina and Chile
HABITAT: rocky slopes
SIZE: 12 cm (4¾ in)

The neck and throat plumage of the male of this species varies but usually includes some glittering green or violet and sometimes both. The female bird has a dull olive-green back and head, white throat and grayish underparts.

Crimson Topaz (male)

Sword-billed
Hummingbird

Long-tailed
Sylph Hummingbird (male)

Ruby-topaz
Hummingbird (male)

Frilled
Coquette

Marvelous
Spatule-tail (male)

White-tipped
Sicklebill

Bee Hummingbird

Giant Hummingbird

Andean Hillstar (male)

Ruby-throated
Hummingbird (male)

Trogons, Mousebirds

ORDER TROGONIFORMES
TROGONIDAE: Trogon Family

The trogons make up a family that is placed in its own order. The 35 or 36 species of trogon are among the most resplendently colorful birds in the world; males are always more brilliantly marked than females. They are found in forest habitats in three quite separate tropical areas: the southern regions of Africa; India and Southeast Asia; and Central and South America.

Trogons are between 23 and 35.5 cm (9 and 14 in) in length and possess short, rounded wings and long tails. Their feet are zygodactyl, that is, they have two toes pointing forward and two pointing backward, an adaptation possessed by many tree-living birds. However, in trogons the first and second digits point forward, while in all other birds with such feet, it is the first and fourth digits that do so.

Primarily woodland and forest birds, trogons spend much of their time perching in trees. They feed on insects and other small invertebrates and also on berries and fruit.

NAME: Quetzal, *Pharomachrus mocinno*
RANGE: Mexico, Central America
HABITAT: high-altitude rain forest
SIZE: 30 cm (11¾ in)
   tail feathers: 61 cm (24 in) Ⓥ

The strikingly colored quetzal has greatly extended upper tail coverts (feathers overlying the tail), which form a magnificent train and are shed and regrown after each breeding season. These feathers were highly prized for ceremonial use by ancient Mayan and Aztec civilizations, and the quetzal itself was regarded as a sacred bird and was associated with the plumed serpent god, Quetzalcoatl. The quetzal is now the national bird of Guatemala. Females are plainer than males, and their upper tail coverts extend only to the end of the tail proper and do not form a train.

Quetzals are arboreal, somewhat solitary birds which inhabit the lower layers of the tropical forest trees. They feed on fruit, of which they seem particularly fond, as well as on insects, small frogs, lizards and snails, and flutter from branch to branch, seizing food items as they go.

They nest in a hole in a tree and 2 or 3 eggs are laid. The male bird takes his turn at incubating the clutch and must sit on the nest with the tail plumes bent forward over his head and hanging out of the hole. By the end of the breeding season, the feathers are damaged and broken from many maneuvers in and out of the nest.

NAME: Elegant/Coppery-tailed Trogon, *Trogon elegans*
RANGE: extreme S.W. USA to Costa Rica
HABITAT: forest, woodland
SIZE: 28–30.5 cm (11–12 in)

This brilliantly plumaged trogon has a stout yellow bill and a distinctive broad, blunt tail. The tail is coppery-red, seen from above, but gray and white below, with a black band at the base. The female bird is patterned like the male but is duller, with a brownish head. This is the only species in the trogon family to occur in the USA.

Elegant trogons are solitary, generally quiet birds, but they do make monotonous, froglike calls. They perch for long periods in the trees and then take to the air to dart about the branches in search of insects, small animals and fruit. Most of their feeding is done in flight, and the birds will sometimes hover in front of a cluster of leaves to glean food from their surfaces. The trogon's legs and feet are weak and are used almost entirely for perching, only rarely for walking.

Both partners of a breeding pair help to excavate a hole in a tree for use as a nest, or they take over an existing hollow or an abandoned woodpecker hole. The 3 or 4 eggs are incubated by both male and female, probably for a total of 17 to 19 days. The young hatch naked and helpless and are cared for and fed by both parents. They leave the nest when 15 to 17 days old.

NAME: Red-headed Trogon, *Harpactes erythrocephalus*
RANGE: Nepal: Himalayas, S. China; S.E. Asia, Sumatra
HABITAT: forest
SIZE: 34 cm (13¼ in)

There are 11 species of trogon in Asia, all in the genus *Harpactes*. All are beautiful birds with broad, squared-off tails. The male red-headed trogon has distinctive dark-red plumage on its head, while the female has a brownish head, throat and breast. Like the American trogons, they are mainly solitary birds which perch on trees and dart out to catch food. Insects form the bulk of their diet, but they also eat leaves, berries, some frogs, and lizards; they do not appear to eat fruit. Twilight is their main period of activity.

The 3 or 4 eggs are laid in an unlined hole in a tree, usually an existing hollow, and are incubated by both parents for about 19 days.

NAME: Narina Trogon, *Apaloderma narina*
RANGE: southern Africa: S. and E. coastal regions
HABITAT: forest, scrub
SIZE: 29 cm (11½ in)

One of the 3 African trogon species, the narina trogon lives in the lower levels of dense forest and will perch for long periods on a branch or creeper in a characteristically hunched posture. It feeds mainly on insects, which it catches among the branches or by darting out from the perch, and only rarely eats fruit.

The 2 or 3 eggs are laid in a hollow tree trunk and are incubated for about 20 days.

ORDER COLIIFORMES
COLIIDAE: Mousebird Family

The 6 species of mousebird, or coly, constitute a distinctive family that modern taxonomists place in an order of its own. All the forms are of very similar appearance, and the sexes look alike in all species. The body of the mousebird is about the size of that of a house sparrow, but it has extremely long tail feathers of graduated lengths. The plumage is soft and loosely attached to the skin. All species have crests, and their bills are short, curved and quite strong.

Mousebirds are distributed in the savanna regions of Africa, south of the Sahara. They are sociable birds which live in small groups and roost together, huddling close for warmth.

NAME: Speckled Mousebird, *Colius striatus*
RANGE: Africa, south of the Sahara
HABITAT: savanna, dense forest
SIZE: body: 12 cm (4¾ in)
   tail: 18–20 cm (7–7¾ in)

The speckled mousebird has a tail almost twice the length of its body. It spends much of its life in trees and climbs expertly among the branches, using its strong, adaptable feet — the hind toes can be turned forward — and long, sharp claws. Like all mousebirds, this species is extremely gregarious and feeds and roosts in small groups. Fruit and any soft vegetable matter, particularly young shoots, are its normal diet, but it occasionally eats insects.

The speckled mousebird makes a nest of twigs and rootlets, lined with leaves, in a tree or bush. Usually 3 eggs are laid, and they are then incubated by both parents for a total of 12 to 14 days. Young are able to leave the nest a few days after hatching and fly at 16 to 18 days old.

Speckled Mousebird

Quetzal

Elegant Trogon

Red-headed Trogon

Narina Trogon

Kingfishers

NAME: Kingfisher, *Alcedo atthis*
RANGE: Europe, N. Africa to Asia, New Guinea and Solomon Islands
HABITAT: inland waterways, marshes. mangrove swamps, seashores
SIZE: 16 cm (6¼ in)

The only European kingfisher, this bird has a wide range and is unmistakable, with its brilliant plumage and long, daggerlike bill. A solitary bird, it lives in the vicinity of water. When hunting, it perches on branches overhanging the water, watching for prey, or flies low over it, often hovering for a few seconds before diving for fish and other small aquatic animals.

In the breeding season, a pair makes a slightly upward-sloping tunnel, up to 61 cm (24 in) long, in the bank of a stream, with a nesting chamber about 15 cm (6 in) across at the end of it. They start the tunnel by repeatedly hurling themselves against the riverbank so that their sharp bills always strike the same spot. Here the female lays 4 to 8 eggs which both parents incubate in shifts for 19 to 21 days. They share in the care and feeding of the young.

NAME: Shovel-billed Kingfisher, *Clytoceyx rex*
RANGE: New Guinea
HABITAT: forest
SIZE: 30.5 cm (12 in)

The soberly colored shovel-billed kingfisher is a solitary bird which inhabits forest at altitudes of up to 2,350 m (7,700 ft). It perches for long periods on tree stumps and branches, swooping down suddenly to catch large insects, larvae and small mice. Using its short, heavy bill as a shovel, it also probes in the mud beside streams and rivers, searching for worms, crabs and reptiles. Little is known about its breeding habits, but it is thought to make its nest on the ground.

NAME: White-collared/Mangrove Kingfisher, *Halcyon chloris*
RANGE: Ethiopia to India, S.E. China, Australia, S.W. Pacific islands
HABITAT: mangrove swamps, estuaries, rivers, forest clearings
SIZE: 25.5 cm (10 in)

This widely distributed kingfisher is found in a variety of habitats but most commonly in mangrove swamps. Perching on branches, it watches for prey, then swoops down to the swamp mud or dives into the water in pursuit of crabs and small fish, its main foods. Before swallowing a crab, the kingfisher will dash it against a branch a few times to crush the shell. These kingfishers nest in holes in trees, among the roots of an arboreal fern or in termite or ant nests. The female lays 3 or 4 eggs.

ORDER CORACIIFORMES

There are 10 families in this order: kingfishers, todies, motmots, bee-eaters, rollers, cuckoo-rollers, ground rollers, hoopoes, woodhoopoes and hornbills. Most species in the order have large bills in proportion to their body size and brightly colored plumage.

ALCEDINIDAE: Kingfisher Family

Although kingfishers are found all over the world, the majority of the 86 or so known species inhabit the hotter regions of the Old World. They range in length from 10 to 46 cm (4 to 18 in) and have stocky bodies, large heads and short necks. The beak is almost always straight, with a pointed tip, and is large in proportion to the body. Wings are short and rounded, and tail length is variable. Most kingfishers have multicolored plumage, with patches of iridescent blue, green, purple or red. Male and female differ slightly in appearance in some species.

As the group name suggests, several kingfishers are fish-eaters. They are usually found near inland waters and catch aquatic invertebrates as well as fish by diving headlong from a perch just above the water. Unusually for diving birds, they do not actually swim. The majority of species, however, feed on dry land on insects, lizards, snakes and even birds and rodents, catching prey by swooping down from a high vantage point.

Kingfishers nest in tunnels, often in riverbanks, or in cavities in trees or termite nests; there is little or no nesting material. Some northern populations migrate south in winter.

NAME: Beautiful/Common Paradise Kingfisher, *Tanysiptera galatea*
RANGE: New Guinea to the Moluccas
HABITAT: forest
SIZE: 28 cm (11 in)

This handsome kingfisher has greatly elongated tail feathers, thought to be used in courtship display. Deep in the forest understory, it perches on branches to watch for its prey, mainly millipedes and lizards but also insects and other invertebrates, and it may dig in the forest litter for earthworms.

Beautiful paradise kingfishers are normally solitary birds, but in the breeding season both partners of a breeding pair help to dig a hole in an arboreal termite nest in which to lay their eggs. Alternatively, the birds will nest in patches of vegetation at the forest edge. The female lays 3 to 5 eggs, which are incubated by both parents.

NAME: Laughing Kookaburra, *Dacelo novaeguineae*
RANGE: Australia; introduced in Tasmania
HABITAT: dry forest fringe, savanna, any open country with trees
SIZE: 46 cm (18 in)

The largest of the kingfishers, the kookaburra is renowned for its noisy, laughlike call; when one bird starts calling, all the others near by will join in, particularly at dawn or at dusk. Kookaburras eat practically anything, including large insects, crabs, small reptiles, mammals and birds, and are beneficial to humans in that they prey on rodents and other harmful vermin.

Kookaburras nest in holes in trees or sometimes in arboreal termite nests, in cavities in banks or even on buildings. The female lays 3 or 4 eggs.

NAME: African Pygmy Kingfisher, *Ispidina picta*
RANGE: Africa, south of the Sahara to Zambia
HABITAT: bush, woodland
SIZE: 12.5 cm (5 in)

One of the smallest kingfishers, this species has the curious habit of diving from its perch into grass, much as other kingfishers dive into water. Grasshoppers, caterpillars, beetles and other insects, as well as some lizards, make up its diet. The insects are caught in the air or on the ground. The pygmy kingfisher's nest is made at the end of a tunnel in a riverbank or in a termite mound or anthill, and the female lays 3 to 5 eggs.

NAME: Belted Kingfisher, *Ceryle alcyon*
RANGE: Alaska, Canada, USA, south to Mexico and Panama; West Indies
HABITAT: fresh water, coasts
SIZE: 28–35.5 cm (11–14 in)

The only American kingfisher to occur north of Texas and Arizona, this common bird inhabits any territory near water. Male and female birds look similar, but the female has a chestnut band across the breast and extending down the flanks, which the male lacks. Solitary birds out of the breeding season, each individual holds its own territory and has a series of habitual perches overlooking water. They feed on small fish, crabs, crayfish, tadpoles, frogs, lizards and some insects and generally hover above the water before diving for prey.

Using their bills and feet, both members of a breeding pair dig a nesting tunnel 1.2 to 2.4 m (4 to 8 ft) long in the riverbank, at the end of which they make a nesting chamber. The female lays 5 to 8 eggs, which are incubated for about 23 days.

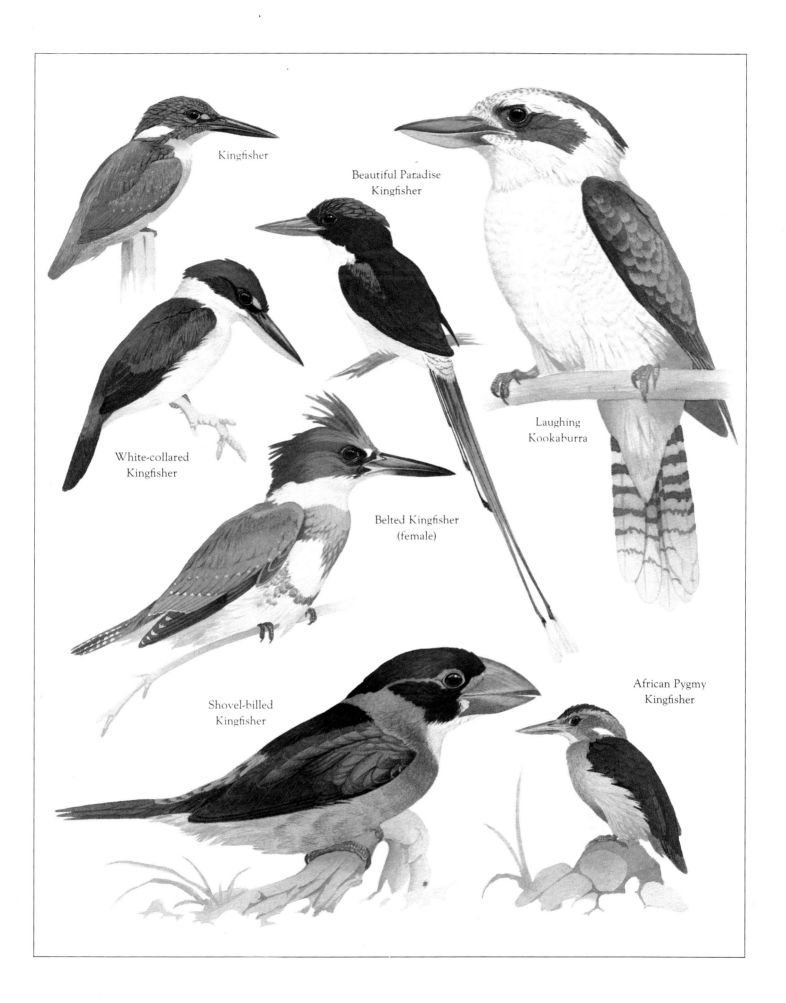

Kingfisher

Beautiful Paradise
Kingfisher

White-collared
Kingfisher

Belted Kingfisher
(female)

Laughing
Kookaburra

Shovel-billed
Kingfisher

African Pygmy
Kingfisher

Motmots,
Bee-eaters and relatives

MOMOTIDAE: Motmot Family
Motmots are beautifully plumaged birds, with decorative, elongated tail feathers. There are 9 species of motmot, found from Mexico to northeastern Argentina. All have slightly downward-curving bills with serrated edges, which they use to seize prey from the dense vegetation among which they live. Male and female look alike or nearly so.

NAME: **Blue-crowned Motmot,** *Momotus momota*
RANGE: **Mexico, Central America, South America to N.W. Argentina; Trinidad and Tobago**
HABITAT: **rain forest, plantations**
SIZE: **38–41 cm (15–16 in)**

The blue-crowned motmot has two greatly elongated central tail feathers, with racket-shaped tips. Although the feathers are initially fully vaned, the vanes just above the ends of the feathers are loosely attached and fall away as the bird preens or brushes against vegetation, leaving the racket tips. The motmot perches to watch for prey, such as insects, spiders or lizards, often swinging its tail from side to side like a pendulum while it waits. It darts out from the perch to seize prey, then returns to consume the item, having briefly beaten it against a branch.

Motmots nest in a burrow, which is dug by both members of a breeding pair, in a bank or opening off the side of a mammal's burrow. The burrow may be up to 4 m (13 ft) long and have several sharp turns. In the enlarged chamber at the end of the tunnel, the female lays her 3 eggs on bare ground. Both parents incubate the eggs for about 21 days.

MEROPIDAE: Bee-eater Family
The 24 species of bee-eater are brightly plumaged birds, with streamlined bodies, long wings and small, weak legs. They occur in tropical and warm temperate areas of the Old World. As their name suggests, they are adept at the aerial capture of insects, such as bees and wasps, which they seize with their long, downward-curving bills. While they are considered a menace by beekeepers, these birds are much appreciated in the tropics, where they consume large numbers of locusts.

Bee-eaters are gregarious birds, feeding together and nesting in colonies of sometimes hundreds of pairs. Males and females look alike. Many species are migratory.

NAME: **(European) Bee-eater,** *Merops apiaster*
RANGE: **breeds in Europe, USSR, N. Africa, S.W. Asia; winters in tropical Africa and Middle East**
HABITAT: **open country, woodland**
SIZE: **28 cm (11 in)**

One of the most tropical-looking European birds, the gaudy bee-eater makes swift darts from a perch to catch prey, mainly bees and wasps. It rubs its prey against a branch or the ground before swallowing it, presumably to destroy the sting.

Bee-eaters nest in colonies. Each pair makes a tunnel 1 to 3 m (3¼ to 9¾ ft) long, often in a riverbank. The female lays 4 to 7 eggs at the end of the tunnel, and both parents incubate the clutch for about 20 days. Together, they care for and feed their young.

TODIDAE: Tody Family
The 5 species of tody all live in the West Indies and are extremely similar in size and appearance, with mostly green and red plumage. Males and females look alike. They are insect-eating birds which catch their prey, flycatcher-fashion, in the air.

NAME: **Jamaican Tody,** *Todus todus*
RANGE: **Jamaica**
HABITAT: **wooded hills and mountains**
SIZE: **10.75 cm (4¼ in)**

The Jamaican tody is typical of its family, with its small, compact body, relatively large head and long, sharp bill. It hunts close to the ground, catching flying insects and, occasionally, baby lizards.

Todies live in pairs or singly and are strongly territorial. They nest in burrows, which they dig with their bills, usually in the sides of banks. The nest tunnel is about 30 cm (11¾ in) long, with a tiny entrance just big enough for the birds to squeeze through, but it opens out at the end into a breeding chamber. The female lays 3 or 4 eggs, and both parents incubate the clutch and care for the young.

CORACIIDAE: Roller Family
Most of the 11 species of roller live in Africa, although they occur in warm temperate and tropical parts of the Old World, from Europe to Australia. They are brightly colored, stocky birds, with large heads, long, downward-curving bills and long wings. Their common name originates from their tumbling, aerobatic courtship displays. Males and females look alike.

NAME: **Roller,** *Coracias garrulus*
RANGE: **breeds in Europe, N. Africa, S.W. Asia; winters in E. and S. Africa, Middle East**
HABITAT: **forest, woodland, open country**
SIZE: **30 cm (11¾ in)**

Robust, gregarious birds, rollers like to perch, particularly on telephone wires, to watch for prey such as insects, small lizards, frogs and birds, They dart out to seize the prey and return to the perch to feed. Fruit is also part of their diet.

The male roller courts his mate with extraordinary flight displays in which he dives to the earth from high in the air, tumbling and rolling as he descends. The nest is made in an existing hole in a tree, wall or bank, or an abandoned nest of another bird species may be used. Both parents incubate the 4 to 7 eggs for a total of 18 or 19 days and share the care of the young.

LEPTOSOMATIDAE: Cuckoo-roller Family
The single species in this family is related to the true rollers and ground rollers. It differs from them, however, in that male and female look unalike.

NAME: **Cuckoo-roller,** *Leptosomus discolor*
RANGE: **Madagascar, Comoro Islands**
HABITAT: **forest, savanna**
SIZE: **41–46 cm (16–18 in)**

Cuckoo-rollers are noisy birds which live in trees, feeding on insects, especially hairy caterpillars, and on lizards. Their legs are short and weak, but they are strong fliers and perform spectacular maneuvers over the treetops. The female is plainer than the male, with rufous plumage and black markings.

BRACHYPTERACIIDAE: Ground Roller Family
The 5 species of ground roller all live in Madagascar. Sometimes classified as a subfamily of rollers (Coraciidae), they differ from the latter in that they are ground-living rather than arboreal.

NAME: **Short-legged Ground Roller,** *Brachypteracias leptosomus*
RANGE: **E. Madagascar**
HABITAT: **dense forest to 1,800 m (6,000ft)**
SIZE: **25.5–30.5 cm (10–12 in)** ®

Typical of its family, the short-legged ground roller is a squat bird, with short wings, strong legs and a stout, downward-curving bill. It lives on the forest floor, feeding on insects and reptiles, and flies up into trees only when alarmed.

Jamaican Tody

Bee-eater

Blue-crowned Motmot

Cuckoo-roller
(male)

Short-legged Ground Roller

Roller

Hoopoe, Woodhoopoes, Hornbills

UPUPIDAE: Hoopoe Family
The single species of hoopoe is a ground-living bird, distinct enough in structure to merit a family of its own. Male and female birds look more or less alike, but females may sometimes be smaller and duller.

NAME: **Common Hoopoe**, *Upupa epops*
RANGE: **Europe (except Scandinavia and, usually, Britain), N. Africa, central and S. Asia; winters tropical Africa, S. Asia**
HABITAT: **open country with trees, forest edge, parks, gardens, orchards**
SIZE: **28 cm (11 in)**

An unusual, striking bird, the hoopoe has pinkish to cinnamon body plumage, boldly barred wings and tail and a huge crest, which is usually held flat. The hoopoe's legs are strong, and it walks and runs swiftly as it searches for worms, insects and invertebrates to eat, probing the ground with its curved, slender bill. Although primarily a ground bird, the hoopoe does perch and roost in trees and flies efficiently, if slowly, occasionally hunting insects in the air.

The female lays 5 to 8 eggs, sometimes as many as 12, in a hole in a tree, wall or building. The male bird feeds his mate while she incubates the clutch for 16 to 19 days.

PHOENICULIDAE: Woodhoopoe Family
Wooded grassland, forest and forest edge in central and southern Africa are the habitats of the 8 species of woodhoopoe. Male and female birds look similar, but the female is often smaller and sometimes browner than the male.

NAME: **Green Woodhoopoe**, *Phoeniculus purpureus*
RANGE: **Africa, south of the Sahara**
HABITAT: **woodland, often near rivers, forest**
SIZE: **38 cm (15 in)**

The slender green woodhoopoe has glossy dark-green and purple plumage and a long, deep-purple tail; its distinctive red bill is long and downward-curving. Male and female look alike, but young birds have brownish neck and breast plumage and black bills. Noisy, gregarious birds, woodhoopoes fly from tree to tree in small parties, searching for insects to eat and calling harshly.

The female woodhoopoe lays her 3 to 5 eggs in a hole in a tree or may use an old woodpecker or barbet hole. She incubates the clutch, but her mate helps her tend and feed the young.

BUCEROTIDAE: Hornbill Family
The 44 species of hornbill occur in Africa, south of the Sahara, and in tropical Asia, south to Indonesia. Most have brown or black and white plumage but are instantly recognizable by their huge bills, topped with horny projections, or casques. Despite its heavy appearance, the hornbill's beak is actually a light honeycomb of bony cellular tissue, encased in a shell of horn. While a few hornbills are ground-feeding birds of open country, most live and feed in trees in forest and savanna. Most are omnivorous, feeding on fruit, insects, lizards and even small mammals. Male and female look similar in some species but differ in others.

Hornbills are probably best known for their extraordinary nesting habits. Once the female has laid her eggs in a suitable nest hole, the entrance is walled up with mud, leaving a small slitlike opening. The male may do this or the female may barricade herself in, using material that the male brings her. She remains there throughout the incubation and part of the fledgling period, totally dependent on her mate for food supplies but perfectly protected from predators. The male brings food, which he passes to her through the slit — a task to which his long, laterally compressed bill is admirably suited.

While she is a captive, she undergoes a molt, but by the time the appetites of the young are too much for the male to cope with, her feathers have regrown. Using her beak, she hacks her way out of the nest, and the young repair the barricade. Both parents then bring food until the young hornbills are able to fly. Details vary slightly from species to species, but all hornbills keep their nests clean, throwing out food debris and excreting through the slit.

NAME: **Red-billed Hornbill**, *Tockus erythrorhynchus*
RANGE: **W., E. and S.E. Africa**
HABITAT: **bush, open woodland**
SIZE: **46 cm (18 in)**

Although brightly colored, the beak of the red-billed hornbill has little, if any, casque. Male and female look similar, with gray and brownish-black plumage and light markings on the wings. The female does not always have a black base to the lower bill. Usually in pairs or small family parties, red-billed hornbills feed on the ground and in trees on insects, such as grasshoppers, locusts and beetles, and on fruit.

The female lays her 3 to 6 eggs in a hole in a tree, which is barricaded with mud in the usual manner of hornbills.

NAME: **Southern Ground Hornbill**, *Bucorvus leadbeateri*
RANGE: **Africa: Lake Tanganyika, south to South Africa: Cape Province**
HABITAT: **open country**
SIZE: **107 cm (42 in)**

The southern ground hornbill and the closely related Abyssinian ground hornbill, *B. abyssinicus*, are the largest of the African hornbills. Both are primarily ground-living, turkey-sized birds, which walk about in pairs or small family parties, feeding on insects and small reptiles and other animals.

The female lays 1 to 3 eggs in a hole in a tree or stump, lined with leaves. She is not walled up in the nest and comes and goes freely, covering the eggs with leaves when she is not sitting.

NAME: **Helmeted Hornbill**, *Rhinoplax vigil*
RANGE: **Malaysian Peninsula, Sumatra, Borneo**
HABITAT: **forest**
SIZE: **1.2 m (4 ft)** ①

The greatly elongated central tail feathers of this huge hornbill may add as much as 50 cm (20 in) to its length. The female is slightly smaller than the male. This bird is unusual in that while all other hornbills have bills that are deceptively light, its casque is formed of solid ivory, making its skull the heaviest of any bird's. This heavy head could cause problems for the bird when in flight, but the elongated central tail feathers help to counterbalance the skull. Unfortunately the attributes of the helmeted hornbill have created much demand for it, and it has long been hunted both for its ivory casque and its tail feathers.

Helmeted hornbills feed on fruit, lizards, birds and their eggs. The breeding procedure is believed to be similar to that of other hornbills.

NAME: **Great Indian Hornbill**, *Buceros bicornis*
RANGE: **India, S.E. Asia, Sumatra**
HABITAT: **forest**
SIZE: **1.5 m (5 ft)**

Although a large bird, the great Indian hornbill has a top-heavy appearance, with its huge bill and casque. The female bird is much smaller, particularly her bill and casque, and has white instead of red eyes, but she is otherwise similar to the male. These hornbills spend much of their time in trees, feeding on fruit, especially figs, as well as on insects, reptiles and other small animals.

The female bird lays 1 to 3 eggs in an unlined hole in a tree and walls up the entrance from within, using her own feces and material brought to her by the male. She incubates the eggs for about 31 days.

Green Woodhoopoe

Red-billed Hornbill

Common Hoopoe

Helmeted Hornbill

Great Indian Hornbill

Southern Ground
Hornbill

Jacamars, Barbets and relatives

ORDER PICIFORMES

This order includes 6 families: jacamars, puffbirds, honey guides, woodpeckers, toucans and barbets. Most of the birds in these families are tree-dwelling and have in common a zygodactyl foot (a foot with two toes pointing forward and two pointing backward), which aids climbing up vertical tree trunks.

GALBULIDAE: Jacamar Family

The 17 species of jacamar are graceful, long-billed birds, which resemble bee-eaters in appearance and in their technique of catching insects in the air, although they are unrelated. Males are usually brightly plumaged, with some glossy or iridescent feathers, while females are a little duller. Jacamars nest in tunnels, which they dig in the ground. They occur from Mexico to Brazil.

NAME: **Rufous-tailed Jacamar**, *Galbula ruficauda*
RANGE: **Mexico, Central America, through tropical South America to Brazil; Trinidad and Tobago**
HABITAT: **forest clearings, second-growth forest, scrub woodland**
SIZE: **23–28 cm (9–11 in)**

The rufous-tailed jacamar is a brightly plumaged bird, with gleaming, iridescent upperparts. The female differs in that she has a buff throat, and young birds are generally duller. Perching on a branch, the jacamar watches for insect prey to fly past, then darts after it in agile, swooping flight, snapping the insect out of the air with great expertise. It returns to its perch to consume the catch, and if the insect is large, beats it against the branch to kill it and to remove any hard, horny legs or wing cases before swallowing.

Jacamars excavate their own breeding tunnel in the ground, the female of the pair doing most of the work. Both birds share the incubation of 19 to 23 days, the female sitting at night, and the male taking over in the daytime. They feed their young until they are able to fly, about 3 weeks after hatching.

BUCCONIDAE: Puffbird Family

Closely related to jacamars, the 34 species of puffbird and nunbird are also insect-eating birds, found from Mexico south through Central and tropical South America. Puffbirds are, however, stouter, more lethargic birds than the agile jacamars, although they do make aerial sallies after prey. Male and female look more or less alike, both with large heads for their size and sober plumage.

NAME: **White-necked Puffbird,** *Notharchus macrorhynchos*
RANGE: **Central and South America to N.E. Argentina**
HABITAT: **open forest, forest edge, savanna with trees**
SIZE: **25.5 cm (10 in)**

Like all puffbirds, this species has a habit of fluffing out its plumage as it perches watching for prey, thus creating a bulky appearance, which is the origin of the common name. Once an insect is sighted, the puffbird flies out to catch it in flight with its broad, hook-tipped bill.

Breeding white-necked puffbirds excavate a tunnel in the ground and then camouflage the entrance with leaves and twigs. The female lays 2 or 3 eggs in a leaf-lined chamber at the end of the tunnel, and both birds incubate the clutch.

NAME: **Black-fronted Nunbird,** *Monasa nigrifrons*
RANGE: **Colombia, east to the Andes, south to Bolivia, Brazil**
HABITAT: **forest**
SIZE: **29 cm (11½ in)**

Puffbirds of the genus *Monasa* have black or black and white plumage, hence their common name of nunbirds. Nunbirds are more gregarious than other puffbirds and often gather in flocks, but they are otherwise similar in their habits. They perch on branches to watch for insects and then fly out to seize the prey in the air.

Breeding pairs excavate tunnels in which to nest, and the female of this species is thought to lay 2 or 3 eggs.

CAPITONIDAE: Barbet Family

The 81 species of barbet are chunky, generally brightly colored little birds, with large heads, and bills often fringed with tufts of bristles. They occur in tropical areas of the Americas, Asia and Africa, but the majority live in Africa. Most are solitary, tree-dwelling birds, and they feed on insects and fruit. Male and female look alike in most species.

NAME: **Double-toothed Barbet,** *Lybius bidentatus*
RANGE: **Africa: S. Sudan, Ethiopia, south to Uganda, W. Kenya, Tanzania**
HABITAT: **light forest, wooded savanna, cultivated land**
SIZE: **23 cm (9 in)**

Identified by its deep-red throat and breast, the double-toothed barbet feeds on fruit, particularly figs and bananas, and will invade plantations.

The nest is excavated in a dead branch of a tree, and the female is thought to lay 3 or 4 eggs. Like all barbets, both partners of a pair share the nesting duties.

NAME: **Coppersmith/Crimson-breasted Barbet,** *Megalaima haemacephala*
RANGE: **India, Sri Lanka, S.E. Asia, Sumatra, Java, Bali, Philippines**
HABITAT: **woodland, gardens, urban areas**
SIZE: **15 cm (6 in)**

A stocky bird, the coppersmith barbet is identified by the patches of bright red and yellow plumage on the throat and head, and the streaked belly. Alone, or sometimes in pairs or small groups, the coppersmith hunts in the trees for fruit, particularly figs, or may make clumsy aerial dashes after insects.

The breeding season lasts from January to June, and the barbets excavate a hole in a dead or rotting branch, which their beaks can penetrate easily. Both parents incubate the 2 to 4 eggs and tend the young birds.

INDICATORIDAE: Honey Guide Family

There are 14 species of honey guide, found in Africa, Asia and Indonesia. Honey guides feed on wax and larval bees, and some species have developed the habit, for which the family is named, of leading man and other mammals to bee's nests in the hope that they will break the nests open. The birds are unique in being able to feed on wax, which they can digest by means of symbiotic bacteria in their intestines. They also feed on other insects, some of which they catch in the air. As far as is known, all species are brood parasites and lay their eggs in the nests of barbets and woodpeckers. Male and female look slightly different in most species.

NAME: **Greater/Black-throated Honey Guide,** *Indicator indicator*
RANGE: **Africa, south of the Sahara**
HABITAT: **varied: forest edge, arid bush, acacia woodland, cultivated land**
SIZE: **20 cm (7¾ in)**

The greater honey guide is one of the 2 species in the family that actively lead other creatures to bee's nests. Chattering loudly, the bird approaches a human being or another honey-eating mammal, such as the ratel, and having attracted the attention, leads the way to the nest, flying a short distance at a time. The honey guide needs the help of another creature to break open the nest and, once this has been done, will feed on the remains of the honey, the wax and larval bees. The skin of this bird is particularly thick and must guard it against stings. Like all honey guides, this bird also feeds on other insects.

The honey guide lays its eggs in the nests of other birds and its young are reared by their foster parents.

Rufous-tailed Jacamar

Double-toothed Barbet

Black-fronted Nunbird

Coppersmith Barbet

White-necked Puffbird

Greater Honey Guide

Toucans

NAME: Emerald Toucanet,
Aulacorhynchus prasinus
RANGE: S. Mexico to Nicaragua,
Venezuela, Colombia, Ecuador and
Peru
HABITAT: humid mountain forest, open
country with trees
SIZE: 35.5 cm (14 in)

The shy emerald toucanet lives at altitudes of between 1,800 and 3,000 m (6,000 and 10,000 ft). The birds sit inconspicuously among the foliage or fly for short distances in pairs or small groups to forage for food, calling to one another as they do so with a variety of noisy sounds. Their diet is wide-ranging and includes insects, small reptiles and amphibians, and the eggs and young of other bird species, as well as the more usual fruit and berries. Striking birds, emerald toucanets are unmistakable, with their bright green plumage and bold yellow and black bills.

The nest is made in a hole in a tree, often an old woodpecker hole; emerald toucanets have even been known to harass woodpeckers until they give up their nests. Both parents incubate the 3 or 4 eggs and bring food, mostly fruit, to the nestlings. The young of the emerald toucanet, like all toucans, hatch naked and develop their first feathers at about 2 weeks. Their beaks, however, grow faster than their bodies, and the young toucanet has a full-sized, 7.5-cm (3-in) bill before its body is even half the size of that of the adult.

NAME: Saffron Toucanet, *Baillonius*
bailloni
RANGE: S.E. Brazil
HABITAT: forest
SIZE: 35.5 cm (14 in)

The saffron toucanet has fine, gold-colored plumage, which is especially lustrous on the cheeks and breast. Shy, graceful birds, they live in small groups and feed mainly on berries, preferring to forage high in the treetops rather than in the lower levels of the forest.

NAME: Laminated Toucan, *Andigena*
laminirostris
RANGE: Andes in Colombia, W. Ecuador
HABITAT: forest
SIZE: 43 cm (17 in)

Also known as the plate-billed mountain toucan, this species lives at altitudes of between 1,000 and 3,000 m (3,300 and 10,000 ft). The bill is about 10 cm (4 in) long and extremely unusual in shape: on each side of the upper bill there is a horny yellow plate, which grows out from the base of the bill. The function of these plates is not clearly understood, since little is known of the habits of these toucans.

RAMPHASTIDAE: Toucan Family

The toucans and aracaris are among the most extraordinary birds in the world. All 37 species are found living in the canopy layers of the dense rain forests of the Amazon basin and in neighboring forested areas of South America. They are medium-sized birds, ranging in size from 30 to 61 cm (12 to 24 in), and have enormous, boldly colored beaks that account for almost half the total body length. These bills are constructed of a honeycomb of bony material and are consequently light but very strong. The gaudy coloration varies greatly, not only between species but within a species. The plumage is usually dark, often black, with patches of boldly contrasting color on head and neck, which accentuates the bill colors. Toucans' wings are short and rounded and their flight weak. The legs are strong and the claws well adapted for grasping branches, with two toes pointing forward and two backward. Male and female look alike in most species.

The specific functions of the toucan's remarkable beak are poorly understood. It may act as an important visual signal in territorial or courtship behavior, or, it has been suggested, it may help the bird to obtain food otherwise out of its reach. Many other birds, however, manage without such bills. The bill may even help to intimidate other birds when the toucan raids their nests for young. Toucans feed on fruit of many types and on large, tree-living insects; occasionally they take larger prey such as nestling birds, eggs and lizards. The toucan seizes food with the tip of its bill and then throws its head back to toss the morsel into its mouth. An extremely long, narrow tongue with a bristlelike appendage at the tip aids manipulation of the food.

Toucans nest in tree cavities, either in natural holes or abandoned woodpecker holes. A few species line their nests with leaves, but in others, regurgitated seeds from fruit form a layer on the nest floor. The 2 to 4 eggs are incubated by both parents, who are able to flex their long tails forward over their backs to fit within the confines of the nesting cavity. Young toucans hatch naked and blind and develop slowly: at 3 weeks their eyes are only just opening, and they are not fully fledged for more than 6 weeks. They have specialized pads on their heels, on which they sit, which may be a form of protection against the rough floor of the nest. Both male and female feed and care for the young during this period.

NAME: Spot-billed Toucanet, *Selenidera*
maculirostris
RANGE: tropical Brazil, south of the
Amazon to N.E. Argentina
HABITAT: lowland rain forest
SIZE: 33 cm (13 in)

An uncommon toucanet, this species has a patch of feathers, usually orange or yellow, behind each eye — a feature peculiar to the *Selenidera* genus and thought to be important in the male's courtship display. The bill of the male is distinctive, with a yellowish tip and black markings on the upper mandible; the female's bill is less clearly marked. This toucanet feeds on berries and large fruit, swallowing them whole and then disgorging the skins and stones. All toucans aid the seed dispersal of a number of fruit-bearing plants in this way.

Once their eggs are hatched, spot-billed toucanets often visit citrus plantations in groups to feed and find termites and other small insects to take to their young.

NAME: Toco Toucan, *Ramphastos toco*
RANGE: E. South America: the Guianas
to N. Argentina
HABITAT: woodland, forest, plantations,
palm groves
SIZE: 61 cm (24 in)

A common toucan and one of the largest of its family, the toco toucan lives in small groups and frequents coconut and sugar plantations, as well as the normal toucan habitats. Its golden-yellow bill is about 19 cm (7½ in) long, and it feeds on a wide range of fruit but has a particular preference for capsicums. Toco toucans are not at all shy and will enter houses, steal food and tease domestic pets.

NAME: Curl-crested Aracari, *Pteroglossus*
beauharnaesii
RANGE: Amazonian Peru, W. Brazil,
N. Bolivia
HABITAT: forest
SIZE: 35.5 cm (14 in)

This toucan is normally shy and nervous but can be aggressive and active. It has some curious plumage quite unlike that of any other toucan: the feathers on its crown are like shiny, curly scales, and those on the cheeks and throat have black scaly tips. Like other aracaris, it has pronounced jagged notches in its beak.

Groups of 5 or 6 adult aracaris roost together in an abandoned woodpecker hole or in a hollow in a tree, folding their tails over their backs to fit into the confined space.

Laminated Toucan

Curl-crested Aracari

Spot-billed Toucanet

Emerald Toucanet

Toco Toucan

Saffron Toucanet

Woodpeckers

NAME: Wryneck, *Jynx torquilla*
RANGE: Europe, N. Africa, N. Asia;
winters in Africa and S. Asia
HABITAT: open deciduous forest,
cultivated land
SIZE: 16–20.5 cm (6¼–8 in)

A skulking, solitary bird, the wryneck is an unusual member of the woodpecker family, with a shorter, weaker bill than the true woodpeckers have. Although it can cling to tree trunks, it does not have the stiff, supporting tail of the typical woodpecker and more often perches. It does not bore into trees for its food but picks ants and other insects off leaves or from the ground, using its long, fast-moving tongue. The common name comes from its habit of twisting its head into strange positions while feeding and in courtship display.

The wryneck breeds in summer in Europe, north Africa and central Asia. It does not excavate its own nest but uses an existing cavity in a tree trunk, an abandoned woodpecker hole or a crevice in a wall or bank. The female lays 7 to 10 eggs, and both parents, but mainly the female, incubate the eggs for 13 days. Both parents feed insects and larvae to the young, which leave the nest about 3 weeks after hatching. After breeding, some populations of wrynecks migrate south to tropical Asia and Africa for the winter.

NAME: Great Spotted Woodpecker,
Picoides **(=** *Dendrocopos*) **major**
RANGE: Europe, N. Africa, Asia
HABITAT: mixed forest, woodland
SIZE: 23 cm (9 in)

The most common European woodpecker, the great spotted woodpecker is an adaptable species, living in all types of woodland, including parks and gardens. As it bores into tree trunks to extract its food — wood-boring insects and their larvae — it makes a characteristic drumming noise, which it also makes in spring in place of a courtship song. It supplements its diet with nuts, seeds and berries and has a habit of wedging a pinecone into a crevice and chipping out the kernels with its bill. The male bird has a red band at the back of his head, which the female lacks, and the juvenile has a red crown.

In Europe the breeding season begins in mid-May, and both partners help to excavate a hole in a tree, 3 m (10 ft) or more above ground. The female lays 3 to 8 eggs in this unlined nest and, with some assistance from the male, incubates them for 16 days. Both parents care for the young, bringing them insects in their bills. Most great spotted woodpeckers are resident birds, but some northern populations may migrate south in winter to find food.

PICIDAE: Woodpecker Family

Woodpeckers and their relatives the wrynecks and piculets must be among the best-known of all specialized tree-living birds. There are about 208 species, found almost worldwide except in Madagascar, Australia, the Papuan region and most oceanic islands. Males and females have slight plumage differences in many species.

Woodpeckers are highly adapted for climbing in trees, extracting insects from bark and wood and making holes in tree trunks. The woodpecker clings tightly to the bark of the trunk with its sharply clawed feet, on which two toes face forward and two backward, giving it maximum grip. The stiff tail acts as an angled strut and gives the bird additional support as it bores into the wood with hammerlike movements of its strong, straight beak. A few woodpeckers are ground-living.

NAME: Ivory-billed Woodpecker,
Campephilus principalis
RANGE: S.E. USA, Cuba
HABITAT: swamps, forest
SIZE: 51 cm (20 in) Ⓔ

The largest North American woodpecker, this species is characterized by its pointed crest and long, ivory-colored bill. A seriously endangered species, it is now confined to a very few localities and may already be extinct in the USA.

It feeds on the larvae of insects, especially of the wood-boring beetles that live between the bark and wood of dying or newly dead trees, and also eats some fruit and nuts. Both members of a breeding pair help to excavate a nest cavity, and the female lays 1 to 3 eggs. The clutch is incubated for about 20 days, the male taking a turn at night, and both parents feed the young.

NAME: White-barred Piculet, *Picumnus*
cirratus
RANGE: South America: Guyana to
N. Argentina
HABITAT: forest, woodland, parks
SIZE: 9 cm (3½ in)

A small, busy woodpecker, the white-barred piculet scrambles over trees, hanging upside down, moving over, under and around the branches in search of larvae to feed on. Predators are deterred from attacking this piculet because of its curious and particularly offensive odor.

The nest is made in a bamboo stem, and to excavate it, the piculet clings to the bamboo in true woodpecker fashion, speedily chipping it away with its beak.

NAME: Rufous/White-browed Piculet,
Sasia ochracea
RANGE: Himalayas, to mountains of
S.E. Asia and S.E. China
HABITAT: woodland, especially bamboo
forest
SIZE: 9 cm (3½ in)

This tiny, dumpy, stub-tailed woodpecker is an active, restless bird, usually seen singly or in pairs. With jerky movements, it creeps over thin twigs of low trees and bushes or hops around the litter of the woodland floor, searching for its food — mainly ants and their larvae. The female bird looks similar to the male but lacks his golden forehead.

The piculet's nest is a tiny hole about 2.5 cm (1 in) across, which is drilled in a decaying, hollow bamboo stem or an old tree. The female lays 3 or 4 eggs.

NAME: Yellow-bellied Sapsucker,
Sphyrapicus varius
RANGE: central Canada, E. USA; winters
in Central America, West Indies
HABITAT: forest, woodland
SIZE: 20.5 cm (8 in)

The sapsucker migrates northward in the spring from its wintering grounds in Central America and the West Indies. On reaching its breeding range, it drills rows of holes in the bark of trees and returns from time to time to drink the oozing sap and to eat the insects that are attracted to it. The bird also collects many other insects in and around the trees, using its brushlike tongue.

A breeding pair bores a nest hole, usually in a dead tree, with the male doing most of the work. The female lays 5 to 7 eggs, which both birds incubate for about 12 days.

NAME: Common Flicker (Yellow- and
Red-shafted Flickers), *Colaptes auratus*
RANGE: Alaska to Mexico, Cuba, Grand
Cayman Island
HABITAT: woodland, open country
SIZE: 25.5–35.5 cm (10–14 in)

The flicker is a ground-feeding bird which lives on ants and other insects; it also eats fruit and berries. There are 2 forms, now considered to be subspecies of the same species: the eastern birds have yellow wing linings, and the western birds red wing linings. The yellow-shafted flicker, *C. a. auratus*, is illustrated. In the Midwest, the forms meet and interbreed.

During courtship, or to communicate possession of its territory, the flicker drums with its bill on a tree or metal roofing. The male flicker selects a site for the nest hole, usually a hole in a tree trunk, stump or telephone pole, and does most of the excavation work. Both parents incubate the eggs.

Wryneck

Ivory-billed
Woodpecker

White-barred
Piculet

Rufous
Piculet
(male)

Great Spotted
Woodpecker
(male)

Common Flicker

Yellow-bellied Sapsucker

Woodpeckers

NAME: Green Woodpecker, *Picus viridis*
**RANGE: Europe, N. Africa, Turkey to
    Iran, W. USSR**
**HABITAT: open deciduous woodland,
    gardens, parks**
SIZE: 32 cm (12½ in)

A large, vividly plumaged woodpecker, this species has a short tail and a long, pointed bill. The male has a characteristic red mustache stripe with a black border; in the female the stripe is all black. Like other woodpeckers, the green woodpecker feeds in trees on the larvae of wood-boring insects, but it also feeds on the ground, where it hops along ponderously, searching for ants. It eats fruit and seeds as well. The flight of this species is typical of the woodpeckers, being deeply undulating, with long wing closures between each upward sweep.

The breeding season starts in April in the south of the range and May in the north. Both partners of a breeding pair help to excavate a nest cavity, often in a rotten tree trunk and usually at least 1 m (3¼ ft) above ground. The female lays 4 to 7 eggs, sometimes as many as 11, which both parents incubate for 18 or 19 days. The chicks hatch naked and helpless and must be fed by their parents on regurgitated food for about 3 weeks, when they are able to fend for themselves.

In a hard winter, as they do not migrate, green woodpeckers can suffer severe food shortages, which cause large drops in population.

NAME: Golden-tailed Woodpecker,
    Campethera abingoni
RANGE: Africa, south of the Sahara
**HABITAT: woodland, brush, mountain
    forest**
SIZE: 20.5 cm (8 in)

The golden-tailed woodpecker can be identified by the broad black streaks on the white plumage from its chin to its belly and by the yellow-tipped tail feathers. There are some dark-red and black markings on the nape and head, and the rest of the plumage is largely green with white flecks. Usually seen in pairs, these woodpeckers are noisy birds and utter calls like derisive laughter; they also give a screeching alarm signal. They are restless birds, continuously on the move with swift, deeply undulating flight, searching for the arboreal ants and the larvae of other insects, such as beetles, that form their main foods.

The nest hole is usually excavated in the soft wood of a dead tree, and the female lays 2 or 3 eggs.

NAME: Great Slaty Woodpecker,
    Mulleripicus pulverulentus
**RANGE: Asia: N. India to S.W. China,
    Sumatra, Java, Borneo, Palawan**
HABITAT: forest, swamp forest
SIZE: 51 cm (20 in)

The great slaty woodpecker is a large species that associates in groups of about 6 birds, which follow one another from one treetop to the next, calling noisily with loud cackles as they fly. Their flight is leisurely, without the normal woodpecker arcs and undulations. The larvae of wood-boring beetles and other insects are the main foods of this woodpecker, and it drills into trees with its powerful bill to find them. Both males and females of this species have some buffy-brown plumage on the chin and neck, but males also have mustache streaks, which the females lack. Juvenile birds resemble the female but are darker and duller in color, with more pale spots on the underparts.

In the breeding season, the groups break up into pairs, which then excavate their nests high up in tree trunks, often in dead or decaying wood. Both parents incubate the 3 or 4 eggs, which are laid in the unlined nest cavity, and share in the care and feeding of the nestlings.

NAME: Ground Woodpecker, *Geocolaptes
    olivaceus*
RANGE: South Africa
HABITAT: dry, open hill country
SIZE: 28 cm (11 in)

True to its name, this woodpecker lives almost entirely on the ground and hops everywhere. On the rare occasions when it does take to the air, it flies heavily and only for short distances, its red rump feathers showing conspicuously. Male and female look alike, with gray plumage on the head, olive-brown upperparts flecked with white, and rose-pink chest and belly. Juvenile birds are duller, with mottled olive and off-white plumage on the belly. Ground woodpeckers live in small groups of up to 6 or so and are usually found on high ground above 600 m (2,000 ft), where they perch on rocks or boulders or, very occasionally, on the low branches of trees and bushes. They feed on ants and other ground-living insects and their larvae, which they find by probing under rocks and stones. Their call is sharp and metallic, and they may also utter high-pitched whistles.

Unlike most woodpeckers, this species nests on the ground in a long tunnel that it excavates in a bank of clay or sand. Both partners of a breeding pair help to dig the burrow, which ends in a small chamber, where the female lays 4 or 5 eggs.

**NAME: Greater Goldenback/Large
    Golden-backed Woodpecker,**
    Chrysocolaptes lucidus
**RANGE: India, S.E. Asia to the
    Philippines**
**HABITAT: woodland, forest fringe,
    mangrove swamps**
SIZE: 33 cm (13 in)

This medium-sized woodpecker is widespread in the wooded areas of India and Southeast Asia, where many races of the species inhabit a variety of forest types. Often found near flocks of other woodpeckers, drongos, bulbuls and babblers, these birds usually associate in pairs. After flying noisily from tree to tree, with characteristic woodpecker arcs and undulations, they alight on a trunk and, working their way up in jerky spirals, bore into the wood to feed on insect larvae. Goldenbacks have also been observed catching winged termites in the air. They seldom feed on the ground but are known to drink the nectar of some flowers. Although this is an extremely variable species, greater goldenbacks can generally be identified by the two black mustache streaks, separated by a patch of white plumage, on each side of the bill. The female bird lacks the male's distinctive red crest and has a flat black crown, spotted with white.

In the breeding season, the male drums particularly energetically as a courtship signal. The birds nest in a hole in a tree trunk, and the hole may be used many times; a fresh entrance to the breeding chamber is cut each season. It is not known whether the same birds return to the same hole every year. The female lays 4 or 5 eggs, which are incubated for 14 or 15 days, and the young woodpeckers remain in the nest until they are able to fly at 24 to 26 days old.

NAME: Blond-crested Woodpecker,
    Celeus flavescens
**RANGE: South America: Amazonian
    Brazil, E. Bolivia, Paraguay,
    N.E. Argentina**
HABITAT: forest
SIZE: 28 cm (11 in)

With its long, shaggy crest, this woodpecker appears rather larger than it is. The yellow feathers of the crest are narrow and soft, so that when erect they blow freely in the breeze. Particularly widespread in southeast Brazil, the blond-crested woodpecker is not confined to the lowlands but has been found at altitudes of up to 900 m (3,000 ft).

Green Woodpecker (male)

Great Slaty Woodpecker

Golden-tailed Woodpecker

Blond-crested Woodpecker

Greater Goldenback

Ground Woodpecker

Ovenbirds

NAME: **Rufous Hornero,** *Furnarius rufus*
RANGE: **Brazil, Bolivia, Paraguay, Uruguay, Argentina**
HABITAT: **trees, often near habitation**
SIZE: **19–20.5 cm (7½–8 in)**

There has been an increasing tendency to refer to the ovenbirds by their South American name (hornero), to avoid confusion with an American wood warbler which is also called the ovenbird. The rufous hornero is a dignified-looking bird, which walks with long, deliberate strides, holding one foot aloft as it hesitates between steps. It feeds on insect larvae and worms and is vocal throughout the year.

Pairs stay together all year round, often for life, and breed during the wettest months. Each year they build a domed, ovenlike nest on a branch, post or building, using clay, with a little plant material mixed into it, which is then baked hard by the hot sun. A small entrance leads to the interior chamber, lined with soft grass, where up to 5 eggs are laid. Both parents incubate the clutch, and, after leaving the nest, the young birds stay with their parents for a few months.

NAME: **Plain Xenops,** *Xenops minutus*
RANGE: **S. Mexico, through Central and South America to N. Argentina**
HABITAT: **tall forest, plantations, clearings with scattered trees**
SIZE: **12.5 cm (5 in)**

One of several species of xenops, the plain xenops is distinguished by its unstreaked back. An active little bird, it forages in shrubs and thin branches of trees in search of insects to eat.

The nest is made by both partners of a breeding pair in a hole in an old, decaying tree and is lined with fine pieces of plant material. Alternatively, the birds may take over a hole abandoned by another bird. The 2 eggs are incubated by both parents for about 16 days.

NAME: **Stripe-breasted Spinetail,** *Synallaxis cinnamomea*
RANGE: **Venezuela, Colombia; Trinidad and Tobago**
HABITAT: **forest edge, coffee plantations**
SIZE: **16.5 cm (6½ in)**

Distinguished by its streaked cinnamon breast, this spinetail moves jerkily and makes low, short flights as it forages for small insects and spiders. It may also jump into the air to catch flying ants.

Both partners of a breeding pair help to build the nest, which is a round structure, made of twigs and placed in the fork of a branch in low scrub or on the ground. The nest is lined with soft plant material and has an entrance tunnel. The 2 or 3 eggs are incubated by both parents.

ORDER PASSERIFORMES

Usually known as the perching birds, or songbirds, this is the largest of all bird orders. It includes about half of the approximately 8,600 living bird species. There are about 60 families in the order, and the most advanced 44 or so of these are grouped together as the oscine perching birds, or songbirds. The other families are known as the suboscines; these birds have a simpler organ of song. Perching birds are usually small — the lyrebirds are the largest species — but they have become adapted to almost all types of land-based habitat.

The group as a whole is identified by a number of structural and behavioral features. The foot is particularly characteristic and is excellently adapted for grasping any thin support such as a twig or grass stem: there are always four toes, all on the same level, with the hallux (big toe) pointing backward. The toes are never webbed.

Male perching birds are normally able to sing complex songs and give voice when courting mates or when defending territory.

FURNARIIDAE: Ovenbird Family

The 219 or so known species in this family occur from southern Mexico through Central and South America, in a wide variety of habitats. As well as the ovenbirds proper, the family includes birds such as spinetails, plainsrunners and leafgleaners.

All the birds in the family have gray, brownish or russet plumage and are between 12 and 28 cm (4¾ and 11 in) long. They tend to be quick-moving, yet secretive birds, which generally remain well hidden within vegetation.

The diversity of this family is best shown by their breeding behavior. The true ovenbirds, for which the family is named, construct ovenlike mud nests, which are baked hard by the sun. Others build domed nests of grass or sticks, while some make well-lined nests in holes in the ground or in trees. Females generally lay from 2 to 5 eggs, and both parents care for the young. In most species, male and female look more or less alike.

NAME: **Red-faced Spinetail,** *Certhiaxis (= Cranioleuca) erythrops*
RANGE: **Costa Rica to Ecuador**
HABITAT: **humid mountain forest**
SIZE: **14–16.5 cm (5½–6½ in)**

Adult red-faced spinetails have reddish markings on the crown and sides of the head; juveniles have brownish crowns. They are active, acrobatic birds and much of their life is spent in the low levels of the forest, foraging in thickets and undergrowth for insects and other small invertebrates. They tend to move alone or in pairs but sometimes join in a flock of other highland birds.

The bulky, ball-shaped nest is made from vines and hangs from the end of a slender branch, well above ground. Both sexes incubate the 2 eggs and feed the young.

NAME: **Larklike Bushrunner,** *Coryphistera alaudina*
RANGE: **S. Brazil, Bolivia, Paraguay, Uruguay, N. Argentina**
HABITAT: **dry scrub regions**
SIZE: **15 cm (6 in)**

Identified by its prominent crest and streaked breast plumage, the larklike bushrunner generally moves in groups of 3 to 6, which are, possibly, family groups. Active both on the ground and in bushes and low trees, they stride along in the open, but if alarmed, they take to the trees and tall bushes.

A rounded nest is made in a low tree from interwoven thorny twigs. A small entrance tunnel leads to the central chamber, where the eggs are laid.

NAME: **Point-tailed/Pintailed Palmcreeper,** *Berlepschia rikeri*
RANGE: **Amazonian Brazil, Venezuela, Guyana**
HABITAT: **palm groves, often near water**
SIZE: **21.5 cm (8½ in)**

An elegant little bird, the point-tailed palmcreeper has distinctive black, white and chestnut plumage and pointed tail feathers. In pairs or small groups, it frequents palm trees of the genus *Mauritia* and forages for insects on the trunks and leaves of the trees. When it catches an insect, the palmcreeper bangs it sharply against the trunk or branch before swallowing it.

NAME: **Des Murs' Spinetail,** *Sylviorthorhynchus desmursii*
RANGE: **W. Argentina, adjacent Chile**
HABITAT: **humid forest with thick undergrowth**
SIZE: **24 cm (9½ in)**

Over two-thirds of the length of this species is taken up by its long and decorative tail, which consists of only two pairs of feathers, plus a vestigial pair. Otherwise this spinetail is an inconspicuous little bird, revealed only by its persistent calls. It frequents the densest parts of the forest and seems to move ceaselessly in search of food.

A globular nest is made just off the ground amid twigs and grass. It is constructed from dry plant material, lined with soft feathers, and has a side entrance. Usually 3 eggs are laid. The bird holds up its tail when in the nest.

Rufous Hornero

Point-tailed Palmcreeper

Stripe-breasted Spinetail

Des Murs' Spinetail

Plain Xenops

Red-faced Spinetail

Larklike Bushrunner

Antbirds

NAME: **Ocellated Antbird,** *Phaenostictus mcleannani*
RANGE: **tropical Nicaragua to Panama; S. Colombia, N.W. Ecuador**
HABITAT: **undergrowth of humid, lowland forest**
SIZE: **19–20 cm (7½–7¾ in)**

The dark markings in the plumage of the ocellated antbird give it an overall spotted appearance, and it has a fairly long tail for its size. The eyes are surrounded with an area of bright-hued bare skin, and it is these two colored circles, one within the other, that give the bird its common name. Male and female look alike.

It is a generally uncommon, timid species and is often found in association with bicolored antbirds. It is seldom seen away from the columns of army ants that march through the forests of its habitat, for it feeds on the invertebrates, such as cockroaches and spiders, which are disturbed by their destructive passage. Its call is a fast series of whistles, running up the scale.

Ocellated antbirds form lasting pair bonds, and before mating, the male feeds the female with tidbits, at some distance from the nest.

NAME: **Bicolored Antbird,** *Gymnopithys leucaspis*
RANGE: **Honduras to Panama; N. Peru, Amazonian Brazil**
HABITAT: **forest undergrowth up to 2,000 m (6,600 ft)**
SIZE: **14 cm (5½ in)**

Although there is some disagreement, this bird is generally considered conspecific with the white-cheeked antbird, G. *bicolor,* of the western Amazon area. The plumage of male and female is alike, and there are patches of bare skin around the eyes. It is a fairly common species and usually the most numerous and noisy of the several that follow the army ants. It spends much of the time on the ground but will perch just above the forest floor, watching for insects, spiders and other invertebrates which are driven out of the leaf litter as the ants advance. It will occasionally even take a small frog.

The nest of the bicolored antbird is usually sited a few feet from the ground in the stump of a decaying palm tree and is made from small pieces of leaf, especially palm leaf, and lined with rootlets and plant fibers. The female lays 2 eggs, which both parents incubate for about 15 days.

FORMICARIIDAE: Antbird Family

The antbirds are found exclusively in Central and South America, mostly on the floor and in the lower levels of the tropical rain forests of the Amazon basin, as well as in some drier and more open habitats. About 220 to 230 species of small to medium-sized birds are known. Many species of antbird do actually feed on ants and other social insects; some eat the invertebrates disturbed by columns of army ants which they follow through the forest, while others, although insectivorous, have no particular predilection for ants.

Their plumage is usually dull, and there are normally clear-cut differences between that of male and female birds. Little is known of their breeding biology, but open, cup-shaped nests seem to be the rule, and both sexes appear to incubate the clutch, which usually contains 2 eggs, for about 15 or 16 days.

NAME: **Chestnut-crowned Antpitta,** *Grallaria ruficapilla*
RANGE: **tropical and subtropical areas, Venezuela to N.W. Peru**
HABITAT: **dense cloud forest, damp woodland and open grassland**
SIZE: **20 cm (7¾ in)**

The chestnut-crowned antpitta is a long-legged bird, with a short tail and a noticeably large head; the feathers on head and neck are reddish brown, hence its common name. It is a ground-living bird, usually found alone, looking for the insects that make up its diet. Even though difficult to see, it is not shy, and its three-note call is often heard. In fact, it will respond to imitations of its call and has a number of local names that suggest it, such as "Seco estoy."

NAME: **Streaked Antwren,** *Myrmotherula surinamensis*
RANGE: **Amazonian Brazil, west to Pacific coast of South America**
HABITAT: **clearings in rain forest, forest edge, woodland**
SIZE: **10 cm (4 in)**

The male of this species is largely black and white, while the female has a bright orange-red head and nape and pale orange-buff underparts. Both sexes have two white bars on the wings. Streaked antwrens are fairly common birds, often found near rivers and on wet ground, where they can generally be seen in pairs, busily searching for grasshoppers and spiders among the undergrowth, vines and leaves. They have a fast, rising, chipping call.

The nest is made in a tree, and the female lays 2 eggs.

NAME: **Great Antshrike,** *Taraba major*
RANGE: **tropical S. Mexico, Central and South America to N. Argentina**
HABITAT: **undergrowth in brush and grassland up to 2,000 m (6,600 ft)**
SIZE: **20 cm (7¾ in)**

The great antshrike is a fairly large bird with a thick, hooked bill and a crest; males and females have quite dissimilar coloration. Although common, these shy birds are usually found only in pairs or, occasionally, alone. They move stealthily through the bushes and low branches of small trees, searching for beetles, grasshoppers, bees and even small lizards to eat. When disturbed, the male performs a threat display, pointing his bill straight upward and raising his crest so that the normally concealed dorsal patch shows clearly.

The flimsy nest is cup shaped, made of dried grass and roots, sometimes lined with leaves, and is about 6.5 cm (2½ in) deep. The female lays 2 or 3 eggs, which both parents incubate for 2 to 3 weeks; they then feed the young until they are ready to leave the nest, about 2 weeks after hatching.

NAME: **Barred Antshrike,** *Thamnophilus doliatus*
RANGE: **tropical Mexico, Central and South America to N. Argentina; Trinidad and Tobago**
HABITAT: **varied: forest, brush, savanna, gardens; rarely above 2,000 m (6,600 ft)**
SIZE: **15 cm (6 in)**

As its name implies, the plumage of this antshrike is conspicuously barred and streaked. The male is mainly black and white, while the female is chestnut, shading to buff, with black barring. Both birds have a crest, which the male always carries partially erect, and a toothed beak. Barred antshrikes are common birds, usually found in pairs; but as they are always on the move through bushes and branches in thickets and forest edge about 4.5 m (15 ft) up, they are usually heard calling to one another before they are seen. They feed on insects, such as beetles, grasshoppers, bees and caterpillars, and on berries.

There seems to be no clearly defined mating season, but the male feeds the female during courtship and they may form a permanent pair bond. The female lays 2, rarely 3, eggs in a deep cup-shaped nest, made of grass and plant fibers and suspended by the rim in the fork of a low branch of a tree. Both parents incubate the eggs for about 14 days; only the female incubates at night. The young leave the nest 2 to 3 weeks after hatching.

Ocellated Antbird

Barred Antshrike (male)

Great Antshrike (male)

Streaked Antwren (male)

Bicolored Antbird

Chestnut-crowned Antpitta

Woodcreepers, Gnateaters, Tapaculos

DENDROCOLAPTIDAE:
Woodcreeper Family

The 48 species or so of woodcreeper, found in wooded areas of Central and South America, from Mexico to Argentina, are in many ways the New World equivalent of the treecreepers of the Old World. These birds, also known as woodhewers, vary in length from 15 to 38 cm (6 to 15 in), and male and female look very much alike. They have laterally compressed beaks, which range in shape from short and straight to long and curved, and strong legs and feet.

Woodcreepers are insectivorous and peck their food from crevices in the bark as they climb up the trunks of trees, with the aid of their sharp claws and the strong propping shafts of their tail feathers. They are generally solitary birds but may join in mixed flocks.

NAME: **Red-billed Scythebill,**
Campylorhamphus trochilirostris
RANGE: **E. Panama to N. Argentina**
HABITAT: **swampy and humid forest,
woodland**
SIZE: **20.5–30.5 cm (8–12 in) including bill
of 7.5 cm (3 in)**

These shy, arboreal birds live in the middle to upper stories of forest trees. They are usually found alone, although they may feed among other types of insectivorous birds. Their strong legs and stiff tail feathers help them to climb quickly, and with their long, curved bills, they probe for insects under the bark of trees and inside bromeliads.

The female scythebill lays 2 or 3 eggs in a hole in a tree or in a crevice, and they are incubated for about 14 days.

NAME: **Barred Woodcreeper,**
Dendrocolaptes certhia
RANGE: **tropical S. Mexico, through
Central America to Bolivia,
Amazonian Brazil**
HABITAT: **lowland rain forest to 1,400 m
(4,600 ft), forest edge**
SIZE: **26.5 cm (10½ in)**

Both male and female barred woodcreepers are strongly built and have light olive-brown, barred plumage. The medium-length beak is heavy and slightly curved. These birds live in the undergrowth and tall secondary growth of the rain forest; they are not timid and can be seen alone or in twos and threes, feeding on the trunks of trees. Like the antbirds, they are constant followers of army ants and will come near the ground to feed on the insects disturbed by the ants' progress.

The female lays 2 eggs, in a hole or crevice in a tree; they are incubated for 14 or 15 days.

NAME: **Long-billed Woodcreeper,** *Nasica
longirostris*
RANGE: **tropical northern South America
to Brazil and Bolivia**
HABITAT: **rain forest at 100–200 m
(330–650 ft)**
SIZE: **35.5 cm (14 in) including bill of
6.5 cm (2½ in)**

The solitary, long-billed woodcreeper is an agile bird that climbs about in the trees, looking for its insect food under the bark. It has a long, slightly curved bill, and male and female look similar.

The female makes her nest in a tree hole and lays 2 eggs, which are incubated for about 2 weeks.

NAME: **Olivaceous Woodcreeper,**
Sittasomus griseicapillus
RANGE: **tropical and subtropical Mexico,
through Central and South America to
N. Argentina; Tobago**
HABITAT: **deep forest, forest edge, open
woodland, to 2,300 m (7,500 ft)**
SIZE: **15–16.5 cm (6–6½ in)**

These active little woodcreepers have buff bands on the wings that are conspicuous when they fly. Male and female look alike. They are more or less solitary, but may associate with other types of birds. They forage busily for insects on the trunks of trees with soft bark, in the under and middle stories of the forest, and will sometimes fly out and catch insects in the air.

Only one nest has been found, in a hole in a tree, but it contained no eggs.

CONOPOPHAGIDAE:
Gnateater Family

The gnateaters, or antpipits as they are sometimes called, are a small group of forest-dwelling birds, quite closely related to the antbirds and ovenbirds. Approximately 11 species are recognized, all living in Central and South America. Most are long-legged brown birds with round bodies and short tails. They live largely on the forest floor, capturing insect food on the ground with their flycatcherlike bills. Male and female are alike in some species but differ in others.

NAME: **Black-cheeked Gnateater,**
Conopophaga melanops
RANGE: **E. Brazil**
HABITAT: **rain forest**
SIZE: **12.5 cm (5 in)**

This South American gnateater has long legs and appears almost neckless; the female is more olive-brown than the male. The birds are quite tame but are not often seen because they prefer the undergrowth, where they find their insect food, mainly on the ground.

Black-cheeked gnateaters make an open, cup-shaped nest on the ground, using big leaves, and line it with plant fibers. The female lays 2 eggs, which both parents incubate. If danger threatens the bird on the nest, it will leave the eggs and lure the predator away by pretending to be injured.

RHINOCRYPTIDAE:
Tapaculo Family

The approximately 28 described species of tapaculo are found among low-growing plants in habitats as varied as dense forest, grassland and semiopen arid country in Central and South America. They are ground-living birds, with poor powers of flight, but can run fast on their strong legs. Tapaculos vary in size from 12.5 to 25.5 cm (5 to 10 in) and have rounded bodies; they often cock their tails vertically, as wrens do. They have a curious feature, to which the scientific name refers, of movable flaps covering the nostrils; the exact function of these is not known, but they are presumed to protect the openings against dust. Males and females look alike or nearly so.

NAME: **Elegant Crescentchest,**
Melanopareia elegans
RANGE: **W. Ecuador to N.W. Peru**
HABITAT: **arid scrub**
SIZE: **14 cm (5½ in)**

These small birds seldom fly, but they have long legs and large feet and run about rapidly, gathering up insects; when excited, they cock up their tails. Elegant crescentchests are shy birds that are not often seen, although their calls can be heard.

No information is available about the breeding biology of these birds.

NAME: **Chestnut-throated Huet-huet,**
Pteroptochos castaneus
RANGE: **Chile**
HABITAT: **forest**
SIZE: **25.5 cm (10 in)**

This is a medium-sized bird, with a rounded body, long legs and quite a long tail for its size — about 10 cm (4 in). The upperparts are mostly blackish-brown, but the throat and underparts are a dark reddish-brown, with some black and buff bars. Male and female look alike. These huet-huets are ground-dwellers which rarely fly, and they run, rather than hop, about looking for their insect food.

The nest is made from roots and soft grasses in a hole in the ground or in a tree stump, and the female lays 2 eggs.

Barred Woodcreeper

Red-billed Scythebill

Long-billed Woodcreeper

Olivaceous Woodcreeper

Elegant Crescentchest

Black-cheeked Gnateater (male)

Chestnut-throated Huet-huet

Manakins, Cotingas

PIPRIDAE: Manakin Family

This intriguing and showy family contains about 56 species, all found in the tropical forests of Central and South America. They are small, colorful birds, rarely more than 12.5 to 15 cm (5 to 6 in) in length. Males and females are dramatically different in appearance. Males, typically, have a solid background color, commonly black, brilliantly counterpointed with areas of contrasting primary colors; females are generally olive-green. The decorative males utilize their plumage in intricate courtship dances.

NAME: **Blue-backed Manakin,** *Chiroxiphia pareola*
RANGE: **northern South America to S.E. Brazil, N. Bolivia; Tobago**
HABITAT: **rain forest, secondary growth**
SIZE: **10 cm (4 in)**

These lively, agile little birds forage in pairs or small groups for insects and fruit in low bushes, often near wet ground or streams. They are square tailed, with the male showing dazzling patches of pale blue and red feathers on back and crown.

Male manakins have display perches or "bowers," which they keep clear by plucking at the surrounding leaves while on the wing and pecking at the bark while perching. They wear the perch smooth by continually moving around. Before display, the dominant male summons a subordinate male by calling and then duets with him, the subordinate following a fraction of a second behind. The males dance together, but the dance only becomes fully developed if a female appears. The other bird drops out, leaving the dominant male to mate with the female after a quite different solo display. She lays 2 eggs in a nest, made of fine plant fibers, so cobwebby and transparent that eggs and young can be seen through it.

NAME: **Wire-tailed Manakin,** *Teleonoma* (= *Pipra*) *filicauda*
RANGE: **Venezuela to N.E. Peru, W. Brazil**
HABITAT: **rain forest, plantations**
SIZE: **11.5 cm (4½ in)**

The male wire-tailed manakin has dramatic black, red and yellow patches, typical of the family, and the tails of both male and female end in long wiry filaments, from which the common name is derived. These birds prefer humid areas and are found from the middle story to the forest canopy, as well as in clearings and cocoa plantations. Solitary birds, they forage alone for insects and fruit.

COTINGIDAE: Cotinga Family

The 73 species of cotinga, all found in the New World, constitute a colorful and varied family, with common names such as bellbird, umbrellabird, tityra, fruiteater and cock-of-the-rock, as well as the cotinga itself. This variety of nomenclature mirrors an equal diversity in body form and habit.

Cotingas are nonmigratory birds in forested areas and often spend most of their time in the canopy layers, feeding on fruit and insects.

NAME: **Andean Cock-of-the-rock,** *Rupicola peruviana*
RANGE: **Andes, N. Venezuela to N. Bolivia**
HABITAT: **forest along river gorges**
SIZE: **38 cm (15 in)**

The male of this species is one of the most brilliantly colored of all birds, with its flashing orange or red plumage and strong, golden-colored beak. On its head is a crest of feathers that almost conceals the beak. Both male and female have powerful legs and sharp claws.

The Andean cock-of-the-rock lives in the lower levels of the forest, where its swift, weaving flight and good maneuverability enable it to move about easily as it searches for fruit to eat. Females also catch frogs and lizards to feed to their young. The males live an independent existence — they roost alone at night, forage in pairs and display in pairs at dawn and dusk at traditional leks, where each male has his own place near to that of his paired male. Only the dominant male of the lek mates with females. The female alone builds the nest — on a rocky cliff face — and often several nests are grouped together. The nest is a large truncated cone, made of mud, with a deep, 6.5 cm (2½ in), lined nest cup, in which 2 eggs are laid.

NAME: **Barred Fruiteater,** *Pipreola arcuata*
RANGE: **Andes, N.W. Venezuela to N.W. Bolivia**
HABITAT: **cloud forest at 1,200–3,350 m (4,000–11,000 ft)**
SIZE: **21.5 cm (8½ in)**

This heavy-bodied bird is the largest of the fruiteaters and is found at higher altitudes than any other. The male's coloration is striking, while the female is mostly olive-green; both birds have rather weak, slightly hooked beaks and red legs and feet. Barred fruiteaters live in the middle and lower layers of the forest, where they feed mainly on fruit and some insects, either singly or in pairs. No information is available about breeding and nesting behavior.

NAME: **Bearded Bellbird,** *Procnias averano*
RANGE: **parts of Colombia, Guyana, Venezuela, N. Brazil; Trinidad**
HABITAT: **high-altitude forest**
SIZE: **25.5 cm (10 in)**

The fringe of black wattles hanging from the throat of both male and female gives this species its common name. They are shy birds, feeding singly or in pairs on large, single-seeded berries, particularly laurel, which they take on the wing and then sit on a branch to eat.

In the breeding season, male bearded bellbirds display to other males and to females on special "visiting" perches in the lower forest layers. They jump as high as 1.2 m (4 ft) into the air and land crouched, on another perch, with tail spread. After mating, the female builds a light, thin, cup-shaped nest of twigs from specific trees, about 2.4 to 15.25 m (8 to 50 ft) up, in the horizontally forked outer branch of a tree. She lays 1 egg, which she incubates for about 23 days.

NAME: **Spangled Cotinga,** *Cotinga cayana*
RANGE: **Amazon and Orinoco basins; the Guianas**
HABITAT: **forest up to 1,200 m (4,000 ft)**
SIZE: **21.5 cm (8½ in)**

The blue plumage of the male spangled cotinga is iridescent, hence the name. These are gregarious birds, usually feeding in groups on large berries, sometimes with birds of other species.

The female alone builds the flimsy, shallow nest, using twigs and rootlets and coating the whole structure in white fungal threads. She lays and then incubates 1 large egg, sometimes 2.

NAME: **Amazonian/Ornate Umbrellabird,** *Cephalopterus ornatus*
RANGE: **northern South America to Amazonian Brazil, N. Bolivia**
HABITAT: **virgin forest to 1,400 m (4,600 ft), islands in larger rivers**
SIZE: **40.5–48 cm (16–19 in)**

The largest of the cotingas, the ornate umbrellabird is distinguished by its erect crest of long, silky feathers and by the wattle at the base of the neck. The female is much duller than the male, with a smaller wattle and "umbrella." The wings are short. These strange birds live in the forest canopy and spring noisily through the branches, looking for fruit and insects.

Males have their preferred calling trees, where they perch, spread their umbrellas and, filling two specially modified sacs in the trachea with air, make loud booming noises. The shallow, open nest is built of twigs in the fork of a fairly low tree, and the female lays 1 egg, which she incubates alone.

Wire-tailed Manakin
(male)

Blue-backed
Manakin
(male)

Barred Fruiteater
(male)

Andean
Cock-of-the-rock
(male)

Spangled
Cotinga
(male)

Bearded Bellbird

Amazonian
Umbrellabird
(male)

Sharpbill, Plantcutters, Tyrant Flycatchers

OXYRUNCIDAE: Sharpbill Family

The sharpbill family contains only 1 species, which is a neotropical form, found in the upper layers of humid forests from Costa Rica south to Paraguay.

NAME: **Sharpbill**, *Oxyruncus cristatus*
RANGE: **patchy distribution in Costa Rica, Panama to Paraguay, Amazonian Brazil**
HABITAT: **humid tropical forest**
SIZE: **16.5–18 cm (6½–7 in)**

The sharpbill has a straight, pointed beak, which gives it its common name. It is a strong flier, with rather rounded, long wings. Male and female look similar, but the male has a black and scarlet crest, bordered with black, while the female may have a pale crest. Sharpbills are secretive birds which forage actively for fruit in the middle to canopy layers of the forest.

PHYTOTOMIDAE: Plantcutter Family

The 3 known species of plantcutter are found in the more open areas of western South America. They form a small, homogeneous family, closely related to the cotinga family (Cotingidae). In appearance, however, with their strong, conical beaks, they bear more resemblance to the finches of the Old World. The edges of their bills are finely serrated and used for cropping the buds, fruit and leaves that make up much of their diet. The plantcutters' fruit-eating habits mean that they are often regarded as pests by fruit farmers. Male and female do not look alike.

NAME: **Rufous-tailed Plantcutter**, *Phytotoma rara*
RANGE: **central Chile, Argentina**
HABITAT: **open scrub, orchards, gardens, mountain valleys**
SIZE: **20.5 cm (8 in)**

These short-legged birds have bright reddish-orange eyes and stout, serrated beaks. The male has reddish-chestnut underparts and tail; the female is paler, with a buff throat and underparts. Plantcutters are usually seen singly or in small groups, flying sluggishly among fruit trees, where they eat the buds, shoots and young leaves and often destroy the fruit. In spring, the plantcutters move to high mountain valleys, where they mate between October and December.

The female lays 2 to 4 eggs in a cup-shaped nest, made of twigs and lined with fine twigs and rootlets.

TYRANNIDAE: Tyrant Flycatcher Family

The 370 species of tyrant flycatcher constitute one of the largest families of perching birds. They are found only in the Americas, where they replace, and in several respects are similar to, the Old World flycatchers, Muscicapinae. The center of the wide range of the family is within the rain forests of the Amazon basin, but species have spread wherever food is available; consequently forms are found as far apart as Alaska and Tierra del Fuego.

Most species catch insects on the wing, but forms are known which feed on fruit, small mammals, reptiles, amphibians and fish, as well as on insects. The insect-eaters' beaks are rather flattened and slightly hooked, with well-developed bristles at the base. The sexes look alike in most species.

NAME: **Scissor-tailed Flycatcher**, *Muscivora forficata*
RANGE: **south–central USA; winters S. Texas, Mexico to Panama**
HABITAT: **open grassland (prairie), ranchland**
SIZE: **28–38 cm (11–15 in) including tail of up to 23 cm (9 in)**

When these elegant birds fly, the black feathers of their remarkably long tails open and close like the blades of a pair of scissors; but when they perch, the birds close up the blades. The female is smaller than the male, with a shorter tail. Scissor-tailed flycatchers spend much of their time perching on fences, telephone wires and trees, darting out swiftly to catch insects in the air or on the ground. They take mainly grasshoppers and crickets, which make up 50 percent of their food, but also eat bees, wasps, moths, caterpillars and spiders, as well as berries and seeds.

The bulky nest is built from weeds, rootlets and cotton, lined with hair and rootlets. The female lays 4 to 6 eggs, usually 5, and incubates them for about 14 days.

NAME: **White-headed Marsh Tyrant**, *Arundinicola leucocephala*
RANGE: **South America, east of the Andes, to N. Argentina; Trinidad**
HABITAT: **riverbanks, marshes, wet grassland**
SIZE: **11.5 cm (4½ in)**

Sociable birds, these marsh tyrants live in pairs or family groups and feed on insects, which they catch on the wing. They make their nests in low bushes or clumps of grass, using boll cotton in their construction. The female lays 2 or 3 eggs.

NAME: **Eastern Phoebe**, *Sayornis phoebe*
RANGE: **eastern N. America; winters in S. USA and Mexico**
HABITAT: **woodland near water, rocky ravines, wooded farmland**
SIZE: **16–18.5 cm (6¼–7¼ in)**

The distinguishing features of this flycatcher are its erect posture and the way it appears to wag its tail when it alights, sweeping it from side to side. Its name is derived from its frequently repeated two-note call, "fee-bee." Phoebes are not timid birds and, in summer, can be seen on farmland and wooded country roads, searching for the beetles, ants, bees, wasps and other invertebrates that make up their diet.

Their cup-shaped nests are made from mud and moss and sited on rocky ledges, or even on rafters or window sills in farm buildings. The female lays 3 to 8 eggs, usually 5, which are incubated for 16 days.

NAME: **Kiskadee Flycatcher**, *Pitangus sulphuratus*
RANGE: **S.E. Texas, Central and South America to central Argentina**
HABITAT: **groves, orchards, wooded banks of streams**
SIZE: **23–26.5 cm (9–10½ in)**

A large bird with a big head, the kiskadee flycatcher is active and noisy, advertising its presence with its loud call, "kis-ka-dee." It is conspicuous at dawn and dusk and behaves much like a kingfisher, perching quite still above water and then plunging into it after fish and tadpoles. Its plumage needs to dry out after three dives, so it turns to catching flying insects such as beetles and wasps. In winter, when these are scarce, it feeds on fruit and berries.

Kiskadee flycatchers make their large, oval nests about 6 m (20 ft) up in trees. The female lays 2 to 5 eggs, usually 4.

NAME: **Eastern Kingbird**, *Tyrannus tyrannus*
RANGE: **central Canada, through USA to Gulf of Mexico; winters in Central and South America to N. Argentina**
HABITAT: **open country with trees, orchards, gardens**
SIZE: **20.5–23 cm (8–9 in)**

The eastern kingbird is a noisy and aggressive bird and will attack other birds, such as hawks, vultures and crows, sometimes landing on the other bird's back. It has even been known to attack low-flying aircraft. It has been observed to eat more than 200 types of insect, which it takes in the air or from the ground or scoops up from water. It will also pick berries, while hovering.

Both male and female kingbirds incubate the 3 to 5 eggs for about 2 weeks and both feed the young.

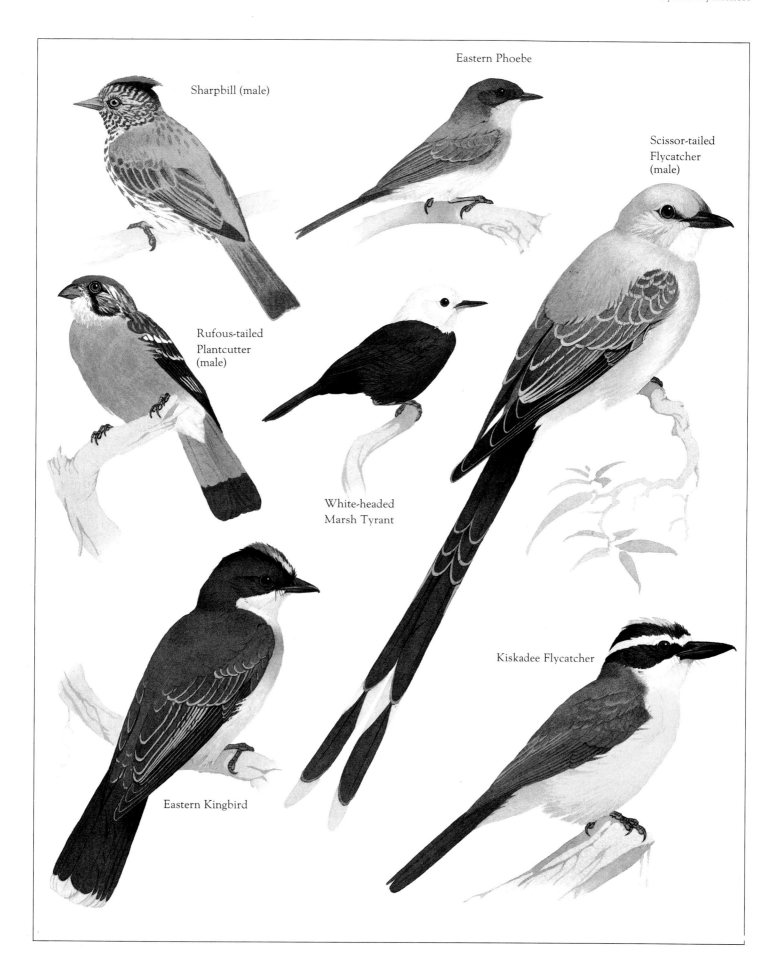

Sharpbill (male)

Eastern Phoebe

Scissor-tailed
Flycatcher
(male)

Rufous-tailed
Plantcutter
(male)

White-headed
Marsh Tyrant

Kiskadee Flycatcher

Eastern Kingbird

Tyrant Flycatchers

NAME: **Willow Flycatcher,** *Empidonax*
traillii
RANGE: **S. Canada, USA: Maine to**
Virginia, west to Arkansas and
California
HABITAT: **open country near water to**
2,400 m (7,900 ft)
SIZE: **13.5–15 cm (5¼–6 in)**

True to its common name, this bird is most frequently encountered where willow trees abound — on islands in rivers, in shrubs along streams and in beaver meadows. In appearance it is similar to the alder flycatcher (*E. al-norum*), but it has a slightly longer bill and more rounded wings. It is a prodigious insect-eater and is known to catch at least 65 species of beetle, as well as aphids, scale insects, bees, wasps and crane flies, all of which it takes in flight. It also eats caterpillars, spiders and millipedes, as well as some berries.

Willow flycatchers usually build their nests about 2.5 m (8 ft) above the ground in the upright fork of a bush or tree, in an area where willows or plants of the rose family grow. The shredded bark of milkweed, cattail and the silky catkins of aspen and willow are used in its construction, and it is softly lined with grass and feathers. The female lays 3 or 4 eggs, which are incubated for about 12 days. The young leave the nest when they are about 2 weeks old.

NAME: **Many-colored Rush-tyrant,**
Tachuris rubrigastra
RANGE: **South America: Peru,**
S.E. Brazil, Paraguay, Uruguay,
Argentina, Chile
HABITAT: **fields, meadows near water,**
swampy ground
SIZE: **10.5 cm (4¼ in)**

There are seven colors visible in the plumage of these pretty little birds — yellow, blue, white, bronze, black, carmine and green. The birds are sprightly and flit about constantly among the stems of tall grasses, particularly cattails, searching for small insects to eat. Although they are so active, many-colored tyrants are seldom seen and often can be located only by their frequently repeated, sharp, ringing calls.

The cone-shaped nest is attached to the stalk of a cattail or reed, 50 to 80 cm (20 to 30 in) above the water. It is intricately woven from small pieces of dry reed, with the point of the cone at the bottom, and the reeds are cemented with a sticky substance, which gives the nest a smooth, shiny surface. The female lays her eggs in multiples of three: 3, 6 or 9.

NAME: **Royal Flycatcher,**
Onychorhynchus coronatus
RANGE: **South America: Amazon basin**
HABITAT: **rain and cloud forest, forest**
edge
SIZE: **16.5 cm (6½ in)**

The royal flycatcher is a showy bird, with a large crest of crimson feathers that end in disks with a metallic blue luster; in the female the crest is orange. Normally the crest lies flat, but in display it is opened and closed like a fan. The bill is broad and flat and quite wide, well suited to the bird's diet of insects, which they take on the wing. These flycatchers are usually found singly or in pairs in secondary growth or at the forest edge.

The long, bag-shaped nest is built in a tree, often near a stream, and the female lays 2 eggs.

NAME: **Eastern Wood Peewee,** *Contopus*
virens
RANGE: **breeds S.E. Canada, E. USA;**
winters Central America, northern
South America
HABITAT: **deciduous or mixed woodland,**
tall shade trees in gardens
SIZE: **15–17 cm (6–6¾ in)**

The eastern wood peewee is so similar in appearance to the western species (*C. sordidulus*) that in western Manitoba and Nebraska, where their ranges overlap, it is possible to distinguish it only by its plaintive, whistling call. It perches in the deep shade of tall trees, darting out to catch flying insects, beetles and tree-hoppers.

Eastern wood peewees build thick-walled, cup-shaped nests high up on the horizontal branches of trees. The nest is made of weeds and fibers, lined with wool, grass and hair, and well covered with lichen, which makes it invisible from the ground. Normally 3 eggs are laid, which are incubated until they hatch after about 13 days.

NAME: **Short-tailed Pygmy-tyrant,**
Myiornis ecaudatus
RANGE: **northern South America, east of**
the Andes, Amazonian Brazil; Trinidad
HABITAT: **high open rain forest, clearings**
in forest, plantations
SIZE: **6.5 cm (2½ in)**

The smallest of the tyrants, this tiny bird has an exceptionally short tail, scarcely longer than the tail coverts. Male and female look alike. Alone or in pairs, the birds dart about in the forest trees, from the bottom branches to the canopy, looking for insects to feed on. Pygmy-tyrants are not shy, but because they live in such dense vegetation, they are hardly ever seen, and no information is available about their breeding or nesting behavior.

NAME: **White-crested Spadebill,**
Platyrinchus platyrhynchos
RANGE: **northern South America to**
Amazon basin
HABITAT: **rain forest, forest edge**
SIZE: **7.5 cm (3 in)**

A tiny, stout-bodied bird, with a round head and a wide, short bill, the white-crested spadebill is distinguished by the white feathers on its head. Pairs remain together throughout the year, flitting busily through the bushes and the lower branches of forest trees in their search for insects and spiders to eat. Occasionally they may even be seen among the many birds that follow the columns of army ants.

The female spadebill builds a bulky, cup-shaped nest, rather like a humming-bird's, from tree ferns, plant fibers and cobwebs. The nest is usually sited in the vertical fork of a tree about 2 m (6½ ft) from the ground. Two eggs are laid, two days apart, and they are incubated for about 17 days by the female alone. Both parents feed the young, which can fly at about 2 weeks old.

NAME: **Yellow-bellied Elaenia,** *Elaenia*
flavogaster
RANGE: **Central and South America:**
S. Mexico to N. Argentina; Trinidad,
Tobago
HABITAT: **shady pasture, savanna, parks,**
plantations, to 1,800 m (6,000 ft)
SIZE: **16 cm (6¼ in)**

Despite its name, the most remarkable characteristic of this flycatcher is the double crest of stiff gray feathers that stands up on each side of the head, revealing the white patch between. The bird's breast and belly are pale yellow, the tail long and the bill short. Male and female look alike. Elaenias live in pairs all year round, always in open country with trees, where they feed on insects taken on the wing and on many different types of berries.

Both birds help to build the nest in the fork of a tree, generally about 2 to 4.5 m (6½ to 15 ft) above the ground. It is a shallow, open structure, made from rootlets, plant fibers and cobwebs, covered with lichen and moss and lined with feathers. The female lays 2 eggs, which she incubates for about 15 days. The nestlings are fed by both parents and leave the nest 17 or 18 days after hatching. There are often two broods produced in a year.

Willow Flycatcher

White-crested Spadebill

Yellow-bellied Elaenia

Royal Flycatcher (male)

Eastern Wood Peewee

Many-colored
Rush-tyrant

Short-tailed Pygmy-tyrant

Tyrant Flycatchers

NAME: Common Tody-flycatcher,
Todirostrum cinereum
RANGE: S. Mexico, Central and South
America to Bolivia and Brazil
HABITAT: open country, plantations,
parkland
SIZE: 10 cm (4 in)

The long, straight bill and the narrow, graduated tail feathers make up over half of this bird's body length. Avoiding dense woodland, it feeds wherever there are scattered trees, making short darts from branch to branch and seizing insects and berries from foliage and bark. It hops sideways along branches, continuously wagging its tail as it goes. Male and female look alike and live in pairs throughout the year.

Both partners of a breeding pair help to make the nest, which is suspended from a slender twig or vine. They do not weave the nest but mat together plant fibers and then excavate an entrance hole and central cavity in the resulting mass. The female lays 2 or 3 eggs, which she incubates for 17 or 18 days, and both parents feed the young.

NAME: Ocher-bellied Flycatcher,
Pipromorpha oleaginea
RANGE: S. Mexico, through Central and
South America to Peru and Brazil
HABITAT: forest, clearings
SIZE: 12 cm (4¾ in)

A slender, long-tailed bird, the ocher-bellied flycatcher is mainly olive-green, with grayish plumage on the throat and ocher-yellow underparts. Its bill is long and slender, with a hooked tip. An active little bird, it has a characteristic mannerism of constantly twitching its wings above its back, one at a time. Unlike other flycatchers, this species does not make aerial dashes after prey but seizes insects and spiders from foliage as it flits from tree to tree. It also feeds on fruit and berries, particularly mistletoe berries. An extremely solitary bird, it never gathers in flocks or even pairs, except during the brief period of courtship and mating.

Normally silent, in the breeding season male ocher-bellied flycatchers take up territories in which they perch and sing tirelessly to attract mates. Several males may sing within hearing of each other. They do not assist females in nest-building or rearing of young. A pear-shaped nest, covered with moss, is suspended from a slender branch or vine or from the aerial root of an air plant. It takes the female about 2 weeks to build this nest. She incubates the 2 or 3 eggs for 19 to 21 days and feeds the young for 2 to 3 weeks.

NAME: Cliff Flycatcher, *Hirundinea*
ferruginea
RANGE: northern South America to
Brazil and N. Argentina
HABITAT: arid hillsides, ravines, cliffs,
open woodland
SIZE: 18.5 cm (7¼ in)

A mainly brown and black bird, this flycatcher has bright chestnut underparts and wing patches, which are conspicuous in flight. Its wings are long and swallowlike, and it catches much of its insect prey in skillful aerial dashes.

The nest is made in a crevice in a rock or cliff.

NAME: Great Shrike Tyrant, *Agriornis*
livida
RANGE: South America: S. Argentina,
Chile
HABITAT: open scrub, fields
SIZE: 28 cm (11 in) including tail of
11 cm (4¼ in)

This silent bird avoids woodland and populated regions and frequents lonely, open areas. It has a powerful beak and feeds on insects, small animals, such as newts, toads and mice, and eggs of other birds.

On the coast, the birds begin nesting in October, but farther inland, in the Andean foothills, breeding does not start until November. A bulky nest, made of grass and sticks and lined with sheep's wool, is built in a thick bush. The female lays 2 to 4 eggs, usually 3.

NAME: Vermilion Flycatcher,
Pyrocephalus rubinus
RANGE: S.W. USA, Mexico, Central and
South America to Argentina;
Galápagos Islands
HABITAT: scrub, desert
SIZE: 14–17 cm (5½–6¾ in)

A striking bird, the male vermilion flycatcher has a bright red head and underparts. The female is brownish above, with a lighter, streaked belly and breast. These flycatchers feed on flying insects, particularly bees, darting into the air from a high perch in pursuit of their prey. They also feed on the ground on grasshoppers and beetles, especially in areas of sparse vegetation.

The courting male flies up from a tree, singing ecstatically, his vermilion crest erect and his breast feathers puffed out. He hovers briefly, then flutters down to the female. A flattish, cup-shaped nest, made of twigs, grass and rootlets, is built on a horizontally forked branch. While the female incubates the 2 to 4 eggs, the male fearlessly defends the nest. The young leave the nest about 2 weeks after hatching.

NAME: Piratic Flycatcher, *Legatus*
leucophaius
RANGE: S. Mexico, Central and South
America to N. Argentina
HABITAT: open woodland
SIZE: 14.5 cm (5¾ in)

A dully colored bird, the piratic flycatcher makes itself conspicuous by being one of the noisiest flycatchers, with a wide range of calls. It feeds on insects, especially dragonflies, caught on the wing, and berries.

Piratic flycatchers appear to be the only members of the tyrant flycatcher family to depart from normal nest-building habits, and this departure earns them their common name. They do not build their own nests but usurp the freshly built nests of other birds, often other species of flycatcher. Having chosen their victims, the pair of piratic flycatchers perch nearby to watch the building progressing. They chatter noisily and make their presence felt but do not usually attack until the nest is complete. Then they harass the rightful owners until they finally abandon the nest to their attackers. Any eggs are thrown out, and the female piratic flycatcher lays 2 or 3 eggs, which she incubates for about 16 days. Both parents feed the nestlings on berries and insects until they leave the nest almost 3 weeks after hatching. Central American and northern South American populations of piratic flycatchers migrate south after breeding.

NAME: Torrent Tyranulet, *Serpophaga*
cinerea
RANGE: Central and South America:
mountains of Costa Rica and Panama,
Andes from Venezuela to Bolivia
HABITAT: rocky streams
SIZE: 10 cm (4 in)

The torrent tyranulet lives amid the fast-flowing waters of mountain streams, and its gray and black plumage echoes its wild, rocky habitat. With great skill, it plucks insects not only from the air but also from slippery boulders surrounded by foaming water, often becoming drenched with spray in the process. It even alights on wet rocks to search for other tiny invertebrates. Male and female look alike and live together throughout the year, holding a stretch of river as their territory.

A cup-shaped nest, covered with moss, is made in vegetation overhanging water, rarely over the bank. The 2 eggs are incubated by the female for 17 or 18 days, but the male stays nearby. Both parents feed the young on insects for 2 or 3 weeks, and even after leaving the nest, the young birds stay with their parents for a further 5 or 6 weeks before seeking their own territory.

Common
Tody-flycatcher

Ocher-bellied Flycatcher

Vermilion Flycatcher
(male)

Great Shrike Tyrant

Cliff Flycatcher

Torrent Tyranulet

Piratic Flycatcher

Broadbills, Pittas and relatives

EURYLAIMIDAE: Broadbill Family
There are about 14 known species in the broadbill family, all found in Africa, southern and Southeast Asia in forest and woodland. They are rather rotund little birds, with bright plumage, heavy, wide bills and short legs and tails. Male and female look unalike in most species. Broadbills feed on insects, fruit, seeds and other plant material. Most build pear-shaped nests, suspended from branches or twigs, often over water.

NAME: **Green Broadbill,** *Calyptomena viridis*
RANGE: **Malaysia, Sumatra, Borneo**
HABITAT: **forest on lowland and hills**
SIZE: **19 cm (7½ in)**

The green broadbill spends much of its life foraging for fruit, its main food, high in the forest trees, where it is hard to spot among the leaves. The male is bright and iridescent, but the female is a duller green and often larger than the male.

The nest is made of coarse, matted plant fibers and is suspended from thin twigs just above the ground. It is wider at the top than at the bottom, and there is an entrance hole near the top. The female bird lays 2 eggs, which both parents are believed to incubate.

PITTIDAE: Pitta Family
The 24 species of pitta occur in Africa, Asia and Southeast Asia to Australia. They are stout birds, with long legs, and most species have bright plumage. Male and female look alike in some species but differ in others.

NAME: **Indian Pitta,** *Pitta brachyura*
RANGE: **N. and central India; winters in S. India and Sri Lanka**
HABITAT: **varied, including semi-cultivated land and forest**
SIZE: **18 cm (7 in)**

This brightly plumaged little bird forages on or close to the forest floor, searching among leaves and debris for food such as insects and spiders; it will also eat worms and maggots found near excrement. If alarmed, it flies up into a tree with a whirring sound and then sits still, with only its tail moving slowly up and down.

The nest, built in a tree, is a domed, globular structure, made of moss and covered with twigs. It is lined with plant material and has a side entrance. Both parents incubate the 4 to 6 eggs and feed the helpless, naked young. Large flocks of Indian pittas migrate south in winter.

NAME: **Garnet Pitta,** *Pitta granatina*
RANGE: **Malaysia, Sumatra, Borneo**
HABITAT: **lowland forest, swamps**
SIZE: **15 cm (6 in)**

Both male and female garnet pittas have brilliant, jewel-like plumage, while juveniles are brownish and acquire the adult coloration only gradually. Much of the garnet pitta's life is spent running about on the ground, foraging for ants, beetles and other insects, as well as snails and seeds, but it will also fly short distances.

Its nest, typical of the pitta family, is made on the ground and is a domed structure of rotting leaves and fibers, roofed with twigs and leaves. There is a small entrance to the chamber in which the female lays 2 eggs.

XENICIDAE:
New Zealand Wren Family
This family of 4 species of small wren-like birds is confined to forest and scrubland in New Zealand.

NAME: **Rifleman,** *Acanthisitta chloris*
RANGE: **New Zealand and neighboring islands**
HABITAT: **forest and modified habitats with remnants of forest**
SIZE: **7.5–10 cm (3–4 in)**

The tiny rifleman feeds mainly in the trees, searching in crevices and over trunks and branches for insects and spiders; it may occasionally come down to the forest floor. Male and female differ in plumage, the female having dark- and light-brown striped upper-parts, instead of yellowish-green.

The nest is made in a crevice in a tree, and both parents incubate the 4 or 5 eggs and feed the young.

PHILEPITTIDAE: Asity Family
The 4 species in this family are divided into two distinct groups: the asities and the false sunbirds. They are plump, tree-dwelling birds, all found in Madagascar. Male and female differ in plumage.

NAME: **Wattled False Sunbird,** *Neodrepanis coruscans*
RANGE: **E. Madagascar**
HABITAT: **forest**
SIZE: **9 cm (3½ in)**

The long, downward-curving bill of the wattled false sunbird gives it a strong superficial resemblance to the true sunbirds (Nectariniidae), hence the common name. The bill is used for the same purpose, that is, to drink nectar from flowers. The false sunbird also feeds on fruit, insects and spiders.

MENURIDAE: Lyrebird Family
The 2 species of lyrebird both live in the mountain forests of southeastern Australia. Both sexes have brownish plumage, but the males have extraordinarily long and elaborate tails.

NAME: **Superb Lyrebird,** *Menura novaehollandiae*
RANGE: **Australia: S.E. Queensland to Victoria; introduced in Tasmania**
HABITAT: **mountain forest**
SIZE: **male: 80–95 cm (31½–37½ in); female: 45–50 cm (17¾–19¾ in)**

Although male and female lyrebirds are similar in body size and general appearance, the male's tail is up to 55 cm (21½ in) long and is a flamboyant mix of boldly patterned, lyre-shaped feathers and fine, filamentous feathers. The lyrebirds are mainly ground-living and rarely fly but hop and flap up into trees to roost. They search on the ground for insects and larvae, scratching around with their large, strong legs and feet.

Prior to mating, the male makes several earth mounds and displays near them before the female, spreading his shimmering tail right over himself and dancing. The nest is a large, well-camouflaged dome, made of grass and plant fiber and lined with rootlets. It is built on the ground near rocks or logs or sometimes in a tree. The female incubates her 1 egg for about 6 weeks and cares for the nestling.

ATRICHORNITHIDAE:
Scrub Bird Family
There are 2 species of scrub bird, both found in Australia; they are the closest relatives of lyrebirds. They have small wings, long, broad tails and strong legs. Male and female differ slightly in coloration and females are smaller.

NAME: **Noisy Scrub Bird,** *Atrichornis clamosus*
RANGE: **S.W. Australia: Two People's Bay**
HABITAT: **coastal scrub, vegetated gullies**
SIZE: **23 cm (9 in)**   Ⓔ

Now an extremely rare bird, the noisy scrub bird was thought to be extinct for more than 70 years until it was rediscovered, in 1961, at Two People's Bay. It is now protected by law.

Noisy scrub birds live among dense vegetation on or near the ground and feed on insects and seeds. They usually live alone and rarely move far afield. The female bird builds a domed nest of dried rushes, in which she lays 1 egg. She incubates the egg for 36 to 38 days.

Rifleman (male)

Green Broadbill (male)

Superb Lyrebird (male)

Wattled
False
Sunbird
(male)

Indian Pitta

Garnet Pitta

Noisy Scrub Bird
(male)

Larks

NAME: **Desert Lark,** *Ammomanes deserti*
RANGE: **Africa: Sahara; Middle East, through Iran to Afghanistan**
HABITAT: **stony, hilly desert, dry wooded slopes**
SIZE: **15 cm (6 in)**

The plumage of the desert lark perfectly matches the color of the desert soil — the best example of soil camouflage in birds. The very dark subspecies, *A. d. annae*, blends with the black larval sand of central Arabia, while the pale race, *A. d. isabellina*, does not stray from areas of white sand.

The nest is usually built up against a rock or tuft of grass and is reinforced on the windward side by small decorative pebbles. In the harsh desert interior, 3 eggs are laid, while 4 or 5 may be produced at the desert edge.

NAME: **Singing Bushlark,** *Mirafra javanica*
RANGE: **central and E. Africa, Middle East, S.E. Asia, New Guinea, Australia**
HABITAT: **open bush or scrub, rice fields**
SIZE: **15 cm (6 in)**

The vibrant songs of the singing bushlark can often be heard issuing from bushes or the air, even on bright moonlit nights. Darker and more evenly colored than other larks, this plump, gregarious bird has a heavy, finchlike bill, which it uses to pick up grass seeds and insects. With its shape, its strong, rapid gait and weak flight, the singing bushlark is well suited to life on the ground.

The igloo-shaped grass nest is built in the shelter of a rock or tuft of grass and has a side entrance and soft, grass lining. The female lays 3 to 5 eggs.

NAME: **Thick-billed/Clotbey Lark,** *Ramphocoris clotbey*
RANGE: **N. Africa to Syria**
HABITAT: **stony desert**
SIZE: **17 cm (6¾ in)**

True to its name, this lark is distinguished by its large, powerful bill. The bird uses it to crush tough seed cases and hard-shelled desert insects and carries its head very straight or thrown backward, to counteract the weight of the bill. The male is sandy colored, with black spots on the underparts; the female has a redder tinge and fewer spots.

Although this species is normally sedentary, some birds move away from the heat of the desert outside the breeding season. The nest is sited up against a stone or grass tussock and starts out as a small hollow, filled with soft plant material. As it begins to overflow, the nesting material is supported by a collection of small pebbles. The female lays 2 to 5 eggs.

ALAUDIDAE: Lark Family

The larks, about 75 species in all, are concentrated in the Old World except for the horned lark and the introduced skylark, found also in North America. Typically, the wings are fairly long and pointed and the beak rather long and slightly down-curved. Males and females look more or less alike, but the female is often smaller.

Most species favor an open habitat with low vegetation, such as tundra, meadowland or desert, where they are commonly seen walking or running along the ground. The diet consists of seeds, buds, insects and small underground invertebrates, obtained by bill-probing or digging.

NAME: **Short-toed/Red-capped Lark,** *Calandrella cinerea*
RANGE: **Mediterranean area, Africa, Asia to Mongolia; occasional visitor to N. Europe and Britain**
HABITAT: **open sandy or stony plains**
SIZE: **14 cm (5½ in)**

The tiny short-toed lark is a widespread species with about 14 races. It varies in color throughout its range, from sandy to reddish — the South African race, for example, has a rufous cap on its head and reddish patches on the sides of its breast. In spite of its name, the ground-dwelling short-toed lark is a speedy runner. When alarmed, however, it escapes by flying low, then lands abruptly and sprints away. Short-toed larks feed on the ground on seeds and insects but perform prolonged, undulating song flights at a height of about 15 m (50 ft).

Northern populations migrate to their breeding grounds, south of the Sahara and in central India, in autumn. All races gather in large flocks out of the breeding season but disperse to mate, when they are seen singly or in pairs. The nest, deep and cup-shaped, holds two clutches of 3 to 5 eggs each in a year. Incubation lasts for 11 to 13 days.

NAME: **Horned Lark,** *Eremophila alpestris*
RANGE: **N. America, Europe, N. Africa, Asia**
HABITAT: **varied: rocky alpine meadows up to 5,275 m (17,300 ft), stony steppe, tundra and desert, open grassland**
SIZE: **16 cm (6¼ in)**

One of only two larks found in the Americas, the horned lark comprises 40 widespread races. The male has a distinctive black and yellow head with short black tufts, or horns, of feathers; the female and juveniles are less black. In winter, northern groups migrate to southern breeding grounds, and most populations winter in lowland fields, where they sometimes form flocks with buntings. In summer, they feed on seeds, buds, insects and their larvae, supplementing these with small crustaceans and mollusks in winter.

The nest is a simple structure of plant stems, lined with soft plant material; it is built on the ground and surrounded with sheep droppings, plant debris and pebbles. The female usually lays two broods of 4 eggs each, which she incubates for 10 to 14 days.

NAME: **Skylark,** *Alauda arvensis*
RANGE: **Europe, Asia, N. Africa; introduced in Australasia and Canada**
HABITAT: **moorland, marshes, sand dunes, arable and pasture land**
SIZE: **18 cm (7 in)**

The skylark has dark wings and a long tail, both with a white fringe, a boldly streaked breast and a short, but prominent, crest. It is a terrestrial bird and roosts on the ground; it walks rather than hops and crouches when uneasy, emitting a liquid chirrup when flushed. Skylarks enjoy dust baths and prefer to perch on low walls, fences or telephone wires. They usually sing early in the morning and have a characteristic song flight, fluttering high in the sky and sustaining their song for long periods. Their diet consists of seeds and ground-living invertebrates.

The female builds a well-concealed grass nest in which she lays 3 to 5 eggs; she then incubates them for 11 days. Two or three broods are raised each year. Northern races migrate south of their range for the winter.

NAME: **Greater Hoopoe Lark/Bifasciated Lark,** *Alaemon alaudipes*
RANGE: **Cape Verde Archipelago, across the Sahara to Middle East, W. India**
HABITAT: **open sandy desert**
SIZE: **20.5 cm (8 in)**

One of the larger species, the greater hoopoe lark is long legged, long billed and distinguished by its white eyebrow tufts. It uses its sturdy, down-curved bill to dig up to 5 cm (2 in) into the desert soil in search of grubs, locust pupae and seeds. This bold bird is not easily upset by human observers and defends its territory against competitors. It has a long, melodious call, but its song is a series of pipes and whistles, and it normally only flies during its extremely high, rising and falling song flight.

Like most larks, it nests on the ground, although in the hottest areas, the nest, which may be scanty or quite substantial, is placed a few inches off the ground in the shady lower branches of a bush. The female usually lays 2 eggs.

Skylark

Desert Lark

(dark race)

(pale race)

Horned Lark (male)

Greater Hoopoe Lark

Thick-billed Lark
(male)

Short-toed Lark

Singing Bushlark

Swallows

NAME: **Barn Swallow**, *Hirundo rustica*
RANGE: **almost worldwide; breeds between 30°N and 70°N; winters in southern hemisphere**
HABITAT: **open cultivated country with buildings, near water**
SIZE: **19.5 cm (7¾ in)**

The barn swallow is absent only from very high latitudes and some oceanic islands. The male is metallic blue, with a deeply forked tail covered in white spots and a white breast. Females and young birds have shorter tails and less vibrant plumage. They feed on insects, caught on the wing or plucked from the surface of water.

In summer, barn swallows are seen in pairs and small groups, but in autumn they form huge flocks and roost in reedbeds before migrating south. The Old World races winter in Africa, south of the Sahara, the Indian subcontinent and northern Australia; the North American birds fly down to Panama, central Chile and northern Argentina.

Both sexes help to build the open nest, using mud and straw and lining it with feathers. They now seem to prefer ledges on buildings to the original cave or cliff sites. The female lays 4 or 5 eggs and incubates them for about 15 days, with some help from the male. Both parents feed the nestlings, which can fly at about 3 weeks old. There are two, sometimes three, broods a year.

NAME: **Bank Swallow**, *Riparia riparia*
RANGE: **temperate regions of Eurasia, N. America**
HABITAT: **steep sand or gravel banks, near water**
SIZE: **12–14 cm (4¾–5½ in)**

The tiny bank swallow is the smallest swallow in North America, with a wingspan of only 25.5 to 28 cm (10 to 11 in). This energetic little bird darts, twists and zigzags in flight, snapping up a variety of winged insects, including termites, leafhoppers and mosquitoes.

Bank swallows live in burrows, which they dig straight into sand or gravel banks, often by water or alongside roads and railway tracks. The birds start the burrow with their bills, and both male and female take turns to kick out the soil until the burrow is about 1 m (3¼ ft) long. Each spring, the bank swallows flock north, often returning to the previous year's hole, and fights over ownership are not unusual. The nest is built at the end of the burrow from soft grass, feathers, hair and rootlets. The female lays up to 8 eggs, usually 4 or 5, which are incubated alternately by both parents for 16 days. The young fly at 3 weeks old.

HIRUNDINIDAE: Swallow Family

The 78 species of swallow and martin are all swift-flying birds, which display great agility in the air. They are found almost worldwide, and many make regular migrations between breeding and wintering areas, sometimes traveling as much as 13,000 km (8,000 mi). There is little consistent difference between the swallows and martins. All forms have smallish bodies, short necks and long, pointed wings. They are fast, agile fliers and catch their prey on the wing in their wide, gaping beaks. Swallows and martins are the passerine equivalents of swifts. The two families have become alike by adapting to a similar way of life in the air; swifts, however, do have longer wings and tend to fly higher than swallows.

On the ground, their short legs and weak feet are ill suited to locomotion, but the birds do perch. They frequently nest close to or in human dwellings or use natural hollows in trees, caves or cliffs in which to construct a burrow. Clutches of 3 to 7 eggs are laid, which both parents incubate.

Swallows and martins are generally gregarious birds and feed, nest and migrate in large flocks. Males and females look more or less alike, but in some species there may be minor differences, such as the male having longer tail feathers.

NAME: **White-eyed River Martin,**
Pseudochelidon sirintarae
RANGE: **winters central Thailand**
HABITAT: **reedbeds in marshes**
SIZE: **24 cm (9½ in) including tail streamers of 9 cm (3½ in)** ①

The white-eyed river martin is identified by its distinctive white spectacles and rump and by the long streamers flowing from its rounded tail. It also has a large, swollen, yellow bill, unusual for a swallow. The juvenile has a darker head and only very short streamers.

This rare species was discovered only in 1968 and is believed to be a migrant from the north. Its nearest relative, and the only other member of its subfamily, is *P. eurystomina*, which lives in Africa, in Zambia. The white-eyed river martin winters in central Thailand, at Bung Boraphet, where it roosts at night in large lakeside reedbeds in flocks with other species of swallows. By day, it perches on trees and wires and catches insects in flight.

Its summer migration and breeding habits remain a mystery, although it may breed in holes in riverbanks in Thailand or China.

NAME: **Purple Martin**, *Progne subis*
RANGE: **breeds Canada to Mexico; winters south to West Indies, Venezuela, Brazil**
HABITAT: **suburban gardens and farmland**
SIZE: **18 cm (7 in)**

The purple martin is one of the tamest birds of the family. The male's metallic blue plumage gradually fades out to brown on the wings and tail; the female is mainly brown, and the juvenile is a grayish-brown. This species supplements its diet of insects, taken on the wing, with snails, probably as a source of calcium.

These birds build their nests in trees or cliff holes, using grass, feathers and often green leaves, which may help to keep the nest cool and moist. The 3 to 5 eggs are incubated for 13 days, mainly by the female, and the young leave the nest within a month of hatching.

There are 2 races of purple martin. *P. s. subis* breeds in southern Canada, down the west coast of the USA to central Mexico and east to the Gulf Coast and Florida; it winters in Venezuela and southeast Brazil. *P. s. hesperia* breeds in the lowlands of Arizona, Baja California and the Mexican coast, but it is not known where it winters.

NAME: **Blue Rough-winged Swallow,**
Psalidoprocne pristoptera
RANGE: **Africa: Ethiopia**
HABITAT: **high plateaus**
SIZE: **18 cm (7 in)**

The blue rough-winged swallow has glossy blue-black plumage above, with an oily green look to its wings and tail. The broad tail is not as deeply forked in the female as in the male. The juvenile is a dull, dark brown and blue. These birds are often seen in pairs, swooping over streams in search of insects, which they take on the wing.

The nesting hole is at the end of a tunnel, chiseled into a riverbank or cliff face, and is padded with layers of soft grass. The female lays 3 eggs, which are glossy white and thin shelled.

NAME: **Golden Swallow**, *Kalochelidon euchrysea*
RANGE: **Jamaica, Hispaniola**
HABITAT: **dry, wooded, limestone hills**
SIZE: **12.5 cm (5 in)**

This delicate, graceful bird earns its name from the bright golden gloss over its olive-green plumage. The juvenile keeps its duller colors and gray chest band until maturity. The Jamaican race is now believed to be rare, although there is insufficient information available at present to classify it as such.

Golden swallows feed entirely on the wing and nest in tree holes or under the eaves of houses. The female lays 3 eggs.

Barn Swallow (male)

Bank Swallow

Golden Swallow

Purple Martin
(male)

Blue
Rough-winged
Swallow
(male)

White-eyed River Martin

Pipits

NAME: **Yellow-throated Longclaw,**
Macronyx croceus
RANGE: **Africa, south of the Sahara**
HABITAT: **wet grassland, open woodland,**
swamps, cultivated land
SIZE: **20.5 cm (8 in)**

The hind claw of this widespread species is nearly 5 cm (2 in) long. Male and female look alike, but the juvenile lacks the black chest marking of the adults and has only black spots. These birds live in pairs and are often seen perching in trees or on farmland. In flight they flap, rather like the larks, and occasionally dive into the grass to rummage for insects.

The male's courtship flight is leisurely, and he fans out his tail and sings at the same time. The loosely constructed nest, made of grass and roots, is usually hidden among long grass or under a tussock. The female lays 3 or 4 eggs.

NAME: **Golden Pipit, Tmetothylacus**
tenellus
RANGE: **Africa: Ethiopia, Somalia, Sudan**
to Tanzania
HABITAT: **dry scrub**
SIZE: **15 cm (6 in)**

The shy golden pipit is bright yellow, but the darker bars and mottling help it to blend with its arid scrub habitat. The female and juvenile are browner and paler than the male. All have a long hind claw. These birds are usually seen alone or in small family groups, wagging their tails as they perch above the ground, watching for the insects that form their food.

In his courtship display, the male flies down from a tree, with wings raised in a V-shape over his back, whistling as he goes. The female makes a grass nest, lined with rootlets, just off the ground in a clump of grass, and lays 2 to 4 eggs.

NAME: **Forest Wagtail, Dendronanthus**
indicus
RANGE: **E. Asia: breeds Siberia to N.**
China; winters south to India and Java
HABITAT: **glades and clearings in**
montane forest, near water
SIZE: **20.5 cm (8 in)**

The forest wagtail can be identified by the loud chirruping sound it makes as it flies, perches or runs about looking for the snails, slugs, worms and insects on which it feeds. When standing, by rotating its body, it wags its tail from side to side, rather than up and down as other wagtails do.

Bundles of plant material are bound together with spider's webs to form a compact nest, which is usually built on a horizontal branch overhanging water. The female lays 4 eggs.

MOTACILLIDAE: Pipit Family

The family of longclaws, pipits and wagtails is absent only from the extreme north and small oceanic islands. Most of the 54 species are characterized by a long tail, which they wag up and down, and some by a long hind claw. All forms are essentially ground-living birds, with strong feet, and have narrow, pointed beaks and slender bodies, which, among the wagtails, have an elongated appearance. Males and females look alike in some species, unalike in others.

NAME: **Meadow Pipit, Anthus pratensis**
RANGE: **Europe, Asia; winters in**
N. Africa, Middle East
HABITAT: **tundra, grassland, heaths**
SIZE: **15 cm (6 in)**

The meadow pipit has the normal pipit plumage pattern, with white outer tail feathers, although its body coloration is very variable. In their southern, winter home, meadow pipits gather in small, loose groups; in the summer, individuals can be seen either perching high — on telephone wires for instance — or on the ground in open grassland or alpine meadows. The diet is varied and generally includes flies, mosquitoes, spiders, worms and some seeds.

To attract a female, the male displays by flying up from the ground and then, with wings stretched out and tail lifted, gliding down while he sings a simple song. The nest is made and lined with soft grasses and is often tucked into a tussock of heather or grass to hide it. The female lays two clutches of 4 or 5 eggs and incubates them for 2 weeks. The male helps to feed the young.

NAME: **Water Pipit, Anthus spinoletta**
RANGE: **widespread in N. America,**
Europe, N. Asia
HABITAT: **summers in marshy areas of**
tundra, mountain and coast; winters in
plains and lowlands
SIZE: **15–18 cm (6–7 in)**

The water pipit has a slender body and thin, pointed bill. Male and female look alike, both with grayish-brown plumage and creamy-white underparts. When walking, they nod their heads up and down and swing their tails from side to side. Water pipits feed on aquatic worms and insects, which they obtain by wading in shallow pools and from mud flats and mats of drifting seaweed. They also take seeds and insects such as weevils, aphids, grasshoppers and ants. In spring, flocks of up to 500 birds can be seen feeding together before they fly off to their breeding grounds.

The female alone builds the nest of dried grass and twigs in the shelter of a rock, mossy bank or tussock of grass; sometimes it may be only a scraped hollow on the ground. She also incubates the 4 or 5 eggs for about 2 weeks, and the young fly 2 weeks after hatching.

In America, northern populations migrate to Mexico in vast numbers for the winter.

NAME: **Yellow Wagtail, Motacilla flava**
RANGE: **Europe, Asia to W. Alaska;**
winters in tropical Africa and Asia
HABITAT: **marshy grassland, heaths,**
moors, steppe, tundra
SIZE: **16.5 cm (6½ in)**

The yellow wagtail is the most pipitlike of the wagtails. All forms are greenish and black, with yellow underparts, but the males display a variety of head colors such as black, green and gray. The female has a pale patch above the eye, and the juvenile has dark throat spots. Several races flock together to migrate to the tropics, where the birds settle by rivers and lakes for the winter. They feed on insects on the ground or in the air, particularly those flushed out by grazing animals.

During his courtship display flight, the male puffs up his feathers, fans out his tail, which he holds bowed, and vibrates his wings until they seem to shiver. The nest is made of plant fibers, softly lined with hair and wool, and is well hidden on the ground. The female lays 5 or 6 eggs, which she incubates for 13 days.

NAME: **Pied/White Wagtail, Motacilla**
alba
RANGE: **Europe, Asia, N. Africa; winters**
south to S. Africa, S. Asia
HABITAT: **riverbanks, steppe, tundra,**
alpine meadows, cultivated land,
gardens, near water
SIZE: **18 cm (7 in)**

This wagtail has two distinct races, both of which have similar black and white markings and develop a white throat in winter. The mantle and rump of the white wagtail, M. a. alba, of continental Europe, however, are gray, while those of the pied wagtail, M. a. yarrellii, of the British Isles, are black, or dark gray in the female. These wagtails often roost in hundreds in trees and reedbeds and occasionally wade in shallow water. They take off from a fast, tail-bobbing run into undulating flight and snap up insects in the air with dexterity.

The cup-shaped, grassy nest, lined with wool, hair and feathers, is usually made in a hollow in a steep bank, on a building or on flat ground. It houses two, or sometimes three, broods of 5 or 6 eggs, which the female incubates for 2 weeks.

Pied Wagtail

Forest Wagtail

Yellow Wagtail

races of
Yellow
Wagtail

Golden Pipit

Meadow Pipit

Yellow-throated
Longclaw

Water Pipit

Cuckoo-shrikes and Minivets

RANGE: Australia
HABITAT: dry, open country
SIZE: 33 cm (13 in)

The ground cuckoo-shrike is far more terrestrial than other cuckoo-shrikes, which only occasionally forage on the ground. A stout-legged bird, it walks and runs well as it searches for insects to eat. It usually lives in family groups.

The nest, usually placed in the fork of a tree, is made of grass, stems and rootlets, and spider's webs may be used to bind the plant material together. It may sometimes be built on top of the old nest of another bird species. The female usually lays 2 or 3 eggs; more than one female may lay eggs in the same nest.

NAME: Cicadabird, *Coracina tenuirostris*
RANGE: Sulawesi to Solomon Islands,
    New Guinea, Australia
HABITAT: forest edge, grassland,
    mangrove swamps
SIZE: 25.5 cm (10 in)

Known as the cicadabird because of its high, shrill song, this bird is rather shy and is more often heard than seen; it is usually silent, however, outside the breeding season. Insects, such as beetles, caterpillars and cicadas, are its main foods, and most are caught up in the trees.

The nest of the cicadabird is only about 7.5 cm (3 in) across and is made of twigs and spider's webs, camouflaged with lichen; it is usually placed on a horizontal, forked branch. The female lays only 1 egg, and the male defends the nest and his territory against any intruders. He feeds his mate while she incubates the egg.

NAME: Large/Black-faced Cuckoo-shrike,
    Coracina novaehollandiae
RANGE: India to S.E. Asia and Australia
HABITAT: light forest, gardens, suburbs,
    plantations
SIZE: 33 cm (13 in)

The large cuckoo-shrike is a heavily built, mostly gray bird. The male has some black, shrikelike markings on his head; the female looks similar in most respects, but her head markings are dark gray. Small groups of cuckoo-shrikes forage high in the treetops for food, mainly fruit such as figs, insects and insect larvae. They sometimes take insects in the air or dive to pick up food from the ground.

Large cuckoo-shrikes tend to return to the same breeding site, even the same branch, year after year. The nest is saucer shaped and made of twigs and spider's webs, usually in the fork of a branch. The female lays 2 or 3 eggs.

CAMPEPHAGIDAE:
Cuckoo-shrike and Minivet Family

Cuckoo-shrikes are not cuckoos, nor are they shrikes and, in fact, they are not even related to these two families, even though in plumage coloration and body form there are a number of similarities. Together, cuckoo-shrikes and minivets make up a family of about 70 species, found for the most part in the tropics of the Old World, including Australia.

Cuckoo-shrikes are rather drab, dull-colored birds, with strong, notched beaks, long pointed wings and strong bristles around the base of the bill. Most are arboreal. Minivets have brightly colored plumage, often red and black in males and yellow or orange and gray in females. Like cuckoo-shrikes, they are mainly forest and woodland birds.

Many of the birds in this family have densely packed erectile feathers on the back and rump. These have stiff, sharp-pointed shafts and are easily shed, possibly as a defensive measure against predators. The nest is usually cup shaped and built in a tree, and there are 2 to 5 eggs, which may be incubated by both parents or by the female alone. Male and female look alike in some species, unalike in others.

NAME: Pied/Bar-winged Flycatcher-
    shrike, *Hemipus picatus*
RANGE: India, Sri Lanka, S.E. Asia,
    Sumatra, Borneo
HABITAT: woodland, forest, forest edge
SIZE: 12.5 cm (5 in)

The pied flycatcher-shrike is a small cuckoo-shrike, which pursues insects in the air as skillfully as a true flycatcher. It also finds food by hopping around the branches, gleaning insects from leaves, and may sometimes feed on the ground, although it is primarily a tree-living bird. Small groups of about 6 birds usually live together out of the breeding season and may also join in mixed flocks. Male and female look similar, but the black plumage of the male is replaced by dark brown in the female in some races.

The shallow, saucer-shaped nest is built on a branch of a tree and is made of grass and rootlets, bound together with spider's webs. Lichen is used to camouflage the outside, and the sitting bird appears to be on a clump of lichen rather than a nest. The female lays 2 or 3 eggs. Once hatched, the young birds sit still, with their eyes closed and their heads raised together, and can easily be mistaken by the casual observer for a spur of dead wood.

NAME: Red-shouldered/Black Cuckoo-
    shrike, *Campephaga phoenicea*
RANGE: Africa, south of the Sahara
HABITAT: forest, woodland
SIZE: 20.5 cm (8 in)

Some races of this species have the distinctive red markings they are named for, but others have small yellow shoulder patches or none at all. Males have glossy black plumage, while females are mainly olive-brown or gray, with yellow-edged wings and tail. Restless, active birds, they are always on the move in pairs or in parties of several species. They feed on caterpillars and insects, gleaned from foliage or found on the ground.

A cup-shaped nest, made of moss and lichen bound together with spider's webs, is built in the fork of a tree, and the female lays 2 or 3 eggs. She incubates the eggs for about 20 days, and both parents then feed the newly hatched nestlings.

NAME: White-winged Triller, *Lalage
    sueurii*
RANGE: Java, Lesser Sunda Islands,
    Sulawesi, Australia, New Guinea
HABITAT: open forest, woodland
SIZE: 18 cm (7 cm)

The white-winged triller makes its melodious calls as it flies from tree to tree, taking insects from leaves and branches. Male and female differ in plumage, the female being largely brown, while the male is glossy black, gray and white.

Both partners of a breeding pair help to build a nest of plant material, usually in the fork of a branch. They both incubate the 1 to 3 eggs for about 14 days and feed the young.

NAME: Scarlet Minivet, *Pericrocotus
    flammeus*
RANGE: India, Sri Lanka, S. China, S.E.
    Asia to Philippines, Bali and Lombok
HABITAT: forest, woodland
SIZE: 23 cm (9 in)

One of the 10 species of minivet, the scarlet minivet, with its bright plumage, is typical of the group. The male is red and black, while the female has dark-gray and yellow plumage, distributed in the same manner. Both can be identified by the oval patch on each wing that is red in males and yellow in females. Strictly arboreal, scarlet minivets search among the treetops for large, soft-bodied insects to eat, often catching them in flight.

The shallow, cup-shaped nest is made on the branch of a tree from twigs, roots and grass stems, bound together with spider's webs. A covering of lichen and fragments of bark camouflages the nest. The female lays 2 or 3 eggs and incubates them alone. Both parents feed the young.

White-winged Triller (male)

Scarlet Minivet (male)

Pied
Flycatcher-shrike

Ground Cuckoo-shrike

Red-shouldered
Cuckoo-shrike
(male)

Large Cuckoo-shrike
(male)

Cicadabird

Bulbuls

NAME: Yellow-bellied/Yellow-breasted Greenbul, *Chlorocichla flaviventris*
RANGE: Africa: Tanzania to Namibia
HABITAT: forest, woodland with heavy undergrowth, coastal scrub
SIZE: 22 cm (8½ in)

Unexpectedly shy and skulking birds for their family, the greenbuls are found only in pairs or small parties, although they are widespread throughout their range. Male and female look alike, with yellowish underparts and olive-green plumage on the back, wings and head; in juveniles, the head and mantle are the same color. These birds creep through undergrowth and dense vegetation in search of seeds and berries to eat and will also cling to the trunks of trees like woodpeckers, looking for insects under the bark.

The flimsy nest is neatly made from tendrils, grass and some stems and is well hidden in dense cover. The female lays 2 eggs.

NAME: Leaflove, *Phyllastrephus scandens*
RANGE: Africa: Senegal to Sudan, Uganda, Tanzania
HABITAT: forest
SIZE: 22 cm (8½ in)

The charmingly named leaflove is a mostly dusky, gray-green bird, with creamy-white and yellow underparts. Male and female look alike; the juvenile is duller and paler. These birds are completely arboreal, frequenting thickets, often near streams, and climbing among the foliage, looking for insects to eat. They move about in small parties, chattering incessantly; when disturbed they become extremely noisy.

The cup-shaped nest is made from fine grass and leaves and is often slung between the stems of a vine or creeper. There are normally 2 eggs.

NAME: Black-eyed/White-vented Bulbul, *Pycnonotus barbatus*
RANGE: Africa
HABITAT: gardens, woodland, coastal scrub, open forest
SIZE: 18 cm (7 in)

Both male and female black-eyed bulbuls have grayish-white plumage on breast and belly and white undertail coverts. In fact, albinism is not uncommon in this species. The head appears slightly crested when the feathers are raised on the nape. These are tame, lively birds and have a habit of warbling briefly and slightly raising their wings when they land. They seem to eat equal quantities of fruit and insects.

The nest is neatly cup shaped, lightly made from grass and a few dead leaves, and is often suspended in the fork between two twigs. The female normally lays a clutch of 2 or 3 eggs.

PYCNONOTIDAE: Bulbul Family

The bulbuls are a family of about 120 species, found in forest, orchards and cultivated land in tropical regions of Africa in particular but also in Madagascar, southern Asia and Southeast Asia. With a few exceptions, they are noisy, gregarious birds of medium size, with shortish wings and comparatively long tails. Beaks are long and notched, with stiff bristles at the base. Some forms possess a crest. Males and females look alike, although occasionally the male is larger.

Their food consists mainly of fruit, berries, buds, flower nectar and insects removed from vegetation.

NAME: Red-whiskered Bulbul, *Pycnonotus jocosus*
RANGE: India, S.E. Asia, S. China, Andaman Islands; introduced in USA, Australia, Nicobar Islands, Mauritius
HABITAT: low scrub, cultivated land near villages, gardens, orchards
SIZE: 20.5 cm (8 in)

This widespread bird is locally abundant throughout its range. It is named for the tufts of deep-red feathers that sprout, like a mustache, on each side of the head; it also has red undertail feathers. Male and female look alike, but the tufts are white in the juvenile. It is a sprightly, cheerful bird, with a musical call, and in the summer, dozens can be seen feasting together in fruit trees. They do a great deal of damage to the crop, since they eat both green and ripe fruit; they also eat the insects they come across when feeding.

The cup-shaped nest is made from grass, roots and stalks, lined with fine grass, and, characteristically, some dry leaves and pieces of fern are woven into the bottom of it. The female lays 2 to 4 eggs.

NAME: Crested Finchbill, *Spizixos canifrons*
RANGE: Assam to S.W. China, Burma, Laos, Tonkin
HABITAT: deciduous and evergreen forest
SIZE: 20.5 cm (8 in)

This handsome bird has a black crest, which, when erected, hangs forward, and a thick, finchlike beak; these characteristics give it its common name. Male and female look alike. Also known as the crested finch-billed bulbul, this bird is a typical bulbul in its habits, traveling in flocks of up to 100 through the trees and undergrowth and calling constantly with a typically chattering note. It feeds on seeds and fruit and on insects, which it often takes in the air, flycatcher-fashion. It is one of the few birds to profit by the slash-and-burn agricultural methods of the seminomadic tribes in its habitat, for it flourishes where scattered low trees grow through dense undergrowth.

The distinctive cup-shaped nest is always made from corkscrew tendrils of a vine, sometimes with a few twigs added, and is placed low in a tangle of bushes and brambles. There are 2 or 3, rarely 4, eggs.

NAME: Black Bulbul, *Hypsipetes madagascariensis*
RANGE: Madagascar, Seychelles, S. and S.E. Asia to Taiwan, S. China
HABITAT: mountain forest up to 3,000 m (10,000 ft)
SIZE: 25.5 cm (10 in)

The bold, noisy black bulbul lives entirely in the trees, scarcely coming down even to the undergrowth. Its flight is swift and agile, but its legs and feet are weak, so it does not hop about in the branches but flies everywhere. It feeds on berries and may catch flies or other insects, which it snaps up when they visit flowers for their nectar.

The nest is cup shaped and made of coarse grass, dry leaves and moss, bound outside with spider's webs and lined with fine grass, moss roots and pine needles. Male and female birds appear to be very attached to each other, and while the female is sitting on her 2 to 4 eggs, the male remains close to her.

NAME: White-throated Bulbul, *Criniger flaveolus*
RANGE: Himalayas in India, China: Yunnan Province, Burma
HABITAT: humid forest with thick undergrowth
SIZE: 23 cm (9 in)

These large, crested bulbuls are usually found in rowdy parties of 6 to 15 birds. They behave rather like laughing-thrushes, chattering to each other as they climb about in the trees and bushes or fly in a stream from one dense patch of jungle undergrowth to another. They are seldom found more than about 3 m (10 ft) from the ground, where they forage for berries, wild figs and insects, which they sometimes take on the wing. Their flight is strong and direct, and when they perch, they fan out their tails.

Both male and female help to build a substantial nest from fine roots, bamboo leaves and dead leaves; the nest is well concealed in the cover of vines or brambles about 1 m (3¼ ft) from the ground. The female lays 3 or 4 eggs, which both parents incubate for 13 days.

Red-whiskered Bulbul

White-throated Bulbul

Crested Finchbill

Yellow-bellied Greenbul

Black-eyed Bulbul

Leaflove

Black Bulbul

Bulbuls, Leafbirds

NAME: **Bristlebill**, *Bleda syndactyla*
RANGE: **Africa: S. Sudan, Kenya, Uganda, Zaire**
HABITAT: **dense forest**
SIZE: **21.5 cm (8½ in)**

The bristlebill is a large, heavily built bird, with olive-brown plumage on the upperparts and a yellow throat and belly. Like all bulbuls, it has tufts of bristles near the bill base. Male and female look alike; the juvenile is duller and more rusty colored. The bill of the male is larger and more hooked than that of the female. These uncommon birds are shy and alert and difficult to observe as they move around in small trees and forest undergrowth; consequently little is known of their habits.

They are known to build a shallow, cup-shaped nest from leaves, sticks and plant fibers and to lay 2 eggs.

NAME: **Nicator**, *Nicator chloris*
RANGE: **Africa, south of the Sahara**
HABITAT: **tropical forest, thick woodland, scrub**
SIZE: **21.5 cm (8½ in)**

This shy forest bird is inconspicuous, often revealing itself only by a burst of clear, chattering song or by grunting, almost squirrel-like calls. It lives among the lower branches of trees or in dense undergrowth, feeding on plant matter and insects. Male and female look alike, but the juvenile has paler plumage on the upperparts and narrower, more pointed tail feathers.

Normally 2 eggs are laid in a nest that is either a shallow grass cup or a flat platform of stalks and tendrils, sited in the cover of thick vegetation.

NAME: **Hook-billed Bulbul**, *Setornis criniger*
RANGE: **Borneo, Sumatra, Bankga Island**
HABITAT: **primary lowland forest**
SIZE: **19 cm (7½ in)**

This bold and busy bird shows itself clearly as it moves about among the branches, searching for beetles, dragon-fly nymphs, and small, stoneless berries. Usually seen alone, sometimes in pairs, hook-billed bulbuls are silent, only occasionally calling with loud, harsh cries. Males, females and juveniles look alike, the plumage of the young birds merely being duller.

No information is available on the birds' mating and nesting behavior.

IRENIDAE: Leafbird Family

This family consists of 14 species, divided into 3 relatively distinct groups of songbirds: ioras, leafbirds and fairy bluebirds. All occur in southern and Southeast Asia, generally in forest, but in inhabited areas they are also found in gardens and orchards.

The family is probably closely related to the bulbuls. All forms have short legs, a moderately long bill and long, dense, somewhat fluffy plumage. The 4 species of iora are the smallest members of the family, some no bigger than 12.5 cm (5 in) long; they are mostly insect eaters and tend to be solitary birds. The leafbirds are larger and, as their name suggests, bright green in color. The 8 species consume fruit and berries, as well as insects, pollen and nectar. They are gregarious birds, moving in flocks through the forest canopy. The remaining group, the fairy bluebirds, consists of only 2 species of 25.5-cm (10-in) long, brilliant blue birds. They are highly arboreal and gregarious in their habits and gather in small flocks; they feed on fruit. In all species in the family, male and female look unalike, females usually being duller than males.

NAME: **Common Iora**, *Aegithina tiphia*
RANGE: **India to S.E. Asia, Java, Sumatra, Borneo**
HABITAT: **open country and gardens up to 1,700 m (5,600 ft)**
SIZE: **12.5 cm (5 in)**

There are considerable variations in coloration in this species, according to both sex and season. The male, in winter, tends to lose almost all his black feathers, and the yellow ones become paler; the female is green above and yellow below throughout the year, merely becoming paler in winter. Both sexes have noticeably soft and abundant feathers on their rumps. Ioras are frequently found in gardens, hopping inconspicuously about among the branches of trees and shrubs. They feed on insects, such as caterpillars, ants and beetles, and also on seeds.

In the breeding season, the male displays by flying up, fluffing out his feathers — particularly those on the rump — until he looks like a ball, then spiraling down to a perch. At the same time, he makes a strange croaking noise, rather like a frog. The nest is a neat structure, finely made from soft grass, covered in spider's webs, in which 2 to 4 eggs are laid.

NAME: **Gold-fronted Leafbird**, *Chloropsis aurifrons*
RANGE: **India, Sri Lanka, S.E. Asia, Sumatra**
HABITAT: **forest fringe, open country, gardens, damp hill country to 900 m (3,000 ft)**
SIZE: **18 cm (7 in)**

Despite their bright coloration, these arboreal birds are seldom seen, except when they fly briefly from clump to clump of trees or attract attention by calling or imitating other birds. The male is brilliant green, with a blue throat patch and a bright orange crown. With this primarily green plumage, leafbirds blend well with foliage. They are extremely agile and acrobatic in the trees, even swinging from the branches as if on a trapeze. They live in pairs or small groups, feeding among the leaves on insects, particularly caterpillars, spiders, berries and the nectar of the flowers of the coral tree (*Erythrina*), loranthus and the silk cotton tree. As they search for nectar, they may incidentally pollinate plants.

The small, cup-shaped nest is built among thickly growing foliage at the outer end of a branch, high up in a tree, and consequently is rarely found. The female lays 2 or 3 eggs and is thought to incubate them alone.

NAME: **Fairy Bluebird**, *Irena puella*
RANGE: **India to S.E. Asia, Greater Sunda and Andaman Islands, Philippines: Palawan**
HABITAT: **hill forest to 1,700 m (5,600 ft)**
SIZE: **25.5 cm (10 in)**

Fairy bluebirds are almost totally arboreal, preferring to spend their time high up in the branches of evergreen trees near running water. Males, particularly, are shy birds, not often clearly seen except when they come down to drink or bathe, when their striking coloration — bright ultramarine upperparts, with velvety black below — and red eyes make them conspicuous. Females are duller, with peacock-green and blackish-brown plumage. These birds feed mainly on the nectar of the flowers of the coral tree (*Erythrina*), and on fruit, especially ripe figs, often in the company of hornbills and pigeons.

The nest is built 3 to 6.5 m (10 to 21 ft) up in a small tree, in the darkest part of the forest, and is made of roots and twigs, covered with moss. Usually 2 eggs are laid.

Bristlebill

Common Iora (male)

Nicator

Gold-fronted
Leafbird
(male)

Hook-billed Bulbul

Fairy Bluebird
(male)

Shrikes

NAME: **Bornean Bristlehead**, *Pityriasis gymnocephala*
RANGE: **Borneo**
HABITAT: **lowland forest to 1,200 m (4,000 ft), peat swamp, forest**
SIZE: **25.5 cm (10 in)**

This rare shrike has a large, extremely heavy, hooked bill and relatively short tail feathers, which gives it a top-heavy look. In keeping with their massive appearance, these birds are ponderous fliers, which keep to the middle layers of the forest. They feed on insects and their larvae, mainly beetles, grasshoppers and cockroaches, and also some spiders, noisily snapping them up with their large bills.

NAME: **Black-backed Puffback**, *Dryoscopus cubla*
RANGE: **Africa: Kenya, west and south to Angola and South Africa**
HABITAT: **open woodland, gardens, scrub**
SIZE: **15 cm (6 in)**

There are 4 races of black-backed puffback; the race illustrated here is found in South Africa, and the other 3 occur throughout the rest of the range. The female is duller and paler than the male, with pale yellow eyes. When excited, this bird puffs up the feathers on its back and rump until it looks like a ball. These sociable little birds are usually found in pairs or in small parties with other bird species, hunting among the leaves of shrubs and trees for insect larvae. They often take insects in flight and, in the breeding season, eat the eggs and young of small birds.

The cup-shaped nest is made from bark fiber and rootlets, well hidden and bound to the fork of a tree with spider's webs. There are 2 or 3 eggs.

NAME: **Gray-headed Bush-shrike**, *Malaconotus blanchoti*
RANGE: **Africa, south of the Sahara (not extreme south)**
HABITAT: **woodland, acacia trees, often near water (East Africa)**
SIZE: **25.5 cm (10 in)**

Despite their size and quite bright coloration, these birds are not easily seen in the thick foliage of the trees and bushes they frequent. Most often they can be located by their calls — either a brisk, chattering sound or a two- or three-note whistle. They have big, hooked bills and, in South Africa, are known to take prey as large as mice and lizards, which they find among leaf litter on the ground. Male and female look alike.

The conspicuous nest is built close to the ground. It is either a rough heap of grass and leaves or a platform of twigs with an inner cup, in which 2 or 3, rarely 4, eggs are laid.

LANIIDAE: Shrike Family

This family of 65 species of songbird is divided into 4 subfamilies: the bush-shrikes and helmet shrikes of Africa, the aberrant bristlehead of Borneo and the true shrikes of North America, Europe, Africa and Asia.

Shrikes are aggressive, insectivorous or carnivorous birds. They have strong, hooked beaks, with which they kill large insects and small reptiles, birds and mammals. Many species impale prey on thorns or hang it in the forks of branches, to be eaten later, hence one of their common names — butcherbird. They have strong legs and feet with sharp claws, which are used for manipulating prey during dismemberment. The tail is long and often rounded. Male and female look alike in some species, unalike in others.

Most shrikes inhabit areas with a mixture of tall vegetation and open spaces. Typically they keep watch from a high vantage point, swooping down to the ground to take prey or else catching it flycatcher fashion, on the wing, then returning to the perch.

NAME: **Northern Shrike**, *Lanius excubitor*
RANGE: **widespread in N. America, Asia, Europe, N. Africa; winters south of breeding range**
HABITAT: **varied: woodland, open country, marsh, tundra, savanna, desert**
SIZE: **24 cm (9½ in)**

Northern shrikes perch in a prominent position and from there fly out to capture their prey: mainly insects, although small birds, mammals, reptiles and frogs are also taken. Normally they return to the perch to eat, but will sometimes store food and eat it later. They defend their territory strongly against all intruders, even hawks, and like hawks, they hover when hunting. The female looks like the male but is duller, with crescent-shaped markings on the underparts; the juvenile is even more heavily marked.

The bulky nest is built by both birds from twigs, moss and grass and is usually placed about 12 m (40 ft) from the ground. In the north, the female lays 5 to 7 eggs, which she incubates for 14 to 16 days. Fewer eggs are laid at a time in the south, but there may be two clutches in a year. This shrike is one of only 2 species found in North America; the other is the loggerhead shrike, *L. ludovicianus*, which is fairly similar to the northern shrike both in its appearance and its habits.

NAME: **White/Straight-crested Helmet Shrike**, *Prionops plumata*
RANGE: **Africa: S. Ethiopia to Angola, Namibia, northern South Africa**
HABITAT: **open bush country, woodland**
SIZE: **20.5 cm (8 in)**

The tame and gregarious white helmet shrikes live in small flocks of 8 to 12 birds. They always move close together through the lower branches of trees and bushes, where they forage for insects, often in company with birds of other species. Male and female look alike.

Even when breeding, white helmet shrikes are sociable, and a number of birds will share the brooding and feeding at a single nest. Normally 3 or 4 eggs are laid.

NAME: **Crimson-breasted Shrike**, *Laniarius atrococcineus*
RANGE: **Africa: southern E. Africa to Angola, South Africa**
HABITAT: **thorn veld, acacia bush**
SIZE: **20.5 cm (8 in)**

Surprisingly, these strikingly marked birds are not easy to see in the dense cover of the thornbushes they prefer, but they are not timid and, as soon as they come out into the open, they are conspicuous. Male and female look alike, the juvenile is duller, with crimson feathers only under the tail. Crimson-breasted shrikes usually travel in pairs, keeping in touch by calling, the male with a clear, deep whistle that the female answers with a throaty, growling sound. They feed mainly on insects.

The nest is a shallow cup, made from grass, plant fibers and dry bark, and is sited in the forked branch of a thorn tree. The female lays 2 or 3 eggs.

NAME: **Long-tailed Shrike**, *Corvinella melanoleuca*
RANGE: **Africa: Kenya, Tanzania, Mozambique across to S. Angola**
HABITAT: **open country with scattered trees and bush**
SIZE: **35.5–38 cm (14–15 in)**

The black and white plumage of this large bird resembles that of a magpie, and it is also known as the magpie shrike. Male and female look alike; the juvenile is duller. Despite its striking coloration and its habit of sitting conspicuously on the tops of trees, this shrike is a rather shy bird. It usually moves in pairs or small parties, often with other bird species, and feeds on insects, which it catches on the ground by dropping down on them from a high perch. Long-tailed shrikes often skewer their prey on a thorn before eating it.

The nest is a bulky, untidy structure, sited among thorny branches, and is usually made of thorny twigs. There are normally 3 or 4 eggs.

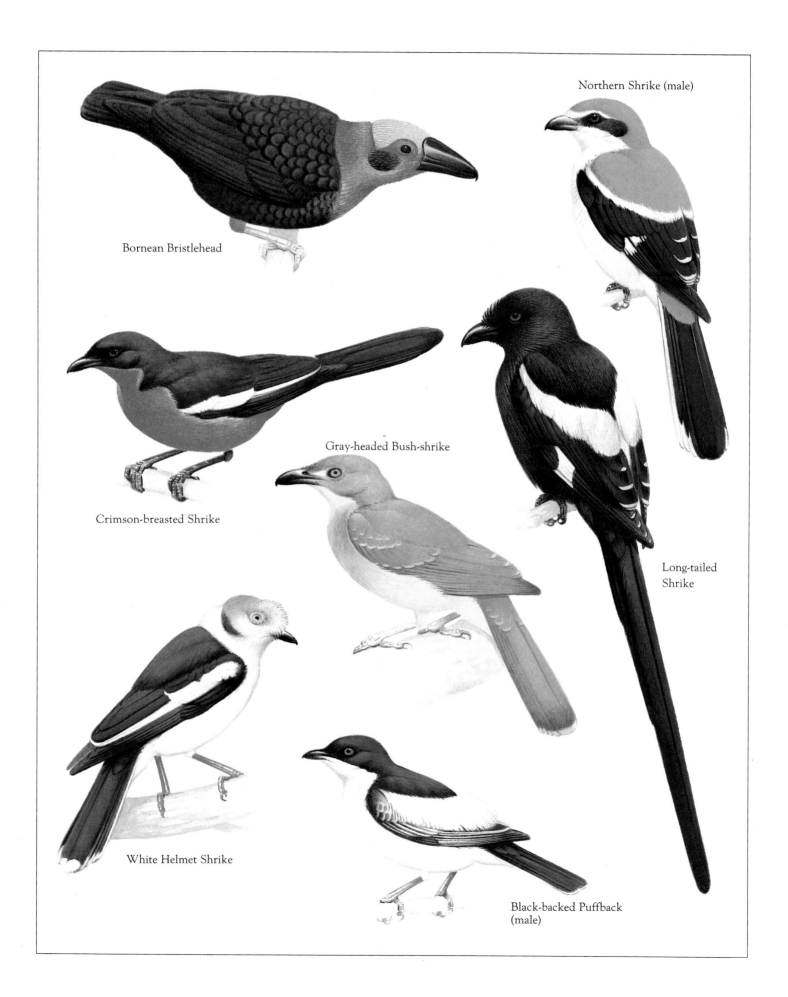

Northern Shrike (male)

Bornean Bristlehead

Crimson-breasted Shrike

Gray-headed Bush-shrike

Long-tailed
Shrike

White Helmet Shrike

Black-backed Puffback
(male)

Vangas, Waxwings, Palm Chat

VANGIDAE: Vanga Family

There are about 12 species of vanga, which are restricted to the island of Madagascar. They seem to have evolved from a shrikelike ancestor and are predators in the shrike fashion. Male and female do not look alike.

NAME: **Coral-billed Nuthatch,** *Hypositta corallirostris*
RANGE: **E. Madagascar**
HABITAT: **humid forest**
SIZE: **13 cm (5 in)**

The coral-billed nuthatch has been a taxonomical problem for ornithologists. It feeds like a treecreeper and looks somewhat like a nuthatch, but, more recently, it has been regarded as a close, but highly aberrant relative of the vangas. A brightly colored little bird, it clings with its feet to the bark on the upper part of tree trunks while it searches diligently in cracks and crevices for insects to eat. The female and young are blue above, with gray underparts.

NAME: **Hook-billed Vanga,** *Falculea palliata*
RANGE: **Madagascar**
HABITAT: **forest and secondary brush to 1,800 m (6,000 ft), mangrove swamps**
SIZE: **25 cm (9¾ in)**

These birds are usually seen alone or in pairs among the larger branches of trees, where they move about slowly and deliberately, searching for their prey. Their strong beaks, with sharply hooked tips, and the fact that they respond to squeaks and cheeping sounds suggest that they may eat small mammals and young birds, in addition to the chameleons, lizards, frogs and insects that are known to be part of their diet.

NAME: **Sicklebill,** *Vanga curvirostris*
RANGE: **Madagascar**
HABITAT: **woodland, dense savanna, forest edge, mangrove swamps**
SIZE: **32 cm (12½ in) including bill**

This vanga is more like the woodhoopoe, *Phoeniculus,* in appearance and habits than it is like the vangas, shrikes or sturnids, with which it has been classed. A party of up to 25 birds will suddenly appear in a patch of woodland, where, like woodhoopoes, they run about on the tree trunks and branches. They even hang upside down by their claws while they poke their long, curved beaks into crevices in the bark in search of large insects to eat.

The female builds a well-hidden nest from twigs some 12 m (40 ft) up in a tall, isolated tree. It is not known how many eggs are laid, since none has yet been found.

BOMBYCILLIDAE: Waxwing Family

This complex family of songbirds is sometimes divided into 3 separate families, although it is here considered as a single rather heterogeneous assemblage. The waxwings proper, with 3 species, are found in high latitudes of the northern hemisphere, but they occasionally migrate south to Europe, central China, Japan and even Central America in the winter. Male and female look almost alike, with soft, silky plumage and crested heads. They feed on fruit and berries.

The silky flycatchers of the New World are a group of 7 species which also have prominent crests and eat berries. The gray hypocolius from southwest Asia is the only member of its group. It feeds on fruit and berries, and some insects are also taken.

NAME: **Gray Silky Flycatcher,** *Ptilogonys cinereus*
RANGE: **N. Mexico to Guatemala**
HABITAT: **oak and pine forest at 1,200–3,000 m (4,000 to 10,000 ft)**
SIZE: **21 cm (8¼ in)**

With their soft, silky plumage, these flycatchers resemble the waxwings, but their long, narrow tails are like those of the flycatchers, and it is this that gives them their common name. In fact, they live largely on fruit and berries, especially mistletoe berries, although they do also capture flying insects in the air. Silky flycatchers are usually found in small flocks outside the breeding season.

The female builds the nest high in a tree, using twigs and fibers bound together with spider's webs. She lays 2 or 3 eggs.

NAME: **Bohemian Waxwing,** *Bombycilla garrulus*
RANGE: **circumpolar regions of N. America, Europe and Asia**
HABITAT: **tall coniferous forest of the taiga**
SIZE: **18 cm (7 in)**

The name "waxwing" is derived from the drop-shaped and waxlike tips of the secondary wing feathers that are, in fact, elongations of the feathers' shafts. The sexes look much alike, except that the female's plumage is duller. Waxwings normally live on fruit and berries, although they will catch insects on the wing during the breeding season. In winter they sometimes migrate south of their range.

During his courtship display, the male presents the female with a berry or ant pupa, which the birds then pass back and forth from beak to beak but never swallow. The bulky nest is made from twigs, moss and plant fibers, mainly by the female, who lays 3 to 7 eggs, which she alone incubates.

NAME: **Gray Hypocolius,** *Hypocolius ampelinus*
RANGE: **N. Africa to Iran and India**
HABITAT: **semidesert**
SIZE: **23 cm (9 in)**

The unique gray hypocolius is generally a sociable bird, and outside the breeding season small parties of them are found eating fruit and berries, such as nightshade, mulberries, figs and, particularly, dates. They also take some insects. The female looks very much like the male, lacking only the black feathers on the head that can be erected into a small crest; juveniles are a buffy-brown, with no black on the tail. These are shy, slow-moving birds, like the waxwings, but their flight is strong and straight.

Both male and female hypocolius help to build the large, cup-shaped nest, which is usually well hidden among the leaves of a palm tree. It is roughly constructed from twigs and lined with soft plant matter and hair; the female lays 4 or 5 eggs. If the birds are disturbed, they will desert the nest and are reputed to return and destroy it, only to build a new one a week or so later.

DULIDAE: Palm Chat Family

Previously considered as a member of the waxwing group, the palm chat from the West Indies is now regarded as constituting a family of its own.

NAME: **Palm Chat,** *Dulus dominicus*
RANGE: **West Indies: Hispaniola, Île de la Gonâve**
HABITAT: **open country with Royal Palms (*Roystonea*)**
SIZE: **17.5 cm (6¾ in)**

The plumage of the palm chat is thick and rough, quite different from that of the waxwings. Male and female look alike, but the juvenile has a dark throat and neck and a buff-colored rump. Palm chats are sociable birds which live in pairs or in groups of 2 to 5 pairs in a large communal nest about 1 m (3¼ ft) in diameter. The nest is loosely made from dry twigs, woven around the trunk and the base of the fronds of a royal palm tree. Within this structure, each pair of birds has a separate area, divided off from the others and with its own entrance. Here they roost and, in an inner chamber, raise their 2 to 4 young.

Palm chats feed on berries from the palms and other plants and also eat flowers.

Coral-billed Nuthatch (male)

Sicklebill (male)

Hook-billed Vanga

Bohemian
Waxwing

Gray Silky Flycatcher (male)

Gray Hypocolius (male)

Palm Chat

Wrens

NAME: Winter Wren, *Troglodytes troglodytes*
RANGE: Iceland, Europe, N.W. Africa, Middle East, east to E. China, Japan; S. Canada, E. USA and Pacific coast
HABITAT: undergrowth in coniferous forest, gardens, heaths and parks
SIZE: 9.5–11.5 cm ($3\frac{3}{4}$–$4\frac{1}{2}$ in)

The only wren to occur in the Old World, this species is a plump bird with a short tail, which is almost always held cocked up, and a loud, vibrant song. An extremely active little bird, the winter wren forages in dense undergrowth for insects, mainly larvae, as well as for spiders and a few berries.

The breeding season begins in April in most of the range. These wrens are polygamous in some areas, and the male makes several nests, in which he may install mates. The nest is a bulky, domed structure, made of twigs, moss, grass and rootlets and situated in a protected cavity in a bank or among tree roots or in a hollow stump. The male may also make "dummy" nests, which are not actually used but may help to divert potential predators. Having lined her chosen nest with hair and feathers, the female bird lays 4 to 16 eggs (usually 5 or 6), which she incubates for 14 to 16 days. The young are fed by the female and fly at 16 or 17 days. Some populations migrate south of the breeding range in winter.

NAME: House Wren, *Troglodytes aedon*
RANGE: S. Canada through USA and Central and South America; Trinidad and Tobago
HABITAT: woodland, gardens, parks
SIZE: 11–14 cm ($4\frac{1}{4}$–$5\frac{1}{2}$ in)

The common, widespread house wren is one of the plainest wrens, with gray-brown plumage and a faint stripe above each eye. It feeds on a wide variety of insects, such as crickets, beetles, ants, flies and caterpillars, as well as on some spiders and snails. House wrens winter to the south of their breeding range and migrate north again in spring.

Males arrive at breeding areas before females and build nests of twigs, leaves and other plant material. Nests are usually sited in cavities in trees or rocks but may be built almost anywhere that there is some degree of shelter and protection. When the females arrive, each selects a nest, which she lines with feathers, wool and hair. The female lays up to 9 eggs, usually 6 to 8, which she incubates for 13 to 15 days. The young leave the nest 12 to 18 days after hatching.

There are many subspecies of house wren; two Caribbean races are endangered and thought to be near extinction.

TROGLODYTIDAE: Wren Family

There are about 60 species of wren in the world, all except one confined to the Americas. The exceptional species is the bird known as the wren in Europe and the winter wren in North America.

The wren family is closely related to the dipper and mockingbird families. Most wrens are between 10 and 23 cm (4 and 9 in) long and are generally brown in color, with barred patterning. Wings are short and bodies plump, and a number of forms have stumpy tails, which can be cocked upward. Male and female look alike or nearly so.

Wrens occur in a wide range of habitats, including rain forest, cooler wooded areas, marshes, deserts, moorland and mountains. Where possible, they frequent dense, low vegetation, where they hunt for insects and other invertebrate prey with great agility and speed. They are excellent and varied songsters, often with loud vocal repertoires for birds of their size. In many species both sexes sing (not just the males), and some tropical wrens are known to perform "duets." Wrens generally produce two or more broods a season. The eggs are incubated by the female in most species, but both parents care for the young until they are able to fly, 2 or 3 weeks after hatching.

NAME: Cactus Wren, *Campylorhynchus brunneicapillus*
RANGE: S.W. USA to central Mexico
HABITAT: desert, arid scrubland
SIZE: 18–22 cm (7–$8\frac{1}{2}$ in)

The largest North American wren, the cactus wren has a distinctive white stripe over each eye and a longer-than-usual tail, which it does not normally cock up. Cactus wrens frequent areas with thorny shrubs, cacti and trees and forage mostly on the ground around vegetation for insects, such as beetles, ants, wasps and grasshoppers, and occasionally lizards or small frogs. Some cactus fruit and berries and seeds are also eaten. The wrens can run swiftly but usually fly if traveling any distance. Nests are made for roosting in at night and for shelter in bad weather.

The breeding season begins in March or April, and there may be two or three broods. The nest is a bulky, domed structure, made of plant fibers, twigs and dead leaves, with a tubelike side entrance that can be up to 15 cm (6 in) long; it is lined with fur or feathers. The nest is situated on a prickly cholla cactus or amid the sharp leaves of a yucca or other thorny bush. From 3 to 7 eggs, usually 4 or 5, are laid and then incubated by the female for about 16 days.

NAME: Long-billed Marsh Wren, *Cistothorus palustris*
RANGE: S. Canada, USA, Mexico
HABITAT: marshes
SIZE: 10–14 cm (4–$5\frac{1}{2}$ in)

The distinctive little marsh wren has a dark head, stripy markings on its back and a white streak above each eye. It lives among dense vegetation in marshland and feeds on aquatic insects.

The male builds several "dummy" nests before the female arrives in the breeding area. She, however, does most of the building of the nest that is actually used — a large coconut-shaped structure, which is lashed to bulrushes or other upright vegetation and which is made of water-soaked sedges and grasses, woven with rootlets and stems. There is a tubelike side opening, and the interior cavity is lined with feathers and shredded plant material. The 3 to 10, usually 5 or 6, eggs are incubated by the female for 13 to 16 days.

NAME: Bewick's Wren, *Thryomanes bewickii*
RANGE: S.W. and central Canada, USA, Mexico
HABITAT: open woodland, thickets, gardens, pastures
SIZE: 14 cm ($5\frac{1}{2}$ in)

Bewick's wren has a long, slim bill, which it uses to forage on the ground and on vegetation for insects, such as beetles, ants and caterpillars, as well as for spiders. It will also delve into crevices in buildings for food.

The nest is made by both partners of a breeding pair in almost any available cavity in a tree, rock or building, or in any hollow object, natural or man-made. It is cup shaped and constructed with sticks, bark, leaves, moss and other plant material and lined with feathers. The female lays 4 to 11, usually 5 to 7, eggs, which she incubates for 14 days.

NAME: Rock Wren, *Salpinctes obsoletus*
RANGE: S.W. Canada, W. USA, south to Costa Rica
HABITAT: dry rocky valleys, cliffs
SIZE: 13–15 cm (5–6 in)

A pale-plumaged bird, the rock wren blends well with its habitat. It frequents arid, bare country, where it clambers with great agility among rocks, searching for insects and spiders.

The nest is built by both members of a pair in a crevice in a rock, a pile of stones or a burrow and is made of grass, rootlets and stems, lined with fur and feathers. Although the nest is carefully concealed, there may be a path of small pebbles leading up to it, and the entrance to the nest cavity itself may be lined with stones, bones and other debris. The female usually lays 5 or 6 eggs, which she incubates.

Winter Wren

Cactus Wren

House Wren

Bewick's Wren

Long-billed
Marsh Wren

nest of
Rock
Wren

Rock Wren

Mockingbirds, Dippers, Accentors

MIMIDAE: Mockingbird Family

Only about half of the 31 or so members of this family are called mockingbirds, the others are known as catbirds, tremblers and thrashers. All live in the Americas, from Canada to Argentina, usually in wooded country and scrub, and feed on or near ground level on insects and other invertebrates, as well as on fruit and seeds. Typically, they are slim-bodied birds, with long legs and tails, and are well known for their ability to mimic the songs of other birds and sounds such as piano notes, barking dogs and sirens. Male and female look alike or nearly so.

NAME: **Galápagos Mockingbird,** *Nesomimus trifasciatus*
RANGE: **Galápagos Islands**
HABITAT: **varied**
SIZE: **25.5 cm (10 in)**

There are 9 subspecies of Galápagos mockingbird, one of which is now rare and found only on Champion and Gardner islets. Some ornithologists group these subspecies into 4 separate species. The birds appear to use all available habitats on the islands and to feed on anything they can find, mainly insects, fruit and berries, but also carrion and seabird's eggs.

The twig nest is built in a cactus or low tree and 2 to 5 eggs are laid.

NAME: **Mockingbird (Northern Mockingbird),** *Mimus polyglottos*
RANGE: **USA, south to Mexico; West Indies; introduced in Hawaii**
HABITAT: **open woodland, gardens, orchards**
SIZE: **23–28 cm (9–11 in)**

One of the best-known American songbirds and the state bird of five US states, the male mockingbird sings night and day, often mimicking other birds and other sounds. Mockingbirds are aggressive and hold territories, which they defend vigorously against all enemies; in winter, female birds hold their own separate territories. They feed on insects, particularly grasshoppers and beetles, and also on spiders, snails and small reptiles. Fruit, too, is an important part of the diet.

At the onset of the summer breeding season, males court mates, flashing the white markings on the wings as they make display flights. Both partners help to build the nest, from twigs, leaves and bits of debris such as paper and wool; the nest is placed in a low tree or bush. The female incubates the 3 to 6 eggs for 12 days, and both parents help to feed the young. There may be two or three broods a year.

NAME: **California Thrasher,** *Toxostoma redivivum*
RANGE: **USA: California; Mexico: Baja California**
HABITAT: **chaparral, mountain foothills, parks, gardens**
SIZE: **28–33 cm (11–13 in)**

This large thrasher has a distinctive, downward-curving, sickle-shaped bill, which it uses to rake through leaves and dig in the soil for insects and berries. Its wings are rather short, and it is an awkward bird in flight, so it lives mainly on the ground, where it runs with its long tail raised. The male bird sings for prolonged periods from a perch on a bush and is an excellent mimic; females also sing.

Both parents help to build a large, cup-shaped nest of plant material a meter or so off the ground, in a low tree or bush. They incubate the 2 to 4 eggs for about 14 days. The young leave the nest 12 to 14 days after hatching, but the male continues to feed them for a little longer, even while the second brood is being incubated by the female.

NAME: **Gray Catbird,** *Dumetella carolinensis*
RANGE: **S. Canada, USA (not S.W.); winters Central America and West Indies**
HABITAT: **woodland, forest edge, thickets, gardens**
SIZE: **20.5–24 cm (8–9½ in)**

Named for its mewing, catlike call, the gray catbird usually lives in dense vegetation, where it forages for insects and berries, mainly on the ground. At the end of the winter, catbirds migrate north to breeding grounds in huge flocks, often at night.

The males arrive at breeding areas and sing to attract females. They display to, and chase, their mates. Both partners of a pair help to build a ragged nest of plant material in a low tree or bush. The 2 to 6 eggs, usually 4, are incubated for 12 to 15 days, mostly by the female, but the male helps to feed the newly hatched young. There are usually two broods a season.

NAME: **Trembler,** *Cinclocerthia ruficauda*
RANGE: **West Indies**
HABITAT: **rain forest, woodland**
SIZE: **23–25.5 cm (9–10 in)**

Tremblers vary from dark brown to olive-gray, the Saint Lucia birds being the palest and grayest. They are identified by, and named for, their characteristic habit of violently shaking the wings and body. Their main foods are insects and invertebrates, most of which are found on the forest floor.

A nest is made in a cavity in a tree or tree fern, and the female lays 2 or 3 eggs.

CINCLIDAE: Dipper Family

The 5 species of dipper live in Europe, Asia and North and South America, usually in upland country near swift mountain streams. They are the only passeriform birds to have adopted a truly aquatic way of life, yet they have no webs on their feet and few obvious special adaptations other than movable flaps to close off the nostrils when underwater. Propelling themselves with their wings, they swim and dive underwater, and they also appear to be able to walk on the bottoms of streams. Male and female look alike.

NAME: **Dipper,** *Cinclus mexicanus*
RANGE: **Alaska, through N.W. America to Panama**
HABITAT: **mountain streams**
SIZE: **18–22 cm (7–8½ in)**

A wren-shaped bird, the dipper has a compact body, long, stout legs and a short, square-tipped tail. Its bill is hooked and is notched at the tip. Like all dippers, it frequents mountain streams and walks or dives into the water, swims underwater and even walks on the bottom, to obtain insect and invertebrate prey, especially caddis fly larvae.

A bulky, domed nest, made of moss and grass, is built by the female on a rock in a stream or beside a stream among tree roots or rocks; it has a side entrance. The female lays 3 to 6 eggs, which she incubates for 15 to 17 days.

PRUNELLIDAE: Accentor Family

Accentors are small, sparrowlike birds, with inconspicuous plumage, found in Europe and Asia. There are 12 species, all in the genus *Prunella*. Male and female birds look similar.

NAME: **Dunnock/Hedge Sparrow,** *Prunella modularis*
RANGE: **Europe, Asia, east to Urals, south to Lebanon**
HABITAT: **woodland, scrub, gardens**
SIZE: **15 cm (6 in)**

The little brown dunnock is distinguished by its slender bill and gray underparts. Mainly a ground-living species, it forages among fallen leaves and other debris for insects, larvae and, particularly in winter, seeds.

The neat, cup-shaped nest is made of twigs, grass and roots and is situated in a bush. The female lays from 3 to 6 eggs, which she incubates for 12 to 14 days; the male helps to feed the young. There may be two broods a season.

Dipper

Gray Catbird

Galápagos
Mockingbird

Trembler

Mockingbird

Dunnock

California Thrasher

Thrushes

NAME: **White-browed/Blue Shortwing,**
Brachypteryx montana
RANGE: **E. Nepal to W. and S. China,**
south to S.E. Asia and Indonesia
HABITAT: **forest undergrowth**
SIZE: **15 cm (6 in)**

The male of this species is a distinctive
little bird with dark-blue plumage and
conspicuous, long white eyebrows;
females have brownish plumage, with
rusty-red markings on the forehead and
indistinct eyebrows. In some areas,
males are colored like females but with
white eyebrows. Shy, retiring birds,
they skulk around in the densest undergrowth, searching for insects, especially
beetles, and usually staying on or close
to the ground.

The globular nest is made on a tree
trunk or rock face, and the female lays
3 eggs.

NAME: **Karroo Scrub-robin,**
Erythropygia coryphaeus
RANGE: **Africa: Namibia to South Africa:**
Cape Province
HABITAT: **arid, sandy regions**
SIZE: **16 cm (6¼ in)**

An abundant, lively bird, the karroo
scrub-robin spends much of its time on
the ground, where it searches for insects,
as well as for seeds and berries when
available. It runs swiftly and darts for
cover if alarmed, after dancing around
and flicking its tail for a moment or two.

A cup-shaped nest, made of grass, is
built in a hollow in the ground, in a bush
or under vegetation. The female lays 2
or 3 eggs, which are incubated for 14 or
15 days.

NAME: **Nightingale, Erithacus**
(= Luscinia) megarhynchos
RANGE: **Europe: S.E. England to**
Mediterranean and N. Africa; east to
S.W. Siberia, Afghanistan; winters in
tropical Africa
HABITAT: **woodland, thickets, hedgerows**
SIZE: **16 cm (6¼ in)**

The nightingale sings from dawn to
dusk or even to midnight, and its
melodious song is its most characteristic
feature. Male and female look alike,
with brownish and creamy plumage. A
sturdy, solitary bird, the nightingale
skulks among dense vegetation, foraging for food, such as worms, insects and
larvae and berries on the ground. It
moves around with long hops, rarely
flying for other than short distances.

The breeding season begins in May,
and the female builds a nest of leaves on
or close to the ground, amid vegetation.
She lines the nest with grass or hair and
lays 4 or 5 eggs, which she incubates for
13 or 14 days. Both parents feed the
young, which are able to fly at about 11
or 12 days.

MUSCICAPIDAE

This huge family of songbirds contains
over 1,000 species, formerly organized
in separate families. These are now
regarded as 13 closely related subfamilies of the Muscicapidae.

TURDINAE: Thrush Subfamily

There are over 300 species in this subfamily, found almost all over the world
except on the polar ice caps and some
Pacific islands; formerly absent from
New Zealand, they have now been
introduced there. The group contains
not only the thrushes proper, in the
genus *Turdus*, but also robins, redstarts,
chats, wheatears, nightingales and
solitaires, among others. Male and
female look alike in some species but
differ in others.

Most members of the subfamily are
small to medium-sized songbirds — 10
to 33 cm (4 to 13 in) long — with slender
beaks. They are strong fliers, many
forms making regular, long migrations.
Insects and other invertebrates, such as
slugs, snails, worms and crustaceans,
make up the bulk of the diet for most
thrushes, but berries and other plant
foods are also eaten.

NAME: **Eurasian Robin, Erithacus**
rubecula
RANGE: **Europe, Mediterranean islands,**
N. Africa, east across Asia to Mongolia
HABITAT: **forest, woodland, gardens**
SIZE: **14 cm (5½ in)**

The familiar robin is easily identified by
its orange-red breast and face, separated
from the olive-brown upperparts by a
gray-blue border. Male and female look
alike. Although a shy forest bird over
much of its range, the robin has learned
to make use of humans and their gardens
in Britain and parts of western Europe
and has become a bold, easily tamed
species. Aggressive little birds, robins
live alone in winter, each defending its
territory against any intruders by presenting the red breast, with feathers erected, and emphasizing the warning color
by swaying from side to side. Robins
usually feed on the ground on small insects, larvae, spiders, worms and snails,
and on berries and small fruit in season.

In the breeding season, robins form
pairs, and males court before mating,
using a less aggressive form of the threat
display. The female then builds the cup-
shaped nest on an ivy-covered bank, in
a bush or hedge, in a hole in a tree or
stump or on a building or ledge. She lays
5 to 7 eggs, which she incubates for 12
to 14 days, and both parents feed the
young. There may be two or even three
broods a year.

NAME: **Red-flanked Bluetail, Erithacus**
(= Tarsiger) cyanurus
RANGE: **Lapland, across N. Asia; winters**
in S. Asia; separate population in
Himalayas and W. China
HABITAT: **swampy coniferous forest,**
open woodland
SIZE: **14 cm (5½ in)**

An attractive little bird, the red-flanked
bluetail has characteristic reddish-
orange patches on its sides. The male
has largely blue plumage, and this is
replaced in the female, except on the
tail, by olive-brown. It forages for food,
mainly insects, on the ground and in low
vegetation, quivering its tail as it moves;
it may also catch insects in the air.

The nest is made of moss and situated
in a hollow in the ground among moss
or tree roots. The female lays 3 to 7 eggs,
which she alone incubates.

NAME: **Robin Chat/Cape Robin,**
Cossypha caffra
RANGE: **E. and S. Africa: S. Sudan to**
Cape of Good Hope
HABITAT: **forest, bush, cultivated areas,**
town shrubberies
SIZE: **18 cm (7 in)**

Rather like the Eurasian robin, the
robin chat is usually a shy, retiring bird
but has become tame and accustomed to
man in inhabited areas. Male and female
look alike, and both have distinctive
white eye stripes. They feed mainly on
the ground on insects, spiders, worms,
small frogs and lizards and berries, but
dart for cover at any sign of danger.

The nest is made of moss and rootlets
and is situated in an overgrown tree
stump or on a well-vegetated bank. The
female lays 2 or 3 eggs, which she incubates for 13 to 19 days. Both parents
feed the nestlings for 14 to 18 days.

NAME: **Fire-crested Alethe, Alethe**
diademata
RANGE: **Africa: Nigeria to Zaire and**
Uganda
HABITAT: **lowland forest**
SIZE: **18 cm (7 in)**

One of 7 or so species of alethe living in
Africa, the fire-crested alethe is a bird of
dense forest and shady undergrowth.
Although it does not actually feed on
ants, it frequently watches army ants as
they march through the forest, in order
to catch the other insects that flee from
their path. Male and female birds look
alike, both with dark-brown plumage
and an orange streak of feathers along
the crown. When the bird is excited, it
erects this crest, while spreading its tail.

The cup-shaped nest is made of moss
and roots, lined with soft rootlets, and
is situated in a tree stump or among
heaps of debris on the forest floor. The
female lays 2 or 3 eggs.

White-browed Shortwing (male)

Red-flanked Bluetail (male)

Karroo Scrub-robin

Robin Chat

Eurasian Robin

Fire-crested Alethe

Nightingale

Thrushes

NAME: **Black Redstart,** *Phoenicurus ochruros*
RANGE: **Europe, N. Africa, Asia, east to China and just into N. India**
HABITAT: **open rocky areas, near human habitation**
SIZE: **14 cm (5½ in)**

An adaptable bird, the black redstart has learned to live alongside humans in some areas. Both sexes have rusty-red tails, although the male's is brighter, and the male has dull black upperparts, while the female is brownish. The black redstart spends much of its time on the ground and also perches on rocks and buildings. Insects, caught on the ground and in flight, are its main food, but it also eats some berries. Holes in rocks and buildings are used as nighttime roosts.

The breeding season starts in early to late April, depending on the area. The female constructs a loose, cup-shaped nest from dry grass, moss and fibers, lined with hair, wool and feathers; it is situated on a cliff, rock or building or in a hollow tree. The female lays 4 to 6 eggs, which she incubates for 12 to 16 days. Both parents feed the young until they leave the nest 12 to 19 days after hatching. There are usually two broods, sometimes three.

NAME: **Eastern Bluebird,** *Sialia sialis*
RANGE: **N. America: S. Canada, east of the Rockies to Gulf Coast, USA; Mexico, Central America**
HABITAT: **open country, farmland, gardens, parks**
SIZE: **16.5–19 cm (6½–7½ in)**

A beautiful bird, the male eastern bluebird has distinctive, bright blue plumage on its upperparts; the female looks similar but has paler, duller plumage. The bluebird is beloved not only for its attractive appearance but also for its melodious song. It often perches in a hunched posture on wires and fences but takes most of its insect prey on the ground. Berries are also an important item of diet.

The male bluebird performs flight displays to court his mate and then both birds build a nest of grass, twigs and other plant material, lined with hair, fine grass and feathers. The nest is situated in a natural hole in a tree or stump, in an abandoned woodpecker hole or even in a bird box. The female lays 3 to 7 eggs, usually 4 or 5, which she incubates for 13 to 15 days, sometimes with assistance from her mate. The young are fed by both parents and leave the nest 15 to 20 days after hatching. There are usually two broods. Some northern populations migrate south for the winter.

NAME: **Magpie Robin,** *Copsychus saularis*
RANGE: **India, S. China, S.E. Asia, much of Indonesia, east to the Philippines**
HABITAT: **brush, gardens, cultivated land**
SIZE: **21.5 cm (8½ in)**

The male magpie robin has distinctive black and white plumage; the female looks similar but has dark-gray instead of black plumage. This widespread, common bird often lives near human habitation and feeds in the open, usually near or on the ground. A good mimic, the magpie robin imitates other birds but also has a loud, melodious song of its own, which it uses to announce its presence. Insects, such as crickets, beetles and ants, are its main foods.

The large, cup-shaped nest is made of fine roots and is situated among tree roots or branches or in any protected hole. The female lays 3 to 6 eggs, usually 5, which both parents incubate for 12 or 13 days.

NAME: **White-crowned Forktail,** *Enicurus leschenaulti*
RANGE: **Sikkim to S. China and Hainan, S.E. Asia to Bali**
HABITAT: **rocky streams in forest**
SIZE: **20.5–28 cm (8–11 in)**

Both male and female white-crowned forktails have similar, sharply contrasting plumage and long tails. These long-legged birds frequent streams and feed on aquatic insects, which they take from the water surface or the streambed. They wade from stone to stone, searching for food and occasionally dipping under the water in pursuit of prey.

The cup-shaped nest is always built in a damp area, often near a stream, and is generally sited on a rock, in a crevice or among stones or tree roots. The female lays 2 eggs.

NAME: **Andean Solitaire,** *Myadestes ralloides*
RANGE: **Central and South America: Costa Rica to N. Bolivia, Venezuela**
HABITAT: **mountain forest**
SIZE: **18 cm (7 in)**

The shy, secretive Andean solitaire usually lives between altitudes of 900 and 4,500 m (3,000 and 15,000 ft). It is an excellent songster and sings more or less throughout the year in a pure, clear voice. True to its name, the solitaire tends to live alone for much of the time, but birds are also found in pairs. Its bill is rather short and wide, and it feeds on fruit and insects.

A nest is made on the ground or in a tree, and about 3 eggs are laid and incubated for 12 or 13 days.

NAME: **Stonechat,** *Saxicola torquata*
RANGE: **Europe, Africa, W. and central Asia**
HABITAT: **moors, fields, hill scrub, agricultural land**
SIZE: **13 cm (5 in)**

The plump little stonechat is a lively, restless bird. It seldom moves on the ground but flies fast and perches in exposed spots, such as on a post or on top of a bush, to watch for insect prey; it also eats plant matter and grain. The female has paler, browner plumage than the male and her white markings are less distinct.

The breeding season begins between late March and early June, depending on area. The male displays to the female, spreading his wings and tail to show off his markings. The nest is usually made by the female from coarse grass, moss and plant stems, lined with hair, fine grass or feathers. It is sited in an open area on the ground, under cover of a bush or actually in a bush. The female lays 5 or 6 eggs, which she incubates for about 14 days, sometimes assisted by the male. The young remain in the nest for 12 or 13 days, being fed on insects by both parents. Some northern populations may migrate south in winter.

NAME: **Wheatear,** *Oenanthe oenanthe*
RANGE: **Europe, N.W. Africa, W. and central Asia, arctic N. America; winters mainly in Africa**
HABITAT: **open country, moors, tundra, heaths**
SIZE: **14 cm (5½ in)**

A widely distributed species, this is the only wheatear to have become established in the New World. In summer breeding plumage, the male has a grayish crown, black marks on the cheeks and a white stripe above each eye. Both sexes have distinctive white rumps, but the female is brownish and buff; in winter the male resembles the female. Primarily a ground-dweller, the wheatear finds much of its food, such as insects, spiders, centipedes and small mollusks, on the ground. It flits from one perch to another and may sometimes fly up to catch an insect on the wing.

In display, the male reveals his white rump to the female and dances with spread wings. The nest is made in open country in a hole on the ground, in a rock or wall, or in debris such as a can or drainpipe. The female lays 5 or 6 eggs, occasionally up to 8, which are incubated for about 14 days. She does most of the incubation, although the male may assist. Both parents feed the young, which remain in the nest for about 15 days.

Magpie Robin (male)

White-crowned Forktail

Andean Solitaire

Eastern Bluebird
(male)

Stonechat
(male)

Black Redstart
(male)

Wheatear
(male in breeding plumage)

Thrushes

NAME: **Cape Rock-thrush,** *Monticola rupestris*
RANGE: **South Africa: Transvaal to Cape Province**
HABITAT: **scrub, rocky country**
SIZE: **22 cm (8½ in)**

The male Cape rock-thrush is recognized by his blue-gray head, neck and throat, while the female's head is mottled brown and black. They are fairly common birds, seen in pairs or small groups, often perching on rocks, boulders or the tops of bushes. Insects and small mollusks are their main foods, mostly found on the ground.

The shallow, cup-shaped nest is made of grass, small twigs and plant fibers, lined with rootlets; it is usually situated in a rock crevice or even under a roof. The female lays 3 to 5 eggs.

NAME: **White's Thrush,** *Zoothera dauma*
RANGE: **USSR (stragglers as far west as Britain), India, China, Taiwan, Philippines, Sumatra and Java, south to Australia, N. Melanesia**
HABITAT: **forest, woodland**
SIZE: **11 cm (4¼ in)**

White's thrush is characterized by the crescent-shaped, scalelike markings on its back and underparts. Juveniles have barred, rather than scaly, markings. A shy, retiring bird, white's thrush spends much of its life on the ground, feeding on insects and berries. Some birds migrate in winter, and vagrants may even stray into Europe.

The nest is rather different from that of most thrushes. Situated up to 4 m (13 ft) above ground in a tree, it is large and flat and made mostly from pine needles, with a base of mud and moss to fix it to the branch. The female lays 3 to 5 eggs.

NAME: **Veery,** *Catharus fuscescens*
RANGE: **S. Canada; USA: Oregon to New Mexico, Great Lakes area and New England, south to Georgia; winters in South America**
HABITAT: **moist woodland**
SIZE: **16–18 cm (6¼–7 in)**

More often heard than seen, the veery is an inconspicuous little bird with a beautiful, musical song. It feeds on insects, spiders and earthworms, as well as on fruit and berries, which it finds by foraging in the trees and by searching under leaves on the woodland floor.

The bulky, cup-shaped nest is made of weed stems, grass, pieces of bark and twig, lined with dry leaves and rootlets, and is situated on or near the ground in a bush or clump of plants. The female lays 3 to 6 eggs, usually 4, which she incubates for 11 or 12 days. Both birds care for the young, which leave the nest 10 to 12 days after hatching.

NAME: **American Robin,** *Turdus migratorius*
RANGE: **N. America, Mexico, Guatemala**
HABITAT: **open woodland, forest edge, gardens, city parks**
SIZE: **23–28 cm (9–11 in)**

The adaptable American robin has learned to live alongside man in urban areas, and city birds have become bolder than the shy, forest robins. The coloration is variable, but in the breeding season, the male is generally gray above, with a black head and tail and reddish breast. The female is duller and paler, with a gray head and tail. Robins feed in open areas and in vegetation on insects, earthworms, fruit and berries.

Although some robins winter in the northern states, generally they are migratory birds, breeding north of the Gulf Coast. Males arrive first in small flocks and begin singing and courting when the females arrive. Nests are made in a variety of sites: in a tree or bush, on a post, a ledge on a building or cliff, or even on the ground. The inner part of the nest is a deep cup of mud, which is surrounded by twigs, weeds and stems and lined with grass. The female lays 3 to 6 eggs, usually 4, which she incubates for 12 to 14 days.

NAME: **Blackbird,** *Turdus merula*
RANGE: **Europe, N. Africa, Asia (except N.E. and S.); introduced in New Zealand**
HABITAT: **forest, woodland, scrub, gardens, parks**
SIZE: **25.5 cm (10 in)**

One of the most familiar European birds, the blackbird has adapted well to man's environments, finding the short grass of lawns, parks and recreation areas ideal for foraging for insects and worms. It also feeds on many kinds of fruit and berries. Much of its time is spent on the ground, but the blackbird finds a prominent, often exposed perch from which to sing. While the male is black, with a yellowish-orange bill and eye-ring, the female has dark-brown plumage with paler underparts.

A variety of nest sites is used, such as branches of low trees and bushes, ledges on or in buildings, and crevices in rocks or walls. The female builds the nest, which has an outer layer of plant stems, twigs and leaves covering the inner cup of mud and plant material and is lined with fine grass or dead leaves. The female lays up to 9 eggs, usually 3 to 5, at daily intervals. She incubates the clutch for 12 to 15 days. Both parents care for the young during their 12 to 15 days in the nest and continue to feed them for a further 3 weeks.

NAME: **Cape/Olive Thrush,** *Turdus olivaceus*
RANGE: **Africa, south of the Sahara**
HABITAT: **forest, cultivated land**
SIZE: **24 cm (9½ in)**

Several races of Cape thrush, which vary in coloration, occur over its range. Male and female look alike, but juveniles have streaked upperparts and dusky spots on underparts. It is an adaptable bird and has taken well to life in urban gardens, where it tends to dominate other birds. Much of its food is found by scratching around on the ground to uncover insects and invertebrates such as snails and earthworms. It also feeds on fruit.

The courting male puffs himself up, spreads his tail, then shuffles around the female with his wings trailing. The nest is made of grass, on a foundation of twigs, roots and earth, and is situated on a branch, tree stump or bush. The female lays 2 or 3 eggs, which are incubated for about 14 days.

NAME: **Austral Thrush,** *Turdus falcklandii*
RANGE: **South America: S. Argentina, S. Chile; Falkland and Juan Fernandez Islands**
HABITAT: **open country with shrubs**
SIZE: **28–29 cm (11–11½ in)**

The southern counterpart of the robin of North America, the austral thrush is common on both sides of the Andes up to about 2,000 m (6,600 ft). It is similar to the robin in its habits, digging for earthworms and other invertebrates on grassland and in damp places. It also feeds on fruit.

The cup-shaped nest is made of twigs, bound with grass and mud, and is usually well concealed in dense vegetation. The female produces two, sometimes three, clutches a season, each containing 2 or 3 eggs.

NAME: **Island Thrush,** *Turdus poliocephalus*
RANGE: **islands from Christmas Island through Indonesia, New Guinea to New Caledonia, Fiji and Samoa**
HABITAT: **forest edge**
SIZE: **23–25.5 cm (9–10 in)**

There may be 50 or more forms of island thrush, all varying slightly in appearance, some found on only one island or on a small group of islands. Most males have largely black plumage, and females look similar, but usually duller, in color. Generally a shy, solitary bird, the island thrush takes refuge in trees but feeds on the ground in the open, on plant matter, such as seeds and fruit, and on a few insects.

The female normally lays 1 egg in a nest on a bush or rocky ledge.

American Robin (male)

Austral Thrush

Blackbird
(male)

Cape Thrush

Island Thrush
(male)

Cape Rock-thrush (male)

Veery

White's Thrush

Babblers

NAME: White-necked/White-eared Babbler, *Stachyris leucotis*
RANGE: Malaysian Peninsula, Sumatra, Borneo
HABITAT: forest
SIZE: 15 cm (6 in)

The white-necked babbler is identified by its white eyebrow streaks, linked to the row of white spots on the sides of its neck. Male and female look similar. It is mainly a ground-living bird, found in the undergrowth of forest, and does not fly well. It feeds on insects such as black beetles and flies.

The neat, cup-shaped nest is made of grass, roots and plant fibers, in a tree or dense undergrowth. The female is thought to lay 3 eggs, but few nests have been observed.

NAME: Large Wren-babbler, *Napothera macrodactyla*
RANGE: Malaysian Peninsula, Sumatra, Java
HABITAT: lowland forest
SIZE: 19 cm (7½ in)

A big, plump, short-tailed babbler, the large wren-babbler has white patches between the beak and eyes, a white throat and characteristic scalelike markings on breast and upperparts. The bill is stout and the feet large and strong. An uncommon bird, this babbler lives in undergrowth and feeds near or on the ground on insects. It perches on bushes to sing.

Little is known of its nesting habits, but it is thought to lay 2 eggs.

NAME: Scaly-breasted Illadopsis, *Trichastoma albipectus*
RANGE: Africa: S. Sudan, Zaire, east to Kenya
HABITAT: forest, dense high bush
SIZE: 14 cm (5½ in)

The scaly-breasted illadopsis lives on the floor or in the undergrowth of thick forest, often side by side with the pale-breasted illadopsis, *T. rufipennis*, which it closely resembles. A rather quieter bird than most babblers, it moves in small groups, close to or on the ground, searching for ants, beetles and other insects. Male and female look alike, both with pale chest feathers edged with gray, which creates a scaly appearance.

The cup-shaped nest is made of dead leaves and hidden among leaves or on an overgrown tree stump. The female lays 2 eggs.

TIMALIINAE: Babbler Subfamily

This large, diverse subfamily of the family Muscicapidae includes about 250 species of babbler, all found in the warmer parts of the Old World, with the greatest diversity in Africa and South Asia. A notoriously confusing group to classify, the babbler subfamily includes several species that are probably not closely related. As their name suggests, most are extremely vocal, noisy birds, and some are fine songsters.

Babblers tend to have short, rounded wings and are poor fliers, spending much of their time on the ground or clambering around in the low levels of trees and bushes. Their feathers are soft, and the plumage varies from dull browns to bright colors, often with bold markings on the head and neck. Most have thickset bodies and fairly long tails when compared to thrushes. Their legs and feet are strong, enabling them to probe and dig in thick vegetation and ground litter for invertebrate prey and small berries and fruit. Feeding activity is generally accompanied by the loud, varied "babbling" calls that give the group its common name. Much of this calling behavior may be linked to keeping the small feeding flocks together in dense vegetation.

Males and females look alike in some species but differ in others. The nest is generally cup shaped or domed, and the female lays up to 7 eggs. In some species both parents incubate the clutch, but in others only the female incubates. Both parents care for the young.

NAME: Rufous-crowned Babbler, *Malacopteron magnum*
RANGE: Malaysian Peninsula, Sumatra, Borneo
HABITAT: forest
SIZE: 18 cm (7 in)

The rufous-crowned babbler is identified by its reddish-brown crown and the black plumage at the back of the neck. Its wings and tail are longer than those of many babblers. An arboreal bird, it rarely descends to the ground but frequents the lower branches of tall trees and the forest undergrowth, where it forages for insects such as black beetles and grasshoppers. It also feeds on seeds.

The cup-shaped nest, made of twigs and rootlets and lined with fungal threads, is built in a small tree. The female lays 2 eggs.

NAME: Coral-billed Scimitar-babbler, *Pomatorhinus ferruginosus*
RANGE: Himalayas, northern S.E. Asia to Thailand
HABITAT: forest undergrowth
SIZE: 24 cm (9½ in)

This large babbler has a distinctive stout red bill and characteristic black face markings on either side of the white eyebrow streaks. In noisy flocks, it searches for insects and larvae on the forest floor or in the undergrowth. It hops from perch to perch and rarely flies unless forced to do so.

The domed nest is made on the ground or in a low bush and is built from bamboo leaves, grass and plant fibers, bound together with plant stems or vines and lined with fine grass and fibers. The female lays 3 to 5 eggs.

NAME: Chestnut-capped Babbler, *Timalia pileata*
RANGE: Nepal, S.E. Asia (not Malaysian Peninsula), Java
HABITAT: bamboo thickets, forest, scrub
SIZE: 18 cm (7 in)

Small parties of chestnut-capped babblers forage for insects in dense undergrowth, remaining well within cover. They tend to stay just above ground. If alarmed, the birds scatter and dive for shelter, regrouping once the danger is past. This babbler is identified by its reddish-brown crown, black bill and white feathers on forehead, throat and breast.

The female lays 3 or 4 eggs in a ball-shaped nest, made of bamboo leaves or grass and lined with fine grass or hair. The nest is often situated at the base of a bamboo clump.

NAME: Yellow-eyed Babbler, *Chrysomma sinense*
RANGE: E. Pakistan, India through S.E. Asia (not Malaysian Peninsula) to S. China
HABITAT: bamboo thickets, scrub, cultivated land
SIZE: 18 cm (7 in)

True to its name, the yellow-eyed babbler has yellowish eyes and orange markings ringing the eyes. Pairs or small parties of these babblers forage together in the undergrowth, searching for insects and larvae among the foliage. Much of their time is spent in cover, but they will emerge into the open to sun themselves for a moment and perhaps to sing.

A compact nest is made from grass and strips of bark and covered with spider's webs; it may be lined with finer grass and stems. It is usually built above ground in a bush or tree, or it may be attached to thick grass stems. The female lays 5 eggs.

White-necked Babbler

Rufous-crowned Babbler

Scaly-breasted
Illadopsis

Large Wren-babbler

Chestnut-capped Babbler

Yellow-eyed Babbler

Coral-billed Scimitar-babbler

Babblers

NAME: Brown-cheeked Fulvetta, *Alcippe poioicephala*
RANGE: India to S.W. China, S.E. Asia
HABITAT: forest, scrub, bamboo scrub
SIZE: 15 cm (6 in)

The brown-cheeked fulvetta is a rather plain little bird, with mainly buffy-brown plumage. Both male and female have gray plumage on the top of the head. In small groups of 4 to 20, these babblers forage in the forest under-growth for insects. They rarely, if ever, descend to the ground but may climb farther up trees into the canopy layers. The birds keep in touch by calling to one another and are extremely wary of any danger.

The nest is made on a branch of a tree or bush a few meters above ground or is suspended from a few twigs. It is cup shaped and built of moss and dead leaves, lined with fine moss and ferns. The female usually lays 2 eggs, which are incubated by both parents.

NAME: Stripe-throated Yuhina, *Yuhina gularis*
RANGE: Himalayas to northern S.E. Asia and W. China
HABITAT: forest
SIZE: 15 cm (6 in)

A distinctive little babbler, the stripe-throated yuhina has a prominent crest, dark streaks on its throat and an orange-rufous streak on the wings. Male and female look alike. Small parties of these active little birds forage in the trees for insects, such as beetles and wasps, and sometimes join in mixed flocks with other species of babbler. They also feed on seeds and nectar, and their crests become coated with pollen as they fly from flower to flower.

Little is known of the breeding habits of these birds, but nests made of roots and of moss have been described. The female is thought to lay 4 eggs.

NAME: Brown Babbler, *Turdoides plebejus*
RANGE: Africa: Senegal, east to Sudan, Ethiopia and W. Kenya
HABITAT: bush, savanna
SIZE: 23 cm (9 in)

Both male and female brown babblers have mainly grayish-brown plumage, with some white markings and light underparts. Typical babblers, they form noisy flocks, flying from one bush to another while making chattering, bab-bling calls. They feed on insects and some fruit, which they find in the low levels of bushes or by scratching about on the ground.

The cup-shaped nest is made of root-lets, lined with fine plant material, and is situated in a dense bush. The female lays 2 to 4 eggs.

NAME: White-crested Laughingthrush, *Garrulax leucolophus*
RANGE: Himalayas, S.W. China, S.E. Asia, W. Sumatra
HABITAT: forest
SIZE: 30.5 cm (12 in)

One of the larger babblers, the white-crested laughingthrush has an erectile crest on its white head, a white throat and breast and characteristic black masklike markings on its head. There are several races within the range, which may differ slightly in the shade of the darker areas of plumage. Like most laughingthrushes, they are sociable birds, which move in small flocks, foraging in the undergrowth and on the ground. Insects, berries and seeds are their main foods, but they take nectar and small reptiles as well. Large items of prey are held down with the foot while being torn to pieces with the bill. The laughingthrushes seem to prefer densely vegetated areas, and birds in the flock communicate by chattering calls, often followed by wild, cackling sounds, which resemble laughter and are the origin of the common name.

The nest is well hidden in a low tree or bush. It is cup shaped and made of grass, bamboo leaves, roots and moss, all bound together with tendrils of vine and lined with rootlets. The female lays 3 to 6 eggs, usually 4, and both parents incubate the clutch for about 14 days. The chestnut-winged cuckoo, *Clamator coromandus*, is known to lay its eggs in the nest of the white-crested laughingthrush, making it an unwitting foster parent.

NAME: Red-billed Leiothrix/Peking Robin, *Leiothrix lutea*
RANGE: Himalayas, mountain areas of northern S.E. Asia and S. China; introduced in Hawaii
HABITAT: forest undergrowth, scrub, grass
SIZE: 15 cm (6 in)

The male red-billed leiothrix is an attractive bird, with an orange-red bill and bright yellow and orange plumage on the throat, breast and wing feathers; his bill has a blackish base in winter. The female has duller plumage, with a paler throat and breast, and she lacks the bright wing feathers. These birds live in many different types of forest where they forage in the undergrowth for in-sects. They are lively, gregarious birds, usually seen in small groups, except in the breeding season when they form pairs.

The courting male perches on top of a bush and delivers what has been described as "a delightful song," while fluffing out his feathers to attract his mate. The cup-shaped nest is made of

leaves, moss and lichen, of moss only or of bamboo leaves, depending on what plant material is available, and it is lined with fine threads of fungal material. Usually rather conspicuous, the nest is placed on a horizontally forked branch or in an upright fork, or is bound to several twigs or stems. The female lays 3 eggs and there is usually more than one brood. This leiothrix is a familiar cage bird, under the name of the Peking robin.

NAME: Fire-tailed Myzornis, *Myzornis pyrrhoura*
RANGE: Himalayas from Nepal to Burma; S.W. China
HABITAT: bush, forest
SIZE: 12.5 cm (5 in)

An exquisite little bird, the fire-tailed myzornis has touches of black, white and red on its mainly green plumage. The female looks similar to the male, but her red plumage is duller, and the throat and belly tend toward buff-brown. Generally found in forest above 1,800 m (6,000 ft), the myzornis lives alone or in small groups of 3 or 4, which may sometimes join with mixed flocks of other babblers and warblers. It is a most adaptable bird in its feeding techniques: it forages on foliage and flowers for insects and spiders, like other babblers, but can also run up mossy tree trunks to find prey or hover like a sunbird in front of flowers. Using its bristly tongue, it will probe the flowers of shrubs, such as rhododen-drons, for nectar and also feeds on sap, which it obtains from trees.

Little is known of the breeding habits of this bird, the only representative of its genus. The one nest that has been found was in dense, mossy forest, and both parents appeared to be feeding the young.

NAME: Bush Blackcap, *Lioptilus nigricapillus*
RANGE: South Africa: E. Cape Province, Natal, N.E. Transvaal
HABITAT: damp forest
SIZE: 16.5–18 cm (6½–7 in)

A rare, little-known babbler, the bush blackcap is a quieter, less conspicuous bird than many of its relatives. Alone or in pairs, it forages for berries and other fruit, much of which it finds on or near the ground in dense undergrowth. Both male and female birds have characteris-tic black markings on the head, and the rest of the plumage is brownish and gray.

The neat, cup-shaped nest is made of twigs and moss, lined with rootlets, and is usually situated just above the ground in a bush. The female lays 2 eggs.

Brown Babbler

Brown-cheeked Fulvetta

Stripe-throated Yuhina

Fire-tailed Myzornis (male)

Red-billed Leiothrix
(male)

White-crested Laughingthrush

Bush Blackcap

Babblers, Parrotbills and relatives

NAME: **Wrentit,** *Chamaea fasciata*
RANGE: **USA: Pacific coast, Oregon to California; Mexico: coast of Baja California**
HABITAT: **scrub, chaparral**
SIZE: **15–17 cm (6–6¾ in)**

The single species of wrentit is included in the main babbler subfamily, the Timaliinae, or, sometimes, placed in its own subfamily. Believed to be closely related to babblers and to parrotbills, the Panurinae, its relationships and classification have been the subject of much dispute.

An elusive, inconspicuous little bird, the wrentit spends all its life within its selected territory, which it defends throughout the year, seldom flying across any distance of open country. Pairs mate for life and forage and roost together. Insects, spiders and berries are their main foods.

Together the paired wrentits build a neat, cup-shaped nest from bark, plant fiber and grass, bound together with spider's webs. The nest is usually above ground in a bush or small tree. The female lays 3 to 5 eggs, generally 4, which she incubates for 15 or 16 days although the male may take a turn.

PANURINAE: Parrotbill Subfamily

The 19 species of parrotbill are closely related to the babblers, which are sometimes included in the same subfamily, but they have short, heavy, usually yellowish bills, resembling those of parrots. They feed on insects, seeds and berries. All the species occur in Asia, and 1, the bearded tit, also lives in Europe. Male and female look alike in some species but differ in others.

NAME: **Spot-breasted/White-throated Parrotbill,** *Paradoxornis guttaticollis*
RANGE: **N.E. India (Assam), S.W. China, northern S.E. Asia**
HABITAT: **scrub, grass, bamboo clumps**
SIZE: **20.5 cm (8 in)**

The spot-breasted parrotbill can be identified by its yellow, parrotlike bill, the reddish-brown plumage on its head and the dark, arrowhead markings on its throat and breast. Male and female look alike. In noisy flocks, parrotbills forage in dense vegetation for insects, seeds and berries.

The cup-shaped nest is made above ground, from bamboo leaves and grass, bound with spider's webs. The female lays 2 to 4 eggs.

NAME: **Bearded Tit/Reedling,** *Panurus biarmicus*
RANGE: **scattered locations in S. and central Europe, east across USSR and S. central Asia to Manchuria**
HABITAT: **reedbeds, swamps, near lakes and streams**
SIZE: **16 cm (6¼ in)**

The only babblerlike bird to occur in Europe, the bearded tit has a long tail for its size and a smaller, weaker bill than other parrotbills. The male has a distinctive gray head, with black mustache markings, while the female has a brown head and no black markings. An active little bird, it moves with agility through reed stems, often straddling two stalks as it picks off insects. It may also come to the ground to scratch for insects and in winter feeds on seeds. Though their flight seems labored, bearded tits do often wander great distances, and northern populations may migrate in winter.

The male displays to court his mate, raising his head feathers, puffing out his "mustaches" and spreading his tail. The pair builds a nest of reed and grass stalks, lined with flowering reed heads, which is concealed among reeds or aquatic vegetation. The female lays 5 to 7 eggs, which are incubated for 12 or 13 days by both parents. The nestlings are fed by their parents for 9 to 12 days. There may be two or more broods a season.

PICATHARTINAE: Bare-headed Rockfowl Subfamily

The 2 species of bare-headed rockfowl, also called picathartes or bald crows, are thought by most authorities to be close relatives of the babblers, being similar in many respects to laughingthrushes. Both species are large, long-tailed birds, found in the forests of West Africa, and they are similar in their biology and habits. The common name comes from the characteristic bare patch on the head.

NAME: **Guinea Bare-headed Rockfowl,** *Picathartes gymnocephalus*
RANGE: **W. Africa: Guinea and Sierra Leone to Togo**
HABITAT: **forest**
SIZE: **38–41 cm (15–16 in)** Ⓥ

Recognizable by the bare, yellow head, with two black patches at the back, both male and female rockfowls have gray and white plumage and powerful legs and feet. Rockfowls spend much of their life on the ground, where they move with graceful hops, searching for insects, snails, crustaceans and small frogs. The species is becoming rare,

partly because of forest clearance and partly from trapping to fulfill the demands of zoos and private collectors. It is protected by law in Ghana.

Rockfowls nest colonially in caves, in nests made of mud and fibrous plant materials and attached to the walls of the caves. Unfortunately, this habit of colonial nesting in often easily identified sites makes the birds easy prey for collectors. Both parents incubate the 2 eggs for about 21 days and then feed their young with insects.

ORTHONYCHINAE: Quail Thrush Subfamily

In this diverse group are 17 species of whipbird, logrunner and quail thrush, all but 1 found in Australia and New Guinea; the exception occurs farther north, in Malaysia. They are babblerlike birds, often included with the babbler group.

NAME: **Eastern Whipbird,** *Psophodes olivaceus*
RANGE: **Australia: Queensland to Victoria**
HABITAT: **thickets in or near forest**
SIZE: **25–28 cm (9¾–11 in)**

The eastern whipbird has mainly dark plumage, with some touches of white, and a long, broad tail; male and female look alike. It lives on or near the ground but usually stays in dense undergrowth, searching for insects, larvae and spiders among the leaf litter. It hops and runs swiftly and can climb up into bushes but flies rarely and only for short distances.

The nest of twigs and rootlets is made near the ground in dense undergrowth. The female lays 2 eggs.

NAME: **Cinnamon Quail Thrush,** *Cinclosoma cinnamomeum*
RANGE: **Australia: drier areas, Western Australia to Queensland and Victoria**
HABITAT: **semidesert, scrub**
SIZE: **20 cm (7¾ in)**

Alone or in small family groups, the cinnamon quail thrush skulks among bushes or hides in holes and burrows to escape predators and the heat of the day. It usually feeds in the cool of dawn and dusk, on seeds and insects. It may also hunt for insects over open country, flying low with noisy, whirring wings. Male and female differ in plumage, the female lacking the male's characteristic black markings.

The nest is sited in a shallow dip in the ground or under a bush or fallen branch and is made of grass and twigs, lined with bark and leaves. The female lays 2 or 3 eggs.

Wrentit

Eastern Whipbird

Bearded Tit
(male)

Cinnamon
Quail Thrush
(male)

Spot-breasted
Parrotbill

Guinea Bare-headed Rockfowl

Gnatcatchers, Old World Warblers

POLIOPTILINAE:
Gnatcatcher Subfamily

There are 12 species in this subfamily of the family Muscicapidae, found in North, Central and South America. They are small, dainty birds, related to and resembling Old World warblers but with bluish-gray and white plumage. Male and female may differ slightly in appearance.

NAME: **Blue-gray Gnatcatcher,** *Polioptila caerulea*
RANGE: **USA, Mexico, Cuba and Bahamas**
HABITAT: **forest, woodland, swamps, inhabited areas**
SIZE: **10–13 cm (4–5 in)**

The blue-gray gnatcatcher is a slender, lively, little bird with a long tail, often held cocked like a wren's. Male and female look similar, but the female tends to be less blue in color and lacks the black head markings developed by the breeding male. They search for insects, larvae and spiders in the trees, sometimes launching themselves into the air to catch prey.

The cup-shaped nest is usually sited on a horizontal branch and is made from plant fibers lined with fine bark, grass and feathers. The parents incubate the 3 to 6 eggs in shifts for about 14 days and care for the young.

SYLVIINAE:
Old World Warbler Subfamily

Small, often dull-colored birds, many of the 350 or so species of Old World warbler are noted for their marvelous songs. Most of the species occur in Europe, Asia and Africa, but there are 3 species in North America and about 20 in Australia.

Almost without exception, warblers are active, quick-moving birds, found in woodland, moorland, marshes and reedbeds feeding on insects and fruit. Male and female generally look alike.

NAME: **Long-tailed/Common Tailorbird,** *Orthotomus sutorius*
RANGE: **India, S. China, S.E. Asia to Java**
HABITAT: **scrub, bamboo thickets, gardens**
SIZE: **12 cm (4¾ in)**

Distinguished by their rufous caps, both male and female have similar plumage, but in the breeding season, the male's two central tail feathers grow much longer than the others, adding about 4 cm (1½ in) to his length. The tailorbird is a common, widespread species, which spends much of its time hopping about in bushes and low trees, searching for insects, larvae and small spiders; it will also feed on nectar.

Pairs mate for life and nest on a bush or low branch. The nest is made in a cradle, formed by sewing together the edges of a large leaf or two smaller leaves of the tree. The tailorbird makes a series of small holes in the edges of the leaf with its beak and then pulls through strands of wool, spider's web or cocoon silk, to draw them together. Each stitch is separate. The 2 or 3 eggs are laid inside this cradle, on a nest of soft fibers. Both parents incubate the eggs and tend the young.

NAME: **Blackcap,** *Sylvia atricapilla*
RANGE: **breeds in Europe, Britain and Scandinavia to Mediterranean countries, east to Iran and Siberia; winters south of range and in Africa**
HABITAT: **woodland, gardens, orchards**
SIZE: **14 cm (5½ in)**

The male blackcap is distinguished from other *Sylvia* warblers by his black crown and gray neck; females and juveniles have rusty-brown caps and are otherwise similar to males but browner. An active, lively bird, it forages in trees and bushes for insects and eats more fruit than most other warblers.

The male courts his mate by raising his head and back feathers and drooping and flapping his wings. The nest is made in a low bush or other low cover and is constructed from dry stems, spider's webs and wool. Both parents incubate the 3 to 6 eggs for 10 to 15 days and feed their young.

NAME: **Fan-tailed Warbler/Zitting Cisticola,** *Cisticola juncidis*
RANGE: **Africa, south of the Sahara; S. Europe; India, China, Japan; S.E. Asia to N. Australia**
HABITAT: **grassland, scrub, rice fields, cultivated land**
SIZE: **10 cm (4 in)**

A ground-living bird, the fan-tailed warbler skulks in grass, feeding on insects, and flies only when disturbed or in courtship. Males and females look similar, but breeding males have more strongly defined streaks on the head.

In the breeding season, males perform various courtship displays, including a jerky, dipping flight, accompanied by a particular song. The unique nest is built amid grass taller than itself, for camouflage. It is pear shaped, with the entrance at the top, and is made of soft grass stems, bound together with spider's webs and lined with plant down. Some blades of the surrounding grass are woven into the nest for support. The 3 to 6 eggs are incubated by both parents for about 10 days.

NAME: **Graceful/Striped-backed Prinia,** *Prinia gracilis*
RANGE: **E. Africa: Egypt to Somalia; east across S. Asia to N. India**
HABITAT: **scrub, bushy areas**
SIZE: **10 cm (4 in)**

As much as half the length of this little warbler is accounted for by its tail of graduated feathers, the outer ones of which are tipped with white. The graceful prinia tends to frequent sandy ground near rivers, where there is some grass and bushy cover. It forages for insects in the vegetation and comes into the open only to fly clumsily from one patch of cover to the next.

The courting male sings a somewhat monotonous song from a perch on a tall grass stem. The tiny, domed nest is made of fine grass and is woven into a thick clump of grass stems, a meter or so above ground; there is an entrance at one side. Both parents incubate the 3 or 4 eggs for about 12 days. There are usually two broods a year.

NAME: **Yellow-breasted/Black-breasted Apalis,** *Apalis flavida*
RANGE: **Africa, south of the Sahara to South Africa: Transvaal**
HABITAT: **forest, bush**
SIZE: **11 cm (4¼ in)**

The yellow-breasted apalis occurs in a variety of well-vegetated areas. It usually moves in pairs or small family groups, carefully searching through the foliage for insects.

The domed, pear-shaped nest is made of moss, lichen and spider's webs and is bound to a twig of a low bush with spider's webs; there is a side opening. Alternatively, this apalis may take over an old domed nest abandoned by another bird species. The female lays 2 or 3 eggs.

NAME: **Long-billed Warbler,** *Acrocephalus (= Conopoderas) caffra*
RANGE: **Society and Marquesas Islands**
HABITAT: **woodland bordering rivers, hillside forest**
SIZE: **22 cm (8½ in)**

One of the largest warblers, the long-billed warbler has a distinctive beak that can be 4 cm (1½ in) long. Subspecies on the different islands vary in coloration, and on Tahiti alone, there are some birds with olive upperparts and yellow underparts and other birds that are blackish-brown all over.

Long-billed warblers forage in trees and bushes for insects; they do not feed on the ground. They have a musical, varied song, performed from a high perch. The nest is usually made in a bamboo thicket, 9 m (30 ft) or more above ground.

Blue-gray Gnatcatcher

Fan-tailed Warbler (male)

Blackcap (male)

Long-tailed Tailorbird

Graceful Prinia

Long-billed Warbler

Yellow-breasted Apalis

Old World Warblers

NAME: Chestnut-headed Warbler,
Seicercus castaneiceps
RANGE: Himalayas, S. China, S.E. Asia,
Sumatra
HABITAT: forest
SIZE: 10 cm (4 in)

An attractive little bird, the chestnut-headed warbler has a reddish-brown crown, with dark bands at the sides of the head, and yellow underparts. Male and female look alike. They live in dense forest and, outside the breeding season, move in mixed flocks, searching for insects in the middle to canopy layers of the forest. In the Himalayas, the birds breed at between 1,800 and 2,400 m (6,000 and 7,900 ft), moving down the mountains in winter.

The compact, oval nest is situated on the ground, well hidden by moss or creepers in a hollow at the base of a tree or bush or in a bank or hillside. Both partners help to build the nest, which is made of densely woven moss, and incubate the 4 or 5 eggs. The emerald cuckoo, *Chalcites maculatus*, often lays its eggs in the nests of this warbler.

NAME: Willow Warbler, *Phylloscopus*
trochilus
RANGE: N. Europe and Asia: Britain and
Scandinavia, south to central France,
east to USSR; winters in Africa and
S. Asia
HABITAT: open woodland, cultivated land
with scattered trees and bushes
SIZE: 11 cm (4¼ in)

Typical of the many species in the genus *Phylloscopus* in appearance, the willow warbler is extremely hard to distinguish from the chiffchaff, *P. collybita*, except by its song. It is said to look "cleaner" than the chiffchaff, and its eyebrow streak is more marked. Male and female birds look similar, but juveniles have much more yellow on their underparts. Willow warblers search in the vegetation for insects and also sometimes catch prey in the air. In autumn, they feed on berries, before migrating south for the winter. Some northern birds travel as far as 12,000 km (7,500 mi) to winter in African forest and savanna.

Willow warblers nest on the ground, in vegetation under a bush, tree or hedge, or sometimes a little above ground in a bush or on a creeper-covered wall. The female builds the domed nest from grass, moss, stems and roots, lined with finer stems and feathers. She lays 6 or 7 eggs, which she incubates for 13 days. Both parents tend the young, which spend 13 to 16 days in the nest. Birds in the south of the range may produce two broods.

NAME: Grasshopper Warbler, *Locustella*
naevia
RANGE: Europe: Britain and S. Sweden,
south to N. Spain and Italy, east to
central Siberia; winters in Africa and
Asia
HABITAT: marsh edge, open woodland
SIZE: 13 cm (5 in)

The grasshopper warbler is a retiring, secretive species, which quickly disappears into thick cover when disturbed. It feeds on insects and larvae. Male and female birds have similar streaked plumage.

The male warbler performs courtship displays, spreading his tail and flapping his wings. The nest, built by both birds, is placed in thick cover on the ground or just above it in grasses or rushes and is made of plant stems and grass on a base of dead leaves. The female lays 4 to 7 eggs, usually 6, which both parents incubate for 13 to 15 days. The young spend 10 to 12 days in the nest, tended and fed by both parents. Birds in the south of the range have two broods, and those in the north usually only one. In autumn, the birds migrate south for the winter.

NAME: Strong-footed/Brownish-flanked
Bush Warbler, *Cettia fortipes*
RANGE: Himalayas, S. China, S.E. Asia,
Indonesia
HABITAT: open forest, swamp-jungle,
gardens
SIZE: 10 cm (4 in)

A small, skulking warbler, the strong-footed warbler has a distinctive whistling call, culminating in a loud, explosive phrase, but is rarely seen. It is a solitary bird and forages for insects in the dense undergrowth found in its habitat. It may hop up into bushes but rarely climbs trees. Mountain birds make seasonal movements, descending to lower altitudes in winter and breeding between 2,000 and 3,000 m (6,600 and 10,000 ft).

The untidy nest is built in a bush, usually less than a meter or so above ground. It may be a cup-shaped or, sometimes, a domed structure, with an entrance near the top. Both parents incubate the 3 to 5, usually 4, eggs.

NAME: Ceylon Bush Warbler,
Bradypterus palliseri
RANGE: Sri Lanka
HABITAT: montane forest undergrowth,
dwarf bamboo thickets
SIZE: 16 cm (6¼ in)

Ceylon bush warblers live at altitudes of over 900 m (3,000 ft). In pairs, they skulk in dense undergrowth, searching under leaves and among stems for insects and worms, and rarely climb more than 2 m (6½ ft) above ground.

The male performs a sketchy courtship, climbing a little farther than usual up a stem to sing a brief song and then flying from one patch of vegetation to another. The nest is relatively large for the size of the birds and is made of moss, grass and bamboo leaves, lined with fine fibers. It is situated in a bush, close to the ground. The female lays 2 eggs.

NAME: Golden-crowned Kinglet,
Regulus satrapa
RANGE: Alaska, S. Canada, USA; winters
Mexico and Central America
HABITAT: forest, usually coniferous
SIZE: 8–10 cm (3–4 in)

This tiny bird is one of the 3 members of the Old World warbler subfamily to occur in North America. The plumage is restrained for the most part, but there is a conspicuous black-bordered crown, which is orange in the male and yellow in the female, hence the common name; juveniles develop the crown patch as they mature. Kinglets join mixed flocks to forage in the trees and bushes for insects and larvae.

The birds nest high in a conifer, usually a spruce. The female builds a globular nest of moss, lichen, pine needles and grass, bound together with spider's webs and lined with fine rootlets, fibers and feathers. This structure has an opening at the top and is suspended from twigs, to which it is bound with spider's webs. The female alone is thought to incubate the 8 to 10 eggs for 14 to 17 days, but both parents tend the young.

NAME: Little Grassbird, *Megalurus*
gramineus
RANGE: Australia (except N.); Tasmania
HABITAT: swamps
SIZE: 14 cm (5½ in)

The little grassbird lives amid the vegetation of coastal and inland swamps. A furtive bird, it stays in cover as it creeps about, foraging for insects and small aquatic animals. It seldom flies in its everyday life, but since it occurs in temporary swamps, it must occasionally make quite long flights to find a new home, when its existing one dries out. Birds occupying permanent swamps are sedentary. Male and female look alike, with streaked brownish plumage and broad white eye stripes. The long tail accounts for almost half of the bird's length.

The nest is made in thick vegetation, sometimes over the swamp water. It is cup shaped and made of grass, lined with feathers. The female lays a clutch of 3 or 4 eggs.

Chestnut-headed Warbler

Strong-footed Bush Warbler

Willow Warbler

Little Grassbird

Grasshopper Warbler

Ceylon Bush Warbler

Golden-crowned Kinglet (male)

Australian Warblers

NAME: **Superb Blue Wren,** *Malurus cyaneus*
RANGE: **Australia: Victoria to Queensland; Tasmania**
HABITAT: **woodland, savanna, parks**
SIZE: **13 cm (5 in)**

Only in the male breeding plumage is this little bird superb. The breeding male has attractive, shiny blue plumage around the head and neck, contrasting with some bold black markings; older, dominant males tend to keep this plumage all year. Nonbreeding males and females are mainly brownish and dull white. The birds live in groups, ruled by a dominant pair, and together defend a territory from intruders. Hopping about with tails cocked, they forage for insects on the ground and among the vegetation.

All members of the group combine to build the dome-shaped nest, which is situated near the ground in a bush or on a tussock and is made of grass, rootlets and bark, bound with spider's webs. The dominant female lays 3 or 4 eggs, and again, all the group members assist with the 14-day incubation and the rearing of the young.

NAME: **Eyrean Grass Wren,** *Amytornis goyderi*
RANGE: **South Australia: Lake Eyre area**
HABITAT: **cane grass on sandhills, spinifex grassland**
SIZE: **14 cm (5½ in)** Ⓘ

The Eyrean grass wren is apparently a rare bird, but the exact state of the population is not known. In 1976, it was recorded in some numbers in the sandhills of Simpson Desert, in South Australia, but by the following year, the habitat had deteriorated, and the birds had largely gone. Prior to 1976, it had been recorded only at its discovery in 1874, in 1931 and in 1961.

A furtive little bird, the Eyrean grass wren stays well hidden as it forages among the tussocks of vegetation. Little is known of its breeding habits, but the observed nests have been partly domed, made of interwoven grass and stems.

NAME: **White-browed Scrubwren,** *Sericornis frontalis*
RANGE: **E. and S.E. Australia, islands in Bass Strait**
HABITAT: **bushy coastal vegetation**
SIZE: **11 cm (4¼ in)**

The white-browed scrubwren lives on or near the ground, keeping hidden in the thick undergrowth while it hops about in search of insects and other small invertebrates.

The domed nest is built in the undergrowth on or near the ground. It is made of leaves and fibers and has a side entrance. The female lays 3 eggs.

MALURINAE:
Australian Warbler Subfamily

Within this somewhat uncertain assemblage are 3 main tribes of birds: the Australian warblers (Acanthizini), the Australian wrens (Malurini) and the Australian chats (Epthianurini).

In the Australian warbler tribe are about 67 species of bird, with diverse common names such as gerygone, thornbill, bristlebird and scrubwren. Most are small birds, with sober plumage, which live in forest undergrowth.

Of the 30 species of Australian wren, one or two are also found in New Guinea. Male birds are brightly or boldly plumaged, with long, slender tails. Some have strange social and reproductive habits, which may be their way of dealing with the often harsh conditions of their habitat. Groups of birds hold a territory together, which they defend from other birds, and each group builds a single, spherical nest, in which one dominant female lays her eggs. All other adult members of the group then assist in the incubation and care of the young. Sometimes pairs nest alone, but they tend to have a high failure rate.

The 5 species of Australian chat are boldly marked little birds, which make erratic, nomadic migrations, according to the unpredictable rains in their arid range.

The position of the silktail within the huge family Muscicapidae is uncertain, and it has even been placed among the birds of paradise.

NAME: **Yellow-rumped Thornbill,** *Acanthiza chrysorrhoa*
RANGE: **Australia, south of Tropic of Capricorn**
HABITAT: **open woodland, savanna**
SIZE: **10 cm (4 in)**

The male and female of this species both have somewhat sober plumage but with deep-yellow rump feathers, the origin of their common name. They feed on insects and plant matter, such as seeds, which they find on the ground and by foraging in bushes and trees.

The large, untidy nest is made of grass and plant fibers and has a hooded brood chamber with a low, overhung entrance. It is usually situated in a low bush or other foliage. The female lays 3 eggs, which she incubates for 18 to 20 days; both parents then tend the young. The birds produce up to four broods a season, and young from earlier broods assist in the care of subsequent nestlings. This unusual habit is common to many members of this subfamily.

NAME: **White-throated Warbler,** *Gerygone olivacea*
RANGE: **S.E. New Guinea, coastal N. and E. Australia**
HABITAT: **open forest, woodland**
SIZE: **11 cm (4¼ in)**

An arboreal bird, the white-throated warbler forages for insects on bark and foliage and occasionally pursues prey on the wing. It usually occurs alone or in scattered, loosely knit groups. Male and female look alike, both with grayish-brown upperparts and yellow underparts.

The long, oval-shaped nest is suspended from twigs up to 15 m (50 ft) above ground. It is made of plant fiber and strips of bark, interwoven with spider's webs and lined with feathers or plant down; it has a hooded entrance near the top. The female lays 2 or 3 eggs.

NAME: **Crimson Chat,** *Epthianura tricolor*
RANGE: **Australia**
HABITAT: **grassy plains with some bush cover**
SIZE: **10–11 cm (4–4¼ in)**

The male crimson chat is a vividly plumaged little bird, with his red, white and brownish-black markings. The female bird is plainer, with more brown plumage, but she does have a crimson rump. The birds forage on or near the ground in grass or low trees and bushes and may poke their bills into flowers to find insects. If a large insect is caught, the chat wedges it in a forked twig and then tears it apart as it devours it.

Breeding takes place after heavy rainfall, when food supplies are assured; the birds usually breed in loose colonies. Courting males perform display flights, with crimson crown feathers erect. The cup-shaped nest, made of grass and twigs, is situated in a bush or on a tussock, and the female lays 3 or 4 eggs. Both parents incubate the eggs and tend the young.

NAME: **Silktail,** *Lamprolia victoriae*
RANGE: **Fiji**
HABITAT: **mature mountain forest**
SIZE: **12 cm (4¾ in)**

The silktail is a striking bird, with dark, velvety plumage, scattered with metallic blue spangles, and a white rump. It forages for its insect prey on the foliage of the forest understory and also goes down to the ground to find food. Swift and agile in flight, it darts between the trees and may also pursue slow-flying insects.

The nest is made in a tree, of fibers, rootlets, vines and slivers of bark and is lined with feathers. The female lays a single egg.

Silktail

Superb Blue Wren (male)

White-browed Scrubwren

Eyrean Grass Wren

Yellow-rumped Thornbill

White-throated Warbler

Crimson Chat (male)

Old World Flycatchers

NAME: **Flame Robin,** *Petroica phoenicea*
RANGE: **Tasmania and adjacent Australian mainland**
HABITAT: **dry forest, woodland, open country**
SIZE: **13–14 cm (5–5½ in)**

The flame robin is so called because of the bright red throat and belly of the male bird, reminiscent of those of the European robin. The female has pale buff underparts, with sometimes a touch of orange-red on the belly. The birds feed on insects, taken on the ground and in trees, and continually flit from perch to perch. Normally solitary, they may form flocks, sometimes of one sex, outside the breeding season.

The nest is made of grass and bark strips, bound together with spider's webs. It may be in a tree fork or hollow, on a bank or among tree roots. The female lays 3 eggs.

NAME: **Spotted Flycatcher,** *Muscicapa striata*
RANGE: **Europe: Scandinavia, south to Mediterranean countries; N. Africa to central Asia; winters tropical Africa and S.W. Asia**
HABITAT: **forest edge, woodland, scrub, gardens, parks**
SIZE: **14 cm (5½ in)**

The spotted flycatcher feeds in the manner typical of its group, perching in exposed spots and making swift aerial sallies after insects. While perched, it constantly flicks its wings and tail. Male and female look alike, both with mainly grayish-brown plumage.

The female does most of the work of nest-building, making a neat structure of moss, bark and fibers, lined with rootlets and feathers. The nest may be in a variety of sites such as on a ledge, in a cavity or tree fork or on a wall or rock. Both parents incubate the 4 to 6 eggs for 12 to 14 days and tend the young. They often produce two broods.

NAME: **Rufous-tailed Jungle Flycatcher,** *Rhinomyias ruficauda*
RANGE: **Philippines, Borneo**
HABITAT: **forest**
SIZE: **14 cm (5½ in)**

A rather rare bird, the rufous-tailed jungle flycatcher frequents dense undergrowth, where it feeds on insects and spiders. Much of its food is gleaned from foliage, but it makes swift flights into the air to catch winged insects. The subspecies of this bird vary slightly in coloration, but all have the distinctive chestnut tail. The female looks similar to the male in most respects.

The breeding habits of this species are not known.

MUSCICAPINAE: Old World Flycatcher Subfamily

This large subfamily of the family Muscicapidae includes nearly 150 species of insect-eating songbirds. All occur in the Old World, with the greatest diversity in Africa, Asia and Australasia. Some are brightly plumaged, others are dull, and flycatchers have diversified into a wide range of body forms and habits to fit different niches. Males and females look alike in some species and differ in others.

The "typical" flycatchers, which include some examples that occur in Europe, have a flat, wide beak, the base of which is surrounded by prominent bristles. Their method of insect capture is extremely characteristic: the feeding bird sits on a perch in a good vantage position for observing prey; if an insect passes, the bird launches itself into the air for a brief, agile, hunting flight and deftly captures the prey in its bill; it takes the prey back to its perch to eat. Some birds, of course, do use other methods of catching prey and feed on the ground or on foliage.

NAME: **Blue-throated Flycatcher,** *Niltava rubeculoides*
RANGE: **Himalayas through northern S.E. Asia to China; winters south of range**
HABITAT: **forest, gardens**
SIZE: **14 cm (5½ in)**

The blue-throated flycatcher lives in well-wooded areas with plenty of undergrowth. It does make aerial dashes after insect prey but hardly ever returns to the same perch, or even the same tree, to consume the catch. It may also drop down to the ground to find food and may flush out a concealed cricket or grasshopper with its open wings. Male and female differ in plumage, the female having mainly olive-brown and buff feathers instead of the distinctive blue of the male.

The nest is made in a hollow in a mossy bank, in a rock crevice or in a hole in a tree or bamboo stem. The female lays 3 to 5 eggs, usually 4, which both birds incubate for 11 or 12 days.

NAME: **Citrine Canary Flycatcher,** *Culicicapa helianthea*
RANGE: **Philippines, Sulawesi**
HABITAT: **forest, woodland**
SIZE: **about 10 cm (4 in)**

Also called the sunflower flycatcher, this bird has mostly yellow plumage of various shades; the upperparts of juvenile birds tend to be darker and more green than those of adults. It perches on the outer branches of trees and makes short aerial dashes after passing insects in true flycatcher fashion; it also sometimes feeds in mixed flocks.

NAME: **Maroon-breasted Flycatcher,** *Philentoma velata*
RANGE: **Malaysia, Sumatra, Java, Borneo**
HABITAT: **forest**
SIZE: **20.5 cm (8 in)**

A noisy, active bird, the maroon-breasted flycatcher frequents the lower to middle layers of the forest, often perching on low branches, vines and creepers. It catches all its prey on the wing and does not forage on foliage. It normally lives in pairs, and both sexes have loud, harsh calls. Male and female differ slightly in plumage: the female is a darker blue than the male and lacks his maroon chest patch. Nearly always found near water, these flycatchers love to bathe.

The nest is made on a forked branch of a tree.

NAME: **Pale/Mouse-coloured Flycatcher,** *Bradornis pallidus*
RANGE: **Africa, south of the Sahara**
HABITAT: **woodland, coastal scrub, gardens, cornfields**
SIZE: **15–18 cm (6–7 in)**

The pale flycatcher has largely grayish-brown plumage and is less conspicuous than many flycatchers; juvenile birds have some streaked and spotted plumage. In pairs or small, loosely knit groups, they forage on the ground for much of their food, such as spiders and termites, but also catch flies and moths in the air. They are quiet birds, making only an occasional twittering call.

Breeding begins at the start of, or just before, the rainy season. The small, neat, cup-shaped nest is made of rootlets and sited on a forked branch of a tree or bush. The female lays 2 or 3 eggs. Families remain together for a prolonged period, and there is some evidence that birds other than the parents help to rear broods.

Citrine Canary Flycatcher

Flame Robin (male)

Rufous-tailed Jungle
Flycatcher

Spotted
Flycatcher

Maroon-breasted
Flycatcher (male)

Blue-throated Flycatcher (male)

Pale Flycatcher

Monarch Flycatchers

MONARCHINAE: Monarch Flycatcher Subfamily

Monarchs and paradise flycatchers are boldly plumaged birds of forest areas. Some dart out from perches to catch prey, while others search the foliage of the trees.

NAME: Black-naped (Blue) Monarch, *Hypothymis azurea*
RANGE: India, S. China, S.E. Asia to Lesser Sunda Islands and Philippines
HABITAT: forest, scrub, bamboo thickets, cultivated land
SIZE: 16.5 cm ($6\frac{1}{2}$ in)

The male black-naped monarch has bright blue plumage, with a little patch of black feathers on the nape of the neck that can be erected when the bird is excited. There is also a narrow black band across his chest. The female looks similar to the male but has grayish-brown plumage on the upperparts and lacks the black nape and chest markings.

This flycatcher tends to perch in higher trees than other species and makes agile looping flights after insect prey such as butterflies and moths; it also forages in undergrowth and on the ground. When a large insect is caught, the bird will hold it down with its foot and tear it apart before eating it. Usually seen alone or in pairs, the black-naped monarch is an extremely active, lively bird, constantly on the move as it flits from perch to perch.

The neat, cup-shaped nest is built on a forked branch, to which it is bound with spider's webs, or in a bush, sapling or bamboo clump. The female bird does most of the work, using grass and bark for the cup and covering the outside with moss, spider's webs and egg cases; the male attends her closely throughout the nest-building. She lays 3 or 4 eggs, which she incubates for 15 or 16 days. Both parents tend the young.

NAME: White-tailed Crested Flycatcher, *Trochocercus albonotatus*
RANGE: Africa: Uganda, W. Kenya to Malawi, Zambia, Zimbabwe
HABITAT: highland forest
SIZE: 10 cm (4 in)

The white-tailed crested flycatcher is an attractive little bird, with black, gray and white plumage; male and female look alike. It feeds on insects, making short, jerky flights after prey or foraging rapidly over foliage.

The male bird displays to his mate, hopping around her with his tail raised and his wings trailing. The neat little nest is made of woven moss, bound with cobwebs, and is built around a fork of a low tree. The female lays 2 eggs.

NAME: Asian Paradise Flycatcher, *Terpsiphone paradisi*
RANGE: Turkestan to N.E. China; S.E. Asia, Indonesia
HABITAT: open forest, mangrove swamps, gardens, cultivated land
SIZE: 22.5 cm ($8\frac{3}{4}$ in)

The male Asian paradise flycatcher is a beautiful bird, with extremely long central tail feathers, which add 25.5 cm (10 in) or more to his length. Males occur in two color phases: white and rufous. The white male has white body and tail plumage, with a black head, crest and throat; the rufous male is more variable, according to race, but has rufous tail, back and wings. The female is similar to the rufous male but lacks the crest and long tail feathers.

Alone, or sometimes in pairs or mixed hunting parties, the paradise flycatcher frequents the higher branches of trees, flitting from perch to perch. Its flight is swift and it makes brief sallies from a perch to catch insect prey, returning to the same tree or to another to consume the item. It may also flush out insects on the ground. Flies, dragonflies, beetles, moths and butterflies are its main prey.

The courting male displays to his mate by arching his tail streamers gracefully, while singing and beating his wings. Both sexes help to build the nest, which is a deep, inverted cone, made in a horizontal forked branch of a tree, often near or overhanging water. The 3 or 4 eggs are incubated mostly by the female for 15 or 16 days; unusually for such a decorative bird, the male may sometimes assist and sits with his long tail hanging out behind him. The male bird also helps tend the nestlings.

NAME: Boat-billed Flycatcher, *Machaerirhynchus flaviventer*
RANGE: Australia: N.E. Queensland; New Guinea and adjacent islands
HABITAT: rain forest
SIZE: 12 cm ($4\frac{3}{4}$ in)

The broad, flat bill is the distinctive feature of this flycatcher and the reason for its common name. Male and female differ slightly in appearance, the female having yellowish-olive upperparts, with areas of brownish-black, and fewer yellow and more white markings than the male has. A tree-living bird, it gleans insects from the foliage, moving busily from branch to branch, and also makes short flights to catch prey on the wing.

The shallow, cup-shaped nest is made of strips of bark, bound together with spider's webs and decorated with lichen; the interior is lined with vine tendrils. It is usually built fairly high up on a slender, forked branch. The female lays 2 eggs.

NAME: Spectacled Monarch, *Monarcha trivirgata*
RANGE: E. Australia, New Guinea, the Moluccas, Timor, Flores
HABITAT: wet forest, mangrove swamps, woodland
SIZE: 15 cm (6 in)

Both male and female spectacled monarchs have the black, masklike markings on the face that are the origin of their common name. A solitary, arboreal species, this monarch frequents low, dense vegetation, where it moves swiftly, yet quietly, hunting for insect prey. It may sometimes feed on the ground.

The cup-shaped nest is made of bark strips, lined with spider's webs, and is usually situated low in a bush or sapling. The female lays 2 eggs.

PLATYSTEIRINAE: African Monarch Flycatcher Subfamily

These are chunky, boldly patterned flycatchers with short tails and strong bills. Many species have brightly colored wattles on the face.

NAME: Black-headed Puffback, *Batis minor*
RANGE: Africa: Sudan to Somalia, south to Cameroon and Angola
HABITAT: open woodland, bush
SIZE: 10 cm (4 in)

A small, rather stumpy flycatcher, the puffback can erect the plumage on its back, making itself appear rotund and fluffy — hence the common name. Male and female look alike in most respects, but the female lacks the male's black head plumage and has a dark chestnut, instead of black, band on the chest. They are restless little birds and move in pairs, searching the foliage for insect prey or making brief hunting flights in true flycatcher fashion.

The nest is made of fibers and lichen, bound with spider's webs, and is usually placed in a forked branch of a tree. The female lays 2 or 3 eggs.

NAME: (Common) Wattle-eye, *Platysteira cyanea*
RANGE: W., central and N.E. Africa
HABITAT: forest, woodland, crop fields
SIZE: 13 cm (5 in)

Distinctive red wattles over the eyes make the common wattle-eye easily recognizable. Wattle-eyes behave more like warblers than flycatchers, foraging in pairs over foliage and twigs for insect prey. In noisy, chattering flocks they make some seasonal migrations.

The cup-shaped nest is made of fine grass, plant fibers and lichen and is bound to a forked branch with spider's webs. The female lays 2 eggs.

Black-headed Puffback (male)

Asian Paradise
Flycatcher (male)

White-tailed
Crested
Flycatcher

Black-naped Monarch
(male)

Boat-billed Flycatcher
(male)

Spectacled
Monarch

Wattle-eye

Fantail Flycatchers, Whistlers

Fantail Flycatcher Subfamily

Most fantails occur in Australasia, with a few species in Asia. Their common name comes from their habit of continually spreading and wagging their tails as they move through low vegetation.

NAME: Yellow-bellied Fantail, *Chelidorhynx hypoxantha*
RANGE: Himalayas to S.W. China; northern S.E. Asia: Burma, Thailand, Laos
HABITAT: forest
SIZE: 13 cm (5 in)

The yellow-bellied fantail has bright yellow underparts and distinctive white tips to some of the tail feathers. Male and female birds look similar, but the male has black, masklike markings on the face, which are dark olive-brown in the female.

A lively, restless little bird, this fantail frequents the undergrowth up to the lower levels of the forest canopy, where it prances around with its tail fanned out, foraging for insects. It also feeds on tiny insects, which it takes in the air during brief, aerobatic flights, and it may flush insects out of vegetation with its spread wings.

The nest is made the same width as the horizontal branch on which it is sited, which provides a measure of camouflage. It is built from moss, covered with lichen and spider's webs and lined with hair and feathers. The female lays 3 eggs.

NAME: Willie Wagtail, *Rhipidura leucophrys*
RANGE: Australia, New Guinea, Solomon Islands, the Moluccas, Lesser Sunda Islands
HABITAT: forest edge to desert edge, parks, gardens, cultivated land
SIZE: 20 cm (7¾ in)

A common, adaptable bird, the willie wagtail has learned to take advantage of man-made environments. Male and female birds look alike, and their black and white plumage gives them a resemblance to the European pied wagtail, hence the common name. The willie wagtail generally lives alone, outside the breeding season, and finds food on the ground as well as in flight. It also sometimes sits on the backs of cattle and feeds on the insects disturbed by their hoofs.

The nest is made of grass, bark strips or plant fiber, bound tightly with spider's webs. It is usually built on a horizontal branch but may be made almost anywhere above ground. The female lays 4 eggs.

NAME: Rufous Fantail, *Rhipidura rufifrons*
RANGE: Lesser Sunda and W. Papuan Islands, N. and E. Australia, coastal areas of New Guinea, Louisiade Archipelago, Solomon and Santa Cruz Islands, Micronesia
HABITAT: forest, mangrove swamps
SIZE: 16.5 cm (6½ in)

With its tail fanned out, this flycatcher flies with speed and dexterity through the undergrowth, catching insects in flight and picking them off the foliage. Although a tree-living bird, it also feeds on the ground.

A pear-shaped nest, made of coarse plant material bound together with spider's webs, is built on a thin, forked branch as much as 9 m (30 ft) from the ground. Both parents incubate the 2 eggs for about 15 days and feed the young. The young fantails are able to fly about 15 days after hatching. Breeding birds may produce two to five broods a year, depending on food supplies.

PACHYCEPHALINAE:

Whistler Subfamily

The whistlers occur in Australia, New Guinea and Southeast Asia and have a variety of common names. Most of these flycatchers have attractive songs, and many pairs perform duets.

NAME: Golden Whistler, *Pachycephala pectoralis*
RANGE: Indonesia: Java to the Moluccas; Bismarck Archipelago to Fiji and Tonga; E., S. and S.W. Australia, Tasmania
HABITAT: forest, woodland, mallee (eucalyptus) scrub
SIZE: 18 cm (7 in)

Divided into perhaps 70 or 80 races, distributed among the many islands in its range, the golden whistler may have more subspecies than any other bird, some of which are as distinct as species. There is enormous variation between the races, particularly of head plumage, but the male bird is generally olive-green, yellow and black or gray. Females usually have olive-brown to olive-gray upperparts, with grayish throat and breast and whitish belly plumage.

A tree-dwelling bird, the golden whistler feeds in the trees on insects and sometimes on berries. It perches for long periods and is rather inactive compared to most flycatchers.

Both partners of a breeding pair help to build the nest, which is usually in a fork of a small tree or bush. It is made of grass, bark and leaves, lined with fine grass. Both birds incubate the 2 or 3 eggs and tend the young.

NAME: Rusty Pitohui, *Pitohui ferrugineus*
RANGE: New Guinea area, Aru Islands
HABITAT: lowland forest
SIZE: 25.5–28 cm (10–11 in)

One of the largest flycatchers, the rusty pitohui is a gregarious bird which lives in pairs or small parties. It moves slowly through the low levels of the forest, feeding on insects and fruit and often uttering soft calls. Male and female birds look alike, with mainly brown and rufous plumage.

The deep, cup-shaped nest is built on a multiple-forked branch, several meters up in a tree. It is made of twigs, pieces of vine and fiber and is lined with dead leaves, with a further lining of fine plant material. The female lays 1 egg.

NAME: Gray Shrike-thrush, *Colluricincla harmonica*
RANGE: Australia, Tasmania, islands in Bass Strait, S.E. New Guinea
HABITAT: forest, woodland, grassland, suburban parks
SIZE: 23 cm (9 in)

The gray shrike-thrush is a widespread species, common in Australia but found only in a restricted area in New Guinea. A solitary bird, it feeds in undergrowth and among lower branches of trees, as well as on the ground. Unusually for a flycatcher, it eats other small invertebrates, as well as insects. It sings beautifully, with clear, musical notes. The female differs slightly from the male in plumage, having a touch of brown on the upperparts, less distinct white facial markings and streaks on the breast.

The bowl-shaped nest is built on the ground, in a tree or bush or on a rock ledge and is made of bark strips and grass. Alternatively, the birds may take over an old nest of another species. The female lays 2 or 3 eggs, and there may be more than one brood.

NAME: Crested Shriketit, *Falcunculus frontatus*
RANGE: Australia (patchy distribution)
HABITAT: dry forest, woodland
SIZE: 17–19 cm (6¾–7½ in)

The crested shriketit has a rather unusual bill for a flycatcher: it is deep, laterally compressed and slightly hooked. The bird often clings to tree trunks and uses its bill to strip off bark in its search for insects and larvae. It also forages among foliage for insects and is beneficial to mankind in that it eats many larvae of the codlin moths that attack orchards.

The deep, cup-shaped nest is built in a fork of a tree, such as a eucalyptus sapling, and the male often clears the area around it by breaking twigs above the nest. The female lays 2 or 3 eggs.

Crested Shriketit

subspecies showing plumage variations

Golden Whistler
(male)

Gray Shrike-thrush
(male)

Rufous Fantail

Yellow-bellied Fantail (male)

Willie Wagtail

Rusty Pitohui

Penduline Tits, Titmice

AEGITHALIDAE: Long-tailed Titmouse Family

The 8 species of long-tailed titmouse are closely related to the true tits, Paridae, and occur in Europe, Asia and North and Central America. They are small birds, with tails often as long or longer than their bodies and tiny bills.

NAME: **Long-tailed Tit,** *Aegithalos caudatus*
RANGE: **Europe (not N. Scandinavia or Iceland); Asia to Japan**
HABITAT: **woodland, scrub, bushy heaths, hedgerows, parks**
SIZE: **14 cm (5½ in)**

The plumage of the tiny long-tailed tit varies over its wide range but is usually a mixture of black, white and pink feathers. Male and female look alike. A restless, active bird, it feeds in trees and undergrowth on insects and their larvae and on spiders, seeds and buds.

A long, oval nest, with a side entrance near the top, is made in a tree, thorny bush or other vegetation. Both parents help with the construction of this fine nest, using moss bound together with spider's webs and covered with lichen. The 8 to 12 eggs are incubated mostly by the female, but the male may help and does take a share in feeding the young.

REMIZIDAE: Penduline Tit Family

The 10 species of penduline tit are related to the other 2 tit families, even though sometimes classified far from them; they differ from those birds in possessing finely pointed beaks. Most live in Africa or Asia, but there is 1 species each in Europe and North America. They tend to inhabit more open country than the other tit families, which favor woodland. Male and female generally look alike.

NAME: **Yellow Penduline Tit,** *Anthoscopus parvulus*
RANGE: **Africa: Lake Chad to S. Sudan**
HABITAT: **dry savanna and acacia woodland**
SIZE: **7.5 cm (3 in)**

A rare, little-known species, the yellow penduline tit is an active, yet quiet, bird. It feeds on caterpillars and on other insects and larvae, which it finds by carefully foraging over foliage and large flowers.

The elaborate nest is suspended from a branch and takes some time to build. It is made of felted plant matter and has a short, tubelike opening near the top that is self-closing. The female usually lays 4 eggs.

NAME: **Verdin,** *Auriparus flaviceps*
RANGE: **S.W. USA: S.E. California to S. Texas; central Mexico**
HABITAT: **desert**
SIZE: **10–11 cm (4–4¼ in)**

The tiny verdin has a distinctive yellow head and throat and a chestnut patch at the bend of the wing, conspicuous only when the wings are open. The female's yellow plumage is slightly duller than the male's, and juveniles lack both yellow and chestnut plumage. It lives in the thorny bushes and cactus plants of its arid habitat and behaves like its relatives the tits and chickadees as it flits about, searching for insects and their eggs and larvae. Some berries and fruit are also eaten for moisture.

The globular nest is made of thorny twigs, lined with softer material such as feathers and leaves, and has a tiny entrance in the side. It is suspended from the prickliest branches or a crotch of a tree or cactus and gains some protection from predators both from its surroundings and the outward-facing thorns of the nest itself. The female lays 3 to 6 eggs, which are thought to be incubated for 10 days.

PARIDAE: Titmouse Family

The familiar titmice are small, stocky songbirds, found throughout the northern hemisphere and Africa, usually in wooded areas. There are 47 species. Many titmice have adapted well to living alongside human habitation and have learned to take full advantage of any extra food supplied by man. Their normal diet is insects and seeds. Active birds, tits are constantly on the move, flitting around the trees in search of food. Male and female may look alike or differ slightly in plumage.

NAME: **Black-capped Chickadee,** *Parus atricapillus*
RANGE: **Alaska, Canada, south to central USA**
HABITAT: **coniferous forest, woodland**
SIZE: **12–15 cm (4¾–6 in)**

Identified by its "chickadee-dee-dee" call, the black-capped chickadee has a black throat and cap and a white face. It is always on the move and hops nimbly over twigs and branches, searching for caterpillars and other insect larvae, spiders, snails, seeds and berries.

Both partners of a pair help to excavate the nest cavity in a soft, rotting stump or branch, and the female lines the nest with plant fibers, moss or feathers. Sometimes chickadees nest in an abandoned woodpecker hole or even in a nesting box. The 5 to 10 eggs are incubated for 11 to 13 days.

NAME: **Sultan Tit,** *Melanochlora sultanea*
RANGE: **Himalayas, mountains of S. China and S.E. Asia; Sumatra**
HABITAT: **forest on foothills, trees near cultivated land**
SIZE: **20 cm (7¾ in)**

A striking, showy bird, the sultan tit is large for its family and has a distinctive yellow crest. Male and female look similar, but the female has olive, not black, plumage on the throat and an olive tinge to her back plumage. In behavior, however, the sultan tit is typical of its family: in pairs or small parties it searches for insects, seeds and berries in foliage, often hanging upside down to peer into crevices or under leaves.

The female bird lays 6 or 7 eggs on a thick pad of moss and plant material, placed in a hole in a tree.

NAME: **Red-throated Tit,** *Parus fringillinus*
RANGE: **Africa: S. Kenya, Tanzania**
HABITAT: **savanna with scattered trees**
SIZE: **11.5 cm (4½ in)**

The red-throated tit lives in pairs or small family groups, foraging on vegetation for insects and larvae. Typical of its family in its habits, it is an agile, lively little bird.

The female lays her 3 eggs in a cavity in a tree, which is lined with down and plant fibers.

NAME: **Great Tit,** *Parus major*
RANGE: **Europe, N.W. Africa, Asia (except N.), S.E. Asia, Indonesia**
HABITAT: **forest, woodland, cultivated land, parks, gardens**
SIZE: **14 cm (5½ in)**

Many forms of great tit, with varying plumage, occur over its vast range, but typically, this tit has blue and yellow plumage, with a black cap and a black stripe down the middle of the chest; this stripe is broader on the belly of the male than of the female. A noisy, sometimes rather dominant and aggressive bird, the great tit lives in large family groups after the breeding season and may also join mixed flocks. It feeds in trees and on the ground, eating insects, spiders, worms and small mollusks, as well as seeds, fruit, nuts and buds. It will use its strong bill to hammer at nuts.

The male courts and chases the female before mating. Both partners help to make a nest of moss and grass in a hole in a tree or wall, or in a nest box or other object, and line it with hair or down. The 5 to 11 eggs are incubated by the female for 13 to 14, rarely 12 to 16, days, and the male helps her to feed the young. There are sometimes two broods in a season.

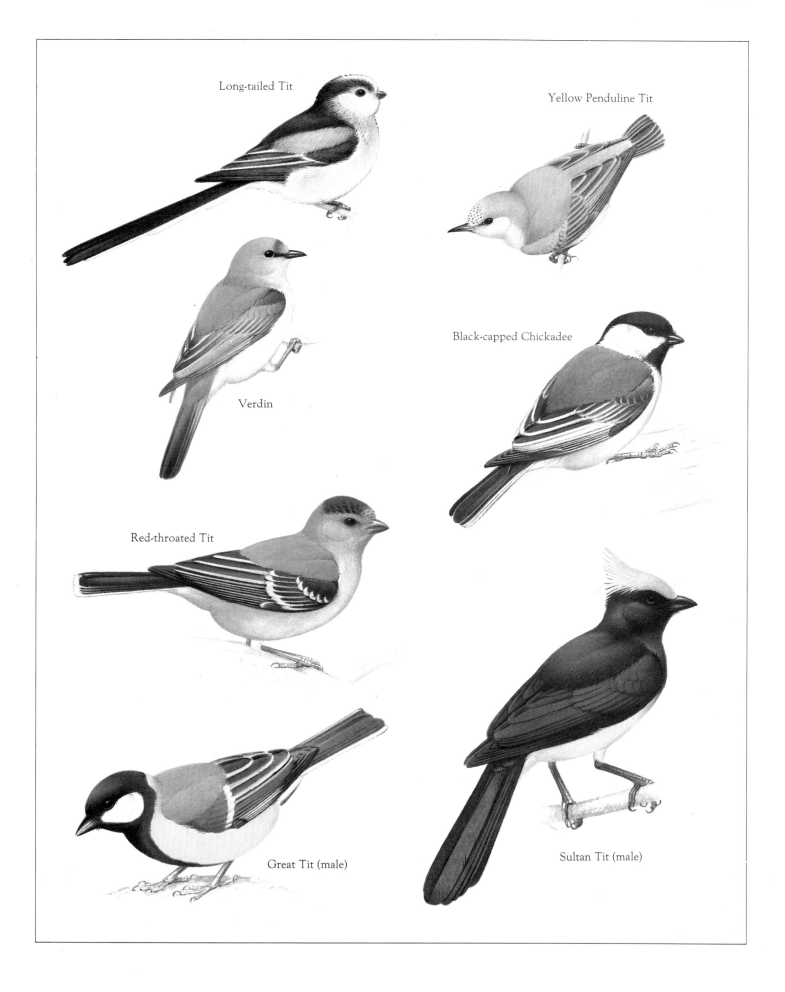

Long-tailed Tit

Yellow Penduline Tit

Verdin

Black-capped Chickadee

Red-throated Tit

Great Tit (male)

Sultan Tit (male)

Treecreepers, Philippine Creepers, Nuthatches

CERTHIIDAE: Treecreeper Family

The 6 species of treecreeper occur throughout the northern hemisphere in North and Central America, Europe, North Africa and Asia; and 1 species, the spotted creeper, lives in Africa, south of the Sahara. This bird is sometimes placed in its own separate family. Treecreepers are arboreal birds which clamber up tree trunks searching for insects to eat. They have sharp claws, enabling them to cling to bark, and long, thin bills, used for probing insect holes. All but the spotted creeper have stiff tails, which help to support them as they climb. Male and female look alike or nearly so.

NAME: **Brown Creeper, *Certhia familiaris***
RANGE: **Canada, USA, Mexico, Central America; Europe and Asia, from Britain to Japan, south to the Himalayas**
HABITAT: **forest, parks**
SIZE: **13–15 cm (5–6 in)**

Using its stiff tail feathers as a prop, the brown creeper slowly makes its way up a tree trunk in a spiral path, searching every crevice in the bark for insects. When it reaches the top of one tree, it flies off to another and begins again at the base of that trunk. It also feeds on nuts and seeds. Male and female look alike, and both have long claws and slender, curved bills.

The nest is usually made behind a piece of loose bark and lined with moss and feathers. The female incubates the 5 or 6 eggs for 14 or 15 days, sometimes assisted by the male.

NAME: **Spotted Creeper, *Salpornis spilonotus***
RANGE: **Africa: irregular distribution south of the Sahara to Angola and Zimbabwe; N. India**
HABITAT: **forest, savanna, woodland**
SIZE: **15 cm (6 in)**

The spotted creeper differs from other treecreepers in its soft tail, which it holds away from the tree trunk as it clambers up, searching for insects. With its long, curved bill, it probes every crevice in the bark for insects.

The cup-shaped nest is made in a vertically forked branch. Both parents incubate the 2 or 3 eggs.

RHABDORNITHIDAE: Philippine Creeper Family

Both species in this small family live in the Philippines. Male and female look unalike.

NAME: **Stripe-headed Creeper, *Rhabdornis mysticalis***
RANGE: **Philippines**
HABITAT: **forest**
SIZE: **15 cm (6 in)**

The stripe-headed creeper has strong legs and feet, well suited to climbing tree trunks, and a long, slightly curved bill with which it probes the bark for insects. It feeds in the same manner as the treecreepers, gradually working its way up a tree. It also licks up nectar from flowers with its brush-tipped tongue and feeds on fruit. The female has lighter plumage than the male and is brown where he is black.

Little is known of the breeding habits of this bird other than that it makes its nest in a hole in a tree.

CLIMACTERIDAE: Australian Treecreeper Family

The 6 species of Australian treecreeper resemble the treecreepers of the family Certhiidae in their appearance and habits. With the aid of their long, curved bills, they feed primarily on bark-dwelling insects, but some species also feed on the ground. They occur in New Guinea as well as Australia. Male and female differ slightly in plumage.

NAME: **Brown Treecreeper, *Climacteris picumnus***
RANGE: **Australia: Queensland to Victoria**
HABITAT: **forest, woodland**
SIZE: **15 cm (6 in)**

The brown treecreeper feeds largely on insects, which it picks from crevices in the bark of a tree trunk as it climbs upward in a spiral path. It makes short, fluttering flights from tree to tree and occasionally feeds on the ground. Male and female look more or less alike, but the female has a chestnut, not black, patch on the throat.

A cup-shaped nest is built in a hole, low down on a tree or in a rotting stump or post, and the female lays 3 or 4 eggs.

SITTIDAE: Nuthatch Family

There are about 25 species in this family, which includes the nuthatches and the wallcreeper, found in North America, Europe and Asia, and the 3 species of sitella, all of which occur in Australasia. They are all robust little birds, with strong legs and feet and sharp claws to help them climb. Their strong, pointed bills are ideal for probing crevices in bark or rocks for insects. Male and female look alike in many species but differ slightly in others.

NAME: **Red-breasted Nuthatch, *Sitta canadensis***
RANGE: **Alaska, Canada, USA**
HABITAT: **coniferous or mixed woodland**
SIZE: **11–12 cm ($4\frac{1}{4}$–$4\frac{3}{4}$ in)**

The male red-breasted nuthatch is identified by his white-edged black cap, black eye stripe and rusty-colored breast. The female has a dark-gray cap. The birds move rapidly over tree trunks and branches, searching for seeds and insects, and deftly investigate pinecones with their bills and extract any food items. Very large insects may even be wedged into bark crevices so that the nuthatches can bite off pieces. They also pursue insects in the air and collect seeds on the ground.

The breeding season begins in April or May. The nest is made in a tree hole, or a cavity is excavated in the stump or branch of a dead tree. Resin from coniferous trees is smeared around the entrance. Both parents incubate the 4 to 7 eggs for about 12 days.

NAME: **Varied Sitella, *Neositta chrysoptera***
RANGE: **Australia**
HABITAT: **open forest, woodland**
SIZE: **10–12 cm (4–$4\frac{3}{4}$ in)**

An agile little bird, the varied sitella runs up or down tree trunks with equal ease. Most of its life is spent in the trees, and it flits from place to place, probing crevices in the bark for insects. It is a gregarious bird and usually moves in small groups. There are many forms, all now included in this one species, which differ greatly in coloration.

The cup-shaped nest is made on a forked branch and camouflaged with pieces of bark. Both parents incubate the 3 or 4 eggs and feed the young.

NAME: **Wallcreeper, *Tichodroma muraria***
RANGE: **central and S. Europe, across Asia to Mongolia and W. China**
HABITAT: **mountain cliffs**
SIZE: **16.5 cm ($6\frac{1}{2}$ in)**

An unusual bird with similiarities to both nuthatches and treecreepers, the wallcreeper is sometimes placed in its own monotypic family. It has a long, curved bill and broad, rounded wings with distinctive red patches. In its search for insects to feed on, it climbs up cliff faces, investigating every crevice, and then flits down to the bottom and starts again on another section of rock. It also forages on the ground under stones but is rarely seen on trees.

The male courts the female with display flights, which show off his wing colors. He helps the female build a nest of moss, grass and rootlets in a rock crevice. The female incubates the 3 to 5 eggs, and both parents feed the young.

Red-breasted Nuthatch

Varied Sitella

Brown
Creeper

Wallcreeper

Spotted Creeper

Stripe-headed Creeper

Brown Treecreeper

Flowerpeckers, White-eyes

DICAEIDAE: Flowerpecker Family

The 58 species of flowerpecker live in Asia, from India to China, and south to Australasia. The greatest diversity of species occurs in the New Guinea area and the Philippines. Flowerpeckers are small birds with short legs and tails. Their bills vary in shape but are partially serrated, which perhaps helps them deal with sticky fruit. The tongue is forked, with the edges rolled into almost complete tubes, an adaptation probably linked to nectar-feeding. Fruit and berries are the flowerpeckers' most important foods, but the birds are often seen on flowers and do take some nectar as well as insects.

Some flowerpeckers have rather drab plumage, and in these species the sexes are similar. In others, however, the males are brightly colored. The 7 species of pardalote, which may not actually belong to this family, have bold, spotted plumage.

NAME: **Crimson-breasted Flowerpecker,** *Prionochilus percussus*
RANGE: **Burma, Malaysia, Borneo, Java, Sumatra and adjacent small islands**
HABITAT: **forest, secondary growth**
SIZE: **10 cm (4 in)**

A red patch on the breast and one on the crown are characteristics of the male of this species, which also has a bright yellow belly and blue upperparts. The female is mainly olive-green, with some grayish plumage and an indistinct orange patch on the crown. An active little bird, the crimson-breasted flowerpecker flies with quick, darting movements and feeds high in the trees, mostly on berries.

The purse-shaped nest is suspended from a branch of a tree and is made of pieces of tree fern. Little is known of the laying habits of this species, but it is thought to produce 1 egg.

NAME: **Black Berrypecker,** *Melanocharis nigra*
RANGE: **New Guinea, Japen and other associated islands, including Aru Islands**
HABITAT: **lowland forest**
SIZE: **11.5 cm (4½ in)**

An agile, quick-moving bird, the black berrypecker usually feeds in the lower levels of the forest, eating mainly berries and fruits but also spiders and insects; it will occasionally drink nectar. It may fly to an isolated tree outside the forest to feed. Although usually solitary, black berrypeckers do sometimes congregate at feeding trees. Male and female differ in appearance: the male is all black or black and green, while the female is dull green and gray.

NAME: **Mistletoe Bird,** *Dicaeum hirundinaceum*
RANGE: **Australia, Aru Islands**
HABITAT: **forest, scrub**
SIZE: **10 cm (4 in)**

The handsome male mistletoe bird has shiny, blue-black, red and white plumage, while the female is a duller brownish-gray. A tree-dwelling species, the mistletoe bird forages high in the trees for berries, particularly those of the mistletoe; the young also feed on insects. The soft part of the berry passes to the stomach, while the hard seeds bypass the specialized digestive system and are quickly expelled. Thus the bird is of great aid to the plant in dispersing its seeds. A solitary bird, this flowerpecker wanders wherever it can find mistletoe in fruit.

The female makes a nest in the shape of an inverted cone, which hangs from a branch of a tree. She lays 3 eggs and incubates them for about 12 days. Both parents feed the young.

NAME: **Spotted Pardalote,** *Pardalotus punctatus*
RANGE: **Australia, Tasmania**
HABITAT: **forest, woodland**
SIZE: **9 cm (3½ in)**

The colorful spotted pardalote has characteristic spots on its plumage that are mostly white in the male and yellow in the female. It feeds on insects, which it finds on the ground and in trees; an agile climber, it clings to twigs in almost any position as it makes a thorough search of the foliage. Outside the breeding season, these pardalotes live alone or in small flocks, sometimes including other species.

A breeding pair excavates a tunnel in a bank or slope and makes a globular nest of bark and grass in a chamber at the end of it. There are usually 4 eggs, incubated by both parents for 14 to 16 days.

ZOSTEROPIDAE: White-eye Family

The 80 or so species of white-eye are a remarkably uniform group of birds. Most are small, with rounded wings and short legs, and have a greenish back, yellow underparts and characteristic rings of white feathers around the eyes. There are some exceptions which are larger in size and duller in plumage. The center of their distribution is Indonesia, but white-eyes also extend into Africa, New Zealand, Japan and the islands of the Pacific. They tend to live in wooded country and gardens, rather than forest, and they feed on insects, fruit and nectar. Male and female look alike.

NAME: **Japanese White-eye,** *Zosterops japonica*
RANGE: **Japan, E. and S. China, Taiwan, Hainan, Philippines; S.E. Asia; Burma, Thailand, Laos**
HABITAT: **woodland, scrub**
SIZE: **11.5 cm (4½ in)**

The Japanese white-eye has some gray plumage on the lower part of its belly; its beak is slender and pointed. A small, active bird, it forages in flocks over trees and bushes, searching for insects, particularly ants, and their eggs and larvae; it also feeds on buds, seeds and fruit. It flits from tree to tree, constantly making its faint, plaintive call, and never comes to the ground.

A cup-shaped nest is made of grass stems and fiber, lined with moss, and is placed in the fork of a thin branch. The female lays 3 or 4 eggs.

NAME: **Gray-breasted White-eye (Silver-eye),** *Zosterops lateralis*
RANGE: **E. and S.E. Australia, Tasmania, New Zealand, Vanuatu, Fiji**
HABITAT: **varied, with trees**
SIZE: **12 cm (4¾ in)**

An adaptable bird, the gray-breasted white-eye tolerates almost any habitat at any altitude, particularly on the islands in its range. It forages at any level of trees, on agricultural land or in gardens, feeding on fruit, insects and nectar from flowers. It occasionally comes to the ground to feed and even into open country. Male and female look alike, both with sharply pointed and slightly curved bills.

The nest is made of plant fiber and grasses, bound together with cobwebs, and is attached to twigs of a tree or bush by its rim. The female lays 2 to 4 eggs, which are incubated by both parents for about 11 days.

NAME: **Príncipe Island Speirops,** *Speirops leucophoea*
RANGE: **Príncipe Island (Gulf of Guinea)**
HABITAT: **forest**
SIZE: **13.5 cm (5¼ in)**

One of the few African species of white-eye, this speirops has largely buff-gray plumage, with some white on throat and belly. In small parties, these restless, active little birds feed in the trees, searching the foliage for insects and also consuming seeds. Their movements are quick and agile, with much flicking of the wings.

The nest is made of grass and bound to a branch with cobwebs or fine plant fiber. The female lays 2 eggs.

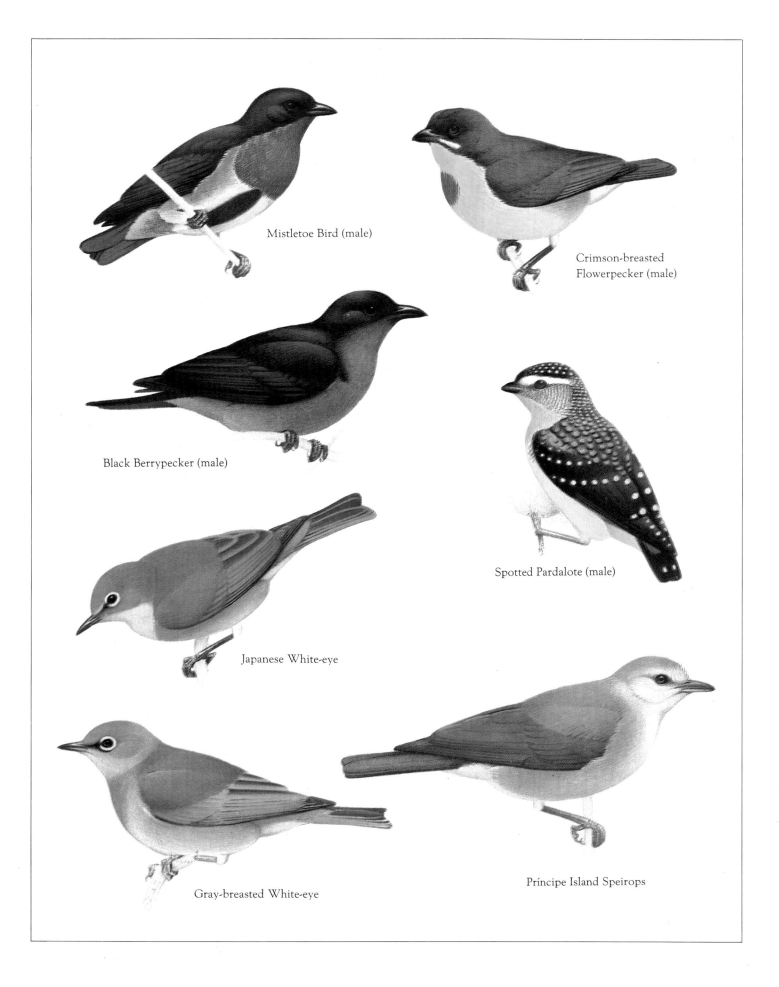

Mistletoe Bird (male)

Crimson-breasted
Flowerpecker (male)

Black Berrypecker (male)

Spotted Pardalote (male)

Japanese White-eye

Gray-breasted White-eye

Príncipe Island Speirops

Sunbirds

NAME: Crimson/Yellow-backed Sunbird,
Aethopyga siparaja
RANGE: India, S.E. Asia, Sumatra, Java,
Borneo, Sulawesi, Philippines
HABITAT: forest, cultivated land
SIZE: 11 cm (4¼ in)

The elongate central feathers of the male's metallic green tail add another few centimeters to his length. The female lacks his bright crimson plumage and is olive-green, with yellowish underparts. These sunbirds forage among flowers of trees, shrubs and garden plants, clinging to the stems and twigs while they suck nectar from the blooms. A few insects and spiders are also eaten.

A pear-shaped nest, made of plant down, rootlets, moss and grass, is suspended from a branch or twig. The female lays 2 or 3 eggs.

NAME: Ruby-cheeked Sunbird,
Anthreptes singalensis
RANGE: E. Himalayas to Burma,
Thailand, Malaysia, Sumatra, Java,
Borneo and adjacent islands
HABITAT: open forest, scrub
SIZE: 11.5 cm (4½ in)

Both male and female ruby-cheeked sunbirds have pale orange throats and yellow bellies, but the female is otherwise less brilliantly colored than the male, with largely olive-green plumage. These sunbirds flit quickly around the foliage, searching for insects and probing blossoms for nectar.

The pear-shaped nest is suspended in a bush from twigs not far from the ground. It is made of fine plant fiber and stalks and has a side entrance, sheltered by an overhanging porch. The female lays 2 eggs.

NAME: Long-billed Spiderhunter,
Arachnothera robusta
RANGE: Thailand, Malaysia, Sumatra,
Java, Borneo
HABITAT: forest
SIZE: 19–21.5 cm (7½–8½ in)

The long-billed spiderhunter is a large sunbird, with an extremely long, thick bill. Like all spiderhunters, it has duller plumage than other sunbirds; male and female look similar, but the male has small orange-yellow tufts at each side of his breast. This spiderhunter usually forages at the tops of tall trees, darting from one to another in search of insects and spiders or perching on high branches. Its flight is strong and direct.

The nest is made under a large leaf, such as a banana leaf, which forms the top of the nest. This structure of coarse plant fiber is attached to the leaf by threads of fiber, passed through the leaf and twisted into knots on its upper surface. An entrance is left near the tip of the leaf. The female lays 2 eggs.

NECTARINIIDAE: Sunbird Family

With their brilliantly colorful, glossy, iridescent feathers, fluttering, rapid flight and sharp, metallic calls, the sunbirds are distinctive and conspicuous. In ecological terms, sunbirds are the Old World counterparts of the hummingbirds of the Americas, but they are less skillful in flight and far more uniform in their appearance.

There are 116 species of sunbird. More than half of these live in Africa, south of the Sahara, but others occur in southern Asia and Australasia. In all species (except for the group known as spiderhunters, which are all soberly colored) males have much more showy plumage than their mates, although some females, too, have patches of iridescence. The female bird generally incubates the eggs for a period of 13 or 14 days and cares for the young; in some species the male may help to find food. The typical sunbird has short, rounded wings, strong legs and feet and a long, downward-curving bill. Using their specialized bills, almost all forms feed on nectar and also on insects. The beak is inserted into the flower, and the sugary liquid is sucked out through the tubular, split-tipped tongue. If it cannot reach the nectar, the sunbird will pierce the flower base to obtain it. Unlike the hummingbirds, sunbirds can hover only briefly, so they use their sturdy legs and feet to perch while they feed.

NAME: Olive-backed Sunbird, *Nectarinia*
jugularis
RANGE: Hainan, S.E. Asia, Indonesia,
New Guinea, Bismarck Archipelago,
Solomon Islands; Australia:
N.E. Queensland
HABITAT: forest, scrub, mangrove
swamps, gardens
SIZE: 12 cm (4¾ in)

The only sunbird found in Australia, this species is common throughout its range. Darting from tree to tree, it searches flowers for insects and nectar, sometimes also catching insects in the air. It will hover briefly before a flower but normally clings to the foliage. Male and female differ in appearance, the female having a bright yellow throat and underparts but the same olive back as the male. Nonbreeding males sometimes look similar to females but have a blue-black band down the center of the throat and an orange tinge to the throat and upper breast.

The nest is made of plant fibers and bark, bound with cobwebs and suspended from a twig of a bush or low tree. The female lays 2 or 3 eggs.

NAME: Purple-throated Sunbird,
Nectarinia sperata
RANGE: Assam, Bangladesh, Burma,
Thailand, Laos, Malaysia, Sumatra,
Java, Borneo, Sulawesi, Philippines
HABITAT: scrub, second growth forest,
mangrove swamps, gardens
SIZE: 10 cm (4 in)

The colorful male purple-throated sunbird is distinguished by his glittering amethyst throat. The female has olive upperparts and a yellow belly. This sunbird does eat small insects, but its main food is nectar, which it extracts from flowers with its slender, curved bill. It hops and climbs with ease around trees and bushes, but its flight is weak.

An oval nest, made of plant fiber and rootlets bound with spider's webs, is suspended from a branch or palm frond up to 6 m (20 ft) above ground. The female lays 2 eggs.

NAME: Scarlet-tufted Malachite Sunbird,
Nectarinia johnstoni
RANGE: Africa: mountain ranges in
E. Zaire, W. Uganda, Kenya,
Tanzania, Malawi, Zambia
HABITAT: alpine zone of mountains up to
the limits of plant growth
SIZE: male: 25.5–30.5 cm (10–12 in)
female: 14–15 cm (5½–6 in)

The elongate central tail feathers of the male of this species account for much of the difference in length between the sexes. In nonbreeding plumage the male's gleaming, metallic feathers are dark brown, but the long tail feathers are retained. The female is dark brown but, like the male, has red tufts at each side of the breast. This sunbird is attracted to the flowers of the protea bushes and giant lobelias found in its alpine habitat. Its main food, however, is insects, particularly flies, which it often catches on the wing.

Its oval nest is made in a low shrub from plant down, dried stems and rootlets. The female lays 1 or 2 eggs.

NAME: Superb Sunbird, *Nectarinia*
superba
RANGE: Africa: Sierra Leone to Angola,
Uganda
HABITAT: forest edge, clearings
SIZE: 14 cm (5½ in)

The superb sunbird forages in the forest canopy for insects and also sucks nectar from flowers. It is partial to the flowers of erythrina trees, which occur near forest, and also to the flowers of forest creepers. The male bird has multicolored plumage, some of it with a metallic sheen, while the female is olive-green with greenish-yellow underparts.

An untidy nest is made of grass, leaves and lichen and suspended from a branch. The female lays 1 or 2 eggs.

Scarlet-tufted Malachite Sunbird
(male)

Crimson Sunbird
(male)

Purple-throated Sunbird
(male)

Ruby-cheeked Sunbird
(male)

Long-billed Spiderhunter
(male)

Superb Sunbird
(male)

Olive-backed Sunbird
(male)

Honey Eaters

NAME: **Kauai O-o**, *Moho braccatus*
RANGE: **Hawaiian Islands: Kauai**
HABITAT: **montane rain forest**
SIZE: **19–21.5 cm (7½–8½ in)**   Ⓔ

Thought to be extinct, like the other 3 species of Hawaiian o-o, the Kauai species was rediscovered in 1960 in the Alakai Swamp. Its relatives were taken in large numbers for their colorful yellow feathers and eventually wiped out, but the more sober coloration of this species saved it from exploitation. It has, however, suffered from the introduction of avian competitors and predators and seems to be intolerant of any alteration in its rain forest habitat. Thus changes, such as the introduction of herbivores and exotic plants, pose a serious threat to the bird's survival. The present population is protected but very small, perhaps only a few birds.

The Kauai o-o feeds on nectar, berries, spiders, insects and snails. It makes its nest in a cavity in an ohia tree and lays 2 eggs on a bed of dead plant material. Both parents feed the young.

NAME: **Brown Honey Eater**, *Lichmera indistincta*
RANGE: **Australia, New Guinea, Aru Islands, Lesser Sunda Islands to Bali**
HABITAT: **forest, woodland, mangrove swamps, cultivated land, gardens**
SIZE: **12–15 cm (4¾–6 in)**

A restless, active bird, the brown honey eater feeds among flowering trees and bushes on nectar and insects; it also catches insects on the wing. It lives alone, in small groups or in larger flocks and is always found near water. It has one of the most beautiful voices of all Australian songbirds

The nest is cup shaped and made of tightly packed bark shreds and grass, bound with cobwebs. It is suspended from a twig or placed among the foliage of a bush or tree. The female lays 2 eggs.

NAME: **Strong-billed Honey Eater**, *Melithreptus validirostris*
RANGE: **Tasmania, islands in Bass Strait**
HABITAT: **open forest, woodland**
SIZE: **14 cm (5½ in)**

Popularly known as the bark-bird, this honey eater has the unusual habit of hopping about on tree trunks, stripping off the bark in its eager search for insects. It is often seen on eucalyptus trees, some of which have loose bark. Nectar, so important to most of the honey eaters, forms only a small part of this bird's diet, and it is rarely seen among tree blossoms. Male and female look alike.

The nest is suspended from a drooping branch and is made of bark strips and grass. The female lays 2, or sometimes 3, eggs.

MELIPHAGIDAE:
Honey Eater Family

With a few exceptions, the 167 species of honey eater occur in the Australian and southwest Pacific regions; 1 species, *Lichmera indistincta*, occurs in Bali. There are, however, 2 species of sugarbird which occur in Africa; both are in the genus *Promerops*. These birds are included with the honey eaters or sometimes classified in their own family. There is some argument as to whether they are a related, but separate group of birds or a part of the main honey eater stock that became isolated millions of years ago.

As their name indirectly suggests, the honey eaters consume nectar from flowers in a manner similar to sunbirds. They are usually larger than sunbirds, however, and most have duller, green or brownish plumage; they are also much more diverse, having adapted to a variety of habitats. Honey eaters have remarkable specializations for nectar-feeding. Despite the variation in body size and beak shape among honey eaters, all have a highly modified, long, protrusible tongue. At its base, this tongue can be curled up to form two long, nectar-transporting grooves; and at its tip, it splits into four parts, each of which is frilled, making the entire end of the tongue an absorbent brush for nectar collection. Honey eaters also eat insects, for protein, and fruit.

Generally tree-dwelling, honey eaters are gregarious birds, aggressive to other species. Male and female look alike in some species, unalike in others.

NAME: **Cardinal Honey Eater**, *Myzomela cardinalis*
RANGE: **Loyalty Islands, Vanuatu, Samoa, Torres and Santa Cruz Islands, Palau Islands, Mariana and Caroline Islands, Solomon Islands (marginally)**
HABITAT: **forest, open woodland, cultivated land**
SIZE: **9 cm (3½ in)**

The cardinal honey eater is one of the smallest honey eaters, and with its bright coloration, does resemble a sunbird. It forages for small insects and nectar and will often form large groups at favored feeding sites. Its flight is fast and direct. Male and female differ in appearance; the male has vivid red and black plumage, while the female is mainly olive-gray, with some red on her rump and lower back.

A small, cup-shaped nest, made of grass stems, is built on a forked branch. The female lays 1 or 2 eggs.

NAME: **Fuscous Honey Eater**, *Meliphaga fusca*
RANGE: **S.E. New Guinea, E. and N. Australia**
HABITAT: **open forest**
SIZE: **15 cm (6 in)**

The fuscous honey eater forages busily among the foliage at various heights, searching for nectar and insects. It also makes aerial dashes to catch insects on the wing. It is a fairly common bird and generally lives alone or in small parties. Male and female look alike, with olive-brown plumage enlivened by touches of yellow and dark markings on the cheeks.

The female lays 2 or 3 eggs in a cup-shaped nest, made of plant fiber and grass and suspended in a tree.

NAME: **Little Friarbird**, *Philemon citreogularis*
RANGE: **E. and N. Australia, S. New Guinea, islands in Banda Sea**
HABITAT: **open forest, woodland**
SIZE: **25–28 cm (9¾–11 in)**

Like all friarbirds, the little friarbird has an area of bare skin on its head, the origin of its common name. Male and female look similar and, despite the name "little," are not much smaller than any other friarbirds. The little friarbird forages in all kinds of trees and bushes for fruit, insects and nectar. It makes a variety of harsh cries, particularly when feeding in a squabbling flock, but also has a more attractive musical song. In the south of Australia, these birds are thought to make regular seasonal movements.

The cup-shaped nest is made of bark strips and plant fiber and is built on a forked branch or suspended from a branch, often overhanging water. The female lays 2 to 4 eggs.

NAME: **Long-bearded Honey Eater**, *Melidectes princeps*
RANGE: **New Guinea**
HABITAT: **mountain forest, alpine grassland**
SIZE: **26.5 cm (10½ in)**

Distinguished by the white "whiskers" on its throat, the long-bearded honey eater has largely black plumage, with some light-colored bare skin around the eyes. Less arboreal than other honey eaters, this bird spends much of its time on the ground, probing the leaf litter with its long, curved bill to find insects and sedge seeds. It also flies jerkily from tree to tree and will climb trees occasionally to feed on berries and fruit.

A bulky nest, made of moss and fungal threads, is built in a bush or tree a meter or so off the ground. The female lays 1 egg.

Brown Honey Eater

Cardinal
Honey Eater
(male)

Long-bearded Honey Eater

Fuscous
Honey Eater

Kauai O-o

Strong-billed
Honey Eater

Little Friarbird

Honey Eaters

NAME: **Common Melipotes,** *Melipotes fumigatus*
RANGE: **mountains of central New Guinea**
HABITAT: **forest at 1,300–2,700 m (4,300–9,000 ft)**
SIZE: **21.5 cm (8½ in)**

A quiet, slow-moving bird, the common melipotes moves about the trees in search of insects, particularly the sedentary, rather than the active varieties. It may, however, chase any flying insects that it disturbs. The common melipotes also feeds on fruit but is rarely seen on a flowering tree; its tongue has no brush-tip for nectar feeding. It lives alone or in pairs or sometimes gathers in flocks. Male and female look alike, with short bills and some bare, orange-yellow skin on the face.

The nest is a deep cup, made of mosses and plant fibers and lined with dead leaves and ferns. It is attached by its rim to the end of a branch. Like many mountain-dwelling honey eaters with sparse food supplies, this species lays only 1 egg. The young bird is fed with berries.

NAME: **Tui,** *Prosthemadera novaeseelandiae*
RANGE: **New Zealand and coastal islands; Kermadec, Chatham and Auckland Islands**
HABITAT: **forest, suburban areas**
SIZE: **29–32 cm (11½–12½ in)**

Also aptly known as the parson bird, the tui has a bib of white tufts at the throat and a ring of fine, lacy feathers which form a collar. The female tui has smaller throat tufts than the male and a paler belly. Juveniles develop throat tufts within a month of hatching and have full adult plumage by about 3 months.

Tuis are noisy, vigorous birds; they fly around in the trees at high speed, sometimes plummeting down from considerable heights. They feed on insects, fruit and, using their brushlike tongues, on nectar. Tuis are aggressive, defending their food and nests against intruders.

In the breeding season, male tuis make spectacular aerial dives, rolling and looping as they descend. The nest is usually made in the fork of a tree and is built with sticks and twigs and lined with fine plant material. The female incubates the 2 to 4 eggs for about 14 days. Throughout the incubation period, the male seems to sing almost continuously from a nearby tree but helps the female to feed the young once they hatch. There are often two broods a season.

NAME: **Red Wattlebird,** *Anthochaera carunculata*
RANGE: **Australia: New South Wales to Western Australia**
HABITAT: **open forest, woodland, suburban parks and gardens**
SIZE: **32–35 cm (12½–13¾ in) including tail of 16 cm (6¼ in)**

The aggressive, noisy red wattlebird is the largest honey eater in mainland Australia. It is very active in the trees, preferring banksia and eucalyptus, and feeds on nectar, fruit and insects. It lives alone or wanders in small parties; in the west of its range it makes regular north-south movements. Male and female look alike, both with fleshy red wattles behind the eyes.

The nest is made of sticks and twigs on a horizontal branch of a bush or tree; it is sometimes lined with grass. The female lays 2 or 3 eggs.

NAME: **Pygmy Honey Eater,** *Oedistoma pygmaeum*
RANGE: **New Guinea and adjacent islands**
HABITAT: **forest**
SIZE: **7.5 cm (3 in)**

One of the smallest of New Guinea birds, the pygmy honey eater bears little resemblance to other members of its family. The male has olive plumage with lighter underparts and an off-white throat; the female is slightly smaller and has duller plumage. Both sexes have short tails and curved bills. The pygmy honey eater frequents the lower levels of the forest but also forages in the tallest flowering trees. It feeds on nectar, insects and spiders.

NAME: **Noisy Miner,** *Manorina melanocephala*
RANGE: **Australia: Queensland to Victoria; Tasmania, islands in Bass Strait**
HABITAT: **woodland, suburban parks**
SIZE: **26–28 cm (10¼–11 in)**

The noisy miner spends much of its life in trees and bushes but will also forage on the ground; it feeds on insects, fruit and nectar. An active, inquisitive bird, it often harasses other birds and, in groups, will attack an owl or hawk. Noisy miners nearly always live in colonies, which forage, feed and roost together.

A cup-shaped nest, made of grass, twigs and pieces of bark, is built on a forked branch of a tree or sapling and lined with soft plant material, on which the female lays 2 to 4 eggs.

NAME: **Eastern Spinebill,** *Acanthorhynchus tenuirostris*
RANGE: **Australia: Queensland to Victoria; Tasmania, islands in Bass Strait**
HABITAT: **rain forest, scrub, cultivated land and gardens**
SIZE: **12–15 cm (4¾–6 in)**

The eastern spinebill is a restless, swift-flying bird which flits from tree to tree, searching for insects and nectar. It will often hover beside a flower while it probes the bloom with its spinelike bill and takes nectar. Primarily an arboreal bird, the eastern spinebill lives alone or in groups and seems to make regular seasonal movements. The female has duller plumage than the striking male.

The cup-shaped nest is built by the female, using grass, bark and moss. The nest is suspended from a thin forked twig in a bush or small tree. The female incubates the 2 or 3 eggs while the male guards the territory. Both parents feed the young, and they may produce two broods a season.

NAME: **Cape Sugarbird,** *Promerops cafer*
RANGE: **South Africa: Cape Province**
HABITAT: **mountain slopes where protea bushes grow**
SIZE: **male: 43 cm (17 in); female: 23–28 cm (9–11 in)**

The male Cape sugarbird's extremely long tail feathers account for the difference in size between the sexes. Male and female otherwise look similar in plumage. Cape sugarbirds are generally associated with protea bushes, where they forage for insects and take nectar from the flowers. They do, however, visit many other trees and bushes and take some insects in the air. Their flight is swift and direct, the tail held straight out behind. Outside the breeding season, sugarbirds are gregarious and live in small groups.

Breeding takes place in the winter months, particularly April to June. The male bird establishes a territory and perches on top of a protea bush to sing and warn off other males. He performs a courtship display for the female over the nesting site, twisting and turning the tail feathers, which are held curved over his back, and clapping his wings. The female bird builds a cup-shaped nest of twigs, grass and stems, lined with fine plant material and the down from protea leaves. The nest is positioned in the fork of a bush, usually protea. She incubates the 2 eggs for about 17 days and does most of the work of feeding the young on insects, spiders and nectar. The young are able to fly about 20 days after hatching but are tended by their parents for another 2 weeks. There are usually 2 broods a season.

Common Melipotes

Cape Sugarbird (male)

Red Wattlebird

Tui (male)

Pygmy Honey Eater (male)

Noisy Miner

Eastern Spinebill

Buntings

NAME: Reed Bunting, *Emberiza schoeniclus*
RANGE: Europe, N. Africa, central and N. Asia
HABITAT: reedbeds, swamps; in winter, farmland and open country
SIZE: 15 cm (6 in)

The male reed bunting is identified by his black head and throat and white collar, while the female has a brown and buff head, with prominent black and white mustache streaks. The reed bunting forages on low vegetation and reed stems and hops briskly on the ground while it searches for food such as the seeds of marsh plants, grasses and grain. In spring and summer, it also feeds on insects and larvae.

The female makes a nest on the ground or in low vegetation and lays 4 or 5 eggs. She does most of the 13- or 14-day incubation, but the male helps to feed the young.

NAME: Yellowhammer, *Emberiza citrinella*
RANGE: Europe, W. Asia to Urals
HABITAT: grassland, farmland, open country with bush and scrub
SIZE: 16 cm (6¼ in)

The yellowhammer feeds for the most part on the ground on seeds, grains, berries, leaves and some insects and invertebrates. The male bird is distinguished by his mainly yellow head and chestnut rump, while the female is duller, with less yellow plumage.

After a courtship chase and display, a nest is made on or near the ground, often in a hedge or under a bush. The female lays 3 or 4 eggs, which she incubates, mostly on her own, for 12 to 14 days. There may be two or three broods.

NAME: Song Sparrow, *Zonotrichia melodia*
RANGE: N. America: Aleutian Islands, east to Newfoundland, south through Canada and USA to Mexico
HABITAT: forest edge, scrub with nearby water, cultivated and suburban areas
SIZE: 13–18 cm (5–7 in)

An extremely widespread and familiar North American bird, the song sparrow occurs in more than 30 subspecies, which vary in appearance from the small sandy-colored scrub and desert birds to the larger, dark-plumaged northern varieties. The song sparrow feeds on insects, particularly in summer, but also eats wild fruit and berries and forages on the ground for seeds.

The male bird establishes a territory, and his mate builds a neat nest, concealed among vegetation on the ground or in a bush. She incubates her 3 to 6 eggs for 12 or 13 days. There may be two or three broods a season.

EMBERIZIDAE: Bunting Family

The taxonomic and evolutionary relationships between the buntings and their allies on the one hand and the finches (Fringillidae) on the other are complex and disputed by authorities on these birds. Here, the Emberizidae is taken to include the buntings, the plush-capped finch, cardinals and grosbeaks, the swallow-tanager and tanagers, all described as subfamilies.

EMBERIZINAE: Bunting Subfamily

Common names for the approximately 290 species of songbird in this subfamily are confusing. Species occur in both the Old and New Worlds, and while most of those in the Old World are called buntings, many of the North American forms are termed sparrows or finches, the name "bunting" being reserved for a number of species in the subfamily Cardinalinae.

There is little doubt that this group of birds originated in the Americas and has subsequently colonized many parts of the Old World. They are small to medium-sized songbirds, usually about 15 cm (6 in) in length, with somber brown or black plumage, occasionally enlivened with patches of yellow and orange-brown. Their beaks are short and conical, well suited for handling their seed-dominated diet. Males and females usually look unalike.

Included in the Emberizinae are the Darwin's finches, sometimes considered to be a separate subfamily.

NAME: Snow Bunting, *Plectrophenax nivalis*
RANGE: breeds in Iceland, Scandinavia, N. Scotland, Arctic and subarctic Asia, N. America; winters south of breeding range
HABITAT: open stony country, tundra, mountains; winters also on coasts and open country
SIZE: 16 cm (6¼ in)

In breeding plumage, the male snow bunting is almost pure white, except for his black back, central tail and primary wing feathers. In winter, his white plumage becomes mottled with rusty brown. The female has a gray-brown head and back in summer and is simply paler and duller in winter. The snow bunting spends much of its time feeding on seeds and insects on the ground, where it can run quickly and hop.

The nest is made from dead grass, moss and lichen and is concealed among stones. The female lays 4 to 6 eggs, which she incubates for 10 to 15 days. The male bird feeds his mate during the incubation period and helps to feed the young.

NAME: Dark-eyed Junco, *Junco hyemalis*
RANGE: N. America: Alaska, east to Newfoundland, south through Canada and USA to Mexico
HABITAT: clearings, woodland edge, roadsides, parks, gardens
SIZE: 13–16 cm (5–6¼ in)

There are 4 subspecies of this junco, with considerable variations in color; the subspecies illustrated here is *J. h. insularis*. Females of all races are less colorful than males. A lively little bird, this junco feeds largely on the ground, eating mainly seeds in the winter and seeds, berries, insects and spiders in summer.

The male establishes a breeding territory, and his mate builds a nest on the ground, near vegetation or tree roots or in the shelter of a bank or ledge. She lays 3 to 6 eggs and incubates them for 11 or 12 days. There are usually two broods. Northernmost populations migrate to southern USA in winter.

NAME: Savannah Sparrow, *Ammodramus sandwichensis*
RANGE: Alaska, Canada, much of USA (does not breed in S.E.), Mexico, Guatemala
HABITAT: tundra, open grassland, marshes
SIZE: 11–15 cm (4¼–6 in)

There are many subspecies of savannah sparrow, each differing slightly in coloration and song. Primarily a ground-feeder, the savannah sparrow hops about, while scratching and foraging, or runs, mouselike, through the grass; its main foods are seeds and insects such as beetles, grasshoppers and ants.

The female makes a grassy nest on the ground, usually in a natural hollow, and lays 4 or 5 eggs. Both parents take turns to incubate the eggs for about 12 days. Northern populations migrate south to winter in southern USA and Central America.

NAME: Chipping Sparrow, *Spizella passerina*
RANGE: Canada, USA, Mexico, Central America to Nicaragua
HABITAT: open woodland, clearings in forest, gardens, parks
SIZE: 13–15 cm (5–6 in)

Both sexes of chipping sparrow have distinctive chestnut caps, edged by white eyebrow stripes. They are inconspicuous little birds and often live in suburban and inhabited areas. Grass seeds are their main food, but they also eat weed seeds, insects and spiders.

The female bird makes a nest in a vine or on a branch of a bush or tree. She lays 3 to 5 eggs, and her mate feeds her while she incubates the eggs for 11 to 14 days. There may be two broods in a season.

Reed Bunting (male)

Dark-eyed Junco

Savannah Sparrow

Yellowhammer (male)

Snow Bunting (male)

Chipping Sparrow

Song Sparrow

Buntings

NAME: Patagonian Sierra-finch,
Phrygilus patagonicus
RANGE: South America: Chile, central
Argentina to Tierra del Fuego
HABITAT: heavily vegetated ravines
SIZE: 15–16 cm (6–6¼ in)

This highly specialized bunting prefers areas with plenty of seed-bearing bushes, and rocky outcrops smothered with vines. It feeds mainly on seeds, but also on some insects. The female differs slightly from the male in plumage, having mainly dark-olive upperparts and yellowish-green underparts.

The nest is concealed among tangled roots and detritus and is made of grass, lined with soft plant material. The female lays 2 to 4 eggs.

NAME: Variable Seedeater, *Sporophila*
americana
RANGE: Central and South America:
Mexico to Peru and Brazil
HABITAT: forest, grassland, parks,
gardens
SIZE: 11.5 cm (4½ in)

Small flocks of variable seedeaters often associate with other seedeater species as they hop about on grass stems and weeds or perch on bushes or small trees. With fast-beating wings, they also make short flights in the open. These birds feed on grass seeds and insects and also share the thick, fruiting catkins of *Cecropia* trees with many other birds. Males may vary in plumage but are generally black and white, while females are olive-brown, with some buffy-white on the lower belly.

The female makes a nest of rootlets and fibers, placed in a tree or bush and fastened to a branch with cobwebs. She usually lays 2 eggs, which she incubates for about 12 or 13 days. The male may occasionally feed her during this period, and both parents feed the young with regurgitated seeds. There are at least two broods a year.

NAME: White-naped Brush Finch,
Atlapetes albinucha
RANGE: Mexico, through Central
America to Colombia
HABITAT: forest edge, scrub
SIZE: 18 cm (7 in)

Male and female of this species look alike, both with distinctive black and white heads. Basically terrestrial birds, they flutter and hop about on the ground and up on to stems and low branches. They forage in the litter of the forest floor by flicking leaves aside with sweeps of the bill as they search for grass seeds and some insects.

A grassy nest is built by the female in a low bush. She usually lays 2 eggs.

NAME: Rufous-sided Towhee, *Pipilo*
erythrophthalmus
RANGE: S. Canada, USA, Mexico,
Guatemala
HABITAT: forest edge, woodland, parks,
gardens
SIZE: 18–22 cm (7–8½ in)

The male rufous-sided towhee is recognized by his mainly black and white plumage and the distinctive rufous patches on each side of the belly. The female has a similar plumage pattern but is brown where the male is black. Both sexes have red eyes. The birds scratch around on the ground and under vegetation for a wide variety of food, including insects, such as caterpillars, beetles and ants, snails, small lizards, snakes and salamanders, spiders, millipedes, seeds and berries.

The courting male chases the female and fans his tail to expose the white markings; he sings to her from a perch in a bush or tree. The female builds the nest on or close to the ground, using grass, rootlets, leaves, bark shreds and twigs. She lays 3 to 4 eggs, which she incubates for 12 or 13 days. The young leave the nest some 10 to 12 days after hatching, and there may be a second brood. Birds from the north of the range and mountainous areas migrate south in winter.

NAME: Grassland Yellow-finch, *Sicalis*
luteola
RANGE: S. Mexico, through Central and
South America to Argentina east of
Andes
HABITAT: grassland, open pasture, cliffs
SIZE: 11.5–14 cm (4½–5½ in)

Primarily a ground-dweller, the grassland yellow-finch hops about, rather than runs. Sometimes it perches on low branches of shrubs and trees, and it will also fly in the open. It feeds on the seeds of a variety of plants. In Chile and Argentina, it is the most numerous small bird, and in winter and spring, large flocks will gather and sing. The female has duller plumage than the male; her upperparts are tinged with brown, and her underparts are pale gray, washed with yellow.

The male courts the female with a display flight and song. She lays 3 to 5 eggs in a cup-shaped nest, concealed among grass or small plants. There are two, sometimes three, broods. Birds in the south of the range migrate north in winter.

NAME: Large Ground Finch, *Geospiza*
magnirostris
RANGE: Galápagos Islands
HABITAT: arid zones
SIZE: 16.5 cm (6½ in)

The large ground finch is one of the 14 species known as Darwin's finches, found only on the remote Galápagos and Cocos islands; they were a key factor in the formation of Darwin's theories. It is almost certain that all species are derived from a single finchlike form that colonized the islands less than a million years ago. As there are few passerine species in the Galápagos, there were plenty of vacant ecological niches for the birds to adapt to, hence the gradual separation into different species. Although most species are similar in plumage, they differ in their ways of life and feeding habits, and this is reflected in their varying bill shapes. Some have huge bills for cracking hard seeds; others have parrotlike bills, used for tearing soft plants; another, a slender bill for seizing insects.

The massive, powerful bill of the large ground finch is ideally suited to coping with its diet of hard seeds; this bird only rarely eats insects. Male and female differ in appearance, the male being largely black and the female gray.

The breeding habits of the large ground finch are similar to those of all Darwin's finches. The male establishes a territory and builds several dome-shaped nests. He displays to the female, and she selects a nest or helps to build another one. The male feeds the female during the period before she lays her 2 to 5 eggs and for about 12 days while she incubates them. Both parents feed the young birds until they leave the nest 13 or 14 days after hatching. There may be several broods, depending on food supplies.

NAME: Warbler Finch, *Certhidea olivacea*
RANGE: Galápagos Islands
HABITAT: humid to dry zones
SIZE: 10 cm (4 in)

The most agile and lively in flight of all the Darwin's finches, the warbler finch maneuvers well as it flits through the vegetation, searching for insects and spiders. Its bill is thin and pointed like that of a warbler, and its manner of picking its food from the foliage is distinctly warblerlike. Some males have orange throat patches, but otherwise males and females look alike.

The male bird selects a territory and builds several nests in bushes or low trees for the female to choose from. She lays 2 to 5 eggs, which she incubates for about 12 days.

Patagonian Sierra-finch (male)

White-naped Brush Finch

Grassland Yellow-finch (male)

Rufous-sided
Towhee (male)

Variable Seedeater (male)

Warbler Finch

Large Ground Finch (male)

Plush-capped Finch, Cardinals and Grosbeaks, Swallow-tanager

CATAMBLYRHYNCHINAE: Plush-capped Finch Subfamily

The single species of South American songbird in this family represents a puzzle for taxonomists. It is finchlike, but its relationships with other bird groups are obscure. Here it is treated as a distinct subfamily of the Emberizidae but in the opinion of some ornithologists, it should have its own family.

NAME: **Plush-capped Finch,** *Catamblyrhynchus diadema*
RANGE: Andes, from Venezuela to N.W. Argentina
HABITAT: cloud forest, forest edge, clearings
SIZE: 14 cm (5½ in)

A golden-yellow crest of short, erect feathers is the distinguishing feature of this bird. Male and female have similar plumage. Little is known of the plush-capped finch, which occurs in inaccessible mountain forest, but it appears to live alone or in pairs, foraging in low vegetation and on the ground for its insect food.

CARDINALINAE: Cardinal and Grosbeak Subfamily

The 39 species of cardinal and grosbeak occur in the New World, from Canada in the north to Argentina in the south. All are stocky birds with short, strong bills, which enable them to feed on very hard seeds. Males have brightly colored plumage, ranging from the fiery red of the cardinal to the bright blue of the blue grosbeak. Females have duller, plainer plumage.

NAME: **Rose-breasted Grosbeak,** *Pheucticus ludovicianus*
RANGE: S. Canada, central and E. USA, south to N. Georgia; winters from Mexico to northern South America
HABITAT: woodland, borders of swamps and streams, cultivated land
SIZE: 20.5 cm (8 in)

The male rose-breasted grosbeak is a handsome bird, easily identified by his black and white plumage and his red breast patch; the female has streaked brown and white plumage. This grosbeak forages in trees, searching for seeds, buds, blossoms and insects. It is particularly fond of beetles and is a popular bird with farmers because of its habit of feeding on the harmful potato beetles and their larvae.

The nest is made on a low branch of a small tree or bush, usually by the female. She lays 3 or 4 eggs, which are incubated by both parents for 12 or 13 days.

NAME: **(Northern) Cardinal,** *Cardinalis cardinalis*
RANGE: Canada: S. Ontario; E. USA: Great Lakes and New England, south to Gulf Coast, S. Texas and Arizona; Mexico, Guatemala
HABITAT: woodland edge, thickets, parks, gardens
SIZE: 20–23 cm (7¾–9 in)

The male cardinal is an unmistakable, brilliant red bird, while the female is buffy-brown, with a reddish tinge on wings and crest and a red bill. Cardinals are strongly territorial and aggressive birds and have a rich and varied repertoire of songs; both sexes are heard singing at all times of year. They feed on the ground and in trees on seeds and berries and, in the breeding season, also take insects.

The female builds the nest on a branch of a small tree or bush, usually among tangled foliage and vines. She incubates the 3 or 4 eggs for 12 or 13 days. Two or more broods may follow.

NAME: **Buff-throated Saltator,** *Saltator maximus*
RANGE: Mexico; Central and South America: Panama to Brazil
HABITAT: forest edge, tangled secondary growth, plantations
SIZE: 20.5 cm (8 in)

A long-tailed, thick-billed bird, the buff-throated saltator is identified by the black-bordered buff patch on its throat. Male and female look alike. They forage in pairs or small flocks in the treetops, feeding on berries and fruit such as the fruiting catkins of *Cecropia* trees.

The female builds a bulky nest in a tree or bush close to the ground. The male stays near her, singing and feeding her from time to time. She incubates the 2 eggs for 13 or 14 days, and both parents feed the young. There may be two or more broods.

NAME: **Painted Bunting,** *Passerina ciris*
RANGE: S. USA, Mexico; winters from Gulf states to Central America
HABITAT: woodland edge, thickets beside streams, gardens, roads
SIZE: 13–14 cm (5–5½ in)

An extremely colorful bird, the male painted bunting would look quite at home in a tropical forest; the female is bright yellowish-green. Painted buntings feed on a variety of grass seeds, and also on spiders and insects such as grasshoppers, caterpillars and flies. The male is strongly territorial and will battle fiercely with intruders.

The cup-shaped nest, made of grasses, stalks and leaves, is built in a bush, low tree or vine a meter or so above ground. The female incubates her 3 or 4 eggs for 11 or 12 days.

NAME: **Dickcissel,** *Spiza americana*
RANGE: USA: Great Lakes, south through Midwest to Gulf states; winters from Mexico to northern South America
HABITAT: grassland, grain and alfalfa fields
SIZE: 15–18 cm (6–7 in)

The common name of this little bird is derived from its constantly repeated call, which sounds like "dick-dick-cissel." The male is characterized by his heavy bill, yellow breast and black bib and chestnut wing patches. The female is sparrowlike, with streaky plumage, but has a yellowish breast and small chestnut wing patches. Dickcissels feed mainly on the ground on weed seeds, grain, spiders and insects such as crickets and grasshoppers.

The male establishes the nesting territory by calling from a conspicuous perch. The cup-shaped nest, made of weed stems, grasses and leaves, is built on the ground, often in the shelter of alfalfa or grain crops, or in a tree or bush. The female usually lays 4 eggs, which she incubates for 12 or 13 days. There are generally two broods a year.

TERSININAE: Swallow-tanager Subfamily

Like the plush-capped finch, the swallow-tanager is an enigmatic member of the assemblage of buntinglike birds. Found in South America, it is similar to the true tanagers, with which it is sometimes grouped, but differs from them in a number of respects. Male and female are unalike in plumage.

NAME: **Swallow-tanager,** *Tersina viridis*
RANGE: E. Panama to Bolivia, Paraguay, N.E. Argentina, S.E. Brazil
HABITAT: open forest, clearings, parks
SIZE: 14 cm (5½ in)

The swallow-tanager is a gregarious bird out of the breeding season and moves in pairs or small groups. It forages at all levels, from the ground to the highest branches of trees, feeding on fruit and catching insects on the wing. Both male and female are eye-catching birds, the male having mainly turquoise and black plumage, and the female bright green, with a brownish face and throat and touches of yellow on flanks and belly.

The male bird establishes and defends the breeding territory, and the female makes a cup-shaped nest in a hole in a wall or at the end of a burrow, which she digs in a bank. She lays 3 eggs, which she incubates for 14 to 17 days. In some parts of their range, swallow-tanagers breed in highland regions, descending to lowlands for the rest of the year.

Painted Bunting (male)

Cardinal (male)

Rose-breasted Grosbeak

Plush-capped Finch

Buff-throated Saltator

Dickcissel (male)

Swallow-tanager (male)

Tanagers

NAME: **Scarlet Tanager,** *Piranga olivacea*
RANGE: **extreme S.E. Canada, E. central
states of USA; winters in E. South
America**
HABITAT: **woodland, parks and gardens**
SIZE: **19 cm (7½ in)**

In his summer breeding plumage, the
male scarlet tanager is unmistakable,
with his gleaming red head and body
and black wings and tail; in winter, he is
similar to the female, with mainly olive-
green plumage, but retains his black
wings and tail. Despite his brilliance, the
scarlet tanager is hard to see when he
moves slowly or perches high in the
trees, feeding on berries and fruit. The
scarlet tanager also feeds on insects,
slugs, snails and spiders, many of which
it catches on the ground.

Male birds return from the wintering
grounds a few days before females, and
each establishes a territory in the trees.
When the female birds arrive, they are
courted by the singing males. The female
builds a nest in a large tree, using twigs,
rootlets, weed stems and grass. She lays
3 to 5 eggs, which she incubates for 13
or 14 days.

NAME: **Magpie Tanager,** *Cissopis
leveriana*
RANGE: **northern South America, south
to Brazil and N.E. Argentina**
HABITAT: **rain forest, scrub, cultivated
land, clearings**
SIZE: **28 cm (11 in)**

As its common name suggests, this large
tanager resembles a magpie and is certainly different from all other tanagers.
It is a black and white bird, with long,
graduated tail feathers, tipped with
white. Male and female look alike, and
both have black eyes. Little is known of
this tanager, which inhabits areas up to
2,000 m (6,600 ft) in some parts of its
range. In pairs or small groups of 4 or 5
birds, it frequents the middle layers of
the forest, flying from tree to tree, feeding on insects and berries.

There is no information available
about the breeding habits of this
tanager.

NAME: **Black-capped Hemispingus,**
Hemispingus atropileus
RANGE: **Andes, from N.W. Venezuela to
Bolivia**
HABITAT: **forest at 2,300–3,000 m
(7,500–10,000 ft)**
SIZE: **16.5 cm (6½ in)**

The black-capped hemispingus inhabits
the high-altitude cloud forests and the
sparse, stunted woods above this zone.
Alone or in small groups, it forages
among the trees for fruit and insects.
Male and female look similar, both with
black crowns and largely olive plumage.
The cup-shaped nest is made in a tree.

THRAUPINAE: Tanager Subfamily

The approximately 238 species of
tanager occur in the New World, mostly
in the tropics, and are among the most
vividly colored and conspicuous of all
the thousands of bird species found
in the tropical zone of the Americas.
Although a few species are soberly
plumaged, most are brilliant, often with
a combination of many contrasting
plumage colors. In many species, male
and female birds share the same
spectacular appearance, but in the 4
species that have penetrated the temperate zones of North America, male
and female differ.

Tanagers are finch- or bunting-shaped
songbirds which frequent the upper
layers of forests and woods and also the
clearings and fringes of such vegetation.
Their feet and legs are well developed
for their essentially tree-dwelling life.
The diet of a typical tanager consists of
both fruit and insects. Tanagers capture
the latter by plucking them from foliage
or catching them in the air, or by following army ant columns to seize the insects
they disturb. Tanagers are not noted
as songsters; only a few species, such
as the rose-breasted thrush tanager,
Rhodinocichla rosea, are known to have
well-developed singing abilities.

Most tanagers make open, cup-
shaped nests in trees and bushes.
Clutches contain 1 to 5 eggs and are incubated by the female bird. The male
brings his mate food while she incubates, and he helps with the feeding of
the nestlings.

Honeycreepers are similar to tanagers
but feed on nectar, as well as on fruit
and insects. Most male honeycreepers
are brightly colored, but females are
duller in plumage. Some honeycreepers
are included with the tanagers, and
others with the American wood warblers, Parulidae; they are sometimes all
placed in a subfamily of their own.

NAME: **White-shouldered Tanager,**
Tachyphonus luctuosus
RANGE: **Honduras to Panama, south to
N. Bolivia, Amazonian Brazil**
HABITAT: **rain forest, open woodland,
plantations, clearings**
SIZE: **13 cm (5 in)**

The white-shouldered tanager varies
slightly in coloration over its range —
for example, males in western Panama
have yellow or tawny crowns — but in
most instances, males are bluish-black,
with the white shoulders of their common name, while females are gray, olive
and yellow. These active, noisy birds
live in pairs or small groups or may join
in mixed flocks. They forage for fruit

and insects from the treetops down to
the undergrowth, calling to each other
with harsh, loud calls.

The open, cup-shaped nest is made of
leaves and grasses and is built in a tree,
not far from the ground. The female
incubates the 2 eggs, and both parents
feed the young.

NAME: **Blue-gray Tanager,** *Thraupis
episcopus*
RANGE: **S.E. Mexico, Central and South
America to Brazil and Bolivia;
Trinidad and Tobago**
HABITAT: **open and cleared woodland,
cultivated land, parks, gardens**
SIZE: **16.5 cm (6½ in)**

An adaptable, widespread bird, the
blue-gray tanager is equally at home in
humid and dry areas, in coastal lowlands and at altitudes up to 2,200 m
(7,200 ft). Birds remain paired throughout the year, and together or in small
flocks, they forage in the trees for berries, fruit such as wild figs and bananas,
and insects, which they take from foliage or catch on the wing.

The cup-shaped nest may be made in
a variety of sites: high in a tree, in a low
bush, even in an open shed or the abandoned nest of another bird species. It is
made of rootlets, plant fibers, moss and
grass, matted together and bound with
cobwebs. The blue-gray tanager may
even take over the nest of another
tanager and incubate the eggs with its
own. Normally the female lays 2 or 3
eggs, which she incubates for 13 or 14
days. Both parents feed the young until
they leave the nest about 17 to 20 days
after hatching. There are at least two
broods in a year.

NAME: **Common Bush-tanager,**
Chlorospingus ophthalmicus
RANGE: **Mexico, Central and South
America to N. Argentina**
HABITAT: **rain and cloud forest,
woodland**
SIZE: **14.5 cm (5¾ in)**

The common bush-tanager is a noisy,
active bird, common in many areas. In
small groups, these birds roam the
forest, foraging for insects and fruit,
mainly in low vegetation but also in the
treetops. They may join mixed flocks of
birds. Males and females are similar in
appearance.

The female may build her nest in a
tree or on the ground. The top of the
nest is usually concealed by the vegetation among which it is built. The female
lays 2 eggs, which she incubates for 14
days, and both parents feed the young.

Scarlet Tanager (male)

Blue-gray Tanager

Common Bush-tanager

Black-capped Hemispingus

Magpie Tanager

White-shouldered Tanager (male)

Tanagers

NAME: **Blue-crowned/Turquoise-naped Chlorophonia, *Chlorophonia occipitalis***
RANGE: S.E. Mexico to W. Panama
HABITAT: forest, usually over 1,500 m (5,000 ft)
SIZE: 14 cm ($5\frac{1}{2}$ in)

The male blue-crowned chlorophonia is a beautiful little bird, with bright green and blue plumage set off by touches of yellow. The female is largely green, with less blue and yellow, and young males resemble females until they acquire full adult plumage at about a year old. Arboreal birds, these chlorophonias frequent the treetops, where they feed on fruit; when fruit is scarce in their high-altitude habitat, they may sometimes descend to lower levels. For a few months after the end of the breeding season in July, the birds move in flocks of up to 12, but for the rest of the year, they live in pairs.

The breeding season begins in March. Both partners of a pair help to build a neat, domed nest high in a tree, usually among camouflaging moss and epiphytic plants — profuse in these high forests. The nest is made of moss, roots of epiphytes and spider's webs. There are believed to be 3 or more eggs in a typical clutch, and these are incubated by the female alone. Whenever she leaves the nest to feed, she drops almost to the ground before flying off, in order to confuse predators. Once hatched, the young are fed by both parents on regurgitated food, and they remain in the nest for 24 to 25 days. A second brood may follow.

NAME: **Blue Dacnis, *Dacnis cayana***
RANGE: E. Nicaragua to Panama, tropical South America to N. Argentina
HABITAT: open forest, secondary growth, orange groves
SIZE: 11.5 cm ($4\frac{1}{2}$ in)

The blue dacnis is one of the honeycreeper group of tanagers but differs from them in having a short, conical bill. The male bird is bright blue and black, while the female is bright green, with some blue, gray and black plumage. These active little birds forage in the treetops, alone or in small groups, sometimes joining mixed flocks of tanagers and other honeycreepers. They feed on fruit, nectar and insects, some of which they catch in the air, and are particularly partial to the large flower heads of mango trees and wild figs.

The female makes an open, cup-shaped nest in a tree, using fine plant material. She incubates the 2 or 3 eggs and does most of the work of feeding the young, although the male does help with this. The young leave the nest about 12 days after hatching.

NAME: **White-vented Euphonia, *Euphonia minuta***
RANGE: Mexico, Central and northern South America to Amazonian Brazil
HABITAT: rain forest, secondary growth, scrub, clearings
SIZE: 9 cm ($3\frac{1}{2}$ in)

The white-vented euphonia lives in pairs or small groups and forages high in the trees, feeding primarily on mistletoe berries but also on insects and spiders. The birds may have to travel considerable distances to find the berries. The hard seeds of the mistletoe are excreted in due course, usually up in the trees, where they stick to the branches and germinate. All the euphonia species feed on mistletoe berries, and they are the birds most responsible for the spread of this parasitic plant. The male bird is a colorful mixture of yellow, white, black and gray-blue, while the female is green, gray and yellowish. Both have short bills and tails.

Like the chlorophonias, the white-vented euphonia builds a rounded nest with a side entrance. The nest is made of moss or dry plant material and is placed in a cleft in bark or rock or in a hole in a tree trunk. The female incubates her 2 to 5 eggs for 14 to 18 days, and both parents feed the young with regurgitated food.

NAME: **Silver-beaked Tanager, *Ramphocelus carbo***
RANGE: northern South America east of Andes, south to Bolivia, Paraguay, Brazil
HABITAT: woodland, secondary growth, cultivated land
SIZE: 18 cm (7 in)

The distinguishing feature of this tanager is the conspicuous silvery-white base to the lower mandible of its black beak. The plumage of male birds varies slightly from area to area, being either black or dark maroon on the upperparts, with a red throat and breast. Females seem always to be a dark maroon. Often found near water, silver-beaked tanagers tend to live on or near the edge of wooded areas, rather than inside them. Alone or in small groups, they forage actively for insects and fruit, from the lowest branches to the middle story of trees.

The female bird builds a large nest in a bush or thicket. Her mate brings food to her while she incubates the 2 eggs for about 12 days. The young birds are able to leave the nest about 11 to 13 days after hatching.

NAME: **Paradise Tanager, *Tangara chilensis***
RANGE: northern South America east of the Andes, south to Bolivia and Amazonian Brazil
HABITAT: rain forest
SIZE: 14 cm ($5\frac{1}{2}$ in)

An extremely beautiful bird, the paradise tanager has gleaming, multicolored plumage; males and females look alike. In groups that often include other species, paradise tanagers forage for berries, spiders and insects in the middle and upper layers of the forest.

The breeding habits of this species are probably similar to those of other tanagers.

NAME: **Purple Honeycreeper, *Cyanerpes caeruleus***
RANGE: Trinidad; northern South America to Bolivia, Paraguay, Brazil
HABITAT: rain forest, forest edge, mangrove swamps, plantations
SIZE: 10 cm (4 in)

Groups of purple honeycreepers frequent flowering trees in many different types of wooded areas. Fruit, especially bananas, and insects are important foods, but these birds also perch by flowers and suck nectar from them with their long, curved bills. Male and female differ in plumage, but both are attractive birds; the male is largely bluish-purple and black, with yellow legs, while the female is rich green, with buff and blue patches on the head and breast.

The female builds a cup-shaped nest in the fork of a tree or bush and lays 2 eggs, which she incubates for 12 to 14 days. The young leave the nest about 14 days after hatching.

NAME: **Giant Conebill, *Oreomanes fraseri***
RANGE: South America: Andes in S. Colombia to Bolivia
HABITAT: forested and scrub slopes
SIZE: 17–18.5 cm ($6\frac{3}{4}$–$7\frac{1}{4}$ in)

Although not really a giant, this conebill is distinctly larger than other conebills. It has fairly sober, mainly gray and chestnut plumage and a straight, sharp bill about 1.25 cm ($\frac{1}{2}$ in) long. Little is known about this bird, which inhabits the *Polylepsis* woods at high altitudes in the Andes — between 3,000 and 4,000 m (10,000 and 13,000 ft). These woods are cold and impoverished, with only the *Polylepsis* trees and little vegetation other than mosses and ferns. The giant conebill explores the trunks and branches of the trees for insects, its plumage providing good camouflage against the bark of the trees. It is usually found in chattering groups, sometimes with mixed flocks of flycatchers and finches.

Silver-beaked Tanager (male)

Paradise Tanager

Blue-crowned
Chlorophonia
(male)

Purple Honeycreeper
(male)

Blue Dacnis (male)

White-vented Euphonia (male)

Giant Conebill

American Wood Warblers

NAME: Bananaquit, *Coereba flaveola*
**RANGE: Mexico, Central and South
America to N. Argentina; West Indies**
**HABITAT: forest, mangrove swamps,
gardens, parks, plantations**
SIZE: 9.5 cm (3¾ in)

An extremely adaptable, widespread bird, the bananaquit is equally at home in dense rain forest or dry coastal areas but must have some cover. It lives alone or in pairs and never forms flocks. Bananaquits feed mainly on insects and fruit but also on nectar, probing blossoms with their curved bills or piercing large blooms at the base to obtain the nectar.

A globular nest is built, usually suspended from a branch or vine. The female incubates the 2 or 3 eggs for 12 or 13 days, and both parents feed the nestlings with nectar or insects. There are at least two broods a year.

NAME: Black-and-White Warbler,
Mniotilta varia
**RANGE: breeds S. Canada, USA, east of
Rockies; winters S. USA to
N.W. South America**
**HABITAT: deciduous and mixed forest,
parks, gardens**
SIZE: 11.5–14 cm (4½–5½ in)

Both male and female of this species are boldly striped with black and white, but the male has a black throat while the female's is white. Insects are their main food, and these warblers creep over branches and tree trunks, searching for caterpillars, ants, flies and beetles and also spiders.

The cup-shaped nest is made on the ground at the foot of a tree or by a rock, and the female incubates the clutch of 4 or 5 eggs for 10 to 12 days. The young are tended by both parents until they leave the nest 8 to 12 days after hatching.

NAME: Golden-winged Warbler,
Vermivora chrysoptera
**RANGE: breeds N.E. USA; winters south
to Central America and Venezuela**
HABITAT: woodland, thickets
SIZE: 11–14 cm (4¼–5½ in)

Identified by their bright yellow wing patches and crowns, male and female golden-winged warblers look similar, but the female has a lighter throat and eye patch. They forage at all levels of trees and bushes, searching the foliage for insects and spiders.

The nest is made on the ground or just above it in vegetation, and the female incubates the 4 or 5 eggs, sometimes 6 or 7, for about 10 days. Both parents feed the young, which leave the nest about 10 days after hatching. This warbler often interbreeds with the blue-winged warbler, *V. pinus*, where their ranges overlap.

PARULIDAE:
American Wood Warbler Family

There are approximately 125 species of American wood warbler, found from Alaska and northern Canada to the south of South America. Some of these birds, such as the conebills and the bananaquit, are of uncertain affinity, and there are arguments for placing them in other families.

Despite their name, wood warblers have no close connection with the Old World warblers and, indeed, do not have particularly tuneful songs. Small, slender birds, most are brightly colored, particularly in breeding plumage. Those species that breed in the more tropical zones tend to be sedentary in their habits, but species breeding in the north of the range are highly migratory and form a spectacular part of the north-south bird migrations of the New World. Male and female look alike in some species and differ in others.

NAME: Northern Parula, *Parula
americana*
**RANGE: breeds S.E. Canada, eastern
USA; winters S. Florida, West Indies,
Mexico to Nicaragua**
**HABITAT: coniferous forest, swamps,
mixed woodland in winter**
SIZE: 11 cm (4¼ in)

A sedate little warbler, the northern parula forages for insects, especially caterpillars, in the trees, creeping over the branches and hopping from perch to perch; it also feeds on spiders. Male and female look similar, but the female is slightly duller.

The nest is usually built in hanging tree lichen or Spanish moss. The female incubates the 4 or 5 eggs for 12 to 14 days. Both parents tend the young.

NAME: Yellow Warbler, *Dendroica
petechia*
**RANGE: Alaska, much of Canada, USA;
Mexico, Central and South America to
Peru; West Indies**
HABITAT: damp thickets, swamps
SIZE: 11–13 cm (4¼–5 in)

An extremely widespread species, the yellow warbler varies considerably over its range, but the male breeding plumage is, typically, bright yellow with chestnut or orange streaks; males are duller outside the breeding season, and females are generally more greenish in color. Yellow warblers forage in the foliage of trees and shrubs for insects, feeding largely on caterpillars but also on bark beetles and moths, as well as spiders.

The female builds a cup-shaped nest in a tree or bush and incubates the 4 or 5 eggs for about 11 days.

NAME: Ovenbird, *Seiurus aurocapillus*
**RANGE: breeds central and E. Canada and
USA to N. Gulf states; winters Gulf of
Mexico to northern South America**
HABITAT: forest
SIZE: 14–15 cm (5½–6 in)

The ovenbird is distinguished by its brownish-orange crown, edged with black, and its white eye rings. It finds most of its food on the forest floor by searching under fallen leaves and other debris for insects, spiders, slugs, snails and other small creatures; it also eats seeds and berries.

The female builds a domed, oven-shaped nest on the ground; it has a side entrance. She lays 4 or 5 eggs, which she incubates for 11 to 14 days.

NAME: Mourning Warbler, *Geothlypis
philadelphia*
**RANGE: breeds central and E. Canada,
N.E. USA; winters from Nicaragua to
Ecuador and Venezuela**
HABITAT: thickets, wet woodland
SIZE: 12.5–14.5 cm (5–5¾ in)

Male and female mourning warblers both have gray hoods, and the male has a black patch on the throat. An elusive, skulking warbler, it forages among low vegetation for insects and spiders.

The bulky nest is made on the ground or in a low bush, and the female incubates the 3 to 5 eggs for 12 to 13 days.

NAME: Painted Redstart, *Myioborus
pictus*
RANGE: S.W. USA, Mexico to Nicaragua
HABITAT: woodland, mountain canyons
SIZE: 12.5–14.5 cm (5–5¾ in)

Lively little birds, both male and female painted redstarts have bright red breasts and white bellies. They feed entirely on insects, most of which they catch in the air by darting out from a perch.

The nest is made in a small hollow in the ground near a boulder or clump of grass. The female incubates the 3 or 4 eggs for 13 or 14 days.

NAME: Golden-crowned Warbler,
Basileuterus culicivorus
**RANGE: Mexico, through Central and
South America to N. Argentina;
Trinidad**
HABITAT: rain forest, plantations, scrub
SIZE: 12.5 cm (5 in)

A yellow or rufous-orange patch on the crown, bordered with black, is the distinguishing feature of this warbler. Alone or in pairs, it forages in the lower levels of dense vegetation and rarely flies into the open. Insects are its main food — caught among the foliage or on the wing.

The female builds a domed, oven-shaped nest on the ground and incubates her clutch of 3 eggs for 14 to 17 days.

Bananaquit

Golden-winged
Warbler (male)

Black-and-white
Warbler (male)

Northern Parula

Yellow Warbler (male)

Ovenbird

Mourning Warbler (male)

Painted Redstart

Golden-crowned Warbler

Hawaiian Honeycreepers, Vireos

DREPANIDIDAE:
Hawaiian Honeycreeper Family

Even Darwin's finches on the Galápagos Islands do not surpass the Hawaiian honeycreepers as an object lesson in the ability of a single bird type to differentiate into a range of species when released from competition and provided with a wide diversity of habitats. It seems highly likely that the 15 or so existing Hawaiian honeycreepers, as well as forms now extinct, are all derived from a single colonization of the island cluster by a single type of migratory American wood warbler (Parulidae).

The existing forms divide into two distinct groups: first, the nectar-feeders, which also consume insects and have reddish and black plumage; and second, a group of finchlike birds, which feed mostly on seeds and have yellowish-green plumage. Species differ most dramatically in bill shape, in accordance with their different feeding habits. Male and female differ in some species and look alike in others.

NAME: **Palila,** *Psittirostra bailleui*
RANGE: **Hawaii: Mauna Kea**
HABITAT: **forest**
SIZE: **15 cm (6 in)**   Ⓔ

Previously more widely distributed in Hawaii, the palila is now found only on the western slope of Mauna Kea. It is a seriously endangered bird, largely because of disturbance and the destruction of its forest habitat. It is dependent on the mamani tree of its native forest for its existence and feeds principally on the seeds and flowers of this tree. The bird nips off a seedpod and holds it down on a branch with its claw while it extracts the seeds.

The female builds a nest in a mamani tree and lays 2 eggs, which she incubates for 21 to 27 days. Both parents feed the young with regurgitated food, probably insects on which adults also feed in the breeding season.

NAME: **Akepa,** *Loxops coccinea*
RANGE: **Hawaii, Maui, Kauai**
HABITAT: **forest**
SIZE: **10–12.5 cm (4–5 in)**   Ⓔ

Abundant in some areas of the Hawaiian Islands up to the end of the nineteenth century, the akepa population is in serious decline, and the Oahu Island race is already extinct. An active, sprightly little bird with a short, conical bill, the akepa feeds largely on caterpillars and spiders, which it usually finds on leaves and small twigs. It also drinks nectar. The female lays 3 eggs in a cavity in a tree.

NAME: **Akiapolaau,** *Hemignathus wilsoni*
RANGE: **Hawaii**
HABITAT: **forest**
SIZE: **14 cm (5½ in)**   Ⓔ

Formerly widespread and common on Hawaii, this honeycreeper is now found only in small numbers in a few areas. Two major reasons for its decline are the deterioration of its forest home and the introduction of predators, particularly arboreal rats. The akiapolaau forages on large branches and tree trunks, creeping up and down with equal ease. It has a unique bill: the upper mandible is long and curved and the lower short, straight and wedge-shaped. Using this extraordinary bill, the bird opens up the burrows of wood-boring insects and then uses its thin, brushlike tongue to extract its prey.

VIREONIDAE: Vireo Family

There are about 43 species in this family, all found in the New World. The true vireos dominate the group — there are about 38 species. They all feed on insects among the foliage in wooded areas. Similar to the American wood warblers, Parulidae, in appearance, vireos are more stoutly built, have heavier bills and tend to be more deliberate in their movements.

The remaining birds in the family are divided into two groups, sometimes classified as separate families: the 2 species of peppershrikes and the 3 of shrike-vireos. All are slightly larger birds than vireos and have heavy, hooked bills; they feed in the trees, mainly on insects and fruit.

In all species of this family, male and female look alike or nearly so.

NAME: **Red-eyed Vireo,** *Vireo olivaceus*
RANGE: **Canada, much of USA (not S.W.), Central and South America to Argentina; West Indies**
HABITAT: **deciduous forest and woodland, gardens, parks, orchards**
SIZE: **14–17 cm (5½–6¾ in)**

This widespread vireo is distinguished by its ruby-red eyes; immature birds have brown eyes. It occurs almost anywhere that there are deciduous trees and moves slowly through the lower levels and undergrowth, foraging for insects and berries. A persistent singer, it sings more than any other bird on hot summer days.

The neat, cup-shaped nest is suspended between the twigs of a horizontal fork in a tree or bush. There are usually 4 eggs, which the female incubates for 11 to 14 days. The young leave the nest some 10 to 12 days after hatching.

NAME: **Tawny-crowned Greenlet,** *Hylophilus ochraceiceps*
RANGE: **S. Mexico, Central and South America to Bolivia**
HABITAT: **rain forest, woodland**
SIZE: **11 cm (4¼ in)**

This little vireo has mainly yellowish and brown plumage, with a tawny forehead and crown. It forages among the leaves of bushes and saplings for insects and other small invertebrates. It usually moves in small groups, often with other forest birds.

The female lays 2 eggs in a strongly built, cup-shaped nest, attached by its rim to a forked twig. Both parents feed their young with insects and larvae until they leave the nest at about 14 days old.

NAME: **Rufous-browed Peppershrike,** *Cyclarhis gujanensis*
RANGE: **N.E. Mexico, through Central and South America to N. Argentina; Trinidad**
HABITAT: **forest, woodland, cultivated land**
SIZE: **15 cm (6 in)**

A heavy-bodied bird with a large head and strong legs and feet, this peppershrike is a good climber and forages in trees, but it is weak in flight. It is slow and deliberate in its movements as it searches for insects and berries, particularly at the ends of branches and twigs. If a large insect is caught, the bird holds it down with its foot and tears it apart with its strong, hooked bill. A secretive bird, this peppershrike rarely comes into the open but is often heard singing loudly and persistently from a perch. It usually lives alone or in pairs.

The nest is woven from bark and grasses and suspended in the fork of a branch in a bush or tree. Both parents incubate the 2 or 3 eggs and feed the young.

NAME: **Chestnut-sided Shrike-vireo,** *Vireolanius melitophrys*
RANGE: **Mexico to Guatemala**
HABITAT: **forest**
SIZE: **18 cm (7 in)**

All 3 species of shrike-vireo are more brightly plumaged than typical vireos, and the chestnut-sided shrike-vireo is particularly attractive, with its green back, chestnut flanks and boldly striped head. It has a stout, hooked bill and strong legs and feet. Seldom seen, this bird lives high up in the canopy and rarely flies in the open or perches in exposed spots. It feeds on insects, holding down large ones with its foot and tearing them apart with its bill, and it also eats some fruit.

The nest is suspended from a forked branch of a tree, but the breeding habits of this shrike-vireo are not known.

Palila

Chestnut-sided Shrike-vireo

Akiapolaau

Red-eyed Vireo

Akepa

Rufous-browed Peppershrike

Tawny-crowned Greenlet

Icterids

NAME: **Wagler's Oropendola,** *Psarocolius wagleri*
RANGE: **S. Mexico, through Central America to N.W. Ecuador**
HABITAT: **forest, clearings**
SIZE: **28–35.5 cm (11–14 in)**

Wagler's oropendola has dark plumage, with a characteristic chestnut head and yellow tail feathers. The male is larger than the female and has a crest of a few hairlike feathers. A tree-dwelling bird, it hops and flutters in the middle and upper layers, searching for fruit, seeds and insects.

Colonies of these oropendolas nest together, 50 to 100 pairs making their nests in the same isolated or well-exposed tree or clump of trees. The female bird weaves a long, pouchlike nest, which hangs from an outer branch.

NAME: **Northern Oriole,** *Icterus galbula*
RANGE: **S. Canada, much of USA except Gulf Coast and Florida, N. Mexico; winters from S. Mexico to Colombia**
HABITAT: **woodland, parks, gardens**
SIZE: **18–21 cm (7–8¼ in)**

There are two forms included in this species: the Baltimore oriole, found in the east, and Bullock's oriole, found in the west. Previously they were thought to be separate species. The Baltimore oriole is the subspecies illustrated, and while the western race is similar in many respects, the male Bullock's has a largely orange head and a white wing patch. The two forms interbreed at the center of their range. Northern orioles forage in trees and bushes for caterpillars, beetles, ants and other insects, as well as for fruit and berries.

The female bird makes the nest, which is a deep pouch, woven from plant fiber and other long strands of material and hung from a forked twig. She lays 3 to 6 eggs, usually 4 or 5, which she incubates for about 14 days. Both parents tend the young.

NAME: **Yellow-rumped Cacique,** *Cacicus cela*
RANGE: **Panama, south to N. Bolivia, E. Brazil; Trinidad**
HABITAT: **rain forest, secondary growth, open country with scattered trees**
SIZE: **23–28 cm (9–11 in)**

The yellow-rumped cacique is a gregarious bird, which feeds, nests and roosts in groups. Much of its food, such as fruit and insects, is found in the trees, but it may also dart after flying termites and catch them in the air.

A colonial nester, the female cacique weaves a long, pouchlike nest, from grass and plant fibers, which is suspended from a branch, close to other nests of the colony. She lays 2 eggs, which she incubates for about 12 days.

ICTERIDAE: Icterid Family

There are about 93 species of icterid, found throughout the Americas. An extremely successful and diverse family, it includes many different groups of birds such as oropendolas, caciques, grackles, American blackbirds and American orioles, cowbirds and meadowlarks. The majority of icterids live in woodland or forest, but others occur in all types of habitat, including marshes, desert and open country. Females are usually duller in plumage and smaller than males.

NAME: **Common Grackle,** *Quiscalus quiscula*
RANGE: **S. Canada; USA, east of Rockies**
HABITAT: **open woodland, fields, parks, gardens, orchards**
SIZE: **28–34 cm (11–13½ in)**

The common grackle is a glossy black bird, with an iridescent sheen of purple or other colors, depending on the race. Females are smaller than males. Always gregarious birds, common grackles gather in large, noisy flocks and roost in groups. The diet of the common grackle is extremely varied. It forages in trees and bushes for nuts, fruit and the eggs and young of small birds. On the ground, it probes for worms and chases insects, mice and lizards, and it will even wade into ponds or streams to catch aquatic creatures such as frogs and crayfish.

A bulky nest of twigs, stalks and grass is made in a bush or tree or on a building. The birds usually nest in colonies. The female incubates the 5 or 6 eggs for 13 or 14 days, and both parents tend the young. Most populations winter just south of their breeding range, but some are resident.

NAME: **Bobolink,** *Dolichonyx oryzivorus*
RANGE: **S. Canada; USA, south to Pennsylvania, Colorado, California; winters in South America**
HABITAT: **prairie, cultivated land**
SIZE: **15–20 cm (6–7¾ in)**

In breeding plumage the male bobolink is largely black, with a white rump, a white streak on the back and a yellow nape. In winter, he looks like a larger version of the female, with yellow-brown plumage. Insects are the main diet of the bobolink in summer, but in winter, as it migrates south, it feeds on grain crops — in former times particularly on rice.

The bobolink performs the longest migration of any member of its family, traveling at least 8,000 km (5,000 mi) from Argentina to northern USA and Canada. Once at the breeding grounds,

males court females with display flights and bubbling songs; males may have many mates. The female makes a nest on the ground and lays 5 or 6 eggs, which she incubates for 13 days.

NAME: **Brown-headed Cowbird,** *Molothrus ater*
RANGE: **S. Canada, USA; winters south of breeding range, from Maryland to Texas and California; Mexico**
HABITAT: **woodland, farmland, fields, open country**
SIZE: **15–20 cm (6–7¾ in)**

As the common name suggests, the male of this species is distinguished by his shiny brown head; the female is uniformly gray. They are gregarious birds, forming large flocks in winter and gathering in small groups of up to 6 in the breeding season. They feed largely on plant matter, such as grain, seeds, berries and fruit, and on some insects, spiders and snails.

These cowbirds are brood parasites: the female lays her eggs in the nests of other birds. She lays up to 12 eggs a season, each in a different nest, which need to be incubated for 11 or 12 days. This cowbird has been known to use over 185 different species as hosts, most with smaller eggs than its own. The young cowbirds hatch more quickly and are bigger than the hosts' young, which usually perish.

NAME: **Eastern Meadowlark,** *Sturnella magna*
RANGE: **S.E. Canada; USA: New England to Minnesota, south to Florida, Texas and New Mexico; Mexico, Central and South America to Brazil**
HABITAT: **open country: prairie, fields, grassland**
SIZE: **21.5–28 cm (8½–11 in)**

The eastern meadowlark bears a close resemblance to the yellow-throated longclaw, *Macronyx croceus*, of the wagtail and pipit family. The two are not related but have adapted to a similar way of life in a similar habitat. The eastern meadowlark often perches in conspicuous spots on wires and posts but finds much of its food on the ground. It eats insects, such as grasshoppers, ants, beetles and caterpillars, grain and weed seeds. It will also consume the remains of birds killed by traffic.

After wintering just south of their breeding range, eastern meadowlarks return in the spring, the male birds arriving before females to establish territories. Each male may have more than one mate. The grass nest is made in a dip in open ground and is often dome-shaped. The female usually lays 5 eggs, which she incubates for 13 or 14 days. Both parents feed the young.

Wagler's Oropendola (male)

Northern Oriole (male)

Bobolink (male)

Brown-headed Cowbird (male)

Yellow-rumped Cacique (male)

Eastern Meadowlark

Common Grackle

Finches

NAME: Chaffinch, *Fringilla coelebes*
**RANGE: Europe, across Asia to
Afghanistan, Mediterranean region,
N. Africa, Canary Islands, Azores**
HABITAT: forest, woodland, gardens
SIZE: 15 cm (6 in)

The abundant, widespread chaffinch varies in plumage coloration over its range, and its attractive song exists in many different dialects. The female has duller plumage than the male, being mostly grayish and olive-brown. The chaffinch searches for food in the trees and on the ground, where it hops or moves with short, quick steps; it flies in the undulating manner typical of the finches. Three-quarters of its food intake is plant material, mostly seeds, fruit and corn, but it also eats insects, spiders and earthworms.

A neat, well-constructed nest is made in a tree or bush, and the female lays 4 or 5 eggs, which she incubates for 11 to 13 days. Northern populations migrate south for the winter.

NAME: Purple Finch, *Carpodacus
purpureus*
**RANGE: N. America: British Columbia,
south to Baja California, east to
Newfoundland and N.E. USA; winters
in W. and E. USA and Mexico**
HABITAT: woodland, coniferous forest
SIZE: 14–16 cm (5½–6¼ in)

The male purple finch is distinguished by his rich, reddish coloration, while the female is mainly brown and gray. Outside the breeding season, these finches form large feeding flocks and search out seeds of weeds and trees. In spring and summer, they also feed on beetles and caterpillars.

In the breeding season, the male displays to the female, dancing around her and beating his wings while he sings his rich, warbling song. A nest is made of twigs and grasses, usually in a conifer, and the female lays 4 or 5 eggs, which she incubates for 13 days.

NAME: Canary, *Serinus canaria*
**RANGE: Canary Islands, Madeira, Azores;
introduced in Bermuda**
HABITAT: wooded areas, gardens
SIZE: 12.5 cm (5 in)

All races of domestic canaries are descended from this species, which was first made popular as a cage bird by the Spanish conquerors of the Canary Islands. The female is generally brown and duller than the bright yellow and brown male. Canaries feed on seeds and usually remain hidden in the trees, but their attractive song is often heard.

A cup-shaped nest is made in a tree or bush, and the female lays 4 or 5 eggs, which she incubates for 13 or 14 days.

FRINGILLIDAE: Finch Family

The finches are a successful and widely distributed group of small, seed-eating songbirds. They are most numerous in Europe and northern Asia, but some species occur in other parts of the Old World and in the Americas.

Finches generally live in trees and feed on seeds and nuts in the trees or under them. Their bodies are unspecialized, but, in keeping with their different diets, there is a great diversity of bill shapes within the family. These include the thin, pointed bill of the goldfinches, used for extracting tiny seeds from thistle and teasel heads; the stout, conical bill of generalist finches; and the heavy, "nutcracker" beak of hawfinches and grosbeaks, which enables them to crack cherry stones.

Male and female usually differ in appearance, and young resemble females.

NAME: Red/Common Crossbill, *Loxia
curvirostra*
**RANGE: Europe, Asia, south to
Himalayas; N. America, south to
Nicaragua**
HABITAT: coniferous forest
SIZE: 13–16 cm (5–6¼ in)

This crossbill feeds almost entirely on conifer seeds, which it extracts from the cones by using its specialized crossed mandibles. The bird may hang upside down to feed at cones or tear off the cone and hold it in its foot. It rarely comes down to the ground, where it moves awkwardly. In summer, it also eats insects. Male and female differ in plumage, the female being greenish-gray.

After a pair-forming gathering, a cup-shaped nest is made in a conifer. The female lays 3 or 4 eggs, which she incubates for 13 to 16 days; both parents feed the young, which hatch with symmetrical bills.

NAME: European Goldfinch, *Carduelis
carduelis*
**RANGE: Europe, N. Africa, Azores,
Canary Islands, Madeira; Asia, east to
Lake Baikal, south to Himalayas**
**HABITAT: open woodland, gardens,
orchards, cultivated land**
SIZE: 12 cm (4¾ in)

Unmistakable birds, both male and female goldfinches have red faces and black and white heads. Their wings are long and pointed and their strong bills almost conical. Outside the breeding season, goldfinches often fly to open country to feed near the ground on thistles and other weed seeds, especially small seeds; they also eat some insects.

The female builds a nest on a branch of a tree and lays 5 or 6 eggs.

NAME: Pine Grosbeak, *Pinicola
enucleator*
**RANGE: N. Scandinavia, USSR, Asia;
Alaska, Canada, N. USA**
HABITAT: coniferous and mixed forest
SIZE: 20 cm (7¾ in)

A large, long-tailed finch, the pine grosbeak uses its stout, heavy bill to crush the stones of fruit such as cherries and plums; it also feeds on seeds, buds and insects in summer. It finds its food in trees and on the ground and is a strong flier. Male and female differ in plumage, the female being largely a bronzy color.

The nest is usually made in a conifer or a birch tree, and the female lays 4 eggs, which she incubates for 13 or 14 days. The male feeds her during this period and later on helps to feed the young by regurgitating food for them.

NAME: Common Redpoll, *Acanthis
flammea*
**RANGE: breeds in Iceland, Ireland,
Britain, Scandinavia, central European
mountains, N. Asia to Bering Sea,
northern N. America; winters south of
breeding range**
HABITAT: woodland, forest, tundra
SIZE: 13–15 cm (5–6 in)

The redpoll is able to survive lower temperatures than any songbird other than its close relative the arctic, or hoary, redpoll, *A. hornemanni*. It feeds on seeds, particularly those of birch and alder, and will hang upside down to reach the catkins. It also scratches on the ground to find seeds and in summer feeds on insects.

At the start of the spring breeding season, males perform display flights. The female builds a nest on a forked branch, usually of an alder, willow or spruce, and lays 4 or 5 eggs. She incubates the eggs for 10 or 11 days.

NAME: Bullfinch, *Pyrrhula pyrrhula*
**RANGE: Scandinavia, Britain, south to
Mediterranean regions (not S. Spain);
Asia to Japan**
**HABITAT: coniferous forest, woodland,
parks, gardens, cultivated land**
SIZE: 14–16 cm (5½–6¼ in)

The male bullfinch is identified by his black cap, rose-red underparts and black and white wings; the female looks similar but has pinkish-gray underparts. A shy bird, it usually perches in cover in a bush or tree and does not often come to the ground. In spring, it feeds largely on the buds of fruit trees and can cause considerable damage; buds of other trees are also eaten, as well as berries and seeds.

A nest of twigs and moss is built by the female in a bush or hedge. She lays 4 or 5 eggs, which she incubates for 12 to 14 days.

Chaffinch (male)

Purple Finch (male)

Canary (male)

Red Crossbill (male)

European Goldfinch

Pine Grosbeak (male)

Common Redpoll

Bullfinch (male)

Waxbills

NAME: Red-billed Fire-finch,
Lagonosticta senegala
RANGE: Africa, south of the Sahara (not extreme south)
HABITAT: scrub, thickets, cultivated land, near habitation
SIZE: 9 cm (3½ in)

One of the most widespread and common of African birds, the red-billed fire-finch often feeds on grass and other seeds on the ground in towns and villages. The female is much plainer than the male, having only a touch of red on the face and rump; her underparts are buff, with white spots on the breast. Outside the breeding season, these birds gather in small flocks.

The globular nest, usually made of dry grass, is built on a low wall or in a bush or thatched roof. The female lays 3 to 6 eggs, usually 4, which are incubated by both parents.

NAME: Red-cheeked Cordon-bleu,
Uraeginthus bengalus
RANGE: Africa: Senegal to Ethiopia, south through E. Africa to Zambia
HABITAT: open country, cultivated land
SIZE: 12.5 cm (5 in)

The male red-cheeked cordon-bleu is easily recognized by his crimson cheek patches; females and juveniles are duller in plumage and lack the red markings. A widespread, common bird, it feeds on the ground on various kinds of grass seeds and often comes close to human habitation. Cordon-bleus live in pairs or small family groups.

The globular or oval-shaped nest is made of dry grass and has an entrance hole at the side. It is built in a bush, tree or thatched roof. The female lays 4 or 5 eggs.

NAME: Red Avadavat, *Amandava amandava*
RANGE: India, Pakistan, S.W. China, Hainan, S.E. Asia (introduced in Malaysia), Java, Lesser Sunda Islands
HABITAT: scrub, grassland, reedbeds, cultivated land
SIZE: 9–10 cm (3½–4 in)

A distinctive bird in breeding plumage, the male red avadavat sports bright crimson plumage, dotted with many characteristic white spots; his dark wings, too, are spotted with white. Outside the breeding season, he resembles the female, with a grayish-buff throat and breast. Both sexes have red bills and a patch of red at the base of the tail. Often found in swampy land, the red avadavat feeds on grass seeds. It lives in pairs or groups of up to 30, often with other waxbill species.

The ball-shaped grass nest has an entrance at the side; it is built low in a bush or among rushes or grass. The female incubates the 6 to 10 eggs.

ESTRILDIDAE: Waxbill Family

The range of types of specialist seed-eating songbirds in the Old World is confusing with respect to the inter-relationships of the various groups. Various taxonomical treatments have been proposed, but the one adopted here places the weavers, finches, buntings and warblers all in separate families. Common names, too, are confusing in these groups, for many species of estrildid are called sparrow, finch or weaver.

All members of the waxbill family are small, predominantly seed-eating birds. There are about 126 species, distributed throughout tropical regions of Africa, southern Asia, Australasia and the Pacific islands. The family includes several distinct groups: the waxbills themselves, the grassfinches and the mannikins (a totally separate group from the New World manakins). Most are very colorful birds with striking patches of bright plumage. The bill is typically short and stubby, suited to the diet of seeds. Generally gregarious, flocking birds, many species of waxbill nest socially. Nestlings have remarkable patterns inside their mouths, and the sight of their gapes, marked with black lines and spots, stimulates parents to feed the young. Male and female look alike in some species, different in others.

NAME: Java Sparrow, *Padda oryzivora*
RANGE: Java, Bali; introduced in Sri Lanka, Burma, some Indonesian islands, Seychelles, Zanzibar, St. Helena, Hawaii
HABITAT: rice fields, scrub, mangrove swamps, urban areas
SIZE: 16 cm (6¼ in)

One of the mannikin group, the Java sparrow has become widely established outside its native range, in some places by deliberate introduction, in others by the escape from captivity of large numbers of caged birds. Male and female look alike, both with pinkish-red bills and boldly marked black and white heads. The Java sparrow feeds largely on rice and is thus considered a pest in many areas. It also feeds on fallen seeds of other plants and climbs with great agility on stalks and trees. A gregarious bird, it moves in flocks.

The domed nest is made of grass and built on a wall, under the roof of a building or in a tree. The female lays up to 7 or 8 white eggs, which are incubated for 13 or 14 days. The young are fed on insects until they are able to adopt the adult diet of rice and seeds, which is hard to digest.

NAME: Gouldian Finch, *Chloebia gouldiae*
RANGE: tropical N. Australia
HABITAT: savanna
SIZE: 14 cm (5½ in)

A most beautifully plumaged bird, the gouldian finch occurs in 3 forms that vary in the color of the forehead and face, which may be black, scarlet or, rarely, yellow. Male and female look similar, but the females have duller plumage. The gouldian finch feeds primarily on seeds, which it takes directly from grass heads. It seldom flies down to the ground but clings to grass stems or to the low twigs of bushes and trees within reach of grass heads. It also eats insects in the breeding season. A gregarious bird, it lives in flocks when not breeding. It is seldom far from water and in a drought may become nomadic, wandering in search of water.

The gouldian finch lays its 4 to 8 eggs in a hole in a tree or in a termite mound, sometimes on a sketchy, globular nest.

NAME: Blue-faced Parrot-finch,
Erythrura trichroa
RANGE: Sulawesi, the Moluccas, New Guinea, Bismarck Archipelago, Solomon Islands: Guadalcanal; N.E. Australia, Caroline Islands, Vanuatu, Loyalty Islands
HABITAT: rain forest, mangrove swamps
SIZE: 12 cm (4¾ in)

The blue-faced parrot-finch lives alone or in small groups, frequenting bushes, low trees and vegetation, where it feeds on seeds of various kinds. Male and female look alike, both with blue, green, scarlet and black plumage.

The domed or pear-shaped nest is made of moss and plant fiber and has a side entrance; it is built in a tree or bush. There are 3 to 6 eggs in a clutch.

NAME: Zebra Finch, *Poephila guttata*
RANGE: Australia, Lesser Sunda Islands,
HABITAT: woodland, dry, open country with bushes and trees
SIZE: 9 cm (3½ in)

A common bird throughout Australia, the zebra finch is gregarious and sometimes occurs in large flocks. It feeds in the trees and on the ground on seeds and also on insects, particularly in the breeding season. Male and female differ in appearance: the female lacks the male's facial markings and chestnut flanks and has a grayish-brown throat, with no gray barring.

The timing and frequency of the breeding season depend on rainfall, and in times of drought, birds may wander in search of better conditions. A domed nest is made of grass and twigs low in a tree or bush. There are usually 4 to 6 eggs in a clutch.

Blue-faced Parrot-finch

Red-billed Fire-finch (male)

Red Avadavat
(male)

Red-cheeked
Cordon-bleu
(male)

plumage
variations

Gouldian Finch (male)

Java Sparrow

Zebra Finch (male)

Weavers

NAME: Red-headed Weaver, *Malimbus rubriceps*
RANGE: Africa, south of the Sahara
HABITAT: open woodland, bush country, savanna, cultivated land
SIZE: 14 cm (5½ in)

In the breeding season, the male of this species has bright red plumage on the head, neck and breast; the female looks similar but is yellow where the male is red. The nonbreeding male resembles the female. A rather shy, quiet bird compared to most weavers, the red-headed weaver lives in pairs or small groups and forages in the branches of trees for insects; it also eats seeds.

The polygamous male builds a pendulous woven nest for each of his mates. The nests hang from the ends of high branches and have long entrance tubes. Females lay 2 or 3 eggs.

NAME: Grosbeak/Thick-billed Weaver, *Amblyospiza albifrons*
RANGE: Africa, south of the Sahara
HABITAT: bush country, marshes
SIZE: 19 cm (7½ in)

Identified by its thick, heavy bill, the grosbeak weaver is a fairly common species which lives in small parties or pairs. It feeds mainly on seeds and on some berries when available. The male usually has a white forehead and white wing patches but is otherwise various shades of brown; the female is brown, with heavily streaked underparts.

The birds usually nest in small colonies of about 6 nests. Males may be polygamous. The male weaves a neat nest of fine grass, which is strung between two reed or grass stems. The 3 eggs are incubated by the female.

NAME: Cuckoo/Parasitic Weaver, *Anomalospiza imberbis*
RANGE: Africa: Sierre Leone to Ethiopia, south to South Africa: Transvaal
HABITAT: grassland, bush, cultivated land
SIZE: 11.5 cm (4½ in)

A gregarious bird, the cuckoo weaver congregates in large flocks outside the breeding season. It feeds mainly on grass seeds. Male and female differ in plumage, the female lacking the male's bright yellow markings and having buff and brown plumage. Juvenile birds are quite different in plumage from adults, being dull olive-green streaked with black, with dusky edges to the feathers.

Cuckoo weavers are brood parasites: they lay their eggs in the nests of other birds and leave the foster parents to incubate and rear their young. With plumage markedly different from that of their true parents, the young cuckoo weavers resemble the young of *Cisticola* warblers, birds often used as foster parents.

PLOCEIDAE: Weaver Family

The weavers, buffalo weavers, sparrows and whydahs form a large and successful family of approximately 143 species of seed-eating birds. The group contains birds able to live in close association with humans, one of the most common of these being the house sparrow, which has probably thrived precisely because of this ability. Although originally a native of the Old World, like all of its family, the house sparrow, *Passer domesticus*, has become firmly established in the New World.

This family is so diverse that it is hard to generalize about its members, other than to state that they are seed-eaters, with stout, sharp bills, and that most are gregarious. Male and female look alike in some species but differ in others.

NAME: Baya Weaver, *Ploceus philippinus*
RANGE: India, Sri Lanka to S.W. China, parts of S.E. Asia, Sumatra, Java
HABITAT: cultivated land, grassland, secondary scrub
SIZE: 15 cm (6 in)

A common, gregarious bird, the baya weaver lives in flocks all year round and nests in colonies. It hops around on the ground, feeding on grass and weed seeds and also raids grain crops; this damage is compensated for by its huge consumption of insects, some of them pest species. In breeding plumage, the male has a yellow cap and blackish face mask, but in winter he resembles the female, which has a buff-brown crown.

The male builds a globular nest with a long entrance tube at the bottom, suspended from a branch. There may be up to 200 nests in a single tree. There are usually 3 eggs, which the female incubates for 14 or 15 days. Males are polygamous and may have several mates and nests.

NAME: Village Weaver, *Ploceus cucullatus*
RANGE: Africa, south of the Sahara (not extreme south), Príncipe Island
HABITAT: forest, bush, cultivated and inhabited areas
SIZE: 18 cm (7 in)

Noisy, conspicuous birds, the village weavers live in flocks and breed in colonies. They generally frequent the lower levels of trees in areas near water. Although they damage grain crops, these weavers compensate to some degree by feeding on vast quantities of weed seeds, as well as on some insects. The brightly plumaged male bird is largely yellow, with a black throat and mask and characteristic mottling on the back. The female is duller, with olive-brown on the upperparts and yellowish-white below.

Village weavers breed in colonies, with as many as 100 nests in the same tree. Males are polygamous and may mate several times. The nest is woven from long grass stems and hangs from an outer branch; it has an entrance low down. The female incubates the 1 to 3 eggs.

NAME: Red-billed Quelea, *Quelea quelea*
RANGE: Africa, south of the Sahara
HABITAT: savanna, cultivated land, almost anywhere with trees
SIZE: 12.5 cm (5 in)

An extremely abundant and gregarious species, the red-billed quelea flies in cloudlike flocks of thousands of birds, which descend to feed on grain crops and do incredible damage. They also feed on weed seeds. These birds were one of the main agricultural problems in Africa and have been destroyed on a huge scale, but their numbers have recently decreased, apparently due to natural causes, to the point where controls have been relaxed. In breeding plumage the male bird has a reddish tinge to his crown and chest; his face, chin and throat may be white, buff or black. Out of the breeding season, the male's bill is still red, but he otherwise resembles the female, which has streaky brown and buff plumage and a brownish crown.

Red-billed queleas form monogamous pairs and breed in dense colonies. The male builds the kidney-shaped nest, which hangs from a branch and has a side entrance. The 2 or 3 eggs are incubated by the female for 12 days, and both parents feed the young.

NAME: Red Bishop, *Euplectes orix*
RANGE: Africa, south of the Sahara
HABITAT: open grassland, often near water
SIZE: 12.5 cm (5 in)

Outside the breeding season, these abundant weavers form huge flocks, which are capable of doing enormous damage to grain crops. They also feed on grass seeds. In breeding plumage the male bird is largely red and black, while the female is streaked buff and brown; the nonbreeding male resembles the female but is darker.

Each male red bishop has 3 or 4 mates, which all nest within his defined territory. He weaves an oval grass nest among bulrushes or reeds or in sugarcane plantations or cornfields. The female lines the nest and lays 3 eggs, which she incubates for 11 to 14 days. She feeds her young with insects until they fly, 13 to 16 days after hatching.

Village Weaver (male)

Red-billed Quelea (male)

Baya Weaver (male)

Cuckoo Weaver (male)

Red-headed Weaver (male)

Grosbeak Weaver (male)

Red Bishop (male)

Weavers

NAME: **Buffalo Weaver,** *Bubalornis albirostris*
RANGE: **Africa, south of the Sahara**
HABITAT: **savanna, scrub, cultivated land**
SIZE: **24 cm (9½ in)**

Usually seen in small flocks, the buffalo weaver feeds mainly on the ground on a variety of grass seeds and insects. The plumage of the male is black, but with white bases to the feathers, and he has a black and white or reddish bill. The female has mottled brown plumage and a blackish or red bill.

Up to 8 pairs of buffalo weavers make a huge communal nest in a tree; it is kept in good order all year round and used for years. The framework of the nest is made of thorny sticks, and each individual nest within it is lined with fine grass and rootlets. Females usually lay 2 to 4 eggs and feed their young on insects.

NAME: **Gray-headed Sparrow,** *Passer griseus*
RANGE: **Africa, south of the Sahara**
HABITAT: **bush, cultivated land, near human habitation**
SIZE: **15 cm (6 in)**

A bold little bird, the gray-headed sparrow is common in towns and villages and is similar to the house sparrow in its behavior. It feeds on almost any grain, plant matter and insects and does some damage to crops. The male is slightly larger than the female, but the two look alike, both with distinctive gray heads and mottled wings.

An untidy nest made of grass is built in a tree, in a thatched roof or at any other suitable site, or the birds may use an old nest of another species. There are usually 2 to 4 eggs in a clutch.

NAME: **House Sparrow,** *Passer domesticus*
RANGE: **temperate Europe and Asia, Africa, north of the Sahara; introduced worldwide**
HABITAT: **cultivated land, human habitation**
SIZE: **14.5 cm (5¾ in)**

An extremely adaptable and successful bird, the house sparrow lives in close association with humans all over the world and is one of the most familiar of all birds. House sparrows were first introduced into the USA in 1850, when a few birds were released in Central Park, New York City. Since then, the species has spread all over North and South America, and the birds seem able to adapt remarkably quickly to new environments.

House sparrows often perch on trees and buildings but feed mainly on the ground. They eat almost anything: grain, weed seeds, insects, refuse and food scraps put out by humans.

Gregarious birds, they usually move in flocks and roost in closely packed groups. The male bird is identified by his gray crown, edged with chestnut, his black bib and brown and black-striped back and wings. The female is brownish-gray, with gray underparts.

Both members of a breeding pair help to build the nest, although the male does most of the work. Built in any hole or crevice in a building or wall, such as under eaves or in pipes, or sometimes in a tree or creeping plants, the nest is made of straw, plant stems, paper, cloth or any other available material. The 3 to 5 eggs are incubated, mostly by the female, for 11 to 14 days. Both parents feed the young, mainly on insects. There may be two or three broods a year.

NAME: **Rock Sparrow,** *Petronia petronia*
RANGE: **N. Africa, Madeira and Canary Islands; S.W. Europe, east through Balkans and central Asia to N. China**
HABITAT: **stony mountain slopes, ruined buildings, semidesert**
SIZE: **14 cm (5½ in)**

Although not as bold with humans as the house sparrow, the rock sparrow often lives near villages and dwellings. It is a gregarious bird and moves in flocks, searching for seeds, insects and berries to eat. Male and female look alike.

The nest is made in a crevice in a rock, wall or building or sometimes in a tree or a rodent's burrow. The female lays 4 to 8 eggs, usually 5 or 6. Both parents tend and feed the young, and there may be a second brood.

NAME: **Sociable Weaver,** *Philetairus socius*
RANGE: **Africa: Namibia, South Africa**
HABITAT: **dry scrub**
SIZE: **14 cm (5½ in)**

Sociable weavers move in flocks of anything up to a few hundred birds. They feed on insects and seeds, all of which they take on the ground. Male and female look alike and are identified by their grayish-brown crowns, black bibs and the cream-edged dark feathers on the back that give the plumage a scaly look.

The most remarkable feature about these birds is their enormous communal nest, usually made in a large acacia tree, which may be a home for up to a hundred pairs. The birds do not use the nest just for breeding but live and roost in it all year round. Nests are constantly repaired and rebuilt and may be used for years. Sociable weavers are monogamous birds, and within the communal nest, each pair has its own chamber and entrance. The average clutch contains 3 or 4 eggs.

NAME: **Snow Finch,** *Montifringilla nivalis*
RANGE: **S. Europe, across central Asia to the Himalayas**
HABITAT: **barren, stony ground on mountains at 1,800–2,100 m (6,000–7,000 ft)**
SIZE: **18 cm (7 in)**

Although it seldom leaves its mountain habitat, the snow finch may descend to alpine valleys in bad winter weather. It perches on rocks and buildings and hops and walks quickly on the ground as it forages for insects and, in summer, the seeds of alpine plants. A bold little bird, it is often seen by skiers in alpine resorts and readily approaches to collect crumbs of food. The male is identified by his gray head, black throat and black and white wing and tail feathers. The female has a brownish head and less white on the wings and tail. Adults have black bills in the breeding season and orange-yellow bills in the autumn and winter.

The nest of feathers, dead grass and moss is made in a hole in a rock or building, where these exist, or in a mammal's burrow. The female lays 4 or 5 eggs on a warm lining of feathers and hair. Both parents incubate the eggs for 13 to 14 days and feed the young; a second brood may follow.

NAME: **Paradise Whydah,** *Vidua paradisaea*
RANGE: **E. and S. Africa: Sudan to Angola; South Africa: Natal**
HABITAT: **dry open country**
SIZE: **male: 38 cm (15 in)
female: 15 cm (6 in)**

The elongated central tail feathers of the male account for the discrepancy in size between male and female paradise whydahs. The female bird has mottled brown and buff plumage similar to, but duller than, that of the male in non-breeding plumage. Often gathering in small flocks, paradise whydahs usually feed on the ground on seeds.

In his courtship display, the male bird flies with his long central tail feathers raised almost at a right angle and may also hover near the female, slowly beating his wings. Like all whydahs, this species is a brood parasite: it lays its eggs in the nests of other bird species, usually the melba finches of the waxbill family, Estrildidae. The young of the melba finch have complex patterns on the lining of their mouths which stimulate their parents to feed them, and the association between brood parasite and host has become so strong that the young whydahs have similar mouth patterns. They can also mimic the calls and postures of their foster siblings.

communal
nest

Sociable Weaver

Paradise
Whydah
(male)

Buffalo
Weaver
(male)

Rock Sparrow

House Sparrow
(male)

Gray-headed Sparrow

Snow Finch (male)

Starlings

NAME: Starling, *Sturnus vulgaris*
RANGE: Europe, Asia; introduced almost
worldwide
HABITAT: near habitation, cultivated land
SIZE: 21.5 cm (8½ in)

One of the most familiar birds in city areas, starlings roost in huge numbers on buildings, often performing spectacular massed flights over the site prior to settling. In breeding plumage both male and female are blackish, with a green or purple iridescent sheen. In winter, the plumage is heavily spotted with white, particularly in the female. Juveniles are grayish-brown with pale throats. Starlings are adaptable birds and take to a wide variety of habitats, although deciduous woodland and built-up areas are preferred in the breeding season. They feed on the ground on insects, larvae, earthworms, slugs, snails and centipedes, among other invertebrates, constantly probing the surface with their bills. Fruit, grain, berries and seeds are also included in their widely varying diet. Starlings may sometimes feed in the trees, and they also pursue insect prey in the air with swift, wheeling flight.

Starlings breed in colonies or in separate pairs. The nest is usually built in a hole in a tree or building or among rocks and is made of stems, leaves and other plant material. The female lays 4 to 9 eggs, usually 5 to 7, which both parents incubate for 12 or 13 days. They feed their young for about 3 weeks, but even after leaving the nest, the young starlings follow their parents and solicit food. There may be one or two broods a season. Northernmost populations migrate south in winter.

NAME: Red-winged Starling,
Onychognathus morio
RANGE: Africa: Senegal to Sudan, south
through E. Africa to South Africa:
Cape Province
HABITAT: rocky hills and cliffs, cultivated
and city areas, woodland
SIZE: 30.5 cm (12 in)

A noisy, conspicuous bird, the red-winged starling moves in pairs or small flocks, searching for fruit and insects. Its flight is fast and dipping, and it makes a constant whistling call while in the air. The male bird is mainly blue-black, with brown-tipped, rufous flight feathers; the female has a gray head and neck and a gray-streaked breast but otherwise looks similar to the male.

The nest is made of grass and mud and is built in a hole in a cliff, cave or building or in the roof of a hut. The female lays 3 to 5 eggs, which she incubates for 12 to 23 days.

STURNIDAE: Starling Family

Apart from the species introduced into other places by humans, all 108 species of starling occur in the Old World, with the greatest diversity in Asia. As well as the starlings, the family includes the mynas and the 2 species of oxpecker. Starlings are medium-sized songbirds, 18 to 43 cm (7 to 17 in) in length, with a sturdy appearance and active habits. Most have long bills and strong legs and feet; wings may be rounded and short or long and pointed, and although tails are usually short and square, they are long and graduated in some species. Typically the plumage is dark, often enlivened with a beautiful iridescent sheen of blue, green or purple, particularly in the breeding season. Male and female look alike in some species and differ slightly in others.

Many starlings live in open country and feed on the ground, although some occur in more wooded areas and are arboreal. They feed on almost anything, but largely on insects, fruit, grain, bird's eggs and lizards. Starlings fly swiftly and run or walk on the ground. Generally gregarious birds, they roost communally, often making characteristic loud whistles while flying to roosting sites in huge flocks. Most starlings nest in holes in trees or buildings, but some dig nesting burrows in riverbanks or build domed nests in trees.

NAME: Hill Myna, *Gracula religiosa*
RANGE: India, Sri Lanka, Andaman and
Nicobar Islands, S. China, Hainan, S.E.
Asia, Indonesia; introduced elsewhere
HABITAT: forest
SIZE: 30.5 cm (12 in)

A stockily built bird, the hill myna has glossy black plumage, with bright golden-yellow wattles on the head and a conspicuous white patch on each wing. Male and female look similar. A noisy, sociable bird, it lives in small groups of up to 6 outside the breeding season, occasionally gathering in larger groups at feeding trees. It spends most of its life in trees or bushes and feeds on fruit, particularly figs, berries, buds, nectar, and some insects and lizards. It rarely descends to the ground. Hill mynas have a wide repertoire of calls, but although "myna birds" are first-rate mimics in captivity, they do not mimic sounds in the wild.

The nest is made in a hole in a tree trunk, often an old woodpecker hole. Both parents incubate the 2 or 3 eggs and feed the young.

NAME: Superb Starling, *Spreo superbus*
RANGE: Africa: Ethiopia, Sudan to
Tanzania
HABITAT: scrub, near habitation
SIZE: 18 cm (7 in)

One of the most brilliantly colored starlings, the superb starling has metallic green and blue plumage. Male and female look alike, but juveniles have dull black plumage on head, neck and breast. The superb starling is a gregarious bird, quite fearless of humans where it occurs near villages and towns. It feeds on the ground on insects and berries.

The ball-shaped nest is made of grass and thorny twigs and is usually situated on a branch of a thorn tree or in a bush. A hole in a tree may sometimes be used or the old nest of another bird. There are usually 4 eggs in a clutch.

NAME: Metallic/Shining Starling, *Aplonis metallica*
RANGE: the Moluccas, across New Guinea
region to Bismarck Archipelago and
Solomon Islands; migrates to N. coast
of Australia
HABITAT: rain forest
SIZE: 25 cm (9¾ in)

The black plumage of the metallic starling has a purple and green sheen, and the bird is also characterized by its long, sharply graduated tail and its red eyes. A gregarious, noisy bird, it is mainly tree-dwelling but does sometimes feed on the ground. Fruit and insects are its main foods.

Metallic starlings nest in large colonies of as many as 300 pairs. The large, domed nests are made of plant tendrils and suspended from branches. The usual clutch is 2 to 4 eggs.

NAME: Yellow-billed Oxpecker,
Buphagus africanus
RANGE: Africa, south of the Sahara (not
extreme south)
HABITAT: dry open country
SIZE: 23 cm (9 in)

Common sights in African game reserves, the yellow-billed oxpecker and the similar red-billed oxpecker, *B. erythrorhynchus*, both specialize in feeding on ticks, which they pull off buffaloes, zebras and other large mammals. Their heavy bills are well suited to this habit, and they have strong, sharp claws with which they cling to the animal's skin. They clamber nimbly all over the body in their search, even probing ears and nostrils. Flies are also eaten. Oxpeckers give a warning call when alarmed, often alerting the mammal to danger. Male and female birds look alike.

The nest is made in a hole in a tree or rock or under the eaves of a building. The female lays 2 to 5 eggs, which are incubated for about 12 days.

Yellow-billed Oxpecker

communal nests of
Metallic Starling

Metallic Starling

Superb Starling

Starling

Hill Myna

Red-winged Starling
(male)

Orioles, Drongos, Wattlebirds

ORIOLIDAE: Oriole Family

There are about 28 species of oriole, found mainly in tropical regions from Africa through Asia to Australia. They are noted for their clear, melodious calls. Only 1 species, the golden oriole, occurs in Europe in summer, when it migrates there to breed. Orioles are arboreal birds, and they feed in trees on insects and fruit. They have strong, pointed bills and short, but powerful legs. Males and females look unalike in most species, females usually having duller, streaked plumage.

NAME: **Golden Oriole**, *Oriolus oriolus*
RANGE: **breeds in Europe as far north as S. Finland, Sweden and Britain, N. Africa, Asia; winters in Africa and N.W. India**
HABITAT: **forest, woodland, orchards**
SIZE: **24 cm (9½ in)**

The golden oriole frequents the tree-tops, feeding on insects and fruit, and even the brightly plumaged male is seldom seen. Females and juveniles are duller, with yellowish-green upperparts and lighter, grayish-white underparts. Golden orioles rarely descend to the ground, and their flight is swift and undulating. Although they may remain in family groups for a while after breeding, they usually live alone or in pairs.

The courting male chases the female at top speed through the branches. She does most of the work of building the hammocklike nest, which is suspended by its rim from a forked branch. Both parents, but mainly the female, incubate the 3 or 4 eggs for 14 to 15 days and feed the young for a further 14 days or so.

NAME: **Yellow Figbird**, *Sphecotheres viridis*
RANGE: **N. and E. Australia, S. New Guinea, Kai Islands**
HABITAT: **forest, savanna, fruiting trees**
SIZE: **28 cm (11 in)**

Formerly regarded as a separate species (*S. flaviventris*), the yellow figbird has been proved to be conspecific with the southern figbird (formerly, *S. vieilloti*). The new species name *viridis* now applies to all forms of *Sphecotheres*, from Timor to southern New Guinea and New South Wales. Females of all forms have duller plumage than males. An arboreal bird, the yellow figbird moves in noisy flocks, feeding on figs and other fruit. It also feeds on insects, which it takes on the wing.

The flimsy, saucer-shaped nest is made of twigs and plant tendrils and is built on a high outer branch. There are normally 3 eggs in a clutch.

DICRURIDAE: Drongo Family

The tree-dwelling drongos occur in tropical regions of Africa, Asia and Australasia. There are 20 species, most of which have dark plumage, pointed wings and square or forked tails, often with long, decorative feathers. Drongos spend much of their time perched, on the lookout for insect prey, which they catch in the air; they are skillful, but not sustained fliers.

Males and females look alike, but females are usually slightly smaller.

NAME: **Fork-tailed Drongo**, *Dicrurus adsimilis*
RANGE: **Africa, south of the Sahara, Bioko, Príncipe Island**
HABITAT: **open bush, woodland**
SIZE: **23–25.5 cm (9–10 in)**

A typical drongo, with its black plumage and deeply forked tail, this bird is a common inhabitant of almost any type of woodland, including coconut plantations. It darts out from a perch to catch insects and then returns to the same perch; a wide range of insects is eaten, including butterflies. This drongo is fast and highly maneuverable in flight.

The nest, woven from plant stems, is made on a forked branch of a tree, and there are usually 3 eggs. Like all drongos, this bird is extremely aggressive in defense of its nest and will chase away even much larger birds.

NAME: **Greater Racket-tailed Drongo**, *Dicrurus paradiseus*
RANGE: **India, Sri Lanka, Andaman and Nicobar Islands, S.W. China, Hainan, S.E. Asia, Sumatra, Java, Borneo**
HABITAT: **forest, cultivated land**
SIZE: **33 cm (13 in)**

The male's elongated, racket-tipped, outer tail feathers may add another 32 cm (12½ in) or more to his total length. The female has slightly shorter tail streamers but otherwise resembles the male. This drongo is also identified by its prominent crest, which is smaller in young birds. A bold, noisy bird, it hunts for its insect prey mainly at dusk, when it darts out from the treetops to seize creatures such as moths, termites and dragonflies. It also picks larvae off tree trunks and branches and sometimes eats lizards and even small birds. Nectar from flowers is another important item of diet.

The nest is a loosely built cup, sited on a forked branch of a tree. There are usually 3 eggs, and both parents are believed to incubate the clutch and feed the young. They are extremely pugnacious in their defense of the nest and young.

NAME: **Pygmy Drongo**, *Chaetorhynchus papuensis*
RANGE: **New Guinea**
HABITAT: **forest on mountain slopes**
SIZE: **20.5 cm (8 in)**

Rather different from other drongos and the only species in its genus, the pygmy drongo has a heavier, more hooked bill than other species and twelve, instead of ten, tail feathers. It perches to watch for insect prey and then darts out to seize it in the air. This unusual drongo can be mistaken for a monarch flycatcher, which it resembles.

CALLAEIDAE: Wattlebird Family

The wattlebirds, named for the fleshy, colorful wattles at the sides of the bill, live in the forests of New Zealand. They have large, strong legs and are thought to be related to starlings. There are 3 species, but one, the huia, *Heteralocha acutirostris*, is now believed to be extinct. Like many island birds, the wattlebirds suffered from the colonization of New Zealand and the resulting introduction of foreign animals. The remaining species need careful conservation if they are to survive.

NAME: **Kokako**, *Callaeas cinerea*
RANGE: **New Zealand**
HABITAT: **forest**
SIZE: **38 cm (15 in)**   Ⓥ Ⓔ

The kokako has suffered severely from the introduction into New Zealand of predators, such as rats, mustelids and cats, all likely to prey on the birds and their eggs and nestlings. The race on South Island is critically endangered and may even be extinct, but on North Island, kokakos, although vulnerable, are still fairly well distributed. They are under continued pressure from predators and the destruction of forest, however, and must be actively conserved. Competition for food from introduced herbivores may also be a factor in their decline. The South Island race has orange wattles, and the North Island, blue wattles.

Kokakos, like all wattlebirds, rarely fly but feed on the ground and in trees, hopping energetically from branch to branch. They do occasionally glide from one tree to another. They feed on leaves, flowers, fruit and insects. Usually in pairs or small flocks, kokakos reveal their presence by their varied musical calls.

The nest is made of sticks lined with plant material on a forked branch of a tree. The female incubates the 2 or 3 eggs for about 25 days, and both parents feed the young until they leave the nest some 27 or 28 days after hatching.

Golden Oriole
(male)

Pygmy
Drongo

Greater Racket-tailed Drongo

Yellow Figbird
S. vieilloti (male)

S. flaviventris (male)

Fork-tailed Drongo

Kokako

Butcherbirds, Wood Swallows, Mudnest Builders

CRACTICIDAE:
Butcherbird Family

The 8 species in this Australasian family are strongly built birds, with heavy, hooked bills and, generally, black, gray and white plumage. Primarily tree-dwelling birds, they are noisy and gregarious. Males and females look alike in some species, unalike in others.

NAME: **Black Butcherbird, *Cracticus quoyi***
RANGE: **Australia: Queensland, coast of Northern Territory; New Guinea, Japen and Aru Islands**
HABITAT: **forest**
SIZE: **32–36 cm (12½–14¼ in)**

A bold, often aggressive bird, the black butcherbird feeds mostly on the ground, where it hops along on its short legs. Using its sharp, hooked bill, it tears up prey too large to be swallowed whole such as large insects, particularly grasshoppers, and small vertebrates. Male and female look alike and live alone or in small family groups.

A nest of twigs is made on a forked branch, and the female lays 3 or 4 eggs.

NAME: **Australian Magpie, *Gymnorhina tibicen***
RANGE: **S. New Guinea, Australia, Tasmania; introduced in New Zealand**
HABITAT: **open woodland, grassland, parks, gardens**
SIZE: **36–40 cm (14¼–15¾ in)**

Although it roosts and nests in trees, the Australian magpie does much of its feeding on the ground, searching for larvae, beetles and grasshoppers. Fruit and vegetation are also part of its diet. Australian magpies are gregarious birds and live in groups consisting of two pairs of adults or a larger number of birds, led by a dominant, polygamous male. Males and females look more or less alike.

The nest is made in a tree, and the female lays 3 eggs, which she incubates for 20 to 21 days. She also does most of the feeding of the young.

NAME: **Pied Currawong, *Strepera graculina***
RANGE: **Australia: Queensland to Victoria; Lord Howe Island**
HABITAT: **forest, clumps of trees in parks, suburban land**
SIZE: **45 cm (17¾ in)**

Primarily an arboreal bird, the pied currawong climbs in the trees in search of insects, larvae and fruit; it will also feed on the young and eggs of other bird species. It flies between feeding areas and sometimes feeds on the ground, turning over debris to find insects.

Noisy, gregarious birds, pied currawongs live in flocks. Their name is derived from the similar sounding call the birds make, often while in flight.

The nest is made in a tree, and the female lays 3 or 4 eggs.

ARTAMIDAE:
Wood Swallow Family

The 10 species of wood swallow are essentially Australasian birds, which have extended their range as far as India and southern China. They have stocky bodies and long, pointed wings and are skilled fliers. Launching themselves from frequently used perches, they chase and catch insect prey in the air. Male and female look alike or nearly so.

NAME: **White-breasted Wood Swallow, *Artamus leucorhynchus***
RANGE: **Australia and New Guinea, Philippines, Andaman, Palau and Fiji Islands**
HABITAT: **woodland, mangrove swamps**
SIZE: **17 cm (6¾ in)**

A gregarious bird, the white-breasted wood swallow lives in groups of 10 or more birds, which often sit huddled together on a branch, waiting for prey. Together they will attack passing birds, and individuals dart off in pursuit of insect prey. They return to the perch to consume the catch. If there is a shortage of flying insects, these wood swallows feed on ground insects and larvae.

Both members of a breeding pair help to build a cup-shaped nest in the fork of a tree, a hole in a trunk or branch or a disused magpie lark's nest. The female lays 3 or 4 eggs, which both parents incubate for about 19 days.

NAME: **White-browed Wood Swallow, *Artamus superciliosus***
RANGE: **Australia: breeds Victoria, New South Wales to S.E. Queensland; winters throughout continent**
HABITAT: **arid scrub, savanna**
SIZE: **18–20 cm (7–7¾ in)**

A highly nomadic bird, the white-browed wood swallow disperses over much of the continent out of the breeding season, often moving in mixed flocks with other species of wood swallow. Like them, white-browed wood swallows perch in groups on branches and fly out to catch insects in the air. The female is duller in plumage than the male, and her "eyebrow" streaks are less distinct.

The nest is built in a tree or on a tree stump and is made of sticks and dry grass. Both parents incubate the 2 or 3 eggs for about 16 days.

GRALLINIDAE:
Mudnest Builder Family

The mudnest builders are a small family of medium to large songbirds that live in Australia and New Guinea. There are only 4 species, divided into 2 subfamilies, which are linked merely by their method of building nests; all build large mud nests in trees. One subfamily contains the magpie lark and the torrent lark, both strikingly marked black and white birds; the other contains the apostlebird and the white-winged chough. Male and female magpie larks differ slightly in appearance, but in the other species the sexes look similar.

NAME: **Magpie Lark, *Grallina cyanoleuca***
RANGE: **Australia**
HABITAT: **open woodland, parks**
SIZE: **25–28 cm (9¾–11 in)**

A distinctive black and white bird, the magpie lark spends much of its time on the ground, feeding on insects. It is not shy and is common near human settlements and by roadsides. Many of the insects it consumes are considered pests; it also feeds on the freshwater snails that harbor the liver fluke, so often transmitted to cattle and sheep. The female differs from the male in having a white throat and forehead and has no patches of white plumage above or below her eyes.

Magpie larks pair for life and tend to nest in the same tree year after year, several pairs nesting near one another. The bowl-shaped nest is made from mud lined with grass and is situated on a branch. The female lays 3 to 5 eggs, which are incubated by both parents. The young are also fed by both parents and are independent at 4 weeks.

NAME: **Apostlebird, *Struthidea cinerea***
RANGE: **Australia: Victoria, New South Wales, Queensland**
HABITAT: **open woodland, scrub, cultivated land**
SIZE: **33 cm (13 in)**

The gregarious apostlebird usually lives in groups of about 12 birds — hence its common name — which keep together even in the breeding season. The group may be led by a dominant pair. The birds feed mostly on the ground on insects and seeds, but they will also jump from branch to branch in the trees and fly for short distances.

The bowl-shaped mud nest is lined with grass and made in a tree, usually near several other nests. The female lays 4 or 5 eggs, sometimes more than one female laying in the same nest; the eggs are incubated for 19 days. The young are fed by the group.

White-breasted
Wood Swallow

White-browed
Wood Swallow
(male)

Black Butcherbird

Australian Magpie

Pied Currawong

Magpie Lark
(male)

Apostlebird

Bowerbirds, Birds of Paradise

PTILONORHYNCHIDAE: Bowerbird Family

The 18 species of bowerbird all occur in New Guinea and Australia and are closely related to the birds of paradise, also from those regions. Bowerbirds have stout bills, straight or curved, and strong legs and feet. Much of their life is spent on the ground, but they feed and nest in trees. Females have much duller plumage than males, usually brownish and gray.

The family gets its common name from the "bower-building" activities of all but a few species: the males build ornate bowers on the ground, which they decorate with colorful objects to attract the attention of females.

NAME: **MacGregor's/Gardener Bowerbird,** *Amblyornis macgregoriae*
RANGE: **mountains of New Guinea (not N.W.)**
HABITAT: **forest**
SIZE: **25.5 cm (10 in)**

The male MacGregor's bowerbird is distinguished by his spectacular crest but otherwise has sober plumage. The female looks similar but lacks the crest. They are common, but shy birds and feed on fruit. The male's bower consists of a saucer-shaped platform of moss with a central column of twigs, both decorated with berries, flowers and bright objects such as shiny dead beetles. The bird attends his bower daily, repairing it and cleaning away any debris. Once he has attracted a mate, he displays and then chases her before mating.

The female builds a practical, cup-shaped nest in a tree and incubates her single egg herself.

NAME: **Satin Bowerbird,** *Ptilonorhynchus violaceus*
RANGE: **Australia: Queensland to Victoria**
HABITAT: **forest**
SIZE: **27–33 cm (10½–13 in)**

The male satin bowerbird has a violet sheen to his black plumage — hence the common name — while the female is mainly olive-green, tinged with yellow. Noisy, gregarious birds outside the breeding season, they feed on fruit and insects and often raid orchards. They make a variety of calls and also mimic other sounds. The male's display bower is an "avenue" of twigs, which sweeps upward at both ends and is liberally decorated with berries, flowers and any other bright objects. This bowerbird is particularly attracted to anything blue and will collect items such as bits of blue glass, paper or plastic. If a female shows interest, the male dances in his bower, alternately drooping and raising his wings and puffing up his feathers.

The female builds a nest of twigs and leaves in a tree and lays 2 eggs, which she alone incubates for 19 to 23 days.

PARADISAEIDAE: Bird of Paradise Family

There are 42 known species of bird of paradise, and this aptly named group probably contains the most visually spectacular of all birds. They inhabit the rain forests of New Guinea, the Moluccas and northern Australia and feed on fruit, berries, insects, frogs and lizards.

The males are renowned for their extraordinarily varied and colorful plumage and often have long, decorative tail and head feathers. They use this ornate plumage in the complex courtship dances they perform to attract females. Female birds have dull, usually brown, plumage and look quite different from males.

NAME: **King of Saxony Bird of Paradise,** *Pteridophora alberti*
RANGE: **mountains of New Guinea**
HABITAT: **rain forest**
SIZE: **23 cm (9 in)**

The male King of Saxony bird of paradise has two unique head plumes, one extending from each side of its head. These plumes are two or three times the body length and consist of wirelike shafts bearing a series of horny plates. The bird chooses a display site on a high branch, holds his head plumes up, and bounces up and down while expanding and retracting his back feathers and hissing. The whole effect is quite spectacular. As the female approaches, the male sweeps the long head plumes in front of her and then follows her, and they mate.

The female bird is brownish-gray, with black-barred white underparts. The birds live in the middle and upper layers of the forest and feed on fruit.

NAME: **Crinkle-collared Manucode,** *Manucodia chalybatus*
RANGE: **New Guinea, Misoöl Island**
HABITAT: **rain forest**
SIZE: **37 cm (14½ in)**

The crinkle-collared manucode is a glossy purplish-black bird with curly green feathers adorning its head and neck. Male and female look alike and have none of the spectacular adornments associated with other birds of paradise. They live in the middle to upper stories of the forest and feed on fruit.

These manucodes form monogamous pairs and nest on forked branches. The female is thought to lay 1 egg.

NAME: **King Bird of Paradise,** *Cicinnurus regius*
RANGE: **New Guinea; Japen, Misoöl, Salawati and Aru Islands**
HABITAT: **lowland rain forest**
SIZE: **30.5 cm (12 in) including tail**

A spectacular crimson bird, the king bird of paradise has two wirelike, lyre-shaped tail feathers tipped with metallic green and a fanlike plume at each shoulder. The female lacks the male's long tail wires and has brown plumage edged with chestnut and olive. These birds feed mainly on fruit at all levels of the forest. The male chooses a horizontal branch as his display ground and spends much time there. He adopts various display postures to attract a mate, including raising his tail wires, hanging upside down, and vibrating his wings.

The female makes her nest in a hole in a tree — the only bird of paradise to do so. She lays 2 eggs, which she is thought to incubate for about 12 days.

NAME: **Ribbon-tailed Astrapia/Bird of Paradise,** *Astrapia mayeri*
RANGE: **mountains of central New Guinea**
HABITAT: **rain forest**
SIZE: **1.2 m (4 ft) including tail of up to 91.5 cm (36 in)**

Ribbonlike central tail feathers are the main identifying feature of the male of this species, which is mainly black with patches of green iridescence. The tail feathers play a central role in the male's courtship display, when they are twitched from side to side. The female bird has a much shorter tail and glossy black, green and brown plumage.

One of the last birds of paradise to be discovered, this species lives in a very restricted area of the central highlands. It frequents the branches of tall trees and feeds on fruit. The shallow, cup-shaped nest is made on a base of leaves from moss and vine tendrils.

NAME: **Blue Bird of Paradise,** *Paradisaea rudolphi*
RANGE: **mountains of S.E. New Guinea**
HABITAT: **rain forest**
SIZE: **28 cm (11 in) excluding tail**

The male blue bird of paradise has a velvety black breast and long, lacy flank plumes. His distinctive tail feathers, are narrow and straplike and play an important part in the display dance he performs to attract the much plainer female. The male hangs upside down from a branch, with the flank plumes spread out and the tail straps held in graceful curves. In this position, he swings to and fro, all the while making a strange, grating call.

A nest is made by the female in a low tree, and she is thought to lay 1 egg.

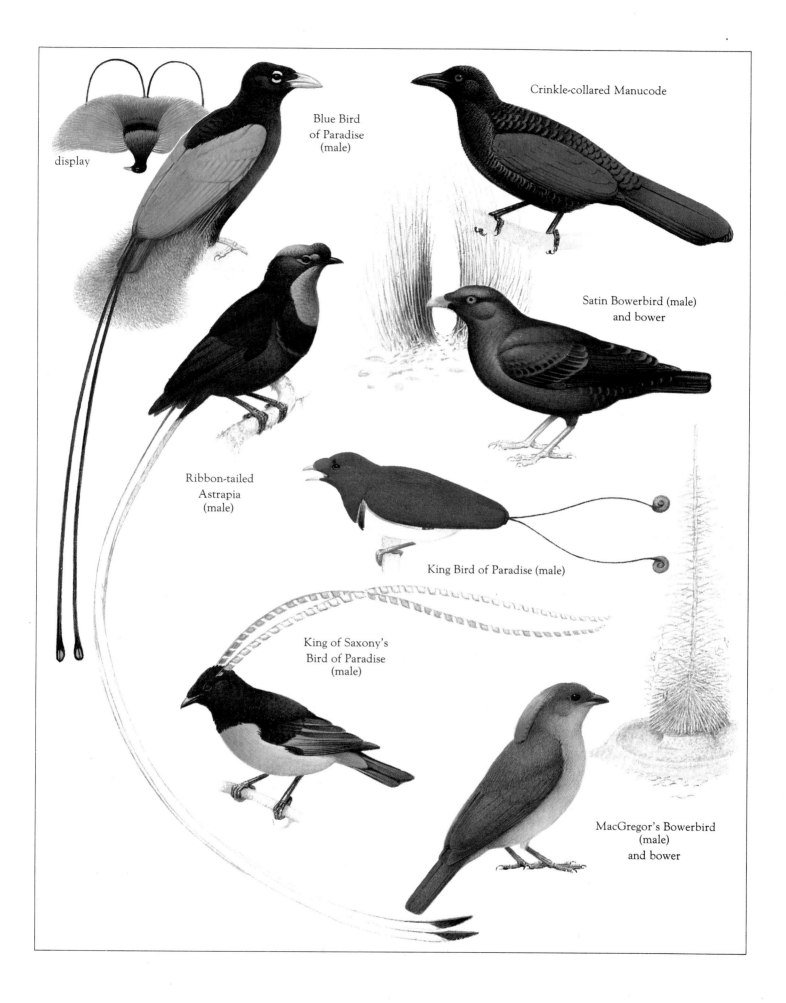

display

Blue Bird
of Paradise
(male)

Crinkle-collared Manucode

Satin Bowerbird (male)
and bower

Ribbon-tailed
Astrapia
(male)

King Bird of Paradise (male)

King of Saxony's
Bird of Paradise
(male)

MacGregor's Bowerbird
(male)
and bower

Crows

NAME: Common Crow, *Corvus brachyrhynchos*
RANGE: S. Canada, USA
HABITAT: open country, farmland, open woodland, woodland edge, parks
SIZE: 43–53 cm (17–20¾ in)

This stocky, black-plumaged crow is extremely abundant and widespread and adapts well to most habitats. Almost omnivorous, it feeds largely on the ground, but also in trees, on insects, spiders, frogs, reptiles, small mammals, birds and their eggs and carrion. It also eats grain, fruit and nuts and scavenges on refuse. These crows usually forage in pairs, although lone males are seen in the breeding season; in winter, they gather in huge flocks to fly to communal roosts.

A nest of sticks and twigs is made in a tree, bush or, occasionally, on a telephone pole. The 3 to 6 eggs are incubated for about 18 days, probably by the female alone. Northern populations migrate south in winter.

NAME: Rook, *Corvus frugilegus*
RANGE: Europe, N. Asia, east to China
HABITAT: open country and farmland with clumps of trees, small woods
SIZE: 45 cm (17¾ in)

The glossy black rook is distinguished by the patch of bare skin on its face in front of the eyes and the shaggy, loose feathers on its thighs. It feeds largely on grain crops and earthworms, which it obtains by driving its bill into the earth (hence the bare forehead, which avoids soiled plumage) and then forcing it open to seize the worm. Insects and other invertebrates, small mammals, young birds, eggs, nuts and fruit are also included in its diet. Primarily a ground-feeder, the rook will fly up into trees to take nuts or other specific items. Rooks live in pairs but in autumn and winter gather in large communal roosts.

Colonies of rooks nest at the tops of tall trees, each pair making a nest of sticks and twigs. The male bird feeds the female while she incubates the 3 to 5 eggs for 16 to 18 days. Both parents tend and feed the young. Northern birds migrate south in winter.

NAME: Hume's Ground Jay, *Pseudopodoces humilis*
RANGE: China
HABITAT: open, sandy country
SIZE: 20 cm (7¾ in)

One of a distinct group of ground-living corvids, Hume's ground jay runs speedily on its long legs and has a heavy bill, with which it probes and digs in the ground for its insect food.

It digs its own nest in the earth, and the female lays 4 to 6 eggs.

CORVIDAE: Crow Family

The 105 species of crow, jay and magpie constitute an advanced and highly successful family of tough, intelligent and adaptable songbirds. They occur worldwide except in New Zealand and some oceanic islands.

All members of the family are large for songbirds, with powerful, often hooked bills. Their legs are strong, and crows are able to move fast on the ground as well as in the air. The woodland-living jays are the most brightly colored of the family; the nutcrackers are spotted, while magpies and the crows themselves are predominantly black. Male and female generally look alike or nearly so.

NAME: (Black-billed) Magpie, *Pica pica*
RANGE: Europe to N. Africa; Asia to Himalayas and just into S.E. Asia; Alaska, W. Canada and USA to Utah
HABITAT: open country with trees, woodland edge, grassland
SIZE: 44–57 cm (17½–22½ in)

This sprightly magpie has black and white plumage and a long tail; the many subspecies show slight variations in plumage, some having a pronounced green, purple or golden sheen. It feeds mainly on the ground on insects, snails, slugs and spiders, but also takes grain, small mammals and carrion and will fly up into a tree to take fruit, nuts and young birds. Some magpies remain in their breeding territory all year round, usually in pairs or small groups, while others gather in communal roosts out of the breeding season.

The large, domed nest is made in a tree or bush by both members of a pair. The male feeds the female while she incubates the 5 to 8 eggs for 17 or 18 days.

NAME: Blue Jay, *Cyanocitta cristata*
RANGE: S.E. Canada, E. USA to Gulf of Mexico
HABITAT: woodland, city parks, gardens
SIZE: 30 cm (11¾ in)

This colorful jay is mainly blue but has black and white plumage on the wings and tail and black markings on the face. It feeds on the ground and in trees on nuts, seeds, grain, fruit, berries, insects and invertebrates, and the eggs and young of other birds. Seen in family parties in summer, blue jays gather in larger groups in autumn. They are noisy birds, and groups have the habit of attacking predators or intruders.

The nest is made in a tree or bush, and the female incubates the 2 to 6 eggs for 16 to 18 days. The male feeds her and helps to tend the brood.

NAME: Green Jay, *Cyanocorax yncas*
RANGE: USA: S. Texas; through Mexico and Central and South America to Brazil and Bolivia
HABITAT: forest, woodland, thickets
SIZE: 30 cm (11¾ in)

The green tail feathers of this bright green, yellow and blue bird help to identify it in flight. The many subspecies found over the wide range show slight variations in plumage. Green jays usually live in pairs or small groups, and feed largely on insects. They also eat acorns and seeds and sometimes the eggs and young of other birds.

The 3 to 5 eggs are laid in a nest in a tree or bush and are incubated by the female. Both parents tend the young.

NAME: Jay, *Garrulus glandarius*
RANGE: Europe to N. Africa; Asia, south to Burma, China and Taiwan
HABITAT: forest, woodland, orchards
SIZE: 34 cm (13¼ in)

An extremely variable species over its wide range, the European jay has a pinkish-brown body, with brilliant wing patterns of blue and black bars. Alone or in pairs, it feeds in trees and on the ground on insects and other small invertebrates, such as spiders, snails and slugs, and also on acorns, berries and grain.

The female lays 3 to 7 eggs in a nest made in a tree and incubates her clutch for 16 to 19 days. The male feeds his mate while she incubates and brings all the food for the brood until the female is able to leave the nest and assist him.

NAME: Ceylon Magpie, *Urocissa ornata*
RANGE: Sri Lanka
HABITAT: forest, gardens
SIZE: 46 cm (18 in)

A handsome bird with chestnut-red and blue plumage, the Ceylon magpie lives alone, in pairs or in small groups. It feeds in trees and on the ground on insects, invertebrates and fruit.

The nest is made in a small tree, and the female lays 3 to 5 eggs.

NAME: Piapiac, *Ptilostomus afer*
RANGE: Africa: Senegal to Nigeria, east to Ethiopia
HABITAT: open country, palm groves
SIZE: 46 cm (18 in)

A slender, long-tailed bird with a thick bill, the piapiac lives in flocks of 10 or more. It feeds mainly on the ground on insects and invertebrates, often following herds of large animals to pick up the insects they disturb; it also takes insects from the backs of large mammals and eats the fruit of the oil palm.

The nest is made in a palm or other tree, and the female lays 3 to 7 eggs.

Common Crow

Magpie

Green Jay

Rook

Jay

Piapiac

Ceylon Magpie

Blue Jay

Hume's Ground Jay

Reptiles – survivors from a prehistoric age

The reptiles that still walk, burrow, climb and swim on our planet represent the survivors in a dramatic evolutionary history of reptilian experimentation. From amphibian beginnings some 300 million years ago, a wide range of more thoroughly terrestrial forms of vertebrate developed. These reptile starting points have had far-reaching implications for the rest of vertebrate evolution. From these early reptile stocks our modern reptiles came. From them, too, however, came a plethora of magnificent dead ends, including the once-mighty dinosaurs, the winged pterosaurs and the swimming ichthyosaurs and plesiosaurs. And from the midst of the complex early family tree of reptile prototypes developed the ancestors of the remaining two groups of terrestrial higher vertebrates: the mammals and the birds. Reptiles thus link the beginnings of life on land, the amphibians, with the most advanced and sophisticated vertebrates.

Different systems exist for classifying the class Reptilia. Most, however, recognize about 16 or 17 orders, known by fossils alone or from fossils and still-existing animals. Only four orders persist today: first, the chelonians — turtles and tortoises; second, the crocodilians; third, the Squamata, which includes all lizards, snakes and the amphisbaenids; fourth, with only one living representative, the Rhynchocephalia, or tuatara, order. Even though these four orders represent only a small fraction of past reptilian diversity, they still show something of the interesting variation of which the reptile body form is capable.

The chelonians are a varied and successful assemblage of reptiles, with about 230 known species. They have short, broad bodies, enclosed by a bony box into which, to a variable extent, head, tail and limbs can be retracted for protection. The protective box consists of internal bony plates, upon which is superimposed tough, horny material, similar to the scales of other reptiles. Chelonians have no teeth but consume vegetation or prey by grasping the foods with the sharp edges of a beak, developed from the upper and lower jaws.

Crocodiles and their allies are the only remaining representatives of the archosaurian reptiles. The archosaurs, in the form of dinosaurs and pterosaurs, were the dominant terrestrial animals on earth from about 200 million years ago to approximately 63 to 70 million years ago. The characteristic elongate, heavy-headed crocodilians have been effective amphibious predators on earth for around 200 million years and are the largest living reptiles today. They are all carnivores, equipped with rows of sharp, peg-like teeth, which are continually replaced as they become worn.

Lizards, snakes and the burrowing amphisbaenids make up the order Squamata, meaning the scaly ones. The elongate, slim, long-tailed bodies of lizards have become modified to enable them to live in a wide range of habitats. Lizards can be expert burrowers, runners, swimmers and climbers, and a few can manage crude, short-distance gliding on rib-supported "wings." Most are carnivores, feeding on invertebrate and small vertebrate prey, but others feed on vegetation. The elongate, limbless snakes have some of the most highly modified skulls to be found among vertebrates, with a high degree of flexibility to accommodate large prey and sometimes effective fang and venom systems. Other snakes use their long, powerful bodies to constrict and suffocate their prey in their embrace.

The final order of reptiles includes only the tuatara of New Zealand. It seems to have changed little in its essential details in the past 200 million years or so.

Each of the four orders of living reptiles shows different adaptations which mark a distinct advance from the amphibians. Perhaps the most crucial of these modifications relate to temperature control, skin structure and methods of reproduction.

Like the amphibians, reptiles seem not to have any significant ability to control their body temperature independently of external heat sources. They do, however, have a set of behavior patterns which enable them to regulate the effect of external heat sources (sun, hot rocks) on their own temperature. By the use of specific postures and activities in or on the heat sources, reptiles can attain high body temperatures and regulate them to some degree. But their ultimate reliance on the sun for body heat means that the majority of reptile species occur in tropical and warm temperate climates.

The moist skin of the amphibians is important as a respiratory surface. Reptiles, in contrast, have waterproofed themselves with a scaly outer layer that is physically and chemically tough and relatively impermeable to water.

Compared with amphibian methods of reproduction, those of all reptiles show a great leap forward in solving the problem of sexual reproduction on land. Instead of having to return to water to breed and being dependent on the water to bring eggs and sperm together, male reptiles fertilize their mates internally by means of their one or two penises.

The great reproductive advance of the reptiles, however, is their eggs, with their tough shells, sometimes doubly strengthened with mineral salts, to protect them from abrasion, damage and water loss in the soil, where they are normally laid. The egg contains enough yolky food reserves and enough liquid to allow the reptile to develop directly into a miniature adult, instead of passing through an intermediate larval phase, as do the amphibians. Systems of blood vessels, running in special membranes enclosing the embryo, transfer the food reserves to it, exchange oxygen and carbon dioxide with the outside air via the shell, or transfer nitrogenous waste products, to be deposited in a special sac, which is left behind in the shell when the reptile hatches out. The hatchling has an egg tooth, which it uses to slit open the shell and which it sheds afterward.

In some reptiles, eggs are retained within the female's body and hatch within it or as they are laid, so that the female produces fully formed live young. In these species the shell is only a thin transparent membrane. A few reptiles and snakes have advanced still further, and their young develop inside the body with no shell membrane, having instead a primitive form of placenta. Young which develop inside the mother have many advantages in that they are protected from predators and physical dangers. By sunning herself, the mother can keep her body temperature as high as possible, in turn ensuring that the embryos develop rapidly. The live-bearing species often occur in particularly harsh climates or at high altitudes.

Reptiles in their evolution have produced all the basic adaptations necessary for efficient terrestrial life that the more advanced birds and mammals carry to higher levels of sophistication. Successful in their own right, they have provided the springboard for the even greater adaptive modifications of the body plans and abilities of the vertebrate animal.

Emydid Turtles

NAME: Pond Slider, *Pseudemys scripta*
RANGE: USA: Virginia to N. Florida,
west to New Mexico; Central America
to Brazil
HABITAT: slow rivers, ponds, swamps
SIZE: 13–30 cm (5–11¾ in)

Pond sliders are highly aquatic animals, which rarely move far from water. They bask on floating logs, often lying on top of one another. The carapace is oval and the markings variable. Males are usually smaller than females and have elongated, curved claws. Young pond sliders feed on insects, crustaceans, mollusks and tadpoles, but as they mature they feed more on plants.

In June and July pond sliders lay up to three clutches of 4 to 23 eggs each. Millions of these turtles are raised on farms and sold as pets. There are 4 subspecies; the subspecies illustrated is the yellow-bellied turtle.

NAME: False Map Turtle, *Graptemys*
pseudogeographica
RANGE: USA: Minnesota to Sabine River
area of Louisiana and Texas
HABITAT: rivers, lakes, ponds
SIZE: 8–25 cm (3–9¾ in)

False map turtles have intricate shell patterns and clear markings on their small heads. Males are smaller than females and have enlarged foreclaws. These turtles prefer habitats with plenty of vegetation and feed on aquatic plants as well as on crustaceans and mollusks.

After a courtship ritual, during which the male swims above the female, then faces her and drums her snout with his claws, the pair mate. The nesting period is from May to July. The female turtle digs a pit in the soil of the riverbank or lakeshore with her hind feet and deposits her 6 to 15 eggs. Up to three clutches are laid in a season.

NAME: Diamondback Terrapin,
Malaclemys terrapin
RANGE: USA: Atlantic and Gulf coasts
HABITAT: salt marshes, estuaries, lagoons
SIZE: 10–23 cm (4–9 in)

This terrapin is the only North American emydid adapted for life in brackish and salt water. It is a strong, fast-swimming turtle with large hind limbs. Females are bigger than males.

Diamondbacks spend their days on mud flats or tidal marshes, feeding on snails, clams and worms and on some plant shoots. At night they bury themselves in mud, and in the northern part of their range they hibernate during the winter, buried in the mud. Diamondbacks mate in the spring and lay 5 to 18 eggs in cavities which they dig in the marshes or dunes.

ORDER CHELONIA

This order contains all forms of turtles and tortoises, perhaps the most familiar of reptiles. There are about 230 living species. A typical chelonid has its body enclosed in a shell made of modified horny scales and bone. The shell is in two parts: the upper part on the animal's back is the carapace, and the shell underneath the body is the plastron. The ribs and most of the vertebrae are attached to the shell. Both pelvic and pectoral girdles lie within the shell, and the limbs emerge sideways. The neck is long and flexible and can usually be withdrawn into the shell. In most families the neck bends up and down to retract, but in 2 families, the greaved turtles (Pelomedusidae), and the matamata and snake-necked turtles (Chelidae), the neck bends sideways when being retracted.

Chelonids have no teeth, but their jaws are equipped with horny beaks of varying strength. All lay eggs, usually burying them in a pit in sand or earth. Hatchlings must dig their own way out to the surface.

EMYDIDAE: Emydid Turtle Family

A varied group of freshwater and semi-terrestrial turtles, the emydid family is the largest group of living turtles, with around 85 species. The family is closely related to the land tortoises (Testudinidae); indeed, some authorities group them together as one family. A clear distinguishing feature of the emydid group is the adaptation of the hind feet for swimming rather than walking. Most species live in the northern hemisphere.

Emydid turtles have a varied diet and generally eat both plants and animals. Some species start life as carnivores but feed mainly on plants as adults.

NAME: Wood Turtle, *Clemmys insculpta*
RANGE: USA: Nova Scotia to
N. Virginia; Great Lakes region
HABITAT: woods, marshy meadows,
swamps
SIZE: 12.5–23 cm (5–9 in)

The rough-shelled wood turtle spends most of its life on land but is usually in the vicinity of water. It is a good climber and feeds on fruit as well as on worms, slugs and insects. In May or June females lay 6 or 8 eggs, which usually hatch by October but which may overwinter and hatch the following spring in the north. Adults hibernate in the north of the range. Wood turtles are popular pets, but they have been overhunted and are now rare and protected in some states of the USA.

NAME: Eastern Box Turtle, *Terrapene*
carolina
RANGE: USA: E. states, west to Texas
HABITAT: moist forested areas
SIZE: 10–20 cm (4–8 in)

A poor swimmer, the box turtle rarely enters any other than shallow water and spends most of its life on land. Its carapace is nearly always domed in shape, and it is variable in coloration and pattern. Box turtles eat almost anything, but slugs, earthworms and fruit are favored foods; they are able to eat mushrooms that are poisonous to humans, and anyone then eating the turtle is poisoned. Usually active early in the day or after rain, box turtles may take refuge in swampy areas in the heat of the summer.

In the spring, after hibernating throughout the winter, box turtles perform prolonged courtship rituals. The female lays 3 to 8 eggs in a flask-shaped pit which she digs. The hatchlings may remain in the nest over the following winter. Females can store sperm and lay fertile eggs several years after mating.

NAME: European Pond Turtle, *Emys*
orbicularis
RANGE: central France, south to
N. Africa, east to Iran
HABITAT: ponds, marshes, rivers
SIZE: 13–15 cm (5–6 in)

An aquatic species, the European pond turtle prefers water with plenty of vegetation but suns itself on riverbanks and hunts prey on land as well as in water. It is entirely carnivorous and feeds on prey such as fish, frogs, snails and worms.

In winter these turtles hibernate, burying themselves in mud or in specially built chambers in the riverbank. They mate in spring, and, having dug an egg pit with her tail, the female lays 3 to 16 eggs. She generally uses the same nest site every year.

NAME: Batagur, *Batagur baska*
RANGE: S.E. Asia from Bengal to
Vietnam
HABITAT: tidal areas, estuaries
SIZE: 58 cm (23 in)   Ⓔ

A large herbivorous turtle with a smooth heavy shell, the batagur is often found in brackish or even salt water. It has only four claws on each foot.

Batagurs nest on sandbanks and usually lay three clutches in a season, making a total of 50 to 60 eggs. Excessive collecting of eggs and killing of adults for food has led to a decline in the population, and this turtle has now been eliminated in some parts of its range.

Pond Slider

False Map Turtle

Batagur

Eastern Box Turtle

European Pond Turtle

Diamondback Terrapin

Wood Turtle

Land Tortoises

NAME: African Pancake Tortoise,
Malocochersus tornieri
RANGE: Africa: Kenya, Tanzania
HABITAT: rocky outcrops in arid land
SIZE: 15 cm (6 in) Ⓘ

The African pancake tortoise is one of the world's most unusual and extraordinary species. Its shell is extremely flat and soft, and rather than retreating into its shell when disturbed, the tortoise runs to hide in a rock crevice. Once there, it inflates its lungs, thus increasing its size, so that it is wedged in and almost impossible to remove. It sometimes falls when clambering over rocks but can right itself easily because of its flat shell and slender, flexible limbs. Females are slightly larger than males.

The pancake tortoise feeds on dry grass. It nests in July and August, laying 1 egg at a time, and it may lay two or more times in a season. The eggs hatch after about 6 months.

NAME: Gopher Tortoise, *Gopherus*
polyphemus
RANGE: USA: South Carolina to Florida,
west to Louisiana
HABITAT: sandy areas between grassland
and forest
SIZE: 23.5–37 cm (9¼–14½ in)

The gopher tortoise has a domed shell and heavily scaled front legs, flattened for efficient digging. An excellent burrower, this tortoise makes an unusually long tunnel, ending in a chamber which serves as a refuge where humidity and temperature remain relatively constant. One tunnel recorded was over 14 m (46 ft) long. Other small animals may move in and share the tortoise's burrow.

Gopher tortoises emerge from their burrows during the day to bask in the sun and feed on grass and leaves. They mate in spring and nest from April to July. Several clutches of 2 to 7 eggs are laid in a shallow pit during the nesting period.

NAME: Bowsprit Tortoise, *Chersine*
angulata
RANGE: South Africa
HABITAT: coastal areas
SIZE: 15–18 cm (6–7 in)

The bowsprit tortoise has distinctive triangular markings on its carapace. The front opening of the carapace is particularly small, providing good protection against predators. Males are bigger than females and aggressive toward one another. Bowsprits are believed to feed on plant material. They nest in August and lay 1 or 2 eggs in a hole about 10 cm (4 in) deep. The eggs usually take about a year to hatch.

TESTUDINIDAE:
Land Tortoise Family

There are about 39 species of land tortoise, found in North America, Europe and Asia, and in Africa and Madagascar. All are strictly terrestrial and have stumpy, elephantine hind legs; on the front legs are thick, hard scales. These tortoises can retract head and limbs completely inside the shell, leaving only the soles of the hind feet, tail region and scaly fronts of the forelimbs exposed. Thus most depend on their armor for protection and do not usually show aggression or attempt to flee when disturbed. All species are predominantly herbivorous.

NAME: Galápagos Giant Tortoise,
Geochelone elephantopus
RANGE: Galápagos Islands
HABITAT: varied: cool, moist forest to
arid land
SIZE: up to 1.2 m (4 ft) Ⓔ

There are at least 13 subspecies of these giant tortoises, which may weigh over 225 kg (500 lb). Subspecies have evolved because the populations are isolated from one another on separate islands and, over thousands of years, have adapted to suit the particular conditions. The discovery of these subspecies on the different islands was one of the major observations that stimulated Darwin to start his speculations on the origin of species.

The tortoises vary in size, length and thickness of limbs and, most importantly, in the shape of the carapace. Some species have a "saddleback" shell which rises up above the head, allowing the tortoise to lift its head straight up and thus graze on a greater range of vegetation. These species occur only on those islands with high-growing vegetation. Males are always markedly larger than females.

Galápagos tortoises feed on almost any vegetation, which they seek in the more fertile highlands. They mate at any time of year, and males are easily able to overcome the smaller females and bear them to the ground for mounting. Nesting has been closely observed on Indefatigable Island where there is a tortoise reserve. After mating, the female descends to the lowland area, where there is bare soil in full sun; she then urinates to soften the earth and digs a pit up to 30.5 cm (12 in) deep with her hind feet. After laying up to 17 eggs, she plasters the excavated soil over the cavity so that it is well closed; the soil dries again in the sun. As usual with tortoises, the young must hatch and dig themselves out of the cavity unaided.

NAME: Leopard Tortoise, *Geochelone*
pardalis
RANGE: Africa: Sudan and Ethiopia to
South Africa
HABITAT: savanna, woodland
SIZE: 61 cm (24 in)

The leopard tortoise has a markedly domed, boldly patterned carapace. It feeds on a great variety of plant material, including fruit and beans. Courting males compete for females, butting at each other until one is overturned. They nest in September and October in South Africa, but the season is longer in tropical Africa. The female prepares a nest cavity by urinating on the soil to soften it, then excavating a pit with her hind limbs. She lays 5 to 30 eggs, and there may be several clutches in a season.

NAME: Schweigger's Hinged-back
Tortoise, *Kinixys erosa*
RANGE: W. and central Africa
HABITAT: rain forest, marshes, riverbanks
SIZE: 33 cm (13 in)

A unique hinge on the carapace of this tortoise, located in line with the junction of the second and third back plates, allows the rear of the carapace to be lowered, if the tortoise is attacked, to afford some protection to its hindquarters. This hinge is not present in young tortoises. By digging itself into plant debris, the hinged-back remains hidden for much of its life. It feeds on plants and may also eat small animals. There are usually 4 eggs in a clutch.

NAME: Spur-thighed Tortoise, *Testudo*
graeca
RANGE: N. Africa; extreme S.E. and
S.W. Europe; Middle East
HABITAT: meadows, cultivated land,
woodland
SIZE: 15 cm (6 in) Ⓥ

This tortoise has a moderately domed shell and a small spur in the thigh region of each front limb. Females are larger than males. The tortoises hibernate in winter but, in coastal areas, will emerge as early as February. They court in spring, the male butting and biting the female before mating with her. The eggs, usually 2 or 3 in a clutch, are laid in May and June and generally hatch in September and October, although this varies with the local climate. The young tortoises are similar to adults but have more rounded shells and clearer markings.

Thousands of these tortoises are collected and exported as pets, many of which die because of unsuitable climate and conditions.

African Pancake Tortoise

Schweigger's Hinged-back Tortoise

Gopher Tortoise

Galápagos Giant Tortoise

Bowsprit Tortoise

Leopard Tortoise

Spur-thighed Tortoise

Snapping Turtles, Mud Turtles, River Turtles

CHELYDRIDAE: Snapping Turtle Family

The 2 species in this family are both large predatory freshwater turtles. They have massive nonretractile heads and strong jaws.

NAME: **Snapping Turtle,** *Chelydra serpentina*
RANGE: **S. Canada to Ecuador**
HABITAT: **marshes, ponds, rivers, lakes**
SIZE: **20–47 cm (8–18½ in)**

A highly aggressive species, the snapping turtle shoots its head forward with surprising speed while snapping its strong jaws. It feeds on all kinds of aquatic and bankside life, including fish, amphibians, mammals and birds, as well as on aquatic plants. Usually found in water with plenty of aquatic vegetation, the snapping turtle lies at the bottom, concealed among plants. It is an excellent swimmer. Males and females are alike in appearance, but males grow slightly larger.

Snapping turtles hibernate in winter and begin nesting in early summer. The average clutch is 25 to 50 eggs, laid in a flask-shaped cavity dug by the female. As the eggs are laid, she pushes each one into place with movements of her hind feet. The eggs incubate for 9 to 18 weeks, depending on the area and the weather; in cooler areas, the hatchlings may remain in the nest through the winter.

NAME: **Alligator Snapping Turtle,** *Macroclemys temmincki*
RANGE: **central USA**
HABITAT: **deep rivers, lakes**
SIZE: **33–66 cm (13–26 in)**

The alligator snapping turtle has three strong ridges on the carapace and a rough-textured head and neck. The carapace is shaped, allowing the head to be raised. A resident of dark, slow-moving water, this turtle is so sedentary that algae grow on its shell, contributing to the existing camouflage of the lumpy irregular outline. It rests, practically invisible to passing fishes, with its huge mouth gaping open to reveal a pink, fleshy appendage. Unsuspecting fish come to investigate the "bait" and are swallowed whole or sliced in half by the turtle's strong jaws. Alligator snappers also eat crustaceans.

These turtles continue to grow after maturity, and some old specimens, at over 76 cm (30 in) long and 91 kg (200 lb) in weight, are the largest freshwater turtles in the USA. They nest between April and June and lay from 15 to 50 eggs in a flask-shaped pit dug near water. The young are born with a rough-surfaced shell and the lure already in place.

KINOSTERNIDAE: Mud and Musk Turtle Family

The 18 species in this family are mainly aquatic turtles living in North and Central America and northern South America. They give off a musky odor from 2 pairs of glands, positioned on each side of the body where skin and shell meet. Their heads are retractile.

NAME: **Yellow Mud Turtle,** *Kinosternon flavescens*
RANGE: **USA: Nebraska to Texas; Mexico**
HABITAT: **slow streams**
SIZE: **9–16 cm (3½–6¼ in)**

The yellow mud turtle does indeed seem to prefer water with a mud bottom, but it may also be found in artificial habitats such as cattle drinking troughs and ditches. It feeds on both aquatic and terrestrial invertebrates. Breeding females lay 2 to 4 eggs.

NAME: **Common Musk Turtle,** *Sternotherus odoratus*
RANGE: **USA: E. states, west to Texas**
HABITAT: **slow, shallow, muddy streams**
SIZE: **8–13 cm (3–5 in)**

Also known as the stinkpot, this turtle exudes a strong-smelling fluid from its musk glands when molested. It is a highly aquatic species, rarely found far from water, but it does emerge to bask on branches overhanging water. It feeds on carrion, insects and mollusks as well as on small amounts of fish and plants. Nesting is from February to June, depending on the latitude; females lay 1 to 9 eggs under trees, logs or dead leaves.

CARETTOCHELYIDAE: Plateless River Turtle Family

This was once a widespread family, as proved by fossils found in Europe, Asia and North America. There is now only 1 species with a restricted distribution.

NAME: **New Guinea Plateless River Turtle,** *Carettochelys insculpta*
RANGE: **New Guinea: Fly River area**
HABITAT: **rivers**
SIZE: **46 cm (18 in)**

This New Guinea species, now also discovered to be living in northern Australia, is better adapted for aquatic life than most freshwater turtles. Its limbs are modified into long paddles but retain two claws and resemble the limbs of sea turtles. There are few details about the nesting habits of this species, but it lays 17 to 27 eggs and the hatchlings are about 6 cm (2¼ in) long.

PLATYSTERNIDAE: Big-headed Turtle Family

The single living species in this family is a freshwater turtle found in Southeast Asia.

NAME: **Big-headed Turtle,** *Platysternon megacephalum*
RANGE: **Burma, Thailand, S. China**
HABITAT: **mountain streams, rivers**
SIZE: **15–18 cm (6–7 in)**

Although a relatively small species in carapace length, this turtle has a huge head, almost half the width of the carapace. The head is not retractile, and the carapace is slightly shaped to allow the head and the short, thick neck to be raised. The feet of this turtle are small and only partially webbed, and there are enlarged, flattened scales on the forelimbs.

The big-headed turtle is an unusually agile climber, and, using its outstretched claws, it clambers over branches and rocks in search of food or a basking spot. It lays only 2 eggs at a time.

DERMATEMYIDAE: Central American River Turtle Family

A single species survives from this once widespread family, formerly found in North and Central America, Europe and Africa.

NAME: **Central American River Turtle,** *Dermatemys mawi*
RANGE: **Mexico to Guatemala and Belize (not Yucatán)**
HABITAT: **clear rivers and lakes**
SIZE: **46 cm (18 in)** Ⓥ

This turtle has long been hunted for its meat and is now scarce throughout much of its range. Although protected to some degree by conservation laws, there is still concern for its future.

A smooth-shelled turtle, it has a relatively small head with a pointed, projecting snout and large nostrils. Males have a golden-yellow patch on the head, but the females and juveniles have grayish heads. It has large webbed feet and is one of the most aquatic of all freshwater turtles; it rarely climbs out on the bank to bask but floats on the water instead. On land this turtle is awkward, but it swims well and is able to stay submerged for long periods. Aquatic vegetation is its main food source. It nests in the flood season and lays its 6 to 16 eggs in mud near the water's edge.

Snapping Turtle

Yellow Mud Turtle

Alligator Snapping Turtle

Central American River Turtle

Common Musk Turtle

Big-headed Turtle

New Guinea Plateless
River Turtle

Leatherback, Marine Turtles

DERMOCHELYIDAE: Leatherback Family

There is a single living species in this family. It has many distinctive features but resembles other sea turtles in many details of skull structure and has similar nesting habits.

NAME: **Leatherback,** *Dermochelys coriacea*
RANGE: **worldwide, usually in warm seas**
HABITAT: **oceanic**
SIZE: **1.5 cm (5 ft)** Ⓔ

The world's largest turtle, the leatherback has an average weight of 360 kg (800 lb) and a maximum of 590 kg (1,300 lb). Its foreflippers are extremely long, with a span of about 2.7 m (9 ft). It has no horny shields on its shell, no scales and no claws. The carapace resembles hard rubber and has three longitudinal ridges. Leatherbacks feed mainly on jellyfish, a diet in keeping with their weak, scissorlike jaws.

Leatherbacks apparently perform long migrations between nesting and feeding sites. Most breed every other year and lay clutches of about 80 to 100 eggs. The nesting procedure is much the same as that of the other sea turtles, but, after laying, the leatherback always turns one or more circles before returning to the sea. Several clutches are laid in a season at roughly 10-day intervals. Hatchlings are 6 cm (2¼ in) long and have scales on shell and skin which disappear within the first 2 months of life.

CHELONIDAE: Marine Turtle Family

The larger of the 2 families of marine turtles, Chelonidae contains 6 species, all generally found in tropical and subtropical waters. All have nonretractile heads and limbs. The forelimbs are modified into long, paddlelike flippers with one or two claws; the turtles swim by making winglike beats of the foreflippers. On land, the green turtle moves particularly awkwardly, heaving itself forward with both flippers simultaneously, but the others move with alternating movements of the limbs, as most four-legged animals do.

The 6 species have become specialized for different niches and diets, to compensate for the inevitable overlap of their ranges in many oceans.

NAME: **Green Turtle,** *Chelonia mydas*
RANGE: **worldwide in seas where temperature does not fall below 20°C (68°F)**
HABITAT: **coasts, open sea**
SIZE: **1–1.2 m (3¼–4 ft)** Ⓔ

This large, thoroughly aquatic turtle rarely comes to land except to bask and sleep and to lay eggs. Males have slightly longer, narrower carapaces than females and enlarged curved claws on the front flippers for gripping the female when mating.

Green turtles are primarily herbivorous animals and have serrated jaw surfaces, well suited to feeding on sea grasses and seaweed; some crustaceans and jellyfish may also be eaten. The best feeding grounds, where there are vast underwater pastures of plants, are often far away from the best nesting beaches, and green turtles have evolved astounding migratory habits. At nesting time they travel hundreds of miles to the beach of their birth to lay eggs, and as a result, there tend to be a limited number of important nesting sites, to which hundreds of turtles go. One such site is Ascension Island in the mid-Atlantic.

Every second or third year, green turtles travel to their nesting site and mate. The female heaves herself up the beach well away from the tidal area. With her foreflippers she sweeps away sand to create a hollow to lie in, her shell flush with the beach. She then uses her hind flippers to dig a hole about 40 cm (16 in) deep, immediately beneath her tail. She deposits her eggs into the hole, covers the area with sand and returns to the sea. The average clutch contains about 106 eggs. Sometimes a female lays several clutches in a season at 2-week intervals.

After a 2- to 3-month incubation period, the young turtles hatch and dig their way through the sand to the surface. Having oriented themselves, they rush for the sea, past a horde of eager predators. Mortality is high, and those which do reach the sea will have to face yet more predators.

The green turtle is now an endangered species, and the population has been eliminated in some areas, although it is still reasonable in others. The turtles have been overexploited for their meat, hides and eggs, and the predictability of their nesting habits has made them easy victims. Exploitation is now strictly controlled, and imports are banned in many countries.

The closely related flatback turtle, *C. depressa*, is a little smaller than the green turtle and lives off the coast of Northern Australia.

NAME: **Loggerhead,** *Caretta caretta*
RANGE: **temperate and tropical areas of the Pacific, Indian and Atlantic Oceans**
HABITAT: **coasts, open sea**
SIZE: **76–102 cm (30–40 in)** Ⓥ

A large turtle with a long, slightly tapering carapace, the loggerhead has a wide chunky head housing powerful jaws. It can crush even hard-shelled prey and feeds on crabs and mollusks as well as on sponges, jellyfish and aquatic plants.

Loggerheads usually breed every other year and lay three or four clutches of about 100 eggs each in a season.

The loggerhead population has been reduced by overcollection of eggs and lack of hunting controls, but in southeast Africa, where the turtles have been protected for more than 10 years, their numbers have increased by over 50 percent.

NAME: **Olive Ridley,** *Lepidochelys olivacea*
RANGE: **tropical Pacific, Indian and S. Atlantic Oceans**
HABITAT: **coasts, open sea**
SIZE: **66 cm (26 in)** Ⓔ

The olive ridley is small and lightly built for a sea turtle. It feeds on small shrimp, jellyfish, crabs, snails and fish, which it crushes with strong jaws. Like its close relative Kemp's ridley, *L. kempi*, the olive ridley breeds every year and always returns to the same nesting beaches. The female lays about 100 eggs in a pit in the sand and covers them. She then begins a strange movement peculiar to ridleys, rocking from side to side so that each edge of the shell thumps the sand in turn. Both ridleys are in grave danger due to overexploitation by man.

NAME: **Hawksbill,** *Eretmochelys imbricata*
RANGE: **tropical Atlantic, Pacific and Indian Oceans; Caribbean**
HABITAT: **coral reefs, rocky coasts**
SIZE: **76–91 cm (30–36 in)** Ⓔ

The hawksbill's beautiful carapace provides the best tortoiseshell and is the reason for the endangered status of the species. Conservation controls have been introduced after many years of hunting, and imports are banned in some countries. The carapace is serrated at the back and has particularly thick, horny plates. The tapering head of the hawksbill is an adaptation for searching out food, such as mollusks and crustaceans, in rocky crevices and reefs.

In many areas hawksbills are opportunistic breeders, nesting on any beach convenient to feeding grounds. They lay more eggs at a time than any other turtle, usually about 150.

Leatherback

Green Turtle

Hawksbill

Olive Ridley

Loggerhead

Softshell Turtles, Greaved Turtles, Matamatas

TRIONYCHIDAE:
Softshell Turtle Family

This family contains 32 species of aquatic turtles which have only three claws on each foot. All species have rounded, flexible carapaces with no horny plates, hence their pancakelike appearance and their common name. Most species have long mobile necks. Softshells move fast in water and on land but spend most of their lives in water. Species are found in eastern North America and Southeast Asia, and there is a single species in the Middle East.

Softshells lay up to three clutches of hard-shelled eggs each year. Females usually grow larger than males, and as they mature, their carapace patterns become obscured by blotches. Males tend to retain clear carapace patterns.

NAME: **Spiny Softshell,** *Trionyx spiniferus*
RANGE: **N. America: Ontario and Quebec, south to Florida and Colorado**
HABITAT: **rivers, creeks, ponds**
SIZE: **15–46 cm (6–18 in)**

Conical projections, or tubercles, around the front edge of this turtle's shell are the origin of its common name. There are about 6 geographically distinct races, and some have more pronounced spines than others. Females are notably larger than males.

Spiny softshells are highly aquatic; they feed on insects, crayfish, and some fish and plant matter. They nest in summer and lay about 20 eggs.

NAME: **Narrow-headed/Indian Softshell,** *Chitra indica*
RANGE: **India, Pakistan, Thailand**
HABITAT: **rivers**
SIZE: **91 cm (36 in)**

A large, fast-swimming turtle with flipperlike limbs, this softshell does indeed have an elongated narrow head, with eyes placed far forward near the snout. It seems to prefer clear, sandy-bottomed water and is carnivorous, feeding in the main on fish and mollusks.

NAME: **Nile Softshell,** *Trionyx triunguis*
RANGE: **Africa: Egypt to Senegal**
HABITAT: **ponds, lakes, rivers**
SIZE: **91 cm (36 in)**

The Nile softshell can weigh up to 45 kg (100 lb) and is hunted for food by man in many parts of its range. Although it is a freshwater species, groups have been found living off the coast of Turkey. It is omnivorous and feeds on mollusks, fish, insects and fruit. In Egypt it breeds in April and lays 50 to 60 eggs; elsewhere clutches may be smaller.

NAME: **Zambesi Softshell,** *Cycloderma frenatum*
RANGE: **Africa: Tanzania, Mozambique, Zambia, Malawi**
HABITAT: **ponds, lakes, rivers**
SIZE: **51 cm (20 in)**

A carnivorous turtle, the Zambesi softshell feeds mainly on mollusks. It lays its 15 to 20 eggs from December to March and is most active in rainy weather. Hatchlings have pale green carapaces and dark lines on their heads. In adults these lines are outlined with white dots and become fainter with age. The only other species in this genus is Aubry's softshell, *C. aubryi*, found in West Africa.

PELOMEDUSIDAE:
Greaved Turtle Family

This family of 19 species is one of the 2 families of side-necked turtles. A sideneck retracts its head by moving it sideways under the carapace. This leaves an undefended area of the head and neck exposed and may have prevented the evolution of any terrestrial sidenecks, since they would be extremely vulnerable to mammalian predators. All these turtles live in fresh water in Africa, Madagascar and South America, east of the Andes.

NAME: **Arrau River Turtle,** *Podocnemis expansa*
RANGE: **northern South America**
HABITAT: **Orinoco and Amazon river systems**
SIZE: **61–76 cm (24–30 in)**　　　　Ⓔ

The largest of the side-necks, the arrau turtle may weigh over 45 kg (100 lb). Females have wide, flattened shells and are larger and more numerous than males. Adults feed entirely on plant matter.

The nesting habits of these turtles are similar to those of sea turtles in that they gather in large numbers to travel to certain suitable nesting areas. They lay their eggs on sandbanks which are exposed only in the dry season, and there are relatively few such sites. The females come out onto the sandbanks at night, and each lays as many as 90 or 100 softshelled eggs. They then return to their feeding grounds. The hatchlings, which are about 5 cm (2 in) long, emerge to the attentions of many predators; even without man's activities, only about 5 percent reach adult feeding grounds.

Uncontrolled hunting of adults and excessive collecting of eggs have seriously reduced the population of this turtle. It is now an endangered species and is protected in most areas.

CHELIDAE: Matamata and Snake-necked Turtle Family

The other family of side-necked turtles contains 30 species, found in South America, Australia and New Guinea. This family shows a number of structural advancements over the more primitive Pelomedusids. They are carnivorous animals and live in rivers and marshes.

NAME: **Matamata,** *Chelus fimbriatus*
RANGE: **northern South America**
HABITAT: **rivers**
SIZE: **41 cm (16 in)**

The matamata is one of the most bizarre of all turtles. Its carapace is exceedingly rough and ridged, and from above, its head is flat and virtually triangular. Its eyes are tiny and positioned close to the thin, tubelike snout. Fleshy flaps at the sides of the head wave in the water, possibly attracting small fish. The matamata's neck is thick and muscular and its mouth extremely wide. Its limbs are small and weak.

Well camouflaged by its irregular outline, the matamata lies at the bottom of the water. It is so sedentary that algae grow on its shell, adding to the camouflage. When a fish swims by, it opens its huge mouth, sucking in both water and fish. The turtle then closes its mouth, leaving only a slit for the water to flow out, and swallows the fish.

Matamatas lay 12 to 28 eggs; the young have light-tan-colored carapaces.

NAME: **Murray River Turtle,** *Emydura macquarri*
RANGE: **S.E. Australia**
HABITAT: **rivers**
SIZE: **30 cm (11¾ in)**

The Murray River turtle is a well-known Australian side-neck. The shape of its carapace alters with age: hatchlings have almost circular carapaces; in juveniles, carapaces are widest at the back; and adults have virtually oval shells. The head of the Murray River turtle is quite small, with bright eyes and a light band extending back from the mouth. It is an active species and feeds on frogs, tadpoles and vegetation. In summer it lays 10 to 15 eggs in a chamber dug in the riverbank. These normally hatch in 10 or 11 weeks.

Spiny Softshell

Narrow-headed Softshell

Nile Softshell

Zambesi Softshell

Matamata

Arrau River Turtle

Murray River Turtle

Crocodiles, Alligators and Caimans, Gavial

NAME: Gavial, *Gavialis gangeticus*
RANGE: N. India
HABITAT: large rivers
SIZE: 7 m (23 ft) Ⓔ

The Indian gavial has an extremely long narrow snout, studded with about 100 small teeth — ideal equipment for seizing fish and frogs underwater. Like all crocodilians, the gavial has been hunted for its skin, and it is now one of the rarest in Asia. Its hind limbs are paddle-like, and the gavial seems rarely to leave the water except to nest. The female lays her eggs at night in a pit dug in the river-bank.

NAME: American Alligator, *Alligator mississipiensis*
RANGE: S.E. USA
HABITAT: marshes, rivers, swamps
SIZE: up to 5.5 m (18 ft) Ⓞ

The American alligator, once struggling for survival against hunters and habitat destruction, has been so effectively protected by conservation laws that the population is now on the increase.

These alligators usually mate in shallow water in April, and courtship is slow and quiet. The male stays with the female for several days before mating, occasionally stroking her body with his forelimbs. As she nears acquiescence, he rubs her throat with his head and blows bubbles past her cheeks. The female finds a nest site near water and scrapes up whatever plant debris is available with sweeping movements of her body and tail. She packs the vegetation together to form a mound, with a cavity for the eggs. She lays 28 to 52 eggs and crawls over the mound to close the cavity with more vegetation. She guards the nest while the eggs incubate for about 65 days. The hatching young call out to their mother, prompting her to open the nest and free them. They remain with her for up to 3 years.

NAME: Spectacled Caiman, *Caiman crocodilus*
RANGE: Venezuela to S. Amazon basin
HABITAT: slow still waters, lakes, swamps
SIZE: 1.5–2 m (5–6½ ft) long Ⓥ

There are several species and subspecies of this caiman, and its name has been the subject of much dispute; it is often known as *C. sclerops*. Its common name derives from the ridge on the head between the eyes, which resembles the bridge of a pair of glasses. The population of wild caimans has declined drastically since they are not only hunted for skins but the young are also collected and sold as pets or stuffed as curios. The female caiman makes a nest of plant debris scraped together into a pile and lays an average of 30 eggs.

ORDER CROCODILIA

The crocodiles, alligators and caimans, and the single species of gavial are the 3 families which together make up this order and include the largest and most dangerous living reptiles. All are powerful amphibious carnivores, preying on a range of vertebrate animals, although juvenile crocodiles also eat insects and some other small invertebrates. The crocodilia are the most direct evolutionary descendants of the archosaurs, the dominant animal life forms from the Triassic to the end of the Cretaceous eras (190 to 65 million years ago). There are 21 species alive today: 13 in the crocodile family, 7 alligators and caimans, and 1 gavial. All are found in tropical and subtropical regions. Males and females look alike in all species, and it is difficult to determine the sex visually. Males do tend to grow larger than females.

All members of the order have elongate, short-limbed bodies covered with horny skin scales. Thickened bony plates on the back give added protection. The crocodilian's predatory armament is a long snout with many conical teeth anchored in deep sockets in the jaw bones. Breathing organs are highly modified for underwater predation; the external nostrils, on a projection at the snout-tip, have valves to close them off, while a pair of flaps in the throat forms another valve which enables the animal to hold prey in its open jaws beneath the surface, without inhaling water.

Both crocodiles and alligators possess a pair of large teeth near the front of the lower jaw for grasping prey. In the crocodiles, these two teeth fit into distinct notches in the upper jaw and are visible when the jaws are closed, while in the alligators, the large teeth are accommodated in bony pits in the upper jaw.

NAME: West African Dwarf Crocodile, *Osteolaemus tetraspis*
RANGE: W. Africa, south of the Sahara
HABITAT: streams and lakes
SIZE: 1.5 m (5 ft) Ⓘ

Also known as the short-nosed crocodile, this animal is indeed characterized by its unusually short snout. It is now extremely rare because of over-exploitation for skins and the destruction of its habitat. It resembles the New World alligators in appearance and size, although it is a member of the crocodile family. Little is known of its biology and breeding habits.

NAME: Estuarine Crocodile, *Crocodylus porosus*
RANGE: S. India through Indonesia; S. Australia
HABITAT: estuaries, coasts, mangrove swamps
SIZE: up to 6 m (19½ ft) Ⓔ

The estuarine crocodile is one of the largest and most dangerous species and has been known to attack man. It is rapidly being exterminated since its hide is considered the most valuable of all crocodiles' for leather. It is now illegal to catch the estuarine crocodile in many areas, but the population is still low. Where hunting is allowed, it is restricted, and skin exports are controlled.

The most aquatic and most marine of all crocodile species, the estuarine crocodile spends little time on land and swims great distances. The female lays 25 to 90 eggs in a mound of plant debris which she scrapes together near water. She guards the eggs for about 3 months while they incubate.

NAME: Nile Crocodile, *Crocodylus niloticus*
RANGE: Africa (not Sahara or N.W.)
HABITAT: large rivers, lakes, marshes
SIZE: 4.5–5 m (15–16½ ft) long Ⓥ

The population and range of the once widespread Nile crocodile is now seriously reduced by both the demand for skins and the destruction of natural habitats. The Nile crocodile preys on large mammals and birds which come to the water's edge to drink. After seizing its catch, the crocodile drowns it by holding it underwater and then twists off chunks of flesh by spinning its own body in the water while holding onto the prey. Adult crocodiles swallow stones, which remain in the stomach and act as stabilizing ballast when the crocodiles are in water.

The Nile crocodile spends its nights in water and comes out onto land just before sunrise in order to bask in the sun during the day. It leads a rather leisurely existence and does not need to feed every day.

The male defends a territory and enacts a courtship display at breeding time. The mated female lays 25 to 75 eggs in a pit near the water. She covers her eggs well and guards them during the 3-month incubation period. When ready to hatch, the young are sensitive to the footfalls of their mother overhead. They call to her from the nest; she uncovers them and carries them inside her mouth to a safe nursery area, where she cares for them assiduously for another 3 to 6 months. The young feed on insects, then progress to crabs, birds and fish before adopting the adult diet.

Spectacled Caiman

Nile Crocodile

Estuarine Crocodile

West African Dwarf Crocodile

Gavial

American Alligator

Tuatara, Iguanas

ORDER RHYNCHOCEPHALIA

Apart from a single species, the tuatara, living in New Zealand, this order of reptiles is known only from fossils.

SPHENODONTIA: Tuatara Family

The sole family in the Rhynchocephalia order contains only 1 species, which is believed to be extremely similar to related species alive 130 million years ago. The scientific name means "the wedge-toothed ones" and refers to the sharp teeth, fused into both jawbones.

NAME: **Tuatara,** *Sphenodon punctatus*
RANGE: **New Zealand**
HABITAT: **woods with little undergrowth**
SIZE: **up to 65 cm (25½ in)** ⃝

A powerfully built reptile, the tuatara has a large head and a crest running from its head down its back. The male is generally larger than the female. Active at dusk and at night, the tuatara has the least need of warmth of any reptile — it is quite content at 12°C (53°F), whereas most reptiles prefer over 25°C (77°F). Its metabolism and growth rate are correspondingly slow. Tuataras are ground-living and shelter in burrows, which they dig in loose soil or take over from shearwaters. They feed on crickets, earthworms, snails, young birds and lizards.

The female tuatara lays up to 15 eggs in a hole she digs in the soil. They hatch 13 to 15 months later — the longest development time of any reptile. She probably does not breed every year. Tuataras are long-lived and probably do not attain sexual maturity until they are about 20 years old. Once in danger of extinction from introduced predators, healthy tuatara populations now live in special island sanctuaries and are protected by conservation laws.

ORDER SQUAMATA

The largest reptilian order, the Squamata includes all the lizards, snakes and amphisbaenids — more than 6,000 species in all.

IGUANIDAE: Iguana Family

There are more than 600 species in this family, the vast majority of which live in the Americas, although there are a few species in Madagascar and Fiji. They are the New World equivalents of the Old World agamid lizards and nowhere do the two families occur together.

Most are ground- or tree-living and feed on insects and small invertebrates. Many are brightly colored and perform elaborate courtship displays.

NAME: **Common Iguana,** *Iguana iguana*
RANGE: **Central and N. South America; introduced into USA: Florida**
HABITAT: **forest, trees near water**
SIZE: **1–2 m (3¼–6½ ft)**

The common iguana has a characteristic crest of comblike spines, longest at the neck area but running all the way down its body and tail. The bands across the shoulders and tail become darker as the iguana gets older — juveniles are bright green. Active in the daytime, these iguanas are agile, tree-dwelling lizards which also swim readily. They are herbivores but will defend themselves with their sharp teeth and claws when they are attacked.

In autumn, the female lays 28 to 40 eggs in a hole she digs in the ground. The eggs hatch in about 3 months.

NAME: **Eastern Fence Lizard,** *Sceloporus undulatus*
RANGE: **USA: Virginia to Florida, west to New Mexico; Mexico**
HABITAT: **open woodland, grassland**
SIZE: **9–20 cm (3½–7¾ in)**

This iguana occurs in many subspecies, with varying coloration over its range, but it always has a characteristic roughened surface because of its keeled scales. Either arboreal or terrestrial, depending on its habitat, it is active during the day and feeds on most insects, particularly beetles, as well as spiders, centipedes and snails.

The courting male holds a territory, which he vigorously defends against competitors while he attracts his mate. The female lays 3 to 12 eggs under a log or other debris and may produce up to four clutches a season.

NAME: **Chuckwalla,** *Sauromalus obesus*
RANGE: **USA: S. California, Nevada, Utah, Arizona; Mexico**
HABITAT: **rocky desert**
SIZE: **28–42 cm (11–16½ in)**

A dark-skinned, plump-bodied lizard, the chuckwalla has a thick, pale yellow tail with a blunt tip. The male tends to be darker than the female, with some red or yellow speckling on the body, while females and juveniles often have dark crossbands. The chuckwalla hides under a rock or in a crevice during the night and emerges in the morning to bask in the sun and warm its body. An herbivorous lizard, it then searches for leaves, buds and flowers to eat, often feeding on the creosote bush.

The chuckwalla is well adapted for desert life: in the folds of skin on its sides are accessory lymph glands in which it can store liquid, when it is available, for use in prolonged dry seasons. The female is thought to breed every other year and lays 5 to 10 eggs at a time.

NAME: **Green Anole,** *Anolis carolinensis*
RANGE: **USA: Virginia to Florida, west to Texas**
HABITAT: **forest edge, roadsides**
SIZE: **12–20 cm (4¾–7¾ in)**

The green anole has a slender body and long toe pads as an adaptation for its tree-dwelling habits. Although usually green, it can turn brown in seconds. It is active during the day and feeds on insects and spiders.

The remarkable pink, fanlike flap on the throat of the male is used in courtship display. His display triggers sexual receptivity and ovulation in the female. She lays her eggs, one at a time, at 2-week intervals throughout the breeding season, from April to September. The eggs hatch in 5 to 7 weeks.

NAME: **Collared Lizard,** *Crotaphytus collaris*
RANGE: **USA: Utah, Colorado, south to Texas; Mexico**
HABITAT: **rocky hillsides, forest**
SIZE: **20–35.5 cm (7¾–14 in)**

The robust collared lizard has a large head and a distinctive collar of dark and light markings. Active in the daytime, it particularly likes to bask around rocks where there are crevices for refuge. It feeds on insects and small lizards.

The female collared lizard lays up to 12 eggs in midsummer. The young, measuring about 9 cm (3½ in), hatch 2 to 3 months later.

NAME: **Texas Horned Lizard,** *Phrynosoma cornutum*
RANGE: **USA: Kansas to Texas, Arizona; introduced in Florida**
HABITAT: **arid country**
SIZE: **6–18 cm (2¼–7 in)**

The well-armored Texas horned lizard has a flattened body with pointed scales fringing each side. Behind its head are two enlarged horns, flanked by enlarged scales. In its arid habitat, it may bury itself under loose soil or seek refuge under bushes. It feeds largely on ants.

The female lizard digs a hole in which she lays her 14 to 36 eggs in midsummer; the eggs hatch in about 6 weeks.

NAME: **Forest Iguana,** *Polychrus gutterosus*
RANGE: **tropical South America**
HABITAT: **forest**
SIZE: **up to 50 cm (19¾ in) including tail of up to 37 cm (14½ in)**

A tree-dwelling iguana, this long-legged lizard lies on a branch, its flattened body pressed inconspicuously to the surface, waiting for insect prey. It climbs well and is able to hold onto a branch with its hind legs alone, but it is slow-moving.

The female forest iguana lays clutches of 7 or 8 eggs.

Green Anole (male)

Forest Iguana

Common Iguana

Chuckwalla (male)

Collared Lizard

Eastern Fence Lizard

Texas Horned Lizard

Tuatara

Iguanas

NAME: Marine Iguana, *Amblyrhynchus cristatus*
RANGE: Galápagos Islands
HABITAT: lava rocks on coasts
SIZE: 1.2–1.5 m (4–5 ft)

The only present-day lizard to use the sea as a major habitat, the marine iguana swims and dives readily as it forages for seaweed, its main food. Vital adaptations to marine life are the nasal glands that remove the excess salt the iguana takes in with its food; the salt is expelled in a thin shower of water vapor which the iguana blows out through its nose. When swimming, the iguana uses its powerful tail for propulsion; its feet are normally held against the body, but they are sometimes used to steer a course. The iguana cannot breathe underwater, but when it dives, its heart rate slows down, reducing the blood flow through the body and thus conserving the limited supplies of oxygen.

Male marine iguanas are highly territorial and fight to defend their own small areas of breeding territory on the shore. The combat is ritualistic, each individual trying to overthrow the other by butting him with his head. In one race of marine iguanas, breeding males develop green crests and red flanks. After mating, the female finds a sandy area in which to bury her eggs. She digs a hole about 30.5 cm (12 in) deep, lays 2 or 3 eggs and covers them with sand. The eggs incubate for about 112 days.

Numbers of these once abundant creatures have been reduced by predators, introduced by settlers and sailors. Previously there were no native mammalian predators to threaten their existence.

NAME: Galápagos Land Iguana, *Conolophus subcristatus*
RANGE: Galápagos Islands
HABITAT: arid land, coasts to volcanoes
SIZE: up to 1.2 m (4 ft)

Once common on all of the Galápagos islands, this iguana is now extinct on some and rare on others. Many have been shot for food or sport, and others have suffered from the ravages of introduced predators. Conservation measures have now been established.

A stout-bodied animal with a rounded tail, the land iguana is generally yellow or brown, sometimes with irregular spots on the body. It has a crest at the back of the neck, and older individuals have rolls of fat around the neck. It lives in arid land where there is some vegetation and where it can dig into the soil to make a burrow for shelter. Plants, including cacti, are its main food; it may also eat some small animals. Breeding females lay clutches of about 9 eggs.

NAME: Basilisk Lizard, *Basiliscus plumifrons*
RANGE: South America
HABITAT: forest
SIZE: 80 cm (31½ in)

Male basilisk lizards sport prominent, impressive crests on back and tail and bony casques on the head. The 5 species in the genus are all extremely alike and can be distinguished only by the characteristic shapes of the head casques of the males; these casques are poorly developed in females and absent in juveniles.

The long-legged basilisks are among the few four-legged animals to run on two legs. They rear up on their hind legs and run in a semierect position, with the long tail held up to help balance. This counterweighting effect is vital, and if too much of the tail is amputated, the iguana is unable to rise up on its hind legs. Adults have achieved speeds of 11 km/h (6.8 mph) but only over short distances. Basilisks can even run a few yards over smooth water, held up by the surface film, and they then swim when it is no longer possible for them to remain on the surface.

Active in the daytime, basilisks feed on fruit and small animals, often climbing into trees to find food. In the breeding season, females lay 10 to 15 eggs, which incubate for about 80 days.

NAME: Rhinoceros Iguana, *Cyclura cornuta*
RANGE: Hispaniola and other islands of the Lesser Antilles
HABITAT: arid scrub
SIZE: up to 1.2 m (4 ft)

The male rhinoceros iguana is easily identified by the characteristic protuberances on the tip of his snout that are formed from enlarged scales. The female has only small, inconspicuous protuberances. A large, powerful species, this iguana has a strong tail and a somewhat compressed body. Some individuals, particularly old males, develop rolls of fat at the back of the head. There are many races of rhinoceros iguana with only minor physical variations. They are among the most primitive iguanas.

Rhinoceros iguanas live on land, among thorn bushes and cacti, and feed on plants, worms and mice. Breeding females lay clutches of about 12 eggs, which incubate for 120 days or more. In some islands of the Lesser Antilles, this iguana has been displaced by the common iguana, which has recently become established.

NAME: Spiny-tailed Iguana, *Ctenosaura pectinata*
RANGE: Mexico, Central America
HABITAT: forest
SIZE: 1 m (3¼ ft)

A land-dwelling lizard, the spiny-tailed iguana is so called because its tail is ringed with spiny scales, making it an effective weapon. These iguanas feed mainly on plant material, particularly on beans, but also catch some small animals. Their diet is rich in potassium salts, and they are equipped with nasal glands to excrete excess salt, which then collects as encrustations around the nostrils.

Highly gregarious and territorial, these iguanas live in colonies, ruled by a strict pecking order. One male in the colony is dominant, and although the other males hold territories, they will only defend them against one another and not against the leader. In the breeding season, females dig burrows in which to lay their clutches of about 50 eggs.

NAME: Fijian Banded Iguana, *Brachylophus fasciatus*
RANGE: islands of Fiji and Tonga
HABITAT: woodland, forest
SIZE: 90 cm (35½ in)

One of the few iguana species found outside the Americas, the Fijian iguana has an extremely long tail, often more than twice the length of its slender body, and a low crest along its back. An arboreal iguana, its elongate fingers and toes are equipped with sharp claws for climbing. The female has a uniformly green body, while the male is banded with lighter green and has light spots on his neck. They feed on leaves and other plant material.

The Fijian iguana is a little-known species that may be nearing extinction because of the destruction of much of its forest habitat and the introduction into its range of mongooses, which prey on the iguana and its eggs.

NAME: Madagascan Iguana, *Oplurus* sp.
RANGE: Madagascar, small offshore islands
HABITAT: forest
SIZE: up to 38 cm (15 in)

There are 2 iguana genera in Madagascar: *Oplurus* and *Chalarodon*. The 6 species of *Oplurus* are all similar in appearance, with rings of spiny scales on their tapering tails. *Chalarodon* species are easily distinguished by their small crests, which *Oplurus* species lack, and their smooth-scaled tails.

Although primarily land-dwelling, these iguanas can climb and often take refuge in bushes and trees.

Fijian Banded Iguana (male)

Basilisk Lizard (male)

Marine Iguana

Madagascan Iguana

Rhinoceros Iguana

Galápagos Land Iguana

Spiny-tailed Iguana

Agamid Lizards

AGAMIDAE:
Agamid Lizard Family

The agamid family contains more than 300 species of plump-bodied lizards, found throughout the warmer regions of the Old World, except in Madagascar and New Zealand.

Most agamids have thin tails, long legs and triangular-shaped heads. They live on the ground, in trees or among rocks and feed mainly on insects and other small invertebrates, but also on some plant matter.

NAME: **Common Agama,** *Agama agama*
RANGE: **central Africa**
HABITAT: **tropical forest**
SIZE: **12 cm (4¾ in)**

Agamas live in groups of 2 to 25 in a defined territory, ruled by one dominant male. They are active during the day, emerging at dawn to bask in the sun and feed, mainly on insects. If the dominant male is challenged by another male, he adopts a threat posture, bobbing his head, raising his body off the ground and spreading the folds of his neck skin as far as possible.

Mating usually coincides with the rainy season, when the earth is sufficiently moist for the female agama to make her nest. She digs a small hole in damp soil in which she lays 4 to 6 eggs. She covers the eggs over and smooths the ground surface to conceal the nest. While they develop, the eggs absorb moisture from the soil. The young hatch in 2 or 3 months.

NAME: **Flying Dragon,** *Draco volans*
RANGE: **Philippines to Malaysia and Indonesia**
HABITAT: **rain forest, rubber plantations**
SIZE: **19–22 cm (7½–8½ in)**

An arboreal lizard, the so-called flying dragon actually glides from tree to tree on winglike skin flaps. At each side of its body, between front and hind limbs, there is a large flap of skin, supported by extended movable ribs. Usually these flaps are held folded at the sides of the body, but they can be extended to carry the lizard in an almost horizontal glide for many meters. The flying dragon feeds on insects, particularly ants.

To breed, the flying dragon descends to the ground and buries its 1 to 4 eggs in the soil.

NAME: **Frilled Lizard,** *Chlamydosaurus kingii*
RANGE: **Australia: N. Western Australia, N. Northern Territory, E. Queensland; New Guinea**
HABITAT: **dry forest, woodland**
SIZE: **66 cm (26 in) including tail of 44 cm (17¼ in)**

This slender, long-tailed lizard has an extraordinary rufflike collar of skin around its neck, which may be as much as 25.5 cm (10 in) in diameter. Normally this collar lies in folds around the neck and shoulders, but if alarmed, the lizard opens its mouth wide, and at the same time, the brightly colored frill erects, giving the animal a startling appearance and making it look larger than it really is, in order to intimidate the enemy.

Active in the daytime, the frilled lizard forages in trees and on the ground for insects and other small animals.

NAME: **Thorny Devil,** *Moloch horridus*
RANGE: **Australia: Western, North and South, Queensland**
HABITAT: **arid scrub, desert**
SIZE: **16 cm (6¼ in)**

The grotesque thorny devil is the only species in its genus and one of the strangest of lizards. Its body bristles with large, conical spines, and it has spines above each eye and a spiny hump behind its head. The tail, too, is spiny. It is a slow-moving creature, which forages for its food, mainly ants and termites, on the ground.

The female thorny devil lays 3 to 10 eggs, usually 8, in November or December. The newly hatched young are tiny, spiny replicas of their parents.

NAME: **Princely Mastigure,** *Uromastyx princeps*
RANGE: **Africa: Somalia**
HABITAT: **rocky, stony land**
SIZE: **about 23 cm (9 in)**

A plump-bodied lizard, the princely mastigure has a short, thick tail, studded with large spines, and a small turtlelike head. It is active by day, sheltering at night in holes or crevices in the rocks. Grass, flowers, fruit and leaves are its main foods. If attacked, it defends itself against the enemy with its spiny tail, lashing it to and fro.

NAME: **Arabian Toad-headed Agamid,** *Phrynocephalus nejdensis*
RANGE: **S.W. Asia**
HABITAT: **desert, semidesert**
SIZE: **up to 12.5 cm (5 in)**

The Arabian toad-headed agamid has a rounded head, long, slender legs and a tapering tail. It is a burrowing lizard and digs short tunnels for shelter; it also buries itself in sand by wriggling from side to side. If alarmed, it adopts a defense posture, with tail raised, and then rolls and unrolls its tail. It feeds mainly on insects and also eats some flowers, fruit and leaves.

Females lay several clutches of eggs during the year.

NAME: **Bearded Dragon,** *Amphibolurus barbatus*
RANGE: **Australia: E. and S.E. (except Cape York Peninsula and Tasmania)**
HABITAT: **arid land to forest**
SIZE: **44.5 cm (17½ in) including tail of 19.5 cm (7¾ in)**

This large, formidable-looking lizard is adorned with spiny scales above its ears, at the back of its head and behind its mouth. On its body are a mixture of small and enlarged keeled scales. Adults have throat pouches, or beards, which are bordered with spiny scales. Most bearded dragons are semiarboreal and feed on insects, flowers and soft plant growth in low vegetation.

The female bearded dragon lays 10 to 20 eggs in a nest which she digs in the soil. She covers the eggs with soil and, warmed by the sun, they incubate in the pit for about 3 months.

NAME: **Soa-soa Water Dragon,** *Hydrosaurus amboinensis*
RANGE: **New Guinea, Moluccas, Sulawesi**
HABITAT: **rain forest**
SIZE: **1.1 m (3½ ft), including tail of 75 cm (29½ in)**

One of the largest agamids, the soa-soa is a powerfully built lizard with strong forefeet. The adult male has a showy crest on the base of the tail, which can be erected, supported by bony extensions of the tail vertebrae. As its name suggests, this is an aquatic lizard, usually found close to rivers. It can swim well, propelling itself with its laterally compressed tail, and run on its hind legs on land.

Despite its formidable appearance, the soa-soa feeds largely on plants, particularly tender leaves; it also consumes insects and millipedes. It reproduces by laying eggs.

NAME: **Eastern Water Dragon,** *Physignathus leseueri*
RANGE: **E. Australia**
HABITAT: **coasts, forested slopes**
SIZE: **73 cm (28¾ in), including tail of 50 cm (19¾ in)**

The eastern water dragon varies in coloration over its wide range but always has a long, powerful tail and a crest running along the length of its body and tail. A semiaquatic, tree-living lizard, it lies on a branch overhanging a river or stream and, if disturbed, will tumble down into the water. It also forages on rocky seashores. Its diet is varied, including insects, small aquatic animals such as frogs, terrestrial animals and fruit and berries. The breeding female lays about 8 eggs under a rock or in a burrow she digs in the soil. The eggs hatch in 10 to 14 weeks.

Thorny Devil

Flying Dragon

Frilled Lizard

Princely Mastigure

Common Agama

Soa-soa Water Dragon (male)

Bearded Dragon

Eastern Water Dragon

Arabian Toad-headed Agamid

Chameleons

NAME: Jackson's Chameleon, *Chamaeleo jacksonii*
RANGE: E. Africa: Uganda, Tanzania to N. Mozambique
HABITAT: savanna vegetation
SIZE: 11–12 cm (4¼–4¾ in)

The three prominent horns on his head make the male Jackson's chameleon instantly recognizable. The female has only one small horn on the snout and rudimentary horns by each eye. Usually colored a drab green, this chameleon resembles lichen on the bark of a tree.

One of the live-bearing species in the chameleon family, the female Jackson's chameleon may carry 20 to 40 eggs, but only 10 or so young ever actually survive. At birth, the young are about 5.5 cm (2¼ in) long and have two tiny horns in front of the eyes and a conical scale in the position of the middle horn.

NAME: Meller's Chameleon, *Chamaeleo melleri*
RANGE: E. Africa: Tanzania, Malawi
HABITAT: savanna vegetation
SIZE: 54–58 cm (21¼–22¾ in) including tail of 28–29 cm (11–11½ in)

The largest chameleon found outside Madagascar, the male Meller's chameleon has only a tiny snout horn, which is also present in the female. Its body is distinctively marked with broad yellow stripes and black spots. As it sits on a branch, the chameleon often sways slightly, as a leaf might do in a breeze, and this, combined with its camouflaging coloration and patterning, makes it extremely hard to detect in foliage, despite its large size. Meller's chameleons feed on small birds, as well as on insects.

NAME: Flap-necked Chameleon, *Chamaeleo dilepis*
RANGE: tropical and southern Africa
HABITAT: forest, scrubland
SIZE: 25–36.5 cm (9¾–14¼ in)

This aggressive chameleon has lobes of membranous skin at the back of its head, which it erects in threat when it meets another member of its own species. It may raise only the lobe on the side of the opponent. A tree- and bush-dwelling species, it descends to the ground only to move from one tree to another or to lay eggs. Its coloration varies with the background, being green when among leaves and yellow or reddish-brown when on bark. When angry or alarmed, for example when confronting the boomslang (tree snake), its main enemy, the chameleon turns dark blackish-green, with yellow and white spots, and makes hissing sounds.

The female lays 30 to 40 eggs in a hole she digs in the ground; she then conceals the nest with grass and twigs. The eggs hatch in about 3 months.

CHAMAELEONIDAE: Chameleon Family

The chameleons are probably the most specialized group of tree-living lizards, superbly adapted in both structural and behavioral ways. About 85 species are known; most live in Africa and Madagascar, but a few occur in Asia, and there is one European species. Although primarily an arboreal group, a few species are ground-living.

Most chameleons are between 15 and 30 cm (6 and 11¾ in) in length, but a few are smaller, and one species in Madagascar reaches 70 to 80 cm (27½ to 31½ in). Whatever their size, all chameleons are recognizable by certain characteristic attributes. The typical chameleon has a body which is flattened from side to side; the head often has prominent crests or horns, and the large eyes are protuberant and can be moved independently of one another to locate insect prey. The toes on hind and forefeet are arranged to provide a pincerlike grip on branches: each foot divides clearly, with three toes on one side and two on the other. The muscular prehensile tail can be curled around a branch and helps the chameleon to stay immobile as it watches for prey.

Although several groups of lizards are able to change the color of their skins, usually for camouflage purposes, the chameleon is the most accomplished. Camouflage helps the chameleon in its slow, stalking approach toward prey and also helps to hide it from predators. The mechanism behind the chameleon's color-change abilities is complex. The pattern of pigmentation in the skin cells is controlled by the nervous system, and pigment can be spread out or contracted, thus lightening or darkening the skin. The strength of the light seems to be the most important influence on the mechanism.

Perhaps, however, the most extraordinary adaptive feature of the chameleons is their protrusible tongue. It can be shot out, from its tongue-bone support, to capture insects a body-length away from the reptile; at the tip of the tongue is a sticky pad to which the insect adheres. The chameleon has superb eyesight, which enables it to take accurate aim at the prey.

Chameleons generally reproduce by laying eggs, which the mother buries in a hole in the ground. A few African species, however, give birth to live young. In these forms, completely developed young chameleons grow inside their egg membranes, but free themselves from these enclosures immediately after the eggs are laid.

NAME: European Chameleon, *Chamaeleo chamaeleon*
RANGE: S. Spain and Portugal, Crete, N. Africa, Canary Islands
HABITAT: bushes in dry country
SIZE: 25–28 cm (9¾–11 in)

The only chameleon to occur in Europe, this species is usually yellowish-brown with dark bands on the body, but may turn green when among grass or other green vegetation. When alarmed, it turns very dark and inflates its body with air so as to appear larger than its true size. In vegetated areas, this chameleon lives in bushes and descends to the ground only to lay eggs. In North Africa, however, in areas of sparse plant growth, it is a ground-dweller and lives in holes, which it digs itself, on the outskirts of oases. It feeds on insects, particularly locusts.

At mating time, males fight one another for females, and paired males and females may also fight. The female lays 20 to 30 eggs, which she buries in the ground.

NAME: *Brookesia spectrum*
RANGE: Cameroon, Gabon to E. Africa
HABITAT: forest floor
SIZE: 7.5–9 cm (3–3½ in)

This tiny, dusty-brown chameleon closely resembles the dead leaves among which it lives on the forest floor. The effect is enhanced by the stumpy tail, little peaks on the head and body and the irregular lines on the body which mimic leaf veins. There are two tiny appendages on the snout. Its legs are extremely thin and bony and the tail is not prehensile — as a ground-living chameleon it has no need of the fifth limb so useful to tree-dwelling species. It rarely changes color; again, it has little need, being so well camouflaged already. Like all chameleons, it moves slowly and deliberately and may remain still for hours. It feeds on insects.

Little is known of the breeding habits, but females are believed to lay 3 to 6 eggs in a clutch.

NAME: *Rhampholeon marshalli*
RANGE: Africa: Zimbabwe, Mozambique
HABITAT: forest on mountain slopes
SIZE: 3.5–7.5 cm (1¼–3 in)

The shape of this chameleon, with its flattened body and highly arched back, contributes to its leaflike appearance as it sits, swaying gently from side to side as if blowing in the wind. Rows of light-colored tubercles scattered over the body are particularly prominent in males. Females are usually twice the size of males. Much of this chameleon's life is spent among the leaf litter of the forest floor.

The female lays 12 to 18 eggs.

Jackson's Chameleon (male)

Brookesia spectrum

Meller's Chameleon

Rhampholeon marshalli

European Chameleon

Flap-necked Chameleon

Geckos

NAME: **Tokay Gecko,** *Gekko gekko*
RANGE: **Asia, Indonesia**
HABITAT: **in or near houses**
SIZE: **28 cm (11 in)**

One of the largest and most common geckos, the tokay gecko is believed to bring good luck to the houses whose walls it frequents. It feeds on insects, particularly cockroaches, and on young lizards, mice and small birds, all of which it seizes in its powerful jaws. The male makes his loud barking call, "tok-eh" or "gek-oh," most frequently in the mating season; the female is mute.

The female tokay gecko lays 2 sticky-surfaced eggs, which are usually stuck fast to a perpendicular object and are almost impossible to remove without breaking. The same locations are used year after year, and it is common to find 8 to 10 sets of eggs together, all laid by different females and in various stages of incubation.

NAME: **White-spotted Gecko,** *Tarentola annularis*
RANGE: **Africa: Libya, Egypt, Sudan, Ethiopia, Somalia**
HABITAT: **trees, rocks, ruins in semidesert**
SIZE: **20.5 cm (8 in)**

The body color of these geckos varies according to the surface they are on: geckos on the black rocks above the first Nile Cataract are black, while those found on white-washed walls are almost white.

Aggressive, active creatures, they feed primarily on insects but also eat spiders and lizards. They are able to survive long periods without water, although they drink eagerly when the opportunity presents itself.

Mating is triggered by the arrival of the rains, and the female gecko lays her eggs in a crevice or hole in a rock or wall.

NAME: **Leopard Gecko,** *Eublepharius macularius*
RANGE: **Afghanistan, S. Turkestan, Pakistan, W. India**
HABITAT: **dry, rocky regions**
SIZE: **up to 30 cm (11¾ in)**

Also known as the panther gecko, this chunky lizard has a spotted body and a large head. Unlike most geckos, which have fused transparent eyelids, this species is one of the few with movable eyelids — a primitive characteristic in the gecko family. Its legs are long and thin and it holds its body well off the ground when it runs. Leopard geckos feed on grasshoppers, scorpions, beetles and spiders. They are nocturnal and hide during the day under rocks or in burrows in the sand.

During the year, the female lays several clutches, each of 2 eggs.

GEKKONIDAE: Gecko Family

Throughout the tropical, subtropical and warm temperate zones of the world are distributed some 675 species of gecko. These lizards may inhabit forests, swamps, deserts or mountainous areas; in fact, any place with sufficient insect life for them to feed on and where nights do not become too cold. They range in size from 5 to 30 cm (2 to 11¾ in), although most are between 7 and 15 cm (2¾ and 6 in) long.

The typical gecko has a flattened head and a body with soft skin, containing many minute scales. Most are nocturnal animals and have enormous eyes, each with a permanently closed transparent eyelid. Many have "friction pads" of specialized scales under the toes, which enable them to climb easily up vertical surfaces and even to walk upside down, on a ceiling for instance.

The males of many of the nocturnal species are among the most vocal lizards and make loud, repetitive calls. Females lay only 1 to 3 eggs at a time but may breed several times a year; the young are already almost half the length of their parents when they hatch. The eggs of most geckos are harder-shelled than those of other lizards; they are quite soft when laid and harden after a period of exposure to air.

NAME: **Web-footed Gecko,** *Palmatogecko rangei*
RANGE: **S.W. Africa: Namib Desert**
HABITAT: **sand dunes, rocks**
SIZE: **12.5 cm (5 in)**

This extremely rare species, which lives on the seaward slopes of the Namib Desert, where rain is almost unknown, absorbs moisture from the sea breezes and from the mists that roll in from the sea. It also laps dew from the stones and licks its own eyes for moisture.

Since this gecko lives on the ground, it has no need of friction pads on its feet for climbing vertical surfaces; instead, its almost clawless toes are connected by webs which act like snowshoes in the soft sand. When running, the gecko holds its body well off the hot ground, and its feet leave little or no trace of its movements. The webbed feet are also used for burrowing into the sand to escape from predators or from the blistering sun. The gecko makes a chamber in which it lies with its head facing the entrance, waiting to pounce on the termites, beetles, flies and worms that are its main food. If a predator should try to pull it out, the gecko clings to the side of the chamber with its strong tail, engaging in a tug-of-war.

NAME: **Kuhl's Gecko,** *Ptychozoon kuhli*
RANGE: **S.E. Asia, Indonesia, Borneo**
HABITAT: **forest**
SIZE: **15 cm (6 in)**

The geckos of this genus, often known as the fringed or even "flying" geckos, have fringes of skin along the sides of the head, limbs, body and tail, and webs between the toes. When jumping or falling from trees, the gecko extends its legs and tail to expand the flaps and uses them like a parachute. Perhaps even more important is the camouflage the fringes give as the gecko rests on the branch of a tree: the gecko presses the skin flaps down against the bark, thus removing any shadows and breaking up its outline.

The female Kuhl's gecko lays her eggs in November. The eggs, coated with a sticky substance when laid, adhere to each other and to the branch of the tree and gradually develop a hard shell. The young geckos hatch the following May.

NAME: **Marbled Gecko,** *Phyllodactylus porphyreus*
RANGE: **South Africa, Australia**
HABITAT: **arid mountain slopes**
SIZE: **11.5 cm (4½ in)**

This active little gecko lives in cracks in rocks or beneath stones and varies in coloration according to its surroundings. It feeds on insects and is often parasitized by mites.

The female marbled gecko lays her eggs under a stone or on a tree, where they remain until they hatch approximately 115 days later. The newly hatched young are about 2 cm (¾ in) long, with tails that are over half their body length.

NAME: **Brook's Gecko,** *Hemidactylus brookii*
RANGE: **Asia, Africa, South America, East and West Indies**
HABITAT: **coastal plains to upland savanna to 2,100 m (7,000 ft)**
SIZE: **15 cm (6 in)**

This unusually widespread gecko lives under stones, in cracks in rocks, in abandoned termite mounds, beneath fallen tree trunks and even under heaps of garden debris.

With its sharply curving claws, it climbs with great agility up even vertical surfaces. It feeds on insects and at night will enter houses to prey on those which are attracted to the light. It is difficult to ascertain the exact length of this species, since adults rarely have their long tails intact; although the tail breaks off easily, muscles in the main tail artery contract speedily to prevent any undue loss of blood.

In the breeding season the female Brook's gecko lays 2 eggs.

Brook's Gecko

White-spotted Gecko

Marbled Gecko

Web-footed Gecko

Tokay Gecko

Leopard Gecko

Kuhl's Gecko

Geckos, Scaly-foot Lizards

NAME: Leaf-tailed Gecko, *Uroplatus fimbriatus*
RANGE: Madagascar
HABITAT: forest
SIZE: 20.5 cm (8 in)

A flat-bodied gecko with large bulging eyes, the leaf-tailed gecko's mottled body blends excellently with bark or lichen. It lies with its body pressed against a branch or trunk of a tree, and the small scales bordering its legs and sides reduce any shadow. In addition to this camouflage, it can change the intensity of its coloration, becoming darker by night and lighter again in the morning. When alarmed, it turns dark brown or black. The broad, flat tail can be rolled up dorsally — toward the back — and is used as a fifth limb for holding onto branches.

Mainly active at night, this gecko feeds on insects. Each individual has a preferred resting place where, after a meal, it retires to clean itself, using its tongue to lick over its whole body, even the eyes.

NAME: Green Day Gecko, *Heteropholis manukanus*
RANGE: New Zealand (Marlborough Sound, Stephens Island)
HABITAT: forest, scrub
SIZE: 12.5–16.5 cm (5–6½ in)

Unlike most geckos, the green day gecko is active in the daytime when it forages in trees for insects and small invertebrates. It is found mainly on the manuka, or tea tree, (*Leptospermum scoparium*). Its bright green coloration has yellow undertones, and the female's belly is yellowish-green, the male's bluish-green. In both sexes the soles of the feet are yellowish. The head is rather large and the snout deep and blunt.

Most geckos lay eggs, but the female of this species gives birth to 2, occasionally only 1, live young. The young are similar in appearance to the adults.

Numbers of these geckos have fallen because large areas of their forest and scrub habitat have been cleared for development.

NAME: *Phelsuma vinsoni*
RANGE: Mauritius and neighboring islands
HABITAT: forest
SIZE: 17.5 cm (6¾ in)

An unusual gecko species with its vivid coloration, the male *Phelsuma vinsoni* has bright red spots on a blue and green back and brown lines on the head and neck region. The female has similar patterning but is less vivid and is tinged with brown or gray. This gecko is also unusual in that it is active during the day; most are nocturnal. A good climber, it is often found on screwpine trees, the fruit of which attracts the insects on which it feeds. Fruit such as bananas and the nectar of flowers sometimes supplement the gecko's diet.

The female gecko lays 2 sticky-surfaced eggs, which are usually left attached to a branch; several females may lay their eggs together. They hatch after 9 to 12 weeks, depending on the temperature, and the young geckos measure about 12 cm (4¾ in), most of which is tail.

PYGOPODIDAE:
Scaly-foot Lizard Family

The scaly-foots, or snake lizards, are one of the groups of lizards which, although they are limbless and snakelike, are anatomically different from true snakes. There are about 14 known species, all found in Australia or New Guinea.

Although externally so similar to snakes, the scaly-foots are, in fact, most closely related to geckos and share certain characteristics with them, such as fused eyelids and their ability to make sounds. Their hind limbs are present as vestigial scaly flaps, and the tail is extremely long. The flat, fleshy tongue is slightly forked and can be extended well out of the mouth.

NAME: Burton's Snake-lizard, *Lialis burtonis*
RANGE: Australia: central areas, Queensland; New Guinea
HABITAT: semidesert, rain forest
SIZE: up to 61 cm (24 in)

The most widespread species of its family, this snake-lizard is able to adapt to the contrasting habitats of rain forest and semidesert. A ground-dweller, it hides in clumps of grass or under plant debris. Its color and pattern vary, but they are not related to geographical distribution, and it always has a distinctive brown stripe on each side of the head. The snout is long and pointed.

Active during both day and night, Burton's snake-lizard feeds on insects, skinks and other small lizards. Its long, pointed, backward-curving teeth enable it to overcome quite large prey, which it seizes with a quick snap of its jaws and swallows whole.

Unlike other snake-lizards, which make geckolike barks or soft squeaks, this lizard emits a long, drawn-out note. The female lays 2 or 3 large elongate eggs which have parchmentlike shells.

NAME: Hooded Scaly-foot, *Pygopus nigriceps*
RANGE: Western Australia
HABITAT: dry inland country, coastal forest
SIZE: 46 cm (18 in)

Also known as the black-headed or western scaly-foot, this species has a tail that is slightly longer than its body and a rounded snout. The hind limbs are present as scaly flaps, each containing miniature leg bones and four toes. These flaps usually lie flat against the body, but when the animal is handled or injured, they are held out at right angles.

If threatened, the hooded scaly-foot mimics the poisonous elapid snake *Denisonia gouldii* to try to deter its enemy: it draws back its head, bends its neck into an S-shape, puffs out its throat slightly and hisses. It feeds on insects and small lizards and is most active at dusk and at night. The female lays 2 eggs.

NAME: *Delma nasuta*
RANGE: Australia: Western and Northern Territories, South Australia
HABITAT: sandy and stony desert, arid scrub
SIZE: 30 cm (11¾ in) including tail of 22 cm (8½ in)

The 3 species of scaly-foot in the genus *Delma* are all slender bodied and move exactly like snakes, resembling the smaller elapid snakes of Australia. They feed on insects and small lizards both at night and during the day, but species living in the hot desert areas of central Australia are strictly nocturnal. The hind limbs are present as tiny but movable flaps, which are held against the body. The female lays 2 eggs.

NAME: *Aprasia striolata*
RANGE: Australia: isolated populations in S.W. Western Australia, S. Australia to W. Victoria; Northern Territory
HABITAT: sandy or loamy soils
SIZE: 15 cm (6 in)

There are 4 species in the genus *Aprasia*, all of which are alike in habits and appearance. A small burrowing creature, this species has a rounded snout and inconspicuous flaps, which are vestiges of its hind limbs. Its tail is short. It feeds on insects and lizards and is mainly active in the daytime. The females of this genus of lizard generally lay 2 eggs at a time.

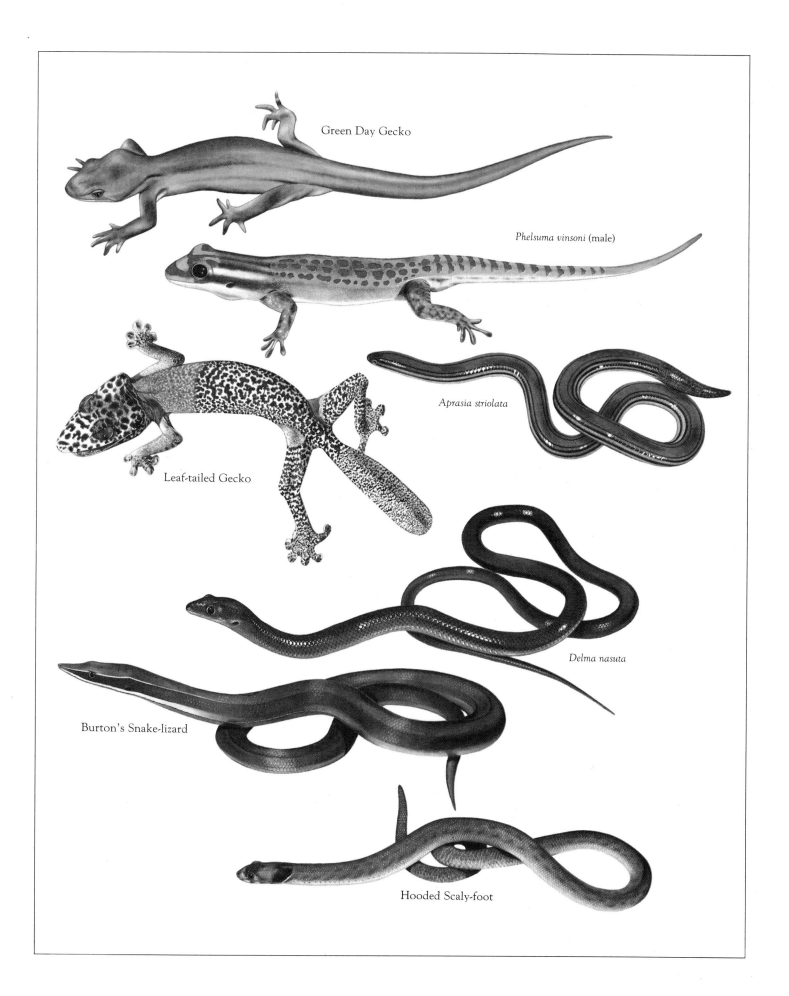

Green Day Gecko

Phelsuma vinsoni (male)

Aprasia striolata

Leaf-tailed Gecko

Delma nasuta

Burton's Snake-lizard

Hooded Scaly-foot

Night Lizards, Teiid Lizards

XANTUSIIDAE: Night Lizard Family

As their name suggests, night lizards are nocturnal, beginning their hunting activities at dusk and spending the daylight hours hidden among rocks and under stones. There are about 18 species in the family, found in the southwest of the USA, Central America and Cuba, mostly in rocky, arid habitats. They feed on nocturnal insects.

Night lizards have a superficial resemblance to geckos, with their immobile eyelids, the lower of which have transparent "windows." Unlike the geckos, they have scales on the back and belly and shields on the head. All night lizards give birth to live young, which develop inside the mother's body, nourished by a form of placenta.

NAME: **Desert Night Lizard, *Xantusia vigilis***
RANGE: **S.W. USA: Nevada, Utah to California; Mexico**
HABITAT: **rocky, arid and semiarid land**
SIZE: **9.5–12.5 cm (3¾–5 in)**

The desert night lizard varies in coloration over its range but is marked with many small dark spots; *X. v. utahensis* is the subspecies illustrated. It frequents yucca plants and agaves and feeds on termites, ants, beetles and flies, which it finds among vegetation or rocks.

Night lizards give birth to live young. They mate in early summer, usually May or June, and 1 to 3 young are born, tail first, a few months later.

TEIIDAE: Teiid Lizard Family

There are about 230 species in this exclusively American family, the majority of which live in South America. Teiids are slender lizards with thin, whiplike tails and characteristic long, deeply divided tongues, which they use to search for food. Most species have scales on the back and belly.

In many ways, teiids represent the New World equivalent of the lacertid lizards. Most species are ground-living, feeding on a variety of small animals, but some have become specialized for a particular way of life, for example the caiman lizard, which is semiaquatic and feeds on snails.

Teiids reproduce by laying eggs. Most must mate first in the normal way, but in a few unisexual species no mating is necessary. In these teiids, all individuals are female and can lay eggs, which do not need to be fertilized and which hatch into more females, so completely dispensing with the need for males.

NAME: **Caiman Lizard, *Dracaena guianensis***
RANGE: **N.E. South America**
HABITAT: **swampy flooded ground, often woodland bordering rivers**
SIZE: **1.2 m (4 ft)**

The large, powerful caiman lizard has an oarlike, laterally flattened tail and rough, horny, platelike scales along its back. It inhabits areas which are flooded for much of the time, except when the rivers are at their lowest, and frequents the resulting pools and ponds. It spends much of the day in water and dives and swims well, using its tail for propulsion. At night, it finds shelter above water level, often in trees or bushes. It feeds almost entirely on aquatic snails, taking the snail in its jaws, then raising its head so that the snail slides back into its mouth, where it is broken up by the huge, crushing back teeth. The pieces of shell are spit out and the soft body swallowed.

The female caiman lizard, having mated, lays eggs which she buries, often in a deserted arboreal termites' nest.

NAME: **Common Tegu, *Tupinambis teguixin***
RANGE: **Central America, N. South America**
HABITAT: **forest, woodland**
SIZE: **1.2–1.4 m (4–4½ ft), including tail of 70–85 cm (27½–33½ in)**

A robust lizard with a long cylindrical tail, the tegu has prominent yellow markings on its dark body. It frequents dense undergrowth and is also found in cultivated areas where food is abundant. Chickens and their eggs are included in its diet, as well as small mammals, frogs, large insects, worms and some fruit and leaves. It hunts by day and hides in a burrow at night and in cool weather. A formidable opponent, the tegu will lash out at an enemy with its powerful tail before attacking with its jaws. However, it will run away from danger when possible, and juveniles are able to run on their hind legs. Local tribespeople catch the tegu and use the yellow body fat as a cure for inflammations.

The female tegu lays her eggs in an inhabited arboreal termite nest, tearing the outer wall open to deposit her 6 to 8 eggs inside. The ever-vigilant termites then come along and repair the wall of their nest, thus sealing the tegu eggs safely away from predators and changes in temperature or humidity while they develop. The newly hatched young must break out of the termite nest by themselves.

NAME: **Jungle Runner, *Ameiva ameiva***
RANGE: **Central America; South America, east of the Andes; introduced in USA: Florida**
HABITAT: **open grassland**
SIZE: **15–20 cm (6–7¾ in)**

A ground-living, extremely active lizard, the jungle runner emerges in the morning to forage for food, flicking out its long forked tongue to search for insects, spiders, snails and other small invertebrates and small lizards. The protrusible tongue is tactile and can also detect scents. In coastal regions, the jungle runner may be found in burrows, such as those made by crabs, and in Panama it is reported to be extending its normal range by moving into areas recently cleared by man.

The male jungle runner is usually larger than the female and is marked with conspicuous light spots, whereas the female has distinctive stripes along her body. After mating, the female lays a clutch of 1 to 4 eggs.

NAME: **Teyu, *Teius teyou***
RANGE: **S.E. Brazil to Argentina**
HABITAT: **open, rocky land**
SIZE: **30 cm (11¾ in)**

One of the most numerous and widespread of South American teiids, the adaptable teyu lives wherever there is open land with some rock cover. For shelter, it makes a tunnel under a large stone that leads down to a small chamber, measuring about 2.5 cm by 4 cm (1 in by 1½ in). Here it lies, curled in a U-shape, its body in the chamber and its head and long tail in the tunnel. It feeds on insects and, occasionally, on spiders.

NAME: **Strand Racerunner, *Cnemidophorus lemniscatus***
RANGE: **Central America to N. South America; Trinidad, Tobago**
HABITAT: **lowland plains, open regions of flood-plain forest**
SIZE: **30 cm (11¾ in)**

One of the fastest-moving of all the lizards, the strand racerunner is always on the move, continually darting off in different directions and sometimes running on its hind legs. Speeds of 24 to 28 km/h (15 to 17 mph) have been recorded over short distances. It is active during the day, and although mainly ground-dwelling, it also climbs low trees and bushes in search of food. A long-bodied lizard, it has an elongate, tapering, ridged tail; its snout may be blunt or pointed.

To mate, the male sits astride the female, holding the skin of her neck in his mouth. He curves his body around hers while copulating. The female lays 4 to 6 eggs, which hatch some 8 to 10 weeks later.

Caiman Lizard

Desert Night Lizard

Strand Racerunner

Common Tegu

Jungle Runner

Teyu

Skinks

NAME: Legless Skink, *Acontias* **sp.**
RANGE: South Africa, Madagascar
HABITAT: sandy regions
SIZE: 10 cm (4½ in)

Legless skinks spend most of their lives in their underground burrows. They are indeed limbless, with long cylindrical bodies and short tails. Their eyes and ears are protected by scales, and their lower eyelids are equipped with transparent "windows," to enable them to see when burrowing without getting soil in their eyes. Their bodies are covered with hard, smooth scales, enabling them to move easily through the earth. They also move quickly on the surface, using snakelike undulations of the body. Legless skinks are largely insectivorous but may also eat small invertebrates and frogs.

Females bear live young, producing litters of 3 or 4 at a time.

NAME: Round-bodied Skink, *Chalcides bedriagai*
RANGE: Spain, Portugal
HABITAT: varied: arid sandy land, hilly areas, grassland
SIZE: up to 16 cm (6¼ in)

An elongate, short-legged species, this skink keeps out of sight in ground vegetation or burrows into loose sand. It is usually a buff or grayish-brown, with dark-edged markings, and its scales are large, smooth and shiny. It varies somewhat in color and proportions over its range: southern individuals, for example, have shorter legs than the western populations, while those in the east have medium-length legs. Round-bodied skinks feed on a variety of small invertebrates.

Females give birth to 2 or 3 fully formed live young, which have developed inside the body, nourished by a form of placenta.

NAME: Sundeval's Skink, *Riopa sundevalli*
RANGE: Africa: Zambia to South Africa
HABITAT: open plains, sandy savanna
SIZE: up to 18 cm (7 in)

A burrowing species, Sundeval's skink has tiny limbs and smooth scales. It comes to the surface in search of food — insects and their larvae, spiders, wood lice and soft snails — and may hide under stones or leaf debris. Termite hills and manure heaps are also favorite spots for these skinks. On the ground, the skink moves in a snakelike fashion, its tiny limbs of little use. The tail breaks away easily, and adults are seldom seen with a complete tail.

Females lay 2 to 6 eggs, usually 4, in a nest underground or in a termite mound. The newly hatched young measure 5 cm (2 in).

SCINCIDAE: Skink Family

One of the largest lizard families, with many hundreds of species, skinks occur on every continent except Antarctica. They are most abundant in Southeast Asia and the Australasian region.

Skinks live on or below the ground and are normally smooth-scaled, with elongate, rounded bodies and tapering tails. Their legs are short, and some burrowing skinks have tiny legs or none at all. Many families of lizards include species with reduced or no limbs, but this is particularly common in the skink family. The majority are between 8 and 35 cm (3¼ and 13¾ in) in length, although there are a few giant forms.

Most skinks feed on insects and small invertebrates; the giant forms, however, are herbivorous. Their reproductive habits vary: most species lay eggs but some give birth to live young.

NAME: Sandfish, *Scincus philbyi*
RANGE: Saudi Arabia
HABITAT: sandy desert
SIZE: up to 21 cm (8¼ in)

Unlike most burrowing skinks, this species retains well-developed legs and feet. Its digits are flattened and have fringes of scales to help it move easily over loose sand. The body of the sandfish is robust and cylindrical, and it has a broad, wedge-shaped snout. The sandfish is active through the heat of the day, for it spends most of its time under the surface of the sand, looking for prey such as beetles and millipedes. It pushes its way along, seeming literally to swim through the sand, hence its name.

The female sandfish gives birth to fully formed live young, which have developed inside her body.

NAME: *Feylinia cussori*
RANGE: tropical Africa
HABITAT: forest
SIZE: 35 cm (13¾ in)

A large burrowing skink, *Feylinia cussori* has a rather flattened head, which merges smoothly with its limbless cylindrical body. There are no external eardrums, and its tiny eyes are protected by transparent scales. It is often found under decaying wood and feeds largely on termites, which it locates by the sounds they make in the wood.

The female bears litters of 2 or 3 live young, which have developed inside her body. There is a local superstition that *Feylinia* can enter the human body whenever it desires, and when it leaves again, the person dies.

NAME: Great Plains Skink, *Eumeces obsoletus*
RANGE: central and S.W. USA: Wyoming and Nebraska to Arizona and Texas; Mexico
HABITAT: rocky grassland, usually near water
SIZE: 16.5–35 cm (6½–13¾ in)

The largest North American skink, the Great Plains skink has well-developed, sturdy limbs, and its body is spotted with dark brown or black; these spots may merge in places to give the impression of lengthwise stripes. Active in the daytime, it feeds on insects, spiders and small lizards. It is an aggressive skink and will bite readily if alarmed.

The Great Plains skink is unusual among lizards for the degree of maternal care it displays. A few weeks after mating in April or May, the female lays 17 to 21 eggs in a nest, which she makes beneath a rock. She guards the eggs while they incubate and turns them regularly to ensure even warming. When, a couple of months later, the eggs begin to hatch, the female rubs them and presses them with her body, stimulating the young to move and then to wriggle free of the shell. For a further 10 days after hatching, she attends her young, cleaning each one regularly. Juvenile Great Plains skinks are generally black with blue tails and some white spots. This coloration gradually fades as the skinks mature.

NAME: Sand Skink, *Neoseps reynoldsi*
RANGE: USA: central Florida
HABITAT: sandhills
SIZE: 10–13 cm (4–5 in)

This small skink is an expert digger and burrower; using its chisel-shaped snout, it burrows speedily into the sand, undulating its body as it goes, as if swimming. Its limbs are tiny, and it has only one digit on each forelimb and two on each hind limb. It feeds on termites and beetle larvae, which it locates by the sound vibrations they cause. Although it is active in the daytime and comes to the surface to shelter under logs and other debris, the sand skink is a secretive species and is rarely seen. If alarmed, it quickly buries itself.

Sand skinks mate in spring, and the female lays 2 eggs.

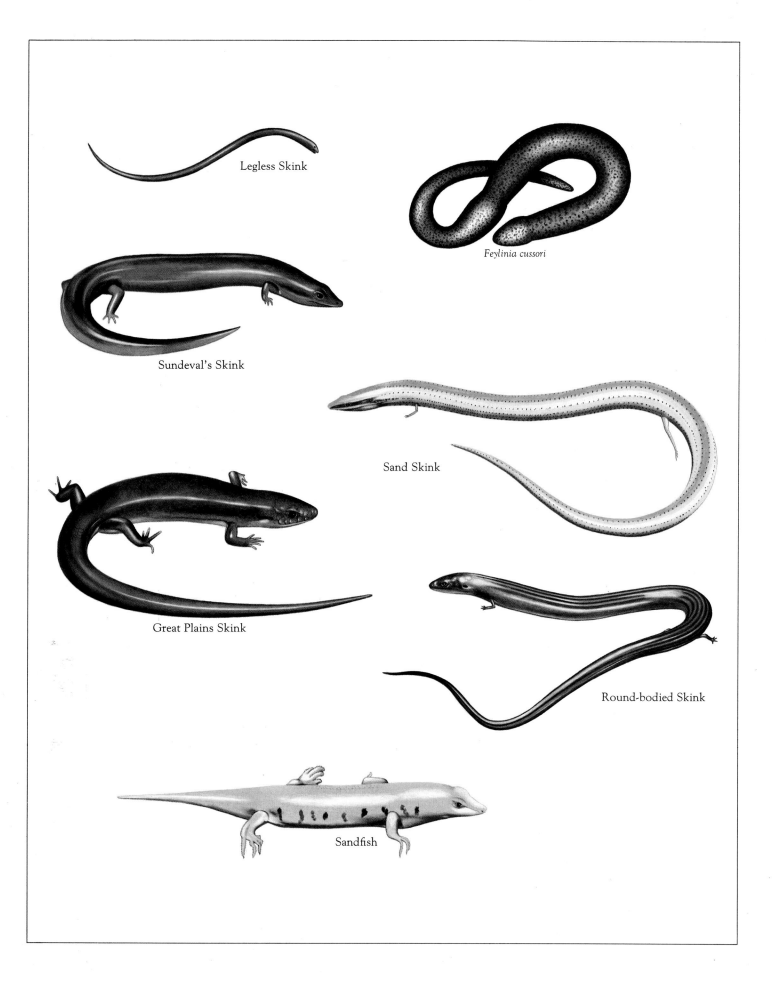

Legless Skink

Feylinia cussori

Sundeval's Skink

Sand Skink

Great Plains Skink

Round-bodied Skink

Sandfish

Skinks

NAME: Mabuya, *Mabuya wrightii*
RANGE: Seychelles
HABITAT: granite islands with guano deposits
SIZE: 31 cm (12¼ in) including tail of up to 18 cm (7 in)

The stocky-bodied mabuya has well-developed hind limbs with long digits. Its snout is slightly elongate and blunt. A fast-moving, ground-dwelling lizard, the mabuya is active in the daytime and has a great need of warmth. Mabuyas are usually found on the smaller islands of the Seychelles, often in close association with the nesting colonies of seabirds. In the breeding season, mabuyas feed on bird's eggs, especially those of terns, which they break by rolling them off rocks or branches. They then lap up the contents. Their diet is not known outside the birds' breeding season.

Most mabuya species give birth to live young, but the exact details of the breeding habits of this particular mabuya have not been observed. One South African mabuya species, *M. trivittata*, is one of the few reptiles to assist her newborn young. She helps the young to escape from the soft membranes in which they are born by tearing the coverings open with her teeth.

NAME: Spiny-tailed Skink, *Egernia stokesii*
RANGE: Western Australia through arid interior to Queensland, New South Wales and South Australia
HABITAT: stony hills, mountains
SIZE: up to 27 cm (10½ in)

The spiny-tailed skink is a most unusual species, with a stout body covered with rough-edged, sometimes spiny, scales. The tail is short and much flattened and particularly well endowed with spinous scales. All four limbs are strong and well developed. This skink frequents rocky areas, where it can shelter in deep crevices or under boulders; the spines on its tail make it virtually impossible to dislodge once it has wedged itself in such a hiding place. It is active during the day, when it basks in the sun and forages for insects within easy reach of its refuge. A gregarious species, it lives in colonies, and the presence of spiny-tailed skinks in an area is signaled by their regular defecation sites, where small piles of feces accumulate.

Spiny-tailed skinks are live-bearers. The female gives birth to about 5 fully formed young, which develop inside her body, nourished by a form of placenta. The young measure about 6 cm (2¼ in) at birth.

NAME: *Emoia cyanogaster*
RANGE: Australia: extreme N. Queensland; Indonesia
HABITAT: forest, banana groves
SIZE: up to 27 cm (10½ in)

A slender, glossy skink with a slim tapering tail, *Emoia cyanogaster* has a pointed, somewhat flattened snout. Its limbs, particularly the hind limbs, are long and well formed, with elongate digits. It is an agile, primarily tree-dwelling species and can jump easily from branch to branch. Much of its day is spent basking on low vegetation or sheltering among the trailing leaves of banana trees, but it often descends to the ground to search for food.

These skinks breed throughout the year, although with some seasonal fluctuations. The female usually lays 2 eggs at a time.

NAME: *Leiolopisma infrapunctatum*
RANGE: New Zealand
HABITAT: open country with some vegetation
SIZE: 24 cm (9½ in)

This smooth-scaled skink has beautiful markings, which may vary slightly in coloration and intensity but are usually constant in pattern. The most striking are the broad, broken bands of reddish-brown, which run from behind each eye, above the limbs, to the tail. The belly is usually yellow, with scattered dark markings. The head and body are elongate and there is no distinct neck.

Active in the daytime, this skink often lives near petrel nesting sites. It basks in the sun but is easily scared and swiftly takes refuge at the least sign of disturbance. It feeds on small land-living invertebrates and insects. Mating takes place in spring, and the female gives birth to a litter of live young about 4 months later.

NAME: Western Blue-tongued Skink, *Tiliqua occipitalis*
RANGE: S. Australia
HABITAT: arid areas
SIZE: 45 cm (17¾ in)

The heavily built western blue-tongued skink has a stout body and large head but relatively small limbs. Bands of dark brown scales pattern its body and tail, and there are characteristic dark streaks behind each eye. It is active in the daytime and forages around on the ground for insects, snails and berries. A rabbit warren may be used for shelter.

The female gives birth to about 5 live young, which have distinct bands of dark brown and yellow.

NAME: Prickly Forest Skink, *Tropidophorus queenslandiae*
RANGE: Australia: N. Queensland
HABITAT: rain forest
SIZE: 13–20 cm (5–7¾ in)

The prickly forest skink is easily distinguished from other Australian skinks by its covering of strongly keeled small scales. Its rounded tail is also covered with keeled scales, and its limbs are well developed. A nocturnal skink, it lives beneath plant debris or rotting logs on the forest floor, where its dark body with irregular pale markings keeps it well camouflaged. It is a slow-moving, sluggish skink which does not like to bask in sunlight and is usually found in a rather torpid state. Worms and soft-bodied insects are its main foods.

Little is known of the breeding biology of this skink, but several of the 20 *Tropidophorus* species are known to produce litters of 6 to 9 live young. These develop inside the mother's body and break from their thin shells as the eggs are laid.

NAME: Ground Skink, *Scincella lateralis* (previously *Lygosoma laterale*)
RANGE: USA: New Jersey to Florida, west to Nebraska and Texas
HABITAT: humid forest, wooded grassland
SIZE: 8–13 cm (3¼–5 in)

This smooth, shiny skink, also known as the brown-backed skink, has dark stripes on the sides of its body and a pale, often yellowish or whitish belly. Its body is long and slender and its legs well developed, with elongate digits on the hind feet. Like many skinks, the ground skink has movable eyelids with a transparent window in each lower lid; this feature enables it to see clearly, even when it must close its eyes to avoid dirt getting into them when it is burrowing into cover. It lives on the ground and prefers areas with plenty of leaf litter in which to take shelter. Active in the daytime, particularly in warm, humid weather, it feeds mainly on insects and spiders. The closest relatives of this species live in Central America and Australia.

A prolific breeder, the female ground skink lays a clutch of 1 to 7 eggs every 4 or 5 weeks, with a maximum of about 5 clutches during the breeding season, which extends from April to August in most areas. Embryonic development is already well advanced when the eggs are laid, and the female does not tend the eggs further.

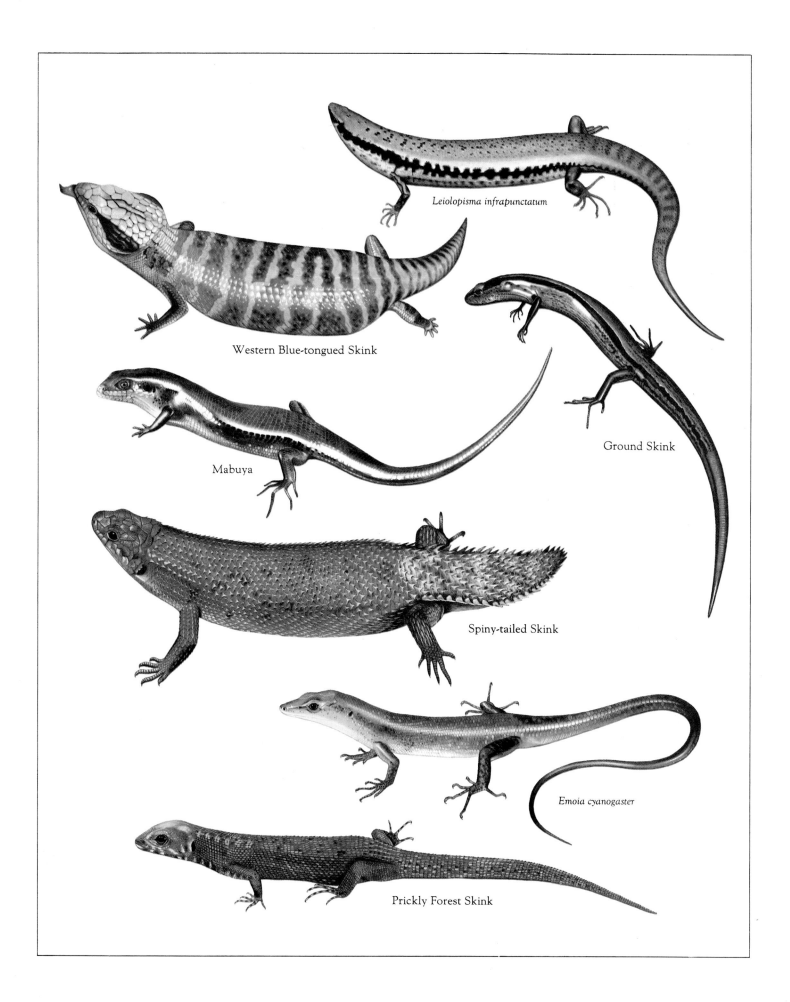

Leiolopisma infrapunctatum

Western Blue-tongued Skink

Ground Skink

Mabuya

Spiny-tailed Skink

Emoia cyanogaster

Prickly Forest Skink

Lacertid Lizards

NAME: Green Lizard, *Lacerta viridis*
RANGE: Europe: Channel Islands, south to N. Spain, Sicily, Greece; east to S.W. Russia
HABITAT: open woodland, field edges, riverbanks, roadsides
SIZE: 30–45 cm (11¾–17¾ in) including tail of 20–30 cm (7¾–11¾ in)

Also known as the emerald lizard, this is the largest lizard found north of the Alps. Males are brilliant green, finely stippled with black, while females are more variable, often duller green or brownish. The coloration of mature adults is most vivid in the spring and fades as the year proceeds.

An adaptable lizard, the green lizard lives almost anywhere that there is dense vegetation but avoids arid areas. It is an agile climber and can move speedily up trees, bushes and walls to find a spot in which to bask in the sun. Insects and their larvae and small invertebrates, particularly spiders, are its main foods.

Solitary creatures for most of the year, green lizards mate in the spring, when males compete fiercely for females. When copulating, the male grasps the female with his jaws. She lays 4 to 21 eggs in a hole she digs in the soil. She covers the eggs with earth, and they incubate for several months. In winter, green lizards hibernate in tree hollows or other crevices.

NAME: Viviparous Lizard, *Lacerta vivipara*
RANGE: Europe: arctic Scandinavia, Britain, south to N. Spain, N. Italy, Yugoslavia; N. Asia
HABITAT: meadows, open woodland, marshes, any grassland
SIZE: 14–18 cm (5½–7 in)

The viviparous lizard is the only lizard found within the Arctic Circle. Its coloration is variable over its wide range, but this lizard is commonly gray or yellowish-brown, with pale spots and dark stripes on the back. In the hotter parts of its range, it is rarely found below 500 m (1,650 ft) except in humid areas, but it likes to bask in the sun for much of the day. Alert and agile, it is a fairly good climber and an excellent swimmer. Insects, spiders, earthworms, slugs and other small invertebrates are all part of its diet. It lives alone, except in the hibernation and breeding seasons.

The breeding habits of this lizard are unique in its family, hence its name, meaning "live-bearing." The 5 to 8 young develop inside the mother, feeding on the yolks of their eggs, and break out of their thin, membranous shells fully formed, as they are expelled from her body or shortly afterward.

LACERTIDAE:
Lacertid Lizard Family

About 180 species of lacertid lizard are distributed throughout Europe, Asia and Africa, excluding Madagascar. Within this range, they occur from the hottest tropical habitats to locations within the Arctic Circle. Most are ground-dwelling, but others live in trees or among rocks.

The elongate, long-tailed lacertids are mostly small to medium-sized lizards, between 10 and 75 cm (4 and 29½ in) in total length. All have large scales on head and belly. Externally, males can generally be distinguished from females by their larger heads and shorter bodies. Almost all species reproduce by laying eggs, depositing their clutches in earth or sand.

Lacertids are highly territorial in their behavior. Males in particular adopt characteristic threat postures to warn off intruders, with the head tilted upward and the throat expanded.

In common with many other lizard families, lacertids feed on small, mainly invertebrate prey. A few species, particularly island-dwelling forms, also consume large amounts of plant material.

NAME: Wall Lizard, *Lacerta muralis*
RANGE: Europe: N. France to N. Spain, S. Italy, Greece, east to Romania
HABITAT: dry, sunny areas; walls, rocks, tree trunks
SIZE: up to 23 cm (9 in)

A slender, flat-bodied reptile, the wall lizard has a tapering tail, which may be up to twice its body length. The coloration and markings of this species are exceedingly variable over its range, but many individuals are brownish-red or gray, with dark markings. A sun-loving lizard, it spends much of the day basking on any type of wall, even near human habitation; in the midday heat, it shelters in the shade. It is extremely active and alert and an expert climber. It feeds on insects, such as flies and beetles, and on invertebrates such as earthworms, spiders, snails and slugs. A gregarious species, it lives in small colonies.

Soon after their winter hibernation, the lizards mate, males competing with one another for females. The female digs a hole and lays 2 to 10 eggs, which she covers with soil. The eggs hatch in 2 to 3 months. In a warm spring, with good food supplies, wall lizards may lay several clutches.

NAME: Bosc's Fringe-toed Lizard, *Acanthodactylus boskianus*
RANGE: Egypt, Saudi Arabia
HABITAT: desert
SIZE: 12.5 cm (5 in)

A sand-colored, desert-living lizard, this species has long toes bordered with broad combs of scales; this enlarges the surface area of the feet and thus improves the grip on the sand. It can run quickly over sand and digs deep burrows for refuge. The female lays 2 to 4 eggs, which she buries in a hole she digs in the sand.

NAME: Algerian Sand Racer, *Psammodromus algirus*
RANGE: Spain, Portugal, S.W. France, N. Africa
HABITAT: dense vegetation in sandy areas, woodland, gardens, parks
SIZE: 30 cm (11¾ in)

The reptile most commonly seen in urban areas within its range, the sand racer is metallic brown, with light stripes down its sides. Its tail is long and stiff and often orange-colored in juveniles. In the morning, the sand racer is sluggish while it basks in the sun after the cool night. When warmed up, it is an agile, fast-moving lizard, which hunts for invertebrate prey among vegetation or on the ground.

The female sand racer lays 6 or more eggs, which hatch in about 2 months.

NAME: Racerunner, *Eremias* sp.
RANGE: Europe, central Asia to Mongolia; Africa
HABITAT: desert, semiarid scrub, grassland, rocky desert
SIZE: 15–22 cm (6–8½ in)

There are many species of *Eremias* lizards, many not yet properly classified. Most have scaly bodies and well-developed legs and are marked with spots, arranged in rows along the body. They tend to live in dry areas, taking refuge among rocks and in crevices, and feed on invertebrates, mainly insects and spiders.

Some *Eremias* lizards reproduce by laying clutches of 2 to 12 eggs, but others give birth to living young.

NAME: Essex's Mountain Lizard, *Tropidosaura essexi*
RANGE: South Africa
HABITAT: mountains
SIZE: 14 cm (5½ in)

A small lizard with a blunt, rounded snout, Essex's mountain lizard has pale stripes, running from behind its head down its body and onto its tail. A ground-dweller, it is active in the daytime and is quick and agile in its movements. It feeds on insects and small invertebrates.

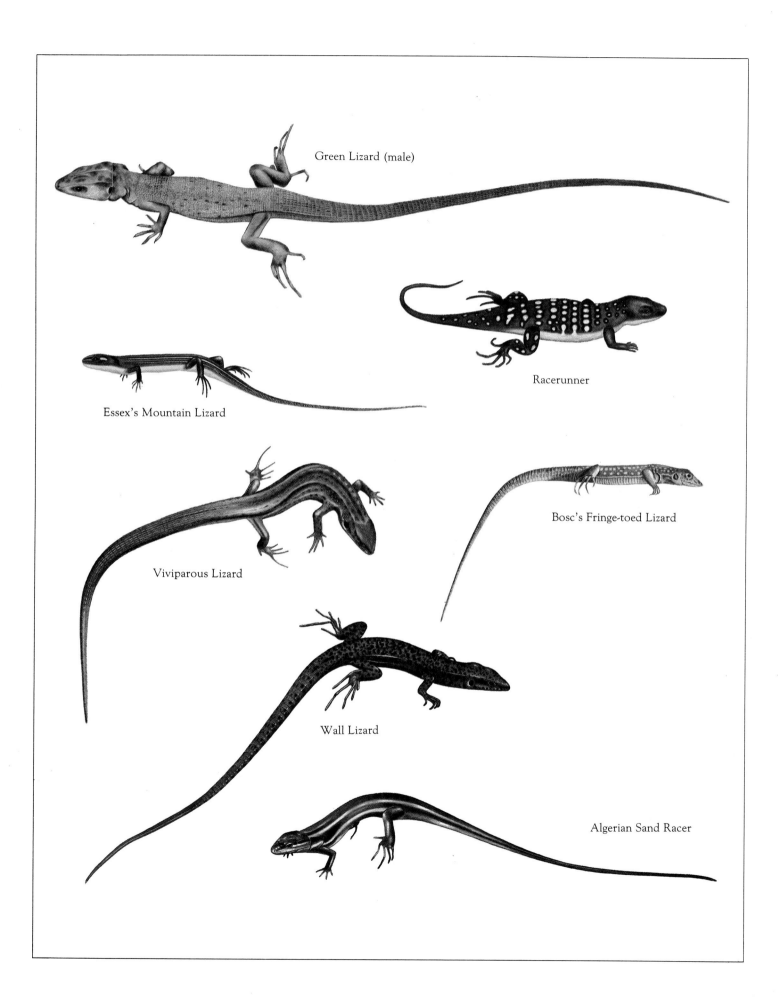

Green Lizard (male)

Racerunner

Essex's Mountain Lizard

Viviparous Lizard

Bosc's Fringe-toed Lizard

Wall Lizard

Algerian Sand Racer

Girdled and Plated Lizards

NAME: *Cordylosaurus subtessellatus*
RANGE: Africa: S. Angola, Namibia
HABITAT: dry, rocky areas
SIZE: 15 cm (6 in)

The greatly compressed head and body of this lizard make it easy for it to take refuge in crevices and crannies in the rocks, where it hides from enemies or shelters from intense heat or nighttime cold. It may also shelter under stones. In each lower eyelid there is a transparent "window," so that the lizard can close its eyes in windy weather, when sand and dust might blow into them, but is still able to see. Under its digits are keeled scales, perhaps to help it grip on rocks. Its tail is easily shed and later regenerated.

An agile, ground-dwelling lizard, it feeds on insects and other small invertebrates. The female reproduces by laying eggs.

NAME: Imperial Flat Lizard, *Platysaurus imperator*
RANGE: Africa: N.E. Zimbabwe, contiguous Mozambique
HABITAT: rocky knolls of granite and sandstone in grassland
SIZE: 39 cm (15¼ in)

The head, body, limbs and tail of this lizard are all flattened laterally; in consequence it can take refuge in narrow cracks and crevices in the rocks among which it lives. As these rocky knolls weather, many crevices are created, ideal as hiding places. Once in a crevice, the lizard expands its body with air and braces itself against the rock, making it virtually impossible for any predator to remove it. This lizard tends to frequent the tops of the knolls, whereas the other platysaurans live at the base.

The biggest species in its genus, the imperial flat lizard has large scales on its neck and a smooth back. The male, with his yellow, red and black body, is larger and more brightly colored than the female, which is largely black, with three distinctive yellow stripes on her head that taper off toward the back. Males hold territories which they compete for and defend against intruders by adopting an aggressive posture, rearing up and displaying throat and chest colors. Active in the daytime, flat lizards hunt insects, particularly locusts and beetles. They shelter from the midday heat and emerge again to hunt in the afternoon.

The female flat lizard lays 2 eggs, elongate in shape, in a crevice in the rocks.

CORDYLIDAE:
Girdled and Plated Lizard Family

The cordylid lizards are an African family of about 40 species, found largely in rocky or arid habitats, south of the Sahara and in Madagascar. Names include plated, whip, girdled, crag, snake and flat lizards; this gives some idea of the range of adaptations within the family.

The typical cordylid lizard has a body covered with bony plates, which underlie the external and visible scales. This undercoat of armor, however, is not continuous over the whole body: on each side there is a lateral groove, without a plate layer, which allows body expansion, when the belly is full of food for example, or, in egg-laying females, when distended with eggs. There are many variations of form within the family: the girdle-tailed lizards have short tails, armored with rings of spines, and often have spines on the head; flat lizards of the genus *Platysaurus* have flattened bodies. and skin covered with smooth granules; snake lizards of the genus *Chamaesaura* are very elongate, with tails up to three-quarters of their body length. Some cordylids have well-developed limbs, while in others the limbs are much reduced or even absent.

Most lizards in the family feed on insects and small invertebrates such as millipedes. Some of the larger forms also consume smaller lizards, and others are almost entirely vegetarian in their habits. Their reproductive habits vary, some species laying eggs and others bearing live young.

NAME: Transvaal Snake Lizard, *Chamaesaura aena*
RANGE: South Africa
HABITAT: grassland
SIZE: 40 cm (15¾ in)

This snakelike lizard has an elongate body and a tail which is about three-quarters of its total length. It has four small limbs, each with five clawed digits; the other 3 species in this genus have at most two digits per limb, and one species, C. *macrolepsis*, has no front limbs at all. Active in the daytime, the Transvaal snake lizard moves quickly through the grass with serpentine undulations of its body, often with its head and forelimbs lifted off the ground. It feeds on insects, spiders, earthworms and other small invertebrates.

The female's 2 to 4 young develop inside her oviduct. The fully formed young break from their soft shells as they are expelled from her body.

NAME: Armadillo Lizard, *Cordylus cataphractus*
RANGE: South Africa: W. Cape Province
HABITAT: arid rocky areas
SIZE: 21 cm (8¼ in)

The armadillo lizard is heavily armored with strong spiny scales which extend from its head right along its back and tail. Its head, body and clublike tail are all flattened, enabling it to wriggle easily into rock crevices for shelter. The nostrils are elongated into little tubes.

A ground-dwelling lizard, it is active in the daytime and feeds on a wide variety of insects, as well as on spiders and other invertebrates. It is fairly slow-moving and, rather than darting for cover when threatened, may adopt a curious defensive posture, which earns it its common name. It rolls itself up like an armadillo, its tail tightly held in its jaws, thus presenting a spiny ring to the predator and protecting the softer, vulnerable belly area.

The 1 to 3 young of the armadillo lizard develop inside the female's body. The tiny, fully formed lizards break from their soft membranous shells as they are expelled from her body.

NAME: Plated Lizard, *Gerrhosaurus flavigularis*
RANGE: Africa: Sudan, Ethiopia, south through E. Africa to South Africa: Cape Province
HABITAT: grassland, scrub
SIZE: 45.5 cm (18 in)

A ground-living and burrowing lizard, this species is usually greenish-gray or brownish, with a red or yellow throat and often a narrow stripe down each side. It is well armored, with hard body plates, and head shields fused to the skull. The tail is generally about two-thirds of the total length. Its limbs are well developed and it has five toes on each foot. These are not specially adapted for digging, and the lizard probably does most of its tunneling after rain, when the ground is soft. Active by day, it hunts insects and is rarely seen, despite its size. It moves rapidly through the grass and at any sign of danger darts into its burrow, usually positioned under a bush.

The female plated lizard lays clutches of 4 or 5 eggs in a shallow pit, which she excavates.

NAME: Girdled Lizard, *Zonosaurus* sp.
RANGE: Madagascar
HABITAT: forest
SIZE: 38–61 cm (15–24 in)

There are 3 *Zonosaurus* species, all large, strong, ground-dwelling lizards. They have well-developed limbs and distinct grooves along their sides to allow for body expansion. Little is known of their habits or biology.

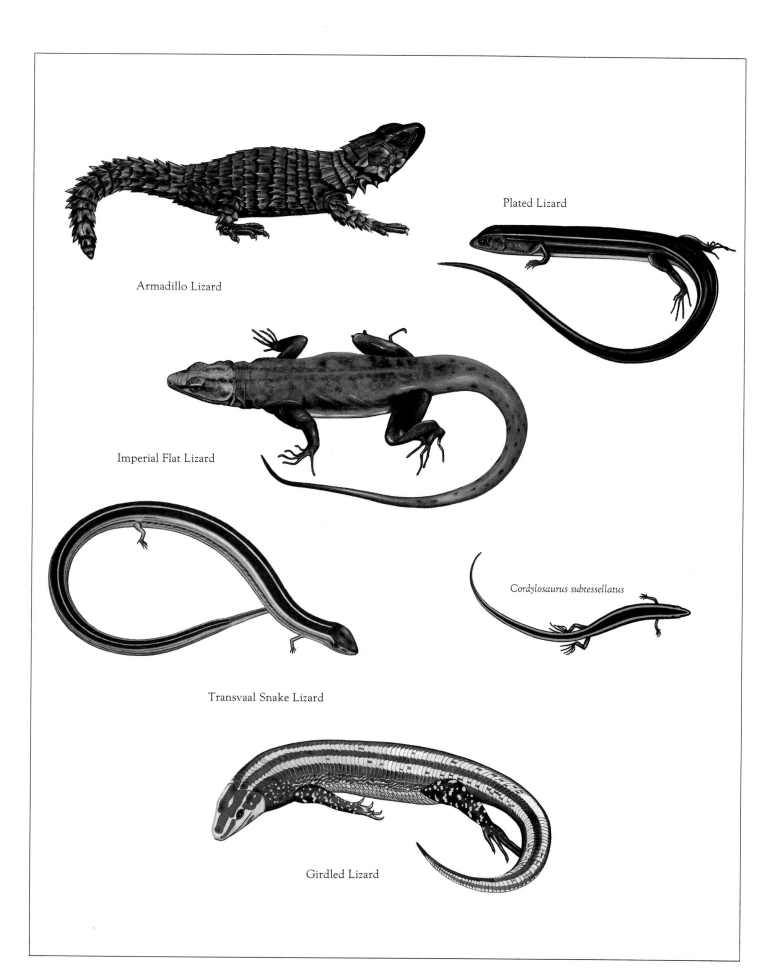

Armadillo Lizard

Plated Lizard

Imperial Flat Lizard

Cordylosaurus subtessellatus

Transvaal Snake Lizard

Girdled Lizard

Old World Burrowing Lizards, Anguid Lizards, Legless Lizards

DIBAMIDAE: Old World Burrowing Lizard Family

This small family contains only 3 species of small, wormlike, limbless lizards, all in the genus *Dibamus*. They live in parts of Southeast Asia, the Philippines and New Guinea.

NAME: *Dibamus novaeguineae*
RANGE: New Guinea
HABITAT: forest
SIZE: up to 30 cm (11¾ in)

All three *Dibamus* species are blind, limbless lizards, specialized for a burrowing, underground life. The body is wormlike, and the eyes and ears are covered by skin. The nostrils are positioned on an enlarged scale at the tip of the snout, and the teeth are small and backward curving. The male has stumplike vestiges of hind limbs that are used for clasping the female when mating. Dibamids will burrow into rotting logs as well as soil.

Little is known of their habits. Eggs which were probably dibamid eggs have been discovered in rotting logs and forest floor humus.

ANGUIDAE: Anguid Lizard Family

There are about 80 species in this family of elongate, snakelike lizards, found in North, Central and South America, the West Indies, Europe, North Africa and Asia. Typically, they have smooth, elongate bodies and tails, movable eyelids and external ear openings. Most are land-dwelling or burrowing animals, and many, such as the slowworms and glass lizards and snakes, are limbless or have only vestigial limbs. The alligator lizards of North and Central America, however, have well-developed limbs.

Many of these lizards have stiff bodies, armored by bony plates under the surface skin. In order that their bodies can expand when breathing, or to accommodate food or eggs, there are grooves of soft scales along their sides. Their long tails easily become detached if seized by an attacker, usually along one of the series of fracture planes. The tail is regrown in a few weeks, but not always completely.

Most anguids feed on insects, small invertebrates and even small mammals and lizards. All but a few species reproduce by laying eggs. The others, mostly species found at high altitudes, give birth to live young.

NAME: Galliwasp, *Diploglossus lessorae*
RANGE: Central America, N. South America
HABITAT: forest
SIZE: up to 35 cm (13¾ in)

The smooth, shiny galliwasp resembles the alligator lizards but has a more elongate body and lacks the expandable grooves along the sides of the body that the heavily armored alligator lizards possess. It is a ground-dwelling species, active in the daytime, and feeds on insects, worms and mollusks. It is believed to reproduce by laying eggs.

NAME: Southern Alligator Lizard, *Gerrhonotus multicarinatus*
RANGE: W. USA: Washington; Mexico: Baja California
HABITAT: grassland, open woodland
SIZE: 25.5–43 cm (10–17 in)

The agile southern alligator lizard has a strong prehensile tail, which it can wrap around branches and use like a fifth limb when climbing in bushes. There are 5 subspecies of this lizard, which vary in coloration from reddish-brown to yellowish-gray, usually with some dark markings, but all have distinct folds along their sides, where flexible scales allow the stiff, armored body to expand. These lizards are active in the daytime, when they hunt for insects and any other small creatures that they are able to catch and swallow, including scorpions and black widow spiders.

Alligator lizards breed in the summer, females laying several clutches over the season. There are usually 12 eggs in a clutch, but there may be up to 40 on occasion.

NAME: Glass Snake, *Ophisaurus apodus*
RANGE: Europe: Yugoslavia, Greece to Black Sea region, east to S.W. and central Asia
SIZE: up to 1.2 m (4 ft)

The largest species of its family, the glass snake is a heavy-bodied, snakelike animal with vestiges of hind limbs. The body is rather stiff, with a bony layer under the smooth scales. Grooves of flexible scales on each side allow the body to expand when necessary. The glass snake is active in the daytime and at dawn and dusk, feeding on lizards, mice and other small animals, which it kills with its powerful jaws.

Males become aggressive and competitive in the breeding season, and there is fierce rivalry for mates. The female lays 5 to 7 eggs in a hollow under a rock or log, or in a pile of rotting vegetation. She curls around her eggs and guards them from predators while they incubate. The young hatch in about 4 weeks and are about 12.5 cm (5 in) long.

NAME: Slowworm, *Anguis fragilis*
RANGE: Europe (not Ireland, S. Spain and Portugal or N. Scandinavia), east to central and S.W. Asia; N.W. Africa
HABITAT: fields, meadows, scrub, heath, up to 2,400 m (7,900 ft)
SIZE: 35–54 cm (13¾–21¼ in)

The slowworm is a smooth, extremely snakelike creature with no visible limbs. It is reddish-brown, brown or gray above; females usually have a dark stripe on the back, while some males may have blue spots. It moves by serpentine undulations and can shed its long tail if seized by an enemy. The tail does not fully regenerate, however, and is then stumplike. The night and heat of the day are spent under rocks or logs, and the slowworm emerges in the morning and evening to hunt for slugs and worms, as well as spiders, insects and larvae. It is slower-moving than most lizards but can disappear into cover with considerable speed.

In late spring, breeding males become aggressive and compete with one another for mates. As they copulate, the male holds the female's neck or head in his jaws. About 3 months later, the female gives birth to live young, usually 6 to 12 but sometimes as many as 20. The young develop in thin-shelled eggs inside her body and break out of the membranous shells as the eggs are laid. They are about 6 to 9 cm (2¼ to 3½ in) long at birth.

ANNIELLIDAE: California Legless Lizard Family

There are only 2 species of these slender, wormlike, burrowing lizards, found only in the USA and Mexico. They are similar to the anguid lizards but lack the bony plates under the skin and have no external ear openings.

NAME: California Legless Lizard, *Anniella pulchra*
RANGE: USA: California; Mexico: Baja California
HABITAT: beaches, sand dunes, banks of streams, soft loamy soil
SIZE: 15–23 cm (6–9 in)

Specialized for burrowing, this legless lizard has a smooth body, which helps it to move easily through soil, and a shovel-shaped snout for digging. Its eyes are small and have movable lids. Most of its life is spent underground or burrowing in leaf litter, searching for insects and insect larvae. It rarely moves in the open. The race illustrated is the silvery legless lizard, *A. p. pulchra*.

These lizards are live-bearing; females produce litters of up to 4 fully formed young.

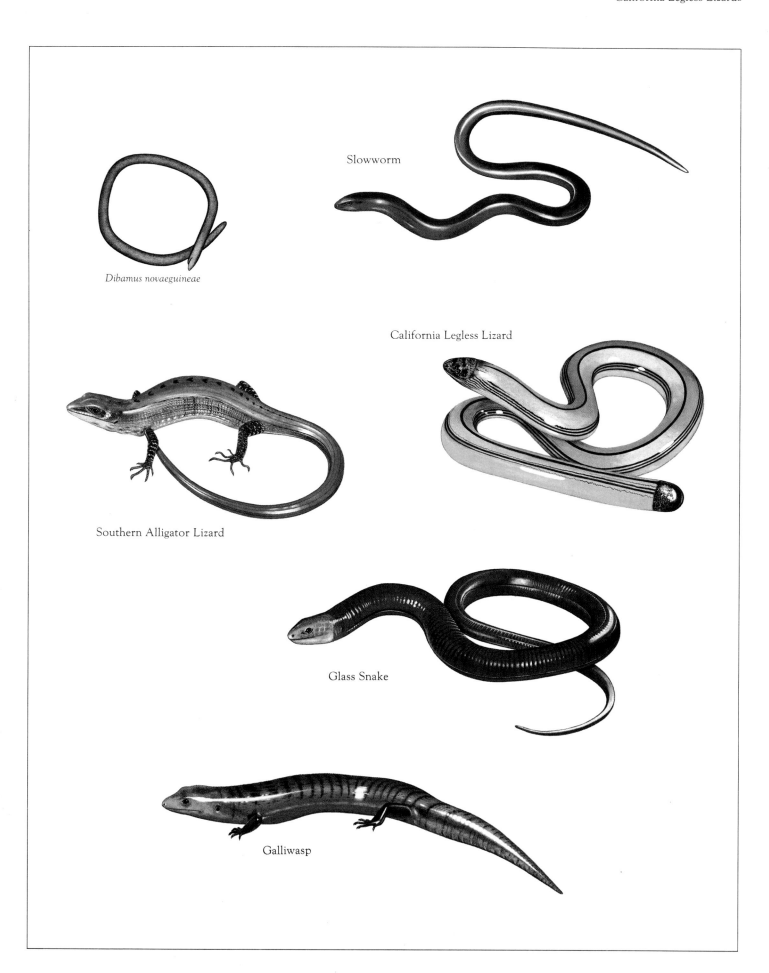

Slowworm

Dibamus novaeguineae

California Legless Lizard

Southern Alligator Lizard

Glass Snake

Galliwasp

Crocodile Lizards, Gila Monster, Monitors

XENOSAURIDAE:
Crocodile Lizard Family

There are 4 species in this family, 3 in Central America and Mexico and 1 in southern China. They are related to the anguid lizards and, under the body scales, have bony plates, which may be tiny or large but are not joined together. Unlike many anguids, however, their limbs are well developed.

NAME: *Xenosaurus* sp.
RANGE: **Mexico, Guatemala**
HABITAT: **rain forest**
SIZE: **about 20 cm (7¾ in)**

These powerful, strong-limbed lizards have flat heads and robust bodies. They are inconspicuous creatures and are not often seen, spending much of their time in refuges beneath tree roots or in rocky crevices. They will also lie in water for long periods. Active at night, they feed on insects, particularly winged termites and ants. If alarmed, *Xenosaurus* adopts a threat posture, with mouth agape, revealing a black membrane.

The females gives birth to litters of 3 fully formed live young, which are about 4 cm (1½ in) long at birth.

VARANIDAE:
Monitor Lizard Family

The monitor lizards of the Old World include within their number the largest of lizards. The Komodo dragon may be 3 m (10 ft) long and weigh 163 kg (360 lb); several other species exceed 2 m (6½ ft) in length. There are about 30 species of monitor in a single genus, all of them elongate lizards with long necks and tails and well-developed limbs. Their snakelike forked tongues can be retracted into the mouth.

Monitors occur in Africa (except Madagascar), the Middle East, southern Asia, Indonesia and Australasia. All are voracious carnivores. Male monitor lizards may perform spectacular ritualized fights to assert their dominance. They rear up on their hind legs and wrestle with their forelimbs until one contestant is pushed over and defeated. Monitors reproduce by laying eggs, and several species are known to dig pits in the ground in which the eggs are buried to incubate.

NAME: **Komodo Dragon,** *Varanus komodensis*
RANGE: **islands of Komodo, Flores, Pintja and Pada, east of Java**
HABITAT: **grassland**
SIZE: **3 m (10 ft)**　　Ⓡ

The awe-inspiring Komodo dragon dwarfs most present-day lizards. It has a heavy body, long, thick tail and well-developed limbs with talonlike claws. Its teeth are large and jagged, and it has a forked tongue that can be flicked in and out of the mouth. Despite its size, it is a good climber, moves surprisingly quickly and swims well; it tends to live near water. It is active during the day and preys on animals as large as hog deer and wild boar, as well as on small deer and pigs.

The female Komodo lays about 15 eggs, which she buries in the ground.

NAME: **Nile Monitor,** *Varanus niloticus*
RANGE: **Africa: south and east of the Sahara to Cape Province**
HABITAT: **forest, open country**
SIZE: **over 2 m (6½ ft)**

The versatile, yet unspecialized, Nile monitor is a strong reptile, typical of the monitor group. Using its broad tail as a rudder, it swims and dives well and can climb trees with the aid of its huge claws and strong prehensile tail, which it uses to hold onto branches. It can also dig burrows. Nile monitors tend to stay near water and do not venture into desert areas. They feed on frogs, fish and snails, as well as on crocodile eggs and young.

One of the most prolific egg-laying lizards, the female Nile monitor lays up to 60 eggs in a termite mound. She tears a hole in the wall, lays her eggs inside and departs. The termites repair their nest, thus enclosing the eggs in the warm, safe termitarium. When they hatch, the young monitors must make their own way out of the nest.

NAME: **Gould's Monitor,** *Varanus gouldi*
RANGE: **Australia**
HABITAT: **coastal forest to sandy desert**
SIZE: **about 1.5 m (5 ft)**

The widespread Gould's monitor, also known as the sand monitor, varies in size, coloration and pattern over its range. Like those of all monitors, its limbs are powerful, and its distinctly ridged tail is laterally compressed, except at the base. It is ground-dwelling, sheltering in burrows, which it digs or takes over from other animals, or under logs and debris. To find food, it must roam over large areas of sparsely populated country, searching for birds, mammals, reptiles, insects, even carrion. Like all monitors, the female reproduces by laying eggs.

HELODERMATIDAE:
Gila Monster Family

There are only 2 species in this family, which is related to the monitor lizards and the rare earless monitor. They are the gila monster, from western North America, and the Mexican beaded lizard.

NAME: **Gila Monster,** *Heloderma suspectum*
RANGE: **S.W. USA: S. Utah, Arizona to New Mexico; Mexico**
HABITAT: **arid and semiarid areas with some vegetation**
SIZE: **45–61 cm (17¾–24 in)**　　Ⓥ

This formidable, heavy-bodied lizard has a short, usually stout tail, in which it can store fat for use in periods of food shortage. It is gaudily patterned and has brightly colored beadlike scales on its back. The gila lives on the ground and shelters under rocks or in a burrow, which it digs itself or takes over from another animal. It is primarily nocturnal but may emerge during the day in spring.

The two members of the gila monster family are the only venomous lizards. The venom is produced in glands in the lower jaw and enters the mouth via grooved teeth at the front of the lower jaw; it flows into the victim as the lizard chews. The gila also eats the eggs of birds and reptiles.

Gila monsters mate in the summer, and the female lays 3 to 5 eggs some time later, in the autumn or winter.

LANTHANOTIDAE:
Earless Monitor Family

The earless monitor, found only in Sarawak, is the only species in its family. Little is known of the biology of this rare, nocturnal lizard.

NAME: **Earless Monitor,** *Lanthanotus borneensis*
RANGE: **Sarawak**
HABITAT: **forest**
SIZE: **up to 43 cm (17 in)**

The earless monitor has an elongate, rather flattened body and short but strong limbs, each with five digits. On each body scale there is a small tubercle. Its eyes are tiny with movable lids, the lower of which have transparent "windows," and there are no external ear openings. Much of the earless monitor's life is spent burrowing underground or swimming; it avoids bright light and does not need intense warmth. In captivity the earless monitor will eat fish, but its natural diet is not known.

Nile Monitor

Komodo Dragon

Gould's Monitor

Gila Monster

Xenosaurus sp.

Earless Monitor

Amphisbaenids

NAME: **Florida Worm Lizard,** *Rhineura floridana*
RANGE: **USA: N. and central Florida**
HABITAT: **sandy, wooded areas**
SIZE: **18–40.5 cm (7–16 in)**

The only blind, limbless lizard in North America, the Florida worm lizard is just over 0.5 cm ($\frac{1}{5}$ in) in diameter and has a shovel-shaped head. It lives underground, feeding on worms, spiders and termites, and rarely comes to the surface unless driven by rain or disturbed by cultivation. Unlike an earthworm, it leaves a tunnel behind it as it burrows, pushing through the earth with its spadelike snout and compacting the soil as it goes, to form the tunnel.

In summer, the Florida worm lizard lays up to 3 long, thin eggs in a burrow. The young hatch in autumn, when they are about 10 cm (4 in) long.

Fossil research has shown that this amphisbaenid was at one time widely distributed in North America.

NAME: **Two-legged Worm Lizard,** *Bipes biporus*
RANGE: **Mexico: Baja California**
HABITAT: **arid land**
SIZE: **20 cm (7$\frac{3}{4}$ in)**

The worm lizards of this genus are the only members of the family to possess limbs. They have two tiny front legs with five clawed toes on each limb. Despite their size, these limbs are powerful, and the digits are adapted for digging and climbing. Like all amphisbaenids, the two-legged worm lizard spends most of its life underground in burrows and uses its limbs to start digging its tunnels. Once the burrow is begun, the worm lizard pushes through with its round head, compacting the soil as it goes. When digging a large tunnel, it may use its limbs as well as its head.

These worm lizards feed on worms and termites. Although little is known of their breeding habits, they are believed to lay eggs.

NAME: **South African Shield Snout,** *Monopeltis capensis*
RANGE: **Africa: central South Africa, Zimbabwe**
HABITAT: **sandy soil**
SIZE: **30 cm (11$\frac{3}{4}$ in)**

The thick horny plates on the shovel-like head of this amphisbaenid enable it to burrow into harder soils than many other species. It tunnels down to depths of 20 cm (7$\frac{3}{4}$ in) and only emerges above ground when driven by rains or if attacked by ants. When they do emerge, shield snouts are preyed on by birds such as ravens and kites. Shield snouts themselves feed on termites, beetles and other ground-living insects.

AMPHISBAENIDAE: Amphisbaenid Family

The 100 or so species of amphisbaenid are extraordinary, wormlike, burrowing reptiles, whose position in the reptile group is not fully understood. Known as worm lizards, they are not true lizards and are given their own suborder within the Squamata order, on a parallel with the much larger lizard and snake groups. Most species occur in Central and South America and Africa, but there are a few species in the warmer parts of North America and Europe. They prefer moist habitats in which they can build semipermanent tunnel systems that will not collapse after the animal has passed through. They soon dehydrate in dry soil. Water is taken into the mouth and swallowed, not absorbed through the skin, as was once believed.

Most species are limbless, only the 3 species in the genus *Bipes* have tiny forelimbs. The skin is loosely attached over the simple cylindrical body, which is ringed with small scales. The tail is pointed in some species and rounded in others but is always covered with horny scales. Amphisbaenids have no external ear openings, and their tiny eyes are covered with scales.

Amphisbaenids live underground in burrows which they dig themselves, often near ant or termite colonies. Bracing their long bodies against the walls of the tunnel, they excavate new lengths by repeated battering strokes of their hard, strong heads. Like worms, they can move backward or forward in a straight line with no body undulations — ideal for life in tunnels. Indeed, the Greek word *amphisbaena* means "goes both ways." This ability, combined with the similar appearance of the head and tail, has caused many to see the amphisbaenid as a two-headed monster, and it is mentioned as such in a Roman epic poem.

Amphisbaenids find all their prey — mostly insects and worms — below ground. Larger species may also attack and eat small vertebrate animals. They are able to hear their prey crawling in the ground and move accurately in its direction. The sense of smell also seems to play a part in locating prey. Once it has found its quarry, the amphisbaenid grabs it and tears it apart with its strong, interlocking teeth, set in powerful jaws.

Little is known of the breeding habits of amphisbaenids, but most species are believed to lay eggs, which incubate and hatch in the underground burrows.

NAME: **White-bellied Worm Lizard,** *Amphisbaena alba*
RANGE: **tropical South America; Trinidad**
HABITAT: **rain forest**
SIZE: **61 cm (24 in)**

The body of this worm lizard, the most widespread in South America, is cylindrical over its entire length, the tail being almost as thick and blunt as the head. Tail and head look similar, and the species is known as the two-headed blind snake in some areas. It is over 2.5 cm (1 in) in diameter.

Although a burrowing, underground animal, this species often crawls over the forest floor, particularly after heavy rain. It feeds on earthworms and ants and is often found in ant nests. Indeed, some tribes call it "ant king" or "mother ant" and believe it to be reared by ants. If in danger, this worm lizard lifts its tail and moves it around as if it were a head. Presumably this tricks the enemy into attacking the tail, thus keeping the vulnerable head area safe and enabling the worm lizard to make a counterattack.

NAME: **Somali Edge Snout,** *Agamodon anguliceps*
RANGE: **Africa: Somalia, S.E. Ethiopia**
HABITAT: **sandy soil**
SIZE: **11 cm (4$\frac{1}{4}$ in)**

The Somali edge snout has a shorter, thicker body than most amphisbaenids. Its tail is short and tapered, and its wedge-shaped head makes it a particularly efficient burrower, even in hard soils. On the front of its head it has a pair of sharp, vertical ridges, and by screwing motions of its specially adapted head, the edge snout excavates its tunnel and compacts the soil. At night, it moves up to within 5 to 7 cm (2 to 2$\frac{3}{4}$ in) of the surface and, as the daytime temperature rises, descends again to depths of about 15 to 30 cm (6 to 11$\frac{3}{4}$ in). It occasionally moves above ground, swinging its head from side to side and pulling itself along.

NAME: **Worm Lizard,** *Blanus cinereus*
RANGE: **Spain, Portugal, N.W. Africa**
HABITAT: **sandy soil or humus, often in woodland**
SIZE: **22–30 cm (8$\frac{1}{2}$–11$\frac{3}{4}$ in)**

The only European amphisbaenid, this worm lizard has a small, pointed head and a tapering tail. It spends most of its life in underground burrows and is only rarely seen above ground except after heavy rain or when it is disturbed by cultivation. It feeds on small invertebrates, particularly ants.

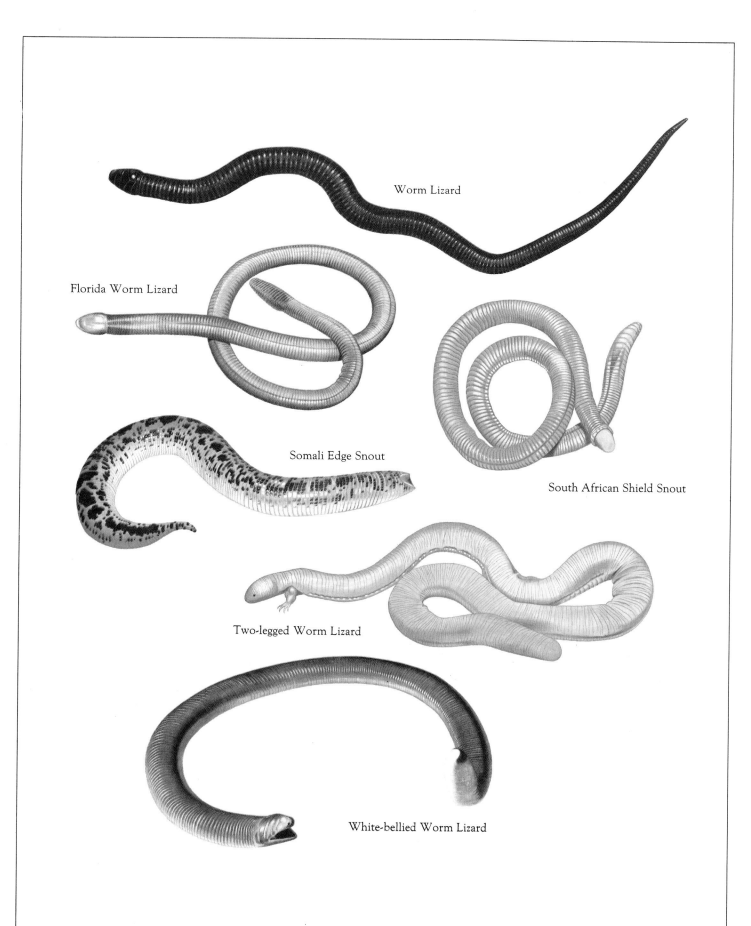

Worm Lizard

Florida Worm Lizard

Somali Edge Snout

South African Shield Snout

Two-legged Worm Lizard

White-bellied Worm Lizard

Slender Blind Snakes, Blind Snakes, Pipe Snakes, Shieldtail Snakes, Sunbeam Snake

LEPTOTYPHLOPIDAE: Slender Blind Snake Family

The slender blind snakes are small, worm-shaped, burrowing snakes that grow to about 38 cm (15 in) long. They possess minute vestiges of a pelvic girdle and hind limbs, and their tiny rudimentary eyes are hidden beneath scales. Like their relatives in the families Typhlopidae and Anomalepidae, these snakes are specialized for their burrowing existence and, in one feature in particular, have evolved in a way which is dramatically different from all other snakes. The size of the mouth has become reduced, and it is only about half the length of the head, whereas in most snakes the mouth is as large as possible in order to accommodate a variety of sizable prey.

Slender blind snakes feed on termites and ants. The approximately 50 species live in Africa, tropical Asia and southern USA, through Central and South America to Argentina.

NAME: **Western Blind Snake,** *Leptotyphlops humilis*
RANGE: **S.W. USA: S.W. Utah; south to northern Mexico and Baja California**
HABITAT: **desert, grassland, scrub, rocky canyons**
SIZE: **18–38 cm (7–15 in)**

A smooth, round-bodied snake, the western blind snake has a blunt head and tail. It lives almost anywhere where there is sandy or gravelly soil suitable for burrowing and spends much of its life below ground, occasionally emerging at dusk on warm evenings or on overcast days. It feeds on ants and termites, which it locates by smell, and with its slender body, it can enter right into their nests.

The snakes mate in spring and the female lays 2 to 6 eggs. She watches over the eggs, which may be laid in a communal nest.

TYPHLOPIDAE: Blind Snake Family

The 180 species in this family of burrowing snakes occur in tropical and warm temperate regions throughout the world. They rarely exceed 60 cm (23½ in) in length. Well adapted for burrowing, they have thin, cylindrical bodies, smooth, polished scales and narrow, streamlined heads. Their eyes are extremely small, and each is covered with a translucent scale. They feed on small invertebrates, particularly ants.

NAME: **Schlegel's Blind Snake,** *Typhlops schlegelii*
RANGE: **Africa: Kenya to South Africa**
HABITAT: **sandy or loamy soil**
SIZE: **60 cm (23½ in)**

Schlegel's blind snake has a spine on the end of its tail, which helps to provide leverage when it is burrowing. Although most of its life is spent underground, it will come near the surface in damp or wet weather.

The female lays 12 to 60 eggs, which are already well advanced in their development when they are laid and take only 4 to 6 weeks to hatch.

ANOMALEPIDAE

Sometimes grouped in the Typhlopidae family, there are about 20 species in this family, all found in Central and South America. They closely resemble the blind and slender blind snakes.

NAME: *Anomalepis* **sp.**
RANGE: **Mexico, tropical Central and South America to Peru**
HABITAT: **forest**
SIZE: **up to 40 cm (15¾ in)**

There are 4 species of *Anomalepis* snakes; all are little-known, wormlike burrowers with cylindrical bodies. They spend much of their lives buried under leaf litter in damp humus and are rarely seen on the surface, except after rain. They feed on termites, ants and other small invertebrates.

ANILIIDAE: Pipe Snake Family

There are 10 species in this family, all of which have a variety of primitive characteristics, including a pelvis and vestigial hind limbs, which appear as spurs, close to the vent. One species lives in northern South America, and the other 9 are found in Southeast Asia. All are excellent burrowers and feed on vertebrates such as other snakes.

NAME: **False Coral Snake,** *Anilius scytale*
RANGE: **N. South America, east of Andes**
HABITAT: **forest**
SIZE: **75–85 cm (29½–33½ in)**

A burrowing species, the false coral snake has a cylindrical body, small head and smooth scales. Its tiny eyes lie beneath transparent scales. Its small mouth is not particularly flexible, and so its diet is restricted to slender prey, such as other snakes, caecilians (limbless wormlike amphibians) and the snakelike amphisbaenids.

The female's young develop inside her body and are born fully formed.

UROPELTIDAE: Shieldtail Snake Family

There are about 40 species in this family of burrowing snakes, all found in India and Sri Lanka.

NAME: **Red-blotched Shieldtail,** *Uropeltis biomaculatus*
RANGE: **India, Sri Lanka**
HABITAT: **mountain forest**
SIZE: **up to 30.5 cm (12 in)**

The red-blotched shieldtail has the typical cylindrical body of a burrowing snake. It tunnels by forming the body into a series of S-bends, which press against the sides of the tunnel, and then thrusting the head forward into the soil. It is a secretive, inoffensive snake and feeds mainly on earthworms and grubs.

The female gives birth to 3 to 8 fully formed live young, which have developed inside her body and hatch from their membranous shells as the eggs are laid.

NAME: **Blyth's Landau Shieldtail,** *Rhinophis blythis*
RANGE: **Sri Lanka**
HABITAT: **forest**
SIZE: **up to 35.5 cm (14 in)**

This small shieldtail burrows through the soil in the same manner as the red-blotched shieldtail. Most of its life is spent beneath the ground, and it feeds on earthworms. Males tend to have longer tails than females. The female gives birth to litters of 3 to 6 fully formed live young, which are about 1 cm (⅜ in) long at birth.

XENOPELTIDAE: Sunbeam Snake Family

Placed in a family of its own, the sunbeam snake of Southeast Asia has both primitive and advanced features. Although much of its skull structure is primitive and inflexible, its lower jaw is flexible, which permits a more varied diet. Like the more advanced snakes, it has no pelvic girdle.

NAME: **Sunbeam Snake,** *Xenopeltis unicolor*
RANGE: **S.E. Asia: Burma to Indonesia**
HABITAT: **rice fields, cultivated land**
SIZE: **up to 1 m (3¼ ft)**

The iridescence of its smooth, blue scales gives the sunbeam snake its name. It spends time both above and below ground and, using its head, can burrow rapidly in soft soil. With its flexible lower jaw, it is able to take a wide range of fair-sized prey, including frogs, small rodents and birds.

Anomalepis sp.

Western Blind Snake

Blyth's Landau Shieldtail

Schlegel's Blind Snake

Red-blotched Shieldtail

Sunbeam Snake

False Coral Snake

Pythons and Boas, Wart Snakes

BOIDAE: Python and Boa Family
There are about 90 species of snake in this family, many of them well known. Most specialists regard the group as a primitive one, since its members retain characteristics which are found in lizards but which have been lost by the more highly evolved, advanced snakes, such as vipers. For example, a pelvic girdle and diminutive hind limbs are discernible in some species, and all possess two working lungs, while in advanced snakes, the left lung has disappeared in the interests of streamlining.

Within the family are 2 groups: the pythons and the boas. The 20 species of python inhabit the more tropical parts of the Old World. They are often found in or near water but also spend much of their time in trees and may have prehensile tails. They reproduce by laying eggs, which develop and hatch outside the body. The boas are found mainly in the New World and live on the ground, in trees or in or near water. They produce live young, which develop inside the body and hatch out of thin-shelled eggs as the eggs are laid.

All boid snakes are predators, but they are nonvenomous, capturing their prey with their teeth or killing it by constriction — wrapping the prey in the powerful body coils until it suffocates.

NAME: **Emerald Tree Boa**, *Boa caninus*
RANGE: **South America: Guyana, south to Brazil and Bolivia**
HABITAT: **rain forest**
SIZE: **1.2 m (4 ft)**
This brilliantly colored boa spends much of its life in trees, where it rests with its body flattened and pressed to a branch, which it grasps with its prehensile tail. From this vantage point, it watches for prey, often birds and bats, which it catches and kills with its strong front teeth. It is the fastest-moving of all boas and is also a good swimmer.

NAME: **Boa Constrictor**, *Constrictor constrictor*
RANGE: **Mexico, Central and South America to N. Argentina; West Indies**
HABITAT: **desert to rain forest**
SIZE: **up to 5.6 m (18¼ ft)**
The second-largest snake in the Americas, the boa constrictor adapts to widely contrasting climatic conditions but seems to prefer swampy rain forest. Primarily a ground-living snake, it does, however, climb trees and has a slightly prehensile tail, which allows it to grasp branches. It kills its prey, mostly birds and mammals, by encircling them in the muscular coils of its body until the prey is suffocated or crushed.

NAME: **Rubber Boa**, *Charina bottae*
RANGE: **W. USA: Washington to S. California, east to Montana and Utah**
HABITAT: **woodland, coniferous forest, meadows, sandy banks of streams**
SIZE: **35–84 cm (13¾–33 in)** Ⓡ
This small boa ranges farther into the temperate zone than any other. It varies in coloration from tan to olive-green, and the confusing appearance of its broad snout and blunt tail are the origin of its other common name of "two-headed snake."

Usually active in the evening and at night, it is a good burrower and swimmer and can climb, using its prehensile tail. During the day, it hides under rocks or logs, or burrows into sand or leaf litter. It feeds on small mammals, birds and lizards, which it kills by constriction. In late summer, the female gives birth to 2 to 8 live young, which measure 15 to 23 cm (6 to 9 in).

NAME: **Anaconda**, *Eunectes murinus*
RANGE: **South America, south to Argentina**
HABITAT: **swampy river valleys, stream banks**
SIZE: **9 m (29½ ft)**
One of the world's longest snakes, the anaconda spends much of its life in sluggish fresh water but also climbs small trees and bushes with the aid of its slightly prehensile tail. It does not pursue its prey but lurks in murky water, waiting for birds and animals to come to the edge to drink. It seizes its victim and then kills it by constriction. It can only remain submerged for about 10 minutes and usually glides along with the top of its head showing above the water.

In the breeding season, males court their mates by making loud booming sounds. Females produce litters of as many as 40 live young, each of which is about 66 cm (26 in) long at birth.

NAME: **Carpet Python**, *Morelia argus*
RANGE: **Australia, New Guinea**
HABITAT: **forest, scrub, bush**
SIZE: **3.4 m (11 ft)**
A common, widely distributed snake, the carpet python is usually found inland, less often on the coast. The dark patterning on its body mimics dead leaves and provides camouflage as it lurks among plant debris. It moves equally well on the ground, in trees or in water. Usually active at night, it rests during the day in a tree or hollow stump and occasionally basks in the sun. A nonvenomous snake, like all pythons, the carpet python kills small mammals, such as mice and rabbits, and birds, such as domestic fowl, using its sharp teeth. The female lays up to 35 eggs.

NAME: **Indian Python**, *Python molurus*
RANGE: **India, S.E. Asia, Indonesia**
HABITAT: **estuarine mangrove swamps, scrub jungle, cool rain forest**
SIZE: **5–6.1 m (16½–20 ft)** Ⓥ
One of the largest species in the world, the Indian python has suffered a reduction in numbers in some areas where it is hunted for its fine skin. It is a thick-bodied, smooth snake with a head shaped like the head of a spear. Like others of its genus, it is believed to have heat sensors near the nostrils to help it find its warm-blooded prey. Coloration varies with locality, but the pale gray race found in western India is reputedly less irritable than others and is used by "snake charmers."

During the day, the Indian python basks in the sun or rests in a cave, abandoned burrow or other refuge. At night it prowls around, looking for prey, or lies in wait at a water hole or other spot where it is sure to encounter its prey — mice, civets, small deer, wild boar and birds. It stalks the animal, then grasps and encircles it with its body coils, restricting the breathing and heartbeat until they fail.

The female python lays up to 100 eggs in a hole, cave or tree hollow and, coiling herself around the eggs, incubates them for 60 to 80 days. She occasionally makes rhythmic contractions of her body muscles, and by this gradual shuffling process, can move the eggs to catch the warmth of the sun or the protection of the shade.

ACROCHORDIDAE: Wart Snake Family
The 2 species in this family are both aquatic, nonvenomous snakes, found in India, Southeast Asia and Australia. They are most unusual, having loose, sagging skin and distinctly tapering bodies. Highly specialized for aquatic life, wart snakes have flaps in the roof of the mouth, which close off the nasal passages when they are underwater. In the same way, the notch on the upper lip, through which the sensory tongue is protruded, can be closed off by a pad on the chin.

NAME: **Elephant-trunk Snake**, *Acrochordus javanicus*
RANGE: **India, S.E. Asia, New Guinea**
HABITAT: **rivers, streams, canals**
SIZE: **1.5 m (5 ft)**
This stout, sluggish snake is almost helpless on land but an expert swimmer. It is generally more active at night and feeds exclusively on fish. The female gives birth to 25 to 30 live young, which are active and able to feed immediately.

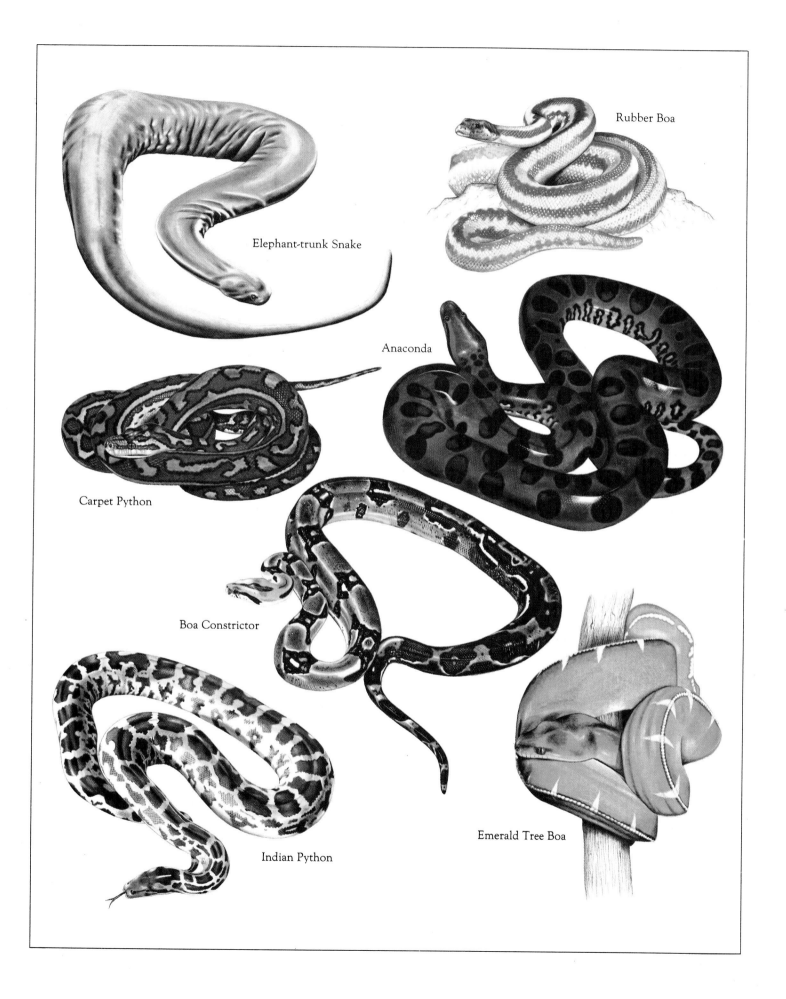

Elephant-trunk Snake

Rubber Boa

Anaconda

Carpet Python

Boa Constrictor

Indian Python

Emerald Tree Boa

Colubrine Snakes

NAME: *Fimbrios klossi*
RANGE: S. Vietnam, Cambodia
HABITAT: mountains with low vegetation
SIZE: 40 cm (15¾ in)

This little-known snake is ground-dwelling and probably nocturnal. It has curious modifications of the scales around the mouth: they are curved, forming a fringe of soft projections, the exact function of which is unknown, although they may be sensory. *Fimbrios* feeds mainly on earthworms.

Like other members of its subfamily, Xenodermatinae, *Fimbrios klossi* probably lays 2 to 4 eggs.

NAME: Slug Snake, *Pareas* sp.
RANGE: S.E. Asia
HABITAT: forest
SIZE: 30.5–76 cm (12–30 in)

The slug snakes, also known as blunt-heads, are mostly nocturnal and have slender bodies and short, wide heads. They feed mainly on slugs and snails, and their lower jaws are adapted for removing the snails from their shells, for they are capable of being extended and retracted independently of the upper jaws. Having seized a snail, the snake inserts its lower jaw into the shell so that the curved teeth at the tip of the jaw sink into the soft body. It then retracts its jaw, extracting the snail from the shell.

These snakes lack the so-called mental groove on the chin, possessed by most snakes, that allows the jaw to be distended when taking in large prey. Thus their diet is restricted to the small items for which they are admirably specialized. As far as is known, these snakes reproduce by laying eggs.

NAME: Snail-eating Snake, *Dipsas indica*
RANGE: tropical South America
HABITAT: forest
SIZE: about 68 cm (26¾ in)

The snail-eating snake is a nocturnal, ground-dwelling species, with a strong body, large head and blunt, short snout. Its upper jaw is short, with few teeth, and its lower jaw long, with elongate, curved teeth. The structure of the jaws is such that the lower jaw can be swung backward and forward without movement of the upper jaw.

It feeds entirely on snails in a manner similar to the *Pareas* snakes, inserting its lower jaw into the snail's shell, twisting it to sink the teeth into the soft body and then pulling it out. As it attempts to defend itself, the struggling snail produces large quantities of slime, which clogs up the snake's nasal openings; to breathe while extracting the snail, the snake relies, therefore, on air stored in its lungs.

COLUBRIDAE:
Colubrine Snake Family

The colubrine family is the largest of the three groups of advanced snakes and contains some 1,800 species — two-thirds of all living snakes. Although a convenient assemblage of species, this large and extremely diverse family may not be a natural one, and it is often divided into subfamilies in an attempt to clarify the relationships. Colubrids are found on all continents except Antarctica.

There is as much variation within the colubrine family as there is between the other two families of advanced snakes, the vipers and elapids, but there are a few shared characteristics. No colubrids have any vestiges of a pelvis or hind limbs, and all have the left lung reduced or even absent (for streamlining of the body). The lower jaw is flexible, but there are no hollow poison-injecting fangs. Instead there are solid teeth on both jaws, and, in some cases, teeth on the upper jaw, with grooves which are connected to a poison gland (rear-fanged snakes).

Most colubrids are harmless; all those which are dangerous, such as the boomslang (*Dispholidus typus*) and the twig snake (*Thelotornis kirtlandii*), occur in Africa.

Colubrids occur in all habitats, and there are ground-dwelling, arboreal, burrowing, even aquatic species. All are predators, feeding on anything from insects to small mammals. Most colubrids lay eggs, but some reproduce by giving birth to fully formed live young.

NAME: Spotted Water Snake, *Enhydris punctata*
RANGE: Australia: coast of Northern Territory
HABITAT: creeks, swamps, rivers
SIZE: 30–50 cm (11¾–19¾ in)

The spotted water snake is one of a subfamily of about 34 colubrids, all specialized for life in water. It is able to move on land as well as in water and comes ashore to bask on riverbanks and shores. Its small eyes are directed upward, and its nostrils, too, are on the upper surface of the head. Pads of skin close off the nostrils completely when the snake is diving.

Mildly venomous, the water snake is rear-fanged — grooved teeth at the back of the upper jaw are connected to a poison gland. It preys on aquatic creatures such as fish and frogs. Females give birth to fully formed live young.

NAME: White-bellied Mangrove Snake, *Fordonia leucobalia*
RANGE: coast of N. Australia, S.E. Asia
HABITAT: mangrove swamps
SIZE: 60 cm–1 m (23½ in–3¼ ft)

A member of the subfamily of aquatic colubrids, the white-bellied mangrove snake has similar adaptations to those of the rest of its group, such as nostrils near the top of its head and upward-facing eyes. Large numbers of these snakes frequent the edges of swamps, where they forage among the roots for food. It is a rear-fanged snake and feeds mainly on crabs, which seem strongly affected by its venom, unlike frogs and mammals, which are not. Fish are also included in its diet. If alarmed, the snake will take refuge in a crab burrow.

NAME: Egg-eating Snake, *Dasypeltis scabra*
RANGE: Africa, south and east of the Sahara
HABITAT: woodland, scrub
SIZE: 75 cm (29½ in)

This slender snake is one of the few snakes to exist entirely on hard-shelled bird's eggs. It hunts for eggs on the ground and in trees, mainly at night, although it is sometimes active during the day. Most other snakes take only the softer-shelled lizard and snake eggs, since they lack the specialized equipment that the snakes of this subfamily have for dealing with their hard, unwieldy food.

The egg-eating snake's mouth and jaws are extremely flexible and are hinged in such a way as to accommodate large eggs. It has only a few small teeth in each jaw, but special projections of the neck vertebrae form a serrated edge of "teeth," which pierce the wall of the esophagus.

When the snake swallows an egg, which may be twice the size of its head, it pushes its mouth against the egg, gradually engulfing it in its jaws by stretching the elastic ligament joining the two halves of the lower jaw. The small neck scales stand apart in rows, so exposing the skin beneath. The esophagus teeth slit the egg open, and the contents pass into the stomach, while a specialized valve rejects the shell, which is regurgitated. When eggs are plentiful, the snake stores up fat in its body; it lives on the fat during those seasons when few eggs are available.

Females of this species lay 8 to 14 eggs, which they deposit singly rather than in a clutch — an unusual habit for an egg-laying snake.

Fimbrios klossi

Egg-eating Snake

Slug Snake

Spotted Water Snake

White-bellied Mangrove Snake

Snail-eating Snake

Colubrine Snakes

NAME: **Grass Snake**, *Natrix natrix*
RANGE: **Europe: Scandinavia, south to Mediterranean countries; N.W. Africa; Asia, east to Lake Baikal**
HABITAT: **damp meadows, marshes, ditches, riverbanks**
SIZE: **up to 1.2 m (4 ft); occasionally up to 2 m (6½ ft)**

One of a group of colubrids adapted for life in water, the grass snake swims well and spends some time in water, even though it is less aquatic than some other *Natrix* species. It is one of the most common and widespread European snakes and 3 subspecies, which differ in coloration and pattern, occur over its large range. Females are generally longer and thicker-bodied than males.

The grass snake is active during the day, hunting for food in water and on land. It preys mainly on frogs, toads and newts but also takes fish and occasionally even small mammals and young birds. Much of its prey is swallowed alive, although it does have a venomous secretion that is toxic to small animals but harmless to man.

Depending on the latitude, grass snakes start to breed from April onward. The male courts the female, rubbing his chin, on which there are many sensory tubercles, over her body. If all goes well, he works his way up to her neck, and they intertwine and mate. Some 8 or more weeks later, the female lays her 30 to 40 eggs, which are already fairly advanced in embryonic development. She deposits the eggs in a warm spot, preferably in decaying organic matter such as manure or compost heaps. The young hatch after 1 or 2 months, depending on the warmth of their surroundings.

NAME: **Dark-green Whipsnake**, *Coluber viridiflavus*
RANGE: **Europe: N.E. Spain, central and S. France, Italy, S. Switzerland, Yugoslavia, Corsica, Sardinia**
HABITAT: **dry, vegetated areas: hillsides, woodland edge, gardens**
SIZE: **up to 1.9 m (6¼ ft)**

A slender, elongate snake, the dark-green whipsnake has a rounded snout, large eyes and a long, tapering tail. Some individuals may, in fact, be almost all black, rather than dark green. Males are generally longer than females. Usually active in the daytime, it is a ground-dwelling snake but can climb well on rocks and bushes. It locates its prey by sight and usually feeds on lizards, frogs, mammals, birds and other snakes.

Males compete fiercely for mates in the breeding season. The female lays her 5 to 15 eggs among rocks or in cracks in the soil. The young hatch in 6 to 8 weeks.

NAME: **Bibron's Burrowing Viper**, *Atractaspis bibroni*
RANGE: **South Africa**
HABITAT: **dry, sandy regions**
SIZE: **up to 80 cm (31½ in)**

Also known as the southern mole viper, this snake is a member of a group of burrowing colubrids called mole vipers, all of which are found in Africa and the Middle East. Like its relatives, it has a shovel-shaped head, no distinct neck, a rounded, slender body and short tail. Its eyes are small.

A venomous snake, the mole viper has a sophisticated venom apparatus similar to that of the true vipers, and because of this, it was originally believed to be a viper. Its fangs are huge, relative to the small head, and can be folded or erected independently of each other. Once swung into the attack position, the fangs eject venom, which is pumped into them from the connected poison glands.

The mole viper burrows into the soil with its strong snout, usually emerging at the surface only at night after rain. If on the surface in sunlight, it coils itself into a ball and hides its head in the coils. It feeds on other reptiles, such as burrowing lizards and blind snakes, which it kills with its venomous bite.

The female mole viper reproduces by laying eggs.

NAME: **Red-bellied Snake**, *Storeria occipitomaculata*
RANGE: **extreme S. Canada; E. USA: Maine to Minnesota, south to Texas and Florida**
HABITAT: **woodland on hills and mountains, bogs**
SIZE: **20–40.5 cm (7¾–16 in)**

There are 3 subspecies of this widely distributed snake, which vary in coloration and the arrangement of the characteristic bright spots on the neck; in the Florida subspecies the spots may be fused, forming a collar. The red-bellied snake lives from sea level to 1,700 m (5,600 ft) and is active mostly at night, when it preys on insects and small invertebrates such as earthworms and slugs. If alarmed, it can curl its upper lip in threat, while discharging a musky secretion from its cloacal opening.

The snakes mate in spring or autumn; before copulation, the male throws his body into a series of waves from tail to head and rubs his chin, equipped with sensory tubercles, over the female's body. He also has sensory tubercles around the cloaca (genital opening) region, which appear to help him position himself correctly. The young develop inside the female's body and are born fully formed and measuring 7 to 10 cm (2¾ to 4 in).

NAME: **Common Garter Snake**, *Thamnophis sirtalis*
RANGE: **S. Canada; USA, except desert regions**
HABITAT: **damp country, often near water: marshes, meadows, ditches, farmland, woodland**
SIZE: **45 cm–1.3 m (17¾ in–4¼ ft)**

The most widely distributed snake in North America and one of the most familiar, the garter snake occurs in many subspecies over its huge range. The coloration is, therefore, extremely variable, but the garter snake nearly always has distinctive back and side stripes. It is active during the day and hunts for frogs, toads, salamanders and small invertebrates among damp vegetation on the ground. One of the few snakes to occur in the far north, the garter snake withstands cold weather well and is found as far north as 67° N. In the south of its range, it may remain active all year round, but in the north it hibernates in communal dens.

Garter snakes usually mate in spring, sometimes communally, as they emerge from hibernation. They may, however, mate in autumn, in which event the sperm spend most of the winter in the female's oviduct and do not move into position to fertilize the eggs until spring. Before copulation, the male snake throws his body into a series of waves and then rubs his chin over the female's body. The tubercles on his chin must receive the right sensory responses before he will mate. As many as 80 young develop inside the female's body, nourished by a form of placenta, and are born fully formed.

NAME: **Rat Snake**, *Elaphe obsoleta*
RANGE: **S. Canada; USA: Vermont to Minnesota, south to Texas and Florida; N. Mexico**
HABITAT: **forest, swamps, farmland, wooded slopes**
SIZE: **86 cm–2.5 m (33¾ in–8¼ ft)**

A large, powerful species, the rat snake tolerates a variety of habitats in wet and dry situations. There are 6 or more subspecies, which occur in one of three main color patterns: plain, blotched or striped. It is an agile snake, good at climbing, and hunts rodents and other small mammals, birds and lizards in trees and in barns or ruined buildings. Usually active during the day, it may tend to be nocturnal in summer. In much of its range, it hibernates throughout the winter.

Rat snakes mate in spring and autumn. The female lays 5 to 30 eggs in leaf debris or under a rock or log. The eggs hatch in 2 to 4 months, depending on the temperature: the warmer the weather, the quicker they hatch.

Red-bellied Snake

Common Garter Snake

Grass Snake

Bibron's Burrowing Viper

Rat Snake

Dark-green Whipsnake

Colubrine Snakes

NAME: **Smooth Snake,** *Coronella austriaca*
RANGE: **Europe: S. Scandinavia, S. England, south to N. Spain, Italy and Greece; east to USSR, N. Iran**
HABITAT: **dry rocky areas, heathland, open woodland**
SIZE: **50–80 cm (19¾–31½ in)**

The slender, round-bodied smooth snake varies in coloration over its wide range but nearly always has a dark streak on each side of its head. The head is fairly small and pointed and there is no clear neck. It is a secretive snake, although active in the daytime, and adapts to a variety of dry habitats up to 1,800 m (5,900 ft); it is even occasionally found in moist areas. Although it rarely basks in full sun, the smooth snake likes to retreat to warm, shady areas under rocks or stones. Lizards, particularly lacertids, make up the bulk of its diet, and it also eats small snakes, young mammals and insects. It holds its prey in a few coils of its body to subdue it while it starts to swallow.

In the breeding season, males fight one another for mates. The female gives birth to 2 to 15 live young in autumn; they emerge in transparent, membranous shells, from which they free themselves immediately. The newly born young measure 12 to 20 cm (4¾ to 7¾ in) in length. Males mature at 3 years and females at 4.

NAME: **Common Kingsnake,** *Lampropeltis getulus*
RANGE: **USA: New Jersey to Florida in east, Oregon to California in west; Mexico**
HABITAT: **varied: forest, woodland, desert, prairie, swamps, marshes**
SIZE: **90 cm–2 m (35½ in–6½ ft)**

A large snake with smooth, shiny scales, the common kingsnake usually has alternating dark and light rings, but some of the many subspecies have more irregular speckled patterns. It is primarily a ground-dwelling species, although it may sometimes climb into small trees or bushes, and is active in the daytime, usually in the early morning and at dusk. Found in almost every type of habitat, it will take refuge under rocks, in vegetation and under logs. It feeds on snakes, including rattlesnakes and coral snakes, lizards, mice and birds which it kills by constriction, holding the prey in the powerful coils of its body until it suffocates.

Kingsnakes mate in spring. The female lays 3 to 24 eggs, which usually hatch in 2 to 3 months, depending on the warmth of the weather.

NAME: **Bullsnake/Pine Snake/Gopher Snake,** *Pituophis melanoleucas*
RANGE: **S.W. Canada; USA: W., central and S.E. states; Mexico**
HABITAT: **dry woodland, grassland, prairie, rocky desert**
SIZE: **1.2–2.5 m (4–8¼ ft)**

These large, robust snakes are found in a variety of habitats and are good climbers and burrowers. The head is small and somewhat pointed. The coloration of the many subspecies varies over the wide range. Different subspecies bear different common names.

Usually active by day, this species may become nocturnal in hot weather. It feeds largely on rodents, as well as on rabbits, birds and lizards, all of which it kills by constriction — throwing its powerful body coils around the victim until it suffocates. It may burrow underground for shelter or take over mammal or tortoise burrows. If alarmed, the snake flattens its head, hisses loudly and vibrates its tail before attacking the enemy.

These snakes mate in spring, and the female lays up to 24 eggs in a burrow or beneath a rock or log. The young hatch in 9 to 11 weeks and are up to 45 cm (17¾ in) long on hatching.

NAME: **Paradise Tree Snake,** *Chrysopelea paradisi*
RANGE: **S.E. Asia: Philippines to Indonesia**
HABITAT: **forest**
SIZE: **up to 1.2 m (4 ft)**

Also known as the flying snake, this species does in fact glide from tree to tree, from one branch down to another. It launches itself into the air, its body stretched out and its belly pulled in to make a concave surface with maximum resistance to the air. In this position it glides downward at an angle of 50 or 60 degrees to the ground for 20 m (65 ft) or more and lands safely without injuring itself. It seems to have little control over its "flight," however, and cannot glide upward or steer with any degree of efficiency.

A further adaptation for its tree-dwelling life are the ridged scales on the snake's belly, which help it to climb almost vertically up tree trunks. The ridges are thrust against the bark and enable the snake to gain a hold on every tiny irregularity of surface. Thus, it can ascend right into the trees, where few other snakes can go, and feed on the abundant tree-dwelling lizards. The closely related oriental tree snake, *C. ornata*, can glide and climb in the same manner.

The female paradise tree snake lays up to 12 eggs.

NAME: **Mangrove Snake,** *Boiga dendrophila*
RANGE: **S.E. Asia: Philippines to Indonesia**
HABITAT: **forest, mangrove swamps**
SIZE: **2.5 m (8¼ ft)**

The beautifully marked mangrove snake has a slender body, with hexagonal scales on its back and sides. Primarily an arboreal species, it hunts birds in the trees but may also descend to the ground to prey on rodents. It is a venomous, rear-fanged snake: the grooved teeth toward the back of the jaw carry venom from the poison gland above the jaw into the prey.

The female mangrove snake lays 4 to 7 eggs.

NAME: **Boomslang,** *Dispholidus typus*
RANGE: **Africa: central to South Africa**
HABITAT: **savanna**
SIZE: **up to 2 m (6½ ft)**

The boomslang is one of only two dangerously poisonous snakes in the colubrid family. It has three large grooved fangs, set farther forward than the usual two fangs of colubrids, and extremely toxic venom, which causes respiratory failure and hemorrhaging and can even kill a human being. Normally, however, it uses its venomous bites on lizards, particularly chameleons, and on frogs and birds.

The boomslang is a tree-dwelling snake, usually active in the daytime. It varies in coloration but is usually predominantly black, brown or green on the upper surface.

The female boomslang lays 10 to 14 eggs.

NAME: **Vine Snake,** *Oxybelis fulgidus*
RANGE: **Central America to N. South America**
HABITAT: **rain forest, cultivated land**
SIZE: **1.5–2 m (5–6½ ft)**

Barely the thickness of a man's finger, about 1.25 cm (½ in) in diameter at the most, the vine snake is a remarkably slender, elongate species. As it lies amid the branches of forest trees, its proportions and greeny-brown coloration make it almost indistinguishable from the abundant creepers and vines. Its head, too, is thin and elongate and equipped with rear fangs and mild venom.

A slow-moving predator, active in the daytime and at night, the vine snake feeds mainly on young birds, which it steals from nests, and on lizards. If threatened, it puffs up the front of its body, revealing vivid coloration usually hidden under scales, and opens its long mouth wide. A frightened snake may also sway from side to side, like a stem in the breeze.

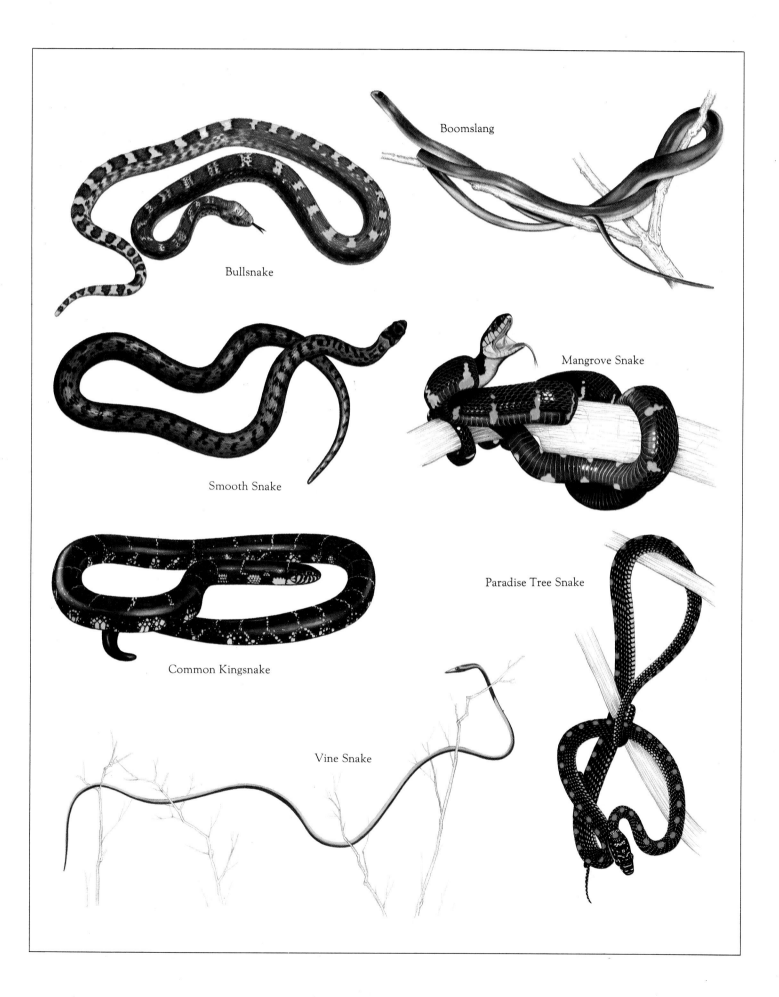

Bullsnake

Boomslang

Smooth Snake

Mangrove Snake

Common Kingsnake

Paradise Tree Snake

Vine Snake

Cobras and Sea Snakes

NAME: Eastern Green Mamba,
Dendroaspis angusticeps
RANGE: E. and S. Africa
HABITAT: savanna
SIZE: 2 m (6½ ft)

The slender, fast-moving mambas spend much of their lives in trees, where they feed on birds and lizards. Their venom is extremely toxic, but these snakes are not generally aggressive unless provoked and tend rather to flee from danger or threat.

In the breeding season, two or three males compete in ritualized fights for females. They wrap their bodies around one another and threaten with their raised heads. Mating may last for many hours. The female lays her 10 to 15 eggs in a hole in the ground or in a hollow tree stump. The young mambas hatch in 17 to 18 weeks.

NAME: De Vis's Banded Snake, *Denisonia devisii*
RANGE: Australia: N. New South Wales, S. Queensland
HABITAT: dry, wooded areas
SIZE: 50 cm (19¾ in)

A nocturnal species, this snake shelters under leaf litter or a log during the day and emerges at night to hunt for food, mainly lizards, which it kills with its toxic venom. It has a distinctive defense posture, which it often adopts when threatened: it flattens its body, which is thrown into a series of stiff curves, and then lashes out and bites if approached.

The female gives birth to about 8 live young, which have developed inside her body, nourished by a form of placenta.

NAME: King Cobra, *Ophiophagus hannah*
RANGE: India, S. China, Malaysia to Philippines and Indonesia
HABITAT: forest, often near water
SIZE: 4–5.5 m (13–18 ft)

The longest poisonous snake in the world, the king cobra has a head as big as a man's hand. It can make itself still more impressive by adopting the cobra threat posture, with the flexible neck ribs and loose skin spread out to form a wide hood. Despite its size, it is an agile, secretive snake and will flee into cover or even water if pursued. It feeds mainly on other snakes — its scientific name means "snake-eater" — but also on monitor lizards.

The female king cobra constructs a nest of vegetation for her eggs, perhaps the only snake to do so. She gathers together twigs, branches and foliage with a coil of her forebody and then makes a chamber in the middle of them by revolving her coiled body. She lays her 18 to 40 eggs in this chamber, covers them and lies coiled on top of the nest while they incubate.

ELAPIDAE:
Cobra and Sea Snake Family

There are about 250 species of highly venomous snake in this family, found mainly in tropical and subtropical areas of Australia, Asia, Africa (except Madagascar) and America. Elapids are most abundant in Australia.

The family is often divided into two groups: the elapids proper, including cobras, kraits, mambas and coral snakes, all of which are land- or tree-dwelling; and the sea snakes. The 50 or so species of sea snake lead entirely aquatic lives; most are marine, but a few live in lakes or enter rivers. All elapids have fangs, situated near the front of the upper jaw, which are either deeply grooved for the transport of venom or have grooves, the edges of which have fused to form a venom canal.

NAME: Indian Cobra, *Naja naja*
RANGE: India, central Asia, S.E. Asia
HABITAT: rain forest, rice fields, cultivated land
SIZE: 1.8–2.2 m (6–7¼ ft)

A large, highly venomous snake, the Indian cobra feeds on rodents, lizards and frogs. As well as biting, the Indian cobra can attack or defend itself from a distance by "spitting" venom, which, if it enters the opponent's eyes, causes severe pain and damage. The snake actually forces the venom through its fangs, by exerting muscular pressure on the venom glands, so that it sprays out in twin jets for 2 m (6½ ft) or more.

In its characteristic threat posture, the Indian cobra raises the front one-third of its body and spreads out its long, flexible neck ribs and loose skin to form a disklike hood, on the back of which there are markings resembling eyes.

Indian cobras pay more attention to their eggs than is usual in snakes. The 8 to 45 eggs (usually 12 to 20) are laid in a hollow tree, a termite mound or earth into which the snakes tunnel. The female guards the clutch throughout the incubation period, leaving them only for a short time each day to feed. The young hatch after about 50 or 60 days.

NAME: Eastern Brown Snake, *Pseudonaja textilis*
RANGE: E. Australia, E. New Guinea
HABITAT: wet forest, rocky hillsides
SIZE: 1.5 m (5 ft)

A fast-moving, venomous snake, this species is equally at home in dry or swampy land. It is active during the day and feeds on small mammals, frogs and lizards. Its coloration varies from yellow to dark brown, with bands of varying intensity.

NAME: Bandy-bandy, *Vermicella annulata*
RANGE: Australia (not extreme S.E., S.W. or N.W.)
HABITAT: varied: damp forest to desert sandhills
SIZE: 40 cm (15¾ in)

A distinctive black and white snake, the rings of the bandy-bandy vary in width and number, according to sex and geographic population. It is a nocturnal snake and feeds mainly, if not exclusively, on blind snakes (Typhlopidae). Although venomous, its fangs and venom supply are too small to cause harm to anything other than small animals.

An egg-laying species, the female deposits her eggs under rocks or logs.

NAME: Eastern Coral Snake, *Micrurus fulvius*
RANGE: USA: North Carolina to Florida, west to Texas; Mexico
HABITAT: forest, often near water, rocky hillsides.
SIZE: 56 cm-1.2 m (22 in-4 ft)

One of the only two elapids in North America, the Eastern coral snake is a colorful species, with red, black and yellow or white bands ringing its body. The bright markings of these poisonous snakes may serve to warn off potential predators. The coral snake is a secretive species, spending much of the time buried in leaf litter or sand. In the morning and late afternoon, it prowls on the surface in search of small lizards and snakes, which it kills with its highly toxic venom.

The female lays 3 to 12 eggs, which hatch in about 3 months.

NAME: Banded Sea Snake, *Hydrophis cyanocinctus*
RANGE: Persian Gulf, Indian Ocean, Pacific Ocean to Japan
HABITAT: coastal waters
SIZE: 2 m (6½ ft)

The banded sea snake is fully adapted to aquatic life and never ventures onto land. Its body is laterally flattened, and its tail is paddle-shaped for propulsion when swimming. It does breathe air but can remain submerged for up to 2 hours. Its nostrils are directed upward and can be closed off by pads of tissue bordering the front of the nostrils. The snake's body muscles have degenerated, and if washed ashore, it collapses helplessly. Like all sea snakes, this species feeds on fish and has extremely toxic venom. The venom of one sea snake, *Enhydrina schistosa*, has been shown in laboratory tests to be more powerful than that of any other snake.

All but one sea snake bear live young in the water. The banded sea snake gives birth to 2 to 6 young.

Eastern Coral Snake

Banded Sea Snake

De Vis's Banded Snake

King Cobra

Indian Cobra

Eastern Brown Snake

Bandy-bandy

Eastern Green Mamba

Vipers

NAME: **Common Viper,** *Vipera berus*
RANGE: **Britain, Europe to Siberia**
HABITAT: **moors, meadows, chalk hills, forest edge**
SIZE: **up to 50 cm (19¾ in)**

The widely distributed common viper, or adder, is active in the daytime in the north of its range, where it takes every opportunity to bask in the sun. Farther south, it is active in the evening and at night. In winter, it must hibernate, often using the abandoned burrow of another creature, until the temperature rises to an average of about 8°C (46°F) — the length of hibernation, therefore, varies with latitude. This viper moves slowly and does not climb but is a good swimmer. Mice, voles, shrews, lizards and frogs, all of which it kills with its venom, are its main foods, and it may occasionally take bird's eggs.

In the mating season, which may occur only every other year in areas where the hibernation period is long, males perform ritualistic aggressive dances before mating. They rear up in front of one another, swaying and trying to push each other over. The female retains her 3 to 20 eggs in the body until they are on the point of hatching. The young are about 18 cm (7 in) long when they hatch and are already equipped with venom and fangs.

NAME: **Desert Sidewinding Viper,** *Vipera peringueyi*
RANGE: **Africa: Namibia**
HABITAT: **desert**
SIZE: **25.5 cm (10 in)**

A small, rare viper, this species is found on the coastal sand dunes of the Namib Desert. It glides over the dunes with a sidewinding motion of lateral waves, leaving tracks like two parallel grooves where two parts of the body touch the sand and support the snake. During the day it half buries itself in the sand — a feat it can accomplish in about 20 seconds — to shelter from the sun or to lie in wait for prey such as rodents or lizards.

NAME: **Horned Viper,** *Vipera ammodytes*
RANGE: **Europe: Austria, Hungary, Balkan Peninsula**
HABITAT: **arid, sandy regions**
SIZE: **76 cm (30 in)**

Identifiable by the small horn on its snout, this viper is also called the sand viper because of its preference for sandy areas. Like many European vipers, it avoids woodland but is found in clearings, paths and often in vineyards. Its movements generally are slow, but it can strike rapidly with its fangs to kill small mammals, lizards, snakes and small birds. Horned vipers hibernate throughout the winter.

VIPERIDAE: Viper Family

There are 40 species of viper, found all over the Old World except in Australia and Madagascar. Most species are short, sturdy snakes which live on the ground; a few species have become arboreal and have prehensile tails.

Vipers do not chase their prey — lizards, small mammals and birds — but wait in a concealed position to ambush and strike. They have a sophisticated fang and venom system: the large hollow fangs, which fold back when the mouth is closed, swing forward and become erect when the mouth is opened wide. Venom is pumped into them from venom glands at the base of the fangs, and as they pierce the victim, the poison is injected.

NAME: **Gaboon Viper,** *Bitis gabonica*
RANGE: **W. Africa, south of the Sahara to South Africa**
HABITAT: **rain forest**
SIZE: **1.2–2 m (4–6½ ft)**

One of the largest vipers, the Gaboon viper is well camouflaged, as it lies among the leaf litter on the forest floor, by the complex geometric patterns on its skin. It has a broad head, slender neck and stout body, tapering to a thin tail. Its fangs, the longest of any viper, are up to 5 cm (2 in) long and are supplied with a venom which causes hemorrhaging in the victim and inhibits breathing and heartbeat.

The Gaboon viper is nocturnal and, although it moves little, manages to find plenty of prey, such as rodents, frogs, toads and ground-living birds, on the forest floor. The female bears live young in litters of up to 30 at a time; each young snake is about 30.5 cm (12 in) long at birth.

NAME: **Aspic Viper,** *Vipera aspis*
RANGE: **Europe: France, Germany, Switzerland, Italy, Sicily**
HABITAT: **warm dry areas up to 3,000 m (9,800 ft)**
SIZE: **up to 76 cm (30 in)**

Also known as the European asp, this species varies in coloration from area to area. A sluggish snake except when alarmed, it spends much of its time basking in the sun on a tree stump or rock, particularly in the early morning or late afternoon. It feeds on small mammals, lizards and nestling birds.

Mating takes place in the spring, after males have performed ritualistic combat displays, and females lay 4 to 18 eggs. In winter, aspic vipers hibernate singly or in groups in underground burrows or in wall crevices.

NAME: **Puff Adder,** *Bitis arietans*
RANGE: **Africa: Morocco, south of the Sahara to South Africa; Middle East**
HABITAT: **savanna up to 1,800 m (6,000 ft)**
SIZE: **1.4–2 m (4½–6½ ft)**

Perhaps the most common and widespread African snake, the puff adder adapts to both moist and arid climates but not to the extremes of desert or rain forest. It is one of the biggest vipers, with a girth of up to 23 cm (9 in), and can inflate its body to an even larger size when about to strike. Its fangs are about 1.25 cm (½ in) long, and the venom causes hemorrhaging in the victim.

Primarily a ground-living snake, the sluggish puff adder relies on its cryptic pattern and coloration to conceal it from both enemies and potential prey. It occasionally climbs into trees and is a good swimmer. Ground-living mammals, such as rats and mice, and birds, lizards, frogs and toads are its main prey.

The female puff adder lays 20 to 40 eggs, which develop inside her body and hatch minutes after laying. The young are 15 to 20 cm (6 to 7¾ in) long when they hatch and can kill small mice.

NAME: **Saw-scaled Adder,** *Echis carinatus*
RANGE: **N. Africa to Syria, Iran, east to India**
HABITAT: **arid, sandy regions**
SIZE: **53–72 cm (20¾–28¼ in)**

An extremely dangerous snake, the saw-scaled adder is responsible for the majority of human deaths from snake bite in North Africa. This adder uses some serrated scales on its sides to make a threatening noise: it coils its body into a tight spiral and then moves the coils so that the scales rub against one another, making a loud rasping sound. It is these scales that give the snake its common name.

The saw-scaled adder often uses a sideways motion, known as sidewinding, when on sandy ground. It throws its body, only two short sections of which touch the ground, into lateral waves. All the adder's weight is, therefore, pushing against the ground at these points, so providing the leverage to push it sideways.

During the day, the saw-scaled adder lies sheltered from the heat under a fallen tree trunk or rock, or flattens its body and digs into the sand by means of the "keeled" lateral scales. It feeds at night on small rodents, skinks, geckos, frogs and large invertebrates such as centipedes and scorpions. Breeding usually takes place in the rainy season, and the female lays about 5 eggs. The young adders are about 20 cm (7¾ in) long when they hatch.

Saw-scaled Adder

Gaboon Viper

Aspic Viper

Common Viper

Horned Viper

Puff Adder

Desert Sidewinding Viper

Pit Vipers

NAME: **Massasauga,** *Sistrurus catenatus*
RANGE: **USA: N.W. Pennsylvania to Arizona; northern Mexico**
HABITAT: **varied: swamp, marshland, woodland, prairie**
SIZE: **45 cm–1m (17¾ in–3¼ ft)**

The massasauga tolerates a wide range of habitat and, although it seems to prefer swampy land, occurs even in arid grassland in the west of its range. It has up to eight rattles on its tail and is distinguished from other rattlers by the nine enlarged scales on its head. It preys on lizards, frogs, insects, small mammals and birds.

In April or May, the massasaugas mate, and a litter of 2 to 19 live young is born in the summer.

NAME: **Sidewinder,** *Crotalus cerastes*
RANGE: **S.W. USA: S. California, Nevada and Utah, south to Mexico**
HABITAT: **desert, rocky hillsides**
SIZE: **43–82 cm (17–32¼ in)**

A small agile snake, the sidewinder has a distinctive hornlike projection over each eye. It is chiefly nocturnal and takes refuge in the burrow of another animal or under a bush during the day. At night it emerges to hunt its prey, mainly small rodents, such as pocket mice and kangaroo rats, and lizards. A desert inhabitant, this snake moves with a sideways motion, known as sidewinding, thought to be the most efficient mode of movement for a snake on sand. It throws its body into lateral waves, only two short sections of it touching the ground. All the snake's weight, therefore, is pushing against the ground at these points, and this provides the leverage to move it sideways. As it travels, the snake leaves a trail of parallel J-shaped markings. An ideal form of movement in open, sparsely vegetated country, sidewinding has the advantage of reducing contact between the snake's body and the hot sand.

Sidewinders mate in April or May, and the female gives birth to 5 to 18 live young about 3 months later.

NAME: **Fer-de-lance,** *Bothrops atrox*
RANGE: **S. Mexico to South America; West Indies**
HABITAT: **low coastal areas**
SIZE: **2.45 m (8 ft)**

A common pit viper, the fer-de-lance varies in color and pattern over its wide range. A sheath of membranous flesh covers its fangs, but when the snake bites, the sheath is pushed back. The fer-de-lance feeds mainly on small mammals, and its venom causes rapid and severe internal bleeding. The female is an unusually prolific breeder for a pit viper, giving birth to up to 50 live young in a yearly litter.

CROTALIDAE: Pit Viper Family

The pit vipers are a group of highly venomous snakes. They occur in eastern Europe and throughout mainland Asia and Japan, but the group is best known for its New World representatives, such as rattlesnakes. Pit vipers are closely related to true vipers (Viperidae) and are considered by some experts to be a subfamily of Viperidae. There are about 123 species. Unlike the true vipers, pit vipers are absent from Africa, and they possess some significant anatomical differences.

The most important of these differences are the organs that give the snakes their common name: sensory pits on each side of the head in front of, and just below, the eyes. These pits can detect heat and are used by these nocturnal snakes to locate warm-blooded prey, the body temperature of which is higher than the surroundings. A pit viper can discern and strike accurately at prey by moving its head from side to side and using both pit organs to discover the distance and direction of the animal. Once it has located its prey, the pit viper kills by a rapid strike, in which the long, curved fangs of the upper jaw impale the target and inject venom. Small or weak creatures may be swallowed whole without poisoning, but larger, more active prey must first be subdued with venom.

One group of pit vipers, the rattlesnakes, has characteristic tail rattles. The rattle is a series of flattened, interlocking hollow segments on the tail which make a noise when the tail is shaken. Each of these segments was once the tip of the tail, and a new one is added each time the snake sheds its skin. However, earlier rattles fall off, and there are rarely more than 14 rattles at any time. The sound produced is used to warn potential enemies to keep their distance.

NAME: **Eastern Diamondback Rattlesnake,** *Crotalus adamanteus*
RANGE: **E. USA: North Carolina to Florida Keys, west to Louisiana**
HABITAT: **woodland, farmland**
SIZE: **91 cm–2.4 m (35¾ in–7¾ ft)**

The largest rattler, the eastern diamondback is the most dangerous snake in North America, with venom that attacks the blood cells. Its striking diamond-patterned skin provides camouflage as it lies coiled in vegetation, watching for prey such as rabbits and birds.

The female diamondback bears 8 to 12 live young, each measuring 30 to 36 cm (11¾ to 14¼ in), in late summer and defends them aggressively.

NAME: **Cottonmouth,** *Agkistrodon piscivorus*
RANGE: **S. and S.E. USA**
HABITAT: **marshes, streams, lakes, swamps**
SIZE: **51 cm–1.9 m (20 in–6¼ ft)**

The heavy-bodied cottonmouth spends much of its life in or near water and swims well, holding its head up out of the water. It is most active at night, when it preys on amphibians, fish, snakes and birds, and it is one of the few snakes to eat carrion. An extremely dangerous species, its venom is hemolytic — it destroys the red blood cells and coagulates the blood around the bite. The venom is actually extracted and used medically for its coagulating properties in the treatment of hemorrhagic conditions.

Female cottonmouths breed every other year and produce litters of up to 15 young which measure 18 to 33 cm (7 to 13 in) at birth.

NAME: **Manushi/Asiatic Pit Viper,** *Agkistrodon halys*
RANGE: **Caspian Sea area, S. USSR, China**
HABITAT: **steppe, semidesert, taiga (coniferous forest)**
SIZE: **46–76 cm (18–30 in)**

One of the few pit vipers in the Old World, the manushi is found as far north as 51°N. Mainly nocturnal, it emerges at sunset to hunt its prey, which consists mostly of small mammals. Its venom is fatal to small creatures, such as mice, but is seldom dangerous to larger animals and causes only mild temporary paralysis in man.

The manushi hibernates during the winter, awaking in March; males usually wake a week or more before females. Mating takes place shortly after the end of hibernation, and the female lays 3 to 10 eggs, which hatch about 3 months later.

NAME: **Bushmaster,** *Lachesis muta*
RANGE: **S. Nicaragua to Amazon basin of South America**
HABITAT: **rain forest**
SIZE: **2.45–3.5 m (8–11½ ft)**

A rare, deadly and formidable pit viper, the bushmaster is the largest of its family. It is strictly nocturnal, hiding during the day in a cave or tree hollow and emerging at night to hunt. It preys on small rodents and other mammals up to the size of small deer. Although its venom is not as poisonous as that of some pit vipers, the bushmaster produces such large quantities of poison, and has such huge fangs with which to inject it, that it is one of the world's most dangerous snakes. The female bushmaster is the only New World viper to lay eggs.

Sidewinder

Manushi

Cottonmouth

Massasauga

Bushmaster

Eastern Diamondback Rattlesnake

Fer-de-lance

Amphibians – the first land vertebrates

Compared with the huge numbers of existing fishes, reptiles, birds and mammals, the total global count of living amphibian species is rather meager. Only about 2,000 forms, divided into about 250 genera, are authoritatively recognized at present.

All modern forms can be accommodated in three major subgroupings, of which two are commonly recognizable animal types: first, the Urodela (newts and salamanders), and second, the Anura (frogs and toads). The third group is the Apoda, which contains several families of limbless, elongate, burrowing amphibians, known as caecilians.

The amphibians were the first group of vertebrates to colonize the land. The distant evolutionary origins of amphibianlike animals from fish ancestors are a key phase in vertebrate evolution, heralding as they do all the subsequent developments of land-living vertebrates. Probably between 375 and 350 million years ago, lobe-fin fishes (crossopterygians), which already possessed lungs and four solidly constructed, downward-directed fins, began, more and more, to move out of freshwater habitats into adjacent terrestrial ones. The development of amphibians had begun.

Almost all the early amphibians must have retained fishlike habits. They were entirely or largely aquatic and were fish-eating animals like their crossopterygian ancestors. (The only known living relative of the crossopterygian fishes is the coelacanth.) Only a few of these early amphibians were truly terrestrial forms.

Of the modern amphibians, it is the newts and salamanders that have kept the most fishlike appearance, with elongate bodies, sinuous swimming movements in water and dorsal and ventral fins on the body. Larval and adult newts and salamanders are relatively similar to one another in these respects, and adults frequently possess some larval characteristics.

The anuran frogs and toads all have a characteristic shortened body with no true tail. This dramatic alteration of the primitive, long-bodied amphibian has opened up a wide range of opportunities for new ways of living. In general, the limbs have become more powerful. Jumping and climbing have been developed to a considerable degree in many species, and others have become efficient burrowers. The caecilians (order Apoda) are extraordinary earthwormlike amphibians which are highly adapted for a burrowing life: the skull of the caecilian is solid and bony, the limbs have completely disappeared.

Amphibians as a group demonstrate an interesting range of methods of locomotion, some very fishlike, others more suitable for life on land. Newts and salamanders have two basic forms of movement on land: when in haste, they move much as they do in water, by a sinuous wriggling of the body with little motion of the limbs; when moving more slowly, the body is lifted off the ground and supported on the four limbs, which move in the typical manner of four-legged vertebrates.

Frogs and toads, having lost their swimming tail, possess a completely different means of progression. Double, synchronized kicks of the long back legs are used for swimming in water and hopping and jumping on land. Both frogs and toads can also walk. Several groups of frogs and toads have independently developed rather similar specializations for moving in trees: they have adhesive pads on elongate toes, enabling them to climb in vegetation. The limbless caecilians move by sinuous undulations similar to those of snakes.

Just as locomotion in amphibians is a fascinating amalgam of fishlike and terrestrial attributes, respiration shows a similar intriguing mix of "technologies." Amphibians may possess gills which are externally visible or tucked away inside a flap of skin. In both instances, the gills are developed from the outer skin and are not equivalent to the more internally placed gills of fishes. The gills are used by larval or adult amphibians for gaseous exchange (oxygen in, carbon dioxide out) in water. Amphibians on land use a mixture of two different mechanisms for the same function. Most possess lungs — paired sacs which open ultimately into the mouth cavity. This buccal cavity is used as a pump chamber to pull air in through the nostrils, push it alternately a few times between lungs and mouth and then expel it through the nostrils. The skin of the buccal cavity is itself well supplied with blood vessels and acts as a minor extension of the respiratory surface of the lungs.

In a similar way, the moist scaleless skin of the amphibians is also important for gaseous exchange. Indeed, the vital need of amphibians to keep their bodies moist for respiration is a major constraint on their utilization of habitats. Only rarely are they able to be active in potentially drying conditions. It also limits their size because, as an animal increases in size, its surface area becomes smaller in proportion to its body volume. A large amphibian, therefore, has a correspondingly less adequate area of respiratory skin to provide for its larger body.

Like the reptiles, amphibians operate on a quite different basis of energy balance from that of birds and mammals. The latter two groups maintain a constant high temperature, somewhere between 36°C and 42°C (96.8°F and 107.6°F). Amphibians and reptiles, on the other hand, have body temperatures close to that of the air or water in which they live and gain heat by basking in the sun. They are dependent on external temperature or sunlight for full activity. They can, however, exist on smaller amounts of food than birds and mammals because of the low energy requirements of the cold-blooded condition.

Although two species of newt are known to be parthenogenetic (capable of virgin birth), all other amphibian species include both male and female forms. The females either lay eggs or produce live young. Almost all amphibians must return to water to breed, even those which are otherwise highly adapted to terrestrial conditions. A few species have sidestepped this constraint in extraordinary ways: for example, by providing a sac on the back in which egg development occurs.

In many amphibians, males and females have different appearances. In many frogs and toads, the males move to the water before the females and attract the latter with loud, species-specific calls. When mating, males cling to the backs of the females by means of roughened pads which develop on the hands, and they fertilize the eggs externally as they are expelled. Newts have complex courtship rituals. The males expel their sperm in packets, called spermatophores, which the females pick up in their genital openings (cloacas); the sperm then fertilizes the eggs internally.

Most amphibians pass through a distinctive tadpole larval stage or series of stages after the hatching of the jelly-covered eggs. During this tadpole phase, the larvae are fully aquatic and possess prominent fins; they progressively acquire adult characteristics such as limbs and lungs. In some species of tailed amphibians, sexual maturity is reached at a stage that in other species would be regarded as larval. This process of neoteny, or paedogenesis (breeding as a larva), is partly connected with the effects of the hormone thyroxine, which is involved in larva-adult metamorphosis.

Although less adaptable and complex than the reptiles, birds and mammals, the amphibians in appropriate habitat conditions are clearly able to hold their own against other vertebrates. Due to their extremely low nutrient requirements, they are successful in conditions where food is sparse, seasonal or intermittent in availability.

Salamanders

ORDER URODELA

There are 8 families of salamanders, newts and allies in this order. All have elongate bodies and long tails.

CRYPTOBRANCHIDAE: Giant Salamander Family

This family contains the largest amphibians alive in the world today. Only 3 species are known: the Chinese and Japanese giant salamanders and the hellbender of the eastern USA. The Asiatic giant salamanders can reach lengths of over 1.5 m (5 ft).

NAME: **Hellbender,** *Cryptobranchus alleganiensis*
RANGE: **E. USA: S. New York to N. Alabama, Missouri**
HABITAT: **rocky-bottomed streams**
SIZE: **30.5–74 cm (12–29 in)**

Despite the implications of its common name, this giant salamander is a harmless creature which feeds on crayfish, snails and worms. It has the flattened head characteristic of its family and loose flaps of skin along the lower sides of its body.

A nocturnal salamander, the hellbender hides under rocks in the water during the day. It depends on its senses of smell and touch, rather than on sight, to find its prey, since its eyes are set so far down the sides of its head that it cannot focus on an object with both eyes at once.

Hellbenders breed in autumn: the male makes a hollow beneath a rock or log on the stream bed, and the female lays strings of 200 to 500 eggs. As she lays the eggs, the male fertilizes them and then guards the nest until the eggs hatch 2 or 3 months later.

HYNOBIIDAE: Asiatic Land Salamander Family

The 30 species in this family are considered the most primitive of living salamanders. All occur in central and eastern Asia.

NAME: **Asian Salamander,** *Hynobius stejnegeri*
RANGE: **Japan**
HABITAT: **mountain streams**
SIZE: **14 cm (5½ in)**

Like all members of its family, the Asian salamander's methods of breeding are primitive, involving external fertilization. The female lays her eggs in water in paired sacs, each sac containing 35 to 70 eggs. The male then takes the sacs and fertilizes the eggs but shows no interest in the female.

SALAMANDRIDAE: Newt Family

There are about 42 species of salamander and newt in this family, found in temperate regions of northwest Africa, Europe, Asia and North America. All have well-developed limbs, with four or five digits, and movable eyelids; adults have fully functional lungs and no external gills. There are aquatic and terrestrial forms, but most are found in or near water, at least in the breeding season.

NAME: **Sharp-ribbed Salamander,** *Pleurodeles waltl*
RANGE: **Portugal and Spain (except N. and N.E.), Morocco**
HABITAT: **slow rivers, ponds, ditches**
SIZE: **15–30 cm (6–11¾ in)**

One of the largest European amphibians, the sharp-ribbed salamander has a stout body and a broad, flat head. Its skin is rough, and there is a row of small protuberances which lie at the tips of the ribs along each side; the ribs are often distinct and may even protrude through the skin. A powerful swimmer, this salamander is usually active at night, when it searches for small invertebrate animals to eat.

A courting male carries his mate on his back in the water before depositing his package of sperm on the bottom. He then lowers the female onto the sperm, and she collects it with her reproductive organ and is fertilized internally. She lays her eggs on a submerged stone.

NAME: **Fire Salamander,** *Salamandra salamandra*
RANGE: **central, W. and S. Europe; N.W. Africa; parts of S.W. Asia**
HABITAT: **forest on hills and mountains**
SIZE: **20–28 cm (7¾–11 in)**

A heavily built species with a rather short tail, the fire salamander is characterized by its bright markings, which may be in the form of spots or stripes. These markings provide warning to potential predators of the salamander's unpleasant body secretions, which irritate the mouth and eyes of enemies and may even be fatal to small mammals. The fire salamander prefers moist areas and is seldom far from water. It emerges from daytime refuges to hunt for its invertebrate prey at night.

Fire salamanders mate on land. The male carries the female around on his back, then deposits his sperm package on the ground and lowers her onto it. She collects the sperm with her reproductive organ and is fertilized internally. The eggs develop inside the female's body, and about 10 months after fertilization, she gives birth to 10 to 50 live young in the water.

NAME: **Warty Newt,** *Triturus cristatus*
RANGE: **Europe (not S. and S.W. France, Iberia, Ireland or S. Greece)**
HABITAT: **still or slow water, woodland**
SIZE: **14–18 cm (5½–7 in)**

A large, rough-skinned newt, the male develops a jagged crest on his back in the breeding season; females are often larger than males but do not develop crests. Warty newts feed on aquatic and land-living invertebrates and may also take small fish and other amphibians and their eggs.

The courting male performs an energetic display for his mate and then deposits sperm, over which the female walks or is led, and which she collects with her reproductive organ. She lays 200 to 300 eggs, one at a time, which hatch in 4 or 5 months.

NAME: **Eastern Newt,** *Notophthalmus viridescens*
RANGE: **S.E. Canada, E. USA: Great Lakes area to Florida and Texas**
HABITAT: **ponds and lakes with vegetation, ditches, swamps**
SIZE: **6.5–14 cm (2½–5½ in)**

The eastern newt occurs in several different patterns and colors over its wide range. Adults are aquatic and are eager predators, searching in shallow water for worms, insects, crustaceans and the eggs and young of other amphibians.

The breeding season begins in late winter or early spring. The female lays from 200 to 400 eggs, one at a time, on submerged plants, and after an incubation of up to 2 months, the eggs hatch into larvae. In later summer, these larvae transform into subadults, known as efts (illustrated), and leave the water to spend up to 3 years living on land and feeding primarily on insects. They then return to the water and become mature, fully developed adults.

NAME: **Rough-skinned Newt,** *Taricha granulosa*
RANGE: **western North America: Alaska to California**
HABITAT: **ponds, lakes, slow streams and surrounding grassland or woodland**
SIZE: **6.5–12.5 cm (2½–5 in)**

The most aquatic of Pacific newts, the rough-skinned newt is identified by its warty skin and its small eyes, with dark lower lids. It searches for its invertebrate prey both on land and in the water, and its toxic skin secretions repel most of its enemies.

In the breeding season, the male's skin temporarily becomes smooth and his vent swells. Unlike other western newts, the female rough-skinned lays her eggs one at a time, rather than in masses, on submerged plants or debris. The eggs hatch into aquatic larvae.

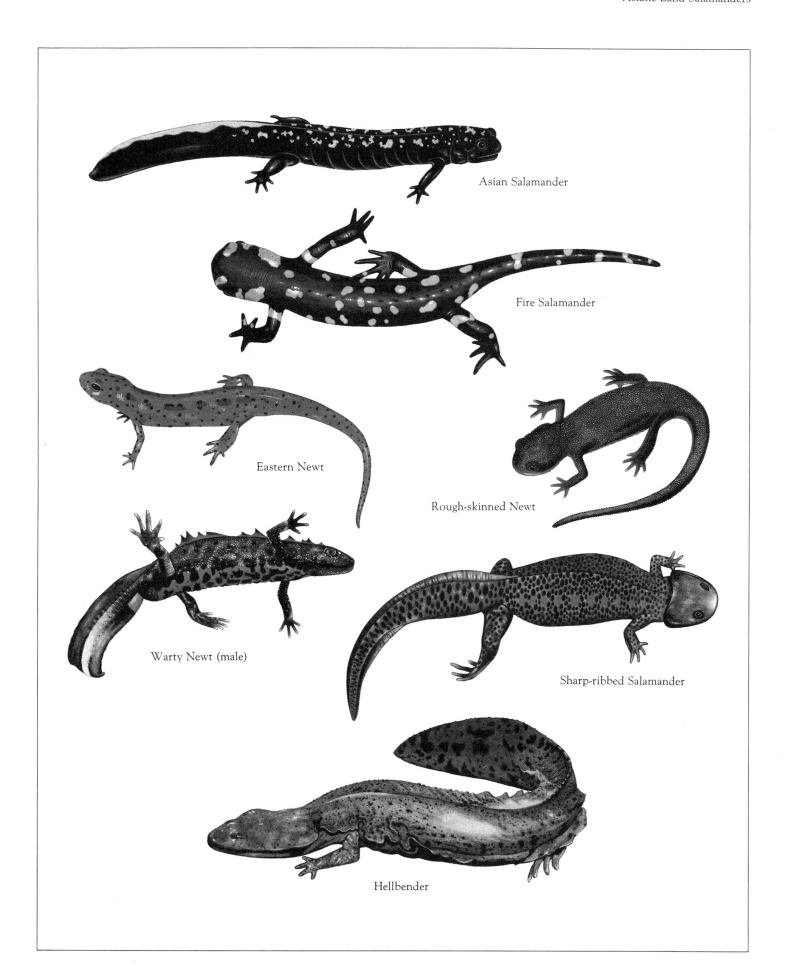

Asian Salamander

Fire Salamander

Eastern Newt

Rough-skinned Newt

Warty Newt (male)

Sharp-ribbed Salamander

Hellbender

Mole Salamanders

NAME: Spotted Salamander, *Ambystoma maculatum*
RANGE: S.E. Canada, E. USA to Georgia and E. Texas
HABITAT: hardwood forest, hillsides near pools
SIZE: 15–24 cm (6–9½ in)

This stout-bodied salamander is identified by the irregular spots on its back, which run from head to tail. Rarely seen, it spends most of its life underground and feeds on slugs and worms.

In early spring, heavy rains stimulate the salamanders to migrate to breeding pools. The female lays about 100 eggs at a time, in a compact mass, which adheres to submerged vegetation in the pond; she may lay more than one such mass. Some 4 to 8 weeks later, the eggs hatch into larvae 1.25 cm (½ in) long, which develop into adult form in 2 to 4 months. Spotted salamanders may live for 20 years.

In some areas, these salamanders are becoming rare because acid rain is polluting their breeding ponds and preventing the successful development of eggs. Acid rain contains dilute sulfuric and nitric acids from the gases released into the atmosphere by the burning of fossil fuels and is a source of increasing anxiety to biologists. In the temporary rain and snow pools used by salamanders for breeding, acidity is often extremely high, causing a high failure rate of eggs and severe deformities in those young that do survive.

NAME: Marbled Salamander, *Ambystoma opacum*
RANGE: E. USA: New Hampshire to Florida, west to Texas
HABITAT: woodland: swamp areas and drier, high ground
SIZE: 9–12.5 cm (3½–5 in)

A dark-colored, stout species, the marbled salamander has some light markings that are the origin of its common name. The male's markings are brighter than the female's; juveniles are dark gray to brown, with light flecks. The salamander emerges at night to hunt for slugs and worms but before morning hides under a log or stone, where it remains for the day.

Marbled salamanders breed from September to December, depending on latitude, and mate and nest on land. The female lays 50 to 200 eggs, one at a time, in a dip on the ground that will later fill with rain. Until the rains come, the salamander curls itself around the eggs to protect them. The larvae hatch a few days after being covered by rain. If there is insufficient rainfall to fill the nest, the eggs may not hatch until the spring. Once hatched, the larvae develop adult form at 4 to 6 months.

AMBYSTOMATIDAE:
Mole Salamander Family

There are about 32 species of mole salamander, all found in North America, from Canada to Mexico. Typically, these salamanders have broad heads and a thick-bodied, sturdy appearance. Many species are ground-living, burrowing animals, rarely seen except in the breeding season, when they migrate to ponds or streams to mate and lay eggs. Others have developed more aquatic habits and live in or near water most of the year. Larvae are aquatic and have feathery external gills and well-developed tail fins.

In most salamanders, the larvae remain permanently in the water, while the adults spend at least part of the time on land. When the larva transforms into a mature, breeding adult, therefore, it loses such features as feathery external gills and the flattened tail, which are only useful in water. The mole salamander family is notable because some species can breed while still living in the water and still retaining these normally larval characteristics. This is known as neotenous breeding. Some geographical races of otherwise normal species are neotenous; for example, western forms of the North American tiger salamander, *Ambystoma tigrinum*, are neotenous, while the eastern relatives are normal.

Insects and small invertebrates are the main foods of all members of the family. Male and female mole salamanders look alike, but males usually have longer tails than females.

NAME: Tiger Salamander, *Ambystoma tigrinum*
RANGE: S. central Canada, central USA, south to N. Florida and Mexico
HABITAT: arid plains, damp meadows, mountain forest
SIZE: 15–40 cm (6–15¾ in)

The world's largest land-dwelling salamander, the tiger salamander has a stout body, broad head and small eyes. Its coloration and pattern vary enormously, and it adapts to a wide variety of habitats, from sea level to 3,350 m (11,000 ft). Tiger salamanders live near water among plant debris or use crayfish or mammal burrows for refuge. They are often active at night, particularly after heavy rain, and feed on earthworms, insects, mice and some small amphibians.

The timing of the breeding season varies according to area, but it is usually prompted by rainfall. The salamanders mate in water, and the female lays her eggs in masses, which then adhere to submerged vegetation or debris.

NAME: Axolotl, *Ambystoma mexicanum*
RANGE: Mexico: principally Lake Xochimilco
HABITAT: permanent water at high altitude
SIZE: up to 29 cm (11½ in) ®

Now rare, the axolotl is threatened by the destruction of its habitat, the introduction of predatory fishes, such as carp, and the collection of specimens for the pet trade. A curious-looking creature, it has a dorsal fin, which extends from the back of its head to the tip and around the underside of its long tail, and three pairs of feathery external gills. Its legs and feet are small and weak.

Axolotls breed in water. The female is attracted to the male by the odor of the secretions of his abdominal glands. He fans his tail in her direction, thus sending the odor through the water. The female approaches and noses the male's glands. He then sheds his sperm in a small packet, known as a spermatophore, which sinks to the bottom of the water. The female settles over it and picks up the sperm packet with her cloaca (the external reproductive chamber) and is thus fertilized internally. In the wild the axolotl lays about 400 eggs, but it may lay thousands in captivity.

The axolotl normally breeds neotenously (in the larval state), retaining its gills and remaining in water. However, some individuals do metamorphose into land-dwelling, gill-less adults.

NAME: Pacific Giant Salamander, *Dicamptodon ensatus*
RANGE: Pacific coast of N. America: British Columbia to California; Idaho, Montana
HABITAT: cool humid forest, rivers, streams and lakes
SIZE: 7–30 cm (2¾–11¾ in)

This smooth-skinned salamander is unusual in that it can make a low-pitched cry — most salamanders are silent. Adults live on land, under logs, rocks and forest debris, and may even climb into trees and bushes. Mainly active at night, they feed on snails, slugs, insects, mice and small snakes, and other salamanders.

In spring, adults breed in water, usually in the headwaters of a spring, and the female lays about 100 eggs on a submerged branch. The larvae live in cold clear lakes or streams; they are highly predatory and cannibalize smaller larvae, as well as feeding on tadpoles and insects. They may mature into adults in their second year or become sexually mature (neotenic) larvae when about 20 cm (7¾ in) long.

Spotted Salamander

Tiger Salamander

Marbled Salamander

Pacific Giant Salamander

Axolotl

Amphiumas, Olm and Mudpuppies, Sirens

AMPHIUMIDAE:
Amphiuma Family

The 3 species of elongate, eel-like creatures in this family are among the world's largest aquatic salamanders; they are all found in the southeastern USA. They have cylindrical bodies and tiny hind and forelimbs, each with one, two or three toes. These limbs are so small that it is doubtful whether they are of any use for locomotion. The skin of these amphibians is smooth and slippery.

Until 1950 there were thought to be only 2 species in this family, but a third species, the one-toed amphiuma, *Amphiuma pholeter*, was then discovered.

NAME: Two-toed Amphiuma,
Amphiuma means
RANGE: USA: S.E. Virginia to Florida,
E. Louisiana
HABITAT: swamps, bayous, drainage
ditches
SIZE: 45 cm–1.2 m (17¾ in–4 ft)

This aquatic salamander has tiny, virtually useless limbs, each with two toes. Mainly active at night, it hunts in water for crayfish, frogs, small snakes and fish and may come onto land in extremely wet weather. It takes refuge during the day in a burrow it digs in the mud or takes over the burrow of another creature.

Two-toed amphiumas mate in water, and the female lays about 200 eggs in a beadlike string. The female coils around the eggs as they lie on the bottom and protects them until they hatch about 5 months after being laid. When the larvae hatch, they are about 5 cm (2 in) long; their tiny limbs are of more use to them at this stage than when they metamorphose to adult form, at about 7.5 cm (3 in) long. The three-toed amphiuma, *Amphiuma tridactylum*, also found in the southern USA, is similar in appearance and habits but has three toes on each of its tiny limbs.

PROTEIDAE:
Olm and Mudpuppy Family

There are 5 species of stream- and lake-dwelling mudpuppies in North America and 1 species of cave-dwelling olm in Europe. Because these amphibians live permanently in the water, they retain the external feathery gills throughout their lives, even into the adult breeding shape. They, therefore, resemble the larvae of other amphibians that do lose their gills when they become adult and leave water for at least part of the time.

NAME: Olm, *Proteus anguinus*
RANGE: Yugoslavia: E. Adriatic coast;
N.E. Italy
HABITAT: streams and lakes in
underground limestone caves
SIZE: 20–30 cm (7¾–11¾ in)   Ⓥ

The olm is a large aquatic salamander with a pale cylindrical body and red feathery gills. Its tail is flattened and its limbs weak and poorly developed. It has three toes on the forelimbs and two on the hind limbs. It lives in total darkness in its cave home and is virtually blind, its eyes hidden beneath the skin. It feeds on small aquatic worms and crustaceans.

The female olm lays 12 to 70 eggs at a time; the eggs are deposited under a stone and guarded by both parents. They hatch in about 90 days. Some females may reproduce in a different manner, retaining a small number of eggs inside the body and giving birth to 2 fully developed young. The young are miniature versions of the parents but have rudimentary eyes.

Once a common species, the olm is now becoming rare because of water pollution in its restricted habitat and the taking of large numbers for the pet trade.

NAME: Mudpuppy, *Necturus maculosus*
RANGE: S. Canada: Manitoba to Quebec;
USA: Great Lakes, south to Georgia
and Louisiana
HABITAT: lakes, rivers, streams
SIZE: 20–43 cm (7¾–17 in)

An aquatic salamander, the mudpuppy inhabits a variety of freshwater habitats, from muddy, sluggish shallows to cold, clear water. It has four toes on each limb and a flattened tail. Its feathery gills vary in size according to the water the individual inhabits: mudpuppies in cold, well-oxygenated water have shorter gills than those in warm, muddy, poorly oxygenated water, which need large, bushy gills to collect all the available oxygen. The mudpuppy hunts worms, crayfish, insects and small fish, mainly at night, but may sometimes catch fish during the day.

The breeding season is from April to June. The female lays 30 to 190 eggs, each of which adheres separately to a log or rock. The male guards the eggs until they hatch some 5 to 9 weeks later. The larvae do not mature until they are 4 to 6 years old.

SIRENIDAE: Siren Family

The 3 species of sirens are aquatic salamanders which retain feathery external gills throughout life. Their bodies are long and eel-like, and they have tiny forelimbs and no hind limbs. All species occur in the USA and northern Mexico.

Sirens swim by powerful undulations of the body and forage among water weeds for food; they are active at night. They breathe by means of external gills, positioned at each side of the neck.

NAME: Dwarf Siren, *Pseudobranchus*
striatus
RANGE: USA: coastal plain of
South Carolina, Georgia, Florida
HABITAT: ponds, swamps, ditches
SIZE: 10–25 cm (4–9¾ in)

The smallest of its family, the dwarf siren is a slender, eel-like creature which lives among dense, submerged vegetation. It has no hind limbs and only tiny forelimbs, with three toes on each foot. The external gills are retained throughout life. A nocturnal creature, the siren feeds on the tiny invertebrate animals it finds among the plant debris near the bottom of the water. If its habitat is in danger of drying up, as in a drought, the siren can burrow into the mud and remain there, dormant, for up to 2 months. Mucus produced by skin glands prevents the body drying out during such a period.

The female lays her eggs, one at a time, on aquatic plants, and the larvae hatch out about 4 weeks later. There are about 5 races of dwarf siren over the range, which vary in coloration and in the shade and distribution of the stripes along the sides of the body.

NAME: Greater Siren, *Siren lacertina*
RANGE: USA: coastal plain from Virginia
to Florida, S. Alabama
HABITAT: shallow, muddy fresh water
with plenty of vegetation
SIZE: 50–97.5 cm (19¾–38¼ in)

The stout-bodied greater siren has permanent external gills and a flattened tail. There are four toes on each of its front feet. During the day, it hides under rocks or plant debris or burrows into the muddy bottom, emerging at night to feed on snails, insect larvae, small fish and some aquatic plants. In drought conditions, the siren undergoes a period of dormancy; it seals itself in a cocoon made from secretions of the skin glands and buries itself in the muddy bottom until the dry spell is ended.

These sirens breed in February or March, laying eggs that hatch 2 or 3 months later into larvae, which are about 1.25 cm (½ in) long.

Dwarf Siren

Olm

Two-toed Amphiuma

Mudpuppy

Greater Siren

Lungless Salamanders

NAME: Texas Blind Salamander,
Typhlomolge rathbuni
RANGE: USA: extreme S. Texas
**HABITAT: underground waters of the
   creek system**
SIZE: 9–13.5 cm (3½–5¼ in)   Ⓔ

A rare species with an extremely restricted distribution, the Texas blind salamander is a typical cave-dweller, with its ghostly pale body and much-reduced eyes. Its external gills are red and feathery and it has long thin legs.

Many bats roost in the caves that are the only entrance to the salamander's habitat. Nutrients in the droppings (guano) of these bats provide food for the invertebrate animals that inhabit the caves, and these creatures, many of which are unique, are in turn eaten by the salamanders.

Nothing is known at present about the breeding habits of this salamander.

NAME: Red-backed Salamander,
Plethodon cinereus
**RANGE: S.E. Canada, N.E. USA, south to
   North Carolina, S. Indiana**
HABITAT: cool, moist forest
SIZE: 6.5–12.5 cm (2½–5 in)

This abundant, widespread salamander lives its whole life on land. The "red back" of its common name is, in fact, a stripe, which may vary greatly from red to gray or yellow; some forms have gray bodies and lack the stripe altogether. A nocturnal creature, it hides during the day under stones or forest litter and emerges at night to search for insects and small invertebrates.

Breeding takes place every other year. The salamanders court and mate during the winter, and in June or July the female lays her 6 to 12 eggs, which hang in a cluster in a crevice, under a rock or in a rotten log. She coils herself around the eggs and protects them until they hatch 8 or 9 weeks later. The larvae do not have an aquatic stage and take 2 years to reach maturity.

NAME: Slimy Salamander, *Plethodon
   glutinosus*
**RANGE: E. and S.E. USA: New York to
   Florida, Missouri, Oklahoma**
HABITAT: floodplains, cave entrances
SIZE: 11.5–20.5 cm (4½–8 in)

A land-dwelling species, the slimy salamander's skin exudes a sticky substance that may have protective properties. By day, it shelters under rocks or logs or in a burrow, but at night, particularly after rain, it searches the forest floor for invertebrate prey.

Southern females breed every year, and northern females only every other year, laying 6 to 36 eggs in a burrow or in a rotten log and guarding them while they develop.

PLETHODONTIDAE:
Lungless Salamander Family

This, the most successful group of living salamanders, includes some 200 of the 300 or so known tailed amphibians. As their name suggests, these salamanders are primarily characterized by their total absence of lungs. The pulmonary artery, which would normally take blood to the lungs, is reduced to minute proportions in a lungless salamander and runs in the body wall. The animal obtains oxygen across its moist skin or through the internal surface of the mouth cavity, both of which are well supplied with blood vessels.

Nearly all lungless salamanders live in North or South America. Two species occur in Europe: the cave salamanders, found in Sardinia and mainland Italy. These forms can be distinguished from all other European salamanders by their partially webbed toes.

NAME: Spring Salamander, *Gyrinophilus
   porphyriticus*
**RANGE: S. Canada: Quebec; USA: Maine,
   to Georgia, Mississippi**
**HABITAT: wet caves, cool clear mountain
   springs**
SIZE: 10–22 cm (4–8¾ in)

The spring salamander is one of the largest species in its family and occurs in several races, with variations of color and pattern. It spends most of its life in water but on rainy nights may come onto land to search for food. Large insects, worms and other salamanders are its main prey.

In July or August, the female spring salamander lays 20 to 60 eggs, which are attached singly to the undersurfaces of submerged rocks. She guards the eggs for 3 months until they hatch. Larvae do not attain adult form and coloration for about 3 years.

NAME: Red Salamander, *Pseudotriton
   ruber*
**RANGE: E. USA: S. New York, west to
   Indiana, south to Louisiana**
**HABITAT: springs, surrounding
   woodland, swamps, meadows**
SIZE: 9.5–18 cm (3¾–7 in)

A brilliantly colored species, the red salamander has a stout body and short tail and legs. It spends much of its life on land, usually in the vicinity of water. Earthworms, insects and small salamanders are its main foods.

After courting and mating in summer, the female red salamander lays 50 to 100 eggs in autumn. The larvae hatch in about 2 months and transform into adult form some 2 years later. Females first breed when 5 years old.

NAME: Yellow-blotched Ensatina,
Ensatina eschscholtzi croceator
RANGE: USA: California
HABITAT: moist forest, canyons
SIZE: 7.5–15 cm (3–6 in)

The yellow-blotched is one of several subspecies of *Ensatina* with a wide variety of colors and patterns. All have the distinguishing feature of a tail which is constricted at its base. The male usually has a longer tail than the female. A land-dwelling species, it shelters under rocks and logs, making forays in search of spiders and large insects such as beetles and crickets.

The female lays from 7 to 25 eggs in spring or early summer in a burrow or rotting log. She guards the eggs while they develop. The larvae live on land and do not have an aquatic phase; they are mature at 2 to 3 years old.

NAME: Dusky Salamander,
Desmognathus fuscus
**RANGE: S. Canada; N.E. USA, south to
   Louisiana**
**HABITAT: springs, woodland creeks,
   floodplains**
SIZE: 6.5–14 cm (2½–5½ in)

Young dusky salamanders have pairs of yellow or red spots on the back, but as they mature, these fade or become obscured. The dusky salamander can jump well when alarmed, leaping several times its own length to escape an enemy. It feeds mainly on insect larvae and earthworms.

In summer, the female lays 12 to 36 eggs in a cluster near water, usually under a rock or log. The larvae hatch in 2 to 3 months and reach maturity in 3 to 4 years.

NAME: California Slender Salamander,
Batrachoseps attenuatus
**RANGE: USA: S.W. Oregon, California,
   western slopes of Sierra Nevada**
**HABITAT: redwood forest, grassland,
   mountains and foothills**
SIZE: 7.5–14 cm (3–5½ in)

True to its name, this salamander has a slim, elongate body and tail. Its legs and feet are tiny and narrow, with four toes on each foot. Coloration varies with area. The most common California salamander, it lives on land and moves with undulating movements of its body, rather than by using its limbs. During the day, it hides in damp vegetation or among tree roots; it emerges at night to hunt for worms and spiders and other invertebrate prey. It is particularly active in rainy periods.

In late autumn or winter, stimulated by rainfall, the female lays 4 to 21 eggs under a rock or log. The eggs hatch in spring and the larvae do not undergo an aquatic phase.

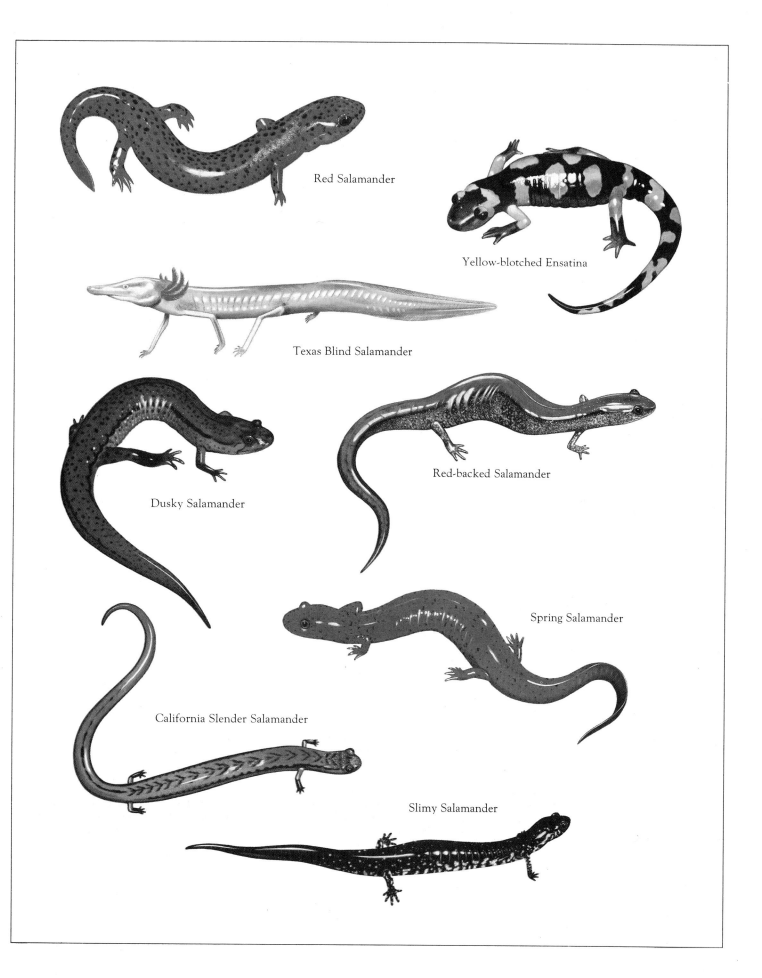

Red Salamander

Yellow-blotched Ensatina

Texas Blind Salamander

Dusky Salamander

Red-backed Salamander

Spring Salamander

California Slender Salamander

Slimy Salamander

Caecilians

ORDER APODA

This order contains 4 families of caecilians, over 150 species in all. Caecilians are limbless amphibians with cylindrical, ringed bodies; they resemble giant earthworms. One family is aquatic, but the others are blind, burrowing creatures, rarely seen above ground. They burrow into the rich, soft soil of tropical or warm temperate forests in search of their prey, usually earthworms, insects and other invertebrates. Adults have a sensory tentacle beneath each eye that is probably used for finding prey. Many species have small scales embedded in the surface of the skin. This is probably a primitive feature, which all other amphibian groups have since lost.

CAECILIIDAE: Caecilian Family

There are 106 species in this family, all of which are land-dwelling burrowers. Many species have scales on the body. Females reproduce either by laying eggs, which develop and hatch outside the body, or by producing eggs which are retained to develop and hatch inside the body and are then born as live young. The young have external gills and may spend some time as free-swimming larvae. Species occur in Old and New World tropics.

NAME: Panamanian Caecilian, *Caecilia ochrocephala*
RANGE: Central and South America: E. Panama, N. Colombia
HABITAT: forest
SIZE: up to 61 cm (24 in)

The Panamanian caecilian has a small, slender head and a wedge-shaped snout. It burrows into soft, usually moist earth and seldom appears above ground except when heavy rains flush it from its burrow. It feeds mainly on insects and earthworms. Snakes often enter the burrows of these caecilians and devour them.

Little is known of the breeding habits of this rarely seen creature, but females are thought to lay eggs, which then develop and hatch outside the body.

NAME: South American Caecilian, *Siphonops annulatus*
RANGE: South America, east of Andes to Argentina
HABITAT: varied, often forest
SIZE: 35 cm (13¾ in)

This widespread caecilian has a short, thick body and no scales. It spends most of its life underground and feeds largely on earthworms. The female lays eggs, but it is not known whether the young pass through a larval stage.

NAME: São Tomé Caecilian, *Schistometopum thomensis*
RANGE: São Tomé Island in Gulf of Guinea, off W. Africa
HABITAT: forest
SIZE: up to 30.5 cm (12 in)

The body of this brightly colored caecilian is usually about 1.25 cm (½ in) in diameter. Its snout is rounded and it has no tail. Like all caecilians, it lives underground, feeding on whatever invertebrate prey it can find, mainly on insects and worms. The female retains her eggs in her body, where they develop and hatch; the young are then born in an advanced state of development.

NAME: Seychelles Caecilian, *Hypogeophis rostratus*
RANGE: Seychelles
HABITAT: swampy coastal regions
SIZE: 20 cm (7¾ in)

The Seychelles caecilian has a slightly flattened body which tapers at both ends. The body color darkens as the caecilian matures. It will burrow wherever the soil is moist and often lives beneath rocks or logs or even digs into rotting trees. It feeds on small invertebrates and on frogs such as *Sooglossus sechellensis*.

Mating takes place at any time of year when there is plenty of rain. The female lays 6 to 30 eggs, which are large and rich in yolk, and coils her body around them to guard them while they develop. The young do not pass through a larval stage but hatch as miniature adults.

ICHTHYOPHIDAE

There are 43 species in this family of terrestrial caecilians, found in Southeast Asia, Central America and tropical South America. They have short tails and scales on the body.

NAME: Sticky Caecilian, *Ichthyophis* sp.
RANGE: S.E. Asia
HABITAT: forest
SIZE: up to 38 cm (15 in)

Adult caecilians of this Southeast Asian genus live in burrows and feed on earthworms and small burrowing snakes. They breed in the spring. The female lays 20 or more eggs in a burrow she makes in moist ground near water. She coils around her eggs while they develop, so as to protect them from predators. As they incubate, the eggs absorb moisture and gradually swell until they are double their original size. On hatching, the larva is four times the weight of a newly laid egg and has a pair of breathing pores on its head. The larvae undergo a prolonged aquatic phase before becoming land-based adults.

TYPHLONECTIDAE

There are 18 species of aquatic caecilian in this family, all found in tropical South America. They live in freshwater streams and ponds, and although they have no tails, the end of the body is laterally flattened for propulsion in water. Caecilians of this family lack primitive body scales.

NAME: *Typhlonectes compressicauda*
RANGE: Guyana, Suriname, French Guiana, Brazil
HABITAT: rivers, streams, pools
SIZE: 52 cm (20½ in)

Typical of its family, this aquatic caecilian swims with eel-like movements of its laterally compressed tail. Like all caecilians, male and female look similar, but the male has a protrusible copulatory organ with which he fertilizes his mate internally. The female retains her eggs inside her body while the young develop.

Having eaten all the yolk that surrounds them in their eggs, the young hatch and distribute themselves along the mother's oviduct. They feed on cells and drops of oil from the uterine wall, which they obtain with the rasping plates in their mouths. More nutrients are obtained through the thin, delicate skin that the young possess at this stage; they also have broad, baglike, external gills, which disappear before they hatch. Once further development has taken place, the young are born; their thin skin is replaced by firmer, stronger skin, and the rasping plates by teeth.

SCOLECOMORPHIDAE

The 6 species of caecilian in this family are all of the same genus and occur only in central Africa. They are tailless and have no primitive body scales. All species live on land in burrows.

NAME: *Scolecomorphus kirkii*
RANGE: Africa: Tanzania, Malawi, Zambia
HABITAT: mountain forest
SIZE: up to 41 cm (16¼ in)

This caecilian lives in burrows it digs under the leaf mold on the forest floor. Unlike other caecilians, it does not even come to the surface after rain. Termites and worms are its main foods.

Little is known of the breeding habits of this family. The male has a protrusible copulatory organ, and the female probably retains her eggs, which then develop inside her body like those of the *Typhlonectes* species and hatch in an advanced state of development.

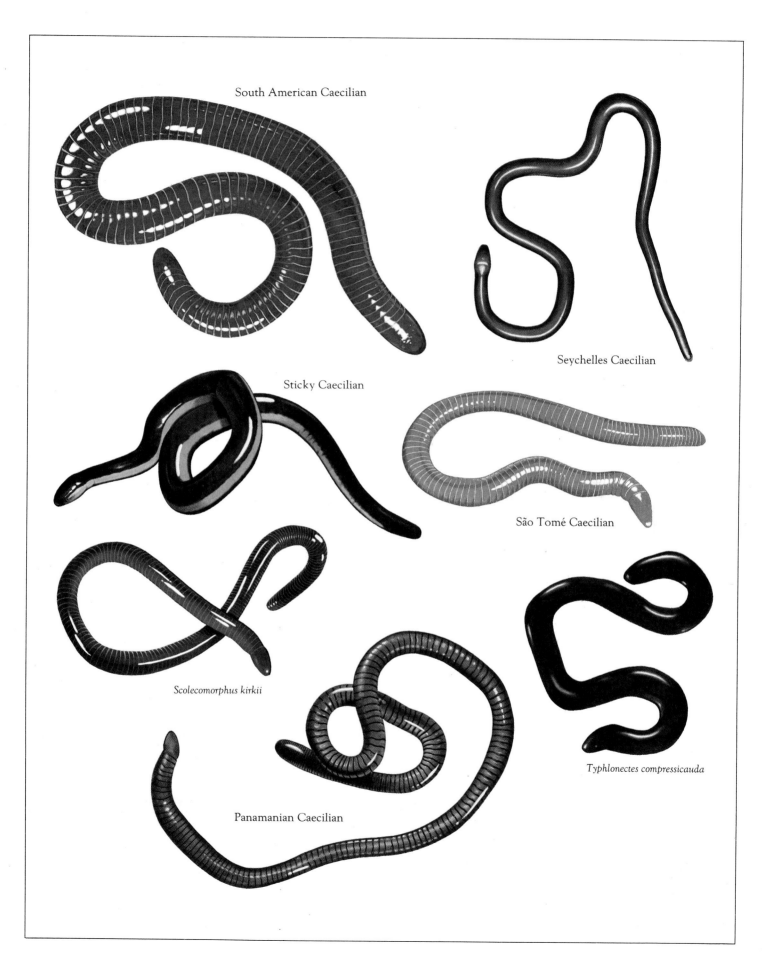

South American Caecilian

Seychelles Caecilian

Sticky Caecilian

São Tomé Caecilian

Scolecomorphus kirkii

Typhlonectes compressicauda

Panamanian Caecilian

Mexican Burrowing Toad, Pipid Frogs, Narrow-mouthed Frogs

ORDER ANURA

There are over 2,500 species of frog and toad, but all are similar in appearance, whatever their habits. As adults they are tailless and have well-developed limbs. Most breed in water, laying eggs which hatch into tailed tadpoles. The tadpoles live in water, feeding on vegetation, and later change to adult form.

The word "frog" was originally used only for members of the family Ranidae, and the word "toad" for members of the family Bufonidae. However, the two words are also used indiscriminately for members of other families, so there is now no taxonomic implication in their use.

RHINOPHRYNIDAE:
Mexican Burrowing Toad Family

The single species in this family, the Mexican burrowing toad is highly specialized for a burrowing existence. It enters water only to breed.

NAME: **Mexican Burrowing Toad,** *Rhinophrynus dorsalis*
RANGE: **Mexico, Guatemala**
HABITAT: **woodland**
SIZE: **6.5 cm (2½ in)**

This unusual frog, equipped with horny, shovel-like appendages on its feet, is an expert burrower. At night, it emerges from its burrow to hunt for termites, which it licks up with its tongue.

When courting, the male frog makes guttural calls to attract a female. They mate in water; he clings to her back and, as she lays her eggs, fertilizes them. The tadpoles have sensory barbels around their mouths and lack the true lips possessed by most other tadpoles.

PIPIDAE: Pipid Frog Family

There are 20 or more species of highly aquatic frogs in this family, found in Central and South America and in Africa, south of the Sahara. All have powerful hind limbs and large, webbed hind feet but only small forelimbs and feet. As they swim, these forelimbs are held out in front of the head, with the fingers spread as sensory probes, to search for food items.

NAME: **Surinam Toad,** *Pipa pipa*
RANGE: **N. South America**
HABITAT: **streams, rivers**
SIZE: **12–20 cm (4¾–7¾ in)**

This active, strong-swimming toad is a voracious predator and will eat almost anything it can find with its slender, tactile fingers, even carrion.

At the beginning of the Surinam toad's extraordinary mating ritual, the male clasps the female from the back, around her hind legs; this stimulates the skin on her back to swell. The clasped pair somersault through the water, and as they flip over, the female lays 3 to 10 eggs on the male's belly. He fertilizes the eggs and, still somersaulting, pushes them onto the female's back. This procedure is repeated until 40 to 100 eggs are laid. The eggs are enveloped in the swollen skin of the female's back, each in its own separate cell. Some 2 to 4 months later, they hatch into fully formed miniature toads.

NAME: **African Clawed Toad,** *Xenopus laevis*
RANGE: **South Africa**
HABITAT: **ponds, lakes**
SIZE: **6.5–12.5 cm (2½–5 in)**

This streamlined toad is as fast and agile in water as any fish and is even able to move backward. It can change its coloration from black to gray to mottled to match its background. The four digits on its forelimbs are tipped with claws, which it uses to forage in the mud for food, and it consumes any animal matter, even its own tadpoles.

The toads mate in water, the male making a soft buzzing sound underwater to attract the female. The eggs, each enclosed in jelly, attach to submerged plants and hatch after 7 days.

MICROHYLIDAE:
Narrow-mouthed Frog Family

There are 300 or more species of burrowing, terrestrial and tree-living frogs in this family, found in tropical regions all over the world and extending into temperate areas in North and South America. Tree-living forms are equipped with adhesive pads on fingers and toes to aid climbing.

NAME: **Sheep Frog,** *Hypopachus variolosus*
RANGE: **USA: S.E. Texas; Mexico**
HABITAT: **margins of damp areas**
SIZE: **2.5–4.5 cm (1–1¾ in)**

A small, stout frog with a pointed snout, the sheep frog is a nocturnal species which hides during the day under rocks or debris or in a rodent burrow; at night, it emerges to feed on ants and termites.

Sheep frogs mate at any time of year when stimulated by sufficient rainfall. The male attracts the female to the breeding pond by making his bleating call — the origin of the common name. He clasps the female's body, and her sticky body secretions help the pair to stay together while they lay and fertilize about 700 eggs.

NAME: **Eastern Narrow-mouthed Frog,** *Gastrophryne carolinensis*
RANGE: **S.E. USA: Missouri and Maryland, south to Florida, Gulf Coast and Texas**
HABITAT: **by ponds and ditches; under moist vegetation**
SIZE: **2–4 cm (¾–1½ in)**

An excellent burrower, this small, smooth-skinned frog can disappear into the soil in a moment. It rests in a burrow during the day and comes out at night to hunt for its insect food, mainly ants.

Breeding is stimulated by rainfall, sometime between April and October. The dark-throated male calls to the female, usually from water, and continues to call as they mate. The eggs float on the water surface for 3 days and then hatch into tadpoles.

NAME: **South African Rain Frog,** *Breviceps adspersus*
RANGE: **South Africa, Namibia, Botswana, Zimbabwe**
HABITAT: **savanna**
SIZE: **3 cm (1¼ in)**

An extremely rotund frog, the South African rain frog has a short snout and small, sturdy limbs. Its back is covered with warty protuberances and coloration and pattern are variable. It burrows well, using its hind feet, and seldom emerges above ground except during rain. It feeds on insects and small invertebrates.

The courting male makes a repeated croaking chirp to attract his mate. They mate in a burrow, held together by sticky body secretions. The few eggs are enclosed in thick jelly and lie in a compact mass in the burrow while they develop. There is no tadpole stage; metamorphosis takes place within the egg capsules, and the young hatch as miniature, land-living frogs.

NAME: **Termite Frog,** *Phrynomerus bifasciatus*
RANGE: **Africa, south of the Sahara**
HABITAT: **savanna**
SIZE: **5 cm (2 in)**

The termite frog has a more elongate body than most members of its family and an unusually mobile head. Its distinctive markings warn of its toxic skin, which contains substances which irritate the skin and mucous membranes of predators. A land-dwelling frog, it may climb up tree stumps and rocks or burrow in search of prey or to shelter from dry weather. Termites and ants are its main foods.

Breeding takes place in shallow pools. The small, jelly-coated eggs are laid in masses and attach to submerged plants or lie at the bottom of the water. They hatch into aquatic tadpoles.

African Clawed Toad

Mexican Burrowing Toad

Eastern Narrow-mouthed Frog

Surinam Toad

South African Rain Frog

Termite Frog

Sheep Frog

Discoglossid Frogs, Tailed Frogs, Spadefoot Toads

DISCOGLOSSIDAE:
Discoglossid Frog Family

The 12 species in this family include the fire-bellied toads, painted frogs and midwife toads, all of which live in the Old World — in Europe, North Africa and parts of Asia. They are characterized by their disk-shaped tongues, which are entirely joined to the floor of the mouth and cannot be flipped forward to capture prey. Most frogs have tongues which are fixed only at the front, leaving the back free to be swiftly flipped over and protruded.

NAME: **Midwife Toad,** *Alytes obstetricans*
RANGE: **W. Europe, south to Alps, Spain and Portugal**
HABITAT: **woodland, cultivated land**
SIZE: **up to 5 cm (2 in)**

The small, plump midwife toad varies in coloration from gray to olive-green or brown, often with darker markings. A nocturnal, land-dwelling animal, it hides by day in crevices in walls or quarries or under logs. Some individuals live in burrows, which they dig with their strong forelimbs. Midwife toads feed on insects and small invertebrates.

The midwife toad is best known for its unusual breeding habits. The toads mate on land at night, the male clasping the female as she lays strings of up to 60 eggs. Once he has fertilized the eggs, he inserts his hind legs among them and twists the strings of eggs around his legs. He carries the eggs in this way while they develop, taking care that they do not dry out and moistening them at intervals in pools. After 18 to 49 days, depending on the temperature, the male deposits his eggs in shallow water, where they hatch into tadpoles.

NAME: **Oriental Fire-bellied Toad,** *Bombina orientalis*
RANGE: **Siberia, N.E. China, Korea**
HABITAT: **mountain streams, rice fields**
SIZE: **5 cm (2 in)**

A brilliantly colored species, the oriental fire-bellied toad's rough skin exudes a milky secretion, which is extremely irritating to the mouths and eyes of predators.

The female toad lays her eggs on the underside of submerged stones in small clumps, each containing 2 to 8 eggs.

ASCAPHIDAE: Tailed Frog Family

There are only 4 species in this family, 3 in New Zealand and 1 in North America. Despite their name, they do not have true tails, but all possess tail-wagging muscles.

NAME: **Hochstetter's Frog,** *Leiopelma hochstetteri*
RANGE: **New Zealand**
HABITAT: **mountains, mountain streams**
SIZE: **4.5 cm (1¾ in)**

The 3 species in the genus *Leiopelma* are the only native frogs in New Zealand, and all are now rare and rigorously protected. Other frogs on the islands are introduced species.

First discovered in 1852, Hochstetter's frog is a robust species with partially webbed hind feet. Although it usually lives in or near water, it has also been found in mountain country some distance from streams. Like its relatives, it is nocturnal and feeds on beetles, ants, earthworms, spiders and slugs.

The breeding habits of this frog are probably an adaptation to its habitat. Groups of 2 to 8 eggs are laid on moist earth under logs or stones, or in tunnels left by dragonfly nymphs. Each egg is surrounded by a water-filled gelatinous capsule, and within this capsule, the embryo passes through all the tadpole stages until it hatches out as a tiny tailed froglet, about 40 days after laying. The tail is resorbed about a month later.

NAME: **Tailed Frog,** *Ascaphus truei,*
RANGE: **Pacific coast of N. America**
HABITAT: **mountain streams, damp forest**
SIZE: **2.5–5 cm (1–2 in)**

The male tailed frog has a unique tail-like structure, which is, in fact, a copulatory organ for internal fertilization of the female. He clasps the female around the waist and deposits sperm directly into her cloaca. She then lays her eggs in a stream, where they attach to rocks. When the tadpoles hatch, they will cling to rocks or any other object with their strong, sucking mouthparts, to avoid being swept away by strong currents. The tadpoles feed on tiny plants and animals and metamorphose to adult form in 1 to 3 years.

PELOBATIDAE:
Spadefoot Toad Family

The 54 species of spadefoot toad are found in North America, Europe, North Africa and southern Asia. Many are highly terrestrial and nocturnal, spending their days in underground burrows. They are known as spadefoots because of the horny tubercle, found on the inner edge of each hind foot, which is used as a digging tool.

Spadefoots breed rapidly after rains, in temporary rainpools. Because the pools will soon dry up, development must be accelerated, and eggs may hatch, pass though the tadpole stage and metamorphose in 2 weeks.

NAME: **European Spadefoot,** *Pelobates fuscus*
RANGE: **W., central and E. Europe to W. Asia**
HABITAT: **sandy soil, cultivated land**
SIZE: **up to 8 cm (3¼ in)**

The plump European spadefoot has a large, pale spade on each webbed hind foot. Males are usually smaller than females and have raised oval glands on their upper forelimbs. Like most spadefoots, this species is nocturnal outside the breeding season.

In the breeding season, however, spadefoots may be active during the day. They breed once a year in spring, usually in deep pools or in ditches. Spadefoots do not develop the rough nuptial pads that males of many other families have to help them grasp their mates, but they still manage to clasp the females and fertilize the eggs as they are laid.

NAME: **Western Spadefoot,** *Scaphiopus hammondi*
RANGE: **W. USA: California, Arizona, New Mexico; Mexico**
HABITAT: **varied: plains, sandy areas**
SIZE: **3.5–6.5 cm (1¼–2½ in)**

An expert burrower, the western spadefoot has a wedge-shaped spade on each hind foot. It is a nocturnal toad and spends the day in its burrow in conditions of moderate temperature and humidity, despite the arid heat typical of much of its range.

Temporary rainpools are used for breeding, any time between January and August, depending on rainfall. The eggs are laid in round clumps, which attach to vegetation and hatch only 2 days later. Since development must be completed before the temporary pool dries up, metamorphosis from tadpole to adult form takes place in under 6 weeks.

NAME: **Parsley Frog,** *Pelodytes punctatus*
RANGE: **Europe: Spain, Portugal, France, W. Belgium, N. Italy**
HABITAT: **various damp areas**
SIZE: **up to 5 cm (2 in)**

A nocturnal, mainly terrestrial creature outside the breeding season, the parsley frog is often found among vegetation near streams or by walls. It is a small, active frog with warty skin and virtually unwebbed hind feet. Parsley frogs climb, swim and jump well and can dig shallow burrows, despite the fact that they lack the spadelike hind foot appendages characteristic of the family.

Parsley frogs mate in spring and may breed more than once a season. Bands of eggs, held together by a thick gelatinous substance, twine around submerged vegetation, where they remain until they hatch into tadpoles.

Hochstetter's Frog

Oriental Fire-bellied Toad

European Spadefoot

Tailed Frog

Parsley Frog

Midwife Toad
(male with eggs)

Western Spadefoot

Myobatrachid Frogs, Ghost Frogs, Leptodactylid Frogs, Mouth-brooding Frog

MYOBATRACHIDAE:
Myobatrachid Frog Family
The species in this small family of frogs appear to have affinities with the bufonid toads and were previously classified with them. Members of the family tend to walk rather awkwardly on the tips of their toes.

NAME: **Corroboree Frog, *Pseudophryne corroboree***
RANGE: **Australia: Victoria, New South Wales**
HABITAT: **mountain forest, grassy marshland**
SIZE: **3 cm (1¼ in)**
A most distinctive species, the corroboree frog has a bright yellow body patterned with irregular black stripes. It lives on land but near water, often at altitudes of more than 1,500 m (5,000 ft), and shelters under logs or in a burrow, which it digs itself.

In summer, the frogs seek out sphagnum bogs, where they dig nesting burrows. Up to 12 large eggs are laid in a burrow, and one parent usually remains with the eggs while they develop. The tadpoles remain in the eggs until there is sufficient rainfall to wash them into a creek, where they hatch at once.

NAME: ***Cyclorana cultripes***
RANGE: **Australia: N. coasts, Western Australia to Queensland**
HABITAT: **underground**
SIZE: **5 cm (2 in)**
This burrowing frog emerges above ground only to breed and to find some of its food — mostly insects and larvae. It has a strong, fairly stout body with warty skin and irregular dark patches on its back.

It breeds after heavy summer rain storms, often in temporary ponds or swollen creeks. The eggs are laid in the water, where they attach to submerged plants until they hatch into fat tadpoles with pointed snouts and deep tail fins.

HELEOPHRYNIDAE:
Ghost Frog Family
Ghost frogs are so called not because of any spectral appearance but because a species was discovered in Skeleton Gorge in South Africa. About 3 or 4 species are known, all found in southern Africa in swift mountain streams. They are long-limbed frogs with flattened bodies, enabling them to squeeze into narrow rock crevices, and expanded digits with which to grip slippery surfaces.

NAME: **Natal Ghost Frog, *Heleophryne natalensis***
RANGE: **N.E. South Africa**
HABITAT: **forest streams**
SIZE: **up to 5 cm (2 in)**
A nocturnal species, the ghost frog takes refuge by day among rocks and pebbles or in crevices, concealed by its mottled, speckled coloration.

In the breeding season, male frogs develop nuptial pads on the forelimbs and small spines on the fingers and armpits for grasping their mates. The eggs are laid in a pool or even out of the water on wet gravel. Once hatched, tadpoles move to fast-flowing streams, where they can withstand the strong currents by holding onto stones with their suckerlike mouths.

LEPTODACTYLIDAE:
Leptodactylid Frog Family
This is a large and varied family with several hundred species, found mainly in Central and South America, Africa and Australia. Their anatomy is similar to that of the true treefrogs (Hylidae), but although the Leptodactylid frogs may have adhesive disks on the digits, they lack the internal structure which makes the treefrogs' digits so flexible.

NAME: **Horned Frog, *Ceratophrys cornuta***
RANGE: **N. and central South America**
HABITAT: **litter on forest floor**
SIZE: **20 cm (7¾ in)**
The extremely stout horned frog is almost as broad as it is long and has a wide, powerful head and large mouth. The eyes are relatively small, with a small protuberance on each upper eyelid. The toes are partially webbed, although the frog spends much of its life half-buried in the ground. Snails, small frogs and rodents are all eaten by this robust frog, and it is believed to cannibalize the young of its own species.

NAME: **Glass Frog, *Centrolenella albomaculata***
RANGE: **N. South America**
HABITAT: **forest**
SIZE: **up to 3 cm (1¼ in)**
The glass frog behaves much like the hylid treefrogs and lives in small trees and bushes, usually near running water. Its digits are expanded into adhesive disks, which give a good grip when it is climbing.

Eggs are laid in clusters on the underside of leaves overhanging running water and are guarded by the male. The tadpoles hatch and tumble down into the water below, where they complete their development.

NAME: **South American Bullfrog, *Leptodactylus pentadactylus***
RANGE: **Central and South America: Costa Rica to Brazil**
HABITAT: **forest, close to water**
SIZE: **up to 20.5 cm (8 in)**
The largest species in its family, the South American bullfrog has extremely powerful hind legs, which are eaten by man in some parts of its range. The male has hard protuberances on each thumb and powerful arm muscles, both of which help him hold the female when mating. The female has ridged horny structures on her body into which the male's thumb-horns fit.

In the spawning season, the sides of the bullfrog's legs turn deep orange or red. The frogs mate in water; the male clasps the female, who secretes a jellylike substance which he then whips into a foam. The foam forms a nest, which floats on or near the water surface and in which the eggs are laid and fertilized. Once they hatch, the tadpoles remain within the protection of the nest until, having metamorphosed into adults, they wriggle out into the water.

RHINODERMATIDAE:
Mouth-brooding Frog Family
This South American family, probably closely related to the Leptodactylidae, contains the unusual mouth-brooding, or Darwin's, frog of the genus *Rhinoderma*. Males of this species carry the developing eggs, and later the tadpoles, in their vocal sacs until they transform into small frogs. The species was discovered by Charles Darwin.

NAME: **Darwin's Frog, *Rhinoderma darwinii***
RANGE: **S. Chile, S. Argentina**
HABITAT: **shallow, cold streams in forest**
SIZE: **3 cm (1¼ in)**
A small, slender frog, Darwin's frog has a pointed extension of skin on its head. Its digits are long and webbed on the hind feet but free on the forefeet.

The breeding habits of *Rhinoderma* are unique among amphibians. The female lays from 20 to 45 eggs on land. They are guarded by several males for 10 to 20 days until the embryos, which are visible from the outside, begin to move around inside the capsules. Each male then gathers up to 15 eggs with his tongue and lets them slide into his large vocal sac. Feeding on their own yolks, the tadpoles develop inside the sac, which expands as they grow. Once they have transformed into small adults about 1.25 cm (½ in) long, the male expels them into water, and his vocal sac shrinks back to its normal size.

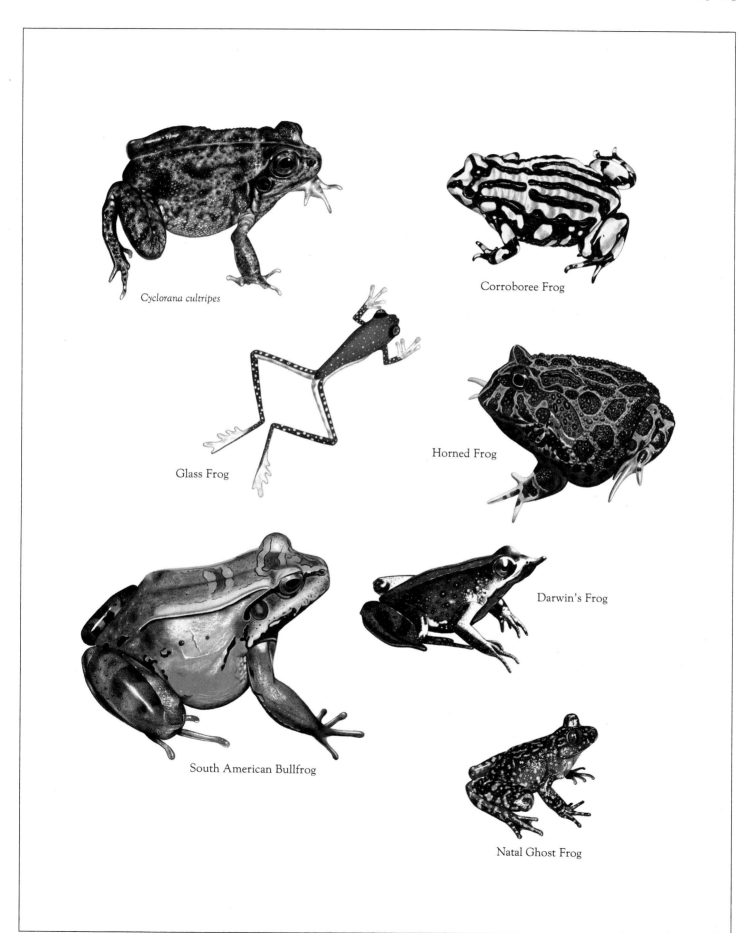

Cyclorana cultripes

Corroboree Frog

Glass Frog

Horned Frog

Darwin's Frog

South American Bullfrog

Natal Ghost Frog

Bufonid Toads, Gold Frog

BUFONIDAE: Toad Family

The name "toad" was originally applied only to the approximately 300 species in this family, although many other anurans with warty skins and terrestrial habits tend to be called toads. Bufonid toads are found over most of the world, except in the far north, Madagascar and Polynesia. A species has now been introduced into Australia, where previously there were no bufonid toads.

The typical bufonid toad has a compact body and short legs. The skin is not moist and is covered with characteristic wartlike tubercles. These contain the openings of poison glands, the distasteful secretions of which protect the toads to some extent, particularly from mammalian predators. With their short legs, toads tend to walk rather than hop and are, in general, slower-moving than frogs. Breeding males develop rough nuptial pads on their three inner fingers for clasping females when mating.

NAME: **Boulenger's Arrow Poison Toad,** *Atelopus boulengeri*
RANGE: **South America: Ecuador, Peru**
HABITAT: **forested slopes of the Andes, near fast-flowing streams**
SIZE: **about 2.5 cm (1 in)**

The contrasting black and orange markings of this toad warn of the poisonous skin secretions that defend it from predators. It is an uncommon, slow-moving species; active during the day, it may climb up into bushes at night. Little is known of its breeding habits, but it is believed to lay its eggs under stones in streams. The tadpoles probably have sucking mouths, with which to anchor themselves to rocks in the fast-flowing water.

NAME: **American Toad,** *Bufo americanus*
RANGE: **S.E. Canada: Manitoba to Labrador, south to Great Lakes; USA: south to Georgia, east to Kansas**
HABITAT: **grassland, forest, gardens**
SIZE: **5–11 cm (2–4¼ in)**

A stout, broad-headed toad, the American toad is liberally covered with warts. Females are usually larger than males. Mainly nocturnal, the American toad takes refuge during the day under stones, logs or other debris or burrows into the soil. It feeds on insects, but also eats small invertebrates such as spiders, snails and earthworms.

American toads usually breed between March and July, in ponds or streams. The female lays two strings of spawn, each containing up to 8,000 eggs, which hatch into tadpoles in 3 to 12 days. The tadpoles metamorphose into adults about 2 months after hatching.

NAME: **Giant Toad,** *Bufo marinus*
RANGE: **USA: extreme S. Texas; Mexico to Central and South America; introduced in many areas, including Australia**
HABITAT: **varied: near pools, swamps**
SIZE: **10–24 cm (4–9½ in)**

One of the largest toads in the world, the giant toad has been introduced widely outside its range, often to feed on, and thus control, insects which destroy crops such as sugarcane. It adapts well to many habitats and feeds on almost anything, including small rodents and birds and many insects, particularly beetles. Toxic secretions from the glands at each side of its body are highly irritating to mucous membranes and may be fatal to mammalian predators.

Giant toads breed at any time of year, given sufficient rainfall and warmth. They lay their strings of eggs in permanent water, where they usually hatch into tadpoles in 3 days. One female may lay up to 35,000 eggs in a year.

NAME: **Green Toad,** *Bufo viridis*
RANGE: **Europe: S. Sweden through Germany to Italy and Mediterranean islands; N. Africa, central Asia**
HABITAT: **varied, often lowland sandy areas, not forest**
SIZE: **8–10 cm (3¼–4 in)**

A thickset species but less plump than the common toad, the green toad has warty skin and distinctive green markings. The female is larger than the male, with brighter markings, and the male has an external vocal sac. Green toads are mainly nocturnal, but they may occasionally emerge during the day to forage for their insect food. Although primarily a land-living toad, the green toad has partially webbed toes and can survive in even brackish water.

Green toads breed from April to June, males courting females with their trilling, musical calls. The mating male clasps the female under her armpits while she lays two long strings of gelatinous spawn, each containing 10,000 to 20,000 eggs.

NAME: **Natterjack Toad,** *Bufo calamita*
RANGE: **W. and central Europe (including Britain), east to Russia**
HABITAT: **varied, often sandy areas**
SIZE: **7–10 cm (2¾–4 in)**

The male natterjack has the loudest call of any European toad: his croak will carry 2 km (1¼ mi) or more. The female is usually larger than the male, but both are robust and relatively short-limbed. Although mainly terrestrial, natterjacks are often found near the sea and may even use brackish water for breeding. They move on land by running in short spurts and are most active at night.

The breeding season lasts from March to August. Natterjacks mate at night and the female lays several strings of gelatinous spawn, each containing up to 4,000 eggs, in shallow water. The eggs hatch in 10 days into tadpoles, which metamorphose to adult form in 4 to 8 weeks. The young frogs are not fully grown and mature until they are 4 or 5 years old.

NAME: **Common Toad,** *Bufo bufo*
RANGE: **Europe (including Britain and Scandinavia); N. Africa; N. Asia to Japan**
HABITAT: **varied, often fairly dry**
SIZE: **up to 15 cm (6 in)**

The largest European toad, the common toad varies in size over its wide range, but females are generally larger than males. It is a heavily built toad with extremely warty skin; males do not have external vocal sacs. A nocturnal species, it hides during the day, often using the same spot time after time, and emerges at dusk to feed on a variety of invertebrate prey. It usually moves by walking but, if distressed, may hop.

In much of their range, common toads hibernate in winter and then congregate in large numbers to breed at about the end of March, frequently returning to the same pond every year. Thousands of eggs are laid in gelatinous strings up to 3 m (10 ft) long. The eggs hatch in about 10 days, and if the weather is warm, the tadpoles metamorphose in about 2 months. In cold weather they take longer.

BRACHYCEPHALIDAE: Gold Frog Family

Closely related to the bufonid toads is the single species of frog in this family, the gold frog.

NAME: **Gold Frog,** *Brachycephalus ephippium*
RANGE: **South America: S.E. Brazil**
HABITAT: **mountain forest**
SIZE: **up to 2 cm (¾ in)**

This tiny, but exquisite, frog is common among the leaf litter of the forest floor, although it may hide in crevices in trees or rocks in dry weather. On its back is a bony shield, made of hard plates fused to the spines of the vertebrae. The frog may use this shield to block the entrance of its hiding place, so maintaining an even humidity.

Its breeding habits are unknown, but since the tadpoles are aquatic, it is presumed that the frog lays its eggs in or near water.

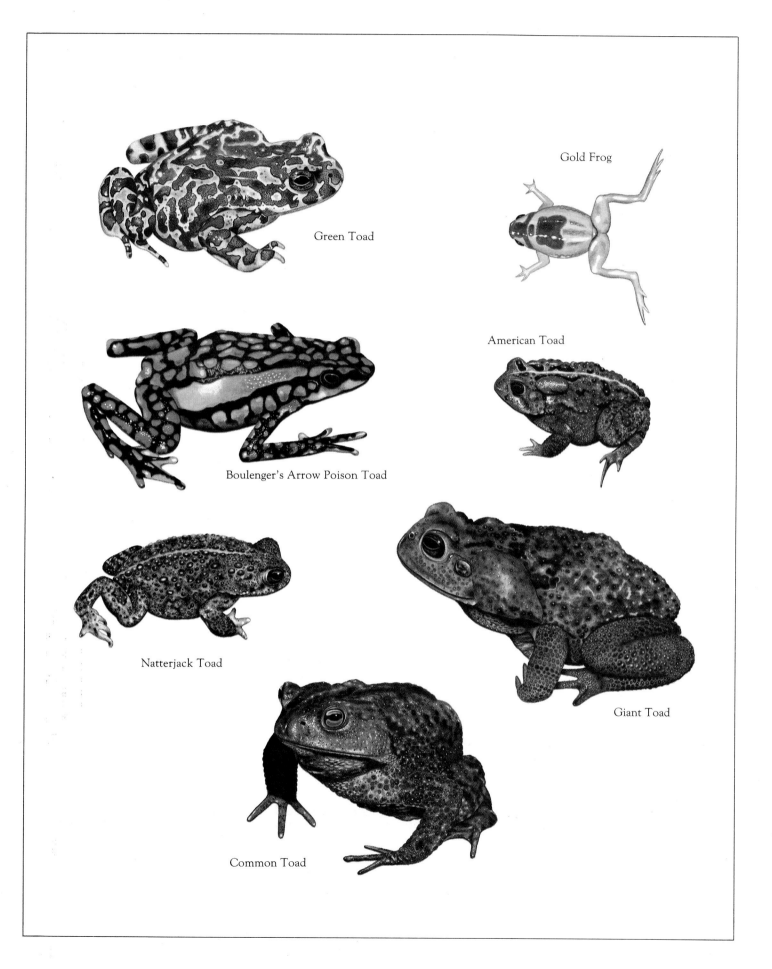

Green Toad

Gold Frog

Boulenger's Arrow Poison Toad

American Toad

Natterjack Toad

Giant Toad

Common Toad

Treefrogs

NAME: **European Green Treefrog,** *Hyla arborea*
RANGE: **most of Europe except N. and parts of S. France and Spain; Turkey, S. USSR to Caspian Sea**
HABITAT: **bushes, trees, reeds near ponds and lakes**
SIZE: **up to 5 cm (2 in)**

The most arboreal of European amphibians, this smooth-skinned treefrog spends most of its life in trees, where it captures flying insects with great skill. It can change color rapidly, from bright green in sunlight to a dark gray in shade.

In early summer, breeding frogs congregate at night in ponds or other small areas of fresh water. The male grasps the female just behind the forelegs and fertilizes her eggs as they are shed into the water. The eggs are laid in clumps of up to 1,000 and float on the water until they hatch into tadpoles.

NAME: **Gray Treefrog,** *Hyla versicolor*
RANGE: **S.E. Canada; USA: North Dakota, east to Maine, south to Texas and Florida**
HABITAT: **bushes, trees near water**
SIZE: **3–6 cm (1¼–2¼ in)**

A rough-skinned frog, the gray treefrog's variable coloration gives good camouflage in trees, and the bright orange areas on the undersurfaces of its thighs can be fleetingly flashed to confuse predators. It lives high up in vegetation and is mainly active at night, when it preys on insects.

Rarely seen on the ground, these treefrogs usually descend only to call and breed. They mate in water, and the eggs are shed in small clusters of 10 to 40. The tadpoles hatch 4 or 5 days later.

NAME: **Spring Peeper,** *Hyla crucifer*
RANGE: **S.E. Canada; USA, south to central Florida, west to Texas**
HABITAT: **woodland, near ponds, swamps**
SIZE: **2–3 cm (¾–1¼ in)**

One of the most abundant frogs in eastern North America, the spring peeper's song does indeed herald the arrival of spring in the north of its range. This agile little frog can climb into trees and bushes, using its well-developed adhesive toe pads, and jump over 17 times its body length. It feeds mainly on small spiders and insects, including flying insects, which it leaps into the air to catch.

Courting males call from trees overhanging water, making a bell-like chorus. The male frog climbs onto a female, who enters water and lays her 800 to 1,000 eggs, one at a time, onto stems of aquatic vegetation. He fertilizes the eggs, which hatch within a few days. The tadpoles metamorphose about 3 months later and leave the pond.

HYLIDAE: Treefrog Family

There are approximately 600 species of treefrog, found on all continents except the Antarctic, but the greatest diversity occurs in tropical areas of the New World. The vast majority live in trees, and they possess a range of anatomical and behavioral adaptations which make them extremely efficient insect-eating, tree-dwelling amphibians.

The most important of these adaptations are on the feet. Each digit is tipped with a sticky adhesive pad to aid climbing, and inside the digit is a disk-shaped zone of cartilage before the claw-shaped end bone. The cartilage allows the digit great mobility, while keeping the adhesive pad flat on the surface which the frog is climbing.

NAME: **Northern Cricket Frog,** *Acris crepitans*
RANGE: **USA: New York, south to N. Florida, west to Minnesota and Texas**
HABITAT: **shallow ponds, slow streams**
SIZE: **1.5–4 cm (½–1½ in)**

This tiny, rough-skinned frog is a poor climber and spends its life on land and in water. Unlike the arboreal treefrogs, which do not jump readily, the cricket frog leaps and hops along and can jump as much as 36 times its own length.

Breeding starts in April in the north of its range or as early as February in the south. Thousands of frogs congregate to call and mate — the male's call is a shrill, metallic clicking sound. The eggs are shed on submerged vegetation or into the water in small clusters or singly. In warm weather, they hatch in 4 days but may take longer if the temperature is below 22° C (72° F).

NAME: **Golden Arrow-poison Frog,** *Dendrobates auratus*
RANGE: **Central and South America: Nicaragua to Panama and Colombia**
HABITAT: **forest**
SIZE: **4 cm (1½ in)**

The brilliant colors of this ground-dwelling frog warn potential enemies of its poisonous glandular secretions. This poison is extracted by local tribesmen and used on the tips of arrows.

Before mating, these frogs fight and contest with each other until they have paired. On land, the female then lays up to 6 eggs, surrounded with a gelatinous substance. The male visits the clutch at intervals until, about 2 weeks after laying, the tadpoles hatch. They then wriggle onto the male frog's back, and he carries them to a hole in a tree where a little water has collected. Here, the aquatic tadpoles complete their development in about 6 weeks.

NAME: **Green and Gold Bell Frog,** *Litoria cyclorhynchus*
RANGE: **W. Australia: south coast**
HABITAT: **large ponds**
SIZE: **up to 8 cm (3¼ in)**

A distinctively marked species, this bell frog climbs only rarely and lives mostly in water or on reeds. It moves on land only in heavy rainfall. Active during the day, it is a voracious predator, feeding on any small animals, including its own tadpoles.

In the breeding season, males call from the water to attract mates, making a sound rather like wood being sawn. The female lays her eggs among the vegetation in the pond.

NAME: **Lutz's Phyllomedusa,** *Phyllomedusa appendiculata*
RANGE: **South America: S.E. Brazil**
HABITAT: **forest, near moving water**
SIZE: **4 cm (1½ in)**

A tree-dwelling frog, Lutz's phyllomedusa has triangular flaps of skin on each heel, which may help to camouflage its outline as it sits on a branch. Areas of red skin inside thighs and flanks can be flashed to confuse predators. It feeds mainly on insects.

The breeding method of this species is an adaptation to arboreal life. The breeding pair selects a leaf which overhangs water. They fold the leaf over, making a nest which is open at both sides, and the 50 or so eggs are laid in a ball of gelatinous mucus inside the nest. When the tadpoles hatch 2 or 3 days later, they drop into the water below.

NAME: **Marsupial Frog,** *Gastrotheca marsupiata*
RANGE: **South America: Ecuador, Peru**
HABITAT: **forest**
SIZE: **up to 4 cm (1½ in)**

This tree-dwelling frog is typical of its family in most respects but has the most extraordinary way of caring for its developing eggs. The female frog is larger than the male and has a special skin pouch on her back. While she lays about 200 eggs, one at a time, the male sits on her back. As each egg is laid, she bends forward so that it rolls down her back; the male then fertilizes the egg before it settles into the skin pouch. When all the eggs are laid, the male helps to pack them into the skin pouch and the edges of the pouch seal over.

A few weeks later the female frog finds some shallow water — a pond or puddle — in which to release her brood. By this time her back is very swollen. She raises one hind leg and, with her fourth and longest toe, slits open the pouch and frees the young tadpoles, which then complete their metamorphosis in water.

Gray Treefrog

Green and Gold Bell Frog

Northern Cricket Frog

Spring Peeper

Lutz's Phyllomedusa

European Green Treefrog

Golden Arrow-poison Frog

Marsupial Frog

True Frogs

NAME: South African Bullfrog,
Pyxicephalus adspersus
RANGE: E. South Africa
HABITAT: open grassland (veld); in temporary puddles when available
SIZE: up to 20 cm (7¾ in)

The largest South African frog, this bullfrog has a stout body and broad head. The male usually has a yellow throat while the female's is cream. On its lower jaw are toothlike projections which it uses to restrain struggling prey such as mice, lizards and other frogs. Its hind toes are webbed, but the front toes are not.

A powerful burrower, it spends much of the year underground but comes to the surface after heavy rain to breed. Males call from a breeding site in shallow water, where females then lay their many eggs, one at a time.

NAME: Striped Grass Frog, *Ptychadena porosissima*
RANGE: Africa: central tropical areas to E. South Africa
HABITAT: marshy areas
SIZE: 4 cm (1½ in)

This small, streamlined frog has a pointed snout and a ridged back. Its hind limbs are powerful, making it a good jumper and strong swimmer. Secretive in its habits, it often lives among dense vegetation.

Breeding males sit among aquatic vegetation and call to females with a rasping sound, which is amplified by their paired external vocal sacs. Their mates lay their eggs, one at a time, in the water. The eggs float at first and then sink to the bottom; the tadpoles swim and feed near the bottom.

NAME: Marsh Frog, *Rana ridibunda*
RANGE: S.W. Europe: S.W. France, Spain and Portugal; E. Europe: Germany, east to USSR and Balkans
HABITAT: ponds, ditches, streams, lakes, rivers
SIZE: up to 15 cm (6 in)

The marsh frog is one of the several noisy, aquatic, gregarious green frogs found in Europe. Apart from its color, this long-legged frog is easily distinguished from the brown frogs by the external vocal sacs at the sides of its mouth. Most of its life is spent in water, but it will come out onto banks or float on lily pads. As well as catching invertebrate prey, these large frogs feed on small birds and mammals.

Marsh frogs sing night and day and are particularly vocal in the breeding season, when they make a variety of sounds. They mate in April or May, and females lay thousands of eggs in several large clusters.

RANIDAE: True Frog Family

There are 500 to 600 species in this family, found almost worldwide on every continent except Antarctica, but sparsely represented in Australasia and the southern parts of South America. Typically, these frogs have slim, streamlined bodies and pointed heads. Their hind legs are long and hind feet extensively webbed. They are usually smooth-skinned and often brown or green in color.

Most ranid frogs live near fresh water and enter it readily to find prey or escape danger. A few species, however, can thrive in brackish waters or warm sulfur springs, and others have become adapted to a ground-living existence and can burrow like spadefoot toads. Some live in trees and have adhesive pads on their toes for grip when climbing, similar to those of the treefrogs (Hylidae). All are carnivorous as adults, feeding mainly on insects, spiders and small crustaceans.

Large numbers of ranid frogs congregate at the start of the breeding season, and males chorus to attract females to the breeding site. The breeding male develops swollen pads on forelimbs and thumbs with which he grasps his mate's body. As she lays her eggs, he fertilizes them by spraying them with sperm. The eggs are usually surrounded by a jellylike substance which protects them to some degree and prevents dehydration. Although females lay thousands of eggs, many of these are destroyed by adverse conditions or eaten by predators, and relatively few survive to adulthood.

NAME: Common Frog, *Rana temporaria*
RANGE: Europe (including Britain and Scandinavia, but excluding much of Spain and Italy), east to Asia
HABITAT: varied: any moist area near ponds, marshes, swamps
SIZE: up to 10 cm (4 in)

European frogs are divided into two groups: green and brown frogs. The brown frogs, of which the common frog is an example, tend to be more terrestrial and have quieter voices than the green frogs. The robust common frog varies in coloration over its wide range, from brown or gray to yellow. It is tolerant of cold and is found up to the snowline in some areas. Much of its life is spent on land, and it rarely enters water except to mate or hibernate.

Breeding occurs from February to April, and males attract females to the breeding sites with their deep, rasping croaks. They mate in water, and females lay 3,000 to 4,000 eggs in large clusters.

NAME: Bullfrog, *Rana catesbeiana*
RANGE: E. and central USA; introduced in western areas and in Mexico, Cuba and N. Italy
HABITAT: lakes, ponds, slow streams
SIZE: 9–20.5 cm (3½–8 in)

The largest North American frog, the bullfrog makes a deep, vibrant call, amplified by the internal vocal sac. Although an aquatic species, it also spends time on land and is often seen at the water's edge. It is most active by night, when it preys on insects, fish, smaller frogs and, occasionally, small birds and snakes. Like all American ranid frogs, it is a good jumper and can leap nine times its own length.

In the north of their range, bullfrogs breed from May to July, but farther south, the season is longer. The female lays 10,000 to 20,000 eggs in water; they may float on the surface or attach to vegetation. The eggs hatch in 5 or 6 days, but the tadpoles take 2 to 5 years to transform into adults.

NAME: Northern Leopard Frog, *Rana pipiens*
RANGE: most of northern N. America except Pacific coast
HABITAT: varied: fresh water to brackish marshes in arid to mountain land
SIZE: 5–12.5 cm (2–5 in)

The slim northern leopard frog is a distinctive species, with large spots on its body and prominent back ridges. It is the most widely distributed North American amphibian, and the pattern and intensity of its spots vary over its large range. It adapts to almost any habitat near a permanent body of water and is equally accommodating in its diet; insects, spiders and crustaceans are its main food, but this voracious frog will eat almost anything it can find. Primarily a nocturnal species, the leopard frog may sometimes search for food during the day. If disturbed on land, it leaps away in a series of zigzagging jumps to seek refuge in water.

In the north of its range, the breeding season usually extends from March to June, but in southern, arid areas, leopard frogs are ready to breed at almost any time of year whenever there has been sufficient rainfall. Males gather at breeding sites and make low grunting calls to attract females. Each female lays about 20,000 eggs, which her mate fertilizes. The eggs then lie at the bottom of the water on submerged vegetation until they hatch about 4 weeks later. The tadpoles metamorphose to adult form in 6 months to 2 years, depending on temperature and conditions.

South African Bullfrog

Common Frog

Striped Grass Frog

Marsh Frog

Northern Leopard Frog

Bullfrog

True Frogs, Hyperoliid Frogs, Sooglossid Frogs

NAME: Wallace's Flying Frog,
Rhacophorus nigropalmatus
RANGE: S.E. Asia
HABITAT: rain forest
SIZE: 10 cm (4 in)

This highly specialized frog is adapted for its habit of gliding from tree to tree in the forest. Its appearance is distinctive, with a broad head, long, slim body and elongate limbs. The feet are greatly enlarged and fully webbed, and the tips of the digits expand into large disks. Flaps of skin fringe the forelimbs and heels. All of these modifications add little to the frog's weight but extend its surface area. It can launch itself into the air, webs and skin flaps outstretched like a parachute, and glide gently down to another branch or to the ground. Experiments have shown that, if dropped from a height of 5.4 m (17¾ ft), the frog glides down diagonally for a total distance of 7.3 m (24 ft).

The breeding habits of this extraordinary frog are little known but are believed to be similar to those of others of its genus. Rhacophorid frogs lay their eggs in a mass of foam, which makes a kind of nest to protect them from excessive heat while they incubate. The male frog grasps the female and fertilizes her eggs as they are laid in the normal way. But the eggs are accompanied by a thick fluid, which the frogs then beat with their hind legs to form a dense, light foam. Surrounded with this substance, the eggs are left on a leaf or branch overhanging water. At hatching time, the bubble nest begins to liquefy, forming a miniature pool for the emerging tadpoles. In some species, the tadpoles complete their development in this custom-made pool, but in others, they drop down into the water beneath.

NAME: Mottled Burrowing Frog,
Hemisus marmoratum
RANGE: N.E. South Africa
HABITAT: open country near pools
SIZE: up to 3 cm (1¼ in)

A stout, squat-bodied frog, this species has a small, pointed head with a hardened snout, used for burrowing. It burrows headfirst, pushing into the soil with its snout and clawing its way forward with its strong forelimbs. It is rarely seen above ground, although it can move rapidly on land.

Breeding males establish themselves in small holes, preferably in a mudbank, and call to attract mates. The female excavates an underground nest and lays her large eggs, each surrounded by a thick, jellylike substance. When her young hatch some 10 to 12 days later, she tunnels to the nearest water, providing a canal for the tadpoles, which then complete their development in water.

NAME: Bush Squeaker, *Arthroleptis*
wahlbergi
RANGE: S.E. South Africa
HABITAT: coastal and inland bush among leaf litter and low vegetation
SIZE: up to 3 cm (1¼ in)

This small, rounded frog is a land-dwelling species. Its legs are short but its digits, particularly the third on each foot, are elongate, well suited to searching through vegetation for prey.

The bush squeaker's breeding habits, too, are adapted to its terrestrial existence. The eggs, each enclosed in a stiff jelly capsule, are laid among decaying vegetation. There is no tadpole stage; metamorphosis takes place within the capsule and tiny froglets emerge about 4 weeks after laying.

HYPEROLIIDAE:
Hyperoliid Frog Family

The hyperoliids are a group of climbing frogs, closely related to the ranid frogs. They differ from them in possessing adaptations for climbing similar to those of the hylid frogs: each digit on the foot has a zone of cartilage, which allows greater flexibility in the use of the adhesive disk at the tip when climbing.

Most of the 52 species in this family live in Africa, often among rushes and sedge near fresh water.

NAME: Arum Lily Frog, *Hyperolius*
horstockii
RANGE: South Africa: S. and W. Cape Province
HABITAT: swamps, dams, streams, rivers, with vegetation
SIZE: up to 6 cm (2¼ in)

The long-limbed arum lily frog has distinctive bands running from its snout along each side. A good climber, its feet are equipped with expanded, adhesive disks and are only partially webbed. The concealed undersurfaces of the limbs are orange, and these bright areas are momentarily revealed if the frog is disturbed by a predator. The frog then freezes in an inconspicuous posture, with its flash colors hidden, while the predator continues to look for the bright orange frog it was hunting. The rest of the body changes color according to conditions, becoming a light cream in bright sun and dark brown in shade. This helps the frog control its body heat by either reflecting or absorbing the sun's rays.

Courting males often climb up onto arum lilies to call to females. They then mate in water, where the small clusters of eggs are laid on submerged water plants.

NAME: Gold Spiny Reed Frog, *Afrixales*
brachycnemis
RANGE: South Africa: E., S.E. and S. coastal regions
HABITAT: pools, swamps
SIZE: 2 cm (¾ in)

Also known as the golden leaf-folding frog, this very tiny, slim amphibian, equipped with adhesive disks on each digit, is a good climber. Its back may be covered with tiny dark spines, hence one of its common names; this feature is common in frogs in the south of the range but rare in the north.

Breeding males take up a position among reeds or on water-lily leaves in pools or *vleis* (temporary, rain-filled hollows) and call to females. The female frog lays a small batch of eggs on a leaf above or below water level. Once the eggs are fertilized, the leaf is folded over and the edges are glued together with sticky secretions from the female's oviduct. When the eggs hatch, the tadpoles emerge from the leaf nest into the water, where they complete their development.

SOOGLOSSIDAE:
Sooglossid Frog Family

The origins and relationships of the frogs of this small family, all found in the Seychelles, have been a matter of contention, but analysis of their anatomy leads most taxonomists to conclude that they are related to the ranid frogs.

NAME: Seychelles Frog, *Sooglossus*
sechellensis
RANGE: Seychelles: Mahé and Silhouette Islands
HABITAT: moss forest on mountains
SIZE: up to 2.5 cm (1 in) ①

The tiny Seychelles frog has thin, weak front limbs but more powerful hind limbs, with long digits on its feet. It is mainly ground-dwelling and lives in rotting plant matter on the forest floor, needing water for only a short phase of tadpole development. It feeds on small invertebrates.

The frogs breed in the rainy season. The female lays her eggs in small clumps of gelatinous substance on moist ground. The male guards the eggs and when they hatch, after 2 weeks incubation, the tadpoles wriggle onto his back. The tadpoles respire through their skin and do not have gills; they are protected from dehydration by mucous secretions on the male frog's back. Most of their development takes place here, but they are later carried to water to spend a brief period there completing their metamorphosis before they return to land as adult frogs.

Wallace's Flying Frog

Gold Spiny Reed Frog

Bush Squeaker

Arum Lily Frog

Seychelles Frog

Mottled Burrowing Frog

Fishes – the first vertebrates

More than half of the 43,500 or so known species of vertebrate animals are fishes, which in their aquatic environment have evolved into a huge range of specialized forms, at least as diverse as that of four-legged animals.

The first major division in this group is between jawless and jawed fishes, with the former group today consisting of only lampreys and hagfishes, remnants of an early stage of vertebrate evolution. The jawed fishes, which arose just under 400 million years ago, are themselves divided into vastly differing groups. First are the cartilage-skeletoned fish (Chondrichthyes), such as sharks, skates and rays, and the ratfish and elephant shark. Second, there are three major types of bony-skeletoned fishes: the ray-finned fishes, with narrow-based fins and fin rays which support them (actinopterygian fishes); and two types of fleshy-finned fishes (sarcopterygians), namely, the lungfishes and the lobe-finned fishes (crossopterygians), the latter represented today only by the coelacanth (*Latimeria*).

Lampreys and hagfishes, like the earliest vertebrates before them, have no jaws. They have only the most rudimentary vertebrae and cylindrical bodies with small unpaired fins at the rear end. Only about 30 lamprey and 32 hagfish species survive today. The former are found in the cool areas of the world both in the sea and in fresh water; the latter are marine fishes of worldwide distribution. Lampreys live parasitically on other fishes, hanging onto their outer surfaces with a sharply toothed sucker that bears a small mouth and a rasping tongue at its center. The lamprey uses its tongue to make a wound in the host's body and then feeds on its blood. Larval lampreys are bottom-dwelling filter-feeders, and lamprey life cycles sometimes involve both marine and freshwater stages. Hagfishes are an entirely marine group; although well known as scavengers which suck out the body contents of dead or dying fishes, they feed mainly on crustaceans and worms.

Both lampreys and hagfishes swim by lateral undulations of the body, produced by the contractions of repeating blocks of muscles along the flanks. These simplest living vertebrates possess what is basically a prototype of the water-breathing gill apparatus used by all higher fishes. The side walls of the pharynx are perforated to provide gill openings from the gut cavity to the outside; there are seven such openings on each side in lampreys. Because of the lamprey's sucker, respiratory water cannot usually pass through the mouth. Instead, when the sucker is in use, water passes both in and out through the gill openings and oxygenates the blood, which is pumped from the heart to the gills through 8 pairs of branchial arteries.

The cartilaginous fishes, of which about 575 species are known, are marine fishes which vary in size between the huge sharks of more than 15 m (49 ft) in length and tiny forms about 30 cm (11¾ in) long. Most are active predators on other fish and are equipped with sharp-edged teeth in both jaws. Although their skeletons are made of cartilage, not bone, these fishes conform to the orthodox body plan of jawed fishes, with paired fins and proper vertebrae. The body is beautifully streamlined, with the greatest width toward the middle, a pointed anterior end and a tapering rear part, terminating in a two-vaned propulsive tail. This is moved from side to side with muscles similar to those which produce body undulations in the jawless fishes.

In many cartilaginous fishes the upper vane of the tail is larger than the lower one, and the front pair of paired fins, the pectorals, act as winglike control surfaces for changing direction. Like the large, unpaired dorsal fins, they also provide directional stability against rolling, pitching and yawing when the fish is swimming. Cartilaginous fishes have between 5 and 7 pairs of gill slits opening to the outside on each side of the head. Typically, the respiratory current passes in through the mouth and out through the gill slits.

There are 20,000 or so species of bony fish — about half the known total of living vertebrate species — and, unlike the cartilaginous fishes, they thrive in fresh as well as salt water. The body plan of these successful animals is similar to that of the cartilaginous fishes, but with some crucial changes. The skeleton, including the fin rays, is made of bone; the tail vanes are characteristically, but not always, equal in size, and there is often a gas-filled swim bladder in the body for buoyancy control. This can be adjusted to make the fish weightless in the water so that it can rest or stay motionless — a great advance over the cartilaginous fishes, which must keep moving or sink. There is also a difference in the gill system. In bony fishes there are usually four respiratory gills on each side of the pharynx, but the openings associated with them are enclosed by a large flap, the operculum, which effectively produces a single, ultimate opening on each side of the fish. The bodies of most bony fishes are covered with overlapping scales, set in the skin, which form a protective armor.

Bony fishes feed in a variety of ways and fill every ecological feeding niche. Some are herbivorous, living on aquatic vegetation and microscopic plant plankton. Others catch small invertebrate animals or strain them from the water by means of gill rakers, comblike structures attached to the gill bars. Still others are active, fast-moving predators equipped with sharp teeth, while species such as flatfishes and anglers rely on their camouflage to keep them hidden while they lie in wait for prey.

Many fishes reproduce by simply shedding vast numbers of eggs into the water, where they are fertilized by the male depositing sperm over them. There is rarely any parental care, and although most eggs hatch, few survive to maturity. Some male fishes, notably sharks, fertilize their mates internally and have clasping organs, developed from modified pelvic fins, which help them hold the female while depositing sperm in her genital opening. These internally fertilized females may retain their eggs, so that the young develop inside the mother's body and are born fully formed.

Most bony fishes are marine and freshwater forms of actinopterygians (ray-finned fishes), but there is also the single marine genus of lobe-finned coelacanth and the 3 surviving genera of lungfishes, which all live in fresh water. Lungfishes breathe air, and most make burrows in which they live when the rivers and lakes of their tropical habitats seasonally dry up. In these fishes the swim bladder is connected to the gut cavity via a tube and operates as an air-breathing lung.

The huge number of fish species and the proportionately large number of fish families have made it impossible to treat them according to families, as the rest of this book is organized. Consequently, the section on fishes is arranged according to order; families are mentioned only in the largest orders.

Lampreys, Hagfishes, Sharks

PETROMYZONIFORMES: Lamprey Order

This order includes only 1 family, the lampreys, with about 30 species. All are primitive fishes which have no true jaws, but only sucking, funnel-like mouths lined with small teeth. Many are parasitic and live on the blood of other fishes. Some are freshwater species, others are anadromous — they live in salt water but travel to fresh water to spawn. Most lampreys occur in the northern hemisphere, but there are some species in and around southern South America, south Australia and New Zealand.

NAME: **Lampern**, *Lampetra fluviatilis*
RANGE: **Britain, N.W. Europe**
HABITAT: **rivers, coastal waters**
SIZE: **30–50 cm (11¾–20 in)**

The parasitic lampern feeds on the blood of other fishes. It attaches itself to the host's body by means of its round suckerlike mouth and rasps away the skin and scales with its sharp teeth.

At spawning time, lamperns leave the coastal waters and migrate upriver. They lay their eggs in spring in shallow pits excavated in the gravel of the riverbed. After hatching, the larvae move downstream and bury themselves in mud, where they remain for up to 5 years, filter-feeding on microorganisms until they reach maturity.

NAME: **Sea Lamprey**, *Petromyzon marinus*
RANGE: **Atlantic coasts of Europe and N. America; W. Mediterranean Sea**
HABITAT: **coastal waters, rivers**
SIZE: **90 cm (35½ in)**

Like lamperns, adult sea lampreys are blood-feeding parasites. The lamprey attaches itself to its victim so firmly that it is almost impossible to remove, and the host must carry this unwelcome burden around until the lamprey moves to a new host. A secretion in the lamprey's mouth prevents the host's blood from clotting, allowing the lamprey to feed freely. Victims often die from blood loss or from infection of the wound.

Adults leave the sea and travel up into rivers to spawn. They make a shallow pit in a stony-bottomed area by moving stones with their sucker mouths; the eggs are deposited in this nest. The blind, toothless larvae live buried in mud, filter-feeding for 4 to 6 years, until, as toothed juveniles, they migrate to the sea. Lampreys also occur in inland lakes, where they prey on valuable commercial fish, but efforts are made to control their numbers in such waters.

MYXINIFORMES: Hagfish Order

The 32 species of hagfishes make up the only living family in this order. They are all marine and occur in temperate and subtropical waters of the Atlantic, Indian and Pacific oceans. They are jawless fishes and have slitlike mouths surrounded with fleshy filaments.

NAME: **Atlantic Hagfish**, *Myxine glutinosa*
RANGE: **N. Atlantic, Arctic Oceans**
HABITAT: **ocean bed**
SIZE: **61 cm (24 in)**

Hagfishes live in fairly deep water where there is a soft muddy bottom into which they can burrow. They have no paired fins nor scales; their eyes are hidden under skin and they are almost blind. The surface of the skin is particularly slimy since it is copiously supplied with mucus-secreting glands. Hagfishes feed on some marine worms and crustaceans, but they are best known for attacking dead and dying fish or fish trapped in nets. Using the toothlike plates on the tongue and the single tooth in the mouth, the hagfish bores into the prey's body and eats away all its flesh and intestines, leaving only skin and bone.

LAMNIFORMES: Shark Order

This order contains 7 families of sharks, 199 species in all. Like all sharks, these fish have skeletons made of cartilage not bone. Almost all these species are large marine fishes with two dorsal fins, one anal fin and five gill slits.

NAME: **Basking Shark**, *Cetorhinus maximus*
RANGE: **worldwide, outside the tropics**
HABITAT: **oceanic**
SIZE: **10.4 m (34 ft)**

The basking shark is the second-largest living species of fish. It shares the streamlined body shape of other sharks but is distinguished by its extra-large gill slits. It feeds entirely on plankton which it sieves from the water by means of comblike bristles on its gill arches. The shark simply swims with its mouth agape, taking in a vast quantity of water and plankton and filtering it through the gill slits. As the name implies, basking sharks often float sluggishly at the surface of the water.

Little is known of the basking shark's breeding habits, but its eggs are believed to develop inside its body, hatching as they are expelled. The young sharks are about 1.5 m (5 ft) long at birth.

NAME: **Whale Shark**, *Rhincodon typus*
RANGE: **all tropical seas**
HABITAT: **surface waters**
SIZE: **15.2 m (50 ft)**

The huge whale shark is the largest living fish; some individuals may grow as long as 18 m (60 ft). It feeds on small fish and plankton which it filters from the water. The shark opens its mouth and takes in a rush of water containing minute organisms. The water is filtered out through the huge gill slits, and the plankton is retained. Little is known of the breeding habits of this giant fish.

NAME: **Sand Tiger**, *Odontaspis taurus*
RANGE: **Atlantic Ocean: N. American and African coasts**
HABITAT: **coastal waters**
SIZE: **3.2 m (10½ ft)**

The sand tiger is a predatory shark which tends to live at the bottom of shallow water, feeding on fish. It has characteristic yellow spots on its body, and dorsal, pelvic and anal fins are much the same size. Its long pointed teeth project forward noticeably. The female sand shark gives birth to 2 young, which develop inside her body for 12 months while feeding on the yolks of unfertilized eggs. The young are about 1 m (3¼ ft) long at birth.

A similar species, the ragged-tooth shark, *O. ferox*, is found in the Mediterranean and off European Atlantic coasts, as well as the Pacific coast of the USA.

NAME: **Thresher Shark**, *Alopias vulpinus*
RANGE: **temperate and tropical oceans**
HABITAT: **surface waters in open sea**
SIZE: **6 m (19½ ft)**

The distinctive thresher shark has a tail as long as the rest of its body, which it uses to advantage when hunting. The sharks feed mainly on schooling fish, and, working in pairs or alone, they lash their tails to herd the fish into a compact mass, where they make easy prey. A thresher may also strike and stun an individual fish with its tail. Threshers sometimes come into coastal waters to hunt, particularly in summer, when they are seen along the American Atlantic coast.

Females give birth to litters of 2 to 4 fully formed young, which may be as long as 1.5 m (5 ft) at birth.

In Australian waters, the thresher shark is known by different scientific names: *A. caudatus* and *A. greyi*.

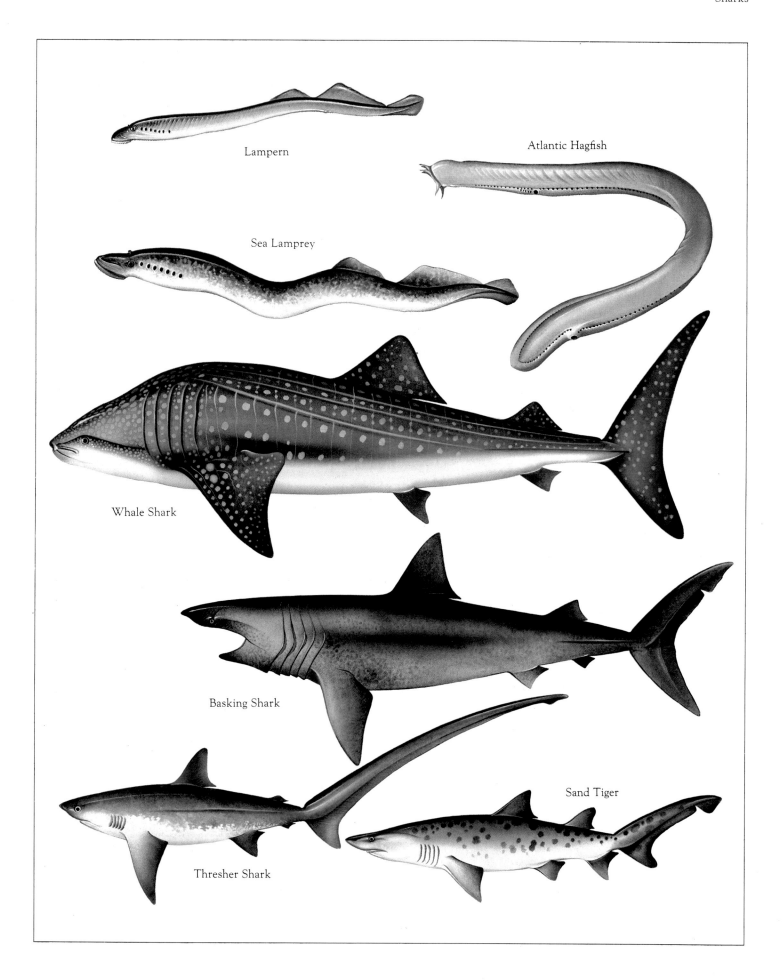

Lampern

Atlantic Hagfish

Sea Lamprey

Whale Shark

Basking Shark

Sand Tiger

Thresher Shark

Sharks

NAME: White Shark, *Carcharodon carcharias*
RANGE: Atlantic, Pacific and Indian Oceans: warm temperate and tropical coastal areas
HABITAT: open sea; seasonally enters coastal waters
SIZE: 6 m (19¾ ft)

The white shark, also known as the great white shark, is not actually white but ranges in color from gray to brown with white underparts. Its long snout is pointed, and its large, powerful teeth are triangular and serrated. The top lobe of its tail is slightly longer than the lower lobe. It feeds on a variety of aquatic animals, such as fish (including other sharks), seals and dolphins, and it also scavenges on dead animals and refuse. An extremely large and aggressive fish, it has acquired the reputation of a man-eater and has, indeed, been involved in many attacks on humans.

Little is known of its breeding habits other than that it bears litters of up to 9 live young.

NAME: Bull Shark, *Carcharhinus leucas*
RANGE: W. Atlantic Ocean: North Carolina to S. Brazil
HABITAT: inshore waters, rivers and connecting lakes
SIZE: 2.5–3.5 m (8¼–11½ ft)

The bull shark has a chunky body, with the first dorsal fin placed well forward. Normally quite a slow-moving shark, it is usually found in shallow water and regularly swims into rivers. These habits make it a species dangerous to humans, since it is frequently encountered. Bull sharks feed on a wide range of fish, including rays and small sharks, and they also eat shrimps, crabs and sea urchins and scavenge on refuse.

The female bull shark produces live young, which are generally born from May to July in brackish, inshore waters.

NAME: Blue Shark, *Prionace glauca*
RANGE: Atlantic, Pacific and Indian Oceans: temperate and tropical areas
HABITAT: open sea, surface waters
SIZE: 2.7–3.8 m (9–12½ ft)

A slender, elongate fish, the blue shark is easily distinguished by its long pectoral fins, pointed snout and bright coloration. It feeds on a range of surface-dwelling fish, such as mackerel, herring and pilchard, and on squid and waste thrown from fishing boats.

Females give birth to live young, and litters of as many as 50 to 60 at a time have been reported. Blue sharks make regular migrations to warmer waters in the winter months.

NAME: Porbeagle, *Lamna nasus*
RANGE: N. Atlantic Ocean: Newfoundland, south to South Carolina; Iceland, south to N. Africa; Mediterranean Sea
HABITAT: open sea; coastal waters
SIZE: 1.8–3 m (6–9¾ ft)

The porbeagle is a swift-swimming, heavy-bodied shark with five gill slits. It feeds on surface-dwelling fish, such as mackerel and herring, and on squid and some bottom-dwelling fish. Identifying characteristics are the position of the dorsal fin (above the base of the pectoral fin) and of the second dorsal fin (directly above the anal fin). This species and the related sharks (mako and white sharks) have body temperatures higher than the surrounding water — an adaptation linked with great muscular activity that improves their swimming efficiency.

The eggs hatch inside the mother and remain there for a short time before she gives birth to fully formed live young. Litters usually contain 1 to 5 young, which are sustained for a few weeks by the yolks of unfertilized eggs that they eat before birth.

The closely related salmon shark, *L. ditropis*, which lives in the Pacific, is similar to the porbeagle in its appearance and habits.

NAME: Shortfin Mako, *Isurus oxyrinchus*
RANGE: Atlantic, Pacific and Indian Oceans: temperate and tropical areas
HABITAT: open sea
SIZE: 3–4 m (9¾–13 ft)

A powerful, streamlined shark with a slender body and a pointed snout, the shortfin mako is a fast-swimming predator. Distinguishing features are the slightly rounded tip to the first dorsal fin, which is positioned in line with the rear edge of the base of the pectoral fin, and the small second dorsal fin, positioned just in front of the anal fin. The shortfin mako is usually deep blue above and white below.

An active surface-dweller itself, the shortfin mako usually feeds on surface-living fish such as tuna, mackerel, herring and sardines, and on squid. It is renowned for its habit of leaping clear of the water, and, although known to be dangerous and aggressive, the shortfin mako is a popular sport fish with shark fishermen because of the spectacular struggle it puts up and the leaps it performs when hooked.

The female shortfin mako gives birth to live young, which develop and hatch inside her body.

NAME: Smooth Hammerhead, *Sphyrna zygaena*
RANGE: Atlantic, Pacific and Indian Oceans: tropical and warm temperate areas
HABITAT: coastal and inshore waters
SIZE: 4.3 m (14 ft)

The smooth hammerhead is one of 10 species of hammerhead shark, all of which have flattened projections at the sides of the head, hence their name. The eyes are positioned on the outer edges of these lobes, and the nostrils also are spread far apart. The advantages of this head shape are not clear, but it may be that the shark gains some improvement of its sensory abilities from the spacing out of eyes and nostrils or that the head shape improves maneuverability or simply increases lift.

The smooth hammerhead feeds on fish, particularly rays, and also scavenges on occasion. In summer, it makes regular migrations to cooler waters. Hammerheads have been known to attack humans and are thought to be aggressive sharks.

NAME: Sandy Dogfish, *Scyliorhinus canicula*
RANGE: N. Atlantic Ocean: coasts of Norway, Britain, Europe, N. Africa; Mediterranean Sea
HABITAT: sandy or gravel bottoms
SIZE: 60 cm–1 m (23½ in–3¼ ft)

A common fish, the sandy dogfish is one of a family of 60 species of small shallow-water sharks. Its dorsal fins are placed well back toward the tail, which is long, with the lower lobe barely developed. Usually light sandy-brown in color, this dogfish is boldly marked with dark-brown spots and has a creamy or white belly. Primarily a bottom-dweller, it occurs in shallow water to depths of 100 m (330 ft) but may sometimes be found in deeper water, down to 400 m (1,300 ft). Its varied diet consists of many types of bottom-living invertebrates, such as crustaceans, mollusks and worms, as well as fish.

Reproduction may take place throughout the year, but in the northern hemisphere most eggs are laid between November and July. The female deposits her eggs among seaweed in shallow water; each is encased in a horny capsule with tendrils at each corner. These tendrils anchor the egg case to weeds or other objects, where it remains during the period of development, which lasts some 5 to 11 months. The newly hatched young are 10 cm (4 in) long; they are sexually mature when about 50 cm (19¾ in) long.

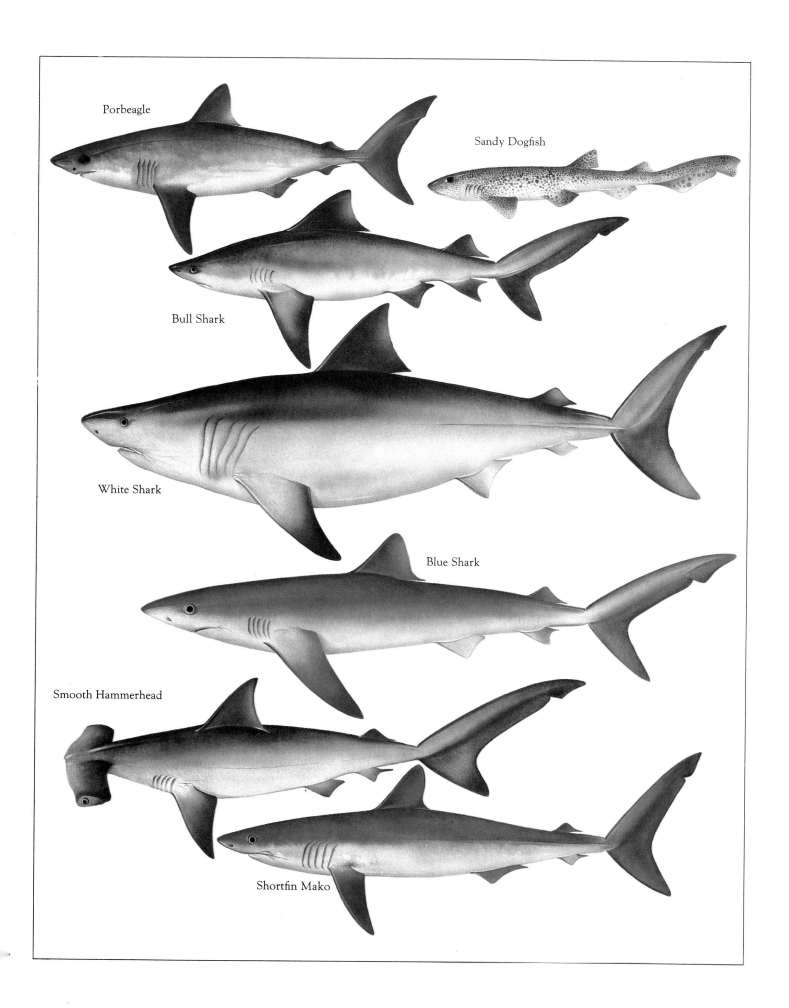

Porbeagle

Sandy Dogfish

Bull Shark

White Shark

Blue Shark

Smooth Hammerhead

Shortfin Mako

Sharks

SQUALIFORMES

This order includes 76 species of shark in 3 families: dogfish sharks, saw sharks and angel sharks. All have two dorsal fins, no anal fin and five or six pairs of gill slits. The species occur worldwide, and the order contains the world's smallest sharks, such as the dwarf shark, *Squaliolus laticaudus*, which is only 23 cm (9 in) long.

NAME: Spiny Dogfish, *Squalus acanthias*
RANGE: N. Atlantic Ocean: coasts of Norway, Britain to N. Africa, W. Greenland to Florida; Mediterranean Sea; N. Pacific Ocean
HABITAT: inshore waters, near seabed
SIZE: 1–1.2 m (3¼–4 ft)

A common shark, easily identified by the large spine in front of each dorsal fin, the spiny dogfish has a long, slender body, a pointed snout and large eyes. Females are longer and heavier than males and are not sexually mature until 19 or 20 years of age; males mature at 11 years. Spiny dogfishes feed on schooling fish, such as herring and whiting, and on bottom-living fish and invertebrates. They themselves move in schools, sometimes numbering thousands of individuals and often of only one sex. These schools may be migrating to warmer or cooler waters or, if females, to shallow water to give birth.

The spiny dogfish bears live young, which develop inside the mother for 18 to 22 months. From 3 to 11 young are born at a time, but the exact number and development time depend on the size of the mother. The combination of a small litter, long gestation and late maturity makes this species particularly vulnerable to fishing pressure, and at one time it was fished in considerable quantities.

NAME: Common Saw Shark, *Pristiophorus cirratus*
RANGE: S. Indian and Pacific Oceans
HABITAT: seabed
SIZE: 1.2 m (4 ft)

The common saw shark, one of 4 species of saw shark, has a distinctive, bladelike snout with sharp teeth, alternately large and small, along each side. The fish's slender body and fin shapes show its relationship to the sharks, despite its strange snout. A sedentary shark, it probes in the mud of the seabed with its saw, searching for invertebrates and bottom-living fish, which it detects with the aid of sensitive barbels on its snout. The young are born well developed, but their teeth do not erupt until after birth.

NAME: Greenland Shark, *Somniosus microcephalus*
RANGE: N. Atlantic Ocean: inside Arctic Circle, south to Cape Cod and Britain
HABITAT: seabed at depths of 180–550 m (600–1,800 ft)
SIZE: 6.4 m (21 ft)

The Greenland shark is the giant of its group, but unlike other Atlantic squalid sharks, it has small dorsal fins with no spines in front of them. It appears to be a sluggish bottom-dweller but will often come to the surface in search of food, particularly in winter. It preys on many kinds of fish, both surface- and bottom-living, and also feeds on mollusks, crustaceans and squid and, reputedly, on seals, porpoises and seabirds. At arctic whaling stations, it was well known as a scavenger.

Female Greenland sharks bear live young from eggs which develop and hatch inside the mother's body. The usual litter is believed to be about 10 young.

NAME: Monkfish, *Squatina squatina*
RANGE: North Sea; E. Atlantic Ocean: Scotland to N. Africa and Canary Islands; Mediterranean Sea
HABITAT: coastal waters, seabed
SIZE: 1.8 m (6 ft)

The monkfish appears to be almost a cross between a shark and a ray, but the gills positioned at the sides, the mouth at the end of its head and well-developed dorsal fins all reveal it to be a true shark. (Rays have mouth and gill slits positioned on their undersides.) Its broad pectoral fins do, however, strongly resemble those of rays. Female monkfishes are larger than males.

A bottom-living shark, the monkfish lies almost buried in sand or mud much of the time, but it can swim well. It feeds on bottom-living fish, such as dab, plaice, sole and rays, and on crabs and mollusks. It bears live young, in litters of 9 to 20, from eggs which develop and hatch inside the mother.

Closely related species are the Atlantic angel shark, *S. dumerili*, and the Pacific angel shark, *S. californica*, which occur off the coasts of North America. They are similar in habits and appearance to the monkfish, although smaller.

HETERODONTIFORMES:
Bullhead Shark Order

This is a small order containing one family of 6 rather primitive species of shark, found in the tropical Indian and Pacific Oceans. All have two dorsal fins, preceded by a thick spine.

NAME: Port Jackson Shark, *Heterodontus portusjacksoni*
RANGE: S. Pacific Ocean, Antarctic Ocean: coasts of Australia from S. Queensland to S.W. Western Australia
HABITAT: coastal waters to depths of 180 m (600 ft)
SIZE: up to 1.5 m (5 ft)

The Port Jackson shark has the large, heavy head, prominent forehead and ridge over each eye that are typical of all bullhead sharks. Other characteristic features are the dark-brown markings encircling its grayish-brown body and the stout spines in front of each dorsal fin. The shark's small mouth is equipped with sharp, pointed teeth at the front and broader crushing teeth farther back, suggesting that it feeds on hard-shelled items such as mollusks, sea urchins and crustaceans. Most feeding takes place at night.

These sharks are believed to migrate year after year to the same shallow, reef areas to breed. Like all bullheads, they are egg-laying sharks, producing eggs that are protected by strong, horny cases with spirally twisted edges. This formation helps the egg case to lodge in a rock crevice, where it remains until the young shark hatches out.

HEXANCHIFORMES:
Cow Shark and Frill Shark Order

The 6 species in this order are all primitive sharks with long bodies and only one dorsal fin. All have six or seven pairs of gill slits — more advanced sharks generally have only five pairs. Most are deep-sea species, and relatively little is known of their habits.

NAME: Sixgill Shark, *Hexanchus griseus*
RANGE: Atlantic, Pacific and Indian Oceans: temperate and warm temperate areas
HABITAT: open sea, inshore waters
SIZE: 1.8–5 m (6–16½ ft)

An elongate shark with a long tail fin and one dorsal fin positioned near the tail, this species has six pairs of gills. Although apparently fairly sedentary and sluggish, it is a powerful shark and feeds on a wide range of bottom-living fish, such as rays, as well as on crustaceans. It is thought to mate in spring; the eggs develop and hatch inside the mother, and the young are 46 to 61 cm (18 to 24 in) long when they are born. There are often 40 or more in a litter, depending on the size of the female.

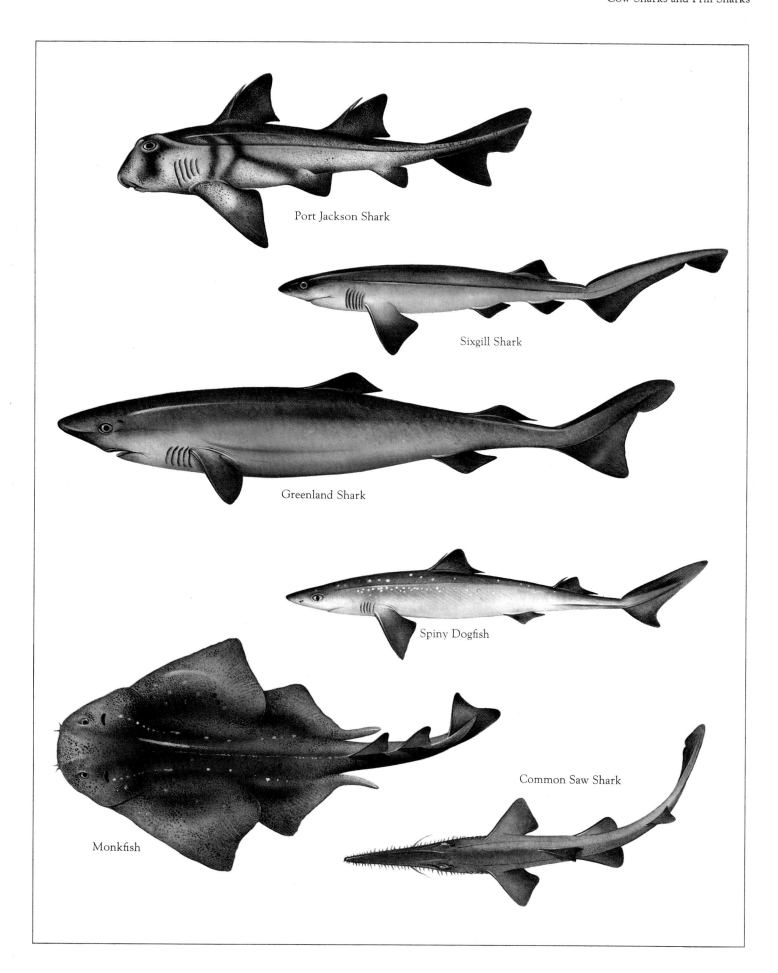

Port Jackson Shark

Sixgill Shark

Greenland Shark

Spiny Dogfish

Common Saw Shark

Monkfish

Skates and Rays

NAME: Smalltooth Sawfish, *Pristis pectinata*
RANGE: temperate and tropical oceans
HABITAT: shallow coastal waters
SIZE: 7.7 m (25 ft)

The smalltooth is the largest of the 6 species of sawfish and is well known off the Atlantic coast of the USA and the East African coast. Like all sawfishes, it has an extraordinary bladelike snout, each side studded with 24 to 32 large teeth of equal size. Its body is more sharklike than raylike, apart from the enlarged pectoral fins and the gill openings on its underside.

Sawfishes live on the seabed in shallow water and use their saws to probe the sand and mud for small invertebrate prey; in doing so they frequently disturb and damage undersea cables. It is claimed that sawfishes also lash out with their snouts at schools of fish to obtain food; while this is unconfirmed, they can certainly cause serious wounds to other fish, and to fishermen, if accidentally caught in fishing nets.

NAME: Atlantic Guitarfish, *Rhinobatus lentiginosus*
RANGE: W. Atlantic Ocean
HABITAT: shallow waters, bays, estuaries
SIZE: 76 cm (30 in)

A common fish along the American Atlantic coast from North Carolina to Yucatán, the guitarfish is halfway between sharks and rays in body shape. Its body is long and rounded with well-developed dorsal fins, but the pectoral fins are enlarged and the gill slits are on the underside of the body. It is a bottom-dweller and feeds mainly on crustaceans and mollusks. There are about 45 species of guitarfish.

NAME: Skate, *Raja batis*
RANGE: E. Atlantic Ocean: Arctic Ocean to Madeira; Mediterranean Sea
HABITAT: deep waters
SIZE: 2.4 m (8 ft)

The skate is a valuable commercial species, and large numbers are caught for food. Skates live in water from 30 to 600 m (98 to 2,000 ft) deep; only young fishes are found in the shallower part of this range. The skate has a flattened body, broad pectoral fins and a tiny tail. There are small spines on the tail and on the underside of the body; adult females also have spines on the front edge of the body, while males have spines on their backs.

Skates are bottom-dwellers; they feed on fish, crabs, lobsters and octopuses. Their eggs, deposited on the seabed, are encased in horny capsules which have long tips at each corner. The young are about 21 cm (8¼ in) long on hatching.

RAJIFORMES:
Skates and Ray Order

There are 8 families of cartilaginous fishes in this order, about 315 species in all. Most are marine fishes of temperate and tropical waters. All, except for the sawfish, have broad, flattened bodies and greatly expanded pectoral fins which extend along the head and trunk, giving the fishes a diamond shape. Tails are small and whiplike and dorsal fins tiny. Gill openings and the slit mouth are on the underside of the body, but there are small openings, or spiracles, on the upper surface through which the fishes can breathe when lying on the seabed. Most species live on or near the seabed and feed on mollusks and crustaceans. When swimming, some rays make flapping movements of the pectoral fins and appear almost to be flying through the water.

They produce eggs, which are either deposited in egg cases to develop in the sea or which develop and hatch inside the mother, who then gives birth to fully formed live young.

NAME: Southern Stingray, *Dasyatis americana*
RANGE: Atlantic coast: New Jersey to Brazil; Gulf of Mexico; Caribbean
HABITAT: shallow coastal waters
SIZE: 1.5 m (5 ft) wide

Stingrays are almost rectangular in shape and have long thin tails; they have no dorsal or anal fins. The stingray's characteristic weapon, and the origin of its common name, is a sharp spine near the base of the tail. This serrated spine has venom-secreting tissue in its underside and can inflict a serious wound that may be fatal, even to humans. Although the stingray cannot move the actual spine independently, it can wield its tail with great speed and force and thus drive the spine into its victim. Some Indo-Pacific tribes use the spines of stingrays as weapons.

Stingrays usually live buried in sand on the seabed; they feed on fish, crustaceans and mollusks which they crush with their strong, flattened teeth. The 3 to 5 young of the stingray develop inside the mother and are about 18 cm (7 in) wide at birth. All stingray species have much the same habits.

Of little commercial importance themselves, stingrays can do immense damage to valuable shellfish beds.

NAME: Eagle Ray, *Myliobatis aquila*
RANGE: E. Atlantic Ocean: Britain to Senegal; Mediterranean and Adriatic Seas
HABITAT: coastal waters
SIZE: 1.8 m (6 ft)

Eagle rays are large, graceful fishes, with pointed, winglike pectoral fins and long thin tails. They feed on the seabed on crustaceans and mollusks but are much more active than stingrays; they swim with supreme grace in mid-water with flying movements of the fins.

In the north of its range, the eagle ray is seen only in summer; in winter it moves south to breed. The female produces up to 7 live young, which are nourished before birth by secretions of her uterine membrane.

NAME: Atlantic Manta, *Manta birostris*
RANGE: Atlantic Ocean: North Carolina to Brazil, Madeira to W. Africa
HABITAT: coastal waters, open sea
SIZE: 5.2 m (17 ft); 6.7 m (22 ft) wide

The gigantic manta, also known as the giant devil ray, is the largest living ray. It has huge pointed pectoral fins, a fairly short tail and a short dorsal fin. The head region is wide, and there are two fleshy appendages at each side of the mouth. These can be rolled or extended to act as scoops for food. The name "manta" originates from the resemblance of the fish's wide, mobile fins to a cloak or mantle.

Like many of the ocean giants, mantas feed on tiny planktonic creatures which they filter from the water onto their gill arches. They also swallow fish and large crustaceans. The young hatch inside their mother and are born well developed.

NAME: Atlantic Torpedo, *Torpedo nobiliana*
RANGE: Atlantic Ocean: Scotland to South Africa, Nova Scotia to North Carolina; Mediterranean Sea
HABITAT: seabed
SIZE: 1.8 m (6 ft)

The torpedo rays are capable of giving electric shocks of 70 to 220 volts, sufficient power to kill or stun a fish or throw a man to the ground. The electric discharges of these fishes are produced by modified muscle cells. Torpedos feed on fish, which they trap and envelop in their pectoral fins while delivering the shock. Although the Atlantic torpedo is one of the largest torpedo rays, it has a small mouth and tiny teeth and would be an inefficient predator without the shock system. Breeding females produce live young which are about 25 cm (9¾ in) long at birth.

Smalltooth Sawfish

Atlantic Guitarfish

Southern Stingray

Atlantic Torpedo

Eagle Ray

Skate

Atlantic Manta

Chimaeras, Lungfishes, Coelacanth

CHIMAERIFORMES: Chimaera Order

This order is the third major group of cartilaginous fishes and includes 25 species of marine fishes distributed throughout the world. Chimaeroids are long-bodied fishes with long thin tails. Their gills open into a single external opening on each side, covered by a flap. Male chimaeroids have pelvic claspers for internal fertilization of females at spawning time.

NAME: **Ratfish/Rabbitfish,** *Chimaera monstrosa*
RANGE: **E. North Atlantic Ocean: Iceland to Azores; Mediterranean Sea**
HABITAT: **deep water**
SIZE: **1.5 m (5 ft)**

The ratfish is a distinctive species, typical of its order with its prominent dorsal fin, large pectoral fins and large eyes. The spine on the dorsal fin is linked to a venom gland. The male has a clublike appendage on its head and is often slightly smaller than the female. Ratfishes are often seen in one-sex schools.

Generally found close to the seabed, the ratfish feeds on starfish, mollusks and crustaceans. In summer it comes into shallower water to breed and lays eggs, each of which is enclosed in a long tapering case. The egg case becomes lodged in the seabed.

NAME: **Elephant Shark,** *Callorhincus milii*
RANGE: **off Australia and New Zealand**
HABITAT: **inshore waters**
SIZE: **1 m (3¼ ft)**

In most respects the elephant shark resembles other chimaeroids, but it is distinguished by its strange, trunklike proboscis, the origin of its common name. There are about 4 species of elephantfish, all found in the southern hemisphere. Fertilization is internal, and females deposit eggs which are enclosed in horny cases.

CERATODIFORMES: Australian Lungfish Order

There is only a single living species in this order, which has some relationship with the other lungfish order. All lungfishes have lunglike breathing organs which they can use to take breaths of air at the surface; when underwater, they inhale water as other fishes do. Lungfishes are related to early air-breathing fishes and are the only remaining representatives of formerly abundant orders.

NAME: **Australian Lungfish,** *Neoceratodus forsteri*
RANGE: **Australia: Queensland**
HABITAT: **rivers**
SIZE: **1.5 m (5 ft)**

First discovered in 1870, the Australian lungfish differs from other lungfishes in that it has only one lung. It lives in permanent waters, so does not generally undergo a period of dormancy to withstand drought. In captivity it is mainly carnivorous and feeds on almost any animal food. The fishes spawn from August to October in shallow water.

The lungfish occurs naturally only in the Burnett and Mary rivers but is being introduced into other rivers in an attempt to protect the species.

LEPIDOSIRENIFORMES: African and South American Lungfish Order

This order contains 2 related families, one with only a single species, the South American lungfish, and the other with 4 species of African lungfishes. The close relationship of these 2 families is one of the pieces of evidence suggesting that Africa and South America were once joined.

NAME: **South American Lungfish,** *Lepidosiren paradoxa*
RANGE: **central South America**
HABITAT: **swamps, weeded river margins**
SIZE: **1.2 m (4 ft)**

The South American lungfish has a pair of lunglike organs connected with its esophagus. This fish usually lives in oxygen-poor, swampy areas, but because of its lungs it is able to supplement the oxygen obtained from the water by breathing air at the surface.

The swamps this lungfish inhabits are periodically flooded and then undergo a dry season. The fish survives the dry period by digging itself a burrow in which it lives, breathing air, while the swamp dries out. Once the surroundings become really arid, the fish closes the burrow entrance with mud, curls up and covers itself with a protective covering of mucus secretion to conserve moisture. Its body slows down to a state of dormancy, but it continues to breathe air. When the rains return, the lungfish emerges from its burrow. This form of inactivity in a hot climate is known as estivation.

During the rainy season, lungfish pairs spawn in burrows made by the male. He guards the eggs and then the young. The newly hatched young have adhesive glands by which they hang from vegetation and which are lost after 6 to 8 weeks.

NAME: **African Lungfish,** *Protopterus aethiopicus*
RANGE: **E. and central Africa**
HABITAT: **rivers, lakes**
SIZE: **2 m (6½ ft)**

The African lungfish has a pair of lungs connected to its esophagus and can breathe air at the water surface. It has normal, but poorly developed, gills. This species lives mostly in permanent waters, but if there is a long dry period and the water level drops, it can burrow and estivate in much the same way as the South American lungfish. The other 3 African species live in swamps and must estivate during the regular dry seasons.

In the breeding season the male makes a hole in which one or more females lay eggs. He then guards the eggs and the young when they hatch.

COELACANTHIFORMES: Coelacanth Order

There is just a single living species in this order, once widespread and abundant. Coelacanths were only known as 90-million-year-old fossils until one was caught by a fisherman off the coast of South Africa in 1938. This living species was so like its fossil relatives as to be unmistakably a coelacanth and has enabled scientists to learn about the bodies of animals hitherto known only from skeletons.

NAME: **Coelacanth,** *Latimeria chalumnae*
RANGE: **Indian Ocean, off Comoro Islands**
HABITAT: **rocky or coral slopes**
SIZE: **1.9 m (6¼ ft)**

Coelacanths are heavy-bodied fishes, with fleshy lobes at the base of all fins except the first dorsal fin; the pectoral fins can be turned through 180 degrees. Such fishes, known as the crossopterygians, were once widespread.

The internal structure of the coelacanth has several features which throw light on the evolution of fishes; for example, the heart is extremely simple compared with that of other fishes and is similar to the early fish heart which theorists had predicated. The kidneys, unlike those of any other vertebrate, are positioned on the underside of the body.

Modern coelacanths are carnivores, believed to feed mainly on fish. There has been much disagreement about their breeding methods, but now, since the discovery of a female with 5 almost fully developed young in her oviduct, they are known to be ovoviviparous: they bear fully formed young by means of eggs that hatch inside the mother.

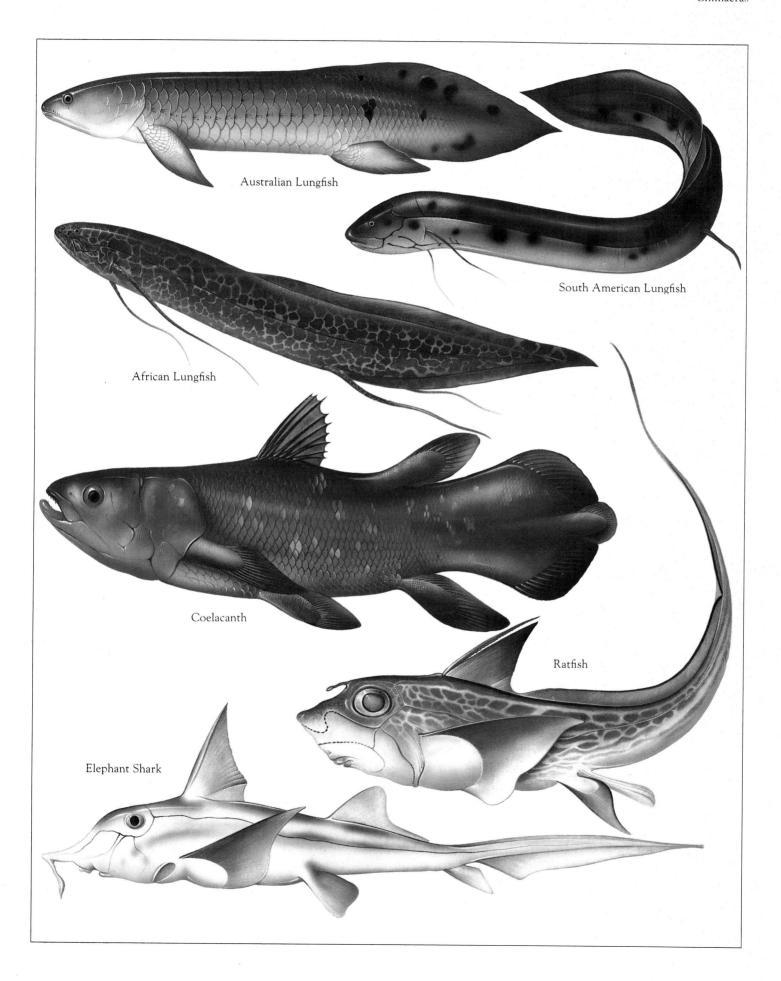

Australian Lungfish

South American Lungfish

African Lungfish

Coelacanth

Ratfish

Elephant Shark

Sturgeons, Gars, Bowfin, Bichirs

ACIPENSERIFORMES: Sturgeon Order

There are 2 families in this order. First, there are the 23 species of sturgeon, which are mainly freshwater and coastal fishes of temperate regions, the marine species of which migrate into rivers to spawn. All have five rows of bony plates along the sides of the body. Second, there is the paddlefish family, in which there are 2 species of sturgeonlike freshwater fishes with long paddlelike snouts and no bony plates.

NAME: **Beluga**, *Huso huso*
RANGE: basins of Caspian and Black Seas; Adriatic Sea, Sea of Azov
HABITAT: **sea, rivers**
SIZE: **5 m (16½ ft)**

Huge heavy fishes, belugas weigh up to 1,200 kg (2,645 lb), sometimes more. They are now relatively uncommon, partly because of river pollution interfering with their migrations and partly because of pressure of fishing. The taking of eggs for caviar from mature females is damaging to stocks, particularly because these fishes mature late, males at 14 years and females at 18 years. A single ripe female may contain up to 7 million eggs.

Belugas migrate into rivers in winter or spring and spawn on rocky riverbeds. The newly hatched young immediately start moving toward the sea, feeding on small bottom-living invertebrates. At sea, the adult belugas feed on fish, particularly herringlike species and members of the carp family.

NAME: **Paddlefish**, *Polyodon spathula*
RANGE: USA: Mississippi River system
HABITAT: **large rivers and lakes**
SIZE: **2 m (6½ ft)**

The paddlefish has a long flattened snout and a large head. It swims with its large mouth agape and lower jaw dropped, filtering any planktonic creatures from the water onto the comblike gill rakers; it closes its mouth periodically to swallow. Its skeleton is mostly cartilage and there are only a few small scales on the skin.

Paddlefish spawn in April and May in gravel or sandy-bottomed areas. As the female deposits the eggs, the male fertilizes them. The eggs then develop an adhesive coating which makes them sink and attach to the first object they touch. The newly hatched larva lacks a long snout, but it starts to develop in 2 to 3 weeks. The only other species, *Psephurus gladius*, lives in China.

NAME: **Sturgeon**, *Acipenser sturio*
RANGE: European coastline: Norway and Baltic Sea to Mediterranean and Black Seas
HABITAT: **shallow sea, rivers**
SIZE: **3 m (10 ft)**

Sturgeons are increasingly rare fishes and are in need of protection in Europe. They have been used by man for centuries as a food fish, and the female's unshed eggs are collected, salted and eaten as caviar. Overfishing, combined with pollution and man-made obstructions in spawning rivers, has led to the sturgeon's decline.

A bottom-dwelling species, the sturgeon feeds on invertebrates, such as worms, mollusks and crustaceans, and on some fish. In spring, breeding sturgeons migrate into rivers to spawn. A large female may contain from 800,000 to 2,400,000 sticky black eggs which she sheds onto the gravel of the riverbed. The eggs hatch in about a week. The young fishes remain in the river for up to 3 years, feeding on insect larvae and crustaceans. A closely related, if not identical, species, *A. oxyrhynchus*, occurs along the Atlantic coast of North America.

SEMIONOTIFORMES: Gar Order

The single surviving family in this previously abundant and widely spread order occurs in North and Central America. It contains 7 species of gars or garpikes, all with some primitive characteristics. They are mostly freshwater fishes, although sometimes found in brackish or salt water. All have long bodies and jaws, and anal and dorsal fins which are placed well back. Their bodies are covered with hard scales.

NAME: **Longnose Gar**, *Lepisosteus osseus*
RANGE: N. America: Quebec and the Great Lakes to Florida and New Mexico
HABITAT: **rivers, lakes**
SIZE: **1.5 m (5 ft)**

The most abundant and widely distributed of the gars, the longnose has particularly long jaws, studded with sharp teeth. It is a predatory fish, waiting concealed among vegetation for fishes and crustaceans to come near; it then thrusts forward and seizes its prey.

In spring, gars congregate in shallow water to spawn. The eggs are adhesive and stick to weeds or stones. The newly hatched young have adhesive suckers under their mouths, and they attach themselves to floating objects until their yolk sacs are absorbed and they must start to hunt for food.

AMIIFORMES: Bowfin Order

Only 1 family with a single species remains in this order that once contained at least 7 other families, all now extinct. The modern bowfin possesses many of the features of its fossil relatives, which have been found in Europe and Asia as well as in North America.

NAME: **Bowfin**, *Amia calva*
RANGE: eastern N. America
HABITAT: **quiet streams and ponds**
SIZE: **91 cm (3 ft)**

A stout-bodied fish with a long dorsal fin and a rounded tail, the bowfin has the primitive feature of two bony plates under the throat. Males are usually smaller than females and have an orange-bordered dark spot at the base of the tail. The bowfin generally lives in densely vegetated, sluggish waters which are poor in oxygen, but by using its swim bladder as a lung and breathing oxygen from the air, it can withstand such conditions. Bowfins feed on fish and some crayfish.

In spring, the male clears a hollow in the riverbed, making a nest of small roots and gravel. The eggs are laid in the nest, and the male guards them for 8 to 10 days until they hatch. Each larva attaches itself to the nest by the cement gland on its head and is nourished by its yolk sac. After about 9 days, the larvae can swim and feed but are still guarded and herded by their male parent until they are about 10 cm (4 in) long.

POLYPTERIFORMES: Bichir Order

This order contains a single family of 11 species, all found in African freshwater habitats. The fishes strongly resemble the earliest fossil fishes and have primitive features, such as a swim bladder which can be used as a means of breathing air.

NAME: **Bichir**, *Polypterus weeksi*
RANGE: central Africa: upper Congo basin
HABITAT: **lakes, rivers**
SIZE: **40 cm (15¾ in)**

A long-bodied fish covered with hard diamond-shaped scales, this bichir, like the rest of its family, inhabits overgrown water margins. Its distinctive dorsal fin is made up of small flaglike fins, each supported by a bony ray. The fan-shaped pectoral fins are mounted on fleshy lobes. Bichirs feed on fish and amphibians.

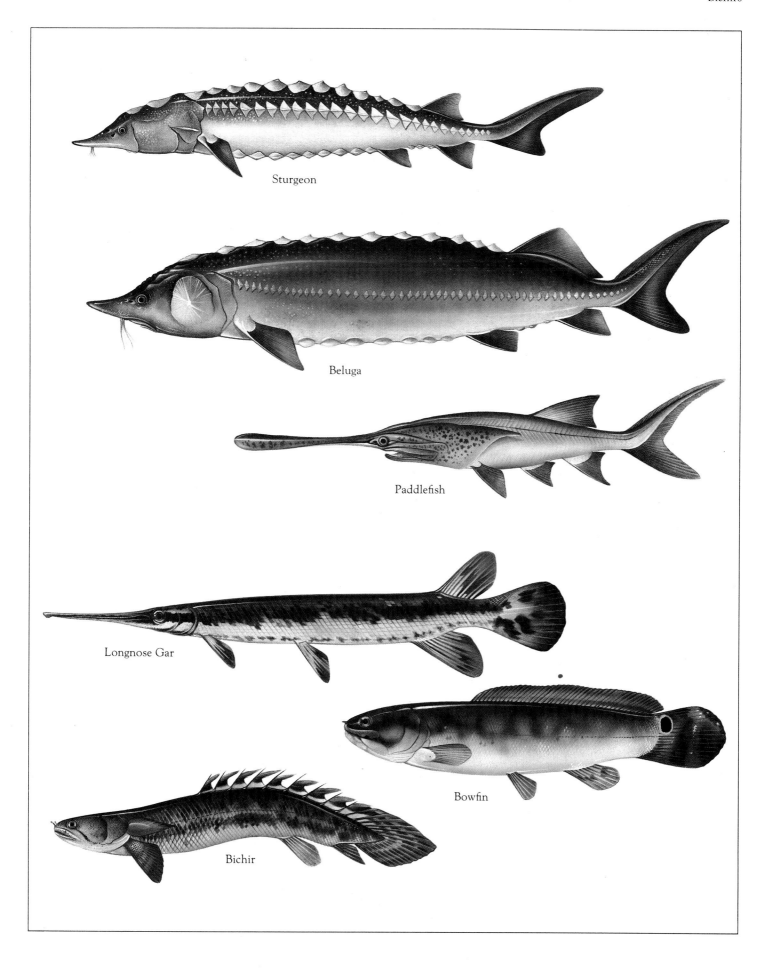

Sturgeon

Beluga

Paddlefish

Longnose Gar

Bowfin

Bichir

Osteoglossiform, Elopiform and Mormyriform Fishes

OSTEOGLOSSIFORMES

The 15 species of bony tongue and their relatives, such as mooneyes, knifefishes and the butterflyfish, are distributed in the fresh waters of South America, West Africa, Southeast Asia and Australasia, with 2 isolated species of mooneye in North America. Principally predatory fishes, they feed on fish and insects and are distinguished by their well-developed bony tongues.

NAME: **Pirarucu**, *Arapaima gigas*
RANGE: **tropical South America**
HABITAT: **rivers, swamps**
SIZE: **up to 4 m (13 ft)** Ⓥ

Said to be the largest freshwater fish in the world, this bony tongue may weigh up to 200 kg (441 lb), and there have been reports of specimens measuring 5 m (16½ ft) in length. It is an elongate fish, with large body scales, but a scaleless head, and long, low dorsal and anal fins set back near the tail. Often found in oxygen-poor swampy water, the pirarucu has a large swim bladder, which is connected to the pharynx and can be used as a lung to breathe air.

Pirarucus breed in sandy-bottomed water and make a small hollow in the riverbed, where the eggs are laid and then guarded until they hatch.

NAME: **Aruana**, *Osteoglossum bicirrhosum*
RANGE: **tropical South America**
HABITAT: **freshwater lakes, quiet rivers**
SIZE: **1 m (3¼ ft)**

The aruana is a fish of unusual appearance, with its prominent chin barbels and dramatically upward-slanting mouth. Its back forms a virtually straight line with the head, and the dorsal and anal fins are long and low.

Thought to incubate its eggs in its mouth, the aruana has a pouchlike structure on its lower jaw similar to that of the related species *Scleropages*, found in Australia and Southeast Asia and known to be a mouth-brooder.

NAME: **Goldeye**, *Hiodon alosoides*
RANGE: **N. America: S. Canada to Mississippi basin**
HABITAT: **rivers, lakes**
SIZE: **30.5–41 cm (12–16 in)**

The goldeye is one of the small family of mooneyes, characterized by their large golden eyes and the many small teeth lining the mouth. It is a silvery fish, somewhat herringlike in appearance, with a long anal fin. Insects and their larvae, as well as small fish, are its main foods, and it is generally active at night; its large eyes are well adapted for night vision.

ELOPIFORMES

There are 11 species in this order, grouped in 3 families: tenpounders, tarpons and bonefishes. All are marine fishes, but some may enter fresh or brackish water. Related to eels and herrings, they are slender-bodied fishes, with deeply forked tails. The order includes several important game fishes.

NAME: **Tarpon**, *Tarpon atlanticus*
RANGE: **W. Atlantic Ocean: Nova Scotia to Gulf of Mexico and Brazil; E. Atlantic: off W. Africa**
HABITAT: **coastal and oceanic waters**
SIZE: **1.2–2.4 m (4–8 ft)**

The tarpon is a huge, silvery fish, its body covered with large scales. It is characterized by its compressed body and flattened sides, protruding lower jaw and pointed dorsal fin, with an elongate last ray. Tarpons feed on many types of fish and on crabs.

Tarpons are most prolific breeders: a large female may contain more than 12 million eggs. These are shed out at sea, but the larvae drift to inshore waters and live in estuaries, swamps and river mouths while they grow. Tarpons are not sexually mature until about 6 or 7 years of age.

NAME: **Ladyfish/Tenpounder**, *Elops saurus*
RANGE: **tropical Atlantic, Indian and W. Pacific Oceans**
HABITAT: **shallow inshore waters, estuaries**
SIZE: **1.2 m (4 ft)**

A slender, silvery-blue fish, with fine scales, the ladyfish has dark, fairly small fins and a deeply forked tail. Fish and crustaceans are its main foods. It is a popular game fish because of its habit of leaping and struggling when hooked.

Ladyfishes spawn offshore, but the larvae drift inshore and live in bays and salt marshes while they develop; they may also enter fresh water.

NAME: **Bonefish**, *Albula vulpes*
RANGE: **worldwide in tropical seas**
HABITAT: **inshore waters, especially over sand flats**
SIZE: **90 cm (35½ in)**

The bonefish has a slender, herringlike body, with dark, silvery scales and a deeply forked tail. Its snout projects slightly beyond its mouth. Shoals of bonefishes feed together, foraging over the seabed with heads down and tails near or above the surface; they feed on bottom-living invertebrates such as clams, crabs and shrimps.

The thin, eel-like larvae drift to inshore waters, where they metamorphose to adult form.

MORMYRIFORMES

There are about 101 freshwater species in this order, 100 of which are in the elephantfish family. The other species, *Gymnarchus niloticus*, is in a separate family. In many species, including *Gymnarchus*, muscles at the base of the tail are modified into electric organs that set up an electric field in the water around the fish. The fish can detect any disturbances in this field, such as an obstruction or the proximity of predators or prey, and so can navigate and hunt even in turbid waters or at night, when sight would be of no use.

NAME: **Elephant-snout Fish**, *Mormyrus kannume*
RANGE: **Africa: Nile River system**
HABITAT: **rivers, lakes**
SIZE: **80 cm (31½ in)**

Like many of its family, the elephant-snout fish has an elongate, proboscislike snout, the origin of its common name. All these mormyrid fishes appear to have good learning abilities and well-developed brains; relative to body size, the brain is comparable in size to that of humans. This species can produce weak electric impulses, which set up an electric field around the body. It can then, via specialized pores in the head region, detect any disturbances caused to this field by obstacles or other animals. It feeds mainly on insect larvae.

NAME: *Gymnarchus niloticus*
RANGE: **Africa: upper Nile, W. Africa**
HABITAT: **swamps, lakes, still water**
SIZE: **90 cm–1.5 m (35½ in–5 ft)**

An elongate, slender fish, *Gymnarchus* has no anal, pelvic or tail fins; the dorsal fin is long and low, and the body tapers to a point. The fish swims by undulations of its dorsal fin and can swim backward by reversing the direction of the undulations. Capable of generating an electric field around its body, *Gymnarchus* is sensitive to any disturbance within the field, so is able to navigate and hunt for fish in turbid waters.

Breeding fishes build a nest of plant fibers, in which about 1,000 eggs are laid. The parents guard the eggs for a few days just before they hatch. The young fishes feed on insects and other small invertebrates.

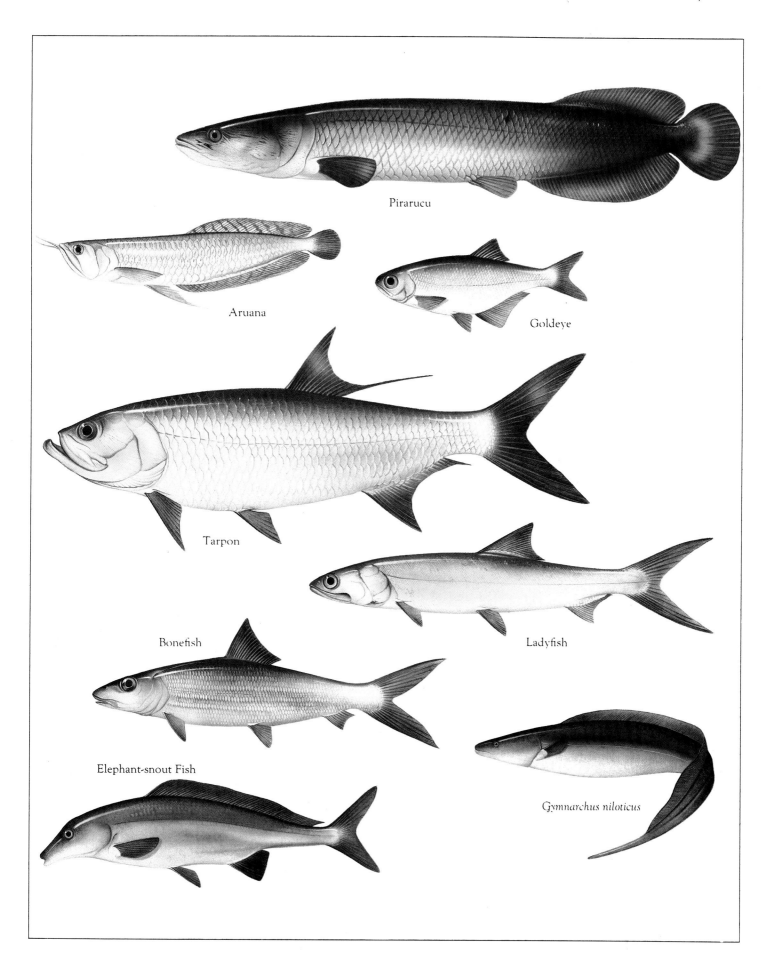

Pirarucu

Aruana

Goldeye

Tarpon

Bonefish

Ladyfish

Elephant-snout Fish

Gymnarchus niloticus

Herrings

NAME: Twaite Shad, *Alosa fallax*
RANGE: Europe, Icelandic coasts, Baltic to Mediterranean Seas
HABITAT: open sea, coastal waters, estuaries
SIZE: 55 cm (22 in)

The twaite shad is a heavy-bodied fish with large fragile scales. It is similar to the allis shad, *A. alosa*, but the species can be easily distinguished by the number of gill rakers on the first gill arch — 40 to 60 in the twaite, and 80 to 130 in the allis. Crustaceans and small fish are the twaite shad's main diet. To spawn, the fishes migrate from coastal waters to the tidal reaches of rivers, but river pollution and man-made obstructions have affected these journeys badly in some areas. The shads spawn at night, and their eggs are spread over the gravel of the riverbed. After hatching, the young fishes move slowly downriver to the sea.

NAME: Alewife, *Alosa pseudoharengus*
RANGE: N. American Atlantic coast, Great Lakes
HABITAT: coastal waters, rivers
SIZE: 38 cm (15 in)

Although primarily a marine fish, the alewife, like all shads, enters rivers to spawn, so it is often found in fresh water. The fishes start their journey in February, and most have returned to the sea by May.

There are some landlocked, freshwater populations which spend their whole lives in lakes, including the Great Lakes. The freshwater alewife is only about half the size of the marine form. Alewife feed mainly on plankton and also take small fish.

NAME: Sardine/Pilchard, *Sardina pilchardus*
RANGE: European coasts; Mediterranean and Black Seas
HABITAT: open sea, coastal waters
SIZE: 25 cm (10 in)

The sardine is a herringlike fish but has a more rounded body and larger scales. Its gill covers are marked with distinct radiating ridges. Shoals of sardines move in surface waters and make seasonal migrations northward in summer, south in winter. They spawn in spring and summer and after spawning generally move farther inshore. Young sardines feed mainly on plant plankton, adults on larger types of animal plankton.

Sardines are extremely valuable food fish. Species of sardine in the closely related genus *Sardinops* are found off Chile and Peru, South Africa, Japan, Australia and along the Pacific coast of the USA.

CLUPEIFORMES: Herring Order

The herring order contains 4 families: 2 have only a single species each — the denticle herring and the wolf herring — the third has the anchovies, and the fourth, and largest, includes all the true herrings, shads, sardines and menhadens. Over 290 species are known. It is one of the most important groups of food fishes — the herring, sardine and anchovy alone account for a large proportion of the total world fish tonnage. Indeed some populations, such as that of the North Sea herring, provide the clearest examples of commercial fish stocks that have been overfished to the point of declining catches.

Most clupeoid fishes are marine and live in schools near the surface of the open sea or in inshore waters. Local populations of some species always return to traditional spawning grounds, and the partial genetic isolation thus produced leads to recognizable races. Typically, clupeoids feed on plankton which they filter from the water through long gill rakers. Their bodies are considerably flattened laterally and are covered with large, reflective, silvery scales. One set of specialized scales found in most clupeoids is the group of enlarged scales (scutes) that form a jagged series of backward-pointing teeth along the middle line of the belly.

NAME: Herring, *Clupea harengus*
RANGE: N. Atlantic Ocean
HABITAT: open sea, coastal waters
SIZE: 41 cm (16 in)

The herring can be divided into a number of races, each with its own characteristics and breeding season. Some races spawn in shallow inshore bays, others offshore on ocean banks, and the eggs form a layer over the seabed. The larvae, which are about 0.5 cm ($\frac{1}{4}$ in) long on hatching, swim in surface waters in large schools and are generally found inshore during the first year of life. Adults, too, swim in surface waters.

Herrings select different items of planktonic food as they grow and also eat other small crustaceans and small fish. The herrings themselves are preyed on by birds, other fishes, dolphins and seals and are an important link in many marine food chains. Atlantic herring has long been an important food fish, and it is one of the top commercial species. The Pacific herring, *C. pallasi*, is closely related to the Atlantic species and has similar habits.

NAME: Wolf Herring, *Chirocentrus dorab*
RANGE: Indian and Pacific Oceans: Red Sea to Australia
HABITAT: surface waters, shallow sea
SIZE: 3.7 m (12 ft)

A herringlike fish of dramatic size, the wolf herring has a long cylindrical body and fanglike teeth. Unlike other members of the order, it does not filter-feed but hunts for its food. Its flesh is of little commercial value.

NAME: Atlantic Menhaden, *Brevoortia tyrannus*
RANGE: N. American Atlantic coast
HABITAT: surface waters
SIZE: 46 cm (18 in)

Menhaden are abundant fishes and travel in huge schools of hundreds of thousands, moving north in spring and summer and south to warmer waters in winter. Also known as the mossbunker, the adult fish has a large head and straight-edged body scales with comblike teeth at their free edge. There is always a definite black spot behind the menhaden's head and a number of smaller spots on its upper sides. The menhaden does not select particular items of plankton but consumes whatever planktonic creatures it filters from the water. It has extremely oily flesh and is used to produce fish meal, oil and fertilizer rather than as food for humans. Many other creatures, such as birds, whales, porpoises, sharks, cod and bluefishes eat the menhaden, and it is used as bait.

NAME: European Anchovy, *Engraulis encrasicolus*
RANGE: European seas
HABITAT: surface waters
SIZE: 20 cm (8 in)

The 110 species of anchovy are found all around the world in temperate to tropical seas. The shape of the anchovy head is distinctive and characteristic, with the snout overhanging the huge mouth; the body is rounded. Anchovies are important food items for many creatures, including tuna, and many species are valuable commercial fish, taken in large quantities, especially off the coast of Peru.

The European anchovy is a slender fish with large, fragile scales. It moves in schools of many thousands of individuals and feeds on plankton, particularly small crustaceans, and the larvae of fish and invertebrates. Found in offshore waters in winter, anchovies move farther inshore in summer to spawn. Eggs and larvae float in surface waters.

The northern anchovy, *E. mordax*, is a common Pacific form, similar to the European species in appearance.

Wolf Herring

Twaite Shad

Herring

European Anchovy

Sardine

Atlantic Menhaden

Alewife

Eels, Spiny Eels

ANGUILLIFORMES: Eel Order

There are more than 600 species of eel, grouped into about 22 families. They occur worldwide, except in polar regions. Most are marine, but there are some freshwater eels. All have long, slender bodies and long dorsal and anal fins; pelvic fins are absent. All species produce eggs which hatch into thin, transparent larvae.

NAME: **Chain Moray, *Echidna catenata***
RANGE: **W. Atlantic Ocean: Bermuda to Brazil, including Caribbean**
HABITAT: **coastal waters**
SIZE: **90 cm (35½ in)**

Moray eels of this genus are most abundant in the Indian and Pacific oceans, but some occur in the tropical Atlantic. The chain moray is common in the Caribbean, where it leads a retiring life among rocks or rocks and sand, usually in shallow water. A striking fish, it is distinctively patterned with brownish-black and yellow or white; young fishes have more light than dark areas.

Unlike most morays, which have sharp, pointed teeth, the chain moray has blunt teeth resembling molars. It feeds mainly on crustaceans and, on occasion, can be seen chasing crabs at the water's edge and even out of water.

NAME: **Moray, *Muraena helena***
RANGE: **Mediterranean Sea; E. Atlantic Ocean: Azores and Cape Verde Islands, north to Bay of Biscay**
HABITAT: **rocky shores**
SIZE: **1.3 m (4¼ ft)**

The most abundant eels, the 100 species of moray are widely distributed in tropical and warm temperate oceans. This moray is typical of the group, with its scaleless, boldly patterned body, which is somewhat laterally compressed. It has no pectoral fins but has well-developed dorsal and anal fins, and its large mouth is equipped with strong, sharp teeth. A voracious predator, the moray habitually lurks in underwater rock crevices with only its head showing, watching for prey — largely fish, squid and cuttlefish. If disturbed, it is a vicious fish and can deliver savage bites.

Morays breed from July to September, and their eggs float at the surface of the sea until they hatch.

NAME: **European Eel, *Anguilla anguilla***
RANGE: **N. Atlantic Ocean: coasts from Iceland to N. Africa; Mediterranean and Black Seas; fresh water in Europe and N. Africa**
HABITAT: **coastal waters, estuaries; fresh water: rivers, streams**
SIZE: **50 cm–1 m (19¾ in–3¼ ft)**

The European eel is easily identified in fresh water, where it is the only eel-like fish, but elsewhere it is characterized by its rounded pectoral fins, the dorsal fin that starts well back from the head, and its small teeth. Its body is covered with tiny scales.

As they approach sexual maturity, European eels migrate from fresh water to the mid-Atlantic, where they spawn and then die. The eggs hatch, and the larvae drift in surface waters for some 3 years, gradually being brought back to coastal waters by ocean currents. Here they metamorphose into elvers and then enter estuaries and rivers, where they grow and mature, feeding on insects, crustaceans and fish. During the freshwater stage, the eels are yellowish-brown in color, but as they mature, they become darker, almost black, with silvery bellies.

The European eel is a valuable food fish and is caught in large quantities. The American eel, *A. rostrata*, found along the Atlantic coasts of North America, closely resembles the European species. It spawns in the west-central Atlantic, and the larvae take only 1 year to drift back to coastal waters.

NAME: **Conger Eel, *Conger conger***
RANGE: **N. Atlantic Ocean: coasts from Iceland to N. Africa; Mediterranean Sea**
HABITAT: **shallow waters, often close to rocks**
SIZE: **2.7 m (9 ft)**

A large, fairly common fish on rocky shores, the conger eel has a scaleless, cylindrical body, prominent pectoral fins and a long-based dorsal fin, which originates well forward near the head. The upper jaw overlaps the lower. The conger feeds on fish, crustaceans, particularly crabs, and octopus.

Usually found in shallow water, adult congers migrate to deeper water to spawn. The eggs hatch into transparent larvae, which drift in surface waters for 1 to 2 years before they develop into small eels.

NAME: **Slender Snipe Eel, *Nemichthys scolopaceus***
RANGE: **Atlantic, Pacific and Indian Oceans: temperate and tropical areas**
HABITAT: **open ocean to depths of 1,000 m (3,300 ft)**
SIZE: **1–1.2 m (3¼–4 ft)**

Slender snipe eels are deep-sea fishes with immensely long, slender bodies and dorsal and anal fins that run most of the length of the body. The narrow, elongate jaws are beaklike and equipped with pointed, backward-facing teeth, which trap prey, such as crustaceans and fish, extremely efficiently. Even though slender snipe eels are fairly common, little is known of their biology.

NAME: **Gulper Eel, *Eurypharynx pelecanoides***
RANGE: **all oceans (particularly Atlantic): warm temperate and tropical areas**
HABITAT: **deep sea at 1,400 m (4,500 ft) or more**
SIZE: **61 cm (24 in)**

The gulper eel is highly unusual in appearance, with its long, delicate body and relatively huge, gaping jaws. Clearly too thin and fragile to be a powerful swimmer, it nevertheless manages to feed on quite large fish. It is thought that the gulper may swim with its jaws wide open, thus engulfing any fish or crustacean that swims unwittingly into its gaping mouth.

NOTACANTHIFORMES: Spiny Eel Order

There are 24 species in this order, found worldwide. All have an eel-like body shape, and most are deep-sea fishes which live on the bottom.

NAME: **Spiny Eel, *Notacanthus chemnitzii***
RANGE: **N. Atlantic Ocean: temperate areas; possibly temperate areas of all other oceans**
HABITAT: **deep sea**
SIZE: **1.2 m (4 ft)**

The spiny eel has a slender, elongate body and a rounded snout that projects beyond the ventrally placed mouth. On its back are a series of short, sharp spines, and there are similar spines preceding the anal fin. The fish is usually brown to grayish-brown in color. Spiny eels are thought to eat bottom-living invertebrates, especially sea anemones, and they probably feed in a head-down position on the seabed. Few details are known of the biology or habits of this rarely seen fish.

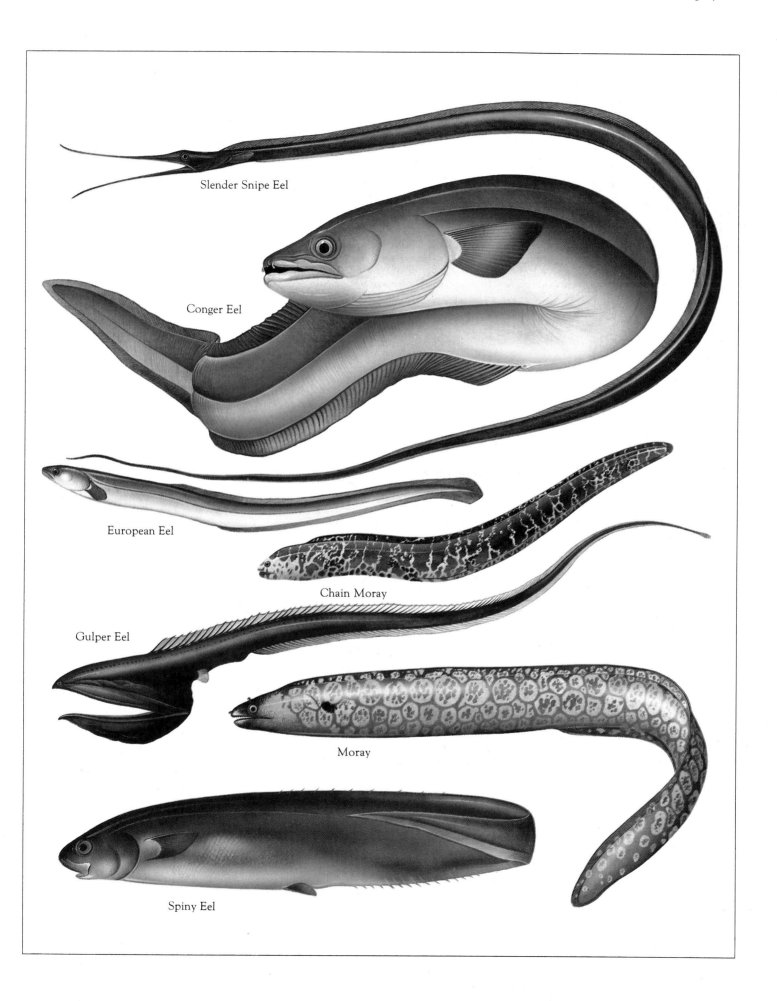

Slender Snipe Eel

Conger Eel

European Eel

Chain Moray

Gulper Eel

Moray

Spiny Eel

Salmon

NAME: Northern Pike, *Esox lucius*
RANGE: circumpolar: Britain, N. Europe, USSR, Alaska, Canada, N. USA
HABITAT: lakes, quiet rivers
SIZE: 1.5 m (5 ft)

The long-bodied northern pike has large jaws with sharp teeth and a pointed snout. The dorsal and anal fins are positioned near the tail and opposite one another, a characteristic of pikes. Females are larger than males, and individuals may weigh 23 kg (50 lb) or more. A predatory species, the pike lurks among vegetation at the water's edge, camouflaged by its mottled coloration, then shoots out to trap prey. It feeds mainly on invertebrates when young and then on fish, but also takes birds and even mammals.

In early spring, as soon as any ice has melted, northern pikes spawn at the water's edge or even in meadows flooded by melted snow. Females shed thousands of eggs over the vegetation.

NAME: Whitefish, *Coregonus lavaretus*
RANGE: Baltic and North Sea basins; Britain, N. Europe, N. USSR, Swiss Alps
HABITAT: marine, brackish water, lakes
SIZE: 20–70 cm (8–27½ in)

Like all members of the whitefish family, this species has large scales, no teeth and a forked tail. Whitefishes tend to vary enormously in size and appearance according to habitat; for example, lake-dwellers are generally much smaller than ocean-dwellers because their food supply is often poor. Many lake populations have been isolated since the last ice age and have evolved their own characteristics.

Whitefishes feed on planktonic crustaceans. They spawn in winter, ocean-dwellers migrating into rivers to spawn.

NAME: Grayling, *Thymallus thymallus*
RANGE: England, N. Europe, Scandinavia, USSR
HABITAT: rivers, large lakes
SIZE: 46 cm (18 in)

The 4 species of grayling are distinctive fishes, all with high sail-like dorsal fins, forked tails and the small fleshy adipose fins near the base of the tail which are typical of salmonlike fishes. Graylings have small teeth in both jaws, and they feed on insects and their larvae, crustaceans and mollusks.

In spring the male oftens displays before breeding; the female makes a hollow in shallow, gravel-bottomed water for her eggs. The eggs hatch 3 to 4 weeks after laying. The American grayling, *T. arcticus*, is similar in appearance and habits.

SALMONIFORMES: Salmon Order

This order contains 24 families with approximately 508 species, including pikes, salmon, whitefishes, graylings, chars, trout and smelts. Members of the order occur in freshwater and marine environments, mainly in the northern hemisphere. Some migrate from the sea into rivers to spawn. Most species are predatory.

NAME: Arctic Char, *Salvelinus alpinus*
RANGE: circumpolar: Arctic and N. Atlantic Oceans, Britain, Europe, USSR, N. America
HABITAT: open sea, rivers, lakes
SIZE: 25–96 cm (10–38 in)

The Arctic char is a highly variable species, according to its environment. In the north of its range, it lives in the sea, growing large on the rich supplies of fish, mollusks and crustaceans, and enters rivers to spawn. Farther south, Arctic char live in mountain lakes, and because of their long isolation, populations have become quite unlike one another and the migratory form. The lake fishes are much smaller and feed on planktonic crustaceans, insects and larvae, and mollusks.

Migratory char breed in gravel-bottomed rivers. The female makes a nest in the male's territory and lays her eggs; he then fertilizes them in the nest. Lake populations spawn in a similar manner on the lake bed or in streams. Growth is slow, although the rate varies from population to population. Migratory fishes do not attain full size until they are about 20 years old.

This char is a good food fish of particular importance to the people of arctic Canada.

NAME: Lake Trout, *Salvelinus namaycush*
RANGE: Canada, N. USA
HABITAT: lakes, rivers
SIZE: 1.2 m (4 ft)

One of the most important commercial freshwater fishes and a popular sport-fishing species in North America, the lake trout is actually a char, not a true trout. It has now been successfully introduced into lakes out of its natural range. A beautiful fish, it has characteristic pale spots on head, back and sides. Lake trout feed on fish, insects, crustaceans and plankton.

From late summer to December, lake trout spawn in shallow, gravel-bottomed water. There is no nest, but males clear the spawning ground of debris. The eggs are laid on the gravel and settle among the stones; they remain there for the winter and hatch in early spring.

NAME: Trout, *Salmo trutta*
RANGE: Europe; introduced worldwide
HABITAT: marine; lakes, rivers
SIZE: 23 cm–1.4 m (9 in–4½ ft)

There are two forms of this well-known food and angling fish: the sea trout, which migrates from river to sea and back to river to breed, and the smaller brown trout, which spends all its life in fresh water. They are alike physically, but sea trout have silvery scales with scattered black markings, and brown trout have numerous dark spots. Both forms feed on fish and crustaceans.

Trout spawn in winter in gravel-bottomed fresh water; the female makes a shallow nest for her eggs. The young hatch in spring and remain in the gravel for a few weeks.

NAME: Rainbow Trout, *Salmo gairdneri*
RANGE: western N. America, E. Pacific; introduced worldwide
HABITAT: marine; rivers
SIZE: up to 1 m (3¼ ft)

Now farmed in large quantities, rainbow trout are extremely popular with anglers and are an important food fish. There is a large migratory form, known as the steelhead, which bears the same relationship to the rainbow as the sea trout does to the brown trout. Both forms feed mainly on insect larvae, mollusks and crustaceans.

In their natural range, rainbow trout spawn in spring in shallow, gravel-bottomed streams. The female makes a shallow nest in the gravel and deposits her eggs, which are then fertilized by the male and covered over.

NAME: Atlantic Salmon, *Salmo salar*
RANGE: N. Atlantic Ocean: Greenland to Cape Cod; Arctic coast of USSR, south to N. Spain
HABITAT: open sea; rivers
SIZE: up to 1.5 m (5 ft)

The best known of its family, the Atlantic salmon is a long-bodied, rounded fish with a slightly forked tail. There are some salmon in inland lakes, but most are migratory, moving from their natal river out to sea and then back to the river to spawn.

The salmon enter the river at different times but all spawn in the winter. Breeding males develop hooked protuberances on their lower jaws. Having excavated a shallow nest in the gravel of the riverbed, the female lays her eggs while the male lies next to her fertilizing them. The eggs overwinter and hatch the following spring. After spending 2 to 6 years in the river, the salmon go out to sea, returning to spawn from 1 to 4 years later. Unlike Pacific salmon, Atlantic salmon can spawn more than once in their lifetime.

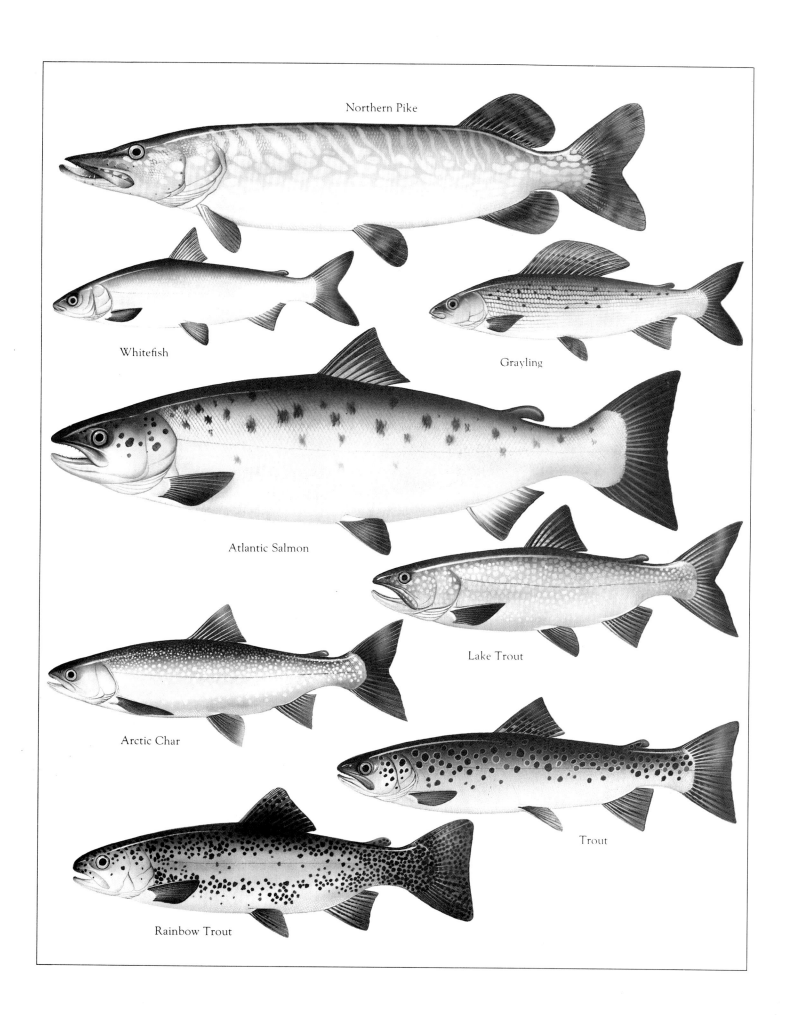

Northern Pike

Whitefish

Grayling

Atlantic Salmon

Lake Trout

Arctic Char

Trout

Rainbow Trout

Salmon, Gonorynchiform Fishes

NAME: **Smelt,** *Osmerus eperlanus*
RANGE: **N. Atlantic Ocean: northern coasts of France, Britain, Holland, Germany, Scandinavia**
HABITAT: **coastal waters, estuaries, rivers; fresh water**
SIZE: **30 cm (11¾ in)**

Small relatives of salmon and trout, smelts are marine fishes which breed in fresh water. This species is similar to the trout in shape and has a small fleshy fin on its back, set well back behind the dorsal fin. A predatory fish, the smelt's mouth is large and its teeth powerful. It feeds on small crustaceans; large smelts may eat young fish.

In winter, mature smelts leave the sea to travel up rivers to breed. In spring, they spawn, shedding the eggs on gravel on the riverbed or on aquatic plants, to which they adhere for a time. Later the eggs may float in the water by means of a parachute of membrane until they hatch. Eventually the young fishes descend to the sea to grow and mature. Smelts have suffered badly in recent decades from river pollution and the erection of structures such as dams, which disturb their migration routes.

There are isolated populations of smelts in freshwater lakes in Scandinavia. These are nonmigratory, slow-growing fishes, smaller than the migratory race.

NAME: **Jollytail,** *Galaxias maculatus*
RANGE: **New Zealand, Tasmania, Australia, southern South America**
HABITAT: **rivers, estuaries, coastal waters**
SIZE: **20 cm (7¾ in)**

The jollytail is one of a family of small, mostly freshwater fishes, found in the southern hemisphere. It is a slender-bodied fish, with a small head and dorsal and anal fins set close to the tail. This fish uses lunar and tidal rhythms to time its spawning. Mature fishes migrate downstream to spawn among estuarine vegetation which is flooded by high spring tides at the time of the new moon. The eggs remain stranded among the vegetation, above the reach of the tides, until the next high spring tides two weeks later. If that tide does not reach them, the young are able to survive inside the eggs for a further 2 weeks. When again immersed in water, they hatch, and the larvae are swept out to sea. After spending some months in the ocean, the young fishes travel up rivers, where they grow and mature, and the cycle begins again.

Even the lake-dwelling jollytails are migratory and travel up small streams to spawn. In these species the hatching of the eggs is triggered by rainfall.

NAME: **Sockeye Salmon,** *Oncorhynchus nerka*
RANGE: **N. Pacific Ocean: N. American coast: Alaska to California; coast of USSR to Japan: Hokkaido**
HABITAT: **open sea, coastal waters, rivers and lakes**
SIZE: **84 cm (33 in)**

The sockeye salmon lives in the ocean, feeding on small shrimplike creatures, until it is 4 to 6 years old. Then, in late spring, mature adults enter rivers to ascend to their breeding areas, sometimes 2,400 km (1,500 mi) inland. They prefer rivers fed by lakes and breed in small adjacent streams or in the lakes themselves. The breeding male develops bright red skin on back and sides; his back becomes humped and jaws markedly hooked. Females also show some red coloration.

When the salmon arrive at their breeding grounds, they pair off. With movements of her tail and body, the female makes a shallow pit in the gravel of the streambed and lays her eggs in it. These are fertilized by the male and drop into the gravel. As the pair repeats the process farther upstream, the eggs become covered with gravel. Once spawning is complete, the adult salmon die. The eggs hatch after 6 to 9 weeks, and the young spend 1 to 3 years in the lake, feeding on crustaceans, before migrating to the sea.

There are nonmigratory populations of sockeye salmon which live all their lives in lakes; these fishes are known as kokanees and are half the size of migratory sockeyes.

NAME: **Hatchetfish,** *Argyropelecus aculeatus*
RANGE: **Atlantic, Pacific and Indian Oceans: tropical and subtropical areas**
HABITAT: **open sea at 100–600 m (330–2,000 ft)**
SIZE: **7 cm (2¾ in)**

The hatchetfish is a common species which forms a major item of diet for many larger fishes. Like all members of its family, the hatchetfish's silvery body is deep and laterally compressed, with a sharp-edged belly. Its eyes are large, and its capacious mouth is nearly vertical. On its belly are rows of light-producing organs, which are arranged in a characteristic pattern in each species, enabling the hatchetfishes to recognize their own kind from below.

Hatchetfishes normally live at depths of 400 to 600 m (1,300 to 2,000 ft) by day but migrate nearer to the surface each night in search of food.

NAME: **Sloane's Viperfish,** *Chauliodus sloani*
RANGE: **Atlantic, Pacific and Indian Oceans: temperate and tropical areas**
HABITAT: **deep sea**
SIZE: **30 cm (11¾ in)**

Sloane's viperfish is one of 6 species of deep-sea viperfishes, all with long, fang-like teeth. The skull is adapted to increase the gape of the mouth, and the jaws open wide to maximize the efficiency of the predatory teeth. The dorsal fin of the viperfish is positioned close behind the head, and the first ray is greatly elongated and bears a light-producing organ to attract prey in the darkness of the deep sea. Viperfishes feed on smaller fish, such as lantern-fishes, following them when they make their nightly migrations to waters nearer the surface to feed on plankton.

GONORYNCHIFORMES

This order contains only about 16 species of marine and freshwater fish, which occur in tropical Africa and the Indian and Pacific oceans. The fishes have a superficial resemblance to herrings, and some authorities have linked the two orders.

The milkfish, of the family Chanidae, is the largest and most important member of the order, which also includes the family Kneriidae, with 12 species of small, minnowlike fish. Kneriids live in tropical areas of Africa in swift-flowing water and feed on plant matter. Males develop horny protuberances on their gill covers, which they rub over the females to stimulate them sexually.

NAME: **Milkfish,** *Chanos chanos*
RANGE: **Indian and tropical Pacific Oceans**
HABITAT: **open sea, coasts, estuaries; occasionally fresh water**
SIZE: **1.8 m (6 ft)**

A large, silvery fish with a pointed tail and a prominent dorsal fin, the milkfish is a fast-swimming species. It is toothless and feeds on minute to small planktonic plant material throughout its life. Normally a fish of the open sea, it enters coastal waters to breed and sometimes ventures into fresh water. One female may shed as many as 6 million eggs in a season.

Milkfishes are an important food fish in Southeast Asia and are the center of a considerable industry in some areas of Indonesia and the Philippines, where newly hatched young are caught and reared in coastal ponds.

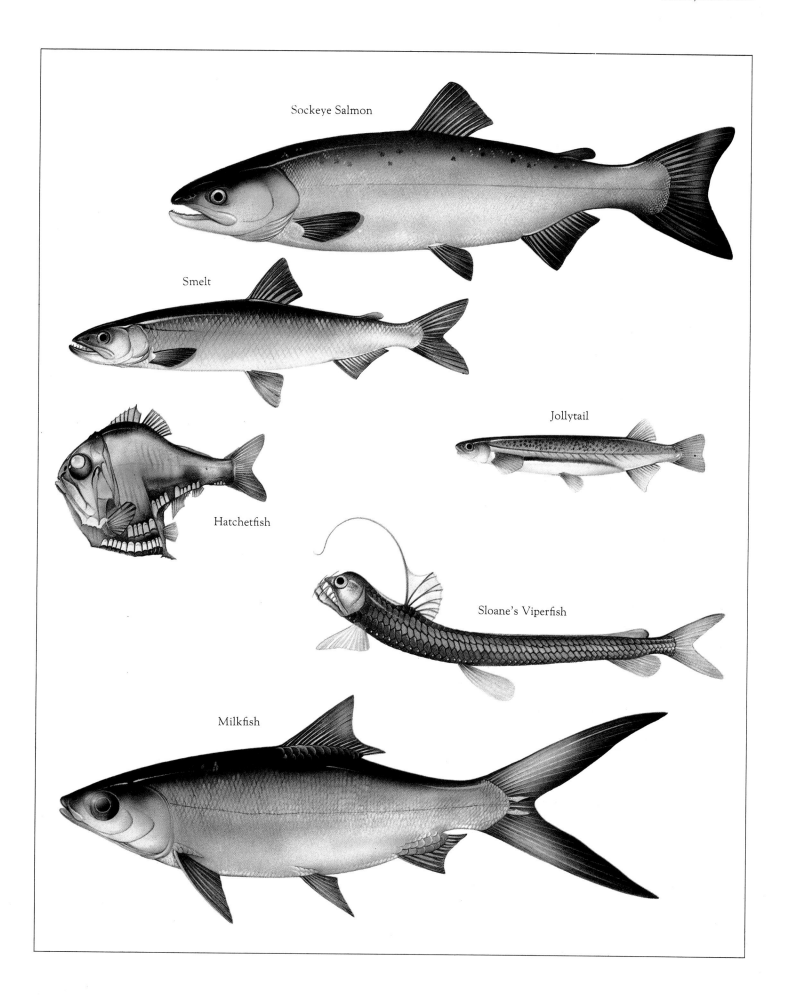

Sockeye Salmon

Smelt

Jollytail

Hatchetfish

Sloane's Viperfish

Milkfish

Cypriniform Fishes

NAME: Jaraqui, *Semaprochilodus insignis*
RANGE: northern South America:
   Amazon basin
HABITAT: rivers, tributaries
SIZE: up to 35.5 cm (14 in)

The jaraqui is one of 30 species of freshwater fish in the South American family Prochilodontidae. The fishes in this family are similar to the related characins but lack their complex dentition. The jaraqui feeds on the bottom on detritus and other fine material.

Around the time of the annual floods, the adults descend from tributaries to spawn in the muddy waters of the main river, where presumably the poorer visibility gives the eggs and young a better chance of escaping the many predatory fishes. They then move back into the tributary, and generally into the flooded forest, to feed. Later in the year, the adults migrate again, this time moving down to the main river and upstream to yet another tributary. The vacated tributary is restocked by the arrival of young fishes, which are swept downstream by strong currents at spawning time.

NAME: Curimbata, *Prochilodus platensis*
RANGE: central South America
HABITAT: rivers
SIZE: 51 cm (20 in)

A member of the family Prochilodontidae, the curimbata is an abundant fish, which lives in huge schools. It feeds on bottom detritus and fine plant matter and has a small mouth with fine teeth well suited to this diet.

Curimbatas make regular migrations upstream to spawn. When the males reach the spawning areas, they emit sounds, which may attract the females, though this is not confirmed. The eggs drift downstream, where young fishes find suitable shallow nursery areas, in which they remain while they grow.

NAME: Red Piranha, *Serrasalmus*
   nattereri
RANGE: northern South America:
   Amazon basin
HABITAT: rivers
SIZE: up to 30.5 cm (12 in)

One of the carnivorous members of the family Characidae, the red piranha is not a large fish but swims in such large shoals that, together, the fishes form a formidable hunting group. They are armed with strong jaws and razor-sharp triangular teeth, which can chop pieces of flesh from a victim with alarming efficiency. Despite their very bloodthirsty reputation, carnivorous piranhas feed largely on fish and on seeds and fruit but will attack larger, usually wounded animals, which they quickly devour by their combined efforts.

CYPRINIFORMES

An enormously successful group of freshwater fish, this order contains 3,000 or so species, divided into 3 main lines of development: the characins — piranhas and their relatives — from Central and South America and Africa; the electric eels from tropical and subtropical Central and South America; and, finally, the carps and their allies of the family Cyprinidae, which gave the order its name. With about 1,600 species, the carp family is the largest of all fish families, and members occur in North America, Africa, Europe and Asia. Besides these main groups, there are many other small families.

The characins have a variety of body forms, but most species have an adipose fin: a small, fleshy fin between the dorsal fin and the tail. Although several of the piranhas are notorious for their carnivorous habits and possess formidable teeth, there are also plant-eating characins among the 1,000 or so recognized species.

About 40 species of electric eel, gymnotid eel and knifefish inhabit the New World tropics. They all possess muscle-derived electric organs, principally used for underwater navigation but also for defense and the capture of prey.

The carplike fishes have scaled bodies and a single dorsal fin. Their swim bladders are connected to the inner ear, which gives them acute hearing abilities.

NAME: Pacu, *Colossoma nigripinnis*
RANGE: N.E. South America
HABITAT: rivers
SIZE: 70 cm (27½ in)

The pacu is a plant-eating characin but is, nevertheless, similar in appearance to the carnivorous piranhas. It has become adapted to feeding on the many fruits and seeds that fall into the forest-bordered water and is equipped with strong jaws and teeth for crushing them.

NAME: Flame Tetra, *Hyphessobrycon*
   flammeus
RANGE: South America: Rio de Janeiro
   area of Brazil
HABITAT: swampy areas
SIZE: 4.5 cm (1¾ in)

One of the many brightly colored species of tetra in the family Characidae, the flame tetra has brilliant red fins and some red coloration on the body. Males and females differ slightly in that the male has a black edge to the anal fin that is either reduced or absent on the female's fin.

NAME: Neon Tetra, *Pracheirodon innesi*
RANGE: northern South America: upper
   part of Amazon River system
HABITAT: rivers, streams
SIZE: 4 cm (1½ in)

A strikingly colored fish, the neon tetra has a bright blue or bluish-green stripe along its body and a band of red toward the tail. Like all tetras, it is a member of the characin family.

NAME: Sardinha, *Triportheus elongatus*
RANGE: northern South America:
   Amazon basin
HABITAT: rivers, streams, flooded forest
SIZE: 20–28 cm (7¾–11 in)

Popularly known as sardinhas because of their resemblance to marine sardines, the fishes of this genus have long, compressed bodies and extended pectoral fins. This species is an adaptable surface-dwelling fish, able to feed on both fruit and seeds and invertebrate animals. Its small mouth, equipped with many fine teeth, fits it well for taking invertebrates from the surface, but means that it is unable to crush hard nuts and seeds and must take softer items. When fruit is scarce, it will also eat leaves and flowers. Much of the sardinha's food is taken during the season when the forest is flooded and it has access to plenty of vegetation. During this period, the fishes lay down body fat, which sustains them in times of shorter supplies.

NAME: *Boulengerella lucius*
RANGE: northern South America:
   Amazon basin
HABITAT: rivers
SIZE: 61 cm (24 in)

Related to the characins, *Boulengerella* is a member of the family Ctenoluciidae, a small group of South American freshwater fishes. It is a predatory fish, with a pointed snout, long jaws, the upper of which has an extended tip, and many sharp teeth.

NAME: Hatchetfish, *Gasteropelecus*
   sternicla
RANGE: northern South America
HABITAT: rivers
SIZE: 6.5 cm (2½ in)

The highly distinctive hatchetfish is a small fish, with an almost straight back but a dramatically curved belly. This body shape makes room for greatly enlarged shoulder muscles, which power the long pectoral fins and enable the fish to fly above the water surface for a short distance, beating its "wings" noisily. These hatchetfishes of the family Gasteropelecidae are the only fishes actually to use propulsive force while in the air.

Hatchetfishes feed at the surface of the water, on insects and crustaceans.

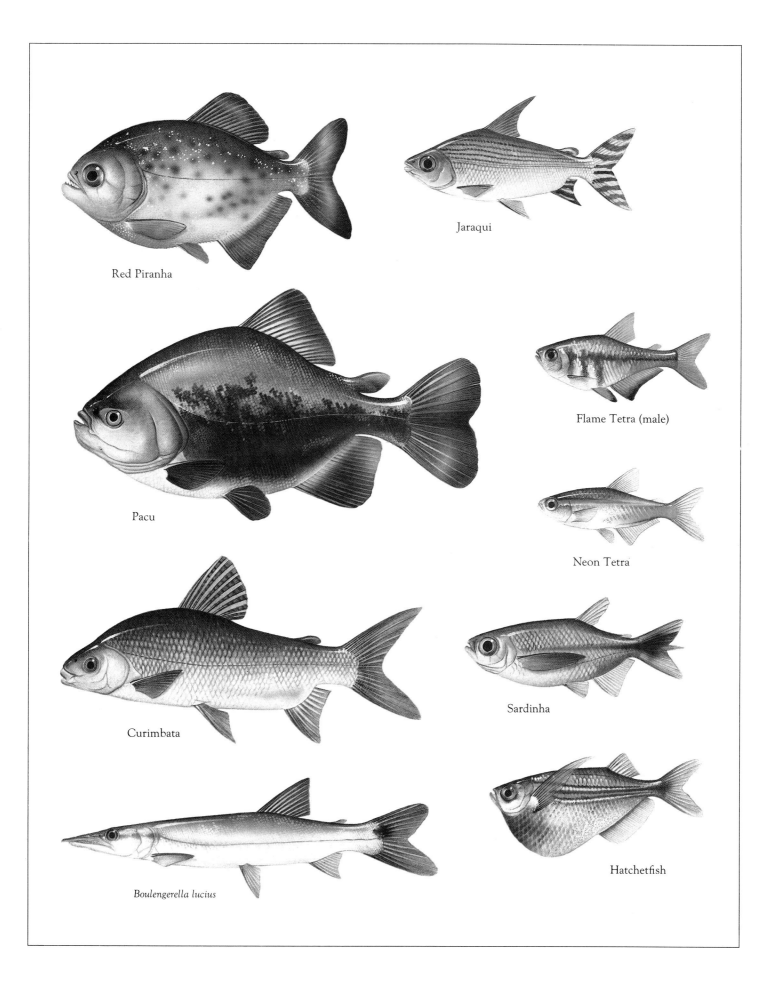

Red Piranha

Jaraqui

Pacu

Flame Tetra (male)

Neon Tetra

Curimbata

Sardinha

Boulengerella lucius

Hatchetfish

Cypriniform Fishes

NAME: **Giant Tigerfish,** *Hydrocynus goliath*
RANGE: **Africa: Congo basin, Lake Tanganyika**
HABITAT: **streams, rivers, lakes**
SIZE: **1.5–1.8 m (5–6 ft)**

One of the largest characins, the giant tigerfish has an elongate, fully scaled body and a well-developed, forked tail fin. It has a small number of large, sharp teeth, with half-grown replacement teeth behind them, and is a voracious predator, taking a wide variety of smaller fish.

NAME: **Mexican Tetra,** *Astyanax mexicanus*
RANGE: **USA: Texas, New Mexico; Mexico, Central America, south to Panama**
HABITAT: **coastal streams**
SIZE: **8–10 cm (3–4 in)**

The only characin to occur in the USA, the Mexican tetra is plain compared to the brilliantly colored tetras from South America. It is sometimes considered to be a subspecies of *A. fasciatus*, some races of which are eyeless fishes, found in caves.

NAME: **Electric Eel,** *Electrophorus electricus*
RANGE: **N.E. South America, including Amazon basin**
HABITAT: **muddy streams and pools**
SIZE: **2.4 m (8 ft)**

The electric eel is the only species in its family, Electrophoridae; it is not, of course, a true eel but has a similar long and cylindrical body. Its anal fin runs much of the length of its body, to the tip of its tail, and it has no dorsal, tail or pelvic fins. An inhabitant of turbid, oxygen-poor water, the fish is able to gulp extra air at the surface, from which it absorbs some oxygen via specialized areas of blood vessels inside its mouth.

Much of its bulky body is occupied by its electric organs: modified muscles, which can release high-voltage charges, used for killing prey or for defense. Each organ is made up of many electroplates, each of which produces only a tiny charge but which together may amount to a charge of 500 volts. Such charges kill smaller fish easily and can give a human being a severe shock. The fish can also produce slow pulses of low voltage to help it navigate in murky water, where vision is of little use. Young electric eels feed on bottom-living invertebrates, but adults consume mostly fish, many of which they stun before eating.

NAME: **Banded Knifefish,** *Gymnotus carapo*
RANGE: **Central and South America: Guatemala to N. Argentina**
HABITAT: **creeks, slow murky water**
SIZE: **61 cm (24 in)**

The banded knifefish is one of 3 species in the South American family Gymnotidae. An elongate, eel-like fish, it has an anal fin running much of the length of its body and small pectorals but no other fins. It moves backward or forward by wavelike motions of the anal fin but is generally a fairly sluggish fish. Usually active at dawn and dusk, in rather cloudy water, it relies on its electrical abilities for navigation, rather than on its poor vision. The electrical pulses it produces are much weaker than those of the electric eel, but they enable it to navigate with ease. Adults feed on fish and crustaceans, and young on crustaceans and insect larvae.

NAME: **Common Carp,** *Cyprinus carpio*
RANGE: **originally S. Europe and Black Sea area; introduced in N. Europe, N. and South America, Australia, New Zealand, parts of Asia and Africa**
HABITAT: **lowland lakes, and rivers**
SIZE: **51 cm–1 m (20 in–3¼ ft)**

Now an extremely widely distributed fish, the common carp belongs to the large, freshwater family Cyprinidae. Carp are robust, fairly deep-bodied fishes; some are fully scaled, but there are other varieties, such as leather carp, which are scaleless, and mirror carp (illustrated here), which have some exceptionally large scales on the sides and at the base of the dorsal fin.

Inhabitants of slow-moving waters with much vegetation, carp tolerate low oxygen levels which would be fatal for many other fishes. They feed mostly on crustaceans, insect larvae, mollusks and some vegetation. Breeding occurs in spring and summer. The eggs are laid in shallow water, where they adhere to aquatic plants until they hatch.

NAME: **Goldfish,** *Carassius auratus*
RANGE: **native from E. Europe across to China; introduced in temperate areas worldwide**
HABITAT: **well-vegetated pools, lakes**
SIZE: **up to 30.5 cm (12 in)**

An extremely familiar species, the goldfish is bred in a variety of forms as an ornamental fish. It is typical of the family Cyprinidae in its body shape and its teeth on the pharyngeal bones, but it has strong spines at the front of both dorsal and anal fins.

Goldfishes spawn in summer over aquatic vegetation. The eggs adhere to the plants and hatch in about a week.

NAME: **Barbel,** *Barbus barbus*
RANGE: **Europe: Britain, south to Alps and Pyrenees, east to Hungary**
HABITAT: **lowland rivers, streams**
SIZE: **50–91 cm (19¾–35¾ in)**

A slender, long-bodied fish, the barbel has a characteristic high dorsal fin and two pairs of sensory barbels around its fleshy lips. It is a bottom-living fish, most active at night and at dusk, and feeds on insect larvae, mollusks and crustaceans. It is a member of the family Cyprinidae.

Barbels breed in late spring, often migrating upstream before spawning. They shed their eggs in shallow, gravel-bottomed water, where they lodge among the stones until they hatch from 10 to 15 days later.

NAME: **Mahseer,** *Barbus tor*
RANGE: **N. India**
HABITAT: **varied: sluggish rivers, fast hill streams**
SIZE: **1.2 m (4 ft)**

A heavily built fish, with large body scales, the mahseer is a member of the family Cyprinidae and is a common species in its range. It feeds on invertebrates, particularly mollusks, as well as on algae and other aquatic plants.

NAME: **Tiger Barb,** *Barbus tetrazona*
RANGE: **Sumatra, Borneo**
HABITAT: **rivers, streams**
SIZE: **7 cm (2¾ in)**

This tiny fish, with four black bands ringing its body, is a distinctive member of the family Cyprinidae. Despite the fact that it is rather aggressive, the tiger barb is a popular aquarium species.

NAME: **Tench,** *Tinca tinca*
RANGE: **Europe: Britain, S. Sweden and Denmark to Mediterranean countries, east to central Asia; introduced in New Zealand, Australia, N. America**
HABITAT: **lakes, ponds; sometimes in slow, lowland rivers**
SIZE: **up to 70 cm (27½ in)**

The tench, a member of the family Cyprinidae, is identified by its thickset body, rounded fins and extremely small scales; these scales are plentifully covered with mucus. In males, the second ray in the pelvic fin is swollen, and the fin may be longer than that of a female, but otherwise the sexes look alike. Tench feed mostly on the bottom on insect larvae, mollusks and crustaceans and are able to thrive in poorly oxygenated water.

Breeding takes place in shallow water in spring and summer. The eggs are often shed onto aquatic vegetation, and they hatch in 6 to 8 days.

Tiger Barb

Giant Tigerfish

Electric Eel

Banded Knifefish

Mexican Tetra

Goldfish
(golden form)

Mahseer

Common Carp
(mirror form)

Tench (male)

Barbel

Cypriniform Fishes

NAME: **Dace,** *Leuciscus leuciscus*
RANGE: N. Europe and Asia: Ireland to Siberia, north to Sweden, south to S. France
HABITAT: rivers, streams
SIZE: 15–30 cm (6–11$\frac{3}{4}$ in)

A slim-bodied fish, the dace has characteristic concave edges to both dorsal and anal fins. It moves in large schools and feeds on insects and their larvae, some plants, and on spiders and other terrestrial invertebrates which fall into the water. Although normally a river fish, some dace occur in lakes.

Dace spawn in spring, often in gravel-bottomed shallow streams, and shoals gather in the breeding areas a few days before spawning. The eggs lodge among the gravel, where they remain until they hatch about 25 days later.

NAME: **Bream,** *Abramis brama*
RANGE: N. Europe: Britain, France, east to central USSR
HABITAT: slow rivers, lakes, ponds
SIZE: 40.5–61 cm (16–24 in)

The bream has a deep body, flattened at the sides, and a curving, high back. Its anal fin has a distinctly concave edge. The bream's head is rather small for its size, and its mouth protrudes into a tubelike structure, with which it gathers insect larvae, mollusks and worms from the river bottom. It lives in shoals and usually feeds at night.

Bream breed in late spring or in summer, usually in shallow water where there is plenty of vegetation. The eggs adhere to submerged plants and take up to 12 days to hatch, depending on the temperature.

NAME: **Roach,** *Rutilus rutilus*
RANGE: Europe, W. Asia: England to central USSR; N. Sweden to Black Sea and Caspian Sea areas
HABITAT: lowland rivers, lakes
SIZE: 35–46 cm (13$\frac{3}{4}$–18 in)

An abundant, adaptable fish, the roach can survive in poorly oxygenated and even slightly polluted water and has an extremely wide distribution; it can also tolerate brackish water. Its abundance and presence in otherwise sparsely populated waters make it an important prey for fish-eating birds and mammals, as well as for other fishes.

An attractively colored fish, the roach has a fairly deep body and small head. Its diet is varied, insects, larvae, crustaceans and other small invertebrates, as well as plants, being consumed. It breeds in well-vegetated shallow water, where its eggs stick to plants while they develop. The eggs hatch in under 2 weeks, but from then on, growth rates of the young vary enormously, according to conditions.

NAME: **Gudgeon,** *Gobio gobio*
RANGE: Europe: Britain to S. Sweden, south to France, east to USSR
HABITAT: rivers, streams, lakes, ponds, marshes
SIZE: 10–20 cm (4–7$\frac{3}{4}$ in)

A round-bodied fish, the gudgeon has a large head for its size and a sensory barbel at each side of its thick-lipped mouth. Found in a wide variety of habitats, it is always a bottom-dweller and feeds on insect larvae, mollusks and crustaceans.

Gudgeons spawn at night in early summer. The sticky eggs adhere to plants or rocks and take up to 4 weeks to hatch. Young gudgeons feed largely on planktonic crustaceans.

NAME: **Bitterling,** *Rhodeus sericeus*
RANGE: N. and E. Europe: N. France, Germany, east to Black and Caspian Sea basins; introduced in N. America
HABITAT: lakes, ponds, slow rivers
SIZE: 6–9 cm (2$\frac{1}{4}$–3$\frac{1}{2}$ in)

The attractively colored bitterling is a small, rather deep-bodied fish. It lives in densely vegetated areas and can tolerate poorly oxygenated water. It feeds on plants and small invertebrate animals.

The breeding habits of the bitterling are most unusual. The female develops a long egg-depositing tube that extends from her genital opening. Using this tube, she lays her eggs inside the gill chamber of a freshwater mussel. The male, who develops brilliant, iridescent coloration in the breeding season, sheds his sperm by the mussel's gills so that it is inhaled by the mussel and fertilizes the eggs. Safe from predators, the eggs develop inside the mussel for 2 or 3 weeks, and the young leave it about 2 days after hatching. The mussel is unharmed by this invasion.

NAME: **Minnow,** *Phoxinus phoxinus*
RANGE: Europe, N. Asia: Britain, east to Siberia, south to the Pyrenees, north to Sweden
HABITAT: streams, rivers, lakes
SIZE: 9 cm (3$\frac{1}{2}$ in); rarely 12 cm (4$\frac{3}{4}$ in)

A small, slender fish, the minnow has a characteristic line of dark blotches along each side. It is an abundant fish, found in schools near the surface of shallow water in summer; it moves to deeper waters in winter. Insect larvae and crustaceans are its main foods, and it will also feed on plants. It forms an important prey item itself for many fish-eating birds and larger fishes.

Breeding takes place in late spring, when courting males develop brilliant red bellies. Minnows spawn in gravel-bottomed water, and the eggs lodge among the stones. They hatch within 5 to 10 days.

NAME: **Grass Carp,** *Ctenopharyngodon idella*
RANGE: China; introduced in S.E. Asia, USSR, parts of Europe and USA
HABITAT: rivers
SIZE: 1–1.2 m (3$\frac{1}{4}$–4 ft)

A native of China, the grass carp has been introduced into many other areas for two reasons. In China and Southeast Asia it is a valuable commercial species, and in Europe and the USSR, this plant-eating fish is used to control vegetation in canals and reservoirs. Although, as an adult, the grass carp is entirely herbivorous, young fishes feed on insect larvae and crustaceans once their egg sacs have been absorbed.

Grass carp spawn in rivers in summer. The eggs float at the surface and must have warm water to grow well.

NAME: **Central Stoneroller,** *Campostoma anomalum*
RANGE: E. USA, west to Minnesota and Texas
HABITAT: clear creeks, streams, rivers
SIZE: 10–18 cm (4–7 in)

Typically, the central stoneroller lives in small streams in riffle areas (shallow water where the flow is broken by the stones and gravel on the streambed). It feeds at the bottom on tiny plants, insect larvae and mollusks.

In spring, the dorsal and anal fins of breeding males turn bright orange and black, and tubercles develop on the upper half of the body. The male makes a shallow nest in the gravel of the streambed, in which the female lays her eggs.

NAME: **Pearl Dace,** *Semotilus margarita*
RANGE: Canada; N. USA, south to Virginia, Wisconsin, Montana
HABITAT: streams, lakes
SIZE: 15 cm (6 in)

The pearl dace is a small fish which, with its blunt, rounded snout, resembles the European minnow. It feeds on insects, planktonic invertebrates and even tiny fish. In the breeding season, males establish territories on the streambed, which they defend against other males. Females are attracted to the territories, where spawning takes place.

NAME: **Northern Squawfish,** *Ptychocheilus oregonensis*
RANGE: N. America: Columbia River system, coastal streams of Oregon and Washington
HABITAT: lakes, slow streams and rivers
SIZE: 90 cm–1.2 m (35$\frac{1}{2}$ in–4 ft)

Squawfishes are the largest North American minnows. A long, slender fish, the northern squawfish lives close to the bottom and is a voracious predator, feeding largely on fish, including young trout and salmon.

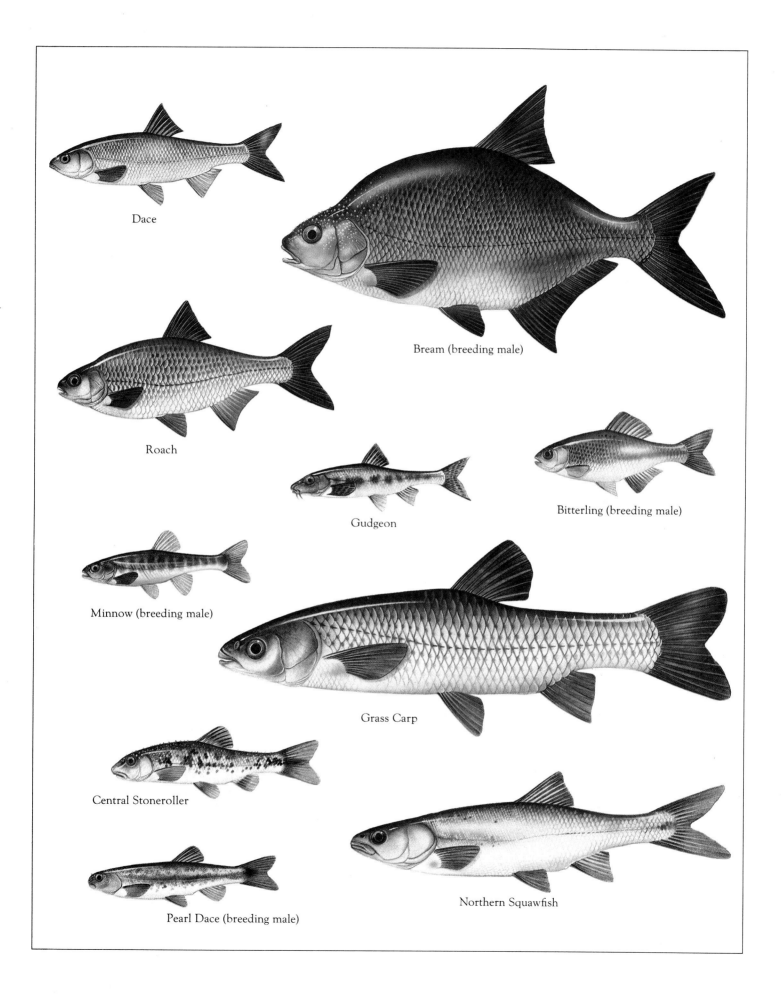

Dace

Bream (breeding male)

Roach

Gudgeon

Bitterling (breeding male)

Minnow (breeding male)

Grass Carp

Central Stoneroller

Northern Squawfish

Pearl Dace (breeding male)

Cypriniform Fishes

NAME: **Common Shiner,** *Notropis cornutus*
RANGE: **S. Canada; N. USA, south to Colorado and Virginia**
HABITAT: **clear streams**
SIZE: 6–10 cm ($2\frac{1}{2}$–4 in)

Shiners are the largest group of American minnows. The common shiner is a round-bodied fish, usually found in fast-flowing water but sometimes occurring in lakes with tributary streams. It feeds on aquatic and terrestrial insects and some algae.

Common shiners spawn in spring or early summer in streams. Schools of breeding adults congregate in breeding areas; male fishes develop bright blue coloration, with pinkish fins, at this time. Females shed their eggs into shallow nests, excavated in the gravel of the streambed, where they are fertilized by the males.

NAME: **Fallfish,** *Semotilus corporalis*
RANGE: **S.E. Canada; USA: Atlantic coast, south to Virginia**
HABITAT: **clear streams, lakes**
SIZE: 10–30.5 cm (4–12 in)

The fallfish is similar in appearance to another American minnow, the creek chub, *S. atromaculatus*, but can be distinguished by the lack of a dark spot on the base of the dorsal fin. Aquatic insects are the main diet of the fallfish, but some small invertebrates are also consumed. Young fallfishes move in schools in shallow waters, while adults are found in deeper waters.

In spring, breeding males develop some pinkish coloration on their sides and small wartlike projections on the head. In a quiet shallow area, each pair makes a nest of stones, which they carry in their mouths. Once the eggs are laid, more stones are added to the nest by the male. The nest protects the eggs while they develop and hatch.

NAME: **Harlequin Fish,** *Rasbora heteromorpha*
RANGE: **Thailand, Malaysia, E. Sumatra**
HABITAT: **streams, lakes**
SIZE: 4.5 cm ($1\frac{3}{4}$ in)

A tiny but attractive fish, the harlequin fish is a popular aquarium species. In its natural habitat, it moves in shoals and feeds on insect larvae.

Having been courted by her mate, the breeding female searches out a broad-leaved water plant and lays her sticky-surfaced eggs on the underside of a leaf, where they remain until they hatch.

NAME: **White Sucker,** *Catostomus commersoni*
RANGE: **Canada: Labrador to Nova Scotia; N. USA, south to Georgia and New Mexico, west to Montana**
HABITAT: **large streams, lakes**
SIZE: 30.5–52 cm (12–$20\frac{1}{2}$ in)

The most common of the suckers, the white sucker is typical of its family, with its mouth positioned behind the point of the snout and its thick, suckerlike lips. Found in a variety of conditions, the white sucker tolerates some pollution and poorly oxygenated waters. It is a bottom-living fish and feeds on insect larvae, crustaceans and mollusks, as well as plant material.

Breeding takes place in spring. White suckers spawn at night, depositing their eggs in rocky- or gravel-bottomed streams. The eggs, which are slightly sticky, sink to the bottom and are lightly covered by gravel, which is stirred up by the vigorous spawning movements.

NAME: **Shorthead Redhorse,** *Moxostoma macrolepidotum*
RANGE: **E. and central Canada; USA: Great Lakes to New York, south to Arkansas and Kansas**
HABITAT: **rivers, streams, lakes**
SIZE: up to 61 cm (24 in)

The shorthead redhorse is one of 18 or more in this genus of sucker. All are silvery to reddish-brown fishes, with round bodies, large heads and suckerlike mouths. They feed mainly on insect larvae and mollusks. Shorthead redhorses have a preference for clear, swift-flowing water and cannot tolerate muddy or polluted rivers — a characteristic which has led to a decline in their population.

In April or May, shorthead redhorses migrate up small streams or into shallow areas of lakes to spawn. Each breeding female lays from 10,000 to 50,000 eggs, which she leaves at the spawning site to develop. The eggs hatch in about 2 weeks. Young redhorses feed on tiny planktonic creatures until they are big enough to take the adult diet.

NAME: **Bigmouth Buffalo,** *Ictiobus cyprinellus*
RANGE: **S. Canada; USA: North Dakota, east to Pennsylvania, south to Gulf Coast**
HABITAT: **large rivers, lakes**
SIZE: 1 m ($3\frac{1}{4}$ ft)

The powerful, deep-bodied bigmouth buffalo is the largest of the American suckers and, in suitable conditions, may become extremely abundant at the expense of other fishes. Distinguishing characteristics are its long-based dorsal fin and its large, slanting mouth, the upper lip of which is almost level with the eyes. It feeds on crustaceans and plant material, as well as on small quantities of insect larvae.

Bigmouth buffalo spawn in April or May. Groups of breeding adults gather in shallow well-vegetated water, where females shed as many as 500,000 eggs randomly into the water. The eggs adhere to plants or other debris and take up to 2 weeks to hatch. The young fishes remain in the shallow breeding areas for some months, feeding on plankton. They are mature at about 3 years old.

NAME: **Stone Loach,** *Noemacheilus barbatulus*
RANGE: **England, south to S. France, across Europe and N. Asia to Siberia and Korea**
HABITAT: **small fast-flowing rivers, lakes**
SIZE: 10–15 cm (4–6 in)

The sluggish stone loach is a bottom-living fish. It spends the day hiding among stones, where it is superbly camouflaged by its irregular markings, and is active at night or in dull daylight. It feeds on bottom-living creatures such as crustaceans, insect larvae and worms.

In April or May, the stone loach breeds, shedding its sticky-surfaced eggs over stones or plants. The eggs usually hatch in just over 2 weeks.

NAME: **Coolie Loach,** *Acanthopthalmus kuhlii*
RANGE: **Thailand, Singapore, Sumatra, Java**
HABITAT: **streams**
SIZE: 8 cm ($3\frac{1}{4}$ in)

A tiny, elongate fish, the coolie loach has striking dark markings, which vary in number. Its eyes are covered with transparent skin. It lives near the bottom, often lurking in dense vegetation, and is a shy, rarely seen fish in the wild.

NAME: **Spined Loach,** *Cobitis taenia*
RANGE: **E. England across Europe (including Mediterranean countries and S. Sweden) and central Asia to China and Japan**
HABITAT: **lakes, canals, slow rivers**
SIZE: 11.5 cm ($4\frac{1}{2}$ in)

The spined loach has a long, laterally compressed body and a small head, with a few sensory barbels around the mouth. Beneath each eye is a tiny spine which is usually buried in the skin. A slow-moving fish, the spined loach spends much of its time buried in mud or weed and feeds on small bottom-living crustaceans. It is thought to be most active at night or at dusk.

The breeding season begins in April. The eggs are shed over plants and algae but few details of the spawning behavior are known.

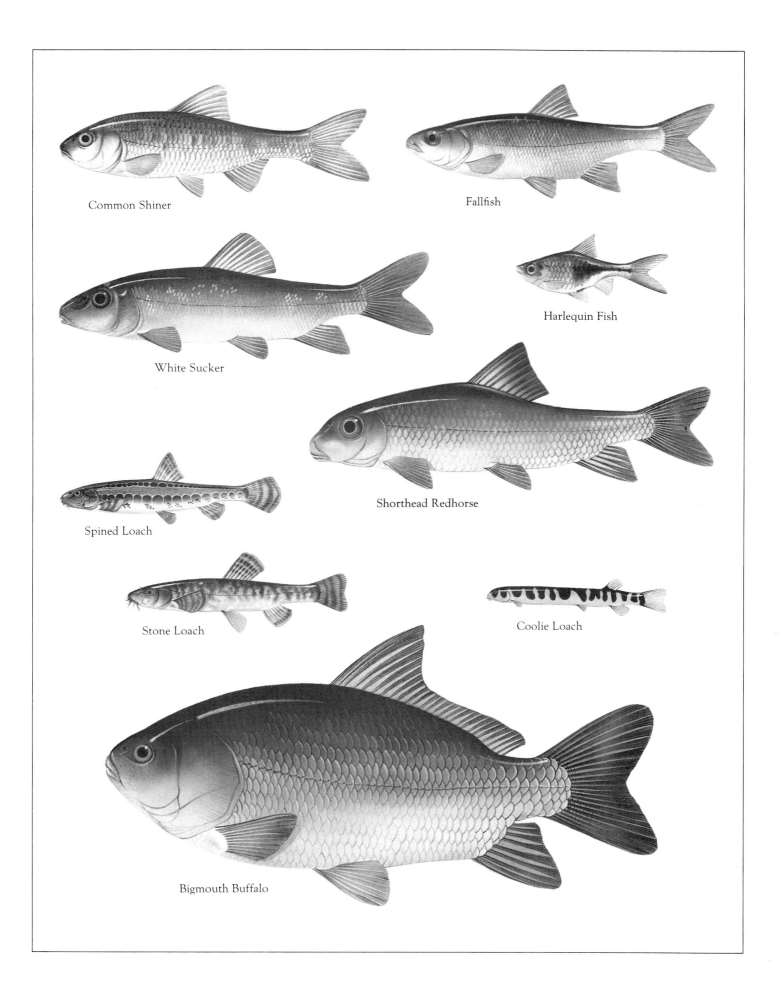

Common Shiner

Fallfish

White Sucker

Harlequin Fish

Spined Loach

Shorthead Redhorse

Stone Loach

Coolie Loach

Bigmouth Buffalo

Siluriform Fishes

NAME: Tadpole Madtom, *Noturus gyrinus*
RANGE: S. Canada, USA: North and South Dakota to Texas, New York to Florida
HABITAT: lakes, quiet streams, ponds, marshes
SIZE: 10 cm (4 in)

Madtoms are small catfishes which have poison glands at the base of the pectoral spines. The tadpole madtom, like other species, has a characteristic long fleshy fin on its back that virtually merges with the upper lobe of the tail. A species which favors muddy-bottomed, well-vegetated water, the tadpole madtom often hunts under stones or logs. It feeds on small fish, crustaceans and insect larvae. In early summer, it spawns, laying its eggs in a shallow hollow which it excavates in the streambed.

NAME: *Bagrus docmac*
RANGE: W. and central Africa
HABITAT: slow-running rivers, backwaters, lakes
SIZE: 1 m (3¼ ft)

This species is one of a family of African and Asian freshwater catfishes, most of which are slender bodied, with well-developed barbels and strong dorsal and pectoral spines. *Bagrus docmac* has a long fleshy fin on its back, a flattened head and a narrow extension of the upper lobe of its tail. A bottom-living predator, the adult feeds mainly on other fish, but the young eat insect larvae and crustaceans. It is a valuable commercial species in its range.

NAME: Blue Catfish, *Ictalurus furcatus*
RANGE: USA: Minnesota and Ohio, south through Mississippi River system and Gulf states; Mexico
HABITAT: rivers, lakes
SIZE: 1.5 m (5 ft)

One of the largest catfishes in North America, the blue catfish can grow to over 45 kg (100 lb) in weight and is an important commercial species. It is a slender-bodied fish, generally a dull silvery-blue in color with a whitish belly. It has a deeply forked tail, a long anal fin and a small adipose fin. There are several pairs of sensory barbels around its mouth. Often found in swifter, clearer waters than is usual for other catfish species, the blue catfish will even frequent rapids and waterfalls; it feeds largely on fish and crayfish.

Blue catfishes shed their eggs in a nest made in the shelter of a rock or submerged log on the river or lake bed. Both parents guard the nest and the young once they hatch.

SILURIFORMES

The bottom-living catfishes, with clusters of sensory barbels around their mouths, have been remarkably successful in their "mud-grubbing" way of life. They have spread into many freshwater habitats throughout the world, being absent only from western Europe, arctic regions of the northern hemisphere, the tip of South America, New Zealand and parts of Australia. Over 2,000 species have been described, ranging from tiny forms only a few centimeters in length to some giant forms which can reach 1.5 m (5 ft) or more and weigh as much as 45 kg (100 lb).

Catfishes do not have ordinary scales, but some have bony plates which cover them like jointed armor. Food is sought by a combination of touch and taste; catfishes probe the bottom sediment until the sensory barbels locate small prey.

NAME: Brown Bullhead, *Ictalurus nebulosus*
RANGE: S. Canada, E. USA to Florida; introduced in W. USA, New Zealand, Europe
HABITAT: muddy-bottomed ponds and rivers
SIZE: 30–46 cm (11¾–18 in)

The brown bullhead is one of a group of North American catfishes known as bullheads; they are most easily distinguished from other catfishes by their rounded tails. A slender, medium-sized catfish, the brown bullhead has a mottled, mainly brownish body, lighter on the underparts. It has a long-based anal fin, a small adipose fin and several sensory barbels around the mouth. Generally a bottom-dwelling fish, it is usually found in well-vegetated waters, where it feeds mainly on invertebrates, such as insect larvae and mollusks, although it will consume anything from plant material to fish. It feeds at night, feeling for prey with its sensitive chin barbels.

In the spring, these catfishes scrape a shallow hollow in the mud, where they spawn, and the male then stands guard over the clusters of sticky-surfaced eggs. Once hatched, the young swim in schools, defended by one or both parents until they are about 2.5 cm (1 in) in length.

Although it is not fished commercially, the brown bullhead has been widely introduced in countries outside its native range.

NAME: Wels, *Silurus glanis*
RANGE: central and E. Europe to S. USSR; introduced in Britain
HABITAT: rivers, lakes, marshes; brackish water in Baltic and Black Seas
SIZE: 1–3 m (3¼–9¾ ft)

A large, long-bodied catfish with a broad head and a long anal fin, the wels lives in slow-moving or still waters. It is chiefly nocturnal, remaining close to the bottom during the day, concealed among vegetation or in a hollow. Fish are its main food, but it also eats frogs, birds and small mammals such as water voles. It spawns in early summer. The male makes a hollow in the river bottom in which the female lays her eggs, and he then guards the eggs until they hatch. Young wels feed on plankton.

NAME: Glass Catfish, *Kryptopterus bicirrhis*
RANGE: Malaysia, Indonesia
HABITAT: rivers, streams
SIZE: 10 cm (4 in)

Unlike most catfishes, the glass catfish moves in small schools in surface and mid-waters during daylight hours. As its common name suggests, its body is virtually transparent, with some iridescent coloration on the sides. It has a long anal fin, a tiny dorsal fin and an apparently lopsided tail fin. Glass catfishes have been observed to balance themselves on the lower lobe of the tail fin, standing either obliquely or vertically in the water. These attractive fishes are a popular aquarium species.

NAME: Butterfish, *Schilbe mystus*
RANGE: W. and central Africa
HABITAT: lakes, rivers
SIZE: 36 cm (14¼ in)

One of a family of catfishes found in Africa and Asia, the butterfish has a scaleless body and four pairs of barbels around its mouth. Its anal fin is long and its dorsal fin tiny. It usually lives in shallow water and feeds on small fish and insect larvae. Spawning takes place during the rainy season.

This species is caught as a food fish, and small specimens are kept in aquariums.

NAME: African Glass Catfish, *Physailia pellucida*
RANGE: Africa: upper Nile basin
HABITAT: fresh water
SIZE: 10 cm (4 in)

The body of the African glass catfish is so transparent that much of its internal structure, such as blood vessels and spine, is clearly visible. The anal fin is long, and there is a tiny fleshy fin on the back but no true dorsal fin. This glass catfish is a popular aquarium species.

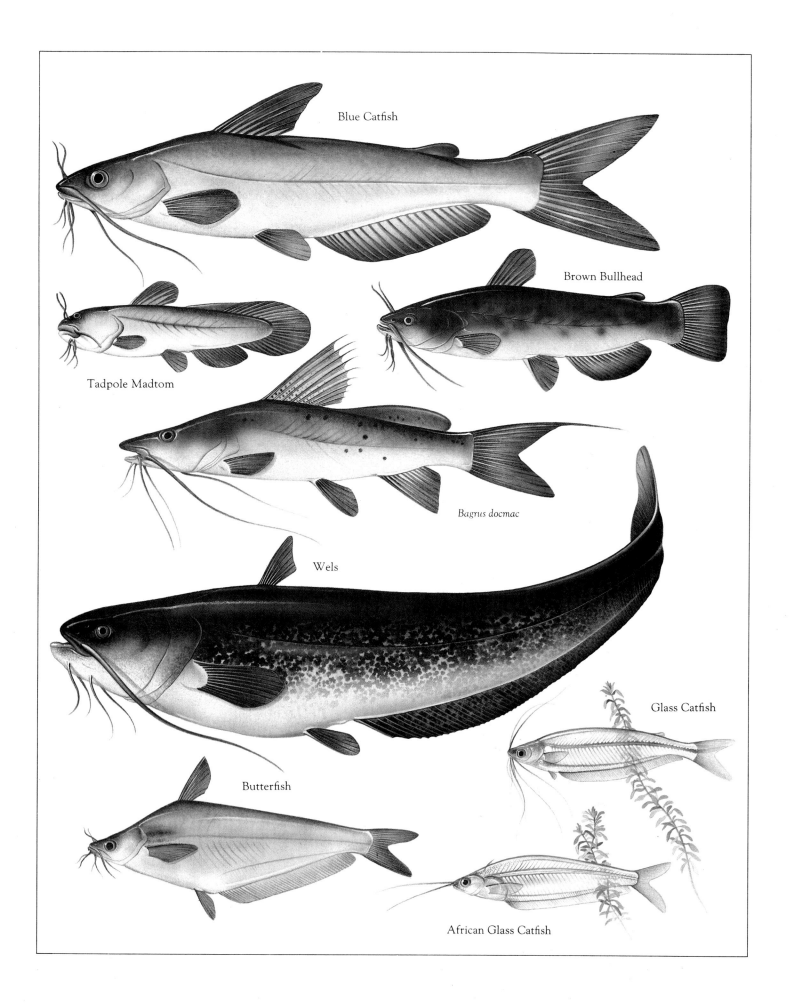

Blue Catfish

Brown Bullhead

Tadpole Madtom

Bagrus docmac

Wels

Glass Catfish

Butterfish

African Glass Catfish

Siluriform Fishes

NAME: Mekong Catfish, *Pangasianodon gigas*
RANGE: China, S.E. Asia
HABITAT: lakes, rivers
SIZE: up to 2.4 m (8 ft) Ⓥ

The huge Mekong catfish is one of about 25 species in the family Pangasiidae, a group of Asian freshwater fishes. It is a distinctive fish, with its flattened back and deeply curving belly, and differs from the rest of its family in having extremely low-set eyes, which give it a rather upside-down look. It has no teeth. These catfishes migrate upstream to breed, spawning in lakes and tributaries.

NAME: Pungas Catfish, *Pangasius pangasius*
RANGE: India, Burma, Thailand, Java
HABITAT: rivers, estuaries
SIZE: 1.2 m (4 ft)

The pungas catfish, a member of the catfish family Pangasiidae, is fairly slender, with a rather flattened back and curving belly. Its dorsal fin is high but short based, and its tail is deeply forked. It has one pair of sensory barbels near its mouth. Believed to be active mainly at night, the pungas catfish feeds on the bottom, on detritus and invertebrate animals.

NAME: Walking Catfish, *Clarias batrachus*
RANGE: India, Sri Lanka, S.E. Asia; introduced in USA: Florida
HABITAT: slow-moving, often stagnant waters
SIZE: 30.5 cm (12 in)

The walking catfish is, indeed, capable of moving on land and, when it does so, is able to breathe air. It belongs to the family Clariidae, whose members have additional, specialized breathing organs opening off the gill arches. These are saclike structures containing many-branched extensions, well supplied with blood vessels for respiration.

An elongate fish, this catfish has long-based dorsal and anal fins and several pairs of sensory barbels; its skin is scaleless but liberally supplied with mucus, which protects the fish when it is out of water. These catfishes live in ponds or temporary pools, some of which may disappear in prolonged dry spells. When this happens, the catfish can move overland to another body of water, making snakelike movements and using its pectoral fins as "legs." If necessary, the walking catfish can bury itself in mud at the bottom of a pond and remain dormant throughout a dry season until the rains return. It feeds on aquatic invertebrates and fish.

NAME: Electric Catfish, *Malapterurus electricus*
RANGE: tropical Africa
HABITAT: swamps, reedbeds in rivers
SIZE: 20.5 cm–1.2 m (8 in–4 ft)

The electric catfish is a plump, scaleless fish, with no dorsal fin; it does, however, have a fleshy adipose fin near the tail. Its body is mottled with irregular black blotches, and its mouth bristles with several pairs of sensory barbels. Young fishes have a conspicuous black band near the tail fin. This catfish belongs to the family Malapteruridae, which is thought to contain only 1 other species, *M. microstoma*, also found in Africa.

Capable of producing charges of several hundred volts, the electric catfish has well-developed electric organs under its skin, which occupy much of the length of the body. This catfish uses its electrical powers to defend itself and can render even a human being unconscious. It is also thought to catch its prey by stunning it and is certainly a sluggish fish that would probably find it hard to catch prey any other way.

NAME: Gafftopsail Catfish, *Bagre marinus*
RANGE: W. Atlantic Ocean: Cape Cod to Panama, including Gulf of Mexico
HABITAT: coastal waters, bays, estuaries
SIZE: 61 cm (24 in)

One of the large family of sea catfishes, Ariidae, the gafftopsail catfish is distinguished by its high dorsal fin, the first ray of which is extended into a long, thin filament. The first rays of the pectoral fins are also extended into spines, which can inflict painful wounds. There are two pairs of barbels, one short and one elongate and ribbonlike. Although a more active fish than many of its freshwater relatives, the gafftopsail catfish still does much of its feeding on the bottom, taking crabs, shrimps and fish.

The breeding habits of this catfish are remarkable. It spawns in summer, and as the eggs are laid, the male fertilizes them and takes them into his mouth, where they remain until they hatch. There may be between 10 and 30 eggs, and the male is not able to eat during the incubation period. Even after hatching, the young use their parent's mouth as a refuge for several weeks.

NAME: Hardhead Catfish, *Arius felis*
RANGE: W. Atlantic Ocean: Cape Cod to Panama (rare north of Virginia)
HABITAT: coastal waters, estuaries
SIZE: 30.5 cm (12 in)

The hardhead catfish, one of the Ariidae family of marine catfishes, is slender and elongate, with a high, but not extended, dorsal fin and a deeply forked tail. It is most active at night, feeding on crabs, as well as on some shrimps and fish. Large shoals swim together, and the fishes are capable of making quite loud sounds by vibrating their swim bladders with specialized muscles.

Spawning takes place in summer, and as the eggs are laid, the male takes them into his mouth, where they incubate. He must fast during the incubation period. The young fishes also use the male's mouth as a refuge after they hatch.

NAME: Upside-down Catfish, *Synodontis nigriventris*
RANGE: Africa: Congo basin
HABITAT: streams
SIZE: 6 cm (2¼ in)

The upside-down catfish belongs to the family Mochokidae, a group of scaleless catfishes found in fresh waters in Africa. There are about 150 species, most with long fins, forked tails and several pairs of sensory barbels. As its name suggests, this fish swims on its back, belly upward, for long periods. Although many others in the family swim this way part of the time, it is the usual method of movement for this species. It is thought to adopt the posture in order to feed on the algae that grow on the underside of leaves; young fishes swim normally at first, gradually spending more and more time in the upside-down position.

The interesting habits of this little catfish have made it a popular aquarium species.

NAME: Cuiu-cuiu, *Oxydoras niger*
RANGE: South America: Amazon basin
HABITAT: rivers, lakes, flooded forest
SIZE: 1.2 m (4 ft)

The cuiu-cuiu is one of about 130 South American catfish species in the family Doradidae. Known as thorny catfishes, these fishes have rows of bony plates, most bearing spines, along the sides of the body and toothed spines at the front of both dorsal and pectoral fins. A slow-moving, bottom-living fish, the cuiu-cuiu is toothless and feeds on detritus, extracting insect larvae from the mud and rotted leaves.

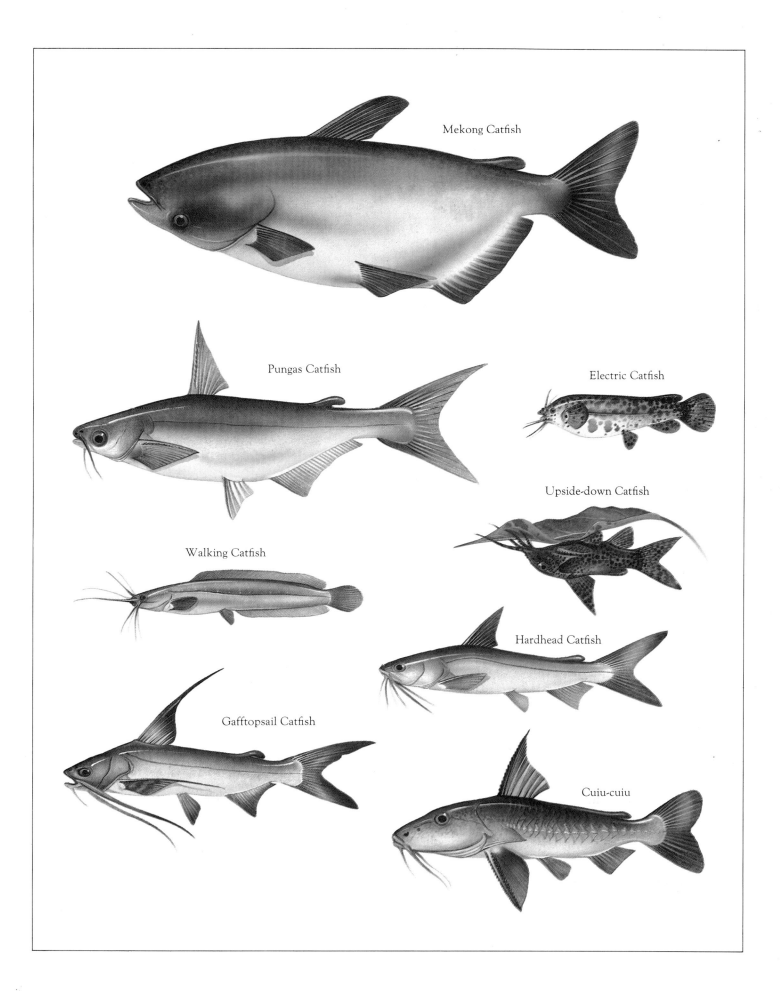

Mekong Catfish

Pungas Catfish

Electric Catfish

Upside-down Catfish

Walking Catfish

Hardhead Catfish

Gafftopsail Catfish

Cuiu-cuiu

Siluriform Fishes

NAME: Barber-eel, *Plotosus lineatus*
RANGE: Indian and Pacific Oceans:
   E. Africa to Sri Lanka and S.E. Asia
HABITAT: coastal waters, estuaries, reefs
SIZE: 30 cm (11¾ in)

The barber-eel is one of a family of 25 or 30 catfishes, all found in Indo-Pacific areas. Its body is elongate and eel-like, and there are two dorsal fins, one just behind the head and the other continuous with the tail and anal fins. As in many other catfishes, spines on the dorsal and pectoral fins can inflict painful wounds. There are several pairs of sensory barbels around the mouth.

Young barber-eels are particularly distinctive fishes, with light bands running the length of the body from snout to tail. Older fishes have brown backs, shading to light brown or white on the belly.

NAME: Australian Freshwater Catfish,
   Tandanus tandanus
RANGE: S. and E. Australia
HABITAT: rivers
SIZE: 61 cm (24 in)

The Australian freshwater catfish is a member of the same family (Plotosidae) as the barber-eel and has a similar fin pattern; its first dorsal fin is high and short based, and the second is continuous with the tail and anal fins. Spines on the dorsal and pectoral fins can cause painful wounds. Its body may be brownish or dull green in color but is always mottled with dark markings.

Several pairs of sensory barbels around the mouth help the catfish find food, mainly invertebrates such as mussels, shrimps and worms. In the breeding season, the eggs are laid in a circular nest made in sand or gravel and tended by one of the parents, usually the male.

NAME: Mandi, *Pimelodus blodii*
RANGE: South America: Amazon basin
HABITAT: rivers, streams, flooded forest
SIZE: 20 cm (7¾ in)

The mandi is a member of a family of about 285 species of South American catfish, known as the fat, or long-whiskered, catfishes (Pimelodidae). Typical of its family, it has a scaleless body and three pairs of sensory barbels, one pair of which is almost as long as the fish itself. Mostly active at night or at dusk, the fish uses these barbels to search for food. Although catfishes are generally bottom-dwellers, the mandi feeds both at the surface, on fruit and seeds which drop into the water, and on detritus and old leaves at the bottom; it also eats invertebrate animals at both levels.

NAME: Surubim, *Pseudoplatystoma*
   fasciatum
RANGE: South America: Amazon basin
HABITAT: rivers, lakes, flooded forest
SIZE: 50–90 cm (19¾–35½ in)

A distinctive fish, the surubim belongs to the Pimelodidae family of South American catfishes. It has an elongate snout, a slender body, marked with irregular dark stripes, and dark blotches on the fins and nose. There is considerable variation in the exact distribution of these markings.

Like most catfishes, the surubim is a bottom-dweller and is thought to feed mostly on invertebrate animals; several pairs of sensory barbels around its mouth help it find food. Unlike many of the Amazonian fishes, the surubim does not appear to have adapted to feeding on the abundant plant material that falls into the water.

NAME: Vieja, *Plecostomus commersonii*
RANGE: South America: S. Brazil,
   Uruguay, Paraguay, N. Argentina
HABITAT: rivers
SIZE: 53 cm (20¾ in)

The vieja is one of a large South American family of heavily armored catfishes (Loricariidae). Its long, slender body is covered with overlapping bony plates, but, unlike other members of its family, it has no such plates on the belly. The fins are well developed, with some dark spots on the high dorsal fin; the tail is large, with the lower lobe longer than the upper. The rounded mouth is on the underside of the snout.

Viejas spawn in spring. Adults feed on worms and crustaceans, as well as aquatic plants, while the young fishes feed on algae.

NAME: Cascarudo, *Callichthys callichthys*
RANGE: tropical South America: Guyana,
   south to Paraguay and Uruguay
HABITAT: rivers
SIZE: 18 cm (7 in)

This widely distributed fish belongs to a South American family of armored catfishes (Callichthyidae). There are about 130 species, and as the name suggests, their bodies are heavily armored with overlapping bony plates. The cascarudo has a more slender body than is usual in its family, a neat, pointed head and two pairs of barbels around the mouth. It lives on the river bottom and is most active at dawn and dusk.

When the cascarudos spawn, the male makes a nest, usually placed among floating plants, by blowing bubbles of air and mucus, which form a foamy mass. The eggs are then deposited in these protective bubbles.

NAME: Cascadura, *Hoplosternum littorale*
RANGE: South America: Venezuela,
   Guyana, south to Peru and Argentina;
   Trinidad
HABITAT: rivers, marshes, swamps
SIZE: 20 cm (7¾ in)

The cascadura belongs to the armored catfish family (Callichthyidae), and its body is covered with neatly overlapping bony plates. It is a heavily built fish, greeny-gray in coloration and with several pairs of long barbels. Like many of its family, it lives on the bottom, often in oxygen-poor, swampy water. In such conditions, it is able to utilize atmospheric oxygen by gulping in air at the water surface, then taking it into its hindgut. It is even believed to be able to travel short distances on land while using the air in its vascular gut. Cascaduras feed on aquatic plants.

Spawning cascaduras blow a bubble nest from air and mucus, which is placed among floating vegetation. The eggs are laid in this protective nest, and the male guards the nest and then the young fishes when they hatch.

NAME: Candirú, *Vandellia cirrhosa*
RANGE: South America: Amazon basin
HABITAT: rivers, streams
SIZE: 2.5 cm (1 in)

The tiny, delicate candirú belongs to a family of parasitic catfishes, Trichomycteridae, all found in South America. Its scaleless body is slender, elongate and virtually transparent, and its dorsal fin is placed well back near the tail. It has two pairs of rather short sensory barbels around the mouth.

Like other members of its family, the candirú is a parasite, living on the blood of other fishes. With small fishes, it simply pierces the skin with its sharp teeth to obtain blood, but it may penetrate the gill system of large fishes and live there, sucking blood. Its tiny body can swell considerably when gorged with food. It is generally active at night or at dawn and dusk and, when not feeding, may bury itself in the sand at the bottom of the river.

The candirú is notorious for its habit of entering the urethra of human bathers or of other mammals which urinate in the water. It is thought that the fish mistakes the urine for the respiratory water flow of a large fish. Once in the urethra, it becomes lodged by the barbs on its gill covers that normally help it stay in the gill chambers of large fishes, and it is extremely difficult and painful to remove.

Barber-eel

Australian Freshwater Catfish

Mandi

Surubim

Candirú

Cascadura

Cascarudo

Vieja

Lanternfishes, Beardfishes, Trout-perches

MYCTOPHIFORMES:
Lanternfish Order

This order includes 390 species of fish, grouped in 16 families and distributed throughout the world. Although there is quite a variety of forms within the order, most species are long bodied, with prominent dorsal fins and large mouths. The order includes families such as lizardfishes, greeneyes, lancetfishes and pearleyes. All species in the order are marine.

Lanternfishes, of which there are about 220 species, are the largest family. They are small deep-sea fishes with many photophores, or light-producing organs, mostly on the lower parts of the body. These are arranged in patterns characteristic to each species and are an important means of distinguishing between species.

NAME: **Red Lizardfish,** *Synodus synodus*
RANGE: **Atlantic Ocean: Florida, through Gulf of Mexico to Uruguay**
HABITAT: **coastal waters**
SIZE: **32 cm (12½ in)**

The red lizardfish is one of a family of about 34 lizardfishes, all found in shallow areas of tropical and warm temperate seas. It has a large head and wide jaws, set with long sharp teeth. With its heavy, shiny scales, it is thought to have a reptilian appearance — hence its common name — and it has some reddish coloration on its tail. The pelvic fins are unusually long, and the fish has the habit of lying on the seabed, supported on these fins; it can also partly bury itself. A voracious carnivore, it catches its prey by darting upward from its hiding place on the seabed.

NAME: **Bummalow,** *Harpadon nehereus*
RANGE: **N. Indian Ocean**
HABITAT: **estuaries, shallow coastal waters**
SIZE: **41 cm (16 in)**

The bummalow is one of a small family of 4 or 5 species, all found in the Indian Ocean. It has an elongate body, large jaws, housing sharp curving teeth, and long pelvic and pectoral fins. It is often found near the mouths of large rivers, such as the Ganges, where it feeds on small fish and crustaceans, although it breeds farther out to sea.

This fish is better known as Bombay duck, as it is called when it has been split and dried in the sun and is served with curries. It is a valuable commercial species for use in this way.

NAME: **Lanternfish,** *Myctophum punctatum*
RANGE: **N. Atlantic Ocean; Mediterranean Sea**
HABITAT: **deep sea**
SIZE: **10 cm (4 in)**

Typical of its family, with its blunt, rounded head and large eyes, the lanternfish has many light-producing organs, or photophores, arranged in short rows and groups on its body. Young fish start to develop their light-producing organs when they are about 2 cm (¾ in) long, and the arrangement differs in males and females. The function and value of these photophores are not yet fully understood. They may help the fish to illuminate the dark depths and find prey, or may be used to confuse predators; the lanternfish has photophores on its tail and is said to lash its tail to and fro to dazzle an enemy.

Lanternfishes feed on tiny planktonic animals, making vertical migrations of as much as 400 m (1,300 ft) or more to follow the nightly movements of the plankton to surface waters. They move in large schools and, in the Mediterranean area, are known to breed from April to July.

POLYMIXIIFORMES:
Beardfish Order

This order contains a single family of 3 rather similar species, all called beardfish. They are marine and are found in tropical and subtropical regions of the Atlantic, Indian and Pacific oceans, usually at depths of 180 to 640 m (600 to 2,100 ft). Beardfishes are all deep bodied, with large eyes and a pair of barbels beneath the chin.

NAME: **Stout Beardfish,** *Polymixia nobilis*
RANGE: **all oceans, tropical areas**
HABITAT: **deep water**
SIZE: **25 cm (9¾ in)**

A deep-bodied fish, the stout beardfish has a pair of long barbels dangling from its lower jaw which may help it to find food on the seabed. The coloration of its fully scaled body is variable, but its tail fin and the tip of the dorsal fin are usually dark, almost black. The almost identical species, *P. japonicus,* is found in the Sea of Japan.

PERCOPSIFORMES:
Trout-perch Order

There are about 8 species, grouped in 3 families, known to belong to this order. All are freshwater fishes, found in North America in larger streams, deep clear lakes and cave water, and have common names such as sandroller, pirate-perch and cavefish. Trout-perches, as their name suggests, show structural similarities to both trout and perch, but are never more than 15 cm (6 in) long and are not related to either. Most species in the order feed on aquatic insects and crustaceans, but the pirate-perch preys on small fish.

NAME: **Northern Cavefish,** *Amblyopsis spelaea*
RANGE: **USA: Kentucky, Indiana**
HABITAT: **fresh water in limestone caves**
SIZE: **10 cm (4 in)**

One of a small family of 5 or 6 species, 4 of which live in limestone caves, the northern cavefish was first discovered in 1842. It is a slender-bodied fish, with no scales on its head but small irregular scales on its body. Its eyes are rudimentary and covered with skin, since it has no need of vision in its dark cave habitat and has adapted accordingly. To compensate for its virtual blindness, its body is covered with tiny sensory protuberances with which it can detect even slight movements in water and thus find its prey and avoid obstacles.

The male cavefish fertilizes the female internally with a specially adapted genital organ. She has an unusual way of guarding her eggs: once they are fertilized and shed, she carries them in her gill chamber until they hatch.

NAME: **Trout-perch,** *Percopsis omiscomaycus*
RANGE: **N. America: Alaska to Quebec; Great Lakes to Kentucky, Missouri, Kansas**
HABITAT: **lakes, muddy rivers**
SIZE: **20 cm (7¾ in)**

One of the 2 species of trout-perch, this fish has a silvery body, translucent in parts. Its head is scaleless, but the rest of its body is covered with rough, saw-toothed scales. Nocturnal in its habits, the trout-perch feeds on aquatic insects, crustaceans and mollusks. It spawns in spring or early summer in streams and shallow lakes. The eggs sink to the bottom, where they remain until they hatch.

The other trout-perch, the sandroller, *P. transmontana,* lives only in the Columbia River system in northwestern USA. It is similar to *P. omiscomaycus* in fin pattern but is usually greenish-yellow in color.

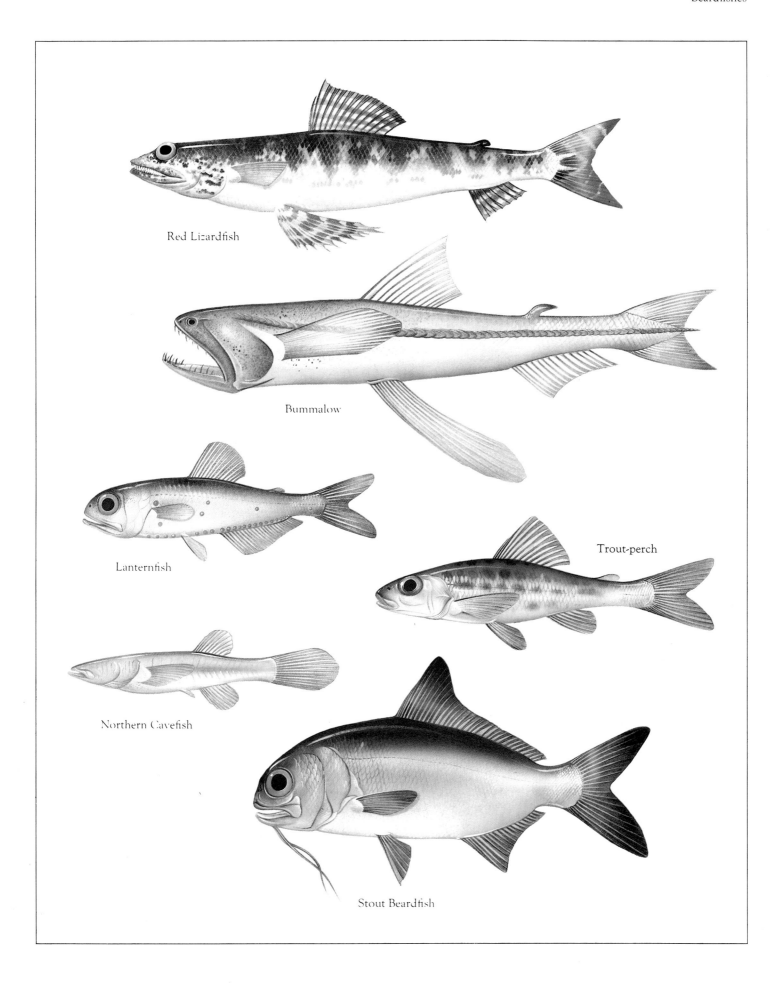

Red Lizardfish

Bummalow

Lanternfish

Northern Cavefish

Trout-perch

Stout Beardfish

Codfishes

NAME: **Atlantic Cod,** *Gadus morhua*
RANGE: **N. Atlantic Ocean: Greenland and Hudson Strait to North Carolina; Baltic Sea to Bay of Biscay**
HABITAT: **coastal waters**
SIZE: **1.2 m (4 ft)**

A stout-bodied fish, the cod is identified by its three dorsal and two anal fins and the single long chin barbel. Its mouth is large, containing many small teeth, and its mottled coloration is variable. Cod usually swim in schools in surface waters but will search for food — crustaceans, worms and fish — at mid-depths or on the seabed.

Breeding takes place between February and April, and some cod populations make long migrations to specific spawning areas. Eggs drift in surface waters, at the mercy of currents and predators, while they develop and hatch into larvae. The young cod feed on small crustaceans.

The cod is an extremely valuable food fish which has been exploited by man for centuries.

NAME: **Haddock,** *Melanogrammus aeglefinus*
RANGE: **N. Atlantic Ocean: Barents Sea and Iceland to Bay of Biscay; Newfoundland to Cape Cod**
HABITAT: **coastal waters, near seabed**
SIZE: **76 cm (30 in)**

The haddock resembles the cod, with its three dorsal and two anal fins, but the first dorsal fin is markedly triangular and pointed and there is a distinct black mark on each dusky side. Haddock live near the seabed and feed on bottom-living animals such as brittle stars, worms, mollusks and some small fish.

Spawning takes place between January and June, and eggs are left to float in surface waters while they hatch into larvae. Young haddock often shelter among the tentacles of large jellyfishes. Some haddock populations migrate south in winter or move from shallow inshore waters to deeper waters.

NAME: **Blue Whiting,** *Micromesistius poutassou*
RANGE: **N. Atlantic Ocean: Barents Sea to Mediterranean and Adriatic Seas**
HABITAT: **oceanic**
SIZE: **35–41 cm (13¾–16 in)**

Shoals of blue whiting move in surface and mid-waters to depths of about 300 m (980 ft). A slender species, they have three well-spaced dorsal fins and two anal fins, the first of which is long based. They feed mainly on crustaceans and some small fish, and are themselves an important item of diet for many larger fishes.

GADIFORMES: Cod Order

This order contains about 684 species, only 5 of which are freshwater fishes. They are grouped into 10 families, and some of the most familiar forms, such as cod, haddock, whiting, hake, pollock and ling, are valuable food fish.

The majority of the cod species live in the northern hemisphere in the relatively shallow waters of the continental shelves. Some species, however, notably the grenadiers, or rat-tails, live in deep oceanic water. All are carnivorous, feeding on fish, crustaceans and other forms of marine life.

The body of the codfish is covered with small scales, and the fins contain soft rays. Many members of the order have a sensory barbel on the chin that is equipped with additional taste buds.

Most cod spawn simply by forming shoals, when both sexes discharge their eggs and sperm into the water. The eggs are then abandoned and, although millions are produced, so many are destroyed by the elements or eaten by other fishes that few survive. In the case of the cod, it is estimated that only one egg in a million survives to adulthood.

NAME: **Whiting,** *Merlangius merlangus*
RANGE: **European coasts, Iceland to Spain, Mediterranean and Black Seas**
HABITAT: **shallow inshore waters to 100 m (330 ft)**
SIZE: **30–40 cm (11¼–15¾ in)**

A slender fish, the whiting has three dorsal and two anal fins, the first of which is long based. The upper jaw is longer than the lower, and there is a characteristic black mark at the base of each pectoral fin. Adult whiting feed on fish and crustaceans, while young feed mainly on small crustaceans. They spawn in spring in shallow water.

A common species, it is a valuable commercial food fish for humans and is also hunted and eaten by many larger fishes and also birds.

NAME: **Walleye Pollock,** *Theragra chalcogramma*
RANGE: **N. Pacific Ocean: N.W. Alaska to California; Sea of Japan**
HABITAT: **surface to mid-waters, 360 m (1,200 ft)**
SIZE: **90 cm (35½ in)**

The widely distributed walleye pollock has a tapering body, three well-spaced dorsal fins and two anal fins. Its head and mouth are large, and its eyes bigger than those of most codfishes. Unlike most codfishes, it spends little time near the seabed and feeds mainly in mid-depths on crustaceans and other marine invertebrates and some small fish.

NAME: **Pollock,** *Pollachius virens*
RANGE: **N. Atlantic Ocean: Iceland, Greenland and Barents Sea to Bay of Biscay; Labrador to North Carolina**
HABITAT: **surface waters: coastal and offshore**
SIZE: **70–80 cm (27½–31½ in)**

Although it has the typical cod fin pattern, the pollock is characterized by its slightly forked tail, the lower jaw, which protrudes slightly beyond the upper, and the lack of a chin barbel. Pollock usually move in small schools and feed on fish, particularly other cod species and herring; young pollock feed on crustaceans and small fish.

Pollock migrate to offshore breeding grounds to spawn in deep water between January and April. The eggs and then the larvae drift at the surface, gradually being carried to shallower inshore waters, where the young fishes are found the following summer. Large numbers are caught commercially, and it is a popular species with sea anglers.

NAME: **White Hake,** *Urophycis tenuis*
RANGE: **N.W. Atlantic Ocean: Gulf of St. Lawrence to North Carolina**
HABITAT: **inshore and offshore waters to depths of 1,000 m (3,300 ft)**
SIZE: **1.2 m (4 ft)**

An elongate fish, the white hake has only two dorsal fins, the second of which is long based, a small rounded tail and one long anal fin. It is commonly found near soft muddy bottoms where it feeds on crustaceans, squid and small fish. Spawning begins in late winter and eggs and larvae float at the surface.

Large quantities of white hake and the closely related red hake, *U. chuss*, are taken by commercial fisheries. Even though, confusingly, their common names are the same, these hakes are a quite separate group from the true hakes (*Merluccius* species).

NAME: **Ling,** *Molva molva*
RANGE: **N.E. Atlantic Ocean: Iceland, Norway to Bay of Biscay**
HABITAT: **deep water, 300–400 m (980–1,300 ft)**
SIZE: **1.5–2 m (5–6½ ft)**

A long slim fish, the ling has two dorsal fins, the second of which is long based, and one long anal fin. It has one barbel on its chin. It is most common in rocky-bottomed areas and feeds on fish and large crustaceans. Although mainly a deepwater species, the ling may be found in shallower areas, where the bottom is suitable. It breeds from March to July, and one female may shed up to 60 million eggs. These eggs float in surface waters while they develop.

Ling are valuable commercial fish in some European waters.

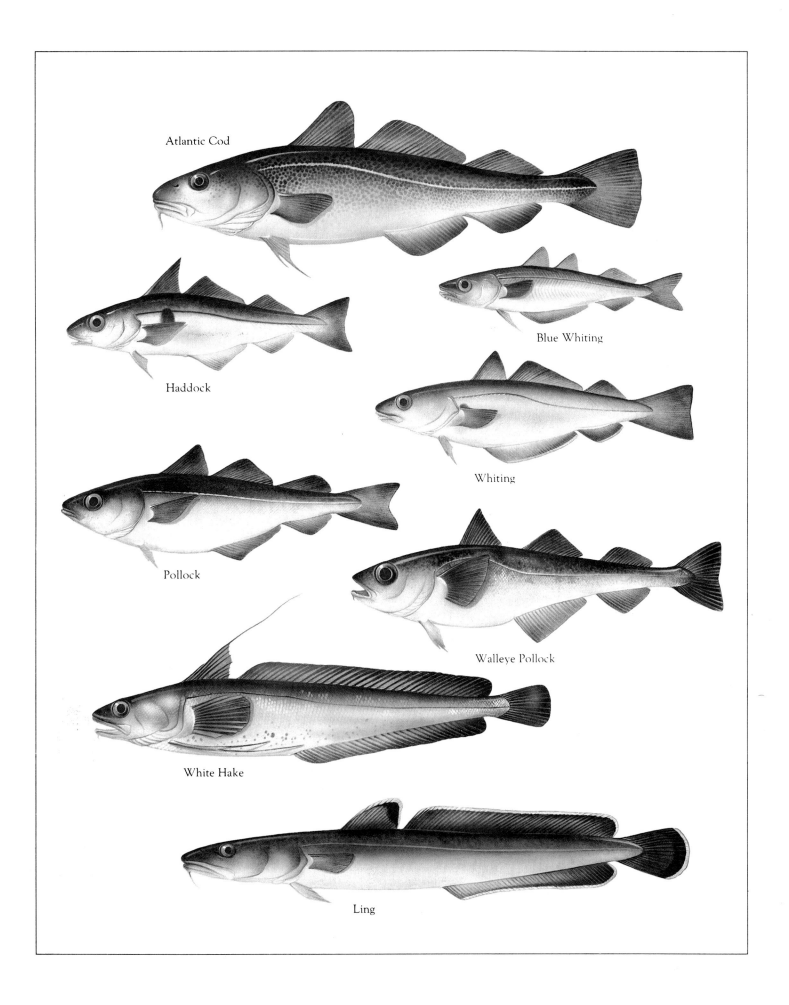

Atlantic Cod

Haddock

Blue Whiting

Whiting

Pollock

Walleye Pollock

White Hake

Ling

Codfishes

NAME: Three-barbed Rockling,
Gaidropsarus mediterraneus
RANGE: European coasts: S. Norway,
W. British Isles to Mediterranean and
Black Seas
HABITAT: rocky shores
SIZE: 15–35 cm (6–13¾ in)

One of several species of rockling, the three-barbed is typical of the group, with its long slender body and two dorsal fins. The first of these has short, fine rays and the second is long based. The anal fin is also long based, and, as the common name implies, there are three barbels, one on the chin and two on the snout.

An abundant fish on many shores, this rockling nearly always occurs on rocky bottoms and feeds on crustaceans, worms and small fish. It spawns offshore, and eggs and larvae float on surface waters. When the young fishes measure about 4 cm (1½ in) long, they adopt the bottom-living habits of the adult rocklings.

NAME: Burbot, *Lota lota*
RANGE: Canada, N. USA, N. Europe,
Asia
HABITAT: rivers, lakes
SIZE: 51–99 cm (20–39 in)

One of the few fishes in the cod order to live in fresh water, the burbot is similar to many marine codfishes, with its long body, chin barbel and long-based dorsal and anal fins. It is a fairly sluggish fish, hiding among aquatic vegetation by day and emerging at dawn and dusk to feed. Adults eat fish, crustaceans and insects, while the young burbot feed on insect larvae and small crustaceans.

Burbot spawn at night in shallow water during the winter. They are prolific egg-layers: one female may shed up to 3 million eggs which sink to the bottom, where they remain while development takes place.

NAME: New Zealand Ling, *Genypterus*
blacodes
RANGE: seas off S. Australia, New
Zealand
HABITAT: coastal waters
SIZE: 90 cm (35½ in)

Not to be confused with the North Atlantic lings (*Molva*), this ling is one of a group known as cusk-eels, which belong to the cod order. A long, tapering fish, its dorsal, tail and anal fins are joined to form one continuous strip around the body. The head is flattened, and there are two thin pelvic fins under the lower jaw. The anus is positioned behind the head.

NAME: European Hake, *Merluccius*
merluccius
RANGE: N. Atlantic Ocean: Iceland,
Norway to N. Africa; Mediterranean
Sea
HABITAT: deep water, 165–550 m
(550–1,800 ft)
SIZE: 1–1.8 m (3¼–6 ft)

The true hakes are a small family of cod-like fishes, all in the genus *Merluccius*. The European hake is a typical species, with its slender body, large head and two dorsal fins, the first of which is triangular and the second long based and curving. It lives near the seabed but migrates upward nightly to feed nearer the surface on fish and squid.

Hakes spawn in spring or summer and the eggs and larvae drift in surface waters, gradually being carried farther inshore, where the young fish remain for their first year, feeding principally on crustaceans.

The Pacific hake, *M. productus*, is similar to the European species in appearance and habits.

NAME: Roughhead Grenadier, *Macrourus*
berglax
RANGE: N. Atlantic Ocean: Nova Scotia
to Greenland, Iceland, Norway
HABITAT: deep water, 200–1,000 m
(650–3,300 ft)
SIZE: 90 cm–1 m (35½ in–3¼ ft)

The roughhead grenadier is one of a family of about 15 species belonging to the cod order which are found in deep water; all are known as grenadiers or rattails. The males of many of these species can make surprisingly loud sounds by vibrating their swim bladders with specialized muscles. Such sounds may be used for communication, particularly during the breeding season.

Characteristic of its family, with its large, heavy head and tapering, pointed tail, the roughhead grenadier has a high first dorsal fin, but its second dorsal fin and anal fin are continuous with the tail. The head is ridged beneath the eyes and the body scales are rough and toothed. The grenadier feeds on crustaceans, mollusks and brittle stars. It is believed to breed in winter to early spring.

NAME: *Lucifuga spelaeotes*
RANGE: Bahamas: near Nassau
HABITAT: freshwater pools in limestone
SIZE: 11 cm (4¼ in)

This species was first discovered in 1967 and is known only from this one location, although it is believed to be related to 2 species in the same genus, found in cave pools in Cuba. A small but distinctive fish, its body curves upward sharply behind the broad, flattened head and its long-based dorsal and anal fins are continuous with the tail fin. Much of its head is scaleless, but the body is covered with small scales. The Cuban species are blind, but *L. spelaeotes* has small yet well-developed eyes.

In view of its apparently extremely restricted distribution, it seems that this species may be in danger of disappearing only years after its discovery.

NAME: Pearlfish, *Carapus acus*
RANGE: Mediterranean and Adriatic Seas
HABITAT: seabed
SIZE: 20 cm (7¾ in)

Pearlfishes are small, slender fishes, with translucent, spotted skin, found in tropical and warm temperate waters. Many of them spend much of their lives inside other marine animals such as clams, sea urchins, starfish, sea cucumbers and even pearl oysters — hence the common name. This species is a typical pearlfish, with its elongate tapering body and long, low dorsal and anal fins which form a continuous border to the body. The adult fish lives inside a sea cucumber. It enters the animal through its anus, inserting its tail first and then wriggling backward until it is inside the body cavity. Several pearlfishes may occupy one host, feeding on its internal organs until the host is destroyed.

Young pearlfishes pass through two larval stages before taking up residence in this way; in the first phase, the young float in surface waters, and in the second, they live near the seabed. Adult pearlfishes can live outside a host, feeding on small crustaceans.

NAME: Ocean Pout, *Macrozoarces*
americanus
RANGE: N. Atlantic Ocean: Labrador to
Delaware
HABITAT: seabed, 15–183 m (50–600 ft)
SIZE: 93 cm (36½ in)

The ocean pout is one of a small family collectively known as eelpouts. Their classification has been the subject of dispute, and some authorities have placed them with the blennies rather than the codfishes.

Typical of the eelpouts, the elongate ocean pout has long anal and dorsal fins, joined to the tail fin. Its head is broad and flattened, and it has very thick, protuberant lips. It is a bottom-living species and feeds on crustaceans, sea urchins, brittle stars and other small invertebrates. In autumn, ocean pouts migrate into deeper, offshore waters to spawn. One female may shed 4,000 or more eggs, massed together in a gelatinous substance, which lie on the bottom and hatch after 2 or 3 months. Some eelpouts, such as the European species *Zoarces viviparus*, give birth to live young.

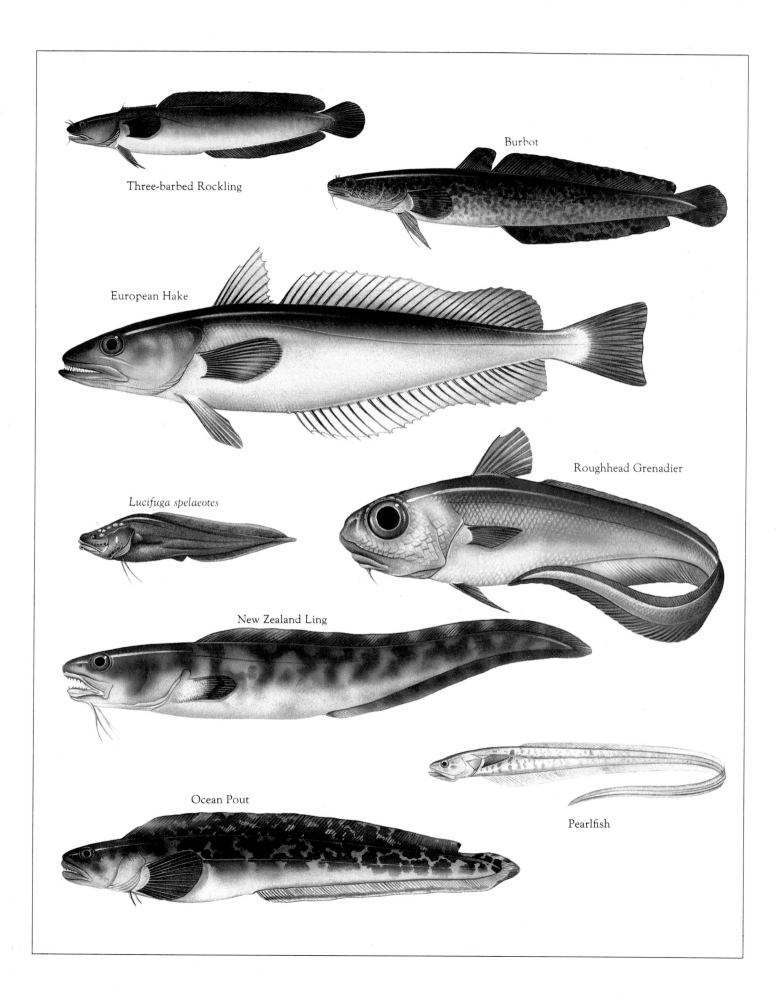

Three-barbed Rockling

Burbot

European Hake

Lucifuga spelaeotes

Roughhead Grenadier

New Zealand Ling

Ocean Pout

Pearlfish

Toadfishes, Angler Fishes

BATRACHOIDIFORMES: Toadfish Order

There are about 55 species of bottom-dwelling toadfish, found in many of the oceans of the world, mostly in tropical or warm temperate areas. There are 2 freshwater species. Their common name arises from the supposed resemblance of the broad, flattened head, with its wide mouth and slightly protuberant eyes, to that of a toad.

NAME: **Atlantic Midshipman,** *Porichthys porosissimus*
RANGE: **W. Atlantic Ocean: coasts of Brazil to Argentina**
HABITAT: **inshore waters**
SIZE: **30 cm (11¾ in)**

The bottom-dwelling Atlantic midshipman has a large, flattened head and eyes that are positioned near the top of the head, looking upward, rather than at the sides. The body is scaleless, and on each side there are rows of several hundred photophores, or small light-producing organs, each resembling a tiny shining dot, which are arranged in a regular, characteristic pattern. Midshipmen are among the few shallow-water fishes to possess such organs.

Also known as the singing fish, this species can make a variety of sounds. Specialized muscles in the walls of the fish's swim bladder contract, vibrating the walls of the bladder to produce grunts and whistles.

LOPHIIFORMES: Angler Fish Order

There are about 215 species of angler fish known; they are found at all depths in tropical and temperate seas. All have large heads, wide mouths filled with many rows of sharp teeth and small gills and gill openings. The body is rounded in deepwater forms and flattened from top to bottom in shallow-water forms.

The majority of anglers have a fishing lure, which is a modification of the dorsal fin spine, tipped with a flap of skin, and which can be moved into a position in front of the mouth. The shallow-water angler lies camouflaged on the seabed, gently moving its lure. Prey, seeing the lure and thinking it a tasty food morsel, comes nearer to investigate and is then engulfed by the angler's huge jaws.

A number of deep-sea anglers have an extraordinary mode of reproduction. The males, which are a fraction of the size of females, attach themselves to the latter so intimately that their tissues fuse; the male then becomes merely a reservoir of sperm.

NAME: **Angler,** *Lophius piscatorius*
RANGE: **European coasts from Scandinavia and Iceland to N. Africa; Black and Mediterranean Seas**
HABITAT: **coastal waters**
SIZE: **1–2 m (3¼–6½ ft)**

A large, highly distinctive fish, the angler has a flattened body, dominated by its broad, flattened head. The mouth is extremely wide and the teeth well developed. The head and mouth are fringed with small skin flaps that help conceal the fish's outline as it lies on the seabed. The pectoral fins are placed on the small fleshy limbs, and on the first elongated dorsal spine is a flap of skin, used as a fishing lure.

The angler is a bottom-living fish, found from shallow water down to 500 m (1,650 ft) or more. Half-buried in the sand or shingle of the seabed, it watches for prey and moves its lure to attract fish within easy reach of its capacious mouth. Once the angler opens its mouth, powerful water currents are created, sucking in the unfortunate prey.

Anglers move farther out to sea in spring and early summer to spawn over deep water. The eggs are shed enclosed in ribbonlike trails of gelatinous mucus which keeps them together as they float near the surface. The larvae, too, float near the surface, aided by their enlarged dorsal fins. The closely related goosefish, *L. americanus,* of the Atlantic coast of North America is similar in appearance and habits.

NAME: **Sargassumfish,** *Histrio histrio*
RANGE: **Atlantic, Indian, Pacific Oceans, tropical areas**
HABITAT: **surface waters among sargassum weed**
SIZE: **19 cm (7½ in)**

The sargassumfish is one of the family of anglers known as frogfishes, which, typically, have a balloon-shaped body covered with bumps and flaps of skin. It is perfectly camouflaged to blend with the sargassum weed in which it lives, and, while its coloration is variable, it always matches its own particular weed patch. Frondlike rays on the snout mimic the weed itself, and white dots on the body resemble the white encrustations of tiny animals that live on sargassum plants. The fish's pectoral fins are flexible and limblike and can be used actually to grasp the weed as it clambers around.

Small invertebrates are the main food of the sargassumfish, and it attracts prey by means of the small lure on its snout. If itself attacked by a predator, the sargassumfish may rapidly take in water, pumping itself into a ball too big for its enemy to swallow.

NAME: **Longlure Frogfish,** *Antennarius multiocellatus*
RANGE: **tropical W. Atlantic Ocean, Caribbean**
HABITAT: **seabed**
SIZE: **15 cm (6 in)**

The longlure frogfish has the stout body characteristic of its family and a particularly pronounced "fishing line" on its snout. Its coloration is variable but always merges well with its surroundings, whether rock, coral or seaweed. A bottom-living, slow-moving fish, it crawls around the seabed with the aid of its limblike pectoral fins, feeding on small fish and crustaceans.

NAME: **Shortnose Batfish,** *Ogcocephalus nasutus*
RANGE: **Caribbean**
HABITAT: **seabed**
SIZE: **28 cm (11 in)**

The shortnose batfish is typical of the 55 or so species of batfish, with its almost triangular body, dramatically flattened from top to bottom. Its pectoral fins are large and flexible and positioned on armlike stalks. Its snout is pointed and mouth small, and the upper surface of its body is studded with hard tubercles — small, rounded projections.

A slow-moving fish and an awkward swimmer, the batfish crawls over the seabed on its pectoral and pelvic fins, using its tail as support. It feeds on fish, mollusks, crustaceans and worms.

NAME: **Atlantic Footballfish,** *Himantolophus groenlandicus*
RANGE: **worldwide (but uncommon)**
HABITAT: **deep sea, 100–300 m (330–980 ft)**
SIZE: **61 cm (24 in)**

The footballfish is a deep-sea angler. Its extremely rotund body is studded with bony plates, each bearing a central spine, and the modified ray on the head makes a thick "fishing rod," tipped with a many-branched lure and with a central luminous bulb. It preys on fish attracted to the lure in the sparsely inhabited dark depths. Males are smaller than females but are not parasitic.

NAME: *Linophryne arborifera*
RANGE: **Atlantic, Pacific, Indian Oceans**
HABITAT: **deep sea**
SIZE: **7 cm (2¾ in)**

One of a family of about 20 deep-sea anglers, *Linophryne* has a rounded body and a distinctive, branched chin barbel, resembling a piece of seaweed. The prominent "fishing rod" on its snout is also branched and bears a luminous lure. The tiny adult males of this species are believed to live parasitically on the females, losing their own powers of vision and smell.

Atlantic Midshipman

Atlantic Footballfish

Sargassumfish

Longlure Frogfish

Shortnose Batfish

Linophryne arborifera

Angler

Atheriniform Fishes

INDOSTOMIFORMES

There is only 1 species in this order, the affinities and classification of which have been the subject of much dispute. The species, however, is thought sufficiently distinct to deserve its own order.

NAME: *Indostomus paradoxus*
RANGE: Burma: Lake Indawgyi; Thailand
HABITAT: lakes, streams
SIZE: 3 cm (1¼ in)

This tiny, rare fish has only ever been found in two sites. It is slender bodied, and the position of its dorsal fin, opposite the similarly shaped anal fin, gives it an unusually symmetrical appearance. The body is covered with hard plates, but despite this is very flexible. The fish lives in shallow water among vegetation and, although it is generally slow-moving and static, can swim fast when necessary, propelling itself with the tail fin. It feeds exclusively on microscopic invertebrate animals.

ATHERINIFORMES

This diverse and successful group includes such species as flyingfishes, halfbeaks, toothcarps and silversides. In all there are over 800 species in the order, grouped in 16 families and found in freshwater and marine habitats.

The 140 or so species of flyingfishes and halfbeaks are unusual members of the fish communities of tropical and subtropical seas. The flyingfishes are tail-powered gliders, different species gaining lift from enlarged, winglike pectoral fins, or pectoral and pelvic fins, but all propelling themselves forward with their rapidly beating tails to glide short distances over the water. The related halfbeaks skip along the surface of the sea but do not become fully airborne like the flyingfishes. Flyingfishes usually "fly" to escape from predators such as dolphin fish.

There are almost 500 species of toothcarp and killifish in fresh and brackish waters in Asia, Africa and the Americas. They have common names such as guppy, killifish and swordtail, and are rarely more than a few centimeters long. There are both carnivorous and herbivorous species.

Silversides are a large family of about 200 species of slim, small fishes which are widely distributed in tropical and warm temperate seas as well as in fresh water. They are often seen in schools and are all carnivorous. Many have shining, silvery lines running along the sides of the body, hence the common name.

NAME: Atlantic Flyingfish, *Cypselurus heterurus*
RANGE: W. Atlantic Ocean: S. Canada to Brazil; E. Atlantic: Denmark to N. Africa; Mediterranean Sea
HABITAT: surface waters: open sea and coastal
SIZE: 30–43 cm (11¾–17 in)

The Atlantic flyingfish is a four-winged flyingfish, with enlarged pectoral and pelvic fins to propel it on its "flights." When swimming underwater, its pectoral fins are kept folded against the body. The dorsal and anal fins are small and positioned near the tail, which has a long lower lobe. The body is fully scaled. Before a flight, the fish builds up speed in the water and then rises into the air, both pairs of fins expanded, and glides up to 90 m (300 ft) at 1.5 m (5 ft) above the surface. Most flights last about 10 seconds.

Flyingfishes breed in the spring and lay their eggs among seaweed or other debris. The eggs bear many fine threads which attach them to one another and anchor them to floating objects. When they hatch, the young flyingfishes have a pair of short barbels on the chin.

NAME: Tropical Two-wing Flyingfish, *Exocetus volitans*
RANGE: all oceans: tropical and subtropical areas
HABITAT: open sea
SIZE: 30 cm (11¾ in)

This species of flyingfish has only one pair of wings: the enlarged pectoral fins. Flights of two-winged flyingfishes are shorter and less controlled than those of four-winged species. Otherwise this species is similar to the Atlantic flyingfish in its habits. Like all flyingfishes it is carnivorous, feeding mostly on other fish.

NAME: Wrestling Halfbeak, *Dermogenys pusillus*
RANGE: Thailand, Malaysia, Singapore, Sunda Islands
HABITAT: fresh water
SIZE: 7 cm (2¾ in)

A small slender fish, with dorsal and anal fins positioned near the broad rounded tail, the wrestling halfbeak has the elongated lower jaw typical of its group. It is one of the few freshwater halfbeaks. Mosquito larvae are its main food source, and it is an important controller of these pests.

Males are aggressive and fight one another by wrestling with their jaws. The anal fin of the male is modified to form a copulatory organ for internal fertilization of the female. About 8 weeks after her eggs have been fertilized, the female gives birth to 12 to 20 live young, each of which is about 1 cm (½ in) long.

NAME: Ballyhoo, *Hemiramphus brasiliensis*
RANGE: Atlantic Ocean: New England to Brazil; Gulf of Mexico, Caribbean; off W. Africa
HABITAT: coastal waters
SIZE: 45 cm (17¾ in)

The ballyhoo is a slender-bodied fish, with a greatly elongated lower jaw and small dorsal and anal fins set back on the body near the tail. It is a typical halfbeak with small pectoral fins; although it cannot glide over the water like its relatives the flyingfishes, it can skim over the surface. It is surface-living and moves in schools, feeding on sea grass and small fish. The form of its jaws may help it to scoop up food from the water surface.

NAME: Freshwater Needlefish, *Belonion apodion*
RANGE: South America
HABITAT: lakes, rivers
SIZE: 5 cm (2 in)

A tiny, fragile fish, first discovered in 1966, the freshwater needlefish is one of a family of about 26 needlefishes and garfishes, most of which are marine. It is typical of its family, with its slender body and small anal and dorsal fins placed near the tail, but unlike most other species, which have elongate upper and lower jaws, only its lower jaw is long.

NAME: Garfish, *Belone belone*
RANGE: N. Atlantic Ocean: Iceland to Spain and Scandinavia; Mediterranean and Black Seas
HABITAT: surface waters, mainly offshore
SIZE: 94 cm (37 in)

The garfish is a long, slim fish with elongate jaws, studded with numerous needlelike teeth. Both dorsal and anal fins are long based and set well back near the tail. An active predator, the garfish feeds on many species of small fish and crustaceans. It spawns in late spring or early summer, in coastal waters. The small, round eggs bear many fine threads which attach to floating debris or seaweed.

NAME: Houndfish, *Tylosaurus crocodilus*
RANGE: all oceans
HABITAT: inshore surface waters
SIZE: 1.5 m (5 ft)

The largest, heaviest needlefish, the houndfish has a shorter, thicker beak than most species. Houndfishes sometimes leap out of the water and skip over the surface and, because of their size and strong, pointed jaws, can be quite dangerous to man. The houndfish feeds on fish, which it seizes cross-wise in its jaws and skillfully turns to swallow headfirst.

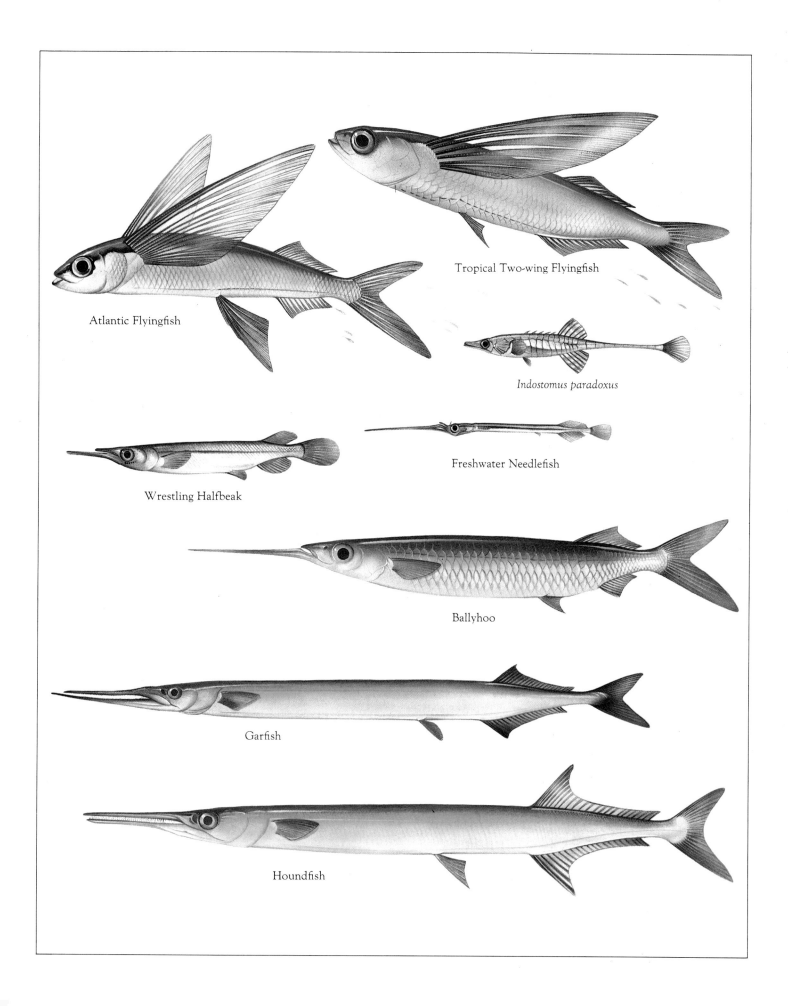

Tropical Two-wing Flyingfish

Atlantic Flyingfish

Indostomus paradoxus

Wrestling Halfbeak

Freshwater Needlefish

Ballyhoo

Garfish

Houndfish

Atheriniform Fishes

NAME: **Atlantic Saury,** *Scomberesox saurus*
RANGE: **N. Atlantic Ocean: N. American to European coasts; Mediterranean Sea; temperate waters in S. hemisphere, around the globe**
HABITAT: **open ocean, coastal waters**
SIZE: **40–50 cm (15¾–19¾ in)**

This distinctive saury is a long, slim fish with elongate, beaklike jaws, the lower of which is longer than the upper. Behind the dorsal and anal fins are further rows of small fins. Sauries swim in shoals in surface waters, feeding on small crustaceans and small fish.

Sauries spawn in open sea. Their eggs, which are small and round and covered with many threads, float at the water surface while they develop. The young fishes hatch with short jaws of equal length; the elongate jaws develop as the fishes grow and mature.

NAME: **Ricefish/Japanese Medaka,** *Oryzias latipes*
RANGE: **Japan**
HABITAT: **coastal marshes, rice fields**
SIZE: **4 cm (1½ in)**

The ricefish is one of a family of 7 species of fish, known as medakas and found in Southeast Asia and Japan. It is a small, slender fish, with a flattened head and an almost straight back. The underside of the body is distinctly curved, and there is a long-based anal fin. In the male the dorsal fin is pointed, but in the female it is rounded. Medakas are useful to mankind in that they feed on mosquito larvae, as well as other small invertebrates.

Medakas breed by laying eggs. At first, the female carries her eggs around in a mucous sheath on her belly, but then moves them to submerged plants, where they complete their development and hatch, up to 12 days after laying.

NAME: **Cape Lopez Lyretail,** *Aphyosemion australe*
RANGE: **Africa: Gabon, Cape Lopez area**
HABITAT: **swamps, ditches**
SIZE: **6 cm (2¼ in)**

The male Cape Lopez lyretail is an attractive, brightly colored fish, with large, pointed dorsal and anal fins and a tail with extended lobes. The female is plainer, and her fins lack the decorative points and extensions.

The lyretail deposits its eggs among the mud and detritus at the bottom of its habitat. If there is then a prolonged dry season, the embryos cease their development and lie dormant in the mud, protected by their drought-resistant egg membrane. Although the parent fishes die in the drought, the eggs resume development with the arrival of rain and hatch shortly afterward.

NAME: **Sheepshead Minnow,** *Cyprinidon variegatus*
RANGE: **USA coasts: Cape Cod to Texas, south to Mexico**
HABITAT: **bays, harbors, salt marshes**
SIZE: **7.5 cm (3 in)**

The sheepshead minnow belongs to a large family of small fishes known as toothcarps. This name refers to their resemblance to the carps and to the tiny teeth that line their jaws. This species has a short, stubby body, a high back and a prominent dorsal fin. Outside the breeding season, males and females appear similar, but females have darker markings. Breeding males develop much brighter coloration, turning steely-blue and green, with orange or red bellies. Sheepshead minnows feed on a wide range of tiny invertebrates and aquatic plants.

Breeding takes place from April to September, and males compete for mates. The female lays her eggs a few at a time, while the male clasps her around the tail and fertilizes the eggs as they are shed. The eggs have sticky threads on their surface, which attach them to each other and to plants or objects on the bottom.

NAME: **Mummichog,** *Fundulus heteroclitus*
RANGE: **N. American coasts: Labrador to Mexico**
HABITAT: **bays, marshes, river mouths**
SIZE: **10–15 cm (4–6 in)**

A member of the toothcarp family, the stout-bodied mummichog is an adaptable, hardy fish that tolerates brackish, salt and fresh water. It is a voracious feeder and eats almost any available plants and animals.

Mummichogs breed from April to August in shallow water. The male chases his mate in an extensive courtship ritual and then clasps her with his fins and fertilizes the eggs as they are laid. The sticky-surfaced eggs sink to the bottom in a cluster.

NAME: ***Aphanius dispar***
RANGE: **Indian Ocean: coasts of E. Africa and Middle East; Red Sea**
HABITAT: **coastal waters**
SIZE: **8 cm (3¼ in)**

This adaptable toothcarp occurs in fresh- and saltwater pools in its range, as well as in the sea. Male and female differ slightly in coloration: males are brownish-blue, with dark markings near and on the tail, while females are grayish-blue, with markings on the sides. They feed on small invertebrates and algae.

The female sheds her eggs onto submerged plants. They hatch in under 2 weeks, and the young fishes feed on plant plankton and algae.

NAME: **Four-eyed Fish,** *Anableps anableps*
RANGE: **S. Mexico, Central America and northern South America**
HABITAT: **coasts, estuaries, lakes**
SIZE: **30 cm (11¾ in)**

The four-eyed fish has, in fact, only two eyes, which project well above the head and are divided into two parts. The top section of each eye is adapted for vision in the air and the lower for vision in water; the sections are separated by a dark band. The fish swims at the surface, the water reaching the level of the dividing bands on the eyes, and is able to watch for insect prey at the surface or in the air and any prey swimming just underwater.

Four-eyed fish bear live young and females are fertilized internally. The male's anal fin is modified into a copulatory organ, which can be moved either to the left or the right, and the female's genital opening is covered by a specialized scale, which opens to the left or right. It is believed that a "left-handed" male must copulate with a "right-handed" female and vice versa; fortunately it seems that the proportion of right and left mating types is more or less equal in both sexes. The eggs develop inside the mother's body, and 4 or 5 live young are born.

NAME: **Guppy,** *Poecilia reticulata*
RANGE: **northern South America to Brazil; Barbados, Trinidad; introduced in many tropical areas**
HABITAT: **streams, pools**
SIZE: **6 cm (2¼ in)**

The guppy occurs naturally over a wide range and has been spread by man as a pest controller, since it feeds on the aquatic larvae of mosquitoes. It is an extremely abundant fish, occurring in huge numbers in brackish as well as fresh water. Females are generally larger than males and are less attractively colored, with dull, brownish bodies. As well as feeding on mosquito larvae, guppies eat other insect larvae, small crustaceans and the eggs and young of other fishes.

Guppies breed throughout the year, bearing litters of live young. The male's anal fin is modified as a copulatory organ for internal fertilization of the female. The young develop inside the mother and their egg membranes burst as they are born. Up to 24 young are born at a time, and they achieve sexual maturity in 4 to 10 weeks, depending on the temperature of their surroundings. This ability to mature fast and breed many times a year leads to such large populations of guppies that they are called millions fish in some areas. Many different, brilliantly colored forms are bred as aquarium fish.

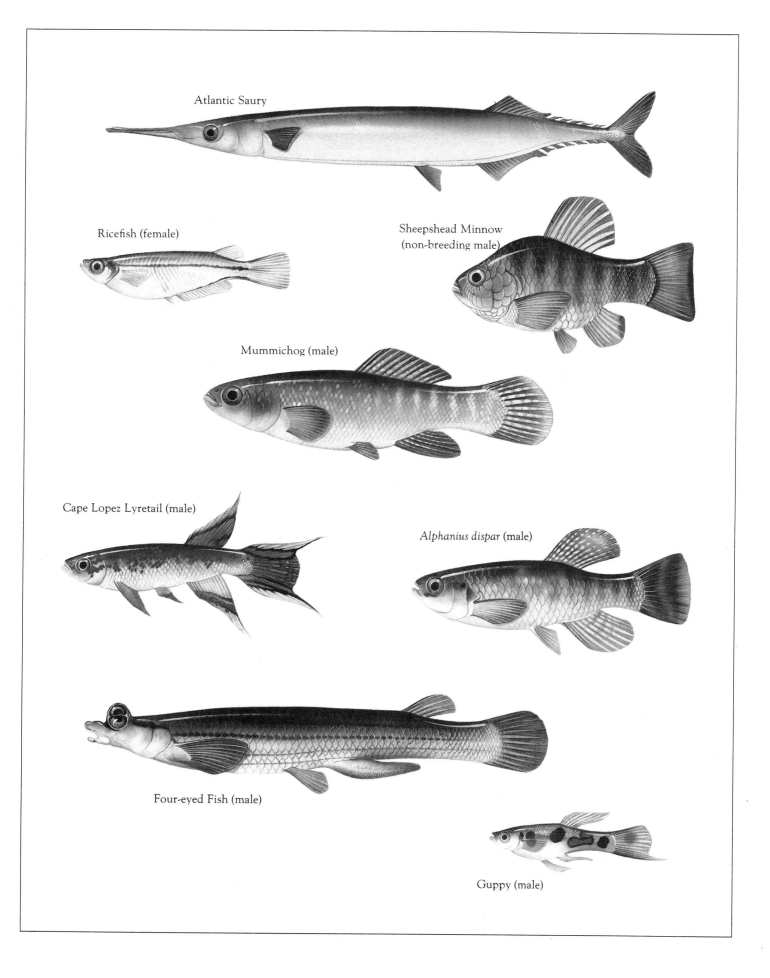

Atlantic Saury

Ricefish (female)

Sheepshead Minnow
(non-breeding male)

Mummichog (male)

Cape Lopez Lyretail (male)

Alphanius dispar (male)

Four-eyed Fish (male)

Guppy (male)

Atheriniform Fishes

NAME: **Hardhead Silverside,** *Atherinomorus stipes*
RANGE: **N. Atlantic Ocean: Florida to Brazil, including Caribbean**
HABITAT: **inshore waters**
SIZE: **12.5 cm (5 in)**

The hardhead silverside has an elongate, cylindrical body and two dorsal fins, the first of which consists of spines. Its eyes are large relative to its body size. Its coloration is variable: during the day it is almost transparent, with a narrow silvery stripe, while at night it darkens.

These silversides are abundant, and they occur in large shoals. They lay eggs bearing threads, which anchor them to aquatic plants.

NAME: *Phenacostethus smithi*
RANGE: **Thailand**
HABITAT: **fresh water: muddy pools, ditches, canals**
SIZE: **2 cm ($\frac{3}{4}$ in)**

One of the tiniest of fishes, this abundant species occurs in small schools and feeds on microscopic planktonic organisms. It has minute scales and two dorsal fins (one of which is just a spine) and a disproportionately long anal fin. Since the body is virtually transparent, the internal organs are visible.

These fishes have no pelvic fins, but the male has a complex copulatory organ, positioned just behind the chin, that involves some of the pelvic structure. The female's urogenital opening is in the same position and is covered by a specialized scale. The fishes spawn from May to December, the male clasping the female and fertilizing the eggs as they are laid.

NAME: **Pike Killifish,** *Belonesox belizanus*
RANGE: **Mexico, Central America to Honduras**
HABITAT: **muddy backwaters, marshes, lakes**
SIZE: **10–20 cm (4–7$\frac{3}{4}$ in)**

A long-bodied fish, the pike killifish has a pointed snout and a large mouth. It does, indeed, resemble a tiny pike and hunts in the same way, lurking among vegetation and dashing out quickly to seize prey. Females of this species are larger than males, sometimes reaching as much as twice their size. These fishes are thought to have suffered considerable reduction in numbers because of the effects of insecticides sprayed on the waters of their habitats to destroy mosquito larvae.

Female pike killifishes produce 20 to 80 live young at a time. Although rather predatory, killifishes are used as aquarium fish.

NAME: **California Grunion,** *Leuresthes tenuis*
RANGE: **Pacific Ocean: coasts of California and Baja California**
HABITAT: **inshore waters**
SIZE: **18 cm (7 in)**

The California grunion is sensitive to tidal and lunar rhythms and uses them to synchronize its spawning activities. These slender little fishes await the extremes of the spring or neap tides to bury their eggs on the sandy shore at the high-water mark. They spawn at night from March until August, but the spawning peaks in May and June. Once the high-water mark is reached by the waves, the grunions swim ashore in huge numbers, mate and lay their eggs in shallow scrapes in the sand. The next wave covers the eggs with sand and carries the fish back out to sea. Two weeks later, at the extreme high of the next high tides, the eggs are exposed, which triggers hatching. The spawning cycle is thus entirely predictable and is associated with the tidal rhythms.

The vast numbers of California grunions that take part in the twice-monthly spawning runs attract many predators, including humans. Fishermen are allowed to take only a limited quantity of the fishes.

NAME: **Sandsmelt,** *Atherina presbyter*
RANGE: **E. Atlantic Ocean: coasts of Britain, Ireland, France, Spain, Portugal and N. Africa**
HABITAT: **inshore waters, estuaries**
SIZE: **15–21 cm (6–8$\frac{1}{4}$ in)**

The sandsmelt is a member of a family of small schooling fishes found worldwide, mostly in tropical and warm temperate seas. This species is one of the few found in northern waters and is fairly typical of its family, with its long, slender body and two widely spaced dorsal fins; the first dorsal fin has seven or eight spines. Schools of sandsmelts are most common on sandy or muddy bottoms, and young fishes may sometimes be found in coastal rock pools. The jaws of sandsmelts are highly protrusible, and small crustaceans form their main food, although they occasionally eat tiny fish. Sandsmelts are themselves preyed upon by larger fishes and by seabirds such as terns.

Breeding starts between late spring and midsummer. Sandsmelts often spawn in shore pools, laying eggs that bear long threads, which anchor them to seaweed. The newly hatched young are about 7 mm ($\frac{1}{4}$ in) long.

NAME: **Least Killifish/Dwarf Topminnow,** *Heterandria formosa*
RANGE: **streams, ponds, ditches, swamps**
HABITAT: **USA: South Carolina, Florida**
SIZE: **2–3.5 cm ($\frac{3}{4}$–1$\frac{1}{4}$ in)**

One of the smallest vertebrates, at only 2 cm ($\frac{3}{4}$ in) long, adult males of this species are smaller than females. The fishes live among dense aquatic vegetation and feed on mosquitoes and minute crustaceans.

Least killifish have unusual breeding habits: after mating, the eggs develop a few at a time and are fertilized inside the female by sperm that were deposited by the male at mating. The young are born over a period of a week or more at the rate of 2 or 3 a day. The least killifish is a popular aquarium species.

NAME: **Crimson-spotted Rainbowfish,** *Melanotaenia fluviatilis*
RANGE: **Australia: South Australia, New South Wales, Queensland**
HABITAT: **rivers, streams**
SIZE: **9 cm (3$\frac{1}{2}$ in)**

The colorful crimson-spotted rainbowfish occurs over a vast area and is one of about 19 species of rainbowfish, all found in Australia or New Guinea. In early summer it lays its eggs, which become safely anchored to aquatic plants by means of fine threads and hatch in about 9 days. This rainbowfish is a popular aquarium species.

NAME: **Green Swordtail,** *Xiphophorus helleri*
RANGE: **Mexico, Guatemala**
HABITAT: **springs, streams, rivers, lagoons, swamps**
SIZE: **12.5 cm (5 in)**

In male green swordtails the lower lobe of the tail is greatly extended into a slim, bladelike projection, hence the common name. Females lack this tail extension and are less brightly colored.

The range of habitats of this species is reflected in the number of forms, differing in coloration, shape and tail development. Green swordtails feed on small aquatic invertebrates.

Like all members of the family Poeciliidae, the green swordtail produces live young. The male fertilizes the female internally, and the young develop inside her ovarian cavity. The female swordtail is known to change sex, but the reasons for this are not clear. She stops producing young, develops the tail extension and male coloration and gradually becomes a totally functional male. Males do not change into females.

These little fishes have become popular aquarium fish and have been bred in a variety of colors.

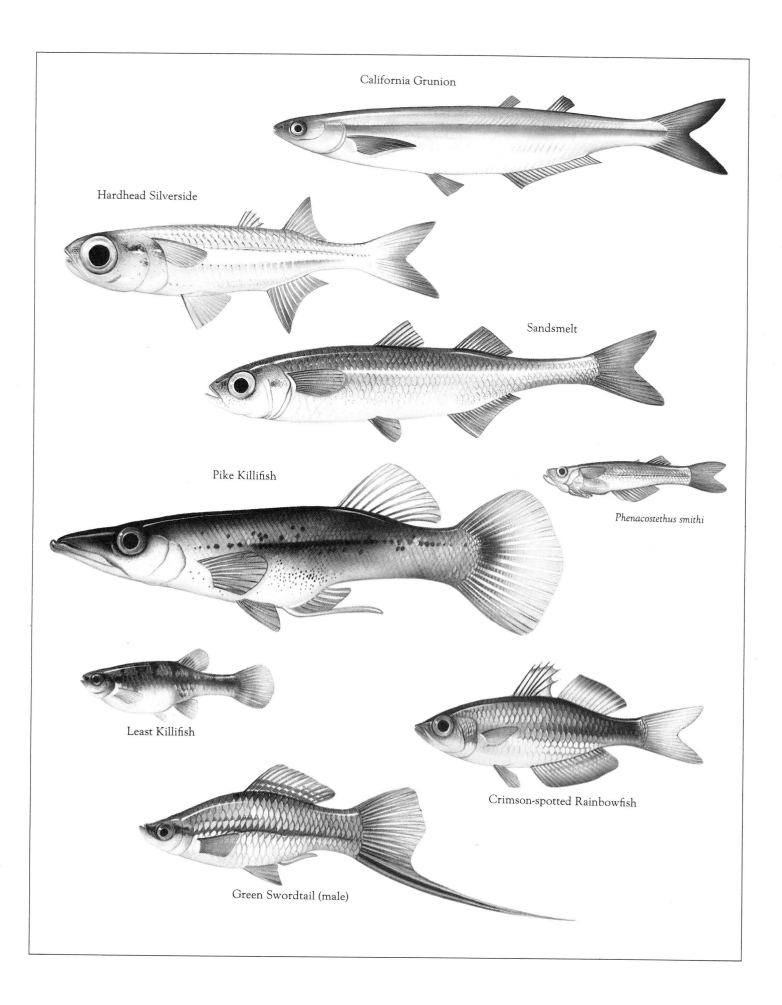

California Grunion

Hardhead Silverside

Sandsmelt

Pike Killifish

Phenacostethus smithi

Least Killifish

Crimson-spotted Rainbowfish

Green Swordtail (male)

Lampridiform Fishes, Zeiform Fishes

LAMPRIDIFORMES

There are about 35 species of marine fish in this little-studied order. They include the opah, crestfishes, oarfishes and ribbonfishes. Many of these are extremely large; for instance, the oarfish reaches 7 m (23 ft).

Most are without scales and have laterally flattened bodies, but some species have fragile, modified scales. The opah is deep-bodied, but most other species are elongate, resembling flattened eels. They have no true spines in their fins.

NAME: Opah, *Lampris guttatus*
RANGE: worldwide except Antarctic; most common in temperate and tropical seas
HABITAT: open sea, mid-waters at 100–400 m (330–1,300 ft)
SIZE: 1.5 m (5 ft)

A striking, colorful fish, the opah is bright blue, dotted with white on the upper part of its body, and has well-developed red fins. An adult may weigh up to 73 kg (161 lb). The opah has a protrusible mouth and is toothless, but despite its lack of armory and its apparently awkward shape, it is a successful predator, feeding mainly on squid and fish such as hake and blue whiting.

Little is known of the biology or habits of this fish, and it is rarely seen.

NAME: Oarfish, *Regalecus glesne*
RANGE: Atlantic, Pacific and Indian Oceans: temperate and tropical areas
HABITAT: open sea at 300–600 m (980–2,000 ft)
SIZE: up to 7 m (23 ft)

A highly distinctive fish, the oarfish has a long, ribbonlike body which is extremely compressed at the sides. The dorsal fin originates just behind the snout and runs the length of the body; its first few rays are elongate and form a crest. There is no anal fin, but the pelvic fins, tipped with flaps of skin, are long and slender. The oarfish swims with rippling, undulating movements and is thought to have given rise to many tales about sea serpents.

The oarfish has a small, protrusible mouth and no teeth and feeds on shrimplike crustaceans. There are thought to be only 1 or 2 species of these strange-looking fishes.

NAME: Dealfish, *Trachipterus arcticus*
RANGE: N.E. Atlantic Ocean: Greenland and Iceland to Madeira and N. Africa
HABITAT: open sea, mid-depths
SIZE: 2.5 m (8¼ ft)

The dealfish has a long, laterally compressed body with a distinctive red dorsal fin running almost its entire length. It has tiny pelvic fins, no anal fin and an unusual upturned tail fin, which looks like a fan. There are several characteristic dark blotches on its silvery sides. Like all members of its family, the dealfish has a protrusible mouth and feeds on fish, squid and crustaceans. It may sometimes move in small schools but is more often found alone.

NAME: *Atelopus japonicus*
RANGE: Indian and Pacific Oceans: E. African coast to Japan
HABITAT: deep sea, 180–550 m (600–1,800 ft)
SIZE: 61 cm (24 in)

This unusual fish has a long, tapering body and a relatively large head. It has threadlike pelvic fins, a high, short-based dorsal fin and a long anal fin, which unites with the reduced tail fin. The body is soft and fragile, and the few specimens found have been damaged. There are teeth only in the upper jaw; the lower jaw is set back under the protruding snout.

The habits of this fish are not well known, but it is thought that it may feed on the seabed on bottom-dwelling invertebrates.

ZEIFORMES

There are about 50 species in this order, which includes the dories, the boarfishes and some lesser-known deep-sea species. All are marine fishes. Typically, the members of this order have laterally compressed, fairly deep bodies and large, prominent eyes. There are usually heavy spines in the anterior parts of the dorsal and anal fins. Most have jaws capable of opening very wide to facilitate the capture of prey.

NAME: Buckler Dory, *Zenopsis ocellata*
RANGE: W. Atlantic Ocean: Nova Scotia to Chesapeake Bay
HABITAT: offshore waters
SIZE: 61 cm (24 in)

The buckler dory, like its European relative, the John Dory, has a deep, greatly compressed body. Its protruding lower jaw is steeply angled, the tip being almost on a line with the eyes. There are nine or ten stout spines in the first dorsal fin; the first three or four are elongate, the remainder becoming progressively shorter. The anal fin bears three or four short, stout spines. Adults are silvery in color, but the young fishes have several irregular dark spots on each side. These gradually disappear as the fishes mature, most adults having only a single spot on each side near the gill opening.

Like all dories, this species catches its prey by slowly stalking it until it can engulf the victim within its vast jaws.

NAME: John Dory, *Zeus faber*
RANGE: E. Atlantic Ocean: N. Scotland to South Africa; Mediterranean Sea
HABITAT: inshore waters at 10–50 m (33–164 ft)
SIZE: 40–66 cm (15¾–26 in)

The John Dory is identified by its deep body and large head with protrusible, steeply sloping jaws. There are nine or ten stout spines in the front portion of the dorsal fin and three or four preceding the anal fin. On each side above the pectoral fin is a characteristic, light-bordered black patch.

Usually a solitary fish, the John Dory may occasionally move in small schools. It is not a fast swimmer and catches prey by stealth rather than speed. Keeping its flattened body head-on and, therefore, harder to spot, it approaches prey slowly until close enough to engulf it in its huge mouth; this is often accomplished by the sudden inrush of water. Small fish and crustaceans make up the bulk of the fish's diet.

Although rarely caught in large numbers, the John Dory is highly thought of as a food fish in Europe. An almost identical species of dory, *Z. japonicus*, occurs in the Indian and Pacific oceans.

NAME: Boarfish, *Capros aper*
RANGE: E. Atlantic Ocean: Ireland to Senegal; Mediterranean Sea
HABITAT: rocky-bottomed open sea at 100–400 m (330–1,300 ft)
SIZE: 10–16 cm (4–6¼ in)

This small relative of the dories also has a deep, laterally compressed body. The head is pointed, with a small mouth, but the jaws are protrusible and lined with fine teeth. Each pelvic fin bears a strong spine, and there are long, stout spines in the first dorsal fin. Small, finely toothed scales cover the body, making it rough to the touch. Like all members of its family, the boarfish is reddish in color.

Boarfishes feed on crustaceans, worms and mollusks. They spawn in the summer, and the eggs float freely in surface waters until they hatch.

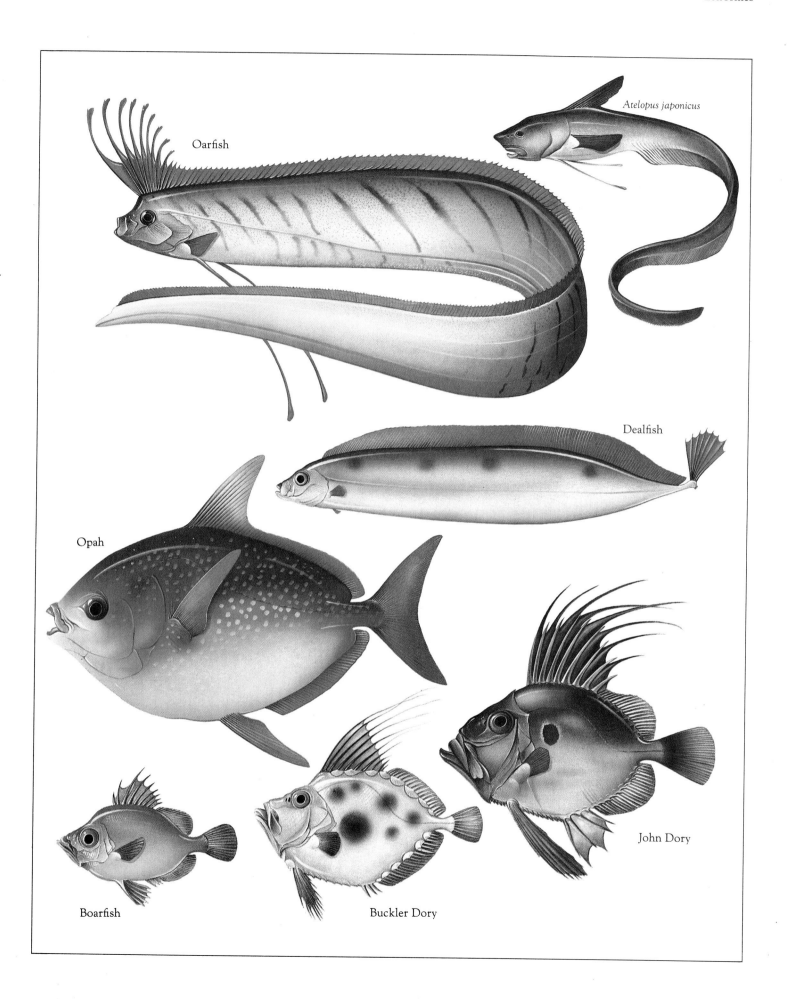

Oarfish

Atelopus japonicus

Dealfish

Opah

Boarfish

Buckler Dory

John Dory

Beryciform Fishes

NAME: Pinecone Fish, *Monocentris japonicus*
RANGE: Indian and Pacific Oceans: South Africa to Japan
HABITAT: open sea at 30–180 m (100–600 ft)
SIZE: 12.5 cm (5 in)

The plump, deep body of the pinecone fish is encased in an armor of heavy, platelike scales which overlap and give the fish a marked resemblance to a pinecone, hence its common name. The dorsal fin consists of stout spines, which are directed alternately to left and right and do not stand vertically, as in other fishes, and this species also has large pelvic spines. Under the lower jaw are two light-producing organs, the luminescence of which is not generated by luminous cells in the fish — as is the case with photophores, light-producing organs possessed by some other fishes — but by the presence of luminous bacteria living symbiotically with the fish.

Pinecone fish move in schools near to the bottom of the sea. There is only 1 other species in the family, also found in the Indian and Pacific oceans.

NAME: Squirrelfish, *Holocentrus ascensionis*
RANGE: Atlantic Ocean: Bermuda, Gulf of Mexico to Brazil; vicinity of Ascension Island
HABITAT: coastal waters in tropical and warm temperate areas
SIZE: 61 cm (24 in)

The brightly colored squirrelfish is particularly common on coral reefs or in rocky-bottomed areas. Its scales are large and rough, and it has a strong spine on the gill cover. A nocturnal fish, it hides in crannies and rock crevices during the day and emerges at night to feed, mainly on small crustaceans.

Squirrelfishes make a variety of sounds by vibrating their swim bladders with the aid of specialized muscles. Such sounds are believed to have a function in territorial and breeding behavior.

NAME: *Adioryx xantherythrus*
RANGE: Pacific Ocean: Hawaiian Islands
HABITAT: coral reefs
SIZE: 18 cm (7 in)

This Hawaiian squirrelfish resembles the other members of its family, with its reddish and pink body and stout dorsal spines. It is a nocturnal fish, remaining hidden in the reef during the day and emerging at night to feed on small invertebrates.

Like the rest of the squirrelfishes, this species is able to produce sounds with its swim bladder which are believed to form part of courtship behavior.

BERYCIFORMES

This order includes about 143 species of marine fishes, grouped in 15 families. Forms include whalefishes, squirrelfishes, lanterneyes, pinecone fishes and slimeheads, and most are deep-bodied, large-eyed fishes with spiny fins. Most of the families contain fewer than a dozen species, many of them deep-sea fishes.

The family of squirrelfishes, Holocentridae, is the largest in the order, with about 70 species. They all have the large eyes and deep bodies characteristic of the order and are usually reddish in color. Most squirrelfishes have a long dorsal fin with a spiny portion that contains up to 13 stout spines, and there is also a spine in each pelvic fin; their bodies are covered with large, rough-surfaced scales. Generally nocturnal, squirrelfishes live in shallow coastal waters and take refuge in rock crevices or among reefs by day. Adults stay close to the bottom, but the young drift in surface waters. These fishes are renowned for the sounds they are able to produce with their resonating swim bladders.

NAME: *Anomalops kaptoptron*
RANGE: S. Pacific Ocean: Indonesian coasts
HABITAT: shallow offshore waters
SIZE: 30 cm (11¾ in)

One of a small family of 3 species known as lanterneyes, this is a heavy, deep-bodied fish with stout dorsal spines. Its head is broad and strong, and it has the large eyes characteristic of the order. Active at night, it swims in small shoals.

Lanterneyes are among the few shallow-water fishes to possess luminous organs. Beneath each eye there is an oval bar which appears white in daylight but shines brightly at night. Inside the bar-shaped organ are many tubes containing luminous bacteria, which live symbiotically with the fish and give off light. If the fish needs to dispense with its light for a while, the organs can be rotated so that the luminous sides are turned downward and masked. The fish blinks its lights as it swims, but it is not known whether this is to communicate with other fishes, to attract prey or to help it navigate.

NAME: Roughie, *Hoplostethus atlanticus*
RANGE: N. Atlantic Ocean
HABITAT: deep sea at 500–1,000 m (1,650–3,300 ft)
SIZE: 30 cm (11¾ in)

The brightly colored roughie has a large head and deep body compressed at the sides, and there are strong spines on its belly and preceding its dorsal fin. Its mouth is large and upturned, and the jaws are equipped with many tiny, close-set teeth. Although little is known of its habits, the roughie is thought to feed mainly on crustaceans.

The family Trachichthyidae, to which the roughie belongs, contains about 14 species. These fishes are known as slimeheads because of the many mucus-secreting cavities on their heads.

NAME: *Photoblepharon palpebratus*
RANGE: Indian and Pacific Oceans
HABITAT: shallow offshore waters
SIZE: 8 cm (3¼ in)

A stout fish with prominent fins and a forked tail, *P. palpebratus* is active only at night. It is a member of the lanterneye family and, like its relatives, has a light organ beneath each eye which appears white in daylight but shines at night. Inside the organ are tubes containing luminous bacteria, which live symbiotically with the fish and in return produce light. To turn the light off, the fish raises a fold of dark skin across the organ.

Local fishermen remove the lanterneye's light organs, which remain luminous for many hours, and use them as fishing lures.

NAME: Whalefish, *Cetomimus indagator*
RANGE: Indian Ocean
HABITAT: deep sea
SIZE: 14 cm (5½ in)

This species belongs to a small family of 10 or more types of deep-sea whalefish. Whalefishes are generally rather stout, with large heads and jaws, and they lack scales and pelvic fins. *C. indagator* is unusual in that its head is smaller and more pointed than normal, but it does have the characteristic whalefish jaws, lined with many tiny teeth. Like all whalefishes, its eyes are rudimentary. Its lateral line — the series of small sensory organs along its sides — is distinctive, being a broad tube with twelve large openings.

At the bases of the dorsal and anal fins, the whalefishes have soft luminous tissue that is believed to glow in the dark. These fishes have soft, fragile bodies and have rarely been caught undamaged, so few details of their biology are known. Only one specimen of *C. indagator* has been found.

Roughie

Pinecone Fish

Squirrelfish

Adioryx xantherythrus

Anomalops kaptoptron

Photoblepharon palpebratus

Whalefish

Syngnathiform Fishes, Sticklebacks and Tube-snouts

SYNGNATHIFORMES

There are 6 families in this order, with a total of about 200 species, all but a few of which are marine fishes. The best-known members of the order are the pipefishes and seahorses — both small fishes of bizarre shape, which normally inhabit shallow marine waters.

NAME: **Winged Dragon,** *Pegasus volitans*
RANGE: **Indian and Pacific Oceans: E. Africa to N. Australia**
HABITAT: **sandy-bottomed shallow waters**
SIZE: **14 cm (5½ in)**

A curious fish, the winged dragon has a broad, flattened body, surrounded with bony rings, and a tapering tail. The snout is long and flattened, with a small mouth on the underside. The pectoral fins are broad and winglike, while the other fins are all relatively small.

NAME: **Shrimpfish,** *Aeoliscus strigatus*
RANGE: **Indian and Pacific Oceans to N. Australia**
HABITAT: **coastal waters, open sea**
SIZE: **15 cm (6 in)**

The shrimpfish has a flat, compressed body with a sharp-edged belly. At the end of its body is a long spine, formed by part of the tail fin. The fish frequently swims in a vertical position, with its elongate snout held downward, propelling itself with its tail and anal fins. It is often found among the spines of sea urchins, where dark stripes along the sides of its body, which mimic the spines, provide camouflage. They also conceal the fish's eyes, which might otherwise reveal its presence.

NAME: **Greater Pipefish,** *Syngnathus acus*
RANGE: **E. Atlantic Ocean: coasts of Norway to N. Africa; Mediterranean and Adriatic Seas**
HABITAT: **shallow waters with sandy or muddy bottoms**
SIZE: **30–47 cm (11¾–18½ in)**

The body of the greater pipefish is encased in bony armor, which forms distinct segments. Its snout is long and tubular, with a small mouth at the tip, and the main means of propulsion is the pronounced dorsal fin. It feeds on small crustaceans and other tiny planktonic creatures, as well as on young fish.

Breeding occurs from May to August. Like all pipefishes, the male incubates the eggs in a brood pouch, which in this species is a double fold of skin positioned under the tail. The eggs are incubated for about 5 weeks, and on hatching, the perfectly formed young are released through a slit, where the folds of the pouch meet.

NAME: **Dwarf Seahorse,** *Hippocampus zosterae*
RANGE: **W. Atlantic Ocean: Florida through Gulf of Mexico to Caribbean**
HABITAT: **shallow waters**
SIZE: **4 cm (1½ in)**

Instantly recognizable, with its head set at an angle to the body and its curling prehensile tail, the dwarf seahorse is the smallest seahorse species. It moves slowly, using gentle movements of its tiny dorsal fin for propulsion, and can attach itself to vegetation by means of its tail. Small crustaceans and larvae are its main foods.

The breeding season extends from February to October, and the female lays 50 or more eggs, which she places in the male's brood pouch.

NAME: **Weedy Seadragon,** *Phyllopteryx taeniolatus*
RANGE: **coasts of S. Australia**
HABITAT: **shallow waters**
SIZE: **46 cm (18 in)**

Although little is known of the habits of this strange seahorse, the many leaflike flaps of skin on its body are presumed to give it a protective resemblance to fronds of seaweed.

As with all seahorses, the male of this species incubates the eggs

GASTEROSTEIFORMES:
Stickleback and Tube-snout Order

The sticklebacks and their relatives the tube-snouts make up an intriguing group of spiny-finned fishes, found in the northern hemisphere. There are 10 species, 3 of which are freshwater; but within 2 species, the threespine stickleback, *Gasterosteus aculeatus*, and the ninespine stickleback, *Pungitius pungitius*, there is enormous diversity over their ranges.

NAME: **Tube-snout,** *Aulorhynchus flavidus*
RANGE: **Pacific Ocean: coast of N. America from Alaska to Baja California**
HABITAT: **inshore waters**
SIZE: **16 cm (6¼ in)**

The tube-snout has a long, cylindrical body which tapers toward the tail. The small mouth is at the tip of the long, rigid snout. There is one normal dorsal fin, placed opposite the anal fin, but in front of this are 24 to 26 isolated spines, which make up the first dorsal fin. Tube-snouts move in large shoals of hundreds or even thousands of individuals and feed on small crustaceans, as well as on other items of plankton.

The female deposits her eggs in a nest of algae, which is stuck together with threads of mucus extruded by the male.

NAME: **Threespine Stickleback,** *Gasterosteus aculeatus*
RANGE: **N. America: Pacific and Atlantic coasts and fresh water; Europe: coasts and fresh water, north to Arctic Circle; N. Asia; N. Pacific Ocean: Bering Strait to Korea**
HABITAT: **coastal waters, lakes, rivers**
SIZE: **5–10 cm (2–4in)**

A small fish with three characteristic spines on its back, this stickleback is scaleless but armored with bony plates. It feeds on almost any available small creatures, such as crustaceans, worms, mollusks, fish eggs and larvae, and even on some plant material.

In the breeding season — spring and early summer in North America and Europe — the male stickleback develops a bright red belly. He makes a nest on the bottom from plant fragments glued together with mucous secretions. He then displays to attract several females to his nest, where they lay eggs, which he immediately fertilizes. He then guards the eggs carefully, driving away predators and fanning water into the nest to aerate the eggs, which hatch in about 3 weeks.

NAME: **Fifteenspine Stickleback,** *Spinachia spinachia*
RANGE: **coasts of Scandinavia, Britain, N. Europe**
HABITAT: **shallow, coastal waters**
SIZE: **15–19 cm (6–7½ in)**

A slender, long-bodied fish with a pointed snout, this stickleback is identified by the 14 to 17 (usually 15) spines on its back. It lives only in the sea, generally in areas where there is abundant seaweed, and feeds on small crustaceans.

The male makes a nest from scraps of marine plants stuck together with his mucous secretions and then attracts a series of females into his nest to lay their eggs. He fertilizes and then guards the eggs until they hatch 18 to 21 days later.

NAME: **Fourspine Stickleback,** *Apeltes quadracus*
RANGE: **W. Atlantic Ocean: E. coast of N. America, Nova Scotia to Virginia**
HABITAT: **coastal waters, brackish and fresh water**
SIZE: **6 cm (2¼ in)**

Found in both salt and fresh water, the fourspine stickleback prefers areas with plenty of seaweed. Its body is naked, lacking the plates of the threespine stickleback, but there are bony ridges on each side of the belly. Small crustaceans are its main food.

Like other sticklebacks, these fishes spawn in spring and early summer, and the male builds a nest in which females lay eggs. The male guards the eggs until they hatch.

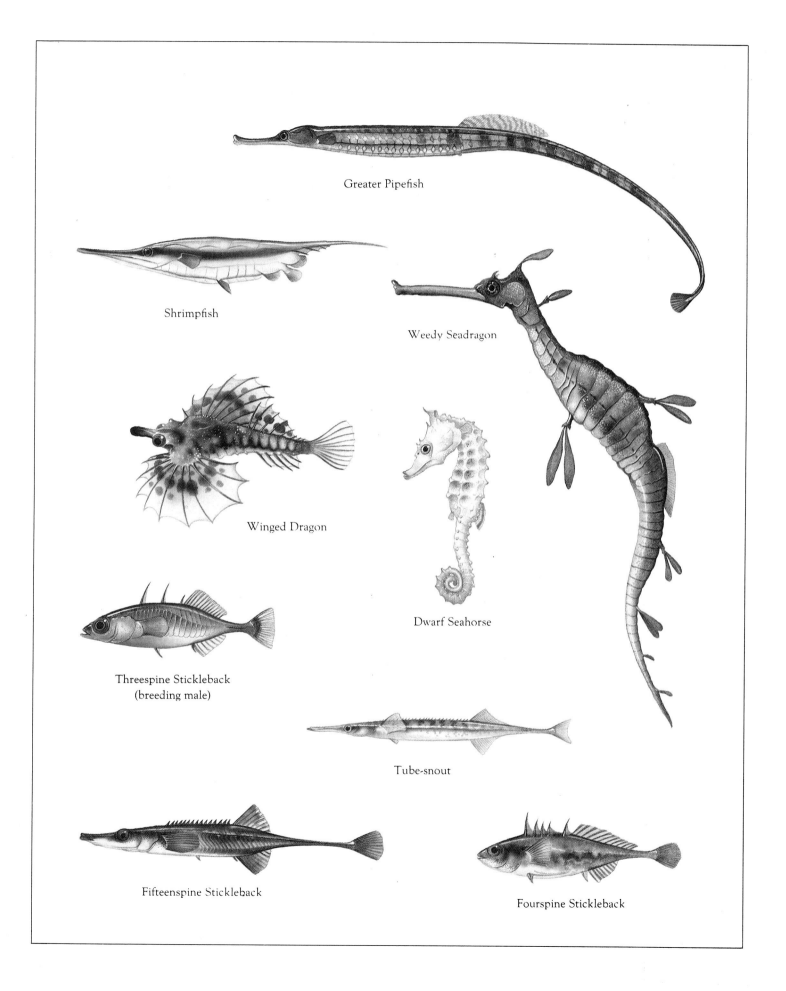

Greater Pipefish

Shrimpfish

Weedy Seadragon

Winged Dragon

Dwarf Seahorse

Threespine Stickleback
(breeding male)

Tube-snout

Fifteenspine Stickleback

Fourspine Stickleback

Flying Gurnards, Scorpaeniform Fishes

SYNBRANCHIFORMES

There are about 13 species in this order, 7 of which are marine. They are grouped in 3 families: the singleslit eels, the swamp-eels and the cuchias. They are not, however, true eels but have an eel-like body shape and extremely reduced fins. Their gill system is minute and is linked with a variety of organs for breathing air.

NAME: **Rice Eel,** *Monopterus alba*
RANGE: **Japan, N. China to Thailand and Burma**
HABITAT: **rivers, ponds, rice fields**
SIZE: **91 cm (35¾ in)**

The rice eel has an elongate, scaleless body and lacks pectoral and pelvic fins. The dorsal and anal fins are low and join with the tail fin. There are one or two gill openings on the throat, but the fish, which commonly lives in stagnant, oxygen-poor water, often breathes air at the surface. In long dry seasons, rice eels can burrow into the mud and remain alive until rains arrive, provided their skin remains moist.

The male rice eel makes a nest by blowing a cluster of bubbles of air and mucus. The eggs are shed among these bubbles, and the whole structure floats freely, guarded by the male.

DACTYLOPTERIFORMES:
Flying Gurnard Order

This small order contains only 1 family of 4 species of marine fishes, found in tropical and warm temperate areas of the Atlantic and Indo-Pacific oceans. Flying gurnards are all slim-bodied fishes with greatly enlarged, winglike pectoral fins. Despite their name, there is no reliable evidence that these fishes can fly above the water surface like the true flyingfishes.

NAME: **Flying Gurnard,** *Dactylopterus volitans*
RANGE: **W. Atlantic Ocean: Bermuda through Caribbean to Argentina; E. Atlantic: Portugal to W. Africa; Mediterranean Sea**
HABITAT: **bottom of shallow waters**
SIZE: **30–40.5 cm (11¾–16 in)**

A bottom-dwelling fish, the flying gurnard uses its pelvic fins to "walk" over the seabed as it searches for its crustacean prey. Its bony head is large relative to its body size, and its pectoral fins are long and winglike. If alarmed, the fish may spread these fins, revealing the bright blue spots on their surfaces and creating an impression of large size to unnerve the opponent.

SCORPAENIFORMES:
Scorpionfish Order

This large, widely distributed order contains 21 families and roughly 1,000 species of fish, about 100 of which are marine. Body form is variable, but most species are thick-set and spiny, often with venom glands connected to the spines.

NAME: **Rascasse,** *Scorpaena porcus*
RANGE: **Mediterranean and Black Seas; N. Atlantic Ocean: Biscay to Madeira**
HABITAT: **shallow waters**
SIZE: **25 cm (9¾ in)**

The rascasse tends to lurk amid seaweed-covered rocks, where the combination of its camouflaging coloration and the weedlike flaps of skin on its head render it almost invisible. Its dorsal fin is spiny, with venom glands at the sides of the spines.

Breeding takes place in spring or early summer, eggs being shed in a mass of gelatinous mucus. Rascasse are an important food fish and are an essential ingredient of bouillabaisse.

NAME: **Redfish/Ocean Perch,** *Sebastes marinus*
RANGE: **N. Atlantic Ocean: Arctic to Scotland and Sweden; USA: New Jersey**
HABITAT: **deep water: 100–400 m (330–1,300 ft)**
SIZE: **81 cm–1 m (31¾ in–3¼ ft)**

A heavy-bodied fish with a large head and a protuberant lower jaw, the redfish has a strongly spined dorsal fin and three spines on the anal fin. During the day, it stays close to the bottom, rising to surface waters at night to feed on fish such as herring and cod.

Redfishes bear live young. In the north of their range, the male fertilizes the female internally in late summer. Females then migrate south during the winter and give birth to up to 40,000 larval young the following May or June. The young are about 8 mm (⅓ in) long at birth. They feed on plankton at first, and then on crustaceans.

NAME: **Lionfish,** *Pterois volitans*
RANGE: **Indian and Pacific Oceans**
HABITAT: **shallow waters, reefs**
SIZE: **38 cm (15 in)**

An extraordinary and decorative fish, the lionfish is immediately identified by its long, fanlike pectoral fins, branched dorsal fin and brightly striped body. This eye-catching coloration warns potential enemies that the lionfish's grooved spines are equipped with potent venom, which can have serious, perhaps fatal, effects, even in humans.

NAME: **Stonefish,** *Synanceia verrucosa*
RANGE: **Indian and Pacific Oceans: Africa and Red Sea to N. Australia**
HABITAT: **shallow water, coral reefs**
SIZE: **30 cm (11¾ in)**

About 20 species of stonefish occur in the Indo-Pacific. All have needlelike dorsal-fin spines, equipped with venom glands that produce the most deadly of all fish venoms. Wounds from a stonefish can kill any human unlucky enough to tread on the spines. This species is typical of its family, with its rough, scaleless body, large, upward-turning head and protuberant eyes. As its name suggests, the stonefish's coloring and shape camouflage it perfectly as it lies half-buried among stones or in rock crevices.

NAME: **Tub Gurnard,** *Trigla lucerna*
RANGE: **E. Atlantic Ocean: Norway, British Isles to N. Africa; coasts of Black, Adriatic and Mediterranean Seas**
HABITAT: **inshore waters, sandy and muddy bottoms**
SIZE: **50–75 cm (19¾–29½ in)**

A member of the searobin family, the tub gurnard has a bony head, pointed snout and well-formed fins. Several rays of the pectoral fins are elongate and free, and they are used by the fish to search for food on the bottom and as props on which to rest. The species feeds on bottom-living crustaceans, mollusks and fish.

Tub gurnards are fished commercially in many areas.

NAME: **Northern Searobin,** *Prionotus carolinus*
RANGE: **W. Atlantic Ocean: Bay of Fundy to Venezuela**
HABITAT: **seabed, coastal waters**
SIZE: **41 cm (16 in)**

The northern searobin is typical of its family, with its large head covered with bony plates and its fanlike pectoral fins. The lowest three rays of the pectoral fins are free, and they are used to feel for prey, such as fish and crustaceans, on the seabed. Coloration varies from grayish to brown, but the searobin always has dark, saddlelike markings across its back. Much of the searobin's life is spent on the bottom; it often supports itself on its pectoral fins and can quickly bury itself if threatened, leaving only the top of its head and its eyes exposed.

Searobins can make loud sounds by vibrating their swim bladders by means of specialized muscles. They are particularly noisy in the breeding season, which lasts from June to September. The eggs are shed and float at the surface until they hatch. The young fishes grow rapidly.

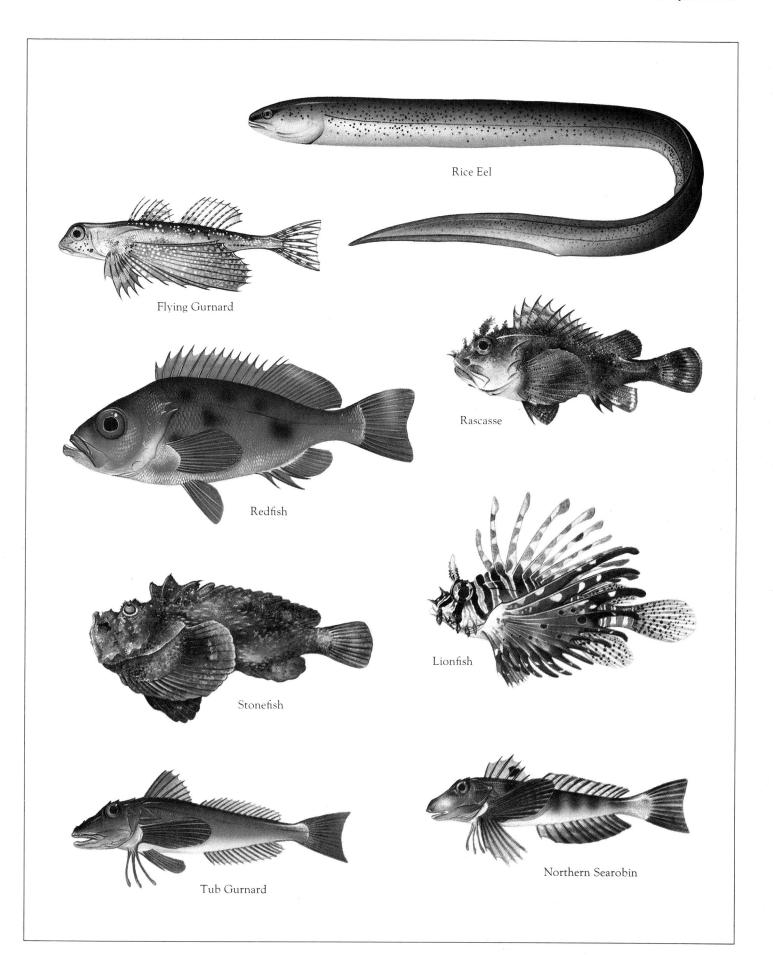

Rice Eel

Flying Gurnard

Rascasse

Redfish

Lionfish

Stonefish

Tub Gurnard

Northern Searobin

Scorpaeniform Fishes

NAME: Sablefish, *Anoplopoma fimbria*
RANGE: Pacific Ocean: Japan to Bering Sea, south to Baja California
HABITAT: inshore waters, open sea
SIZE: up to 1 m (3¼ ft)

The sablefish is a long, slender fish with two well-separated dorsal fins. The head is smooth, lacking the spines and ridges of the related scorpionfishes. Adult sablefishes usually live near the bottom in areas of continental shelf, but young fishes swim in surface waters, often in the open ocean. Sablefishes spawn in winter and early spring.

NAME: Kelp Greenling, *Hexagrammos decagrammus*
RANGE: Pacific coast of N. America: Alaska to California
HABITAT: shallow, rocky-bottomed water, kelp beds
SIZE: 53 cm (20¾ in)

The kelp greenling is one of 11 species of greenling, all found in the North Pacific. Its head is smooth, with no spines or ridges, and it has large pectoral fins and a long-based dorsal fin, which is notched halfway along its length. Males and females differ slightly in appearance, males having blue spots on the foreparts and females reddish-brown spots. Kelp greenlings are unusual in that they have five lateral lines (series of sensory organs) on each side of the body; most fishes have only one.

Kelp greenlings feed on worms, crustaceans and small fish, and they themselves are preyed on by many larger fishes and fish-eating birds. They spawn in autumn, laying clusters of eggs among the rocks. The young fishes swim in the surface waters of the open sea.

NAME: Shorthorn Sculpin, *Myoxocephalus scorpius*
RANGE: N. Atlantic Ocean: Labrador to Cape Cod; N. European coasts: Britain, Scandinavia, Iceland
HABITAT: shallow inshore waters to 60 m (200 ft)
SIZE: 25–60 cm (9¾–23½ in)

Known as the shorthorn sculpin in the USA and the bullrout in Britain, this fish is one of the larger sculpins. It has a broad head, large fins and small spines near its gills and along each side. Females are usually larger than males and have creamy-yellow markings on the belly, where males have orange spots. A bottom-dwelling fish, it feeds mainly on bottom-living crustaceans, as well as on worms and small fish.

It breeds in winter, depositing its sticky-surfaced eggs in clusters among seaweed or in rock crevices. The male guards the eggs until they hatch some 4 to 12 weeks later, depending on the temperature of the water.

NAME: Bullhead, *Cottus gobio*
RANGE: Europe: Sweden and Finland to England and Wales, south to the Pyrenees, Alps, Yugoslavia
HABITAT: streams, small rivers, lakes
SIZE: 10 cm (4 in)

A small, freshwater member of the sculpin family, the bullhead has a broad, flattened head with a small spine at each side. It is most at home in stony-bottomed water and takes refuge during the day under rocks and stones. At night, it emerges to forage for crustaceans and insect larvae.

Bullheads spawn in spring, from March to May. The male makes a shallow cavity under a rock so that the female can shed her eggs on the underside of the rock. The eggs are guarded by the male until they hatch 3 to 4 weeks later. On hatching, the tiny fishes disperse to find shelter among stones.

NAME: Cabezon, *Scorpaenichthys marmoratus*
RANGE: N. Pacific Ocean: Alaska to Baja California
HABITAT: shallow inshore waters to 60 m (200 ft)
SIZE: 76 cm (30 in)

One of the largest sculpins, the cabezon has a heavy body, smooth, scaleless skin and a deeply notched dorsal fin. Its head and mouth are broad, and there is a prominent flap on the snout. Coloration is extremely variable, but the skin is generally mottled with pale patches. Although most common in rocky-bottomed waters, it also lives over sandy bottoms and in kelp beds. Crabs are its main food, and it also eats other crustaceans and small fish.

Cabezons spawn during the winter, from November to March, often using communal sites. A breeding female carries as many as 100,000 eggs, which she deposits in masses on rocks. Males remain at the breeding grounds to guard the eggs until they hatch.

NAME: Baikal Cod, *Comephorus baicalensis*
RANGE: USSR: Lake Baikal
HABITAT: deep water
SIZE: 19 cm (7½ in)

This strange freshwater sculpin is one of a family of only 2 species. It is a long-bodied fish, with no pelvic fins but with long-based dorsal and anal fins. Its head is covered with transparent, delicate skin, and it has a large mouth. Although it lives in deep water, it migrates upward at night to feed near the surface on small crustaceans.

Female baikal cod bear live young in the summer, in the surface waters of the lake. The other species, *C. dybowski*, also lives in Lake Baikal.

NAME: Sturgeon Poacher, *Agonus acipenserinus*
RANGE: N. Pacific Ocean: N. American coast, Bering Sea to California
HABITAT: coastal muddy-bottomed water at depths of 18–55 m (60–180 ft)
SIZE: up to 30 cm (11¾ in)

An elongate, extremely slender fish, the sturgeon poacher has a body armor of nonoverlapping bony plates. It has several spines on its large sturgeonlike head and clusters of slender barbels around its mouth. It lives near or on the seabed and feeds mainly on crustaceans and marine worms. Although a common, abundant species, it has no commercial value.

NAME: Lumpfish, *Cyclopterus lumpus*
RANGE: N. Atlantic Ocean: Arctic to Scandinavia, Iceland, British Isles; Newfoundland to New Jersey, USA
HABITAT: shallow waters to 200 m (650 ft), usually on seabed
SIZE: 30–60 cm (11¾–23½ in)

The lumpfish has a round, deep body studded with rows of spined plates along the sides. Its skin is scaleless. The ventral fins are modified to form the powerful suction disk on its belly, with which the lumpfish attaches itself to the seabed or to rocks and other debris. It feeds on small crustaceans, jellyfishes and other invertebrates, as well as some small fish. Females are usually larger than males.

In late winter or spring, lumpfishes gather in pairs in shallow coastal waters to spawn around the low-tide mark. The female lays as many as 200,000 sticky-surfaced eggs, which sink to the bottom in a spongy mass. The male then guards the egg clusters and keeps water flowing through them until they hatch. The young fishes remain in the coastal shallows during the summer and move out to deeper waters in their first winter.

NAME: Striped Seasnail, *Liparis liparis*
RANGE: N. Atlantic Ocean: Arctic to coasts of Scandinavia, Iceland, British Isles; Greenland to Virginia, USA
HABITAT: inshore waters at 5–150 m (16½–490 ft)
SIZE: 10–18 cm (4–7 in)

A member of the lumpfish family, the striped seasnail is a round-bodied fish with long dorsal and anal fins, both connected with the tail fin. The skin is slimy and scaleless, and on the belly is a strong suction disk with which the seasnail attaches itself to the seabed or to seaweed. It feeds mainly on small crustaceans and worms.

Seasnails spawn in winter or spring. The eggs settle in clusters on seaweed or other objects on the seabed and hatch in 6 to 8 weeks.

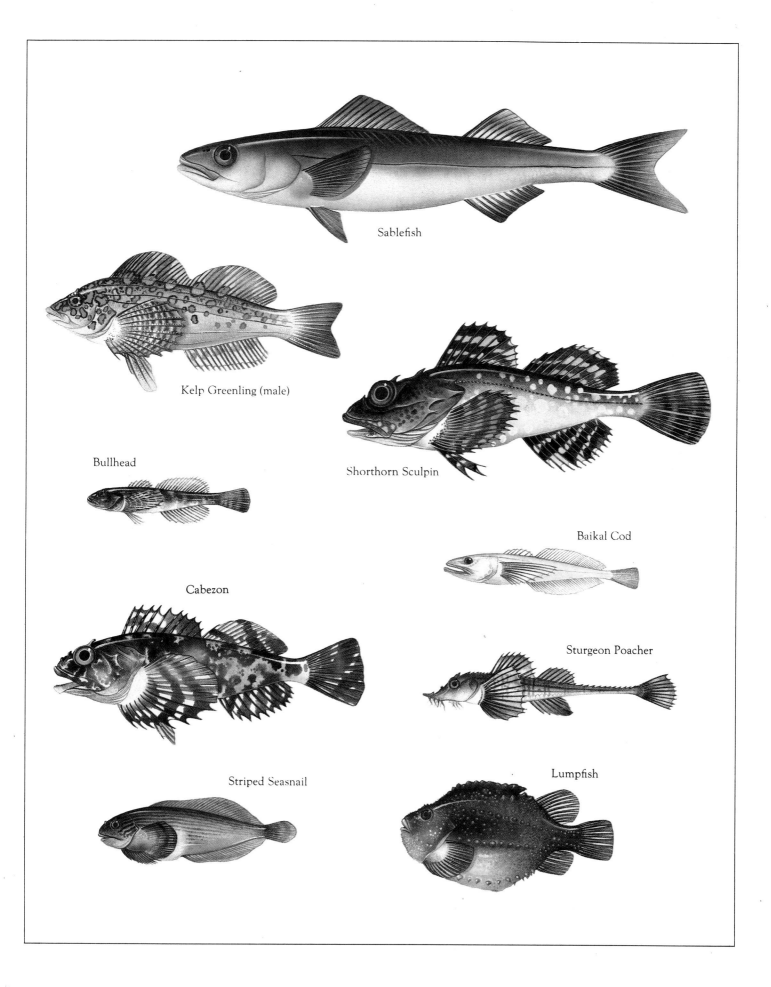

Sablefish

Kelp Greenling (male)

Bullhead

Shorthorn Sculpin

Baikal Cod

Cabezon

Sturgeon Poacher

Striped Seasnail

Lumpfish

Perchlike Fishes

NAME: Snook, *Centropomus undecimalis*
RANGE: Caribbean, north to Florida and South Carolina; south to Brazil
HABITAT: coastal waters, estuaries, bays, brackish water
SIZE: 1.4 m (4½ ft)

One of the largest and most common of the 30 species in the snook family (Centropomidae), this fish has a long, tapering body, a slightly flattened snout and a protruding lower jaw. It feeds primarily on crustaceans and fish, and adults can tolerate a variety of habitats, including almost fresh water.

Snooks spawn from June to November; young fishes, less than a year old, usually live in coastal lagoons and streams. They are mature in their third year. The snook is a popular species with marine fishermen.

NAME: Nile Perch, *Lates niloticus*
RANGE: Africa: Congo, Volta and Niger river systems, Lake Chad
HABITAT: rivers, lakes
SIZE: 2 m (6½ ft)

This widely distributed member of the snook family has been introduced into many man-made lakes and is fished both commercially and for sport. It is one of the most important food fishes in some areas of Africa. A large, heavy-bodied fish, the Nile perch has the spiny first dorsal fin characteristic of the perchlike fishes and three spines on the anal fin. It feeds mostly on fish.

NAME: Striped Bass, *Roccus saxatilis*
RANGE: N. America: Atlantic Coast from Gulf of St. Lawrence to N. Florida; Gulf of Mexico; Pacific Coast from Washington to California
HABITAT: inshore waters, estuaries, bays, deltas
SIZE: up to 1.2 m (4 ft)

A distinctive fish, the striped bass may vary in coloration but always has seven or eight dark stripes along its sides. It has a long head and body, a pointed snout and projecting lower jaw. The female is usually larger and heavier than the male, and large specimens may weigh up to 30 kg (66 lb). They feed on fish and crustaceans. Originally a native of the Atlantic Coast, the striped bass was first introduced to the Pacific Coast in 1886 and is now well established. It is a member of the temperate bass family, Percichthyidae.

In the breeding season, April to July, striped bass enter estuaries and ascend rivers to spawn. The female is courted by a number of males and sheds her eggs into the water, where they drift until they hatch about 3 days later. A mature female may produce several million eggs in a season.

PERCIFORMES:
Perchlike Fish Order

This is the largest and most varied of all fish orders and contains more species than any other vertebrate order. There are 147 families and at least 6,880 species known, of which only 950 are freshwater fishes. The five largest families are the sea basses (Serranidae) with 370 species; cichlids (Cichlidae) with 680 species; gobies (Gobiidae) with 800 species; wrasses (Labridae) with 400 species and combtooth blennies (Blenniidae) with 276 species.

Perciform fishes have found niches for themselves in almost every conceivable aquatic habitat and in so doing have evolved a diverse range of body forms and habits. They include species as different as the barracuda, the angelfish, the swordfish and the Siamese fighting-fish, and it is clearly difficult to generalize about such a widely divergent order. However, there are a few broad similarities. All forms have one or two dorsal fins. In forms with one dorsal fin, it is elongate and spiny at the front, while in fishes with two dorsal fins, the first is generally spiny and the second soft rayed. Most perciform fishes have pelvic fins, which are placed in close proximity to the head. Each pelvic fin usually has a spine and five rays. The body scales are generally of the type known as ctenoid: they have a rounded front edge and a serrated trailing edge.

Perciform fishes are found in marine and freshwater habitats all over the world. Perhaps as many as three-quarters of the species live in waters close to the shore.

NAME: Murray Cod, *Maccullochella macquariensis*
RANGE: Australia: New South Wales, Queensland
HABITAT: rivers, lakes; introduced in reservoirs
SIZE: 1.8 m (6 ft)

One of the largest Australian freshwater fishes, the Murray cod has a long, powerful body, usually with mottled markings on its back and sides, and an elongate snout. It feeds mainly on crustaceans and fish and is itself an important commercial food fish. It is a member of the temperate bass family, Percichthyidae.

Murray cod often spawn over trees and branches, which have fallen into the water, and their eggs adhere to the surface of the bark and branches.

NAME: Giant Sea Bass, *Stereolepis gigas*
RANGE: Pacific Ocean: off coasts of California and Mexico
HABITAT: inshore waters
SIZE: 2.1 m (7 ft)

The giant sea bass is a huge fish, some specimens weighing more than 250 kg (550 lb), and it is known to live for about 70 to 75 years. It feeds on fish and crustaceans and is itself fished both commercially and for sport.

Giant sea bass mature at about 11 to 13 years old, at a weight of about 23 kg (50 lb). They spawn in summer, and the young fishes are reddish in color and deeper bodied than adults. They gradually take on the adult appearance and coloration as they mature.

NAME: Jewfish, *Epinephelus itajara*
RANGE: W. Atlantic Ocean: coasts of Florida, Bermuda, Bahamas, West Indies; Pacific Ocean
HABITAT: coastal waters, around ledges, caves and wrecks
SIZE: 2.4 m (8 ft)

One of the largest of the fishes known as groupers (all members of the sea bass family, Serranidae), the jewfish weighs as much as 318 kg (700 lb). It has a robust body and broad head and is usually dark brown, with irregular dark spots and bars on the body. It lurks around underwater crevices and feeds on crustaceans, fish and even turtles.

Jewfishes are a sought-after food fish and a popular sport fish.

NAME: Black Grouper, *Mycteroperca bonaci*
RANGE: W. Atlantic Ocean: New England, south through Gulf of Mexico and Caribbean to Brazil
HABITAT: coastal waters, deeper waters over rocky bottoms
SIZE: 1.2 m (4 ft)

The black grouper is a large and fairly common grouper which may weigh up to 23 kg (50 lb). With its heavy body and dorsal spines, its appearance is typical of the Serranidae family, to which it belongs. There are irregular dark markings on the sides of its body. It is a good food fish and is caught commercially.

NAME: Coney, *Epinephelus fulvus*
RANGE: W. Atlantic Ocean: Florida, south through the Caribbean and Gulf of Mexico to Brazil
HABITAT: coastal waters, coral reefs
SIZE: 30 cm (11¾ in)

One of the smallest but most abundant groupers, the coney varies from red to yellow or brown in coloration but is usually marked with blue spots. It always has two black spots on its tail. Crustaceans are its main diet, and it is itself highly valued as a food species.

Snook

Nile Perch

Striped Bass

Murray Cod

Jewfish

Giant Sea Bass

Black Grouper

Coney

Perchlike Fishes

NAME: **Greater Soapfish,** *Rypticus saponaceus*
RANGE: **E. Atlantic Ocean: off tropical W. Africa and Ascension Island; W. Atlantic: Florida to Brazil**
HABITAT: **shallow, coastal waters**
SIZE: **30 cm (11¾ in)**

The greater soapfish is one of a family called Grammistidae, which contains 17 species, found in the Atlantic, Pacific and Indian oceans. Its skin is slimy with body mucus, which creates a frothy effect, like soapsuds in the water, hence its name. This mucus is toxic and its presence deters predators. The greater soapfish is usually brownish in coloration, with some gray blotches on the body. There are several spines preceding the dorsal fin. Active at night, it feeds on fish and crustaceans and shelters in rock crevices during the day.

NAME: **Tigerfish,** *Therapon jarbua*
RANGE: **Indian and Pacific Oceans: Red Sea, E. African coast to S. China, Philippines, N. Australia**
HABITAT: **inshore waters, estuaries**
SIZE: **30 cm (11¾ in)**

The tigerfish belongs to a family of about 15 species or more of tigerperch (Theraponidae). A distinctive fish, it is identified by the dark, curving stripes on its sides. Like all tigerperches, it has many small teeth and is predatory, feeding on small fish. Although generally a marine species, it will enter fresh water on occasion. Tigerfishes can produce sounds by vibrating the swim bladder with specialized muscles.

NAME: **Pumpkinseed,** *Lepomis gibbosus*
RANGE: **S. Canada; USA: North Dakota and Great Lakes, east to Atlantic Coast, south to Texas and Florida; introduced on the Pacific Coast and in Europe**
HABITAT: **brooks, clear ponds with plenty of vegetation**
SIZE: **15–23 cm (6–9 in)**

The attractive pumpkinseed is a sunfish, belonging to the Centrarchidae family of about 30 species of sunfish. Aids to its identification are the black gill cover, surrounded with orange or red, the blue lines radiating from the snout and eye region and the three anal spines. It feeds on snails and aquatic insects, as well as small and larval fish.

Breeding takes place between May and July in sandy-bottomed water. The male fish hollows out a shallow nest with his tail and then attracts one or more females to lay eggs in his nest. He guards the eggs while they incubate for 5 to 10 days, depending on the temperature, and continues to look after the young fishes until they are large enough to be able to disperse.

NAME: **Rock Bass,** *Ambloplites rupestris*
RANGE: **S. Canada: Lake Winnipeg, east to coast; USA: Great Lakes, east to Vermont, south to Gulf Coast; introduced in other areas of USA**
HABITAT: **rocky-bottomed streams, lake shallows**
SIZE: **15–25.5 cm (6–10 in)**

True to its name, this sunfish lives among rocks and stones, where it feeds on insects, crayfish and fish. It is a sturdy, deep-bodied fish, with a large mouth and a protruding lower jaw.

The male rock bass excavates a nest at the bottom, often amid the roots of aquatic plants. The female lays about 5,000 eggs in the nest, which is then guarded by the male. He defends the young fishes when they first hatch.

NAME: **Largemouth Bass,** *Micropterus salmoides*
RANGE: **S.E. Canada; USA: Great Lakes area, south to Gulf of Mexico; introduced in other areas of USA and in Europe and Africa**
HABITAT: **shallow lakes, ponds, rivers**
SIZE: **25.5–46 cm (10–18 in)**

A member of the sunfish family, the largemouth bass is usually greenish and silvery in coloration, with a dark band along each side; its dorsal fin is divided almost in two by a notch. A predatory fish, it feeds on crustaceans and other invertebrates when young, gradually progressing to fish, frogs and larger invertebrates when mature.

Spawning takes place in spring or early summer, depending on temperature and latitude. The male excavates a nest in sand or gravel in shallow water and attracts a female to his nest to lay her eggs, usually a few hundred. The male fertilizes the eggs and may then attract more females to his nest. The sticky-surfaced eggs attach themselves to the bottom of the nest and are guarded by the male until they hatch, 7 to 10 days after laying.

NAME: **Conchfish,** *Astrapogon stellatus*
RANGE: **tropical W. Atlantic Ocean, from Bahamas south through Caribbean**
HABITAT: **shallow waters**
SIZE: **5 cm (2 in)**

The conchfish is one of approximately 170 species of cardinalfish (Apogonidae) found in tropical and subtropical seas. It is a tiny fish, with some dark and some silvery coloration and dark spots along its sides. Some cardinalfish live in rock crevices or empty shells, but the conchfish lives in the shell of a live conch, *Strombus gigas*, a large mollusk. The conch is unaffected by the association, but the fish gains the benefit of shelter.

NAME: **Perch,** *Perca fluviatilis*
RANGE: **Europe: Britain, east across Scandinavia and USSR; south to N. Italy, Black and Caspian Seas; introduced in Ireland, Australia, New Zealand and South Africa**
HABITAT: **lakes, ponds, slow rivers**
SIZE: **35–51 cm (13¾–20 in)**

This fish is a member of the perch family (Percidae), which contains 126 freshwater species. It is a deep-bodied fish with two dorsal fins, the first joined to the second only by a membrane at the base. There is a characteristic black mark at the end of the spiny fin. The perch lives among aquatic vegetation, submerged tree roots or other debris, where its barred markings help to camouflage it; it feeds on fish.

Perch spawn in shallow water during April and May. The eggs are shed in long strings, which wind around plants or other objects, and they hatch in about 8 days. Young perch feed on plankton and then on insects and larger crustaceans until they are old enough to adopt the adult diet.

NAME: **Orangethroat Darter,** *Etheostoma spectabile*
RANGE: **central USA: Mississippi and Missouri river systems**
HABITAT: **streams**
SIZE: **8 cm (3¼ in)**

The orangethroat darter is one of the many species of darter found in the USA, all of which are members of the perch family (Percidae). It feeds on insects and planktonic crustaceans.

Breeding males develop some orange coloration on throat and breast, while females and nonbreeding males have pale throats. The male of a pair selects a nesting site, and the female excavates a shallow nest and deposits several hundred eggs, which are fertilized and guarded by the male.

NAME: **Zander,** *Stizostedion lucioperca*
RANGE: **central and E. Europe: Sweden and Finland, south to Black and Caspian Seas, east to USSR; introduced in England and W. Europe**
HABITAT: **large lakes, slow rivers**
SIZE: **60 cm–1.3 m (23½ in–4¼ ft)**

A member of the perch family, the zander has the characteristic two dorsal fins of that group; the first spiny fin is just separated from the second. It prefers cloudy water and does most of its hunting at dawn and dusk, remaining near the bottom at other times; it feeds on almost any species of fish.

Zanders spawn from April to June in sandy- or stony-bottomed water. The eggs are laid in a shallow nest, where they are guarded by the male.

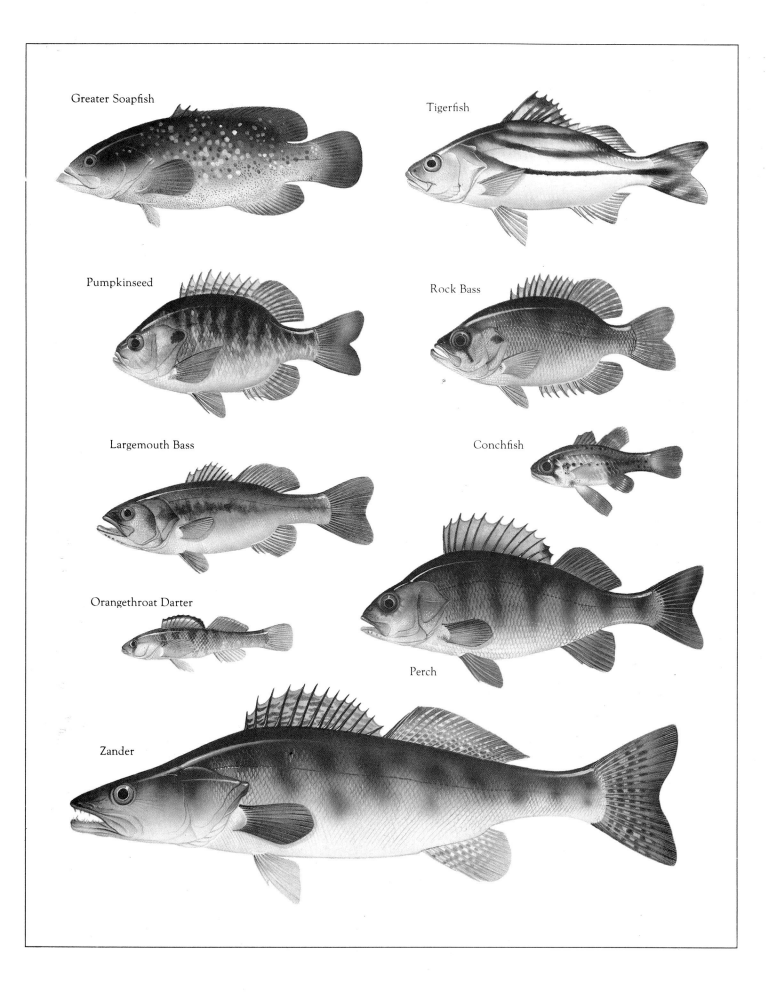

Greater Soapfish

Tigerfish

Pumpkinseed

Rock Bass

Largemouth Bass

Conchfish

Orangethroat Darter

Perch

Zander

Perchlike Fishes

NAME: **Bluefish,** *Pomatomus saltatrix*
RANGE: **Atlantic, Indian and W. Pacific Oceans: tropical and warm temperate areas**
HABITAT: **coastal waters, open ocean**
SIZE: **up to 1.2 m (4 ft)**

The bluefish has the reputation of being one of the most predatory of fishes, killing more prey than it can eat and feeding voraciously on almost any fish, including smaller individuals of its own species. A sturdy fish, it has a forked tail, fully scaled body and large jaws, equipped with formidable teeth.

Schools of bluefishes of a similar size travel together, often following shoals of other fish. Young bluefishes, known as snappers, also form their own shoals, and in general, the smaller the fish, the bigger the shoal.

NAME: **Cobia,** *Rachycentron canadum*
RANGE: **Atlantic, Indian and W. Pacific Oceans: tropical areas**
HABITAT: **open sea, occasionally inshore waters and estuaries**
SIZE: **1.8 m (6 ft)**

The elongate, streamlined cobia is the only species in its family. It is easily recognized by its distinctive coloration of dark-brown bands on a light ground and by the line of dorsal spines on its back before the dorsal fin. It is an active predator, feeding mainly on fish but also taking crabs, squid and shrimps.

NAME: **Remora,** *Remora remora*
RANGE: **Atlantic, Indian and W. Pacific Oceans: tropical and warm temperate areas**
HABITAT: **wherever taken by host, generally offshore**
SIZE: **15–46 cm (6–18 in)**

The remora is one of the 7 or 8 species of sharksucker in the family Echeneidae. By means of a specialized sucking disk on the top of the head, sharksuckers attach themselves to sharks or other large fishes, whales or turtles and travel with them wherever they go. The disk is formed from a modified spiny dorsal fin and contains two rows of slatlike ridges, divided by a central bar. The remora presses the disk flat against the host fish and creates a partial vacuum by moving the ridges, thus making it virtually impossible to remove it.

While some sharksuckers use many different types of host, others, including the remora, are adapted to only a few specific hosts. The remora seems nearly always to be associated with the blue shark. It feeds mainly on the parasites that also live on the shark but may leave its host briefly to catch small fish or crustaceans.

NAME: **Sharksucker,** *Echenis naucrates*
RANGE: **Atlantic, Indian and W. Pacific Oceans: tropical areas**
HABITAT: **wherever taken by host**
SIZE: **up to 92 cm (36¼ in)**

The largest member of the Echeneidae family, the sharksucker is a long-bodied fish, with distinctive white-bordered black stripes down each side of the body, from snout to tail. On top of its rather flattened head is the powerful sucking disk, with which it attaches itself to a host so firmly that it is almost impossible to remove. Attached in this way, the sharksucker rides around effortlessly and presumably gains some protection from the larger animal; this species uses a wide range of hosts, including sharks, large rays and turtles.

Sharksuckers were once used for catching sea turtles. The fish, with a line tied to its tail, was released near the turtle and would generally make straight for it and fasten itself to the tail. The fishermen could then gradually pull in the turtle, the sharksucker holding firm.

NAME: **Greater Amberjack,** *Seriola dumerili*
RANGE: **W. Atlantic Ocean: New England to Brazil; E. Atlantic: Mediterranean Sea to coast of W. Africa**
HABITAT: **surface inshore waters**
SIZE: **up to 1.8 m (6 ft)**

The greater amberjack is one of a large family, Carangidae, which includes about 200 species of fish such as jacks and pompanos. It is a fairly deep-bodied fish, with a dark-blue or green back and lighter, golden or whitish sides. There is a distinctive dark line running from the snout through the eye to the top of the head. It feeds on many species of fish.

NAME: **Crevalle Jack,** *Caranx hippos*
RANGE: **probably worldwide in tropical and subtropical waters**
HABITAT: **juveniles in inshore waters, adults offshore, especially around reefs**
SIZE: **80 cm–1 m (31½ in–3¼ ft)**

The exact distribution of this species is unknown because of confusion between similar species in the Carangidae family. However, it is certainly abundant on both sides of the Atlantic. The crevalle jack has a high, rounded forehead and a prominent dark spot on each gill cover; there are also dark spots on each pectoral fin. Its body is dark blue or metallic green on the back, with silvery or yellowish underparts. Fish are its main food, but crustaceans and some other invertebrates are also eaten.

NAME: **Rainbow Runner,** *Elagatis bipinnulata*
RANGE: **Atlantic, Indian and W. Pacific Oceans: tropical and subtropical waters**
HABITAT: **open sea**
SIZE: **up to 1.2 m (4 ft)**

Identified by its beautiful coloration, the rainbow runner has a blue back and yellow and blue stripes along the sides, shading to a whitish belly. Its body is slender, tapering sharply toward the deeply forked tail. It is a member of the pompano and jack family, Carangidae, and like so many of that family is a popular game fish.

NAME: **Florida Pompano,** *Trachinotus carolinus*
RANGE: **W. Atlantic Ocean: Cape Cod to Brazil**
HABITAT: **shallow waters close to shore**
SIZE: **46–63.5 cm (18–25 in)**

The Florida pompano closely resembles the permit, *T. falcatus*, but has a less strongly arched profile and lacks the elongate dorsal-fin spine of the permit. It has a rounded snout and a fairly deep body, which tapers sharply before the forked tail. Mollusks and crustaceans are its main foods, for which it roots around in the sand and mud of the seabed. It is itself considered an excellent food fish and is caught commercially.

Spawning is believed to take place offshore between March and September, depending on latitude. The young fishes then move inshore, where they feed on bottom-living invertebrates and small fish. The Florida pompano and the permit both belong to the Carangidae family.

NAME: **Lookdown,** *Selene vomer*
RANGE: **W. Atlantic Ocean: New England, south to Bermuda and to Uruguay; E. Atlantic: off W. Africa**
HABITAT: **shallow sandy- or muddy-bottomed waters**
SIZE: **30 cm (11¾ in)**

The lookdown is an extremely unusual-looking fish which has a large head and a small, dramatically tapering body. The head arches up steeply above the snout and is almost one and a half times as deep as it is long. Both dorsal and anal fins have long extensions, which point back toward the sharply forked tail.

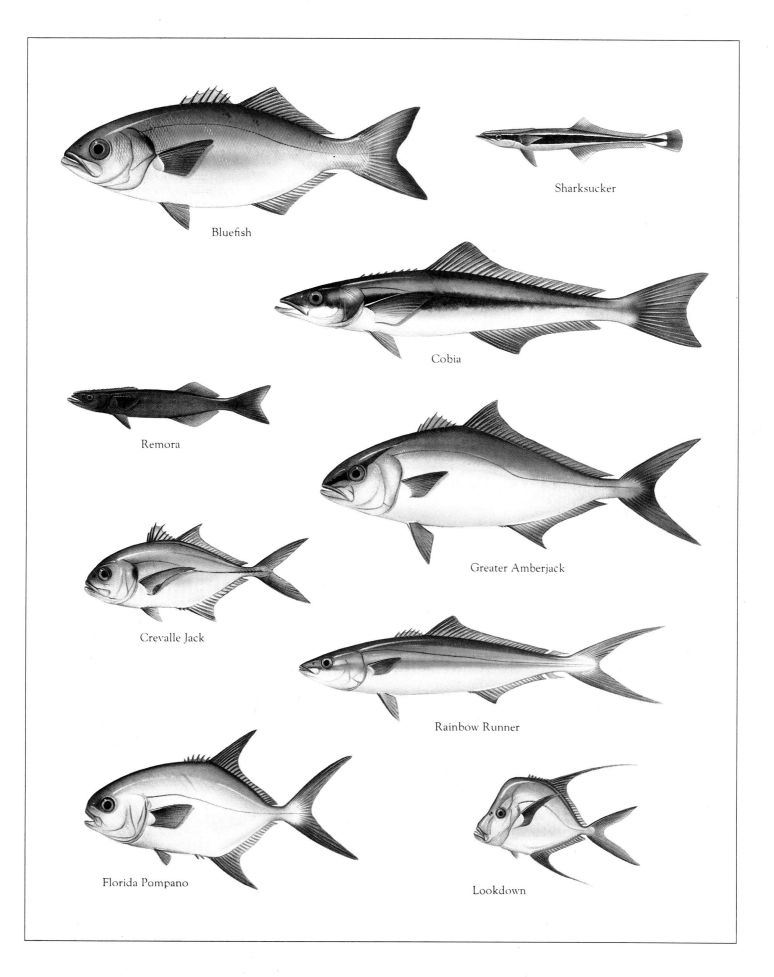

Bluefish

Sharksucker

Cobia

Remora

Greater Amberjack

Crevalle Jack

Rainbow Runner

Florida Pompano

Lookdown

Perchlike Fishes

NAME: **Dolphinfish,** *Coryphaena hippurus*
RANGE: **Atlantic, Pacific, Indian Oceans:**
tropical and warm temperate areas
HABITAT: **open sea**
SIZE: **up to 1.5 m (5 ft)**

Immediately identifiable by the long dorsal fin that originates over its head, the dolphinfish is extremely beautiful, with its vivid blue, green and yellow coloration. As males grow older, their foreheads become increasingly steep, almost vertical, and they may grow larger than females; otherwise males and females look alike. Dolphinfishes move in small schools and feed on a variety of fish, squid and crustaceans. They often frequent the waters around patches of floating seaweed or other debris which may harbor potential prey.

Dolphinfishes are popular game fish and excellent to eat. They belong to the family Coryphaenidae, which contains only 1 other species, the pompano dolphinfish, *C. equisetis*; this fish is similar in appearance but smaller than *C. hippurus*. They are also known simply as dolphins, but the name dolphinfish is preferable in order to distinguish them from mammalian dolphins.

NAME: **Atlantic Pomfret,** *Brama brama*
RANGE: **N. Atlantic Ocean: Iceland and**
Scandinavia to N. Africa;
Mediterranean Sea; off coasts of Chile,
South Africa, Australia, New Zealand
HABITAT: **open sea**
SIZE: **40–70 cm (15¾–27½ in)**

The Atlantic pomfret, a member of the family Bramidae, which contains 18 species, has a deep body that tapers sharply toward the long, deeply forked tail. It migrates into the northern part of its range in summer, but such migrations are irregular and appear to be dependent on suitable water temperatures. An unselective predator, it feeds on almost any fish or crustaceans available.

NAME: **Australian Salmon,** *Arripis trutta*
RANGE: **S. Pacific Ocean: waters around**
S. and W. Australia, Tasmania, New
Zealand
HABITAT: **shallow inshore waters, often**
near river mouths
SIZE: **91 cm (35¾ in)**

The Australian salmon is one of a family (Arripidae) of only 2 species, both confined to Australian waters. It is not related to the salmons of the northern hemisphere. It has a tapering, cylindrical body, a long dorsal fin and distinctive yellow pectoral fins; its sides are spotted with dark markings, which are particularly plentiful on young fishes. Shrimplike crustaceans and small fish are its main foods.

NAME: **Mutton Snapper,** *Lutjanus analis*
RANGE: **W. Atlantic Ocean: Florida and**
Bahamas, south to Caribbean, Gulf of
Mexico and Brazil
HABITAT: **coastal waters, bays**
SIZE: **up to 76 cm (30 in)**

Common off American coasts, the mutton snapper is one of the approximately 230 species in the snapper family, Lutjanidae. It is a brightly colored fish, with a green and reddish or pink body and some blue markings; there is a black spot below the dorsal fin on both sides of the body. Like most snappers, it has large, caninelike teeth. Mutton snappers often frequent shallow waters, where there are mangroves or turtle grass, and feed on the fish and crustaceans found among the vegetation.

Some snappers are among the fishes known to cause the ciguatera type of fish poisoning, which can be fatal to humans who eat the flesh of affected fish. The poison originates in certain algae. Herbivorous fishes may feed on this algae and are in turn eaten by carnivorous fishes, with no apparent ill effects to the predators. Their flesh becomes toxic, however.

NAME: **Yellowtail Snapper,** *Ocyurus*
chrysurus
RANGE: **W. Atlantic Ocean: New**
England to Brazil, including Gulf of
Mexico and Caribbean
HABITAT: **offshore waters, near coral**
reefs
SIZE: **76 cm (30 in)**

One of the snapper family (Lutjanidae), the yellowtail snapper is an attractive fish, with a bright yellow tail and a yellow stripe along each side. Its body is slender and its dorsal fin long and low. Yellowtails feed near the bottom on crustaceans and fish but also occur offshore above reefs. Popular with anglers, they are excellent food fish.

NAME: **Tripletail,** *Lobotes surinamensis*
RANGE: **Atlantic, Indian and W. Pacific**
Oceans: tropical and warm temperate
areas
HABITAT: **coastal surface waters**
SIZE: **1 m (3¼ ft)**

Although never common, the tripletail is a widely distributed fish which occurs on both sides of the Atlantic. It belongs to the tripletail family (Lobotidae), which includes only about 4 species. It has a deep, heavy body and is usually dark brown in color, although some individuals may be yellow and brown. The large, rounded lobes of the dorsal and anal fins project back toward the tail; this gives the fish the appearance of having three tails.

Young tripletails often live close to the shore in bays and estuaries, where they float on their sides among dead mangrove and other leaves. Their curving posture and brownish-yellow coloration imitate the movement and appearance of the surrounding leaves and are an excellent example of protective mimicry.

NAME: **Margate,** *Haemulon album*
RANGE: **W. Atlantic Ocean: Bahamas and**
Florida, south through Caribbean to
Brazil
HABITAT: **shallow inshore waters, often**
near reefs
SIZE: **63 cm (24¾ in)**

The margate is one of about 175 species in the grunt family, Pomadasyidae. These marine fishes occur in tropical waters and are related to the snappers but lack their large teeth. They are known as grunts because of the noise that they make by grinding their pharyngeal teeth together; the resulting sounds are amplified by the swim bladder. The margate is fairly typical of its family, with its high, spiny dorsal fin, which is continuous with the rayed dorsal fin. It is usually grayish in color, with darker dorsal and tail fins, but coloration does vary.

Small groups of margates often frequent reefs and wrecks, where they feed on small fish and also forage on the seabed for bottom-living invertebrates. This is the largest of the Atlantic grunts and is caught commercially.

NAME: **Black Margate,** *Anisotremus*
surinamensis
RANGE: **W. Atlantic Ocean: Florida and**
the Bahamas, south through Gulf of
Mexico and Caribbean
HABITAT: **inshore waters, near rocks and**
reefs
SIZE: **up to 61 cm (24 in)**

The black margate, a member of the grunt family, Pomadasyidae, is typical of its group in its body shape and continuous dorsal fin. It is grayish in color, with a dark spot on each scale on the back; the fins are dark gray. Most active at night, it feeds on crustaceans, sea urchins and fish, often foraging in small groups. By day it shelters in caves or crevices.

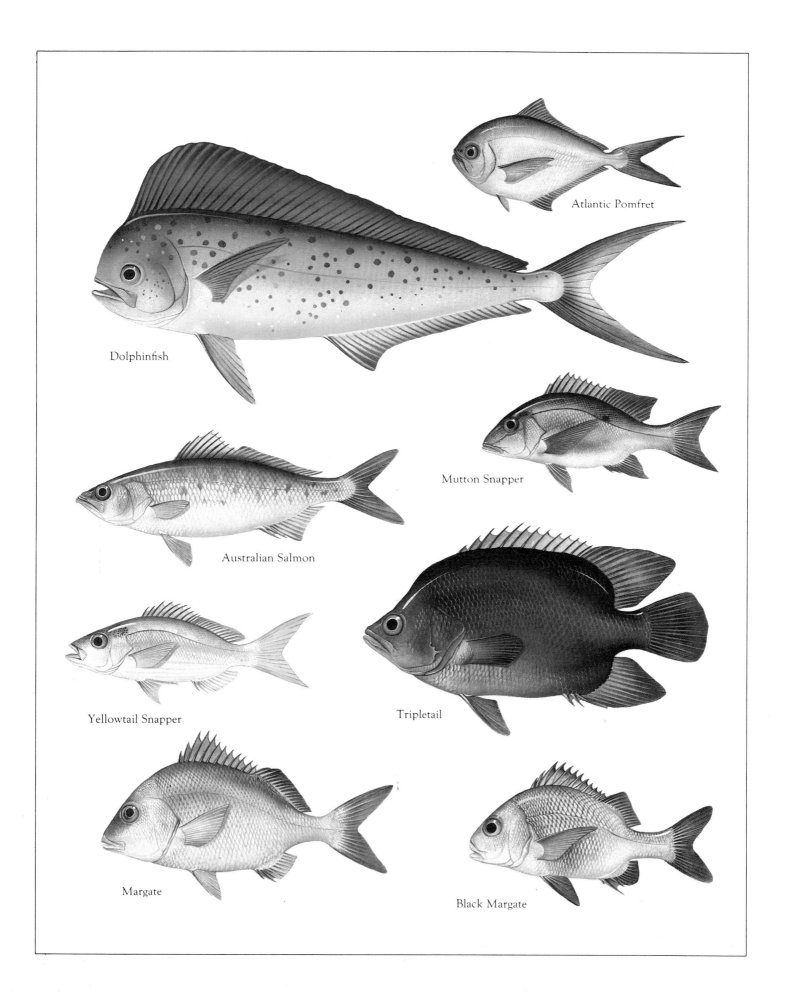

Atlantic Pomfret

Dolphinfish

Mutton Snapper

Australian Salmon

Yellowtail Snapper

Tripletail

Margate

Black Margate

Perchlike Fishes

NAME: Sweetlip Emperor, *Lethrinus chrysostomus*
RANGE: off N. coast of Australia, Great Barrier Reef
HABITAT: inshore waters, reef areas
SIZE: 91 cm (35¾ in)

The sweetlip emperor is one of the 21 or so species in the family Lethrinidae. The fishes in this family, known as scavengers and emperors, are related to the grunts (family Pomadasyidae) and resemble them, with their spiny dorsal and anal fins. The sweetlip has a rather large head for its body, a long snout and scaleless cheeks. Its coloration is striking, with deep-red fins, dark barring on the sides and vivid red patches around the eyes. It can attain a weight of 9 kg (20 lb) and is a valuable food fish.

NAME: Spangled Emperor, *Lethrinus nebulosus*
RANGE: Indian and Pacific Oceans: Red Sea and E. Africa to N. Australia and W. Pacific islands
HABITAT: coral reefs, open ocean
SIZE: 76 cm (30 in)

The name of the attractively colored spangled emperor is well deserved. Identifying characteristics are the scattering of blue spots on its dorsal and anal fins, the blue on many of the scales on its sides and the blue lines on each side of the face, running from the eye toward the snout. A member of the family Lethrinidae, the fish has the long snout, thick lips and dorsal and anal spines typical of the group. Like several of the larger members of this family, it is a valuable food fish.

NAME: Scup, *Stenotomus chrysops*
RANGE: Atlantic coast of N. America: Cape Cod (sometimes Nova Scotia) to Florida
HABITAT: sandy-bottomed inshore and offshore waters
SIZE: 46 cm (18 in)

An abundant fish in the Atlantic, the scup, also called the northern porgy, is one of the 100 species in the porgy family, Sparidae. It has a deep, laterally compressed body, a deeply forked tail and spines on both dorsal and anal fins. Its scales are silvery, with indistinct dark bars on the sides of the body. Most of its feeding is done on the bottom, and the scup takes crustaceans, worms and some bottom-living fish.

In spring, adults spawn in waters close to the shore, often in bays; the eggs float freely until they hatch. In winter, scups move farther offshore and toward the south of their range.

NAME: Jolthead Porgy, *Calamus bajonado*
RANGE: Caribbean, Gulf of Mexico; W. Atlantic Ocean: coasts of N. and South America from New England to Brazil
HABITAT: coastal waters, near reefs
SIZE: 61 cm (24 in)

One of the larger members of the family Sparidae, the jolthead porgy is a distinctive fish, with a high, rounded forehead. Its scales have a silvery sheen, and there are some blue markings around the eyes, which are placed characteristically high. Small schools of jolthead porgies feed near the shore on invertebrates such as sea urchins, mollusks and crustaceans. They are good food fish, prized by anglers and commercial fishermen.

NAME: Sheepshead, *Archosargus probatocephalus*
RANGE: W. Atlantic Ocean: Nova Scotia, south to Gulf of Mexico (now rare in north of range)
HABITAT: tidal streams, bays, seabed near jetties
SIZE: 30–76 cm (11¾–30 in)

Sometimes called the convict fish, the sheepshead is identified by the broad black bars down each of its silvery sides. These bars vary in shape and number and are most prominent in younger fishes. Otherwise the sheepshead is typical in appearance of the porgy family, with its large head, thick lips and spiny dorsal and anal fins. It feeds on crustaceans and mollusks, which it crushes with its broad, flat teeth, and is itself an excellent food fish, caught commercially in large quantities.

Spawning takes place in spring, and the eggs float freely until they hatch only 3 or 4 days later, provided the temperature is sufficiently high.

NAME: Snapper, *Chrysophrys auratus*
RANGE: Pacific Ocean: coasts of New Zealand, Australia, Lord Howe Island
HABITAT: seabed, rocky reefs
SIZE: 1.3 m (4¼ ft)

The snapper, a member of the porgy family, Sparidae, undergoes slight changes of appearance and behavior as it matures. Young snappers are pale pink in color, with dark bands, and live in large schools in shallow water close to the shore, often in bays. Adults are redder, with bright blue spots dotting the fins, back and sides. They frequent the seabed and rocky reefs in deeper waters but may come into shallow coastal waters in summer. In the oldest specimens, the forehead becomes rather humped, and the lips particularly fleshy; these older fishes tend to be solitary. The snapper is a good food fish.

NAME: Red Sea Bream, *Pagellus bogaraveo*
RANGE: Atlantic Ocean: coasts of S. Norway, Britain, Europe, N. Africa, Canary Islands; Mediterranean Sea
HABITAT: inshore waters, deeper waters at 100–200 m (330–650 ft)
SIZE: 35–51 cm (13¾–20 in)

Quite common in the south of its range, the red sea bream is rare in the north, and those fishes which do occur in northern waters are mostly summer migrants. A member of the porgy family, Sparidae, the fish is distinguished by the reddish flush to its body and fins, the dark spot above its pectoral fin and its short, rounded head. Young fishes are paler in color than adults and may lack the dark spot. The young form large schools and frequent shallow inshore waters, feeding on small crustaceans. Adults live farther offshore in deeper waters and form smaller groups; they feed on fish, and also on crustaceans.

Little is known of the breeding habits of the red sea bream, but it is thought to spawn in summer or autumn, depending on the area: the farther south, the earlier it spawns. It is a good-quality food fish and is caught commercially.

NAME: Gilthead Bream, *Sparus aurata*
RANGE: Atlantic Ocean: coasts of Ireland, S. England, Europe, N. Africa, Canary Islands; Mediterranean and Black Seas
HABITAT: shallow sandy- or muddy-bottomed waters at about 30 m (100 ft)
SIZE: up to 70 cm (27½ in)

A golden stripe, which runs between the eyes, is the origin of the common name of this fish; the stripe fades on death. The gilthead is a fairly deep-bodied fish, with a markedly rounded snout and high-set eyes; there is a dark spot on each side, well above the pectoral fin. It feeds largely on mollusks and crustaceans, and its teeth are adapted to deal with this hard-shelled prey: those in the front of the jaws are pointed and curved for breaking into the shells, while those at the sides are broad and flattened for crushing and grinding down food. Because of their diet, giltheads can prove a menace on commercial oyster and mussel beds.

Like all sea breams, the gilthead is a member of the porgy family, Sparidae. Breeding takes place in winter in offshore waters, deeper than the giltheads normally frequent. They are not believed to breed in the north of their range.

Sweetlip Emperor

Scup

Spangled Emperor

Jolthead Porgy

Sheepshead

Snapper

Red Sea Bream

Gilthead Bream

Perchlike Fishes

NAME: **White Seabass,** *Cynoscion nobilis*
RANGE: **Pacific Ocean: Alaska to Mexico**
HABITAT: **near kelp beds, shallow to deep waters**
SIZE: **61 cm–1.8 m (24 in–6 ft)**

The white seabass is not a true sea bass but a member of the drum family, Sciaenidae. There are about 160 species of drum, so called because many of them are capable of making sounds by vibrating their swim bladders with specialized muscles; in some species, only the male makes sounds, and in others, both male and female can "drum." Most species of drum have a deeply, often almost completely, divided dorsal fin.

A large, elongate fish, the white seabass has a rather pointed head and large mouth, with the lower jaw projecting slightly beyond the upper. The two parts of its dorsal fin just touch. It moves in large schools and feeds on many kinds of fish and on crustaceans and squid. Spawning takes place in spring and summer, and young fishes generally live in quiet, inshore waters.

White seabass are important to both sport and commercial fishermen along the Pacific coast of North America. An almost identical but much larger fish, the totuava, *C. macdonaldi*, occurs farther south, off the coast of Mexico.

NAME: **Spotted Seatrout,** *Cynoscion nebulosus*
RANGE: **Atlantic Ocean: coast of USA from New York to Florida; Gulf of Mexico**
HABITAT: **coastal bays, estuaries; deeper waters in winter**
SIZE: **45–61 cm (17¾–24 in)**

Although called "seatrout" because of its scattering of troutlike spots, the spotted seatrout belongs to the drum family, Sciaenidae. It has an elongate body and pointed head, with a slightly protruding lower jaw; its dorsal fin is deeply notched. Like many drums, the spotted seatrout is capable of making sounds by vibrating its swim bladder. It feeds on crustaceans, such as shrimps, and on fish.

Spawning takes place in sheltered coastal bays, from March to November. Once hatched, larval and juvenile fishes stay in the protection of marine vegetation, where they find plentiful supplies of food. In winter, they move into deeper waters. A good food fish, spotted seatrout are caught commercially and also for sport.

NAME: **Black Drum,** *Pogonias cromis*
RANGE: **W. Atlantic Ocean: coasts from New England to Argentina**
HABITAT: **bays, coastal lagoons**
SIZE: **1.2–1.8 m (4–6 ft)**

Identified by its short, deep body, somewhat flattened belly and arched back, the black drum is one of the largest members of the drum family and is known to weigh as much as 66 kg (146 lb). Several short barbels hang from its lower jaw. A bottom-feeding fish, the black drum eats crustaceans and mollusks, which it is able to crush with the large, flat teeth in its throat. Oysters are a particularly favored food, and black drums can do much harm to commercial oyster beds.

NAME: **Jackknife-fish,** *Equetus lanceolatus*
RANGE: **W. Atlantic Ocean: coasts of North and South Carolina, Bermuda to Brazil; Gulf of Mexico, Caribbean**
HABITAT: **rocky- or coral-bottomed waters more than 15 m (50 ft) deep**
SIZE: **23 cm (9 in)**

An unusual member of the drum family, the jackknife-fish is an extremely distinctive species, strikingly marked with three black stripes, bordered with white. One of these stripes curves down from the high dorsal fin to the tail fin, disrupting the normal outline of the fish. Such markings are a form of camouflage, intended to confuse and distract the observer and in this way delay recognition.

A solitary species, the jackknife-fish hides among rocks or in crevices in the coral reef during the day and feeds at night.

NAME: **Freshwater Drum,** *Aplodinotus grunniens*
RANGE: **N. America: S. Canada through the Great Lakes and Mississippi River system to Gulf of Mexico; south to Mexico and Guatemala**
HABITAT: **large rivers, lakes**
SIZE: **up to 1.2 m (4 ft)**

One of the few freshwater species in the drum family, this fish has a humped back and a long-based dorsal fin. As befits a bottom-feeder, its mouth is low slung; its main foods are mollusks, crustaceans and some insect larvae, all of which it crushes with the large, flattened teeth in its throat, spitting out the shells and swallowing the soft bodies. Like many drums, it produces sounds by vibrating its swim bladder and is one of the few freshwater fishes to do so.

Spawning takes place in April, May or June in shallow gravel- or sandy-bottomed water. Each female may shed from 10,000 to 100,000 eggs, which hatch in about 2 weeks.

NAME: **Maigre,** *Argyrosomus regius*
RANGE: **Indian Ocean; E. Atlantic Ocean: Britain to Senegal; Mediterranean Sea**
HABITAT: **shoreline to deeper waters to 350 m (1,150 ft), estuaries**
SIZE: **1.5–2 m (5–6½ ft)**

One of the giants of the drum family, the maigre is an elongate fish, with a rounded snout and large mouth. It is a common fish in southern waters and only occasionally strays to northern European seas. It moves in shoals, feeding on fish, and usually occurs in sandy-bottomed water.

NAME: **Spotted Goatfish,** *Pseudupeneus maculatus*
RANGE: **W. Atlantic Ocean: New Jersey to Brazil; Gulf of Mexico, Caribbean**
HABITAT: **shallow waters, reefs, turtle grass beds**
SIZE: **28 cm (11 in)**

There are 55 species of goatfish, or red mullet, in the family Mullidae, which occur worldwide in tropical and warm temperate seas. Generally these fishes have elongate bodies and two widely separated dorsal fins.

The spotted goatfish is typical of the family and has the characteristic feature of two long, sensory chin barbels, used for finding food on the seabed. With these barbels, the goatfish forages over the substrate for the small invertebrate animals on which it feeds.

NAME: **Red Mullet,** *Mullus surmuletus*
RANGE: **Mediterranean Sea, E. Atlantic Ocean: Britain, south to Canary Islands and N. Africa**
HABITAT: **sandy-, muddy-, sometimes rocky-bottomed waters to 90 m (300 ft)**
SIZE: **40 cm (15¾ in)**

The red mullet is a Mediterranean species, which sometimes occurs farther north, presumably as a summer migrant. It has a steeply rounded forehead and, like the other members of the family Mullidae, two sensory barbels on its chin, which it uses to search the seabed for food, mostly bottom-living invertebrates. Once prey is found, the red mullet will dig to uncover it. Red mullets usually travel in small schools of fewer than 50. They can change color quite dramatically, varying between reddish-brown, red and yellowish-brown. In the daytime, they are usually brownish, with several yellow stripes along the sides; at night, these lines break up into a marbled pattern. In deeper water, red mullets are a deep red, but color variations also occur when the fishes are alarmed.

Spawning takes place between July and September. The female sheds her eggs on the seabed, but once they hatch, the young live at the surface.

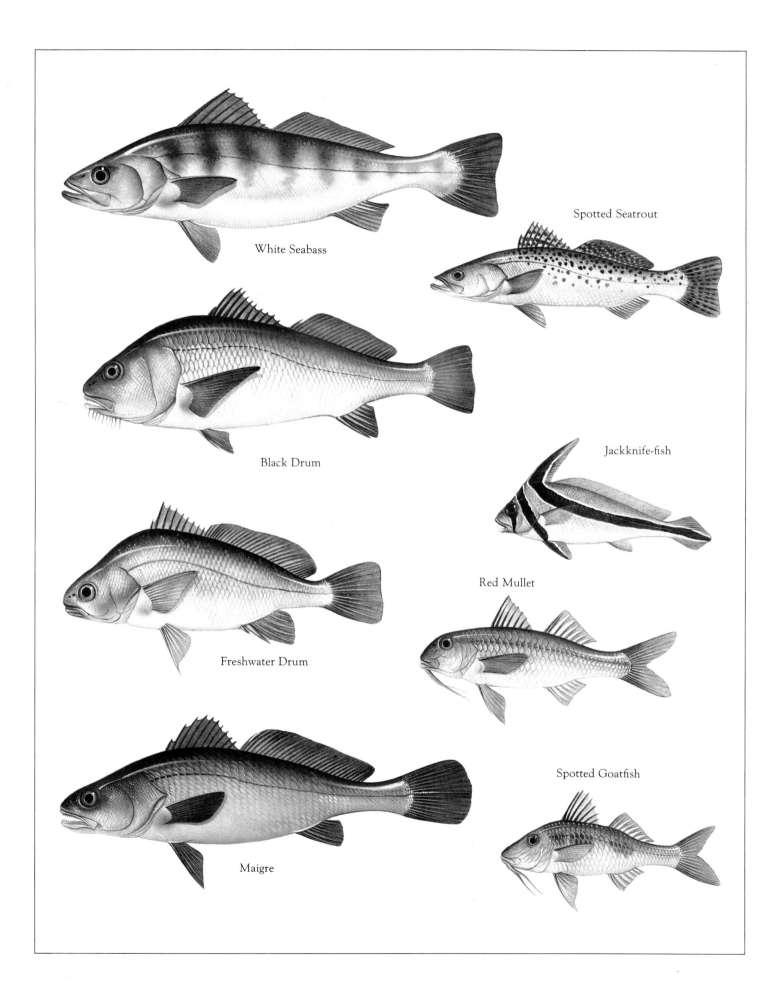

White Seabass

Spotted Seatrout

Black Drum

Jackknife-fish

Freshwater Drum

Red Mullet

Maigre

Spotted Goatfish

Perchlike Fishes

NAME: Bermuda Chub, *Kyphosus sectatrix*
RANGE: W. Atlantic Ocean: Cape Cod, south to Bermuda, Caribbean and Brazil; E. Atlantic: off coast of W. Africa; Mediterranean Sea
HABITAT: rocky-bottomed waters, reefs
SIZE: up to 76 cm (30 in)

The sea chubs of the family Kyphosidae are found worldwide in tropical and warm temperate waters. Most of the 30 or so species live in shallow water and feed on algae. The Bermuda chub is typical of its family, with its deep body and small head and mouth. Its coloration varies, but it is generally gray, with narrow dark bands running the length of the body and yellow markings on the head. Plants are its main food, but it also eats small invertebrates.

Although the range extends to Cape Cod, adult Bermuda chub are rarely found north of Florida. Young fishes are probably carried farther north by the Gulf Stream.

NAME: Archerfish, *Toxotes jaculator*
RANGE: India, S.E. Asia, Philippines, Indonesia, N. Australia
HABITAT: inshore waters, estuaries, lower reaches of rivers
SIZE: 23 cm (9 in)

The 4 species of archerfish in the family Toxotidae are so called because of their habit of shooting down insects by spitting water at them. The archerfish holds water in its throat and, with its tongue, makes the mouth opening into a narrow tube. By then using its tongue as a valve and compressing the gill covers to propel the water, the archerfish ejects the drops with some force and great accuracy. The fish has excellent vision, and its large mobile eyes allow it to look upward above the water surface. It shoots at insects on plants overhanging the water and also feeds on aquatic insects and small invertebrates.

NAME: Atlantic Spadefish, *Chaetodipterus faber*
RANGE: W. Atlantic Ocean: New England, Bermuda, south to Gulf of Mexico, Caribbean to Brazil
HABITAT: rocky-bottomed waters
SIZE: 46–90 cm (18–35½ in)

The Atlantic spadefish has a deep body, much compressed from side to side, and extended dorsal and anal fins. Its coloration changes as it grows: small, young fishes are black, becoming silvery gray as they mature, with dark vertical bars down the sides; these bars become indistinct in large adults. It is a member of the family Ephippidae, which contains about 14 species.

Spadefishes feed primarily on small invertebrate animals.

NAME: Batfish, *Platax pinnatus*
RANGE: Indian and Pacific Oceans: Red Sea, E. Africa to Philippines, Indonesia, Australia
HABITAT: coastal waters; lagoons when young, reefs as adults
SIZE: 76 cm (30 in)

A member of the spadefish family, Ephippidae, the batfish has a deep, laterally compressed body and high dorsal and anal fins. Juvenile batfish are black, with fins outlined in orange. They appear similar to certain aquatic flatworms and mollusks which fishes find unpleasant to eat and presumably gain some protection from this. The resemblance is heightened by the fishes' habit of swimming on their sides, with similar undulatory movements to those of their models.

NAME: Scat, *Scatophagus argus*
RANGE: Indian and Pacific Oceans: E. Africa to India, Indonesia and W. Pacific Islands
HABITAT: coastal waters; fresh and brackish water
SIZE: 30 cm (11¾ in)

The scat is one of the 3 or so species in the family Scatophagidae, which means, literally, "dung-eaters." The scat has obtained this reputation because it is often found near sewer outlets and is thus believed to feed on feces. Normally it feeds on plant material, however. While adults are spotted with brownish blotches, young fishes have dark, barred markings on their sides.

NAME: Foureye Butterflyfish, *Chaetodon capistratus*
RANGE: W. Atlantic Ocean: Cape Cod, south to Caribbean and Gulf of Mexico
HABITAT: coral reefs, rocky- and sandy-bottomed waters
SIZE: 15 cm (6 in)

The approximately 200 species in the family Chaetodontidae are among the most colorful inhabitants of coral reefs. The family divides into 2 groups: butterflyfishes and angelfishes; the main difference between them is that angelfishes have a stout spine near each gill cover.

The foureye butterflyfish is typical of the family, with its deep, laterally compressed body, so thin that it resembles a disk. This body shape is ideal for twisting and turning among the coral "forests" and utilizing the many crevices for shelter. The black spots on each side near the tail presumably mislead predators into thinking that these are the vulnerable eye areas, while the actual eyes have additional protection from the dark bands that run through and help to conceal them. The fishes feed by grazing on the coral reef, eating polyps or pieces of seaweed.

NAME: Copperband Butterflyfish, *Chelmon rostratus*
RANGE: Indian and Pacific Oceans: E. Africa to India, Indonesia, Australia, Japan and Philippines
HABITAT: coral reefs, rocky areas
SIZE: 20 cm (7¾ in)

Also known as the beaked butterflyfish, this fish has a long, beaklike snout, with which it can reach into crevices in the coral to find food. The beak is equipped with tiny, sharp teeth. It is an attractive fish, with coppery bands running down each side of the body, presumably as a camouflaging device. There is a black spot near the dorsal fin, which confuses predators into thinking that this is the vulnerable head area.

NAME: Forceps Butterflyfish, *Forcipiger longirostris*
RANGE: Indian and Pacific Oceans: tropical areas from Hawaii to Indonesia and Comoro Islands
HABITAT: coral reefs, rocky areas
SIZE: 18 cm (7 in)

The forceps butterflyfish has a long, beaklike snout, with a small mouth at the tip, which it pokes into crevices and crannies in the coral to find food. With its jaws like forceps, it picks out tiny invertebrates and polyps from the densely packed coral heads.

NAME: Queen Angelfish, *Holacanthus ciliaris*
RANGE: tropical W. Atlantic Ocean: Florida and Bahamas, south to Brazil including Gulf of Mexico
HABITAT: coral reefs
SIZE: up to 46 cm (18 in)

The brilliantly colored queen angelfish belongs to the same family as the butterflyfishes (Chaetodontidae) but has a characteristic spine near each gill cover. It has a deep, slim body, a blunt snout and greatly elongated lobes to dorsal and anal fins that extend past the tail fin.

NAME: Imperial Angelfish, *Pomacanthus imperator*
RANGE: tropical Indian and Pacific Oceans: Red Sea, E. Africa to Indonesia, Philippines, Australia and Polynesia
HABITAT: coral reefs, rocky areas
SIZE: up to 38 cm (15 in)

The adult imperial angelfish is a striking fish, with attractive yellow and blue markings and a dark, masklike area over the eyes. Young fishes, however, are much darker, with blue and white stripes on the body and a whitish spot near the tail. The stripes are believed to lead a predator's eye toward the light spot and away from the vulnerable head area. The fish's slightly protuberant mouth enables it to graze over the coral.

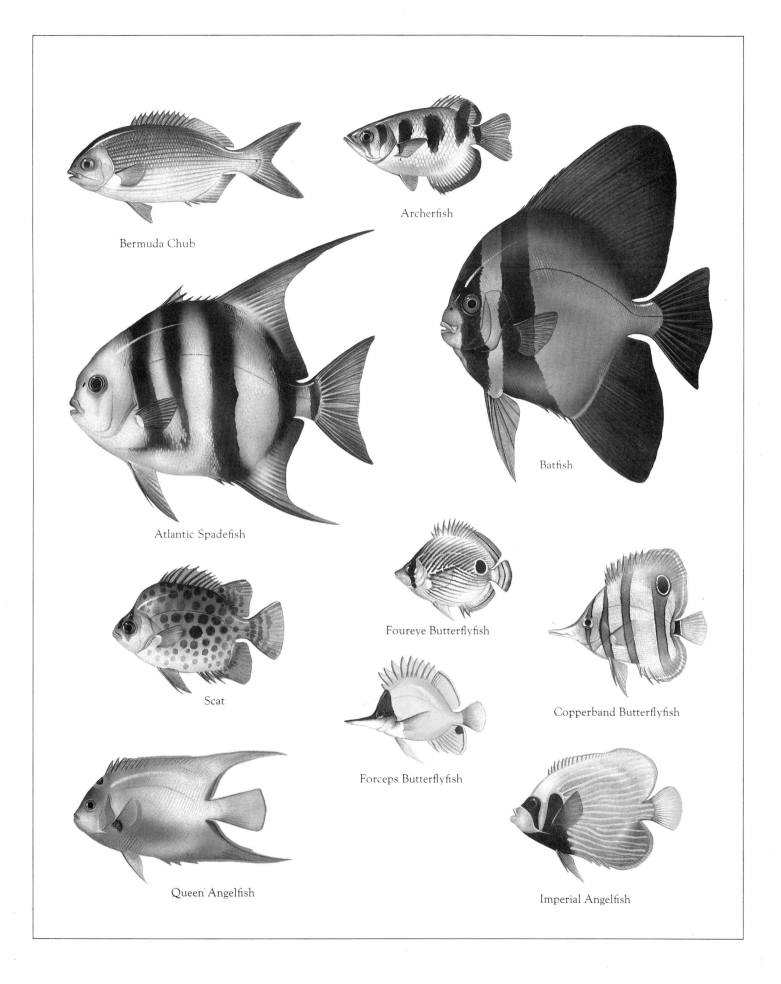

Bermuda Chub

Archerfish

Atlantic Spadefish

Batfish

Scat

Foureye Butterflyfish

Copperband Butterflyfish

Forceps Butterflyfish

Queen Angelfish

Imperial Angelfish

Perchlike Fishes

NAME: Barred Surfperch, *Amphistichus argenteus*
RANGE: USA: California, south to Mexico: Baja California
HABITAT: coastal waters
SIZE: up to 41 cm (16 in)

The barred surfperch belongs to the family Embiotocidae, which contains about 23 species, all but one found in the North Pacific. Most members of the family frequent the surf area of coasts, hence the common name. A deep-bodied fish, its sides are marked with gold or bronze vertical bars and spots. It feeds on small crabs and other crustaceans and mollusks.

Surfperches bear live young. The male fertilizes the female internally by means of the modified front portion of the anal fin, and the young develop inside her body, protected and nourished by ovarian fluid. The litter size varies from 4 to 113, depending on the size of the mother, but the average is about 33. Most young are born between March and July and are mature at about 2 years old, when they are just over 12.5 cm (5 in) long.

NAME: Kelp Perch, *Brachyistius frenatus*
RANGE: Pacific coast of N. America: Vancouver to California
HABITAT: shallow waters along rocky coasts, kelp beds
SIZE: 20 cm (7¾ in)

A member of the surfperch family, Embiotocidae, the kelp perch has handsome coppery coloration on its sides, each scale having a dark spot. It feeds on crustaceans. Like the other members of its family, it bears live young. The male fertilizes the female internally, and the young develop inside her body.

NAME: Discus Fish, *Symphysodon discus*
RANGE: tropical South America: Amazon and other large river systems
HABITAT: heavily vegetated backwaters and pools
SIZE: 20 cm (7¾ in)

One of the most handsome members of the family Cichlidae, the discus fish has a laterally compressed body, marked with irregular red stripes. These stripes, and the dark vertical bars that cross them, help to camouflage the fish among the vegetation and dappled light of its forested habitat.

The discus fish lays its eggs on gravel bottoms and later moves the newly hatched young to submerged vegetation. About 3 days after hatching, the young swim to one of their parents, attach themselves to its body or fins and feed on slime secreted by the adult's skin. They continue to feed in this way for 5 weeks or more.

NAME: Angelfish, *Pterophyllum scalare*
RANGE: South America: Amazon basin
HABITAT: densely vegetated, slow-flowing rivers
SIZE: 15 cm (6 in)

Its popularity with aquarium keepers makes the angelfish one of the most familiar cichlids. In its natural habitat, its compressed body, marked with dark vertical stripes, and its extended fins keep it well concealed in the cloudy plant-filled water, the threadlike fin filaments blending perfectly with the stems of plants.

NAME: Nile Mouthbrooder, *Oreochromis niloticus*
RANGE: N. Africa, south to Congo basin and E. Africa
HABITAT: rivers, dammed-up pools
SIZE: 50 cm (19¾ in)

A large cichlid, the Nile mouthbrooder is a sturdy fish, with a long-based dorsal fin. It has a small mouth and tiny teeth and feeds mainly on plankton, although insects and crustaceans are also part of its diet.

Like many cichlids, this fish carries its developing eggs inside its mouth, thus keeping them safe and aerated at the same time. The female of this species broods the eggs, and even when the young are hatched, they will return to her mouth if danger threatens.

NAME: Ring-tailed Pike Cichlid, *Crenicichla saxatilis*
RANGE: South America: Venezuela, Amazon basin to Paraguay and Uruguay
HABITAT: rivers, pools
SIZE: 36 cm (14¼ in)

A large, elongate fish, the ring-tailed pike cichlid has a distinctive black stripe running the length of its body. Its tail and dorsal fins are black-edged, and there is a black spot on the tail fin. Male and female fishes have the same markings, but males have pointed dorsal and anal fins and females rounded fins. An active predator, it snaps up prey in its large mouth as a pike does.

NAME: Schomburgk's Leaffish, *Polycentrus schomburgkii*
RANGE: N.E. South America; Trinidad
HABITAT: freshwater streams, pools
SIZE: 10 cm (4 in)

This leaffish is a member of the family Nandidae, a group of about 10 species of freshwater fish. Typical of its family, it has a laterally compressed body and many dorsal and anal spines; its mouth is large and protrusible. Although small, it is a voracious predator, lurking among vegetation, where it is well camouflaged by its leaflike appearance, to watch for prey and then dashing out to attack.

NAME: Sergeant Major, *Abudefduf saxatilis*
RANGE: worldwide, warm temperate and tropical seas
HABITAT: inshore waters, coral reefs
SIZE: 23 cm (9 in)

The sergeant major belongs to the damselfish family, Pomacentridae, which contains several hundred species of marine fish, found all over the world in warm temperate and tropical areas. A deep-bodied fish, its coloration changes according to the depth of water it is in; in shallow water, it is yellow with dark barring, but in deeper water or caves, it turns blue with darker-blue vertical bars.

The eggs are laid on a rock or in a rock crevice, on a surface cleared of any algal plant growth. The male fish guards the eggs until they hatch.

NAME: Clown Anemonefish, *Amphiprion percula*
RANGE: W. and central Pacific Ocean
HABITAT: coral reefs
SIZE: 6 cm (2¼ in)

Unmistakable with its broad bands of white and orange and its dark-rimmed fins, the clown anemonefish belongs to the damselfish family, Pomacentridae. Like the others in its genus, it has developed a relationship with large sea anemones, living among their stinging tentacles and even remaining inside when the anemone draws in its tentacles. Thus the fish shelters from predators, and, at the same time, it is protected from the anemone's poison by its own body mucus. It feeds on tiny crustaceans and other organisms taken during brief dashes from its refuge.

The eggs are laid on rock or coral near the anemone and guarded by both parents.

NAME: Beaugregory, *Pomacentrus leucostictus*
RANGE: W. Atlantic Ocean: coasts of Florida and Bermuda; Caribbean; Pacific coast of Mexico
HABITAT: inshore waters, coral reefs
SIZE: 15 cm (6 in)

A member of the family Pomacentridae, the beaugregory is a handsome, rich orange-brown and blue fish, dotted with yellow spots. Like most members of its family, it is an active little fish, darting around coral and rock crevices and feeding on algae, tiny crustaceans, worms and other small invertebrates.

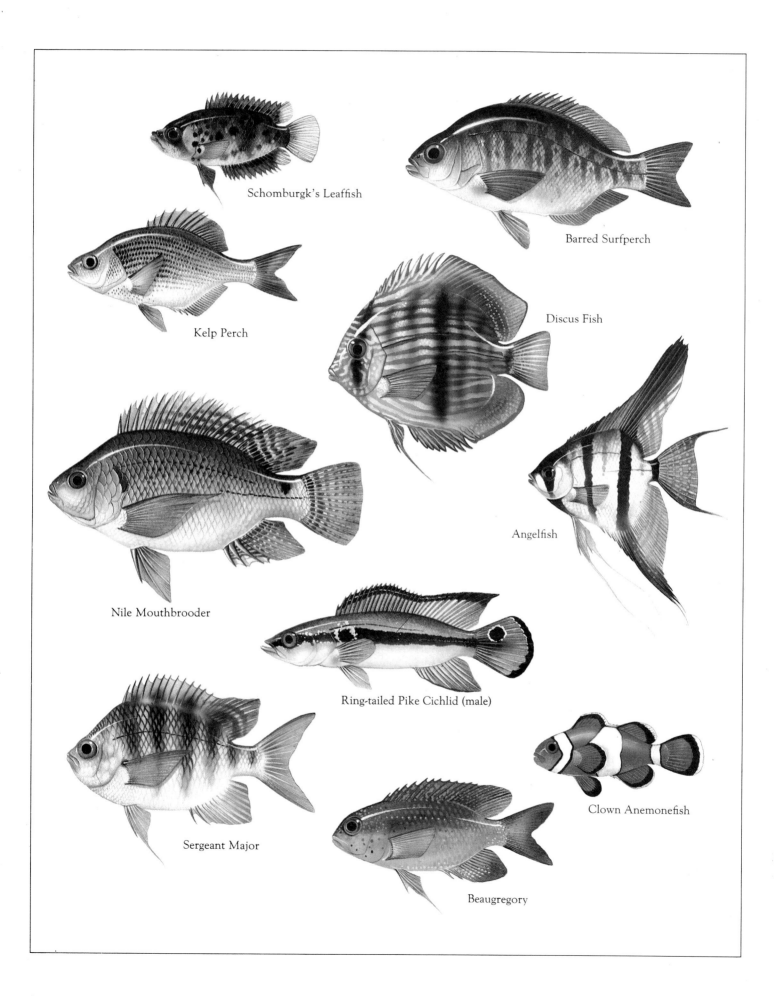

Schomburgk's Leaffish

Barred Surfperch

Kelp Perch

Discus Fish

Nile Mouthbrooder

Angelfish

Ring-tailed Pike Cichlid (male)

Sergeant Major

Beaugregory

Clown Anemonefish

Perchlike Fishes

NAME: **Striped Mullet,** *Mugil cephalus*
RANGE: **worldwide, tropical and warm temperate seas**
HABITAT: **open sea, inshore waters, estuaries**
SIZE: **up to 91 cm (35¾ in)**

The striped mullet is one of the gray mullet family, Mugilidae, which contains species that live in salt, brackish and fresh water. Typical of its family in appearance, it has a rounded, heavily scaled body and widely spaced dorsal fins. It feeds on the minute algae and planktonic animals contained in the bottom detritus, by sucking up the detritus, filtering it through its gills and crushing the remaining material in its muscular stomach. A good deal of sand and mud is also taken into the gut.

NAME: **Great Barracuda,** *Sphyraena barracuda*
RANGE: **worldwide, tropical seas except E. Pacific Ocean; best known in Caribbean and W. Atlantic Ocean**
HABITAT: **coastal lagoons, coral reefs; adults farther offshore**
SIZE: **up to 1.8 m (6 ft)**

There are about 18 species of barracuda, found in tropical and subtropical areas of the Atlantic, Indian and Pacific oceans. The great barracuda is characteristic of the family, with its long, slender body, pointed head and jutting jaw, studded with formidable teeth. An aggressive predator, it preys on fish but has been known to attack humans when disturbed or provoked. Barracudas are generally solitary fishes but may gather in groups before spawning.

NAME: **Ballan Wrasse,** *Labrus bergylta*
RANGE: **E. Atlantic Ocean: Norway and Britain, south to N. Africa; Mediterranean Sea**
HABITAT: **rocky coasts**
SIZE: **50–60 cm (19¾–23½ in)**

There are several hundred species of wrasse in the family Labridae, found all over the world in tropical and warm temperate areas. The ballan wrasse is the largest of the European species and has a fairly deep body, a pointed snout and a large dorsal fin. It feeds on mollusks and crustaceans, particularly crabs, which it breaks into with its pointed jaw teeth and then crushes with the strong, broad teeth in its pharynx.

Like many wrasses, it has interesting breeding behavior. After some pre-spawning displays, the pair builds a nest of weeds, bound together with mucus and lodged in a rock crevice. Once the eggs are laid, the male fertilizes them and guards the nest until the eggs hatch.

NAME: **Tautog,** *Tautoga onitis*
RANGE: **W. Atlantic Ocean: Nova Scotia to South Carolina**
HABITAT: **coastal waters, around rocky shores and mussel beds**
SIZE: **up to 91.5 cm (36 in)**

A member of the wrasse family, Labridae, the tautog is a rather dull-colored fish, with a blunt snout and a well-rounded body. Adults feed on a variety of invertebrates, mostly barnacles, mussels, crabs and snails, which they crush with their strong jaws and teeth. Young fishes feed on worms and small crustaceans.

Spawning occurs in the spring and summer, in deep water. The eggs float at the surface and gradually drift inshore as they develop and hatch. The young spend their first few months in shallow waters where there is plenty of seaweed for protection.

NAME: **Hogfish,** *Lachnolaimus maximus*
RANGE: **W. Atlantic Ocean: Bermuda and North Carolina to Brazil; Gulf of Mexico, Caribbean**
HABITAT: **coastal waters, coral reefs**
SIZE: **91 cm (35¾ in)**

A colorful member of the wrasse family, Labridae, the hogfish is identified by its dorsal fin, the first three spines of which are greatly elongated and thickened. The tips of both dorsal and anal fins are pointed. The hogfish's thick lips protrude slightly, and its forehead curves steeply above the mouth. Although coloration is variable in this species, males always tend to be more intense in hue than females. Hogfishes feed on mollusks, crabs and sea urchins.

NAME: **California Sheephead,** *Pimelometopon pulchrum*
RANGE: **Pacific Ocean: Monterey Bay, California, to Gulf of California**
HABITAT: **rocky coasts, around kelp and mussel beds**
SIZE: **up to 91.5 cm (36 in)**

This distinctive wrasse is easily distinguished from the other members of the family Labridae by its coloration and shape. Its body is deep, and it has a heavy, bulbous head; in the breeding season, the male develops a prominent bump on the forehead. Its dorsal fin spines are shorter than the rayed portion of the fin, and the lobes of the dorsal, anal and tail fins are pointed. The sexes differ in coloration: the middle of the male's body is red and the front and back are black or purple, while the female is reddish all over, sometimes with black markings.

The California sheephead feeds on crustaceans and mollusks and is believed to spawn in the summer.

NAME: **Slippery Dick,** *Halichoeres bivittatus*
RANGE: **W. Atlantic Ocean: Bermuda and North Carolina to Brazil; Caribbean**
HABITAT: **coastal waters, coral reefs**
SIZE: **up to 23 cm (9 in)**

The slippery dick is an extremely common inhabitant of coral reefs, where it feeds on many crustaceans, sea urchins, worms and mollusks. The species is characterized by the two black lines running along the sides of the body.

NAME: **Rainbow Parrotfish,** *Scarus guacamaia*
RANGE: **W. Atlantic Ocean: Bermuda and Florida through Caribbean to Argentina**
HABITAT: **coastal waters, coral reefs**
SIZE: **1.2 m (4 ft)**

The brightly colored rainbow parrotfish is one of approximately 68 species in the family Scaridae. One of the largest of North American parrotfishes, it has a robust, heavy body and a large head. Like all of its family, it has strong, beak-like jaws, formed from fused teeth, with which it scrapes algae and coral off reefs to eat. Farther back in the throat, the fish has large grinding teeth, with which it crushes its food.

In common with some other parrotfish species, the rainbow parrotfish sometimes secretes a cocoon of mucus around its body at night. This natural "sleeping bag" protects the fish from predators while it sleeps.

NAME: **Blue Parrotfish,** *Scarus coeruleus*
RANGE: **W. Atlantic Ocean: North Carolina to Brazil, including Gulf of Mexico and Caribbean**
HABITAT: **coral reefs**
SIZE: **1.2 m (4 ft)**

The beautiful blue parrotfish is distinctive in that its lower jaw is far shorter than the upper; older males develop a prominent bump on the snout, which gives them an unusual profile. The blue parrotfish feeds in the same manner as the rest of the family Scaridae, scraping algae and coral off reefs with its beaklike jaws; the food is then broken down for digestion by the grinding teeth, farther back in the throat.

NAME: **Stoplight Parrotfish,** *Sparisoma viride*
RANGE: **Caribbean**
HABITAT: **coral reefs**
SIZE: **25–50 cm (9¾–19¾ in)**

Males of this common parrotfish species are larger than females and differ in coloration: they are bluish-green, while females are red and reddish-brown. These parrotfishes feed on algae and other plant material, which they scrape from rocks and coral with their teeth.

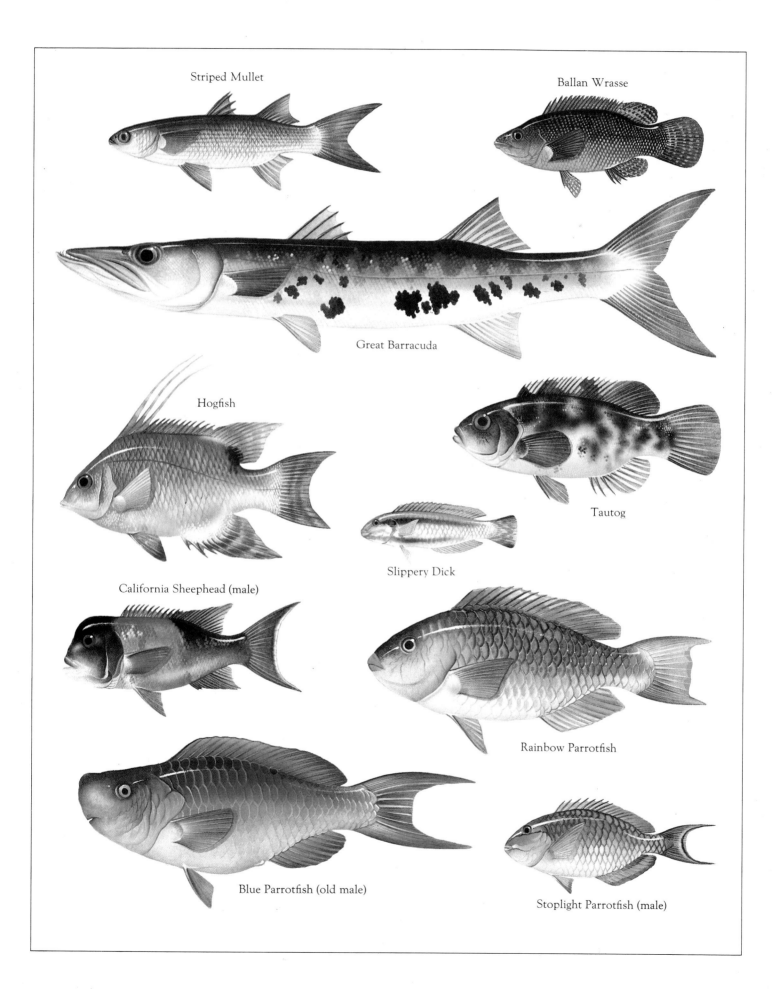

Striped Mullet

Ballan Wrasse

Great Barracuda

Hogfish

Tautog

Slippery Dick

California Sheephead (male)

Rainbow Parrotfish

Blue Parrotfish (old male)

Stoplight Parrotfish (male)

Perchlike Fishes

NAME: **Lesser Weever,** *Echiichthys vipera*
RANGE: **European Atlantic coasts, Britain to N. Africa; Mediterranean Sea**
HABITAT: **shallow, sandy-bottomed waters**
SIZE: **14 cm (5½ in)**

A bottom-living fish, the lesser weever lies half-buried in the sand with only its head visible. If disturbed, it will erect its dorsal fin spines, which contain tissue that produces highly toxic venom; there are more venom-producing spines on the gill covers. These spines can cause extremely painful wounds but are used only in defense and as a warning signal. The lesser weever feeds on small bottom-living crustaceans and fish. It is one of about 6 species in the family Trachinidae, all of which possess venomous spines.

NAME: **Northern Stargazer,** *Astroscopus guttatus*
RANGE: **Atlantic coast of N. America: New York to North Carolina**
HABITAT: **shallow, sandy-bottomed waters**
SIZE: **up to 30.5 cm (12 in)**

The northern stargazer has a robust body and large head, with the mouth directed upward; its eyes, too, are on top of the head, facing upward. This body structure equips the stargazer for its habit of lying partially buried on the seabed with only its eyes and mouth exposed, waiting for prey such as fish and crustaceans. Behind the eyes is a specialized area of electric organs, developed from muscles and capable of producing charges of over 50 volts.

Spawning is believed to take place in spring or early summer, offshore. The young fishes gradually drift inshore to shallower waters, where they settle to the bottom-dwelling life of adults.

NAME: **Antarctic Cod,** *Notothenia coriiceps*
RANGE: **Antarctic coasts**
HABITAT: **coastal waters**
SIZE: **61 cm (24 in)**

The family Nototheniidae, to which the antarctic cod belongs, is the most abundant group in the Antarctic; almost three-quarters of fishes in that region belong to the family. Some members of the family have a specialized protein in their blood, which lowers its freezing point, so that they can live at temperatures as low as −1.9°C (28°F).

The adult antarctic cod has a long, slim, scaled body, with a heavy head, and is generally brownish in color; young fishes, however, are blue and silver at first, becoming reddish as juveniles. This cod is a bottom-dweller and feeds on algae, mollusks, small crustaceans and worms.

NAME: **Icefish,** *Chaenocephalus aceratus*
RANGE: **Antarctic area off South Georgia, South Orkneys, South Shetlands**
HABITAT: **shallow waters to 340 m (1,100 ft)**
SIZE: **60 cm (23½ in)**

The icefish is one of about 16 species in the family Channichthyidae, all found in the antarctic area. They are interesting fishes in that they lack the oxygen-carrying pigment hemoglobin, which is common to all other vertebrate animals. Without red blood cells, their blood appears whitish, almost clear. Oxygen is taken in through the gills in the normal way for fishes but is carried within the body dissolved in the blood plasma. This system is more than adequate, as the cold antarctic waters are rich in oxygen. Furthermore, the icefish requires little oxygen because of its sluggish habits.

An elongate, slender fish, the icefish has a large head, with beaklike jaws. It spends much of its time close to the bottom, feeding on fish and crustaceans.

NAME: **Giant Kelpfish,** *Heterostichus rostratus*
RANGE: **Pacific coast of N. America: British Columbia to Baja California**
HABITAT: **inshore shallow waters, near kelp beds**
SIZE: **up to 61 cm (24 in)**

The giant kelpfish is the largest of the family Clinidae, which contains about 175 species of primarily tropical marine fish. It is distinguished by its elongate body, sharp, pointed head and long-based dorsal and anal fins, but its coloration is extremely variable, according to its surroundings. Fishes living in eelgrass are bright green, others are dark green, brown, orange, yellow or reddish; their coloration always blends with the aquatic vegetation or other background of their habitat.

NAME: **Shanny,** *Lipophrys pholis*
RANGE: **N. European coasts: S. Norway and Scotland, south to Portugal and Madeira**
HABITAT: **rocky shores, rock pools**
SIZE: **up to 18 cm (7 in)**

The combtooth blenny family, Blenniidae, to which the shanny belongs, contains about 276 species of mostly marine shorefish. The shanny is typical of the family, with its scaleless skin, rounded head and rows of fine, sharp teeth — these teeth are the origin of the family's common name. The shanny's diet is wide-ranging, including algae, barnacles, crustaceans and fish.

The eggs are laid in clusters under a rock or in a crevice and are guarded by the male until they hatch.

NAME: **Redlip Blenny,** *Ophioblennius atlanticus*
RANGE: **W. Atlantic Ocean: North Carolina to Bermuda and south to coast of Brazil; Gulf of Mexico, Caribbean**
HABITAT: **rocky- or coral-bottomed waters**
SIZE: **12 cm (4¾ in)**

Characterized by its steep, rounded snout bearing tufts and tentacles, red lips and red-edged dorsal fin, the redlip blenny is a common fish in its range. It is a member of the combtooth blenny family, Blenniidae, and is typical of the family in its bottom-living, secretive habits. It feeds on small invertebrates.

The eggs are laid amid coral or under rocks and are guarded by the male. The young fishes live in surface waters, farther offshore than adults.

NAME: **Wrymouth,** *Cryptacanthodes maculatus*
RANGE: **W. Atlantic Ocean: Labrador to New Jersey**
HABITAT: **muddy seabed**
SIZE: **90 cm (35½ in)**

A bottom-living fish, the wrymouth lives buried in mud, sometimes making a complex system of tunnels. It feeds on fish, crustaceans and mollusks. Rather eel-like in appearance, the wrymouth has an elongate, scaleless body, with dorsal and anal fins continuous with the tail fin but no pelvic fins. Its head is flat-topped, with the eyes set high, and its mouth slants obliquely, the lower jaw extending beyond the upper.

Also known as the ghostfish, the wrymouth is one of the 4 species in the family Cryptacanthodidae.

NAME: **Rock Gunnel,** *Pholis gunnellus*
RANGE: **W. Atlantic Ocean: Labrador to Massachusetts; E. Atlantic: N. coast of France, north to Barents Sea; coasts of Iceland and S. Greenland**
HABITAT: **rocky shores, intertidal pools, sometimes in deeper waters**
SIZE: **25 cm (9¾ in)**

This widely distributed fish has a slender, elongate body, brownish in color, and a distinctive row of white-edged black spots along the bottom of its long-based dorsal fin. It is a member of the family Pholidae, which contains about 13 species of fish found in the cooler waters of the North Pacific and Atlantic. Small crustaceans, worms and mollusks are its main foods, and since the rock gunnel is so abundant near the shore, it is itself an important item of diet for many seabirds.

Spawning takes place in winter, and the eggs are laid in clusters among stones near the shore. The parents guard the eggs until they hatch.

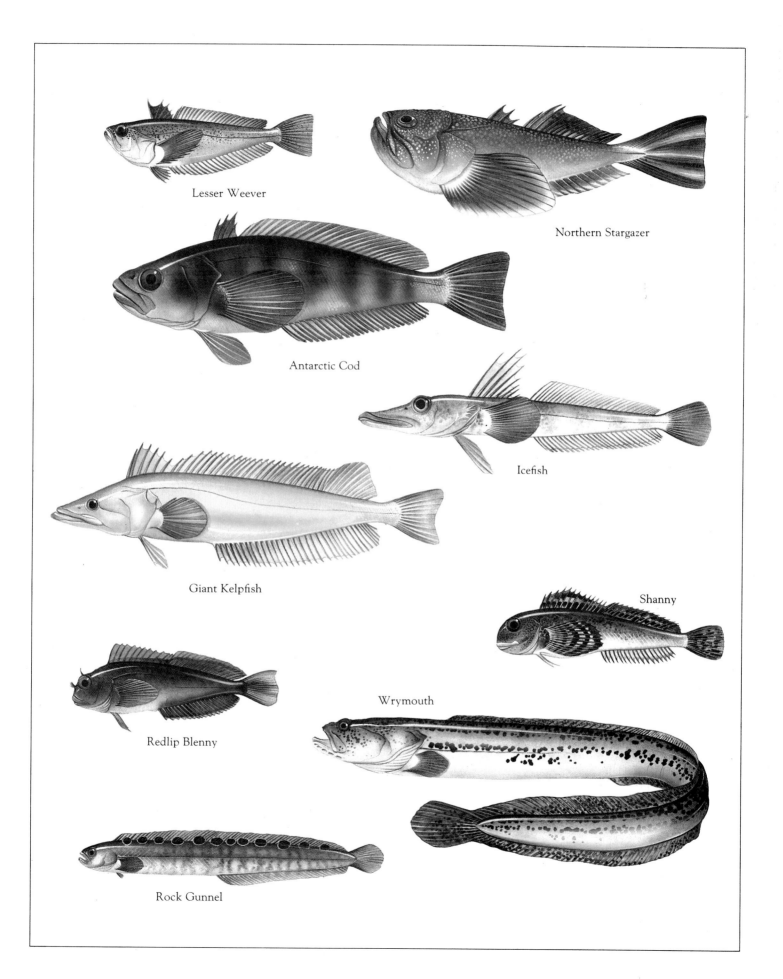

Lesser Weever

Northern Stargazer

Antarctic Cod

Icefish

Giant Kelpfish

Shanny

Redlip Blenny

Wrymouth

Rock Gunnel

Perchlike Fishes

NAME: **Sand Eel/Sand Lance,** *Ammodytes tobianus*
RANGE: **E. Atlantic Ocean: Iceland and Norway to S. Portugal and Spain**
HABITAT: **inshore waters to depths of about 30 m (100 ft)**
SIZE: **20 cm (7¾ in)**

Sand eels are so called because of their habit of burrowing extremely rapidly into clean, sandy bottoms, but they also swim in shoals near the surface. There are about 12 species in the sand eel family, Ammodytidae, all of which are thin, elongate fishes, with long dorsal and anal fins. Typically, the head is pointed, with a protruding lower jaw. The sand eel feeds on plankton and is itself an important food fish for many larger fishes.

Some sand eels spawn in autumn, others in spring, but all shed their eggs on the seabed, where they adhere to the sand.

NAME: **Fat Sleeper,** *Dormitator maculatus*
RANGE: **W. Atlantic Ocean: Bahamas and North Carolina to Gulf of Mexico and Brazil**
HABITAT: **muddy-bottomed shores, brackish pools, river mouths**
SIZE: **46 cm (18 in)**

The fat sleeper and the other species of sleeper are sometimes included in the goby family; otherwise they are placed in a separate family, Eleotridae. The main difference between the two groups is that sleepers have separate pelvic fins, while gobies generally have united pelvics, which form a suckerlike disk. A small, but thickset, little fish, with a large, rounded head, the fat sleeper has the habit of resting motionless on the seabed for long periods, hence the common name.

NAME: **Atlantic Wolffish,** *Anarhichas lupus*
RANGE: **W. Atlantic Ocean: Labrador to Cape Cod, sometimes New Jersey; across to E. Atlantic: Iceland and Spitsbergen to N. France**
HABITAT: **from shallow waters down to 300 m (980 ft)**
SIZE: **1–1.2 m (3¼–4 ft)**

One of about 6 species in the marine family Anarhichadidae, the Atlantic wolffish is characteristic of its family, with its huge head, fanglike teeth and long dorsal and anal fins. It feeds on mollusks, such as clams and mussels, and on crustaceans, all of which it breaks open with its sharp fangs and crushes with the broader teeth farther back in its mouth.

Spawning takes place in winter. The sticky-surfaced eggs are shed in clumps on the seabed, where they may adhere to stones or other debris.

NAME: **Dwarf Goby,** *Pandaka pygmaea*
RANGE: **Philippines**
HABITAT: **lakes, streams**
SIZE: **11 mm (4/10 in)**

The dwarf goby is one of the smallest fishes in the world and is perhaps the smallest vertebrate animal; mature adults as tiny as 6 mm (2/10 in) long have been found. The dwarf goby's head is scaleless, but its slender body is scaled and marked with dark spots.

NAME: **Rock Goby,** *Gobius paganellus*
RANGE: **N. Atlantic Ocean: Britain to N. Africa; Mediterranean coasts**
HABITAT: **rocky shores, coastal pools**
SIZE: **12 cm (4¾ in)**

The goby family, Gobiidae, is one of the largest marine families, with many species also entering fresh water. The rock goby is one of the larger species, but is typical, with its big, blunt head, slender body and rounded tail fin. Its pelvic fins are fused to form a sucking disk, with which it attaches itself to rocks or other surfaces. The goby feeds on crustaceans and other small invertebrates and young fish.

Spawning occurs in the spring and summer. The eggs are shed onto the roof of a hole in the rocks, where they are guarded by the male until they hatch.

NAME: **Blue Tang,** *Acanthurus coeruleus*
RANGE: **W. Atlantic Ocean: New York and Bermuda, south to Caribbean and Brazil**
HABITAT: **coastal waters, coral reefs**
SIZE: **30.5 cm (12 in)**

The brilliantly colored blue tang is one of the 75 or so species in the surgeonfish family, Acanthuridae. The fishes are so called because of the extremely sharp, movable spines on each side of the tail that are thought to resemble a surgeon's scalpels. Normally the spines lie flat in a groove, but if the fish is disturbed or alarmed, they are erected and can inflict serious wounds on an enemy as the tail is lashed to and fro. The blue tang uses these spines only for defensive purposes, since it feeds entirely on algae, which it removes from rocks with its sharp-edged teeth.

Although fairly typical of its family in appearance, the blue tang has a particularly deep body and steep profile. Its coloration changes as it matures: young fishes are bright yellow, with blue spots near the eyes; they then become blue over much of the front of the body, with a yellow tail, while adults are a deep, rich blue all over, with narrow, dark-blue lines running the length of the body.

NAME: **Moorish Idol,** *Zanclus cornutus*
RANGE: **Indian and Pacific Oceans: E. Africa to Hawaiian Islands**
HABITAT: **shallow waters, coral reefs**
SIZE: **18 cm (7 in)**

The spectacular moorish idol is an unmistakable fish, with its extremely bold coloration and projecting snout. Its body is deep and compressed, and its dorsal and anal fins are pointed and swept back, making the fish appear deeper than it is long. The dorsal fin has a long, filamentous extension. Adults develop protuberances over the eyes that enlarge with age.

Although a member of the surgeonfish family, Acanthuridae, the moorish idol lacks the formidable tail spines of its relatives. The young fish, however, has a sharp spine at each corner of the mouth; these spines drop off as the fish matures. Indeed, young and adults appear so different that they were originally thought to be separate species.

NAME: **Striped-face Unicornfish,** *Naso lituratus*
RANGE: **Indian and Pacific Oceans: E. Africa to Australia and Hawaiian Islands**
HABITAT: **coastal waters, coral reefs**
SIZE: **41 cm (16 in)**

The striped-face unicornfish is a member of the surgeonfish family, but it has fixed, forward-pointing spines, not erectile spines, on each side of its tail. Unlike others of its genus, this species does not develop a horn on its forehead as it matures. Males do, however, have long, distinctive streamers on the lobes of the tail fin.

Unicornfishes swim in small schools and graze on algae and coral.

NAME: **Blue-lined Spinefoot,** *Siganus virgatus*
RANGE: **Indian and Pacific Oceans: India and Sri Lanka to Indonesia and N. Australia, north to Philippines, China and Japan**
HABITAT: **inshore waters, edges of coral reefs**
SIZE: **25.5 cm (10 in)**

The blue-lined spinefoot is one of 10 or so species in the rabbitfish, or spinefoot, family, Siganidae, which is closely related to the surgeonfishes. Spinefoots possess many strong, sharp spines capable of inflicting serious wounds on an enemy: two on each pelvic fin, seven on the anal fin, and a forward-pointing spine in front of the spiny dorsal fin. There are venom glands on these spines.

Like all members of its family, this species has a blunt, rounded head and strong jaws. It grazes on algae on reefs and rocks.

Atlantic Wolffish

Sand Eel

Fat Sleeper

Dwarf Goby

Rock Goby

Moorish Idol

Blue Tang (young fish)

Blue-lined Spinefoot

Striped-face Unicornfish (male)

Perchlike Fishes

NAME: Atlantic Cutlassfish, *Trichiurus lepturus*
RANGE: Atlantic Ocean: tropical and temperate waters, including Gulf of Mexico and Caribbean; Mediterranean Sea
HABITAT: surface waters of open sea
SIZE: 1.5 m (5 ft)

A striking fish, with its elongate, ribbon-like body, the Atlantic cutlassfish has a pointed head and large jaws, armed with formidable teeth. Its dorsal fin runs the length of its silvery body to the end of the tapering tail. A voracious predator, it feeds on fish and squid. It is a member of the family Trichiuridae, which contains about 17 species.

NAME: Atlantic Mackerel, *Scomber scombrus*
RANGE: W. Atlantic Ocean: Gulf of St. Lawrence to North Carolina; E. Atlantic: Iceland, Scandinavia, south to N. Africa; Mediterranean Sea
HABITAT: offshore surface waters
SIZE: 41–66 cm (16–26 in)

The abundant mackerel has a slender, but well-rounded, body, marked with irregular black lines. The adults' diet includes crustaceans and small schooling fish, while young fishes feed on planktonic crustaceans and fish larvae. Mackerel seem to make regular seasonal movements, going north, as well as farther inshore, in spring and summer and south again in winter. In winter, the fishes group in deep, but relatively warm, waters along the edge of the continental shelf, where they hardly move and eat little. Mackerel belong to the family Scombridae, which contains about 45 species, many of which are important food fishes.

Spawning takes place in summer. A medium-sized female may produce as many as 450,000 eggs. The eggs float until they hatch, about 4 days after being laid.

NAME: Skipjack Tuna, *Euthynnus pelamis*
RANGE: worldwide in tropical seas, seasonally in temperate areas
HABITAT: offshore surface waters
SIZE: 1 m (3¼ ft)

A member of the family Scombridae, the skipjack has the streamlined body shape typical of the fast-swimming tunas. Dark stripes on the lower half of its body are distinguishing characteristics. An extremely abundant fish, it swims in huge schools, sometimes comprising as many as 50,000 fishes, and is one of the most important commercial fishes, particularly in the Pacific. Skipjacks feed on fish and invertebrates such as squid and crustaceans.

NAME: Yellowfin Tuna, *Thunnus albacares*
RANGE: worldwide, tropical and warm temperate seas
HABITAT: offshore surface waters, inshore waters
SIZE: up to 2 m (6½ ft)

Distinguished by its long pectoral fins, the small, yellow finlets behind the dorsal and anal fins and the yellow markings along its sides, the yellowfin tuna has the typical, spindle-shaped body of the tunas. Large yellowfins have greatly extended anal and second dorsal fins, another point of identification. They feed on fish, crustaceans and squid, and like most members of the Scombridae family, they make seasonal migrations.

Spawning takes place at any time of year in tropical waters and in late spring and summer elsewhere. Females are believed to produce at least two batches of over a million eggs each in a year.

NAME: Wahoo, *Acanthocybium solanderi*
RANGE: worldwide in tropical seas
HABITAT: open sea
SIZE: up to 2 m (6½ ft)

Unlike most other members of the family Scombridae, the wahoo is not a schooling fish and usually occurs alone or in small groups. Its body is more elongate and slender than with most tunas, and it has a long, narrow snout, equipped with many strong teeth. It feeds on a wide range of fish and squid and is capable of bursts of extremely high-speed swimming when in pursuit of prey — reputedly up to 66 km/h (41 mph).

Since it is not an abundant species, the wahoo is not fished commercially but is popular with anglers.

NAME: Sailfish, *Istiophorus platypterus*
RANGE: worldwide, tropical and warm temperate seas
HABITAT: surface waters, open sea and sometimes closer to shore
SIZE: 3.6 m (12 ft)

The high, sail-like dorsal fin is the outstanding characteristic of the sailfish, but it also has elongate jaws, which are rounded, not flattened like those of the swordfish. It is one of the 10 species in the family Istiophoridae, all of which are spectacular, fast-swimming fishes. The sailfish has a varied diet and seems to eat almost any available type of fish and squid. It makes regular seasonal migrations, moving from cooler to more tropical waters in winter.

Sailfishes spawn in open sea, each female shedding several million eggs, which float in surface waters until they hatch. Those few that survive grow extremely quickly.

NAME: Blue Marlin, *Makaira nigricans*
RANGE: worldwide, tropical and warm temperate seas
HABITAT: offshore waters, open sea
SIZE: 3–4.6 m (10–15 ft)

An extremely impressive fish, the blue marlin weighs at least 180 kg (400 lb) on average and can be more than twice as heavy. It has the elongate, rounded snout common to all members of the family Istiophoridae, with which it is thought to stun prey such as schooling fishes and squid.

Blue marlins are among the fastest of all fishes and have perfectly streamlined bodies and the high, crescent-shaped tails characteristic of the high-speed species. They make regular seasonal migrations, moving toward the equator in winter and away again in summer.

NAME: Striped Marlin, *Tetrapturus audax*
RANGE: Indian and Pacific Oceans: warm temperate waters, less common in tropical waters
HABITAT: open sea, inshore waters
SIZE: 3 m (10 ft)

A steely-blue fish, marked with blue or white vertical bars, the striped marlin is distinguished from the blue marlin by its higher dorsal fin. Otherwise it is similar in appearance, with its elongate, beaklike snout and streamlined body. It feeds on fish and occasionally squid, both surface and deepwater species. Like all marlins, it is a member of the family Istiophoridae.

NAME: Swordfish, *Xiphias gladius*
RANGE: worldwide, temperate and tropical seas
HABITAT: open sea, surface and deep waters
SIZE: 2–4.9 m (6½–16 ft)

The huge and spectacular swordfish is the only member of the family Xiphiidae. It has a greatly elongated, flattened snout, and its dorsal fin is sickle-shaped and placed farther back from the head than that of the similar sailfish. Swordfishes can also be distinguished from marlins and sailfishes by their flattened bills and lack of pelvic fins. Adult swordfishes are generally solitary and do not form schools, except in the spawning season. They are fast, active predators and feed on a variety of small fish, as well as squid. The exact function of the sword is not clear; it may be used to strike at schooling fishes, or it may be simply a result of body streamlining.

In the northern hemisphere, swordfishes make seasonal migrations, in winter moving south and into deeper waters. The elongated snout is not present in young fishes but develops gradually, as they mature.

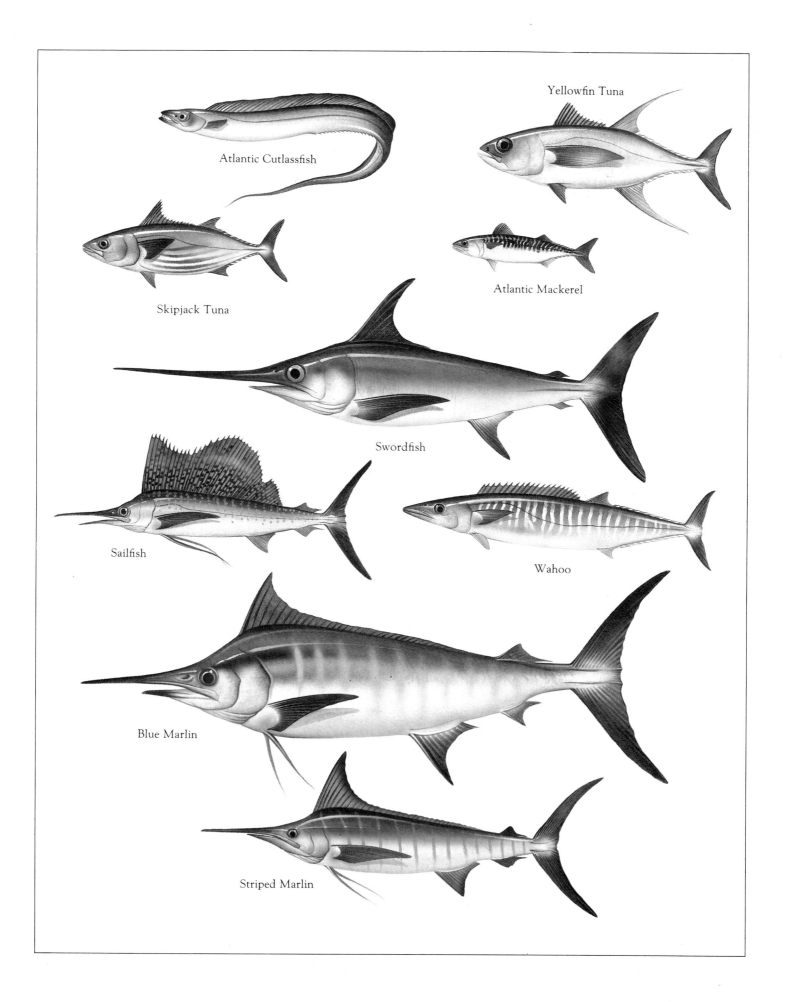

Atlantic Cutlassfish

Yellowfin Tuna

Skipjack Tuna

Atlantic Mackerel

Swordfish

Sailfish

Wahoo

Blue Marlin

Striped Marlin

Perchlike Fishes

NAME: **Man-of-war Fish,** *Nomeus gronovii*
RANGE: **tropical areas of Indian and Pacific Oceans; tropical W. Atlantic Ocean and Caribbean**
HABITAT: **lives in association with the Portuguese man-of-war jellyfish**
SIZE: **22 cm (8½ in)**

Best known for its habit of living among the long, stinging tentacles of the Portuguese man-of-war, *Physalia physalis*, this little fish seems to be immune to the *Physalia*'s stinging cells or may even inhibit their operation. The jellyfish is usually thought to be unaffected by the fish's presence, but the details of the relationship are poorly known, and it is possible that the fish removes debris from its host's body.

The man-of-war fish is one of about 15 species in the family Nomeidae.

NAME: **Butterfish,** *Peprilus triacanthus*
RANGE: **W. Atlantic Ocean: Gulf of St. Lawrence to S. Florida**
HABITAT: **coastal waters, bays, estuaries**
SIZE: **30.5 cm (12 in)**

The attractively colored butterfish has a deep, but laterally compressed, body, a deeply forked tail and long dorsal and anal fins; adults have no pelvic fins. It feeds on crustaceans, squid and small fish. Butterfishes swim in small schools, and some appear to move northward in summer, returning south, but farther offshore, in winter. They belong to the family Stromateidae, which contains about 13 species of marine fish.

NAME: **Climbing Perch,** *Anabas testudineus*
RANGE: **India, Sri Lanka, S.E. Asia, Indonesia, Philippines, S. China**
HABITAT: **rivers, canals, ditches, ponds**
SIZE: **25.5 cm (10 in)**

The climbing perch often inhabits stagnant, poorly oxygenated water, and this fact, combined with its small gills, means that it must obtain some of its oxygen from the air. In each gill chamber is a labyrinthine organ, well supplied with blood vessels. Air taken in through the mouth passes through this auxiliary breathing organ, where oxygen is absorbed. The other unusual feature of this fish is its astonishing capacity for movement on land, made feasible by its capacity for breathing air. Using its tail for leverage and its pectoral fins and spiny gill covers as props, it will haul itself considerable distances between bodies of water, usually because its previous home has dried up. It is thought to feed on insects and small crustaceans.

A member of the family Anabantidae, which contains about 40 species, the climbing perch is an important food fish in much of its range.

NAME: **Paradisefish,** *Macropodus opercularis*
RANGE: **China, S.E. Asia**
HABITAT: **ditches, rice fields**
SIZE: **9 cm (3½ in)**

The paradisefish normally lives in poorly oxygenated water but, like the other members of the family Belontiidae, has auxiliary breathing organs in each gill chamber for extracting oxygen from the air. These operate in a similar manner to those of the climbing perch. An attractive, colorful little fish, it has greatly extended fins, those of the male being particularly long.

Its breeding habits are common to many of its family: the male makes a floating nest by blowing bubbles of air and mucus and then attracts a female to his nest. She sheds her eggs, which he fertilizes and transfers to the nest by spitting them into the bubbles, where they remain until they hatch.

NAME: **Siamese Fightingfish,** *Betta splendens*
RANGE: **Thailand**
HABITAT: **ponds, ditches, slow rivers**
SIZE: **6 cm (2¼ in)**

The Siamese fightingfish has long been bred in captivity, and many forms with extremely long fins, particularly in the male, have been developed. Male fishes may be green, blue or red, but females are usually yellowish-brown. In the wild, males are brown or green. Well known for their aggressive nature, male fightingfish are kept in captivity to take part in staged fights; keen observers bet on the outcome. In natural conditions, however, the fishes fight for dominance or to maintain territory, but much of the contest takes the form of ritualized threat displays, rather than actual combat. The fishes adopt postures, extending their fins and raising their gill covers, one of them usually submitting before an actual fight becomes necessary.

Like many members of the Belontiidae family, to which it belongs, the Siamese fightingfish often lives in stagnant, oxygen-poor water. It is able to take in air at the surface, however, using auxiliary breathing organs within its gill chambers. Mosquito larvae, as well as other aquatic insects, are the main diet of the Siamese fightingfishes, which are consequently extremely important as controllers of these insect pests.

In the breeding season, the male fish selects a suitable nest site and blows a bubble nest from air and mucus, which both protects the eggs and keeps them at the well-oxygenated water surface. As the eggs are shed, they are fertilized by the male, who spits them into the nest. The male guards the nest and replaces the bubbles if necessary.

NAME: **Gourami,** *Osphronemus goramy*
RANGE: **probably Indonesia; introduced in China, S.E. Asia, India, Sri Lanka, Philippines**
HABITAT: **ponds, swamps, streams**
SIZE: **61 cm (24 in)**

A large, heavy-bodied fish, with a greatly extended pelvic fin ray, the gourami is the only species in its family, Osphronemidae. It is related to the Siamese fightingfish family and, like them, has auxiliary breathing organs in its gill chambers, which allow it to take in air at the surface. It often lives in oxygen-poor waters.

The male gourami makes a bubble nest into which the eggs are blown. He guards the eggs and then the developing larvae.

NAME: **Snakehead,** *Ophicephalus striatus*
RANGE: **India, Sri Lanka, S.E. Asia, China, Philippines, Indonesia**
HABITAT: **lakes, rivers, canals, ditches, swamps**
SIZE: **1 m (3¼ ft)**

An elongate fish, with long dorsal and anal fins, the snakehead is one of about 10 species in the family Channidae. It generally lives in oxygen-poor waters but has accessory organs in its gill chambers with which it can utilize oxygen from the air. It can live for prolonged periods out of water and, as long as its skin remains moist, can survive dry spells by burrowing into mud.

Before spawning, parents clear a surface area of vegetation, and the eggs float there for 3 days, guarded by the male until they hatch.

NAME: **Spiny Eel,** *Mastacembelus armatus*
RANGE: **India, Sri Lanka, S.E. Asia, China, Sumatra, Java, Borneo**
HABITAT: **swamps, rivers, lakes**
SIZE: **75 cm (29½ in)**

A slender, eel-like fish, the spiny eel is identified by the row of sharp, individual spines preceding its dorsal fin. It has no pelvic fins, and the dorsal and anal fins are set right back, near the tail. The head is narrow and pointed, and the upper part of the snout extends into a fleshy appendage. The spiny eel usually lives in well-vegetated water and feeds on insects and crustaceans; large adults also eat fish.

The spiny eel is one of about 50 species in the family Mastacembelidae.

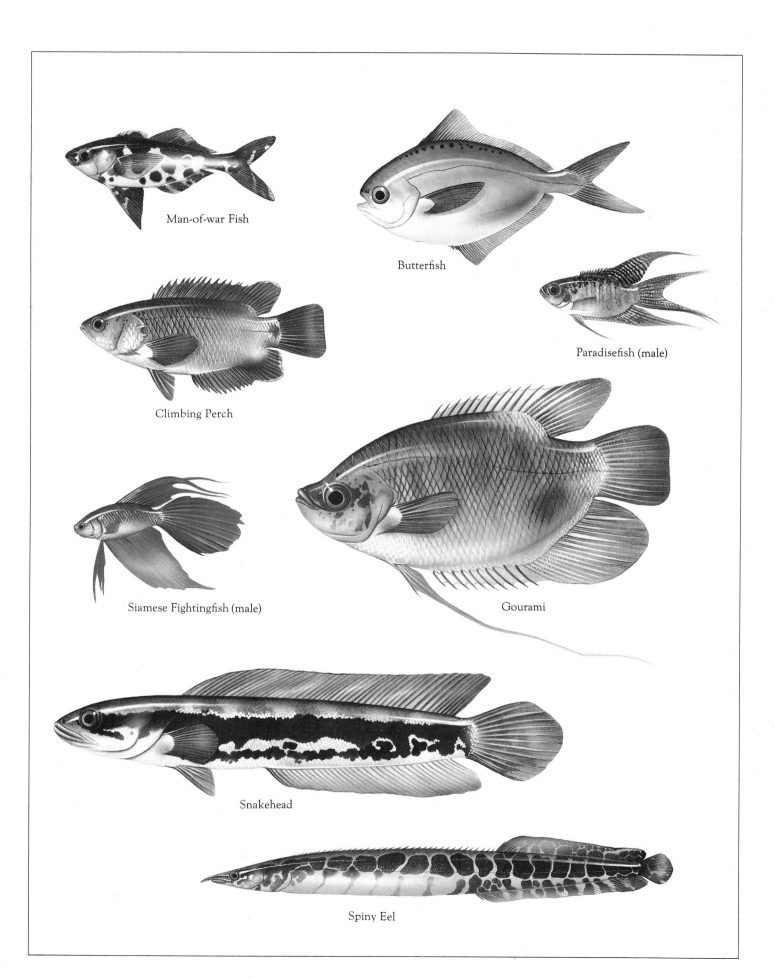

Man-of-war Fish

Butterfish

Paradisefish (male)

Climbing Perch

Siamese Fightingfish (male)

Gourami

Snakehead

Spiny Eel

Gobiesociform Fishes, Flatfishes

GOBIESOCIFORMES

This order contains about 144 species of mostly marine fishes. Typically these fishes are scaleless and live on the bottom in shallow water. The largest of the 3 families in the order, with about 100 species, is the Gobiesocidae, or clingfish family. There are 2 smaller groups: the Callionymidae, or dragonet family, with about 40 species, and the Draconettidae, with 4.

NAME: Shore Clingfish, *Lepadogaster lepadogaster*
RANGE: N. Atlantic Ocean: Scotland to N. Africa; W. Mediterranean coasts
HABITAT: rocky shores, between tide marks
SIZE: 6.5 cm (2½ in)

A small, scaleless fish, with low fins lacking spiny rays, the shore clingfish is fairly typical of its family. On its underside is a strong sucking disk, formed partly from its pelvic fins, with which it can cling to rocks or other surfaces. Its snout is elongate and beaklike and topped with a fringed flap.

Shore clingfishes spawn in summer, attaching their eggs to the underside of a rock, where they are guarded by one of the parents.

NAME: *Diademichthys lineatus*
RANGE: Indian and Pacific Oceans: Mauritius to New Caledonia, north to Philippines
HABITAT: among sea urchin spines
SIZE: 5 cm (2 in)

This extremely slender, long-snouted clingfish lives in association with the sea urchin *Diadema savignyi*, and its body shape is a perfect adaptation for its habit of hanging, head downward, among the urchin's spines. Obviously it gains protection from predators in this prickly refuge, but it also feeds on the tiny tube feet of the urchin.

NAME: Northern Clingfish, *Gobiesox maeandricus*
RANGE: Pacific Ocean: British Columbia to S. California
HABITAT: coastal waters between tide marks
SIZE: 15 cm (6 in)

One of the most common of the Pacific Coast clingfishes, the northern clingfish is identified by its smooth body and broad head. Its dorsal and anal fins are low and set back near the tail. Like all clingfishes, its pelvic fins are modified to form part of a sucking disk on its belly, with which it clings to rocks or other surfaces in the turbulent intertidal zone. It feeds on mollusks and crustaceans.

NAME: Dragonet, *Callionymus lyra*
RANGE: E. Atlantic Ocean: Iceland, Norway, south to N. Africa and Mediterranean Sea
HABITAT: shallow coastal waters and to depths of 200 m (650 ft)
SIZE: 30 cm (11¾ in)

The largest of the European dragonets, the male of this species is particularly striking, with his blue and yellow dorsal fin and extended rays. Females are smaller, lack the fin extensions and are brownish in color. Like all dragonets, this fish has a rather flattened body and large head, with small gill apertures near the top of the head, in keeping with its habit of lying, often half-buried, in sand on the seabed. Bottom-dwelling crustaceans and worms are its main foods.

Dragonets spawn in the spring or summer, depending on the area, and the males perform complex courtship displays, posturing with their decorative fins. The eggs are shed in surface waters, where they float until they hatch.

NAME: Mandarinfish, *Synchiropus splendidus*
RANGE: coasts of Philippines, Queensland and N. Australia
HABITAT: inshore waters, coral reefs
SIZE: 7.5 cm (3 in)

An extremely striking little fish, the mandarinfish has irregular red markings on its greenish-blue body and on its fins; its pectoral fins are bright blue. Its body is rather stouter than that of other dragonets, and it has a bulbous head. The first spine of the dorsal fin is greatly extended. Although it is a popular aquarium fish, little is known of its life in the wild other than that it lives on the seabed among rocks or coral.

PLEURONECTIFORMES:
Flatfish Order

This distinctive group contains 6 families and about 520 species, all but 3 of which are marine. The typical flatfish has a body that is greatly compressed, more rounded on the eyed side than on the blind side, and it spends much of its life lying on the seabed. Young flatfishes swim normally and are as symmetrical as other fishes, but as they develop, the eye on the side destined to be the underside migrates so that both eyes are on the upper surface. From then on, the fishes lie and swim with the eyed side uppermost. Bone structure, nerves and muscles undergo complex modifications to achieve this change.

All flatfishes are bottom-feeding predators, but some of the larger species also move into mid-waters to find prey.

NAME: Adalah, *Psettodes erumei*
RANGE: Red Sea, Indian Ocean from E. Africa to N. Australia, into W. Pacific Ocean
HABITAT: shallow waters down to 90 m (300 ft)
SIZE: up to 61 cm (24 in)

The adalah is one of the 2 species in the most primitive flatfish family, Psettodidae. It is thicker bodied and less dramatically compressed than other flatfishes, and the migrated eye is on the edge of the head, rather than right over on the top side. Some individuals have eyes on the left, some on the right. The adalah and its fellow species, *P. belcheri*, also differ in that they have spiny rays in front of the dorsal fins. These fishes live on the seabed but also swim in mid-waters.

NAME: Turbot, *Scophthalmus maximus*
RANGE: E. Atlantic Ocean: Scandinavia and Britain, south to N. Africa; Mediterranean Sea
HABITAT: shallow inshore waters to depths of 80 m (260 ft)
SIZE: 1 m (3¼ ft)

The turbot is an extremely broad flatfish, with a large head and mouth; the female is bigger than the male. Its scaleless body varies in coloration but is usually brownish, with dark speckles that camouflage it on the seabed. The right eye is generally the one to migrate, so turbots have both eyes on the left side. Adults are active predators, feeding largely on fish. Young turbots feed also on crustaceans.

Spawning takes place in spring or summer, and females produce as many as 10 million eggs, comparatively few of which reach adulthood. Eggs and larvae float in surface waters while they develop, but by the time the young fish is 2.5 cm (1 in) long, it has adopted the adult body form and started its bottom-dwelling life. Turbot is one of the finest and most commercially valuable of all marine food fishes.

NAME: Windowpane, *Scophthalmus aquosus*
RANGE: W. Atlantic Ocean: Gulf of St. Lawrence to South Carolina
HABITAT: coastal waters to depths of about 70 m (230 ft)
SIZE: 46 cm (18 in)

The windowpane is an extremely thin-bodied flatfish, white on the underside and brown with dark spots on the upper. The right eye is generally the one to migrate, so most individuals have both eyes on the left side. Young fishes feed on crustaceans, but adults normally eat fish. Although edible, this species is too thin bodied to be of commercial value.

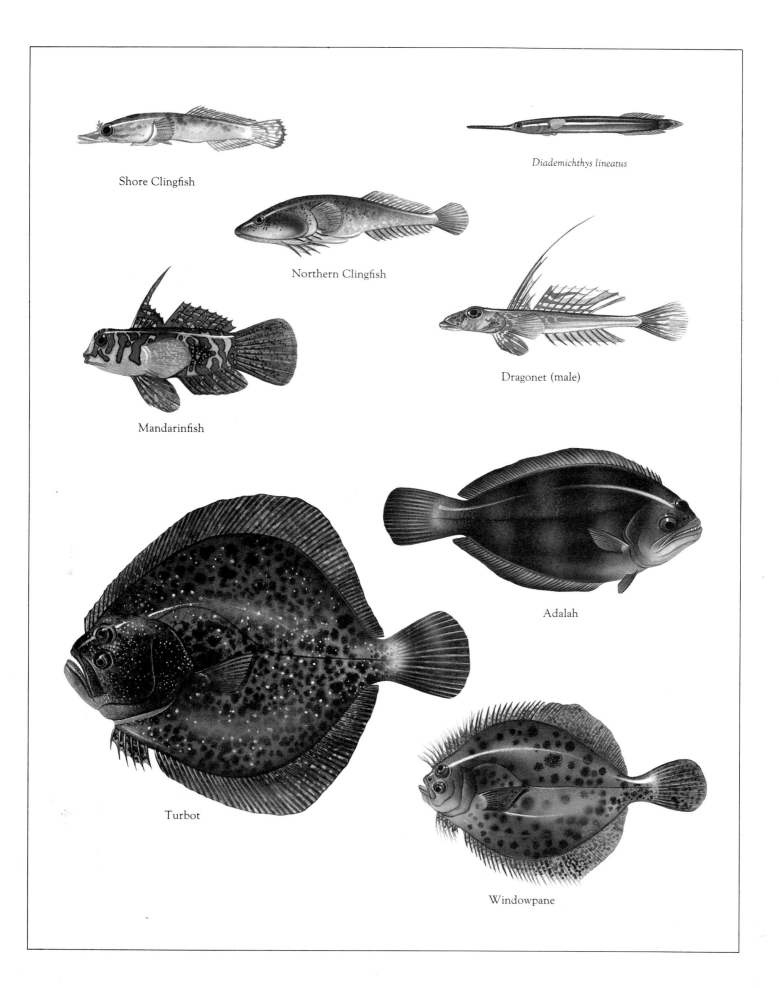

Shore Clingfish

Diademichthys lineatus

Northern Clingfish

Dragonet (male)

Mandarinfish

Adalah

Turbot

Windowpane

Flatfishes

NAME: Peacock Flounder, *Bothus lunatus*
RANGE: W. Atlantic Ocean: Bermuda and Florida through Gulf of Mexico and Caribbean to Brazil
HABITAT: shallow coastal waters
SIZE: 46 cm (18 in)

An attractive fish, with scattered blue markings, the peacock flounder is one of the family of lefteye flounders, so called because both eyes are generally on the left side of the head. The eyes of males are more widely separated than those of females. Another characteristic feature is the dorsal fin, which begins well forward in front of the eyes. Even though it is a fairly common fish, the peacock flounder is rarely seen, spending much of its life partially buried in sand on the seabed.

NAME: Summer Flounder, *Paralichthys dentatus*
RANGE: W. Atlantic Ocean: Maine to South Carolina
HABITAT: coastal waters, bays, harbors; farther offshore in winter
SIZE: up to 1 m (3¼ ft)

The summer flounder is a slender, active flatfish, with both eyes normally on the left side of its head. It feeds on crustaceans, mollusks and fish and will pursue prey in mid-waters and even to the surface. However, despite the fact that it is a relatively fast swimmer, much of its life is spent lying half-buried on the seabed. Its coloration varies according to the type of bottom it is lying on, but it is generally grayish-brown, with dark spots. In summer, it lives in shallow waters close to the shore, moving farther offshore to deeper waters in the winter.

Spawning takes place between late autumn and early spring, depending on the latitude. The eggs are thought to float in surface waters, and the young fishes drift inshore, where they live in shallow water while they develop.

NAME: California Halibut, *Paralichthys californicus*
RANGE: Pacific Ocean: coast of California, sometimes as far north as Oregon
HABITAT: sandy-bottomed coastal waters
SIZE: 1.5 m (5 ft)

The California halibut is a member of the lefteye flounder family, but perhaps as much as half the population have both eyes on the right side. It feeds on fish, particularly anchovies, and has a large mouth and strong teeth. The halibut, in turn, is eaten by rays, sea lions and porpoises and is also an important commercial food fish for man.

Spawning occurs in spring and early summer, and the growth rate of the young is fairly slow.

NAME: Atlantic Halibut, *Hippoglossus hippoglossus*
RANGE: N. Atlantic Ocean: New Jersey, north to Greenland, Iceland and Barents Sea, south to English Channel
HABITAT: sandy-, gravel- and rocky-bottomed waters at 100–1,500 m (330–5,000 ft)
SIZE: 2–2.4 m (6½–8 ft)

One of the largest of all flatfishes, the Atlantic halibut is identified by its size, its relatively elongate, yet thickset, body and its slightly concave tail. It may attain a top weight of 316 kg (700 lb), although fishes of such size are probably rare today. Its mouth and teeth are large, and both eyes are on the right side in almost all individuals. Females are generally larger than males and tend to live longer. Despite its size, the halibut is an active and voracious predator and pursues prey in mid-waters, rather than remaining confined to the seabed. Fish are the main food of adults, but young halibuts also feed on crustaceans.

Spawning occurs in winter and spring, each female shedding as many as 2 million eggs. The eggs drift near the surface of deep water until they hatch after 9 to 16 days. Their growth rate is slow, and halibut are not sexually mature until they are 10 to 14 years of age. Adults migrate northward after spawning.

The Atlantic halibut has long been an important commercial species, but its slow growth rate and late maturity make the population extremely vulnerable to overfishing. Its numbers are now greatly reduced.

NAME: Starry Flounder, *Platichthys stellatus*
RANGE: N. Pacific Ocean: California to Alaska and Bering Sea, south to Japan and Korea
HABITAT: coastal waters, bays, estuaries; also deeper waters down to 275 m (900 ft)
SIZE: 91.5 cm (36 in)

Identified by the distinctive pattern of dark and light bars on the fins, the starry flounder has a dark-brown body on the eyed side, scattered with sharp spines. Although a member of the righteye flounder family, Pleuronectidae, more than half of the population have both eyes on the left side. This flounder feeds on worms, crustaceans, mollusks and fish.

Spawning takes place in late winter and spring, usually in shallow waters. Young fishes may enter brackish water or river mouths. Females are mature in their third year, males in their second. Starry flounders are caught commercially, particularly off the coasts of Japan and Korea.

NAME: Plaice, *Pleuronectes platessa*
RANGE: E. Atlantic Ocean: Scandinavia, south to N. Africa and Mediterranean Sea; coasts of Iceland and S. Greenland
HABITAT: shallow waters down to 50 m (165 ft), sometimes to 200 m (650 ft)
SIZE: 50–91 cm (19¾–35¾ in)

The plaice is characterized by the rich brown color, dotted with prominent orange spots, of its eyed side; the underside is white. A member of the righteye flounder family, Pleuronectidae, the plaice has both eyes on the right side of the body; reversed specimens (those with eyes on the left) are rare. A bottom-dweller, it lives on mud, sand or gravel on the seabed and feeds on mollusks, worms and crustaceans. Even adults often come right inshore to the tidal zone to find food.

Spawning usually takes place between January and March. The eggs hatch in 10 to 20 days, depending on water temperature. The larvae live at the surface for up to 6 weeks before adopting the bottom-dwelling life, when they are about 1.25 cm (½ in) long. By this time, the structural adjustments and the migration of the eye have been completed. Males are mature at 2 to 6 years, females at 3 to 7 years, and they may live for up to 30 years.

Plaice is an important commerical food fish in northern Europe.

NAME: Dab, *Limanda limanda*
RANGE: E. Atlantic Ocean: White Sea, coasts of Scandinavia and Britain to Biscay; coasts of Iceland
HABITAT: shallow sandy-bottomed waters
SIZE: 25–42 cm (9¾–16½ in)

A small flatfish, the dab has toothed scales on its eyed side, which give its body a rough texture. The blind side is white and has toothed scales only at the edges of the body. Both eyes are on the right side and exceptions are rare. The dab feeds on the seabed on almost any bottom-living invertebrates, especially crustaceans, worms and mollusks. It makes seasonal migrations, moving inshore in spring and offshore in autumn.

The dab spawns in spring and early summer, and the eggs and larvae float in surface waters until they adopt the adult form and bottom-dwelling habits, when about 2 cm (¾ in) long. By this time, the structural modifications and migration of the eye to the right side are complete.

This extremely abundant fish is an important commercial species in Europe, despite its small size.

Summer Flounder

Peacock Flounder

California Halibut

Starry Flounder

Atlantic Halibut

Dab

Plaice

Flatfishes

NAME: Greenland Halibut, *Reinhardtius hippoglossoides*
RANGE: N. Atlantic Ocean: Arctic Ocean, Norwegian Sea, Iceland, Greenland, coasts of N. America as far south as New Jersey; N. Pacific Ocean: Bering Sea and Sea of Okhotsk, south to California and Japan
HABITAT: deep waters at 200–2,000 m (650–6,600 ft)
SIZE: 80 cm–1.2 m (31½ in –4 ft)

An active predator, the Greenland halibut hunts in mid-waters rather than on the seabed, feeding on fish, crustaceans and squid. In keeping with its habits, it is more symmetrical in body form than most flatfishes and has a blind side almost as dark as its eyed side. Although both eyes are on the right side, the upper eye is at the edge of the head, giving a larger field of vision than is usual for flatfishes. The large jaws are equipped with strong, fanglike teeth.

Spawning occurs in deep water in summertime; eggs and larvae float freely until the metamorphosis to adult form is complete.

NAME: Winter Flounder, *Pseudopleuronectes americanus*
RANGE: W. Atlantic Ocean: Labrador to Georgia
HABITAT: shallow coastal waters, bays, estuaries, down to 90 m (300 ft)
SIZE: 30–61 cm (11¾–24 in)

The winter flounder is most common in shallow waters over muddy sand, but the fish is also found over gravel or hard bottoms. In normal specimens, both eyes are on the right side, which is usually reddish-brown in color. The underside is white, but there are a few fishes with darker undersides. Winter flounders feed on the sea bottom on worms, crustaceans and mollusks and are thought to damage valuable soft-shelled clams by feeding on their breathing siphons. In autumn, the flounders migrate to inshore waters, moving offshore again in spring.

Spawning takes place in winter and early spring, each female shedding up to half a million eggs. Unlike the eggs of most flatfishes, which float, these eggs sink to the bottom, where they stick to each other and to other objects. They hatch in about 2 weeks.

The winter flounder is an important food fish, caught both commercially and by anglers.

NAME: American Plaice, *Hippoglossoides platessoides*
RANGE: W. Atlantic Ocean: Greenland, Labrador, south to Rhode Island; E. Atlantic: Iceland, Barents Sea, south to English Channel
HABITAT: depths of 40–180 m (130–600 ft)
SIZE: 30–61 cm (11¾–24 in)

Also known as the long rough dab, this plaice has toothed scales on its eyed side, which give the skin a rough texture. Both eyes are on the right side, which is brown or reddish-brown; the underside is white. American plaice live on sand or mud bottoms, feeding on bottom-living invertebrates such as sea urchins, brittle stars, crustaceans, mollusks and worms.

Spawning takes place in summer in the north and in spring in the south. Each female produces up to 60,000 eggs, which are buoyant and float near the surface until they hatch.

NAME: Sole, *Solea solea*
RANGE: E. Atlantic Ocean: Norway and Britain, south to N. Africa and Mediterranean Sea
HABITAT: shallow coastal waters; winters farther offshore in deeper waters
SIZE: 30–60 cm (11¾–23½ in)

The sole is the most abundant member of the family Soleidae in Europe and is an important food fish. Like other flatfishes, soles pass through a symmetrical larval stage, but as they develop, one eye migrates around to the other side of the head — the left eye usually moves to the right side. This, and other structural adaptations, fit the sole for a life spent partially buried on the seabed, eyed side uppermost. The sole is a fairly slender-bodied flatfish, medium-brown on its upper side, white on its blind side. Its dorsal and anal fins extend as far as the tail fin. Normally a nighttime feeder, the sole eats crustaceans, worms, mollusks and sometimes fish, often coming near the surface in search of prey. It may be active during the day in dull weather, but it usually spends daylight hours buried in sand or mud.

Soles make seasonal migrations, moving into shallow waters in spring and offshore again in winter. They spawn in spring and early summer, the eggs floating at the surface of the water until they hatch. Larvae live at the surface at first, but by the time they are about 1.25 cm (½ in) long, they have metamorphosed into adult form and have drifted into shallow coastal waters, where they begin life on the seabed.

NAME: Naked Sole, *Gymnachirus melas*
RANGE: W. Atlantic Ocean: coasts of Massachusetts, south to Florida, Bahamas and Gulf of Mexico
HABITAT: coastal waters, most common in depths of 30–45 m (100–150 ft)
SIZE: 23 cm (9 in)

An unusual member of the sole family, the naked sole is a thickset flatfish, with scaleless skin marked with dark stripes on the eyed side. Both eyes are on the right in most individuals. Much of their life is spent on the sandy seabed, but they can swim well if necessary.

NAME: Long Tongue-sole, *Cynoglossus lingua*
RANGE: Indian Ocean: E. Africa to India and Sri Lanka; W. Pacific Ocean
HABITAT: coastal waters, estuaries
SIZE: 43 cm (17 in)

The long tongue-sole has an extremely narrow body for a flatfish but is well adapted to life on the seabed, where it lives virtually buried in sand or mud, with only its eyes showing. Both eyes are on the left side of the body, and the mouth, too, is situated on the left, low down, just below the eyes. The fish has no pectoral fins, and only the left pelvic fin is developed; the dorsal and anal fins join with the small, pointed tail fin. On the eyed side, the scales have toothed edges, giving a rough texture to the body.

There are about 86 species in the tongue-sole family, Cynoglossidae; most are marine and are found in tropical and subtropical seas.

NAME: Blackcheek Tonguefish, *Symphurus plagusia*
RANGE: W. Atlantic Ocean: New York, south to Florida, Bahamas and Gulf of Mexico
HABITAT: sandy bays, estuaries
SIZE: 20.5 cm (8 in)

A member of the tongue-sole family of flatfishes, this fish is typical of the group, with a body that is broadest at the front and tapers to a pointed tail. Its dorsal and anal fins unite with the tail; it has no pectoral fins, and only the left pelvic fin is developed. Both its eyes are on the left of the head, and the small mouth is set low and is contorted to the left. The eyed side is pale brown, with some dark markings and a dark spot near the eyes. The blind side is creamy-white. Like all flatfishes, the tonguefish passes through a larval stage when its eyes are symmetrical — one on each side of the head — before the metamorphosis to adult form occurs.

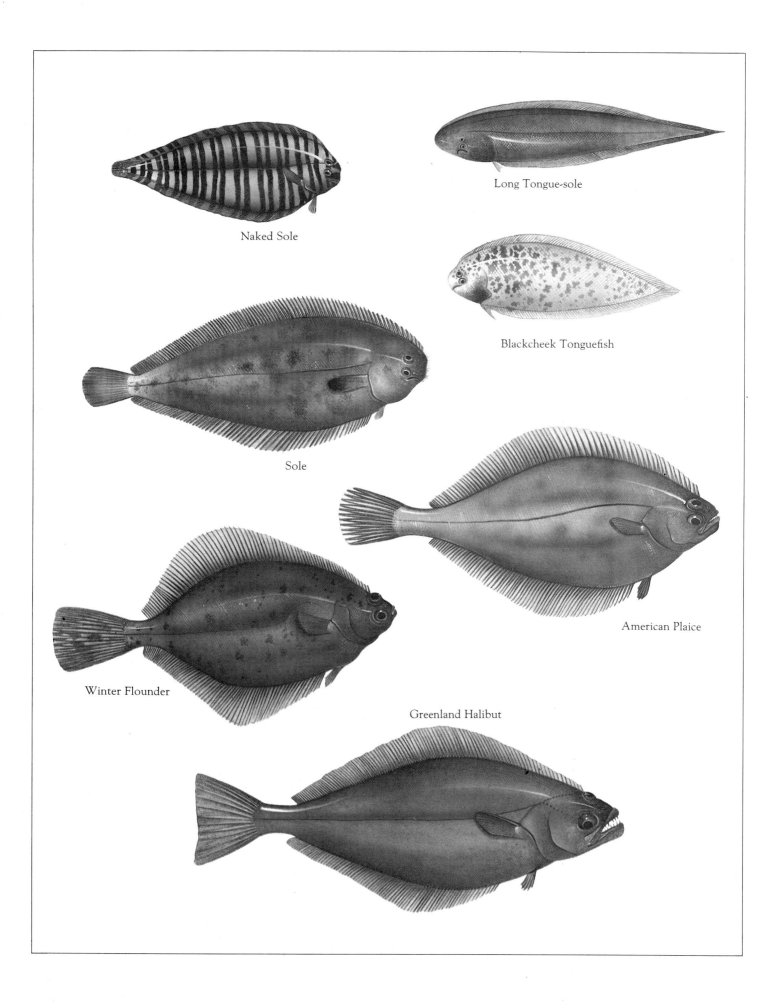

Naked Sole

Long Tongue-sole

Blackcheek Tonguefish

Sole

American Plaice

Winter Flounder

Greenland Halibut

Tetraodontiform Fishes

NAME: **Gray Triggerfish,** *Balistes carolinensis*

RANGE: **Atlantic Ocean: from W. Africa to Portugal in E. (seasonally north to Britain), across to Argentina and north to Nova Scotia in W.**

HABITAT: **open sea**

SIZE: **41 cm (16 in)**

The gray triggerfish, a member of the family Balistidae, has a compressed, but deep, body and a slightly protruding snout, armed with sharp, incisorlike teeth. Its anal and second dorsal fins are prominent, and the first dorsal fin consists of three spines, the first of which is strong and thick and, when erect, is locked into place by the second spine. This "trigger" must be released before the spine can be flattened again. If the triggerfish is alarmed or pursued, it can take refuge in a crevice and wedge itself in by means of this "locking" spine, which makes it extremely hard to remove. It lacks pelvic fins but does possess a pelvic spine. It is thought to feed on crustaceans.

Young gray triggerfishes float among sargassum weed in the open sea and hence become widely distributed.

NAME: **Queen Triggerfish,** *Balistes vetula*

RANGE: **W. Atlantic Ocean: Florida, (sometimes New England) to Brazil, including Gulf of Mexico and Caribbean**

HABITAT: **inshore waters, coral reefs**

SIZE: **56 cm (22 in)**

The attractive queen triggerfish is easily distinguished from other species by the slender extensions on its dorsal and tail fins and by its striking blue and yellow coloration. Like other triggerfishes, it has three dorsal spines, the first of which can be locked into an erect position by the second spine. It feeds on a variety of invertebrates, particularly sea urchins.

NAME: **Clown Triggerfish,** *Balistoides conspicillum*

RANGE: **Indian and Pacific Oceans: E. Africa to India, S.E. Asia, N. Australia and Japan**

HABITAT: **rocky coasts, coral reefs**

SIZE: **33 cm (13 in)**

A dramatically patterned fish, the clown triggerfish has large, light spots on the lower half of its body, contrasting with the dark coloration on its back. Its mouth is circled with bright orange, and there are green markings on its back and on its tail fin. Its second dorsal and anal fins are smaller than those of many triggerfishes, but the first of the dorsal spines is robust and can be locked into an erect position by the second spine, in the manner common to all members of the family Balistidae.

TETRAODONTIFORMES

This order of spiny-finned fishes contains about 320 species, only about 8 of which live in fresh water. Common names, such as pufferfish, porcupinefish, boxfish, trunkfish and triggerfish, give an idea of the strange body forms of the fishes contained in the order; most of them are rotund, deep or boxlike in shape. Some accentuate this plumpness by inflating the body with water as a defensive mechanism, and in species such as the porcupinefish, this swelling erects an array of sharp body spines. Others, such as the triggerfishes, enlarge the body by expanding a flap on the belly.

Many tetraodontiformes produce sounds, either by grinding their teeth or by vibrating the swim bladder with specialized muscles.

NAME: **Black-barred Triggerfish,** *Rhinecanthus aculeatus*

RANGE: **Indian and Pacific Oceans: E. Africa through S.E. Asia to Hawaiian Islands**

HABITAT: **shallow waters on the outer edges of reefs**

SIZE: **30.5 cm (12 in)**

The black-barred triggerfish, a member of the family Balistidae, has a strongly compressed body and a rather elongate snout. Its coloration is distinctive but variable, although there are always dark and light bands running down to the anal fin. In addition to the three dorsal spines, typical of the triggerfish family, there is a patch of spines on each side of its tail, surrounded by an area of black. This triggerfish is capable of making quite loud sounds by rubbing together bones supporting the pectoral fin. The sounds are amplified by the fish's swim bladder.

NAME: **Sargassum Triggerfish,** *Xanthichthys ringens*

RANGE: **W. Atlantic Ocean: North Carolina through Caribbean to Brazil; probably also occurs in tropical areas of Indian and W. Pacific Oceans**

HABITAT: **open sea**

SIZE: **25.5 cm (10 in)**

A small, fairly soberly colored member of the family Balistidae, the sargassum triggerfish is marked with dark, broken stripes along the length of its body. Like other triggerfishes, it has no pelvic fins, but it does have a pelvic spine. The young of this species tend to live under patches of floating sargassum weed at the water surface.

NAME: **Scrawled Filefish,** *Aluterus scriptus*

RANGE: **Atlantic, Pacific and Indian Oceans: tropical seas**

HABITAT: **inshore waters, seabed**

SIZE: **91 cm (35¾ in)**

The scrawled filefish is one of a group of about 85 species of filefish, which make up a subfamily of the triggerfish family. This filefish is long and much more slender than most other members of its family, and its snout is long and sharp-pointed. It has one dorsal spine, and its dorsal and anal fins are small and soft. There are small spines on its scales, giving the body a prickly texture, which is the origin of the fish's common name.

Bottom-living invertebrates and algae are the scrawled filefish's main foods, and it forages on the seabed with its nose down. It often feeds in clumps of eelgrass, where, with its head-down posture, undulating fins and mottled, greenish coloration, it is perfectly camouflaged.

NAME: **Planehead Filefish,** *Monacanthus hispidus*

RANGE: **W. Atlantic Ocean: Cape Cod (sometimes as far north as Nova Scotia) to Florida and Caribbean, south to Brazil**

HABITAT: **inshore waters**

SIZE: **15–25.5 cm (6–10 in)**

The planehead filefish has a compressed, deep body, covered with small, spiny scales, which give it a rough texture. A distinguishing feature is the fish's single dorsal spine, which has a toothed rear edge. There is also a large pelvic spine.

NAME: **Scrawled Cowfish,** *Lactophrys quadricornis*

RANGE: **W. Atlantic Ocean: New England to Brazil, including Gulf of Mexico and Caribbean**

HABITAT: **coastal waters, among beds of eelgrass**

SIZE: **46 cm (18 in)**

A member of the boxfish family, the scrawled cowfish has a bony shell, composed of fused plates, encasing most of its body. Only the mouth, eyes, gill and ventral openings, and fins are free of this rigid shell. On its head is a pair of forward-pointing spines, and there is another, backward-pointing pair at the rear of the shell near the tail — hence the scientific name meaning "four-horned."

Well protected by its body armor, the scrawled cowfish swims slowly, by means of paddlelike movements of the fins, but spends much of its life amid eelgrass or close to the seabed. Bottom-living invertebrates and aquatic plants are its main foods.

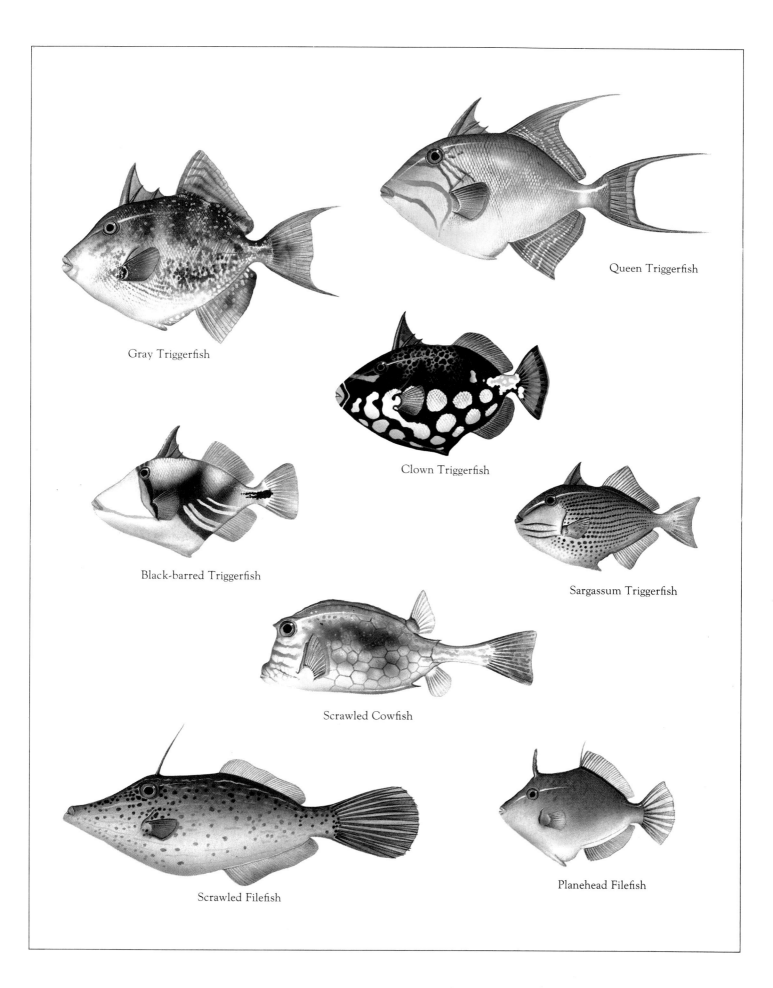

Gray Triggerfish

Queen Triggerfish

Clown Triggerfish

Black-barred Triggerfish

Sargassum Triggerfish

Scrawled Cowfish

Scrawled Filefish

Planehead Filefish

Tetraodontiform Fishes

NAME: **Blue-spotted Boxfish,** *Ostracion tuberculatus*
RANGE: **Indian and Pacific Oceans: E. Africa to S.E. Asia, Australia, Philippines and W. Pacific islands**
HABITAT: **coastal waters, coral reefs**
SIZE: **46 cm (18 in)**

Like all members of the boxfish family, Ostraciontidae, the blue-spotted boxfish has a body encased in a bony shell, composed of fused plates. Mouth, eyes, fins, and gill and ventral openings are the only breaks in this armor, which effectively protects the fish from predators. This boxfish feeds on a variety of bottom-living invertebrates, and although it normally swims quite slowly, it can make a rapid spurt by moving its strong, flexible tail.

NAME: **Sharpnose Puffer,** *Canthigaster rostrata*
RANGE: **W. Atlantic Ocean: Bermuda and Bahamas, south to Brazil, including Gulf of Mexico and Caribbean; E. Atlantic: St. Helena, W. Africa, Canary Islands, Madeira**
HABITAT: **coastal waters, coral reefs, tidal pools, eelgrass beds**
SIZE: **11 cm (4¼ in)**

A member of the pufferfish family, Tetraodontidae, the sharpnose puffer, like most of its relatives, is a stout, round-bodied little fish. A characteristic dark ridge runs along the middle of its back, and its head and body are scattered with blue markings. Its varied diet includes worms, crustaceans, sea urchins, crustaceans and aquatic plants.

NAME: **Oceanic Puffer,** *Lagocephalus lagocephalus*
RANGE: **tropical and subtropical Atlantic Ocean, occasionally as far north as Britain; Indian and Pacific Oceans**
HABITAT: **surface waters in open sea**
SIZE: **61 cm (24 in)**

This pufferfish, a member of the family Tetraodontidae, has a body that is stout behind the head and tapers sharply toward the forked tail. Like most puffers, it is capable of inflating its body with water, and when it does this, the small spines embedded in its belly stand erect as a defensive device. The skin on its back is smooth. Like all puffers, it has beaklike jaws, formed by one pair of partially fused teeth in each jaw. It is believed to feed on fish, crustaceans and squid, although little is known about its habits.

NAME: **Bandtail Puffer,** *Sphoeroides spengleri*
RANGE: **W. Atlantic Ocean: New England to Brazil; E. Atlantic: Azores, Madeira, Canary and Cape Verde Islands**
HABITAT: **shallow inshore waters, sea grass beds, tidal inlets**
SIZE: **30.5 cm (12 in)**

An elongate puffer, the bandtail has a long, blunt snout and large eyes for its size. It is identified by the row of dark spots running from head to tail; there are also barred markings on its tail. Like all puffers, it has the ability to inflate its body enormously with water until it is like a balloon, in order to deter its predators. Any enemy would find it extremely difficult to swallow or even bite the blown-up body. The skin is covered with tiny spines, which stick out when the body is inflated. Once the danger is past, the puffer quickly deflates.

NAME: **Common Pufferfish,** *Tetraodon cutcutia*
RANGE: **India, Burma, Malaysia**
HABITAT: **rivers**
SIZE: **15 cm (6 in)**

One of the few freshwater puffers, the common pufferfish has a rotund body, attractively colored with green and patches of yellow. When threatened, it inflates its body with water until it is virtually globular, but it does not have skin spines. With its plump, rather rigid, body the puffer moves slowly, using undulations of its small dorsal and anal fins, but it compensates for this lack of speed by its defensive techniques. It feeds on bottom-dwelling invertebrates and on fish.

Common puffers are very popular aquarium fishes and have been bred in captivity. The female sheds her eggs on the bottom, where they are guarded by the male, who lies over them until they hatch.

Many members of the puffer family are considered good food fish, despite the fact that their internal organs — and occasionally even the flesh — are extremely toxic and can cause fatal poisoning. In Japan, chefs are specially trained in the cooking of puffers, known as *fugu*, but there are still a number of cases of poisoning.

NAME: **Porcupinefish,** *Diodon hystrix*
RANGE: **Pacific, Indian and Atlantic Oceans: tropical areas**
HABITAT: **most common in shallow waters, turtle grass beds**
SIZE: **91 cm (35¾ in)**

Similar to its relatives the pufferfishes in that it can inflate its body, the porcupinefish is covered with long, sharp spines; these spines normally lie flat but stand out when the body is inflated. It is clearly almost impossible for any predator to tackle this globular pin cushion, and this method of defense compensates the fish for its lack of speed and mobility. It swims slowly, with undulations of its small dorsal and anal fins; it lacks pelvic fins.

The porcupinefish has two fused teeth in each jaw, making a sharp, bird-like beak with which it crushes hard-shelled prey such as crabs, mollusks and sea urchins.

NAME: **Striped Burrfish,** *Chilomycterus schoepfi*
RANGE: **W. Atlantic Ocean: Cape Cod to Florida, south through Gulf of Mexico and Caribbean to Brazil**
HABITAT: **shallow inshore waters**
SIZE: **up to 25.5 cm (10 in)**

One of the approximately 15 species in the porcupinefish family, Diodontidae, the striped burrfish has an oval body, studded with stout, thornlike spines. The body can be inflated with water, but the spines are fixed in an erect position. The upper part of the body is marked with dark, irregular stripes, and there are a couple of dark patches on the sides.

Crustaceans and mollusks are the main foods of the striped burrfish, which has fused, beaklike teeth, strong enough to crush their hard shells.

NAME: **Ocean Sunfish,** *Mola mola*
RANGE: **Atlantic, Pacific and Indian Oceans: temperate and tropical areas**
HABITAT: **open sea**
SIZE: **up to 4 m (13 ft)**

The extraordinary ocean sunfish is a member of the small, largely unstudied family Molidae, which contains 3 to 5 species. Quite unlike any other fish, it has an almost circular body, which ends rather abruptly in a curious frill, consisting of a series of lobes that form a modified tail. Both dorsal and anal fins are short based and high and placed near the end of the body. The ocean sunfish's pectoral fins are rounded, and it lacks pelvic fins. Its mouth is small for so large a fish and contains two fused teeth in each jaw, making a strong beak. The fish feeds largely on small planktonic organisms, such as tiny jellyfishes and comb jellies, but also eats crustaceans and fish.

Although they are so huge and so widely distributed, ocean sunfishes are little known. They are so called because of the belief that they bask in the sun in surface waters, but fishes observed basking thus may, in fact, be sick or disabled.

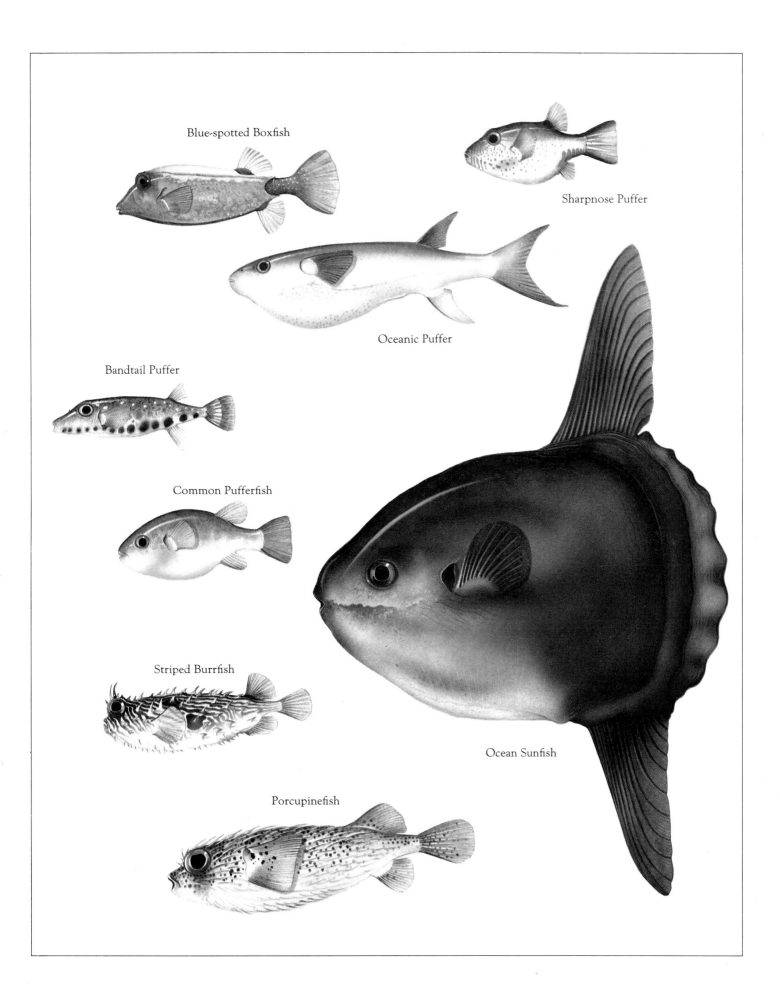

Blue-spotted Boxfish

Sharpnose Puffer

Oceanic Puffer

Bandtail Puffer

Common Pufferfish

Striped Burrfish

Ocean Sunfish

Porcupinefish

Classification

CLASS MAMMALIA: **Mammals**

Subclass Prototheria: Egg-laying Mammals

Order Monotremata: Monotremes
Family Tachyglossidae: Spiny Anteaters
Family Ornithorhynchidae: Platypus

Subclass Theria: Live-bearing Mammals
Infraclass Metatheria: Marsupials

Order Marsupialia: Marsupials
Family Didelphidae: Opossums
Family Microbiotheriidae: Colocolo
Family Caenolestidae: Rat Opossums
Family Dasyuridae: Marsupial Carnivores
        and Insectivores
Family Myrmecobiidae: Numbat
Family Notoryctidae: Marsupial Mole
Family Phascolarctidae: Koala
Family Vombatidae: Wombats
Family Tarsipedidae: Honey Possum
Family Peramelidae: Bandicoots
Family Thylacomyidae: Rabbit-bandicoot
Family Phalangeridae: Phalangers
Family Burramyidae: Pygmy Possums
Family Petauridae: Ringtails
Family Macropodidae: Kangaroos, Wallabies

Infraclass Eutheria: Placental Mammals

Order Edentata: Edentates
Family Myrmecophagidae: Anteaters
Family Bradypodidae: Sloths
Family Dasypodidae: Armadillos

Order Pholidota
Family Manidae: Pangolins

Order Tubulidentata
Family Orycteropodidae: Aardvark

Order Insectivora: Insectivores
Family Solenodontidae: Solenodons
Family Tenrecidae: Tenrecs, Otter-shrews
Family Chrysochloridae: Golden Moles
Family Erinaceidae: Hedgehogs, Moonrats
Family Soricidae: Shrews
Family Talpidae: Moles, Desmans
Family Macroscelididae: Elephant Shrews

Order Dermoptera
Family Cynocephalidae: Flying Lemurs

Order Chiroptera: Bats
Family Pteropodidae: Old World Fruit Bats
Family Rhinopomatidae: Mouse-tailed Bats
Family Emballonuridae: Sheath-tailed Bats
Family Craseonycteridae: Hog-nosed Bat
Family Nycteridae: Slit-faced Bats
Family Megadermatidae: False Vampire Bats
Family Rhinolophidae: Horseshoe Bats
Family Hipposideridae: Old World Leaf-nosed Bats
Family Noctilionidae: Fisherman Bats
Family Mormoopidae: Mustached Bats
Family Desmodontidae: Vampire Bats
Family Molossidae: Free-tailed Bats
Family Phyllostomatidae: American Leaf-nosed Bats
Family Vespertilionidae: Evening Bats
Family Natalidae: Funnel-eared Bats
Family Furipteridae: Smoky Bats
Family Thyropteridae: Disk-winged Bats
Family Myzopodidae: Sucker-footed Bat
Family Mystacinidae: New Zealand Short-tailed Bat

Order Scandentia
Family Tupaiidae: Tree Shrews

Order Primates: Primates
Family Cheirogaleidae: Mouse-lemurs
Family Lemuridae: Lemurs
Family Indriidae: Leaping Lemurs
Family Daubentoniidae: Aye-aye
Family Lorisidae: Lorises
Family Tarsiidae: Tarsiers
Family Callitrichidae: Marmosets and Tamarins
Family Cebidae: New World Monkeys
Family Cercopithecidae: Old World Monkeys
Family Pongidae: Apes
Family Hominidae: Hominids

Order Carnivora: Carnivores
Family Canidae: Dogs, Foxes
Family Ursidae: Bears
Family Ailuropodidae: Pandas
Family Procyonidae: Raccoons
Family Mustelidae: Mustelids
Family Viverridae: Civets
Family Hyaenidae: Hyenas
Family Felidae: Cats

Order Pinnipedia: Pinnipeds
Family Otariidae: Sea Lions
Family Odobenidae: Walrus
Family Phocidae: Seals

Order Sirenia
Family Dugongidae: Dugong
Family Trichechidae: Manatees

Order Cetacea: Whales
Family Platanistidae: River Dolphins
Family Phocoenidae: Porpoises
Family Delphinidae: Dolphins
Family Monodontidae: White Whales
Family Physeteridae: Sperm Whales
Family Ziphiidae: Beaked Whales
Family Eschrichtidae: Gray Whale
Family Balaenopteridae: Rorquals
Family Balaenidae: Right Whales

Order Proboscidea
Family Elephantidae: Elephants

Order Hyracoidea
Family Procaviidae: Hyraxes

Order Perissodactyla: Odd-toed Ungulates
Family Equidae: Horses
Family Tapiridae: Tapirs
Family Rhinocerotidae: Rhinoceroses

Order Artiodactyla: Even-toed Ungulates
Family Suidae: Pigs
Family Tayassuidae: Peccaries
Family Hippopotamidae: Hippopotamuses
Family Camelidae: Camels
Family Tragulidae: Chevrotains
Family Moschidae: Musk Deer
Family Cervidae: Deer
Family Giraffidae: Giraffes
Family Antilocapridae: Pronghorn
Family Bovidae: Bovids

Order Rodentia: Rodents

Family Sciuridae: Squirrels
Family Geomyidae: Pocket Gophers
Family Heteromyidae: Pocket Mice
Family Aplodontidae: Mountain Beaver
Family Castoridae: Beavers
Family Anomaluridae: Scaly-tailed Squirrels
Family Pedetidae: Springhare
Family Muridae:
    Subfamily Hesperomyinae: New World Rats and Mice
    Subfamily Cricetinae: Hamsters
    Subfamily Spalacinae: Blind Mole-rats
    Subfamily Myospalacinae: Eastern Asiatic Mole-rats
    Subfamily Rhizomyinae: Mole-rats and Bamboo Rats
    Subfamily Lophiomyinae: Crested Rat
    Subfamily Platacanthomyinae: Spiny Dormice
    Subfamily Nesomyinae: Madagascan Rats
    Subfamily Otomyinae: African Swamp Rats
    Subfamily Microtinae: Voles and Lemmings
    Subfamily Gerbillinae: Gerbils
    Subfamily Dendromurinae: African Climbing Mice
    Subfamily Cricetomyinae: African Pouched Rats
    Subfamily Hydromyinae: Island Water Rats
    Subfamily Murinae: Old World Rats and Mice
Family Gliridae: Dormice
Family Seleviniidae: Desert Dormouse
Family Zapodidae: Jumping Mice
Family Dipodidae: Jerboas
Family Hystricidae: Old World Porcupines
Family Erithizontidae: New World Porcupines
Family Caviidae: Guinea Pigs
Family Hydrochoeridae: Capybara
Family Dinomyidae: Pacarana
Family Dasyproctidae: Pacas and Agoutis
Family Chinchillidae: Viscachas and Chinchillas
Family Capromyidae: Hutias and Nutria
Family Octodontidae: Octodont Rodents
Family Ctenomyidae: Tuco-tucos
Family Abrocomidae: Chinchilla-rats
Family Echimyidae: American Spiny Rats
Family Thryonomyidae: Cane Rats
Family Petromyidae: Dassie Rat
Family Bathyergidae: Mole-rats
Family Ctenodactylidae: Gundis

Order Lagomorpha: Lagomorphs

Family Ochotonidae: Pikas
Family Leporidae: Rabbits and Hares

CLASS AVES: Birds

Order Struthioniformes
Family Struthionidae: Ostrich

Order Rheiformes
Family Rheidae: Rheas

Order Casuariiformes
Family Casuariidae: Cassowaries
Family Dromaiidae: Emu

Order Apterygiformes
Family Apterygidae: Kiwis

Order Tinamiformes
Family Tinamidae: Tinamous

Order Sphenisciformes
Family Spheniscidae: Penguins

Order Gaviiformes
Family Gaviidae: Loons

Order Podicipediformes
Family Podicipedidae: Grebes

Order Procellariiformes
Family Diomedeidae: Albatrosses
Family Procellariidae: Petrels
Family Hydrobatidae: Storm-petrels
Family Pelecanoididae: Diving-petrels

Order Pelecaniformes
Family Phaethontidae: Tropicbirds
Family Pelecanidae: Pelicans
Family Sulidae: Gannets, Boobies
Family Phalacrocoracidae: Cormorants
Family Anhingidae: Darters
Family Fregatidae: Frigatebirds

Order Ciconiiformes
Family Ardeidae: Herons, Bitterns
Family Balaenicipidae: Shoebill
Family Scopidae: Hammerkop
Family Ciconiidae: Storks
Family Threskiornithidae: Ibises and
    Spoonbills
Family Phoenicopteridae: Flamingos

Order Anseriformes
Family Anhimidae: Screamers
Family Anatidae: Ducks, Geese, Swans

Order Falconiformes: Birds of Prey

Family Cathartidae: New World Vultures
Family Pandionidae: Osprey
Family Sagittariidae: Secretary Bird
Family Accipitridae: Old World Vultures,
    Eagles, Hawks
Family Falconidae: Falcons

Order Galliformes
Family Megapodiidae: Megapodes
Family Cracidae: Curassows
Family Opisthocomidae: Hoatzin
Family Phasianidae:
    Subfamily Phasianinae: Pheasants
    Subfamily Tetraoninae: Grouse
    Subfamily Odontophorinae: American Quail
    Subfamily Meleagridinae: Turkeys
    Subfamily Numidinae: Guineafowl

Order Gruiformes
Family Mesitornithidae: Mesites
Family Turnicidae: Buttonquails
Family Pedionomidae: Plains-wanderer
Family Gruidae: Cranes
Family Aramidae: Limpkin
Family Psophiidae: Trumpeters
Family Rallidae: Rails
Family Heliornithidae: Finfoots
Family Rhynochetidae: Kagu
Family Eurypygidae: Sunbittern
Family Cariamidae: Seriemas
Family Otididae: Bustards

Order Charadriiformes
Family Jacanidae: Jacanas
Family Rostratulidae: Painted-snipes
Family Haematopodidae: Oystercatchers
Family Charadriidae: Plovers
Family Scolopacidae: Sandpipers
Family Recurvirostridae: Avocets
Family Ibidorhynchidae: Ibisbill
Family Dromadidae: Crab Plover
Family Burhinidae: Thick-knees
Family Glareolidae: Pratincoles
Family Thinocoridae: Seedsnipes
Family Chionididae: Sheathbills
Family Stercorariidae: Skuas
Family Laridae: Gulls, Terns
Family Rynchopidae: Skimmers •
Family Alcidae: Auks

Classification

Order Columbiformes
Family Pteroclididae: Sandgrouse
Family Columbidae: Pigeons

Order Psittaciformes: Parrots
Family Loriidae: Lories
Family Cacatuidae: Cockatoos
Family Psittacidae: Parrots

Order Cuculiformes
Family Cuculidae: Cuckoos
Family Musophagidae: Turacos

Order Strigiformes
Family Tytonidae: Barn Owls
Family Strigidae: Owls

Order Caprimulgiformes
Family Steatornithidae: Oilbird
Family Podargidae: Frogmouths
Family Nyctibiidae: Potoos
Family Aegothelidae: Owlet-nightjars
Family Caprimulgidae: Nightjars

Order Apodiformes
Family Apodidae: Swifts
Family Hemiprocnidae: Crested Swifts
Family Trochilidae: Hummingbirds

Order Coliiformes
Family Coliidae: Mousebirds

Order Trogoniformes
Family Trogonidae: Trogons

Order Coraciiformes
Family Alcedinidae: Kingfishers
Family Todidae: Todies
Family Momotidae: Motmots
Family Meropidae: Bee-eaters
Family Coraciidae: Rollers
Family Brachypteraciidae: Ground Rollers
Family Leptosomatidae: Cuckoo-roller
Family Upupidae: Hoopoe
Family Phoeniculidae: Woodhoopoes
Family Bucerotidae: Hornbills

Order Piciformes
Family Galbulidae: Jacamars
Family Bucconidae: Puffbirds
Family Capitonidae: Barbets
Family Indicatoridae: Honey Guides
Family Ramphastidae: Toucans
Family Picidae: Woodpeckers

Order Passeriformes: Perching Birds

Suboscines: Primitive Passerines
Family Furnariidae: Ovenbirds
Family Formicariidae: Antbirds
Family Dendrocolaptidae: Woodcreepers
Family Conopophagidae: Gnateaters
Family Rhinocryptidae: Tapaculos
Family Pipridae: Manakins
Family Cotingidae: Cotingas
Family Oxyruncidae: Sharpbill
Family Phytotomidae: Plantcutters
Family Tyrannidae: Tyrant Flycatchers
Family Eurylaimidae: Broadbills
Family Pittidae: Pittas
Family Xenicidae: New Zealand Wrens
Family Philepittidae: Asities
Family Menuridae: Lyrebirds
Family Atrichornithidae: Scrub Birds

Oscines: Advanced Passerines
Family Alaudidae: Larks
Family Hirundinidae: Swallows, Martins
Family Motacillidae: Pipits
Family Campephagidae: Cuckoo-shrikes
    and Minivets
Family Pycnonotidae: Bulbuls
Family Irenidae: Leafbirds
Family Laniidae: Shrikes
Family Vangidae: Vangas
Family Bombycillidae: Waxwings
Family Dulidae: Palm Chat
Family Troglodytidae: Wrens
Family Cinclidae: Dippers
Family Mimidae: Mockingbirds
Family Prunellidae: Accentors
Family Muscicapidae:
    Subfamily Turdinae: Thrushes
    Subfamily Timaliinae: Babblers
    Subfamily Panurinae: Parrotbills
    Subfamily Picathartinae: Bare-headed
        Rockfowl
    Subfamily Orthonychinae: Quail Thrushes
    Subfamily Polioptilinae: Gnatcatchers
    Subfamily Sylviinae: Old World Warblers
    Subfamily Malurinae: Australian Warblers
    Subfamily Muscicapinae: Old World Flycatchers
    Subfamily Monarchinae: Monarch Flycatchers
    Subfamily Platysteirinae: African Monarch
        Flycatchers
    Subfamily Rhipidurinae: Fantail Flycatchers
    Subfamily Pachycephalinae: Whistlers

Family Aegithalidae: Long-tailed Titmice
Family Remizidae: Penduline Tits
Family Paridae: Titmice
Family Sittidae: Nuthatches
Family Certhiidae: Treecreepers
Family Rhabdornithidae: Philippine Creepers
Family Climacteridae: Australian Treecreepers
Family Dicaeidae: Flowerpeckers
Family Zosteropidae: White-eyes
Family Nectariniidae: Sunbirds
Family Meliphagidae: Honey Eaters
Family Emberizidae:
    Subfamily Emberizinae: Buntings
    Subfamily Catamblyrhynchinae:
        Plush-capped Finch
    Subfamily Cardinalinae: Cardinals and Grosbeaks
    Subfamily Tersininae: Swallow-tanager
    Subfamily Thraupinae: Tanagers
Family Parulidae: American Wood Warblers
Family Drepanididae: Hawaiian Honeycreepers
Family Vireonidae: Vireos
Family Icteridae: Icterids
Family Fringillidae: Finches
Family Estrildidae: Waxbills
Family Ploceidae: Weavers
Family Sturnidae: Starlings
Family Oriolidae: Orioles
Family Dicruridae: Drongos
Family Callaeidae: Wattlebirds
Family Grallinidae: Mudnest Builders
Family Artamidae: Wood Swallows
Family Cracticidae: Butcherbirds
Family Ptilonorhynchidae: Bowerbirds
Family Paradisaeidae: Birds of Paradise
Family Corvidae: Crows

CLASS REPTILIA: Reptiles

Order Chelonia: Turtles and Tortoises
Family Emydidae: Emydid Turtles
Family Testudinidae: Land Tortoises
Family Chelydridae: Snapping Turtles
Family Kinosternidae: Mud and Musk Turtles
Family Carettochelyidae: New Guinea Plateless
    River Turtle
Family Dermatemyidae: Central American
    River Turtle
Family Platysternidae: Big-headed Turtle
Family Chelonidae: Marine Turtles
Family Dermochelyidae: Leatherback Turtle
Family Trionychidae: Softshell Turtles
Family Pelomedusidae: Greaved Turtles
Family Chelidae: Matamatas and
    Snake-necked Turtles

Order Crocodilia: Crocodiles, Alligators and Gavial
Subfamily Crocodylinae: Crocodiles
Subfamily Alligatorinae: Alligators and Caimans
Subfamily Gavialinae: Gavial

Order Rhynchocephalia: Tuatara
Family Sphenodontia: Tuatara

Order Squamata: Lizards and Snakes
Family Iguanidae: Iguanas
Family Agamidae: Agamid Lizards
Family Chamaeleonidae: Chameleons
Family Gekkonidae: Geckos
Family Pygopodidae: Scaly-foot Lizards
Family Xantusiidae: Night Lizards
Family Teiidae: Teiid Lizards
Family Scincidae: Skinks
Family Lacertidae: Lacertid Lizards
Family Cordylidae: Girdled and Plated Lizards
Family Dibamidae: Old World Burrowing Lizards
Family Anguidae: Anguid Lizards
Family Anniellidae: California Legless Lizards
Family Xenosauridae: Crocodile Lizards
Family Helodermatidae: Gila Monster
Family Varanidae: Monitors
Family Lanthanotidae: Earless Monitor
Family Amphisbaenidae: Amphisbaenids

Primitive Snakes:
Family Leptotyphlopidae: Slender Blind Snakes
Family Typhlopidae: Blind Snakes
Family Anomalepidae
Family Aniliidae: Pipe Snakes
Family Uropeltidae: Shieldtail Snakes
Family Xenopeltidae: Sunbeam Snake
Family Boidae: Pythons and Boas
Family Acrochordidae: Wart Snakes

Advanced Snakes:
Family Colubridae: Colubrine Snakes
Family Elapidae: Cobras and Sea Snakes
Family Viperidae: Vipers
Family Crotalidae: Pit Vipers

CLASS AMPHIBIA: Amphibians

Order Urodela: Newts and Salamanders
Family Cryptobranchidae: Giant Salamanders
Family Hynobiidae: Asiatic Land Salamanders
Family Salamandridae: Newts and Salamanders
Family Ambystomatidae: Mole Salamanders
Family Amphiumidae: Amphiumas
Family Proteidae: Olm and Mudpuppies
Family Sirenidae: Sirens
Family Plethodontidae: Lungless Salamanders

Order Apoda: Caecilians
Family Caeciliidae
Family Typhlonectidae
Family Ichthyophidae
Family Scolecomorphidae

Order Anura: Frogs and Toads
Family Rhinophrynidae: Mexican Burrowing
    Toad
Family Pipidae: Pipid Frogs
Family Microhylidae: Narrow-mouthed Frogs
Family Discoglossidae: Discoglossid Frogs
Family Ascaphidae: Tailed Frogs
Family Pelobatidae: Spadefoot Toads
Family Myobatrachidae: Myobatrachid Frogs
Family Heleophrynidae: Ghost Frogs
Family Leptodactylidae: Leptodactylid Frogs
Family Rhinodermatidae: Mouth-brooding Frog
Family Bufonidae: Toads
Family Brachycephalidae: Gold Frog
Family Hylidae: Treefrogs
Family Ranidae: True Frogs
Family Sooglossidae: Sooglossid Frogs
Family Hyperoliidae: Hyperoliid Frogs

SUPERCLASS AGNATHA: Jawless Fishes
CLASS CEPHALASPIDOMORPHA
Order Petromyzoniformes: Lampreys

CLASS PTERASPIDOMORPHA
Order Myxiniformes: Hagfishes

SUPERCLASS GNATHOSTOMATA: Jawed Fishes
CLASS CHONDRICHTHYES: Cartilaginous Fishes
Order Lamniformes: Sharks
Order Heterodontiformes: Bullhead Sharks
Order Hexanchiformes: Cow and Frill Sharks
Order Squaliformes: Dogfish, Saw and
    Angel Sharks
Order Rajiformes: Skates and Rays
Order Chimaeriformes: Chimaeras

CLASS OSTEICHTHYES: Bony Fishes
Order Ceratodiformes: Australian Lungfish
Order Lepidosireniformes: African and South
    American Lungfishes
Order Coelacanthiformes: Coelacanth
Order Polypteriformes: Bichirs
Order Acipenseriformes: Sturgeons
Order Semionotiformes: Gars
Order Amiiformes: Bowfin
Order Osteoglossiformes: Bony Tongues
Order Mormyriformes: Elephantfishes
Order Elopiformes: Tarpons
Order Clupeiformes: Herrings
Order Anguilliformes: Eels
Order Notacanthiformes: Spiny Eels
Order Salmoniformes: Salmon
Order Gonorynchiformes: Milkfishes
Order Cypriniformes: Carps
Order Siluriformes: Catfishes
Order Myctophiformes: Lanternfishes
Order Polymixiiformes: Beardfishes
Order Percopsiformes: Trout-perches
Order Gadiformes: Cod
Order Batrachoidiformes: Toadfishes
Order Lophiiformes: Angler Fishes
Order Indostomiformes
Order Atheriniformes: Toothcarps, Sandsmelts
Order Gasterosteiformes: Sticklebacks and
    Tube-snouts
Order Lampridiformes: Dealfishes
Order Beryciformes: Squirrelfishes
Order Zeiformes: Dories
Order Syngnathiformes: Pipefishes
Order Synbranchiformes: Swamp-eels
Order Scorpaeniformes: Scorpionfishes
Order Dactylopteriformes: Flying Gurnards
Order Perciformes: Perchlike Fishes
Order Gobiesociformes: Clingfishes
Order Pleuronectiformes: Flatfishes
Order Tetraodontiformes: Pufferfishes and
    Triggerfishes

INDEX

A

Aardvark 28
Aardwolf 98
Abramis brama 514
Abrocoma bennetti 186
Abrocomidae 186
Abudefduf saxatilis 562
Acanthis flammea 384
Acanthisitta chloris 310
Acanthiza chrysorrhoa 348
Acanthizini 348
Acanthocybium solanderi 570
Acanthodactylus boskianus 434
Acanthopthalmus kuhlii 516
Acanthorhynchus tenuirostris 366
Acanthuridae 568
Acanthurus coeruleus 568
Accentor family 330
Accipiter cooperii 222
gentilis 222
Accipitridae 218–22
Acinonyx jubatus 102
Acipenser oxyrhynchus 498
sturio 498
Acipenseriformes 498
Acontias sp. 430
Acris crepitans 480
Acrobates pygmaeus 20
Acrocephalus caffra 344
Acrochordidae 446
Acrochordus javanicus 446
Adalah 574
Addax 148
Addax nasomaculatus 148
Adder, puff 456
saw-scaled 456
Adioryx xantherythrus 540
Aegithalidae 356
Aegithalos caudatus 356
Aegithina tiphia 322
Aegotheles cristatus 272
Aegothelidae 272
Aeoliscus strigatus 542
Aepyceros melampus 152
Aepyprymnus rufescens 22
Aeronautes saxatalis 276
Aethia cristatella 250
Aethopyga siparaja 362
African and South American lungfish order 496
African climbing mouse subfamily 176
African monarch flycatcher subfamily 352
African pouched rat subfamily 176
African swamp rat subfamily 170
Afrixales brachynemis 484
Afropavo congensis 230
Afrotis atra 238
Agama, common 420
Agama agama 420
Agamid, Arabian toad-headed 420
Agamidae 420
Agamodon anguliceps 442
Agapornis roseicollis 260
Agkistrodon halys 458
piscivorus 458
Aglaiocercus kingi 278
Agonus acipenserinus 546
Agouti, Brazilian 184
Agriornis livida 308
Ailuropoda melanoleuca 84
Ailuropodidae 84
Ailurus fulgens 84
Aix galericulata 214
sponsa 214
Akepa 380
Akiapolaau 380
Akodon arviculoides 166
Alaemon alaudipes 312
Alauda arvensis 312
Alaudidae 312
Albatross, light-mantled sooty 200
wandering 200
Albula vulpes 500
Alca torda 250

Alcedinidae 282
Alcedo atthis 282
Alcelaphus buselaphus 148
Alces alces 136
Alcidae 250
Alcippe poioicephala 340
Alectoris rufa 228
Alethe, fire-crested 332
Alewife 502
Allactaga major 180
Alle alle 250
Allenopithecus nigroviridis 70
Alligator, American 414
Alligator mississipiensis 414
Alopex lagopus 78
Alopias vulpinus 488
Alosa alosa 502
fallax 502
pseudoharengus 502
Alouatta caraya 64
seniculus 64
Aluterus scriptus 580
Alytes obstetricans 474
Amandava amandava 386
Amazon, yellow-crowned 262
Amazona ochrocephala 262
Amberjack, greater 552
Ambloplites rupestris 550
Amblyopsis spelaea 524
Amblyornis macgregoriae 398
Amblyospiza albifrons 388
Amblyrhynchus cristatus 418
Amblysomus hottentotus 32
Ambystoma maculatum 464
mexicanum 464
opacum 464
tigrinum 464
Ambystomatidae 464
Ameiva ameiva 428
American leaf-nosed bat family 48
American quail subfamily 232
American spiny rat family 188
American wood warbler family 378
Amia calva 498
Amiiformes 498
Ammodorcas clarkei 152
Ammodramus sandwichensis 368
Ammodytes tobianus 568
Ammodytidae 568
Ammomanes deserti 312
Ammotragus lervia 156
Amphibolurus barbatus 420
Amphiprion percula 562
Amphisbaena alba 442
Amphisbaenid family 442
Amphisbaenidae 442
Amphistichus argenteus 562
Amphiuma, two-toed 466
Amphiuma means 466
Amphiumidae 466
Amytornis goyderi 348
Anabantidae, 572
Anabas testudineus 572
Ableps anableps 534
Anaconda 446
Anarhichadidae 568
Anarhichas lupus 568
Anarhynchus frontalis 240
Anas clypeata 214
platyrhynchos 214
Anastomus lamelligerus 210
oscitans 210
Anathana ellioti 54
Anatidae 212–14
Anchovy, European 502
Andigena laminirostris 290
Anemonefish, clown 562
Angelfish 562
imperial 560
queen 560
Angler 530
Anguid lizard family 438
Anguidae 438
Anguilla anguilla 504
Anguilliformes 504
Anguis fragilis 438
Angwantibo 58
Anhimidae 212
Anhinga anhinga 206
Anhinga 206
Anhingidae 206
Ani, smooth-billed 266

Aniliidae 444
Anilius scytale 444
Anisotremus surinamensis 554
Anniella pulchra 438
Anniellidae 438
Anoa 142
Anole, green 416
Anolis carolinensis 416
Anomalepidae 444
Anomalepis sp. 444
Anomalops kaptoptron 540
Anomalospiza imberbis 388
Anomaluridae 164
Anomalurus beecrofti 164
Anoplopoma fimbria 546
Anous stolidus 248
Anser anser 212
Anseranas semipalmata 212
Anseriformes 212
Antbird, bicolored 298
ocellated 298
Anteater, giant 26
long-nosed spiny 12
short-nosed spiny 12
two-toed 26
Antechinus, brown 16
Antechinus stuarti 16
Antelope, beira 150
four-horned 140
roan 146
royal 150
Antennarius multiocellatus 530
Anthochaera carunculata 366
Anthops ornatus 44
Anthoscopus parvulus 356
Anthreptes singalensis 362
Anthus pratensis 316
spinoletta 316
Antidorcas marsupialis 152
Antilocapra americana 138
Antilocapridae 138
Antilope cervicapra 152
Antpitta, chestnut-crowned 298
Antshrike, barred 298
great 298
Antwren, streaked 298
Anura 460, 472
Aonyx capensis 90
Aotus trivirgatus 62
Apalis flavida 344
Apalis, yellow-breasted/black-breasted 344
Apaloderma narina 280
Ape, barbary 66
Ape family 74–6
Aphanius dispar 534
Aphyosemion australe 534
Aplodinotus grunniens 558
Aplodontia rufa 164
Aplodontidae 164
Aplonis metallica 392
Apoda 460, 470
Apodemus sylvaticus 178
Apodidae 276
Apodiformes 276
Apostlebird 396
Aprasia striolata 426
Aptenodytes forsteri 198
Apterygidae 196
Apteryx australis 196
Apus apus 276
Aquila chrysaetos 222
Ara macao 262
Aracari, curl-crested 290
Arachnothera robusta 362
Aramidae 234
Aramides ypecaha 236
Aramus guarauna 234
Arapaima gigas 500
Aratinga aurocapilla 262
jendaya 262
solstitialis 262
Archilochus colubris 278
Archosargus probatocephalus 556
Arctictis binturong 94
Arctocebus calabarensis 58
Arctocephalus australis 106
Arctonyx collaris 88
Ardea cinerea 208
herodias 208
Ardeidae 208
Ardeola ibis 208
Arenaria interpres 242

Argyropelecus aculeatus 508
Argyrosomus regius 558
Ariidae 520
Arius felis 520
Armadillo, giant 28
nine-banded 28
pink fairy 28
Artamidae 396
Artamus leucorhynchus 396
superciliosus 396
Arthroleptis wahlbergi 484
Artibeus jamaicensis 48
Artiodactyla 128
Aruana 500
Arundinicola leucocephala 304
Arvicanthis abyssinicus 178
Arvicola terrestris 172
Ascaphidae 474
Ascaphus truei 474
Asellia tridens 44
Asiatic land salamander family 462
Asio otus 270
Asity family 310
Ass, African 124
Astrapia mayeri 398
Astrapogon stellatus 550
Astroscopus guttatus 566
Astyanax fasciatus 512
mexicanus 512
Ateles paniscus 64
Atelopus boulengeri 478
Atelopus japonicus 538
Athene noctua 270
Atherina presbyter 536
Atheriniformes 532
Atherinomorus stipes 536
Atherurus macrourus 182
Atilax paludinosus 96
Atlapetes albinucha 370
Atractaspis bibroni 450
Atrichornis clamosus 310
Atrichornithidae 310
Auk, great 250
little 250
Auklet, crested 250
Aulacorhynchus prasinus 290
Aulorhynchus flavidus 542
Auriparus flaviceps 356
Australian lungfish order 496
Australian treecreeper family 358
Australian warbler subfamily 348
Australian wrens 348
Avadavat, red 386
Avahi laniger 56
Avocet 244
Axolotl 464
Aye-aye 56
Aythya fuligula 214
marila 214
valisineria 214

B

Babbler, brown 340
chestnut-capped 338
rufous-crowned 338
white-necked/white-eared 338
yellow-eyed 338
Babirusa 128
Baboon, chacma 68
hamadryas 68
olive 68
Babyrousa babyrussa 128
Badger 88
Chinese ferret 88
Eurasian 88
hog 88
Palawan 88
stink 88
Bagre marinus 520
Bagrus docmac 518
Baillonius bailloni 290
Balaena mysticetus 120
Balaeniceps rex 210
Balaenicipidae 210
Balaenidae 120
Balaenoptera acutorostrata 120
borealis 120
musculus 120
Balaenopteridae 120
Balearica pavonina 234
Balistes carolinensis 580
vetula 580

Balistidae 580
Balistoides conspicillum 580
Ballyhoo 532
Bananaquit 378
Bandicoot, brown 20
  Gunn's 20
Bandicota indica 178
Bandy-bandy 454
Banteng 142
Barb, tiger 512
Barbastella barbastellus 50
Barbastelle 50
Barbel 512
Barber-eel 522
Barbet, coppersmith 288
  double-toothed 288
Barbus barbus 512
  tetrazona 512
  tor 512
Bare-headed rockfowl
  subfamily 342
Barn owl family 268
Barracuda, great 564
Basileuterus culicivorus 378
Basiliscus plumifrons 418
Bass, giant sea 548
  largemouth 550
  rock 550
  striped 548
Bassaricyon gabbi 84
Bat, Australian false vampire 42
  big brown 50
  black mastiff 46
  Brazilian large-eared 48
  Brazilian long-nosed 40
  common long-eared 50
  Cuban flower 48
  dog 38
  eastern smoky 52
  Egyptian free-tailed 46
  Egyptian slit-faced 42
  fish-eating 50
  fisherman 46
  flower-faced 44
  Franquet's fruit 38
  greater false vampire 42
  greater fruit 38
  greater horseshoe 44
  greater mastiff 46
  greater mouse-tailed 40
  hammer-headed 38
  harpy fruit 38
  heart-nosed 42
  hog-nosed 42
  Jamaican fruit-eating 48
  large Malay leaf-nosed 44
  lesser horseshoe 44
  lesser white-lined 40
  long-tongued fruit 38
  Mexican funnel-eared 52
  New Zealand short-tailed 52
  northern ghost 40
  Old World sheath-tailed 40
  painted 50
  Pallas' long-tongued 48
  Parnell's mustached 46
  Persian trident 44
  Peters' disk-winged 52
  Peters' ghost-faced 46
  Philippine horseshoe 44
  Queensland blossom 38
  red 50
  Seba's short-tailed 48
  spear-nosed 48
  sucker-footed 52
  tailless leaf-nosed 44
  tent-making 48
  tomb 40
  trident leaf-nosed 44
  tube-nosed fruit 38
  vampire 40
  Wroughton's free-tailed 46
  yellow-shouldered 48
  yellow-winged 42
Batagur 404
Batagur baska 404
Bateleur 220
Batfish 560
  shortnose 530
Bathyergidae 188
Bathyergus suillus 188
Batis minor 352
Batrachoidiformes 530

Batrachoseps attenuatus 468
Batrachostomus moniliger 272
Bdeogale crassicauda 96
Beaked whale family 118
Beamys hindei 176
Bear, Asiatic black 82
  big brown/grizzly 82
  black 82
  polar 82
  spectacled 82
  sun 82
Bearded dragon 420
Beardfish, stout 524
Beardfish order 524
Beaugregory 562
Beaver 164
  Eurasian 164
  mountain 164
Bee-eater, (European) 284
Bellbird, bearded 302
Belone belone 532
Belonesox belizanus 536
Belonion apodion 532
Belontiidae 572
Beluga 116
Beluga 498
Berardius arnouxii 118
  bairdi 118
Berlepschia rikeri 296
Berrypecker, black 360
Beryciformes 540
Betta splendens 572
Bichir 498
Bichir order 498
Big-headed turtle family 408
Bighorn 156
Bipes biporus 442
Bird of paradise, blue 398
  king 398
  King of Saxony 398
  ribbon-tailed astrapia 398
Bishop, red 388
Bison 144
  European 144
Bison bison 144
  bonasus 144
Bitis arietans 456
  gabonica 456
Bitterling 514
Bittern, American 208
Blackbird 336
Blackbuck 152
  bush 340
Blackcap 344
Blanus cinereus 442
Blarina brevicauda 34
Bleda syndactyla 322
Blenniidae 566
Blenny, redlip 566
Blesbok 148
Blind mole-rat subfamily 168
Blind snake family 444
Bluebird, eastern 334
  fairy 322
Bluetail, red-flanked 332
Boa, emerald tree 446
  rubber 446
Boa caninus 446
Boa constrictor 446
Boar, wild 128
Boarfish 538
Boatbill 208
Bobcat 102
Bobolink 382
Bobwhite 232
Boidae 446
Boiga dendrophila 452
Bombina orientalis 474
Bombycilla garrulus 326
Bombycillidae 326
Bonefish 500
Bongo 140
Bontebok 148
Boobook 270
Booby, brown 204
Boomslang 452
Bos gaurus 142
  javanicus 142
  mutus 142
Boselaphus tragocamelus 140
Botaurus lentiginosus 208
Bothrops atrox 458

Bothus lunatus 576
Boulengerella lucius 510
Boutu 112
Bovid family 140–56
Bovidae 140–56
Bowerbird, MacGregor's/
  Gardener 398
  satin 398
Bowfin 498
Bowfin order 498
Boxfish, blue-spotted 582
Brachycephalidae 478
Brachycephalus ephippium 478
Brachyistius frenatus 562
Brachylophus fasciatus 418
Brachypteracias leptosomus 284
Brachypteraciidae 284
Brachypteryx montana 332
Brachyramphus marmoratus 250
Brachyteles arachnoides 64
Bradornis pallidus 350
Bradypodidae 26
Bradypterus palliseri 346
Bradypus tridactylus 26
Brama brama 554
Branta canadensis 212
Bream 514
  gilthead 556
  red sea 556
Breviceps adspersus 472
Brevoortia tyrannus 502
Bristlebill 322
Bristlehead, Bornean 324
Broadbill, green 310
Brookesia spectrum 422
Bubalornis albirostris 390
Bubalus arnee 142
  depressicornis 142
Bubo virginianus 268
Bucconidae 288
Buceros bicornis 286
Bucerotidae 286
Bucorvus abyssinicus 286
  leadbeateri 286
Budgerigar 260
Budorcas taxicolor 156
Buffalo, African 144
  water 142
Buffalo, bigmouth 516
Bufo americanus 478
  bufo 478
  calamita 478
  marinus 478
  viridis 478
Bufonidae 478
Bulbul, black 320
  black-eyed/white-vented 320
  hook-billed 322
  red-whiskered 320
  white-throated 320
Bullfinch 384
Bullfrog 482
  South African 482
  South American 476
Bullhead 546
  brown 518
Bullhead shark order 492
Bullrout 546
Bullsnake 452
Bummalow 524
Bunting, painted 372
  reed 368
  snow 368
Buphagus africanus 293
Burbot 528
Burhinidae 244
Burhinus oedicnemus 244
Burramyidae 20
Burrfish, striped 582
Bush baby, greater 58
  lesser 58
Bush squeaker 484
Bushlark, singing 312
Bushmaster 458
Bushrunner, larklike 296
Bush-shrike, gray-headed 324
Bush-tanager, common 374
Bustard, great 238
  little black 238
Butcherbird, black 396
Buteo buteo 222
  jamaicensis 222

Butterfish 518, 572
Butterflyfish, copperband 560
  forceps 560
  foureye 560
Buttonquail, little 234
Buzzard 222
  fishing 222
  honey 218

C

Cabezon 546
Cacajao calvus 62
Cacatua galerita 258
Cacatuidae 258
Cacicus cela 382
Cacique, yellow-rumped 382
Caecilia ochrocephala 470
Caecilian, Panamanian 470
  São Tomé 470
  Seychelles 470
  South American 470
  sticky 470
Caeciliidae 470
Caenolestes obscurus 14
Caenolestidae 14
Caiman, spectacled 414
Caiman crocodilus 414
  sclerops 414
Cairina moschata 214
Calamus bajonado 556
Calandrella cinerea 312
California legless lizard family 438
Callaeas cinerea 394
Callaeidae 394
Callicebus moloch 62
Callichthyidae 522
Callichthys callichthys 522
Callimico goeldii 60
Callionymus lyra 574
Callithrix argentata 60
Callitrichidae 60
Callorhincus milii 496
Callorhinus ursinus 106
Callosciurus prevosti 158
Caloenas nicobarica 254
Calypte helenae 278
Calyptomena viridis 310
Camel, bactrian 132
Camelidae 132
Camelus dromedarius 132
  ferus 132
Campephaga phoenicea 318
Campephagidae 318
Campephilus principalis 292
Campethera abingoni 294
Campostoma anomalum 514
Campylorhamphus trochilirostris 300
*Campylorhynchus
  brunneicapillus* 328
Canary 384
Candirú 522
Cane rat family 188
Canidae 78
Canis dingo 78
  latrans 78
  lupus 78
Canthigaster rostrata 582
Canvasback 214
Capitonidae 288
Capra ibex 154
Capreolus capreolus 136
Capricornis sumatraensis 154
Caprimulgidae 274
Caprimulgiformes 272
Caprimulgus europaeus 274
Caprolagus hispidus 190
Capromyidae 186
Capromys ingrahami 186
Capros aper 538
Capybara 184
Caracal 100
Caracara 224
Caranx hippos 552
Carapus acus 528
Carassius auratus 512
Carcharhinus leucas 490
Carcharodon carcharias 490
Cardinal, (northern) 372
Cardinal and grosbeak
  subfamily 372
Cardinalinae 372
Cardinalis cardinalis 372

Cardioderma cor 42
Carduelis carduelis 384
Caretta caretta 410
Carettochelyidae 408
Carettochelys insculpta 408
Cariama cristata 238
Cariamidae 238
Caribou 136
Carnivora 78
Carollia perspicillata 48
Carp, common 512
   grass 514
Carpodacus purpureus 384
Cascadura 522
Cascarudo 522
Cassowary, common 196
Castor canadensis 164
   fiber 164
Castoridae 164
Casuariidae 196
Casuarius casuarius 196
Cat, golden 100
   leopard 100
   Pallas's 102
   pampas 100
   wild 102
Catagonus wagneri 130
Catamblyrhynchinae 372
Catamblyrhynchus diadema 372
Catbird, gray 330
Catfish, African glass 518
   Australian freshwater 522
   blue 518
   electric 520
   gafftopsail 520
   glass 518
   hardhead 520
   Mekong 520
   pungas 520
   upside-down 520
   walking 520
Catharacta skua 248
Cathartes aura 216
Cathartidae 216
Catharus fuscescens 336
Catostomus commersoni 516
Cavefish, northern 524
Cavia tschudii 184
Caviidae 184
Cavy 184
   rock 184
Cebidae 62–4
Cebuella pygmaea 60
Cebus albifrons 62
Celeus flavescens 294
Central American river turtle
   family 408
Centrolenella albomaculata 476
Centropomus undecimalis 548
Centropus milo 266
Cephalophus dorsalis 144
   sylvicultor 144
Cephalopterus ornatus 302
Ceratodiformes 496
Ceratophrys cornuta 476
Ceratotherium simum 126
Cercocebus albigena 66
   galeritus 66
Cercopithecidae 66–72
Cercopithecus aethiops 70
   diana 70
   erythrogaster 70
   neglectus 70
Certhia familiaris 358
Certhiaxis (Cranioleuca)
   erythrops 296
Certhidea olivacea 370
Certhiidae 358
Cervidae 134–8
Cervus canadensis 136
Ceryle alcyon 282
Cetacea 112
Cetomimus indagator 540
Cetorhinus maximus 488
Cettia fortipes 346
Chachalaca 226
Chaenocephalus aceratus 566
Chaetodipterus faber 560
Chaetodon capistratus 560
Chaetorhynchus papuensis 394
Chaetura gigantea 276
Chaffinch 384
Chalcides bedriagai 430

Chalcites maculatus 346
Chamaea fasciata 342
Chamaeleo chamaeleon 422
   dilepis 422
   jacksonii 422
   melleri 422
Chamaeleonidae 422
Chamaesaura aena 436
Chameleon, European 422
   flap-necked 422
   Jackson's 422
   Meller's 422
Chamois 154
Channichthyidae 566
Channidae 572
Chanos chanos 508
Char, Arctic 506
Characidae 510
Charadriidae 240
Charadriiformes 240
Charadrius hiaticula 240
Charina bottae 446
Chat, crimson 348
   palm 326
Chauliodus sloani 508
Chauna chavaria 212
Cheetah 102
Cheirogaleidae 56
Chelidae 412
Chelidorhynx hypoxantha 354
Chelmon rostratus 560
Chelonia 404
Chelonia mydas 410
Chelonidae 410
Chelus fimbriatus 412
Chelydra serpentina 408
Chelydridae 408
Chersine angulata 406
Chevrotain, lesser Malay 134
   water 134
Chickadee, black-capped 356
Chiffchaff 346
Chilomycterus schoepfi 582
Chimaera monstrosa 496
Chimaera order 496
Chimaeriformes 496
Chimpanzee 76
   pygmy 76
Chinchilla 186
Chinchilla laniger 186
Chinchilla-rat 186
Chinchillidae 186
Chionididae 246
Chionis alba 246
   minor 246
Chipmunk, eastern 160
Chirocentrus dorab 502
Chironectes minimus 14
Chiroptera 38
Chiroxiphia pareola 302
Chitra indica 412
Chlamydosaurus kingii 420
Chlamyphorus truncatus 28
Chloebia gouldiae 386
Chlorocichla flaviventris 320
Chlorophonia, blue-crowned 376
Chlorophonia occipitalis 376
Chloropsis aurifrons 322
Chlorospingus ophthalmicus 374
Choeropsis liberiensis 130
Choloepus didactylus 26
Chrysochloridae 32
Chrysochloris asiatica 32
Chrysococcyx cupreus 264
Chrysocolaptes lucidus 294
Chrysocyon brachyurus 80
Chrysolampis mosquitus 278
Chrysolophus pictus 230
Chrysomma sinense 338
Chrysopelea ornata 452
   paradisi 452
Chrysophrys auratus 556
Chrysospalax trevelyani 32
Chub, Bermuda 560
Chuckwalla 416
Cicadabird 318
Cichlid, ring-tailed pike 562
Cichlidae 562
Cicinnurus regius 398
Ciconia ciconia 210
Ciconiidae 210
Ciconiiformes 208
Cinclidae 330

Cinclocerthia ruficauda 330
Cinclosoma cinnamomeum 342
Cinclus mexicanus 330
Circus cyaneus 220
Cissopis leveriana 374
Cisticola, zitting 344
Cisticola juncidis 344
Cistothorus palustris 328
Civet, African 92
   African palm 92
   banded palm 94
   Congo water 92
   masked palm 92
Clamator coromandus 340
Clarias batrachus 520
Clariidae 520
Clemmys insculpta 404
Clethrionomys glareolus 172
Climacteridae 358
Climacteris picumnus 358
Clingfish, northern 574
   shore 574
Clinidae 566
Clupea harengus 502
   pallasi 502
Clupeiformes 502
Clytoceyx rex 282
Cnemidophorus lemniscatus 428
Coati 84
Cobia 552
Cobra and sea snake family 454
Cobra, Indian 454
   King 454
Coccyzus americanus 264
Cochlearius cochlearius 208
Cockatiel 258
Cockatoo, sulphur-crested 258
Cock-of-the-rock, Andean 302
Cod, Antarctic 566
   Atlantic 526
   Baikal 546
   Murray 548
Cod order 526–9
Coelacanth 460, 496
Coelacanth order 496
Coelacanthiformes 496
Coelops frithi 44
Coendou prehensilis 182
Coereba flaveola 378
Colaptes auratus 292
Coliidae 280
Coliiformes 280
Colinus virginianus 232
Colius striatus 280
Collocalia fuciphaga 276
Colluricincla harmonica 354
Colobus angolensis 72
   badius 72
Colobus monkey, Angolan black
   and white 72
   olive 72
   red 72
Colocolo 14
Colossoma nigripinnis 510
Coluber viridiflavus 450
Colubridae 448–52
Colubrine snake family 448–52
Colugo 36
Columba fasciata 252
   livia 252
Columbidae 252–6
Columbiformes 252–6
Columbina passerina 252
Comephorus baicalensis 546
Conchfish 550
Condor, California 216
Condylura cristata 36
Conebill, giant 376
Conepatus mesoleucus 90
Coney 548
Conger conger 504
Connochaetes taurinus 148
Conolophus subcristatus 418
Conopophaga melanops 300
Conopophagidae 300
Constrictor constrictor 446
Contopus virens 306
Conure, golden-capped 262
   jendaya 262
   sun 262
Coot, American 236
Copsychus saularis 334

Coracias garrulus 284
Coraciidae 284
Coraciiformes 282
Coracina novaehollandiae 318
   tenuirostris 318
Cordon-bleu, red-cheeked 386
Cordylidae 436
Cordylosaurus subtessellatus 436
Cordylus cataphractus 436
Coregonus lavaretus 506
Cormorant, flightless 206
   great 206
   reed 206
Corncrake 236
Coronella austriaca 452
Corvidae 400
Corvinella melanoleuca 324
Corvus brachyrhynchos 400
   frugilegus 400
Coryphaena equisetis 554
   hippurus 554
Coryphistera alaudina 296
Corythaixoides concolor 266
Cotinga cayana 302
Cotinga, spangled 302
Cotingidae 302
Cottonmouth 458
Cottontail, desert 192
Cottus gobio 546
Coturnix coturnix 228
Coua, running 266
Coua cursor 266
Coucal, buff-headed 266
Cougar 100
Courser, cream-colored 246
Cow shark and frill shark
   order 492
Cowbird, brown-headed 382
Cowfish, scrawled 580
Coyote 78
Coypu 186
Crab plover family 244
Cracidae 226
Cracticidae 396
Cracticus quoyi 396
Crane, crowned 234
   whooping 234
Craseonycteridae 42
Craseonycteris thonglongyai 42
Crax rubra 226
Creeper, brown 358
   spotted 358
   stripe-headed 358
Crenicichla saxatilis 562
Crescentchest, elegant 300
Crested rat subfamily 170
Crested swift family 276
Crex crex 236
Cricetinae 168
Cricetomyinae 176
Cricetomys emini 176
Cricetus cricetus 168
Criniger flaveolus 320
Crocidura miya 34
Crocodile, estuarine 414
   Nile 414
   West African dwarf 414
Crocodile lizard family 440
Crocodilia 414
Crocodylus niloticus 414
   porosus 414
Crocuta crocuta 98
Crossarchus obscurus 96
Crossbill, red/common 384
Crotalidae 458
Crotalus adamanteus 458
   cerastes 458
Crotaphytus collaris 416
Crotophaga ani 266
Crow, common 400
Cryptacanthodes maculatus 566
Cryptacanthodidae 566
Cryptobranchidae 462
Cryptobranchus alleganiensis 462
Cryptoprocta ferox 96
Ctenodactylidae 188
Ctenodactylus gundi 188
Ctenoluciidae 510
Ctenomyidae 186
Ctenomys talarum 186
Ctenopharyngodon idella 514
Ctenosaura pectinata 418
Cuckoo 264

African emerald 264
channel-billed 264
drongo 264
emerald 346
striped 266
yellow-billed 264
Cuckoo-roller 284
Cuckoo-shrike, ground 318
large/black-faced 318
red-shouldered/black 318
Cuckoo-shrike and minivet family 318
Cuculidae 264–6
Cuculiformes 264
Cuculus canorus 264
Cuiu-cuiu 520
Culicicapa helianthea 350
Cuniculus paca 184
Cuon alpinus 80
Curassow, great 226
nocturnal 226
Curimbata 510
Curlew, stone 244
Currawong, pied 396
Cursorius cursor 246
Cusimanse 96
Cutlassfish, Atlantic 570
Cyanerpes caeruleus 376
Cyanocitta cristata 400
Cyanocorax yncas 400
Cyclarhis gujanensis 380
Cycloderma frenatum 412
Cyclopes didactylus 26
Cyclopterus lumpus 546
Cyclorana cultripes 476
Cyclura cornuta 418
Cygnus columbianus 212
Cynocephalidae 36
Cynocephalus volans 36
Cynogale bennetti 94
Cynoglossus lingua 578
Cynomys ludovicianus 160
Cynoscion nebulosus 558
nobilis 558
Cyprinidae 512
Cyprinodon variegatus 534
Cypriniformes 510–16
Cyprinus carpio 512
Cypselurus heterurus 532
Cypsiurus parvus 276
Cystophora cristata 110

D

Dab 576
Dabchick 198
Dace 514
pearl 514
Dacelo novaeguineae 282
Dacnis, blue 376
Dacnis cayana 376
Dactylopteriformes 544
Dactylopterus volitans 544
Damaliscus dorcas 148
lunatus 148
Damselfish family 562
Darter, orangethroat 550
Darter family 206
Dassie rat family 188
Dasyatis americana 494
Dasycercus cristicauda 16
Dasypeltis scabra 448
Dasypodidae 28
Dasyprocta aguti 184
Dasyproctidae 184
Dasypus novemcinctus 28
Dasyuridae 16
Dasyuroides byrnei 16
Dasyurus viverrinus 16
Daubentonia madagascariensis 56
Daubentoniidae 56
Dealfish 538
Deer, Chinese water 134
forest musk 134
Père David's 136
red 136
roe 136
tufted 134
white-tailed 136
Degu 186
Delma nasuta 426
Delphinapterus leucas 116
Delphinidae 114

Delphinus delphis 114
Dendroaspis angusticeps 454
Dendrobates auratus 480
Dendrocolaptes certhia 300
Dendrocolaptidae 300
Dendrocopos major 292
Dendrocygna viduata 212
Dendrogale melanura 54
Dendrohyrax arboreus 122
Dendroica petechia 378
Dendrolagus lumholtzi 24
Dendromurinae 176
Dendromus mesomelas 176
Dendronanthus indicus 316
Denisonia devisii 454
Dermatemyidae 408
Dermatemys mawi 408
Dermochelyidae 410
Dermochelys coriacea 410
Dermogenys pusillus 532
Dermoptera 36
Desert dormouse family 180
Desman, Russian 36
Desmana moschata 36
Desmodontidae 46
Desmodus rotundus 46
Desmognathidae 468
Desmognathus fuscus 468
Dhole 80
Diademichthys lineatus 574
Dibamidae 438
Dibamus novaeguineae 438
Dicaeidae 360
Dicaeum hirundinaceum 360
Dicamptodon ensatus 464
Dicerorhinus sumatrensis 126
Diceros bicornis 126
Dickcissel 372
Diclidurus virgo 40
Dicruridae 394
Dicrurus adsimilis 394
paradiseus 394
Didelphidae 14
Didelphis virginiana 14
Didunculus strigirostris 256
Dik-dik, Kirk's 150
Dingo 78
Dinomyidae 184
Dinomys branicki 184
Diodon hystrix 582
Diodontidae 582
Diomedea exulans 200
Diomedeidae 200
Diploglossus lessorae 438
Diplomys labilis 188
Dipodidae 180
Dipodillus maghrebi 174
Dipodomys deserti 162
Dipper 330
Dipsas indica 448
Dipus sagitta 180
Discoglossid frog family 474
Discoglossidae 474
Discus fish 562
Dispholidus typus 452
Diving-petrel, subantarctic 202
Dog, bush 80
hunting 80
raccoon 80
Dogfish, sandy 490
spiny 492
Dolichonyx oryzivorus 382
Dolichotis patagona 184
Dolphin, Atlantic bottle-nosed 114
common 114
Ganges 112
Indo-Pacific humpbacked 114
Risso's 114
striped 114
whitefin 112
Dolphinfish 554
Doradidae 520
Dorcatragus megalotis 150
Dorcopsis veterum 24
Dormitator maculatus 568
Dormouse, African 180
Chinese pygmy 170
desert 180
fat 180
Japanese 180
Malabar spiny 170
Dory, buckler 538

John 538
Douroucouli, three-banded 62
Dove, collared 254
diamond 254
ground 252
large brown cuckoo 256
mourning 252
rock 252
scaly-breasted ground 252
superb fruit 254
Dovekie 250
Dracaena guianensis 428
Draco volans 420
Dragonet 574
Drepanididae 380
Drill 68
Dromadidae 244
Dromaiidae 196
Dromaius novaehollandiae 196
Dromas ardeola 244
Dromedary 132
Dromiciops australis 14
Drongo, fork-tailed 394
greater racket-tailed 394
pygmy 394
Drum, black 558
freshwater 558
Dryoscopus cubla 324
Duck, Falklands steamer 214
mandarin 214
muscovy 214
ruddy 214
tufted 214
wood 214
Ducula spilorrhoa 254
Dugong 110
Dugong dugon 110
Dugongidae 110
Duiker, bay 144
common/gray 144
yellow 144
Dulidae 326
Dulus dominicus 326
Dumetella carolinensis 330
Dunnart, fat-tailed 16
Dunnock 330
Dusicyon thous 80

E

Eagle, bald 220
crested serpent 220
golden 222
harpy 222
Earless monitor family 440
Eastern Asiatic mole-rat subfamily 168
Echenis naucrates 552
Echidna catenata 504
Echiichthys vipera 566
Echimyidae 188
Echinoprocta rufescens 182
Echinosorex gymnurus 32
Echis carinatus 456
Eclectus roratus 260
Edentata 26
Edge snout, Somali 442
Eel, conger 504
electric 512
European 504
gulper 504
slender snipe 504
spiny 504
Eel order 504
Egernia stokesii 432
Egret, cattle 208
great 208
Egretta alba 208
ardesiaca 208
Eider, common 214
Eira barbara 86
Elaenia flavogaster 306
Elaenia, yellow-bellied 306
Elagatis bipinnulata 552
Eland 140
Elaphe obsoleta 450
Elaphodus cephalophus 134
Elaphurus davidianus 136
Elapidae 454
Electrophoridae 512
Electrophorus electricus 512
Eleotridae 568
Elephant, African 122

Indian 122
Elephant shrew family 36
Elephantidae 122
Elephant-snout fish 500
Elephas maximus 122
Ellobius fuscocapillus 172
Elops saurus 500
Emballonura monticola 40
Emballonuridae 40
Emberiza citrinella 368
schoeniclus 368
Emberizidae 368–76
Emberizinae 368–70
Embiotocidae 562
Emoia cyanogaster 432
Emperor, spangled 556
sweetlip 556
Empidonax alnorum 306
traillii 306
Emu 196
Emydid turtle family 404
Emydidae 404
Emydura macquarri 412
Emys orbicularis 404
Engraulis encrasicolus 502
Enhydrina schistosa 454
Enhydris lutris 90
Enhydris punctata 448
Enicurus leschenaulti 334
Ensatina, yellow-blotched 468
Ensatina eschscholtzi croceator 468
Ensifera ensifera 278
Epinephelus fulvus 548
Epixerus ebii 158
Epomops franqueti 38
Eptesicus fuscus 50
Epthianura tricolor 348
Epthianurini 348
Equetus lanceolatus 558
Equidae 124
Equus africanus 124
burchelli 124
ferus 124
grevyi 124
hemionus 124
kiang 124
Eremias sp. 434
Eremophila alpestris 312
Eretmochelys imbricata 410
Erignathus barbatus 108
Erinaceidae 32
Erinaceus europaeus 32
Erithacus cyanurus 332
megarhynchos 332
rubecula 332
Erithizon dorsatum 182
Erithizontidae 182
Ermine 86
Erythrocebus patas 70
Erythropygia coryphaeus 332
Erythrura trichroa 386
Esacus magnirostris 244
Eschrichtidae 120
Eschrichtius robustus 120
Esox lucius 506
Estrildidae 386
Etheostoma spectabile 550
Eublepharius macularius 424
Eudynamys scolopacea 264
Eudyptula minor 198
Eumeces obsoletus 430
Eumetopias jubata 106
Eumops perotis 46
Eunectes murinus 446
Euphonia, white-vented 376
Euphonia minuta 376
Euplectes orix 388
Eupleres goudoti 94
Eurostopodus macrotis 274
Eurylaimidae 310
Eurypharynx pelecanoides 504
Eurypyga helias 238
Eurypygidae 238
Euthynnus pelamis 570
Eutoxeres aquila 278
Evening bat family 50
Excalfactoria chinensis 228
Exocetus volitans 532

F

Falanouc 94
Falco berigora 224

peregrinus 224
  rusticolus 224
  subbuteo 224
  tinnunculus 224
Falcon, barred forest 224
  brown 224
  peregrine 224
Falconet, collared 224
Falconidae 224
Falconiformes 216
Falculea palliata 326
Falcunculus frontatus 354
Fallfish 516
False vampire bat family 42
Fantail, rufous 354
  yellow-bellied 354
Fantail flycatcher subfamily 354
Felidae 100–4
Felis aurata 100
  bengalensis 100
  caracal 100
  colocolo 100
  concolor 100
  lynx 100
  manul 102
  pardalis 102
  rufus 102
  serval 102
  silvestris 102
Fer-de-lance 458
Ferret, black-footed 86
  domestic 86
Feylinia cussori 430
Figbird, yellow 394
Fightingfish, Siamese 572
Filefish, planehead 580
  scrawled 580
Fimbrios klossi 448
Finch, Gouldian 386
  large ground 370
  plush-capped 372
  purple 384
  snow 390
  warbler 370
  white-naped brush 370
  zebra 386
Finchbill, crested 320
Finfoot, African 238
Fire-finch, red-billed 386
Fisherman bat family 46
Flamingo, American 210
Flatfish order 574
Flicker, common 292
Flounder, peacock 576
  starry 576
  summer 576
  winter 578
Flowerpecker, crimson-
  breasted 360
Flycatcher, alder 306
  Asian paradise 352
  blue-throated 350
  boat-billed 352
  citrine canary 350
  cliff 308
  gray silky 326
  kiskadee 304
  maroon-breasted 350
  ocher-bellied 308
  pale/mouse-coloured 350
  piratic 308
  royal 306
  rufous-tailed jungle 350
  scissor-tailed 304
  spotted 350
  vermilion 308
  white-tailed crested 352
  willow 306
  see also Monarch; Tyrant
Flycatcher-shrike, pied/
  bar-winged 318
Flying dragon 420
Flying gurnard order 544
Flying lemur, Philippine 36
Flying squirrel, Beecroft's 164
  Zenker's 164
  see also Squirrel
Flyingfish, Atlantic 532
  tropical two-wing 532
Footballfish, Atlantic 530
Forcipiger longirostris 560
Fordonia leucobalia 448
Forktail, white-crowned 334

Formicariidae 298
Forpus conspicillatus 262
Fossa 96
Four-eyed fish 534
Fox, arctic 78
  crab-eating 80
  fennec 78
  red 78
Francolin, red-necked 228
Francolinus afer 228
Fratercula arctica 250
Free-tailed bat family 46
Fregata magnificens 206
Fregatidae 206
Friarbird, little 364
Frigatebird, magnificent 206
Fringilla coelebes 384
Fringillidae 368, 384
Frog, arum lily 484
  common 482
  corroboree 476
  Darwin's 476
  eastern narrow-mouthed 472
  glass 476
  gold 478
  gold spiny reed frog 484
  golden arrow-poison 480
  green and gold bell 480
  Hochstetter's 474
  horned 476
  marsh 482
  marsupial 480
  mottled burrowing 484
  Natal ghost 476
  northern cricket 480
  northern leopard 482
  parsley 474
  Seychelles 484
  sheep 472
  South African rain 472
  striped grass 482
  tailed 474
  termite 472
  Wallace's flying 484
Frogfish, longlure 530
Frogmouth, Ceylon 272
  tawny 272
Fruiteater, barred 302
Fulica americana 236
Fulmar, northern 200
Fulmarus glacialis 200
Fulvetta, brown-cheeked 340
Funambulus palmarum 158
Fundulus heteroclitus 534
Funnel-eared bat family 52
Furipteridae 52
Furipterus horrens 52
Furnariidae 296
Furnarius rufus 296

G

Gadiformes 526–8
Gadus morhua 526
Gaidropsarus mediterraneus 528
Galago senegalensis 58
Galaxias maculatus 508
Galbula ruficauda 288
Galbulidae 288
Galictis vittata 86
Gallicolumba luzonica 256
Galliformes 226
Gallinago gallinago 242
Gallinula chloropus 236
Gallinule, common 508
Galliwasp 438
Galloperdix spadicea 228
Gallus gallus 230
Gannet, northern 204
Gar, longnose 498
Gar order 498
Garfish 532
Garrulax leucolophus 340
Garrulus glandarius 400
Gasteropelecidae 510
Gasteropelecus sternicla 510
Gasterosteiformes 542
Gasterosteus aculeatus 542
Gastrophryne carolinensis 472
Gastrotheca marsupiata 480
Gaur 142
Gavia stellata 198
Gavial 414

Gavialis gangeticus 414
Gaviidae 198
Gaviiformes 198
Gazella thomsoni 152
Gazelle, Thomson's 152
Gecko, Brook's 424
  green day 426
  Kuhl's 424
  leaf-tailed 426
  leopard 424
  marbled 424
  tokay 424
  web-footed 424
  white-spotted 424
Gekko gekko 424
Gekkonidae 424–6
Gelada 68
Genet, small-spotted 92
Genetta genetta 92
Genypterus blacodes 528
Geochelone elephantopus 406
  pardalis 406
Geococcyx californianus 266
Geocolaptes olivaceus 294
Geomyidae 162, 186
Geomys bursarius 162
Geopelia cuneata 254
Geospiza magnirostris 370
Geothlypis philadelphia 378
Gerbil, fat-tailed 174
  great 174
  greater short-tailed 174
  Indian 174
  large North African 174
  South African pygmy 174
Gerbillinae 174
Gerbillurus paeba 174
Gerbillus campestris 174
Gerenuk 152
Gerrhonotus multicarinatus 438
Gerrhosaurus flavigularis 436
Gerygone olivacea 348
Ghost frog family 476
Giant salamander family 462
Gibbon, black 74
  Kloss's 74
  lar 74
  pileated 74
Gila monster 440
Giraffa camelopardalis 138
Giraffe 138
Giraffidae 138
Girdled and plated lizard
  family 436
Glareola pratincola 246
Glareolidae 246
Glass snake 438
Glaucidium passerinum 270
Glaucomys sabrinus 160
Glider, greater 20
  pygmy 20
  sugar 20
Gliridae 180
Glirurus japonicus 180
Glis glis 180
Globicephala melaena 114
Glossophaga soricina 48
Gnatcatcher, blue-gray 344
Gnateater, black-cheeked 300
Goat, mountain 154
Goatfish, spotted 558
Go-away bird, common 266
Gobiesocidae 574
Gobiesociformes 574
Gobiesox maeandricus 574
Gobiidae 568
Gobio gobio 514
Gobius paganellus 568
Goby, dwarf 568
  rock 568
Gold frog family 478
Golden mole, Cape 32
  giant 32
  Hottentot 32
Goldenback, greater 294
Goldeye 500
Goldfinch, European 384
Goldfish 512
Gonorynchiformes 508
Goose, Canada 212
  graylag 212
  magpie 212
Gopher, northern pocket 162

plains pocket 162
Gopherus polyphemus 406
Goral, common 154
Gorilla 76
Gorilla gorilla 76
Goshawk 222
  dark chanting 220
Goura victoria 256
Gourami 572
Grackle, common 382
Gracula religiosa 392
Grallaria ruficapilla 298
Grallina cyanoleuca 396
Grallinidae 396
Grampus 114
Grampus griseus 114
Graphiurus murinus 180
Graptemys pseudogeographica 404
Grassbird, little 346
Gray whale family 120
Grayling 506
  American 506
Greaved turtle family 412
Grebe, great crested 198
  little 198
Greenbul, yellow-bellied/yellow-
  breasted 320
Greenlet, tawny-crowned 380
Greenling, kelp 546
Grenadier, roughhead 528
Grison 86
Grosbeak, pine 384
  rose-breasted 372
Ground roller, short-legged 284
Grouse, black 232
Gruidae 234
Gruiformes 234
Grunion, California 536
Grus americana 234
Grysbok 150
Guan, crested 226
Guanaco 132
Gudgeon 514
Guinea pig/cavy family 184
Guineafowl, helmeted 232
Guitarfish, Atlantic 494
Gull, black-headed 248
  herring 248
  ivory 248
Gulo gulo 88
Gundi 188
Gunnel, rock 566
Guppy 534
Gurnard, flying 544
  tub 544
Gymnachirus melas 578
Gymnarchus niloticus 500
Gymnogyps californianus 216
Gymnopithys bicolor 298
  leucaspis 298
Gymnorhina tibicen 396
Gymnotus carapo 512
Gypaetus barbatus 218
Gypohierax angolensis 220
Gyrfalcon 224
Gyrinophilus porphyriticus 468

H

Haddock 526
Haematopodidae 240
Haematopus ostralegus 240
Hagfish, Atlantic 488
Hake, European 528
  Pacific 528
  white 526
Halcyon chloris 282
Halfbeak, wrestling 532
Haliaeetus leucocephalus 220
Haliastur indus 218
Halibut, Atlantic 576
  California 576
  Greenland 578
Halichoeres bivittatus 564
Halichoerus grypus 108
Halietor africanus 206
Hammerhead, smooth 490
Hammerkop 208, 210
Hamster, common 168
  golden 168
  striped 168
Hare, brown 190
  hispid 190

Natal red   190
Hare-wallaby, spectacled   22
Harlequin fish   516
Harpactes erythrocephalus   280
Harpadon nehereus   524
Harpia harpyja   222
Harpyionycteris whiteheadi   38
Harrier, northern   220
Hartebeest   148
Hatchetfish   508, 510
Hawaiian honeycreeper family   380
Hawk, African harrier   220
   brown   224
   Cooper's   222
   marsh   220
   red-tailed   222
Hawksbill   410
Hedgehog, desert   32
   western European   32
Helarctos malayanus   82
Heleophryne natalensis   476
Heleophrynidae   476
Heliornis fulica   238
Heliornithidae   238
Hellbender   462
Heloderma suspectum   440
Helodermatidae   440
Hemicentetes semispinosus   30
Hemidactylus brookii   424
Hemigalus derbyanus   94
Hemignathus wilsoni   380
Hemipode, Andalusian   234
   collared   234
Hemiprocne longipennis   276
Hemiprocnidae   276
Hemipus picatus   318
Hemiramphus brasiliensis   532
Hemispingus, black-capped   374
Hemispingus atropileus   374
Hemisus marmoratum   484
Hemitragus jemlahicus   156
Heron, black   208
   black-crowned night   208
   boat-billed   208
   gray   208
   great blue   208
Herpestes auropunctatus   96
Herring   502
   Pacific   502
   wolf   502
Hesperomyinae   166
Heteralocha acutirostris   394
Heterandria formosa   536
Heterocephalus glaber   188
Heterodontiformes   492
Heterodontus portusjacksoni   492
Heterohyrax brucei   122
Heteromyidae   162
Heteromys anomalus   162
Heteropholis manukanus   426
Heterostichus rostratus   566
Hexagrammos decagrammus   546
Hexanchiformes   492
Hexanchus griseus   492
Hillstar, Andean   278
Himantolophus groenlandicus   530
Himantopus himantopus   244
Hiodon alosoides   500
Hippocampus zosterae   542
Hippoglossoides platessoides   578
Hippoglossus hippoglossus   576
Hippopotamidae   130
Hippopotamus   130
   pygmy   130
Hippopotamus amphibius   130
Hipposideridae   44
Hipposideros diadema   44
Hippotragus equinus   146
Hirundinea ferruginea   308
Hirundinidae   314
Hirundo rustica   314
Histrio histrio   530
Hoatzin   226
Hobby   224
Hog, giant forest   128
Hogfish   564
Hog-nosed bat family   42
Holacanthus ciliaris   560
Holocentrus ascensionis   540
Honey buzzard   218
Honey eater, brown   364
   cardinal   364
   fuscous   364

long-bearded   364
   pygmy   366
   strong-billed   364
Honey guide, greater/black-
   throated   88, 288
Honey possum family   18
Honeycreeper, purple   376
Hoolock   74
Hoopoe, common   286
Hoplomys gymnurus   188
Hoplosternum littorale   522
Hoplostethus atlanticus   540
Hornbill, Abyssinian ground   286
   great Indian   286
   helmeted   286
   red-billed   286
   southern ground   286
Hornero, rufous   296
Horse, Przhevalski's   124
Horseshoe bat family   44
Houndfish   532
Huet-huet, chestnut-throated   300
Huia   394
Hummingbird, bee   278
   giant   278
   long-tailed sylph   278
   ruby-throated   278
   ruby-topaz   278
   sword-billed   278
Huso huso   498
Hutia, Ingraham's   186
Hutia and nutria family   186
Hyaena brunnea   98
   hyaena   98
Hyaenidae   98
Hydrobates pelagicus   202
Hydrobatidae   202
Hydrochoeridae   184
Hydrochoerus hydrochaeris   184
Hydrocynus goliath   512
Hydromyinae   176
Hydromys chrysogaster   176
Hydrophis cyanocinctus   454
Hydropotes inermis   134
Hydrosaurus amboinensis   420
Hydrurga leptonyx   108
Hyemoschus aquaticus   134
Hyena, brown   98
   spotted   98
   striped   98
Hyla arborea   480
   crucifer   480
   versicolor   480
Hylidae   480
Hylobates concolor   74
   hoolock   74
   klossi   74
   lar   74
   pileatus   74
   syndactylus   74
Hylochoerus meinertzhageni   128
Hylophilus ochraceiceps   380
Hynobiidae   462
Hynobius stejnegeri   462
Hyomys goliath   178
Hyperoliid frog family   484
Hyperoliidae   484
Hyperolius horstockii   484
Hyperoodon ampullatus   118
Hyphessobrycon flammeus   510
Hypocolius ampelinus   326
Hypocolius, gray   326
Hypogeophis rostratus   470
Hypopachus variolosus   472
Hypositta corallirostris   326
Hypothymis azurea   352
Hypsignathus monstrosus   38
Hypsipetes madagascariensis   320
Hypsiprymnodon moschatus   22
Hyracoidea   122
Hyrax, large-toothed rock   122
   small-toothed rock   122
   tree   122
Hystricidae   182
Hystrix africaeaustralis   182

I

Ibex   154
Ibidorhyncha struthersii   244
Ibidorhynchidae   244
Ibis, glossy   210
Ibisbill   244

Icefish   566
Ichneumia albicauda   96
Ichthyomys stolzmanni   166
Ichthyophidae   470
Ichthyophis sp.   470
Ictalurus furcatus   518
   nebulosus   518
Icterid family   382
Icteridae   382
Icterus galbula   382
Ictiobus cyprinellus   516
Ictonyx striatus   86
Idiurus zenkeri   164
Iguana, common   416
   Fijian banded   418
   forest   416
   Galápagos land   418
   Madagascan   418
   marine   418
   rhinoceros   418
   spiny-tailed   418
Iguana iguana   416
Iguanidae   416–8
Illadopsis, scaly-breasted   338
Impala   152
Indicator indicator   288
Indicatoridae   288
Indostomiformes   532
Indostomus paradoxus   532
Indri   56
Indri indri   56
Indriidae   56
Inia geoffrensis   112
Insectivora   30
Iora, common   322
Irena puella   322
Irenidae   322
Island water rat subfamily   176
Isoodon obesulus   20
Ispidina picta   282
Istiophoridae   570
Istiophorus platypterus   570
Isurus oxyrinchus   490

J

Jacamar, rufous-tailed   288
Jacana, North American   240
Jacana spinosa   240
Jacanidae   240
Jack, crevalle   552
Jackknife-fish   558
Jackrabbit, black-tailed   190
Jaguar   104
Jaraqui   510
Jay   400
   blue   400
   green   400
   Hume's ground   400
Jerboa, great   180
   northern three-toed   180
Jewfish   548
Jollytail   508
Junco, dark-eyed   368
Junco hyemalis   368
Jungle runner   428
Junglefowl, red   230
Jynx torquilla   292

K

Kagu   238
Kakapo   260
Kalochelidon euchrysea   314
Kangaroo, Lumholtz's tree   24
   red   24
Kangaroo family   22–4
Kea   258
Kelpfish, giant   566
Kerivoula argentata   50
Kerodon rupestris   184
Kestrel   224
Ketupa zeylonensis   268
Kiang   124
Killifish, pike   536
   least   536
Kingbird, eastern   304
Kingfisher   282
   African pygmy   282
   beautiful/common paradise   282
   belted   282
   shovel-billed   282
   white-collared/mangrove   282

Kinglet, golden-crowned   346
Kingsnake, common   452
Kinixys erosa   406
Kinkajou   84
Kinosternidae   408
Kinosternon flavescens   408
Kite, brahminy   218
   Everglade/snail   218
   red   218
Kittiwake, black-legged   248
Kiwi, brown   196
Klipspringer   150
Knifefish, banded   512
Koala   18
Kob, Uganda   146
Kobus ellipsiprymnus   146
   kob thomasi   146
   leche   146
Koel, common   264
Kogia breviceps   116
   simus   116
Kokako   394
Komodo dragon   440
Kookaburra, laughing   282
Kowari   16
Kryptopterus bicirrhis   518
Kudu, greater   140
Kyphosus sectatrix   560

L

Labridae   564
Labrus bergylta   564
Lacerta muralis   434
   viridis   434
   vivipara   434
Lacertid lizard family   434
Lacertidae   434
Lachesis muta   458
Lachnolaimus maximus   564
Lactophrys quadricornis   580
Ladyfishtenpounder   500
Lagocephalus lagocephalus   582
Lagonosticta senegala   386
Lagopus mutus   232
Lagorchestes conspicillatus   22
Lagostomus maximus   186
Lagothrix lagothricha   64
Lagurus curtatus   172
Lalage sueurii   318
Lama guanicoe   132
Lammergeier   218
Lamna ditropis   490
   nasus   490
Lamniformes   488–90
Lampern   488
Lampetra fluviatilis   488
Lamprey, sea   488
Lamprey order   488
Lampridiformes   538
Lampris guttatus   538
Lamprolia victoriae   348
Lampropeltis getulus   452
Land tortoise family   406
Langur   72
Laniarius atrococcineus   324
Laniidae   324
Lanius excubitor   324
Lanternfish   524
Lanternfish order   524
Lanthanotidae   440
Lanthanotus borneensis   440
Lapwing   240
Laridae   248
Lark, desert   312
   greater hoopoe   312
   horned   312
   magpie   396
   short-toed/red-capped   312
   thick-billed/Clotbey   312
Larus argentatus   248
   ridibundus   248
Lasiurus borealis   50
Lates niloticus   548
Latimeria chalumnae   496
Laughingthrush, white-crested   340
Lavia frons   42
Leafbird, gold-fronted   322
Leaffish, Schomburgk's   562
Leaflove   320
Leaping lemur family   56
Leatherback   410
Lechwe   146

Legatus leucophaius 308
Leiolopisma infrapunctatum 432
Leiopelma hochstetteri 474
Leiothrix, red-billed 340
Leiothrix lutea 340
Leipoa ocellata 226
Lemming, Norway 172
    southern bog 172
Lemmus lemmus 172
Lemur, ring-tailed 56
    ruffed 56
    woolly 56
    see also Flying lemur
Lemur catta 56
Lemuridae 56
Leontopithecus rosalia 60
Leopard 104
    clouded 102
    snow 104
Lepadogaster lepadogaster 574
Lepidochelys kempi 410
    olivacea 410
Lepidosiren paradoxa 496
Lepidosireniformes 496
Lepisosteus osseus 498
Leporidae 190–2
Leporillus conditor 178
Leptodactylid frog family 476
Leptodactylidae 476
Leptodactylus pentadactylus 476
Leptonychotes weddelli 110
Leptosomatidae 284
Leptosomus discolor 284
Leptotyphlopidae 444
Leptotyphlops humilis 444
Lepus americanus 190
    californicus 190
    capensis 190
Lethrinidae 556
Lethrinus chrysostomus 556
    nebulosus 556
Leuciscus leuciscus 514
Leuresthes tenuis 536
Lialis burtonis 426
Lichmera indistincta 364
Limanda limanda 576
Limpkin 234
Ling 526
    New Zealand 528
Linophryne arborifera 530
Linsang, African 92
    banded 92
Liomys irroratus 162
Lion 104
    mountain 100
Lionfish 544
Lioptilus nigricapillus 340
Liparis liparis 546
Lipophrys pholis 566
Lipotes vexillifer 112
Litocranius walleri 152
Litoria cyclorhynchus 480
Lizard, armadillo 436
    basilisk 418
    Bosc's fringe-toed 434
    caiman 428
    California legless 438
    collared 416
    desert night 428
    eastern fence 416
    Essex's mountain 434
    frilled 420
    girdled 436
    green 434
    imperial flat 436
    plated 436
    southern alligator 438
    Texas horned 416
    Transvaal snake 436
    viviparous 434
    wall 434
    see also Worm lizard
Lizardfish, red 524
Loach, coolie 516
    spined 516
    stone 516
Lobodon carcinophagus 108
Lobotes surinamensis 554
Locustella naevia 346
Loddigesia mirabilis 278
Loggerhead 410
Longclaw, yellow-throated 316

Long-tailed titmouse family 356
Lookdown 552
Loon, red-throated 198
Lophiiformes 530
Lophiomyinae 170
Lophiomys imhausi 170
Lophius piscatorius 530
Lophornis magnifica 278
Lophortyx californica 232
Loricariidae 522
Loriidae 258
Lorikeet, rainbow 258
Loris, slender 58
    slow 58
Loris tardigradus 58
Lorisidae 58
Lorius lory 258
Lory, black-capped 258
    rainbow 258
Lota lota 528
Lovebird, peach-faced 260
Loxia curvirostra 384
Loxodonta africana 122
Loxops coccinea 380
Lucifuga spelaeotes 528
Lumpfish 546
Lungfish, African 496
    Australian 496
    South American 496
Lungless salamander family 468
Luscinia megarhynchos 332
Lutjanus analis 554
Lutra lutra 90
Lybius bidentatus 288
Lycaon pictus 80
Lynx 100
Lyrebird, superb 310
Lyretail, Cape Lopez 534

M

Mabuya 432
Mabuya wrightii 432
Macaca arctoides 66
    fuscata 66
    radiata 66
    sylvanus 66
Macaque, bonnet 66
    Japanese 66
    stump-tailed 66
Macaw, scarlet 262
Mackerel, Atlantic 570
Macroclemys temmincki 408
Macroderma gigas 42
Macrodipteryx longipennis 274
Macroglossus minimus 38
Macronyx croceus 316
Macropodidae 22–4
Macropus opercularis 572
Macropus rufus 24
Macropygia phasianella 256
Macroscelides proboscideus 36
Macroscelididae 36
Macrotis lagotis 20
Macrourus berglax 528
Macrozoarces americanus 528
Madagascan rat subfamily 170
Madoqua kirki 150
Madtom, tadpole 518
Magpie, (black-billed) 400
    Australian 396
    Ceylon 400
Mahseer 512
Maigre 558
Makaira nigricans 570
Mako, shortfin 490
Malaclemys terrapin 404
Malaconotus blanchoti 324
Malacopteron magnum 338
Malapterurus electricus 520
    microstoma 520
Malimbus rubriceps 388
Malkoha, small green-billed 266
Mallard 214
Malleefowl 226
Malococchersus tornieri 406
Malurinae 348
Malurini 348
Malurus cyaneus 348
Mamba, eastern green 454
Manakin, blue-backed 302
    wire-tailed 302
Manatee, American 110

Mandarinfish 574
Mandi 522
Mandrill 68
Mandrillus leucophaeus 68
    sphinx 68
Mangabey, agile 66
    white-cheeked 66
Manidae 28
Manis gigantea 28
    tricuspis 28
Man-of-war fish 572
Manorina melanocephala 366
Manta, Atlantic 494
Manta birostris 494
Manucode, crinkle-collared 398
Manucodia chalybatus 398
Manushi 458
Mara 184
Margate 554
    black 554
Marine turtle family 410
Martin, blue 570
    striped 570
Marmosa mitis 14
Marmoset, Goeldi's 60
    pygmy 60
    silvery/black-tailed 60
Marmota monax 160
Marsupial mole family 18
Marsupialia 14
Marten 86
Martes americana 86
    zibellina 86
Martin, purple 314
    white-eyed river 314
Massasauga 458
Mastacembelidae 572
Mastacembelus armatus 572
Mastigure, princely 420
Matamata 412
Matamata and snake-necked turtle
    family 412
Meadowlark, eastern 382
Medaka, Japanese 534
Meerkat 94
Megaderma lyra 42
Megadermatidae 42
Megalaima haemacephala 288
Megalurus gramineus 346
Megapode family 226
Megapodiidae 226
Megapodius freycinet 226
Megaptera novaeangliae 120
Megasorex gigas 34
Melanocharis nigra 360
Melanochlora sultanea 356
Melanogrammus aeglefinus 526
Melanopareia elegans 300
Melanotaenia fluviatilis 536
Meleagridinae 232
Meleagris gallopavo 232
Meles meles 88
Melidectes princeps 364
Melierax metabates 220
Meliphaga fusca 364
Meliphagidae 364–6
Melipotes, common 366
Melipotes fumigatus 366
Melithreptus validirostris 364
Mellivora capensis 88
Melogale moschata 88
Melomys cervinipes 178
Melopsittacus undulatus 260
Menhaden, Atlantic 502
Menura novaehollandiae 310
Menuridae 310
Mephitis mephitis 90
Merganser, red-breasted 214
Mergus serrator 214
Merlangius merlangus 526
Merluccius merluccius 528
Meropidae 284
Merops apiaster 284
Mesite, white-breasted 234
Mesitornis variegata 234
Mesitornithidae 234
Mesocricetus auratus 168
Mesoplodon bidens 118
Mexican burrowing toad
    family 472
Micrastur ruficollis 224
Micrathene whitneyi 268
Microbiotheriidae 14

Microcebus rufus 56
Microdipodops pallidus 162
Microgale longicaudata 30
Microhierax caerulescens 224
Microhylidae 472
Micromesistius poutassou 526
Micromys minutus 178
Micronycteris megalotis 48
Micropsitta bruijnii 258
Micropterus salmoides 550
Microtinae 172
Microtus pennsylvanicus 172
Micrurus fulvius 454
Midshipman, Atlantic 530
Milkfish 508
Milvus milvus 218
Mimidae 330
Mimus polyglottos 330
Miner, noisy 366
Minivet, scarlet 318
Minnow 514
    sheepshead 534
Miopithecus talapoin 70
Mirafra javanica 312
Mirounga angustirostris 110
Mistletoe bird 360
Mniotilta varia 378
Mochokidae 520
Mockingbird 330
    Galápagos 330
Moho braccatus 364
Mola mola 582
Mole, coast 36
    eastern 36
    European 36
    hairy-tailed 36
    marsupial 18
    star-nosed 36
    see also Golden mole
Mole salamander family 464
Mole-rat, Cape dune 188
    giant 168
    lesser 168
    naked 188
Mole-rat and bamboo rat
    subfamily 168
Mole-vole, southern 172
Molidae 582
Moloch horridus 420
Molossidae 46
Molossus ater 46
Molothrus ater 382
Molva molva 526
Momotidae 284
Momotus momota 284
Monacanthus hispidus 580
Monachus monachus 110
Monarch, black-naped (blue) 352
    spectacled 352
Monarcha trivirgata 352
Monarchinae 352
Monasa nigrifrons 288
Mongoose, banded 96
    bushy-tailed 96
    Indian 96
    marsh 96
    white-tailed 96
Monitor, earless 440
    Gould's 440
    Nile 440
Monitor lizard family 446
Monkey, Allen's swamp 70
    black howler 64
    black spider 64
    common woolly 64
    De Brazza's 70
    Diana 70
    patas 70
    proboscis 72
    red howler 64
    red-bellied 70
    snub-nosed 72
    squirrel 62
    night 62
    vervet 70
    woolly spider 64
Monkfish 492
Monocentris japonicus 540
Monodelphis brevicaudata 14
Monodon monoceros 116
Monodontidae 116
Monopeltis capensis 442
Monopterus alba 544

Monotremata 12
Monticola rupestris 336
Montifringilla nivalis 390
Moonrat 32
    Mindanao 32
Moorhen, common 236
Moorish idol 568
Moose 136
Moray 504
    chain 504
Morelia argus 446
Morepork 270
Mormoopidae 46
Mormoops megalophylla 46
Mormyriformes 500
Mormyrus kannume 500
Morus bassana 204
Moschidae 134
Moschus chrysogaster 134
Motacilla alba 316
    flava 316
Motacillidae 316
Motmot, blue-crowned 284
Mouflon 156
Mountain beaver family 164
Mouse, African climbing 176
    climbing 166
    deer 166
    eastern shrew 176
    fat 176
    four-striped grass 178
    golden 166
    harvest 178
    hopping 178
    house 178
    meadow jumping 180
    mosaic-tailed 178
    northern birch 180
    northern grasshopper 166
    pale kangaroo 162
    South American field 166
    western harvest 166
    wood 178
    see also Pocket mouse
Mousebird, speckled 280
Mouse-lemur, russet 56
Mouse-oposum, South
    American 14
Mouse-tailed bat family 40
Mouthbrooder, Nile 562
Mouth-brooding frog family 476
Moxostoma macrolepidotum 516
Mud and musk turtle family 408
Mudnest builder family 396
Mudpuppy 466
Mugil cephalus 564
Mugilidae 564
Mulgara 16
Mulleripicus pulverulentus 294
Mullet, red 558
    striped 564
Mullidae 558
Mullus surmuletus 558
Mummichog 534
Mungos mungo 96
Muntiacus reevesi 134
Muntjac, Chinese 134
Muraena helena 504
Murinae 178
Murre, common 250
Murrelet, marbled 250
Mus musculus 178
Muscicapa striata 350
Muscicapidae 332–54
Muscicapinae 350
Muscivora forficata 304
Musk deer family 134
Muskrat 172
Musophagidae 266
Mustached bat family 46
Mustela erminea 86
    nigripes 86
    nivalis (rixosa) 86
    putorius 86
Mustelid family 86–90
Mustelidae 86–90
Myadestes ralloides 334
Myctoperca bonaci 548
Myctophiformes 524
Myctophum punctatum 524
Mydaus javanensis 88
Myioborus pictus 378
Myiopsitta monachus 262

Myiornis ecaudatus 306
Myliobatis aquila 494
Myna, hill 392
Myobatrachid frog family 476
Myobatrachidae 476
Myocastor coypus 186
Myosorex varius 34
Myospalacinae 168
Myospalax fontanieri 168
Myotis, little brown 50
Myotis lucifugus 50
Myoxocephalus scorpius 546
Myrmecobiidae 18
Myrmecobius fasciatus 18
Myrmecophaga tridactyla 26
Myrmecophagidae 26
Myrmotherula surinamensis 298
Mystacina tuberculata 52
Mystacinidae 52
Mystromys albicaudatus 170
Myxine glutinosa 488
Myxiniformes 488
Myzomela cardinalis 364
Myzopoda aurita 52
Myzopodidae 52
Myzornis, fire-tailed 340
Myzornis pyrrhoura 340

N

Naja naja 454
Nandidae 562
Nandinia binotata 92
Nannopterum harrisi 206
Napothera macrodactyla 338
Narrow-mouthed frog family 472
Narwhal 116
Nasalis larvatus 72
Nasica longirostris 300
Naso lituratus 568
Nasua nasua 84
Natalidae 52
Natalus stramineus 52
Natrix natrix 450
Neacomys guianae 166
Nectarinia johnstoni 362
    jugularis 362
    sperata 362
    superba 362
Nectariniidae 362
Necturus maculosus 466
Needlefish, freshwater 532
Needletail, brown 276
Nemichthys scolopaceus 504
Nemorhaedus goral 154
Neoceratodus forsteri 496
Neofelis nebulosa 102
Neophoca cinerea 106
Neophocaena phocaenoides 112
Neophron percnopterus 218
Neoseps reynoldsi 430
Neositta chrysoptera 358
Neotoma albigula 166
Neotragus pygmaeus 150
Nesolagus netscheri 192
Nesomyinae 170
Nesomys rufus 170
Nestor notabilis 258
New World monkey family 62–4
New World porcupine family 182
New World rats and mice
    subfamily 166
New World vulture family 216
New Zealand short-tailed bat
    family 52
New Zealand wren family 310
Newt, eastern 462
    rough-skinned 462
    warty 462
Nicator 322
Nicator chloris 322
Night lizard family 428
Nightingale 332
Nightjar, (European) 274
    greater eared 274
    lyre-tailed 274
    standard-winged 274
Nilgai 138
Niltava rubeculoides 350
Ninox novaeseelandiae 270
Noctilio leporinus 46
Noctilionidae 46

Noctule 50
Noddy, brown 248
Noemacheilus barbatulus 516
Nomeidae 572
Nomeus gronovii 572
Notacanthiformes 504
Notacanthus chemnitzii 504
Notharchus macrorhynchos 288
Nothocrax urumutum 226
Notomys alexis 178
Notophthalmus viridescens 462
Notornis mantelli 236
Notoryctes typhlops 18
Notoryctidae 18
Notothenia coriiceps 566
Nototheniidae 566
Notropis cornutus 516
Noturus gyrinus 518
Numbat 18
Numenius phaeopus 242
Numida meleagris 232
Numidinae 232
Nunbird, black-fronted 288
Nuthatch, coral-billed 326
    red-breasted 358
Nutria 186
Nyala 140
Nyctalus noctula 50
Nyctea scandiaca 268
Nyctereutes procyonoides 80
Nycteridae 42
Nycteris thebaica 42
Nyctibiidae 272
Nyctibius griseus 272
Nycticebus coucang 58
Nycticorax nycticorax 208
Nycticryphes semicollaris 240
Nyctidromus albicollis 274
Nyctimene major 38
Nymphicus hollandicus 258

O

Oarfish 538
Oceanites oceanicus 202
Oceanodroma hornbyi 202
    melania 202
Ocelot 102
Ochotona alpina 190
Ochrotomys nuttalli 166
Octodon degus 186
Octodont rodent family 186
Octodontidae 186
Ocyphaps lophotes 256
Ocyurus chrysurus 554
Odobenidae 106
Odobenus rosmarus 106
Odocoileus virginianus 136
Odontaspis taurus 488
Odontophorinae 232
Oedistoma pygmaeum 366
Oenanthe oenanthe 334
Ogcocephalus nasutus 530
Oilbird 272
Okapi 138
Okapia johnsoni 138
Old World burrowing lizard
    family 438
Old World flycatcher
    subfamily 350
Old World fruit bat family 38
Old World leaf-nosed bat
    family 44
Old World monkey family 66–72
Old World porcupine family 182
Old World rats and mice
    subfamily 178
Old World vultures 218
Old World warbler
    subfamily 344–6
Olingo, bushy-tailed 84
Olm and mudpuppy
    family 466
Onager 124
Oncorhynchus nerka 508
Ondatra zibethicus 172
Onychogalea fraenata 24
Onychognathus morio 392
Onychomys leucogaster 166
Onychorhynchus coronatus 306
O-o, Kauai 364
Opah 538
Openbill 210

African 210
Ophicephalus striatus 572
Ophioblennius atlanticus 566
Ophiophagus hannah 454
Ophisaurus apodus 438
Opisthocomidae 226
Opisthocomus hoazin 226
Oplurus sp. 418
Opossum, rat 14
    short-tailed 14
    Virginia 14
    water 14
Orangutan 76
Orcinus orca 114
Oreamnos americanus 154
Oreochromis niloticus 562
Oreomanes fraseri 376
Oreotragus oreotragus 150
Oreotrochilus estella 278
Oribi 150
Oriole, golden 394
    northern 382
Oriolidae 394
Oriolus oriolus 394
Ornithorhynchidae 12
Ornithorhynchus anatinus 12
Oropendola, Wagler's 382
Ortalis vetula 226
Orthonychinae 342
Orthotomus sutorius 344
Orycteropodidae 28
Orycteropus afer 28
Oryctolagus cuniculus 192
Oryx, Arabian 148
Oryx leucoryx 148
Oryzias latipes 534
Oryzomys peninsulae 166
Oryzorictes hova 30
Osbornictis piscivora 92
Osmerus eperlanus 508
Osphronemidae 572
Osphronemus goramy 572
Osprey 216
Osteoglossiformes 500
Osteoglossum bicirrhosum 500
Osteolaemus tetraspis 414
Ostracion tuberculatus 582
Ostraciontidae 582
Ostrich 196
Otariidae 106
Otididae 238
Otis tarda 238
Otolemur crassicaudatus 58
Otomops wroughtoni 46
Otomyinae 170
Otomys irroratus 170
Otter, African clawless 90
    Eurasian 90
    giant 90
    sea 90
Otter shrew, giant 30
Otter-civet 94
Otus asio 268
Ouakari, bald 62
Ourebia ourebi 150
Ovenbird 378
Ovenbird family 296
Ovibos moschatus 156
Ovis canadensis 156
    orientalis 156
Owl, barn 268
    brown fish 268
    burrowing 270
    elf 268
    Eurasian pygmy 270
    great horned 268
    hawk 270
    little 270
    long-eared 270
    oriental bay 268
    screech 268
    snowy 268
    tawny 270
Owlet-nightjar, Australian 272
Ox, musk 156
Oxpecker, yellow-billed 392
Oxybelis fulgidus 452
Oxydoras niger 520
Oxyruncidae 304
Oxyruncus cristatus 304
Oxyura jamaicensis 214
Oystercatcher, European 240
Ozotoceros bezoarticus 138

P

Paca 184
Paca and agouti family 184
Pacarana 184
Pachycephala pectoralis 354
Pachycephalinae 354
Pachyptila vittata 200
Pachyuromys duprasi 174
Pacu 510
Padda oryzivora 386
Paddlefish 498
Pademelon, red-legged 22
Pagellus bogaraveo 556
Pagophila eburnea 248
Pagophilus groenlandicus 108
Paguma larvata 92
Painted-snipe, greater 240
  lesser 240
Palila 380
Palmatogecko rangei 424
Palmcreeper, point-tailed 296
Pan paniscus 76
  troglodytes 76
Panda, giant 84
  lesser/red 84
Pandaka pygmaea 568
Pandion haliaetus 216
Pandionidae 216
Pangasianodon gigas 520
Pangasiidae 520
Pangasius pangasius 520
Pangolin, giant 28
  tree 28
Panther 104
Panthera leo 104
  onca 104
  pardus 104
  tigris 104
  uncia 104
Panurinae 342
Panurus biarmicus 342
Papio anubis 68
  hamadryas 68
  ursinus 68
Paradisaea rudolphi 398
Paradisaeidae 398
Paradisefish 572
Paradoxornis guttaticollis 342
Paraechinus aethiopicus 32
Parakeet, monk 262
  rose-ringed 260
Paralichthys californicus 576
  dentatus 576
Parascalops breweri 36
Pardalote, spotted 360
Pardalotus punctatus 360
Pareas sp. 448
Paridae 356
Parotomys brantsi 170
Parrot, eclectus 260
  gray 260
  owl 260
  red-breasted pygmy 258
  yellow-headed 262
Parrotbill, spot-breasted 262
Parrot-finch, blue-faced 386
Parrotfish, blue 564
  rainbow 564
  stoplight 564
Parrotlet, spectacled 262
Partridge, red-legged 228
  roulroul 228
Parula, northern 378
Parula americana 378
Parulidae 378
Parus atricapillus 356
  fringillinus 356
  major 356
Passer domesticus 390
  griseus 390
Passeriformes 296
Passerina ciris 372
Patagona gigas 278
Pauraque 274
Pavo cristatus 230
Peacock, Congo 230
Peafowl, Indian 230
Pearlfish 528
Peccary, Chaco 130
  collared 130
  white-lipped 130

Pedetes capensis 164
Pedetidae 164
Pedionomidae 234
Pedionomus torquatus 234
Peewee, eastern wood 306
Pegasus volitans 542
Pelagodroma marina 202
Pelea capreolus 146
Pelecanidae 204
Pelecaniformes 204
Pelecanoides urinatrix 202
Pelecanoididae 202
Pelecanus occidentalis 204
Pelecanus onocrotalus 204
Pelican, brown 204
  great white/rosy 204
Pelobates fuscus 474
Pelobatidae 474
Pelodytes punctatus 474
Pelomedusidae 412
Penduline tit family 356
Penelope purpurascens 226
Penguin, emperor 198
  Galápagos 198
  little blue/fairy 198
Peppershrike, rufous-browed 380
Peprilus triacanthus 572
Perameles gunni 20
Peramelidae 20
Perca fluviatilis 550
Perch 550
  climbing 572
  kelp 562
  Nile 548
  ocean 544
Perchlike fish order 548–72
Percichthyidae 548
Perciformes 548–72
Percopsiformes 524
Percopsis omiscomaycus 524
Pericrocotus flammeus 318
Perissodactyla 124
Permit 552
Pernis apivorus 218
Perodicticus potto 58
Perognathus californicus 162
  flavus 162
Peromyscus maniculatus 166
Petauridae 20
Petaurista petaurista 160
Petaurus breviceps 20
Petrel, scaled 200
  Wilson's 202
  see also Diving petrel; Storm-
  petrel
Petrogale xanthopus 22
Petroica phoenicea 350
Petromus typicus 188
Petromyidae 188
Petromyzon marinus 488
Petromyzoniformes 488
Petronia petronia 390
Phacochoerus aethiopicus 128
Phaenostictus mcleannani 298
Phaethon rubricauda 204
Phaethontidae 204
Phalacrocoracidae 206
Phalacrocorax carbo 206
Phalaenoptilus nuttallii 274
Phalanger family 20
Phalangeridae 20
Phalarope, red 242
Phalaropus fulicarius 242
Pharomachrus mocinno 280
Phascolarctidae 18
Phascolarctos cinereus 18
Phasianidae 228–32
Phasianus colchicus 230
Pheasant, golden 230
  gray peacock 230
  ring-necked 230
Phelsuma vinsoni 426
Phenacostethus smithi 536
Pheucticus ludovicianus 372
Philemon citreogularis 364
Philentoma velata 350
Philepittidae 310
Philetairus socius 390
Philippine creeper family 358
Philomachus pugnax 242
Phoca vitulina 108
Phocidae 108–10
Phocoena phocoena 112

Phocoenidae 112
Phocoenides dalli 112
Phodilus badius 268
Phodopus sungorus 168
Phoebe, eastern 304
Phoebetria palpebrata 200
Phoenicopteridae 210
Phoenicopterus ruber 210
Phoeniculidae 286
Phoeniculus purpureus 286
Phoenicurus ochruros 334
Pholidae 566
Pholidota 28
Pholis gunnellus 566
Photoblepharon palpebratus 540
Phoxinus phoxinus 514
Phrygilus patagonicus 370
Phrynocephalus nejdensis 420
Phrynomerus bifasciatus 472
Phrynosoma cornutum 416
Phyllastrephus scandens 320
Phyllodactylus porphyreus 424
Phyllomedusa, Lutz's 480
Phyllomedusa appendiculata 480
Phyllonycteris poeyi 48
Phyllopteryx taeniolatus 542
Phylloscopus collybita 346
  trochilus 346
Phyllostomatidae 48
Phyllostomus hastatus 48
Physailia pellucida 518
Physeter catodon 116
Physeteridae 116
Physignathus leseueri 420
Phytotoma rara 304
Phytotomidae 304
Piapiac 400
Pica pica 400
Picathartes gymnocephalus 342
Picathartinae 342
Picidae 292–4
Piciformes 288
Picoides major 292
Piculet, rufous/white-browed 292
  white-barred 292
Picumnus cirratus 292
Picus viridis 294
Pig, bearded 128
  bush 128
Pigeon, band-tailed 252
  brown 256
  crested 256
  Luzon bleeding-heart 256
  Nicobar 254
  nutmeg 254
  purple crowned 254
  tooth-billed 256
  Torres Strait 254
  Victoria crowned 256
  yellow-legged green 254
Pika, northern 190
Pike, northern 506
Pimelodus blodii 522
Pimelometopon pulchrum 564
Pinecone fish 540
Pinicola enucleator 384
Pinnipedia 106
Pipa pipa 472
Pipe snake family 444
Pipefish, greater 542
Pipidae 472
Pipilo erythrophthalmus 370
Pipistrelle, common 50
Pipistrellus pipistrellus 50
Pipit, golden 316
  meadow 316
  water 316
Pipridae 302
Pipromorpha oleaginea 308
Piranga olivacea 374
Piranha, red 510
Pirarucu 500
Pitangus sulphuratus 304
Pithecia monachus 62
Pitohui, rusty 350
Pitohui ferrugineus 354
Pitta, garnet 310
  Indian 310
Pitta brachyura 310
Pitta granatina 310
Pittidae 310
Pituophis melanoleucas 452
Pityriasis gymnocephala 324

Pizonyx vivesi 50
Plaice 576
  American 578
Plains-wanderer 234
Planigale, pygmy 16
Planigale maculata 16
Plantcutter, rufous-tailed 304
Platacanthomyinae 170
Platacanthomys lasiurus 170
Platanista gangetica 112
Platanistidae 112
Platax pinnatus 560
Plateless river turtle family 408
Platichthys stellatus 576
Platycercus elegans 260
Platypus 12
Platyrinchus platyrhynchos 306
Platysaurus imperator 436
Platysteira cyanea 352
Platysteirinae 352
Platysternidae 408
Platysternon megacephalum 408
Plecostomus commersonii 522
Plecotus auritus 50
Plectrophenax nivalis 368
Plegadis falcinellus 210
Plethodon cinereus 468
  glutinosus 468
Plethodontidae 468
Pleurodeles waltl 462
Pleuronectes platessa 576
Pleuronectiformes 574–8
Ploceidae 388–90
Ploceus cucullatus 388
  philippinus 388
Plotosidae 522
Plotosus lineatus 522
Plover, American golden 240
  crab 244
  Egyptian 246
  great shore 244
  ringed 240
Plush-capped finch subfamily 372
Pluvialis dominica 240
Pluvianus aegyptius 246
Poacher, sturgeon 546
Pocket mouse, Californian 162
  forest spiny 162
  Mexican spiny 162
  silky 162
Podargidae 272
Podargus strigoides 272
Podica senegalensis 238
Podiceps cristatus 198
Podicipedidae 198
Podicipediformes 198
Podocnemis expansa 412
Podogymnura truei 32
Poecilia reticulata 534
Poephila guttata 386
Pogonias cromis 558
Poiana richardsoni 92
Polecat, western 86
Polioptila caerulea 344
Polioptilinae 344
Pollachius virens 526
Pollock 526
  walleye 526
Polyboroides typus 220
Polyborus plancus 224
Polycentrus schomburgkii 562
Polychrus gutterosus 416
Polymixia nobilis 524
Polymixiiformes 524
Polyodon spathula 498
Polyplectron bicalcaratum 230
Polypteriformes 498
Polypterus weeksi 498
Pomacanthus imperator 560
Pomacentridae 562
Pomacentrus leucostictus 562
Pomatomus saltatrix 552
Pomatorhinus ferruginosus 338
Pomfret, Atlantic 554
Pompano, Florida 552
Pongidae 74–6
Pongo pygmaeus 76
Poor-will, common 274
Porbeagle 490
Porcupine 182
  Asian brush-tailed 182
  crested 182
  Indonesian 182

long-tailed 182
  tree 182
  Upper Amazon 182
Porcupinefish 582
Porgy, jolthead 556
Porichthys porosissimus 530
Porpoise, Dall's 112
  finless 112
  harbor 112
Possum, brush-tailed 20
  honey 18
Potamochoerus porcus 128
Potomogale velox 30
Potoo, common 272
Potoroo 22
Potorous tridactylus 22
Potos flavus 84
Potto 58
Pout, ocean 528
Pracheirodon innesi 510
Prairie chicken, greater 232
Prairie dog, black-tailed 160
Pratincole, collared 246
Presbytis entellus 72
Primates 56
Prinia, graceful 344
Prinia gracilis 344
Priodontes maximus 28
Prion, broad-billed 200
Prionace glauca 490
Prionochilus percussus 360
Prionodon linsang 92
Prionops plumata 324
Prionotus carolinus 544
Pristiophorus cirratus 492
Pristis pectinata 494
Proboscidea 122
Procavia capensis 122
Procaviidae 122
Procellariidae 200
Procellariiformes 200
Prochilodontidae 510
Prochilodus platensis 510
Procnias averano 302
Procolobus verus 72
Procyon lotor 84
Procyonidae 84
Progne subis 314
Promerops cafer 366
Pronghorn 138
Pronolagus crassicaudatus 190
Propithecus verreauxi 56
Prosthemadera novaeseelandiae 366
Proteidae 466
Proteles cristatus 98
Proteus anguinus 466
Protopterus aethiopicus 496
Protoxerus stangeri 158
Prunellidae 330
Prunella modularis 330
Prunellidae 330
Psalidoprocne pristoptera 314
Psammodromus algirus 434
Psammomys obesus 174
Psarocolius wagleri 382
Psephurus gladius 498
Psettodes belcheri 574
  erumei 574
Psettodidae 574
Pseudemys scripta 404
Pseudobranchus striatus 466
Pseudochelidon sirintarae 314
Pseudohydromys murinus 176
Pseudonaja textilis 454
Pseudophryne corroboree 476
Pseudoplatystoma fasciatum 522
Pseudopleuronectes americanus 578
Pseudopodoces humilis 400
Pseudotriton ruber 468
Pseudupeneus maculatus 558
Psittacidae 258–62
Psittaciformes 258
Psittacula krameri 260
Psittacus erithacus 260
Psittirostra bailleui 380
Psophia crepitans 234
Psophiidae 234
Psophodes olivaceus 342
Ptarmigan, rock 232
Pteridophora alberti 398
Pterodroma inexpectata 200
Pteroglossus beauharnaesii 290
Pterois volitans 544
Pteronotus parnelli 46

Pteronura brasiliensis 90
Pterophyllum scalare 562
Pteropodidae 38
Pteropodocys maxima 318
Pteroptochos castaneus 300
Pteropus giganteus 38
Ptilinopus superbus 254
Ptilocercus lowi 54
Ptilogonys cinereus 326
Ptilonorhynchidae 398
Ptilonorhynchus violaceus 398
Ptilostomus afer 400
Ptychadena porosissima 482
Ptychocheilus oregonensis 514
Ptychozoon kuhli 424
Pudu mephistophiles 138
Puffback, black-backed 324
  black-headed 352
Puffbird, white-necked 288
Puffer, bandtail 582
  oceanic 582
  sharpnose 582
Pufferfish, common 582
Puffin, common 250
Puffinus puffinus 200
Pumpkinseed 550
Pycnonotidae 320–2
Pycnonotus barbatus 320
  jocosus 320
Pygathrix roxellana 72
Pygmy possum family 20
Pygmy-tyrant, short-tailed 306
Pygopodidae 426
Pygopus nigriceps 426
Pyrocephalus rubinus 308
Pyrrhula pyrrhula 384
Python, carpet 446
  Indian 446
Python molurus 446
Pyxicephalus adspersus 482

Q

Quail, California 232
  European 228
  painted 228
Quail thrush, cinnamon 342
Quail-dove, blue-headed 252
Quelea, red-billed 388
Quelea quelea 388
Quetzal 280
Quiscalus quiscula 382
Quokka 24
Quoll 16

R

Rabbit, brush 192
  common 192
  pygmy 192
  snowshoe 190
  Sumatran 192
  swamp 192
  volcano 190
Rabbit and hare family 190
Rabbit-bandicoot 20
Rabbitfish 496
Raccoon 84
Racerunner 434
  strand 428
Rachycentron canadum 552
Rail, giant wood 236
  water 236
Rainbowfish, crimson-spotted 536
Raja batis 494
Rajiformes 494
Rallidae 236
Rallus aquaticus 236
Ramphastidae 290
Ramphastos toco 290
Ramphocelus carbo 376
Ramphocoris clotbey 312
Rana catesbeiana 482
  pipiens 482
  ridibunda 482
  temporaria 482
Ranidae 482–4
Rangifer tarandus 136
Raphiceros melanotis 150
Rasbora heteromorpha 516
Rascasse 544
Rat, African grass 178
  Arizona cotton 166

armored 188
  Australian water 176
  Baja California rice 166
  bamboo 168
  black/house 178
  cane 188
  crested 170
  dassie 188
  desert kangaroo 162
  fat sand 174
  fish-eating 166
  giant pouched 176
  gliding spiny 188
  greater bandicoot 178
  karroo 170
  long-tailed pouched 176
  Madagascan 170
  Norway/brown 178
  rough-tailed giant 178
  spiny rice 166
  stick-nest 178
  swamp 170
  white-tailed 170
  white-throated wood 166
  see also Mole-rat
Rat opossum family 14
Ratel 88
Ratfish 496
Ratites 196
Rat-kangaroo, musk 22
  rufous 22
Rattlesnake, eastern
  diamondback 458
Rattus norvegicus 178
  rattus 178
Ratufa bicolor 158
Ray, eagle 494
Razorbill 250
Recurvirostra avosetta 244
Recurvirostridae 244
Redfish 544
Redhorse, shorthead 516
Redpoll, common 384
Redshank 242
Redstart, black 334
  painted 378
Redunca arundinum 146
Reedbuck 146
Reedling, bearded 342
Regalecus glesne 538
Regulus satrapa 346
Reindeer 136
Reinhardtius hippoglossoides 578
Reithrodontomys megalotis 166
Remizidae 356
Remora remora 552
Rhabdomys pumilio 178
Rhabdornis mysticalis 358
Rhabdornithidae 358
Rhacophorus nigropalmatus 484
Rhampholeon marshalli 422
Rhea, greater 196
Rhea americana 196
Rhebok 146
Rheidae 196
Rhincodon typus 488
Rhinecanthus aculeatus 580
Rhineura floridana 442
Rhinobatus lentiginosus 494
Rhinoceros, black 126
  Indian 126
  square-lipped/white 126
  Sumatran 126
Rhinoceros unicornis 126
Rhinocerotidae 126
Rhinocryptidae 300
Rhinoderma darwinii 476
Rhinodermatidae 476
Rhinolophidae 44
Rhinolophus ferrumequinum 44
  hipposideros 44
  philippinensis 44
Rhinomyias ruficauda 350
Rhinophis blythis 444
Rhinophrynidae 472
Rhinophrynus dorsalis 472
Rhinoplax vigil 286
Rhinopoma microphyllum 40
Rhinopomatidae 40
Rhipidomys venezuelae 166
Rhipidura leucophrys 354
  rufifrons 354
Rhipidurinae 354

Rhizomyinae 168
Rhizomys sumatrensis 168
Rhodeus sericeus 514
Rhodinocichla rosea 374
Rhombomys opimus 174
Rhynchocephalia 402, 416
Rhynchonycteris naso 40
Rhynochetidae 238
Rhynochetos jubatus 238
Rice eel 544
Ricefish 534
Ridley, Kemp's 410
  olive 410
Rifleman 310
Right whale family 120
Ringtail family 20
Riopa sundevalli 430
Riparia riparia 314
Rissa tridactyla 248
River dolphin family 112
Roach 514
Roadrunner 266
Robin, American 336
  Eurasian 332
  flame 350
  magpie 334
  Peking 340
Roccus saxatilis 548
Rockfowl, Guinea bare-
  headed 342
Rockling, three-barbed 528
Rock-thrush, Cape 336
Rodentia 158
Roller 284
Rollulus rouloul 228
Romerolagus diazi 190
Rook 400
Rorqual family 120
Rosella, crimson 260
Rostratula benghalensis 240
Rostratulidae 240
Rostrhamus sociabilis 218
Roughie 540
Rousettus aegyptiacus 38
Ruff 242
Runner, rainbow 552
Rupicapra rupicapra 154
Rupicola peruviana 302
Rush-tyrant, many-colored 306
Rutilus rutilus 514
Rynchopidae 248
Rynchops niger 248
Rypticus saponaceus 550

S

Sable 86
Sablefish 546
Saccopteryx leptura 40
Sagittariidae 216
Sagittarius serpentarius 216
Saguinus imperator 60
  nigricollis 60
Saiga 154
Saiga tatarica 154
Sailfish 570
Saimiri sciureus 62
Saki, monk 62
  black-bearded 62
Salamander, Asian 462
  California slender 468
  dusky 468
  fire 462
  marbled 464
  Pacific giant 464
  red 468
  red-backed 468
  sharp-ribbed 462
  slimy 468
  spotted 464
  spring 468
  Texas blind 468
  tiger 464
Salamandra salamandra 462
Salamandridae 462
Salano 94
Salanoia concolor 94
Salmo gairdneri 506
  salar 506
  trutta 506
Salmon 506
  Atlantic 506

Australian 554
sockeye 508
Salmon order 506–8
Salmoniformes 506–8
Salpinctes obsoletus 328
Salpornis spilonotus 358
Saltator, buff-throated 372
Saltator maximus 372
Salvelinus alpinus 506
namaycush 506
Sand eel/sand lance 568
Sand racer, Algerian 434
Sand tiger 488
Sandfish 430
Sandgrouse, Pallas's 252
Sandpiper family 242
Sand-roller 524
Sandsmelt 536
Sapsucker, yellow-bellied 292
Sarcophilus harrisi 16
Sarcoramphus papa 216
Sardina pilchardus 502
Sardine 502
Sardinha 510
Sardinops 502
Sargassumfish 530
Sasia ochracea 292
Sassaby 148
Sauromalus obesus 416
Saury, Atlantic 534
Sawfish 494
smalltooth 494
Saxicola torquata 334
Sayornis phoebe 304
Scalopus aquaticus 36
Scaly-foot, hooded 426
Scaly-tailed squirrel family 164
Scandentia 54
Scapanus orarius 36
Scaphiopus hammondi 474
Scaridae 564
Scarus coeruleus 564
guacamaia 564
Scat 560
Scatophagus argus 560
Scaup, greater 214
Sceloporus undulatus 416
Schilbe mystus 518
Schistometopum thomensis 470
Schoinobates volans 20
Sciaenidae 558
Scimitar-babbler, coral-billed 338
Scincella lateralis 432
Scincidae 430–2
Scincus philbyi 430
Sciuridae 158–60
Sciurus carolinensis 158
vulgaris 158
Scleropages sp. 500
Scolecomorphidae 470
Scolecomorphus kirkii 470
Scolopacidae 242
Scolopax minor 242
Scomber scombrus 570
Scomberesox saurus 534
Scombridae 570
Scophthalmus aquosus 574
maximus 574
Scopidae 210
Scopus umbretta 210
Scorpaena porcus 544
Scorpaenichthys marmoratus 546
Scorpaeniformes 544–6
Scorpionfish order 544–6
Screamer, black-necked/
northern 212
Scrub bird, noisy 310
Scrubfowl, common 226
Scrub-robin, karroo 332
Scrubwren, white-browed 348
Sculpin, shorthorn 546
Scup 556
Scutisorex somereni 34
Scyliorhinus canicula 490
Scythebill, red-billed 300
Scythrops novaehollandiae 264
Sea lion, Australian 106
California 106
Steller 106
Seabass, white 558
Seadragon, weedy 542
Seahorse, dwarf 542
Seal, bearded 108

crabeater 108
gray 108
harbor 108
harp 108
hooded 110
leopard 108
Mediterranean monk 110
northern elephant 110
northern fur 106
South American fur 106
Weddell 110
Searobin, northern 544
Seasnail, striped 546
Seatrout, spotted 558
Sebastes marinus 544
Secretary bird 216
Seedeater, variable 370
Seedsnipe, least 246
Seicercus castaneiceps 346
Seiurus aurocapillus 378
Selenarctos thibetanus 82
Selene vomer 552
Selenidera maculirostris 290
Selevinia betpakdalensis 180
Seleviniidae 180
Semaprochilodus insignis 510
Semionotiformes 498
Semotilus corporalis 516
margarita 514
Sergeant major 562
Sericornis frontalis 348
Seriema, red-legged 238
Serinus canaria 384
Seriola dumerili 552
Serow 154
Serpophaga cinerea 308
Serrasalmus nattereri 510
Serval 102
Setifer setosus 30
Setonyx brachyurus 24
Setornis criniger 322
Shad, allis 502
twaite 502
Shag, long-tailed 206
Shanny 566
Shark, Atlantic angel 492
basking 488
blue 490
bull 490
common saw 492
dwarf 492
elephant 496
Greenland 492
Pacific angel 492
Port Jackson 492
salmon 490
sixgill 492
thresher 488
whale 488
white 490
Shark order 488–90
Sharksucker 552
Sharpbill 304
Shearwater, Manx 200
Sheathbill, black-billed 246
snowy/yellow-billed 246
Sheath-tailed bat family 40
Sheep, Barbary 156
mountain 156
Sheephead, California 564
Sheepshead 556
Shelduck 212
Shield snout, South African 442
Shieldtail, Blyth's landau 444
red-blotched 444
Shiner, common 516
Shoebill 208, 210
Shortwing, white-browed/blue 332
Shoveler, northern 214
Shrew, armored 34
Ceylon long-tailed 34
elephant 36
masked 34
Merriam's desert 34
mouse 34
pygmy white-toothed 34
short-tailed 34
see also Otter shrew; Tree shrew
Shrike, crimson-breasted 324
long-tailed 324
northern 324
white/straight-crested
helmet 324

Shrike-thrush, gray 354
Shriketit, crested 354
Shrike-vireo, chestnut-sided 380
Shrimpfish 542
Sialia sialis 334
Siamang 74
Sicalis luteola 370
Sicista betulina 180
Sicklebill 326
white-tipped 278
Sidewinder 458
Sierra-finch, Patagonian 370
Sifaka, Verreaux's 56
Siganidae 568
Siganus virgatus 568
Sigmodon arizonae 166
Silktail 348
Siluriformes 518–22
Silurus glanis 518
Silverside, hardhead 536
Siphonops annulatus 470
Siren, dwarf 466
greater 466
Siren lacertina 466
Sirenia 110
Sirenidae 466
Sistrurus catenatus 458
Sitella, varied 358
Sitta canadensis 358
Sittasomus griseicapillus 300
Sittidae 358
Skate 494
Skates and ray order 494
Skimmer, black 248
Skink, great plains 430
ground 432
legless 430
prickly forest 432
round-bodied 430
sand 430
spiny-tailed 432
Sundeval's 430
western blue-tongued 432
Skua 248
Skunk, hog-nosed 90
spotted 90
striped 90
Skylark 312
Sleeper, fat 568
Slender blind snake family 444
Slider, pond 404
Slippery dick 564
Slit-faced bat family 42
Sloth, three-toed 26
two-toed 26
Slowworm 438
Smelt 508
Sminthopsis crassicaudata 16
Smoky bat family 52
Snake, banded sea 454
common garter 450
de Vis's banded 454
eastern brown 454
eastern coral 454
egg-eating 448
elephant-trunk 446
false coral 444
gopher 452
grass 450
mangrove 452
oriental tree 452
paradise tree 452
pine 452
rat 450
red-bellied 450
Schlegel's blind 444
slug 448
smooth 452
snail-eating 448
spotted water 448
sunbeam 444
vine 452
western blind 444
white-bellied mangrove 448
Snakebird 206
Snakehead 572
Snake-lizard, Burton's 426
Snapper 556
mutton 554
yellowtail 554
Snapping turtle family 408
Snipe, common 242
Snowcock, Himalayan 228

Soapfish, greater 550
Softshell, narrow-headed 412
Nile 412
spiny 412
Zambesi 412
Softshell turtle family 412
Sole 578
naked 578
Solea solea 578
Soleidae 578
Solenodon, Cuban 30
Solenodon cubanus 30
paradoxus 30
Solenodontidae 30
Solitaire, Andean 334
Somateria mollissima 214
Somniosus microcephalus 492
Sooglossid frog family 484
Sooglossidae 484
Sooglossus sechellensis 484
Sorex cinereus 34
Soricidae 34
Sousa chinensis 114
Spadebill, white-crested 306
Spadefish, Atlantic 560
Spadefoot, European 474
western 474
Spadefoot toad family 474
Spalacinae 168
Spalax leucodon 168
Sparidae 556
Sparrow, chipping 368
gray-headed 390
hedge 330
house 390
Java 386
rock 390
Savannah 368
song 368
Sparus aurata 556
Spatule-tail, marvelous 278
Speirops, Príncipe Island 360
Speirops leucophoea 360
Speothos venaticus 80
Speotyto cunicularia 270
Sperm whale family 116
Spermophilus tridecemlineatus 160
Sphecotheres viridis 394
Spheniscidae 198
Sphenisciformes 198
Spheniscus mendiculus 198
Sphenodon punctatus 416
Sphenodontia 416
Sphoeroides spengleri 582
Sphyraena barracuda 564
Sphyrapicus varius 292
Sphyrna zygaena 490
Spiderhunter, long-billed 362
Spilogale gracilis 90
Spilornis cheela 220
Spinachia spinachia 542
Spinebill, eastern 366
Spinefoot, blue-lined 568
Spinetail, Des Murs' 296
red-faced 296
stripe-breasted 296
Spiny anteater family 12
Spiny dormouse subfamily 170
Spiny eel 572
Spiny eel order 504
Spiza americana 372
Spizella passerina 368
Spizixos canifrons 320
Spoonbill 210
Sporophila americana 370
Spreo superbus 392
Spring peeper 480
Springbok 152
Springhare 164
Spurfowl, red 228
Squaliformes 492
Squaliolus laticaudus 492
Squalus acanthias 492
Squamata 402, 416
Squatina californica 492
dumerili 492
squatina 492
Squawfish, northern 514
Squirrel, African giant 158
African ground 160
African palm 158
black giant 158
European red 158

gray 158
  Indian striped 158
  northern flying 160
  Prevost's 158
  red giant flying 160
  thirteen-lined ground 160
  see also Flying squirrel
Squirrelfish 540
Stachyris leucotis 338
Stargazer, northern 566
Starling 392
  metallic/shining 392
  red-winged 392
  superb 392
Starnoenas cyanocephala 252
Steatomys krebsi 176
Steatornis caripensis 272
Steatornithidae 272
Stenella coeruleoalba 114
Stenotomus chrysops 556
Stercorariidae 248
Stereolepis gigas 548
Sterna hirundo 248
Sternotherus odoratus 408
Stickleback, fifteenspine 542
  fourspine 542
  threespine 542
Stickleback and tube-snout
  order 542
Stilt, black-winged 244
Stingray, southern 494
Stizostedion lucioperca 550
Stonechat 334
Stonefish 544
Stoneroller, central 514
Storeria occipitomaculata 450
Stork, white 210
Storm-petrel 202
  black 202
  ringed 202
  white-faced 202
Strepera graculina 396
Streptopelia decaocto 254
Strigidae 268–70
Strigiformes 268
Strigops habroptilus 260
Strix aluco 270
Stromateidae 572
Struthidea cinerea 396
Struthio camelus 196
Struthionidae 196
Sturgeon 498
Sturgeon order 498
Sturnella magna 382
Sturnira lilium 48
Sturnus vulgaris 392
Sucker, white 516
Sucker-footed bat family 52
Sugarbird, Cape 366
Suidae 128
Sula bassana 204
  leucogaster 204
Sulidae 204
Sunbeam snake family 444
Sunbird, crimson/yellow-
  backed 362
  olive-backed 362
  purple-throated 362
  ruby-cheeked 362
  scarlet-tufted malachite 362
  superb 362
  wattled false 310
Sunbittern 238
Suncus etruscus 34
Sunfish, ocean 582
Sungrebe 238
Surfperch, barred 562
Suricata suricatta 94
Surnia ulula 270
Surniculus lugubris 264
Surubim 522
Sus barbatus 128
  scrofa 128
Swallow, bank 314
  barn 314
  blue rough-winged 314
  golden 314
  see also Wood swallow
Swallow-tanager 368, 372
Swan, tundra 212
Swift, common 276
  crested 276
  palm 276

white-throated 276
Swiftlet, edible-nest 276
Swordfish 570
Swordtail, green 536
Syconycteris australis 38
Sylvia atricapilla 344
Sylvicapra grimmia 144
Sylviinae 344–6
Sylvilagus aquaticus 192
  auduboni 192
  bachmani 192
  idahoensis 192
Sylviorthorhynchus desmursii 296
Symphurus plagiusa 578
Symphysodon discus 562
Synallaxis cinnamomea 296
Synanceia verrucosa 544
Synaptomys cooperi 172
Synbranchiformes 544
Synceros caffer 144
Synchiropus splendidus 574
Syngnathiformes 542
Syngnathus acus 542
Synodontis nigriventris 520
Synodus synodus 524
Syrrhaptes paradoxus 252

T

Tachuris rubrigastra 306
Tachybaptus ruficollis 198
Tachyeres brachypterus 214
Tachyglossidae 12
Tachyoryctes macrocephalus 168
Tachyphonus luctuosus 374
Tadarida aegyptiaca 46
Tadorna tadorna 212
Tahr, Himalayan 156
Tailed frog family 474
Tailorbird, long-tailed/
  common 344
Takahe 236
Takin 156
Talapoin 70
Talpa europaea 36
Talpidae 36
Tamandua 26
Tamandua mexicana 26
Tamarin, black and red 60
  emperor 60
  golden lion 60
Tamias striatus 160
Tanager, blue-gray 374
  magpie 374
  paradise 376
  rose-breasted thrush 374
  scarlet 374
  silver-beaked 376
  white-shouldered 374
Tandanus tandanus 522
Tang, blue 568
Tangara chilensis 376
Tanysiptera galatea 282
Tapaculo family 300
Tapera naevia 266
Taphozous longimanus 40
Tapir, Brazilian 126
  Malayan 126
Tapiridae 126
Tapirus indicus 126
  terrestris 126
Taraba major 298
Tarentola annularis 424
Taricha granulosa 462
Tarpon 500
Tarpon atlanticus 500
Tarsier, western 58
Tarsiger cyanurus 332
Tarsiidae 58
Tarsipedidae 18
Tarsipes spencerae 18
Tarsius bancanus 58
Tasmacetus shepherdi 118
Tasmanian devil 16
Tatera indica 174
Tauraco erythrolophus 266
Tautog 564
Tautoga onitis 564
Taxidea taxus 88
Tayassu pecari 130
  tajacu 130
Tayassuidae 130
Tayra 86

Tegu, common 428
Teiid lizard family 428
Teiidae 428
Teius teyou 428
Teleonoma filicauda 302
Tench 512
Tenrec, greater hedgehog 30
  rice 30
  shrew 30
  streaked 30
  tailless 30
Tenrec ecaudatus 30
Tenrecidae 30
Terathopius ecaudatus 220
Tern, common 248
Terpsiphone paradisi 352
Terrapene carolina 404
Terrapin, diamondback 404
Tersina viridis 372
Tersininae 372
Testudinidae 406
Testudo graeca 406
Tetra, flame 510
  Mexican 512
  neon 510
Tetracerus quadricornis 140
Tetrao tetrix 232
Tetraodon cutcutia 582
Tetraodontidae 582
Tetraodontiformes 580–2
Tetraogallus himalayensis 228
Tetraoninae 232
Tetrapturus audax 570
Teyu 428
Thalarctos maritimus 82
Thamnophilus doliatus 298
Thamnophis sirtalis 450
Thecurus sumatrae 182
Theragra chalcogramma 526
Therapon jarbua 550
Theropithecus gelada 68
Thick-knee family 244
Thinocoridae 246
Thinocorus rumicivorus 246
Thomomys talpoides 162
Thornbill, yellow-rumped 348
Thorny devil 420
Thrasher, California 330
Thraupinae 374–6
Thraupis episcopus 374
Threskiornithidae 210
Thrush, austral 336
  Cape/olive 336
  island 336
  White's 336
Thryomanes bewickii 328
Thryonomyidae 188
Thryonomys swinderianus 188
Thunnus albacares 570
Thylacomyidae 20
Thylogale stigmatica 22
Thymallus thymallus 506
Thyroptera discifera 52
Thyropteridae 52
Tiang 148
Tichodroma muraria 358
Tiger 104
Tigerfish 550
  giant 512
Tiliqua occipitalis 432
Timalia pileata 338
Timaliinae 338–42
Tinamidae 196
Tinamou, great 196
Tinamus major 196
Tinca tinca 512
Tit, bearded 342
  great 356
  long-tailed 356
  red-throated 356
  sultan 356
  yellow penduline 356
Titi, dusky 62
Titmouse family 356
Tmetothylacus tenellus 316
Toad, African clawed 472
  American 478
  Boulenger's arrow poison 478
  common 478
  giant 478
  green 478
  Mexican burrowing 472
  midwife 474

natterjack 478
  oriental fire-bellied 474
  Surinam 472
Toadfish order 530
Tockus erythrorhynchus 286
Todidae 284
Todirostrum cinereum 308
Todus todus 284
Tody, Jamaican 284
Tody-flycatcher, common 308
Tonguefish, blackcheek 578
Tongue-sole, long 578
Topaz, crimson 278
Topaza pella 278
Topi 148
Top-minnow, dwarf 536
Torgos tracheliotus 218
Torpedo, Atlantic 494
Torpedo nobiliana 494
Tortoise, African pancake 406
  bowsprit 406
  Galápagos giant 406
  gopher 406
  leopard 406
  Schweigger's hinged-back 406
  spur-thighed 406
Toucan, laminated 290
  toco 290
Toucanet, emerald 290
  saffron 290
  spot-billed 290
Towhee, rufous-sided 370
Toxostoma redivivum 330
Trachinidae 566
Trachinotus carolinus 552
Trachipterus arcticus 538
Tragelaphus angasi 140
  euryceros 140
  oryx 140
  strepsiceros 140
Tragopan, Temminck's 230
Tragopan temminckii 230
Tragulidae 134
Tragulus javanicus 134
Tree shrew, Bornean
  smooth-tailed 54
  common 54
  feather-tailed 54
  Madras 54
  mountain 54
  Philippine 54
Treecreeper, brown 358
Treefrog, European green 480
  gray 480
Tremarctos ornatus 82
Trembler 330
Treron phoenicoptera 254
Triaenops persicus 44
Trichastoma albipectus 338
Trichechidae 110
Trichechus manatus 110
Trichiuridae 570
Trichiurus lepturus 570
Trichoglossus haematodus 258
Trichomycteridae 522
Trichosurus vulpecula 20
Trichys fasciculata 182
Triggerfish, black-barred 580
  clown 580
  gray 580
  queen 580
  sargassum 580
Trigla lucerna 544
Triller, white-winged 318
Tringa totanus 242
Trionychidae 412
Trionyx spiniferus 412
  triunguis 412
Tripletail 554
Triportheus elongatus 510
Triturus cristatus 462
Trochilidae 278
Trochocercus albonotatus 352
Troglodytes aedon 328
  troglodytes 328
Troglodytidae 328
Trogon, elegant/coppery-tailed 280
  narina 280
  red-headed 280
Trogon elegans 280
Trogonidae 280
Trogoniformes 280
Tropicbird, red-tailed 204

Tropidophorus queenslandiae 432
Tropidosaura essexi 434
Trout 506
  brown 506
  lake 506
  rainbow 506
  sea 506
Trout-perch 524
Trout-perch order 524
True frog family 482
Trumpeter, common 234
Tuatara 402, 416
Tube-snout 542
Tubulidentata 28
Tuco-tuco 186
Tui 366
Tuna, skipjack 570
  yellowfin 570
Tupaia glis 54
  montana 54
Tupinambis teguixin 428
Turaco, Bannerman's 266
  red-crested 266
Turbot 574
Turdinae 332–6
Turdoides plebejus 340
Turdus falcklandii 336
  merula 336
  migratorius 336
  olivaceus 336
  poliocephalus 336
Turkey 232
Turnicidae 234
Turnix sylvatica 234
Turnstone, ruddy 242
Tursiops truncatus 114
Turtle, alligator snapping 408
  arrau river 412
  big-headed 408
  Central American river 408
  common musk 408
  eastern box 404
  European pond 404
  false map 404
  green 410
  Murray River 412
  New Guinea plateless river 408
  snapping 408
  wood 404
  yellow mud 408
Tylosaurus crocodilus 532
Tympanuchus cupido 232
Typhlomolge rathbuni 468
Typhlomys cinereus 170
Typhlonectes compressicauda 470
Typhlonectidae 470
Typhlopidae 444
Typhlops schlegelii 444
Tyrannidae 304–8
Tyrannus tyrannus 304
Tyrant, great shrike 308
  white-headed marsh 304
Tyrant flycatcher family 304
Tyranulet, torrent 308
Tyto alba 268
Tytonidae 268

U

Umbrellabird, Amazonian/
  ornate 302
Unicornfish, striped-face 568
Upupa epops 286
Upupidae 286
Uraeginthus bengalus 386
Uria aalge 250
Urocissa ornata 400
Urodela 460, 462
Uroderma bilobatum 48
Urogale everetti 54
Uromastyx princeps 420
Uropeltidae 444
Uropeltis biomaculatus 444
Urophycis tenuis 526
Uroplatus fimbriatus 426
Uropsalis lyra 274
Ursidae 82
Ursus americanus 82
  arctos 82

V

Vampire, Linnaeus' false 48

Vampire bat family 46
Vampyrum spectrum 48
Vandellia cirrhosa 522
Vanellus vanellus 240
Vanga, hook-billed 326
Vanga curvirostris 326
Vangidae 326
Varanidae 440
Varanus gouldi 440
  komodensis 440
  niloticus 440
Varecia variegata 56
Veery 336
Verdin 356
Vermicella annulata 454
Vermivora chrysoptera 378
  pinus 378
Vespertilionidae 50
Vicugna vicugna 132
Vicuña 132
Vidua paradisaea 390
Vieja 522
Viper, Asiatic pit 458
  aspic 456
  Bibron's burrowing 450
  common 456
  desert sidewinding 456
  Gaboon 456
  horned 456
Vipera ammodytes 456
  aspis 456
  berus 456
  gabonica 456
  peringueyi 456
Viperfish, Sloane's 508
Viperidae 456
Vireo, red-eyed 380
Vireo olivaceus 380
Vireolanius melitophrys 380
Vireonidae 380
Viscacha, plains 186
Viverra civetta 92
Viverridae 92–6
Vole, bank 172
  European water 172
  meadow 172
  sagebrush 172
Vole and lemming subfamily 172
Vombatidae 18
Vombatus ursinus 18
Vulpes vulpes 78
  zerda 78
Vulture, bearded 216
  Egyptian 218
  king 216
  lappet-faced 218
  palm-nut 220
  turkey 216

W

Wagtail, forest 316
  pied/white 316
  willie 354
  yellow 316
Wahoo 570
Wallabia bicolor 24
Wallaby, bridled nail-tailed 24
  New Guinea forest 24
  ring-tailed rock 22
  swamp 24
Wallcreeper 358
Walrus 106
Wapiti 136
Warbler, black-and-white 378
  blue-winged 378
  Ceylon bush 346
  chestnut-headed 346
  fan-tailed 344
  golden-crowned 378
  golden-winged 378
  grasshopper 346
  long-billed 344
  mourning 378
  strong-footed/brownish-
    flanked 346
  white-throated 348
  willow 346
  yellow 378
Wart snake family 446
Warthog 128
Water dragon, eastern 420
  soa-soa 420

Waterbuck, common/defassa 146
Wattlebird, red 366
Wattle-eye 532
Waxbill family 386
Waxwing, Bohemian 326
Weasel, least 86
Weaver, baya 388
  buffalo 390
  cuckoo/parasitic 388
  grosbeak/thick-billed 388
  red-headed 388
  sociable 390
  village 388
Weever, lesser 566
Wels 518
Whale, Arnoux's beaked 118
  Baird's beaked 118
  blue/sulphur-bottomed 120
  bowhead 120
  Cuvier's beaked 118
  dwarf sperm 116
  gray 120
  humpback 120
  killer 114
  long-finned pilot 114
  minke 120
  northern bottle-nosed 118
  pygmy sperm 116
  sei 120
  Shepherd's beaked 118
  Sowerby's beaked 118
  sperm 116
  white 116
Whale bird 200
Whalefish 540
Wheatear 334
Whimbrel 242
Whipbird, eastern 342
Whipsnake, dark-green 450
Whistler, golden 354
Whistler, subfamily 354
Whistling-duck, white-faced 212
White whale family 116
White-eye (silver-eye), gray-
  breasted 360
  Japanese 360
Whitefish 506
Whiting 526
  blue 526
Whydah, paradise 390
Wildebeest, blue 148
Windowpane 574
Winged dragon 542
Wisent 144
Wolf, gray 78
  maned 80
Wolffish, Atlantic 568
Wolverine 88
Wombat 18
Wood swallow, white-
  breasted 396
  white-browed 396
Woodchuck 160
Woodcock, American 242
Woodcreeper, barred 300
  long-billed 300
  olivaceous 300
Woodhoopoe, green 286
Woodpecker, blond-crested 294
  golden-tailed 294
  great slaty 294
  great spotted 292
  green 294
  ground 294

  ivory-billed 292
  large golden-backed 294
Worm lizard 442
  Florida 442
  two-legged 442
  white-bellied 442
Wrasse, ballan 564
Wren, Bewick's 328
  cactus 328
  Eyrean grass 348
  house 328
  long-billed marsh 328
  rock 328
  superb blue 348
  winter 328
Wren-babbler, large 338
Wrentit 342
Wrybill 240
Wrymouth 566
Wryneck 292

X

Xanthichthys ringens 580
Xantusia vigilis 428
Xantusiidae 428
Xenicidae 310
Xenopeltidae 444
Xenopeltis unicolor 444
Xenops, plain 296
Xenops minutus 296
Xenopus laevis 472
Xenosauridae 440
Xenosaurus sp. 440
Xeromys myoides 176
Xerus erythropus 160
Xiphias gladius 570
Xiphiidae 570
Xiphophorus helleri 536

Y

Yak 142
Yellow-finch, grassland 370
Yellowhammer 368
Yuhina, stripe-throated 340
Yuhina gularis 340

Z

Zaglossus bruijni 12
Zalophus californianus 106
Zanclus cornutus 568
Zander 550
Zapodidae 180
Zapus hudsonius 180
Zebra, common 124
  Grevy's 124
Zeiformes 538
Zenaida macroura 252
Zenopsis ocellata 538
Zeus faber 538
Ziphiidae 118
Ziphius cavirostris 118
Zoarces viviparus 566
Zokor, common Chinese 168
Zonosaurus sp. 436
Zonotrichia melodia 368
Zoothera dauma 336
Zorilla 86
Zosteropidae 360
Zosterops japonica 360
  lateralis 360

ACKNOWLEDGMENTS

The Publishers received invaluable help during the preparation of the *Macmillan Illustrated Animal Encyclopedia* from Heather Angel; Angus Bellairs; H. G. Cogger; Rosanne Hooper; Zilda Tandy; Dr. Pat Morris; Dr. Robert Stebbings; Ed Wade; the staff of the Herpetology Department of the British Museum (Natural History), London, particularly Colin McCarthy and Barry Clarke; the staff of the Ornithology Department of the British Museum (Natural History) outstation at Tring, particularly Peter Colston; the staff of the Science Reference Library, London; and the IUCN Conservation Monitoring Centre, Cambridge, England.